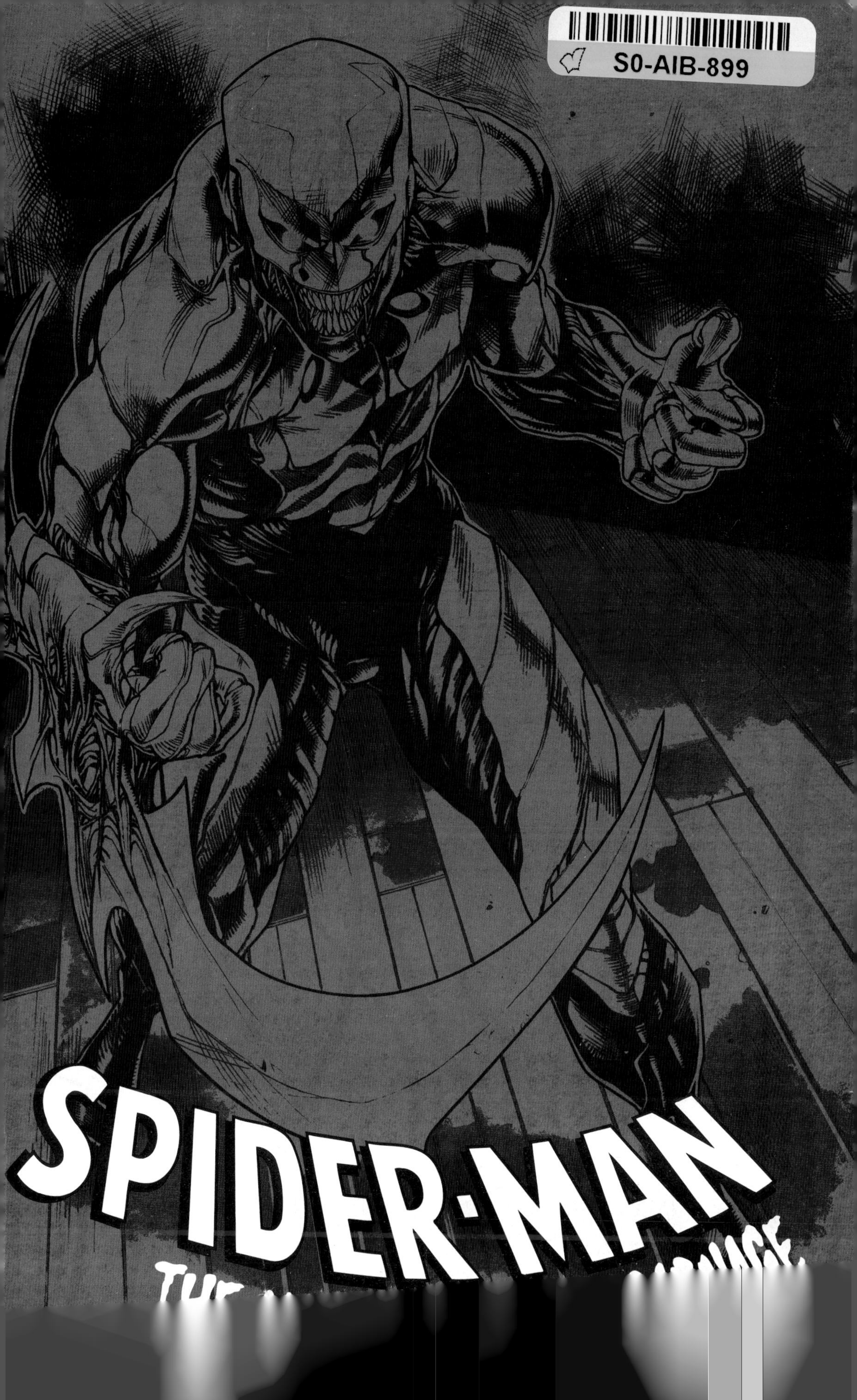
SPIDER-MAN

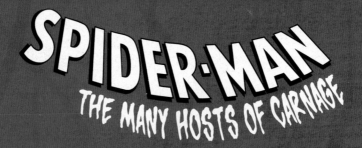

SPIDER-MAN
THE MANY HOSTS OF CARNAGE

AMAZING SPIDER-MAN #361

WRITER: **DAVID MICHELINIE**
PENCILER: **MARK BAGLEY**
INKER: **RANDY EMBERLIN**
COLORIST: **BOB SHAREN**
LETTERER: **JOE ROSEN**
COVER ART: **MARK BAGLEY** & **RANDY EMBERLIN**
ASSISTANT EDITOR: **ERIC FEIN**
EDITOR: **DANNY FINGEROTH**

AMAZING SPIDER-MAN #410, SPIDER-MAN #67 & SPECTACULAR SPIDER-MAN #233

WRITERS: **TOM DeFALCO, HOWARD MACKIE** & **TODD DEZAGO**
PENCILERS: **MARK BAGLEY, JOHN ROMITA JR.** & **SAL BUSCEMA**
INKERS: **LARRY MAHLSTEDT, RANDY EMBERLIN, AL WILLIAMSON, AL MILGROM, ART THIBERT** & **JOHN STANISCI**
COLORISTS: **BOB SHAREN, KEVIN TINSLEY, JOHN KALISZ** & **MALIBU**
LETTERER: **RICHARD STARKINGS** & **COMICRAFT**
COVER ART: **MARK BAGLEY, LARRY MAHLSTEDT** & **ATOMIC PAINTBRUSH**; **JOHN ROMITA JR.** & **AL WILLIAMSON**; **SAL BUSCEMA** & **JOHN BLIGH**
ASSISTANT EDITOR: **MARK BERNARDO**
EDITORS: **BOB BUDIANSKY** & **ERIC FEIN**

AMAZING SPIDER-MAN #431

WRITER: **TOM DeFALCO**
PENCILER: **JOE BENNETT**
INKER: **BUD LaROSA**
COLORIST: **BOB SHAREN**
LETTERER: **RICHARD STARKINGS** & **COMICRAFT's KIFF SCHOLL**
COVER ART: **TOM LYLE**
ASSISTANT EDITOR: **MATT HICKS**
EDITOR: **RALPH MACCHIO**

CARNAGE #3 & CARNAGE, U.S.A. #1-5

WRITER: **ZEB WELLS**
ARTIST: **CLAYTON CRAIN**
LETTERER: **VC's CLAYTON COWLES**
COVER ART: **CLAYTON CRAIN**
ASSOCIATE EDITORS: **ALEJANDRO ARBONA** & **TOM BRENNAN**
EDITOR: **STEPHEN WACKER**

SUPERIOR CARNAGE #3-5

WRITER: **KEVIN SHINICK**
PENCILERS: **STEPHEN SEGOVIA** WITH **DAN MEXIA** (#4-5)
INKERS: **DENNIS CRISOSTOMO** WITH **DAN MEXIA** (#4-5) & **DON HO** (#5)
COLORISTS: **JAY DAVID RAMOS** WITH **VERONICA GANDINI** & **RACHELLE ROSENBERG** (#4) AND **REX LOKUS** (#5)
LETTERER: **VC's JOE CARAMAGNA**
COVER ART: **CLAYTON CRAIN**
ASSISTANT EDITOR: **DEVIN LEWIS**
EDITOR: **SANA AMANAT**
SENIOR EDITOR: **STEPHEN WACKER**

SUPERIOR CARNAGE ANNUAL #1

WRITER: **CULLEN BUNN**
ARTISTS: **KIM JACINTO** (PP. 1-20) & **MIKE HENDERSON** (PP. 21-30)
COLORIST: **JAY DAVID RAMOS**
LETTERER: **VC's JOE CARAMAGNA**
COVER ART: **RAFA GARRES**
ASSISTANT EDITOR: **DEVIN LEWIS**
EDITOR: **SANA AMANAT**
SENIOR EDITOR: **STEPHEN WACKER**

AMAZING SPIDER-MAN #798-799

WRITER: **DAN SLOTT**
PENCILER: **STUART IMMONEN**
INKER: **WADE von GRAWBADGER**
COLORIST: **MARTE GRACIA**
LETTERER: **VC's JOE CARAMAGNA**
COVER ART: **ALEX ROSS**
ASSISTANT EDITOR: **TOM GRONEMAN**
ASSOCIATE EDITOR: **DEVIN LEWIS**
EDITOR: **NICK LOWE**

AMAZING SPIDER-MAN #800

WRITER: **DAN SLOTT**
PENCILERS: **NICK BRADSHAW** (PP. 1-6), **HUMBERTO RAMOS** (PP. 7-30), **GIUSEPPE CAMUNCOLI** (PP. 31-40 & 69-72), **STUART IMMONEN** (PP. 41-68) & **MARCOS MARTIN** (PP. 73-78)
INKERS: **NICK BRADSHAW** (PP. 1-6), **VICTOR OLAZABA** (PP. 7-30), **CAM SMITH** (PP. 31-40 & 69-72), **WADE von GRAWBADGER** (PP. 41-68) & **MARCOS MARTIN** (PP. 73-78)
COLORISTS: **EDGAR DELGADO** (PP. 1-30), **JAVA TARTAGLIA** (PP. 31-40 & 69-72) **MARTE GRACIA** (PP. 41-68) & **MUNTSA VICENTE** (PP. 73-78)
LETTERER: **VC's JOE CARAMAGNA**
COVER ART: **ALEX ROSS**
ASSISTANT EDITOR: **KATHLEEN WISNESKI**
EDITORS: **NICK LOWE** WITH **DEVIN LEWIS**

FRONT COVER ART: **MARK BAGLEY, RANDY EMBERLIN** & **VERONICA GANDINI**
BACK COVER ART: **RAFA GARRES**

SPIDER-MAN CREATED BY **STAN LEE** & **STEVE DITKO**

MARK D. BEAZLEY • ASSISTANT EDITOR: **CAITLIN O'CONNELL** • ASSOCIATE MANAGING EDITOR: **KATERI WOODY**
EDITOR, SPECIAL PROJECTS: **JENNIFER GRÜNWALD** • VP PRODUCTION & SPECIAL PROJECTS: **JEFF YOUNGQUIST**
• PRODUCTION: **JOE FRONTIRRE** • BOOK DESIGNER: **STACIE ZUCKER**

• DIRECTOR, LICENSED PUBLISHING: **SVEN LARSEN**
• PRESIDENT: **DAN BUCKLEY** • EXECUTIVE PRODUCER: **ALAN FINE**

361, #410 and #431; SPIDER-MAN #67; SPECTACULAR SPIDER-MAN #233
ISBN 978-1-302-91964-1. Published by MARVEL WORLDWIDE, INC., a

[redacted]

The Carnage symbiote, Venom's twisted offspring, originally bonded to serial killer Cletus Kasady. The two first encountered one another when the Venom symbiote broke its host Eddie Brock out of jail, in these excerpts from ***Amazing Spider-Man* #344-345**...

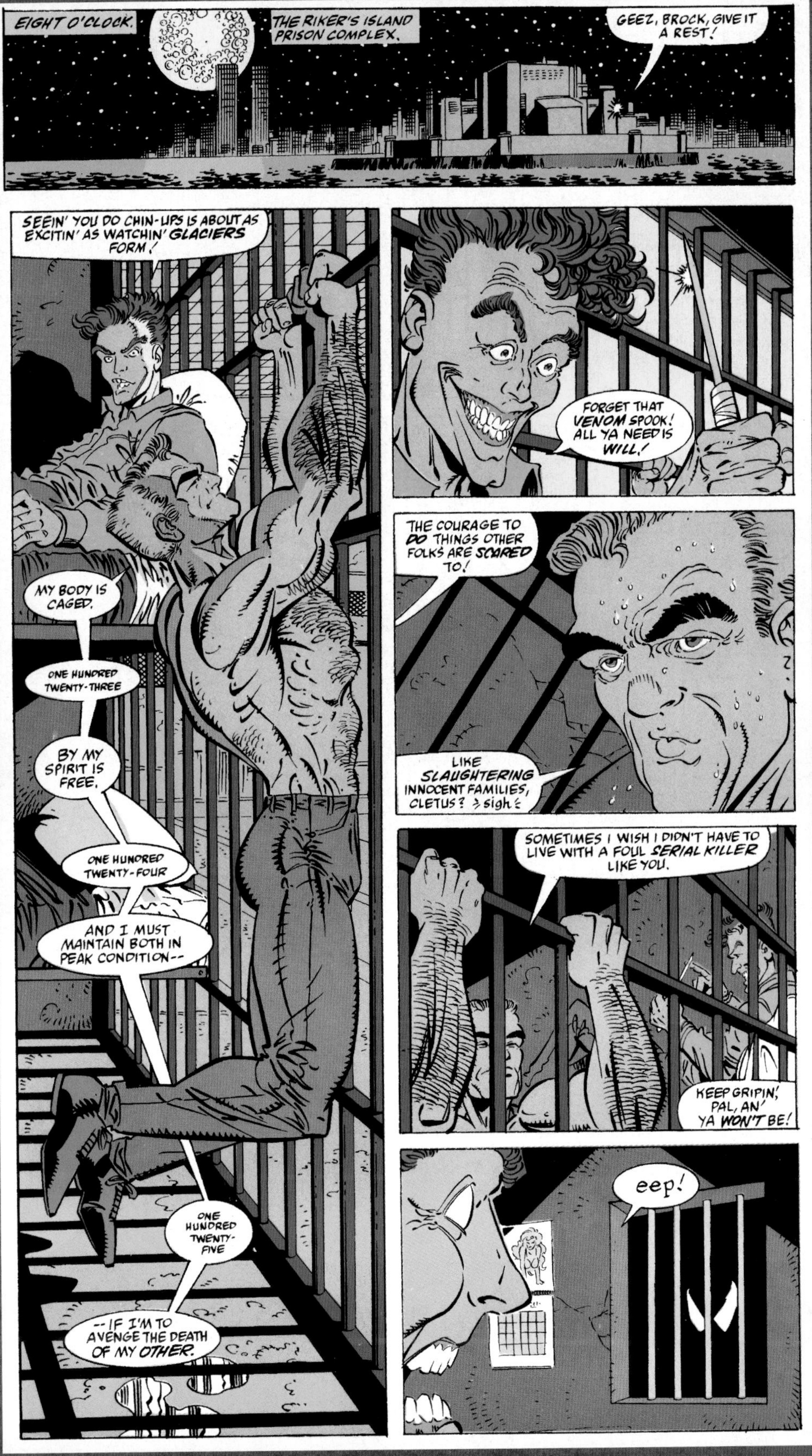
EIGHT O'CLOCK.
THE RIKER'S ISLAND PRISON COMPLEX.
GEEZ, BROCK, GIVE IT A REST!
SEEIN' YOU DO CHIN-UPS IS ABOUT AS EXCITIN' AS WATCHIN' GLACIERS FORM!
MY BODY IS CAGED.
ONE HUNDRED TWENTY-THREE
BY MY SPIRIT IS FREE.
ONE HUNDRED TWENTY-FOUR
AND I MUST MAINTAIN BOTH IN PEAK CONDITION--
ONE HUNDRED TWENTY-FIVE
--IF I'M TO AVENGE THE DEATH OF MY OTHER.
FORGET THAT VENOM SPOOK! ALL YA NEED IS WILL!
THE COURAGE TO DO THINGS OTHER FOLKS ARE SCARED TO!
LIKE SLAUGHTERING INNOCENT FAMILIES, CLETUS? ≷sigh≶
SOMETIMES I WISH I DIDN'T HAVE TO LIVE WITH A FOUL SERIAL KILLER LIKE YOU.
KEEP GRIPIN', PAL, AN' YA WON'T BE!
eep!

WRITER: **DAVID MICHELINIE** • PENCILERS: **ERIK LARSEN** (#344) & **MARK BAGLEY** (#345) • INKER: **RANDY EMBERLIN**
COLORIST: **BOB SHAREN** • LETTERER: **RICK PARKER** • ASSISTANT EDITOR: **DAN CUDDY** • EDITOR: **JIM SALICRUP**

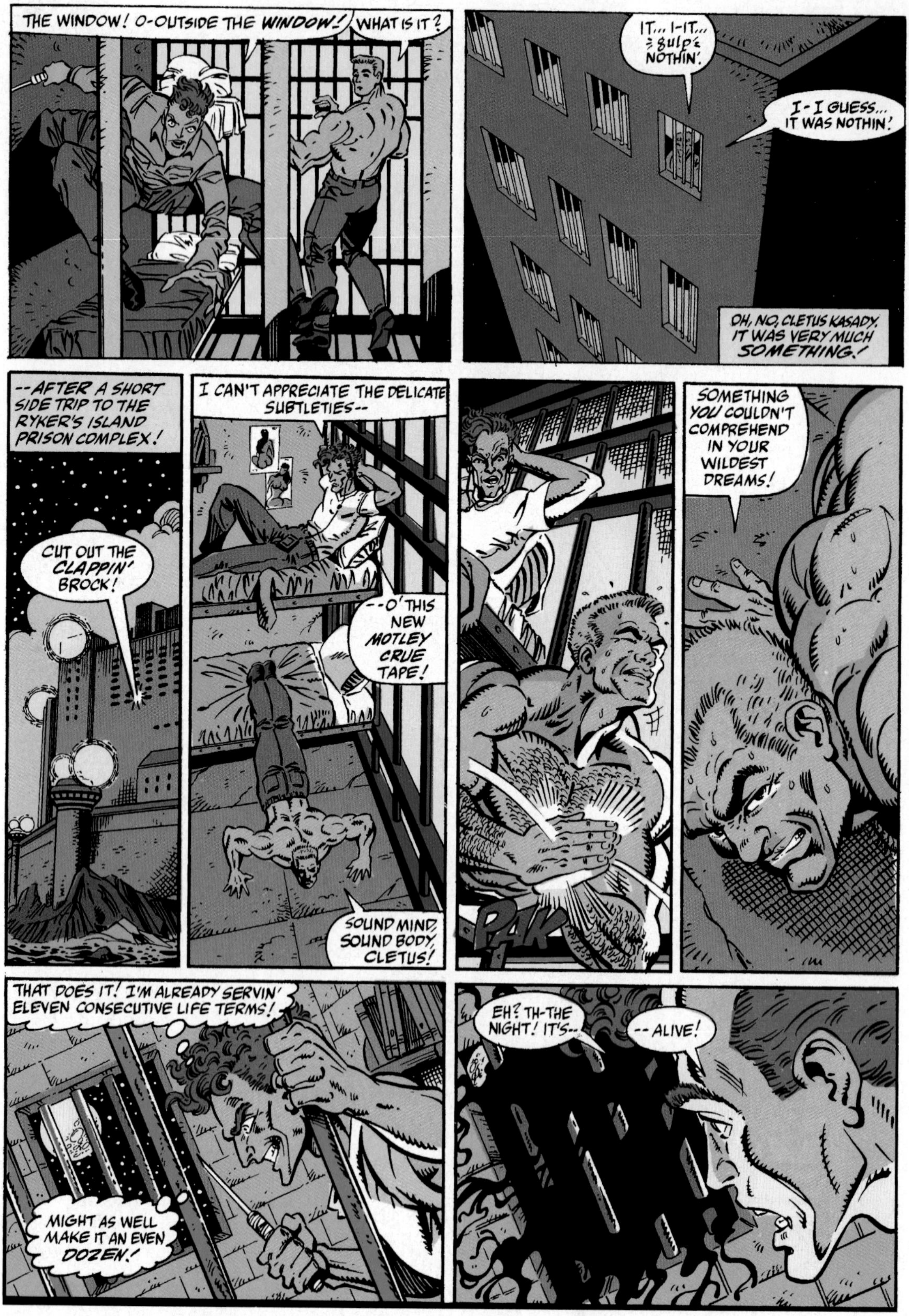
THE WINDOW! O-OUTSIDE THE WINDOW!
WHAT IS IT?
IT... I-IT... gulp NOTHIN'.
I-I GUESS... IT WAS NOTHIN'.
OH, NO, CLETUS KASADY. IT WAS VERY MUCH SOMETHING!
--AFTER A SHORT SIDE TRIP TO THE RYKER'S ISLAND PRISON COMPLEX!
CUT OUT THE CLAPPIN' BROCK!
I CAN'T APPRECIATE THE DELICATE SUBTLETIES--
--O' THIS NEW MOTLEY CRUE TAPE!
SOUND MIND, SOUND BODY, CLETUS!
PAK
SOMETHING YOU COULDN'T COMPREHEND IN YOUR WILDEST DREAMS!
THAT DOES IT! I'M ALREADY SERVIN' ELEVEN CONSECUTIVE LIFE TERMS!
MIGHT AS WELL MAKE IT AN EVEN DOZEN!
EH? TH-THE NIGHT! IT'S--
--ALIVE!

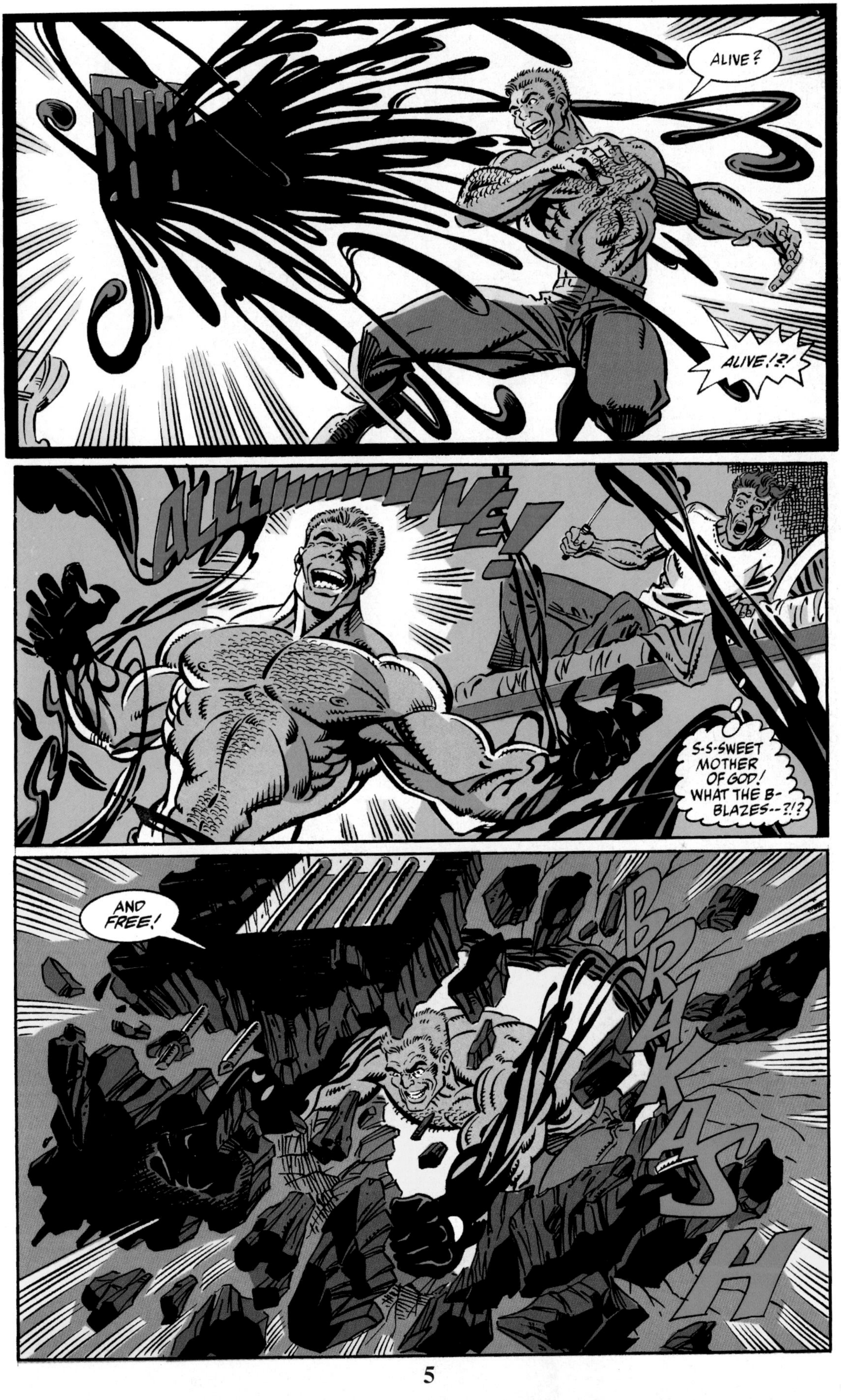
ALIVE?
ALIVE!?!
ALLLIIIIIIIIIVE!
S-S-SWEET MOTHER OF GOD! WHAT THE B-BLAZES--?!?
AND FREE!
K-BRAKASH

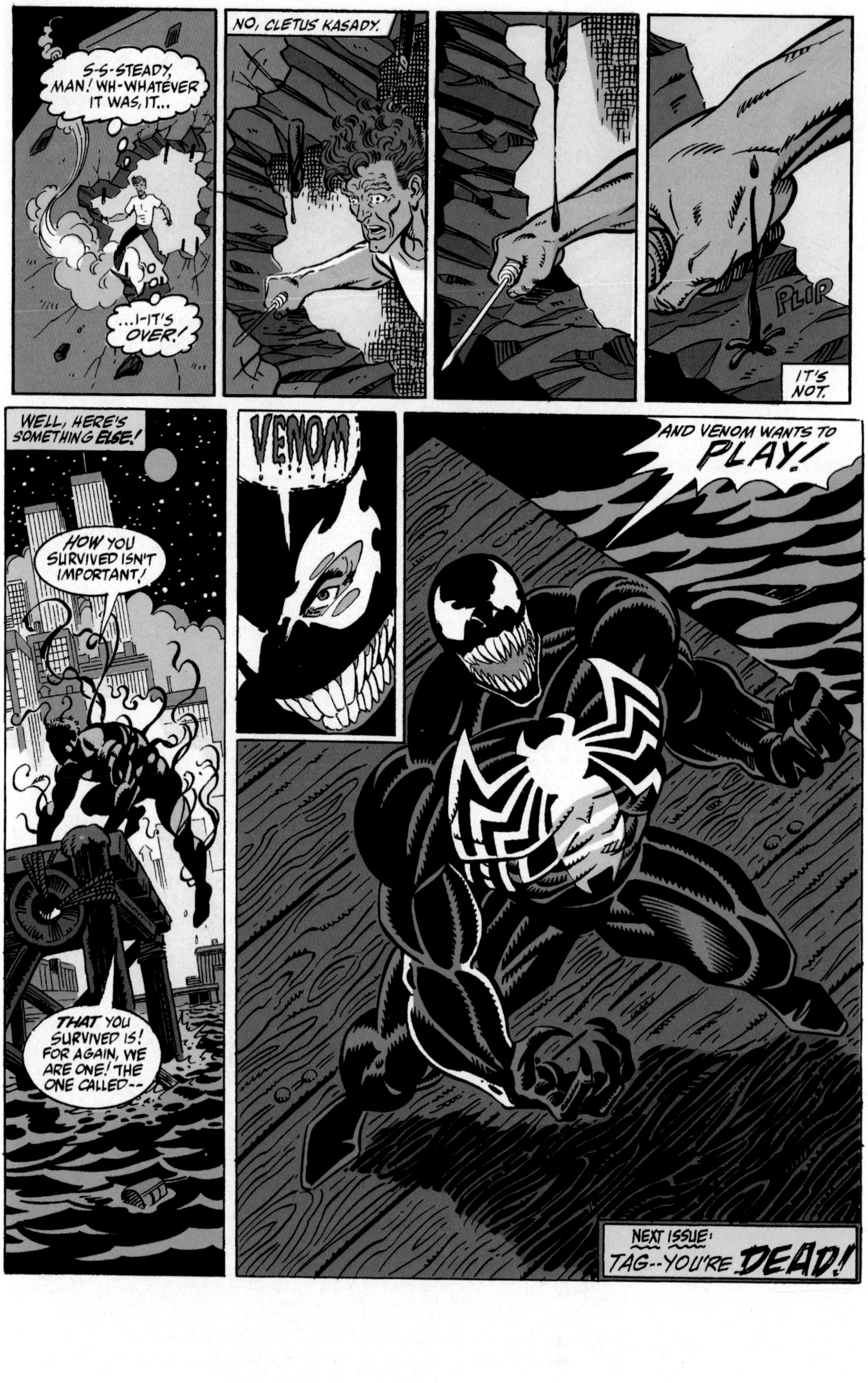
S-S-STEADY, MAN! WH-WHATEVER IT WAS, IT...
...I-IT'S OVER!
NO, CLETUS KASADY.
PLIP
IT'S NOT.
WELL, HERE'S SOMETHING ELSE!
HOW YOU SURVIVED ISN'T IMPORTANT!
THAT YOU SURVIVED IS! FOR AGAIN, WE ARE ONE! THE ONE CALLED--
VENOM
AND VENOM WANTS TO PLAY!
NEXT ISSUE:
TAG--YOU'RE DEAD!

Excerpts from Amazing Spider-Man #359-360

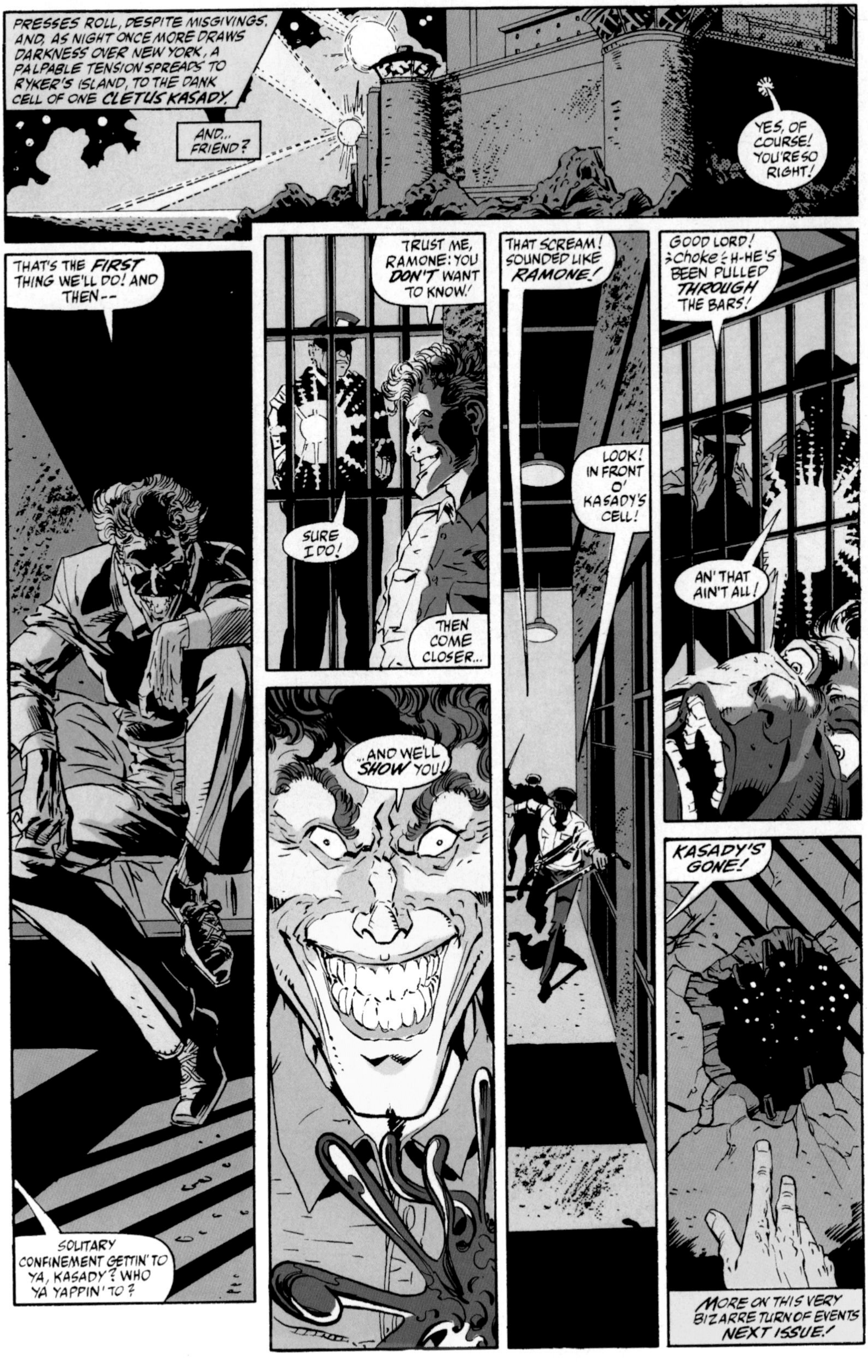

PRESSES ROLL, DESPITE MISGIVINGS. AND, AS NIGHT ONCE MORE DRAWS DARKNESS OVER NEW YORK, A PALPABLE TENSION SPREADS TO RYKER'S ISLAND, TO THE DANK CELL OF ONE CLETUS KASADY.
AND... FRIEND?
YES, OF COURSE! YOU'RE SO RIGHT!
THAT'S THE FIRST THING WE'LL DO! AND THEN--
SOLITARY CONFINEMENT GETTIN' TO YA, KASADY? WHO YA YAPPIN' TO?
TRUST ME, RAMONE: YOU DON'T WANT TO KNOW!
SURE I DO!
THEN COME CLOSER...
...AND WE'LL SHOW YOU!
THAT SCREAM! SOUNDED LIKE RAMONE!
LOOK! IN FRONT O' KASADY'S CELL!
GOOD LORD! :CHOKE: H-HE'S BEEN PULLED THROUGH THE BARS!
AN' THAT AIN'T ALL!
KASADY'S GONE!
MORE ON THIS VERY BIZARRE TURN OF EVENTS NEXT ISSUE!

WRITER: **DAVID MICHELINIE** • PENCILER: **CHRIS MARRINAN** • INKER: **KEITH WILLIAMS**
COLORIST: **BOB SHAREN** • LETTERER: **RICK PARKER** • ASSISTANT EDITOR: **ERIC FEIN** • EDITOR: **DANNY FINGEROTH**

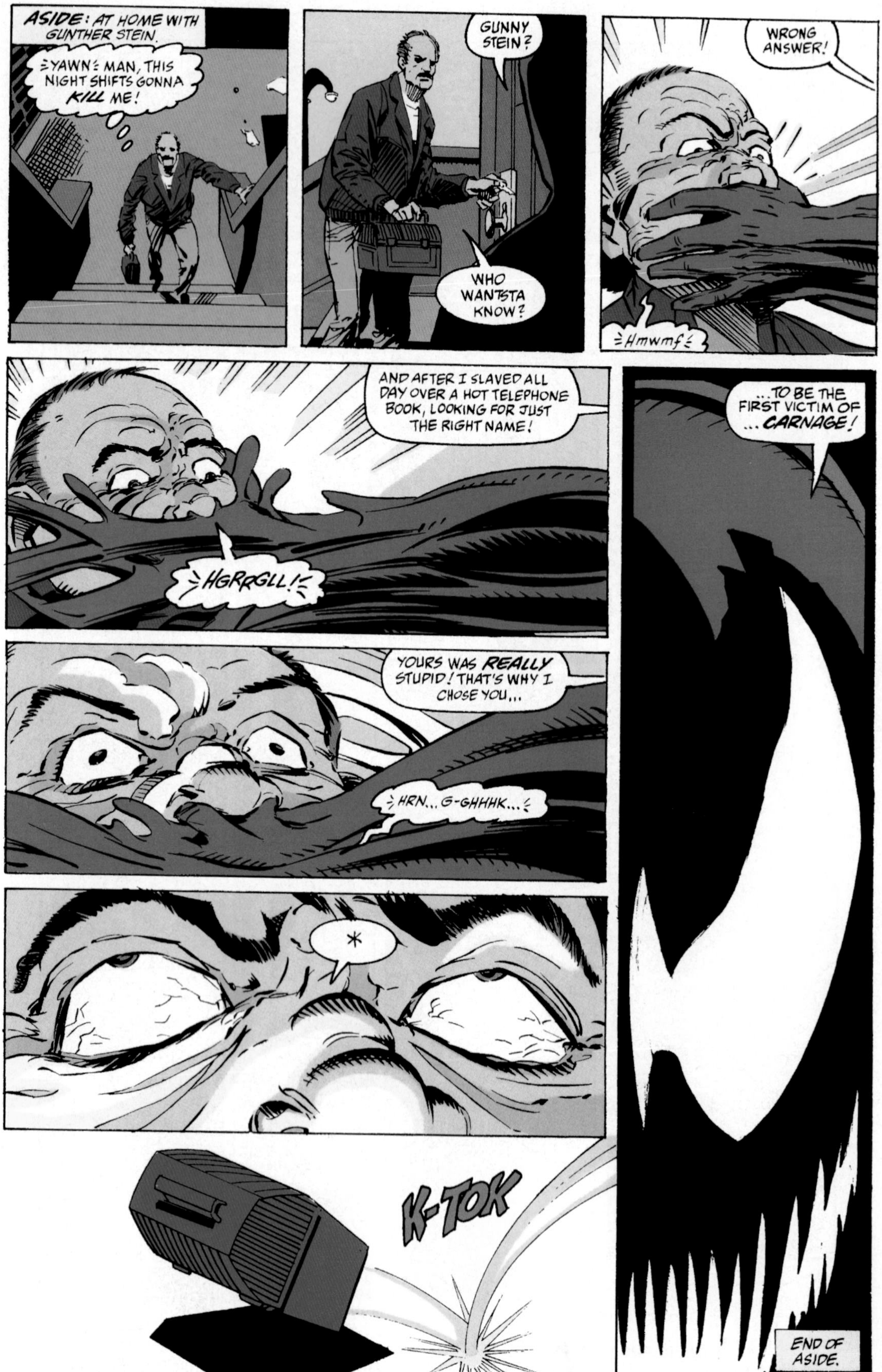
ASIDE: AT HOME WITH GUNTHER STEIN.
YAWN MAN, THIS NIGHT SHIFTS GONNA KILL ME!
GUNNY STEIN?
WHO WANTSTA KNOW?
WRONG ANSWER!
Hmwmf
AND AFTER I SLAVED ALL DAY OVER A HOT TELEPHONE BOOK, LOOKING FOR JUST THE RIGHT NAME!
HGRRGLL!
YOURS WAS REALLY STUPID! THAT'S WHY I CHOSE YOU...
HRN... G-GHHHK...
...TO BE THE FIRST VICTIM OF ...CARNAGE!
*
K-TOK
END OF ASIDE.

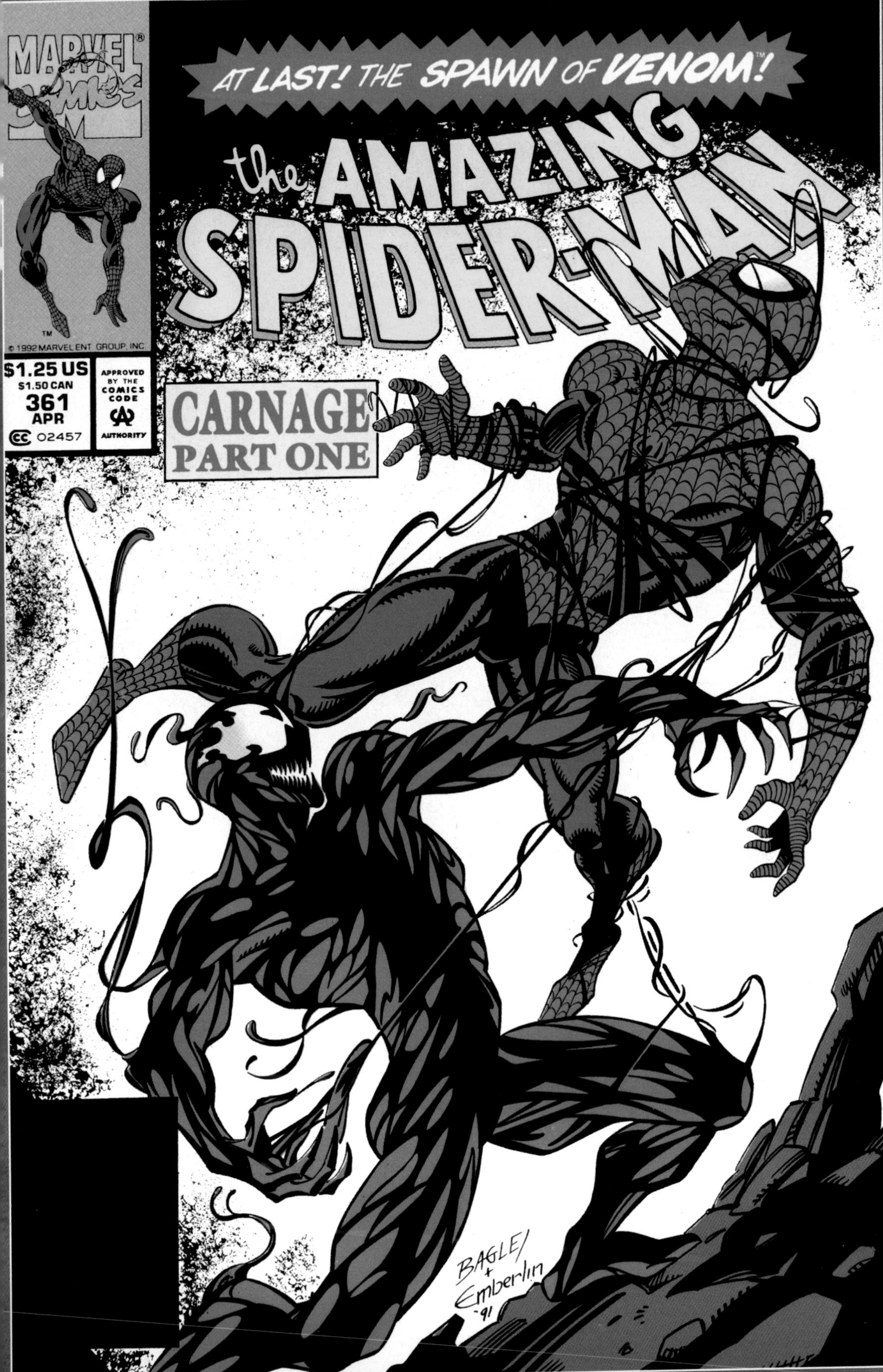
MARVEL COMICS
AT LAST! THE SPAWN OF VENOM!
the AMAZING SPIDER-MAN
© 1992 MARVEL ENT. GROUP, INC.
$1.25 US
$1.50 CAN
361
APR
02457
APPROVED BY THE COMICS CODE AUTHORITY
CARNAGE
PART ONE
BAGLEY + Emberlin '91

BITTEN BY A RADIOACTIVE SPIDER, STUDENT **PETER PARKER** GAINED THE PROPORTIONATE STRENGTH AND AGILITY OF AN ARACHNID! ARMED WITH HIS WONDROUS WEB-SHOOTERS, THE RELUCTANT SUPER HERO STRUGGLES WITH SINISTER SUPER-VILLAINS, MAKING ENDS MEET, AND MAINTAINING SOME SEMBLANCE OF A NORMAL LIFE!

Stan Lee PRESENTS: THE AMAZING SPIDER-MAN®

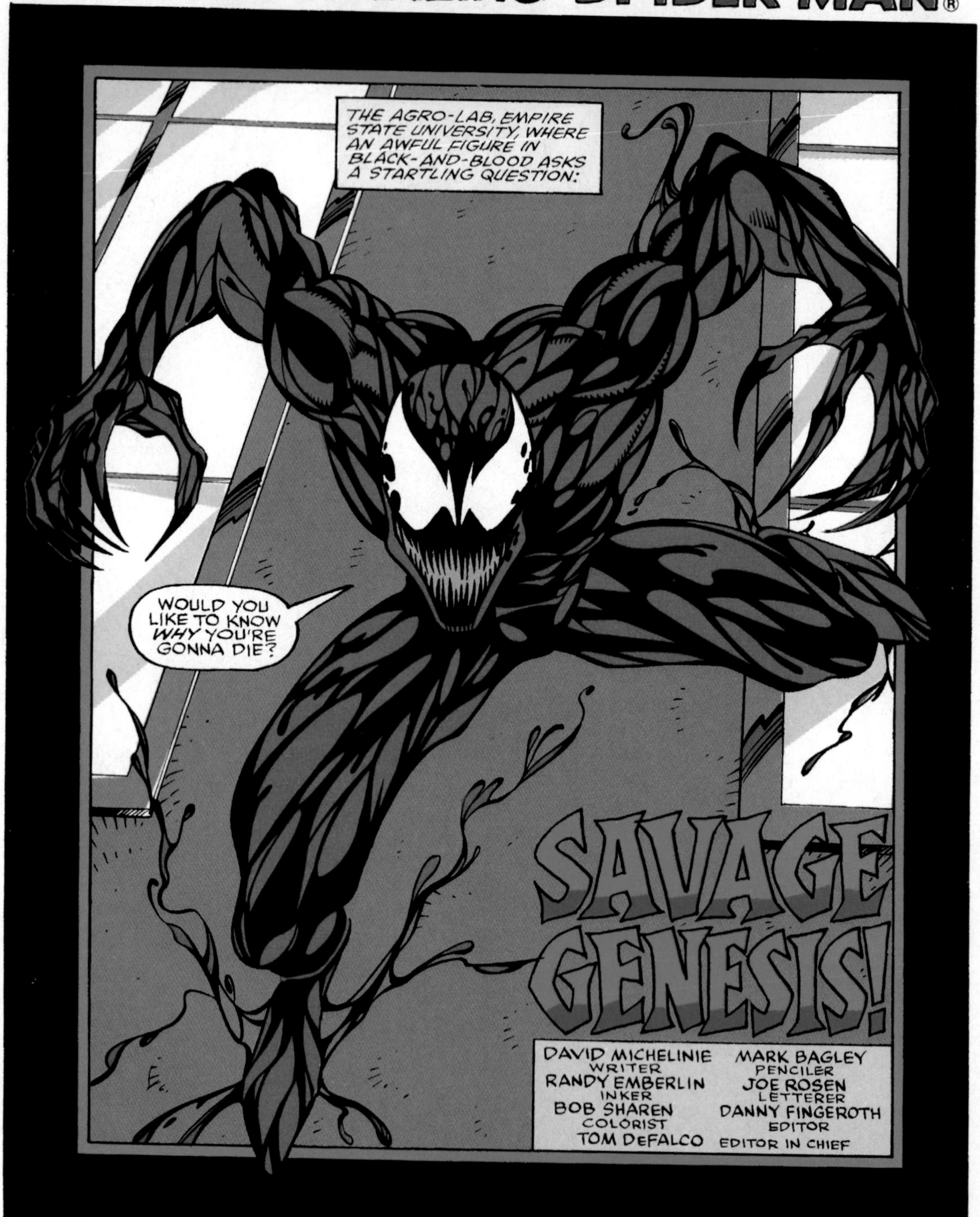
THE AGRO-LAB, EMPIRE STATE UNIVERSITY, WHERE AN AWFUL FIGURE IN BLACK-AND-BLOOD ASKS A STARTLING QUESTION:
WOULD YOU LIKE TO KNOW *WHY* YOU'RE GONNA DIE?
SAVAGE GENESIS!
DAVID MICHELINIE WRITER
MARK BAGLEY PENCILER
RANDY EMBERLIN INKER
JOE ROSEN LETTERER
BOB SHAREN COLORIST
DANNY FINGEROTH EDITOR
TOM DeFALCO EDITOR IN CHIEF

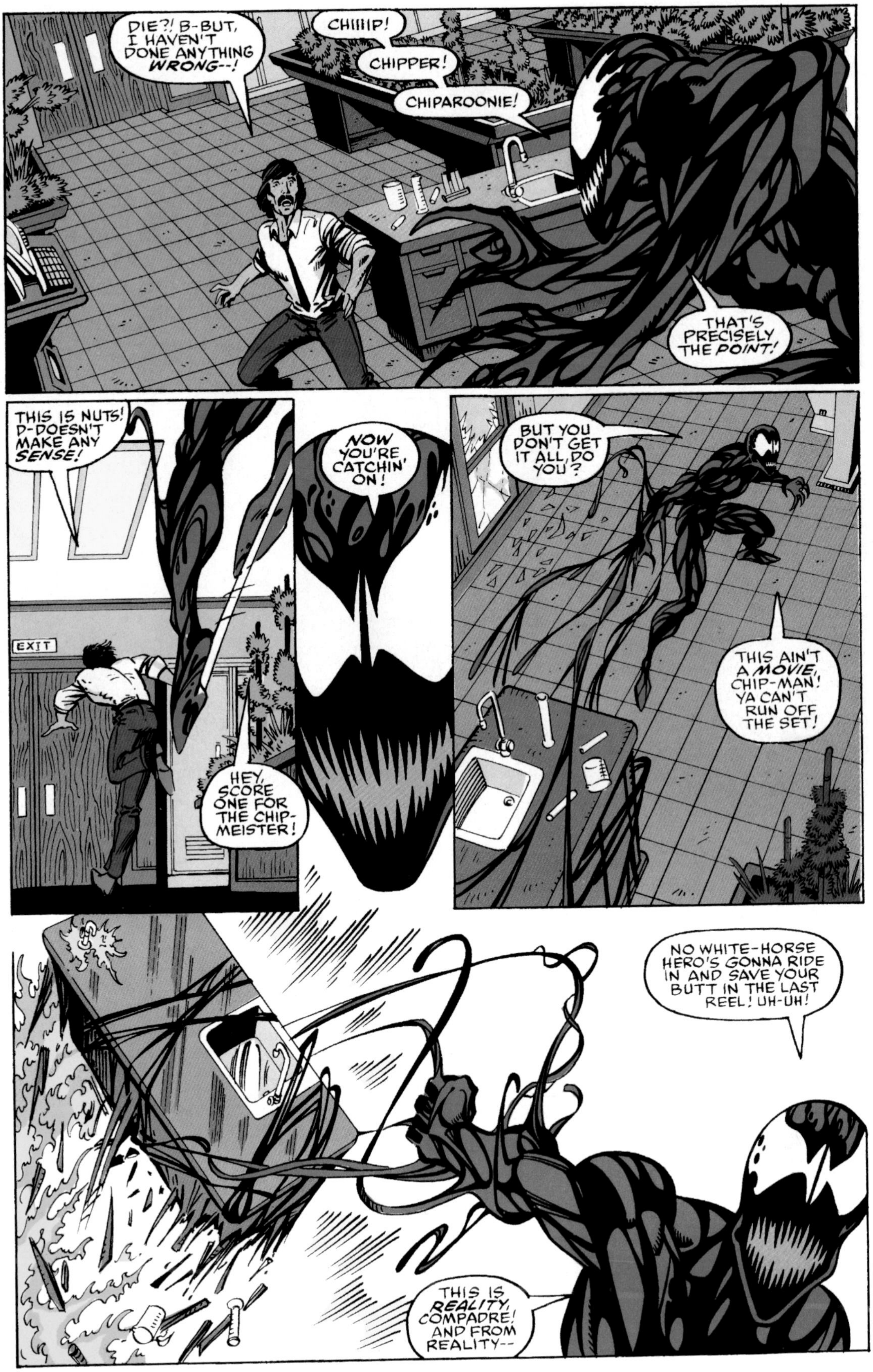
DIE?! B-BUT, I HAVEN'T DONE ANYTHING WRONG--!
CHIIIP!
CHIPPER!
CHIPAROONIE!
THAT'S PRECISELY THE POINT!
THIS IS NUTS! D-DOESN'T MAKE ANY SENSE!
NOW YOU'RE CATCHIN' ON!
HEY, SCORE ONE FOR THE CHIP-MEISTER!
EXIT
BUT YOU DON'T GET IT ALL, DO YOU?
THIS AIN'T A MOVIE, CHIP-MAN! YA CAN'T RUN OFF THE SET!
NO WHITE-HORSE HERO'S GONNA RIDE IN AND SAVE YOUR BUTT IN THE LAST REEL! UH-UH!
THIS IS REALITY, COMPADRE! AND FROM REALITY--

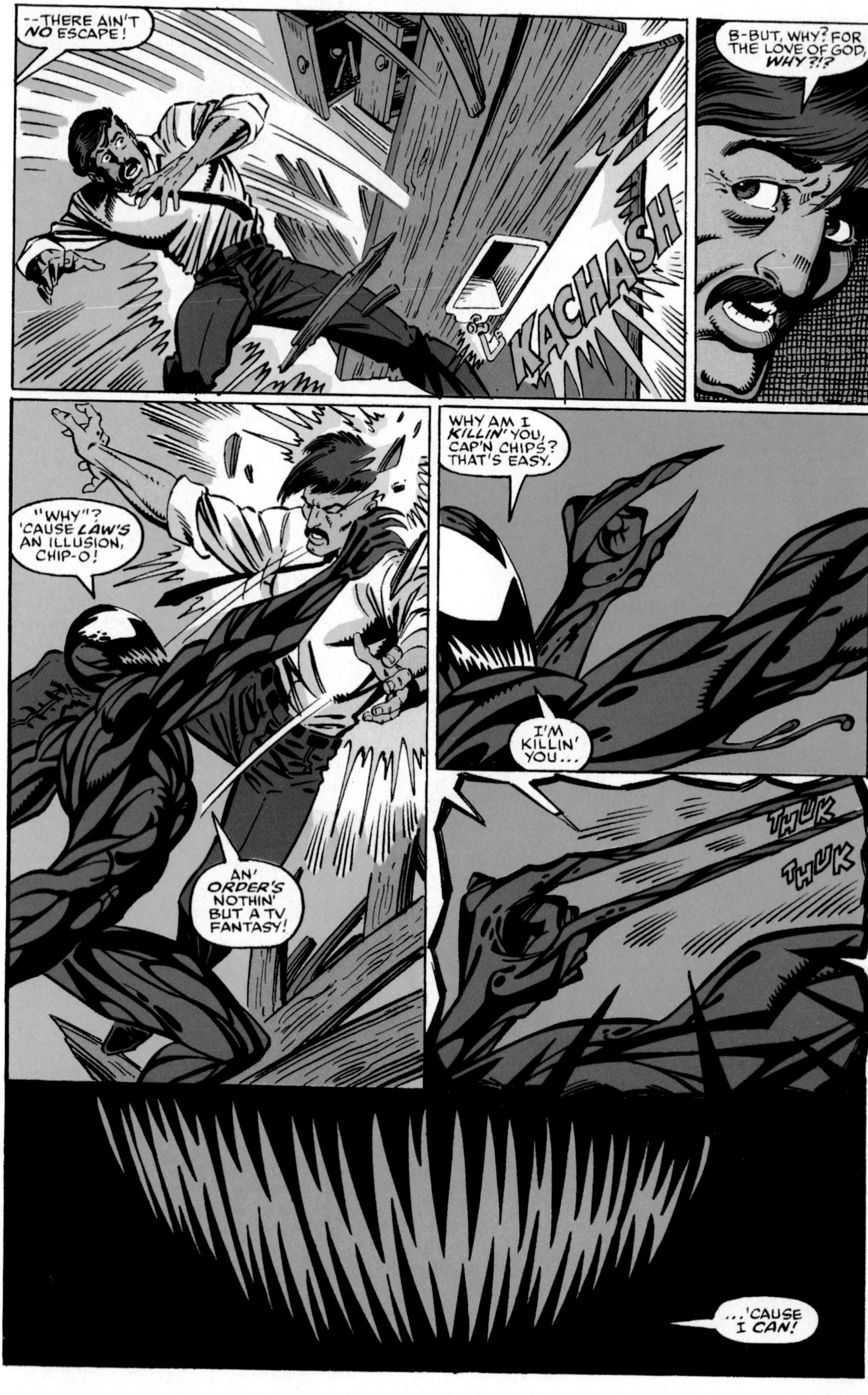
--THERE AIN'T NO ESCAPE!
KACHASH
B-BUT, WHY? FOR THE LOVE OF GOD, WHY?!?
"WHY"? 'CAUSE LAW'S AN ILLUSION, CHIP-O!
AN' ORDER'S NOTHIN' BUT A TV FANTASY!
WHY AM I KILLIN' YOU, CAP'N CHIPS? THAT'S EASY.
I'M KILLIN' YOU...
THUK
THUK
...'CAUSE I CAN!

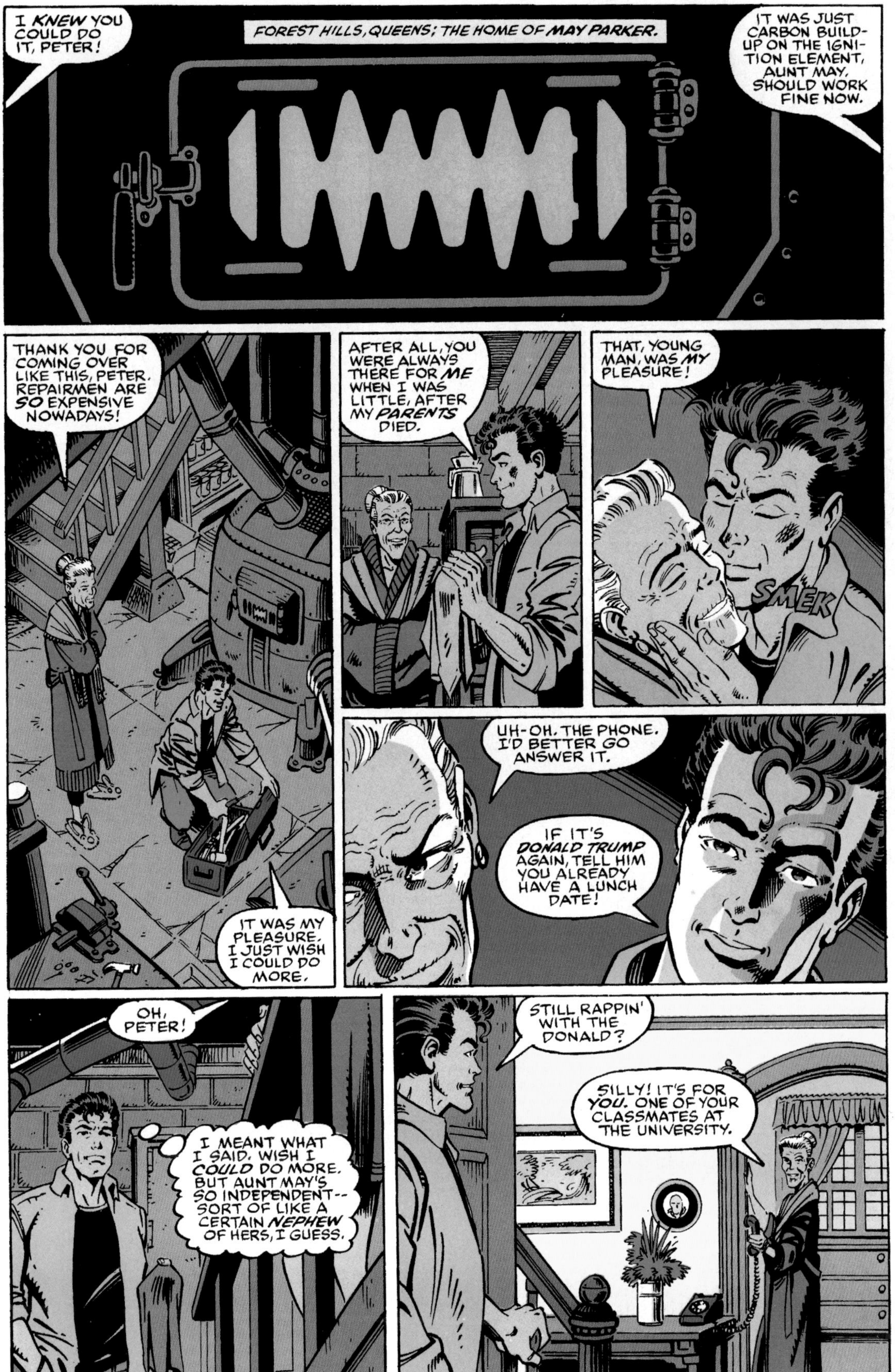
FOREST HILLS, QUEENS; THE HOME OF MAY PARKER.
I KNEW YOU COULD DO IT, PETER!
IT WAS JUST CARBON BUILD-UP ON THE IGNITION ELEMENT, AUNT MAY. SHOULD WORK FINE NOW.
THANK YOU FOR COMING OVER LIKE THIS, PETER. REPAIRMEN ARE SO EXPENSIVE NOWADAYS!
IT WAS MY PLEASURE. I JUST WISH I COULD DO MORE.
AFTER ALL, YOU WERE ALWAYS THERE FOR ME WHEN I WAS LITTLE, AFTER MY PARENTS DIED.
THAT, YOUNG MAN, WAS MY PLEASURE!
SMEK
UH-OH. THE PHONE. I'D BETTER GO ANSWER IT.
IF IT'S DONALD TRUMP AGAIN, TELL HIM YOU ALREADY HAVE A LUNCH DATE!
OH, PETER!
I MEANT WHAT I SAID. WISH I COULD DO MORE. BUT AUNT MAY'S SO INDEPENDENT-- SORT OF LIKE A CERTAIN NEPHEW OF HERS, I GUESS.
STILL RAPPIN' WITH THE DONALD?
SILLY! IT'S FOR YOU. ONE OF YOUR CLASSMATES AT THE UNIVERSITY.

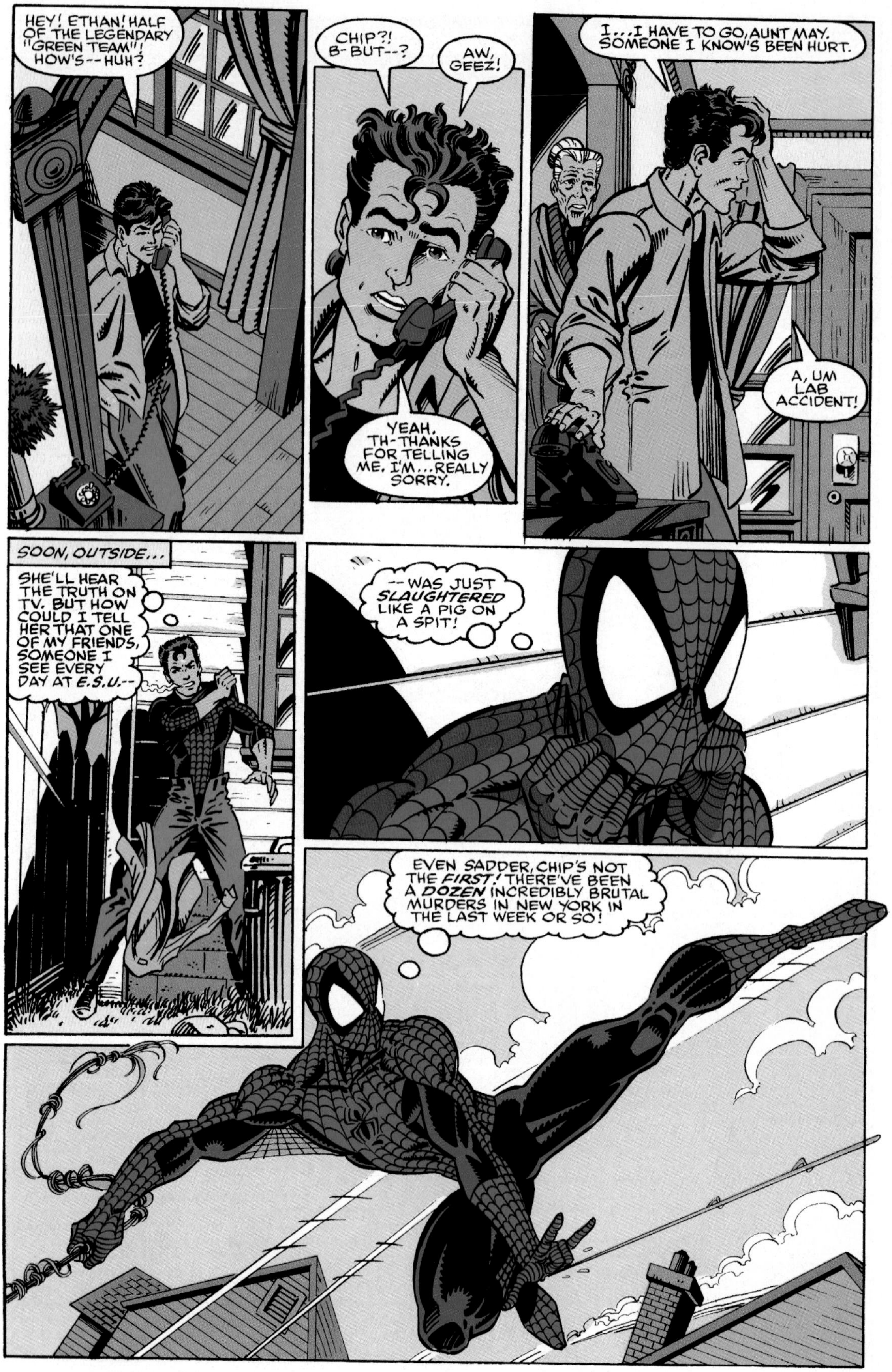
HEY! ETHAN! HALF OF THE LEGENDARY "GREEN TEAM"! HOW'S--HUH?
CHIP?! B-BUT--?
AW, GEEZ!
YEAH. TH-THANKS FOR TELLING ME. I'M...REALLY SORRY.
I...I HAVE TO GO, AUNT MAY. SOMEONE I KNOW'S BEEN HURT.
A, UM LAB ACCIDENT!
SOON, OUTSIDE...
SHE'LL HEAR THE TRUTH ON TV. BUT HOW COULD I TELL HER THAT ONE OF MY FRIENDS, SOMEONE I SEE EVERY DAY AT E.S.U.--
--WAS JUST SLAUGHTERED LIKE A PIG ON A SPIT!
EVEN SADDER, CHIP'S NOT THE FIRST! THERE'VE BEEN A DOZEN INCREDIBLY BRUTAL MURDERS IN NEW YORK IN THE LAST WEEK OR SO!

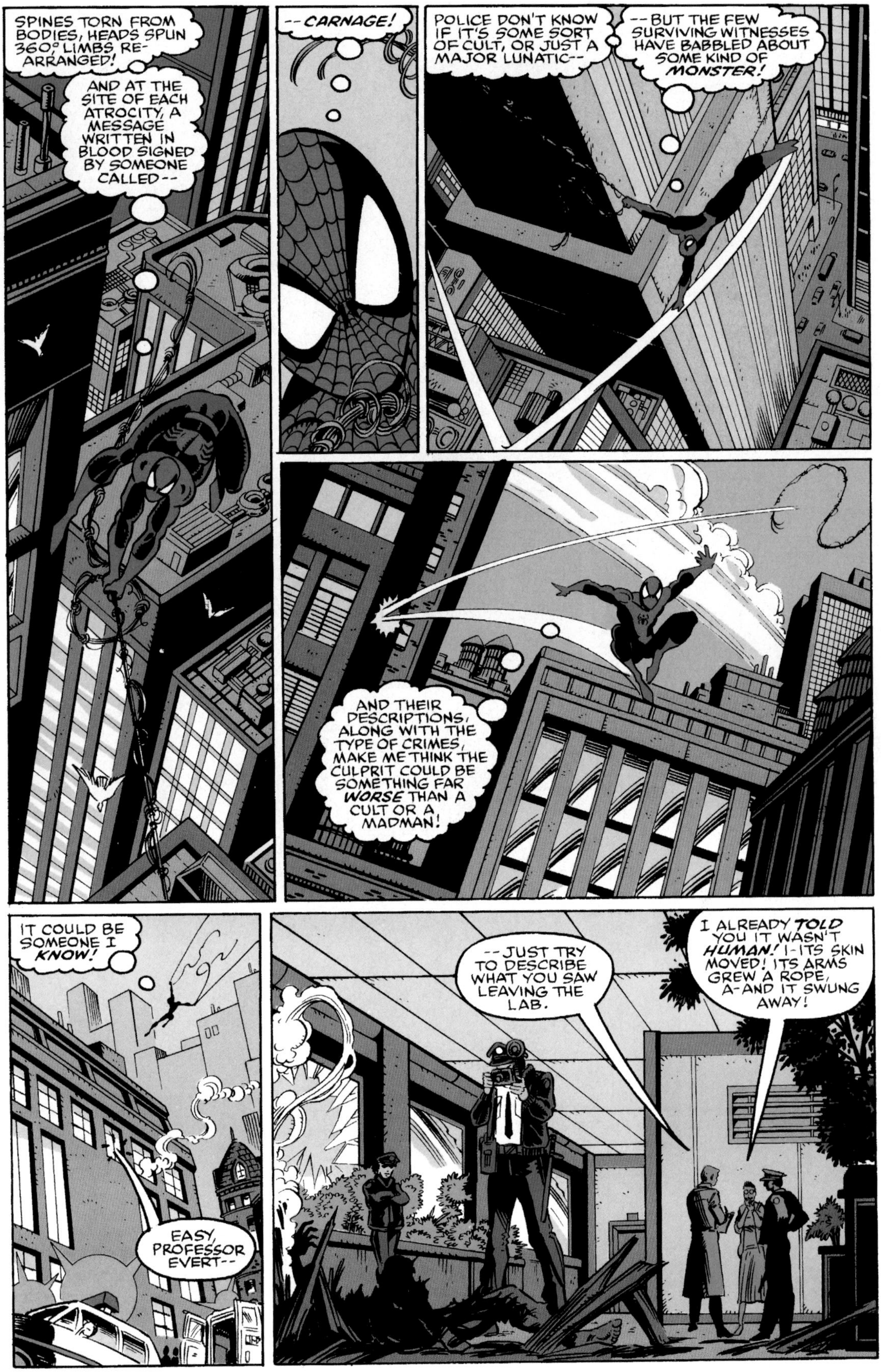

SPINES TORN FROM BODIES, HEADS SPUN 360°, LIMBS RE-ARRANGED!
AND AT THE SITE OF EACH ATROCITY, A MESSAGE WRITTEN IN BLOOD SIGNED BY SOMEONE CALLED--
--CARNAGE!
POLICE DON'T KNOW IF IT'S SOME SORT OF CULT, OR JUST A MAJOR LUNATIC--
--BUT THE FEW SURVIVING WITNESSES HAVE BABBLED ABOUT SOME KIND OF MONSTER!
AND THEIR DESCRIPTIONS, ALONG WITH THE TYPE OF CRIMES, MAKE ME THINK THE CULPRIT COULD BE SOMETHING FAR WORSE THAN A CULT OR A MADMAN!
IT COULD BE SOMEONE I KNOW!
EASY, PROFESSOR EVERT--
--JUST TRY TO DESCRIBE WHAT YOU SAW LEAVING THE LAB.
I ALREADY TOLD YOU IT WASN'T HUMAN! I-ITS SKIN MOVED! ITS ARMS GREW A ROPE, A-AND IT SWUNG AWAY!

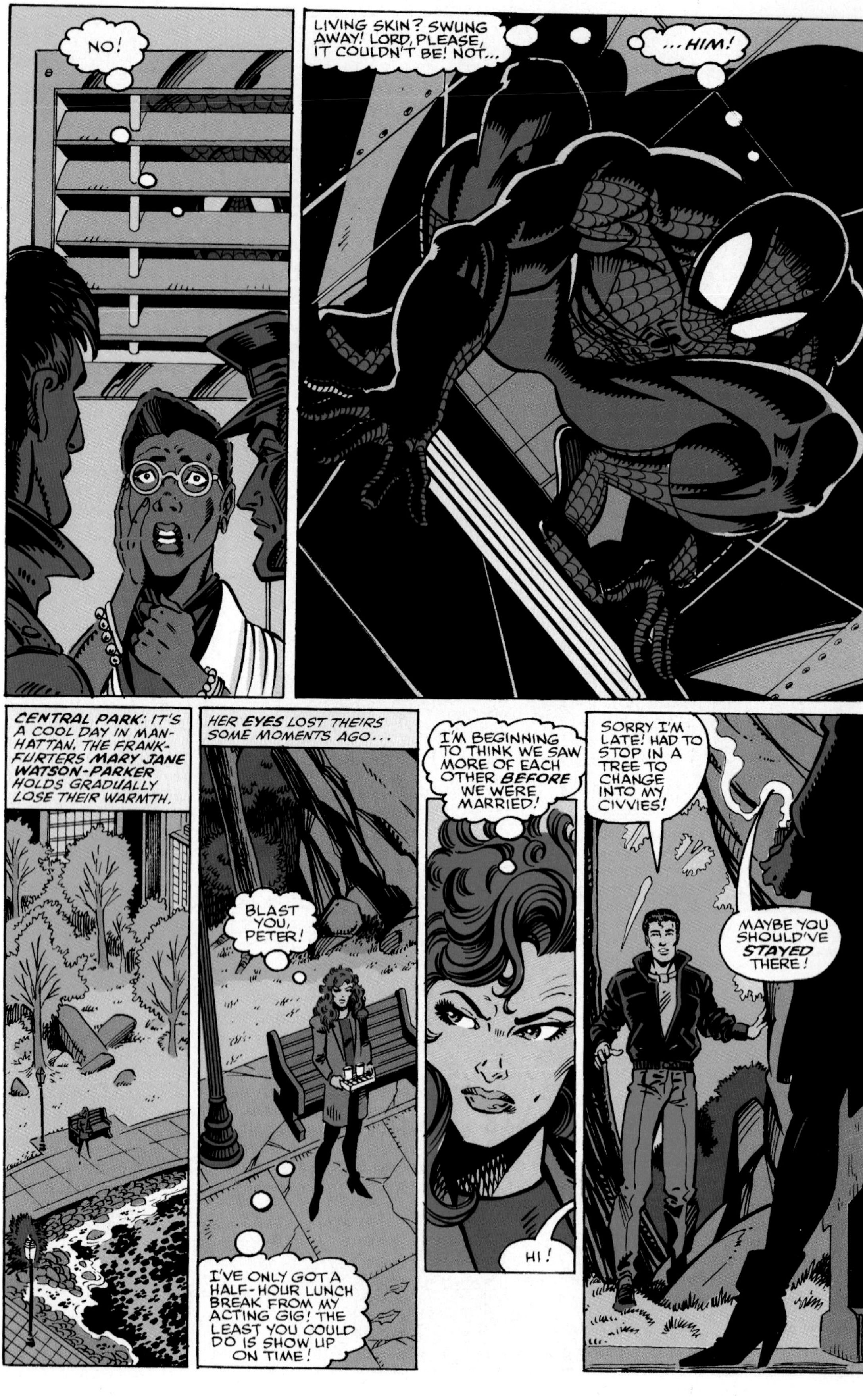
NO!
LIVING SKIN? SWUNG AWAY! LORD, PLEASE, IT COULDN'T BE! NOT...
...HIM!
CENTRAL PARK: IT'S A COOL DAY IN MANHATTAN. THE FRANKFURTERS MARY JANE WATSON-PARKER HOLDS GRADUALLY LOSE THEIR WARMTH.
HER EYES LOST THEIRS SOME MOMENTS AGO...
BLAST YOU, PETER!
I'VE ONLY GOT A HALF-HOUR LUNCH BREAK FROM MY ACTING GIG! THE LEAST YOU COULD DO IS SHOW UP ON TIME!
I'M BEGINNING TO THINK WE SAW MORE OF EACH OTHER BEFORE WE WERE MARRIED!
HI!
SORRY I'M LATE! HAD TO STOP IN A TREE TO CHANGE INTO MY CIVVIES!
MAYBE YOU SHOULD'VE STAYED THERE!

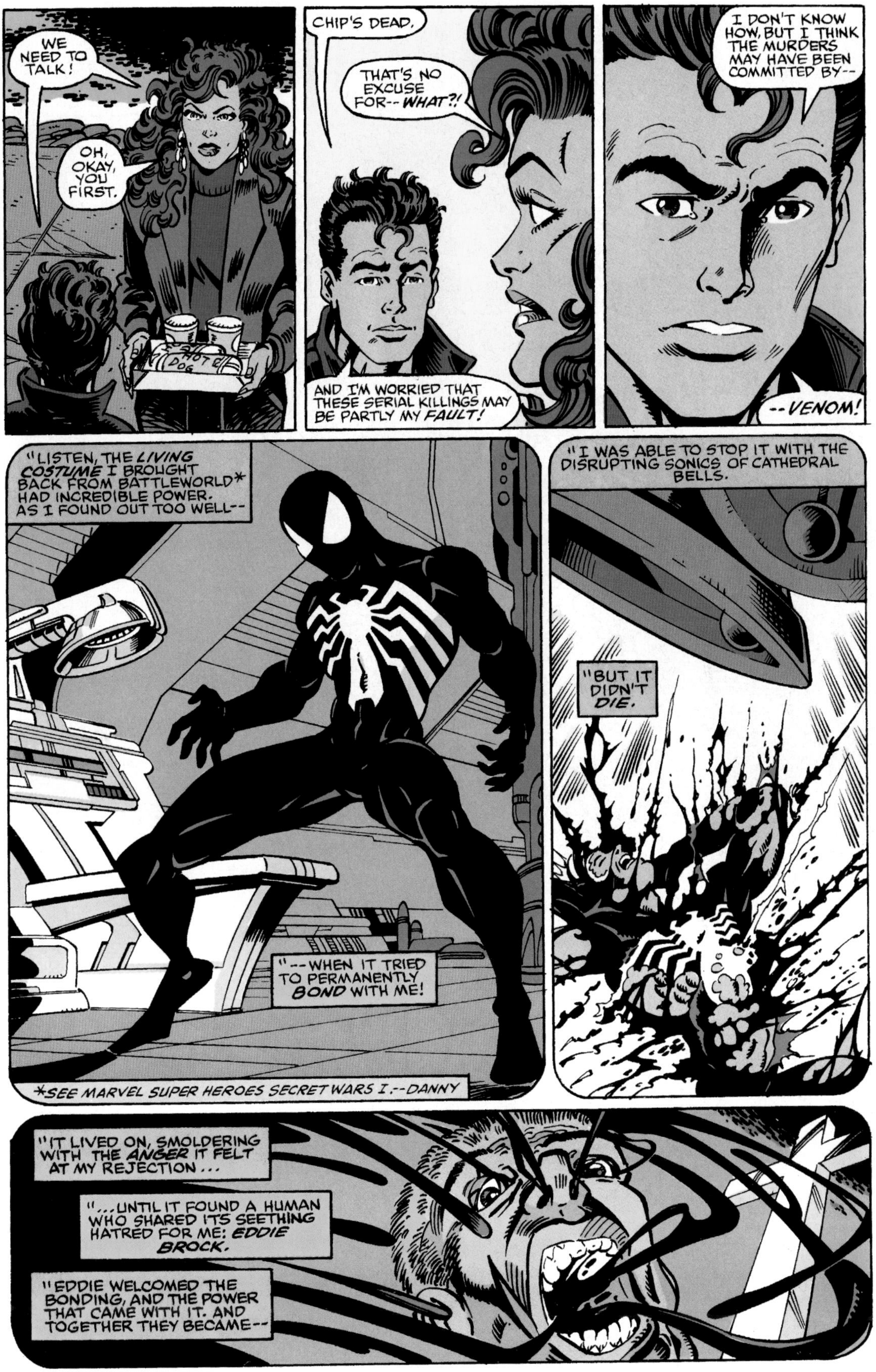

WE NEED TO TALK!
OH, OKAY, YOU FIRST.
HOT DOG
CHIP'S DEAD.
THAT'S NO EXCUSE FOR-- WHAT?!
AND I'M WORRIED THAT THESE SERIAL KILLINGS MAY BE PARTLY MY FAULT!
I DON'T KNOW HOW, BUT I THINK THE MURDERS MAY HAVE BEEN COMMITTED BY--
--VENOM!
"LISTEN, THE LIVING COSTUME I BROUGHT BACK FROM BATTLEWORLD* HAD INCREDIBLE POWER. AS I FOUND OUT TOO WELL--
"--WHEN IT TRIED TO PERMANENTLY BOND WITH ME!
*SEE MARVEL SUPER HEROES SECRET WARS I.--DANNY
"I WAS ABLE TO STOP IT WITH THE DISRUPTING SONICS OF CATHEDRAL BELLS.
"BUT IT DIDN'T DIE.
"IT LIVED ON, SMOLDERING WITH THE ANGER IT FELT AT MY REJECTION...
"...UNTIL IT FOUND A HUMAN WHO SHARED ITS SEETHING HATRED FOR ME: EDDIE BROCK.
"EDDIE WELCOMED THE BONDING, AND THE POWER THAT CAME WITH IT. AND TOGETHER THEY BECAME--

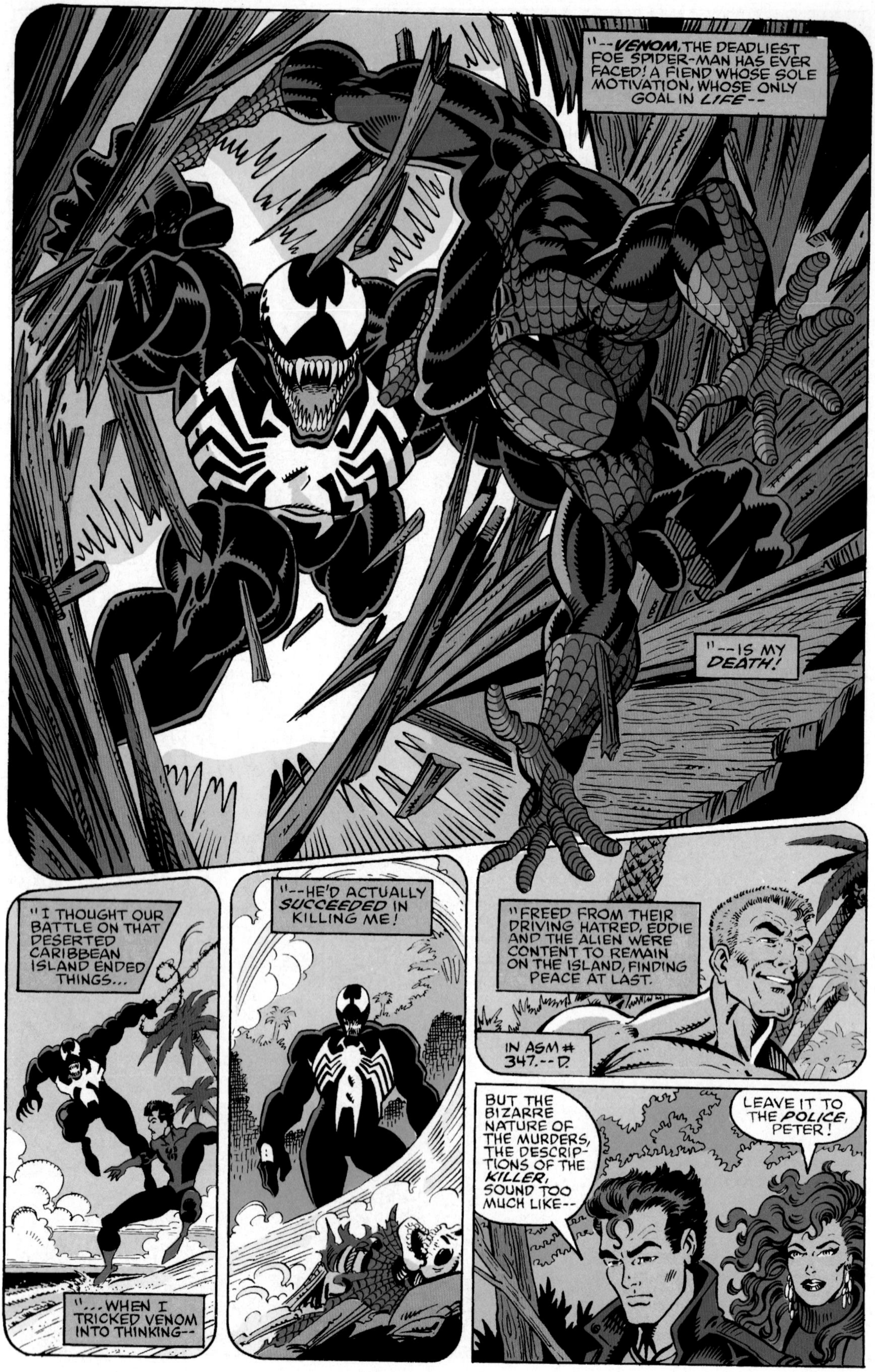
"--*VENOM*, THE DEADLIEST FOE SPIDER-MAN HAS EVER FACED! A FIEND WHOSE SOLE MOTIVATION, WHOSE ONLY GOAL IN *LIFE*--
"--IS MY *DEATH!*
"I THOUGHT OUR BATTLE ON THAT DESERTED CARIBBEAN ISLAND ENDED THINGS...
"...WHEN I TRICKED VENOM INTO THINKING--
"--HE'D ACTUALLY *SUCCEEDED* IN KILLING ME!
"FREED FROM THEIR DRIVING HATRED, EDDIE AND THE ALIEN WERE CONTENT TO REMAIN ON THE ISLAND, FINDING PEACE AT LAST.
IN ASM # 347.--D.
BUT THE BIZARRE NATURE OF THE MURDERS, THE DESCRIPTIONS OF THE *KILLER*, SOUND TOO MUCH LIKE--
LEAVE IT TO THE *POLICE*, PETER!

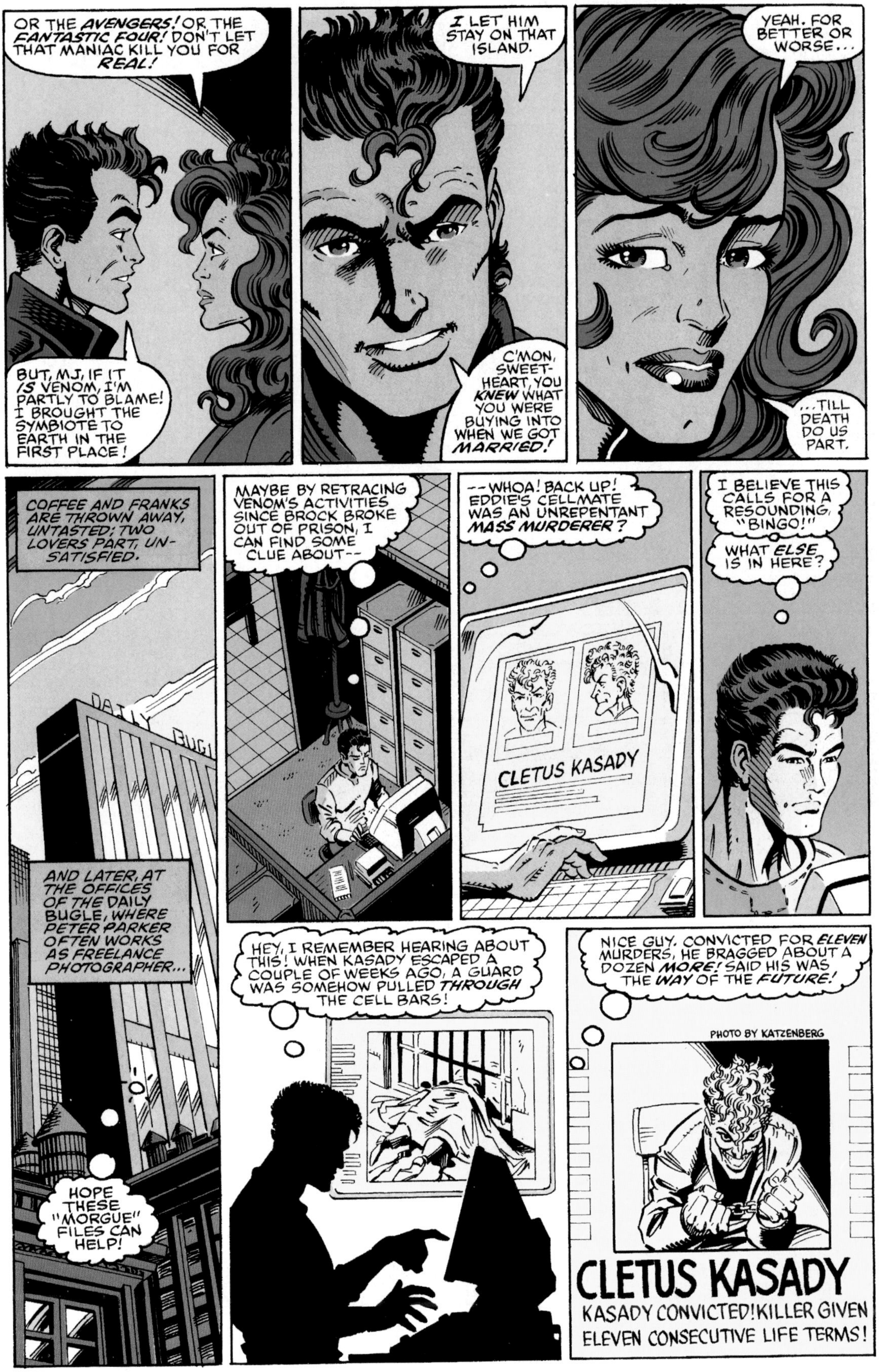
OR THE AVENGERS! OR THE FANTASTIC FOUR! DON'T LET THAT MANIAC KILL YOU FOR REAL!
BUT, MJ, IF IT IS VENOM, I'M PARTLY TO BLAME! I BROUGHT THE SYMBIOTE TO EARTH IN THE FIRST PLACE!
I LET HIM STAY ON THAT ISLAND.
C'MON, SWEET-HEART, YOU KNEW WHAT YOU WERE BUYING INTO WHEN WE GOT MARRIED!
YEAH. FOR BETTER OR WORSE...
...TILL DEATH DO US PART.
COFFEE AND FRANKS ARE THROWN AWAY, UNTASTED; TWO LOVERS PART, UN-SATISFIED.
AND LATER, AT THE OFFICES OF THE DAILY BUGLE, WHERE PETER PARKER OFTEN WORKS AS FREELANCE PHOTOGRAPHER...
HOPE THESE "MORGUE" FILES CAN HELP!
MAYBE BY RETRACING VENOM'S ACTIVITIES SINCE BROCK BROKE OUT OF PRISON, I CAN FIND SOME CLUE ABOUT--
--WHOA! BACK UP! EDDIE'S CELLMATE WAS AN UNREPENTANT MASS MURDERER?
CLETUS KASADY
I BELIEVE THIS CALLS FOR A RESOUNDING, "BINGO!"
WHAT ELSE IS IN HERE?
HEY, I REMEMBER HEARING ABOUT THIS! WHEN KASADY ESCAPED A COUPLE OF WEEKS AGO, A GUARD WAS SOMEHOW PULLED THROUGH THE CELL BARS!
NICE GUY. CONVICTED FOR ELEVEN MURDERS, HE BRAGGED ABOUT A DOZEN MORE! SAID HIS WAS THE WAY OF THE FUTURE!
PHOTO BY KATZENBERG
CLETUS KASADY
KASADY CONVICTED! KILLER GIVEN ELEVEN CONSECUTIVE LIFE TERMS!

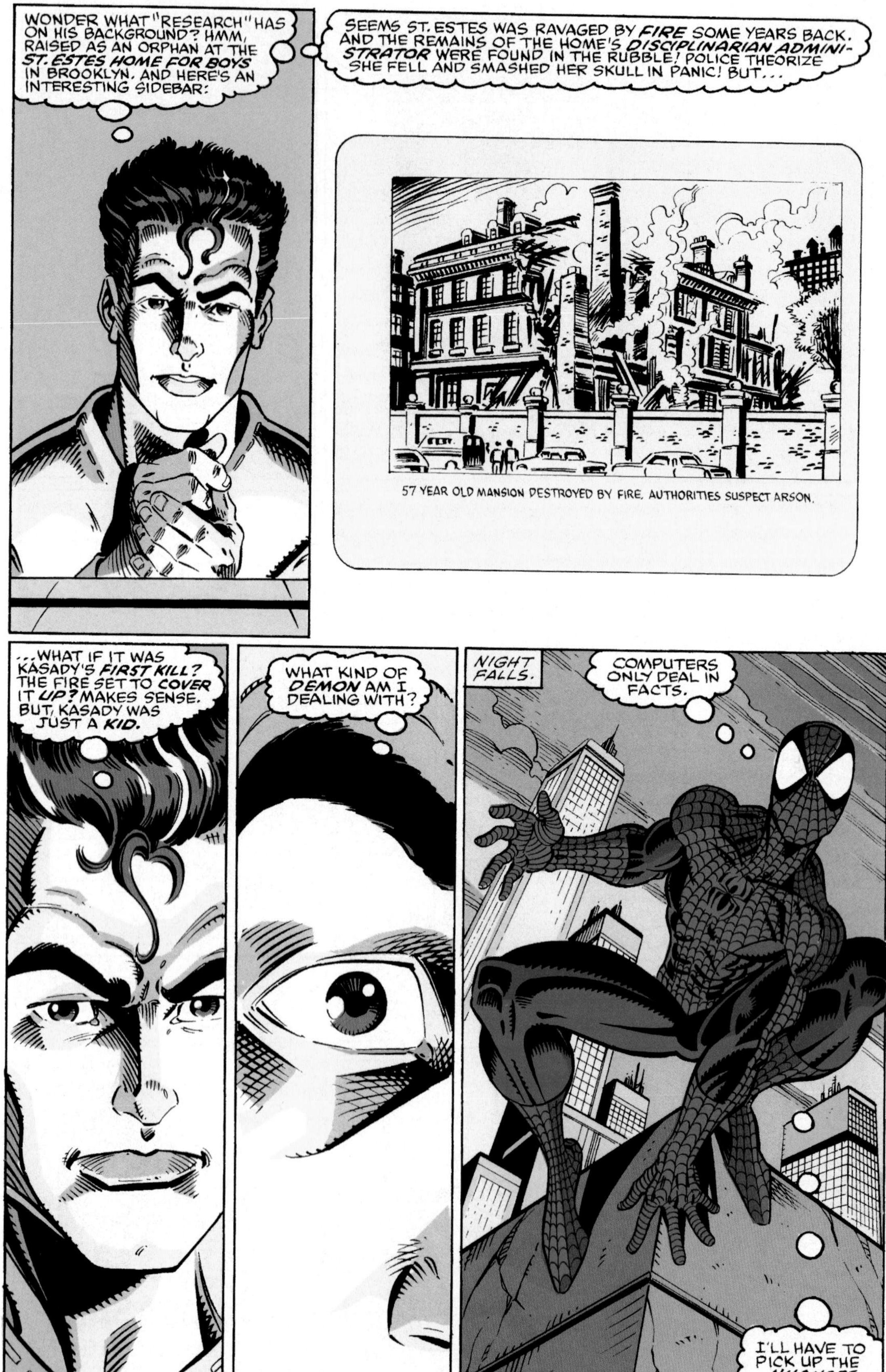
WONDER WHAT "RESEARCH" HAS ON HIS BACKGROUND? HMM, RAISED AS AN ORPHAN AT THE ST. ESTES HOME FOR BOYS IN BROOKLYN. AND HERE'S AN INTERESTING SIDEBAR:
SEEMS ST. ESTES WAS RAVAGED BY FIRE SOME YEARS BACK. AND THE REMAINS OF THE HOME'S DISCIPLINARIAN ADMINISTRATOR WERE FOUND IN THE RUBBLE! POLICE THEORIZE SHE FELL AND SMASHED HER SKULL IN PANIC! BUT...
57 YEAR OLD MANSION DESTROYED BY FIRE, AUTHORITIES SUSPECT ARSON.
...WHAT IF IT WAS KASADY'S FIRST KILL? THE FIRE SET TO COVER IT UP? MAKES SENSE. BUT, KASADY WAS JUST A KID.
WHAT KIND OF DEMON AM I DEALING WITH?
NIGHT FALLS.
COMPUTERS ONLY DEAL IN FACTS.
I'LL HAVE TO PICK UP THE NUANCES FIRST HAND!

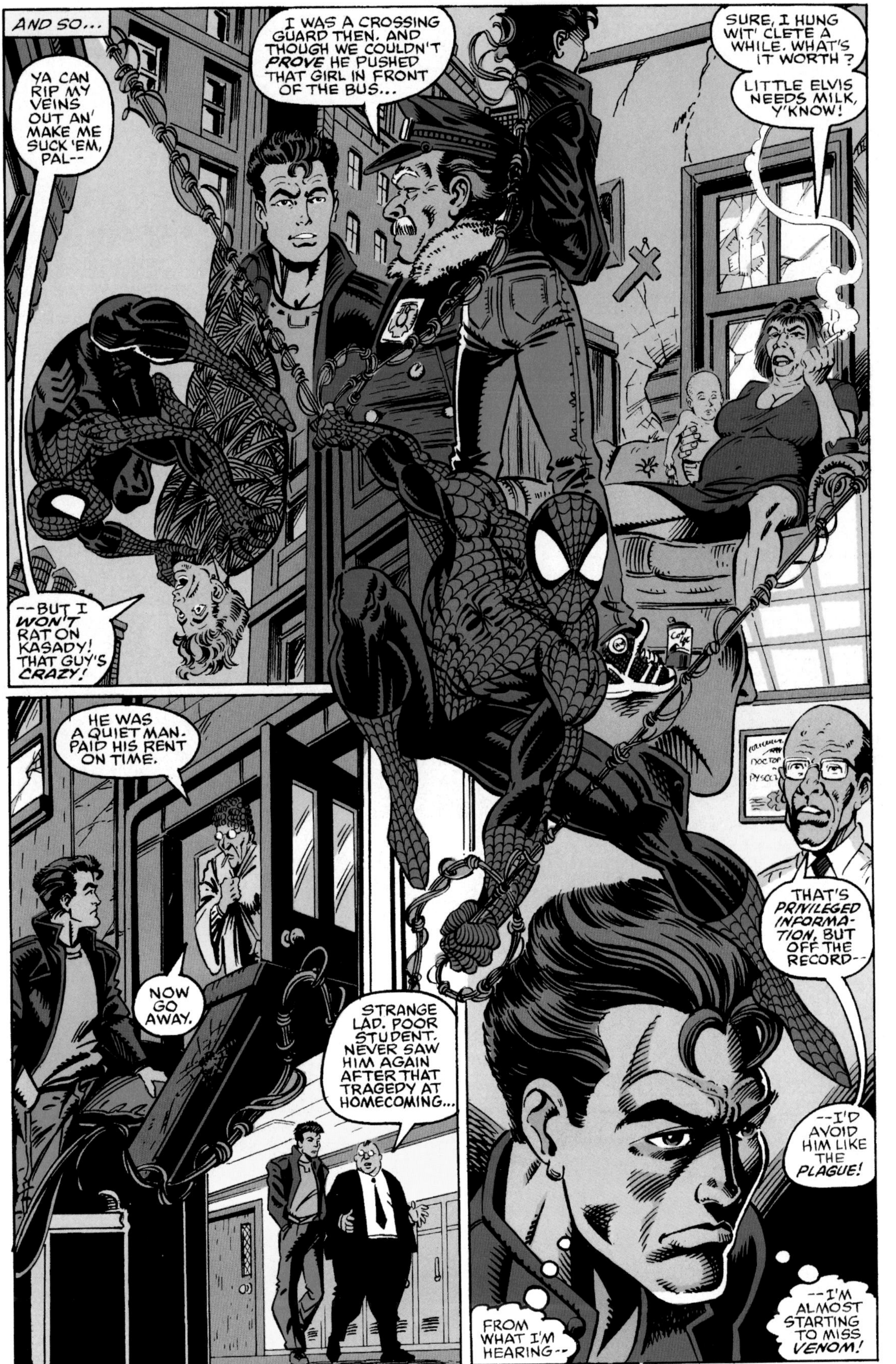
AND SO...
YA CAN RIP MY VEINS OUT AN' MAKE ME SUCK 'EM, PAL--
--BUT I WON'T RAT ON KASADY! THAT GUY'S CRAZY!
I WAS A CROSSING GUARD THEN. AND THOUGH WE COULDN'T PROVE HE PUSHED THAT GIRL IN FRONT OF THE BUS...
SURE, I HUNG WIT' CLETE A WHILE. WHAT'S IT WORTH?
LITTLE ELVIS NEEDS MILK, Y'KNOW!
HE WAS A QUIET MAN. PAID HIS RENT ON TIME.
NOW GO AWAY.
STRANGE LAD. POOR STUDENT. NEVER SAW HIM AGAIN AFTER THAT TRAGEDY AT HOMECOMING...
THAT'S PRIVILEGED INFORMATION, BUT OFF THE RECORD--
--I'D AVOID HIM LIKE THE PLAGUE!
FROM WHAT I'M HEARING--
--I'M ALMOST STARTING TO MISS VENOM!

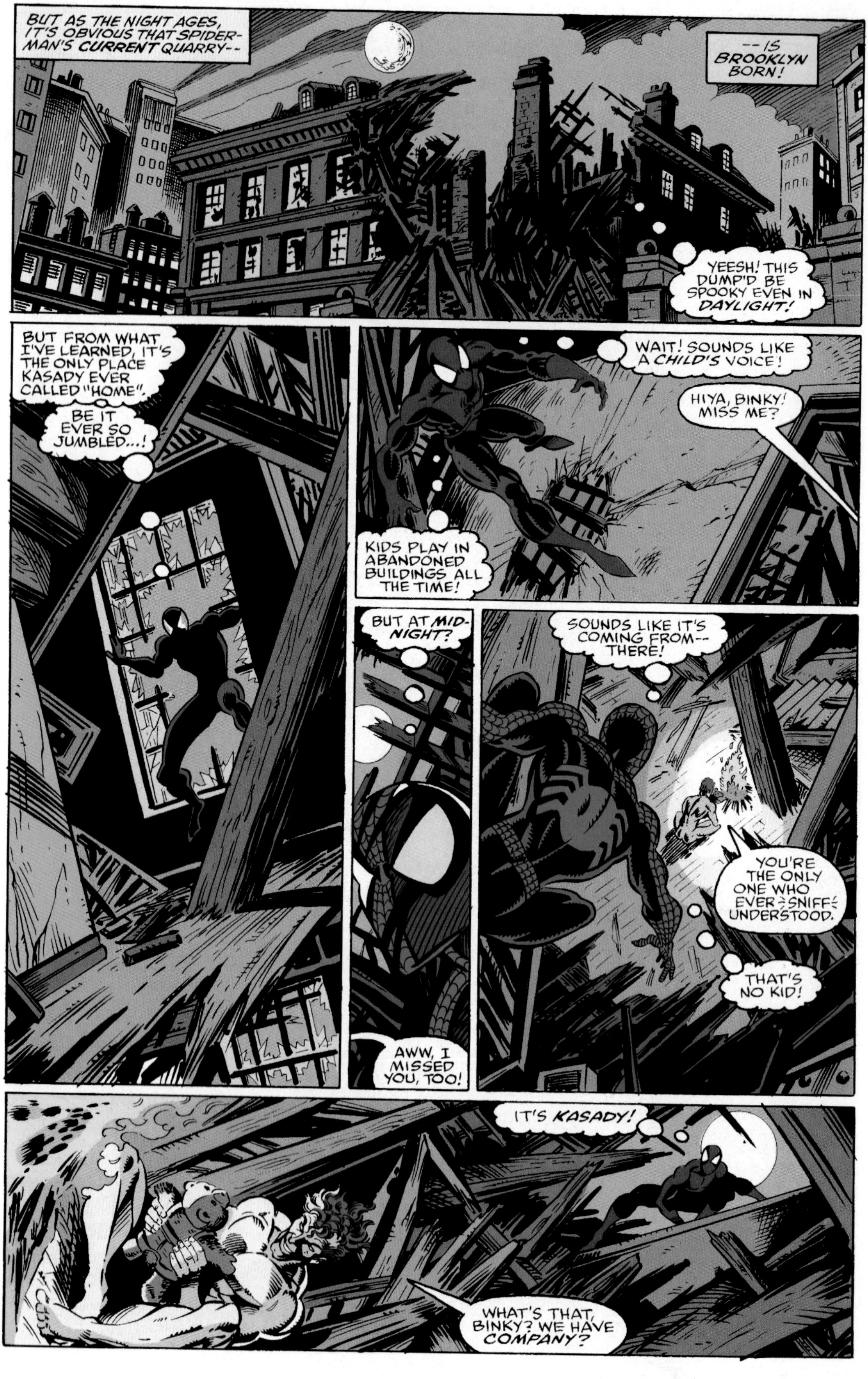

BUT AS THE NIGHT AGES, IT'S OBVIOUS THAT SPIDER-MAN'S CURRENT QUARRY--
--IS BROOKLYN BORN!
YEESH! THIS DUMP'D BE SPOOKY EVEN IN DAYLIGHT!
BUT FROM WHAT I'VE LEARNED, IT'S THE ONLY PLACE KASADY EVER CALLED "HOME".
BE IT EVER SO JUMBLED...!
WAIT! SOUNDS LIKE A CHILD'S VOICE!
HIYA, BINKY! MISS ME?
KIDS PLAY IN ABANDONED BUILDINGS ALL THE TIME!
BUT AT MID-NIGHT?
SOUNDS LIKE IT'S COMING FROM-- THERE!
YOU'RE THE ONLY ONE WHO EVER -SNIFF- UNDERSTOOD.
THAT'S NO KID!
AWW, I MISSED YOU, TOO!
IT'S KASADY!
WHAT'S THAT, BINKY? WE HAVE COMPANY?

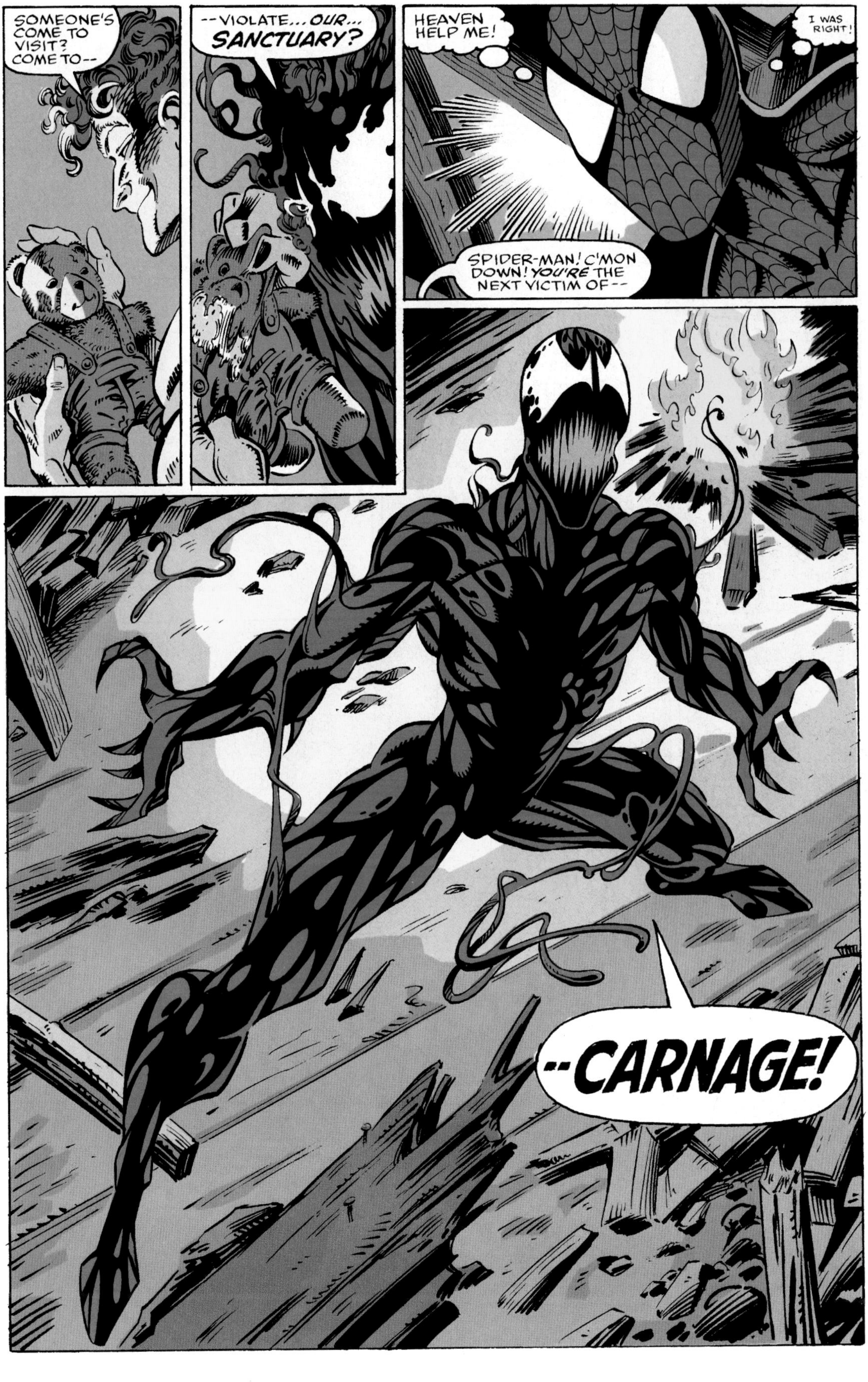
SOMEONE'S COME TO VISIT? COME TO--
--VIOLATE... OUR... SANCTUARY?
HEAVEN HELP ME!
I WAS RIGHT!
SPIDER-MAN! C'MON DOWN! YOU'RE THE NEXT VICTIM OF--
--CARNAGE!

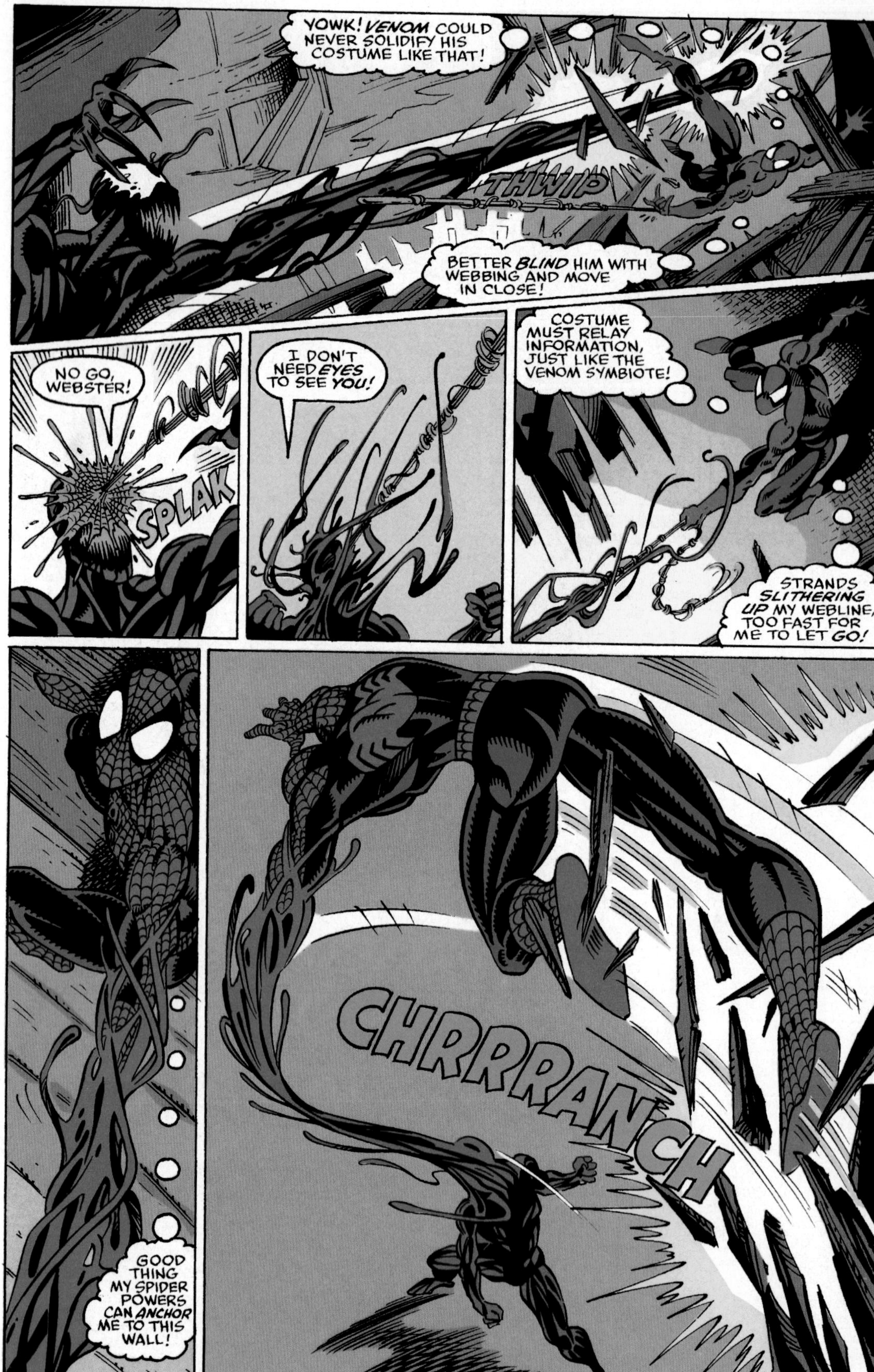
YOWK! VENOM COULD NEVER SOLIDIFY HIS COSTUME LIKE THAT!
THWIP
BETTER BLIND HIM WITH WEBBING AND MOVE IN CLOSE!
NO GO, WEBSTER!
SPLAK
I DON'T NEED EYES TO SEE YOU!
COSTUME MUST RELAY INFORMATION, JUST LIKE THE VENOM SYMBIOTE!
STRANDS SLITHERING UP MY WEBLINE, TOO FAST FOR ME TO LET GO!
GOOD THING MY SPIDER POWERS CAN ANCHOR ME TO THIS WALL!
CHRRRANCH

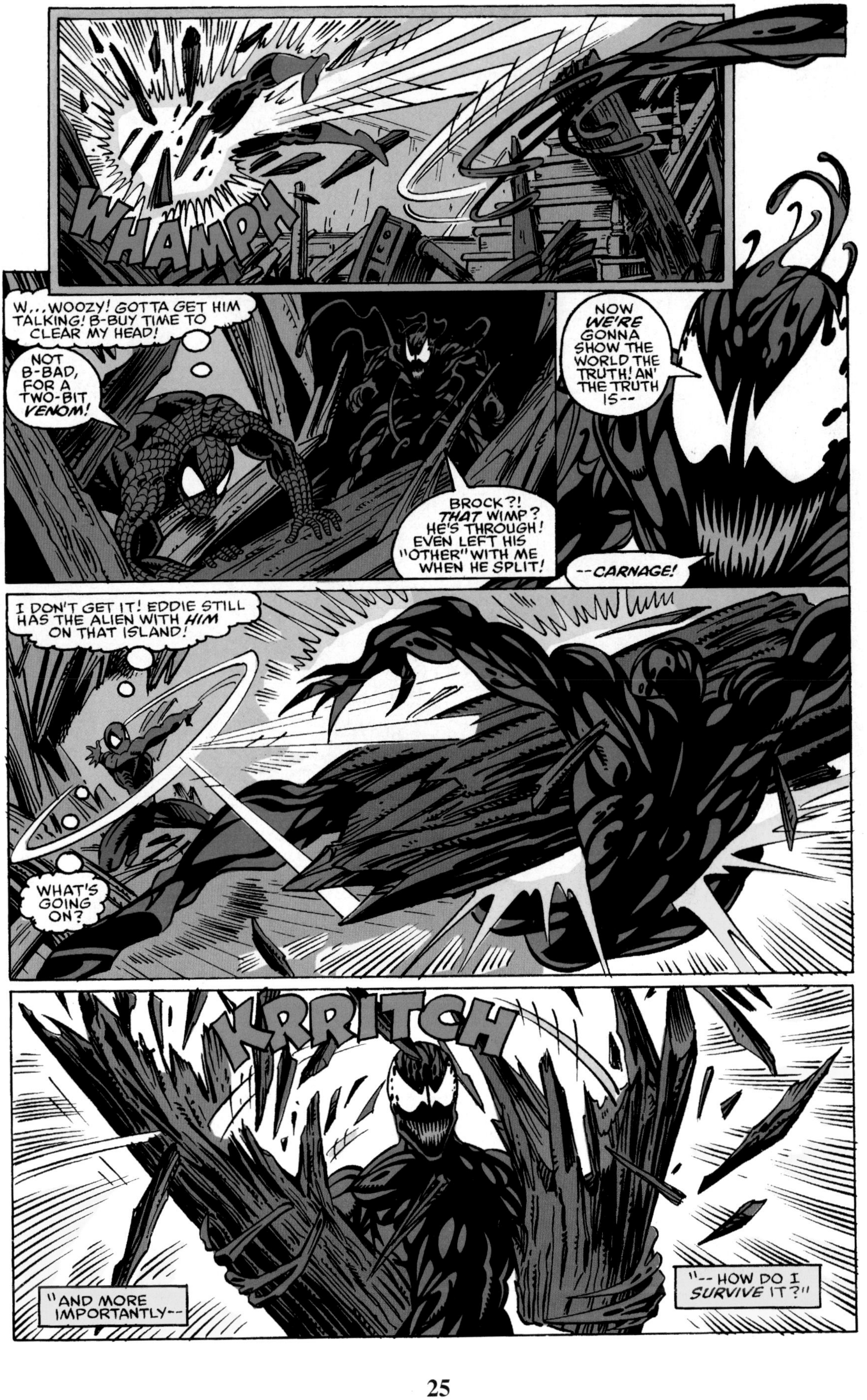
WHAMPH
W...WOOZY! GOTTA GET HIM TALKING! B-BUY TIME TO CLEAR MY HEAD!
NOT B-BAD, FOR A TWO-BIT VENOM!
BROCK?! THAT WIMP? HE'S THROUGH! EVEN LEFT HIS "OTHER" WITH ME WHEN HE SPLIT!
NOW WE'RE GONNA SHOW THE WORLD THE TRUTH! AN' THE TRUTH IS--
--CARNAGE!
I DON'T GET IT! EDDIE STILL HAS THE ALIEN WITH HIM ON THAT ISLAND!
WHAT'S GOING ON?
KRRITCH
"AND MORE IMPORTANTLY--
"--HOW DO I SURVIVE IT?"

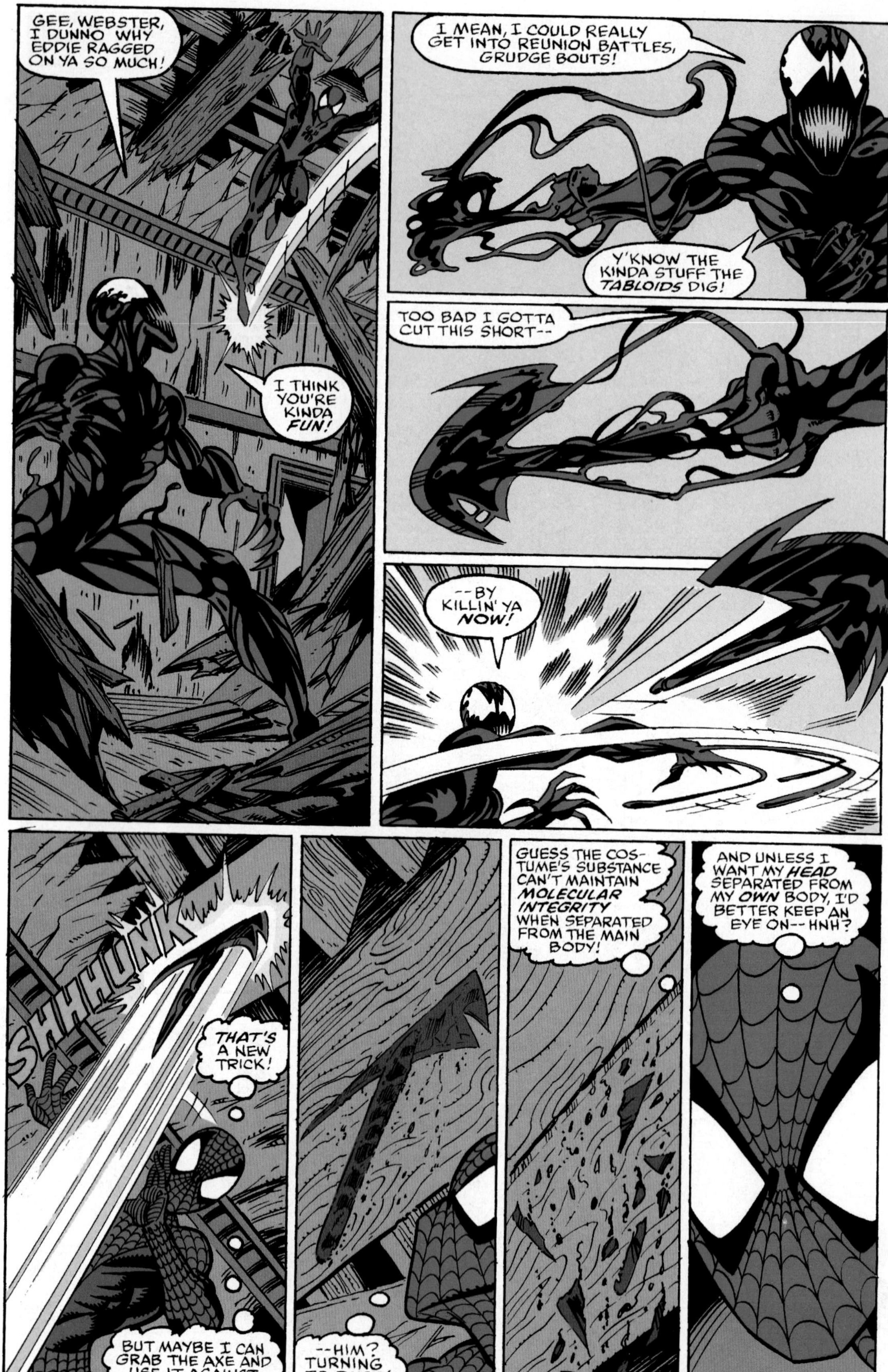
GEE, WEBSTER, I DUNNO WHY EDDIE RAGGED ON YA SO MUCH!
I THINK YOU'RE KINDA FUN!
I MEAN, I COULD REALLY GET INTO REUNION BATTLES, GRUDGE BOUTS!
Y'KNOW THE KINDA STUFF THE TABLOIDS DIG!
TOO BAD I GOTTA CUT THIS SHORT--
--BY KILLIN' YA NOW!
SHHHUNK
THAT'S A NEW TRICK!
BUT MAYBE I CAN GRAB THE AXE AND USE IT AGAINST--
--HIM? TURNING TO DUST!
GUESS THE COSTUME'S SUBSTANCE CAN'T MAINTAIN MOLECULAR INTEGRITY WHEN SEPARATED FROM THE MAIN BODY!
AND UNLESS I WANT MY HEAD SEPARATED FROM MY OWN BODY, I'D BETTER KEEP AN EYE ON-- HNH?

WHERE'D HE GO?

COULDN'T BE HIDING! MY *SPIDER-SENSE* WOULD WARN ME IF HE WAS STILL AROUND!

WOULDN'T IT...?

≶WHMGF≶

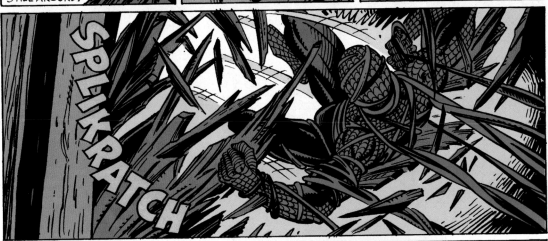

SPLIKRATCH

LOST DOGS, U.F.O. SIGHTINGS, *NOISE COMPLAINTS!*

HOW COME THEY ALL HAPPEN ON *MY* SHIFT!

RELAX, RAMONE. IT'S PROB'LY JUST SOME PUNKS PARTYIN'!

NO BIG DEAL.

VENOM DOESN'T TRIGGER MY SPIDER-SENSE AND APPARENTLY *CARNAGE* DOESN'T EITHER! THEY'RE SIMILAR, BUT DIFFERENT!

AND I DON'T KNOW *THIS* GUY'S RULES!

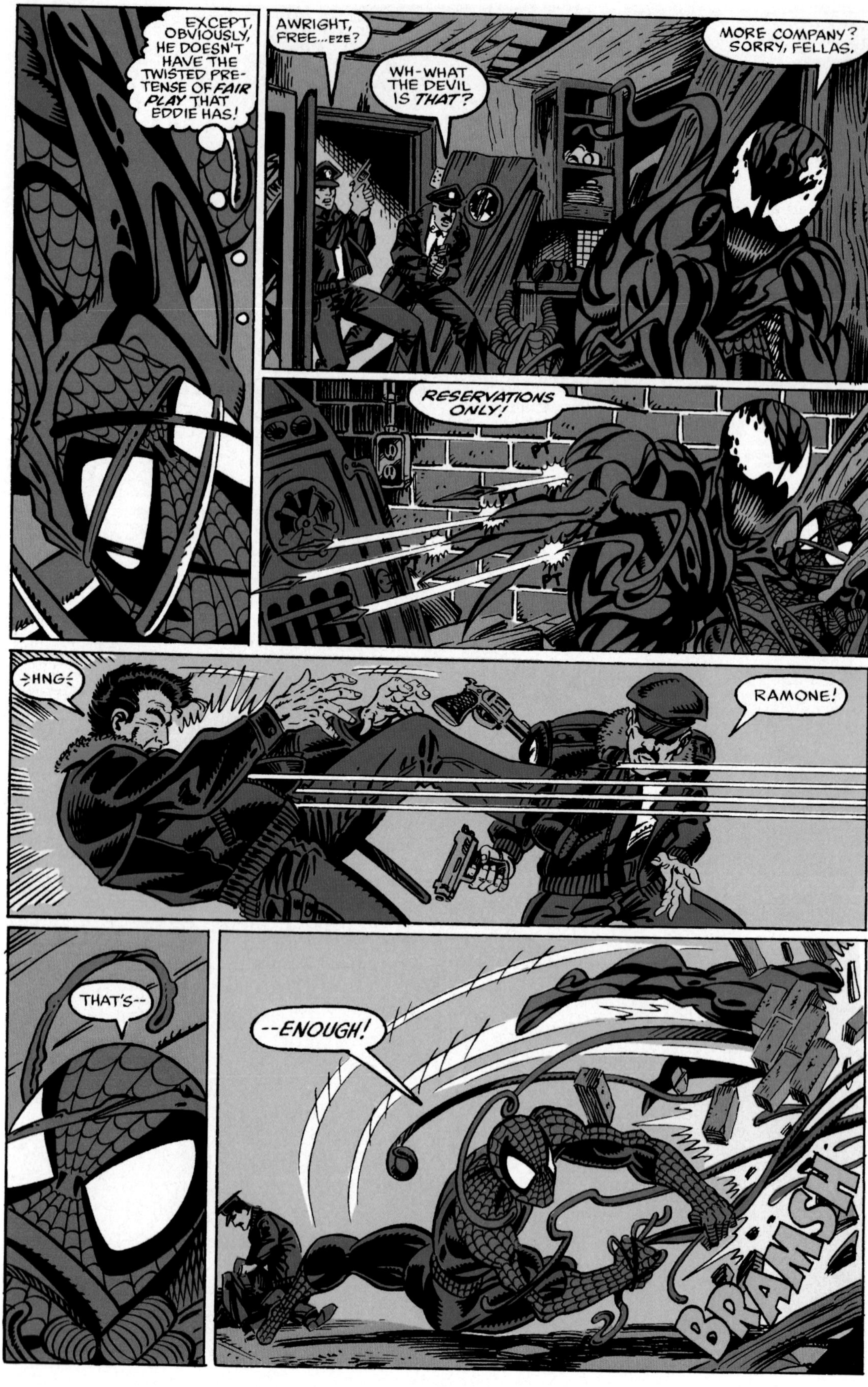
EXCEPT, OBVIOUSLY, HE DOESN'T HAVE THE TWISTED PRETENSE OF FAIR PLAY THAT EDDIE HAS!
AWRIGHT, FREE...EZE?
WH-WHAT THE DEVIL IS THAT?
MORE COMPANY? SORRY, FELLAS.
RESERVATIONS ONLY!
PT
PT
PT
PT
HNG
RAMONE!
THAT'S--
--ENOUGH!
BRAMSH

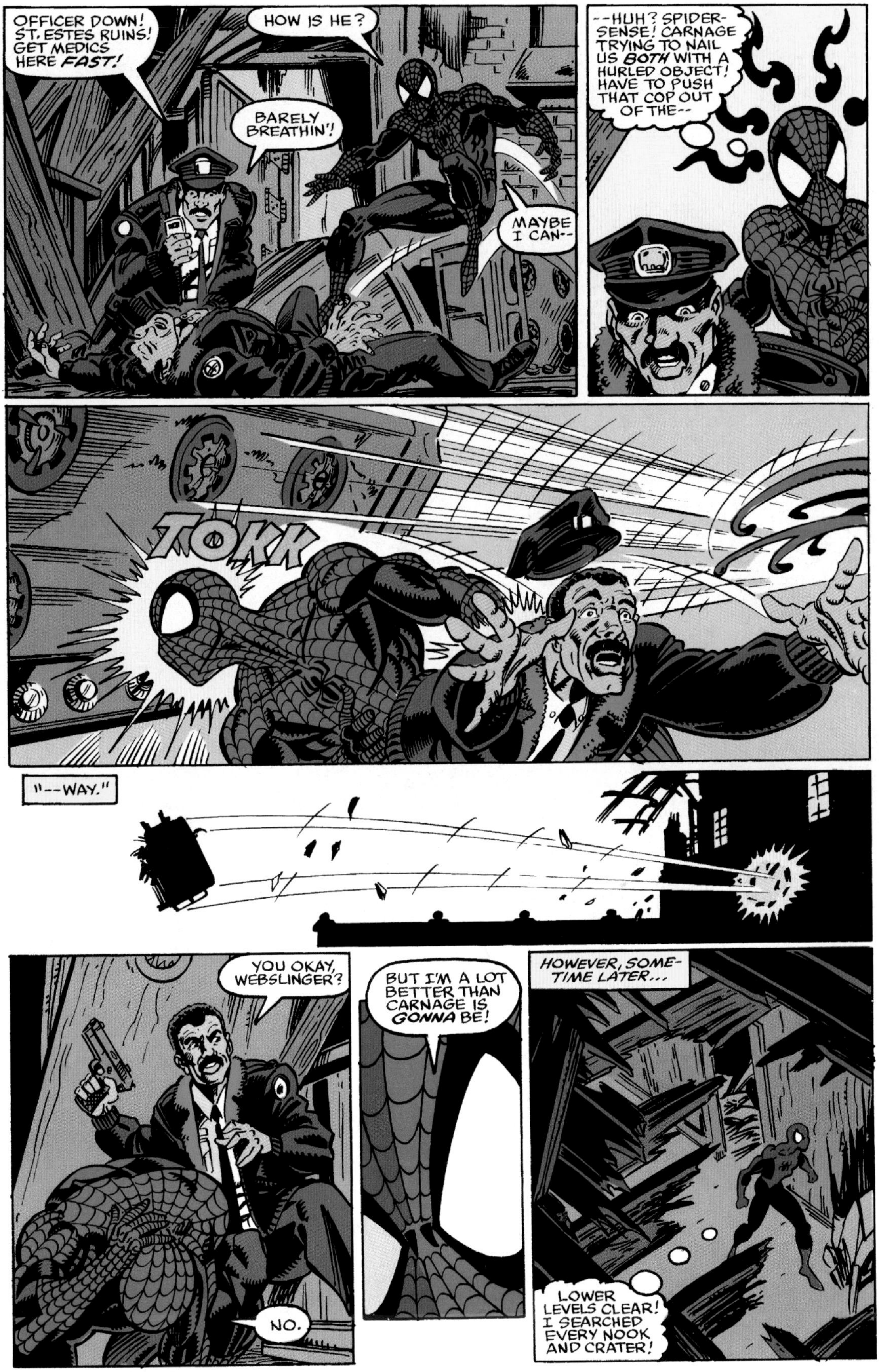
OFFICER DOWN! ST. ESTES RUINS! GET MEDICS HERE FAST!
HOW IS HE?
BARELY BREATHIN'!
MAYBE I CAN--
--HUH? SPIDER-SENSE! CARNAGE TRYING TO NAIL US BOTH WITH A HURLED OBJECT! HAVE TO PUSH THAT COP OUT OF THE--
TOKK
"--WAY."
YOU OKAY, WEBSLINGER?
NO.
BUT I'M A LOT BETTER THAN CARNAGE IS GONNA BE!
HOWEVER, SOME-TIME LATER...
LOWER LEVELS CLEAR! I SEARCHED EVERY NOOK AND CRATER!

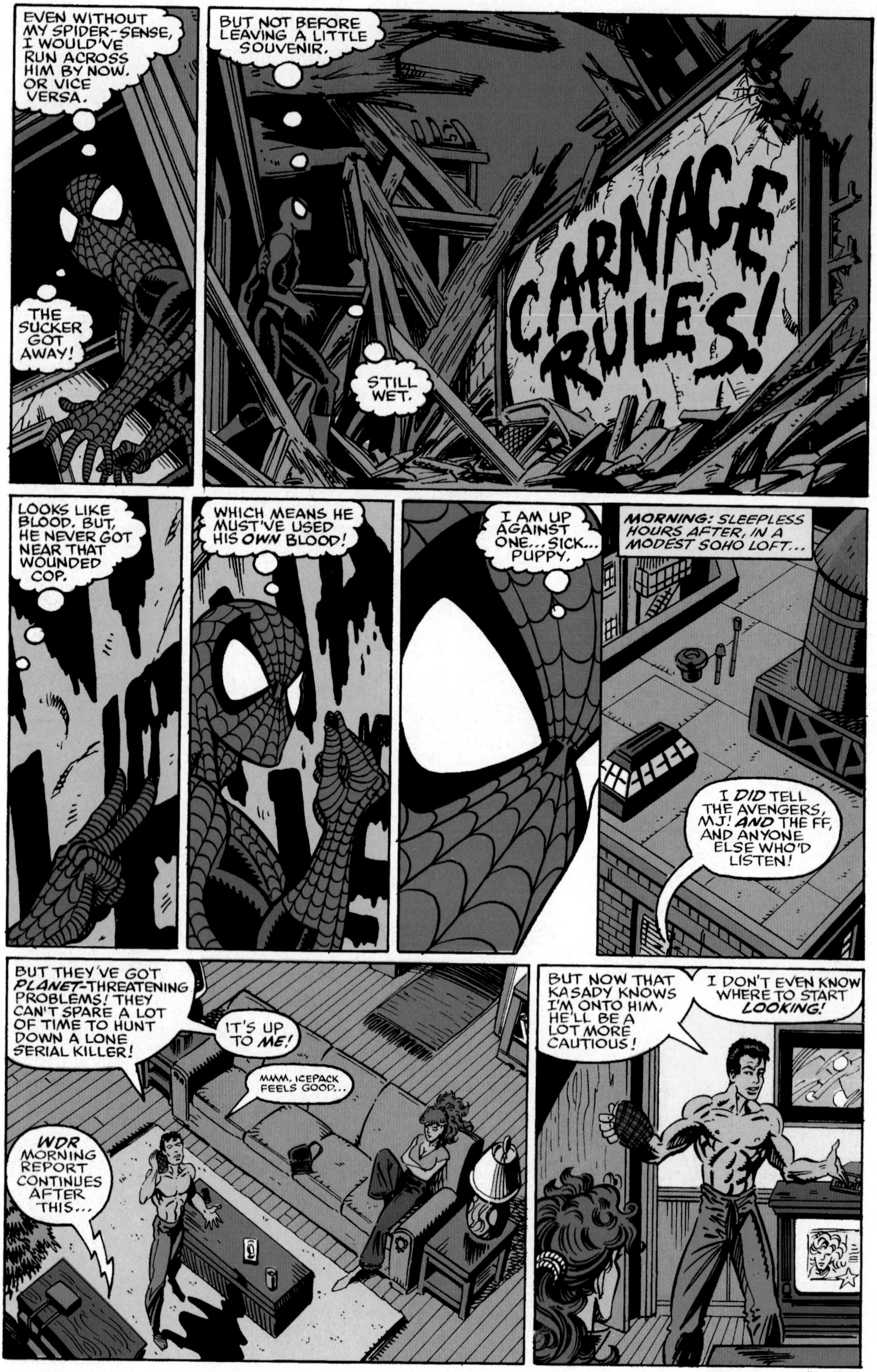

EVEN WITHOUT MY SPIDER-SENSE, I WOULD'VE RUN ACROSS HIM BY NOW. OR VICE VERSA.
THE SUCKER GOT AWAY!
BUT NOT BEFORE LEAVING A LITTLE SOUVENIR.
STILL WET.
CARNAGE RULES!
LOOKS LIKE BLOOD. BUT, HE NEVER GOT NEAR THAT WOUNDED COP.
WHICH MEANS HE MUST'VE USED HIS OWN BLOOD!
I AM UP AGAINST ONE... SICK... PUPPY.
MORNING: SLEEPLESS HOURS AFTER, IN A MODEST SOHO LOFT...
I DID TELL THE AVENGERS, MJ! AND THE FF, AND ANYONE ELSE WHO'D LISTEN!
BUT THEY'VE GOT PLANET-THREATENING PROBLEMS! THEY CAN'T SPARE A LOT OF TIME TO HUNT DOWN A LONE SERIAL KILLER!
IT'S UP TO ME!
MMM, ICEPACK FEELS GOOD...
WDR MORNING REPORT CONTINUES AFTER THIS...
BUT NOW THAT KASADY KNOWS I'M ONTO HIM, HE'LL BE A LOT MORE CAUTIOUS!
I DON'T EVEN KNOW WHERE TO START LOOKING!

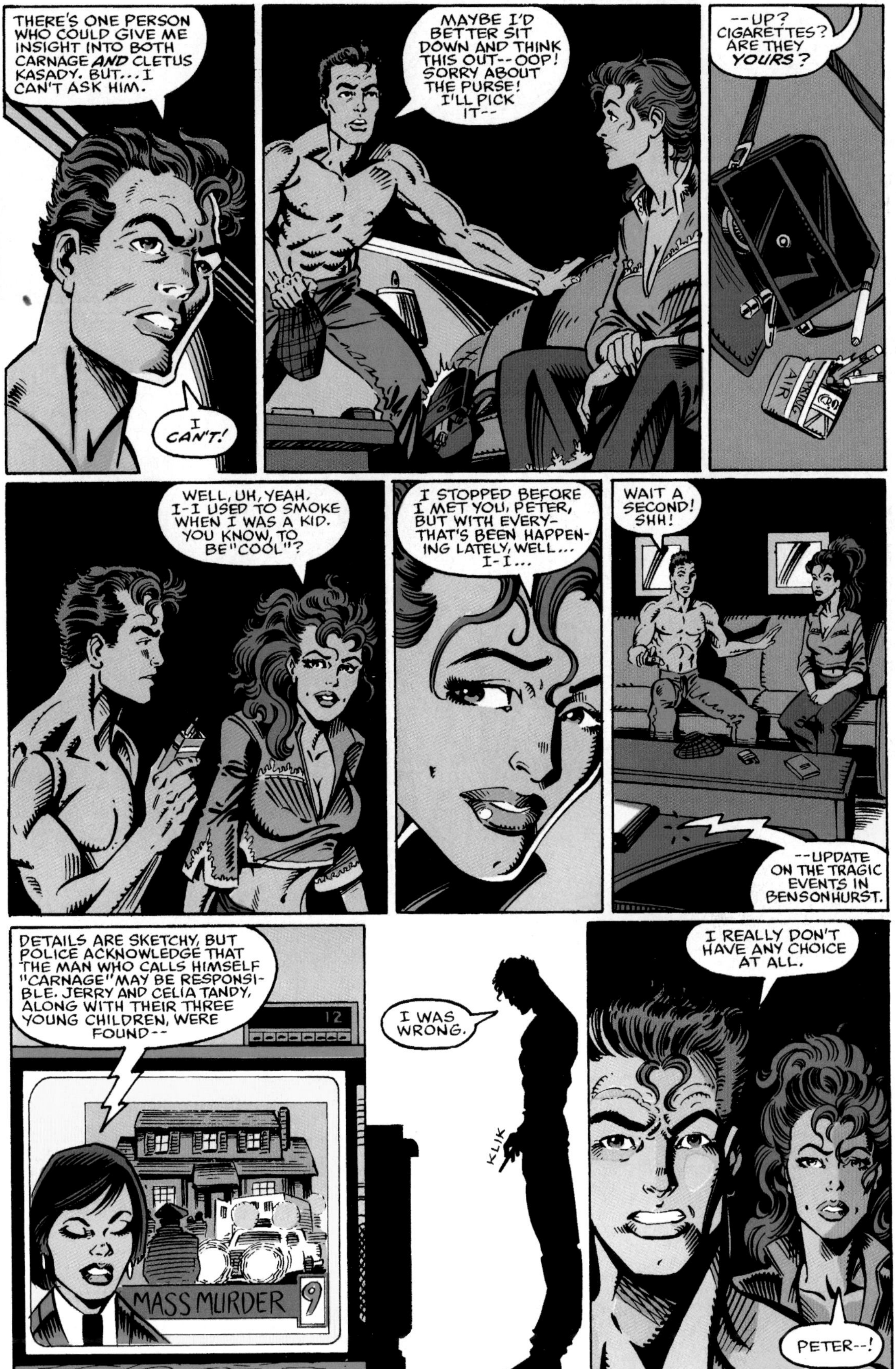
THERE'S ONE PERSON WHO COULD GIVE ME INSIGHT INTO BOTH CARNAGE AND CLETUS KASADY. BUT... I CAN'T ASK HIM.
I CAN'T!
MAYBE I'D BETTER SIT DOWN AND THINK THIS OUT--OOP! SORRY ABOUT THE PURSE! I'LL PICK IT--
--UP? CIGARETTES? ARE THEY YOURS?
WELL, UH, YEAH. I-I USED TO SMOKE WHEN I WAS A KID. YOU KNOW, TO BE "COOL"?
I STOPPED BEFORE I MET YOU, PETER, BUT WITH EVERYTHING THAT'S BEEN HAPPENING LATELY, WELL... I-I...
WAIT A SECOND! SHH!
--UPDATE ON THE TRAGIC EVENTS IN BENSONHURST.
DETAILS ARE SKETCHY, BUT POLICE ACKNOWLEDGE THAT THE MAN WHO CALLS HIMSELF "CARNAGE" MAY BE RESPONSIBLE. JERRY AND CELIA TANDY, ALONG WITH THEIR THREE YOUNG CHILDREN, WERE FOUND--
12
MASS MURDER
9
I WAS WRONG.
KLIK
I REALLY DON'T HAVE ANY CHOICE AT ALL.
PETER--!

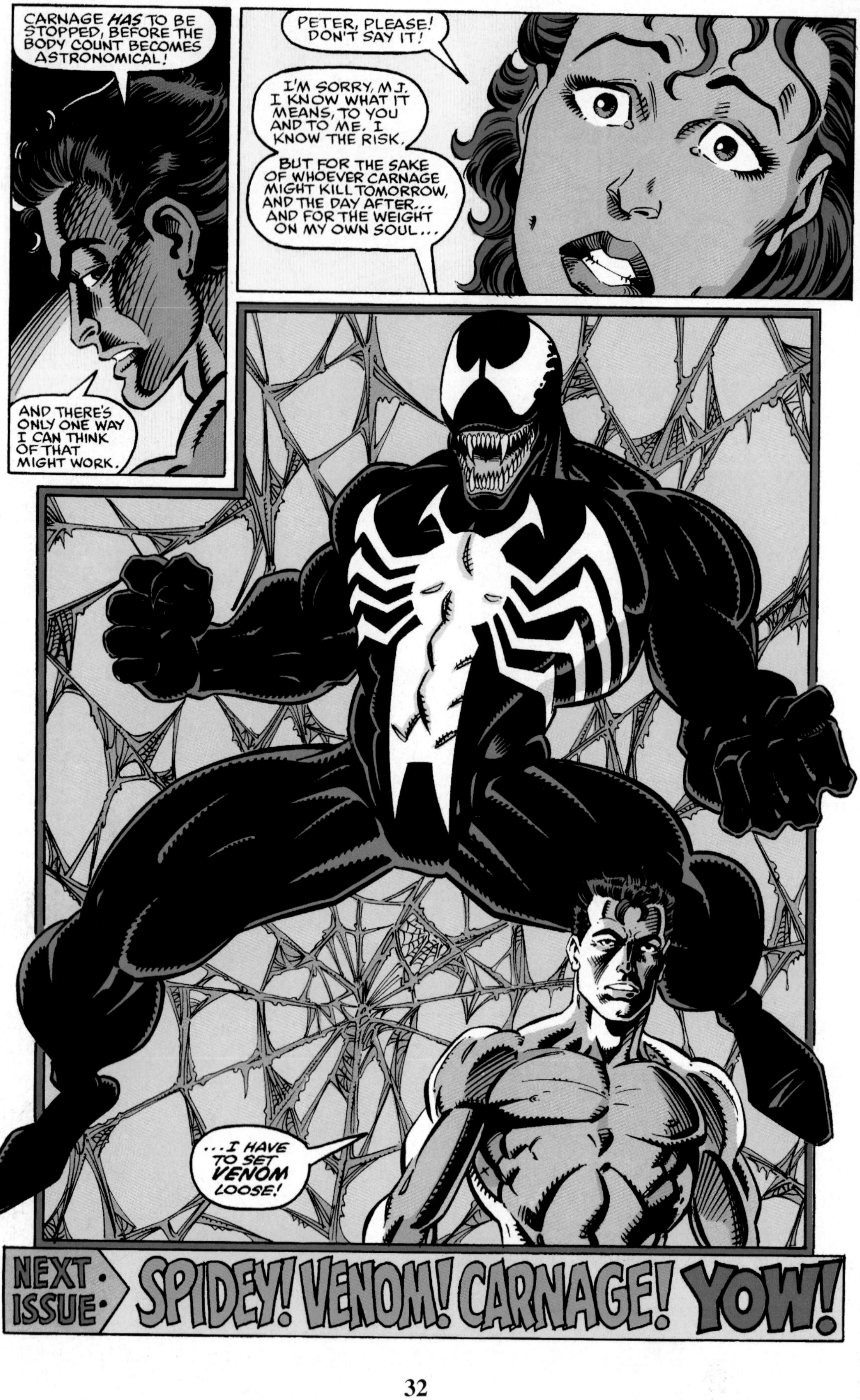
CARNAGE HAS TO BE STOPPED, BEFORE THE BODY COUNT BECOMES ASTRONOMICAL!
AND THERE'S ONLY ONE WAY I CAN THINK OF THAT MIGHT WORK.
PETER, PLEASE! DON'T SAY IT!
I'M SORRY, M.J. I KNOW WHAT IT MEANS, TO YOU AND TO ME. I KNOW THE RISK.
BUT FOR THE SAKE OF WHOEVER CARNAGE MIGHT KILL TOMORROW, AND THE DAY AFTER... AND FOR THE WEIGHT ON MY OWN SOUL...
...I HAVE TO SET VENOM LOOSE!
NEXT ISSUE: SPIDEY! VENOM! CARNAGE! YOW!

Cletus was the symbiote's first and favorite host, but it bonded with several others over the years. It found its next hosts during a time when Spider-Man had been tricked into believing that his clone, Ben Reilly, was actually the original Peter Parker. Reilly took over the role of Spider-Man — and Parker, who had lost his powers, retired to focus on his pregnant wife, Mary Jane...

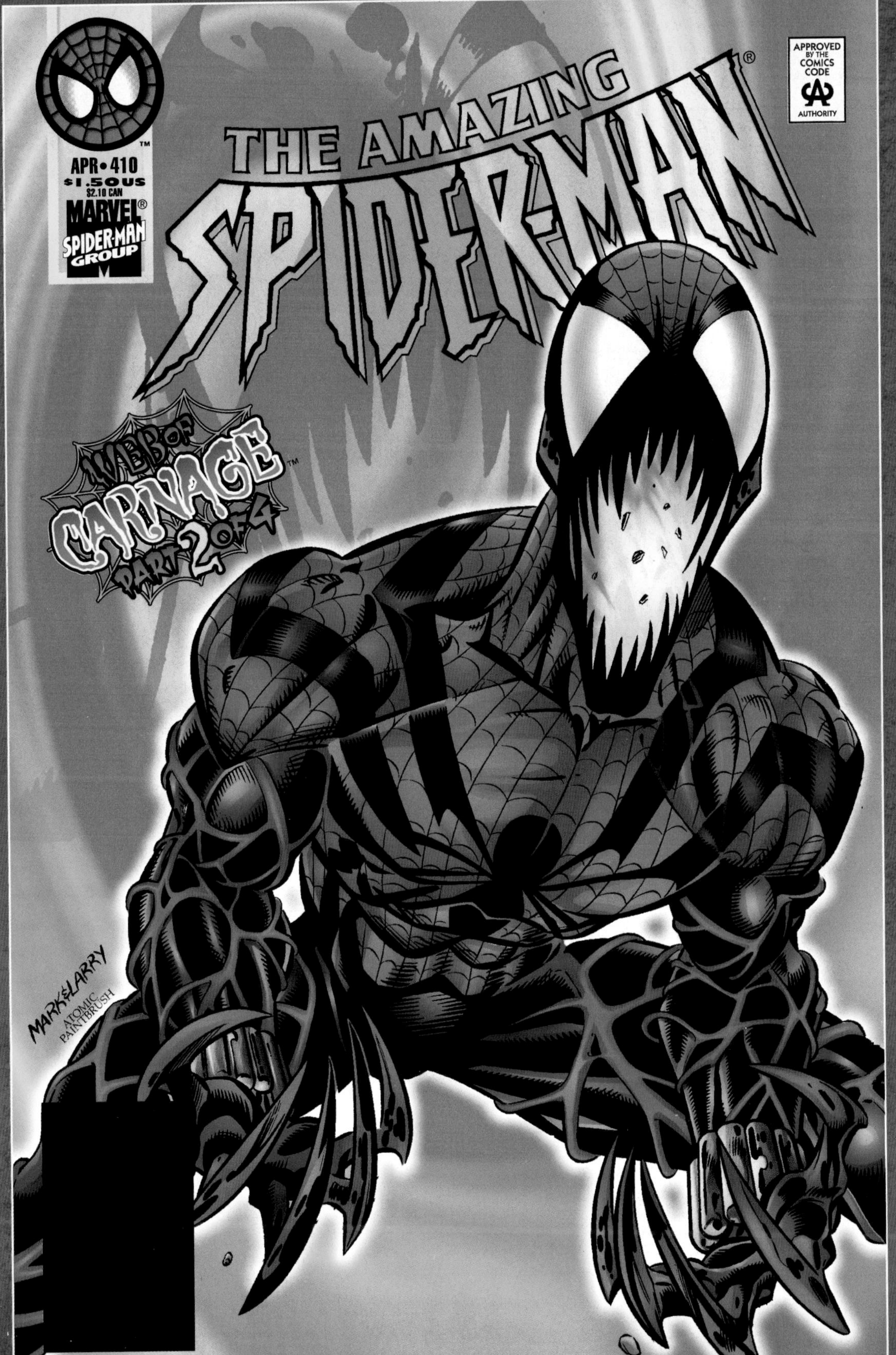

THE AMAZING SPIDER-MAN®
APR • 410
$1.50US
$2.10 CAN
MARVEL®
SPIDER-MAN GROUP
APPROVED BY THE COMICS CODE AUTHORITY
WEB OF CARNAGE™
PART 2 OF 4
MARK&LARRY
ATOMIC PAINTBRUSH

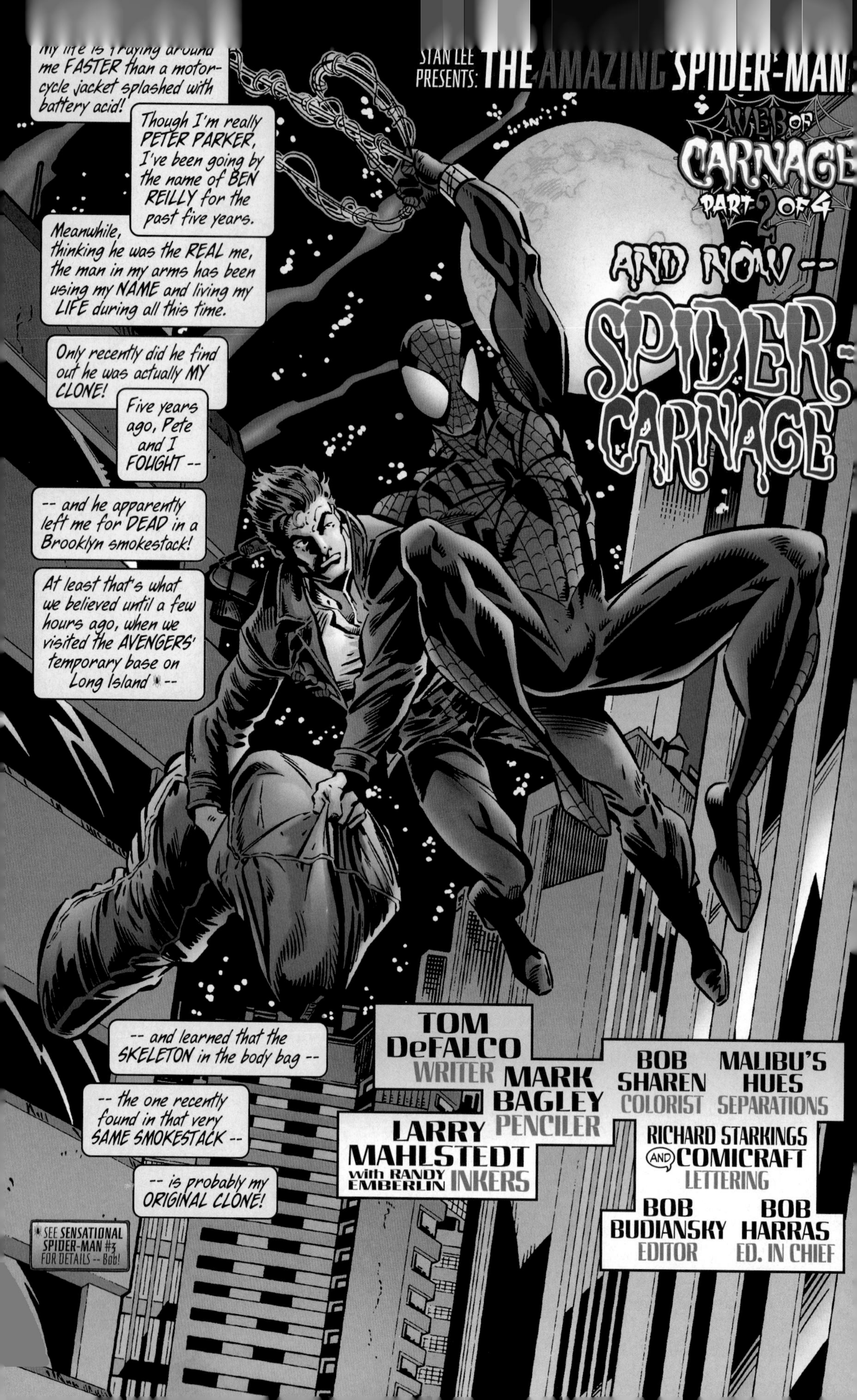

My life is fraying around me FASTER than a motor-cycle jacket splashed with battery acid!
Though I'm really PETER PARKER, I've been going by the name of BEN REILLY for the past five years.
Meanwhile, thinking he was the REAL me, the man in my arms has been using my NAME and living my LIFE during all this time.
Only recently did he find out he was actually MY CLONE!
Five years ago, Pete and I FOUGHT --
-- and he apparently left me for DEAD in a Brooklyn smokestack!
At least that's what we believed until a few hours ago, when we visited the AVENGERS' temporary base on Long Island --
-- and learned that the SKELETON in the body bag --
-- the one recently found in that very SAME SMOKESTACK --
-- is probably my ORIGINAL CLONE!
SEE SENSATIONAL SPIDER-MAN #3 FOR DETAILS -- Bob!
STAN LEE PRESENTS: THE AMAZING SPIDER-MAN
WEB OF CARNAGE PART 2 OF 4
AND NOW --
SPIDER-CARNAGE
TOM DeFALCO WRITER
MARK BAGLEY PENCILER
LARRY MAHLSTEDT with RANDY EMBERLIN INKERS
BOB SHAREN COLORIST
MALIBU'S HUES SEPARATIONS
RICHARD STARKINGS AND COMICRAFT LETTERING
BOB BUDIANSKY EDITOR
BOB HARRAS ED. IN CHIEF

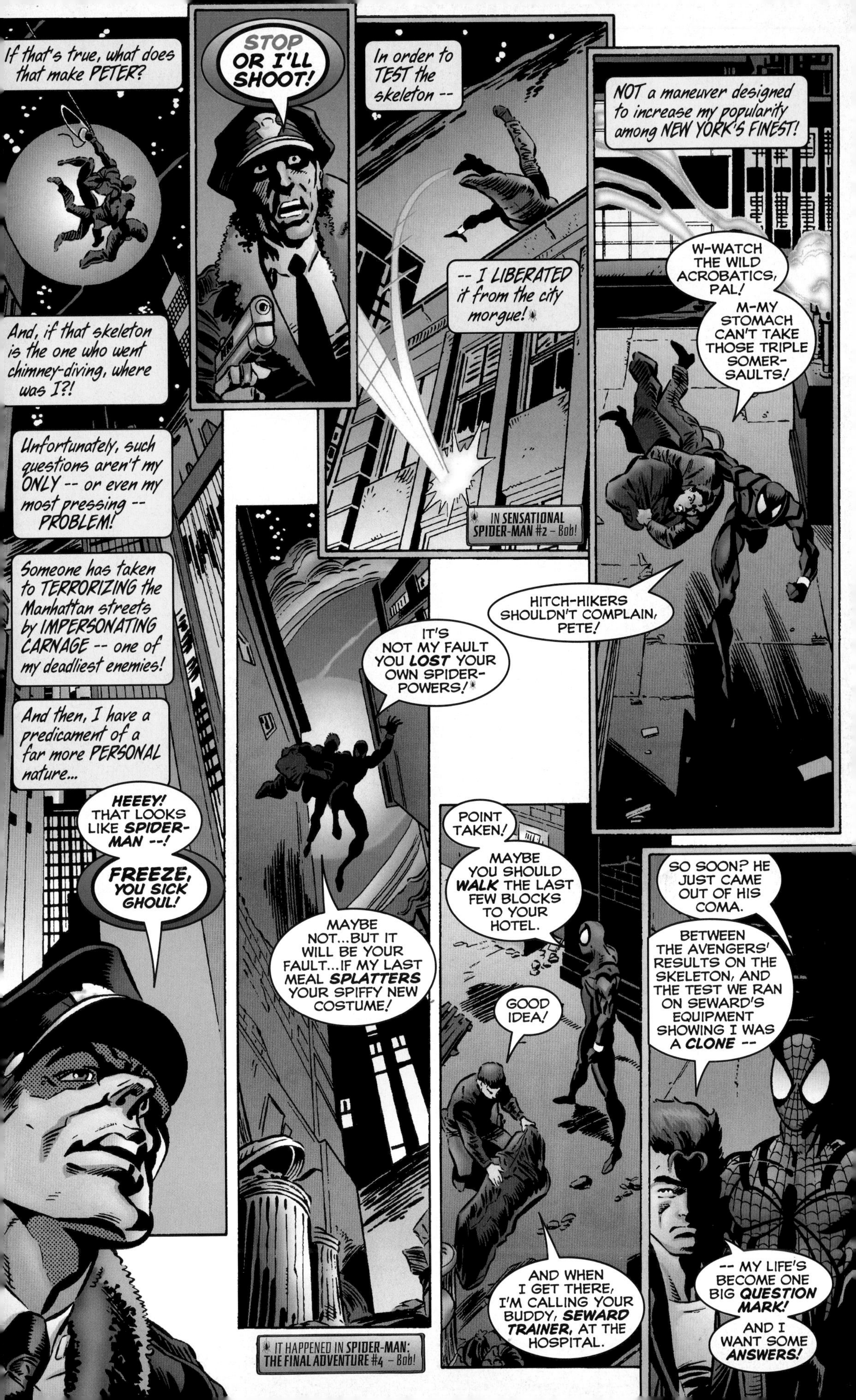

If that's true, what does that make PETER?
And, if that skeleton is the one who went chimney-diving, where was I?!
Unfortunately, such questions aren't my ONLY -- or even my most pressing -- PROBLEM!
Someone has taken to TERRORIZING the Manhattan streets by IMPERSONATING CARNAGE -- one of my deadliest enemies!
And then, I have a predicament of a far more PERSONAL nature...
HEEEY! THAT LOOKS LIKE SPIDER-MAN --!
FREEZE, YOU SICK GHOUL!
STOP OR I'LL SHOOT!
In order to TEST the skeleton --
-- I LIBERATED it from the city morgue!
IN SENSATIONAL SPIDER-MAN #2 – Bob!
NOT a maneuver designed to increase my popularity among NEW YORK'S FINEST!
W-WATCH THE WILD ACROBATICS, PAL!
M-MY STOMACH CAN'T TAKE THOSE TRIPLE SOMER-SAULTS!
HITCH-HIKERS SHOULDN'T COMPLAIN, PETE!
IT'S NOT MY FAULT YOU LOST YOUR OWN SPIDER-POWERS!
MAYBE NOT...BUT IT WILL BE YOUR FAULT...IF MY LAST MEAL SPLATTERS YOUR SPIFFY NEW COSTUME!
IT HAPPENED IN SPIDER-MAN: THE FINAL ADVENTURE #4 – Bob!
POINT TAKEN!
MAYBE YOU SHOULD WALK THE LAST FEW BLOCKS TO YOUR HOTEL.
GOOD IDEA!
AND WHEN I GET THERE, I'M CALLING YOUR BUDDY, SEWARD TRAINER, AT THE HOSPITAL.
SO SOON? HE JUST CAME OUT OF HIS COMA.
BETWEEN THE AVENGERS' RESULTS ON THE SKELETON, AND THE TEST WE RAN ON SEWARD'S EQUIPMENT SHOWING I WAS A CLONE --
-- MY LIFE'S BECOME ONE BIG QUESTION MARK!
AND I WANT SOME ANSWERS!

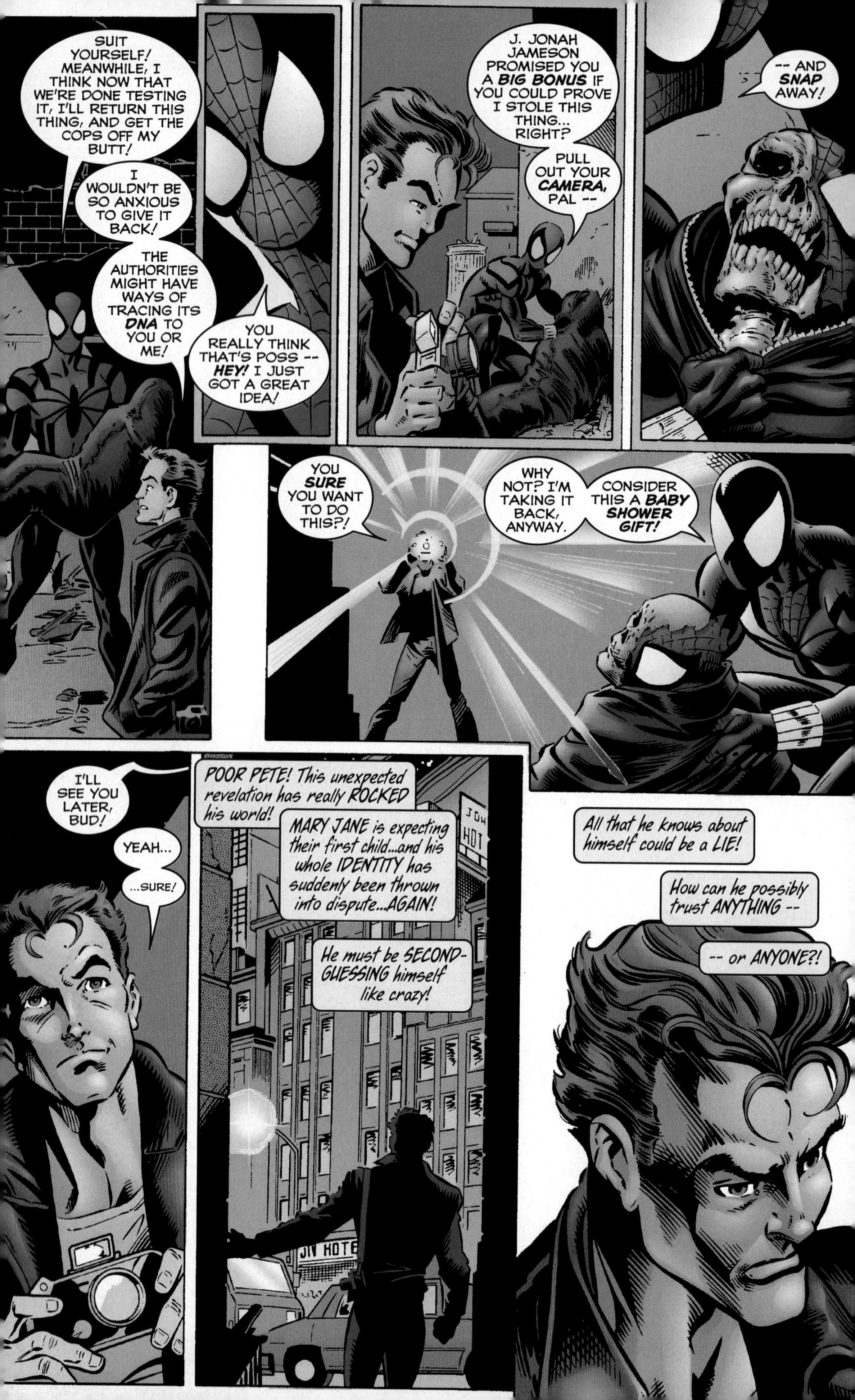

SUIT YOURSELF! MEANWHILE, I THINK NOW THAT WE'RE DONE TESTING IT, I'LL RETURN THIS THING, AND GET THE COPS OFF MY BUTT!
I WOULDN'T BE SO ANXIOUS TO GIVE IT BACK!
THE AUTHORITIES MIGHT HAVE WAYS OF TRACING ITS DNA TO YOU OR ME!
YOU REALLY THINK THAT'S POSS -- HEY! I JUST GOT A GREAT IDEA!
J. JONAH JAMESON PROMISED YOU A BIG BONUS IF YOU COULD PROVE I STOLE THIS THING... RIGHT?
PULL OUT YOUR CAMERA, PAL --
-- AND SNAP AWAY!
YOU SURE YOU WANT TO DO THIS?!
WHY NOT? I'M TAKING IT BACK, ANYWAY.
CONSIDER THIS A BABY SHOWER GIFT!
I'LL SEE YOU LATER, BUD!
YEAH...
...SURE!
POOR PETE! This unexpected revelation has really ROCKED his world!
MARY JANE is expecting their first child...and his whole IDENTITY has suddenly been thrown into dispute...AGAIN!
He must be SECOND-GUESSING himself like crazy!
All that he knows about himself could be a LIE!
How can he possibly trust ANYTHING --
-- or ANYONE?!

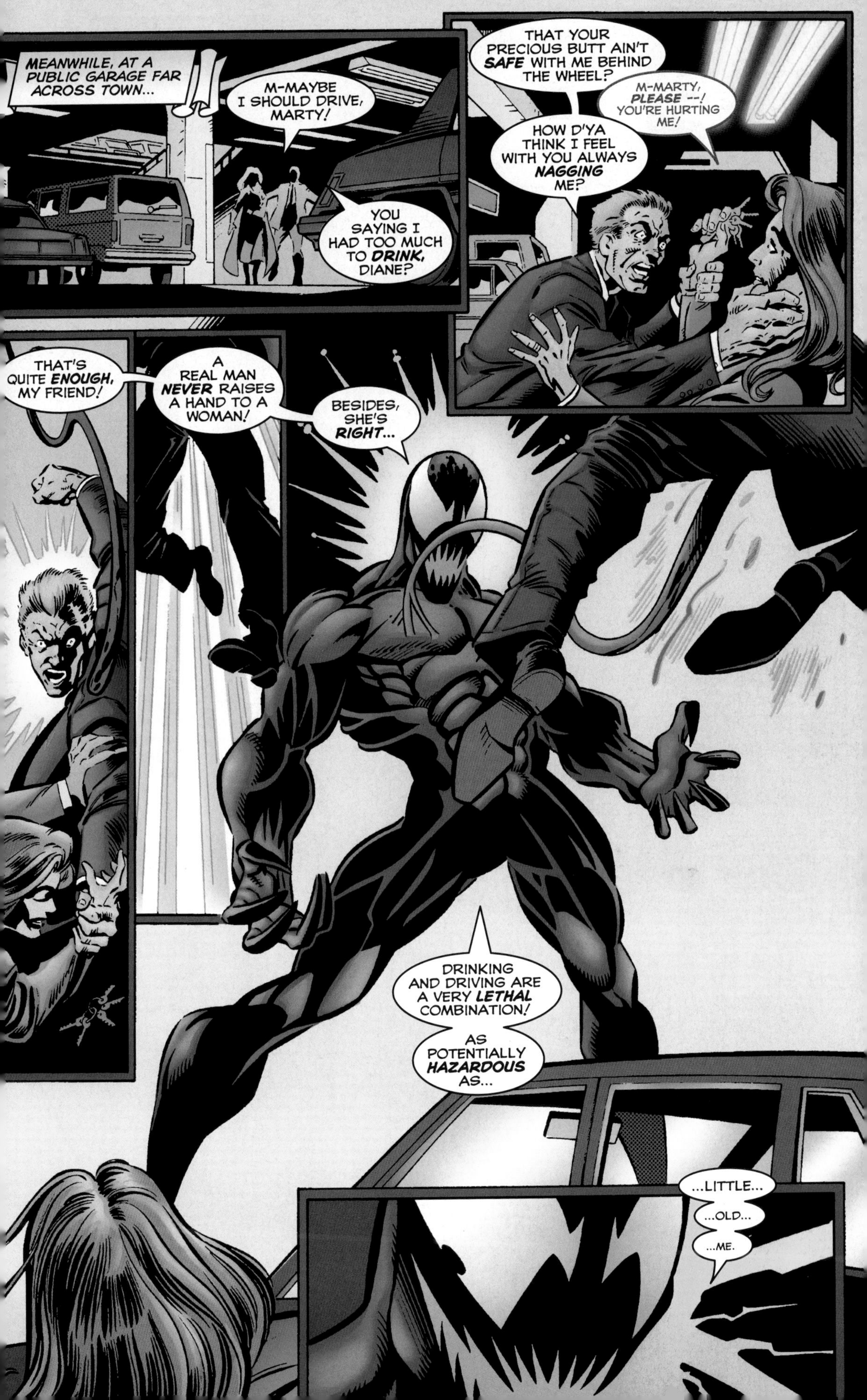
MEANWHILE, AT A PUBLIC GARAGE FAR ACROSS TOWN...
M-MAYBE I SHOULD DRIVE, MARTY!
YOU SAYING I HAD TOO MUCH TO DRINK, DIANE?
THAT YOUR PRECIOUS BUTT AIN'T SAFE WITH ME BEHIND THE WHEEL?
HOW D'YA THINK I FEEL WITH YOU ALWAYS NAGGING ME?
M-MARTY, PLEASE --! YOU'RE HURTING ME!
THAT'S QUITE ENOUGH, MY FRIEND!
A REAL MAN NEVER RAISES A HAND TO A WOMAN!
BESIDES, SHE'S RIGHT...
DRINKING AND DRIVING ARE A VERY LETHAL COMBINATION!
AS POTENTIALLY HAZARDOUS AS...
...LITTLE...
...OLD...
...ME.

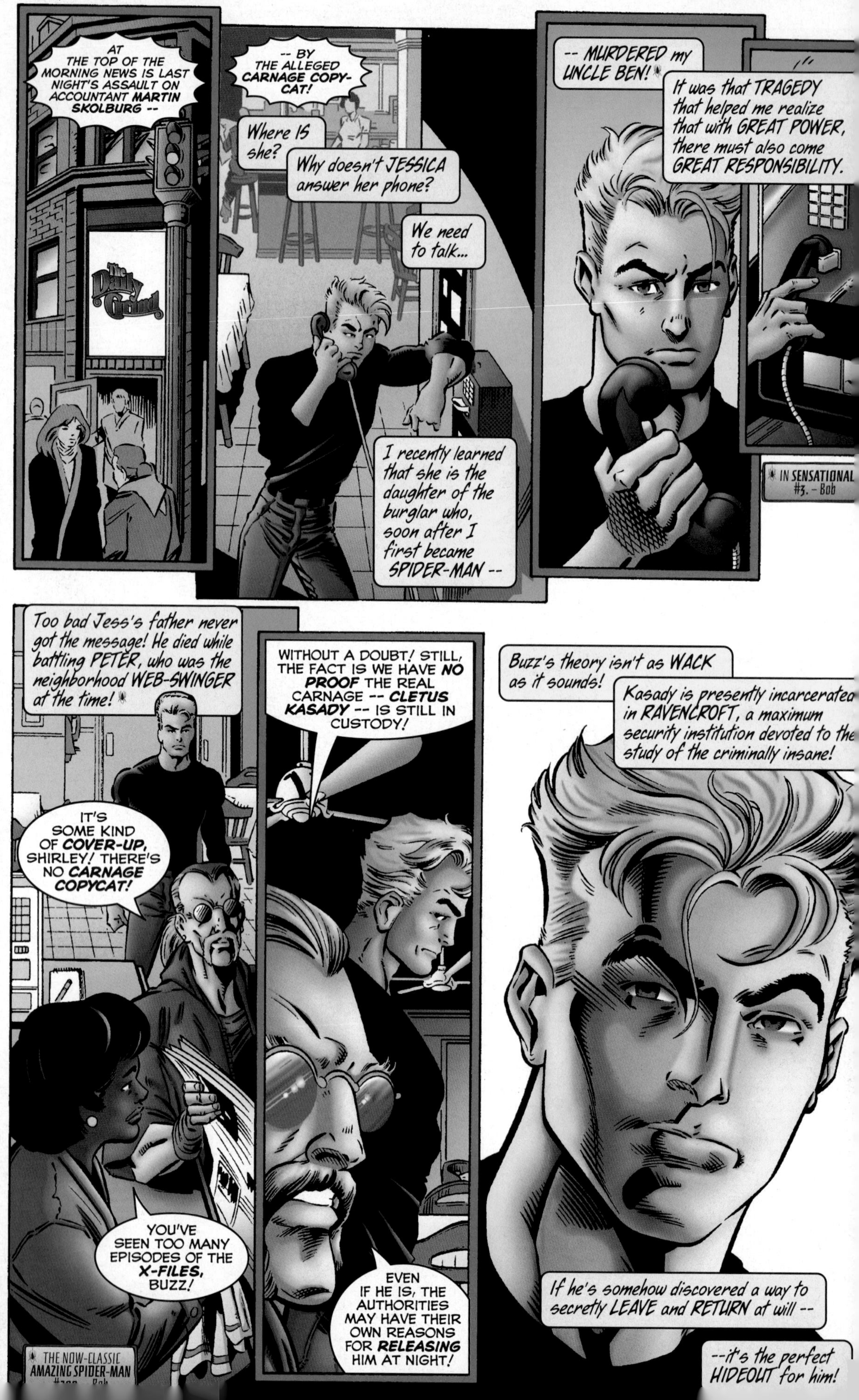
AT THE TOP OF THE MORNING NEWS IS LAST NIGHT'S ASSAULT ON ACCOUNTANT MARTIN SKOLBURG --
-- BY THE ALLEGED CARNAGE COPY-CAT!
The Daily Grind
Where IS she?
Why doesn't JESSICA answer her phone?
We need to talk...
I recently learned that she is the daughter of the burglar who, soon after I first became SPIDER-MAN --
-- MURDERED my UNCLE BEN!
It was that TRAGEDY that helped me realize that with GREAT POWER, there must also come GREAT RESPONSIBILITY.
IN SENSATIONAL #3. – Bob
Too bad Jess's father never got the message! He died while battling PETER, who was the neighborhood WEB-SWINGER at the time!
IT'S SOME KIND OF COVER-UP, SHIRLEY! THERE'S NO CARNAGE COPYCAT!
YOU'VE SEEN TOO MANY EPISODES OF THE X-FILES, BUZZ!
THE NOW-CLASSIC AMAZING SPIDER-MAN
WITHOUT A DOUBT! STILL, THE FACT IS WE HAVE NO PROOF THE REAL CARNAGE -- CLETUS KASADY -- IS STILL IN CUSTODY!
EVEN IF HE IS, THE AUTHORITIES MAY HAVE THEIR OWN REASONS FOR RELEASING HIM AT NIGHT!
Buzz's theory isn't as WACK as it sounds!
Kasady is presently incarcerated in RAVENCROFT, a maximum security institution devoted to the study of the criminally insane!
If he's somehow discovered a way to secretly LEAVE and RETURN at will --
--it's the perfect HIDEOUT for him!

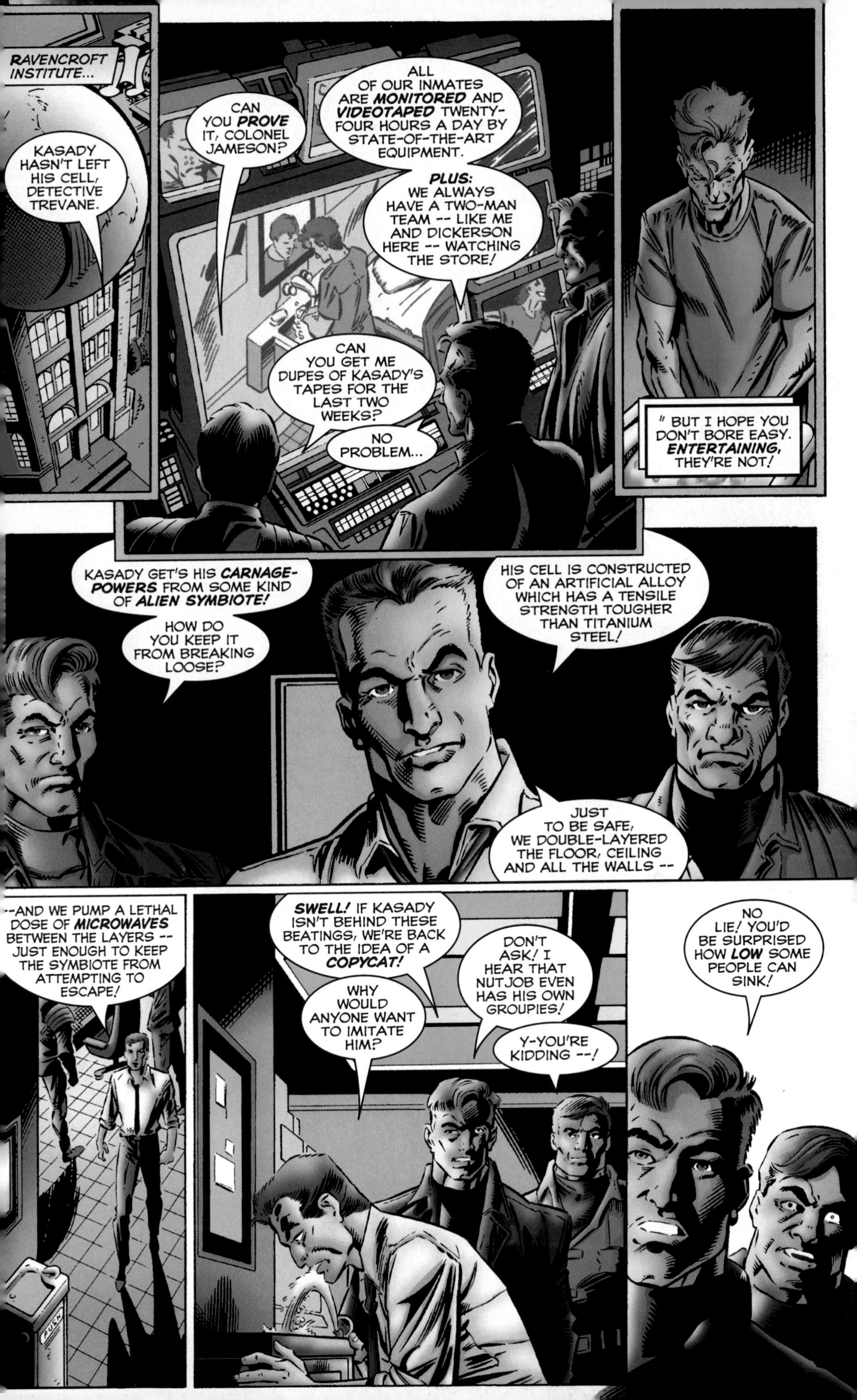
RAVENCROFT INSTITUTE...
KASADY HASN'T LEFT HIS CELL, DETECTIVE TREVANE.
CAN YOU PROVE IT, COLONEL JAMESON?
ALL OF OUR INMATES ARE MONITORED AND VIDEOTAPED TWENTY-FOUR HOURS A DAY BY STATE-OF-THE-ART EQUIPMENT.
PLUS: WE ALWAYS HAVE A TWO-MAN TEAM -- LIKE ME AND DICKERSON HERE -- WATCHING THE STORE!
CAN YOU GET ME DUPES OF KASADY'S TAPES FOR THE LAST TWO WEEKS?
NO PROBLEM...
" BUT I HOPE YOU DON'T BORE EASY. ENTERTAINING, THEY'RE NOT!
KASADY GET'S HIS CARNAGE-POWERS FROM SOME KIND OF ALIEN SYMBIOTE!
HOW DO YOU KEEP IT FROM BREAKING LOOSE?
HIS CELL IS CONSTRUCTED OF AN ARTIFICIAL ALLOY WHICH HAS A TENSILE STRENGTH TOUGHER THAN TITANIUM STEEL!
JUST TO BE SAFE, WE DOUBLE-LAYERED THE FLOOR, CEILING AND ALL THE WALLS --
--AND WE PUMP A LETHAL DOSE OF MICROWAVES BETWEEN THE LAYERS -- JUST ENOUGH TO KEEP THE SYMBIOTE FROM ATTEMPTING TO ESCAPE!
SWELL! IF KASADY ISN'T BEHIND THESE BEATINGS, WE'RE BACK TO THE IDEA OF A COPYCAT!
WHY WOULD ANYONE WANT TO IMITATE HIM?
DON'T ASK! I HEAR THAT NUTJOB EVEN HAS HIS OWN GROUPIES!
Y-YOU'RE KIDDING --!
NO LIE! YOU'D BE SURPRISED HOW LOW SOME PEOPLE CAN SINK!
PUSH

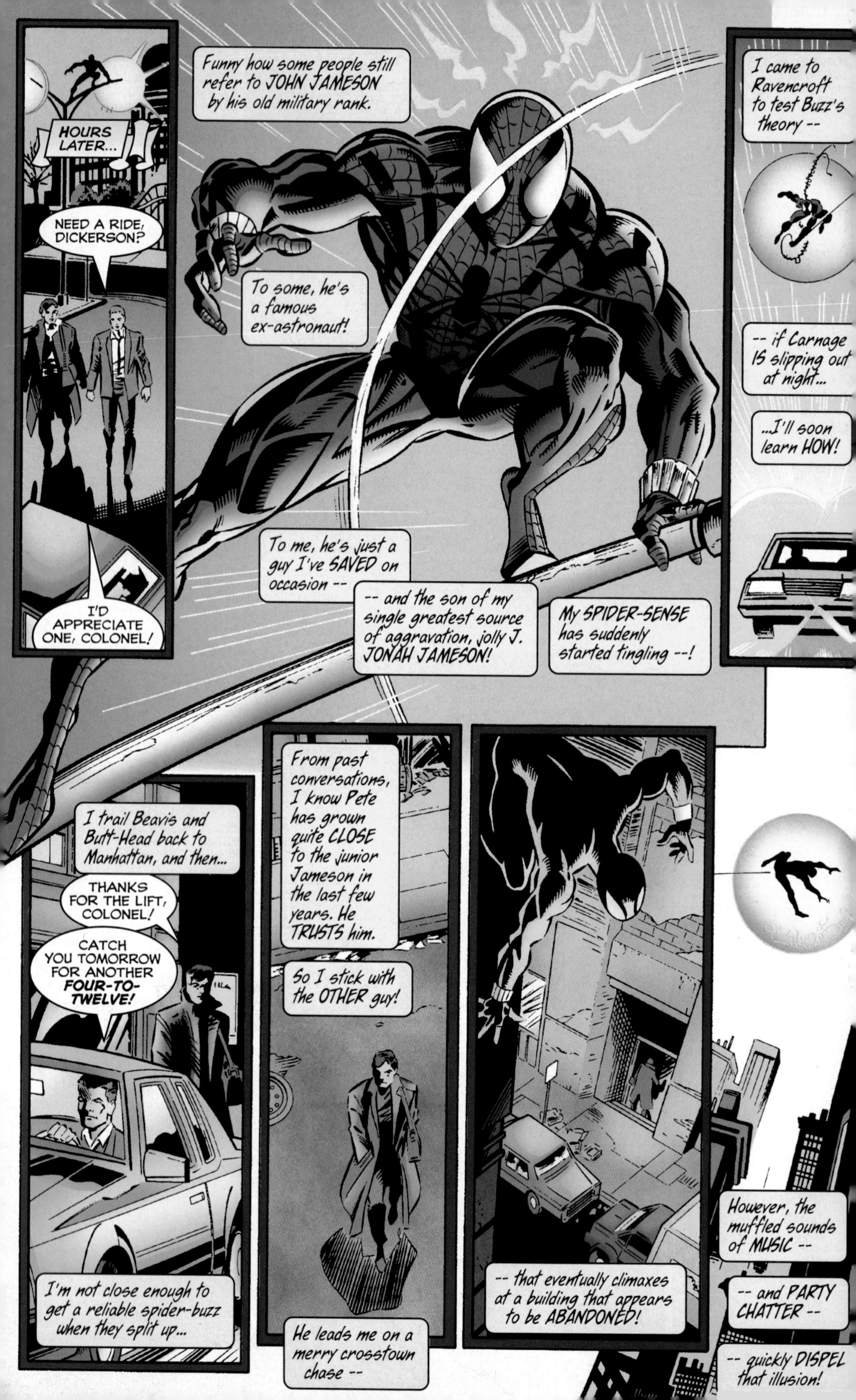
HOURS LATER...
NEED A RIDE, DICKERSON?
I'D APPRECIATE ONE, COLONEL!
Funny how some people still refer to JOHN JAMESON by his old military rank.
To some, he's a famous ex-astronaut!
To me, he's just a guy I've SAVED on occasion --
-- and the son of my single greatest source of aggravation, jolly J. JONAH JAMESON!
My SPIDER-SENSE has suddenly started tingling --!
I came to Ravencroft to test Buzz's theory --
-- if Carnage IS slipping out at night...
...I'll soon learn HOW!
I trail Beavis and Butt-Head back to Manhattan, and then...
THANKS FOR THE LIFT, COLONEL!
CATCH YOU TOMORROW FOR ANOTHER FOUR-TO-TWELVE!
I'm not close enough to get a reliable spider-buzz when they split up...
From past conversations, I know Pete has grown quite CLOSE to the junior Jameson in the last few years. He TRUSTS him.
So I stick with the OTHER guy!
He leads me on a merry crosstown chase --
-- that eventually climaxes at a building that appears to be ABANDONED!
However, the muffled sounds of MUSIC --
-- and PARTY CHATTER --
-- quickly DISPEL that illusion!

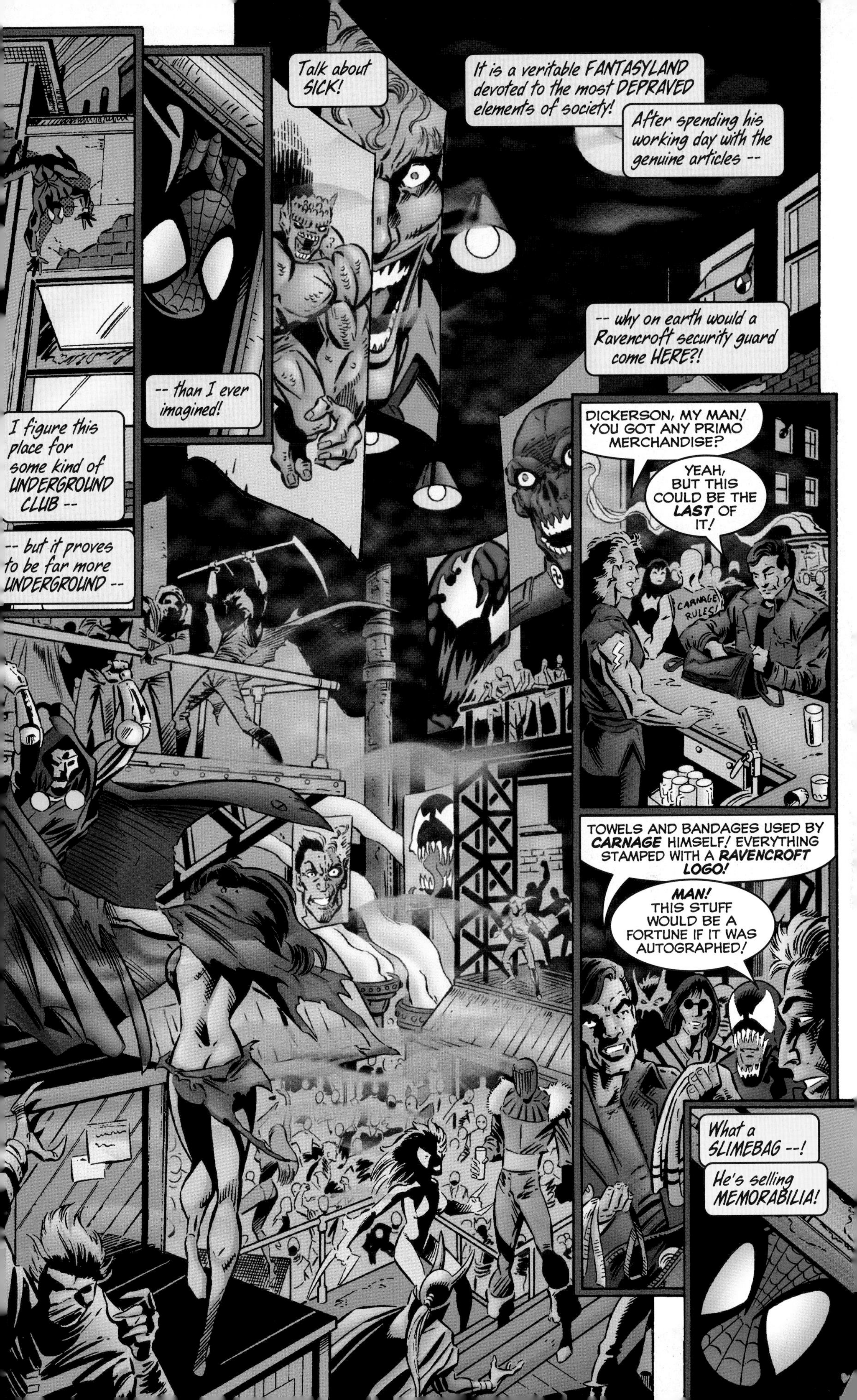

I figure this place for some kind of UNDERGROUND CLUB --
-- but it proves to be far more UNDERGROUND --
-- than I ever imagined!
Talk about SICK!
It is a veritable FANTASYLAND devoted to the most DEPRAVED elements of society!
After spending his working day with the genuine articles --
-- why on earth would a Ravencroft security guard come HERE?!
DICKERSON, MY MAN! YOU GOT ANY PRIMO MERCHANDISE?
YEAH, BUT THIS COULD BE THE LAST OF IT!
CARNAGE RULES!
TOWELS AND BANDAGES USED BY CARNAGE HIMSELF! EVERYTHING STAMPED WITH A RAVENCROFT LOGO!
MAN! THIS STUFF WOULD BE A FORTUNE IF IT WAS AUTOGRAPHED!
What a SLIMEBAG --!
He's selling MEMORABILIA!

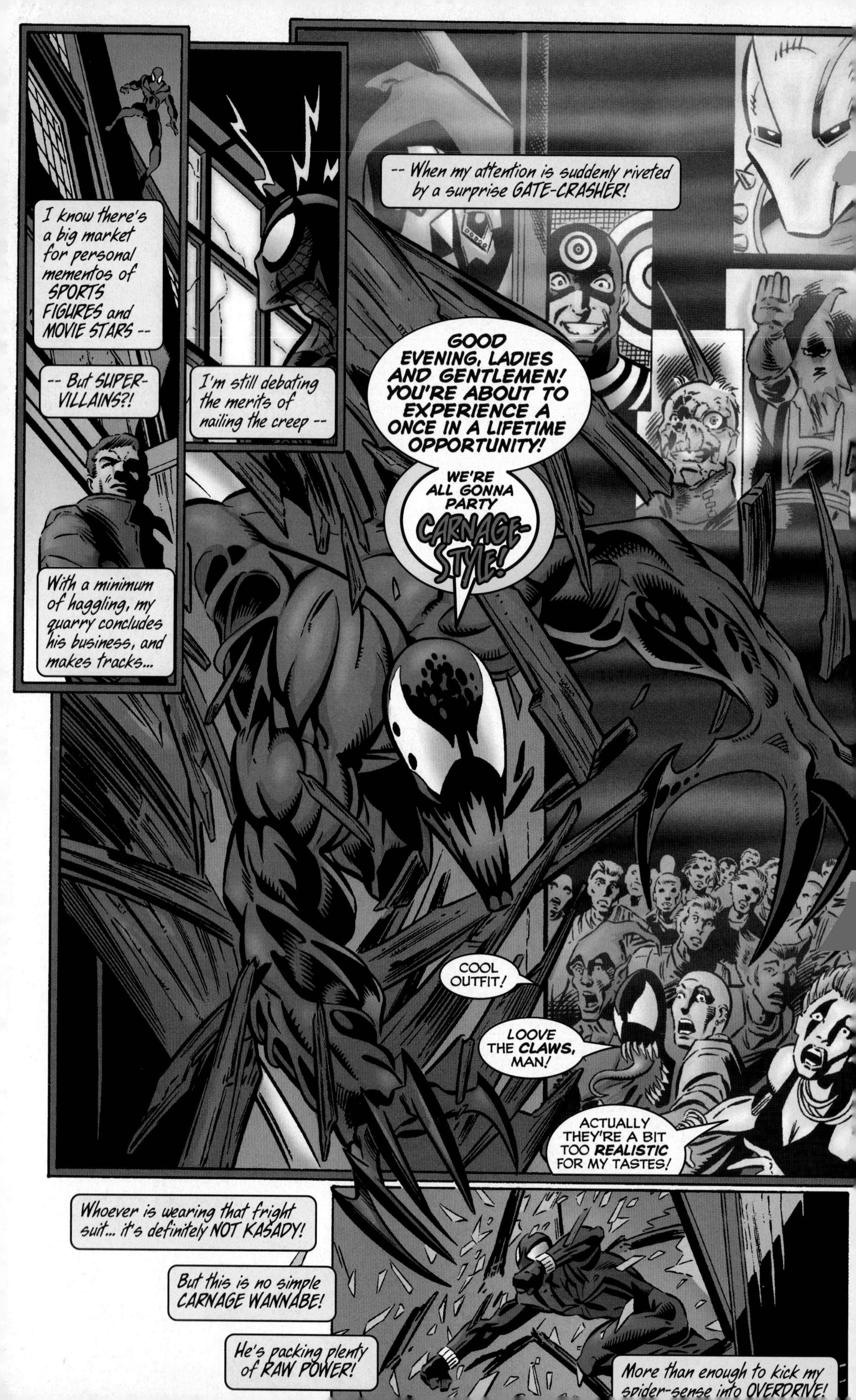
I know there's a big market for personal mementos of SPORTS FIGURES and MOVIE STARS --
-- But SUPER-VILLAINS?!
With a minimum of haggling, my quarry concludes his business, and makes tracks...
I'm still debating the merits of nailing the creep --
-- When my attention is suddenly riveted by a surprise GATE-CRASHER!
GOOD EVENING, LADIES AND GENTLEMEN! YOU'RE ABOUT TO EXPERIENCE A ONCE IN A LIFETIME OPPORTUNITY!
WE'RE ALL GONNA PARTY CARNAGE-STYLE!
COOL OUTFIT!
LOOVE THE CLAWS, MAN!
ACTUALLY THEY'RE A BIT TOO REALISTIC FOR MY TASTES!
Whoever is wearing that fright suit... it's definitely NOT KASADY!
But this is no simple CARNAGE WANNABE!
He's packing plenty of RAW POWER!
More than enough to kick my spider-sense into OVERDRIVE!

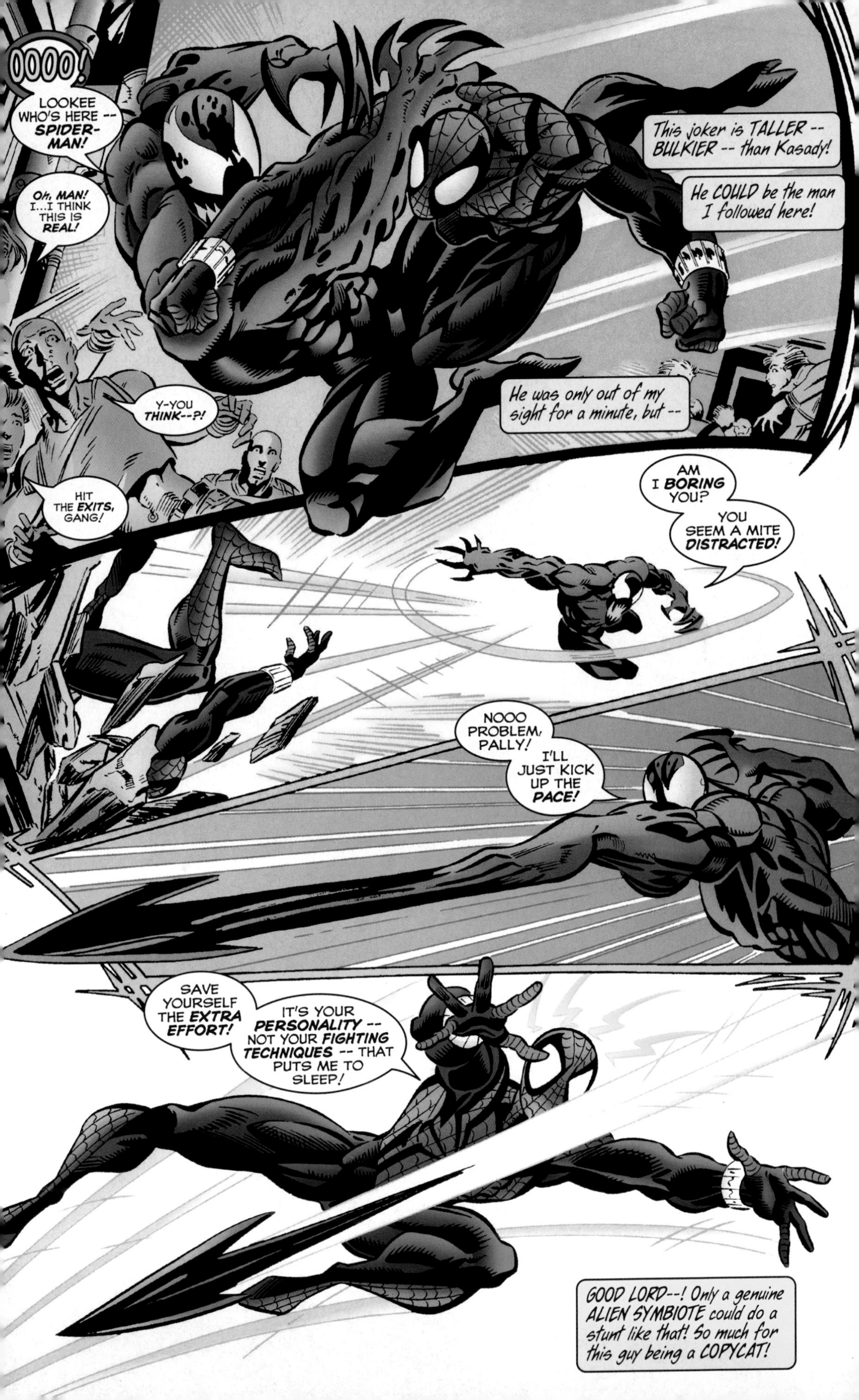

OOOO!
LOOKEE WHO'S HERE -- SPIDER-MAN!
Oh, MAN! I...I THINK THIS IS REAL!
This joker is TALLER -- BULKIER -- than Kasady!
He COULD be the man I followed here!
Y-YOU THINK--?!
He was only out of my sight for a minute, but --
HIT THE EXITS, GANG!
AM I BORING YOU?
YOU SEEM A MITE DISTRACTED!
NOOO PROBLEM, PALLY!
I'LL JUST KICK UP THE PACE!
SAVE YOURSELF THE EXTRA EFFORT!
IT'S YOUR PERSONALITY -- NOT YOUR FIGHTING TECHNIQUES -- THAT PUTS ME TO SLEEP!
GOOD LORD--! Only a genuine ALIEN SYMBIOTE could do a stunt like that! So much for this guy being a COPYCAT!

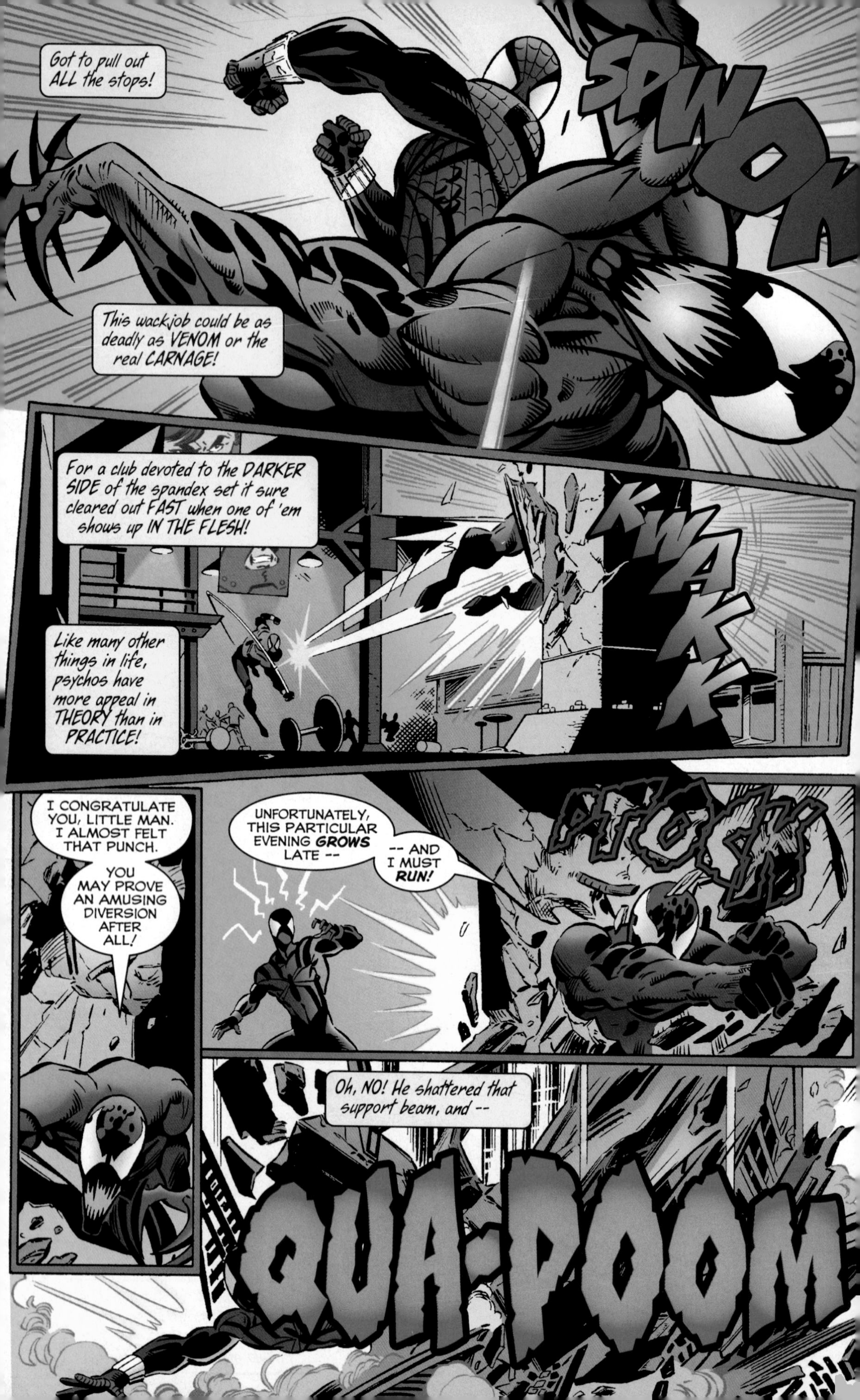

Got to pull out ALL the stops!
SPWOK
This wackjob could be as deadly as VENOM or the real CARNAGE!
For a club devoted to the DARKER SIDE of the spandex set it sure cleared out FAST when one of 'em shows up IN THE FLESH!
KWAKKK
Like many other things in life, psychos have more appeal in THEORY than in PRACTICE!
I CONGRATULATE YOU, LITTLE MAN. I ALMOST FELT THAT PUNCH.
YOU MAY PROVE AN AMUSING DIVERSION AFTER ALL!
UNFORTUNATELY, THIS PARTICULAR EVENING GROWS LATE --
-- AND I MUST RUN!
Oh, NO! He shattered that support beam, and --
QUA-POOM

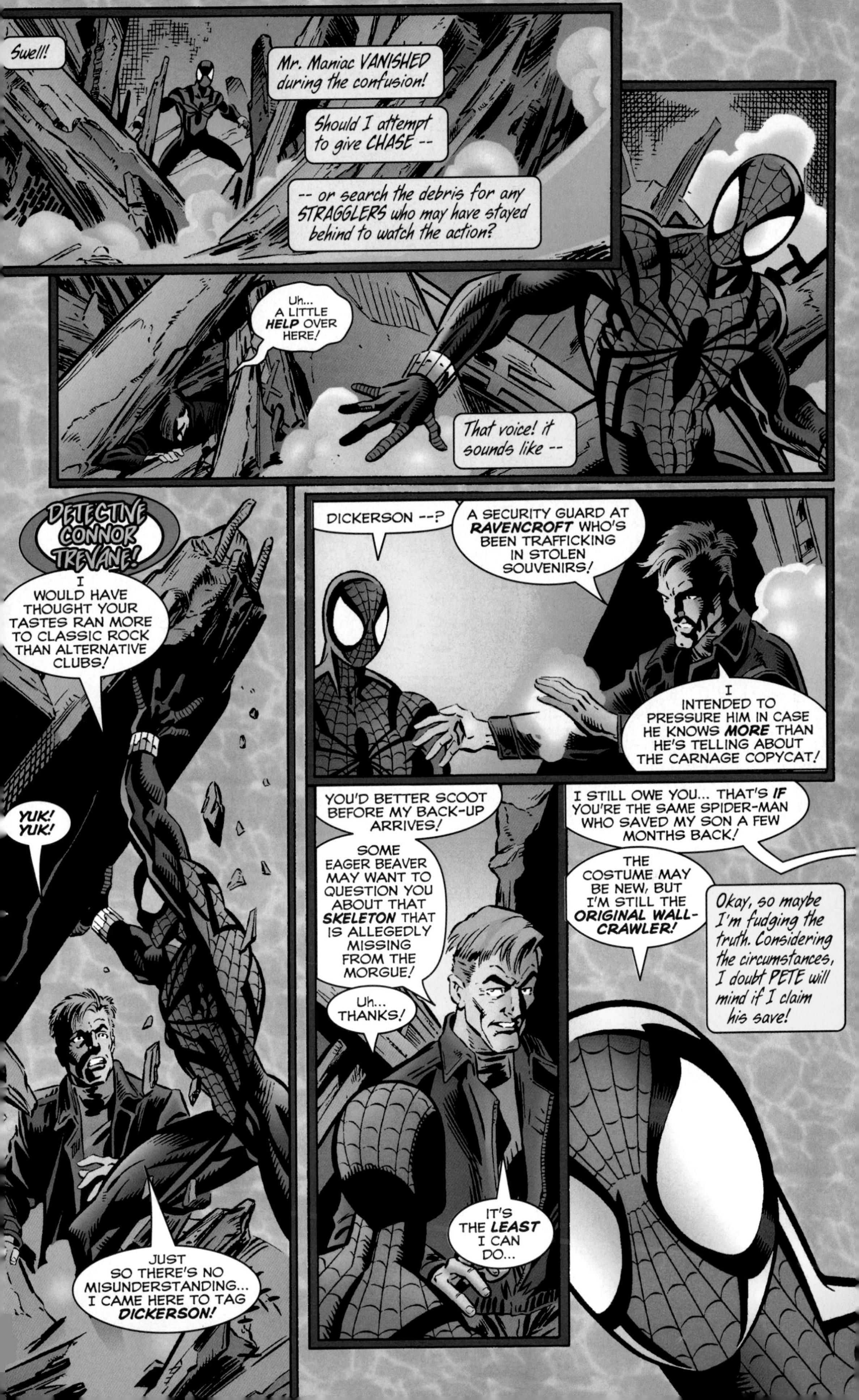
Swell!
Mr. Maniac VANISHED during the confusion!
Should I attempt to give CHASE --
-- or search the debris for any STRAGGLERS who may have stayed behind to watch the action?
Uh... A LITTLE HELP OVER HERE!
That voice! it sounds like --
DETECTIVE CONNOR TREVANE!
I WOULD HAVE THOUGHT YOUR TASTES RAN MORE TO CLASSIC ROCK THAN ALTERNATIVE CLUBS!
YUK! YUK!
JUST SO THERE'S NO MISUNDERSTANDING... I CAME HERE TO TAG DICKERSON!
DICKERSON --?
A SECURITY GUARD AT RAVENCROFT WHO'S BEEN TRAFFICKING IN STOLEN SOUVENIRS!
I INTENDED TO PRESSURE HIM IN CASE HE KNOWS MORE THAN HE'S TELLING ABOUT THE CARNAGE COPYCAT!
YOU'D BETTER SCOOT BEFORE MY BACK-UP ARRIVES!
SOME EAGER BEAVER MAY WANT TO QUESTION YOU ABOUT THAT SKELETON THAT IS ALLEGEDLY MISSING FROM THE MORGUE!
Uh... THANKS!
IT'S THE LEAST I CAN DO...
I STILL OWE YOU... THAT'S IF YOU'RE THE SAME SPIDER-MAN WHO SAVED MY SON A FEW MONTHS BACK!
THE COSTUME MAY BE NEW, BUT I'M STILL THE ORIGINAL WALL-CRAWLER!
Okay, so maybe I'm fudging the truth. Considering the circumstances, I doubt PETE will mind if I claim his save!

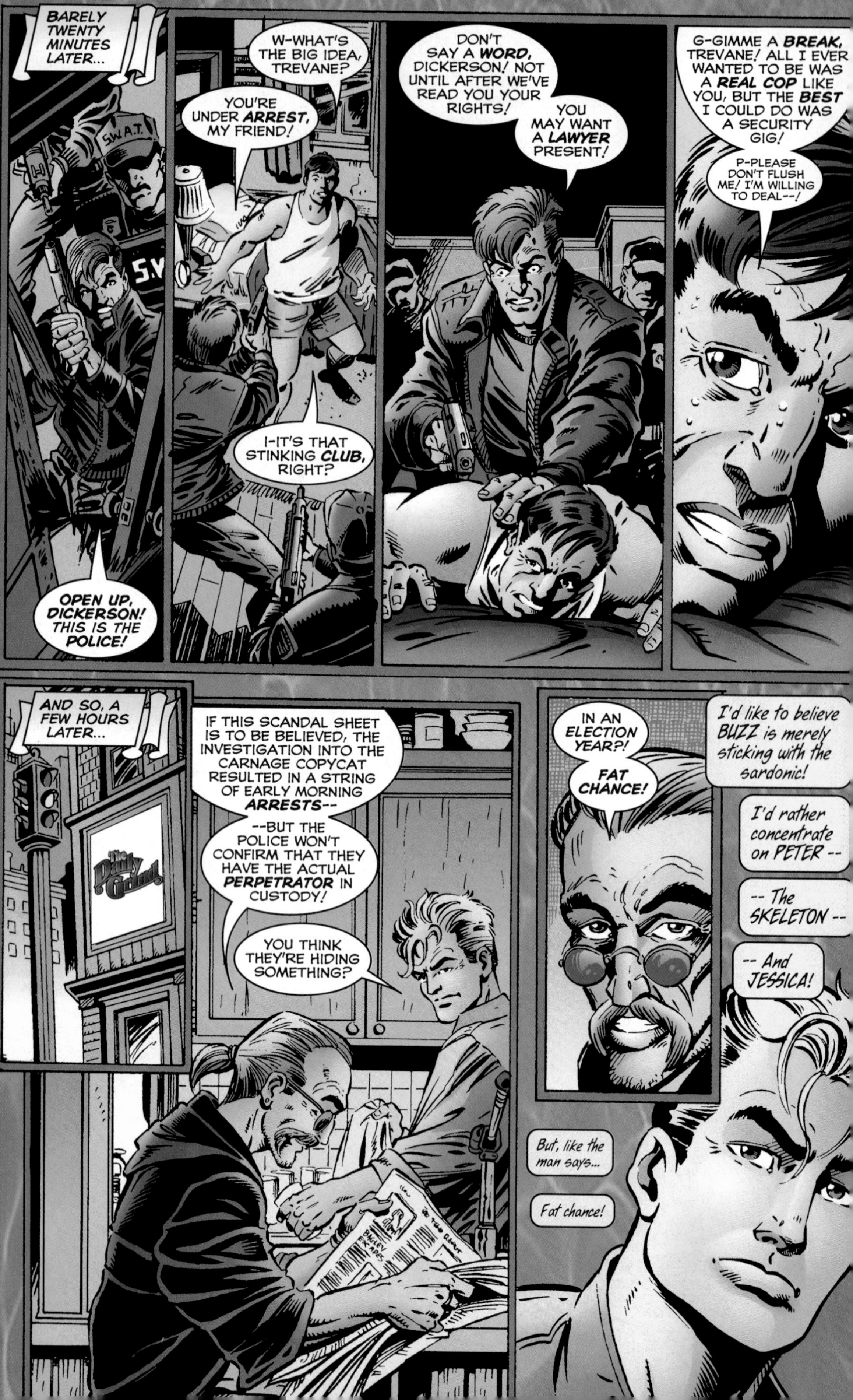
BARELY TWENTY MINUTES LATER...
OPEN UP, DICKERSON! THIS IS THE POLICE!
W-WHAT'S THE BIG IDEA, TREVANE?
YOU'RE UNDER ARREST, MY FRIEND!
I-IT'S THAT STINKING CLUB, RIGHT?
DON'T SAY A WORD, DICKERSON! NOT UNTIL AFTER WE'VE READ YOU YOUR RIGHTS!
YOU MAY WANT A LAWYER PRESENT!
G-GIMME A BREAK, TREVANE! ALL I EVER WANTED TO BE WAS A REAL COP LIKE YOU, BUT THE BEST I COULD DO WAS A SECURITY GIG!
P-PLEASE DON'T FLUSH ME! I'M WILLING TO DEAL--!
AND SO, A FEW HOURS LATER...
The Daily Grind
IF THIS SCANDAL SHEET IS TO BE BELIEVED, THE INVESTIGATION INTO THE CARNAGE COPYCAT RESULTED IN A STRING OF EARLY MORNING ARRESTS--
--BUT THE POLICE WON'T CONFIRM THAT THEY HAVE THE ACTUAL PERPETRATOR IN CUSTODY!
YOU THINK THEY'RE HIDING SOMETHING?
BAGLEY EXPIRES
IN AN ELECTION YEAR?!
FAT CHANCE!
I'd like to believe BUZZ is merely sticking with the sardonic!
I'd rather concentrate on PETER --
-- The SKELETON --
-- And JESSICA!
But, like the man says...
Fat chance!

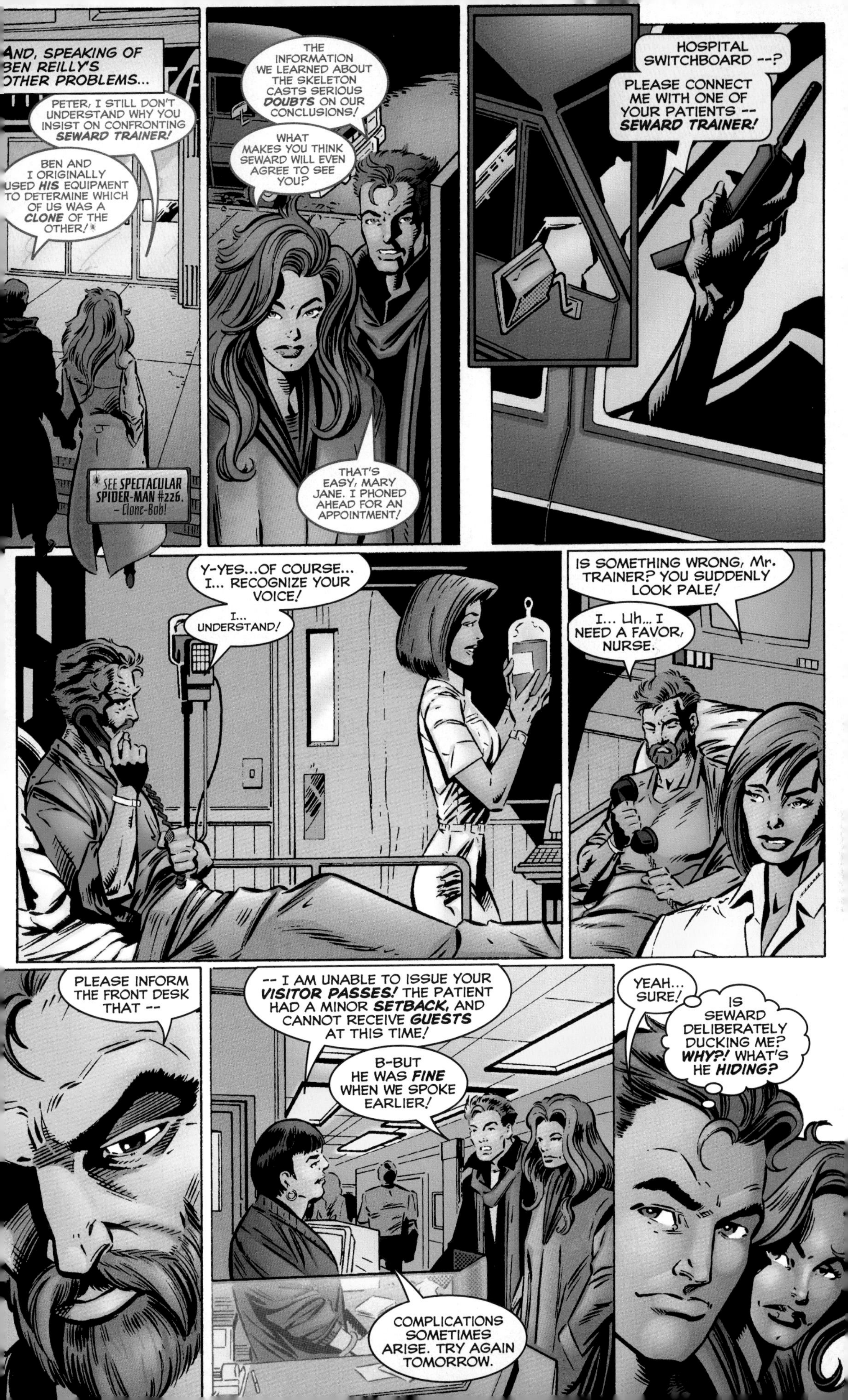
AND, SPEAKING OF BEN REILLY'S OTHER PROBLEMS...
PETER, I STILL DON'T UNDERSTAND WHY YOU INSIST ON CONFRONTING SEWARD TRAINER!
BEN AND I ORIGINALLY USED HIS EQUIPMENT TO DETERMINE WHICH OF US WAS A CLONE OF THE OTHER!
SEE SPECTACULAR SPIDER-MAN #226. –Clone-Bob!
THE INFORMATION WE LEARNED ABOUT THE SKELETON CASTS SERIOUS DOUBTS ON OUR CONCLUSIONS!
WHAT MAKES YOU THINK SEWARD WILL EVEN AGREE TO SEE YOU?
THAT'S EASY, MARY JANE. I PHONED AHEAD FOR AN APPOINTMENT!
HOSPITAL SWITCHBOARD --?
PLEASE CONNECT ME WITH ONE OF YOUR PATIENTS -- SEWARD TRAINER!
Y-YES...OF COURSE... I... RECOGNIZE YOUR VOICE!
I... UNDERSTAND!
IS SOMETHING WRONG, Mr. TRAINER? YOU SUDDENLY LOOK PALE!
I... Uh... I NEED A FAVOR, NURSE.
PLEASE INFORM THE FRONT DESK THAT --
-- I AM UNABLE TO ISSUE YOUR VISITOR PASSES! THE PATIENT HAD A MINOR SETBACK, AND CANNOT RECEIVE GUESTS AT THIS TIME!
B-BUT HE WAS FINE WHEN WE SPOKE EARLIER!
COMPLICATIONS SOMETIMES ARISE. TRY AGAIN TOMORROW.
YEAH... SURE!
IS SEWARD DELIBERATELY DUCKING ME? WHY?! WHAT'S HE HIDING?

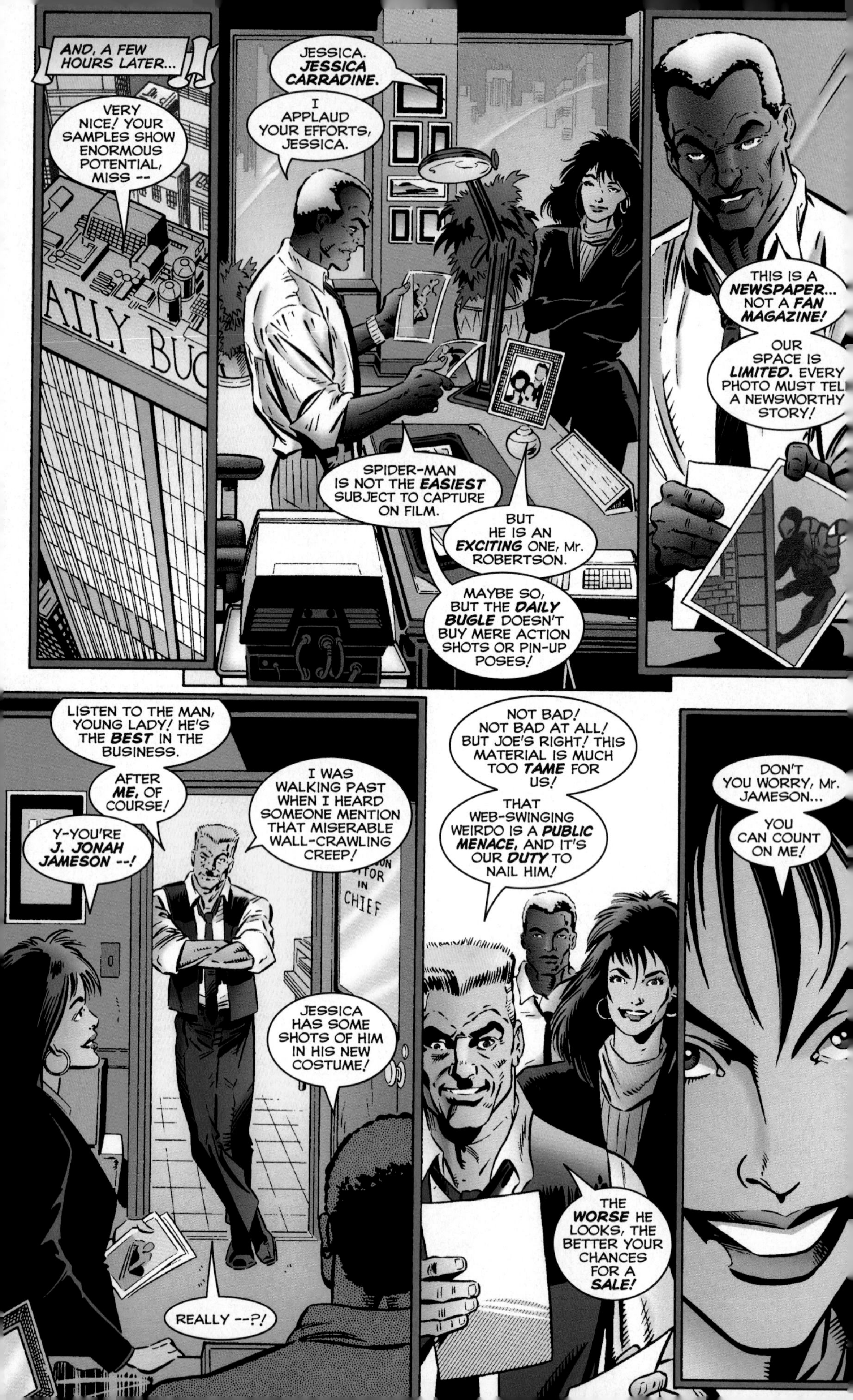
AND, A FEW HOURS LATER...
VERY NICE! YOUR SAMPLES SHOW ENORMOUS POTENTIAL, MISS --
JESSICA. JESSICA CARRADINE.
I APPLAUD YOUR EFFORTS, JESSICA.
SPIDER-MAN IS NOT THE EASIEST SUBJECT TO CAPTURE ON FILM.
BUT HE IS AN EXCITING ONE, Mr. ROBERTSON.
MAYBE SO, BUT THE DAILY BUGLE DOESN'T BUY MERE ACTION SHOTS OR PIN-UP POSES!
THIS IS A NEWSPAPER... NOT A FAN MAGAZINE!
OUR SPACE IS LIMITED. EVERY PHOTO MUST TELL A NEWSWORTHY STORY!
LISTEN TO THE MAN, YOUNG LADY! HE'S THE BEST IN THE BUSINESS.
AFTER ME, OF COURSE!
Y-YOU'RE J. JONAH JAMESON --!
I WAS WALKING PAST WHEN I HEARD SOMEONE MENTION THAT MISERABLE WALL-CRAWLING CREEP!
JESSICA HAS SOME SHOTS OF HIM IN HIS NEW COSTUME!
REALLY --?!
NOT BAD! NOT BAD AT ALL! BUT JOE'S RIGHT! THIS MATERIAL IS MUCH TOO TAME FOR US!
THAT WEB-SWINGING WEIRDO IS A PUBLIC MENACE, AND IT'S OUR DUTY TO NAIL HIM!
THE WORSE HE LOOKS, THE BETTER YOUR CHANCES FOR A SALE!
DON'T YOU WORRY, Mr. JAMESON...
YOU CAN COUNT ON ME!

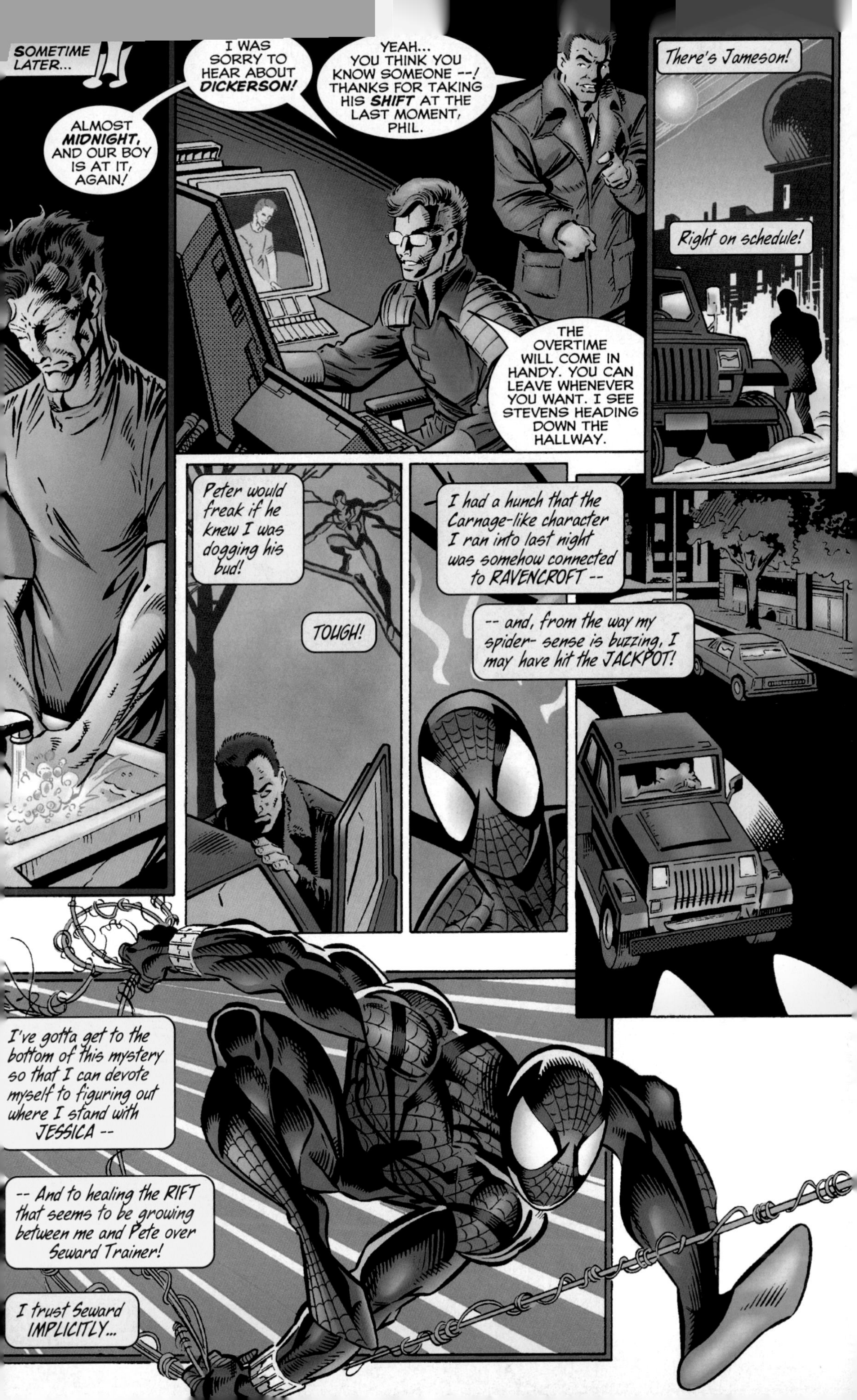

SOMETIME LATER...
ALMOST MIDNIGHT, AND OUR BOY IS AT IT, AGAIN!
I WAS SORRY TO HEAR ABOUT DICKERSON!
YEAH... YOU THINK YOU KNOW SOMEONE --! THANKS FOR TAKING HIS SHIFT AT THE LAST MOMENT, PHIL.
THE OVERTIME WILL COME IN HANDY. YOU CAN LEAVE WHENEVER YOU WANT. I SEE STEVENS HEADING DOWN THE HALLWAY.
There's Jameson!
Right on schedule!
Peter would freak if he knew I was dogging his bud!
TOUGH!
I had a hunch that the Carnage-like character I ran into last night was somehow connected to RAVENCROFT --
-- and, from the way my spider- sense is buzzing, I may have hit the JACKPOT!
I've gotta get to the bottom of this mystery so that I can devote myself to figuring out where I stand with JESSICA --
-- And to healing the RIFT that seems to be growing between me and Pete over Seward Trainer!
I trust Seward IMPLICITLY...

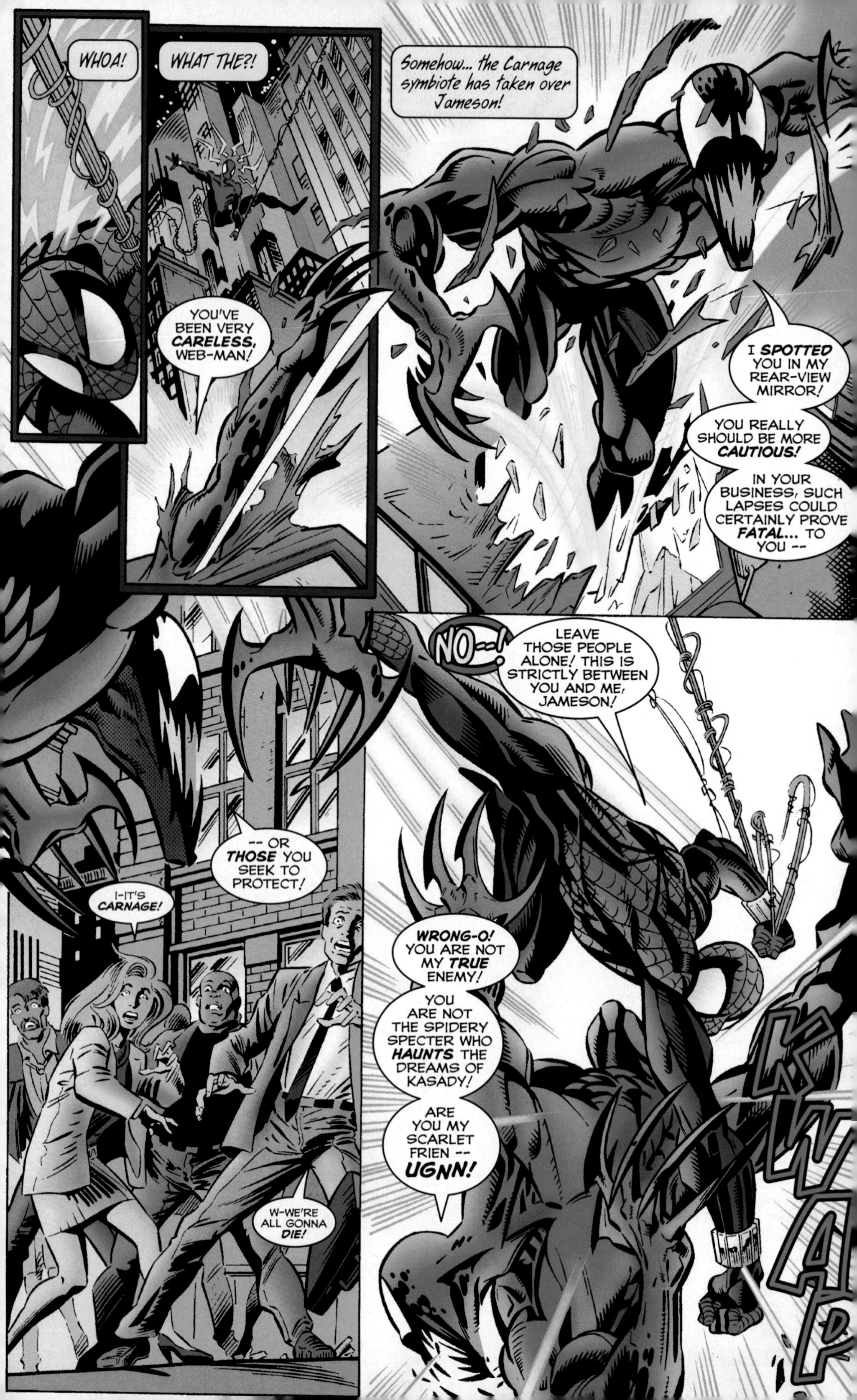
WHOA!
WHAT THE?!
Somehow... the Carnage symbiote has taken over Jameson!
YOU'VE BEEN VERY CARELESS, WEB-MAN!
I SPOTTED YOU IN MY REAR-VIEW MIRROR!
YOU REALLY SHOULD BE MORE CAUTIOUS!
IN YOUR BUSINESS, SUCH LAPSES COULD CERTAINLY PROVE FATAL... TO YOU --
-- OR THOSE YOU SEEK TO PROTECT!
I-IT'S CARNAGE!
W-WE'RE ALL GONNA DIE!
NO--!
LEAVE THOSE PEOPLE ALONE! THIS IS STRICTLY BETWEEN YOU AND ME, JAMESON!
WRONG-O! YOU ARE NOT MY TRUE ENEMY!
YOU ARE NOT THE SPIDERY SPECTER WHO HAUNTS THE DREAMS OF KASADY!
ARE YOU MY SCARLET FRIEN -- UGNN!
KWAP

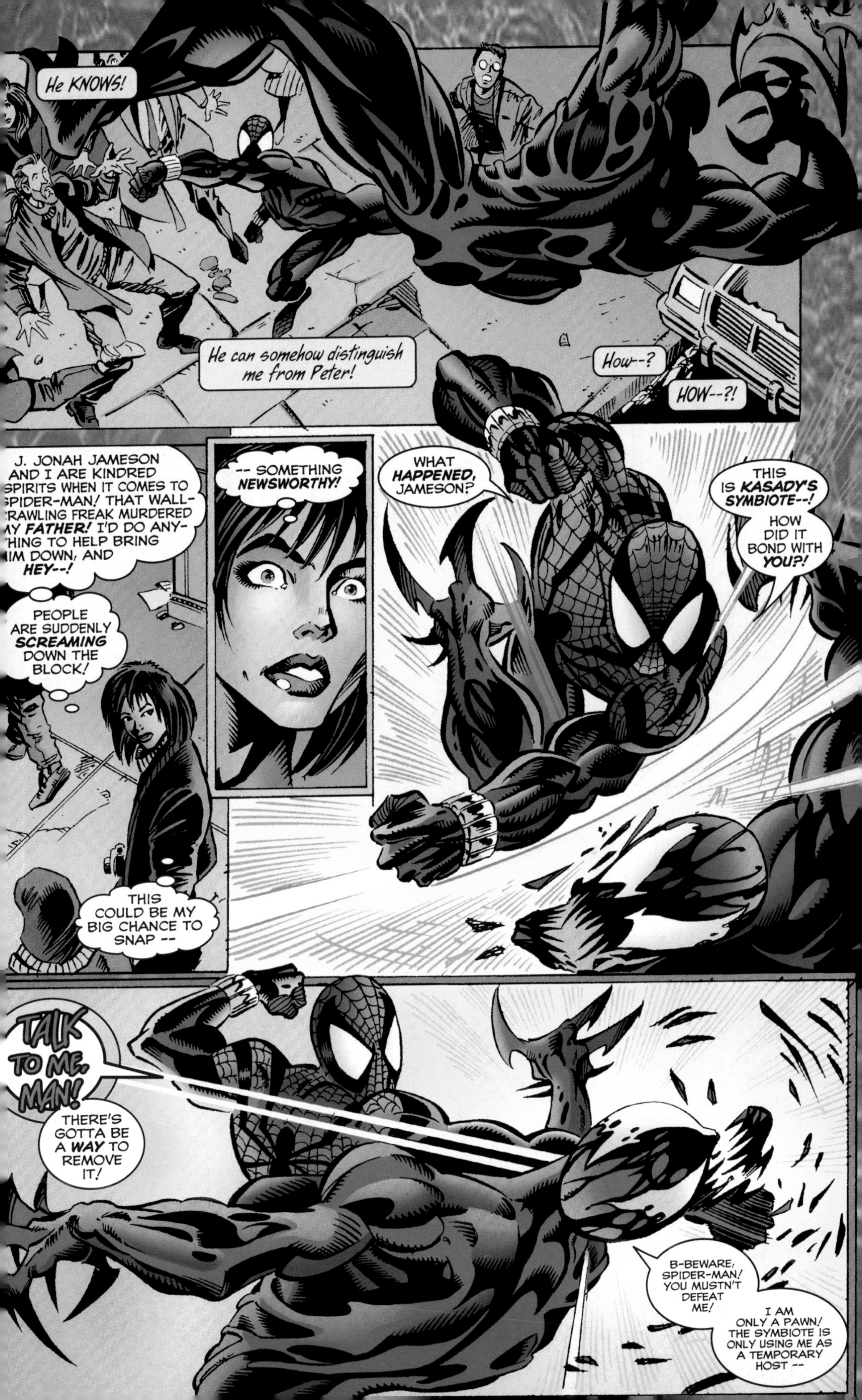
He KNOWS!
He can somehow distinguish me from Peter!
How--?
HOW--?!
J. JONAH JAMESON AND I ARE KINDRED SPIRITS WHEN IT COMES TO SPIDER-MAN! THAT WALL-CRAWLING FREAK MURDERED MY FATHER! I'D DO ANYTHING TO HELP BRING HIM DOWN, AND HEY--!
PEOPLE ARE SUDDENLY SCREAMING DOWN THE BLOCK!
THIS COULD BE MY BIG CHANCE TO SNAP --
-- SOMETHING NEWSWORTHY!
WHAT HAPPENED, JAMESON?
THIS IS KASADY'S SYMBIOTE--!
HOW DID IT BOND WITH YOU?!
TALK TO ME, MAN!
THERE'S GOTTA BE A WAY TO REMOVE IT!
B-BEWARE, SPIDER-MAN! YOU MUSTN'T DEFEAT ME!
I AM ONLY A PAWN! THE SYMBIOTE IS ONLY USING ME AS A TEMPORARY HOST --

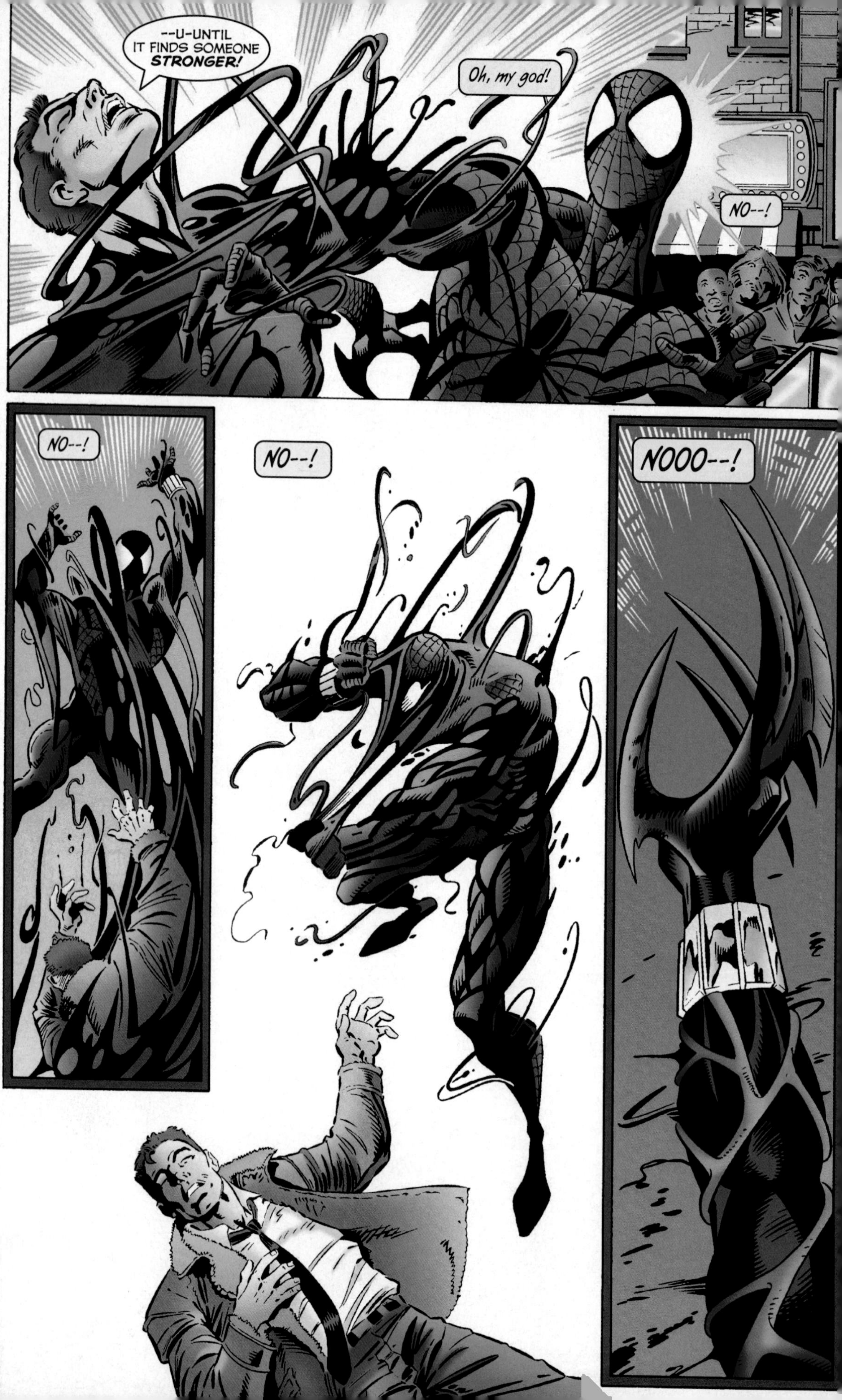
--U-UNTIL IT FINDS SOMEONE STRONGER!
Oh, my god!
NO--!
NO--!
NO--!
NOOO--!

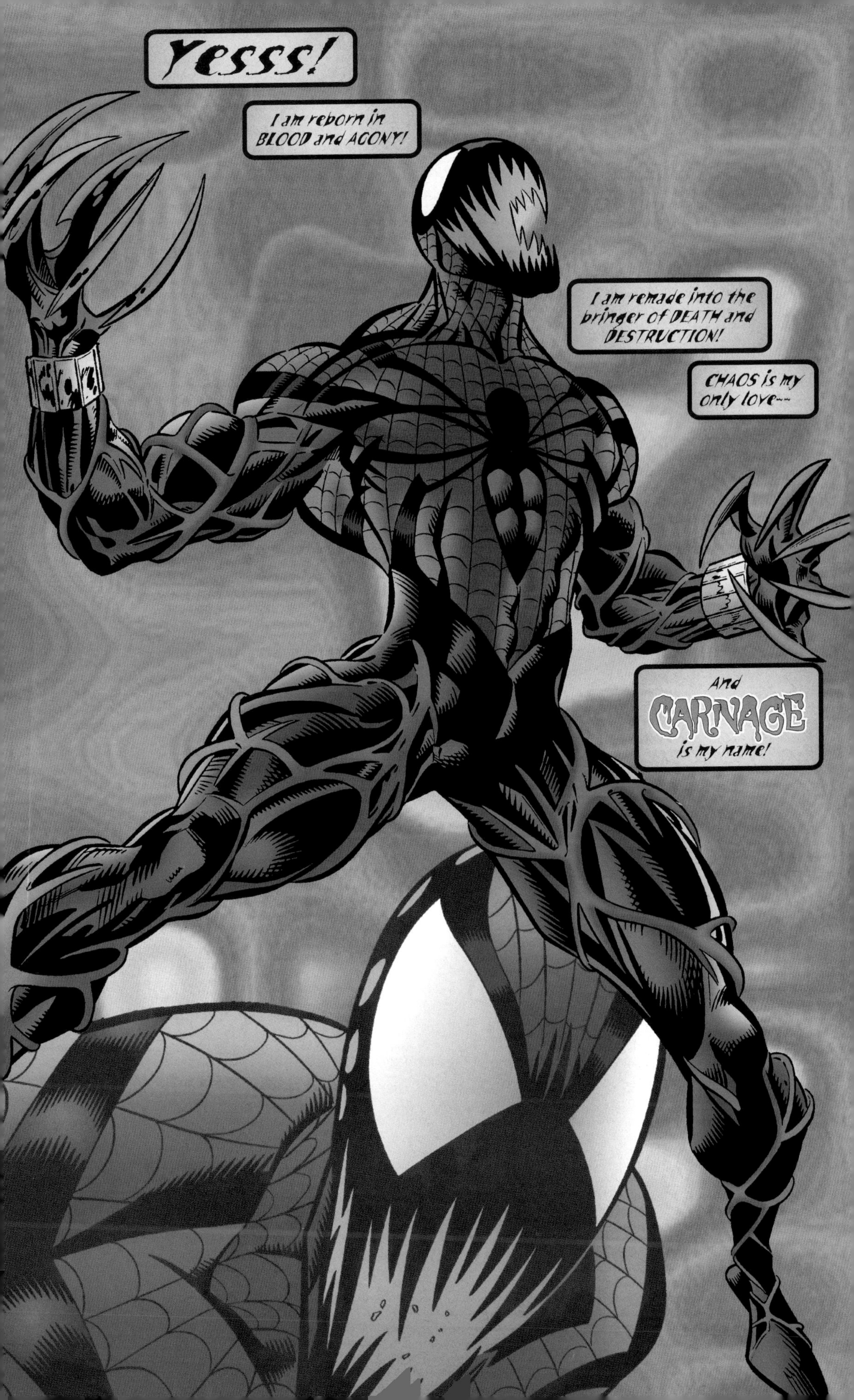
Yesss!
I am reborn in BLOOD and AGONY!
I am remade into the bringer of DEATH and DESTRUCTION!
CHAOS is my only love--
And CARNAGE is my name!

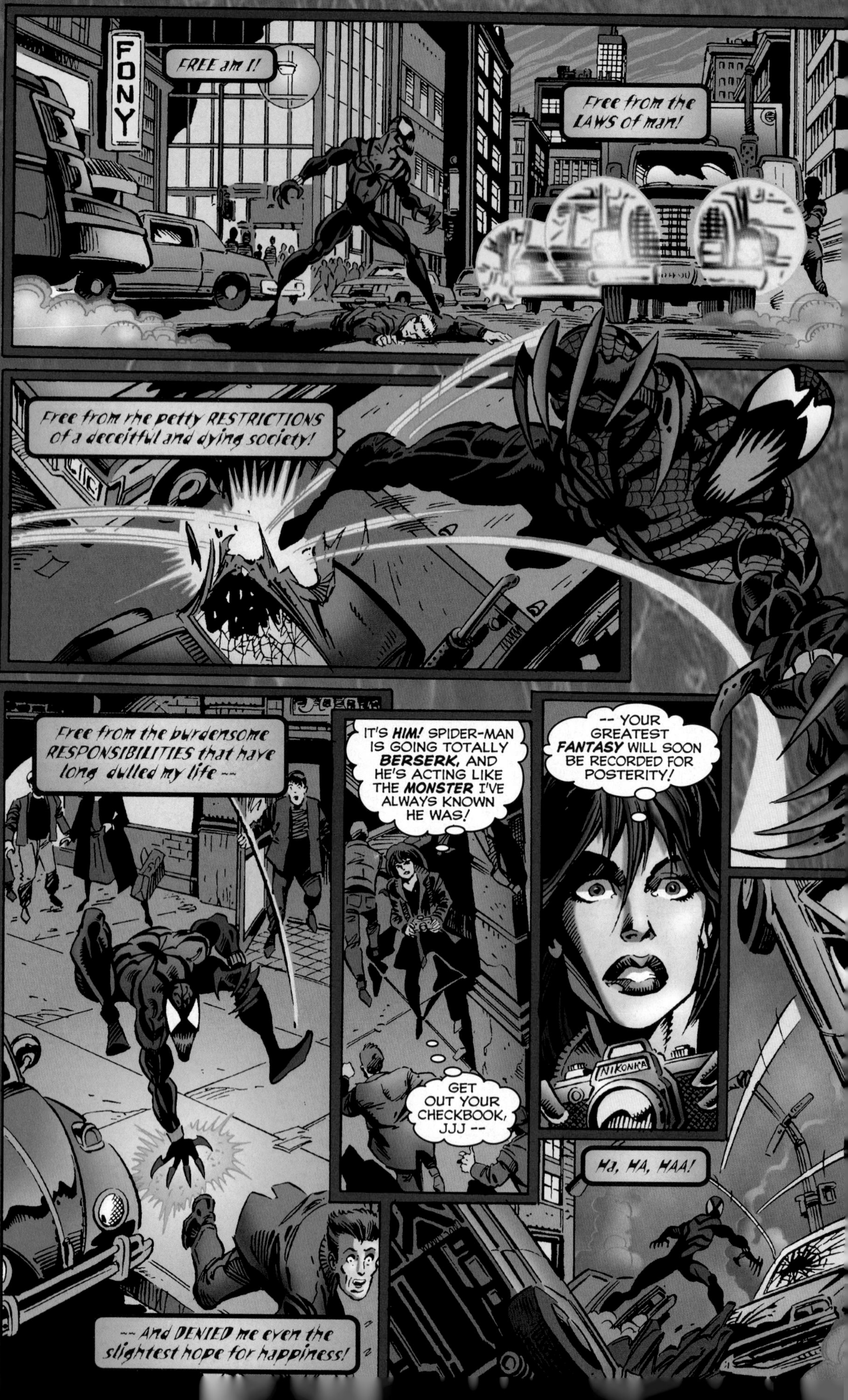
FONY
FREE am I!
Free from the LAWS of man!
Free from the petty RESTRICTIONS of a deceitful and dying society!
Free from the burdensome RESPONSIBILITIES that have long dulled my life --
IT'S HIM! SPIDER-MAN IS GOING TOTALLY BERSERK, AND HE'S ACTING LIKE THE MONSTER I'VE ALWAYS KNOWN HE WAS!
GET OUT YOUR CHECKBOOK, JJJ --
-- YOUR GREATEST FANTASY WILL SOON BE RECORDED FOR POSTERITY!
NIKONKA
Ha, HA, HAA!
-- And DENIED me even the slightest hope for happiness!

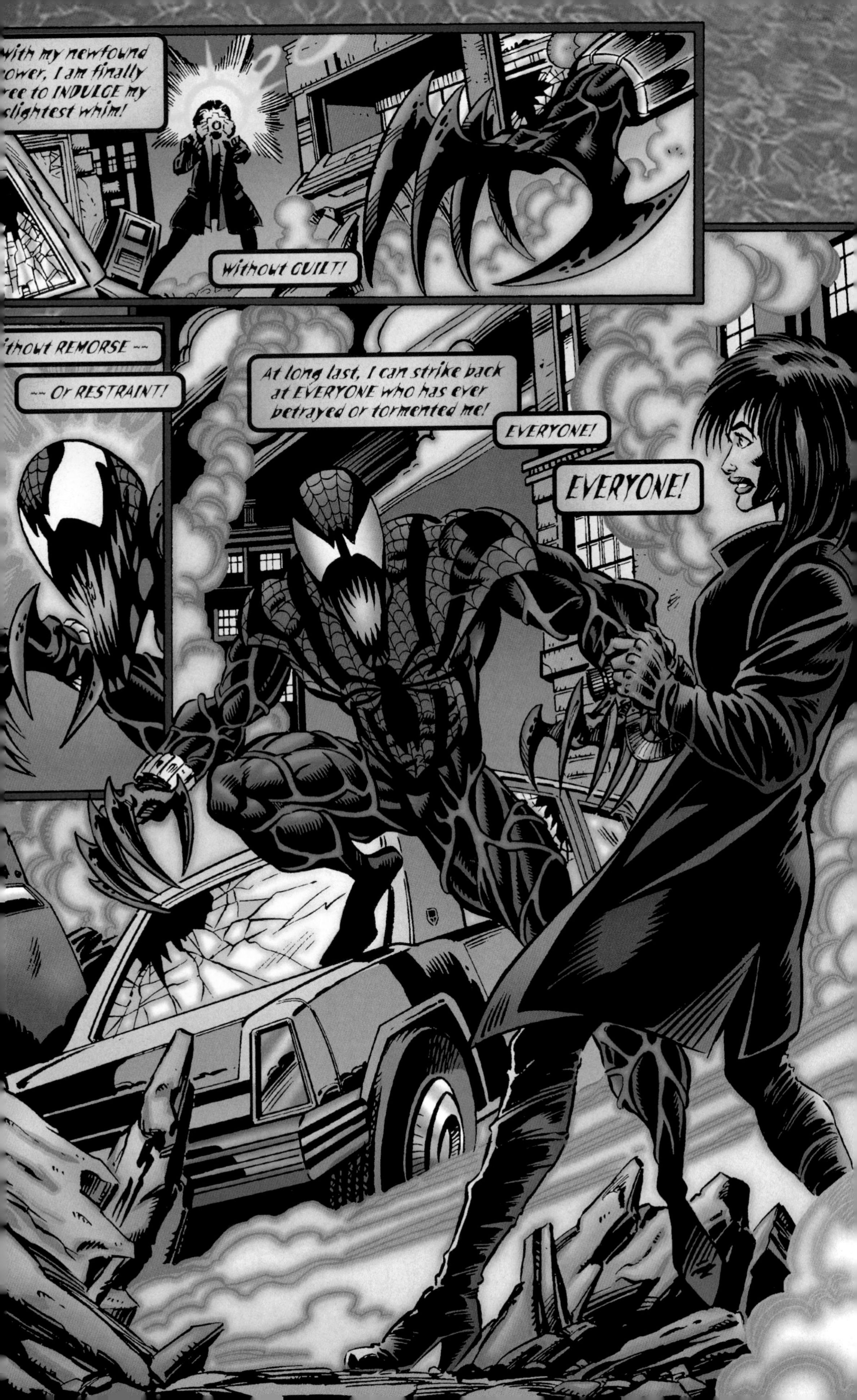

with my newfound ower, I am finally ree to INDULGE my slightest whim!
Without GUILT!
'thout REMORSE --
-- Or RESTRAINT!
At long last, I can strike back at EVERYONE who has ever betrayed or tormented me!
EVERYONE!
EVERYONE!

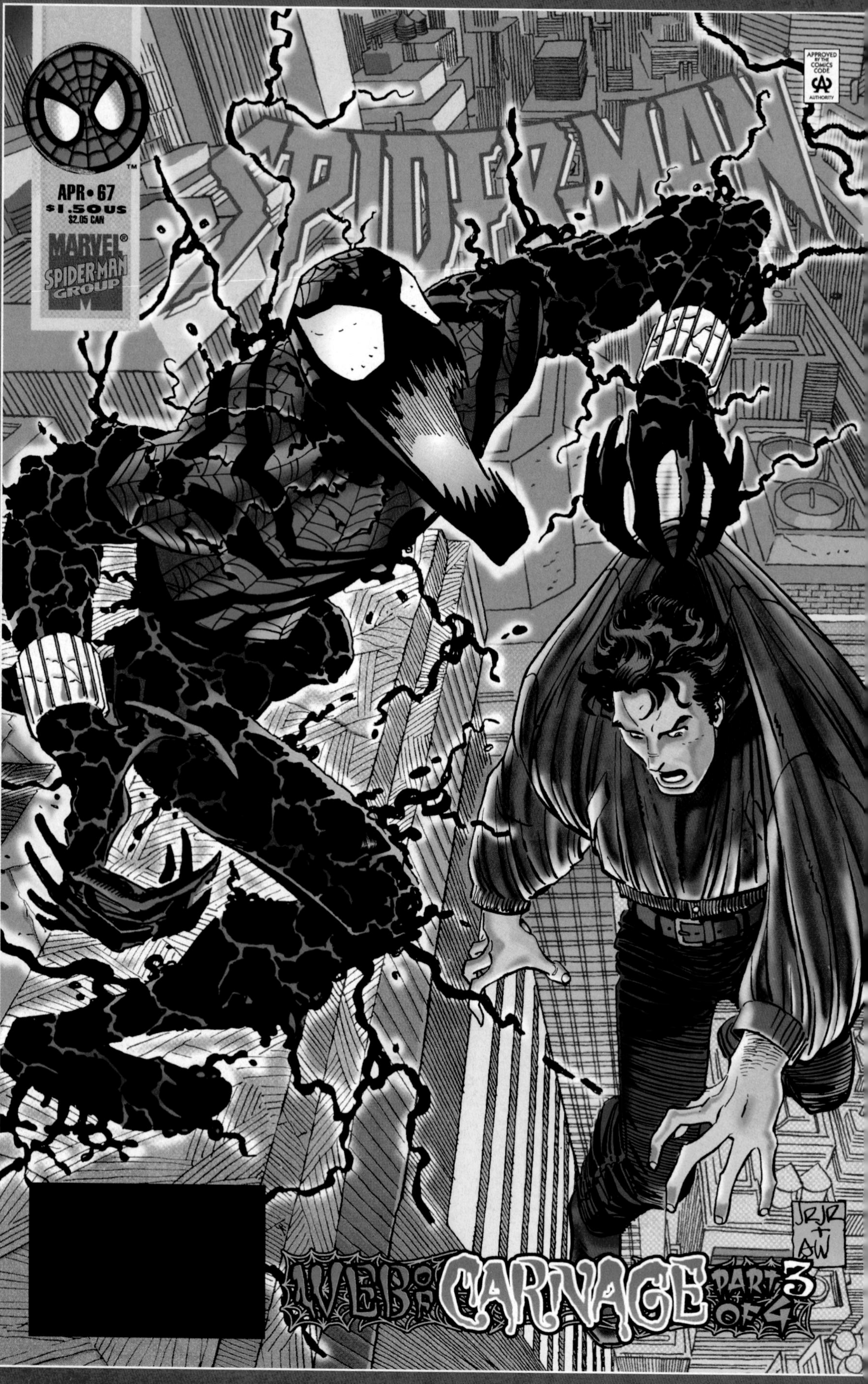
SPIDER-MAN
APR • 67
$1.50US
$2.05 CAN
MARVEL®
SPIDER-MAN GROUP
APPROVED BY THE COMICS CODE AUTHORITY
JRJR + AW
WEB OF CARNAGE PART 3 OF 4

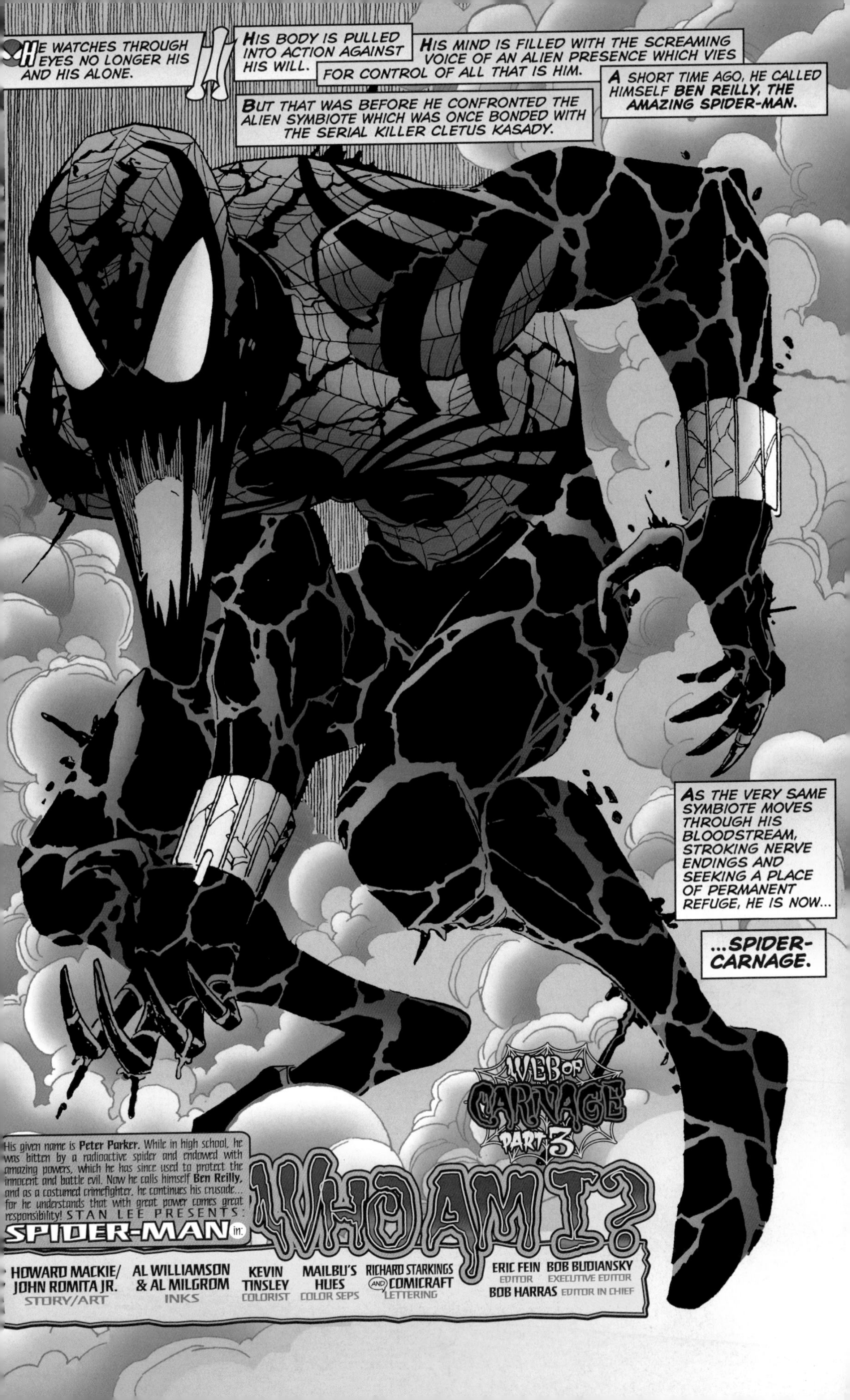

HE WATCHES THROUGH EYES NO LONGER HIS AND HIS ALONE.
HIS BODY IS PULLED INTO ACTION AGAINST HIS WILL.
HIS MIND IS FILLED WITH THE SCREAMING VOICE OF AN ALIEN PRESENCE WHICH VIES FOR CONTROL OF ALL THAT IS HIM.
A SHORT TIME AGO, HE CALLED HIMSELF BEN REILLY, THE AMAZING SPIDER-MAN.
BUT THAT WAS BEFORE HE CONFRONTED THE ALIEN SYMBIOTE WHICH WAS ONCE BONDED WITH THE SERIAL KILLER CLETUS KASADY.
AS THE VERY SAME SYMBIOTE MOVES THROUGH HIS BLOODSTREAM, STROKING NERVE ENDINGS AND SEEKING A PLACE OF PERMANENT REFUGE, HE IS NOW...
...SPIDER-CARNAGE.
WEB OF CARNAGE PART 3
His given name is Peter Parker. While in high school, he was bitten by a radioactive spider and endowed with amazing powers, which he has since used to protect the innocent and battle evil. Now he calls himself Ben Reilly, and as a costumed crimefighter, he continues his crusade... for he understands that with great power comes great responsibility! STAN LEE PRESENTS:
SPIDER-MAN in:
WHO AM I?
HOWARD MACKIE/ JOHN ROMITA JR. STORY/ART
AL WILLIAMSON & AL MILGROM INKS
KEVIN TINSLEY COLORIST
MAILBU'S HUES COLOR SEPS
RICHARD STARKINGS AND COMICRAFT LETTERING
ERIC FEIN EDITOR
BOB BUDIANSKY EXECUTIVE EDITOR
BOB HARRAS EDITOR IN CHIEF

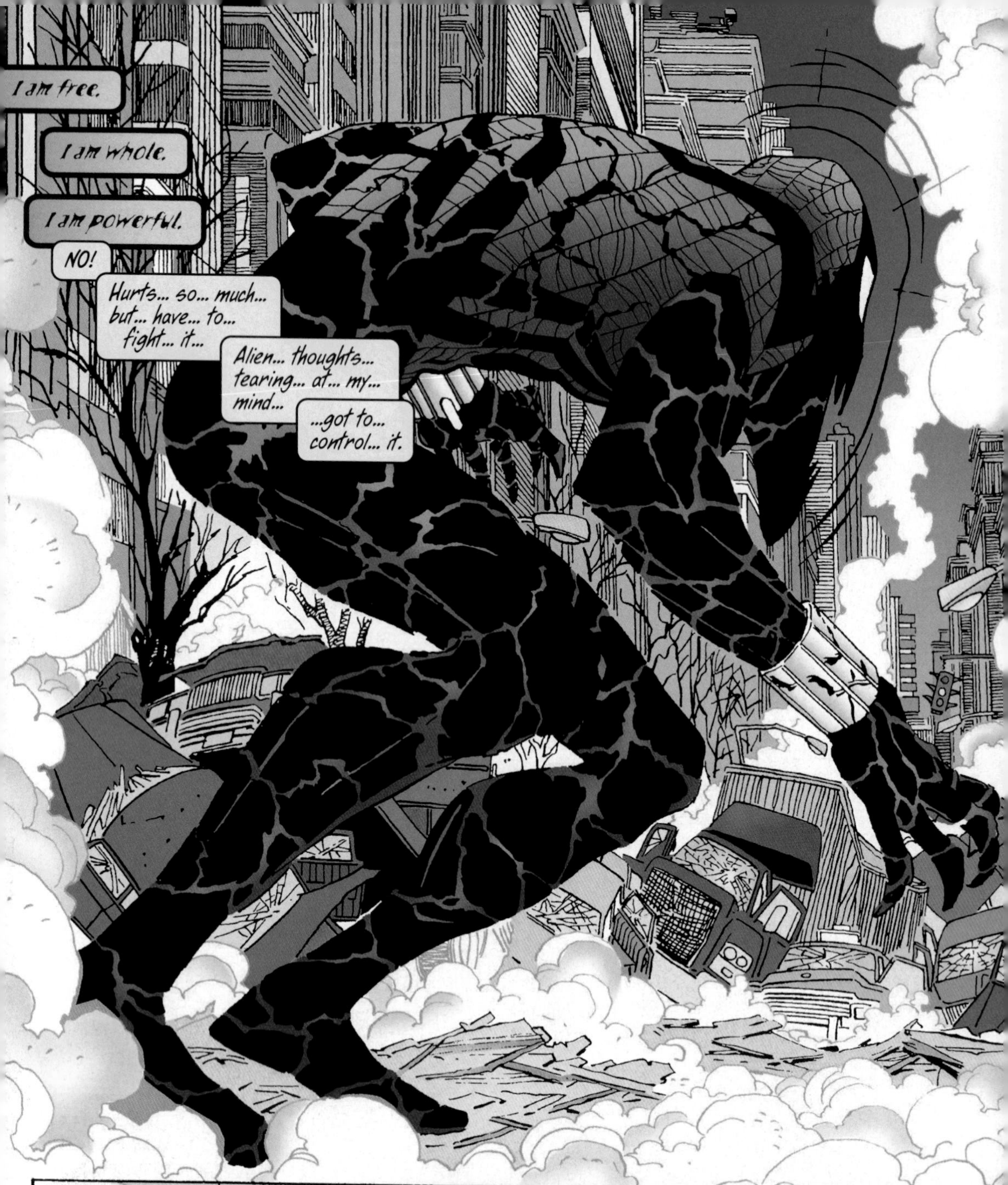
I am free.
I am whole.
I am powerful.
NO!
Hurts... so... much... but... have... to... fight... it...
Alien... thoughts... tearing... at... my... mind...
...got to... control... it.

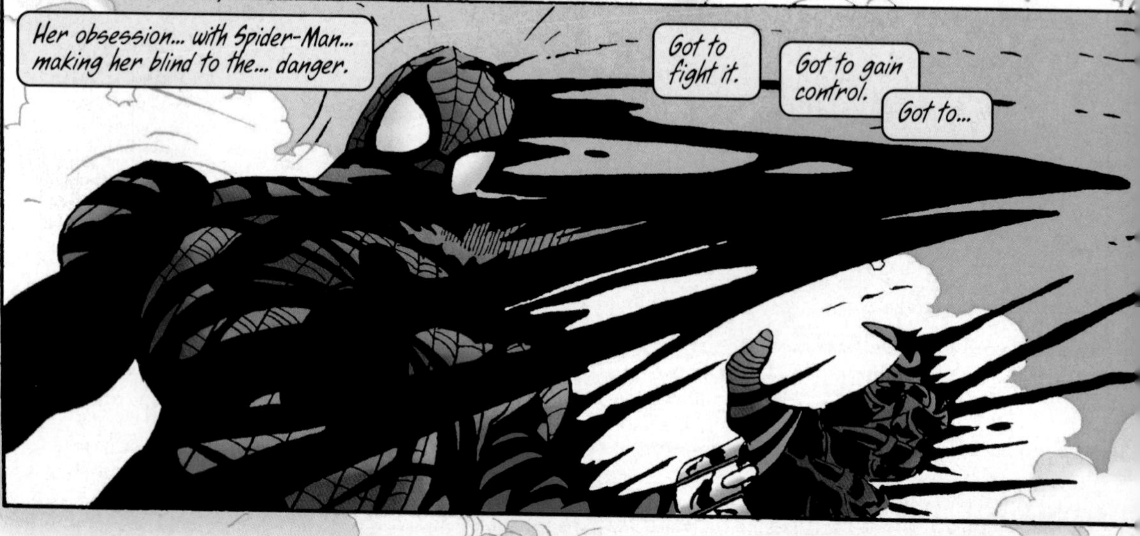
Her obsession... with Spider-Man... making her blind to the... danger.
Got to fight it.
Got to gain control.
Got to...

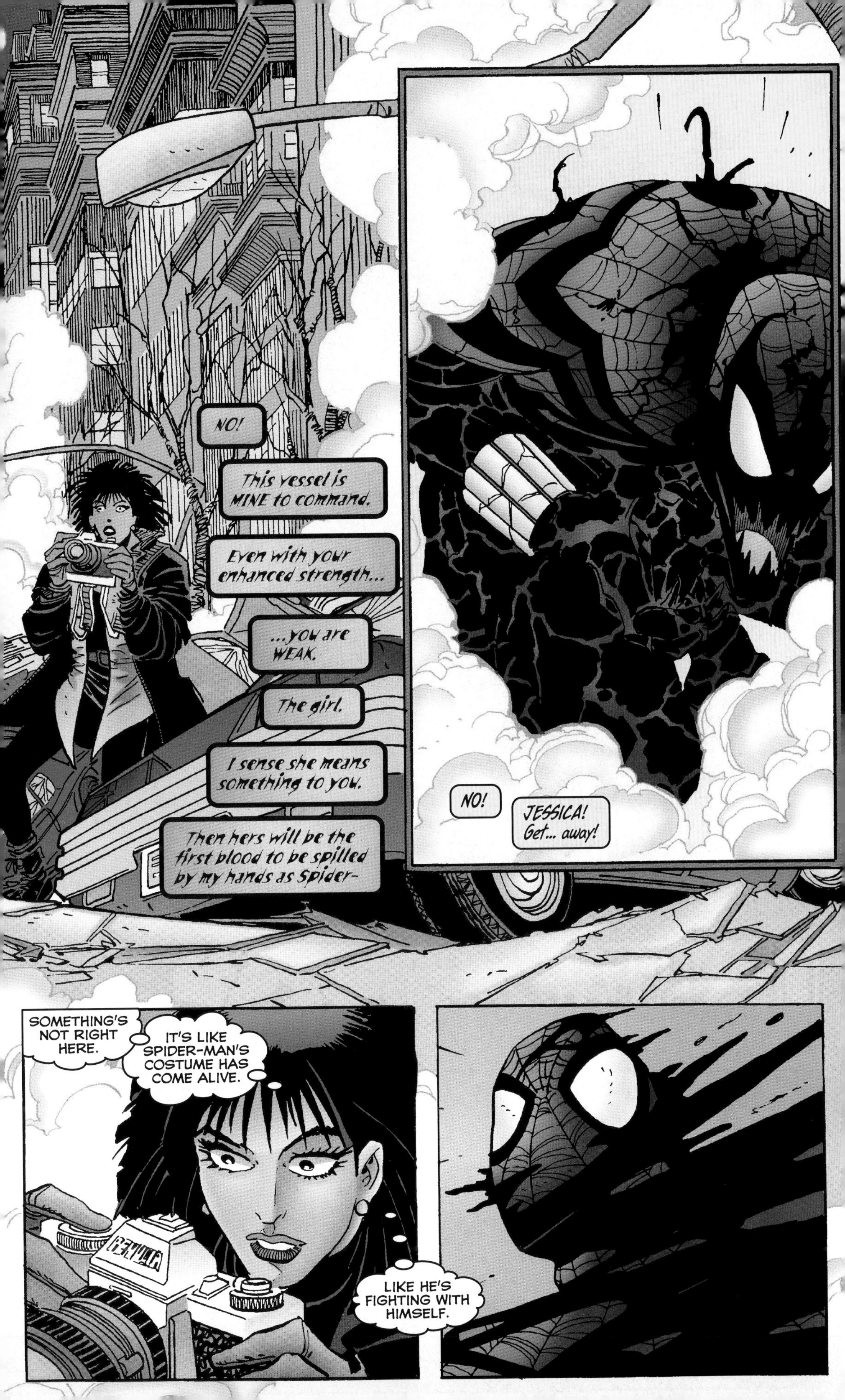
NO!
This vessel is MINE to command.
Even with your enhanced strength...
...you are WEAK.
The girl.
I sense she means something to you.
Then hers will be the first blood to be spilled by my hands as Spider-
NO!
JESSICA! Get... away!
SOMETHING'S NOT RIGHT HERE.
IT'S LIKE SPIDER-MAN'S COSTUME HAS COME ALIVE.
LIKE HE'S FIGHTING WITH HIMSELF.

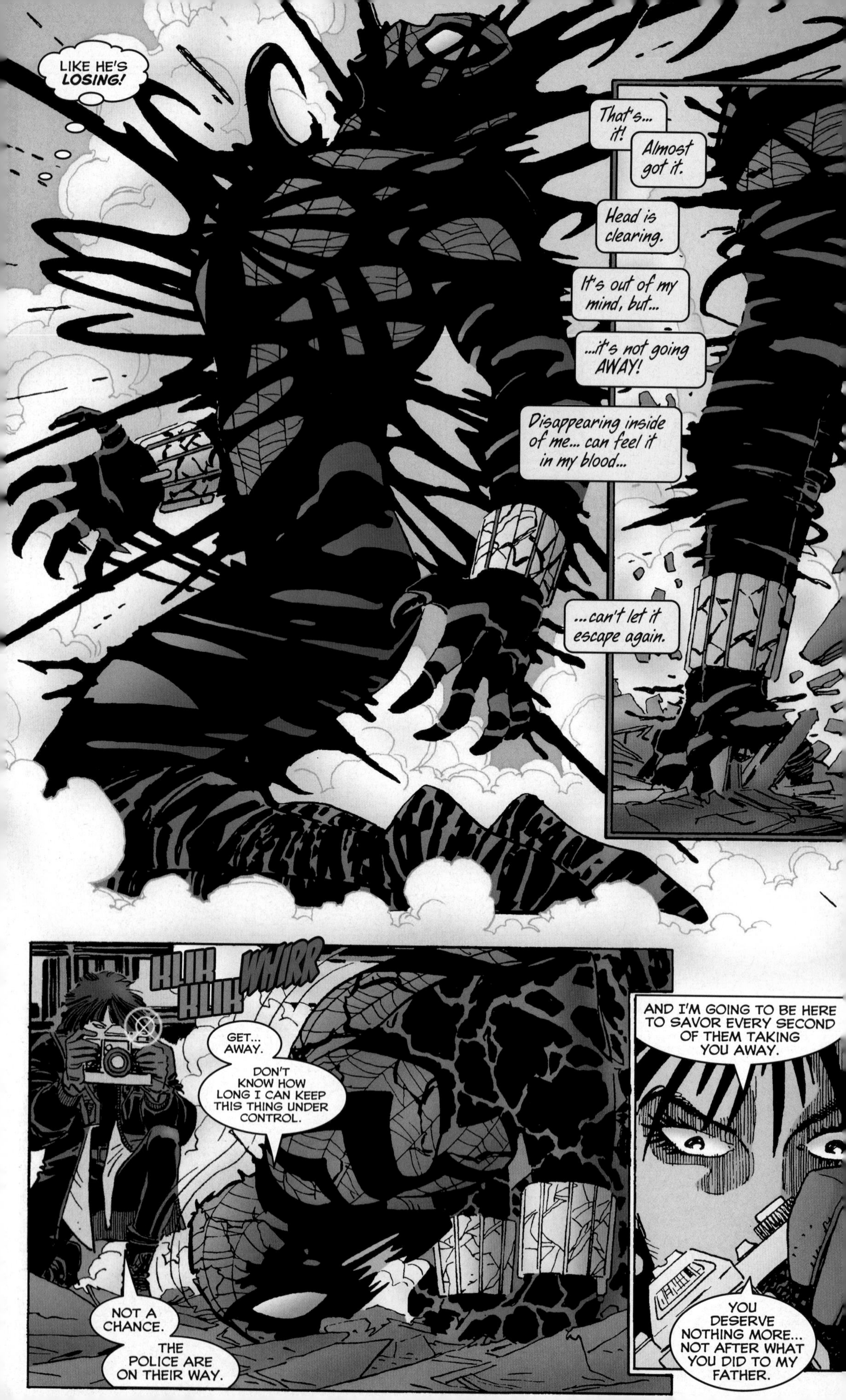
LIKE HE'S LOSING!
That's... it!
Almost got it.
Head is clearing.
It's out of my mind, but...
...it's not going AWAY!
Disappearing inside of me... can feel it in my blood...
...can't let it escape again.
KLIK KLIK WHIRR
GET... AWAY.
DON'T KNOW HOW LONG I CAN KEEP THIS THING UNDER CONTROL.
NOT A CHANCE.
THE POLICE ARE ON THEIR WAY.
AND I'M GOING TO BE HERE TO SAVOR EVERY SECOND OF THEM TAKING YOU AWAY.
YOU DESERVE NOTHING MORE... NOT AFTER WHAT YOU DID TO MY FATHER.

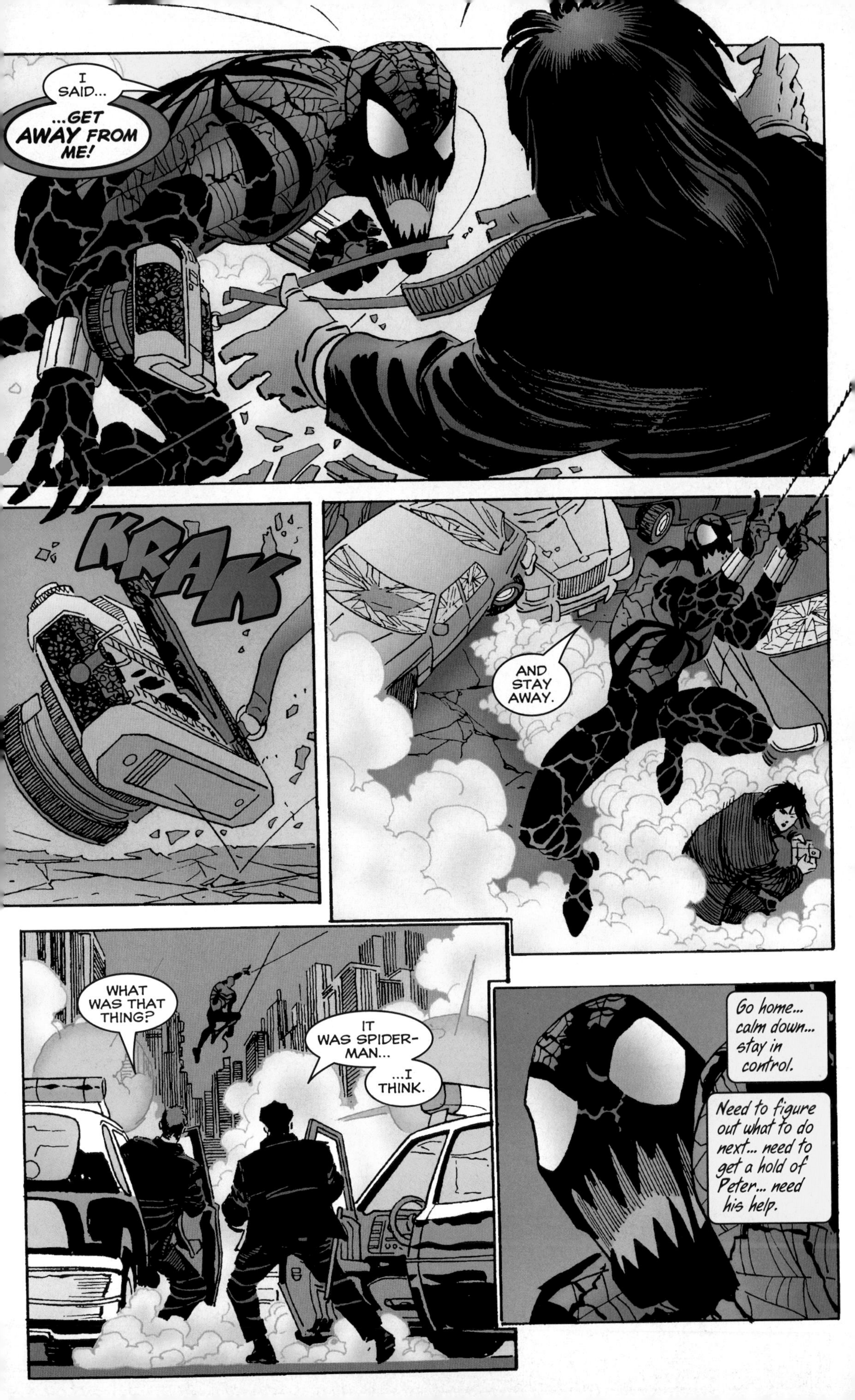
I SAID... ...GET AWAY FROM ME!
KRAK
AND STAY AWAY.
WHAT WAS THAT THING?
IT WAS SPIDER-MAN... ...I THINK.
Go home... calm down... stay in control.
Need to figure out what to do next... need to get a hold of Peter... need his help.

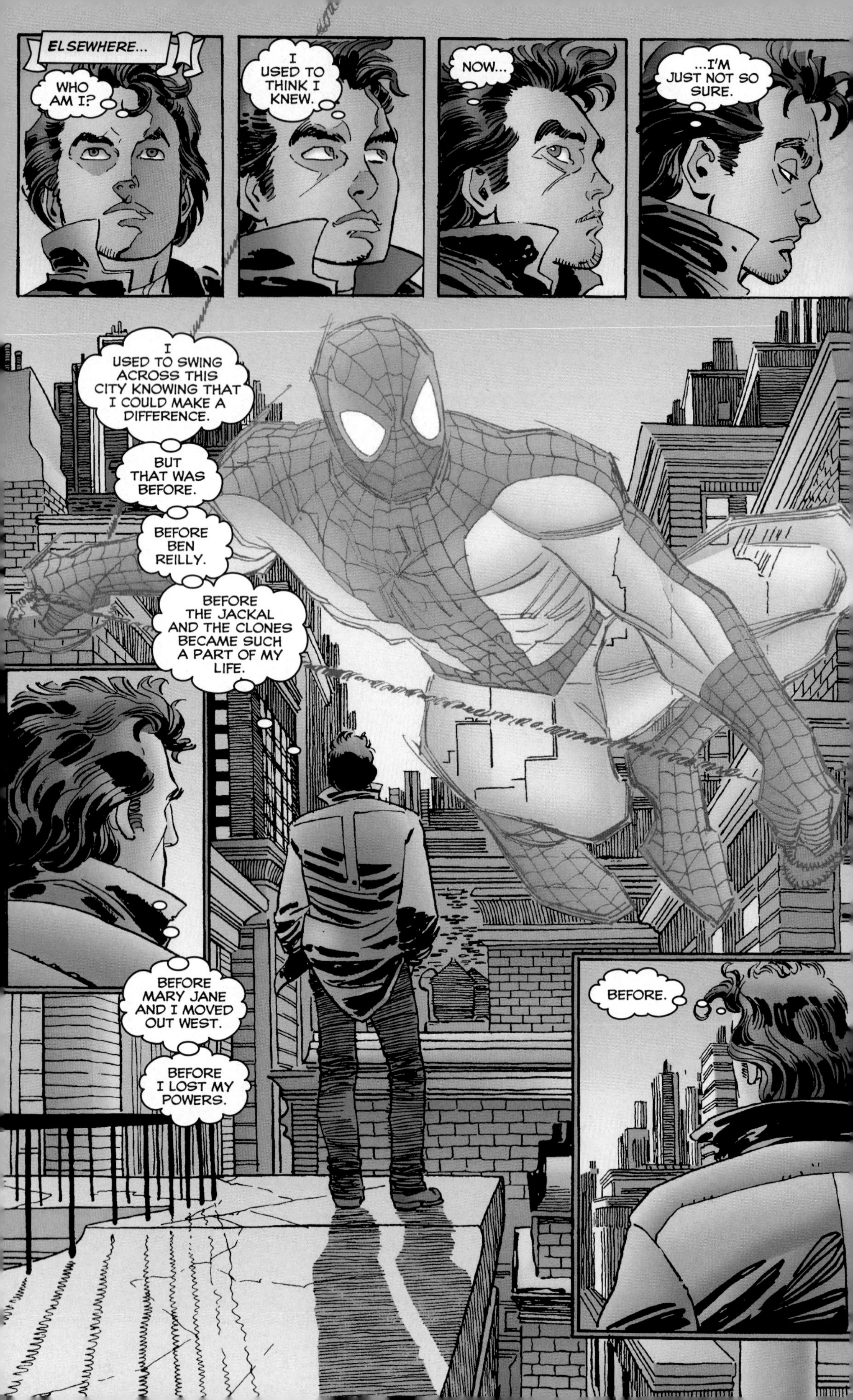
ELSEWHERE...
WHO AM I?
I USED TO THINK I KNEW.
NOW...
...I'M JUST NOT SO SURE.
I USED TO SWING ACROSS THIS CITY KNOWING THAT I COULD MAKE A DIFFERENCE.
BUT THAT WAS BEFORE.
BEFORE BEN REILLY.
BEFORE THE JACKAL AND THE CLONES BECAME SUCH A PART OF MY LIFE.
BEFORE MARY JANE AND I MOVED OUT WEST.
BEFORE I LOST MY POWERS.
BEFORE.

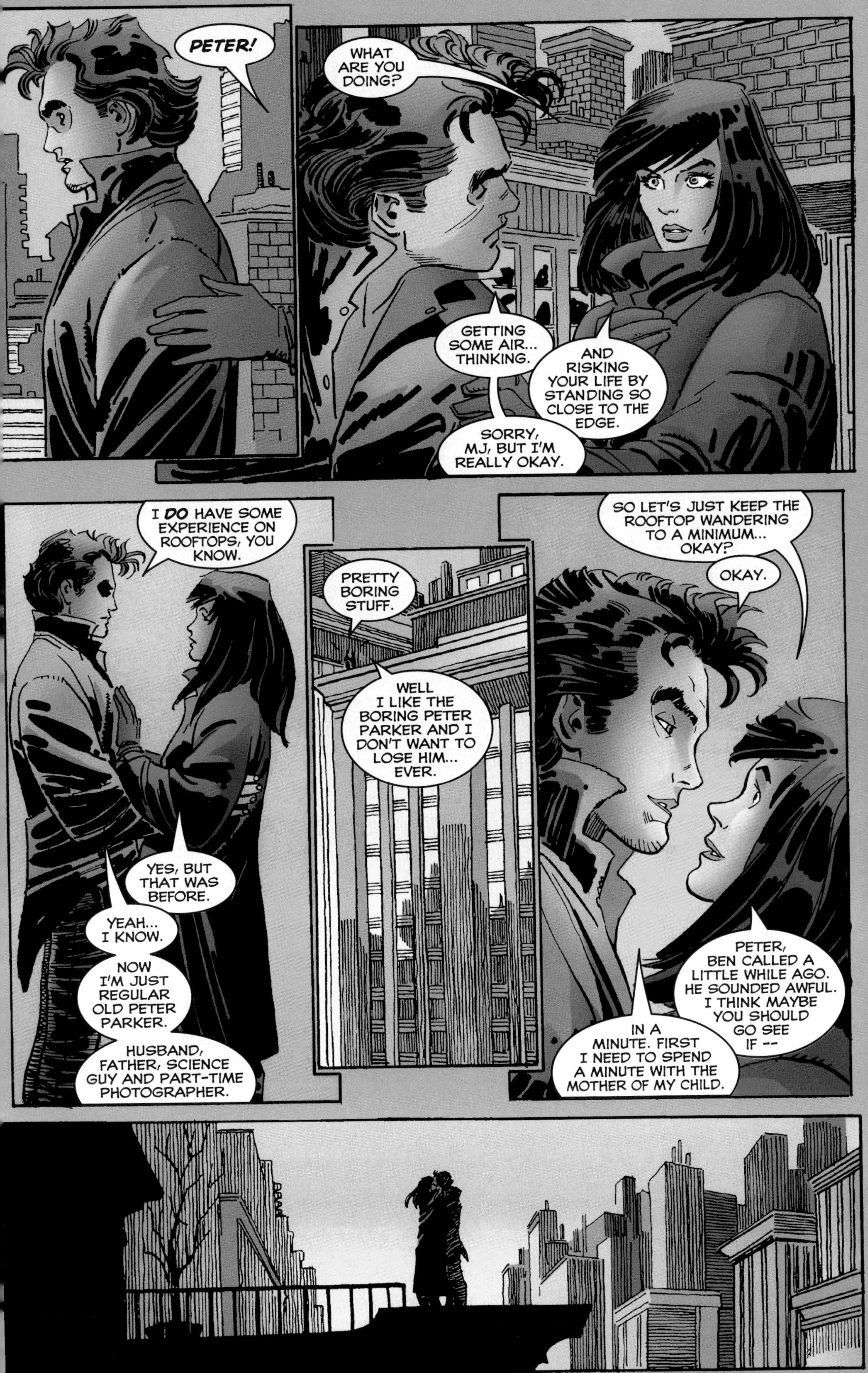
PETER!
WHAT ARE YOU DOING?
GETTING SOME AIR... THINKING.
AND RISKING YOUR LIFE BY STANDING SO CLOSE TO THE EDGE.
SORRY, MJ, BUT I'M REALLY OKAY.
I DO HAVE SOME EXPERIENCE ON ROOFTOPS, YOU KNOW.
YES, BUT THAT WAS BEFORE.
YEAH... I KNOW.
NOW I'M JUST REGULAR OLD PETER PARKER.
HUSBAND, FATHER, SCIENCE GUY AND PART-TIME PHOTOGRAPHER.
PRETTY BORING STUFF.
WELL I LIKE THE BORING PETER PARKER AND I DON'T WANT TO LOSE HIM... EVER.
SO LET'S JUST KEEP THE ROOFTOP WANDERING TO A MINIMUM... OKAY?
OKAY.
PETER, BEN CALLED A LITTLE WHILE AGO. HE SOUNDED AWFUL. I THINK MAYBE YOU SHOULD GO SEE IF --
IN A MINUTE. FIRST I NEED TO SPEND A MINUTE WITH THE MOTHER OF MY CHILD.

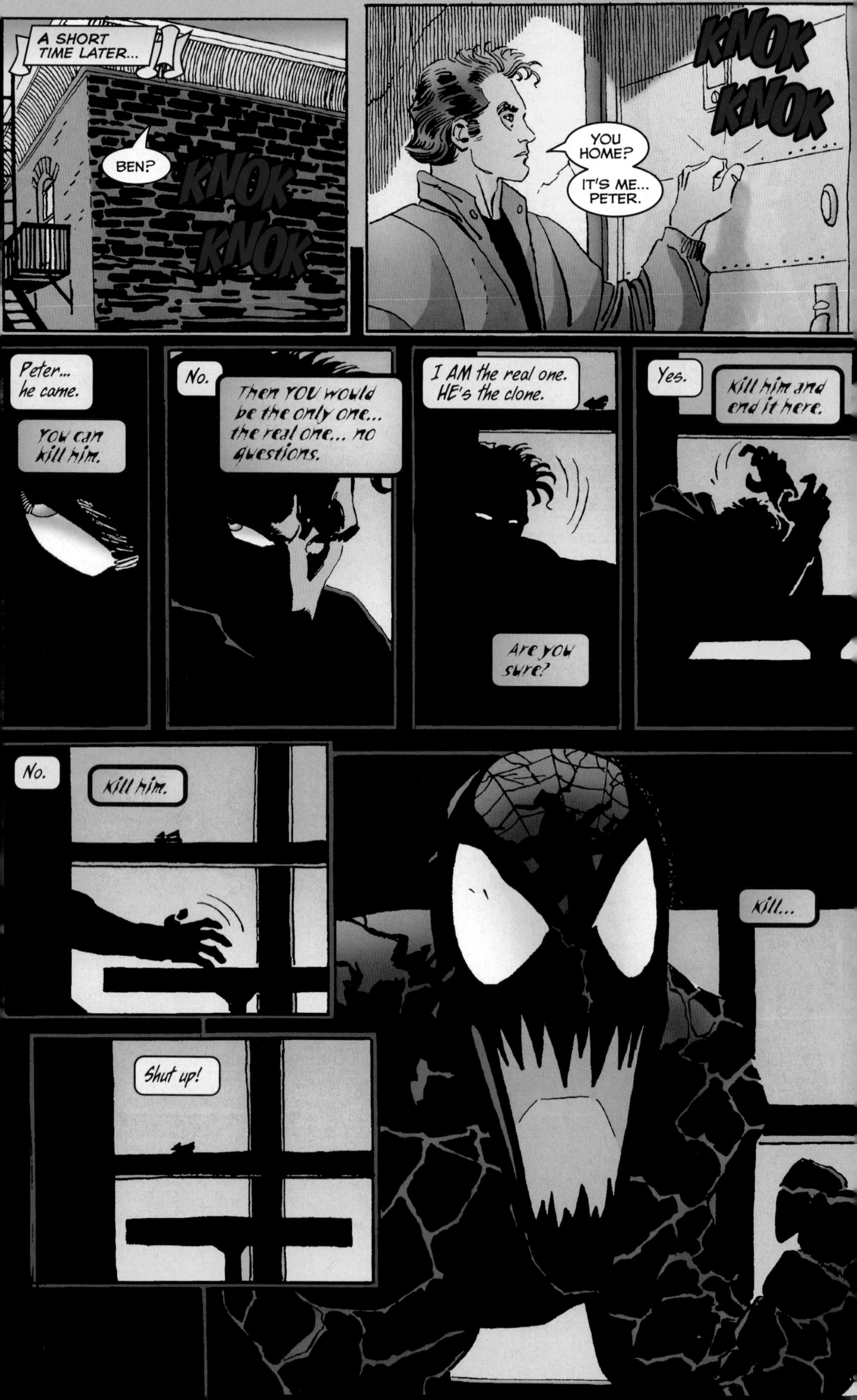
A SHORT TIME LATER...
BEN?
KNOK KNOK
KNOK KNOK
YOU HOME?
IT'S ME... PETER.
Peter... he came.
You can kill him.
No.
Then YOU would be the only one... the real one... no questions.
I AM the real one. HE's the clone.
Are you sure?
Yes.
Kill him and end it here.
No.
Kill him.
Shut up!
Kill...

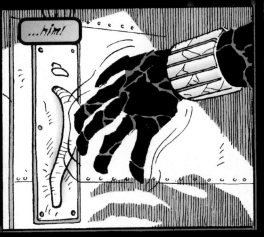

...him!

BEN? MARY JANE SAID YOU CALLED.

ARE YOU FEELING OKAY? YOU LOOK TERRIBLE.

YEAH... WELL... THE LIFE OF A BIG TIME SUPER HERO.

BEEN THERE... DONE THAT... DON'T WANT TO GO THERE AGAIN.

I STILL CAN'T GET OVER THIS APARTMENT.

IT'S A LOT NICER THAN THE FIRST PLACE I HAD IN MANHATTAN.

I'LL TELL THAT TO THE RATS.

SO... WHAT ARE WE GOING TO DO ABOUT IT?

WHAT?

Kill him.

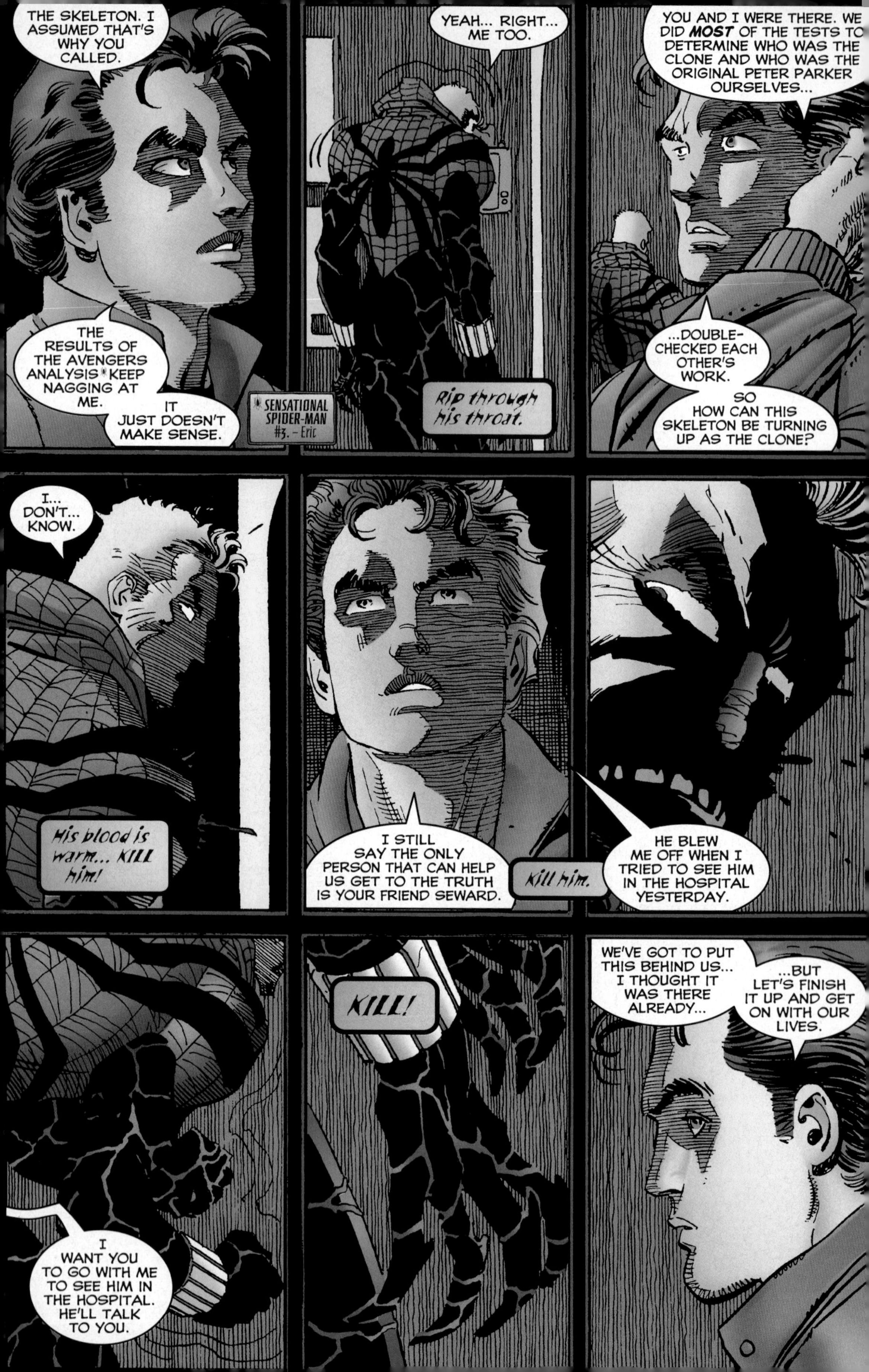
THE SKELETON. I ASSUMED THAT'S WHY YOU CALLED.
THE RESULTS OF THE AVENGERS ANALYSIS KEEP NAGGING AT ME.
IT JUST DOESN'T MAKE SENSE.
SENSATIONAL SPIDER-MAN #3. – Eric
YEAH... RIGHT... ME TOO.
Rip through his throat.
YOU AND I WERE THERE. WE DID MOST OF THE TESTS TO DETERMINE WHO WAS THE CLONE AND WHO WAS THE ORIGINAL PETER PARKER OURSELVES...
...DOUBLE-CHECKED EACH OTHER'S WORK.
SO HOW CAN THIS SKELETON BE TURNING UP AS THE CLONE?
I... DON'T... KNOW.
His blood is warm... KILL him!
I STILL SAY THE ONLY PERSON THAT CAN HELP US GET TO THE TRUTH IS YOUR FRIEND SEWARD.
Kill him.
HE BLEW ME OFF WHEN I TRIED TO SEE HIM IN THE HOSPITAL YESTERDAY.
I WANT YOU TO GO WITH ME TO SEE HIM IN THE HOSPITAL. HE'LL TALK TO YOU.
KILL!
WE'VE GOT TO PUT THIS BEHIND US... I THOUGHT IT WAS THERE ALREADY...
...BUT LET'S FINISH IT UP AND GET ON WITH OUR LIVES.

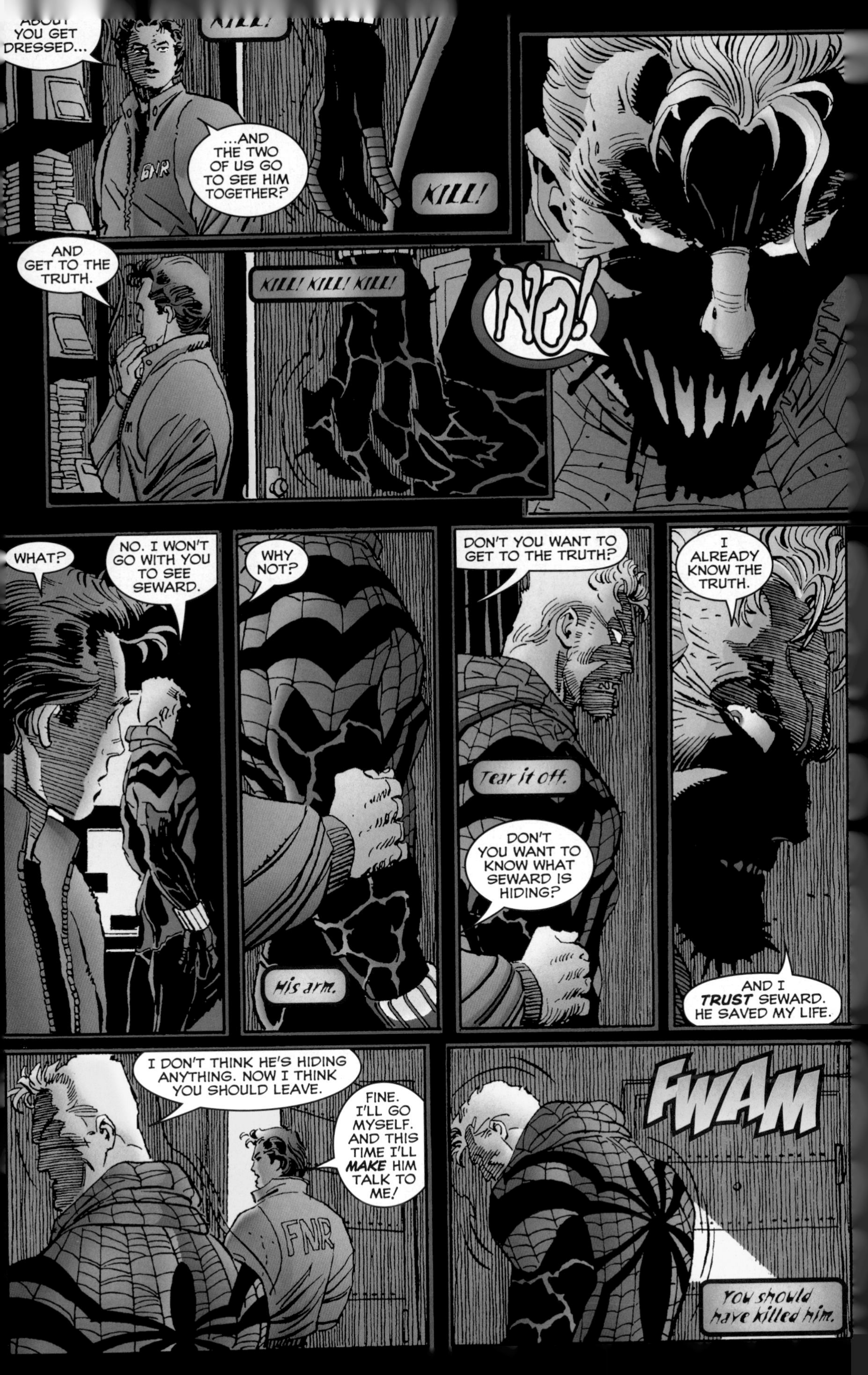

YOU GET DRESSED...
KILL!
...AND THE TWO OF US GO TO SEE HIM TOGETHER?
KILL!
AND GET TO THE TRUTH.
KILL! KILL! KILL!
NO!
WHAT?
NO. I WON'T GO WITH YOU TO SEE SEWARD.
WHY NOT?
His arm.
DON'T YOU WANT TO GET TO THE TRUTH?
Tear it off.
DON'T YOU WANT TO KNOW WHAT SEWARD IS HIDING?
I ALREADY KNOW THE TRUTH.
AND I TRUST SEWARD. HE SAVED MY LIFE.
I DON'T THINK HE'S HIDING ANYTHING. NOW I THINK YOU SHOULD LEAVE.
FINE. I'LL GO MYSELF. AND THIS TIME I'LL MAKE HIM TALK TO ME!
FWAM
You should have killed him.

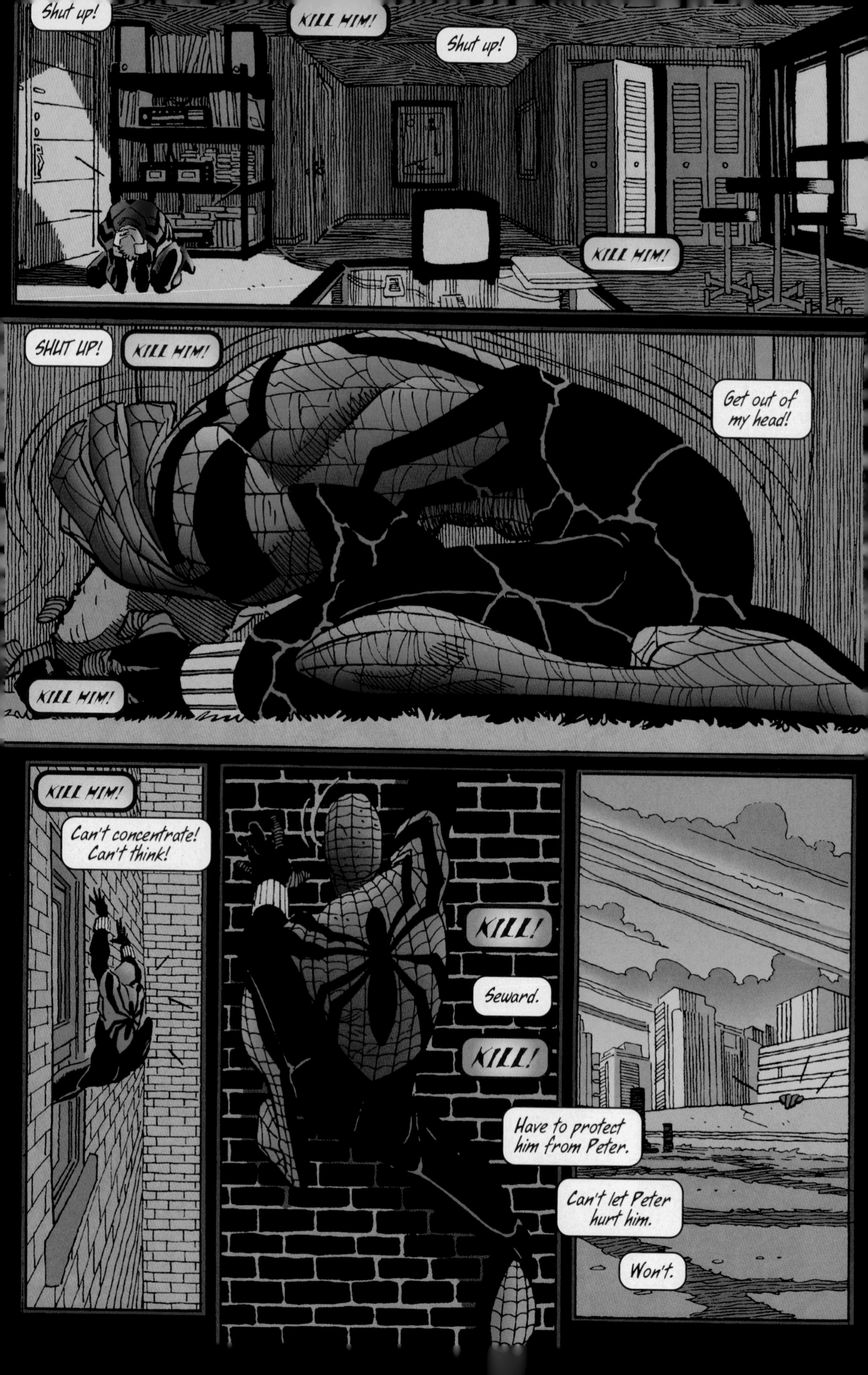
Shut up!
KILL HIM!
Shut up!
KILL HIM!
SHUT UP!
KILL HIM!
Get out of my head!
KILL HIM!
KILL HIM!
Can't concentrate! Can't think!
KILL!
Seward.
KILL!
Have to protect him from Peter.
Can't let Peter hurt him.
Won't.

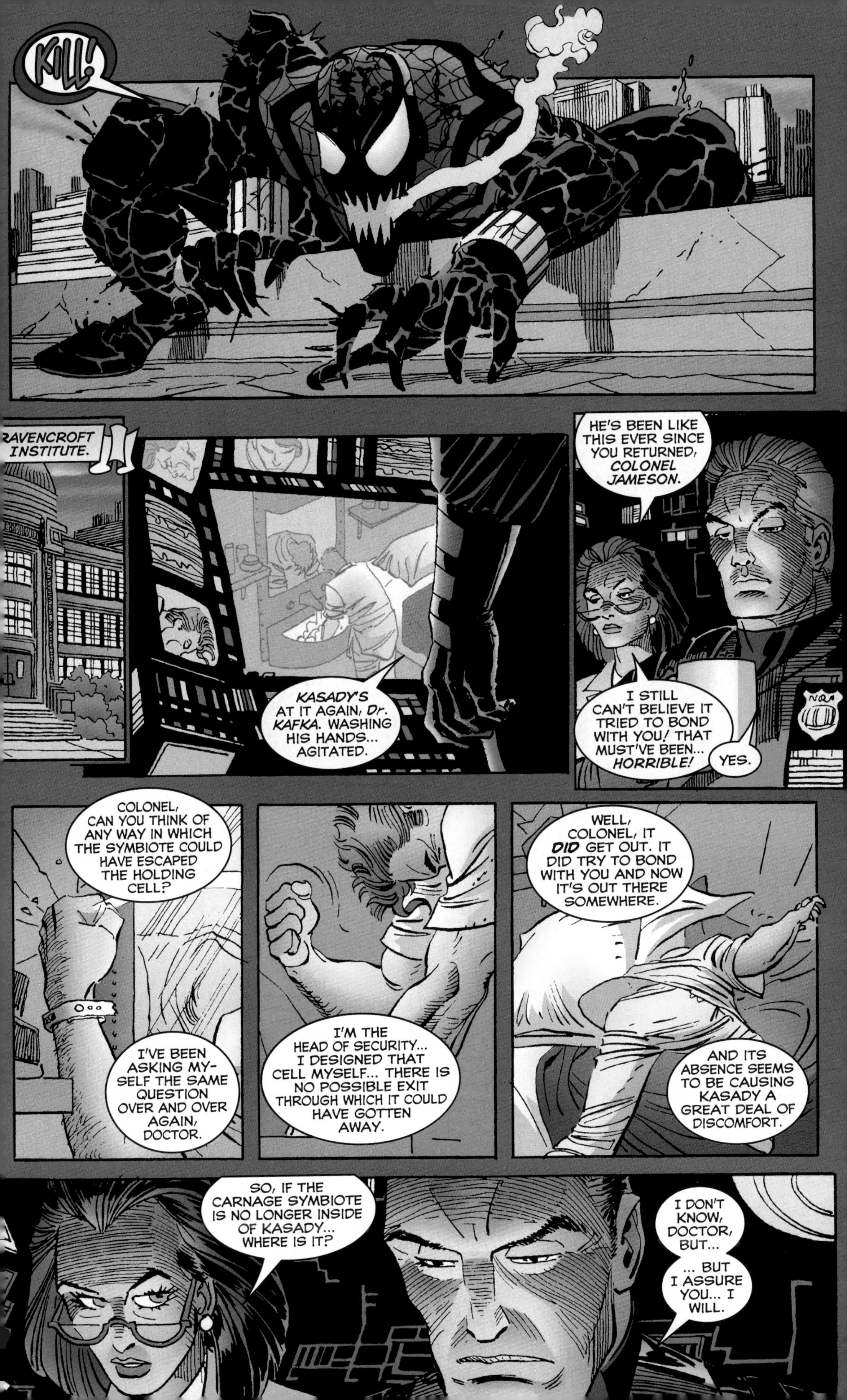
KILL!
RAVENCROFT INSTITUTE.
KASADY'S AT IT AGAIN, Dr. KAFKA. WASHING HIS HANDS... AGITATED.
HE'S BEEN LIKE THIS EVER SINCE YOU RETURNED, COLONEL JAMESON.
I STILL CAN'T BELIEVE IT TRIED TO BOND WITH YOU! THAT MUST'VE BEEN... HORRIBLE!
YES.
COLONEL, CAN YOU THINK OF ANY WAY IN WHICH THE SYMBIOTE COULD HAVE ESCAPED THE HOLDING CELL?
I'VE BEEN ASKING MY-SELF THE SAME QUESTION OVER AND OVER AGAIN, DOCTOR.
I'M THE HEAD OF SECURITY... I DESIGNED THAT CELL MYSELF... THERE IS NO POSSIBLE EXIT THROUGH WHICH IT COULD HAVE GOTTEN AWAY.
WELL, COLONEL, IT DID GET OUT. IT DID TRY TO BOND WITH YOU AND NOW IT'S OUT THERE SOMEWHERE.
AND ITS ABSENCE SEEMS TO BE CAUSING KASADY A GREAT DEAL OF DISCOMFORT.
SO, IF THE CARNAGE SYMBIOTE IS NO LONGER INSIDE OF KASADY... WHERE IS IT?
I DON'T KNOW, DOCTOR, BUT...
... BUT I ASSURE YOU... I WILL.

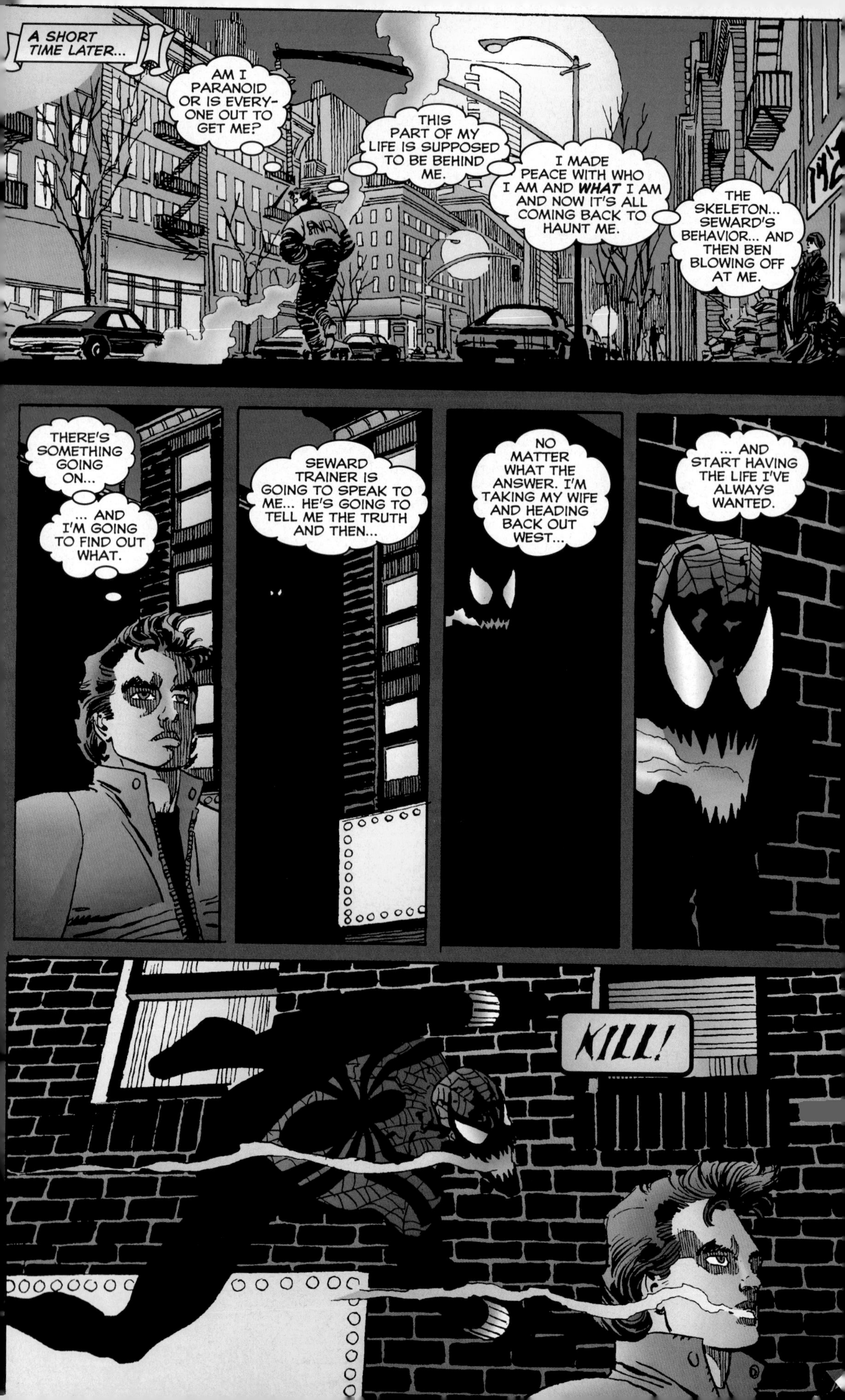
A SHORT TIME LATER...
AM I PARANOID OR IS EVERY-ONE OUT TO GET ME?
THIS PART OF MY LIFE IS SUPPOSED TO BE BEHIND ME.
I MADE PEACE WITH WHO I AM AND *WHAT* I AM AND NOW IT'S ALL COMING BACK TO HAUNT ME.
THE SKELETON... SEWARD'S BEHAVIOR... AND THEN BEN BLOWING OFF AT ME.
THERE'S SOMETHING GOING ON...
... AND I'M GOING TO FIND OUT WHAT.
SEWARD TRAINER IS GOING TO SPEAK TO ME... HE'S GOING TO TELL ME THE TRUTH AND THEN...
NO MATTER WHAT THE ANSWER. I'M TAKING MY WIFE AND HEADING BACK OUT WEST...
... AND START HAVING THE LIFE I'VE ALWAYS WANTED.
KILL!

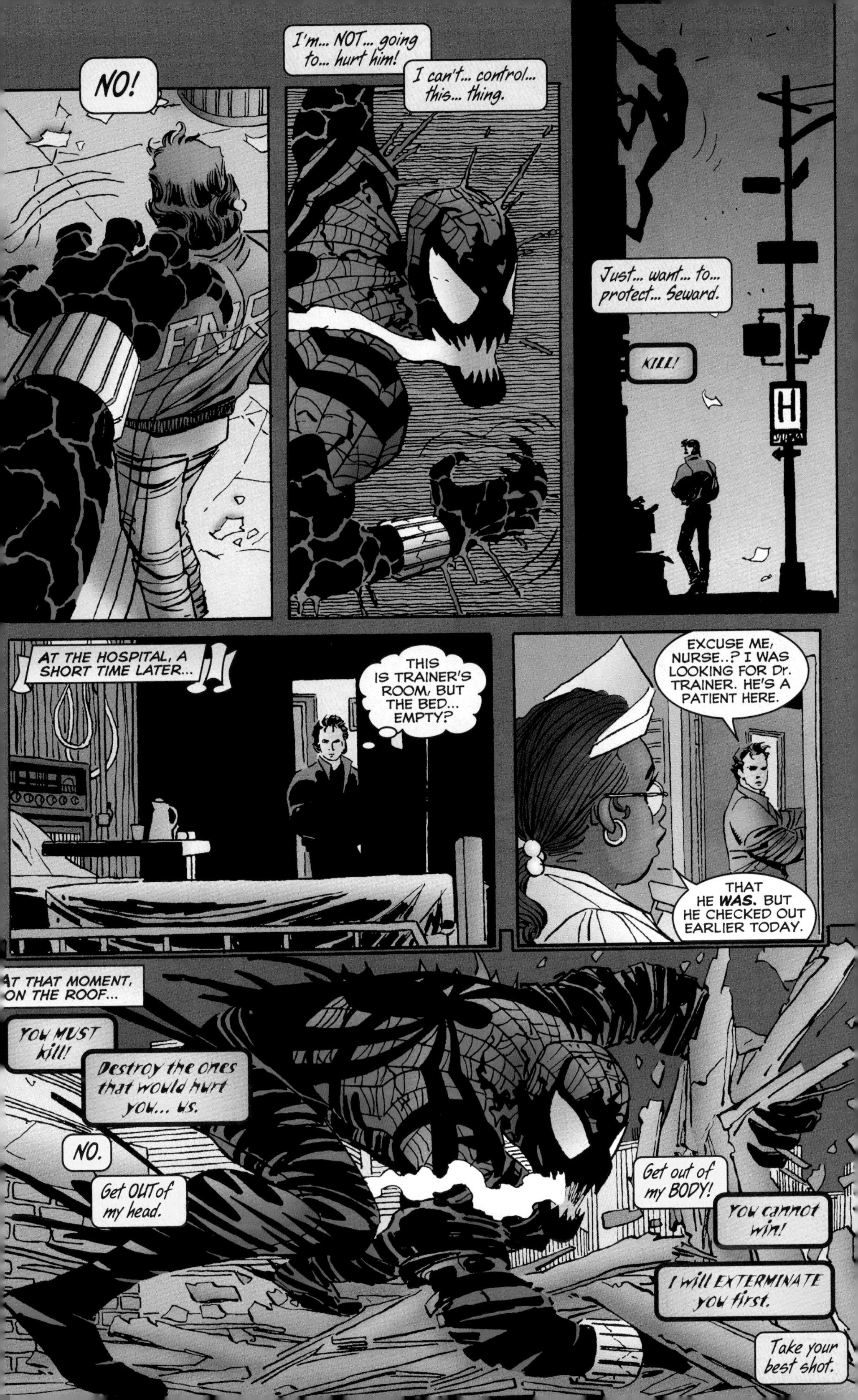
NO!
I'm... NOT... going to... hurt him!
I can't... control... this... thing.
Just... want... to... protect... Seward.
KILL!
AT THE HOSPITAL, A SHORT TIME LATER...
THIS IS TRAINER'S ROOM, BUT THE BED... EMPTY?
EXCUSE ME, NURSE..? I WAS LOOKING FOR Dr. TRAINER. HE'S A PATIENT HERE.
THAT HE **WAS.** BUT HE CHECKED OUT EARLIER TODAY.
AT THAT MOMENT, ON THE ROOF...
YOU MUST kill!
Destroy the ones that would hurt you... us.
NO.
Get OUT of my head.
Get out of my BODY!
You cannot win!
I will EXTERMINATE you first.
Take your best shot.

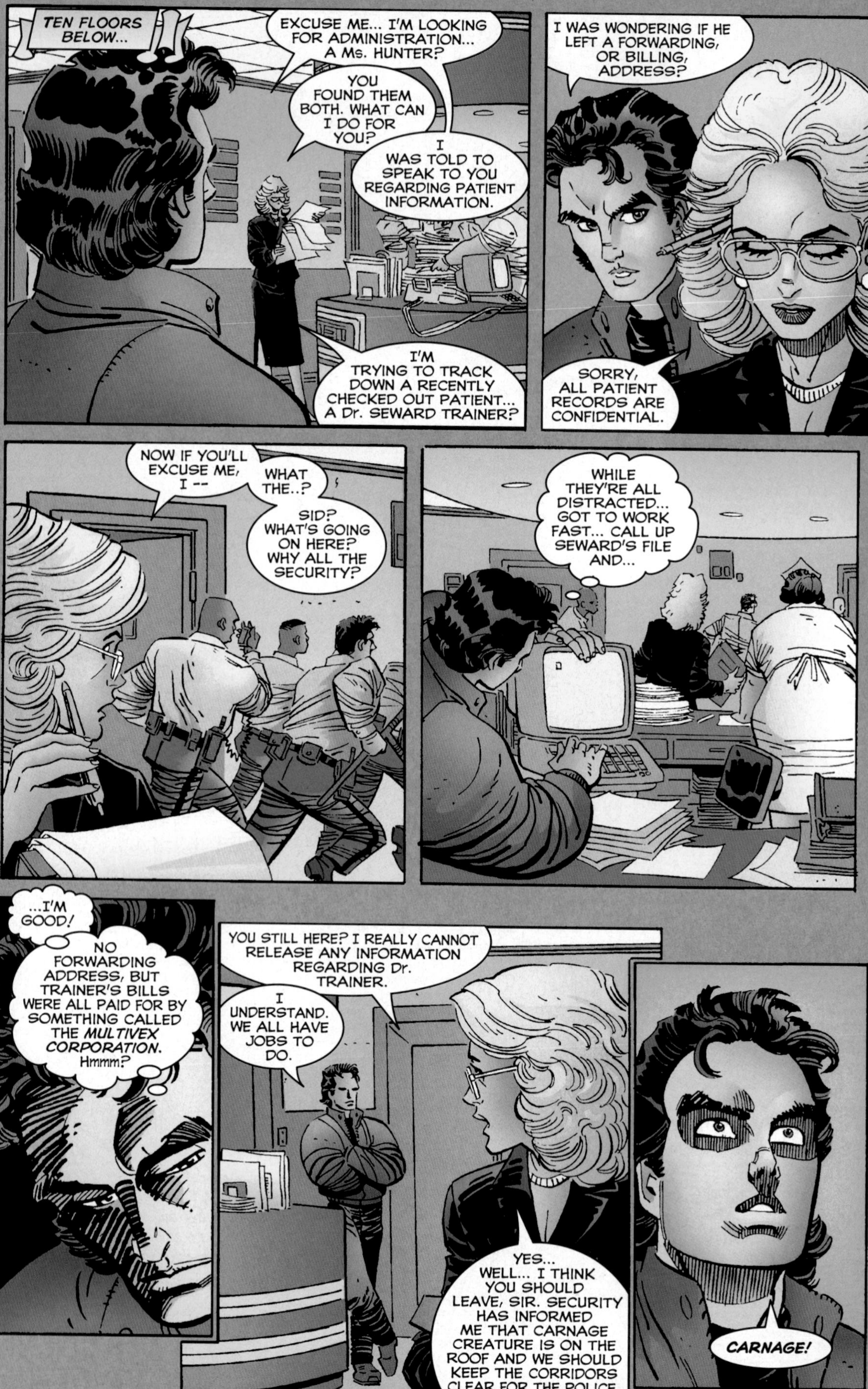
TEN FLOORS BELOW...
EXCUSE ME... I'M LOOKING FOR ADMINISTRATION... A Ms. HUNTER?
YOU FOUND THEM BOTH. WHAT CAN I DO FOR YOU?
I WAS TOLD TO SPEAK TO YOU REGARDING PATIENT INFORMATION.
I'M TRYING TO TRACK DOWN A RECENTLY CHECKED OUT PATIENT... A Dr. SEWARD TRAINER?
I WAS WONDERING IF HE LEFT A FORWARDING, OR BILLING, ADDRESS?
SORRY, ALL PATIENT RECORDS ARE CONFIDENTIAL.
NOW IF YOU'LL EXCUSE ME, I --
WHAT THE..?
SID? WHAT'S GOING ON HERE? WHY ALL THE SECURITY?
WHILE THEY'RE ALL DISTRACTED... GOT TO WORK FAST... CALL UP SEWARD'S FILE AND...
...I'M GOOD!
NO FORWARDING ADDRESS, BUT TRAINER'S BILLS WERE ALL PAID FOR BY SOMETHING CALLED THE *MULTIVEX CORPORATION*. Hmmm?
YOU STILL HERE? I REALLY CANNOT RELEASE ANY INFORMATION REGARDING Dr. TRAINER.
I UNDERSTAND. WE ALL HAVE JOBS TO DO.
YES... WELL... I THINK YOU SHOULD LEAVE, SIR. SECURITY HAS INFORMED ME THAT CARNAGE CREATURE IS ON THE ROOF AND WE SHOULD KEEP THE CORRIDORS CLEAR FOR THE POLICE.
CARNAGE!

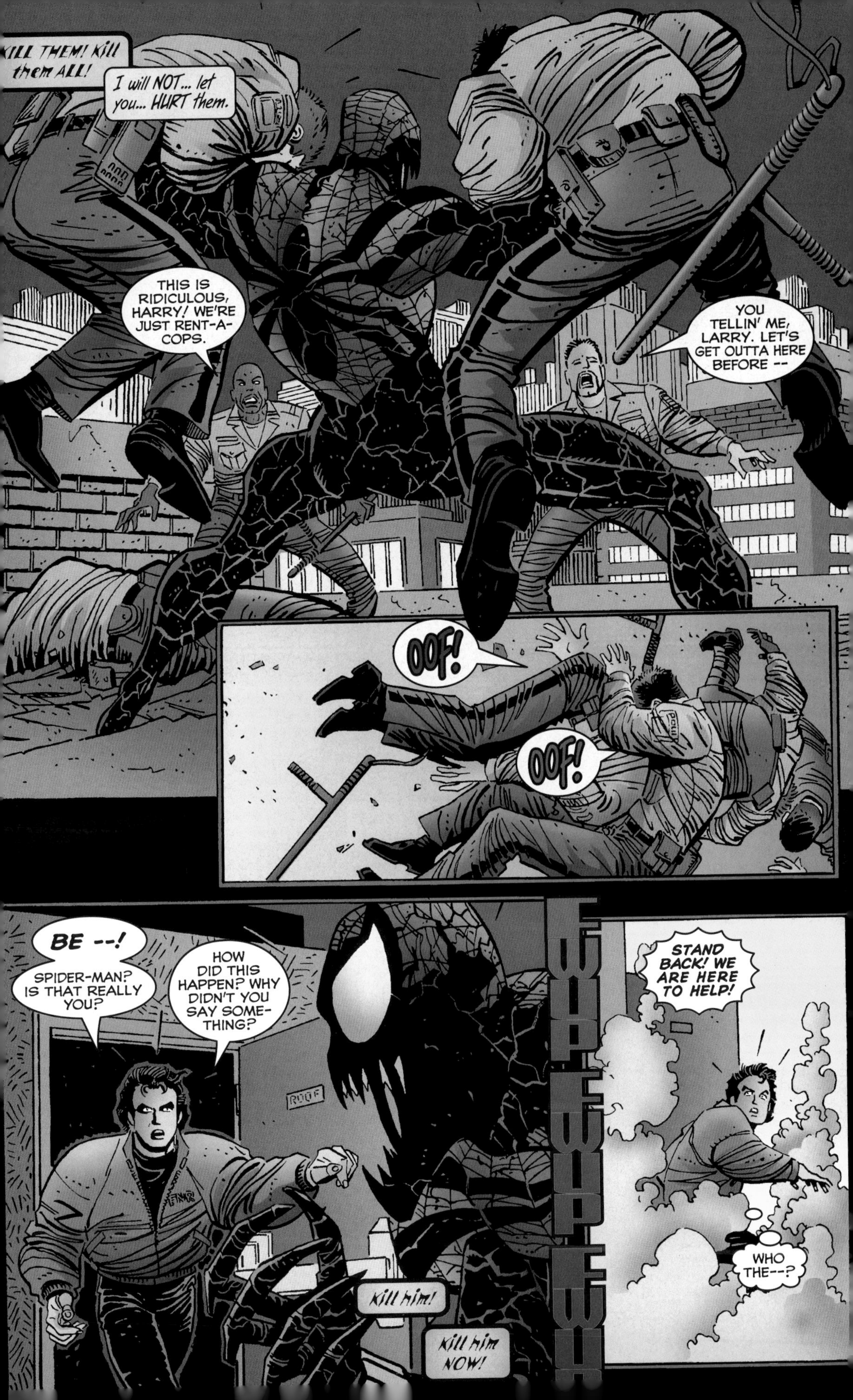
KILL THEM! Kill them ALL!
I will NOT... let you... HURT them.
THIS IS RIDICULOUS, HARRY! WE'RE JUST RENT-A-COPS.
YOU TELLIN' ME, LARRY. LET'S GET OUTTA HERE BEFORE --
OOF!
OOF!
BE --!
SPIDER-MAN? IS THAT REALLY YOU?
HOW DID THIS HAPPEN? WHY DIDN'T YOU SAY SOME-THING?
ROOF
Kill him!
Kill him NOW!
STAND BACK! WE ARE HERE TO HELP!
WHO THE--?

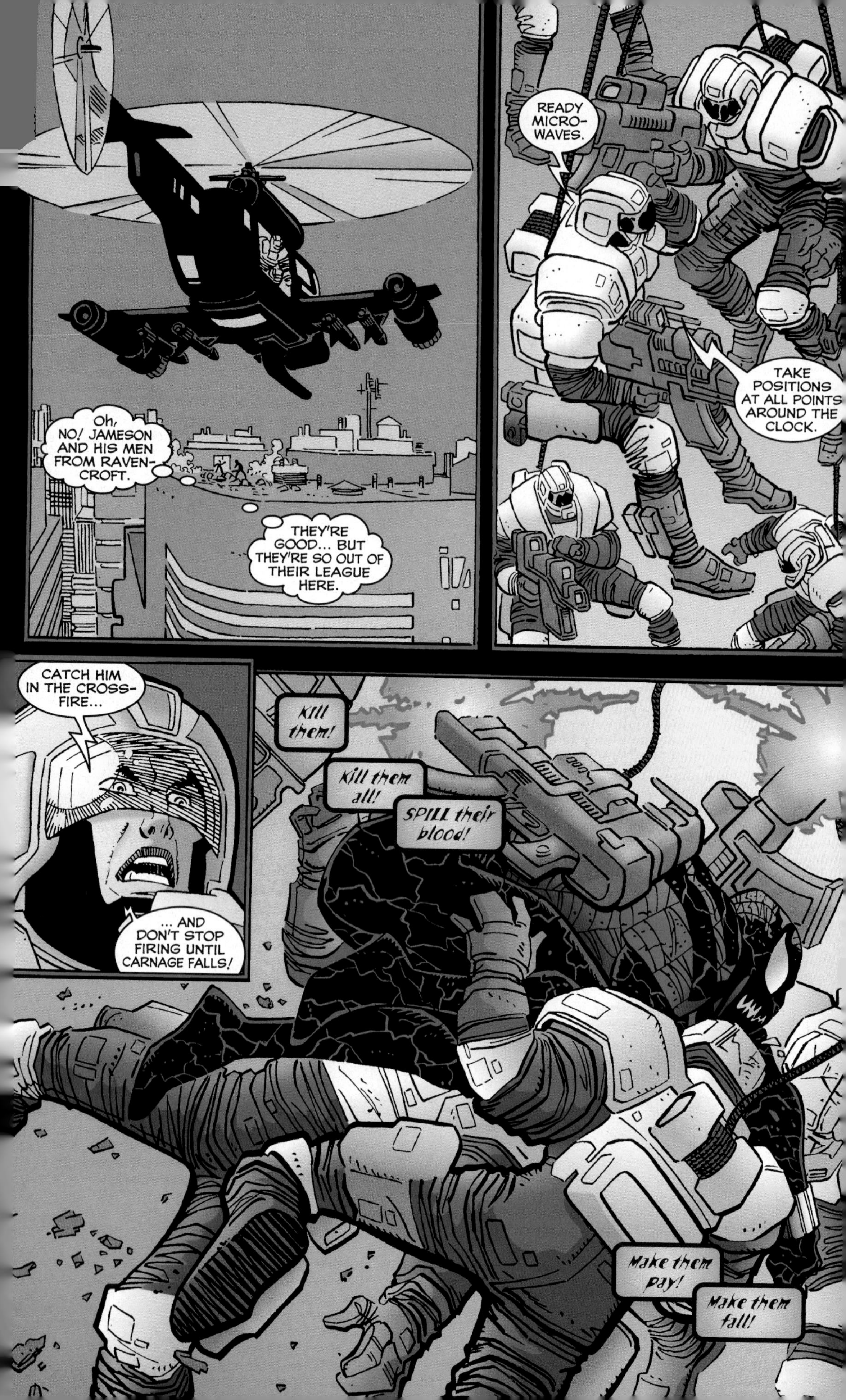
Oh, NO! JAMESON AND HIS MEN FROM RAVEN-CROFT.
THEY'RE GOOD... BUT THEY'RE SO OUT OF THEIR LEAGUE HERE.
READY MICRO-WAVES.
TAKE POSITIONS AT ALL POINTS AROUND THE CLOCK.
CATCH HIM IN THE CROSS-FIRE...
... AND DON'T STOP FIRING UNTIL CARNAGE FALLS!
Kill them!
Kill them all!
SPILL their blood!
Make them pay!
Make them fall!

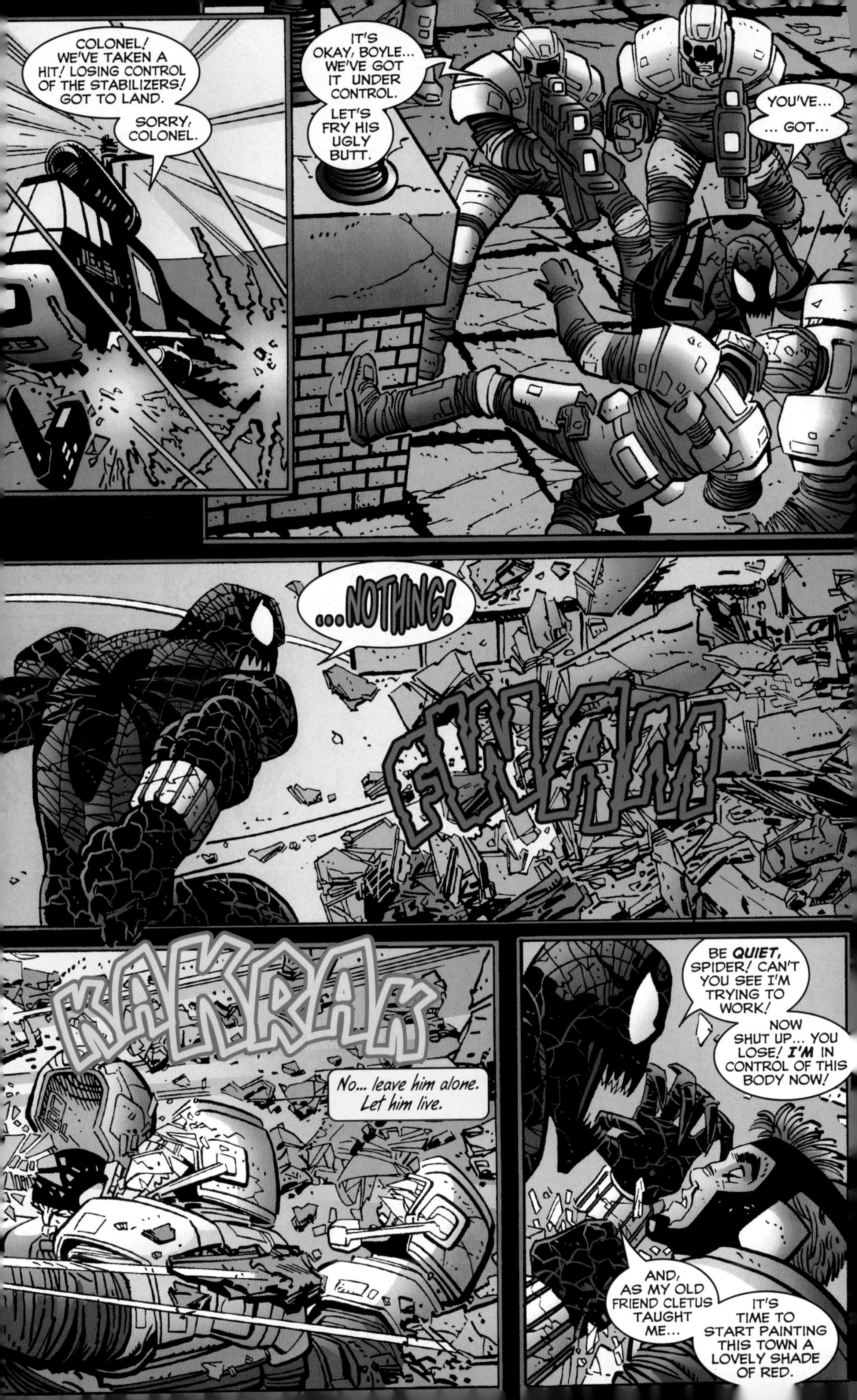
COLONEL! WE'VE TAKEN A HIT! LOSING CONTROL OF THE STABILIZERS! GOT TO LAND.
SORRY, COLONEL.
IT'S OKAY, BOYLE... WE'VE GOT IT UNDER CONTROL.
LET'S FRY HIS UGLY BUTT.
YOU'VE...
... GOT...
...NOTHING!
FWAM
KAKRAK
No... leave him alone. Let him live.
BE QUIET, SPIDER! CAN'T YOU SEE I'M TRYING TO WORK!
NOW SHUT UP... YOU LOSE! I'M IN CONTROL OF THIS BODY NOW!
AND, AS MY OLD FRIEND CLETUS TAUGHT ME...
IT'S TIME TO START PAINTING THIS TOWN A LOVELY SHADE OF RED.

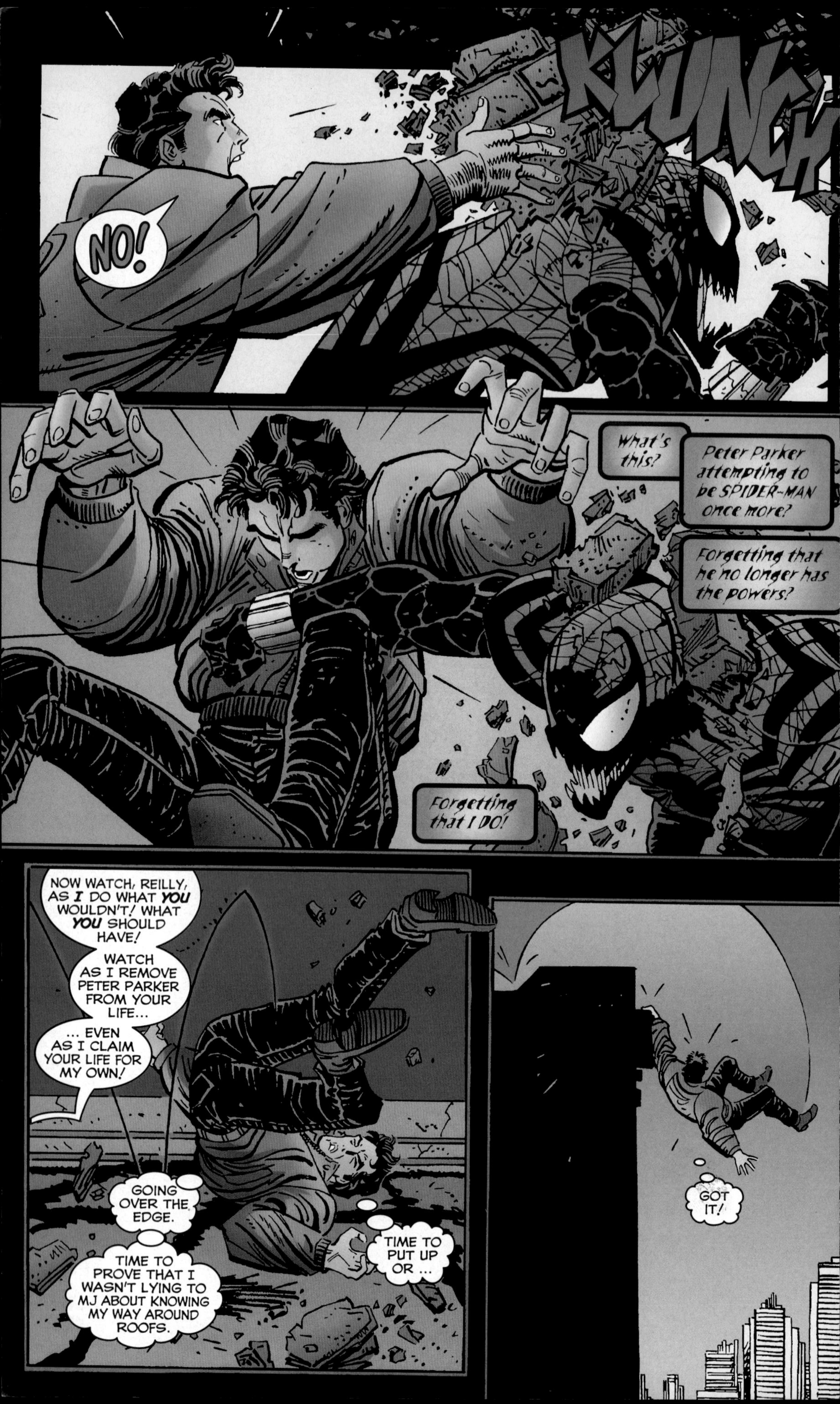
KLUNCH
NO!
What's this?
Peter Parker attempting to be SPIDER-MAN once more?
Forgetting that he no longer has the powers?
Forgetting that I DO!
NOW WATCH, REILLY, AS I DO WHAT YOU WOULDN'T! WHAT YOU SHOULD HAVE!
WATCH AS I REMOVE PETER PARKER FROM YOUR LIFE...
... EVEN AS I CLAIM YOUR LIFE FOR MY OWN!
GOING OVER THE EDGE.
TIME TO PROVE THAT I WASN'T LYING TO MJ ABOUT KNOWING MY WAY AROUND ROOFS.
TIME TO PUT UP OR ...
GOT IT!

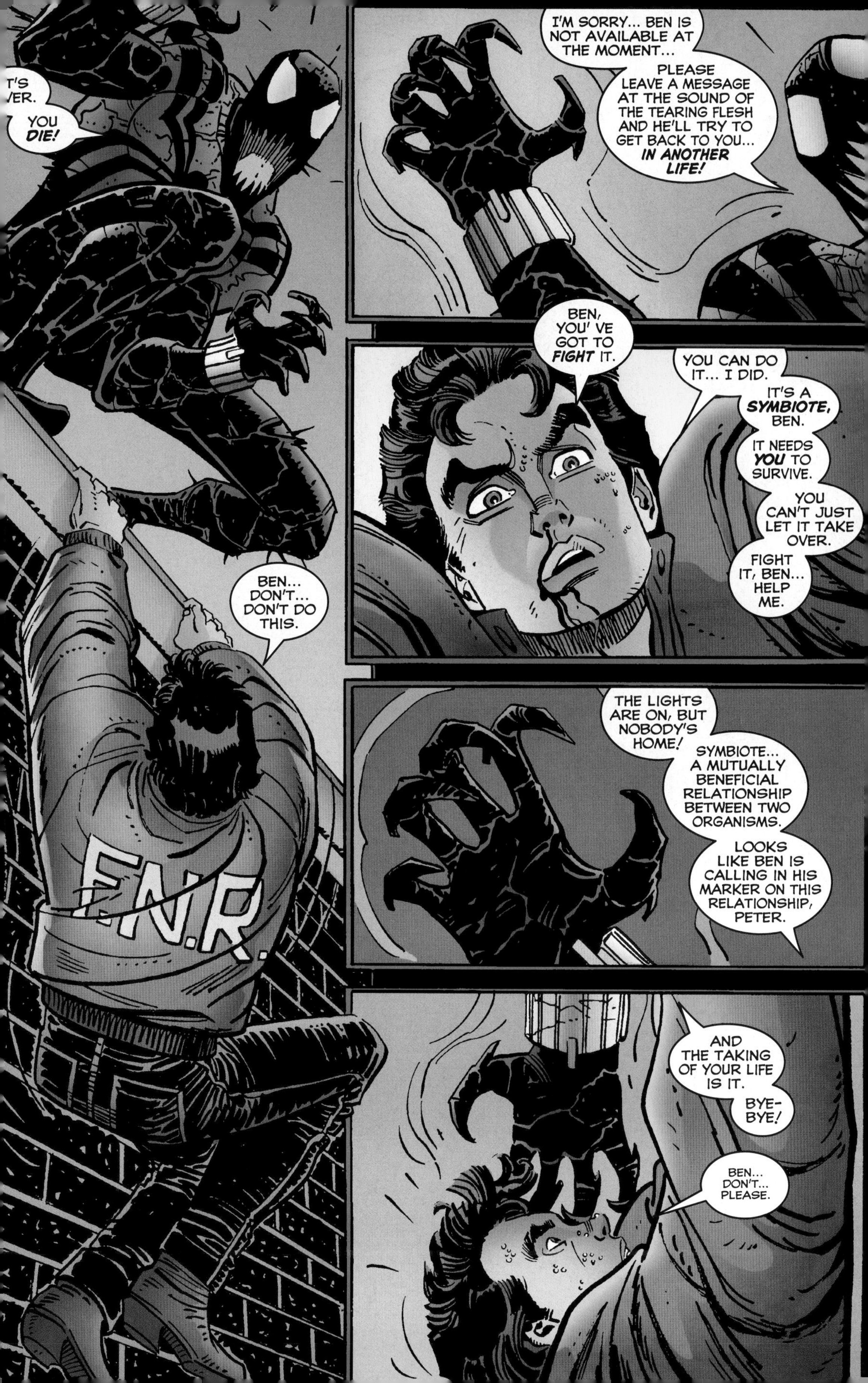

T'S
/ER.
YOU
DIE!
I'M SORRY... BEN IS NOT AVAILABLE AT THE MOMENT...
PLEASE LEAVE A MESSAGE AT THE SOUND OF THE TEARING FLESH AND HE'LL TRY TO GET BACK TO YOU... IN ANOTHER LIFE!
BEN, YOU' VE GOT TO FIGHT IT.
YOU CAN DO IT... I DID.
IT'S A SYMBIOTE, BEN.
IT NEEDS YOU TO SURVIVE.
YOU CAN'T JUST LET IT TAKE OVER.
FIGHT IT, BEN... HELP ME.
BEN... DON'T... DON'T DO THIS.
THE LIGHTS ARE ON, BUT NOBODY'S HOME!
SYMBIOTE... A MUTUALLY BENEFICIAL RELATIONSHIP BETWEEN TWO ORGANISMS.
LOOKS LIKE BEN IS CALLING IN HIS MARKER ON THIS RELATIONSHIP, PETER.
AND THE TAKING OF YOUR LIFE IS IT.
BYE-BYE!
BEN... DON'T... PLEASE.
E.N.R.

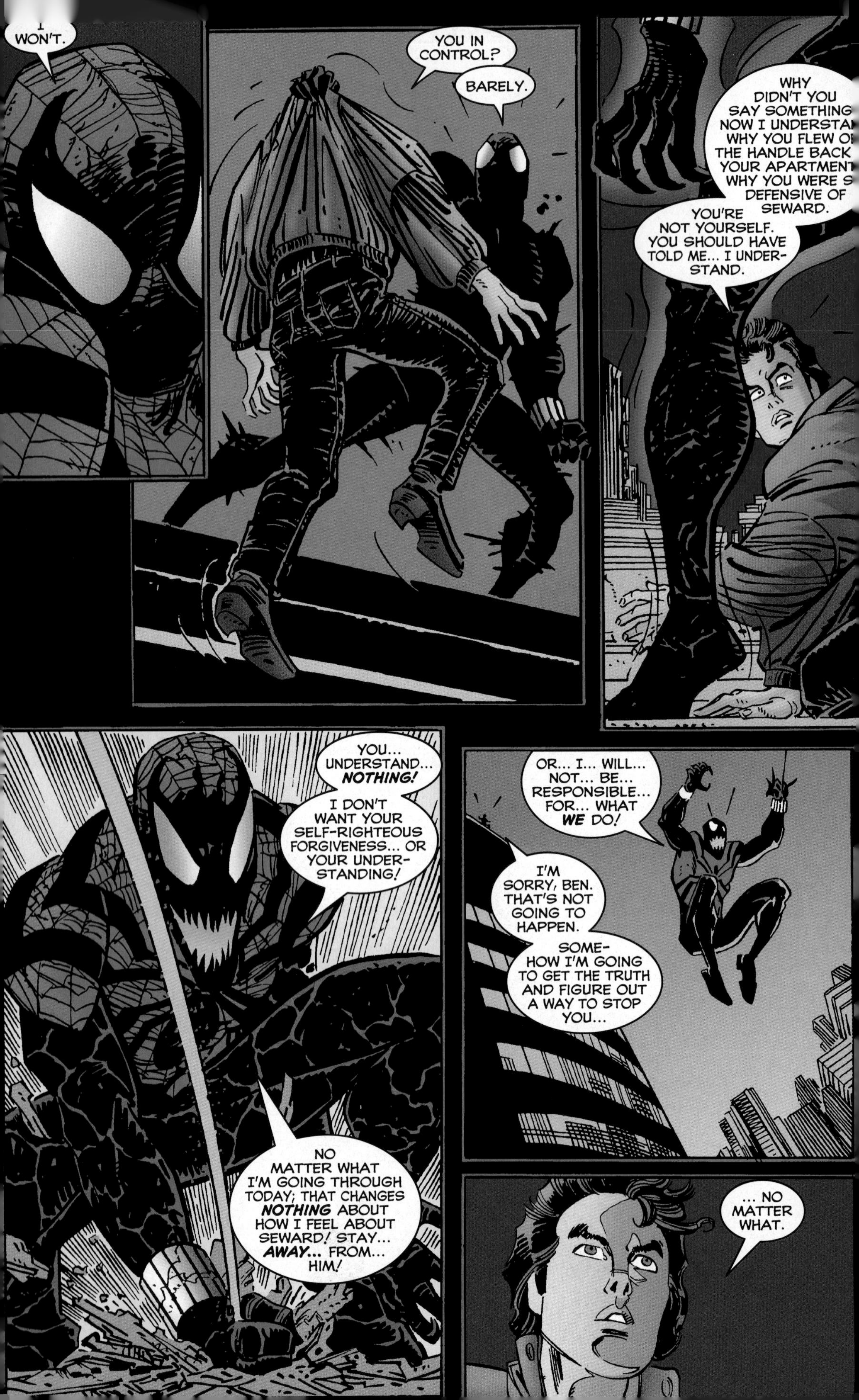
I WON'T.
YOU IN CONTROL?
BARELY.
WHY DIDN'T YOU SAY SOMETHING NOW I UNDERSTA WHY YOU FLEW O THE HANDLE BACK YOUR APARTMENT WHY YOU WERE S DEFENSIVE OF SEWARD.
YOU'RE NOT YOURSELF. YOU SHOULD HAVE TOLD ME... I UNDERSTAND.
YOU... UNDERSTAND... NOTHING!
I DON'T WANT YOUR SELF-RIGHTEOUS FORGIVENESS... OR YOUR UNDERSTANDING!
NO MATTER WHAT I'M GOING THROUGH TODAY; THAT CHANGES NOTHING ABOUT HOW I FEEL ABOUT SEWARD! STAY... AWAY... FROM... HIM!
OR... I... WILL... NOT... BE... RESPONSIBLE... FOR... WHAT WE DO!
I'M SORRY, BEN. THAT'S NOT GOING TO HAPPEN.
SOME-HOW I'M GOING TO GET THE TRUTH AND FIGURE OUT A WAY TO STOP YOU...
... NO MATTER WHAT.

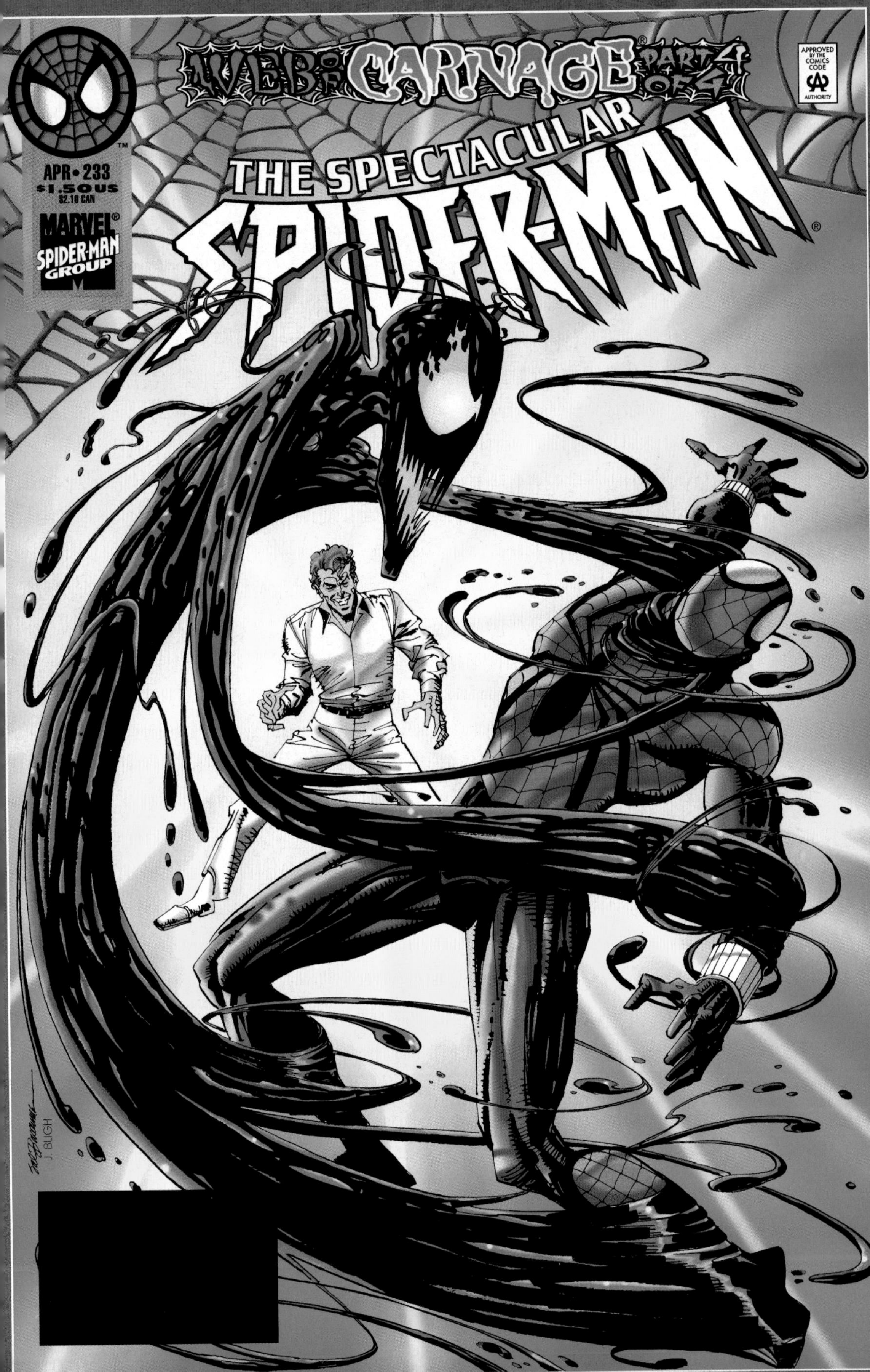
WEB OF CARNAGE PART 4 OF 4
APPROVED BY THE COMICS CODE AUTHORITY
APR • 233
$1.50US
$2.10 CAN
MARVEL
SPIDER-MAN GROUP
THE SPECTACULAR
SPIDER-MAN
J. BUGH

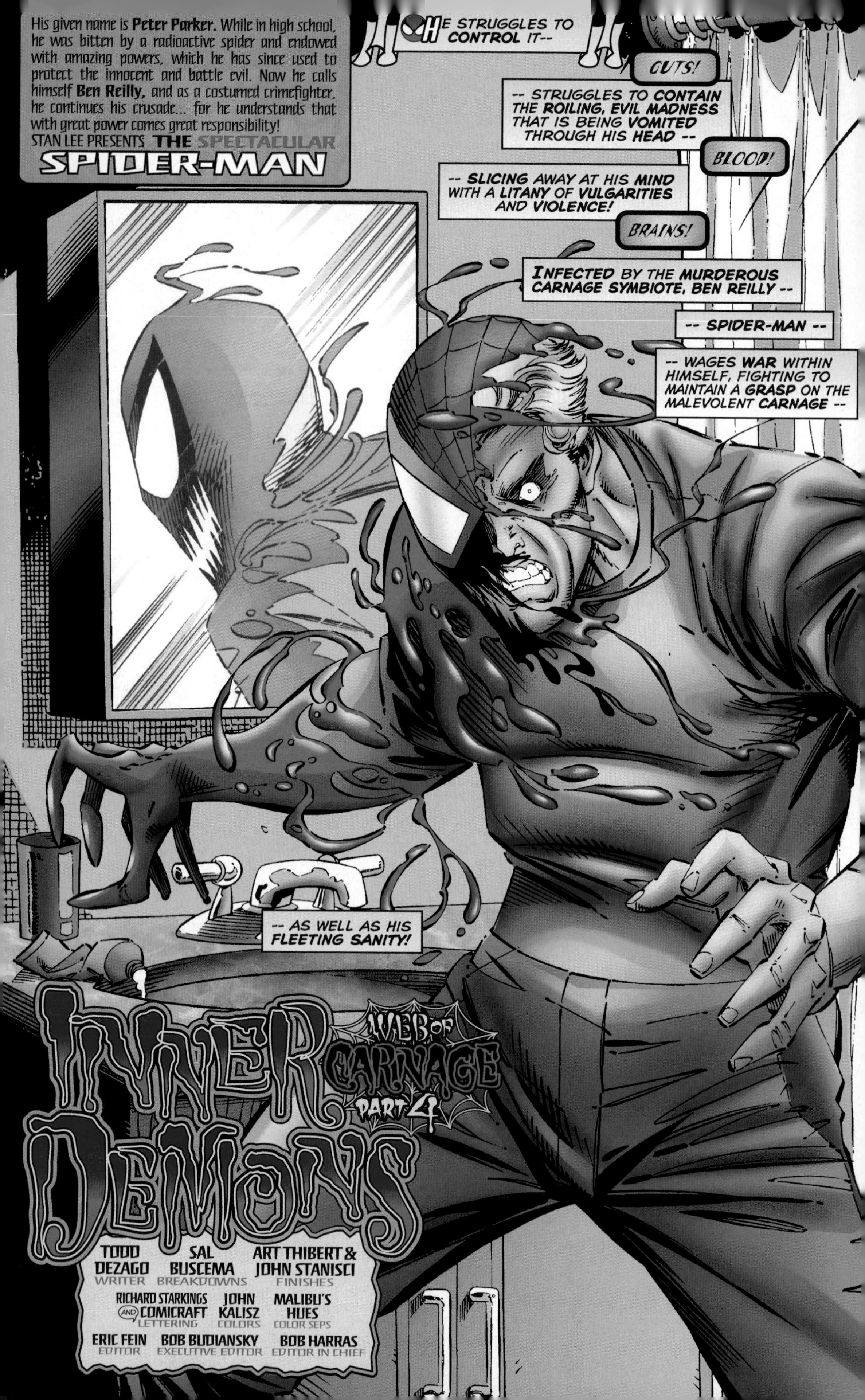

His given name is Peter Parker. While in high school, he was bitten by a radioactive spider and endowed with amazing powers, which he has since used to protect the innocent and battle evil. Now he calls himself Ben Reilly, and as a costumed crimefighter, he continues his crusade... for he understands that with great power comes great responsibility!
STAN LEE PRESENTS THE SPECTACULAR SPIDER-MAN
HE STRUGGLES TO CONTROL IT--
CUTS!
-- STRUGGLES TO CONTAIN THE ROILING, EVIL MADNESS THAT IS BEING VOMITED THROUGH HIS HEAD --
BLOOD!
-- SLICING AWAY AT HIS MIND WITH A LITANY OF VULGARITIES AND VIOLENCE!
BRAINS!
INFECTED BY THE MURDEROUS CARNAGE SYMBIOTE, BEN REILLY --
-- SPIDER-MAN --
-- WAGES WAR WITHIN HIMSELF, FIGHTING TO MAINTAIN A GRASP ON THE MALEVOLENT CARNAGE --
-- AS WELL AS HIS FLEETING SANITY!
INNER DEMONS
WEB OF CARNAGE PART 4
TODD DEZAGO WRITER
SAL BUSCEMA BREAKDOWNS
ART THIBERT & JOHN STANISCI FINISHES
RICHARD STARKINGS AND COMICRAFT LETTERING
JOHN KALISZ COLORS
MALIBU'S HUES COLOR SEPS
ERIC FEIN EDITOR
BOB BUDIANSKY EXECUTIVE EDITOR
BOB HARRAS EDITOR IN CHIEF

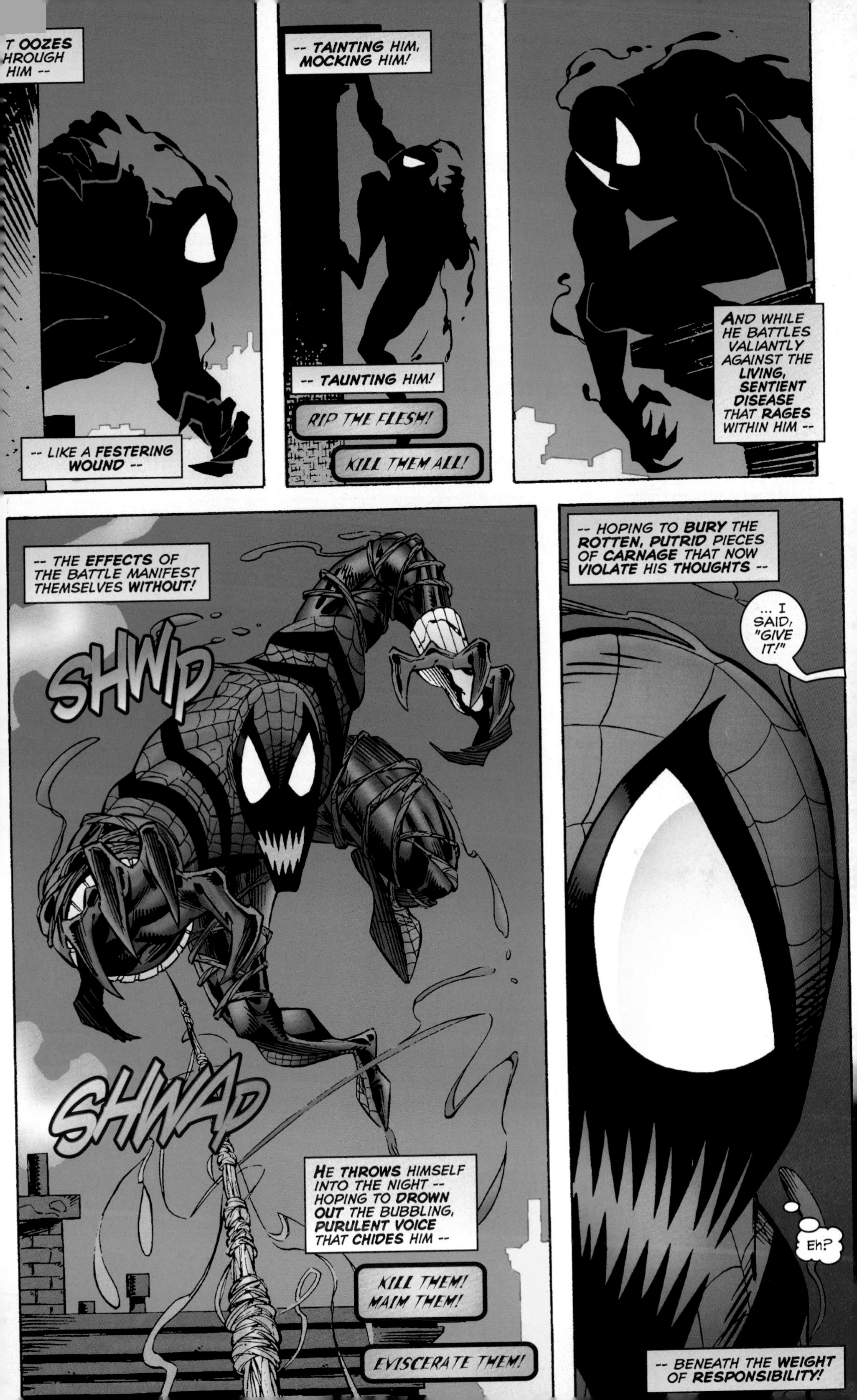
T OOZES HROUGH HIM --
-- LIKE A FESTERING WOUND --
-- TAINTING HIM, MOCKING HIM!
-- TAUNTING HIM!
RIP THE FLESH!
KILL THEM ALL!
AND WHILE HE BATTLES VALIANTLY AGAINST THE LIVING, SENTIENT DISEASE THAT RAGES WITHIN HIM --
-- THE EFFECTS OF THE BATTLE MANIFEST THEMSELVES WITHOUT!
SHWIP
SHWAP
HE THROWS HIMSELF INTO THE NIGHT -- HOPING TO DROWN OUT THE BUBBLING, PURULENT VOICE THAT CHIDES HIM --
KILL THEM! MAIM THEM!
EVISCERATE THEM!
-- HOPING TO BURY THE ROTTEN, PUTRID PIECES OF CARNAGE THAT NOW VIOLATE HIS THOUGHTS --
... I SAID, "GIVE IT!"
Eh?
-- BENEATH THE WEIGHT OF RESPONSIBILITY!

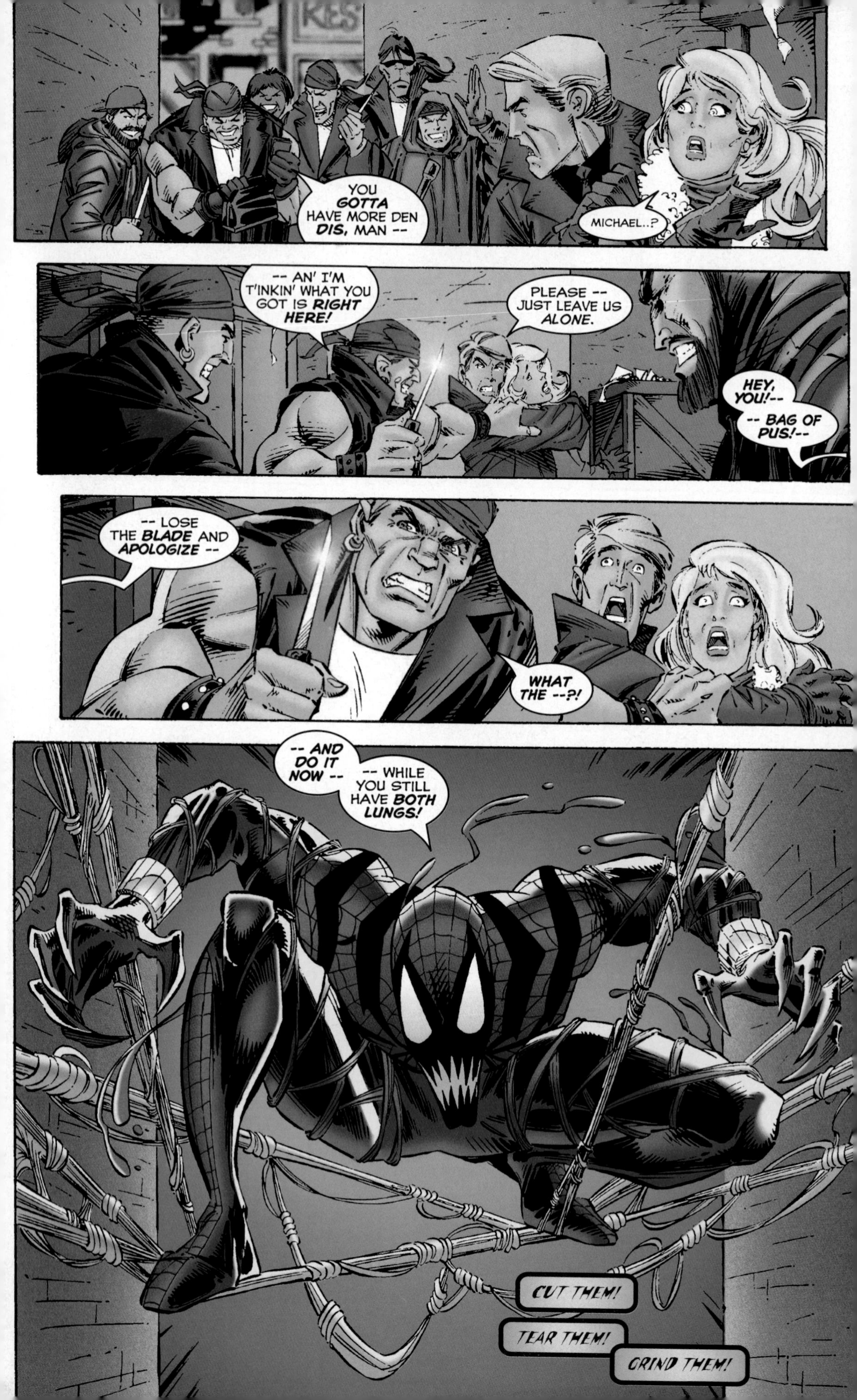
YOU GOTTA HAVE MORE DEN DIS, MAN --
MICHAEL..?
-- AN' I'M T'INKIN' WHAT YOU GOT IS RIGHT HERE!
PLEASE -- JUST LEAVE US ALONE.
HEY, YOU!--
-- BAG OF PUS!--
-- LOSE THE BLADE AND APOLOGIZE --
WHAT THE --?!
-- AND DO IT NOW --
-- WHILE YOU STILL HAVE BOTH LUNGS!
CUT THEM!
TEAR THEM!
GRIND THEM!

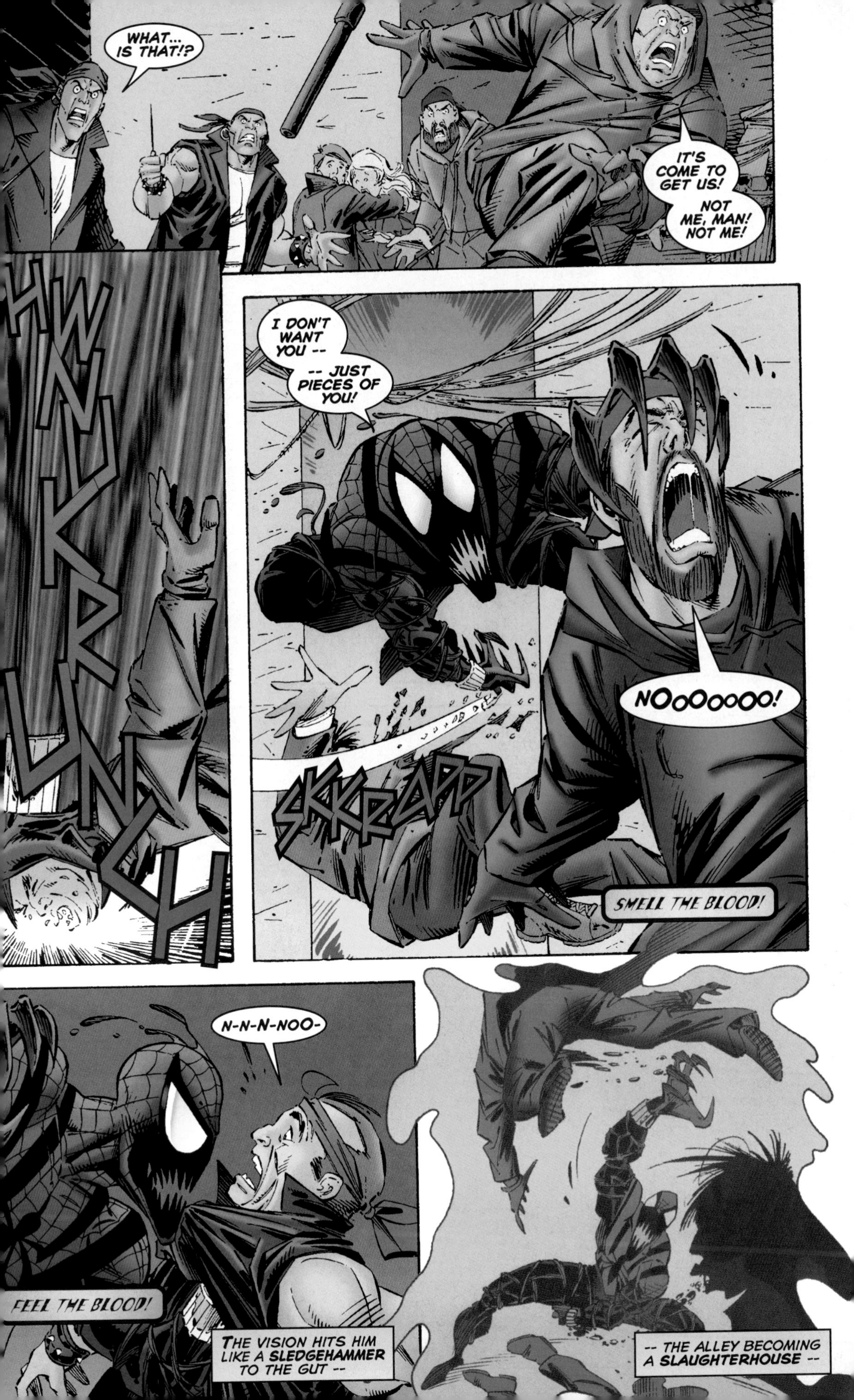
WHAT... IS THAT!?
IT'S COME TO GET US!
NOT ME, MAN! NOT ME!
HWNUKRUNCH
I DON'T WANT YOU --
-- JUST PIECES OF YOU!
NOOOOOOO!
SKKRAPP
SMELL THE BLOOD!
N-N-N-NOO-
FEEL THE BLOOD!
THE VISION HITS HIM LIKE A SLEDGEHAMMER TO THE GUT --
-- THE ALLEY BECOMING A SLAUGHTERHOUSE --

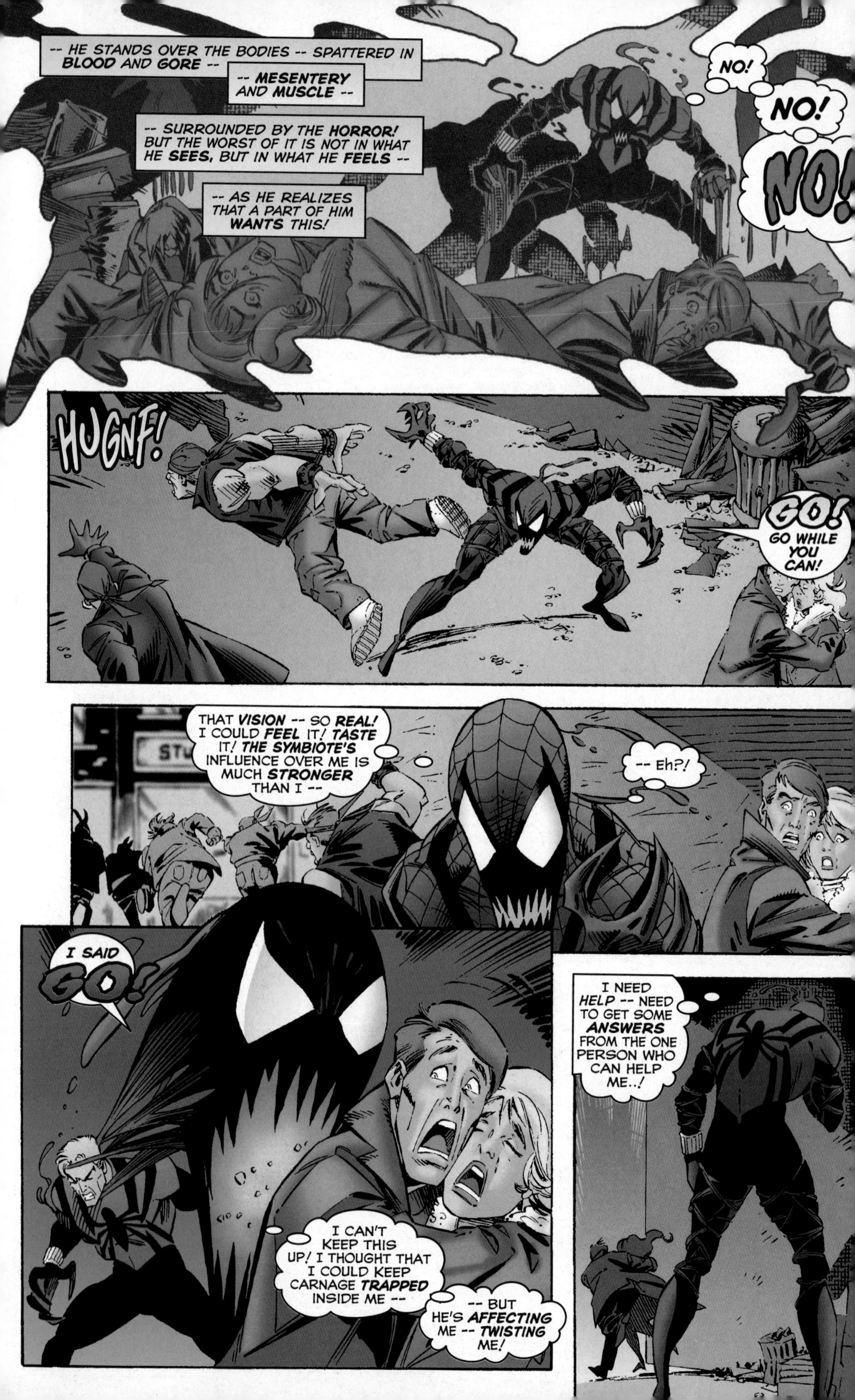
-- HE STANDS OVER THE BODIES -- SPATTERED IN BLOOD AND GORE --
-- MESENTERY AND MUSCLE --
-- SURROUNDED BY THE HORROR! BUT THE WORST OF IT IS NOT IN WHAT HE SEES, BUT IN WHAT HE FEELS --
-- AS HE REALIZES THAT A PART OF HIM WANTS THIS!
NO!
NO!
NO!
HUGNF!
GO! GO WHILE YOU CAN!
THAT VISION -- SO REAL! I COULD FEEL IT! TASTE IT! THE SYMBIOTE'S INFLUENCE OVER ME IS MUCH STRONGER THAN I --
-- Eh?!
I SAID GO!
I CAN'T KEEP THIS UP! I THOUGHT THAT I COULD KEEP CARNAGE TRAPPED INSIDE ME --
-- BUT HE'S AFFECTING ME -- TWISTING ME!
I NEED HELP -- NEED TO GET SOME ANSWERS FROM THE ONE PERSON WHO CAN HELP ME..!

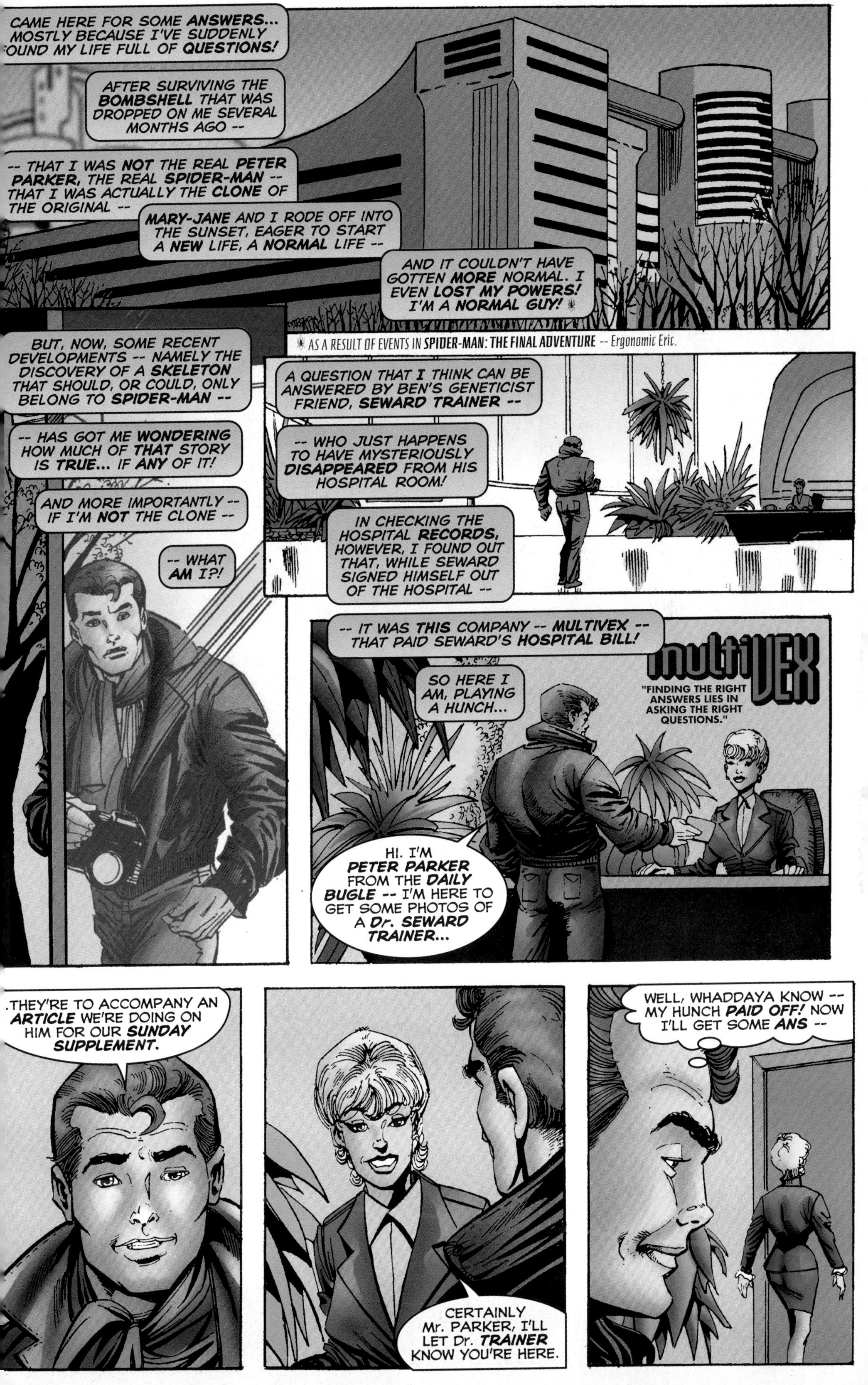

CAME HERE FOR SOME ANSWERS... MOSTLY BECAUSE I'VE SUDDENLY FOUND MY LIFE FULL OF QUESTIONS!
AFTER SURVIVING THE BOMBSHELL THAT WAS DROPPED ON ME SEVERAL MONTHS AGO --
-- THAT I WAS NOT THE REAL PETER PARKER, THE REAL SPIDER-MAN -- THAT I WAS ACTUALLY THE CLONE OF THE ORIGINAL --
MARY-JANE AND I RODE OFF INTO THE SUNSET, EAGER TO START A NEW LIFE, A NORMAL LIFE --
AND IT COULDN'T HAVE GOTTEN MORE NORMAL. I EVEN LOST MY POWERS! I'M A NORMAL GUY!
AS A RESULT OF EVENTS IN SPIDER-MAN: THE FINAL ADVENTURE -- Ergonomic Eric.
BUT, NOW, SOME RECENT DEVELOPMENTS -- NAMELY THE DISCOVERY OF A SKELETON THAT SHOULD, OR COULD, ONLY BELONG TO SPIDER-MAN --
-- HAS GOT ME WONDERING HOW MUCH OF THAT STORY IS TRUE... IF ANY OF IT!
AND MORE IMPORTANTLY -- IF I'M NOT THE CLONE --
-- WHAT AM I?!
A QUESTION THAT I THINK CAN BE ANSWERED BY BEN'S GENETICIST FRIEND, SEWARD TRAINER --
-- WHO JUST HAPPENS TO HAVE MYSTERIOUSLY DISAPPEARED FROM HIS HOSPITAL ROOM!
IN CHECKING THE HOSPITAL RECORDS, HOWEVER, I FOUND OUT THAT, WHILE SEWARD SIGNED HIMSELF OUT OF THE HOSPITAL --
-- IT WAS THIS COMPANY -- MULTIVEX -- THAT PAID SEWARD'S HOSPITAL BILL!
multiVEX
"FINDING THE RIGHT ANSWERS LIES IN ASKING THE RIGHT QUESTIONS."
SO HERE I AM, PLAYING A HUNCH...
HI. I'M PETER PARKER FROM THE DAILY BUGLE -- I'M HERE TO GET SOME PHOTOS OF A Dr. SEWARD TRAINER...
...THEY'RE TO ACCOMPANY AN ARTICLE WE'RE DOING ON HIM FOR OUR SUNDAY SUPPLEMENT.
CERTAINLY Mr. PARKER, I'LL LET Dr. TRAINER KNOW YOU'RE HERE.
WELL, WHADDAYA KNOW -- MY HUNCH PAID OFF! NOW I'LL GET SOME ANS --

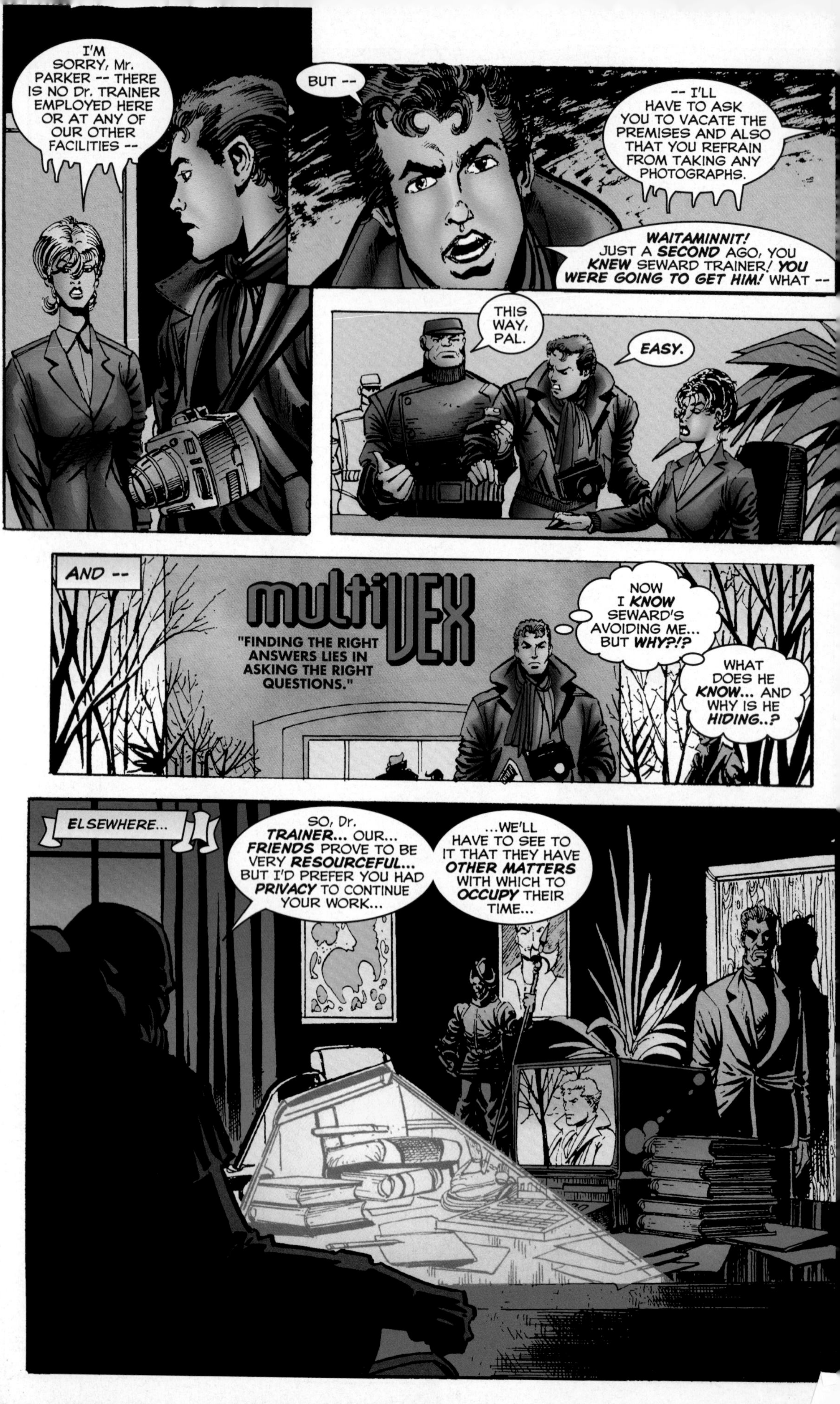
I'M SORRY, Mr. PARKER -- THERE IS NO Dr. TRAINER EMPLOYED HERE OR AT ANY OF OUR OTHER FACILITIES --
BUT --
-- I'LL HAVE TO ASK YOU TO VACATE THE PREMISES AND ALSO THAT YOU REFRAIN FROM TAKING ANY PHOTOGRAPHS.
WAITAMINNIT! JUST A SECOND AGO, YOU KNEW SEWARD TRAINER! YOU WERE GOING TO GET HIM! WHAT --
THIS WAY, PAL.
EASY.
AND --
multiVEX
"FINDING THE RIGHT ANSWERS LIES IN ASKING THE RIGHT QUESTIONS."
NOW I KNOW SEWARD'S AVOIDING ME... BUT WHY?!?
WHAT DOES HE KNOW... AND WHY IS HE HIDING..?
ELSEWHERE...
SO, Dr. TRAINER... OUR... FRIENDS PROVE TO BE VERY RESOURCEFUL... BUT I'D PREFER YOU HAD PRIVACY TO CONTINUE YOUR WORK...
...WE'LL HAVE TO SEE TO IT THAT THEY HAVE OTHER MATTERS WITH WHICH TO OCCUPY THEIR TIME...

"...AND SEE WHAT **DEVELOPS** FROM THERE...!"

C'MON, COME **ON!**

THE DARKROOM OF BEN REILLY'S CURRENT GIRLFRIEND, JESSICA CARRADINE --

PLEASE! LET ME HAVE **SALVAGED** AT LEAST **ONE** OF THE --

NO!

EVERY FRAME IS **OVER-EXPOSED!**

THE **BUGLE'LL** PAY **BIG MONEY** FOR A SHOT OF THIS **SPIDER-MONSTER** THAT'S BEEN **TERRORIZING** THE CITY...

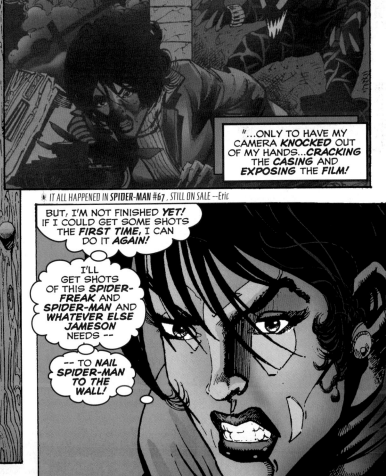

"...AND I HAD MY **CHANCE!**... CLICKED OFF A **WHOLE ROLL** OF THE **UGLY THING**..!"

"...ONLY TO HAVE MY **CAMERA KNOCKED** OUT OF MY HANDS...**CRACKING** THE **CASING** AND **EXPOSING** THE **FILM!**"

★ IT ALL HAPPENED IN **SPIDER-MAN** #67 , STILL ON SALE --Eric

BUT, I'M NOT FINISHED **YET!** IF I COULD GET SOME SHOTS THE **FIRST TIME,** I CAN DO IT **AGAIN!**

I'LL GET SHOTS OF THIS **SPIDER-FREAK** AND **SPIDER-MAN** AND **WHATEVER ELSE JAMESON** NEEDS --

-- TO **NAIL SPIDER-MAN** TO THE **WALL!**

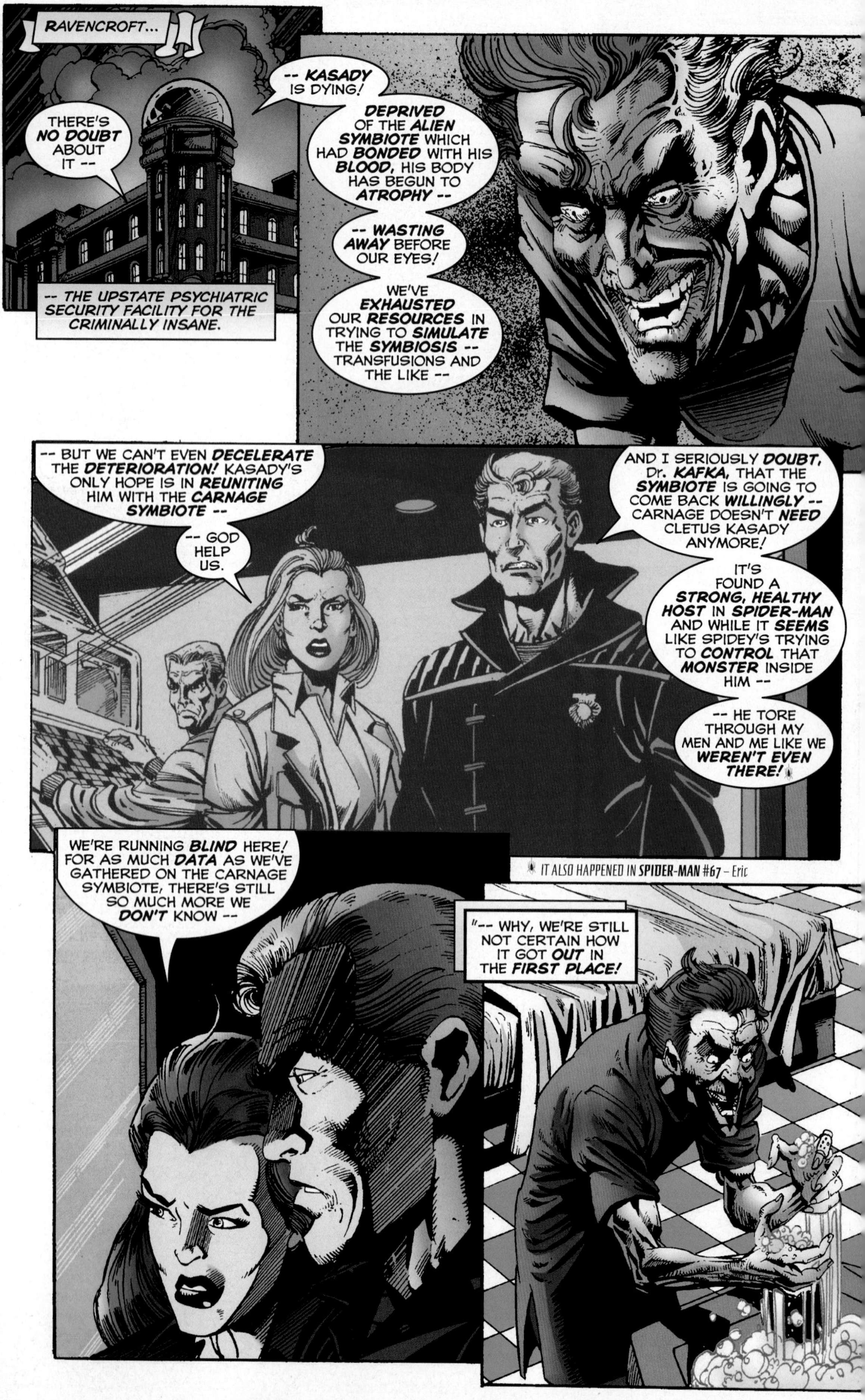

RAVENCROFT...
THERE'S NO DOUBT ABOUT IT --
-- KASADY IS DYING!
DEPRIVED OF THE ALIEN SYMBIOTE WHICH HAD BONDED WITH HIS BLOOD, HIS BODY HAS BEGUN TO ATROPHY --
-- WASTING AWAY BEFORE OUR EYES!
WE'VE EXHAUSTED OUR RESOURCES IN TRYING TO SIMULATE THE SYMBIOSIS -- TRANSFUSIONS AND THE LIKE --
-- THE UPSTATE PSYCHIATRIC SECURITY FACILITY FOR THE CRIMINALLY INSANE.
-- BUT WE CAN'T EVEN DECELERATE THE DETERIORATION! KASADY'S ONLY HOPE IS IN REUNITING HIM WITH THE CARNAGE SYMBIOTE --
-- GOD HELP US.
AND I SERIOUSLY DOUBT, Dr. KAFKA, THAT THE SYMBIOTE IS GOING TO COME BACK WILLINGLY -- CARNAGE DOESN'T NEED CLETUS KASADY ANYMORE!
IT'S FOUND A STRONG, HEALTHY HOST IN SPIDER-MAN AND WHILE IT SEEMS LIKE SPIDEY'S TRYING TO CONTROL THAT MONSTER INSIDE HIM --
-- HE TORE THROUGH MY MEN AND ME LIKE WE WEREN'T EVEN THERE!
IT ALSO HAPPENED IN SPIDER-MAN #67 – Eric
WE'RE RUNNING BLIND HERE! FOR AS MUCH DATA AS WE'VE GATHERED ON THE CARNAGE SYMBIOTE, THERE'S STILL SO MUCH MORE WE DON'T KNOW --
"-- WHY, WE'RE STILL NOT CERTAIN HOW IT GOT OUT IN THE FIRST PLACE!

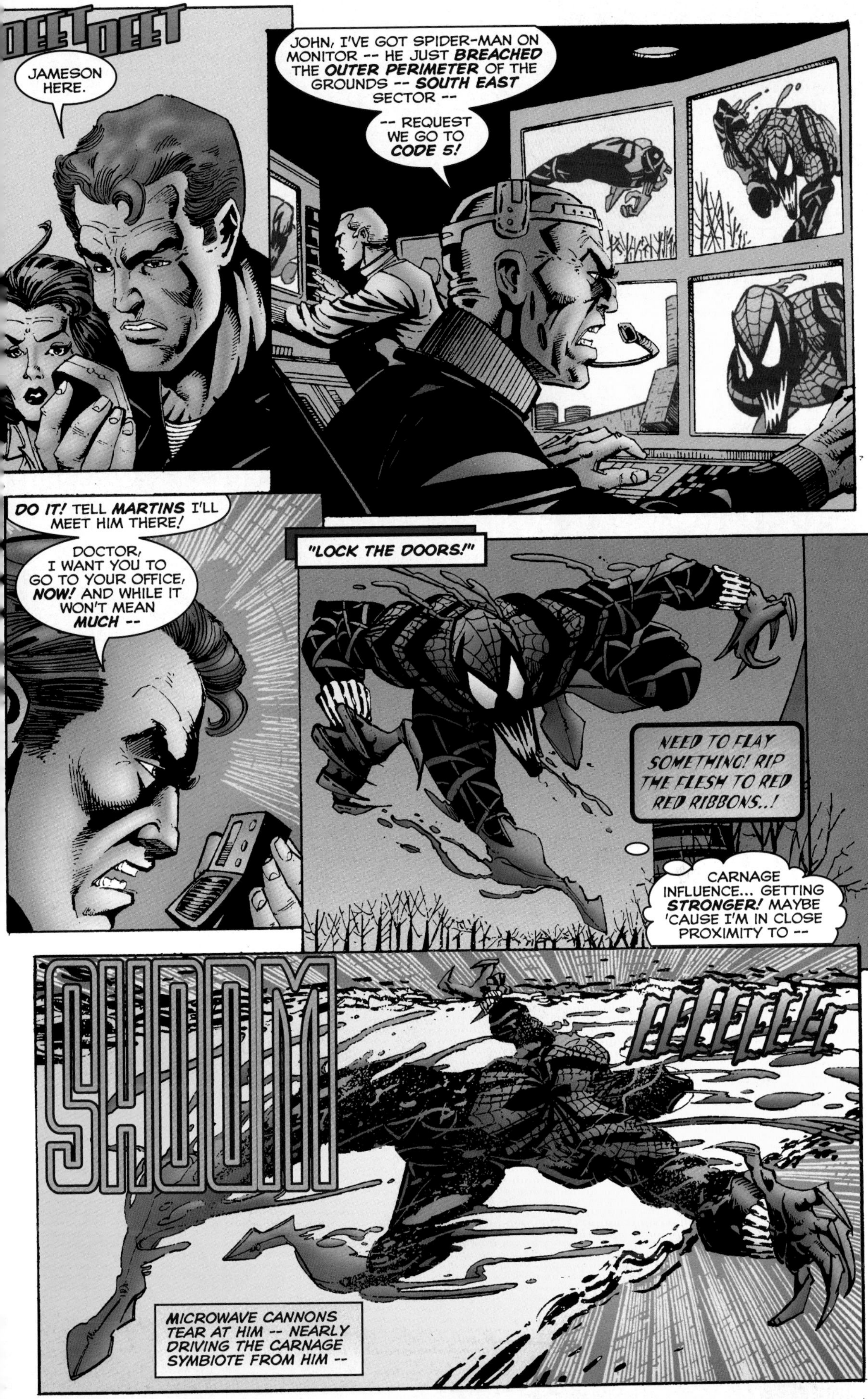

DEET DEET
JAMESON HERE.
JOHN, I'VE GOT SPIDER-MAN ON MONITOR -- HE JUST BREACHED THE OUTER PERIMETER OF THE GROUNDS -- SOUTH EAST SECTOR --
-- REQUEST WE GO TO CODE 5!
DO IT! TELL MARTINS I'LL MEET HIM THERE!
DOCTOR, I WANT YOU TO GO TO YOUR OFFICE, NOW! AND WHILE IT WON'T MEAN MUCH --
"LOCK THE DOORS!"
NEED TO FLAY SOMETHING! RIP THE FLESH TO RED RED RIBBONS..!
CARNAGE INFLUENCE... GETTING STRONGER! MAYBE 'CAUSE I'M IN CLOSE PROXIMITY TO --
SHOOM
EEEEEEE
MICROWAVE CANNONS TEAR AT HIM -- NEARLY DRIVING THE CARNAGE SYMBIOTE FROM HIM --

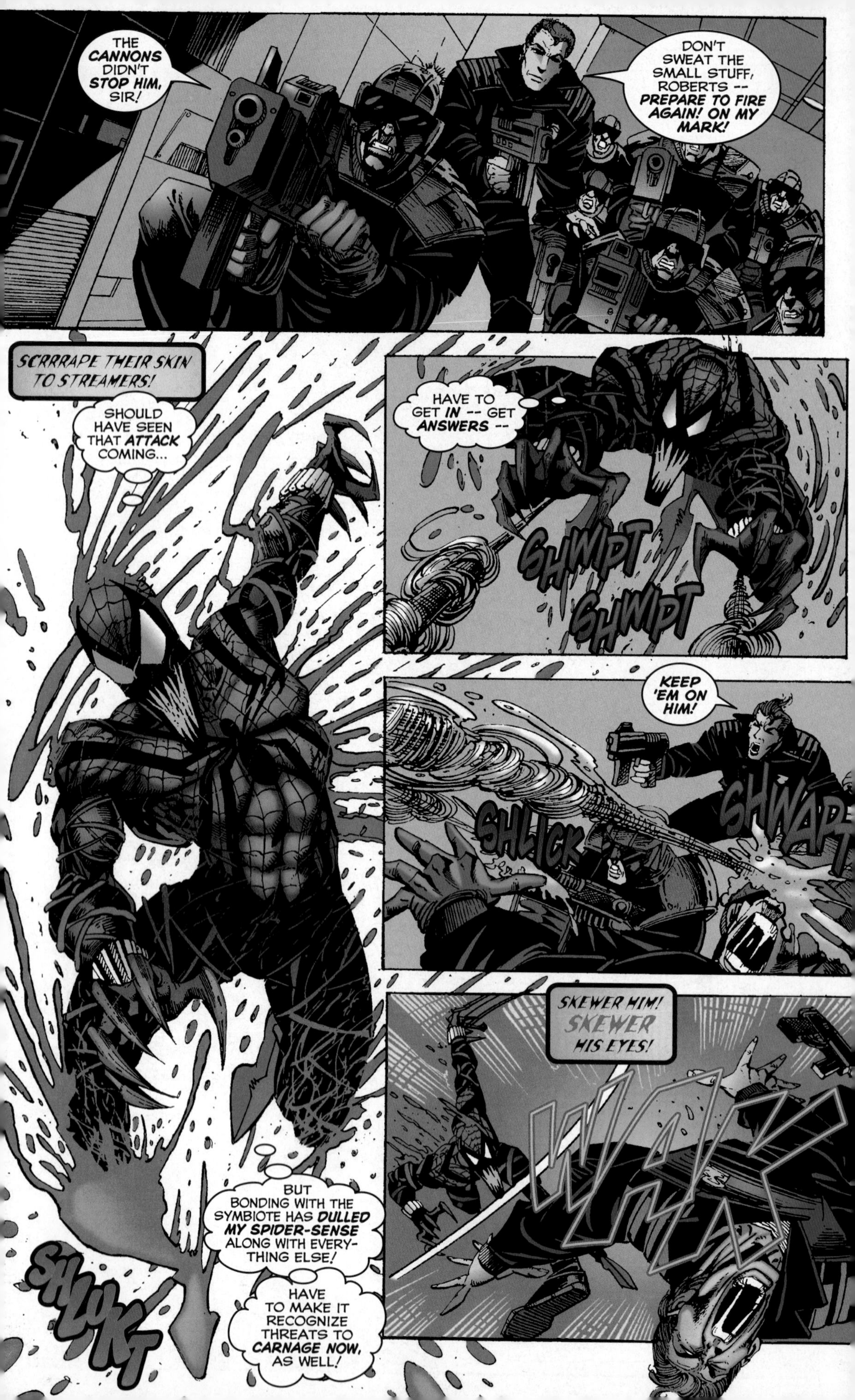
THE CANNONS DIDN'T STOP HIM, SIR!
DON'T SWEAT THE SMALL STUFF, ROBERTS -- PREPARE TO FIRE AGAIN! ON MY MARK!
SCRRRAPE THEIR SKIN TO STREAMERS!
SHOULD HAVE SEEN THAT ATTACK COMING...
HAVE TO GET IN -- GET ANSWERS --
SHWIPT
SHWIPT
KEEP 'EM ON HIM!
SHLICK
SHWAP
SKEWER HIM! SKEWER HIS EYES!
WAK
BUT BONDING WITH THE SYMBIOTE HAS DULLED MY SPIDER-SENSE ALONG WITH EVERY-THING ELSE!
HAVE TO MAKE IT RECOGNIZE THREATS TO CARNAGE NOW, AS WELL!
SHLUKT

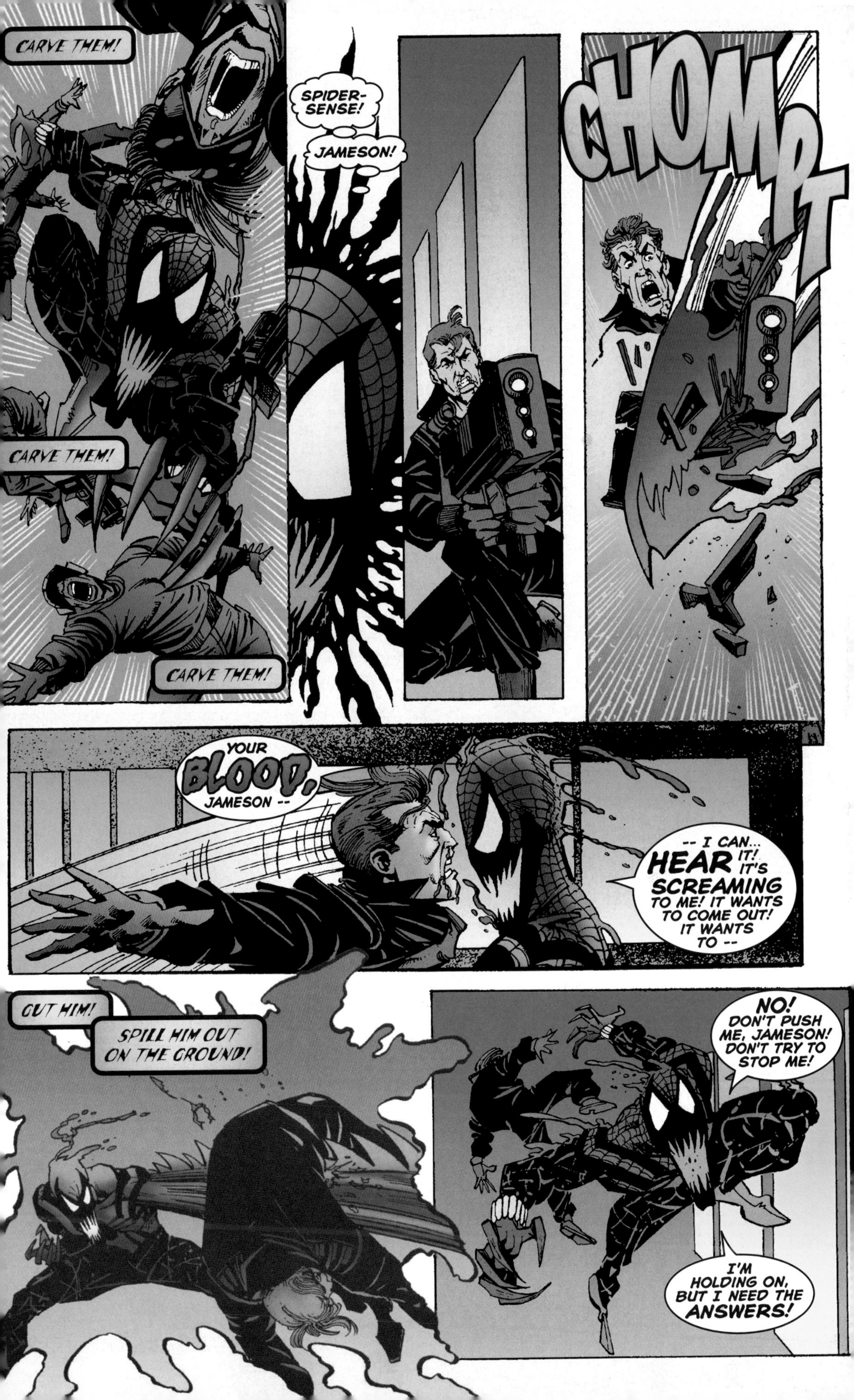
CARVE THEM!
CARVE THEM!
CARVE THEM!
SPIDER-SENSE!
JAMESON!
CHOMPT
YOUR BLOOD, JAMESON --
-- I CAN... HEAR IT! IT'S SCREAMING TO ME! IT WANTS TO COME OUT! IT WANTS TO --
CUT HIM!
SPILL HIM OUT ON THE GROUND!
NO! DON'T PUSH ME, JAMESON! DON'T TRY TO STOP ME!
I'M HOLDING ON, BUT I NEED THE ANSWERS!

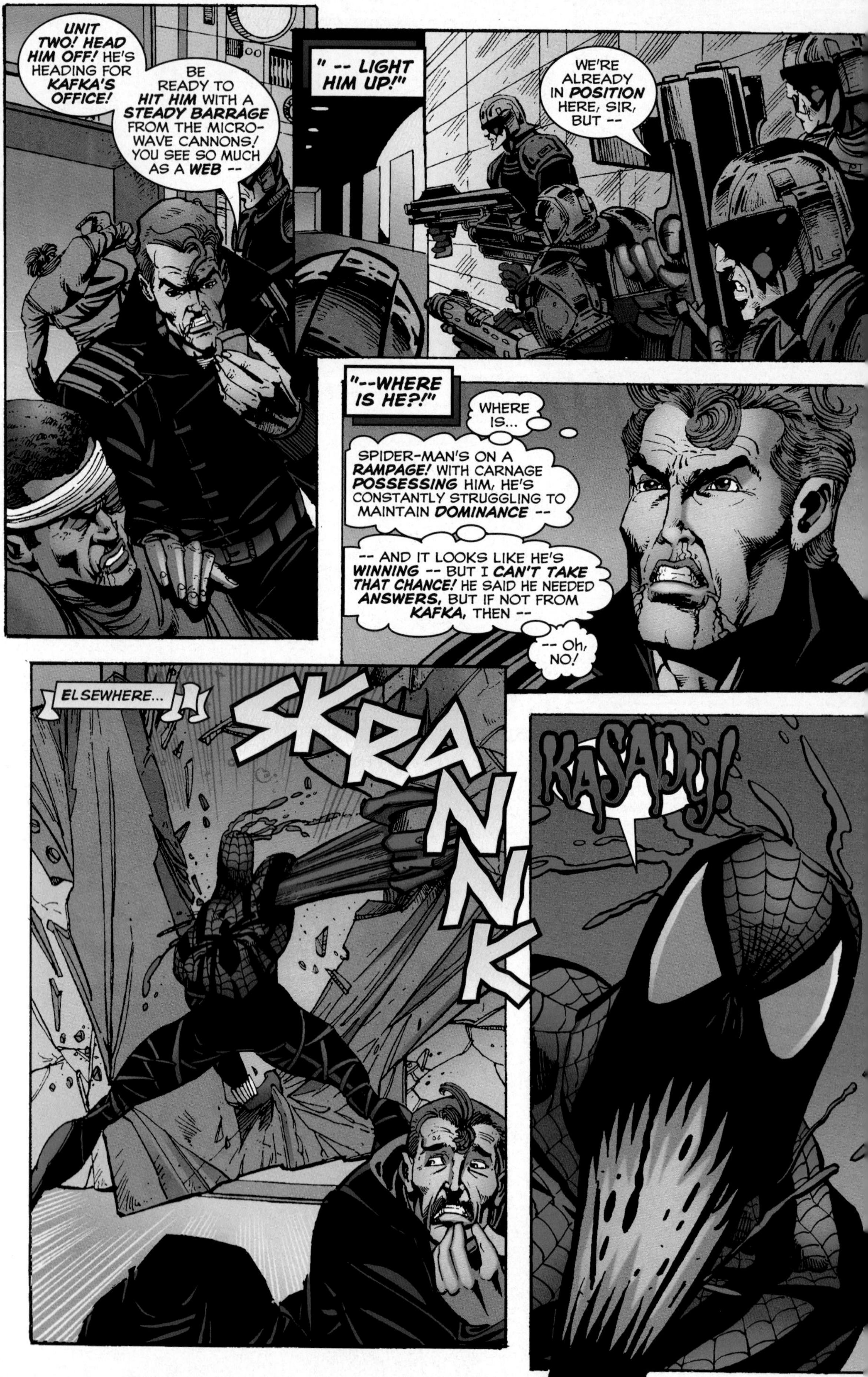
UNIT TWO! HEAD HIM OFF! HE'S HEADING FOR KAFKA'S OFFICE!
BE READY TO HIT HIM WITH A STEADY BARRAGE FROM THE MICRO-WAVE CANNONS! YOU SEE SO MUCH AS A WEB --
" -- LIGHT HIM UP!"
WE'RE ALREADY IN POSITION HERE, SIR, BUT --
"--WHERE IS HE?!"
WHERE IS...
SPIDER-MAN'S ON A RAMPAGE! WITH CARNAGE POSSESSING HIM, HE'S CONSTANTLY STRUGGLING TO MAINTAIN DOMINANCE --
-- AND IT LOOKS LIKE HE'S WINNING -- BUT I CAN'T TAKE THAT CHANCE! HE SAID HE NEEDED ANSWERS, BUT IF NOT FROM KAFKA, THEN --
-- Oh, NO!
ELSEWHERE...
SKRANNK
KASADY!

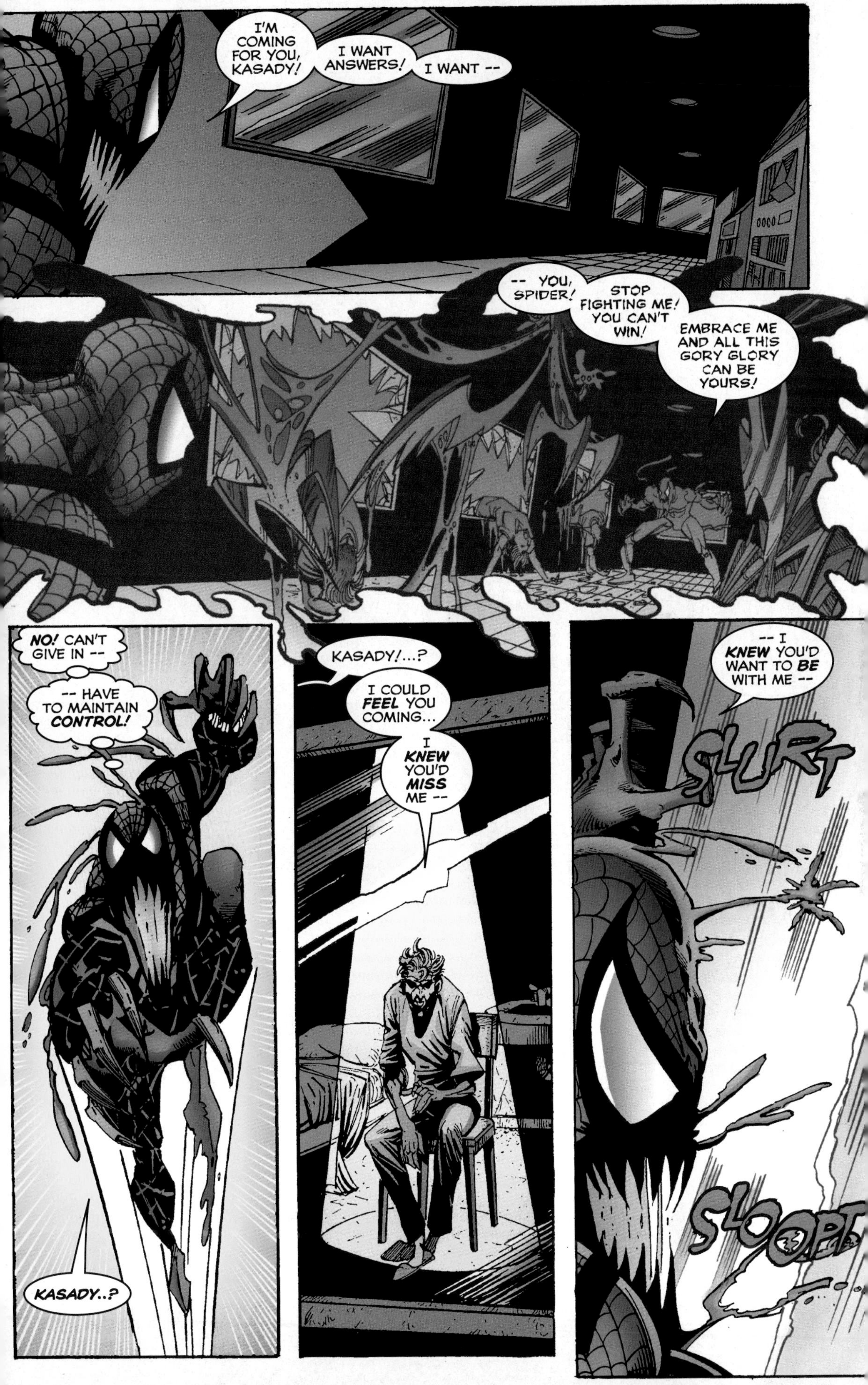
I'M COMING FOR YOU, KASADY!
I WANT ANSWERS!
I WANT --
-- YOU, SPIDER!
STOP FIGHTING ME! YOU CAN'T WIN!
EMBRACE ME AND ALL THIS GORY GLORY CAN BE YOURS!
NO! CAN'T GIVE IN --
-- HAVE TO MAINTAIN CONTROL!
KASADY..?
KASADY!...?
I COULD FEEL YOU COMING...
I KNEW YOU'D MISS ME --
-- I KNEW YOU'D WANT TO BE WITH ME --
SLURT
SLOOPT

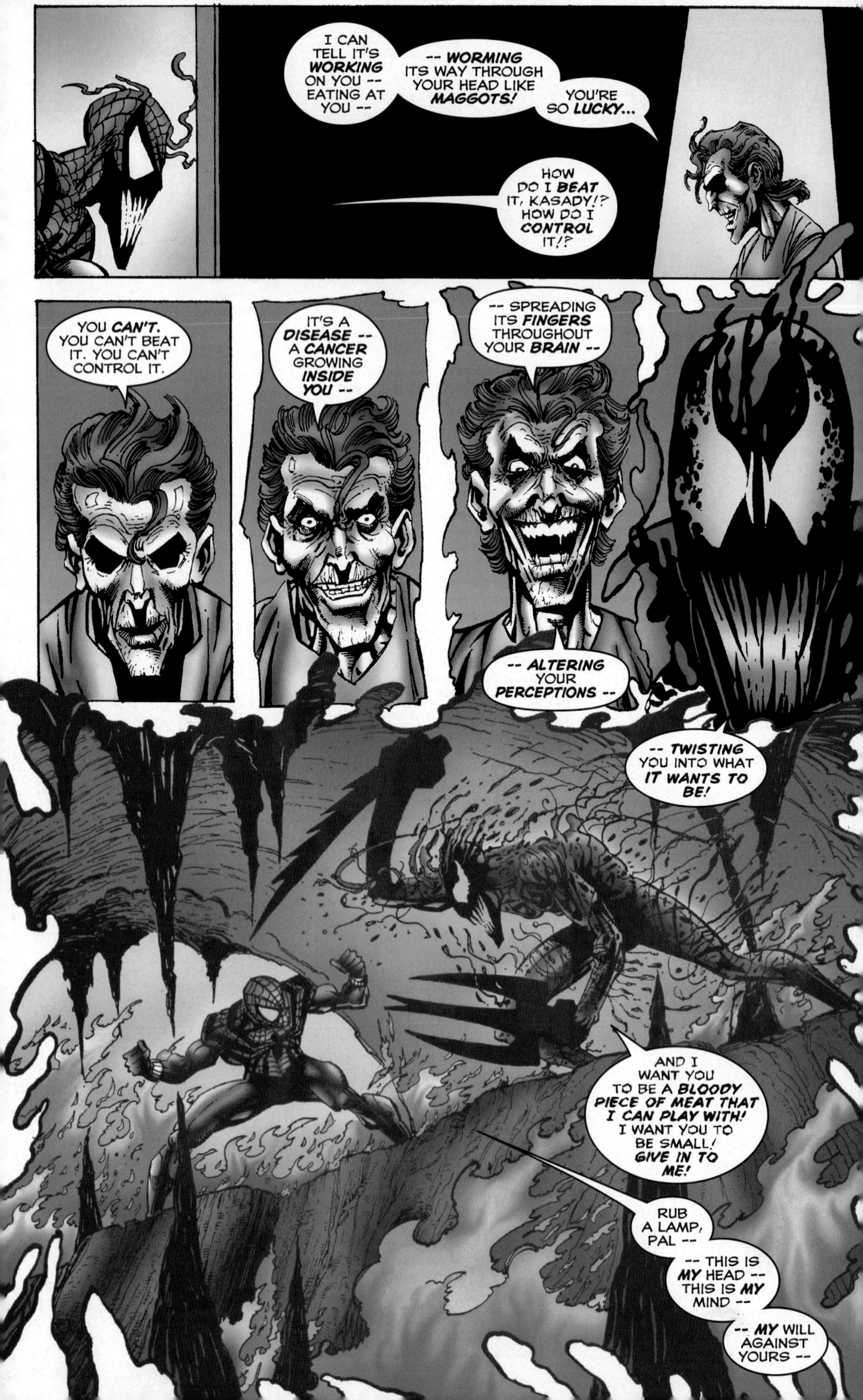
I CAN TELL IT'S WORKING ON YOU -- EATING AT YOU --
-- WORMING ITS WAY THROUGH YOUR HEAD LIKE MAGGOTS!
YOU'RE SO LUCKY...
HOW DO I BEAT IT, KASADY!? HOW DO I CONTROL IT!?
YOU CAN'T. YOU CAN'T BEAT IT. YOU CAN'T CONTROL IT.
IT'S A DISEASE -- A CANCER GROWING INSIDE YOU --
-- SPREADING ITS FINGERS THROUGHOUT YOUR BRAIN --
-- ALTERING YOUR PERCEPTIONS --
-- TWISTING YOU INTO WHAT IT WANTS TO BE!
AND I WANT YOU TO BE A BLOODY PIECE OF MEAT THAT I CAN PLAY WITH! I WANT YOU TO BE SMALL! GIVE IN TO ME!
RUB A LAMP, PAL --
-- THIS IS MY HEAD -- THIS IS MY MIND --
-- MY WILL AGAINST YOURS --

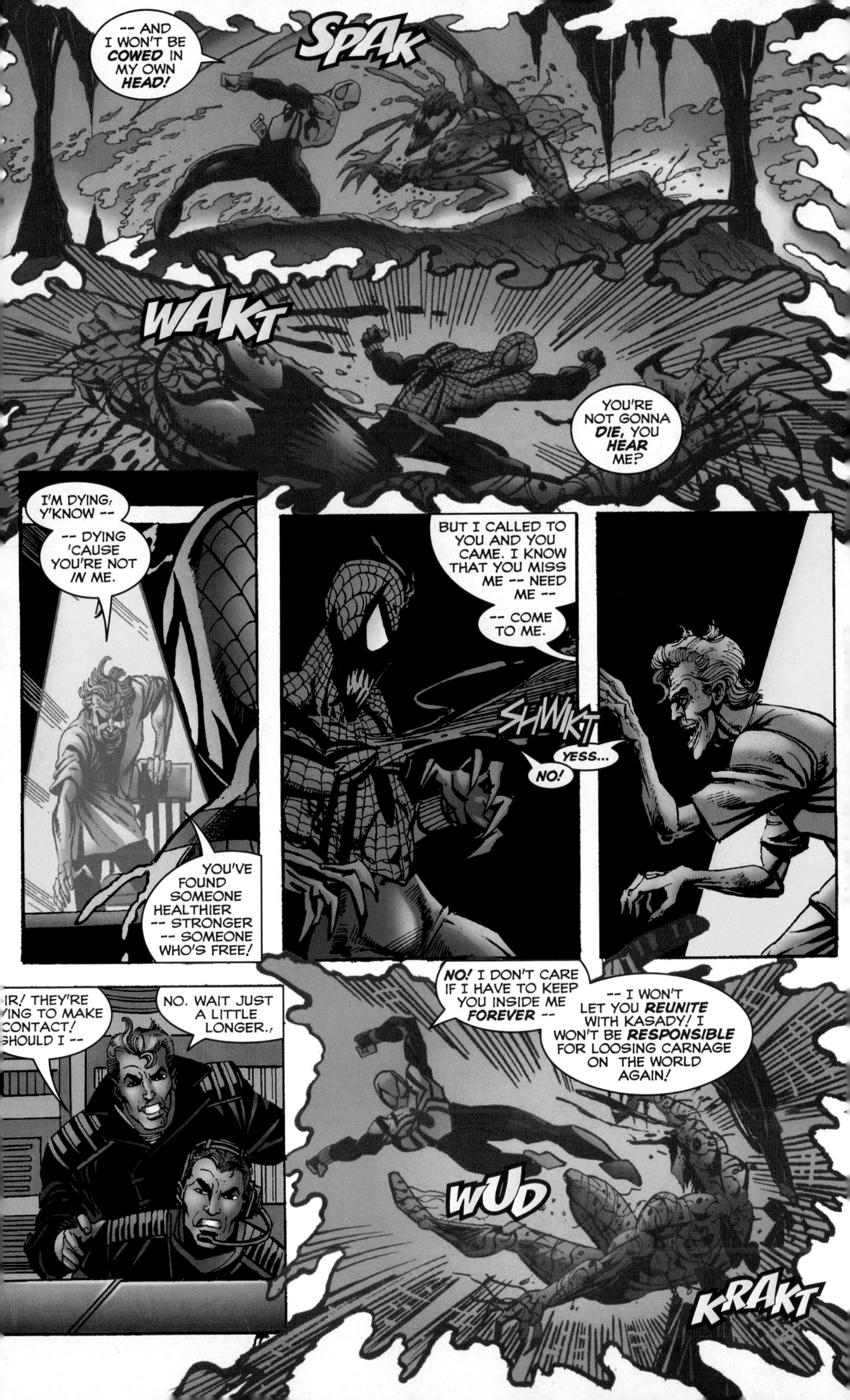

-- AND I WON'T BE COWED IN MY OWN HEAD!
SPAK
WAKT
YOU'RE NOT GONNA DIE, YOU HEAR ME?
I'M DYING, Y'KNOW --
-- DYING 'CAUSE YOU'RE NOT IN ME.
YOU'VE FOUND SOMEONE HEALTHIER -- STRONGER -- SOMEONE WHO'S FREE!
BUT I CALLED TO YOU AND YOU CAME. I KNOW THAT YOU MISS ME -- NEED ME --
-- COME TO ME.
SHWIKT
YESS...
NO!
IR! THEY'RE YING TO MAKE CONTACT! SHOULD I --
NO. WAIT JUST A LITTLE LONGER.
NO! I DON'T CARE IF I HAVE TO KEEP YOU INSIDE ME FOREVER --
-- I WON'T LET YOU REUNITE WITH KASADY! I WON'T BE RESPONSIBLE FOR LOOSING CARNAGE ON THE WORLD AGAIN!
WUD
K-RAKT

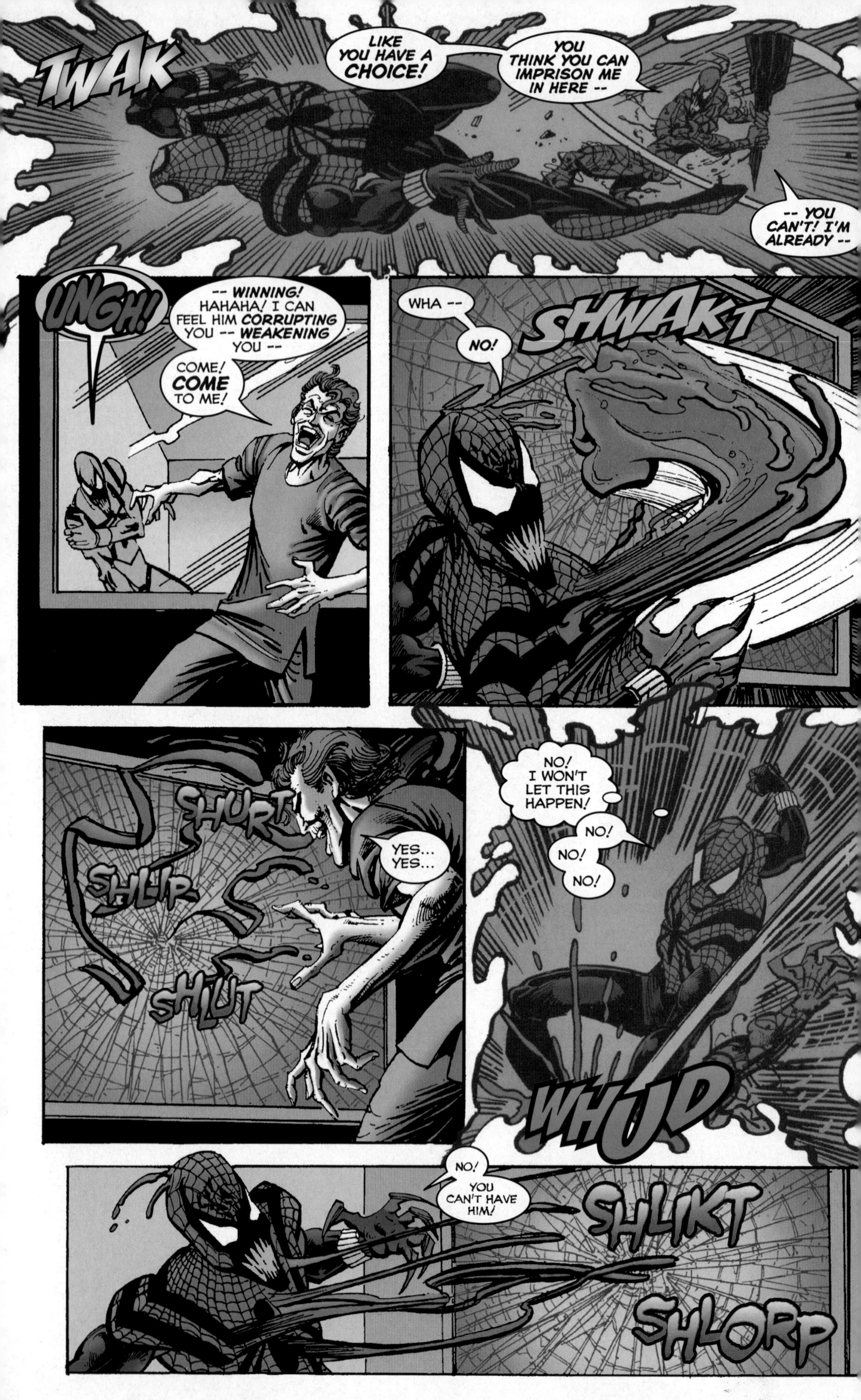
TWAK
LIKE YOU HAVE A CHOICE!
YOU THINK YOU CAN IMPRISON ME IN HERE --
-- YOU CAN'T! I'M ALREADY --
UNGH!
-- WINNING! HAHAHA! I CAN FEEL HIM CORRUPTING YOU -- WEAKENING YOU --
COME! COME TO ME!
WHA --
NO!
SHWAKT
SHURT
SHLIP
SHLUT
YES... YES...
NO! I WON'T LET THIS HAPPEN!
NO!
NO!
NO!
WHUD
NO!
YOU CAN'T HAVE HIM!
SHLIKT
SHLORP

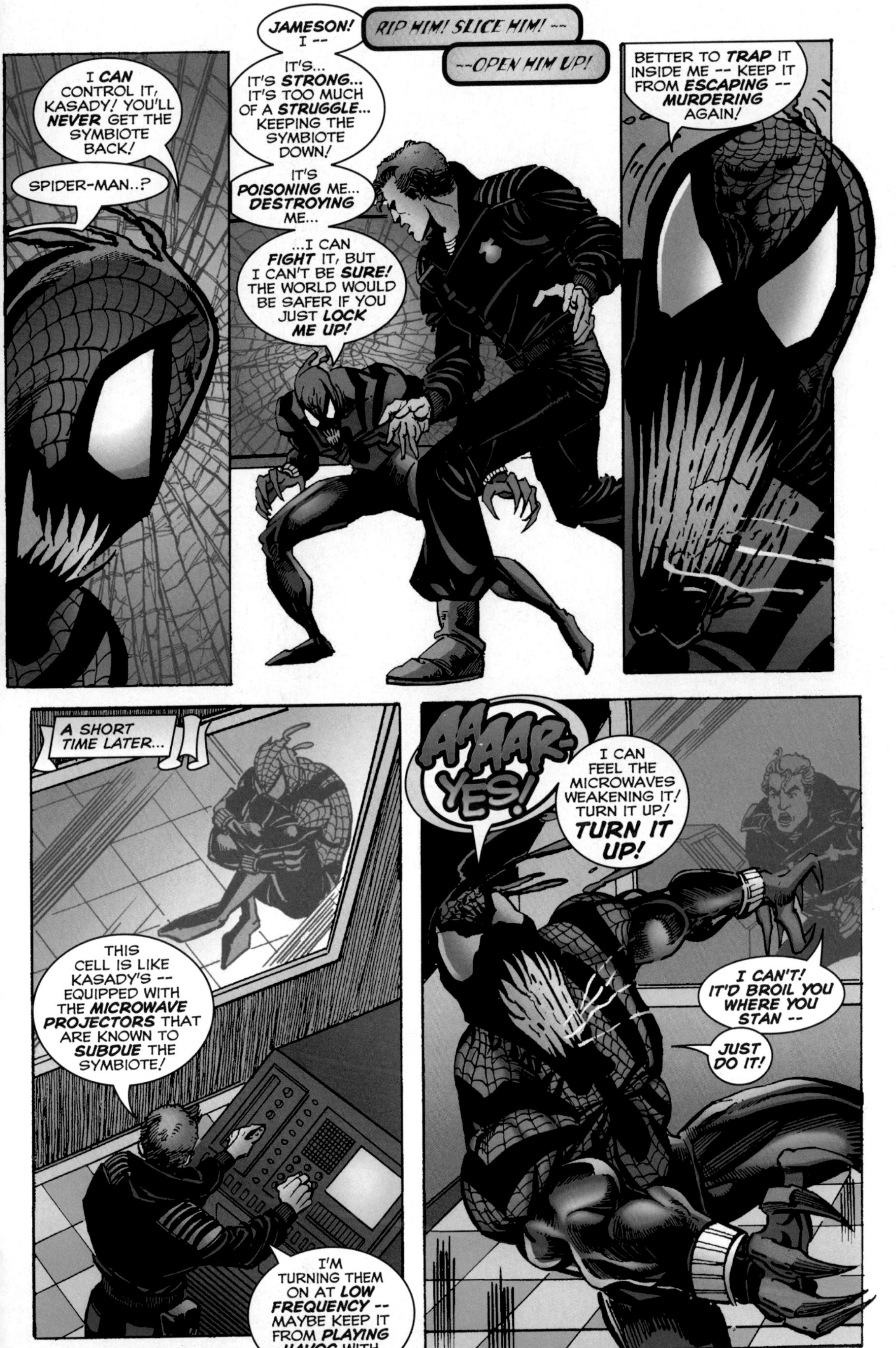
I CAN CONTROL IT, KASADY! YOU'LL NEVER GET THE SYMBIOTE BACK!
SPIDER-MAN..?
JAMESON! I --
RIP HIM! SLICE HIM! --
--OPEN HIM UP!
IT'S... IT'S STRONG... IT'S TOO MUCH OF A STRUGGLE... KEEPING THE SYMBIOTE DOWN!
IT'S POISONING ME... DESTROYING ME...
...I CAN FIGHT IT, BUT I CAN'T BE SURE! THE WORLD WOULD BE SAFER IF YOU JUST LOCK ME UP!
BETTER TO TRAP IT INSIDE ME -- KEEP IT FROM ESCAPING -- MURDERING AGAIN!
A SHORT TIME LATER...
THIS CELL IS LIKE KASADY'S -- EQUIPPED WITH THE MICROWAVE PROJECTORS THAT ARE KNOWN TO SUBDUE THE SYMBIOTE!
I'M TURNING THEM ON AT LOW FREQUENCY -- MAYBE KEEP IT FROM PLAYING HAVOC WITH YOUR --
AAAAR-YES!
I CAN FEEL THE MICROWAVES WEAKENING IT! TURN IT UP! TURN IT UP!
I CAN'T! IT'D BROIL YOU WHERE YOU STAN --
JUST DO IT!

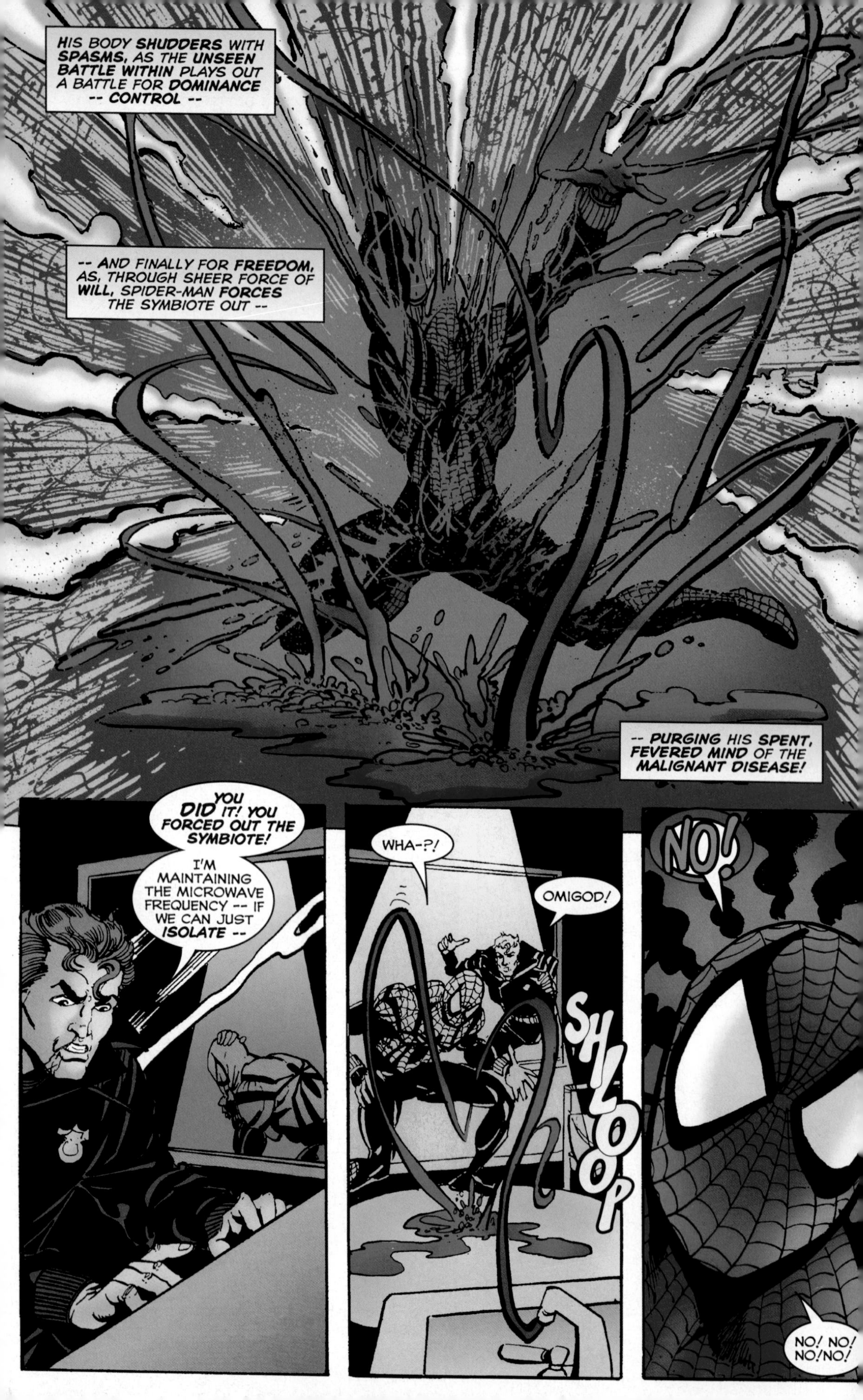
HIS BODY SHUDDERS WITH SPASMS, AS THE UNSEEN BATTLE WITHIN PLAYS OUT A BATTLE FOR DOMINANCE -- CONTROL --
-- AND FINALLY FOR FREEDOM, AS, THROUGH SHEER FORCE OF WILL, SPIDER-MAN FORCES THE SYMBIOTE OUT --
-- PURGING HIS SPENT, FEVERED MIND OF THE MALIGNANT DISEASE!
YOU DID IT! YOU FORCED OUT THE SYMBIOTE!
I'M MAINTAINING THE MICROWAVE FREQUENCY -- IF WE CAN JUST ISOLATE --
WHA-?!
OMIGOD!
SHLOOP
NO!
NO! NO! NO! NO!

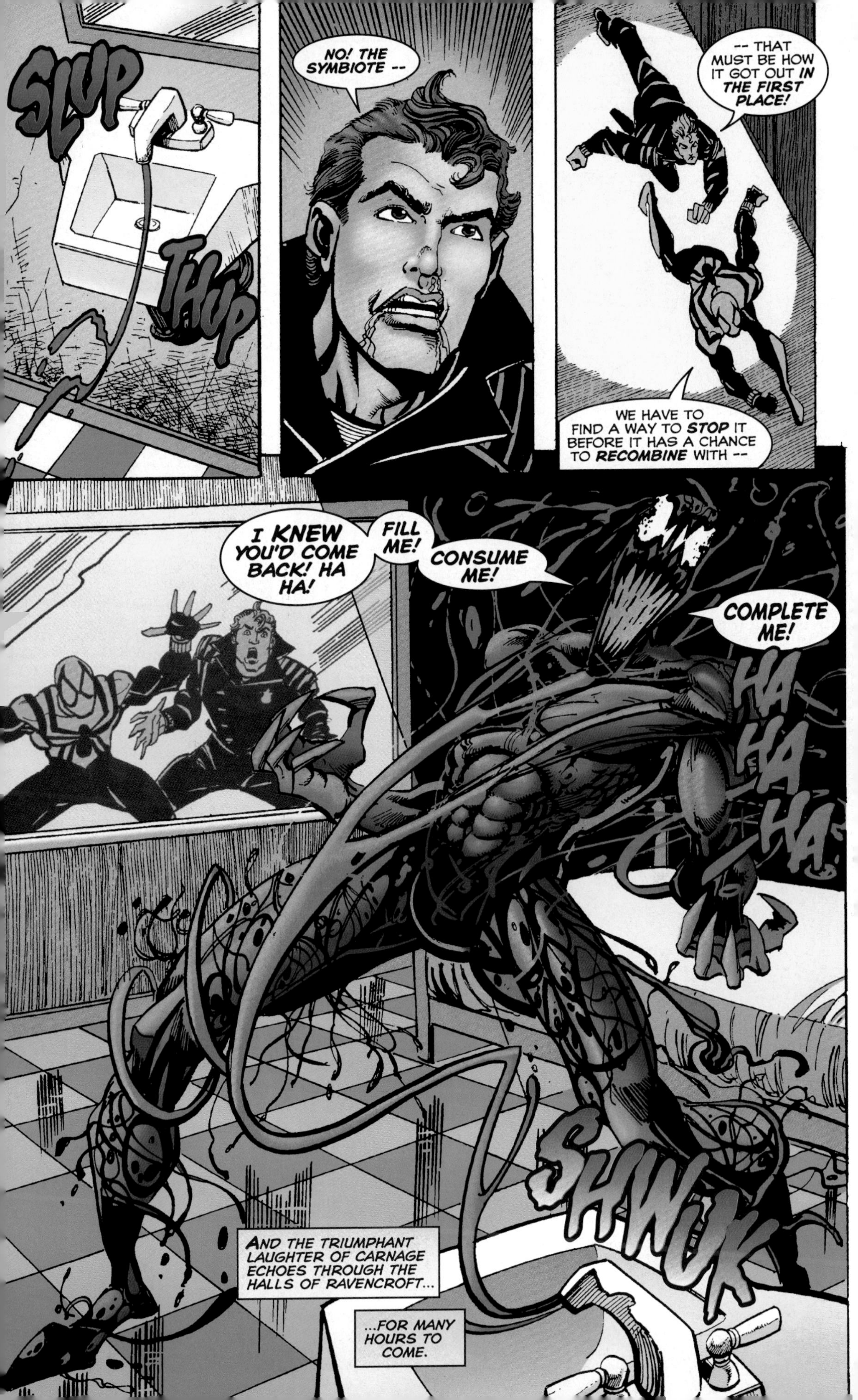
SLUP
THUP
NO! THE SYMBIOTE --
-- THAT MUST BE HOW IT GOT OUT IN THE FIRST PLACE!
WE HAVE TO FIND A WAY TO STOP IT BEFORE IT HAS A CHANCE TO RECOMBINE WITH --
I KNEW YOU'D COME BACK! HA HA!
FILL ME!
CONSUME ME!
COMPLETE ME!
HA HA HA HA
SHNIK
AND THE TRIUMPHANT LAUGHTER OF CARNAGE ECHOES THROUGH THE HALLS OF RAVENCROFT...
...FOR MANY HOURS TO COME.

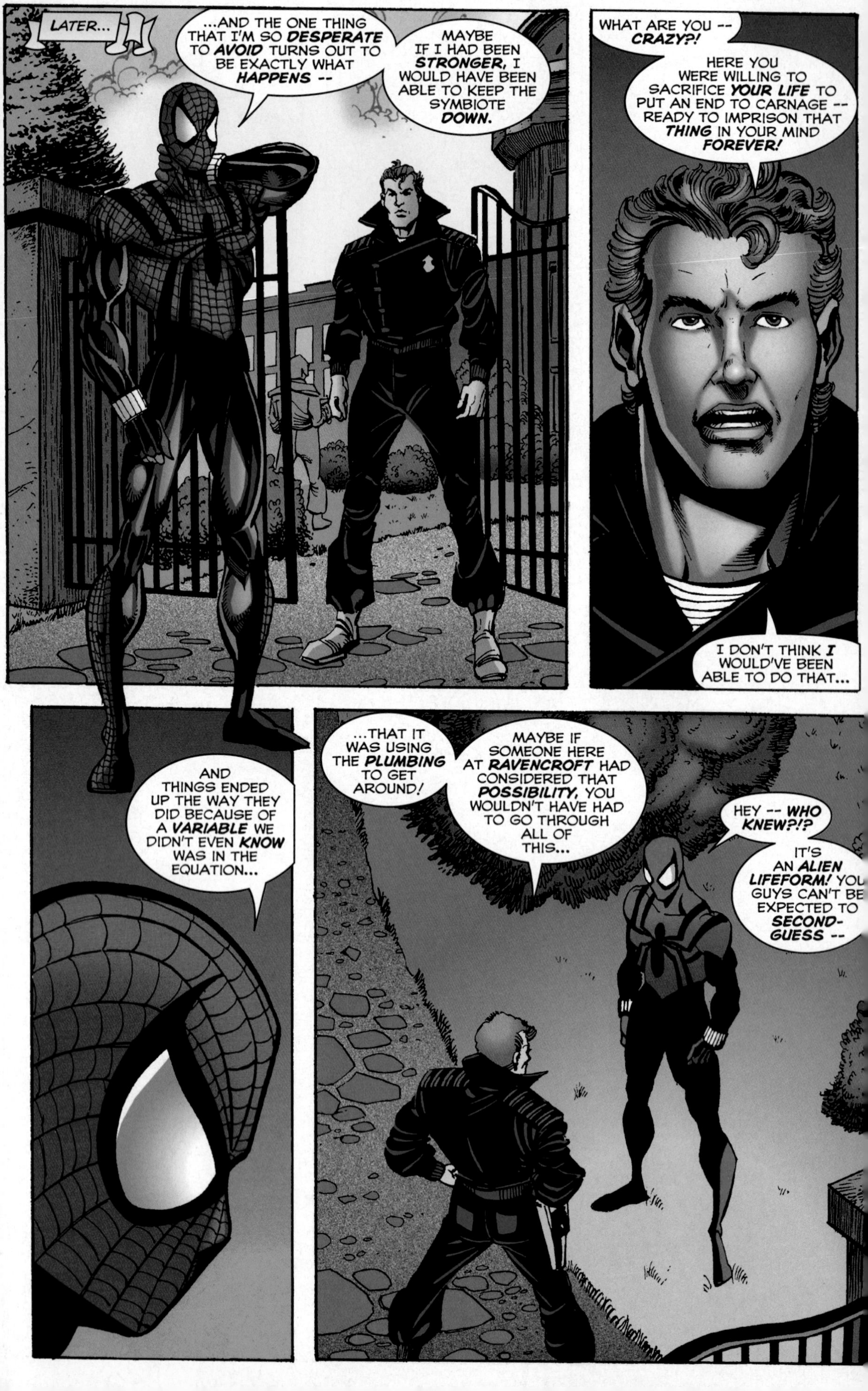
LATER...
...AND THE ONE THING THAT I'M SO DESPERATE TO AVOID TURNS OUT TO BE EXACTLY WHAT HAPPENS --
MAYBE IF I HAD BEEN STRONGER, I WOULD HAVE BEEN ABLE TO KEEP THE SYMBIOTE DOWN.
WHAT ARE YOU -- CRAZY?!
HERE YOU WERE WILLING TO SACRIFICE YOUR LIFE TO PUT AN END TO CARNAGE -- READY TO IMPRISON THAT THING IN YOUR MIND FOREVER!
I DON'T THINK I WOULD'VE BEEN ABLE TO DO THAT...
AND THINGS ENDED UP THE WAY THEY DID BECAUSE OF A VARIABLE WE DIDN'T EVEN KNOW WAS IN THE EQUATION...
...THAT IT WAS USING THE PLUMBING TO GET AROUND!
MAYBE IF SOMEONE HERE AT RAVENCROFT HAD CONSIDERED THAT POSSIBILITY, YOU WOULDN'T HAVE HAD TO GO THROUGH ALL OF THIS...
HEY -- WHO KNEW?!?
IT'S AN ALIEN LIFEFORM! YOU GUYS CAN'T BE EXPECTED TO SECOND-GUESS --

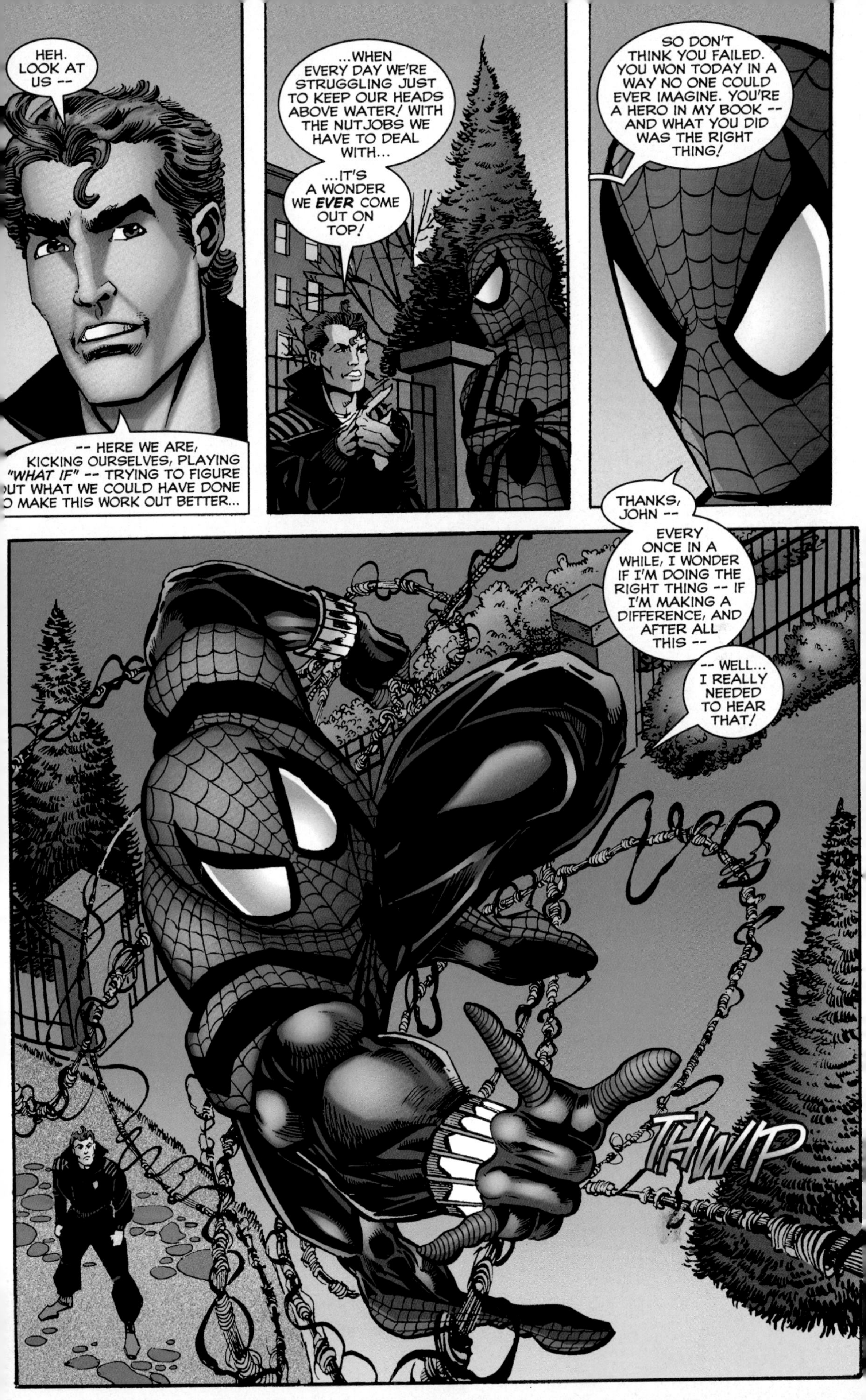
HEH. LOOK AT US --
-- HERE WE ARE, KICKING OURSELVES, PLAYING "WHAT IF" -- TRYING TO FIGURE OUT WHAT WE COULD HAVE DONE TO MAKE THIS WORK OUT BETTER...
...WHEN EVERY DAY WE'RE STRUGGLING JUST TO KEEP OUR HEADS ABOVE WATER! WITH THE NUTJOBS WE HAVE TO DEAL WITH...
...IT'S A WONDER WE EVER COME OUT ON TOP!
SO DON'T THINK YOU FAILED. YOU WON TODAY IN A WAY NO ONE COULD EVER IMAGINE. YOU'RE A HERO IN MY BOOK -- AND WHAT YOU DID WAS THE RIGHT THING!
THANKS, JOHN --
EVERY ONCE IN A WHILE, I WONDER IF I'M DOING THE RIGHT THING -- IF I'M MAKING A DIFFERENCE, AND AFTER ALL THIS --
-- WELL... I REALLY NEEDED TO HEAR THAT!
THWIP

Peter and Ben eventually discovered that Ben was the clone after all. Peter, whose powers had returned, retook the mantle of Spider-Man — though tragically Ben died in battle and Mary Jane suffered a miscarriage. Carnage soon escaped and battled Spider-Man once again. But when the cosmic Silver Surfer interrupted the battle, the symbiote suddenly left Kasady — and attached itself to the Surfer!

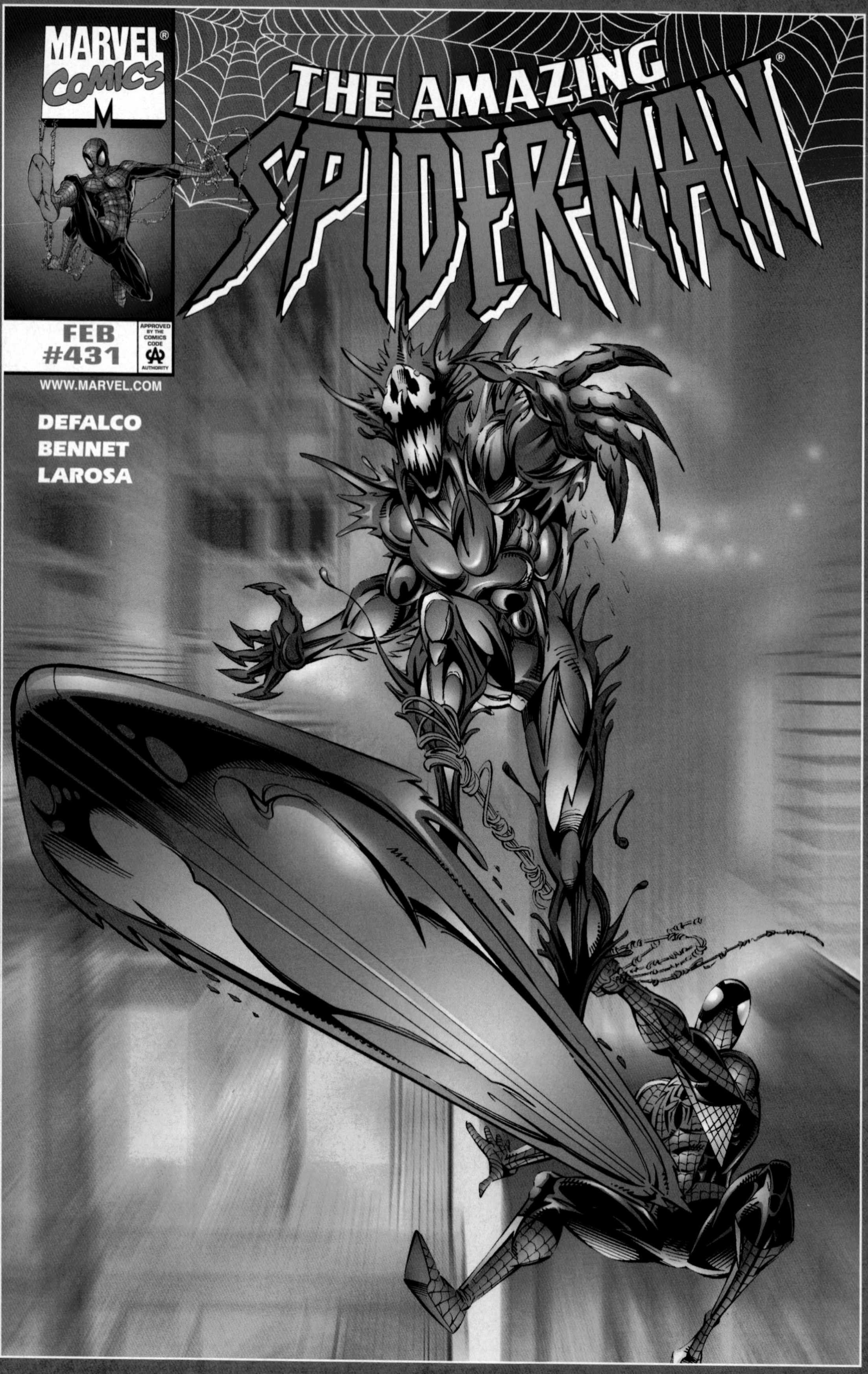
MARVEL® COMICS
THE AMAZING SPIDER-MAN®
FEB #431
APPROVED BY THE COMICS CODE AUTHORITY
WWW.MARVEL.COM
DEFALCO
BENNET
LAROSA

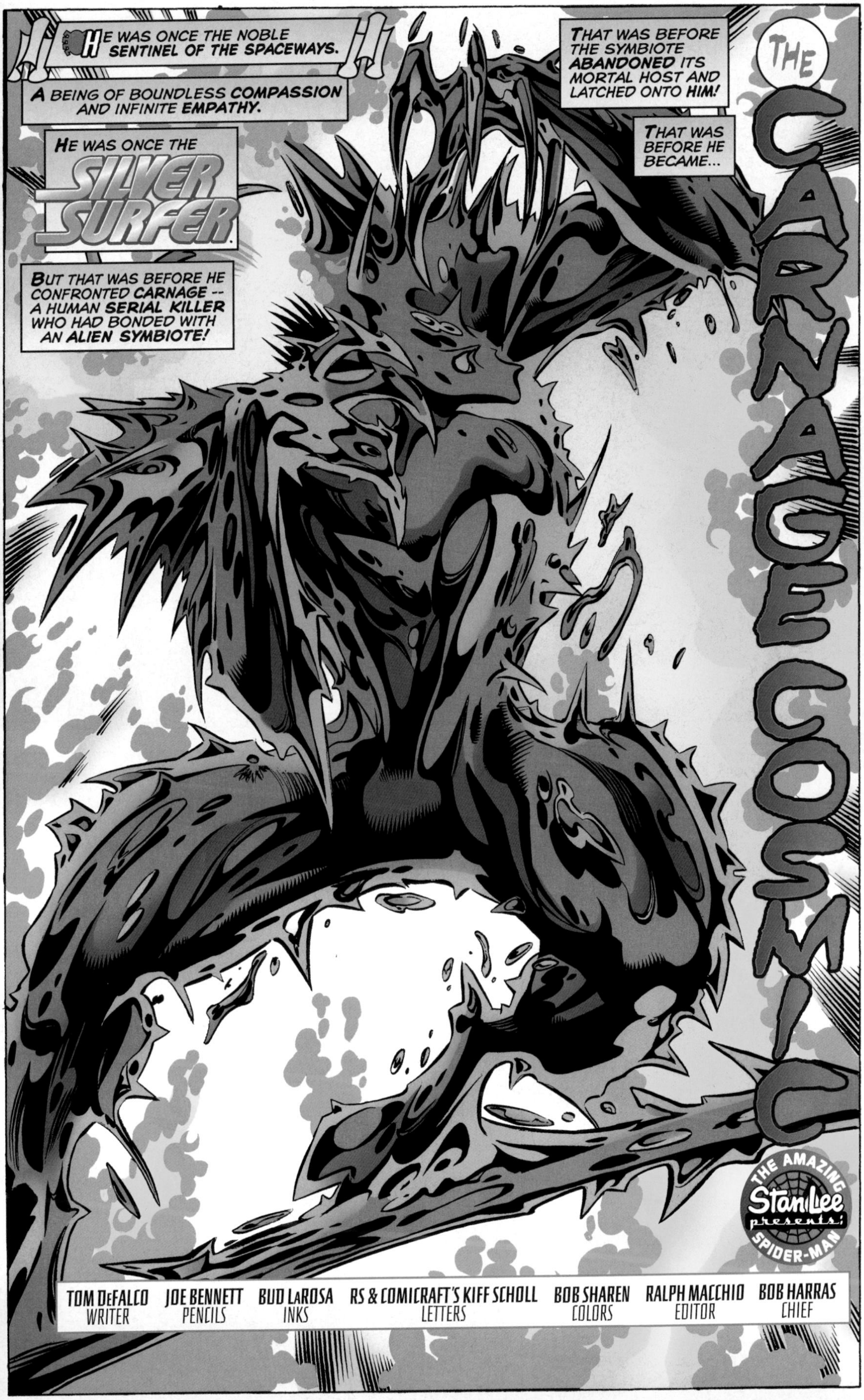
HE WAS ONCE THE NOBLE SENTINEL OF THE SPACEWAYS.
A BEING OF BOUNDLESS COMPASSION AND INFINITE EMPATHY.
HE WAS ONCE THE SILVER SURFER.
BUT THAT WAS BEFORE HE CONFRONTED CARNAGE -- A HUMAN SERIAL KILLER WHO HAD BONDED WITH AN ALIEN SYMBIOTE!
THAT WAS BEFORE THE SYMBIOTE ABANDONED ITS MORTAL HOST AND LATCHED ONTO HIM!
THAT WAS BEFORE HE BECAME...
THE CARNAGE COSMIC
THE AMAZING STAN LEE presents: SPIDER-MAN
TOM DeFALCO WRITER
JOE BENNETT PENCILS
BUD LaROSA INKS
RS & COMICRAFT'S KIFF SCHOLL LETTERS
BOB SHAREN COLORS
RALPH MACCHIO EDITOR
BOB HARRAS CHIEF

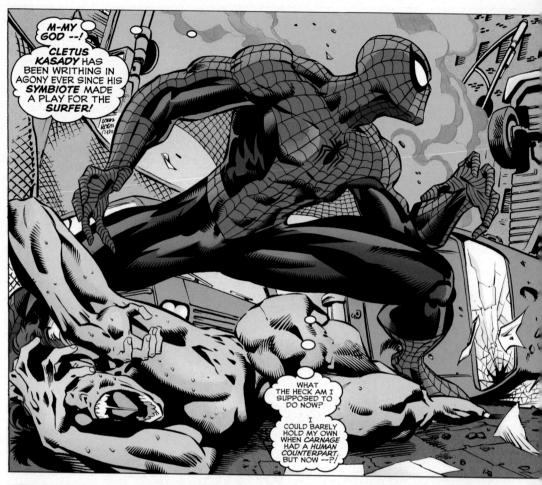

M-MY GOD --!

CLETUS KASADY HAS BEEN WRITHING IN AGONY EVER SINCE HIS SYMBIOTE MADE A PLAY FOR THE SURFER!

WHAT THE HECK AM I SUPPOSED TO DO NOW?

I COULD BARELY HOLD MY OWN WHEN CARNAGE HAD A HUMAN COUNTERPART, BUT NOW --?!

MY ONLY HOPE IS TO STRIKE FAST AND FURIOUS!

I'VE GOT TO PUT HIM DOWN BEFORE THE SYMBIOTE HAS TIME TO INTEGRATE HIS CONFLICTING PERSONALITIES!

YEAH...

...THAT'S ALL I'VE GOTTA DO!

Uh-Oh! I DON'T LIKE THE WAY HE'S SUDDENLY GLARING AT ME AND -- WHOA!

THOSE SPIKEY TENTACLES USED TO BE LETHAL ENOUGH!

ADDING A COSMIC ZAP BLAST IS PURE OVERKILL AS FAR AS I'M CONCERNED.

S-STAY *BACK*, SPIDER-MAN!

T-THE SYMBIOTE SEEKS TO INFLAME MY MIND... WITH OBSCENE LUSTS... AND BASE EMOTIONS!

I-IS THAT REALLY *YOU*, SURFER? *FIGHT 'IM!* DON'T GIVE IN!

WE CAN *BEAT* THIS THING, *I KNOW WE CAN!* THE TWO OF US WILL FIND A WAY!

WE'LL FIND A WAY!

N-NO! I...I FEAR... THIS IS A BATTLE... I MUST FACE...

ALONE!

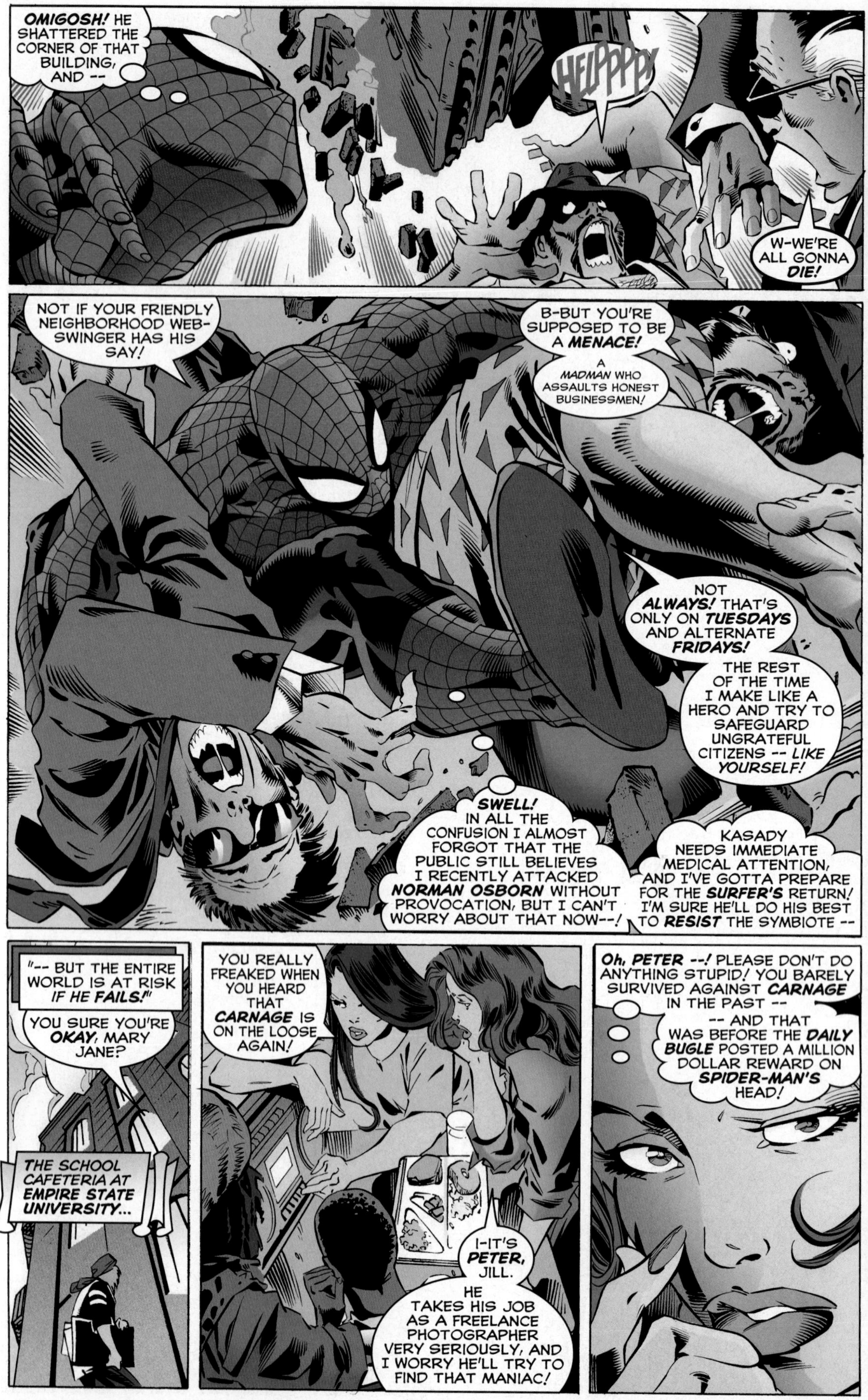
OMIGOSH! HE SHATTERED THE CORNER OF THAT BUILDING, AND --
HELPPPP!
W-WE'RE ALL GONNA DIE!
NOT IF YOUR FRIENDLY NEIGHBORHOOD WEB-SWINGER HAS HIS SAY!
B-BUT YOU'RE SUPPOSED TO BE A MENACE!
A MADMAN WHO ASSAULTS HONEST BUSINESSMEN!
NOT ALWAYS! THAT'S ONLY ON TUESDAYS AND ALTERNATE FRIDAYS!
THE REST OF THE TIME I MAKE LIKE A HERO AND TRY TO SAFEGUARD UNGRATEFUL CITIZENS -- LIKE YOURSELF!
SWELL! IN ALL THE CONFUSION I ALMOST FORGOT THAT THE PUBLIC STILL BELIEVES I RECENTLY ATTACKED NORMAN OSBORN WITHOUT PROVOCATION, BUT I CAN'T WORRY ABOUT THAT NOW--!
KASADY NEEDS IMMEDIATE MEDICAL ATTENTION, AND I'VE GOTTA PREPARE FOR THE SURFER'S RETURN! I'M SURE HE'LL DO HIS BEST TO RESIST THE SYMBIOTE --
"-- BUT THE ENTIRE WORLD IS AT RISK IF HE FAILS!"
YOU SURE YOU'RE OKAY, MARY JANE?
THE SCHOOL CAFETERIA AT EMPIRE STATE UNIVERSITY...
YOU REALLY FREAKED WHEN YOU HEARD THAT CARNAGE IS ON THE LOOSE AGAIN!
I-IT'S PETER, JILL.
HE TAKES HIS JOB AS A FREELANCE PHOTOGRAPHER VERY SERIOUSLY, AND I WORRY HE'LL TRY TO FIND THAT MANIAC!
Oh, PETER --! PLEASE DON'T DO ANYTHING STUPID! YOU BARELY SURVIVED AGAINST CARNAGE IN THE PAST --
-- AND THAT WAS BEFORE THE DAILY BUGLE POSTED A MILLION DOLLAR REWARD ON SPIDER-MAN'S HEAD!

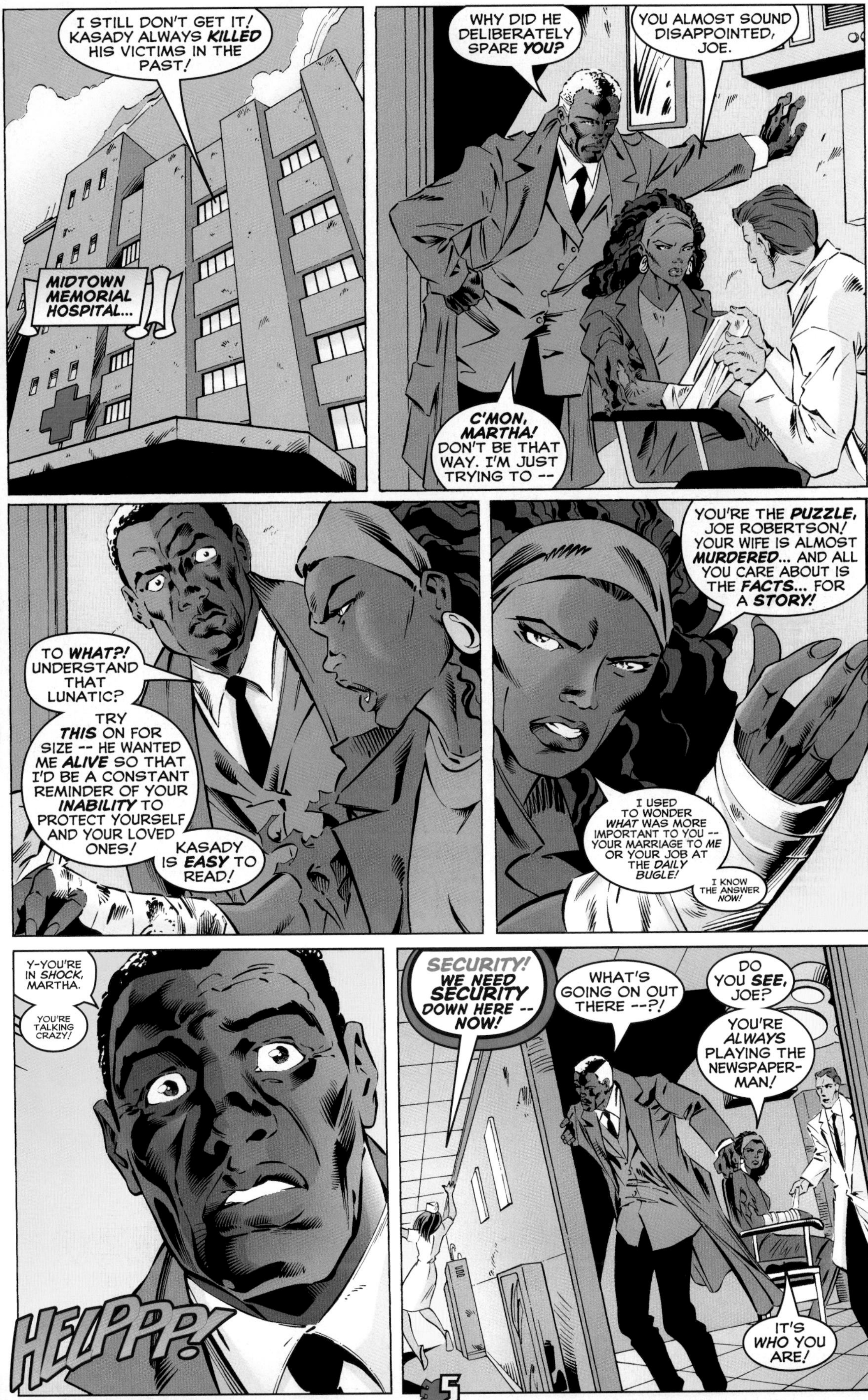

I STILL DON'T GET IT! KASADY ALWAYS KILLED HIS VICTIMS IN THE PAST!
MIDTOWN MEMORIAL HOSPITAL...
WHY DID HE DELIBERATELY SPARE YOU?
YOU ALMOST SOUND DISAPPOINTED, JOE.
C'MON, MARTHA! DON'T BE THAT WAY. I'M JUST TRYING TO --
TO WHAT?! UNDERSTAND THAT LUNATIC?
TRY THIS ON FOR SIZE -- HE WANTED ME ALIVE SO THAT I'D BE A CONSTANT REMINDER OF YOUR INABILITY TO PROTECT YOURSELF AND YOUR LOVED ONES!
KASADY IS EASY TO READ!
YOU'RE THE PUZZLE, JOE ROBERTSON! YOUR WIFE IS ALMOST MURDERED... AND ALL YOU CARE ABOUT IS THE FACTS... FOR A STORY!
I USED TO WONDER WHAT WAS MORE IMPORTANT TO YOU -- YOUR MARRIAGE TO ME OR YOUR JOB AT THE DAILY BUGLE!
I KNOW THE ANSWER NOW!
Y-YOU'RE IN SHOCK, MARTHA.
YOU'RE TALKING CRAZY!
HELPPP!
SECURITY! WE NEED SECURITY DOWN HERE -- NOW!
WHAT'S GOING ON OUT THERE --?!
DO YOU SEE, JOE?
YOU'RE ALWAYS PLAYING THE NEWSPAPER-MAN!
IT'S WHO YOU ARE!

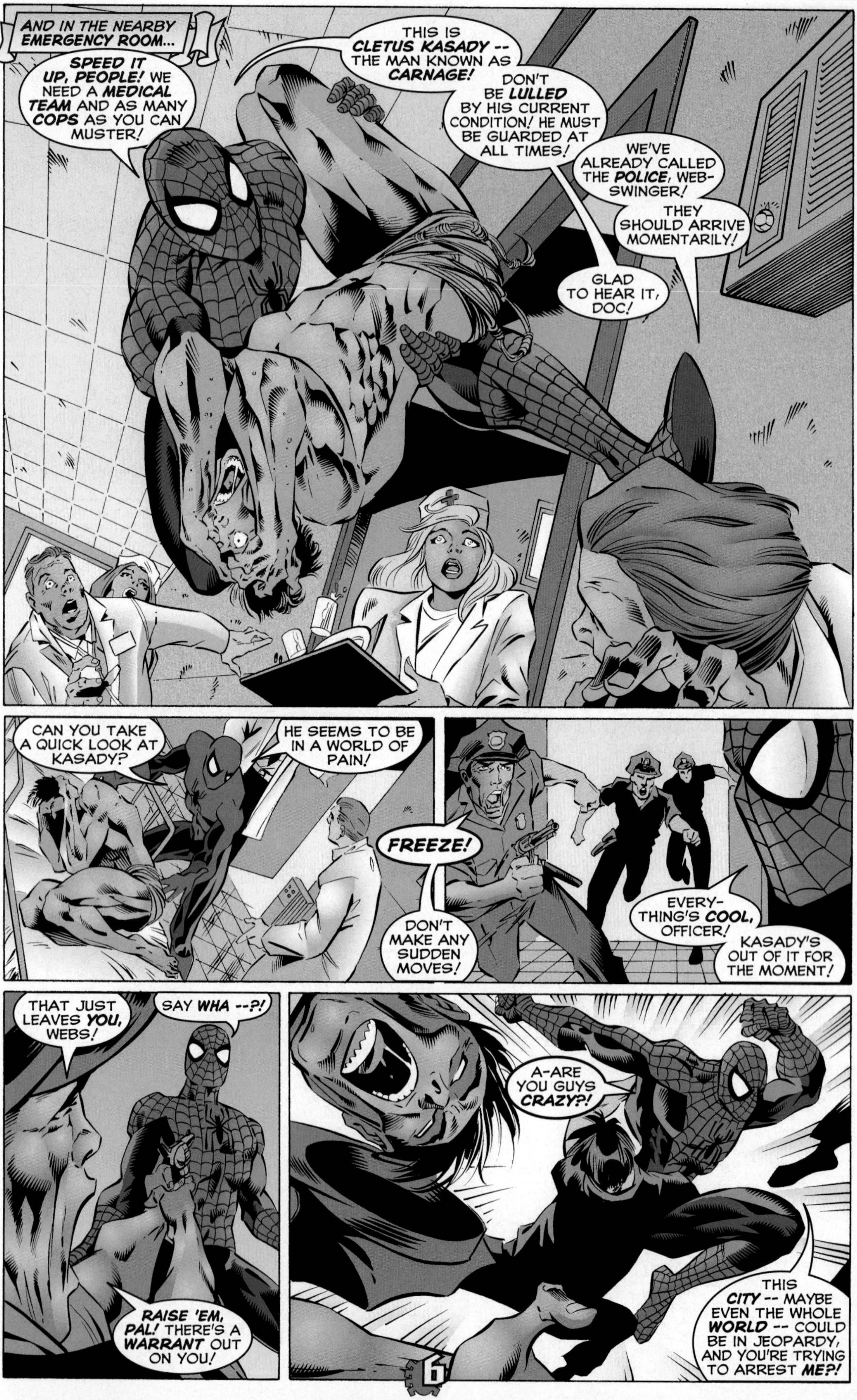
AND IN THE NEARBY EMERGENCY ROOM...
SPEED IT UP, PEOPLE! WE NEED A MEDICAL TEAM AND AS MANY COPS AS YOU CAN MUSTER!
THIS IS CLETUS KASADY -- THE MAN KNOWN AS CARNAGE!
DON'T BE LULLED BY HIS CURRENT CONDITION! HE MUST BE GUARDED AT ALL TIMES!
WE'VE ALREADY CALLED THE POLICE, WEB-SWINGER!
THEY SHOULD ARRIVE MOMENTARILY!
GLAD TO HEAR IT, DOC!
CAN YOU TAKE A QUICK LOOK AT KASADY?
HE SEEMS TO BE IN A WORLD OF PAIN!
FREEZE!
DON'T MAKE ANY SUDDEN MOVES!
EVERY-THING'S COOL, OFFICER!
KASADY'S OUT OF IT FOR THE MOMENT!
THAT JUST LEAVES YOU, WEBS!
SAY WHA --?!
RAISE 'EM, PAL! THERE'S A WARRANT OUT ON YOU!
A-ARE YOU GUYS CRAZY?!
THIS CITY -- MAYBE EVEN THE WHOLE WORLD -- COULD BE IN JEOPARDY, AND YOU'RE TRYING TO ARREST ME?!

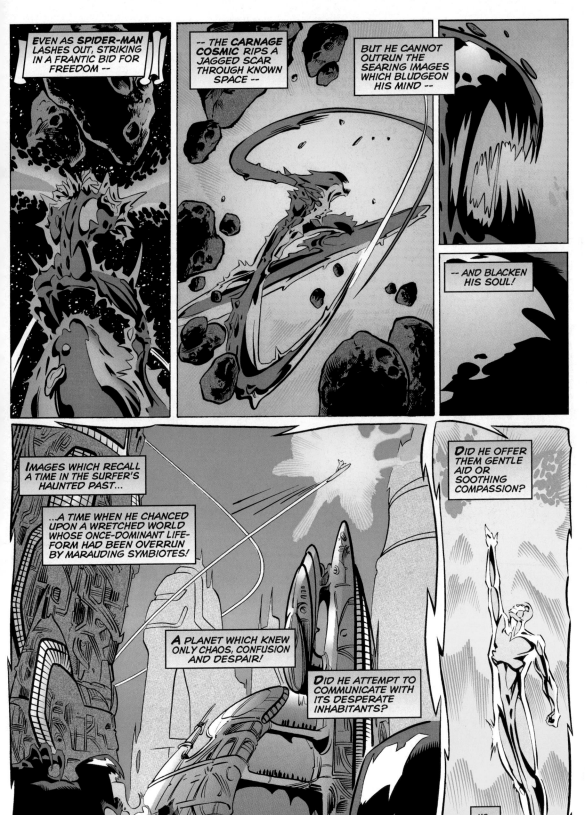

EVEN AS SPIDER-MAN LASHES OUT, STRIKING IN A FRANTIC BID FOR FREEDOM --

-- THE CARNAGE COSMIC RIPS A JAGGED SCAR THROUGH KNOWN SPACE --

BUT HE CANNOT OUTRUN THE SEARING IMAGES WHICH BLUDGEON HIS MIND --

-- AND BLACKEN HIS SOUL!

IMAGES WHICH RECALL A TIME IN THE SURFER'S HAUNTED PAST...

...A TIME WHEN HE CHANCED UPON A WRETCHED WORLD WHOSE ONCE-DOMINANT LIFE-FORM HAD BEEN OVERRUN BY MARAUDING SYMBIOTES!

A PLANET WHICH KNEW ONLY CHAOS, CONFUSION AND DESPAIR!

DID HE ATTEMPT TO COMMUNICATE WITH ITS DESPERATE INHABITANTS?

DID HE OFFER THEM GENTLE AID OR SOOTHING COMPASSION?

NO...

7

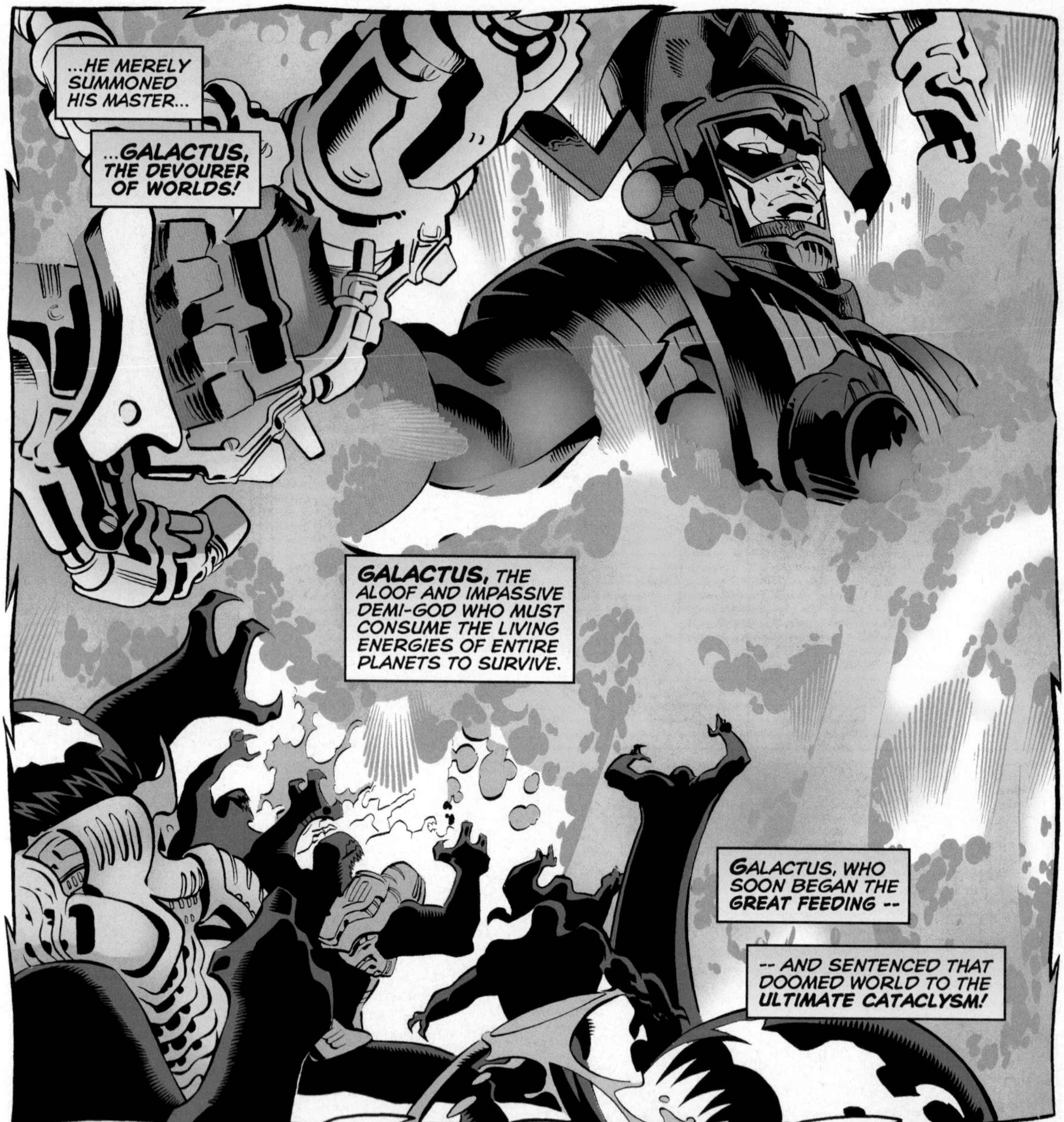
...HE MERELY SUMMONED HIS MASTER...
...GALACTUS, THE DEVOURER OF WORLDS!
GALACTUS, THE ALOOF AND IMPASSIVE DEMI-GOD WHO MUST CONSUME THE LIVING ENERGIES OF ENTIRE PLANETS TO SURVIVE.
GALACTUS, WHO SOON BEGAN THE GREAT FEEDING --
-- AND SENTENCED THAT DOOMED WORLD TO THE ULTIMATE CATACLYSM!

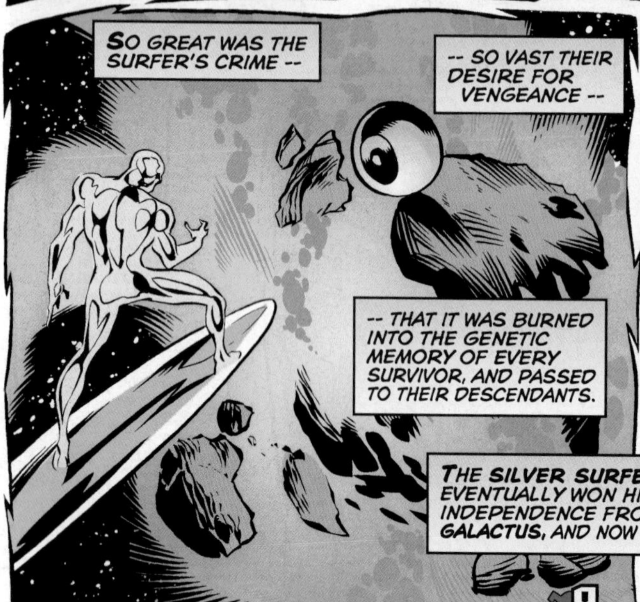
SO GREAT WAS THE SURFER'S CRIME --
-- SO VAST THEIR DESIRE FOR VENGEANCE --
-- THAT IT WAS BURNED INTO THE GENETIC MEMORY OF EVERY SURVIVOR, AND PASSED TO THEIR DESCENDANTS.
THE SILVER SURFER EVENTUALLY WON HIS INDEPENDENCE FROM GALACTUS, AND NOW --

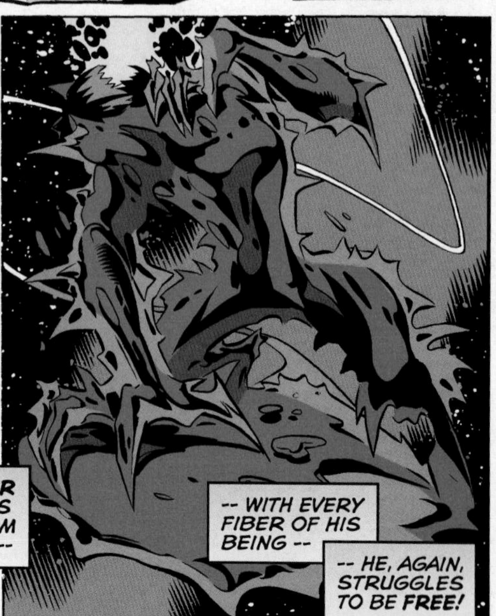
-- WITH EVERY FIBER OF HIS BEING --
-- HE, AGAIN, STRUGGLES TO BE FREE!

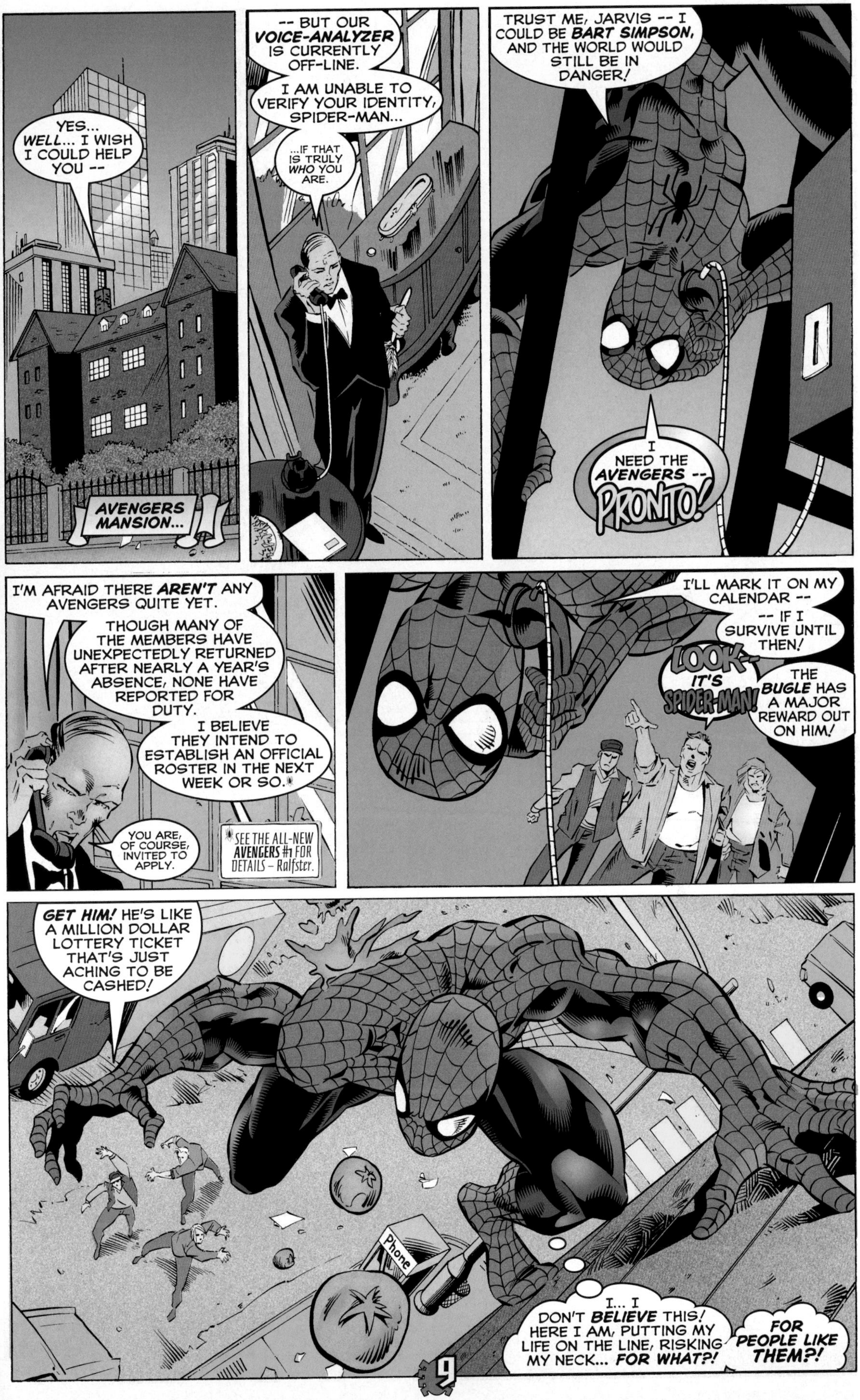
YES... WELL... I WISH I COULD HELP YOU --
AVENGERS MANSION...
-- BUT OUR VOICE-ANALYZER IS CURRENTLY OFF-LINE.
I AM UNABLE TO VERIFY YOUR IDENTITY, SPIDER-MAN...
...IF THAT IS TRULY WHO YOU ARE.
TRUST ME, JARVIS -- I COULD BE BART SIMPSON, AND THE WORLD WOULD STILL BE IN DANGER!
I NEED THE AVENGERS -- PRONTO!
I'M AFRAID THERE AREN'T ANY AVENGERS QUITE YET.
THOUGH MANY OF THE MEMBERS HAVE UNEXPECTEDLY RETURNED AFTER NEARLY A YEAR'S ABSENCE, NONE HAVE REPORTED FOR DUTY.
I BELIEVE THEY INTEND TO ESTABLISH AN OFFICIAL ROSTER IN THE NEXT WEEK OR SO.
YOU ARE, OF COURSE, INVITED TO APPLY.
SEE THE ALL-NEW AVENGERS #1 FOR DETAILS – Ralfster.
I'LL MARK IT ON MY CALENDAR --
-- IF I SURVIVE UNTIL THEN!
LOOK-- IT'S SPIDER-MAN!
THE BUGLE HAS A MAJOR REWARD OUT ON HIM!
GET HIM! HE'S LIKE A MILLION DOLLAR LOTTERY TICKET THAT'S JUST ACHING TO BE CASHED!
Phone
I... I DON'T BELIEVE THIS! HERE I AM, PUTTING MY LIFE ON THE LINE, RISKING MY NECK... FOR WHAT?!
FOR PEOPLE LIKE THEM?!

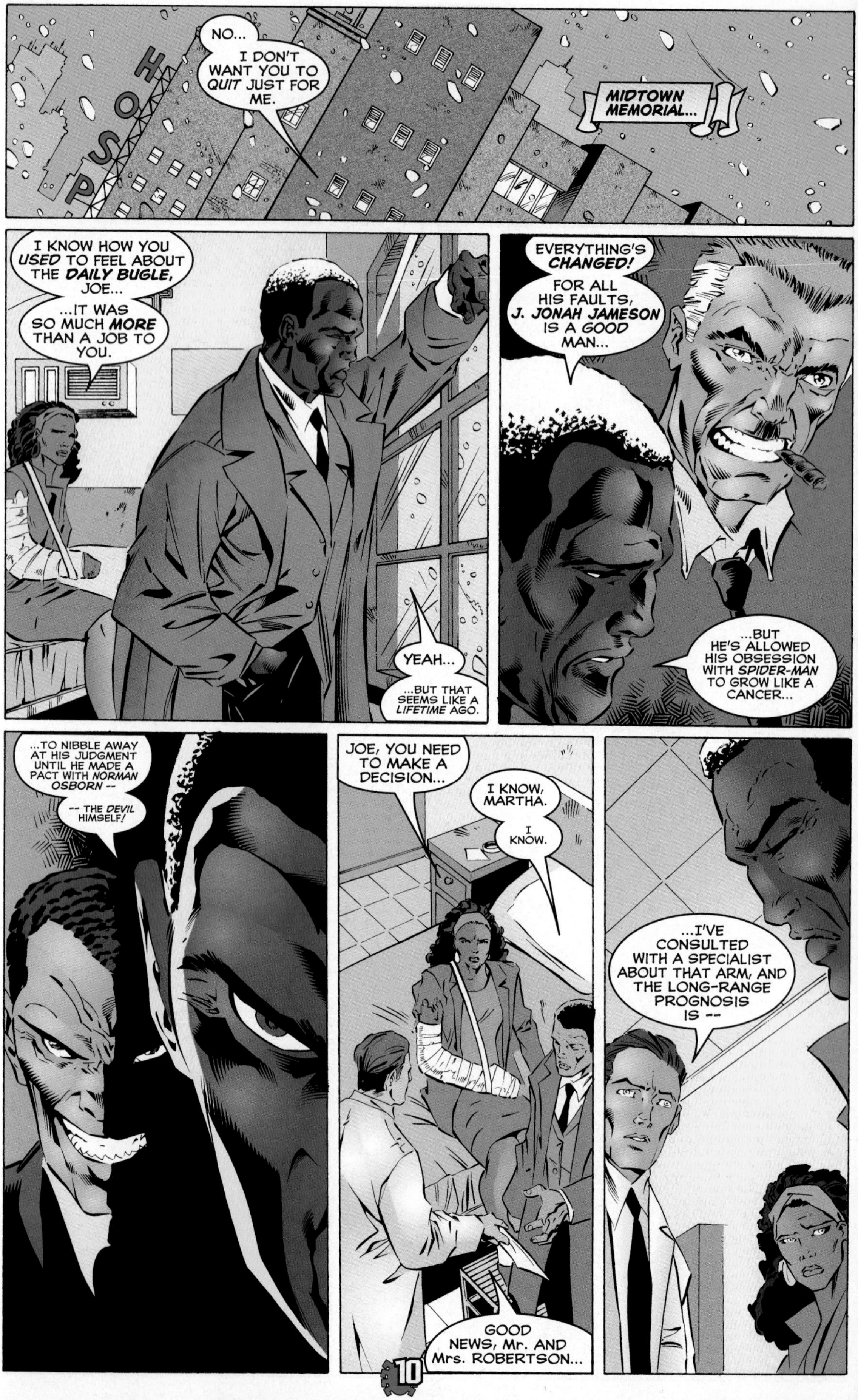
NO...
I DON'T WANT YOU TO QUIT JUST FOR ME.
MIDTOWN MEMORIAL...
I KNOW HOW YOU USED TO FEEL ABOUT THE DAILY BUGLE, JOE...
...IT WAS SO MUCH MORE THAN A JOB TO YOU.
YEAH...
...BUT THAT SEEMS LIKE A LIFETIME AGO.
EVERYTHING'S CHANGED!
FOR ALL HIS FAULTS, J. JONAH JAMESON IS A GOOD MAN...
...BUT HE'S ALLOWED HIS OBSESSION WITH SPIDER-MAN TO GROW LIKE A CANCER...
...TO NIBBLE AWAY AT HIS JUDGMENT UNTIL HE MADE A PACT WITH NORMAN OSBORN --
-- THE DEVIL HIMSELF!
JOE, YOU NEED TO MAKE A DECISION...
I KNOW, MARTHA.
I KNOW.
GOOD NEWS, Mr. AND Mrs. ROBERTSON...
...I'VE CONSULTED WITH A SPECIALIST ABOUT THAT ARM, AND THE LONG-RANGE PROGNOSIS IS --

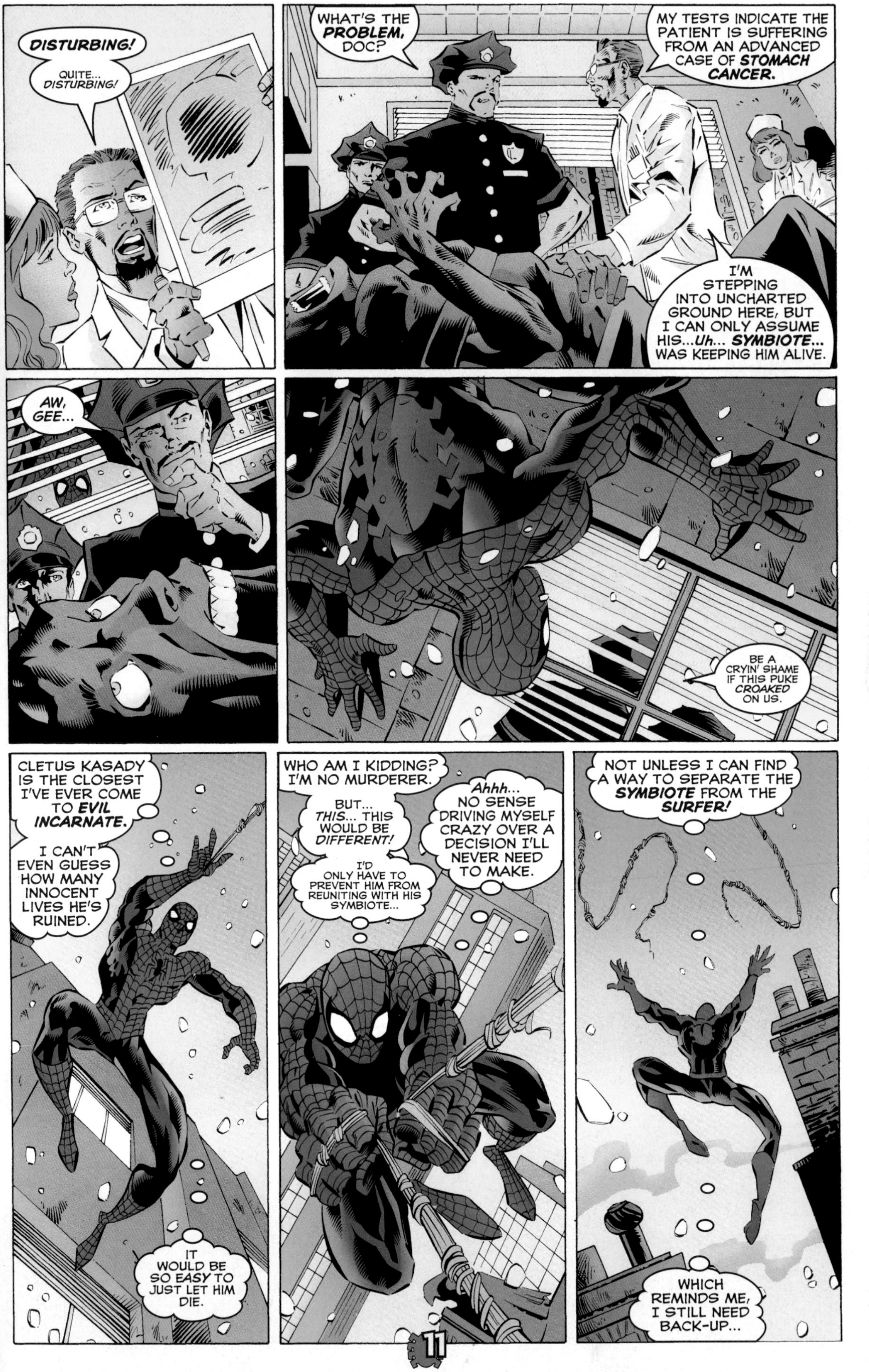

DISTURBING!
QUITE... DISTURBING!
WHAT'S THE PROBLEM, DOC?
MY TESTS INDICATE THE PATIENT IS SUFFERING FROM AN ADVANCED CASE OF STOMACH CANCER.
I'M STEPPING INTO UNCHARTED GROUND HERE, BUT I CAN ONLY ASSUME HIS...Uh... SYMBIOTE... WAS KEEPING HIM ALIVE.
AW, GEE...
BE A CRYIN' SHAME IF THIS PUKE CROAKED ON US.
CLETUS KASADY IS THE CLOSEST I'VE EVER COME TO EVIL INCARNATE.
I CAN'T EVEN GUESS HOW MANY INNOCENT LIVES HE'S RUINED.
IT WOULD BE SO EASY TO JUST LET HIM DIE.
WHO AM I KIDDING? I'M NO MURDERER.
BUT... THIS... THIS WOULD BE DIFFERENT!
I'D ONLY HAVE TO PREVENT HIM FROM REUNITING WITH HIS SYMBIOTE...
Ahhh... NO SENSE DRIVING MYSELF CRAZY OVER A DECISION I'LL NEVER NEED TO MAKE.
NOT UNLESS I CAN FIND A WAY TO SEPARATE THE SYMBIOTE FROM THE SURFER!
WHICH REMINDS ME, I STILL NEED BACK-UP...

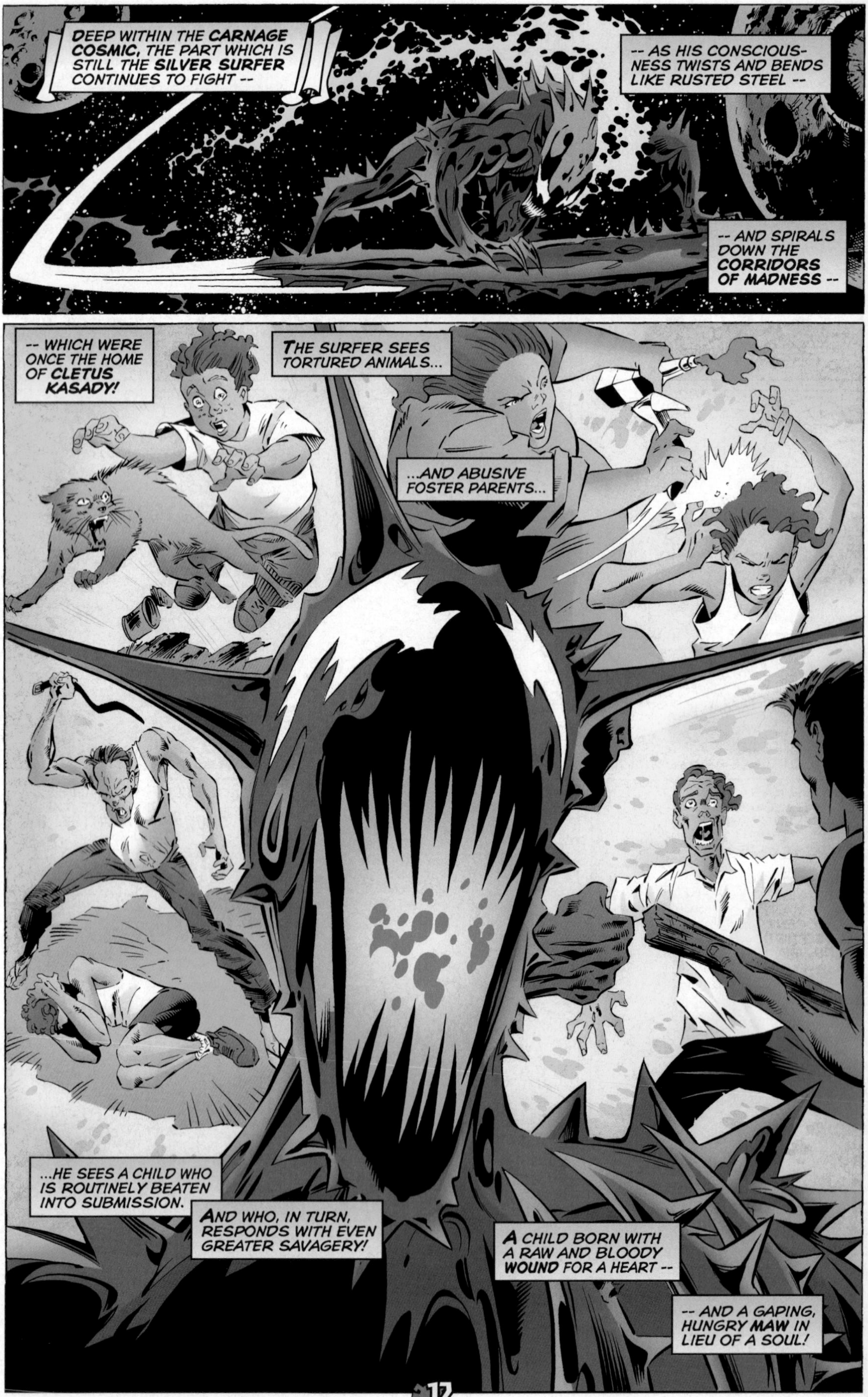
DEEP WITHIN THE CARNAGE COSMIC, THE PART WHICH IS STILL THE SILVER SURFER CONTINUES TO FIGHT --
-- AS HIS CONSCIOUSNESS TWISTS AND BENDS LIKE RUSTED STEEL --
-- AND SPIRALS DOWN THE CORRIDORS OF MADNESS --
-- WHICH WERE ONCE THE HOME OF CLETUS KASADY!
THE SURFER SEES TORTURED ANIMALS...
...AND ABUSIVE FOSTER PARENTS...
...HE SEES A CHILD WHO IS ROUTINELY BEATEN INTO SUBMISSION.
AND WHO, IN TURN, RESPONDS WITH EVEN GREATER SAVAGERY!
A CHILD BORN WITH A RAW AND BLOODY WOUND FOR A HEART --
-- AND A GAPING, HUNGRY MAW IN LIEU OF A SOUL!

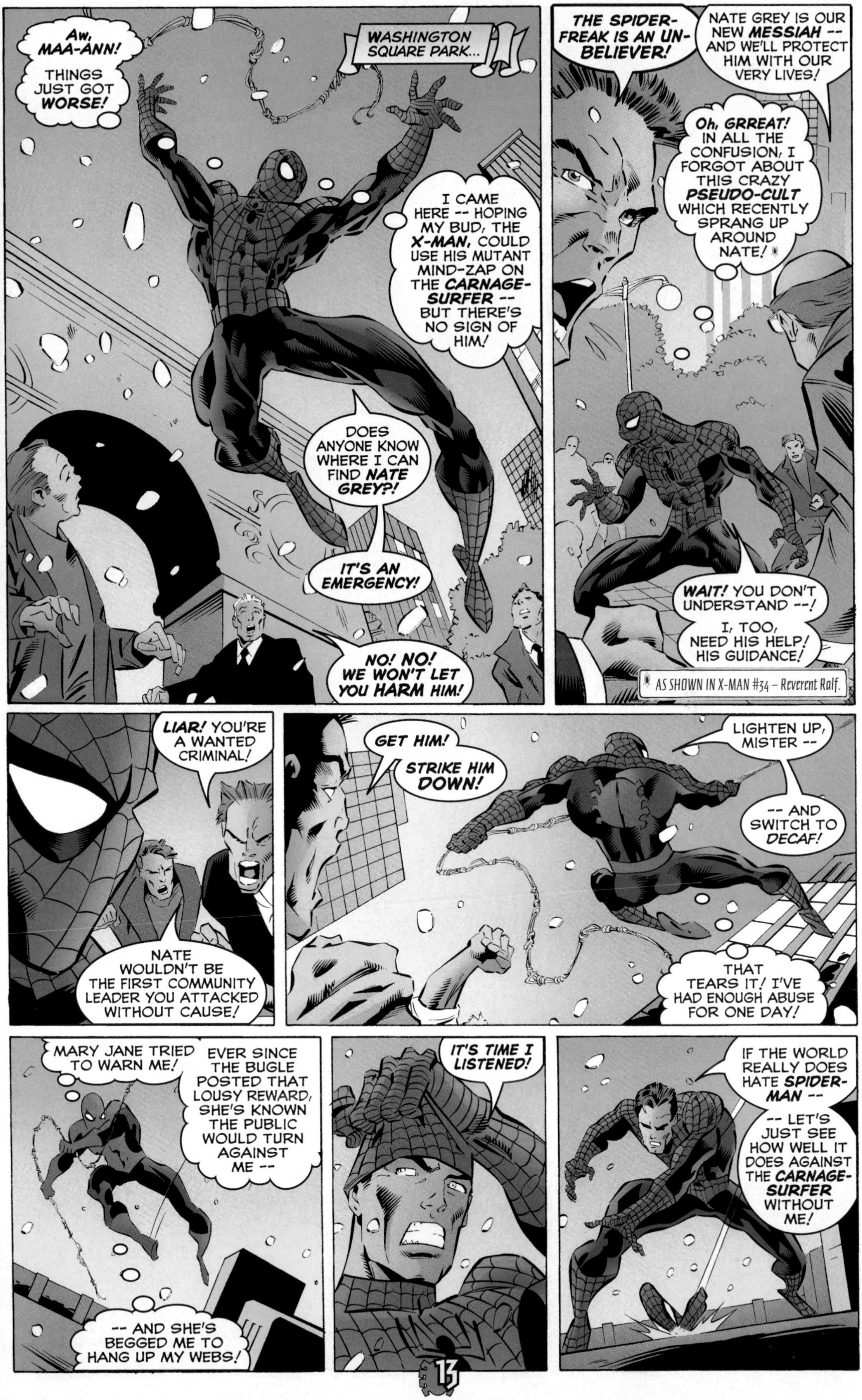
WASHINGTON SQUARE PARK...
Aw, MAA-ANN!
THINGS JUST GOT WORSE!
I CAME HERE -- HOPING MY BUD, THE X-MAN, COULD USE HIS MUTANT MIND-ZAP ON THE CARNAGE-SURFER -- BUT THERE'S NO SIGN OF HIM!
DOES ANYONE KNOW WHERE I CAN FIND NATE GREY?!
IT'S AN EMERGENCY!
NO! NO! WE WON'T LET YOU HARM HIM!
THE SPIDER-FREAK IS AN UN-BELIEVER!
NATE GREY IS OUR NEW MESSIAH -- AND WE'LL PROTECT HIM WITH OUR VERY LIVES!
Oh, GRREAT! IN ALL THE CONFUSION, I FORGOT ABOUT THIS CRAZY PSEUDO-CULT WHICH RECENTLY SPRANG UP AROUND NATE!
WAIT! YOU DON'T UNDERSTAND --!
I, TOO, NEED HIS HELP! HIS GUIDANCE!
AS SHOWN IN X-MAN #34 – Reverent Ralf.
LIAR! YOU'RE A WANTED CRIMINAL!
NATE WOULDN'T BE THE FIRST COMMUNITY LEADER YOU ATTACKED WITHOUT CAUSE!
GET HIM!
STRIKE HIM DOWN!
LIGHTEN UP, MISTER --
-- AND SWITCH TO DECAF!
THAT TEARS IT! I'VE HAD ENOUGH ABUSE FOR ONE DAY!
MARY JANE TRIED TO WARN ME!
EVER SINCE THE BUGLE POSTED THAT LOUSY REWARD, SHE'S KNOWN THE PUBLIC WOULD TURN AGAINST ME --
-- AND SHE'S BEGGED ME TO HANG UP MY WEBS!
IT'S TIME I LISTENED!
IF THE WORLD REALLY DOES HATE SPIDER-MAN --
-- LET'S JUST SEE HOW WELL IT DOES AGAINST THE CARNAGE-SURFER WITHOUT ME!

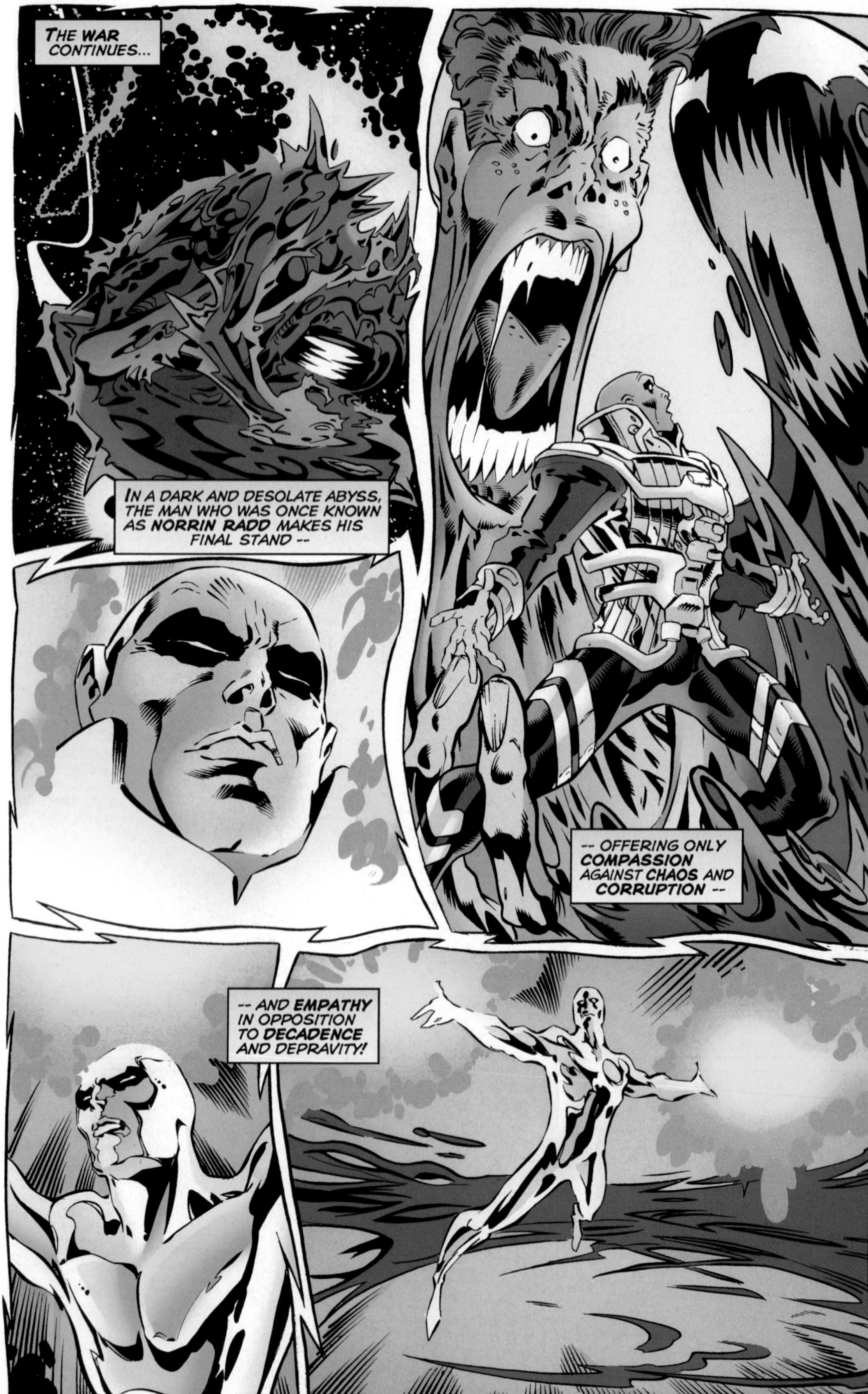
THE WAR CONTINUES...
IN A DARK AND DESOLATE ABYSS, THE MAN WHO WAS ONCE KNOWN AS NORRIN RADD MAKES HIS FINAL STAND --
-- OFFERING ONLY COMPASSION AGAINST CHAOS AND CORRUPTION --
-- AND EMPATHY IN OPPOSITION TO DECADENCE AND DEPRAVITY!

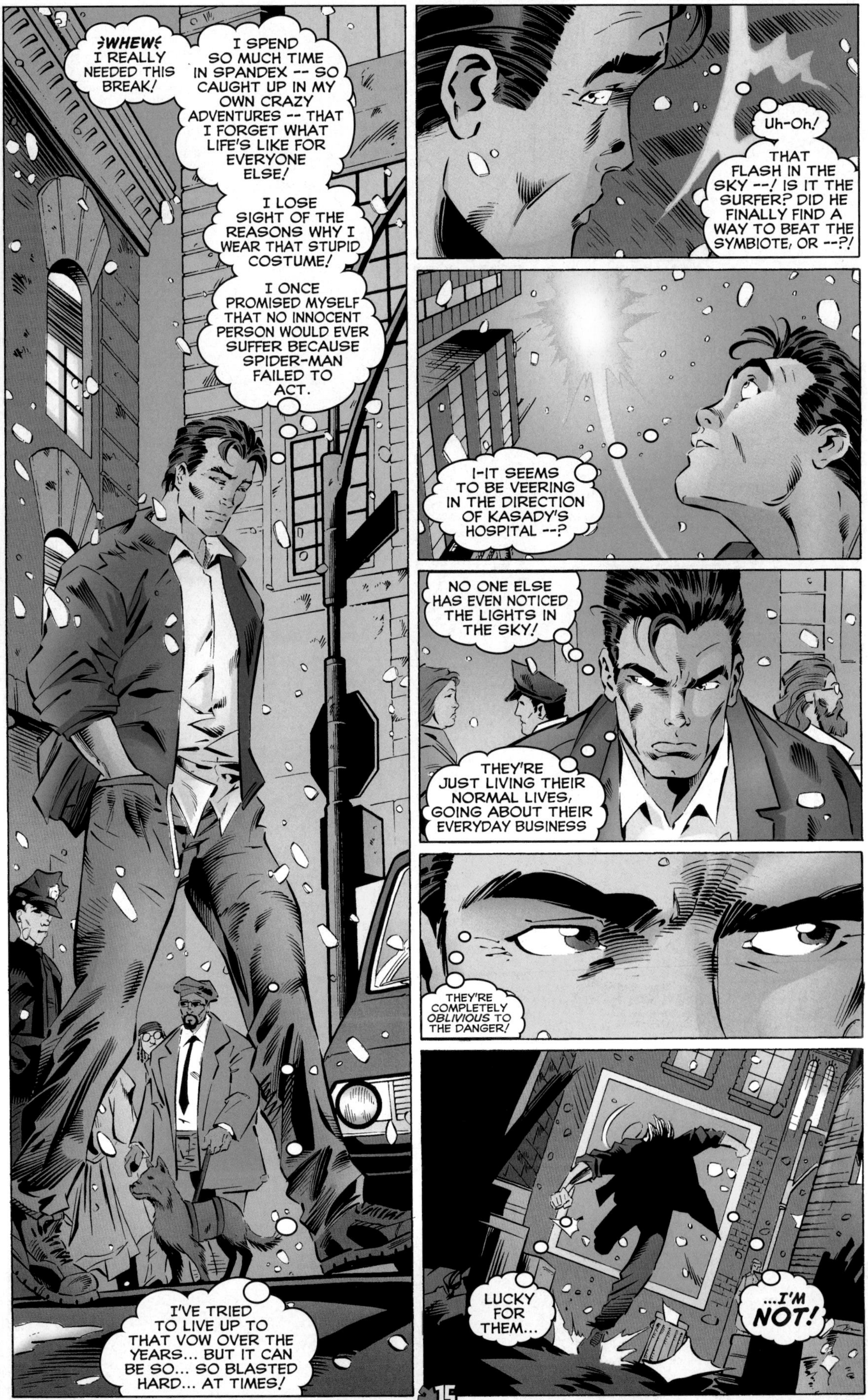

¡WHEW! I REALLY NEEDED THIS BREAK!
I SPEND SO MUCH TIME IN SPANDEX -- SO CAUGHT UP IN MY OWN CRAZY ADVENTURES -- THAT I FORGET WHAT LIFE'S LIKE FOR EVERYONE ELSE!
I LOSE SIGHT OF THE REASONS WHY I WEAR THAT STUPID COSTUME!
I ONCE PROMISED MYSELF THAT NO INNOCENT PERSON WOULD EVER SUFFER BECAUSE SPIDER-MAN FAILED TO ACT.
I'VE TRIED TO LIVE UP TO THAT VOW OVER THE YEARS... BUT IT CAN BE SO... SO BLASTED HARD... AT TIMES!
Uh-Oh!
THAT FLASH IN THE SKY --! IS IT THE SURFER? DID HE FINALLY FIND A WAY TO BEAT THE SYMBIOTE, OR --?!
I-IT SEEMS TO BE VEERING IN THE DIRECTION OF KASADY'S HOSPITAL --?
NO ONE ELSE HAS EVEN NOTICED THE LIGHTS IN THE SKY!
THEY'RE JUST LIVING THEIR NORMAL LIVES, GOING ABOUT THEIR EVERYDAY BUSINESS
THEY'RE COMPLETELY OBLIVIOUS TO THE DANGER!
LUCKY FOR THEM...
...I'M NOT!

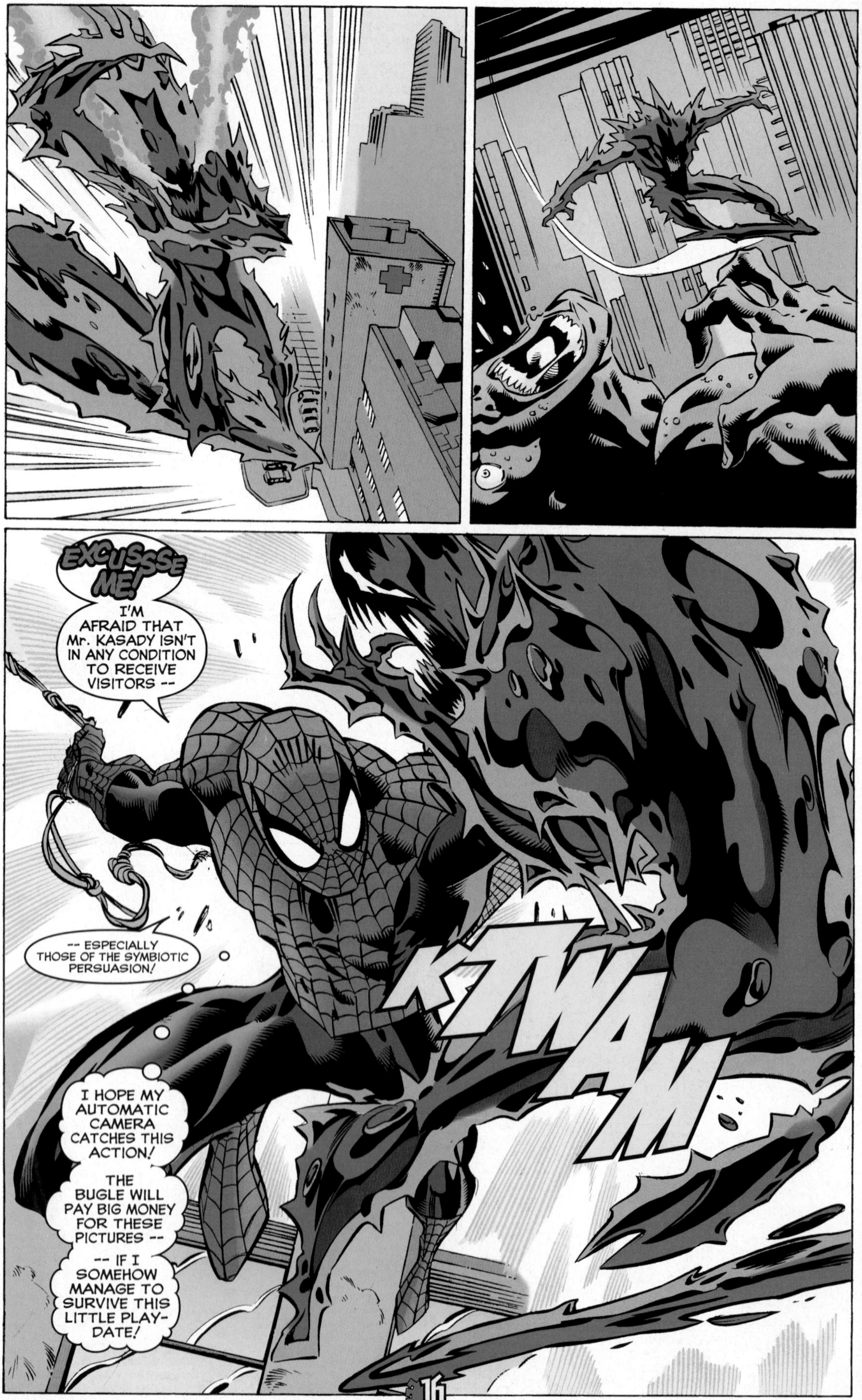
EXCUSSSSE ME!
I'M AFRAID THAT Mr. KASADY ISN'T IN ANY CONDITION TO RECEIVE VISITORS --
-- ESPECIALLY THOSE OF THE SYMBIOTIC PERSUASION!
KTWAM
I HOPE MY AUTOMATIC CAMERA CATCHES THIS ACTION!
THE BUGLE WILL PAY BIG MONEY FOR THESE PICTURES --
-- IF I SOMEHOW MANAGE TO SURVIVE THIS LITTLE PLAY-DATE!

OOPS! DID I MAKE YOU SLAM INTO THAT ROOF?

CLUMSY ME!

I WAS ACTUALLY AIMING FOR THE PARKING LOT!

Y-YOU **MUSTN'T** INTERFERE, SPIDER-MAN...

...I HAVE COME TO REUNITE THIS SYMBIOTE WITH ITS HUMAN HOST!

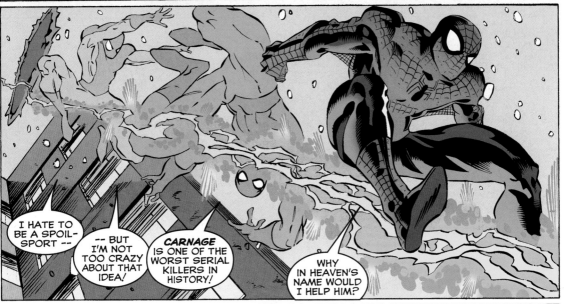

I HATE TO BE A SPOIL-SPORT --

-- BUT I'M NOT TOO CRAZY ABOUT THAT IDEA!

CARNAGE IS ONE OF THE WORST SERIAL KILLERS IN HISTORY!

WHY IN HEAVEN'S NAME WOULD I HELP HIM?

IF YOU CAN REALLY HEAR ME, SURFER... I SAY WE WORK TOGETHER TO DESTROY THE SYMBIOTE AS WELL!

B-BUT KASADY WILL **DIE** WITHOUT IT!

TOUGH! HE SHOULD HAVE THOUGHT ABOUT THAT BEFORE HE BEGAN SLAUGHTERING HELPLESS --

UGNN

K-KASADY IS HELPLESS NOW --

-- AND ONLY WE CAN SAVE HIM!

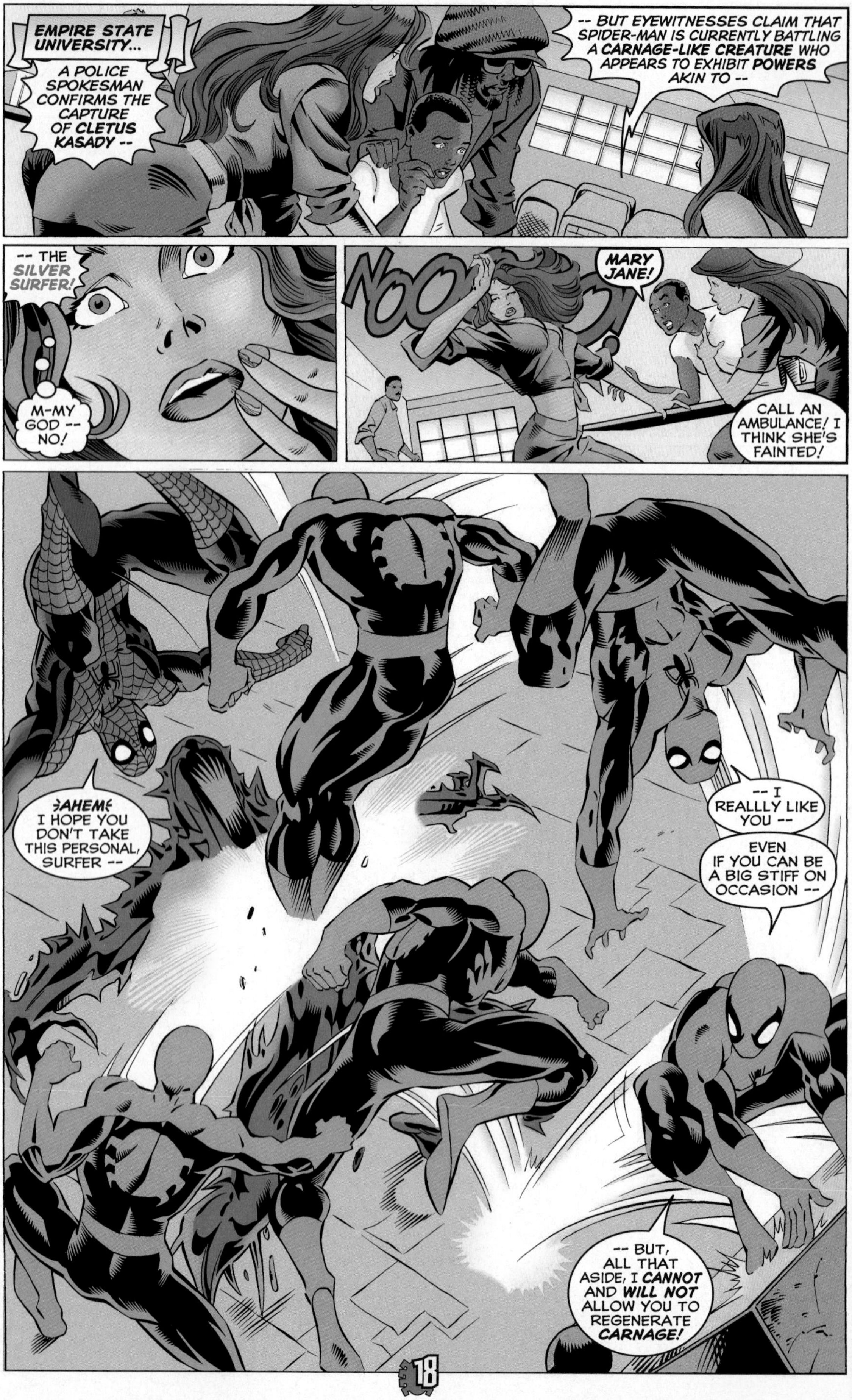

EMPIRE STATE UNIVERSITY...
A POLICE SPOKESMAN CONFIRMS THE CAPTURE OF CLETUS KASADY --
-- BUT EYEWITNESSES CLAIM THAT SPIDER-MAN IS CURRENTLY BATTLING A CARNAGE-LIKE CREATURE WHO APPEARS TO EXHIBIT POWERS AKIN TO --
-- THE SILVER SURFER!
M-MY GOD -- NO!
NOOO
MARY JANE!
CALL AN AMBULANCE! I THINK SHE'S FAINTED!
AHEM
I HOPE YOU DON'T TAKE THIS PERSONAL, SURFER --
-- I REALLLY LIKE YOU --
EVEN IF YOU CAN BE A BIG STIFF ON OCCASION --
-- BUT, ALL THAT ASIDE, I CANNOT AND WILL NOT ALLOW YOU TO REGENERATE CARNAGE!

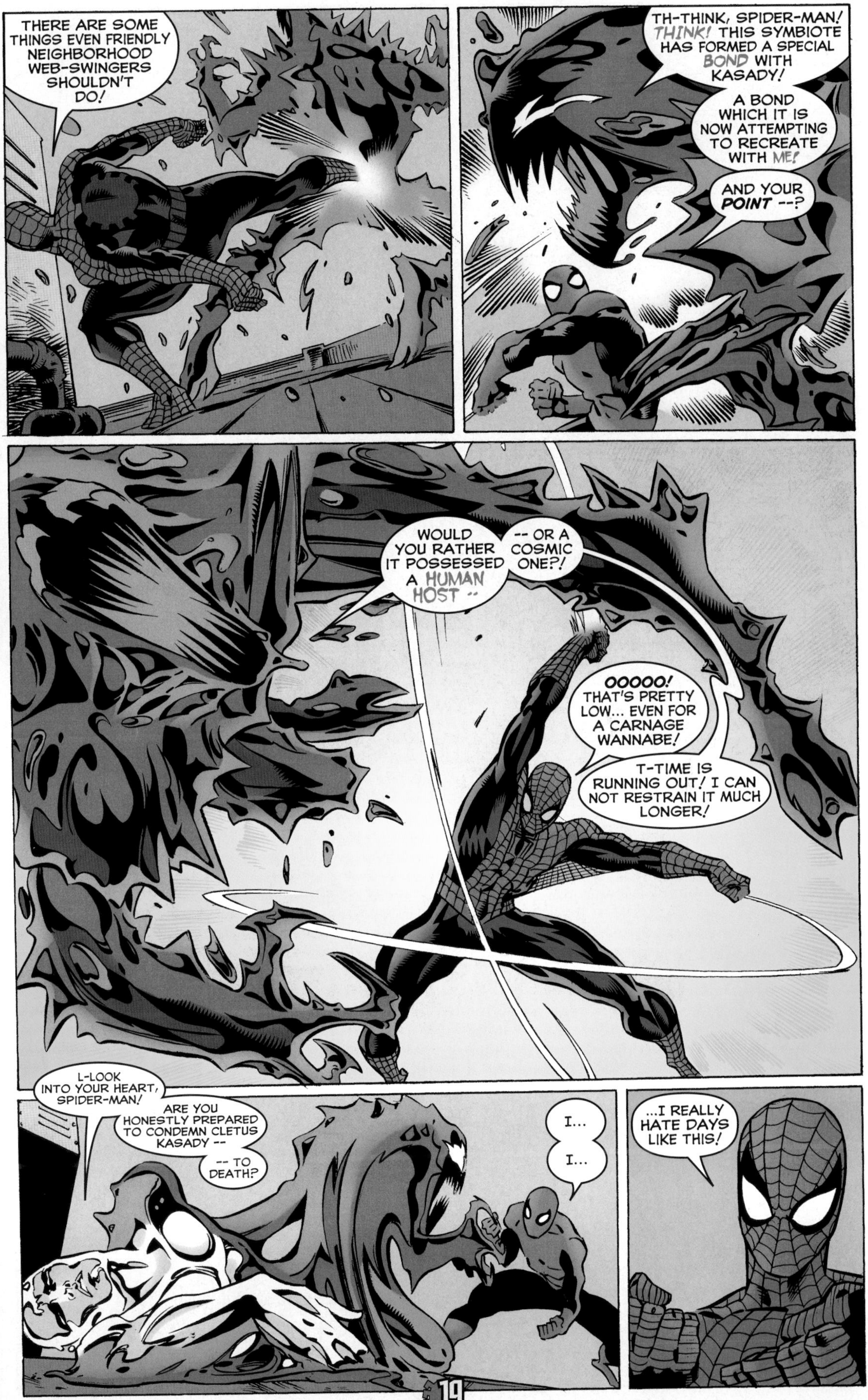
THERE ARE SOME THINGS EVEN FRIENDLY NEIGHBORHOOD WEB-SWINGERS SHOULDN'T DO!
TH-THINK, SPIDER-MAN! THINK! THIS SYMBIOTE HAS FORMED A SPECIAL BOND WITH KASADY!
A BOND WHICH IT IS NOW ATTEMPTING TO RECREATE WITH ME!
AND YOUR POINT --?
WOULD YOU RATHER IT POSSESSED A HUMAN HOST --
-- OR A COSMIC ONE?!
OOOOO! THAT'S PRETTY LOW... EVEN FOR A CARNAGE WANNABE!
T-TIME IS RUNNING OUT! I CAN NOT RESTRAIN IT MUCH LONGER!
L-LOOK INTO YOUR HEART, SPIDER-MAN!
ARE YOU HONESTLY PREPARED TO CONDEMN CLETUS KASADY --
-- TO DEATH?
I...
I...
...I REALLY HATE DAYS LIKE THIS!

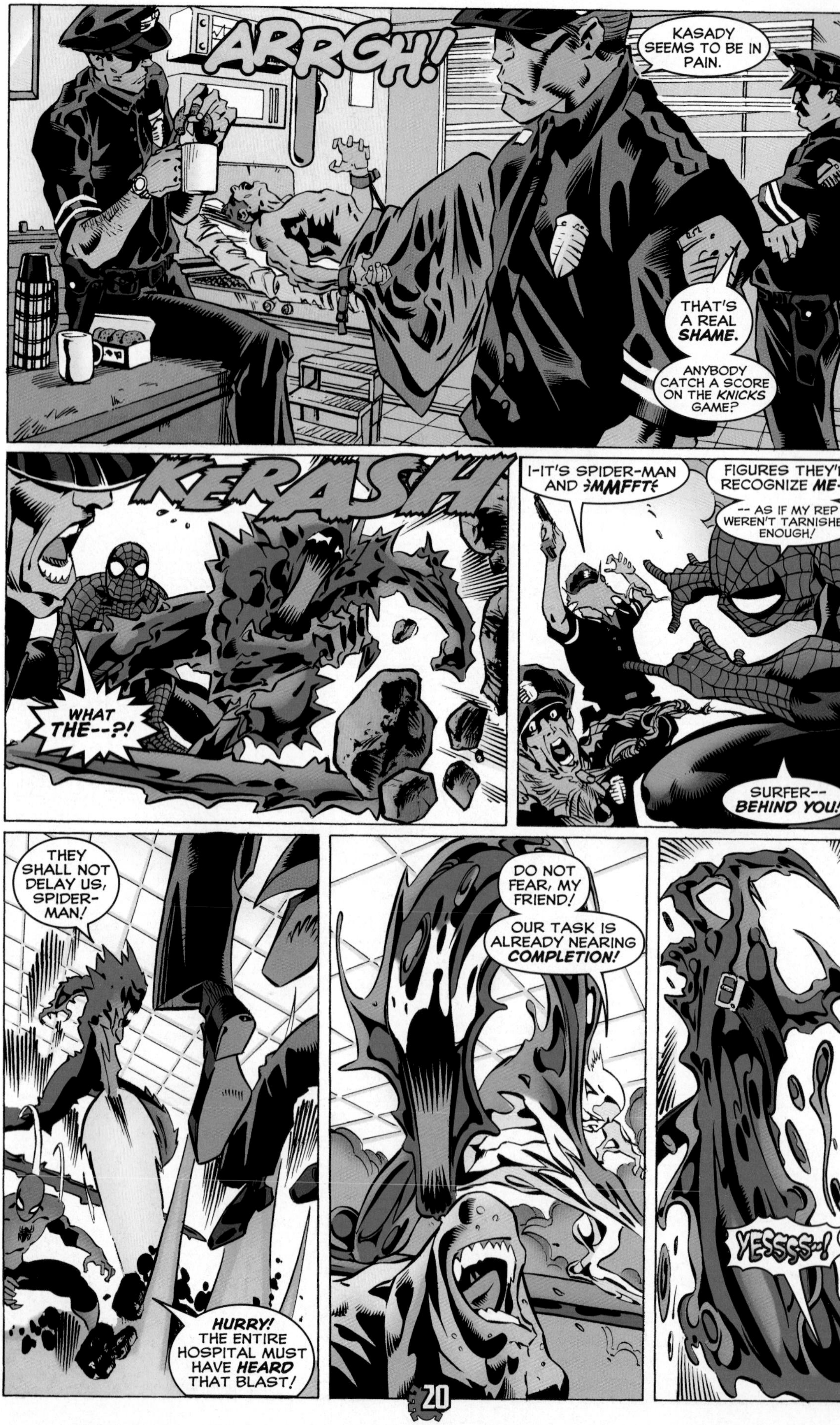
ARRGH!
KASADY SEEMS TO BE IN PAIN.
THAT'S A REAL SHAME.
ANYBODY CATCH A SCORE ON THE KNICKS GAME?
KERASH
WHAT THE--?!
I-IT'S SPIDER-MAN AND MMFFT
FIGURES THEY'D RECOGNIZE ME--
-- AS IF MY REP WEREN'T TARNISHED ENOUGH!
SURFER-- BEHIND YOU!
THEY SHALL NOT DELAY US, SPIDER-MAN!
HURRY! THE ENTIRE HOSPITAL MUST HAVE HEARD THAT BLAST!
DO NOT FEAR, MY FRIEND!
OUR TASK IS ALREADY NEARING COMPLETION!
YESSSS--!

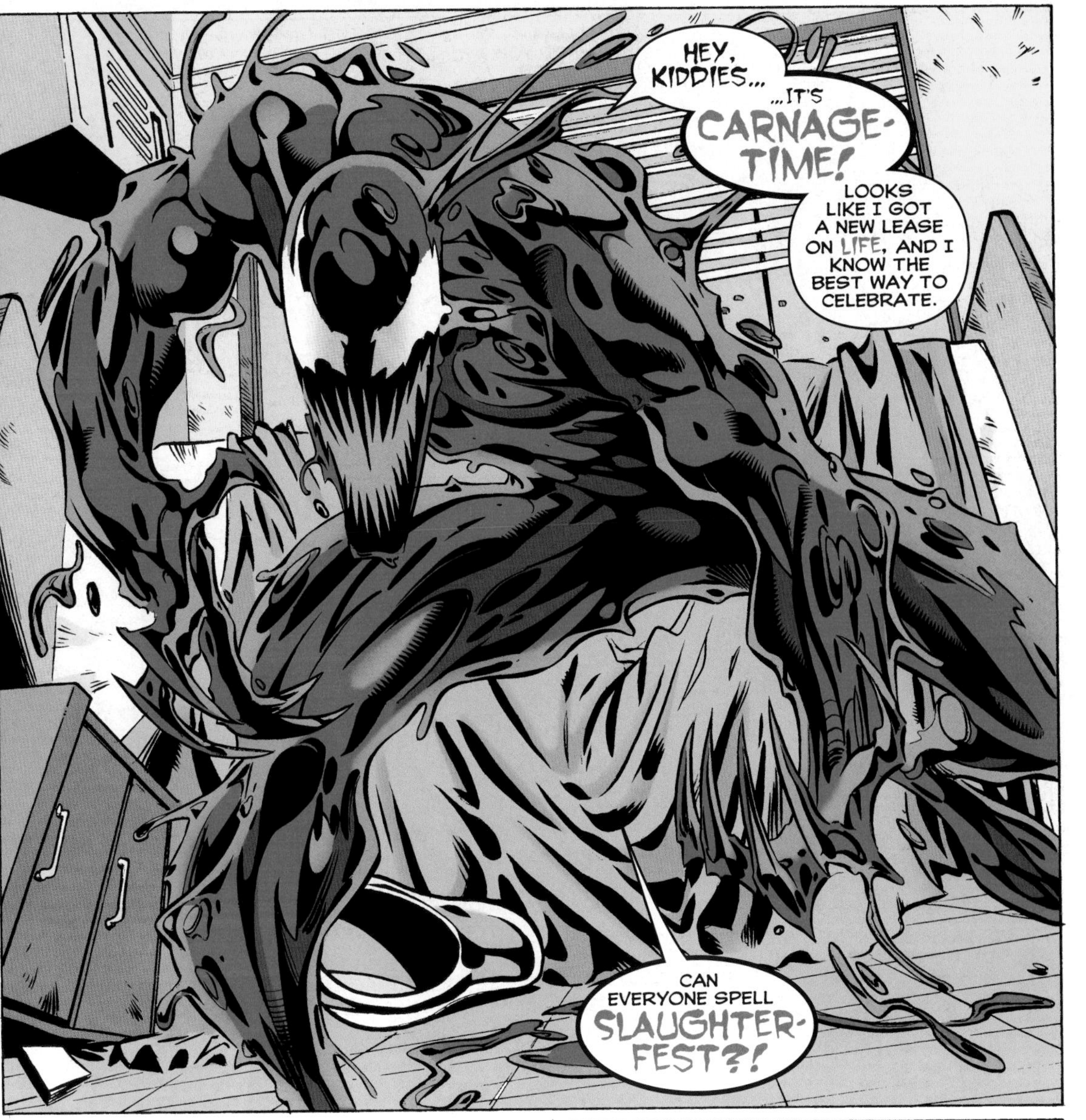
HEY, KIDDIES... ...IT'S CARNAGE-TIME!
LOOKS LIKE I GOT A NEW LEASE ON LIFE, AND I KNOW THE BEST WAY TO CELEBRATE.
CAN EVERYONE SPELL SLAUGHTER-FEST?!

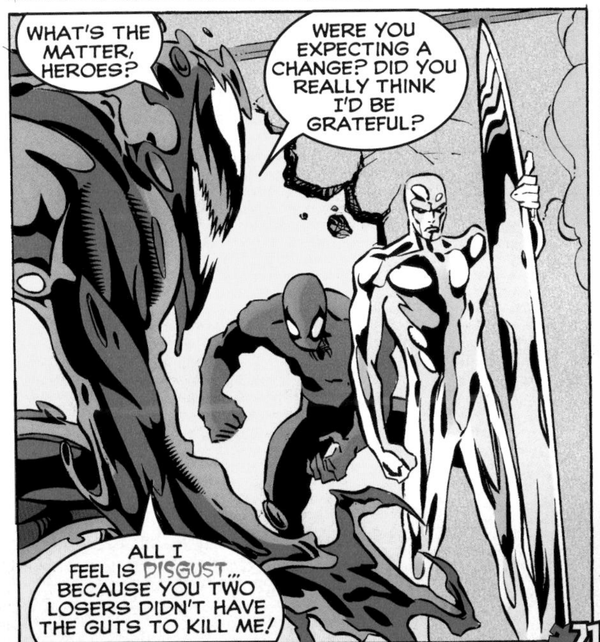
WHAT'S THE MATTER, HEROES?
WERE YOU EXPECTING A CHANGE? DID YOU REALLY THINK I'D BE GRATEFUL?
ALL I FEEL IS DISGUST... BECAUSE YOU TWO LOSERS DIDN'T HAVE THE GUTS TO KILL ME!

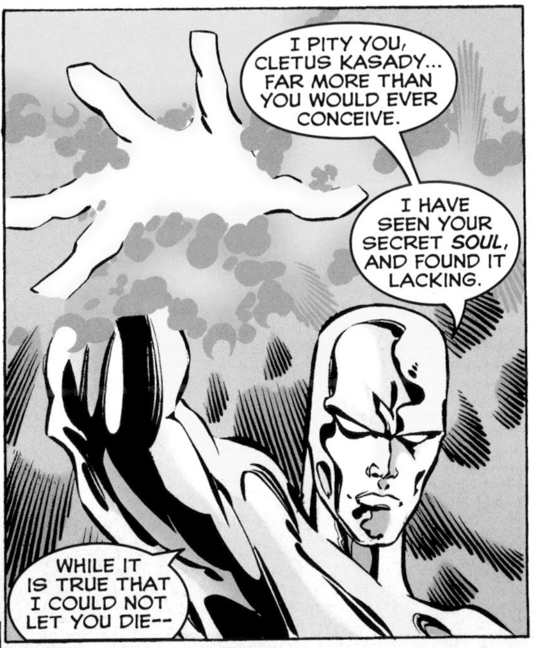
I PITY YOU, CLETUS KASADY... FAR MORE THAN YOU WOULD EVER CONCEIVE.
I HAVE SEEN YOUR SECRET SOUL, AND FOUND IT LACKING.
WHILE IT IS TRUE THAT I COULD NOT LET YOU DIE--

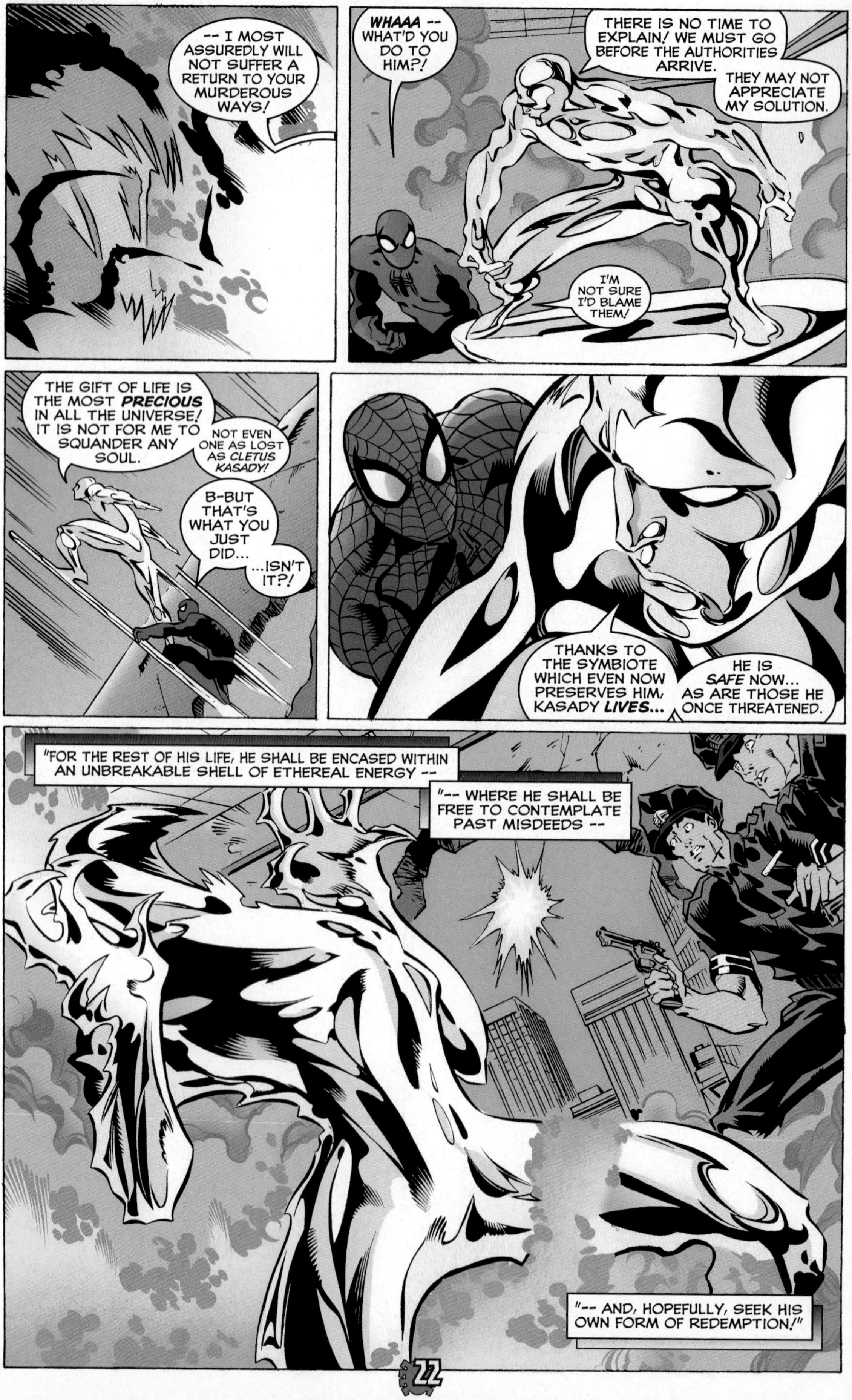
-- I MOST ASSUREDLY WILL NOT SUFFER A RETURN TO YOUR MURDEROUS WAYS!
WHAAA -- WHAT'D YOU DO TO HIM?!
THERE IS NO TIME TO EXPLAIN! WE MUST GO BEFORE THE AUTHORITIES ARRIVE.
THEY MAY NOT APPRECIATE MY SOLUTION.
I'M NOT SURE I'D BLAME THEM!
THE GIFT OF LIFE IS THE MOST PRECIOUS IN ALL THE UNIVERSE! IT IS NOT FOR ME TO SQUANDER ANY SOUL.
NOT EVEN ONE AS LOST AS CLETUS KASADY!
B-BUT THAT'S WHAT YOU JUST DID...
...ISN'T IT?!
THANKS TO THE SYMBIOTE WHICH EVEN NOW PRESERVES HIM, KASADY LIVES...
HE IS SAFE NOW... AS ARE THOSE HE ONCE THREATENED.
"FOR THE REST OF HIS LIFE, HE SHALL BE ENCASED WITHIN AN UNBREAKABLE SHELL OF ETHEREAL ENERGY --
"-- WHERE HE SHALL BE FREE TO CONTEMPLATE PAST MISDEEDS --
"-- AND, HOPEFULLY, SEEK HIS OWN FORM OF REDEMPTION!"

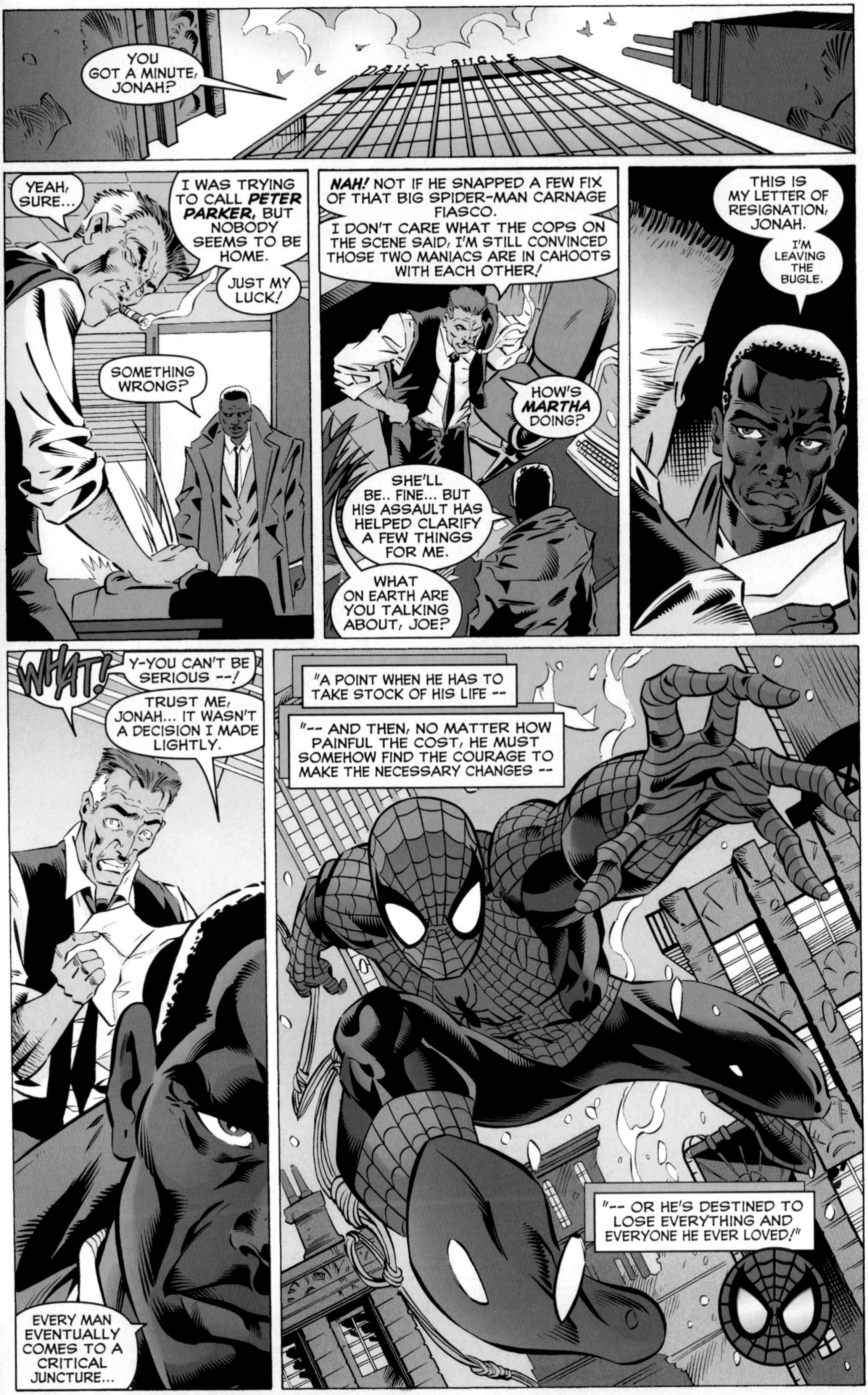
YOU GOT A MINUTE, JONAH?
DAILY BUGLE
YEAH, SURE...
I WAS TRYING TO CALL PETER PARKER, BUT NOBODY SEEMS TO BE HOME.
JUST MY LUCK!
SOMETHING WRONG?
NAH! NOT IF HE SNAPPED A FEW FIX OF THAT BIG SPIDER-MAN CARNAGE FIASCO. I DON'T CARE WHAT THE COPS ON THE SCENE SAID, I'M STILL CONVINCED THOSE TWO MANIACS ARE IN CAHOOTS WITH EACH OTHER!
HOW'S MARTHA DOING?
SHE'LL BE.. FINE... BUT HIS ASSAULT HAS HELPED CLARIFY A FEW THINGS FOR ME.
WHAT ON EARTH ARE YOU TALKING ABOUT, JOE?
THIS IS MY LETTER OF RESIGNATION, JONAH.
I'M LEAVING THE BUGLE.
WHAT!
Y-YOU CAN'T BE SERIOUS --!
TRUST ME, JONAH... IT WASN'T A DECISION I MADE LIGHTLY.
EVERY MAN EVENTUALLY COMES TO A CRITICAL JUNCTURE...
"A POINT WHEN HE HAS TO TAKE STOCK OF HIS LIFE --
"-- AND THEN, NO MATTER HOW PAINFUL THE COST, HE MUST SOMEHOW FIND THE COURAGE TO MAKE THE NECESSARY CHANGES --
"-- OR HE'S DESTINED TO LOSE EVERYTHING AND EVERYONE HE EVER LOVED!"

Carnage was later ripped in half and thrown into space by the Sentry. However, Dr. Michael Hall retrieved Carnage's body and experimented on the symbiote. Dr. Tanis Nieves, therapist to Carnage's old ally Shriek, was injured during an attack by Spider-Man's doppelganger. As Spider-Man and Iron Man investigated the attack, Nieves found herself infected with a piece of the Carnage symbiote — which forced her to free the rest from Hall's lab!

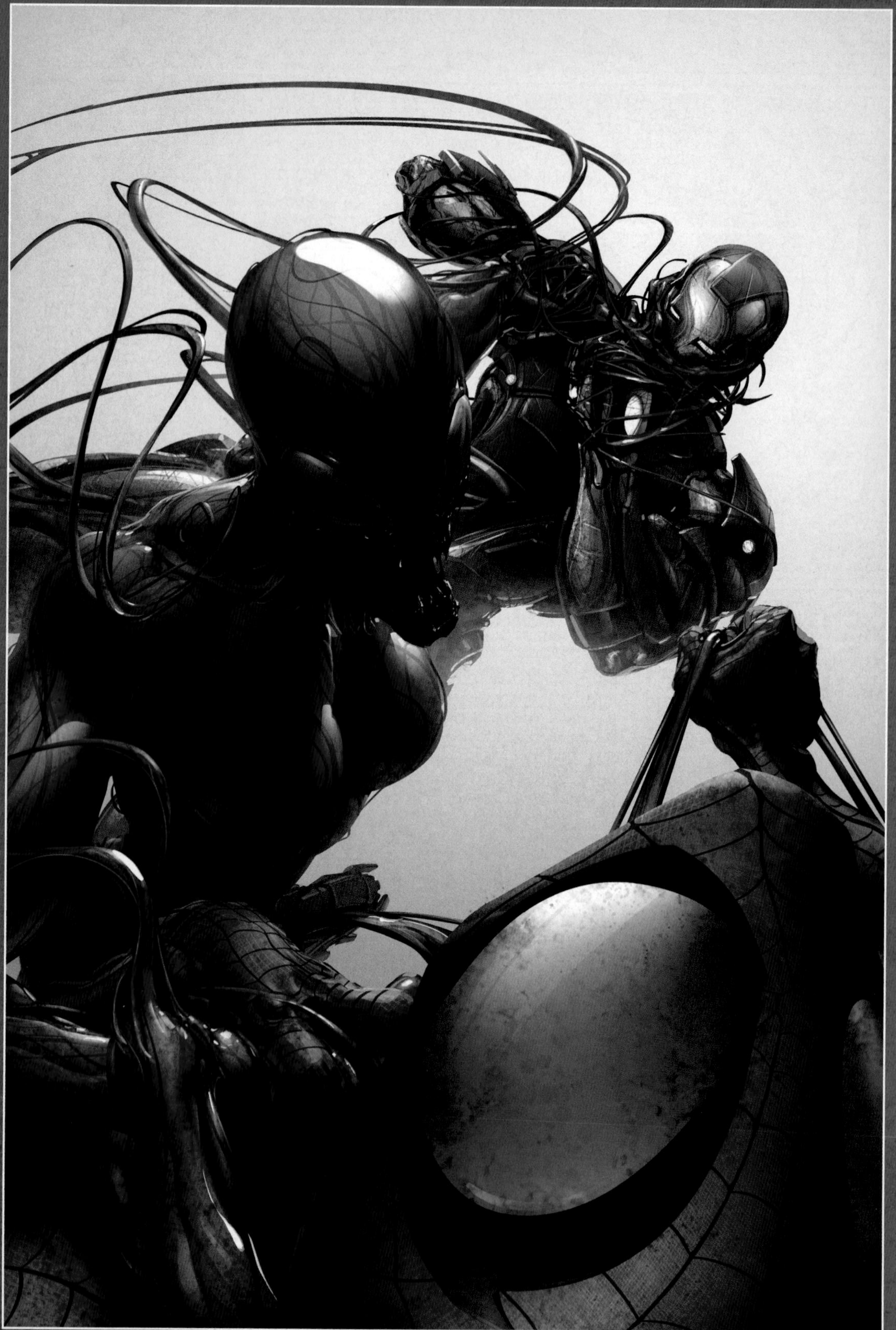

CARNAGE #3

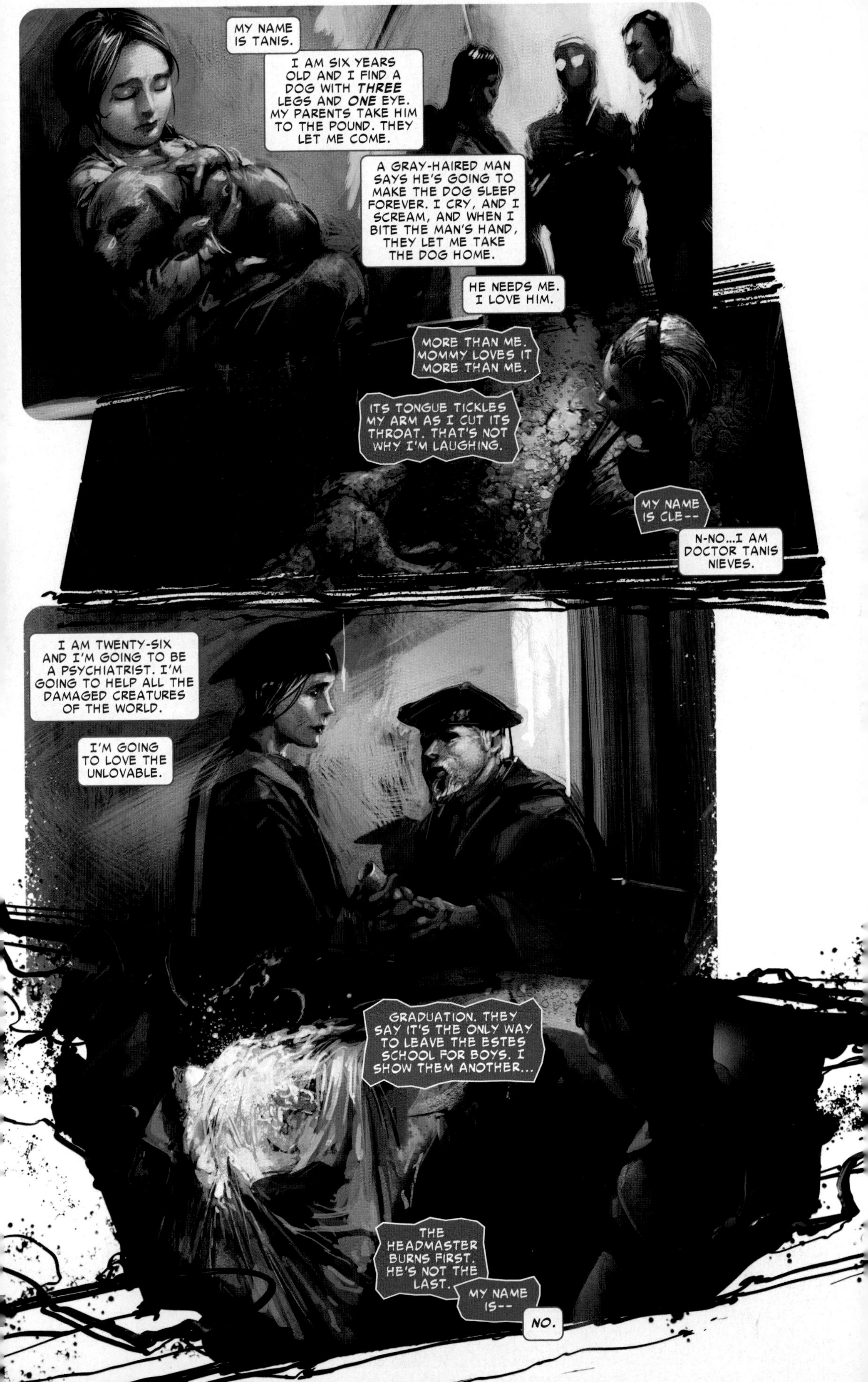

MY NAME IS TANIS.
I AM SIX YEARS OLD AND I FIND A DOG WITH *THREE* LEGS AND *ONE* EYE. MY PARENTS TAKE HIM TO THE POUND. THEY LET ME COME.
A GRAY-HAIRED MAN SAYS HE'S GOING TO MAKE THE DOG SLEEP FOREVER. I CRY, AND I SCREAM, AND WHEN I BITE THE MAN'S HAND, THEY LET ME TAKE THE DOG HOME.
HE NEEDS ME. I LOVE HIM.
MORE THAN ME. MOMMY LOVES IT MORE THAN ME.
ITS TONGUE TICKLES MY ARM AS I CUT ITS THROAT. THAT'S NOT WHY I'M LAUGHING.
MY NAME IS CLE--
N-NO...I AM DOCTOR TANIS NIEVES.
I AM TWENTY-SIX AND I'M GOING TO BE A PSYCHIATRIST. I'M GOING TO HELP ALL THE DAMAGED CREATURES OF THE WORLD.
I'M GOING TO LOVE THE UNLOVABLE.
GRADUATION. THEY SAY IT'S THE ONLY WAY TO LEAVE THE ESTES SCHOOL FOR BOYS. I SHOW THEM ANOTHER...
THE HEADMASTER BURNS FIRST. HE'S NOT THE LAST.
MY NAME IS--
NO.

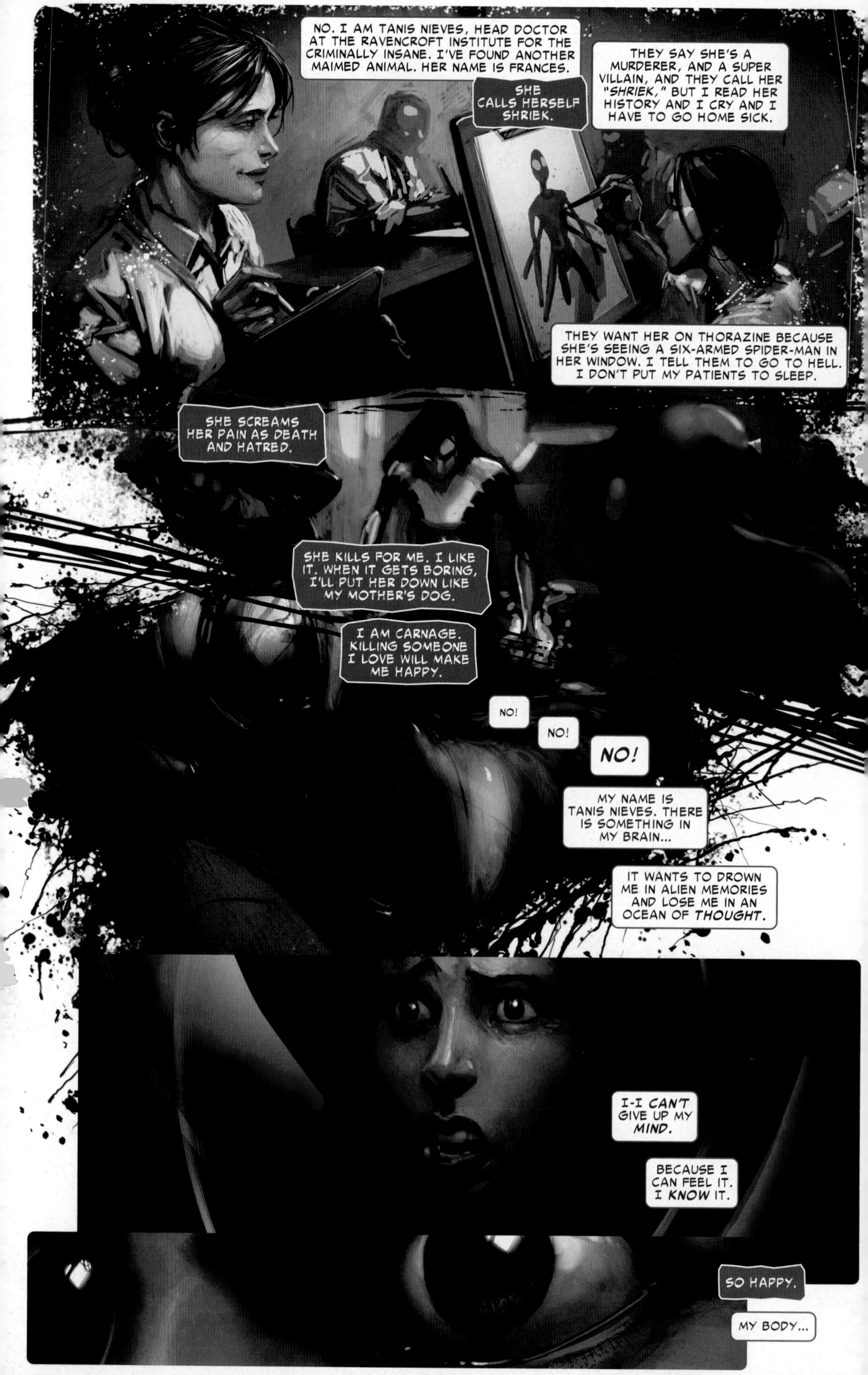
NO. I AM TANIS NIEVES, HEAD DOCTOR AT THE RAVENCROFT INSTITUTE FOR THE CRIMINALLY INSANE. I'VE FOUND ANOTHER MAIMED ANIMAL. HER NAME IS FRANCES.
SHE CALLS HERSELF SHRIEK.
THEY SAY SHE'S A MURDERER, AND A SUPER VILLAIN, AND THEY CALL HER "SHRIEK," BUT I READ HER HISTORY AND I CRY AND I HAVE TO GO HOME SICK.
THEY WANT HER ON THORAZINE BECAUSE SHE'S SEEING A SIX-ARMED SPIDER-MAN IN HER WINDOW. I TELL THEM TO GO TO HELL. I DON'T PUT MY PATIENTS TO SLEEP.
SHE SCREAMS HER PAIN AS DEATH AND HATRED.
SHE KILLS FOR ME. I LIKE IT. WHEN IT GETS BORING, I'LL PUT HER DOWN LIKE MY MOTHER'S DOG.
I AM CARNAGE. KILLING SOMEONE I LOVE WILL MAKE ME HAPPY.
NO!
NO!
NO!
MY NAME IS TANIS NIEVES. THERE IS SOMETHING IN MY BRAIN...
IT WANTS TO DROWN ME IN ALIEN MEMORIES AND LOSE ME IN AN OCEAN OF THOUGHT.
I-I CAN'T GIVE UP MY MIND.
BECAUSE I CAN FEEL IT. I KNOW IT.
SO HAPPY.
MY BODY...

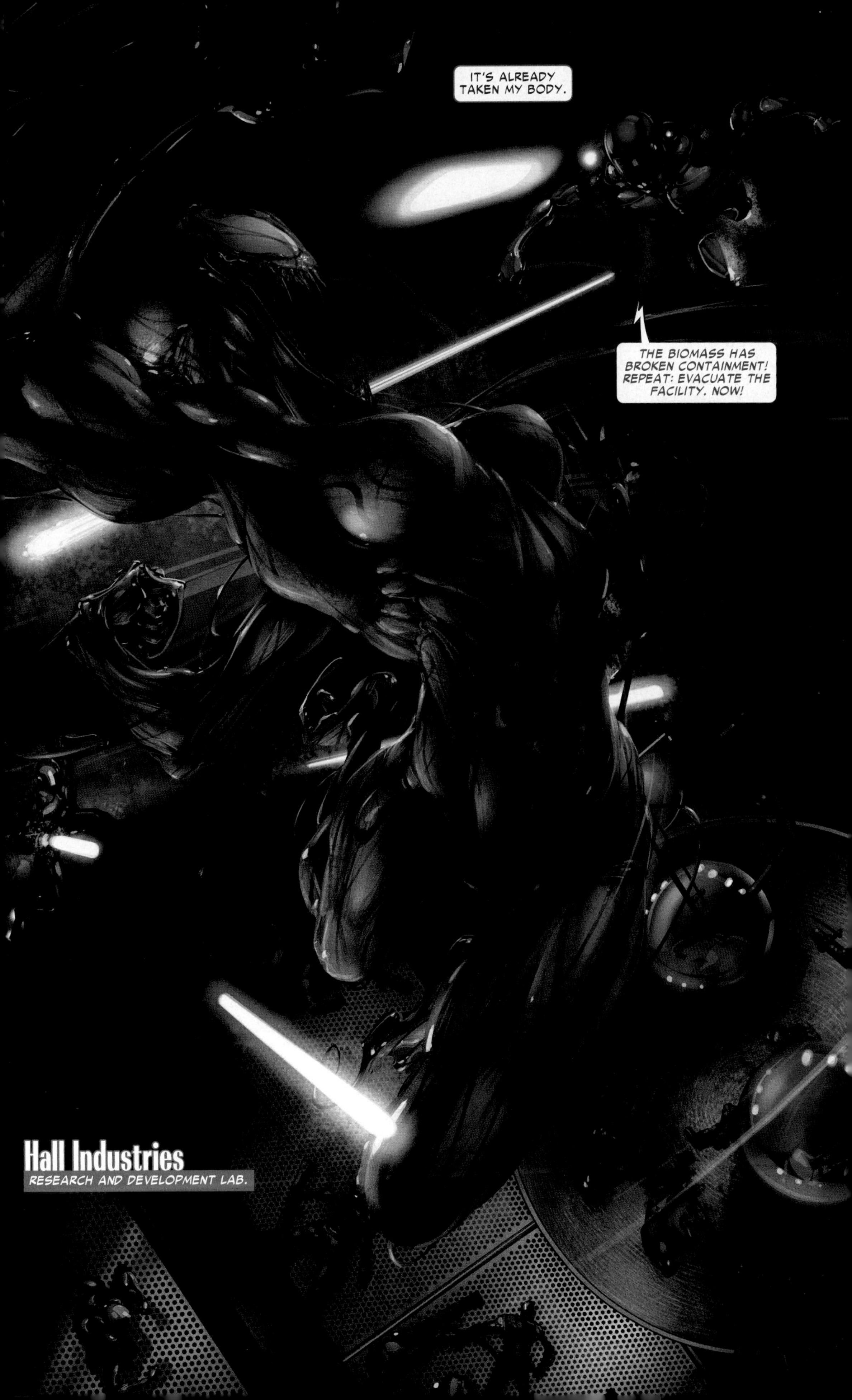
IT'S ALREADY TAKEN MY BODY.
THE BIOMASS HAS BROKEN CONTAINMENT! REPEAT: EVACUATE THE FACILITY. NOW!
Hall Industries
RESEARCH AND DEVELOPMENT LAB.

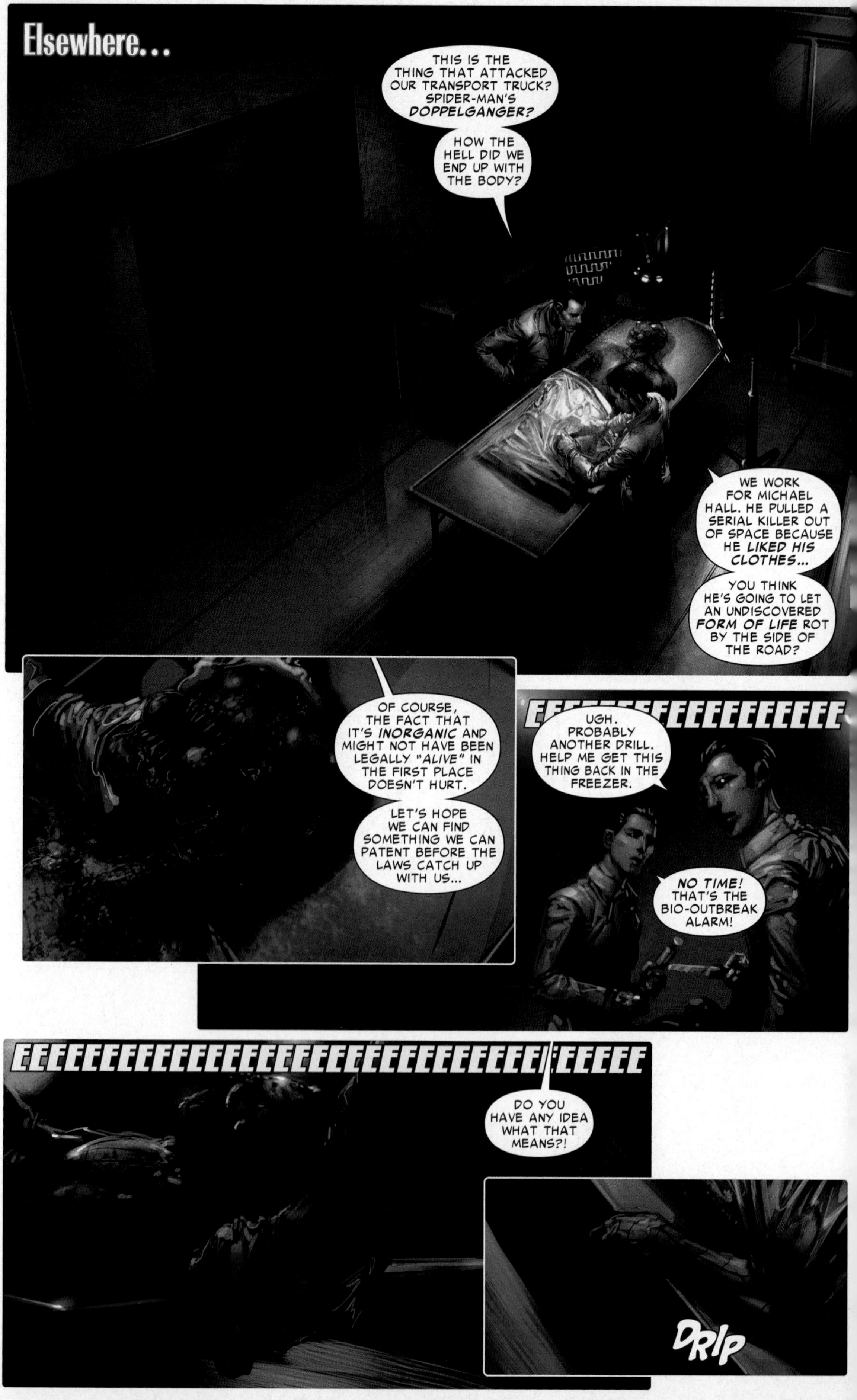
Elsewhere...
THIS IS THE THING THAT ATTACKED OUR TRANSPORT TRUCK? SPIDER-MAN'S DOPPELGANGER?
HOW THE HELL DID WE END UP WITH THE BODY?
WE WORK FOR MICHAEL HALL. HE PULLED A SERIAL KILLER OUT OF SPACE BECAUSE HE LIKED HIS CLOTHES...
YOU THINK HE'S GOING TO LET AN UNDISCOVERED FORM OF LIFE ROT BY THE SIDE OF THE ROAD?
OF COURSE, THE FACT THAT IT'S INORGANIC AND MIGHT NOT HAVE BEEN LEGALLY "ALIVE" IN THE FIRST PLACE DOESN'T HURT.
LET'S HOPE WE CAN FIND SOMETHING WE CAN PATENT BEFORE THE LAWS CATCH UP WITH US...
EEEEEEEEEEEEEEEEEEE
UGH. PROBABLY ANOTHER DRILL. HELP ME GET THIS THING BACK IN THE FREEZER.
NO TIME! THAT'S THE BIO-OUTBREAK ALARM!
EEEEEEEEEEEEEEEEEEEEEEEEEEEEEEEEEEEEEE
DO YOU HAVE ANY IDEA WHAT THAT MEANS?!
DRIP

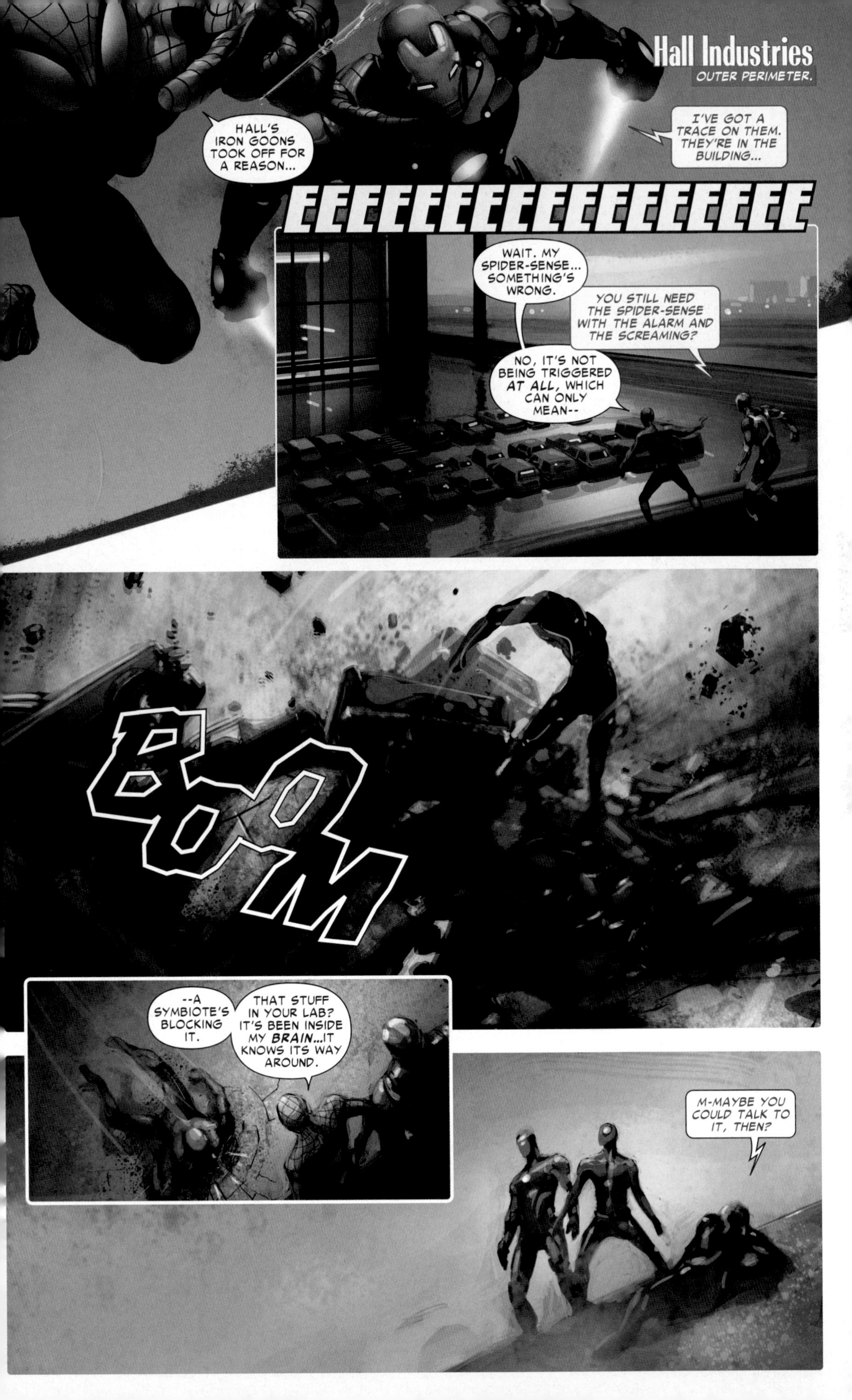
Hall Industries
OUTER PERIMETER.
HALL'S IRON GOONS TOOK OFF FOR A REASON...
I'VE GOT A TRACE ON THEM. THEY'RE IN THE BUILDING...
EEEEEEEEEEEEEEEEEEE
WAIT. MY SPIDER-SENSE... SOMETHING'S WRONG.
YOU STILL NEED THE SPIDER-SENSE WITH THE ALARM AND THE SCREAMING?
NO, IT'S NOT BEING TRIGGERED AT ALL, WHICH CAN ONLY MEAN--
BOOM
--A SYMBIOTE'S BLOCKING IT.
THAT STUFF IN YOUR LAB? IT'S BEEN INSIDE MY BRAIN...IT KNOWS ITS WAY AROUND.
M-MAYBE YOU COULD TALK TO IT, THEN?

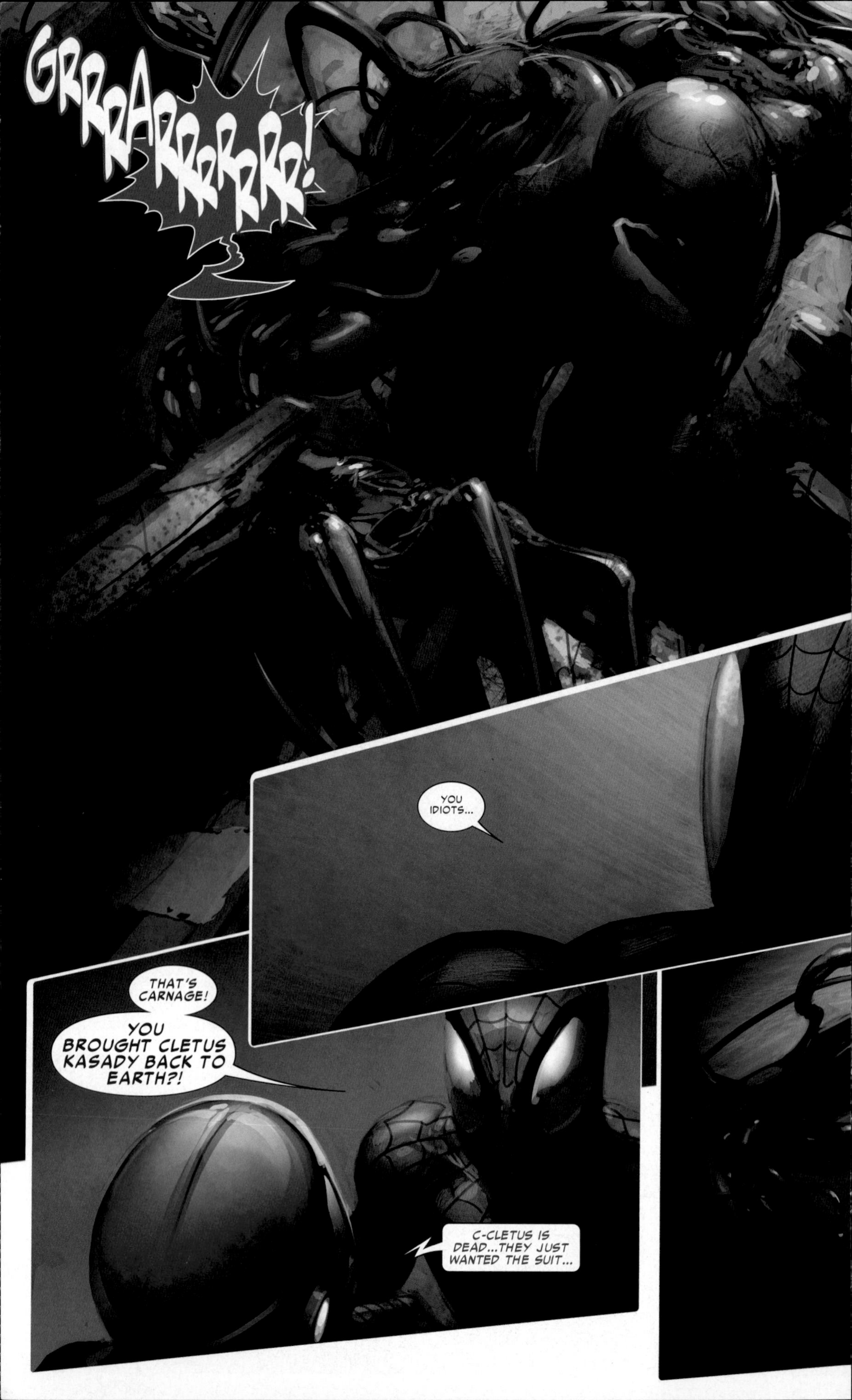
GRRRARRRRRR!
YOU IDIOTS...
THAT'S CARNAGE!
YOU BROUGHT CLETUS KASADY BACK TO EARTH?!
C-CLETUS IS DEAD...THEY JUST WANTED THE SUIT...

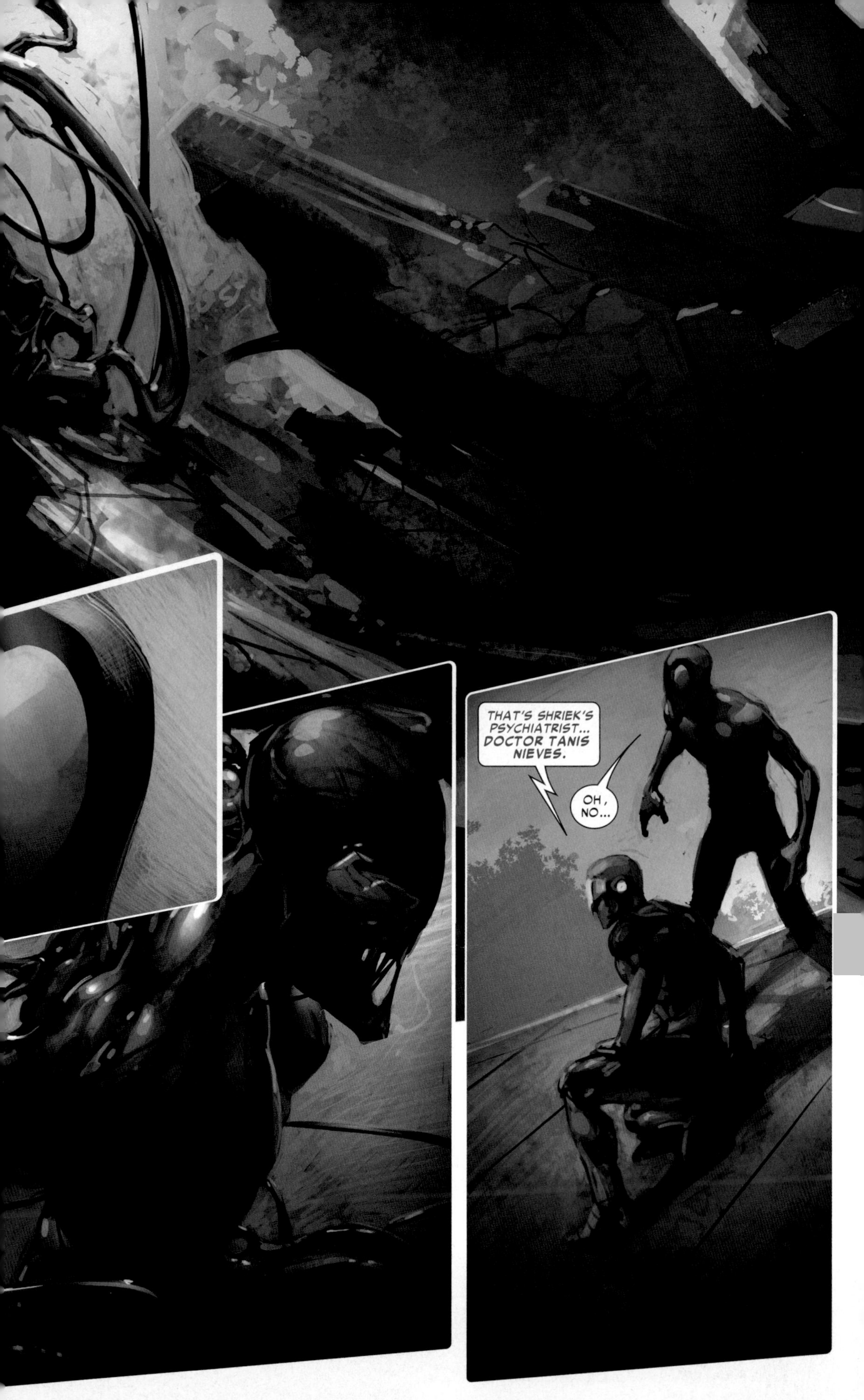
THAT'S SHRIEK'S PSYCHIATRIST... DOCTOR TANIS NIEVES.
OH, NO...

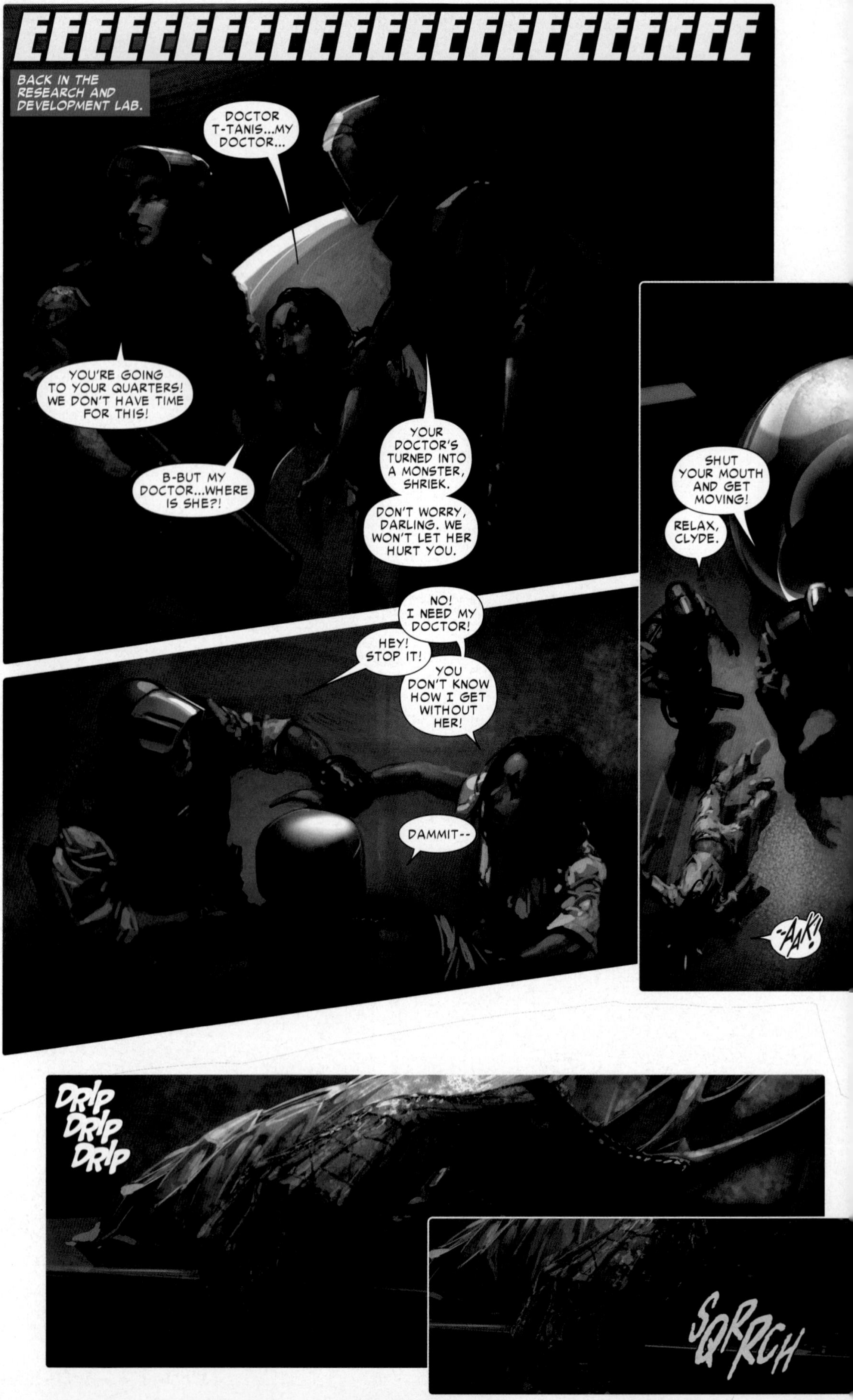
EEEEEEEEEEEEEEEEEEEEEEEE
BACK IN THE RESEARCH AND DEVELOPMENT LAB.
DOCTOR T-TANIS...MY DOCTOR...
YOU'RE GOING TO YOUR QUARTERS! WE DON'T HAVE TIME FOR THIS!
B-BUT MY DOCTOR...WHERE IS SHE?!
YOUR DOCTOR'S TURNED INTO A MONSTER, SHRIEK.
DON'T WORRY, DARLING. WE WON'T LET HER HURT YOU.
NO! I NEED MY DOCTOR!
HEY! STOP IT!
YOU DON'T KNOW HOW I GET WITHOUT HER!
DAMMIT--
SHUT YOUR MOUTH AND GET MOVING!
RELAX, CLYDE.
--AAK!
DRIP DRIP DRIP
SQRRCH

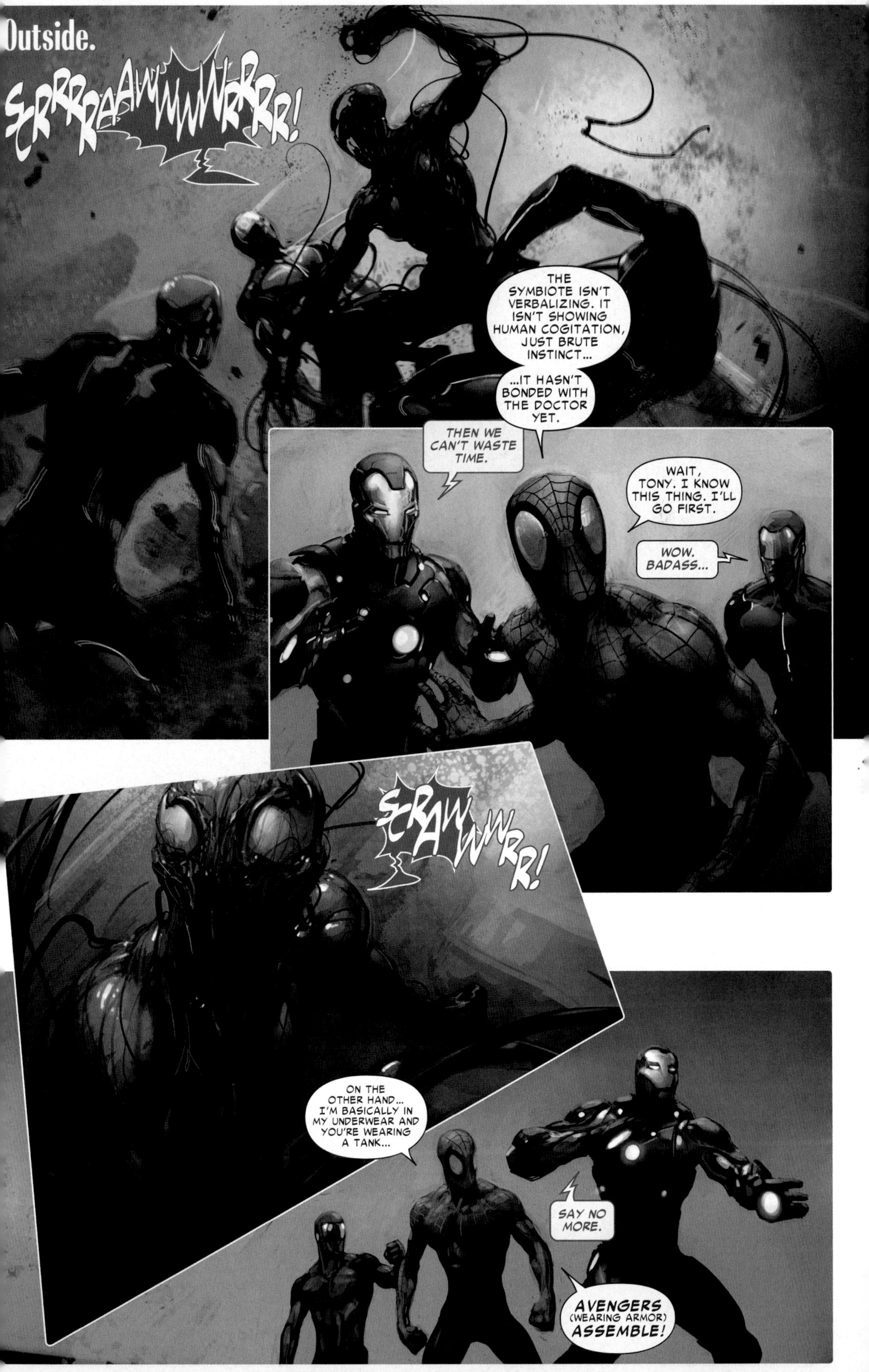
Outside.
SCRRRRAAWWWWRRRR!
THE SYMBIOTE ISN'T VERBALIZING. IT ISN'T SHOWING HUMAN COGITATION, JUST BRUTE INSTINCT...
...IT HASN'T BONDED WITH THE DOCTOR YET.
THEN WE CAN'T WASTE TIME.
WAIT, TONY. I KNOW THIS THING. I'LL GO FIRST.
WOW. BADASS...
SCRAWWRR!
ON THE OTHER HAND... I'M BASICALLY IN MY UNDERWEAR AND YOU'RE WEARING A TANK...
SAY NO MORE.
AVENGERS (WEARING ARMOR) ASSEMBLE!

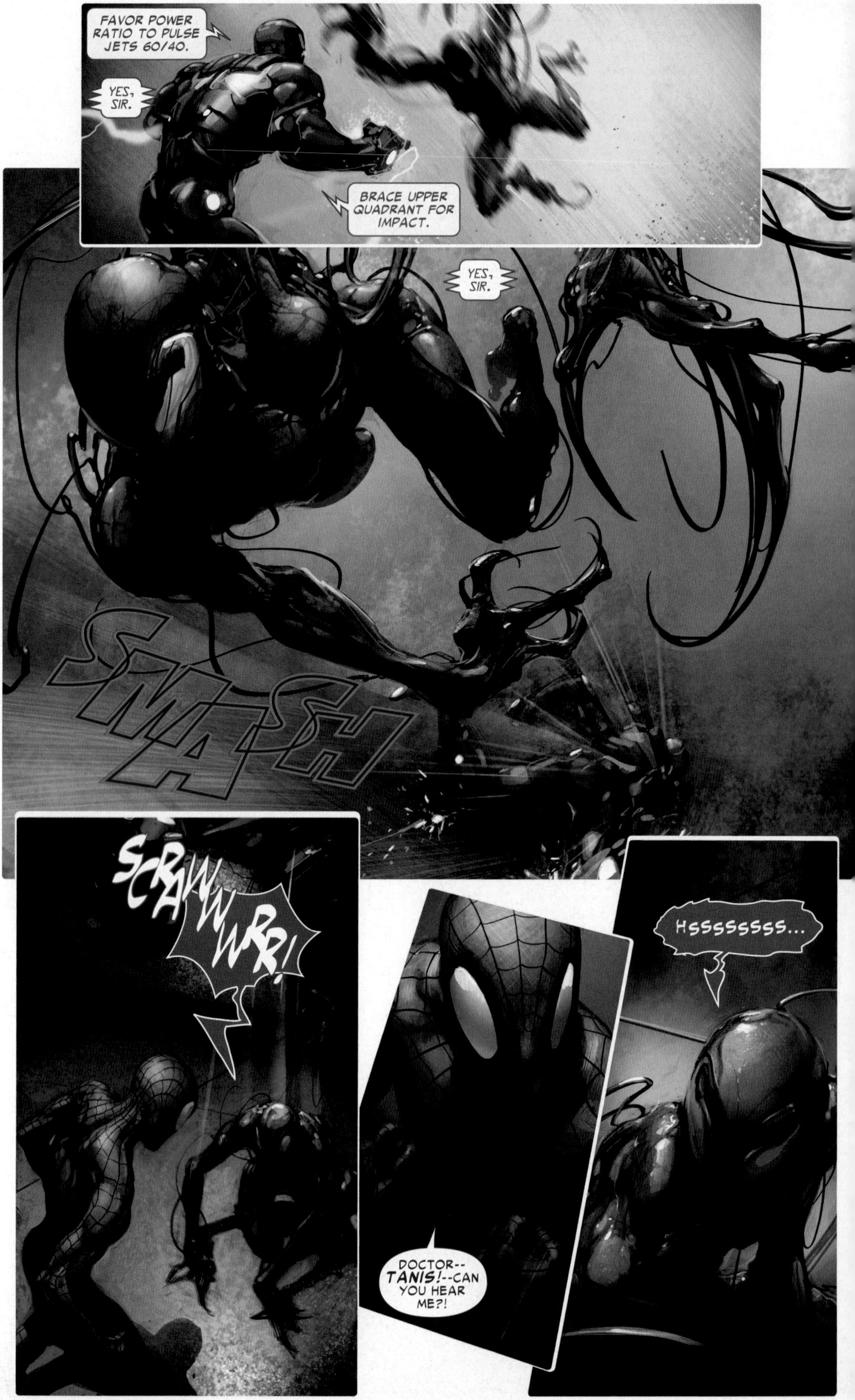
FAVOR POWER RATIO TO PULSE JETS 60/40.
YES, SIR.
BRACE UPPER QUADRANT FOR IMPACT.
YES, SIR.
SMASH
SCRAWWRR!
DOCTOR-- TANIS!--CAN YOU HEAR ME?!
Hsssssss...

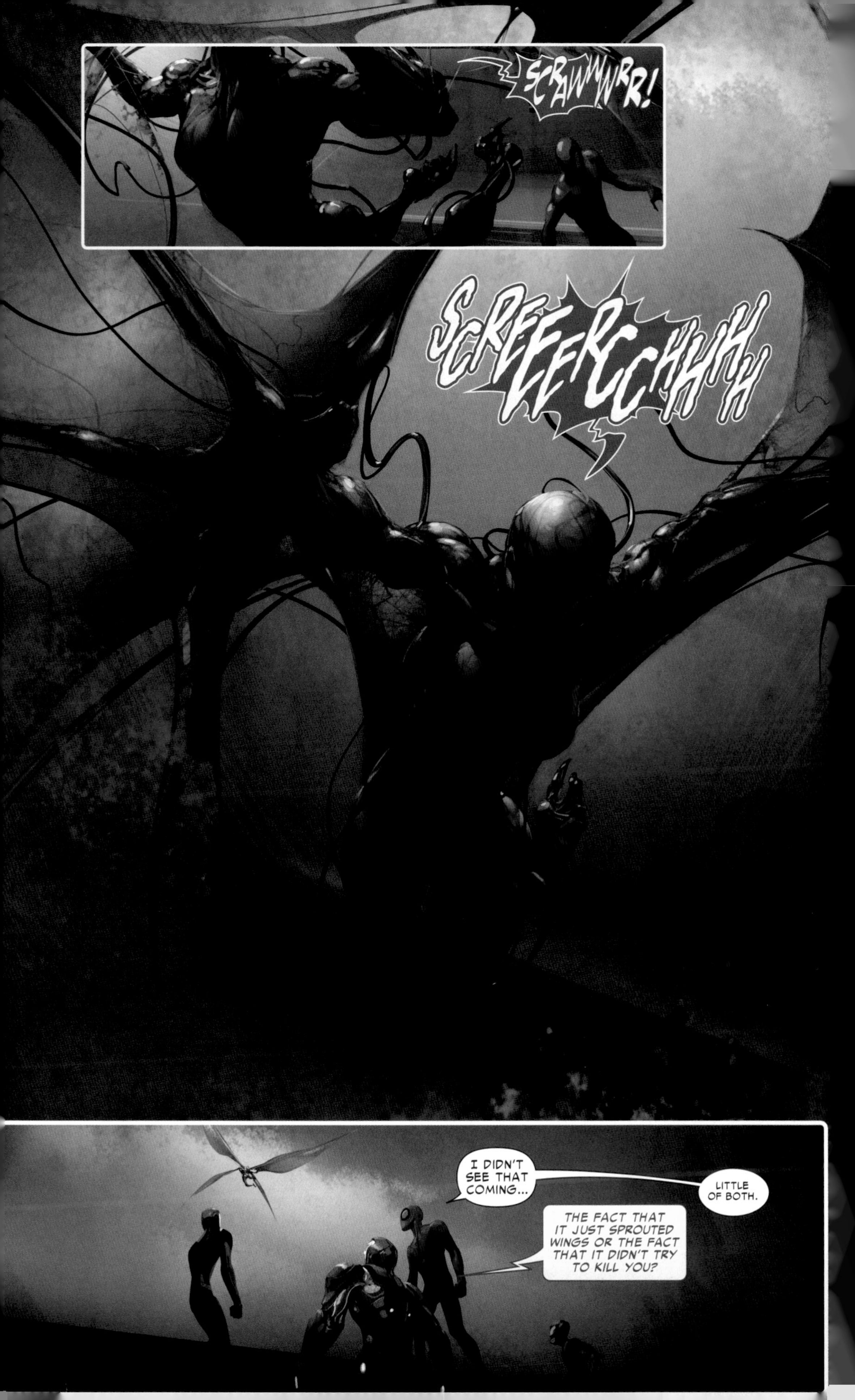
SCRAWWWRR!
SCREEEERCCHHHHH
I DIDN'T SEE THAT COMING...
THE FACT THAT IT JUST SPROUTED WINGS OR THE FACT THAT IT DIDN'T TRY TO KILL YOU?
LITTLE OF BOTH.

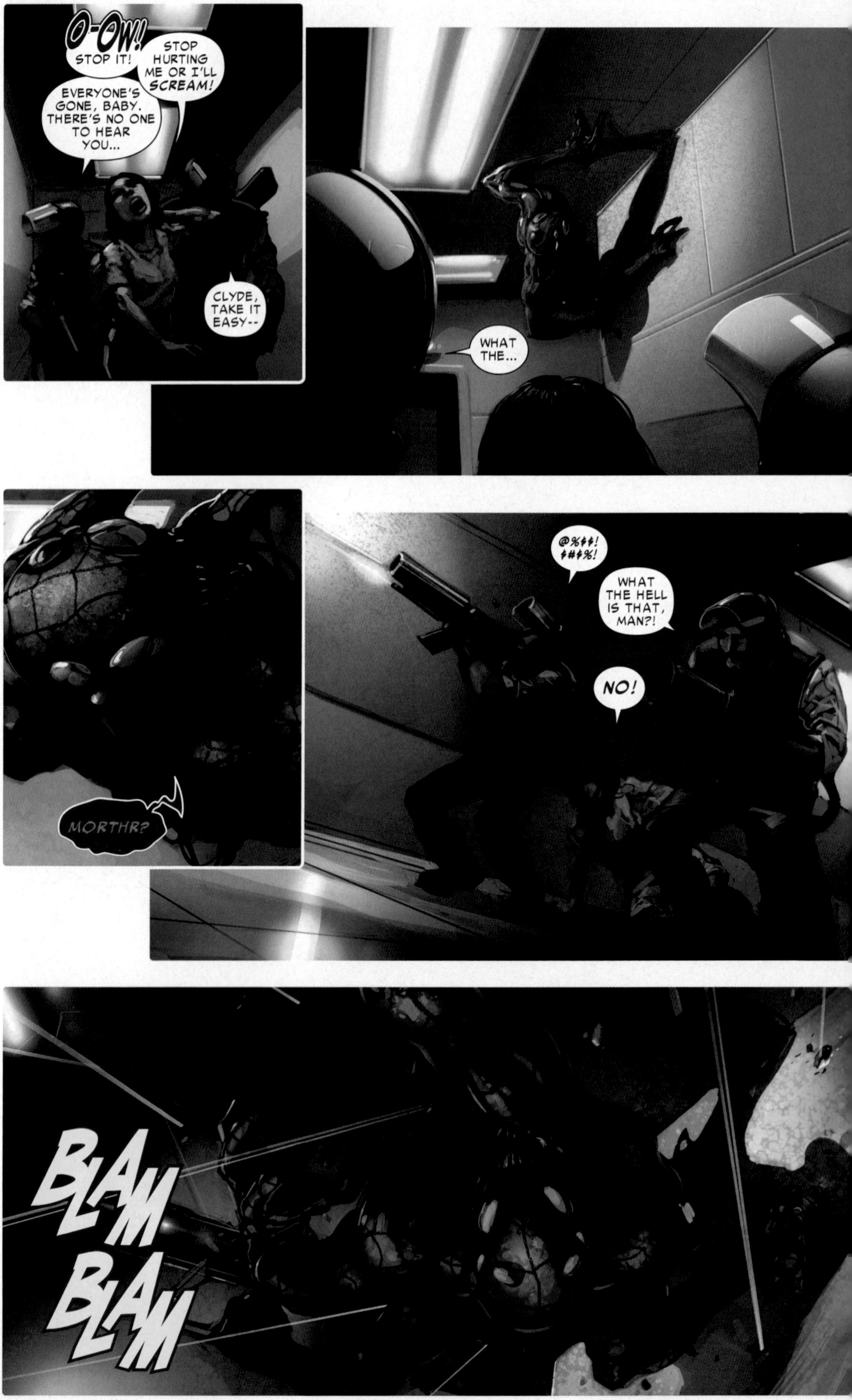
O-OW! STOP IT!
STOP HURTING ME OR I'LL SCREAM!
EVERYONE'S GONE, BABY. THERE'S NO ONE TO HEAR YOU...
CLYDE, TAKE IT EASY--
WHAT THE...
MORTHR?
@%$$! $#$%!
WHAT THE HELL IS THAT, MAN?!
NO!
BLAM
BLAM

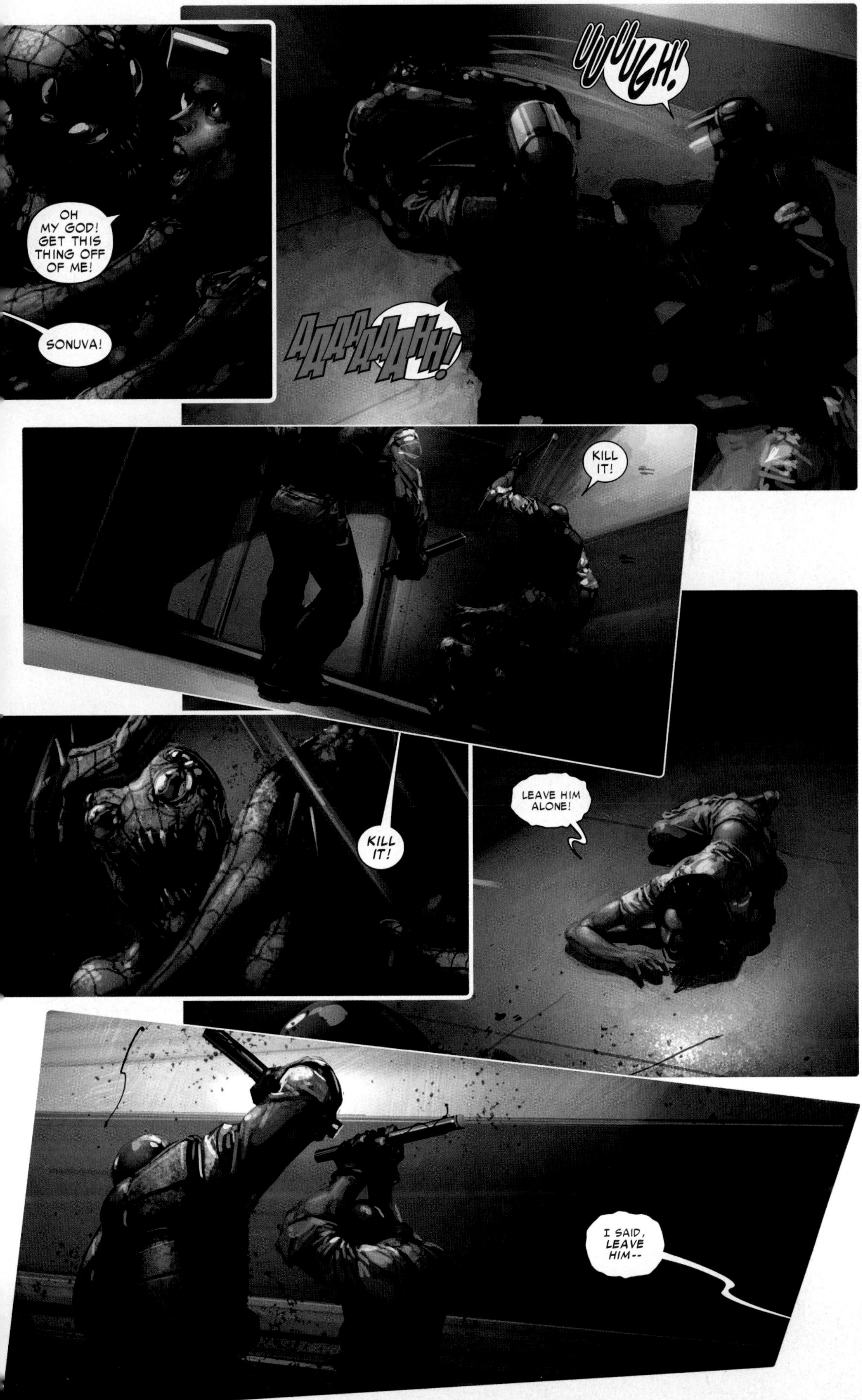
OH MY GOD! GET THIS THING OFF OF ME!
SONUVA!
UUUUGH!
AAAAAAHH!
KILL IT!
KILL IT!
LEAVE HIM ALONE!
I SAID, LEAVE HIM--

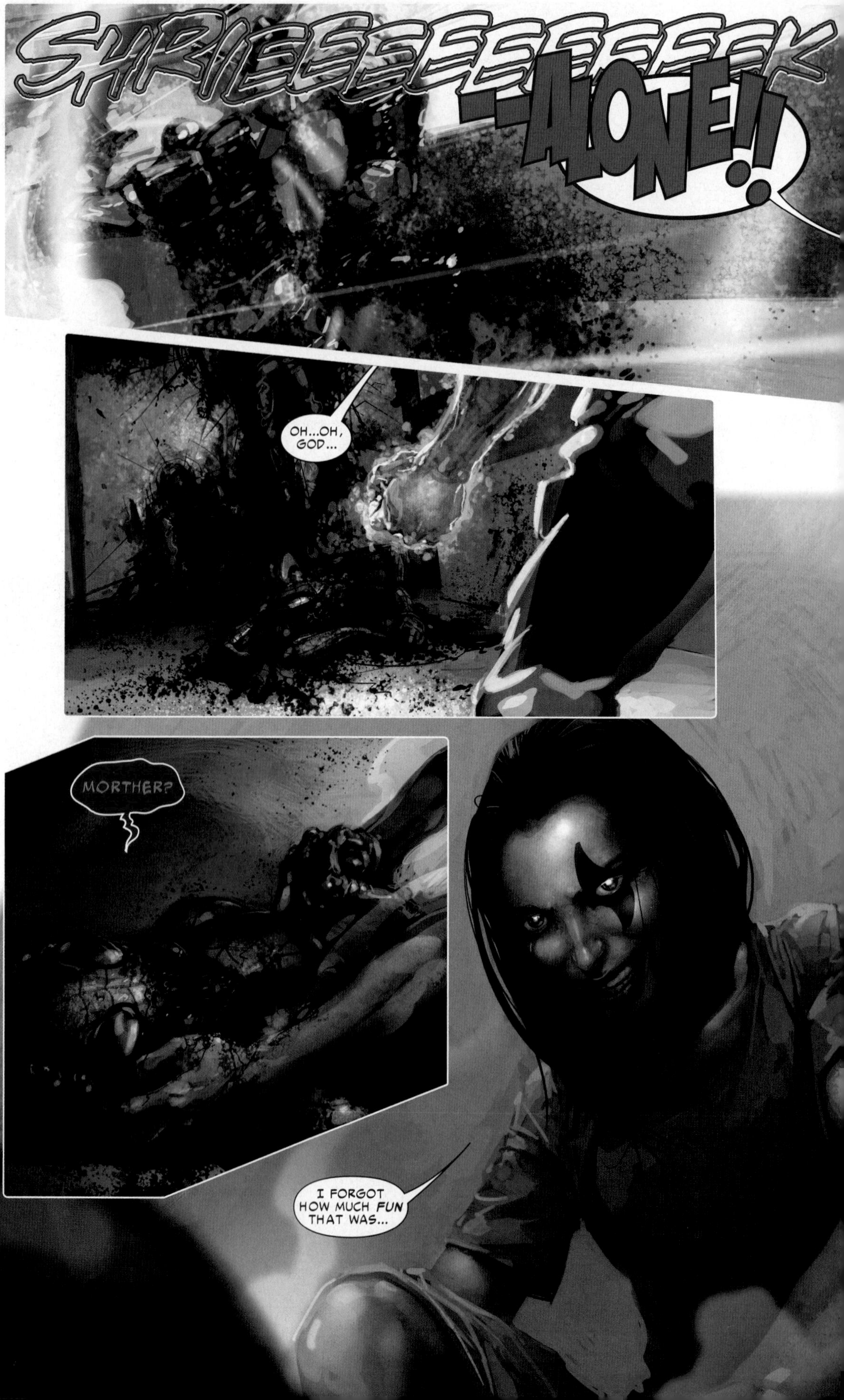
SHRIEEEEEEEEEK
--ALONE!!
OH...OH, GOD...
MORTHER?
I FORGOT HOW MUCH FUN THAT WAS...

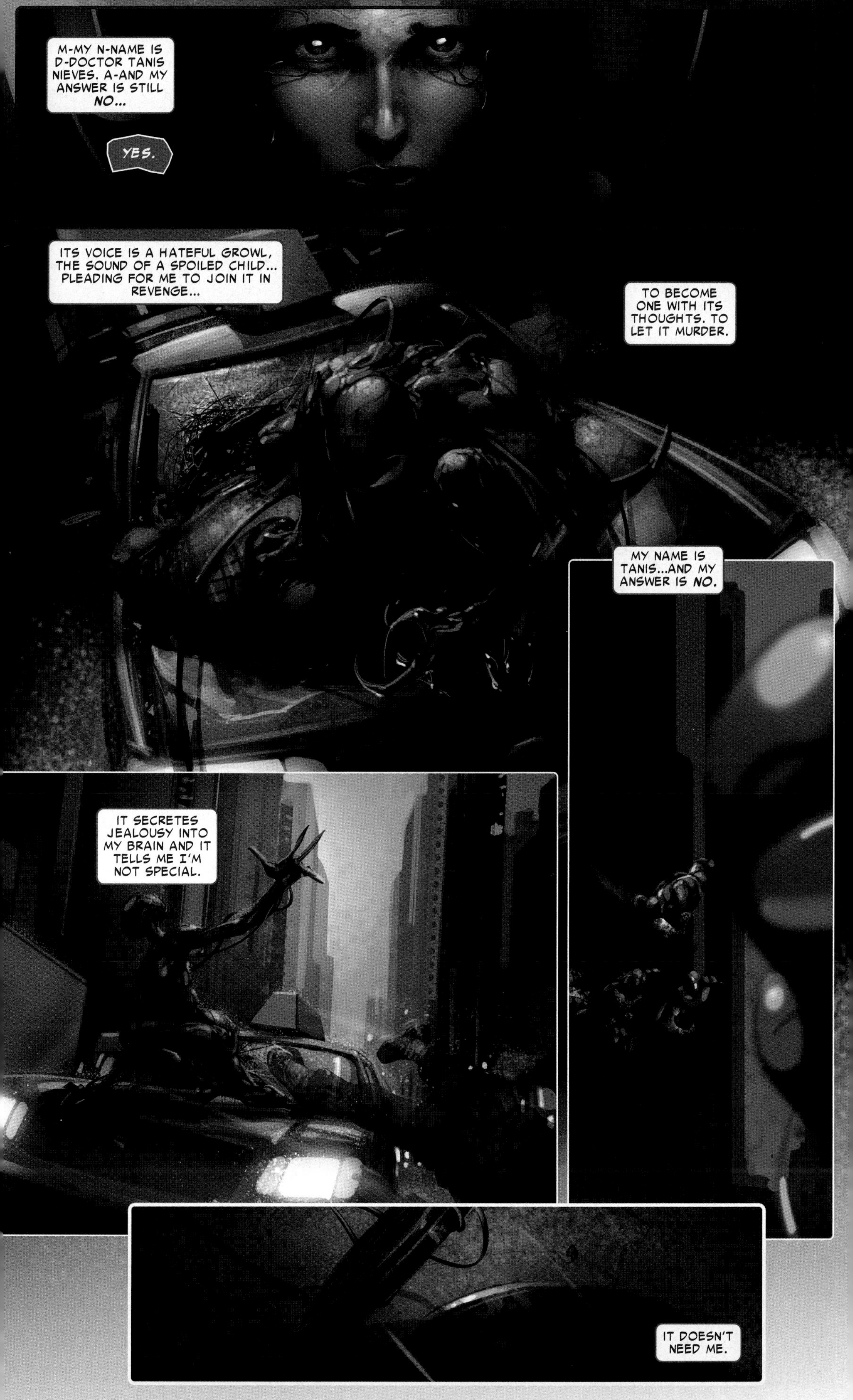
M-MY N-NAME IS D-DOCTOR TANIS NIEVES. A-AND MY ANSWER IS STILL NO...
YES.
ITS VOICE IS A HATEFUL GROWL, THE SOUND OF A SPOILED CHILD... PLEADING FOR ME TO JOIN IT IN REVENGE...
TO BECOME ONE WITH ITS THOUGHTS. TO LET IT MURDER.
IT SECRETES JEALOUSY INTO MY BRAIN AND IT TELLS ME I'M NOT SPECIAL.
MY NAME IS TANIS...AND MY ANSWER IS NO.
IT DOESN'T NEED ME.

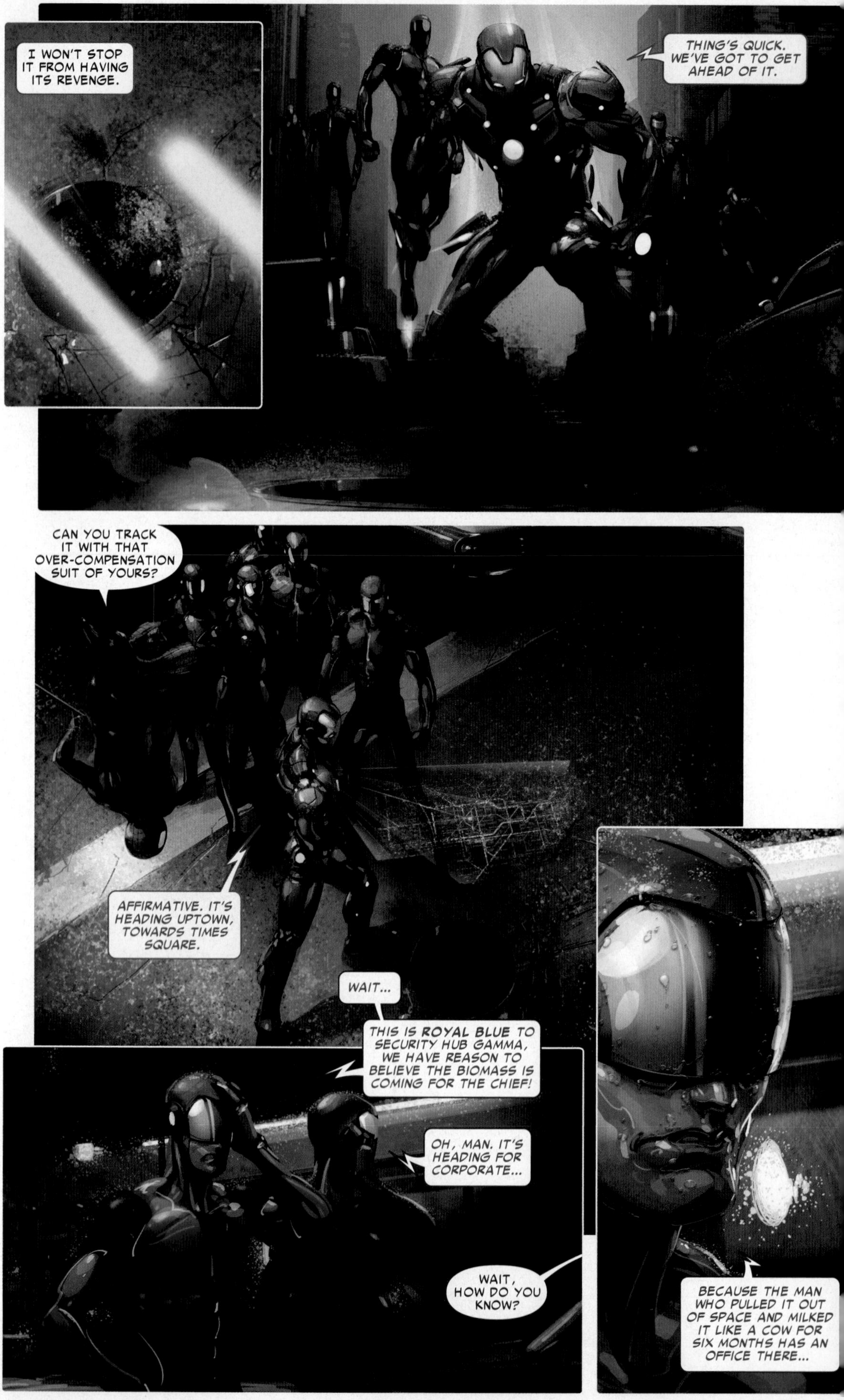
I WON'T STOP IT FROM HAVING ITS REVENGE.
THING'S QUICK. WE'VE GOT TO GET AHEAD OF IT.
CAN YOU TRACK IT WITH THAT OVER-COMPENSATION SUIT OF YOURS?
AFFIRMATIVE. IT'S HEADING UPTOWN, TOWARDS TIMES SQUARE.
WAIT...
THIS IS ROYAL BLUE TO SECURITY HUB GAMMA, WE HAVE REASON TO BELIEVE THE BIOMASS IS COMING FOR THE CHIEF!
OH, MAN. IT'S HEADING FOR CORPORATE...
WAIT, HOW DO YOU KNOW?
BECAUSE THE MAN WHO PULLED IT OUT OF SPACE AND MILKED IT LIKE A COW FOR SIX MONTHS HAS AN OFFICE THERE...

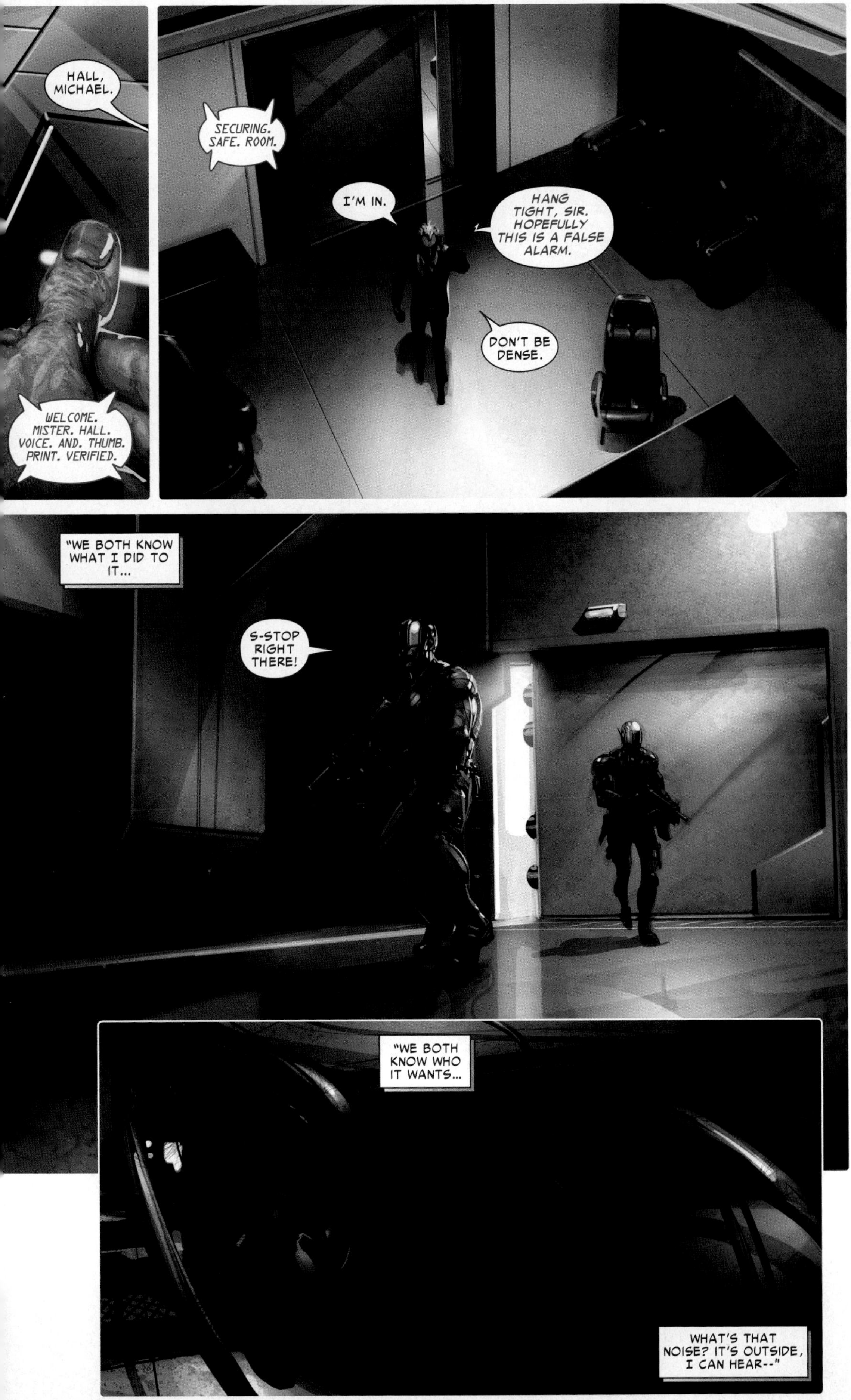
HALL, MICHAEL.
WELCOME. MISTER. HALL. VOICE. AND. THUMB. PRINT. VERIFIED.
SECURING. SAFE. ROOM.
I'M IN.
HANG TIGHT, SIR. HOPEFULLY THIS IS A FALSE ALARM.
DON'T BE DENSE.
"WE BOTH KNOW WHAT I DID TO IT...
S-STOP RIGHT THERE!
"WE BOTH KNOW WHO IT WANTS...
WHAT'S THAT NOISE? IT'S OUTSIDE, I CAN HEAR--"

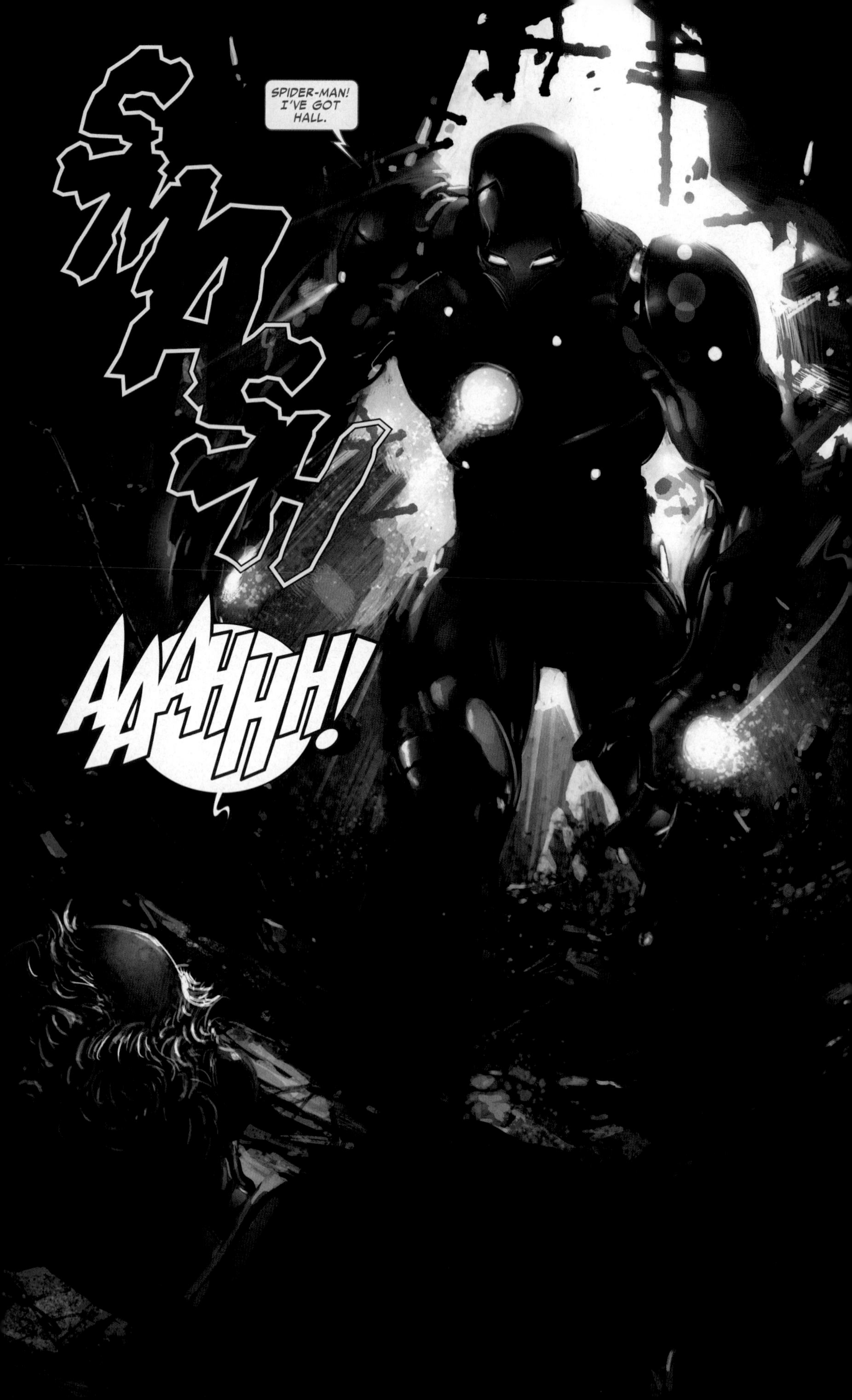
SMASH!
SPIDER-MAN! I'VE GOT HALL.
AAAHHH!

WHA... WHAT?!

THE CARNAGE SYMBIOTE IS AFTER YOU. WE'VE GOT TO MOVE.

GOOD CALL, BY THE WAY, PULLING MY *SCARIEST* BAD GUY OUT OF SPACE AND LOCKING IT IN A SWEATSHOP. IT'S ON ITS WAY TO SAY THANKS.

H-HE'S NOT COMING FOR ME...THAT IS...

I'M NOT THE ONE HE WANTS.

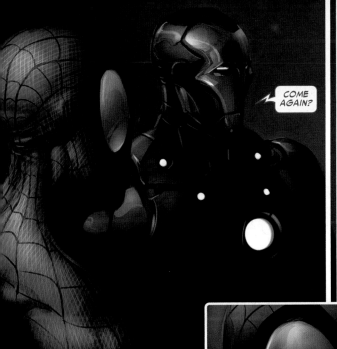

COME AGAIN?

W-WE COULDN'T JUST LET HIM D-DIE--

I'M NOT AN ANIMAL.

OH GOD, HALL...WHAT DID YOU DO?

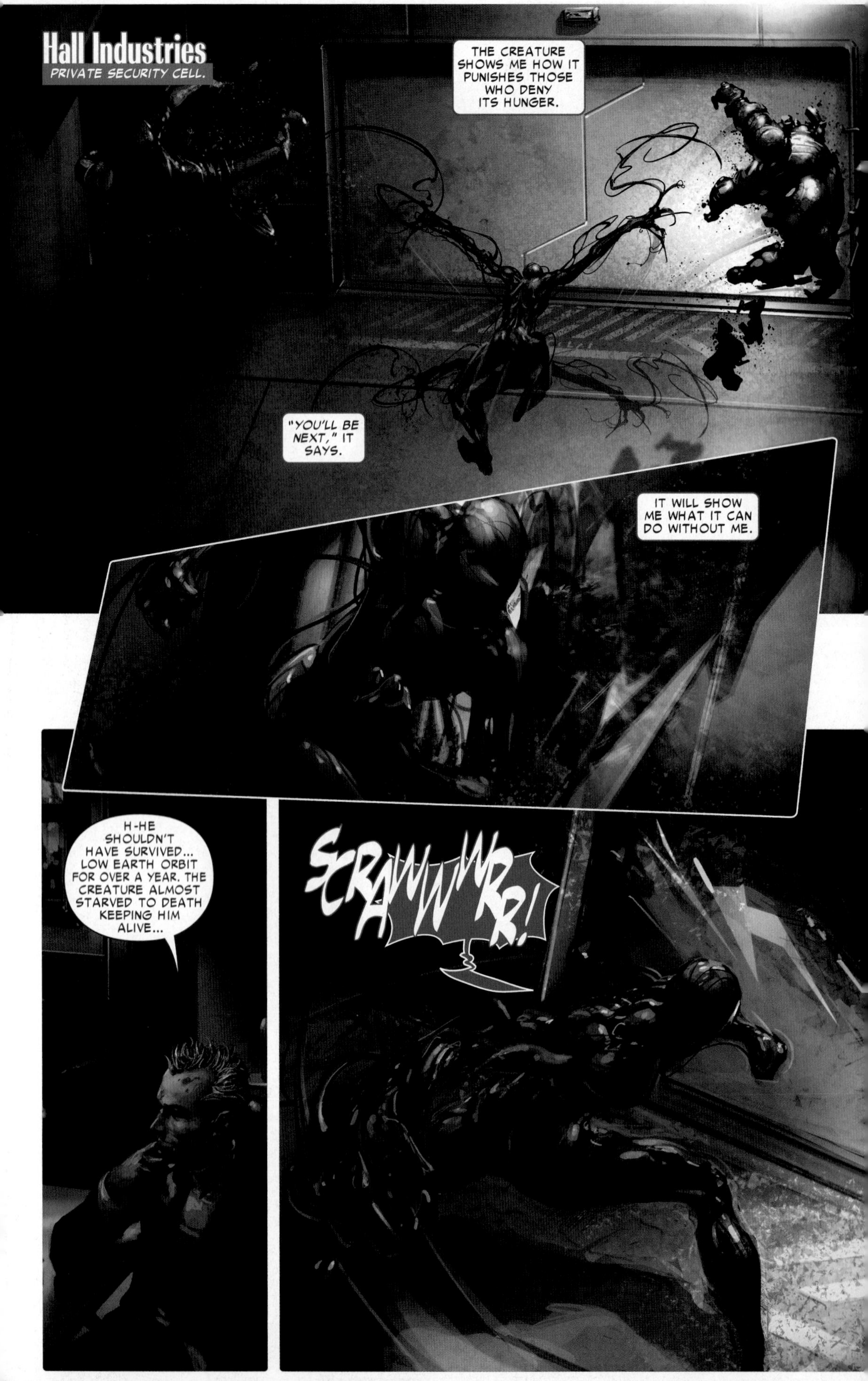
Hall Industries
PRIVATE SECURITY CELL.
THE CREATURE SHOWS ME HOW IT PUNISHES THOSE WHO DENY ITS HUNGER.
"YOU'LL BE NEXT," IT SAYS.
IT WILL SHOW ME WHAT IT CAN DO WITHOUT ME.
H-HE SHOULDN'T HAVE SURVIVED... LOW EARTH ORBIT FOR OVER A YEAR. THE CREATURE ALMOST STARVED TO DEATH KEEPING HIM ALIVE...
SCRAWWWRR!

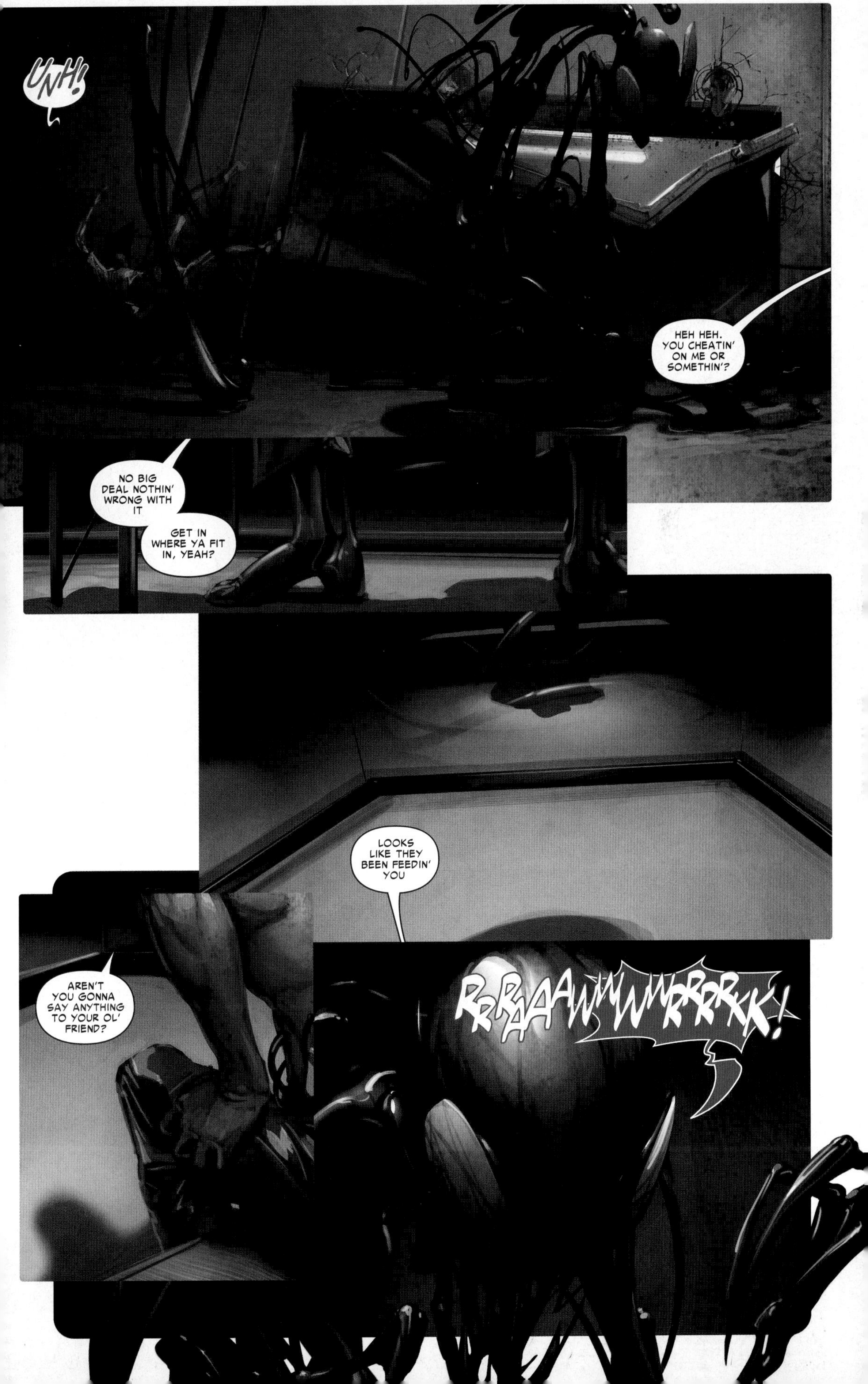
UNH!
HEH HEH. YOU CHEATIN' ON ME OR SOMETHIN'?
NO BIG DEAL NOTHIN' WRONG WITH IT
GET IN WHERE YA FIT IN, YEAH?
LOOKS LIKE THEY BEEN FEEDIN' YOU
AREN'T YOU GONNA SAY ANYTHING TO YOUR OL' FRIEND?
RRRAAAWWWWRRRRKK!

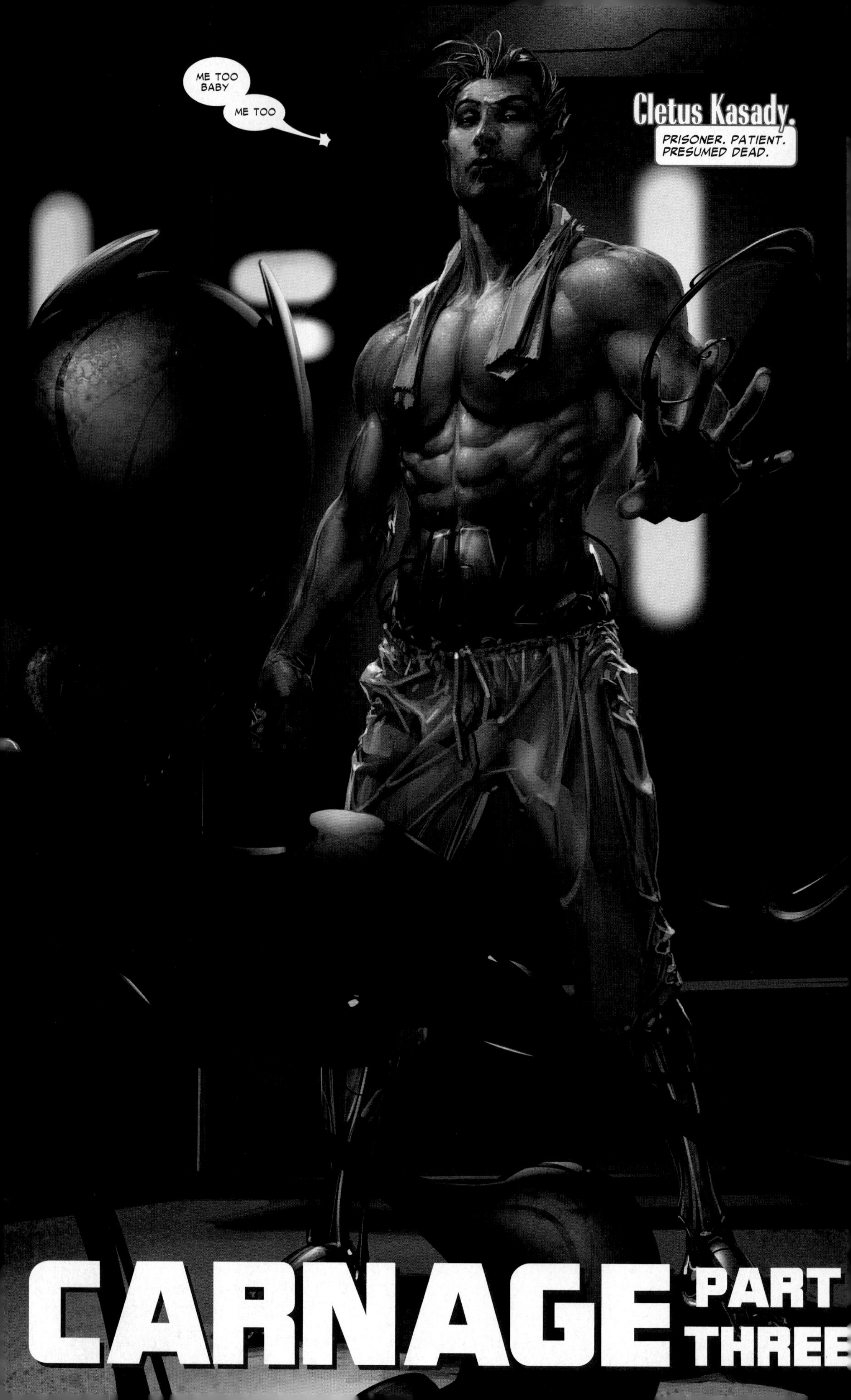
ME TOO BABY
ME TOO
Cletus Kasady.
PRISONER. PATIENT. PRESUMED DEAD.
CARNAGE PART THREE

Kasady, now with prosthetic legs given to him by Hall, re-bonded with the symbiote and escaped with the doppelganger. However, the Carnage symbiote left its offspring inside Dr. Nieves! She eventually tamed this new symbiote and took the name Scorn. Meanwhile, the Venom symbiote passed from Eddie Brock to Spider-Man's old friend Corporal Eugene "Flash" Thompson, who became the hero known as Agent Venom...

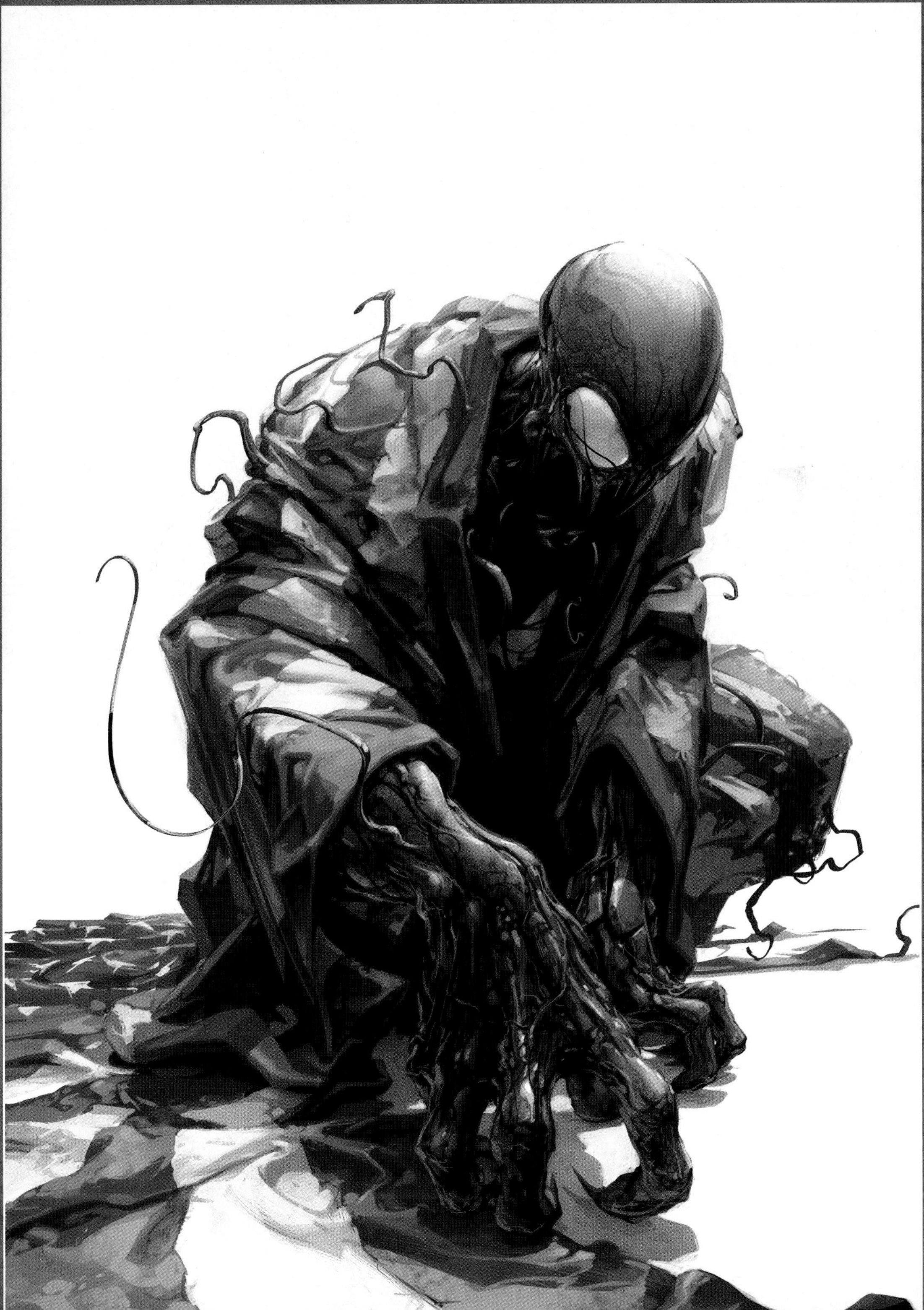

CARNAGE, U.S.A. #1

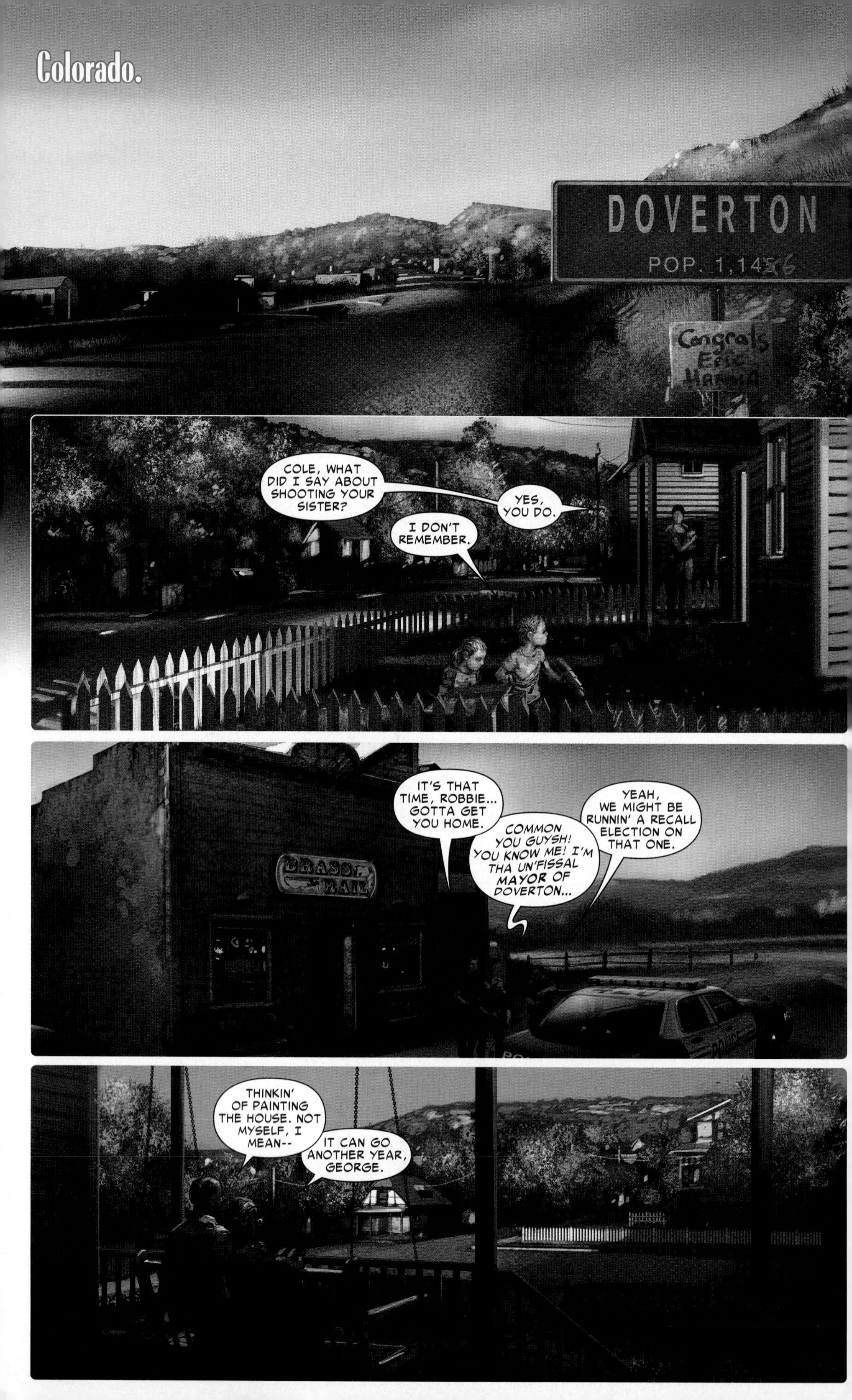
Colorado.
DOVERTON
POP. 1,1456
Congrats Eric Hanna
COLE, WHAT DID I SAY ABOUT SHOOTING YOUR SISTER?
I DON'T REMEMBER.
YES, YOU DO.
IT'S THAT TIME, ROBBIE... GOTTA GET YOU HOME.
COMMON YOU GUYSH! YOU KNOW ME! I'M THA UN'FISSAL MAYOR OF DOVERTON...
YEAH, WE MIGHT BE RUNNIN' A RECALL ELECTION ON THAT ONE.
BRASS RAIL
THINKIN' OF PAINTING THE HOUSE. NOT MYSELF, I MEAN--
IT CAN GO ANOTHER YEAR, GEORGE.

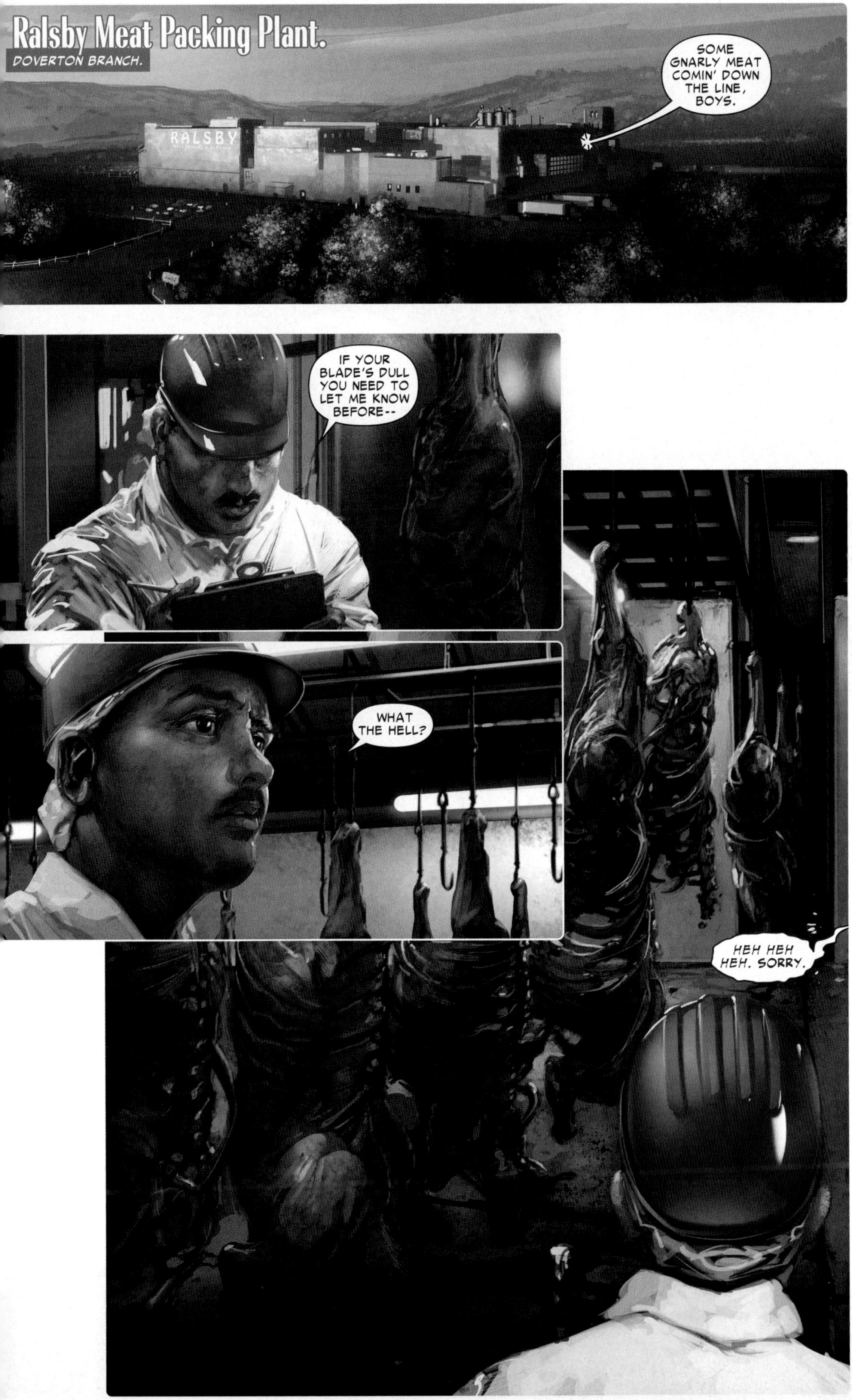
Ralsby Meat Packing Plant.
DOVERTON BRANCH.
RALSBY
SOME GNARLY MEAT COMIN' DOWN THE LINE, BOYS.
IF YOUR BLADE'S DULL YOU NEED TO LET ME KNOW BEFORE--
WHAT THE HELL?
HEH HEH HEH. SORRY.

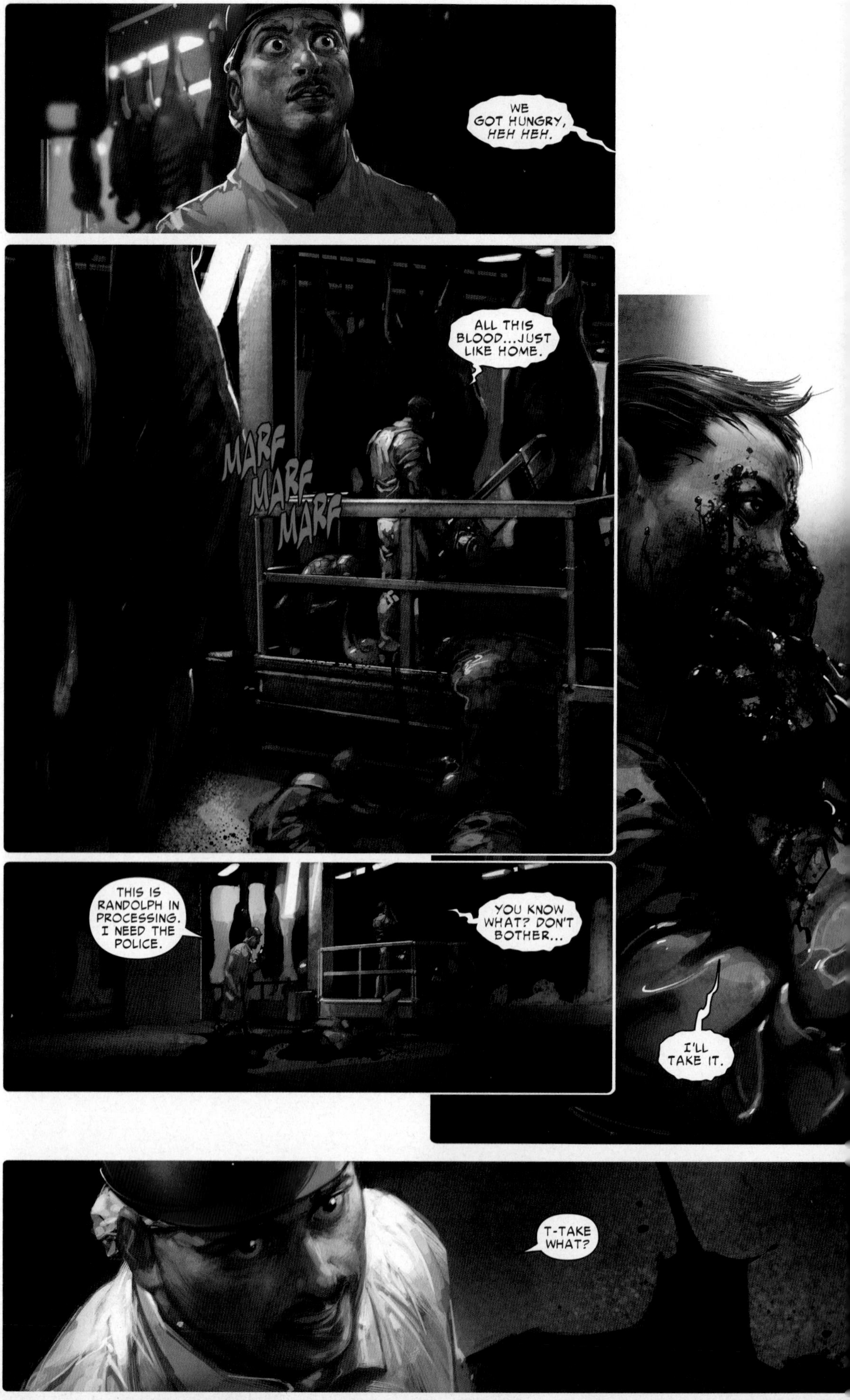
WE GOT HUNGRY, HEH HEH.
ALL THIS BLOOD...JUST LIKE HOME.
MARF MARF MARF
THIS IS RANDOLPH IN PROCESSING. I NEED THE POLICE.
YOU KNOW WHAT? DON'T BOTHER...
I'LL TAKE IT.
T-TAKE WHAT?

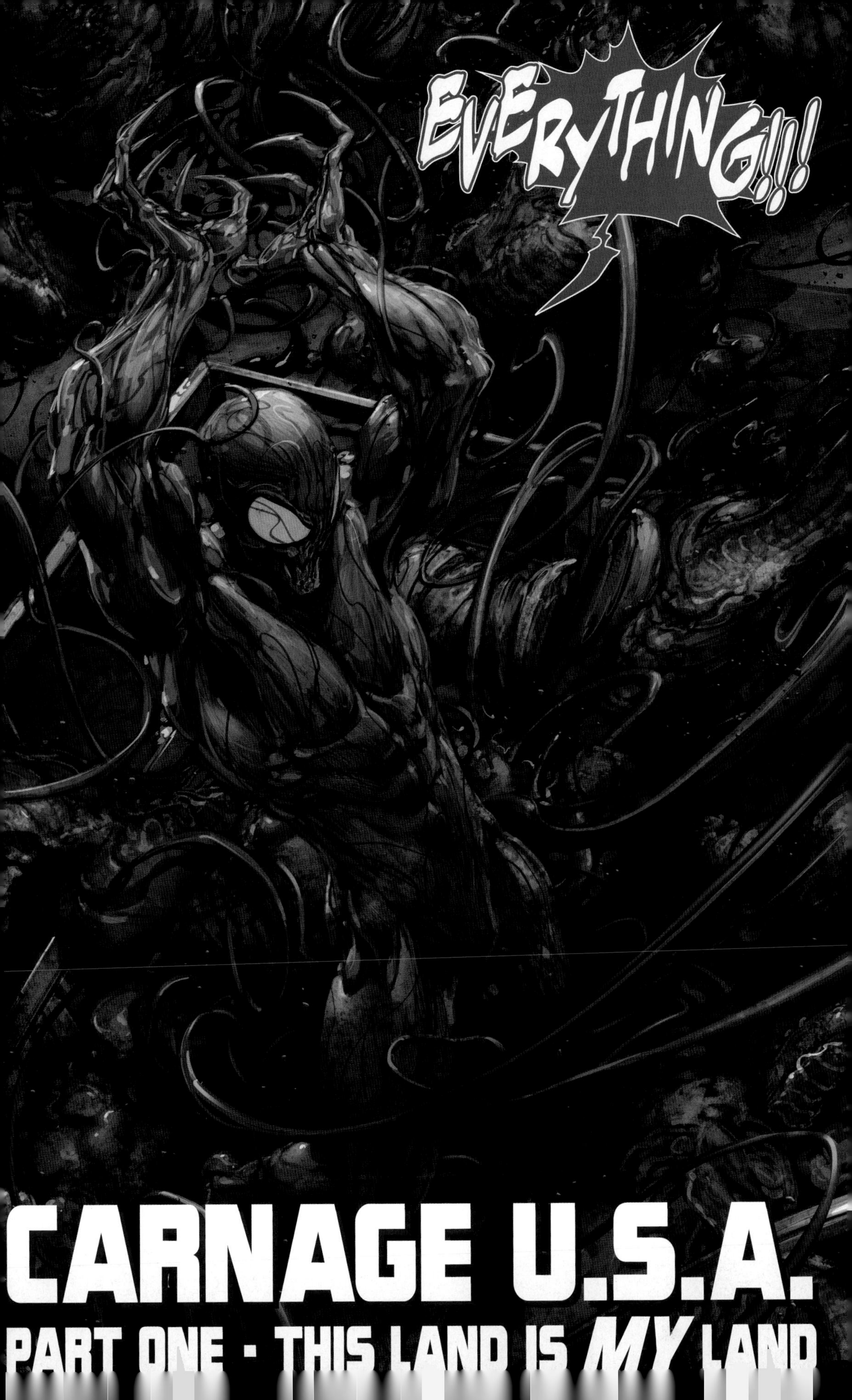
EVERYTHING!!!
CARNAGE U.S.A.
PART ONE - THIS LAND IS MY LAND

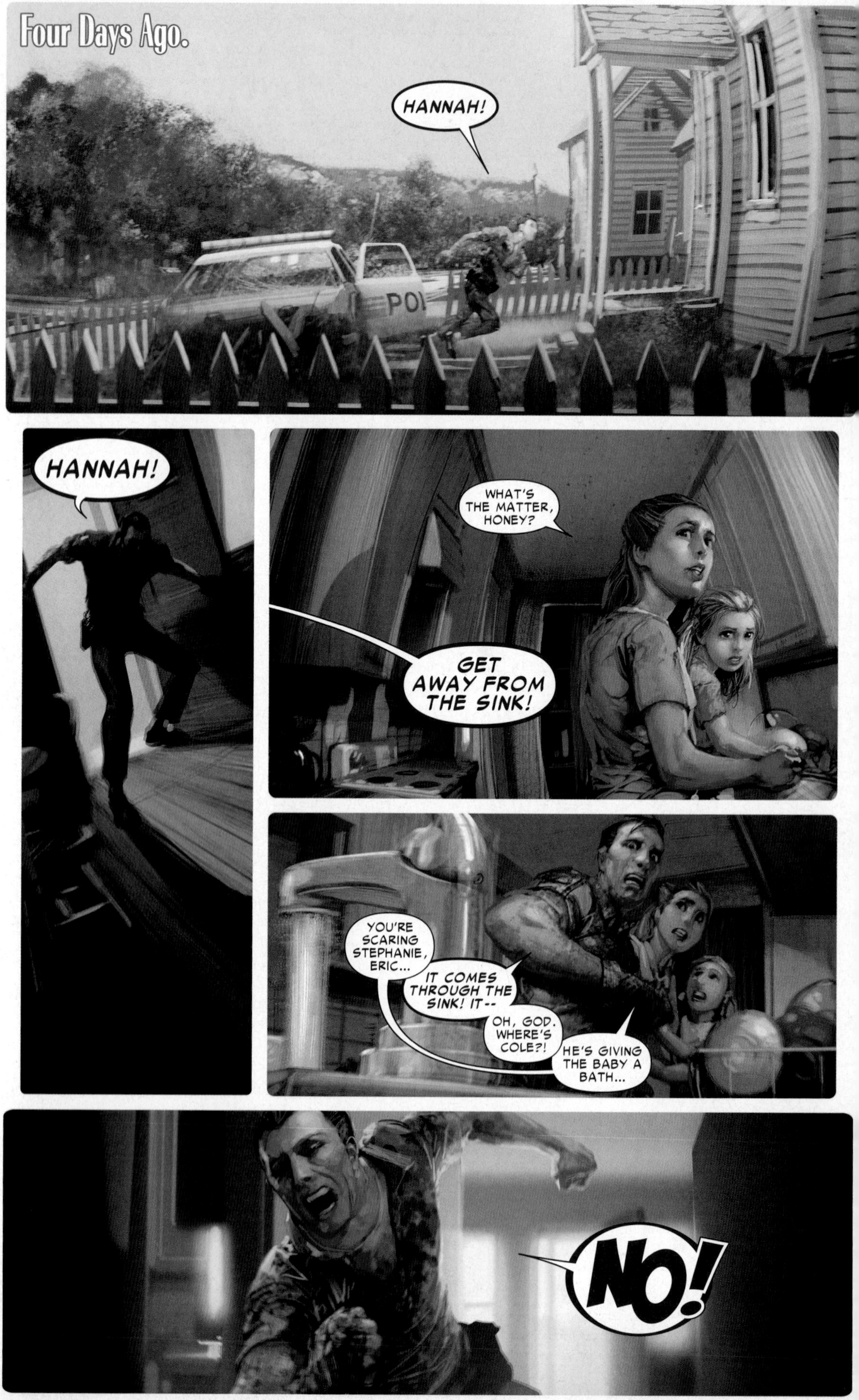
Four Days Ago.
HANNAH!
HANNAH!
WHAT'S THE MATTER, HONEY?
GET AWAY FROM THE SINK!
YOU'RE SCARING STEPHANIE, ERIC...
IT COMES THROUGH THE SINK! IT--
OH, GOD. WHERE'S COLE?!
HE'S GIVING THE BABY A BATH...
NO!

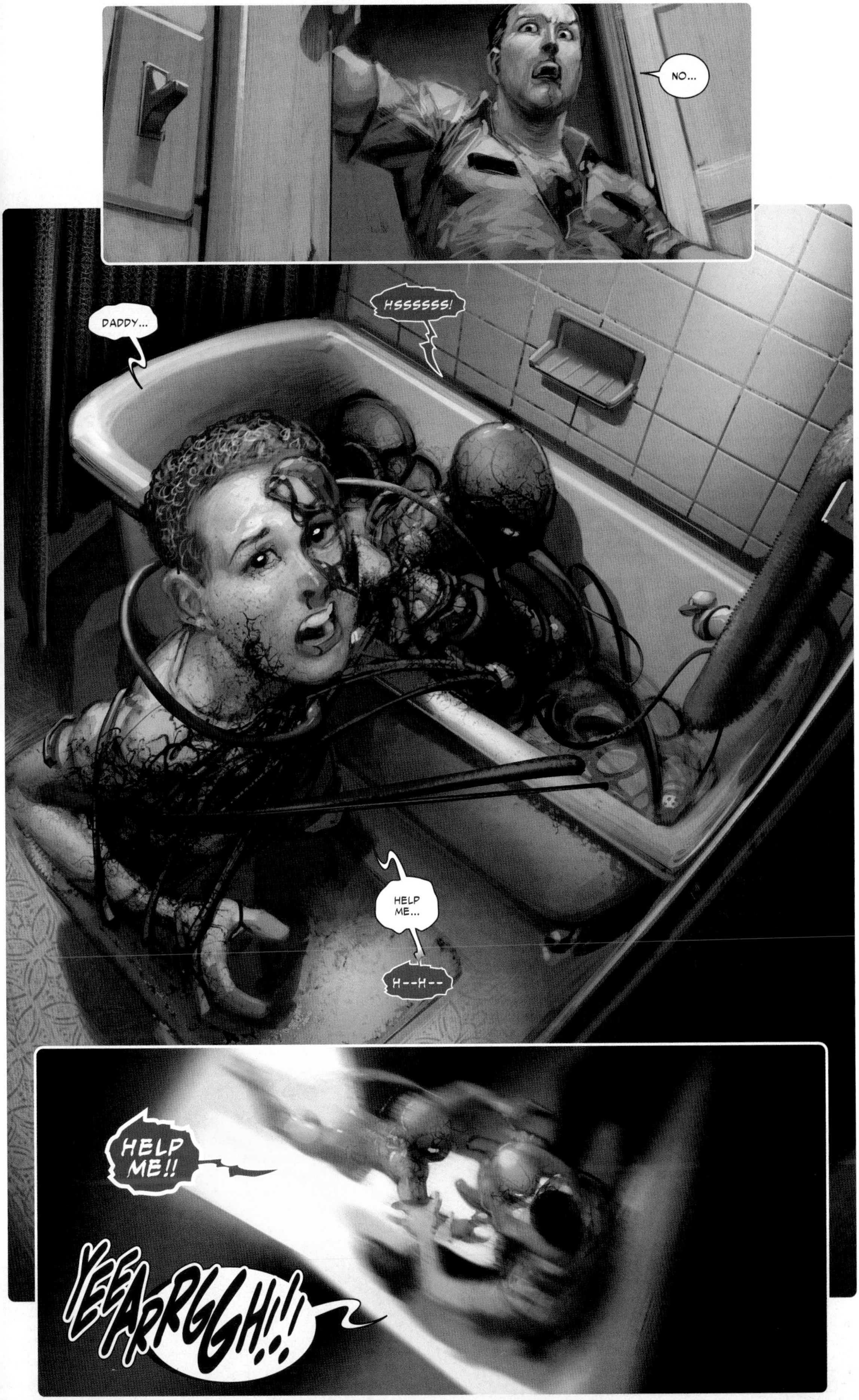
NO...
DADDY...
HSSSSSS!
HELP ME...
H--H--
HELP ME!!
YEEARRGGH!!!

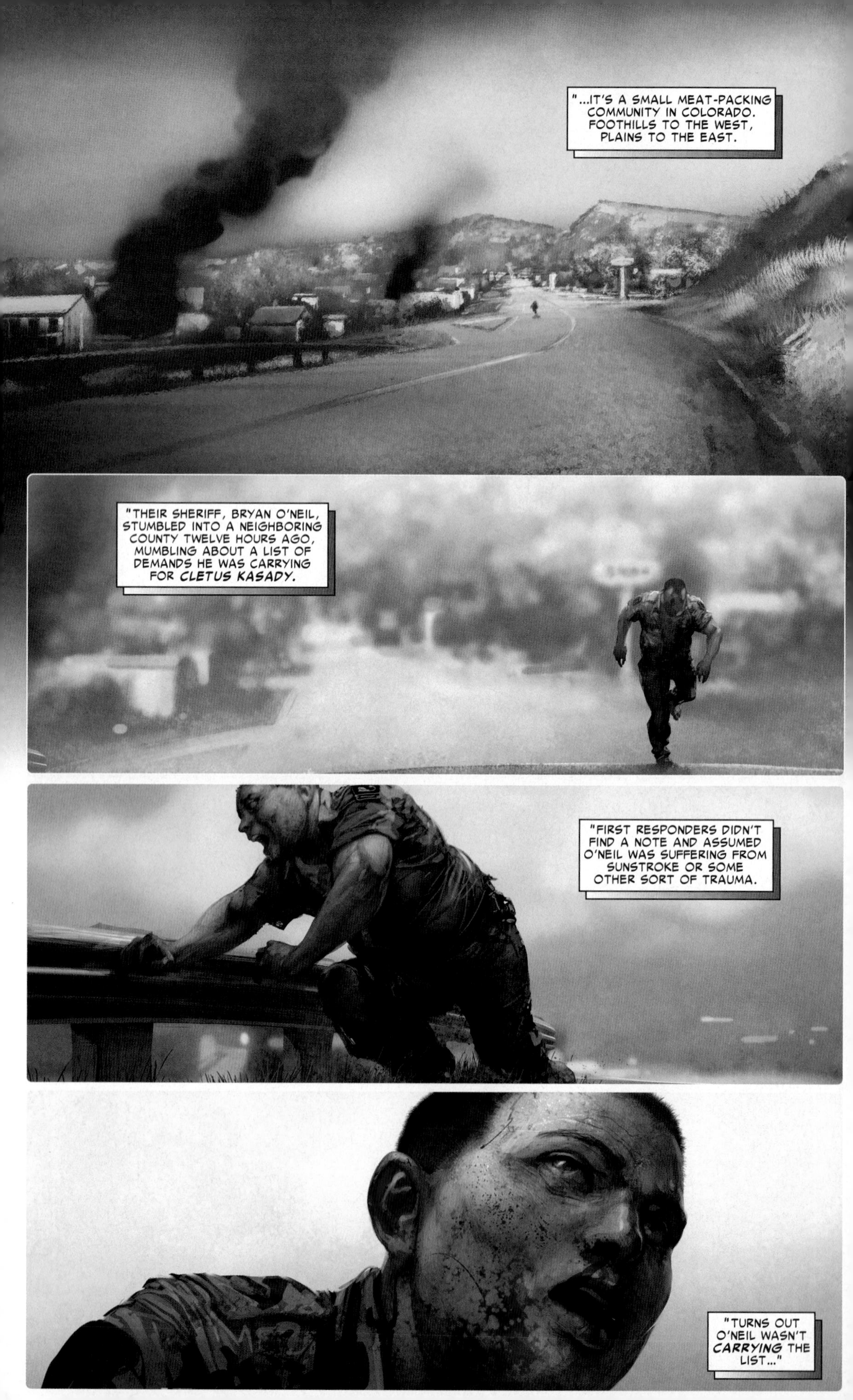
"...IT'S A SMALL MEAT-PACKING COMMUNITY IN COLORADO. FOOTHILLS TO THE WEST, PLAINS TO THE EAST.
"THEIR SHERIFF, BRYAN O'NEIL, STUMBLED INTO A NEIGHBORING COUNTY TWELVE HOURS AGO, MUMBLING ABOUT A LIST OF DEMANDS HE WAS CARRYING FOR CLETUS KASADY.
"FIRST RESPONDERS DIDN'T FIND A NOTE AND ASSUMED O'NEIL WAS SUFFERING FROM SUNSTROKE OR SOME OTHER SORT OF TRAUMA.
"TURNS OUT O'NEIL WASN'T CARRYING THE LIST..."

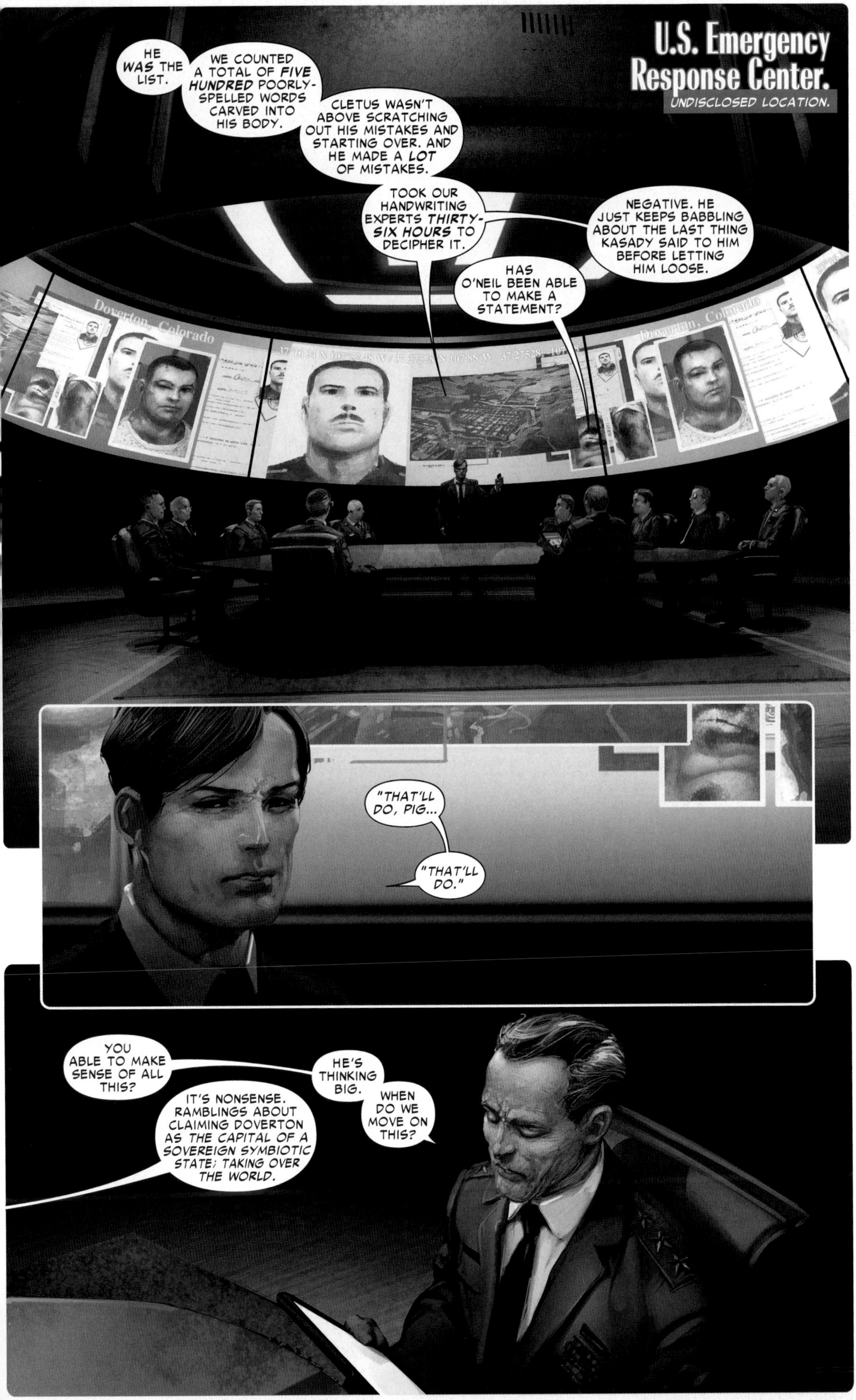
U.S. Emergency Response Center.
UNDISCLOSED LOCATION.
HE WAS THE LIST.
WE COUNTED A TOTAL OF FIVE HUNDRED POORLY-SPELLED WORDS CARVED INTO HIS BODY.
CLETUS WASN'T ABOVE SCRATCHING OUT HIS MISTAKES AND STARTING OVER. AND HE MADE A LOT OF MISTAKES.
TOOK OUR HANDWRITING EXPERTS THIRTY-SIX HOURS TO DECIPHER IT.
HAS O'NEIL BEEN ABLE TO MAKE A STATEMENT?
NEGATIVE. HE JUST KEEPS BABBLING ABOUT THE LAST THING KASADY SAID TO HIM BEFORE LETTING HIM LOOSE.
Doverton, Colorado
"THAT'LL DO, PIG...
"THAT'LL DO."
YOU ABLE TO MAKE SENSE OF ALL THIS?
IT'S NONSENSE. RAMBLINGS ABOUT CLAIMING DOVERTON AS THE CAPITAL OF A SOVEREIGN SYMBIOTIC STATE; TAKING OVER THE WORLD.
HE'S THINKING BIG.
WHEN DO WE MOVE ON THIS?

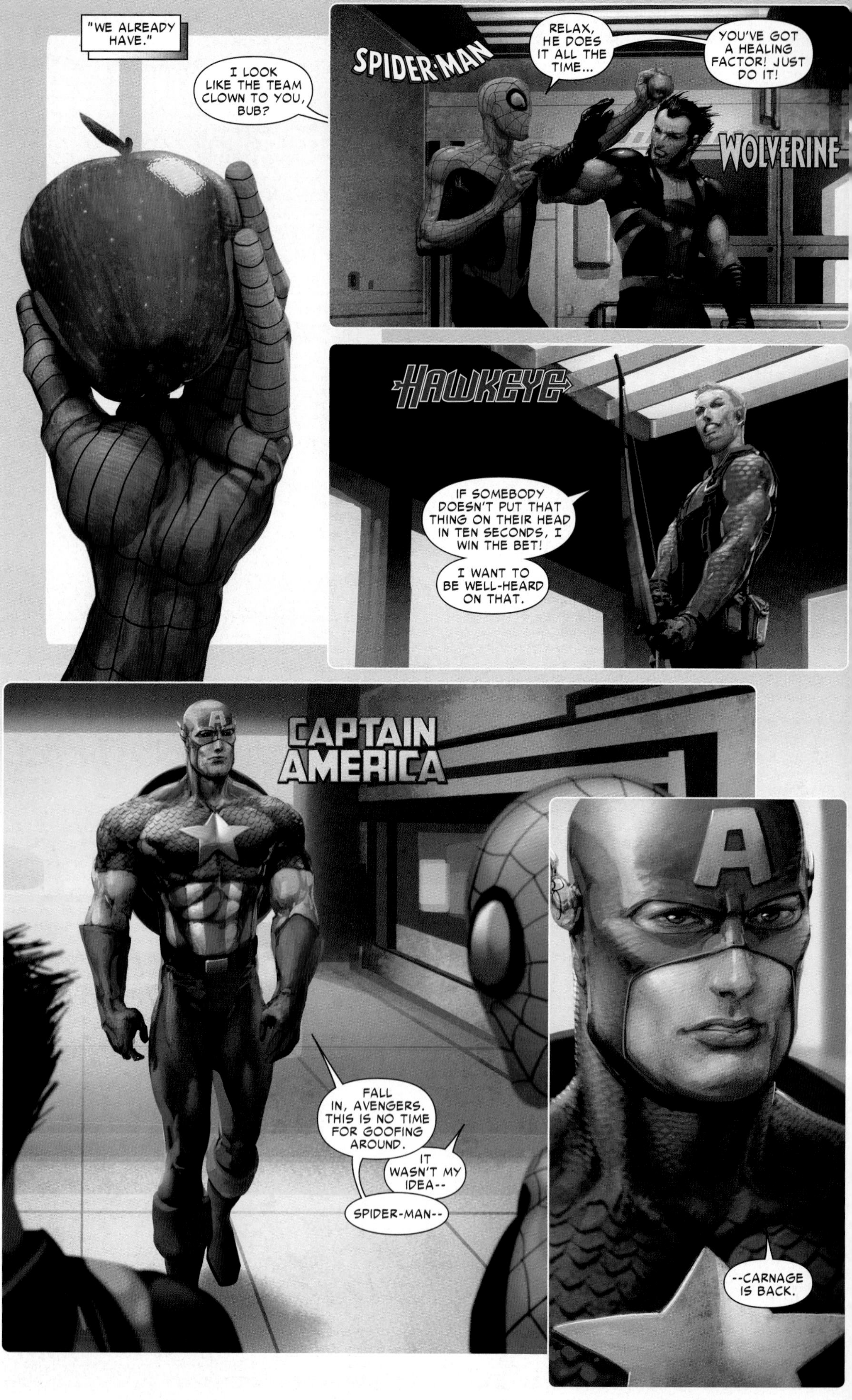
"WE ALREADY HAVE."
I LOOK LIKE THE TEAM CLOWN TO YOU, BUB?
SPIDER-MAN
RELAX, HE DOES IT ALL THE TIME...
YOU'VE GOT A HEALING FACTOR! JUST DO IT!
WOLVERINE
HAWKEYE
IF SOMEBODY DOESN'T PUT THAT THING ON THEIR HEAD IN TEN SECONDS, I WIN THE BET!
I WANT TO BE WELL-HEARD ON THAT.
CAPTAIN AMERICA
FALL IN, AVENGERS. THIS IS NO TIME FOR GOOFING AROUND.
IT WASN'T MY IDEA--
SPIDER-MAN--
--CARNAGE IS BACK.

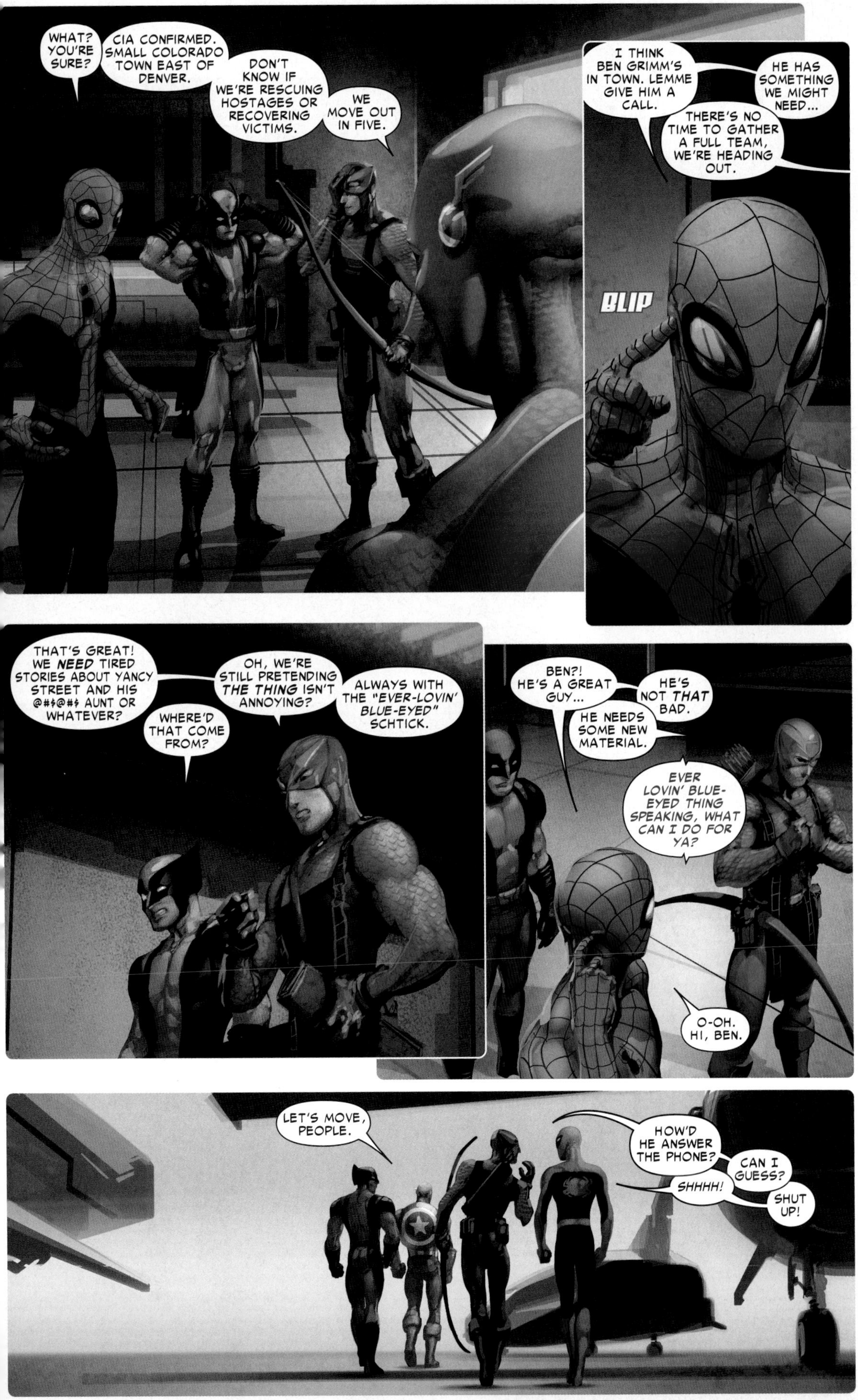
WHAT? YOU'RE SURE?
CIA CONFIRMED. SMALL COLORADO TOWN EAST OF DENVER.
DON'T KNOW IF WE'RE RESCUING HOSTAGES OR RECOVERING VICTIMS.
WE MOVE OUT IN FIVE.
I THINK BEN GRIMM'S IN TOWN. LEMME GIVE HIM A CALL.
HE HAS SOMETHING WE MIGHT NEED...
THERE'S NO TIME TO GATHER A FULL TEAM, WE'RE HEADING OUT.
BLIP
THAT'S GREAT! WE NEED TIRED STORIES ABOUT YANCY STREET AND HIS @#$@#$ AUNT OR WHATEVER?
WHERE'D THAT COME FROM?
OH, WE'RE STILL PRETENDING THE THING ISN'T ANNOYING?
ALWAYS WITH THE "EVER-LOVIN' BLUE-EYED" SCHTICK.
BEN?! HE'S A GREAT GUY...
HE'S NOT THAT BAD.
HE NEEDS SOME NEW MATERIAL.
EVER LOVIN' BLUE-EYED THING SPEAKING, WHAT CAN I DO FOR YA?
O-OH. HI, BEN.
LET'S MOVE, PEOPLE.
HOW'D HE ANSWER THE PHONE?
CAN I GUESS?
SHHHH!
SHUT UP!

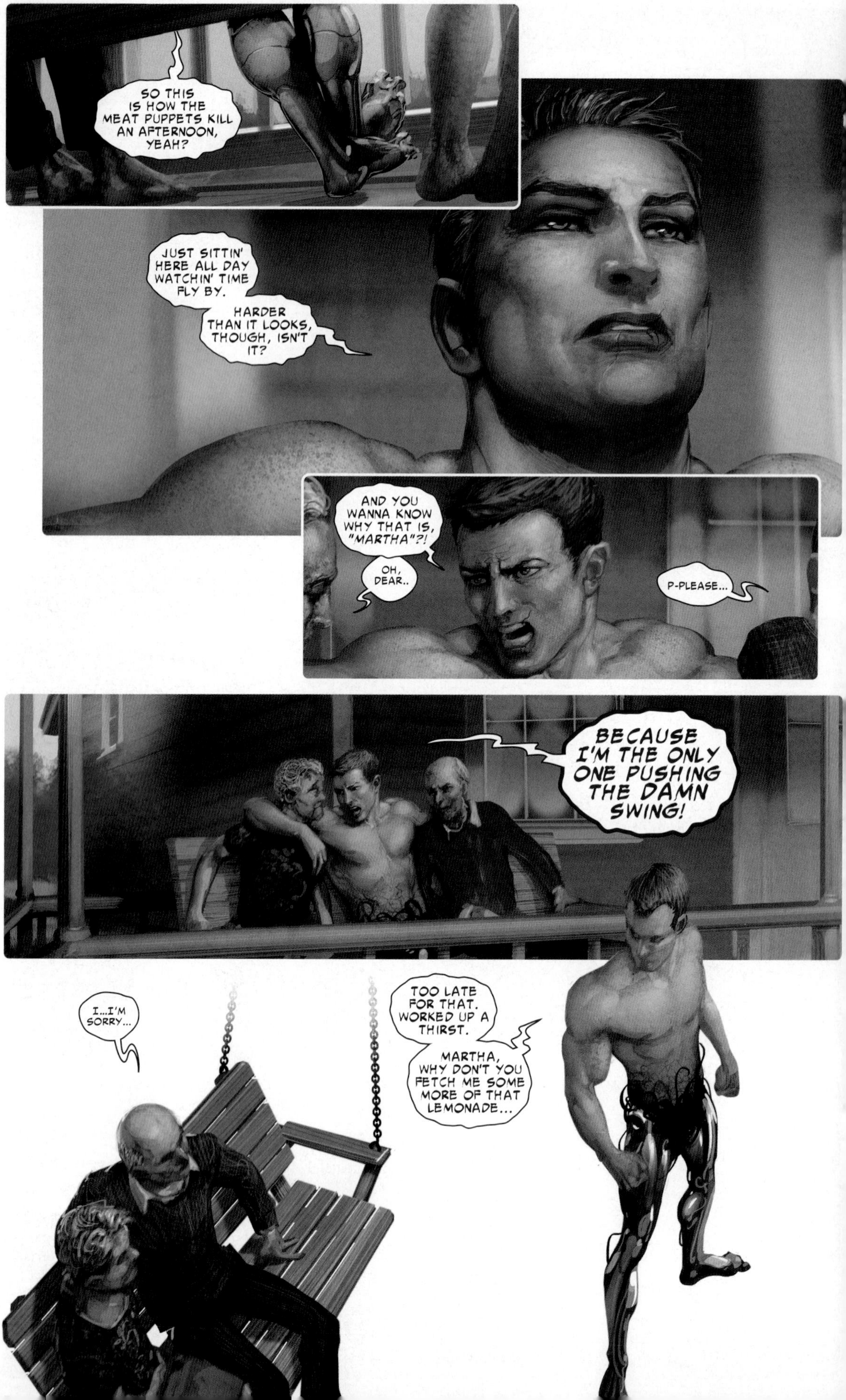

SO THIS IS HOW THE MEAT PUPPETS KILL AN AFTERNOON, YEAH?
JUST SITTIN' HERE ALL DAY WATCHIN' TIME FLY BY.
HARDER THAN IT LOOKS, THOUGH, ISN'T IT?
AND YOU WANNA KNOW WHY THAT IS, "MARTHA"?!
OH, DEAR..
P-PLEASE...
BECAUSE I'M THE ONLY ONE PUSHING THE DAMN SWING!
I...I'M SORRY...
TOO LATE FOR THAT. WORKED UP A THIRST.
MARTHA, WHY DON'T YOU FETCH ME SOME MORE OF THAT LEMONADE...

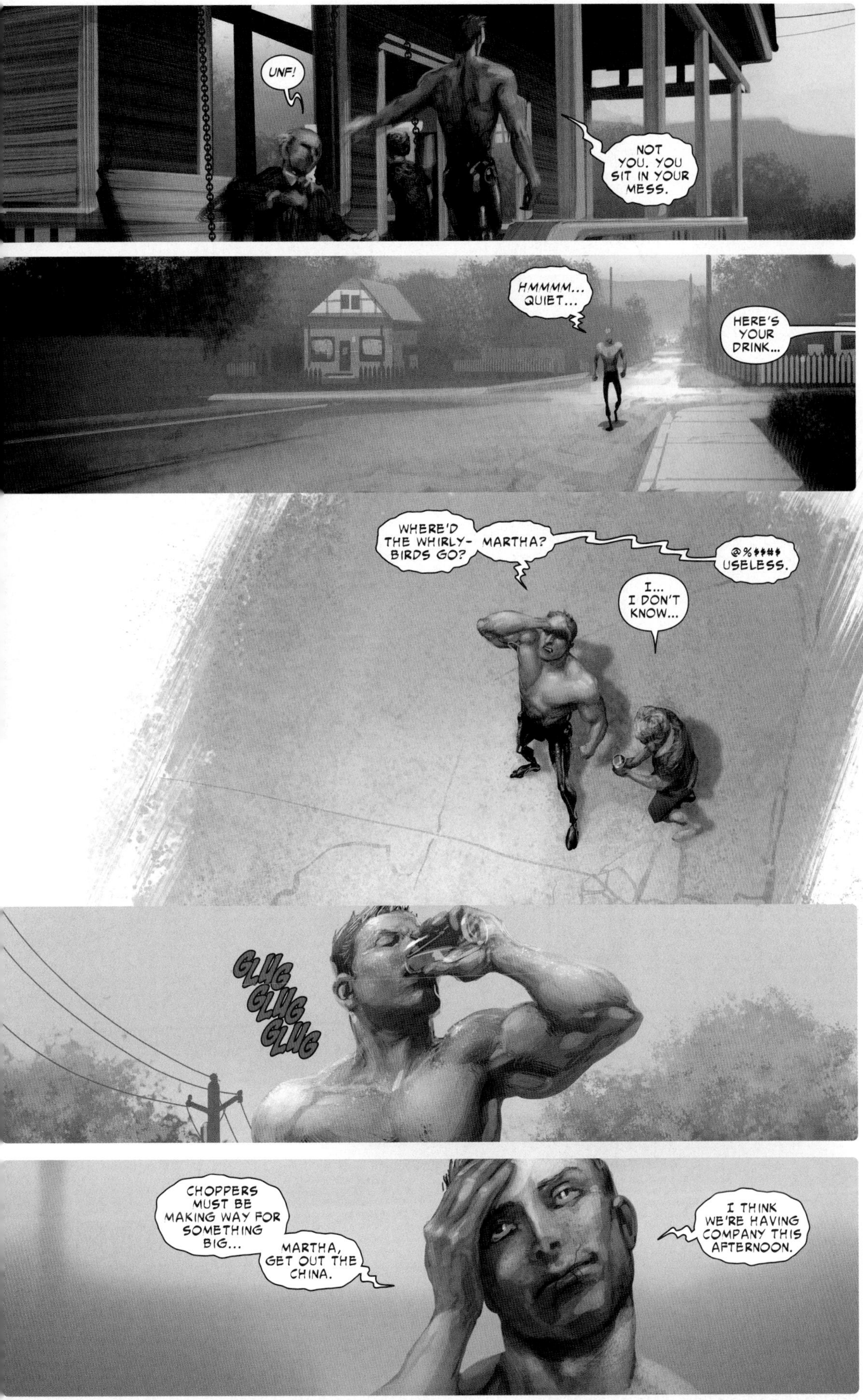
UNF!
NOT YOU. YOU SIT IN YOUR MESS.
HMMMM... QUIET...
HERE'S YOUR DRINK...
WHERE'D THE WHIRLY-BIRDS GO?
MARTHA?
@%$### USELESS.
I... I DON'T KNOW...
GLUG GLUG GLUG
CHOPPERS MUST BE MAKING WAY FOR SOMETHING BIG...
MARTHA, GET OUT THE CHINA.
I THINK WE'RE HAVING COMPANY THIS AFTERNOON.

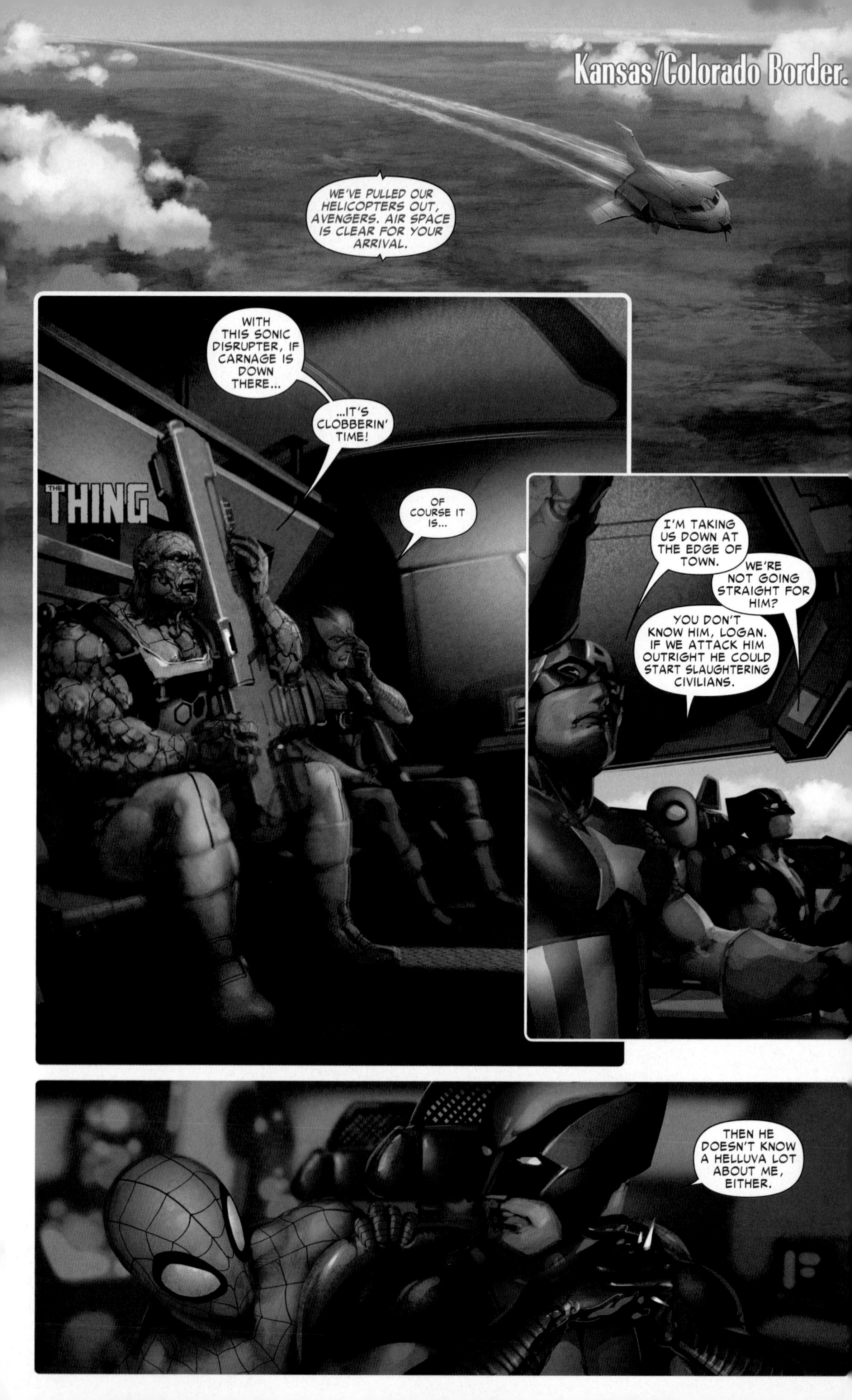
Kansas/Colorado Border.
WE'VE PULLED OUR HELICOPTERS OUT, AVENGERS. AIR SPACE IS CLEAR FOR YOUR ARRIVAL.
WITH THIS SONIC DISRUPTER, IF CARNAGE IS DOWN THERE...
...IT'S CLOBBERIN' TIME!
THE THING
OF COURSE IT IS...
I'M TAKING US DOWN AT THE EDGE OF TOWN.
WE'RE NOT GOING STRAIGHT FOR HIM?
YOU DON'T KNOW HIM, LOGAN. IF WE ATTACK HIM OUTRIGHT HE COULD START SLAUGHTERING CIVILIANS.
THEN HE DOESN'T KNOW A HELLUVA LOT ABOUT ME, EITHER.

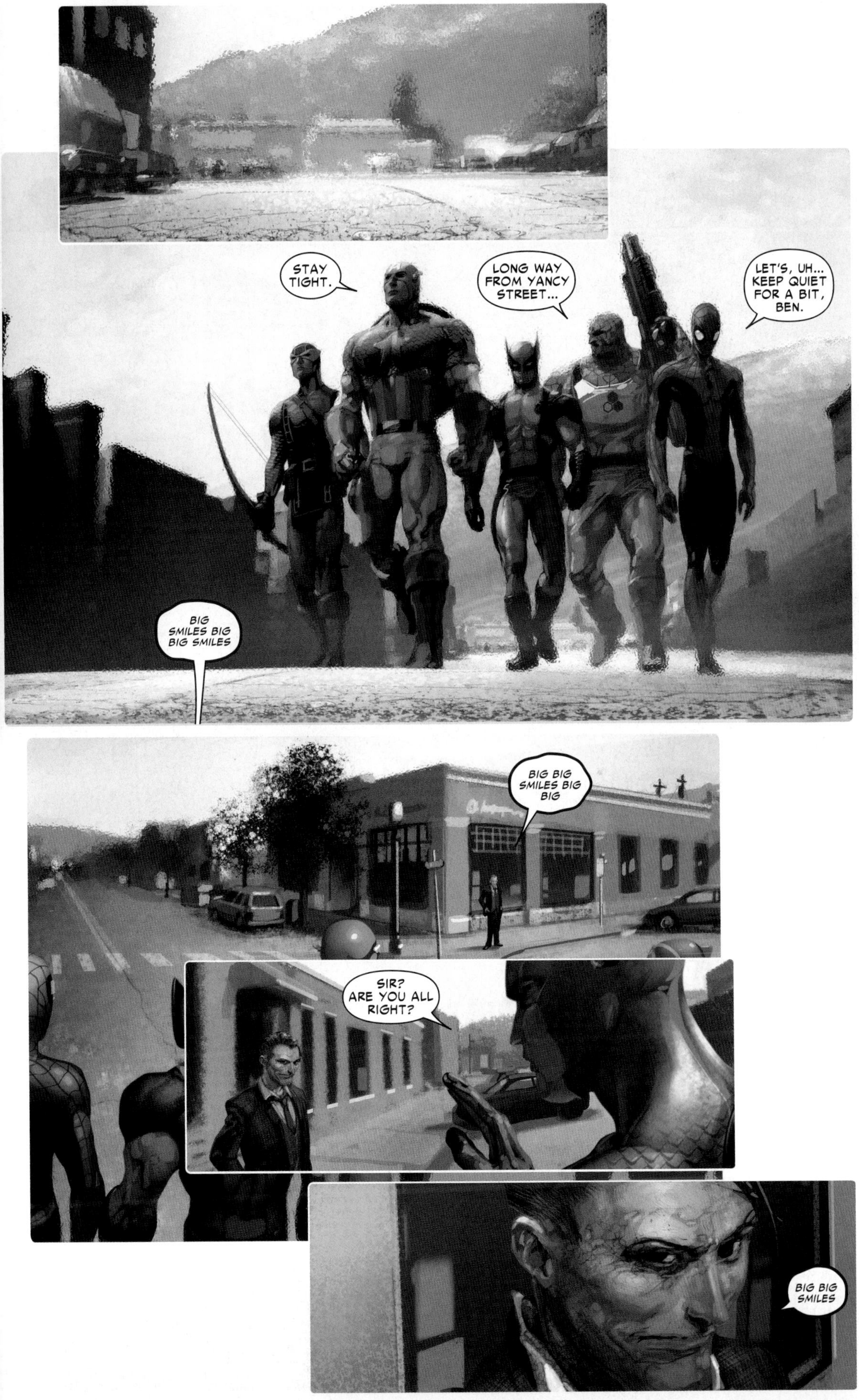
STAY TIGHT.
LONG WAY FROM YANCY STREET...
LET'S, UH... KEEP QUIET FOR A BIT, BEN.
BIG SMILES BIG BIG SMILES
BIG BIG SMILES BIG BIG
SIR? ARE YOU ALL RIGHT?
BIG BIG SMILES

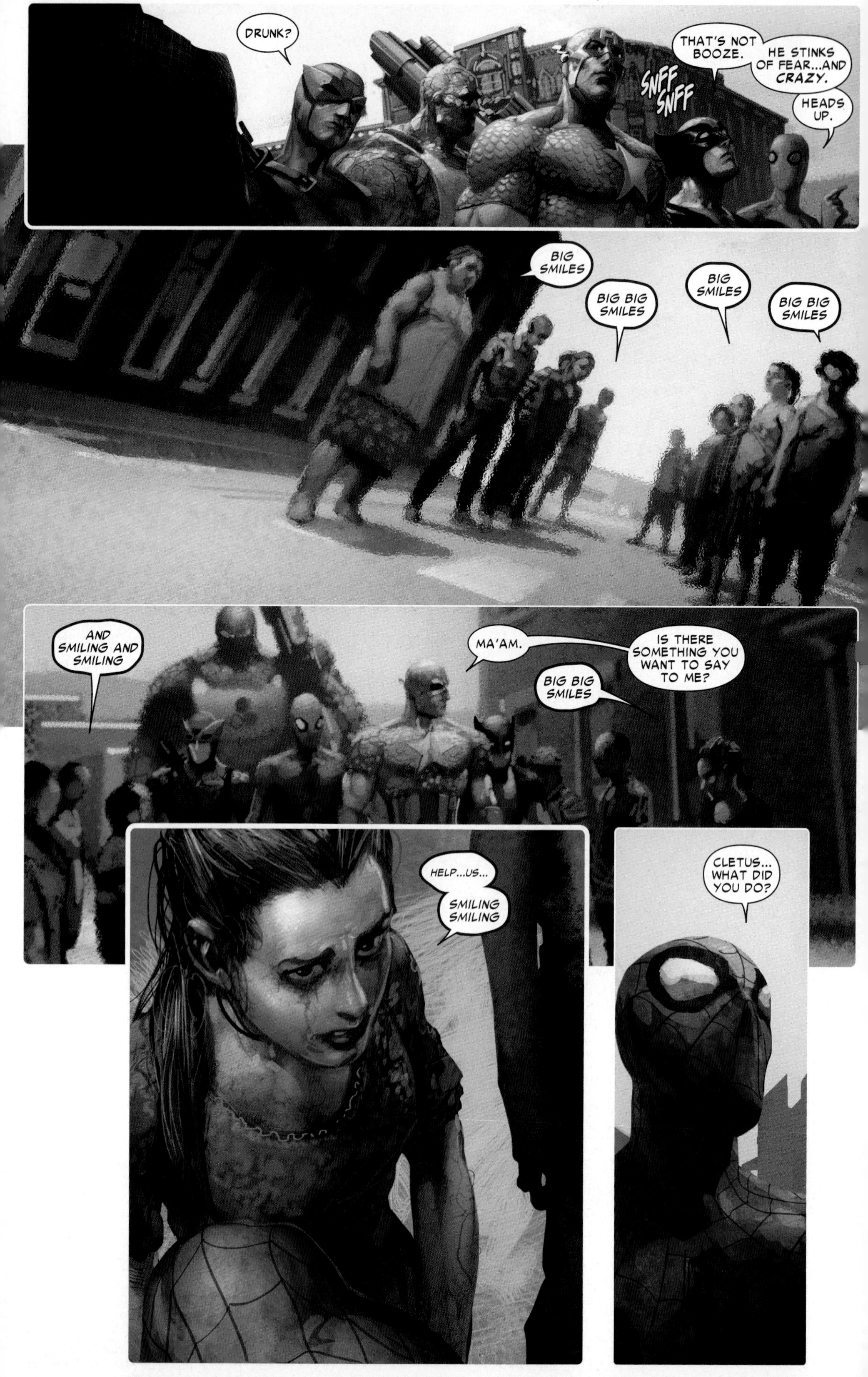

DRUNK?
THAT'S NOT BOOZE.
SNFF SNFF
HE STINKS OF FEAR...AND CRAZY.
HEADS UP.
BIG SMILES
BIG BIG SMILES
BIG SMILES
BIG BIG SMILES
AND SMILING AND SMILING
MA'AM.
IS THERE SOMETHING YOU WANT TO SAY TO ME?
BIG BIG SMILES
HELP...US...
SMILING SMILING
CLETUS... WHAT DID YOU DO?

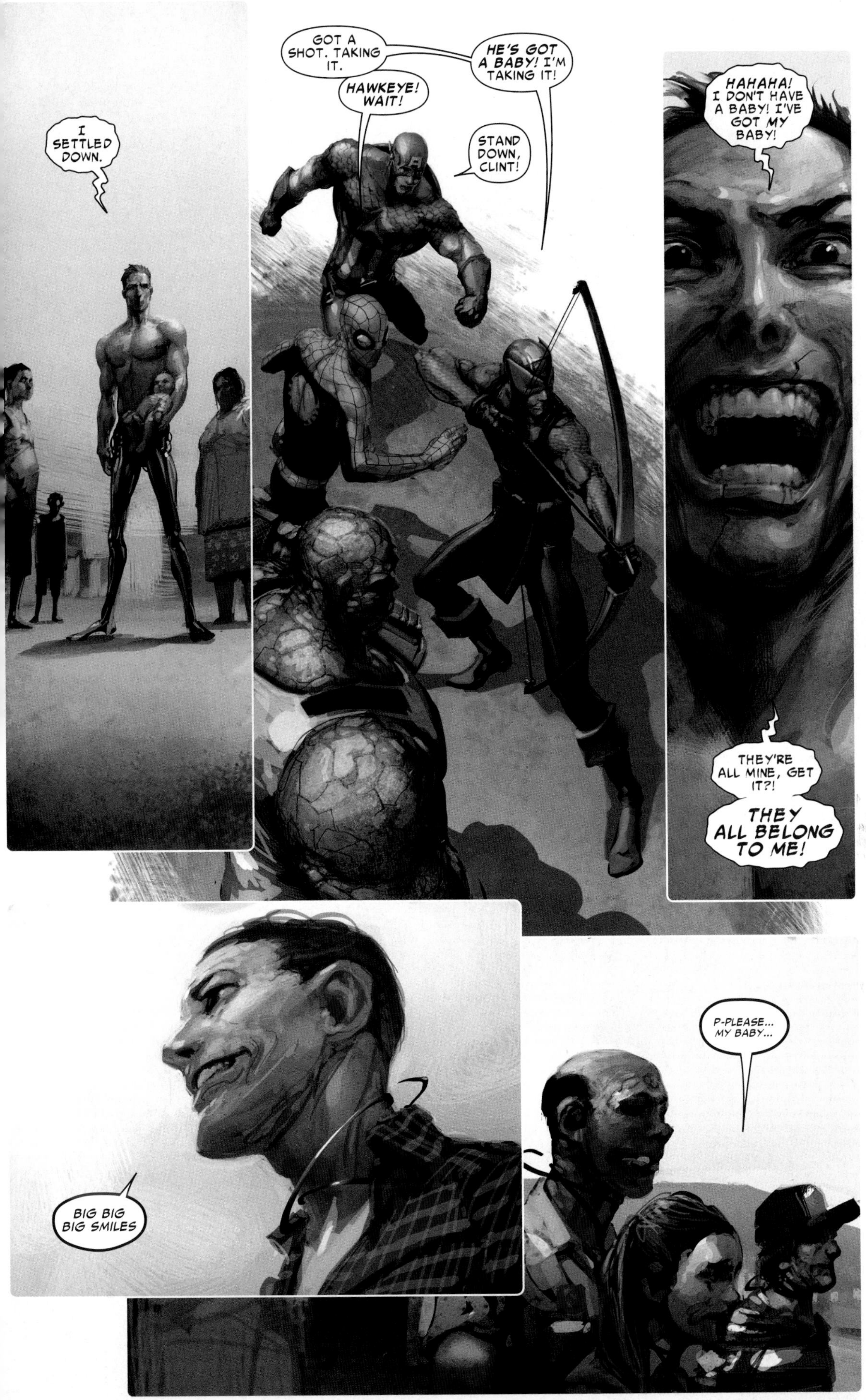
I SETTLED DOWN.
GOT A SHOT. TAKING IT.
HE'S GOT A BABY! I'M TAKING IT!
HAWKEYE! WAIT!
STAND DOWN, CLINT!
HAHAHA! I DON'T HAVE A BABY! I'VE GOT MY BABY!
THEY'RE ALL MINE, GET IT?!
THEY ALL BELONG TO ME!
BIG BIG BIG SMILES
P-PLEASE... MY BABY...

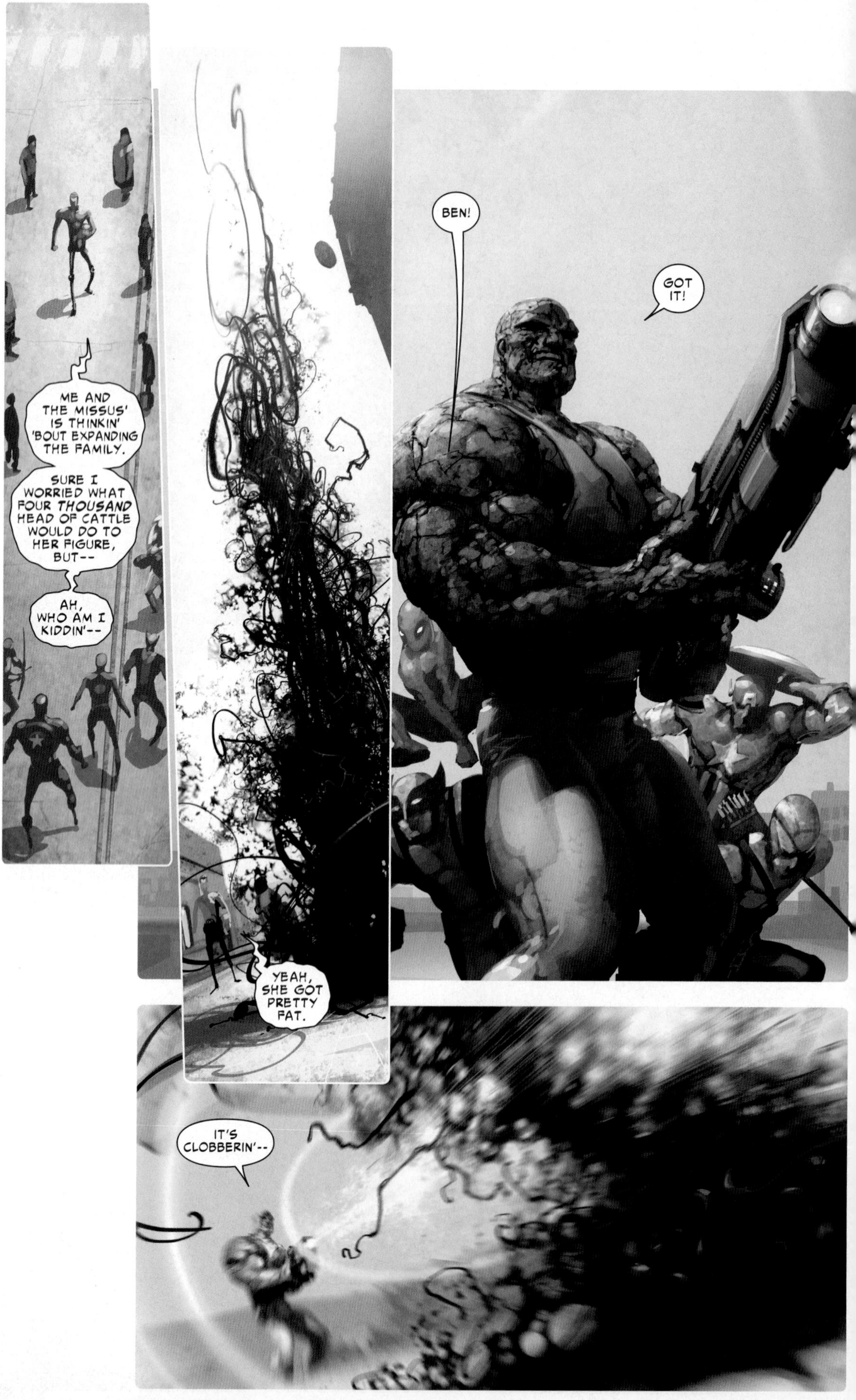

ME AND THE MISSUS' IS THINKIN' 'BOUT EXPANDING THE FAMILY.
SURE I WORRIED WHAT FOUR *THOUSAND* HEAD OF CATTLE WOULD DO TO HER FIGURE, BUT--
AH, WHO AM I KIDDIN'--
YEAH, SHE GOT PRETTY FAT.
BEN!
GOT IT!
IT'S CLOBBERIN'--

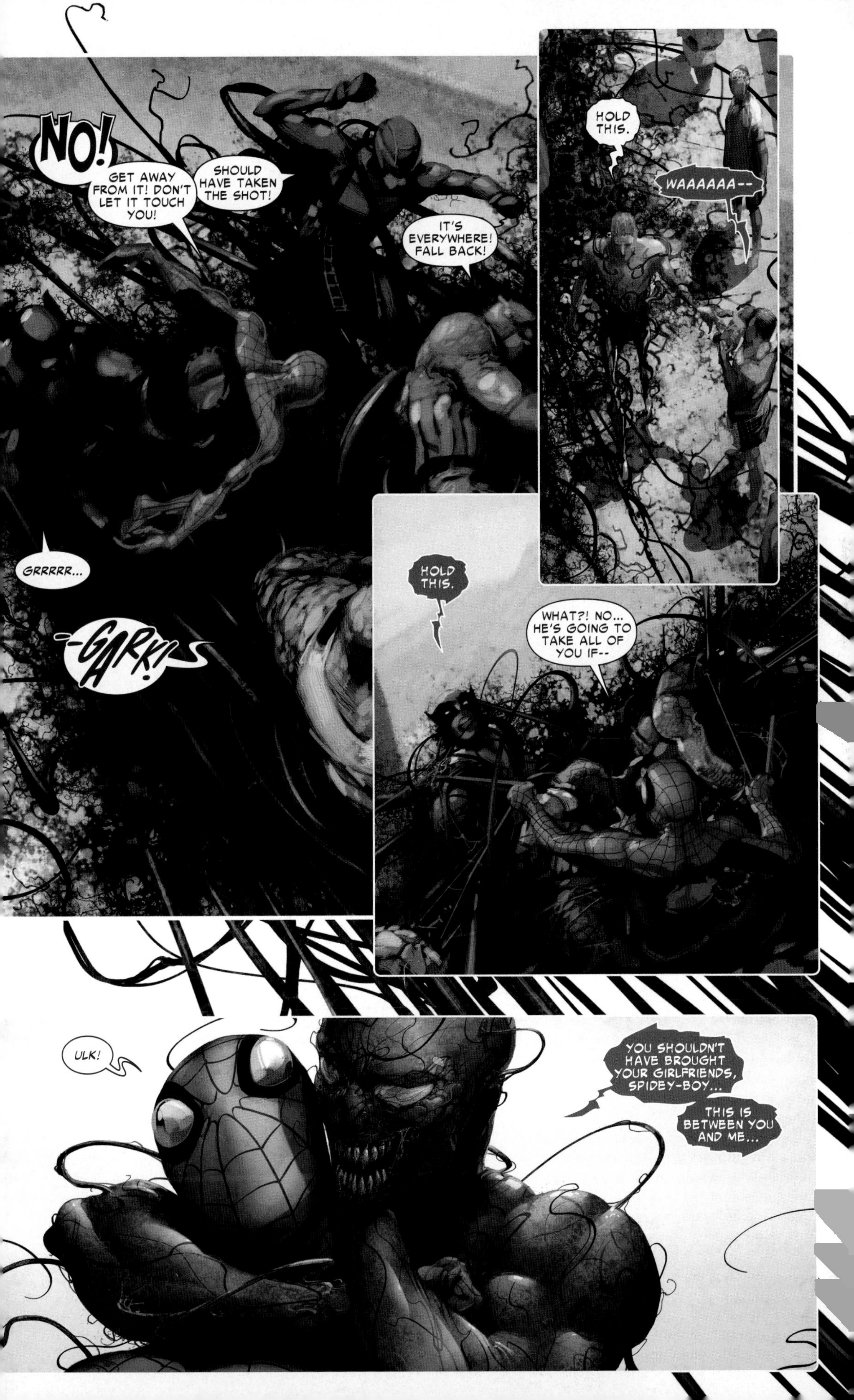
NO!
GET AWAY FROM IT! DON'T LET IT TOUCH YOU!
SHOULD HAVE TAKEN THE SHOT!
IT'S EVERYWHERE! FALL BACK!
HOLD THIS.
WAAAAAA--
GRRRRR...
-GARK!
HOLD THIS.
WHAT?! NO... HE'S GOING TO TAKE ALL OF YOU IF--
ULK!
YOU SHOULDN'T HAVE BROUGHT YOUR GIRLFRIENDS, SPIDEY-BOY...
THIS IS BETWEEN YOU AND ME...

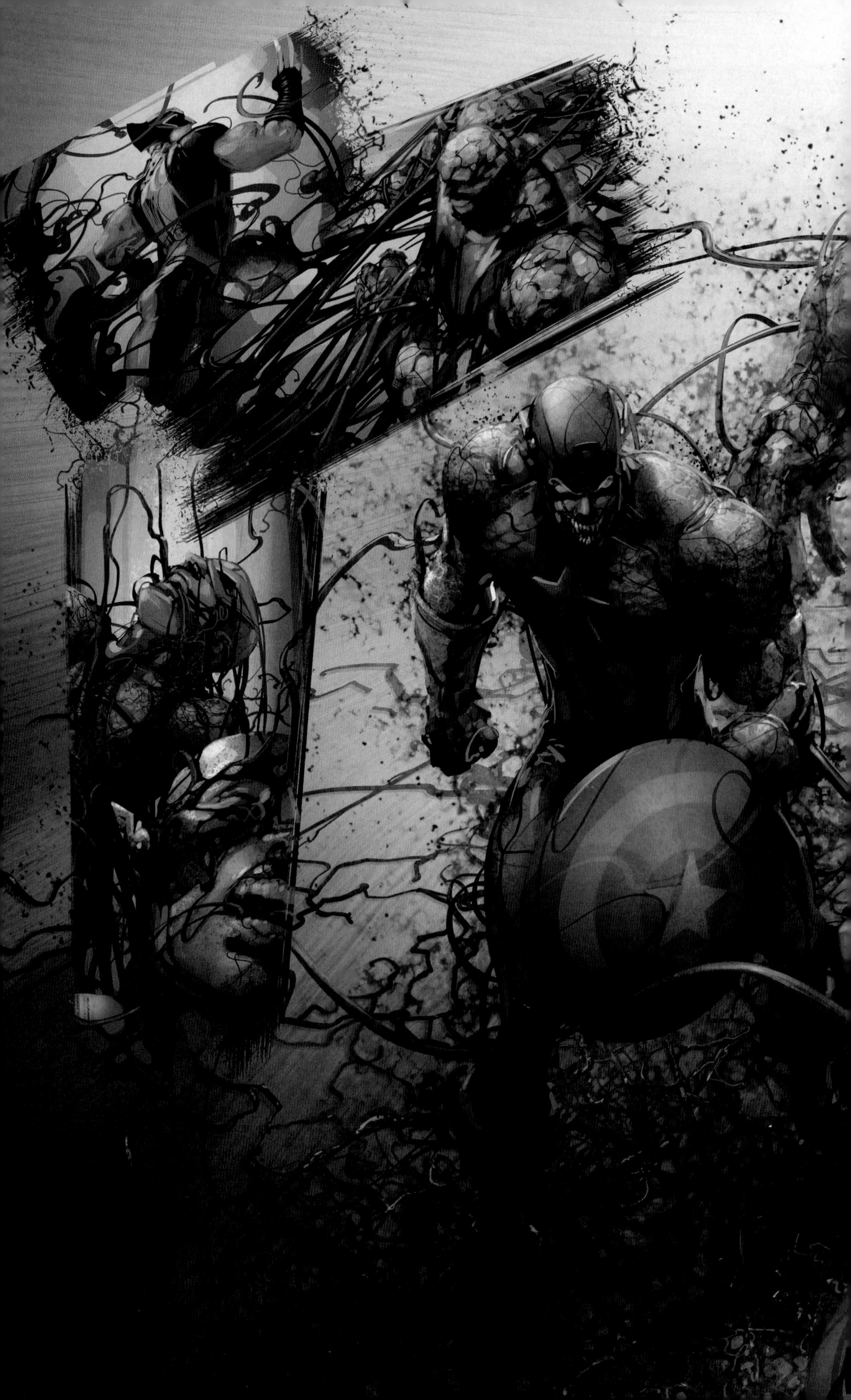

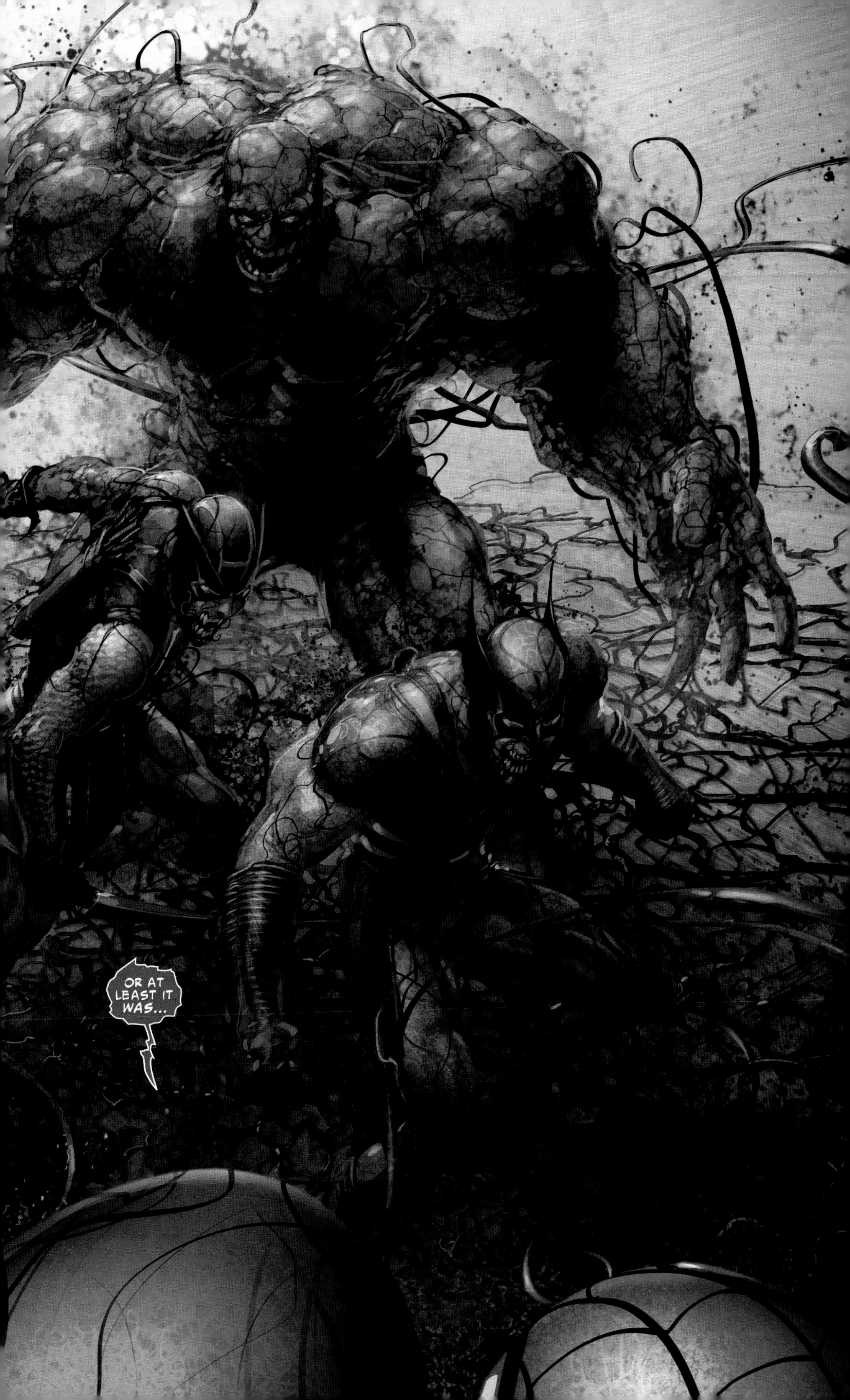
OR AT LEAST IT WAS...

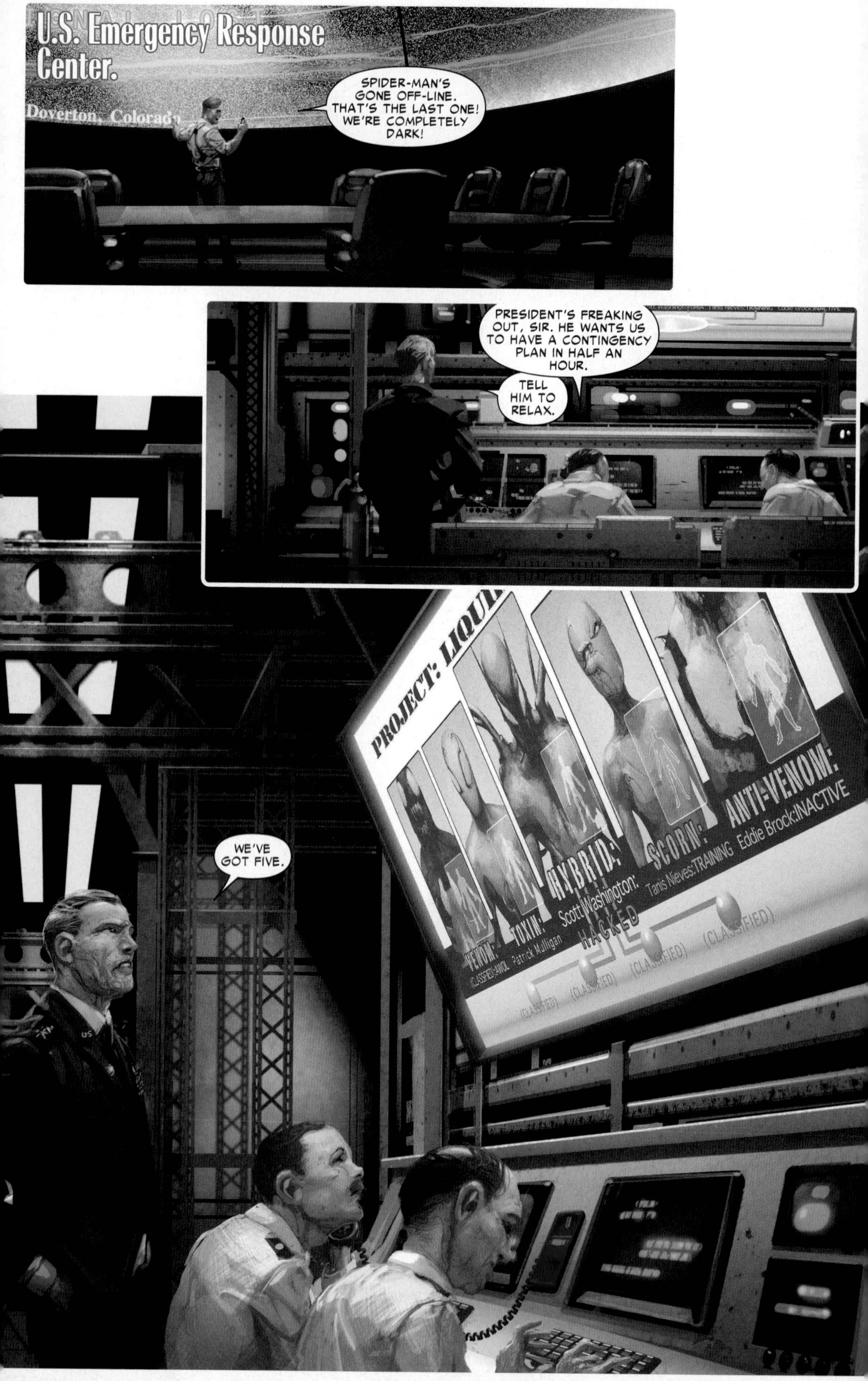
U.S. Emergency Response Center.
Doverton, Colorado
SPIDER-MAN'S GONE OFF-LINE. THAT'S THE LAST ONE! WE'RE COMPLETELY DARK!
PRESIDENT'S FREAKING OUT, SIR. HE WANTS US TO HAVE A CONTINGENCY PLAN IN HALF AN HOUR.
TELL HIM TO RELAX.
WE'VE GOT FIVE.
VENOM:
TOXIN:
Patrick Mulligan
HYBRID:
Scott Washington:
HACKED
SCORN:
Tanis Nieves:TRAINING
ANTI-VENOM:
Eddie Brock:INACTIVE
(CLASSIFIED)
(CLASSIFIED)
(CLASSIFIED)
(CLASSIFIED)

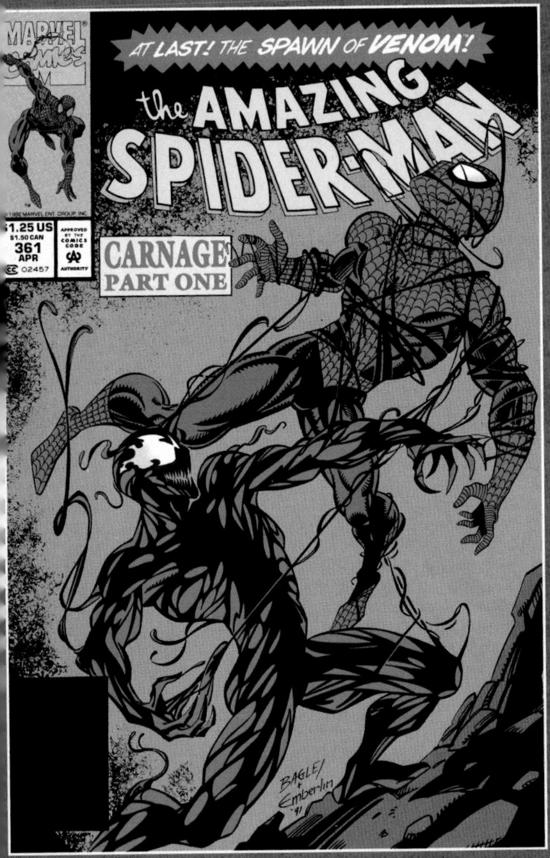
MARVEL COMICS
AT LAST! THE SPAWN OF VENOM!
the AMAZING SPIDER-MAN
$1.25 US
$1.50 CAN
361
APR
APPROVED BY THE COMICS CODE AUTHORITY
CARNAGE PART ONE
BAGLEY/ Emberlin '91

Amazing Spider-Man #361 silver 2nd-printing variant by Mark Bagley & Randy Emberlin

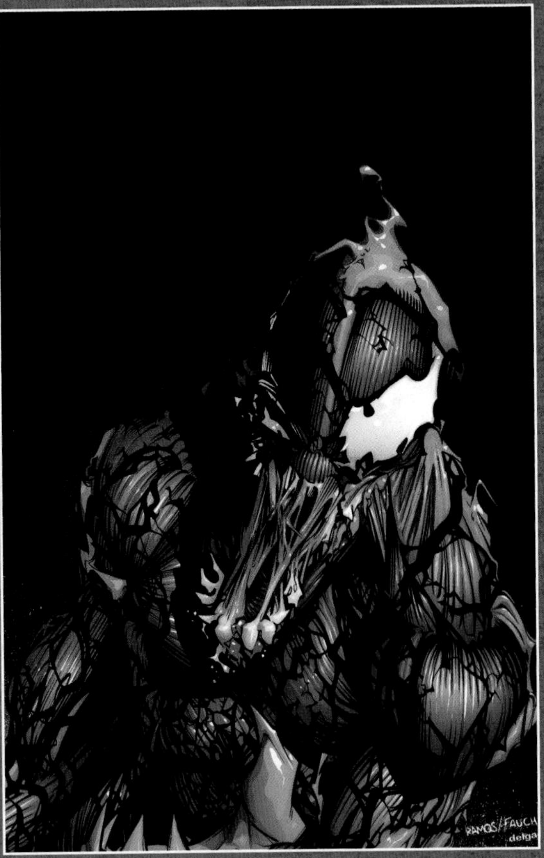
RAMOS/FAUCH
delga

Carnage, U.S.A. #1 variant by Humberto Ramos, Wayne Faucher & Edgar Delgado

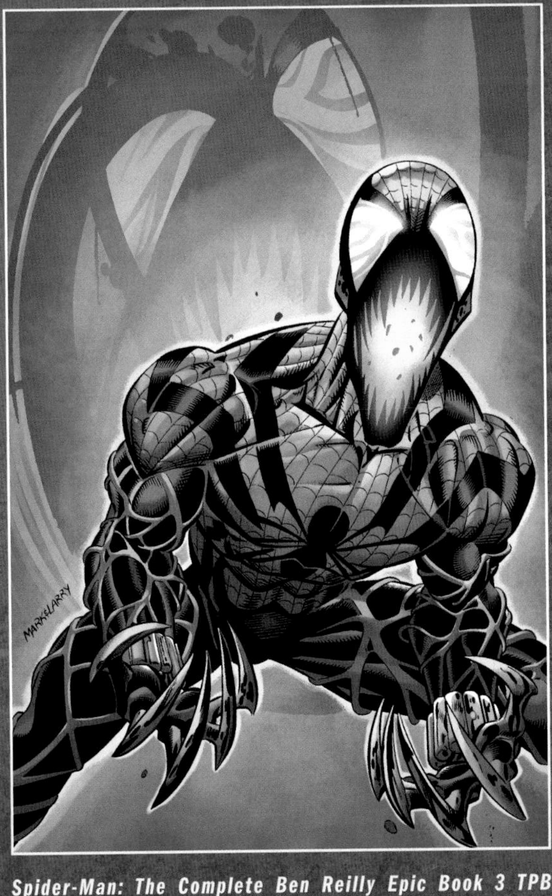
MARK/LARRY

Spider-Man: The Complete Ben Reilly Epic Book 3 TPB
cover art by Mark Bagley, Larry Mahlstedt & Matt Milla

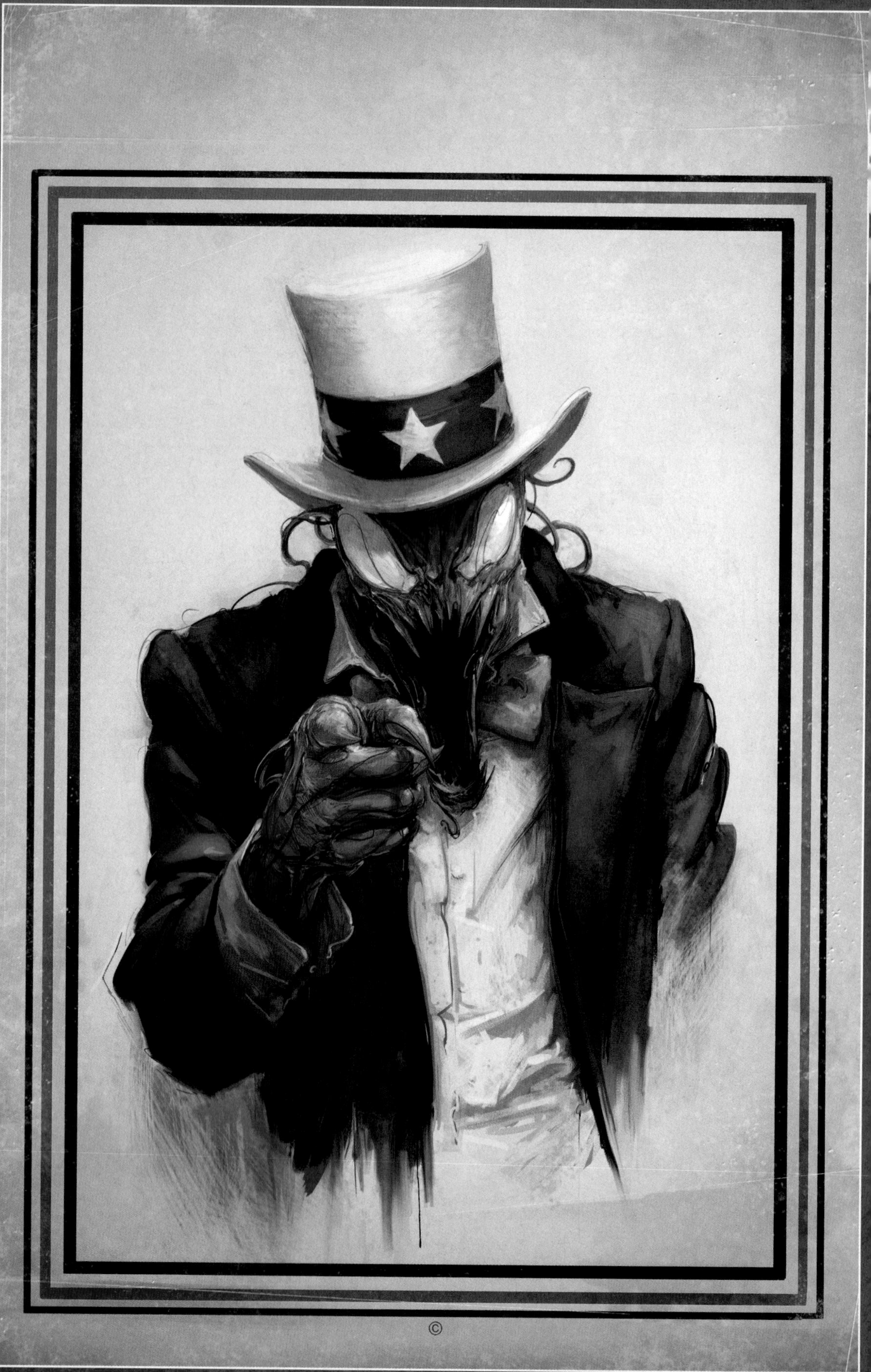

CARNAGE, U.S.A. #2

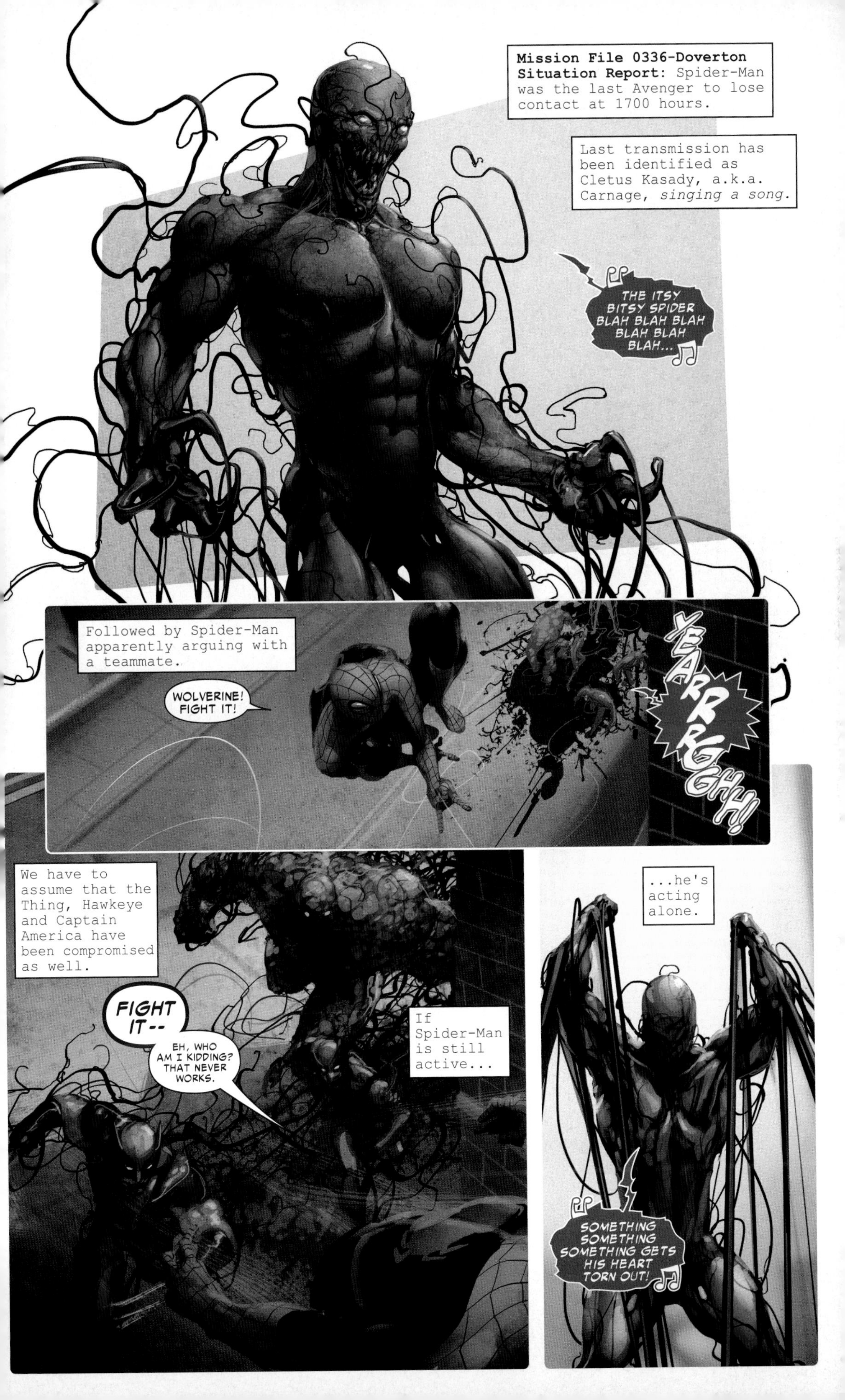
Mission File 0336-Doverton
Situation Report: Spider-Man was the last Avenger to lose contact at 1700 hours.
Last transmission has been identified as Cletus Kasady, a.k.a. Carnage, *singing a song*.
THE ITSY BITSY SPIDER BLAH BLAH BLAH BLAH BLAH BLAH...
Followed by Spider-Man apparently arguing with a teammate.
WOLVERINE! FIGHT IT!
YEARRRGHH!
We have to assume that the Thing, Hawkeye and Captain America have been compromised as well.
FIGHT IT --
EH, WHO AM I KIDDING? THAT NEVER WORKS.
If Spider-Man is still active...
...he's acting alone.
SOMETHING SOMETHING SOMETHING GETS HIS HEART TORN OUT!

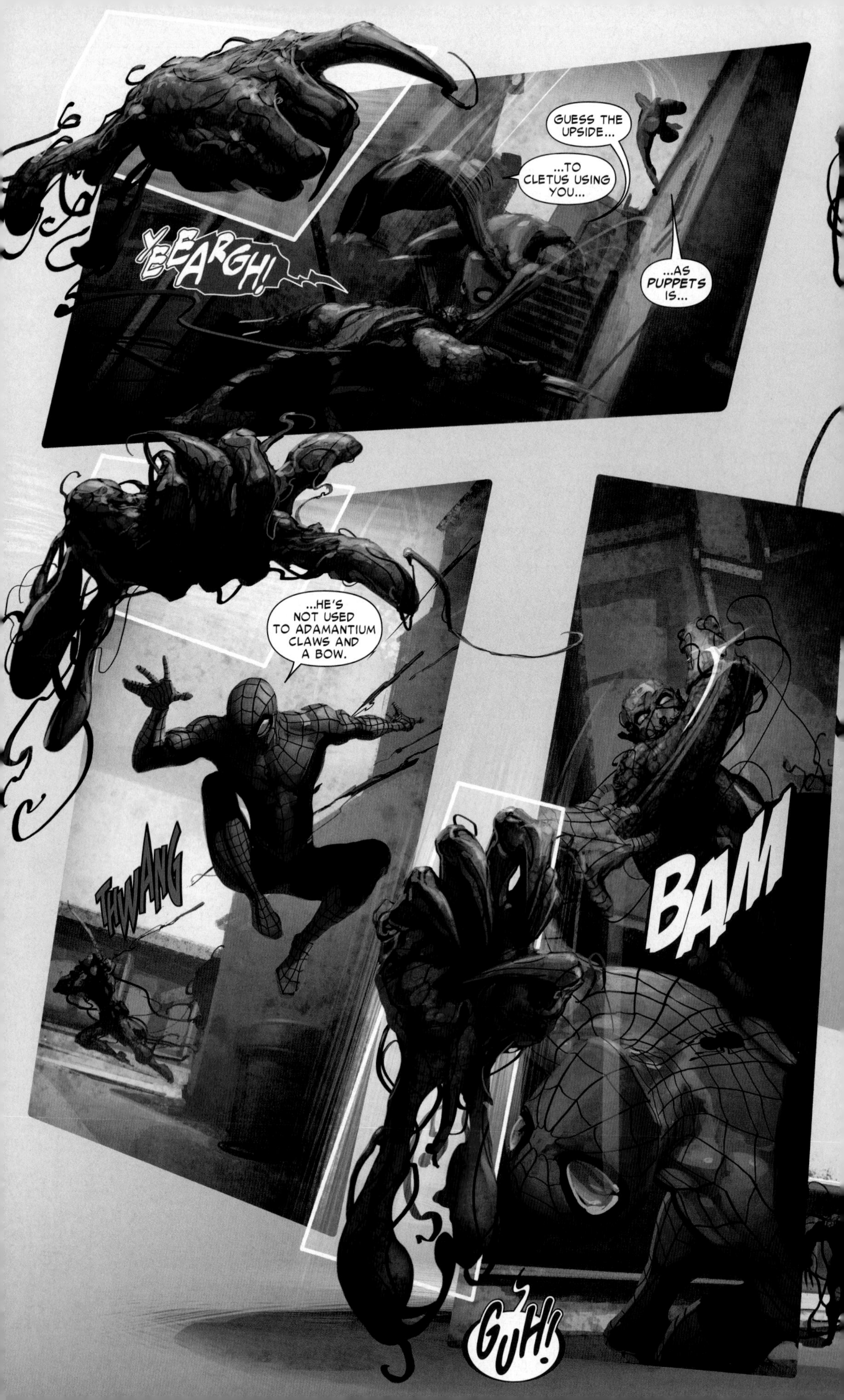
GUESS THE UPSIDE...
...TO CLETUS USING YOU...
...AS PUPPETS IS...
YEEARGH!
...HE'S NOT USED TO ADAMANTIUM CLAWS AND A BOW.
THWANG
BAM
GUH!

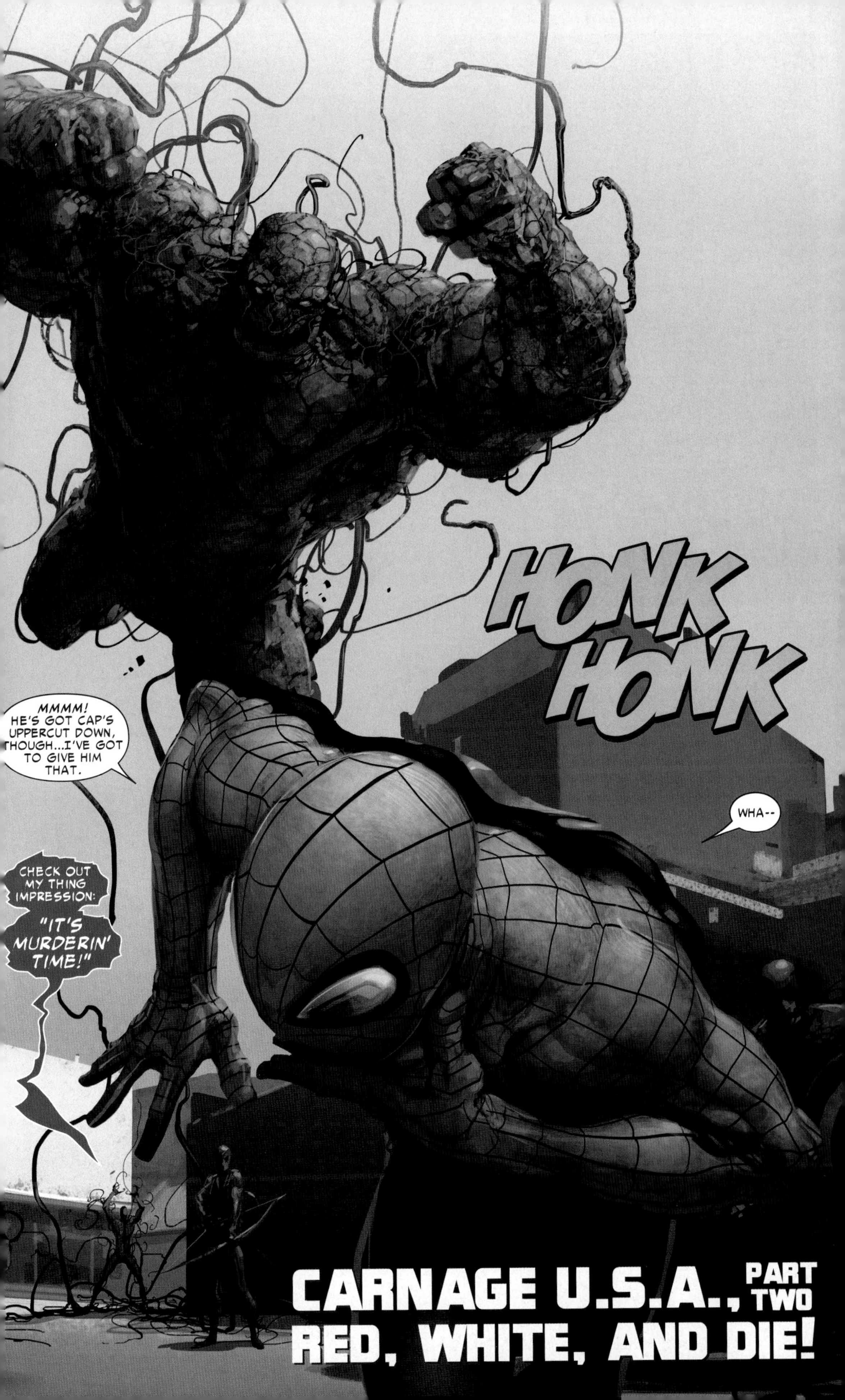
HONK
HONK
MMMM! HE'S GOT CAP'S UPPERCUT DOWN, THOUGH...I'VE GOT TO GIVE HIM THAT.
WHA--
CHECK OUT MY THING IMPRESSION:
"IT'S MURDERIN' TIME!"
CARNAGE U.S.A., PART TWO
RED, WHITE, AND DIE!

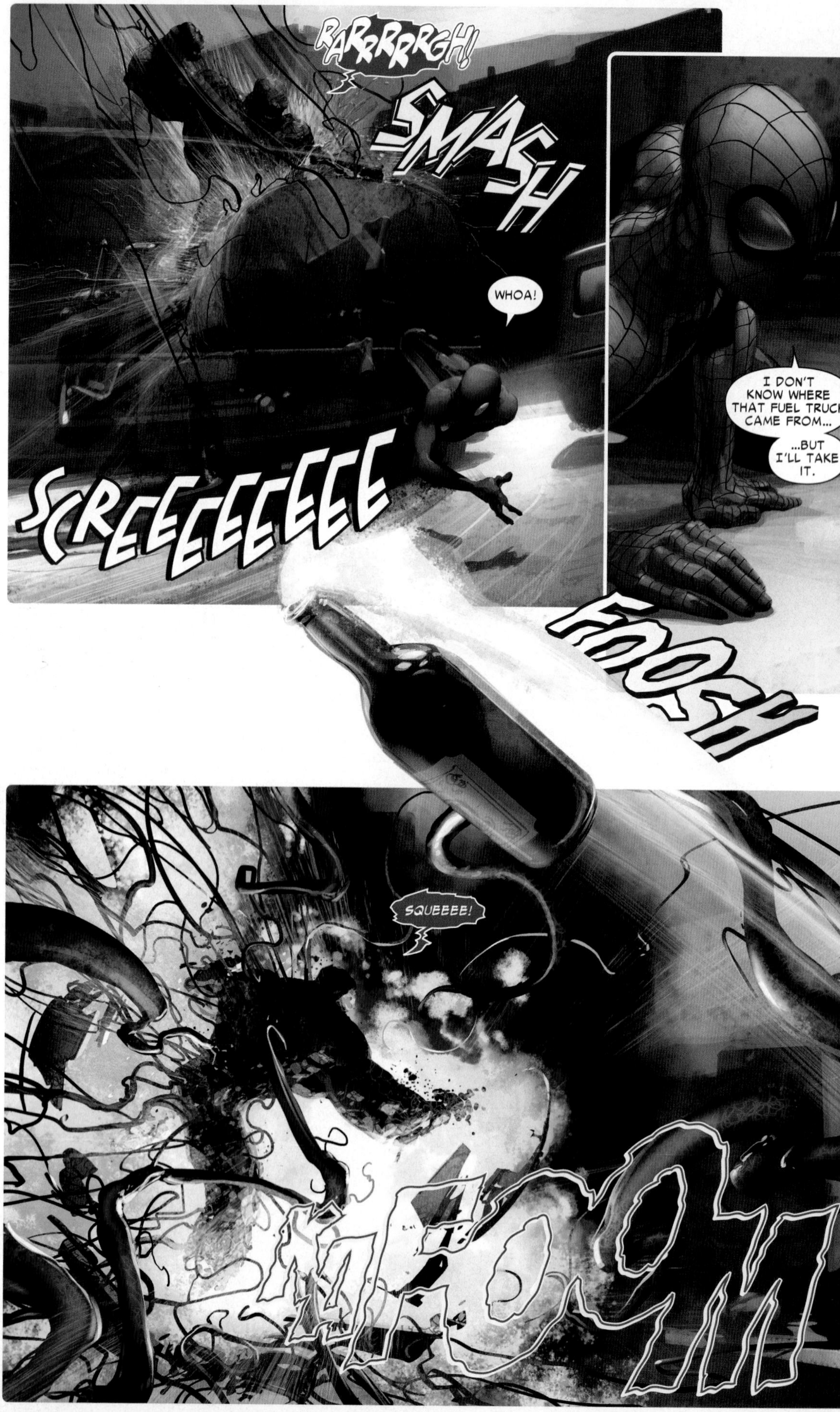

RARRRRGH!
SMASH
WHOA!
SCREEEEEEEE
I DON'T KNOW WHERE THAT FUEL TRUCK CAME FROM...
...BUT I'LL TAKE IT.
FOOSH
SQUBBBE!

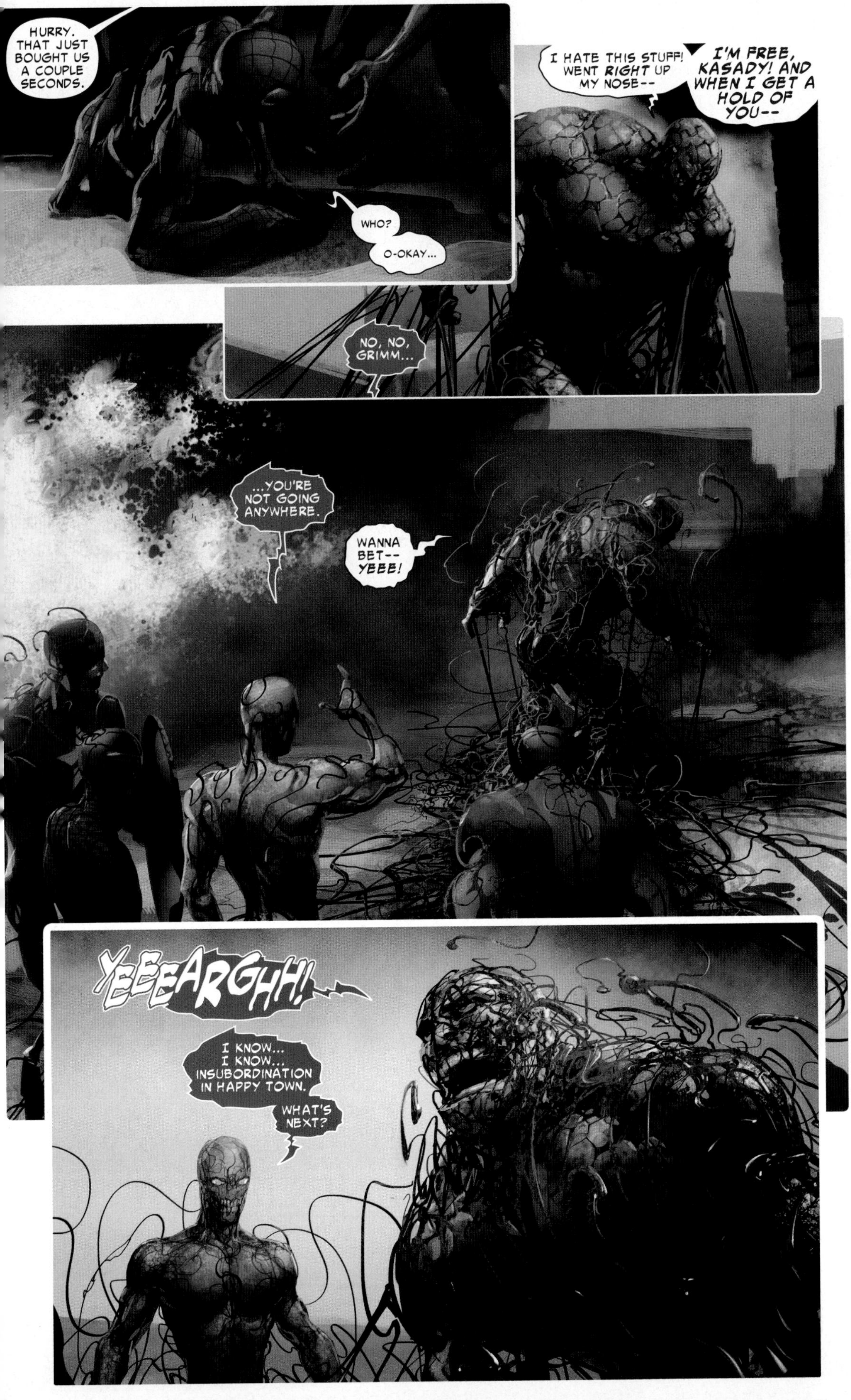
HURRY. THAT JUST BOUGHT US A COUPLE SECONDS.
WHO?
O-OKAY...
I HATE THIS STUFF! WENT RIGHT UP MY NOSE--
I'M FREE, KASADY! AND WHEN I GET A HOLD OF YOU--
NO, NO, GRIMM...
...YOU'RE NOT GOING ANYWHERE.
WANNA BET-- YEEE!
YEEEARGHH!
I KNOW... I KNOW... INSUBORDINATION IN HAPPY TOWN.
WHAT'S NEXT?

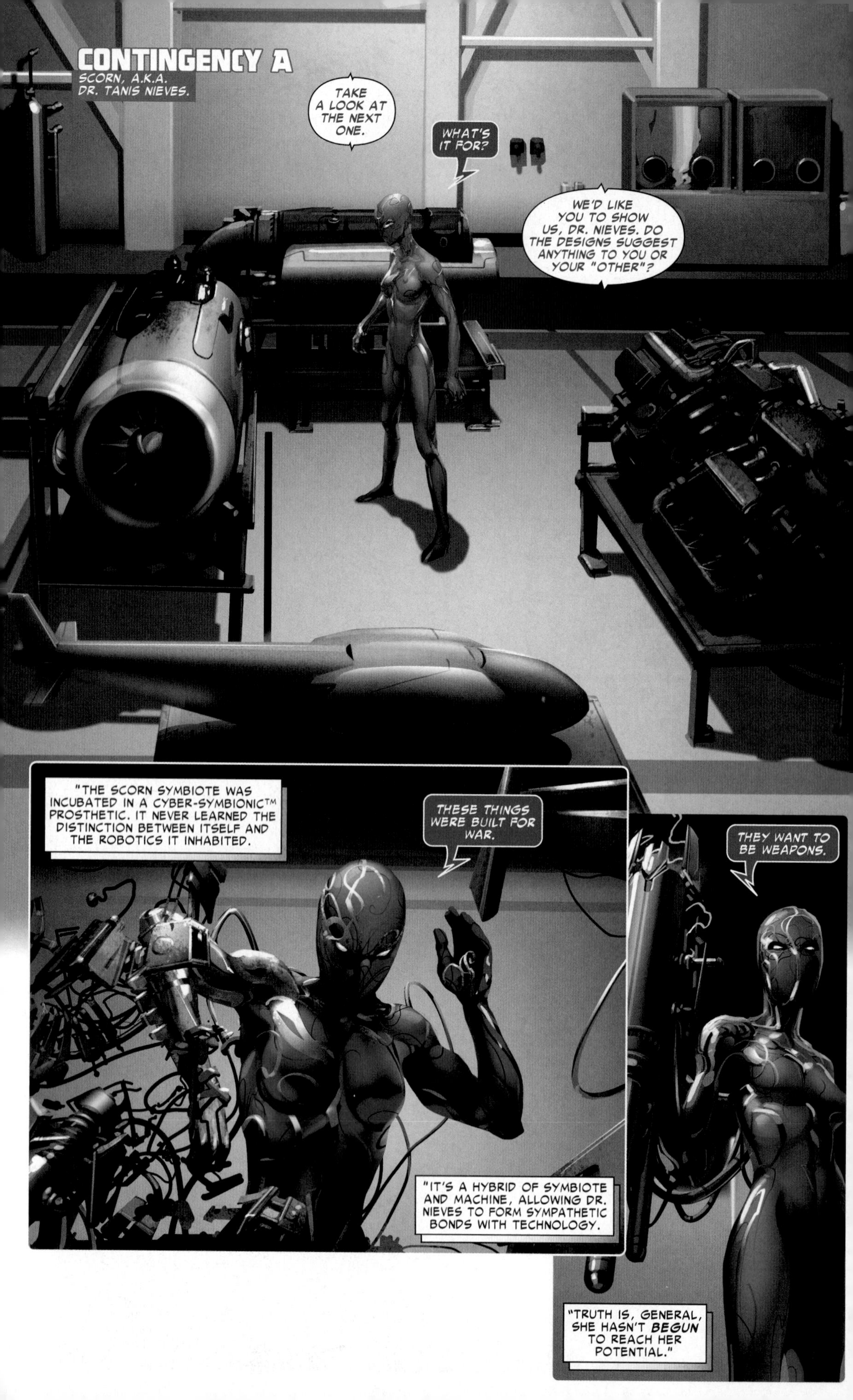
CONTINGENCY A
SCORN, A.K.A. DR. TANIS NIEVES.
TAKE A LOOK AT THE NEXT ONE.
WHAT'S IT FOR?
WE'D LIKE YOU TO SHOW US, DR. NIEVES. DO THE DESIGNS SUGGEST ANYTHING TO YOU OR YOUR "OTHER"?
"THE SCORN SYMBIOTE WAS INCUBATED IN A CYBER-SYMBIONIC™ PROSTHETIC. IT NEVER LEARNED THE DISTINCTION BETWEEN ITSELF AND THE ROBOTICS IT INHABITED.
THESE THINGS WERE BUILT FOR WAR.
"IT'S A HYBRID OF SYMBIOTE AND MACHINE, ALLOWING DR. NIEVES TO FORM SYMPATHETIC BONDS WITH TECHNOLOGY.
THEY WANT TO BE WEAPONS.
"TRUTH IS, GENERAL, SHE HASN'T *BEGUN* TO REACH HER POTENTIAL."

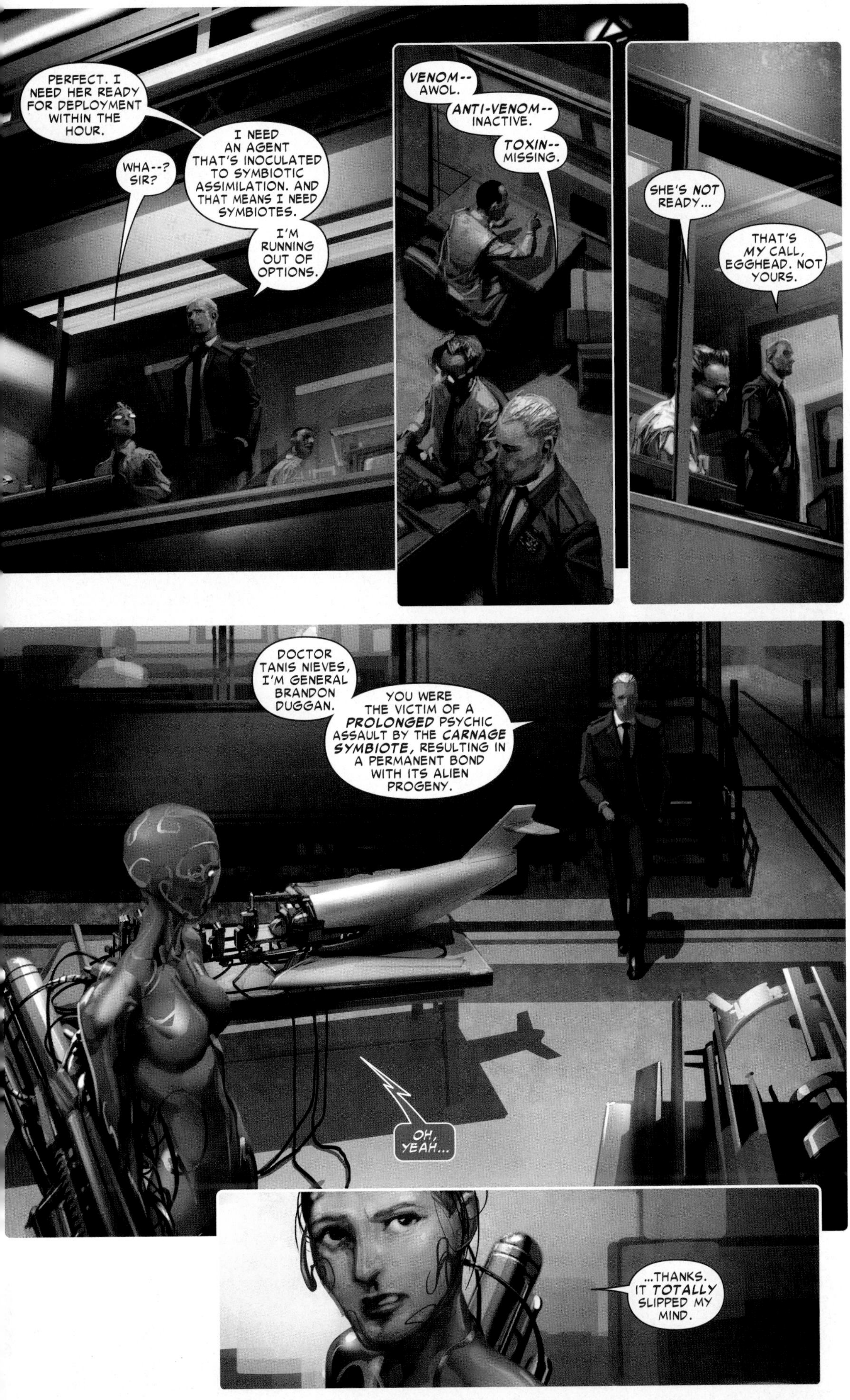
PERFECT. I NEED HER READY FOR DEPLOYMENT WITHIN THE HOUR.
WHA--? SIR?
I NEED AN AGENT THAT'S INOCULATED TO SYMBIOTIC ASSIMILATION. AND THAT MEANS I NEED SYMBIOTES.
I'M RUNNING OUT OF OPTIONS.
VENOM-- AWOL.
ANTI-VENOM-- INACTIVE.
TOXIN-- MISSING.
SHE'S NOT READY...
THAT'S MY CALL, EGGHEAD. NOT YOURS.
DOCTOR TANIS NIEVES, I'M GENERAL BRANDON DUGGAN.
YOU WERE THE VICTIM OF A PROLONGED PSYCHIC ASSAULT BY THE CARNAGE SYMBIOTE, RESULTING IN A PERMANENT BOND WITH ITS ALIEN PROGENY.
OH, YEAH...
...THANKS. IT TOTALLY SLIPPED MY MIND.

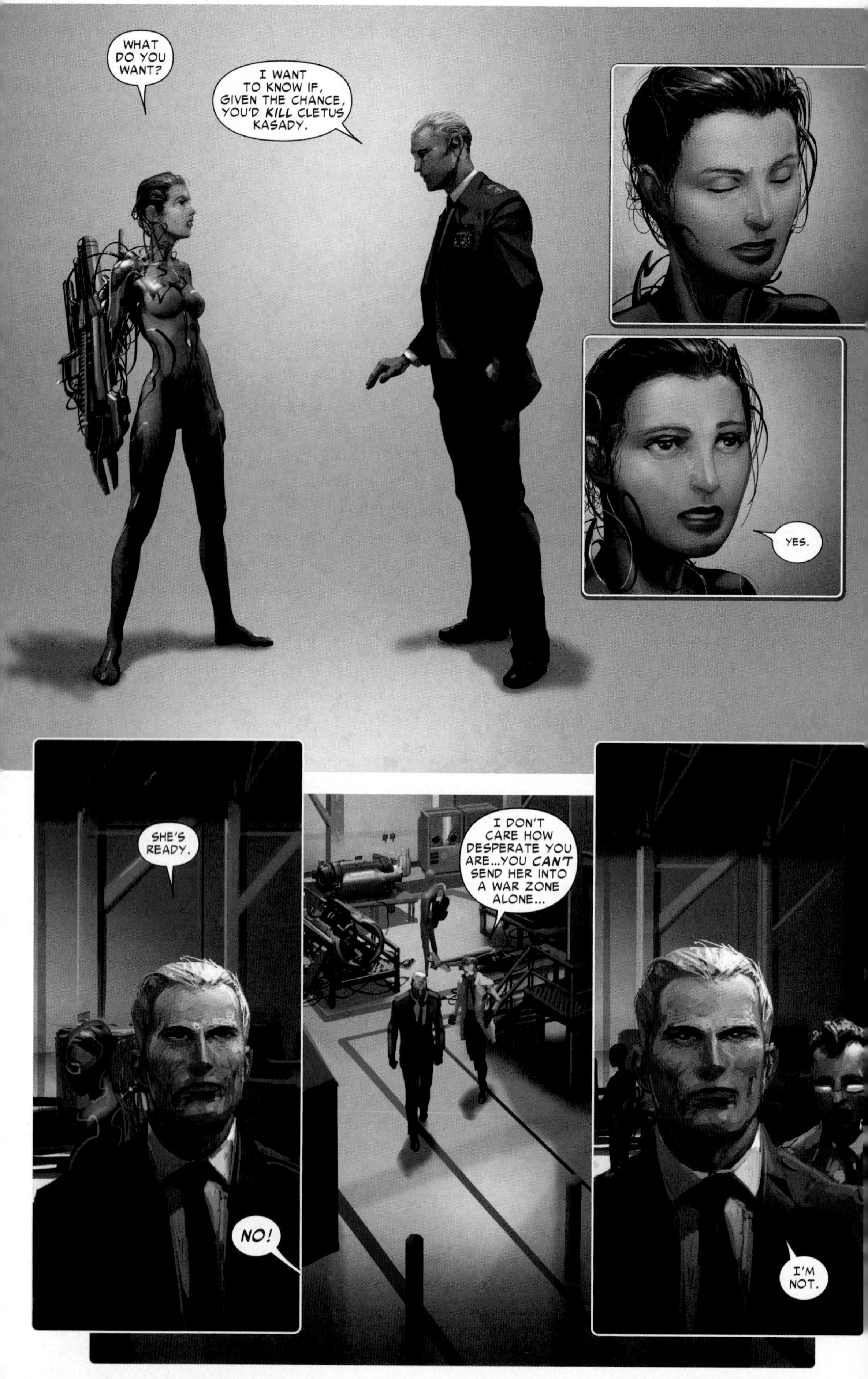
WHAT DO YOU WANT?
I WANT TO KNOW IF, GIVEN THE CHANCE, YOU'D KILL CLETUS KASADY.
YES.
SHE'S READY.
NO!
I DON'T CARE HOW DESPERATE YOU ARE...YOU CAN'T SEND HER INTO A WAR ZONE ALONE...
I'M NOT.

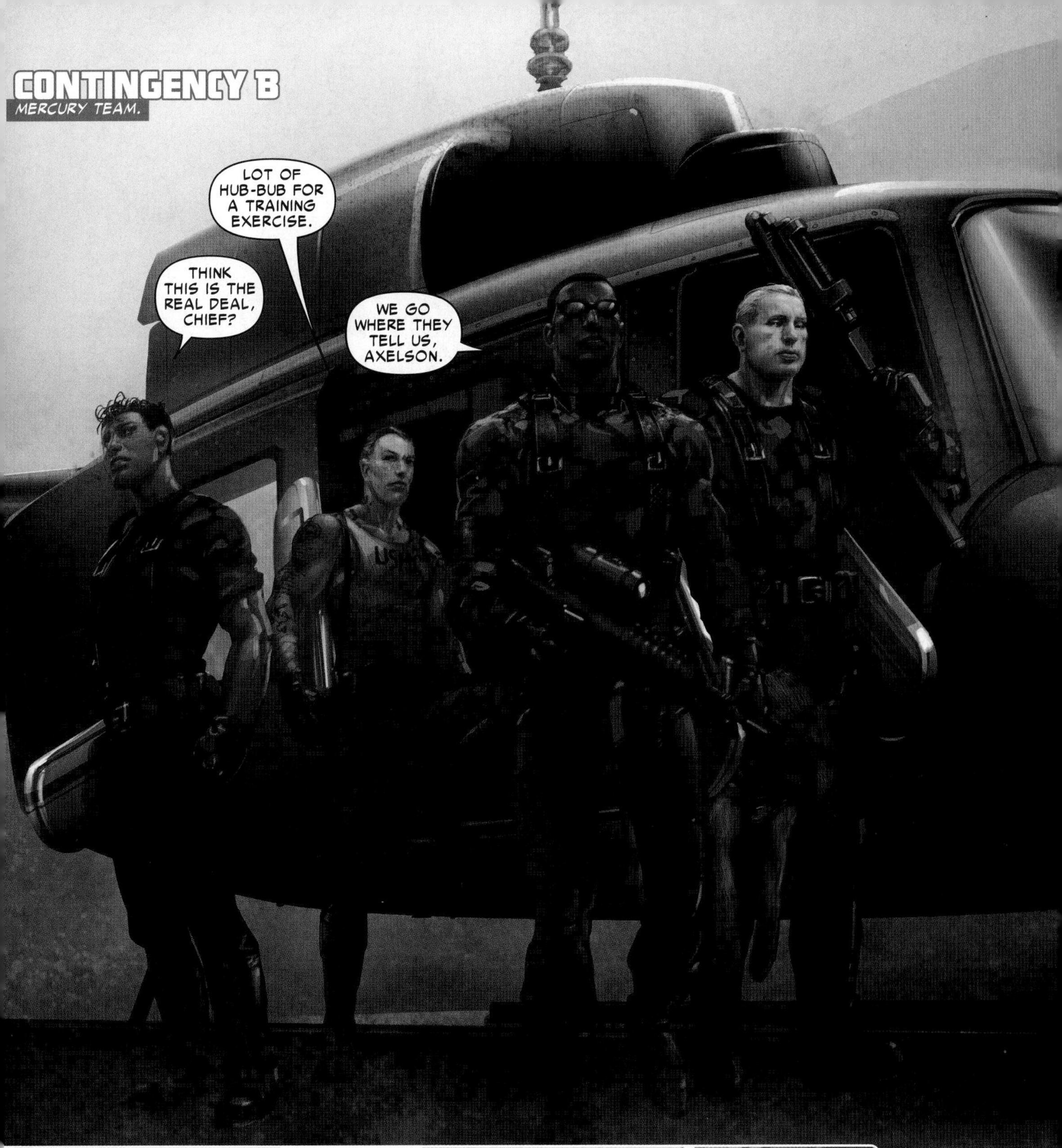
CONTINGENCY B
MERCURY TEAM.
LOT OF HUB-BUB FOR A TRAINING EXERCISE.
THINK THIS IS THE REAL DEAL, CHIEF?
WE GO WHERE THEY TELL US, AXELSON.

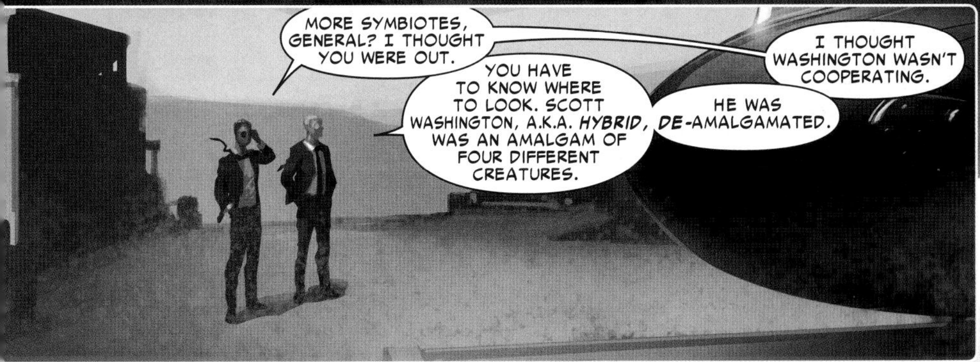
MORE SYMBIOTES, GENERAL? I THOUGHT YOU WERE OUT.
YOU HAVE TO KNOW WHERE TO LOOK. SCOTT WASHINGTON, A.K.A. *HYBRID*, WAS AN AMALGAM OF FOUR DIFFERENT CREATURES.
I THOUGHT WASHINGTON WASN'T COOPERATING.
HE WAS *DE*-AMALGAMATED.

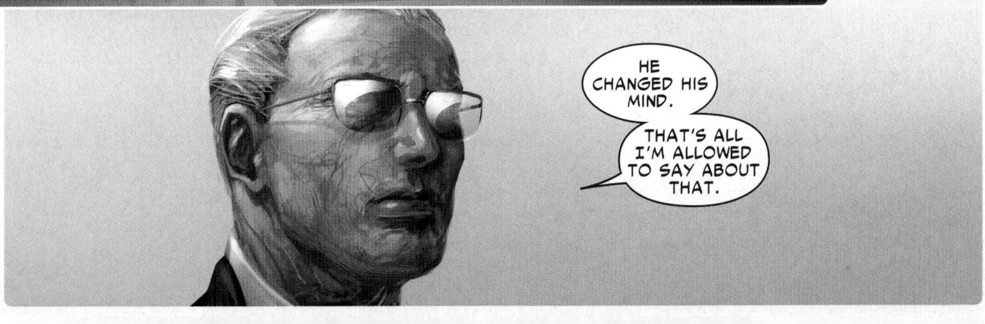
HE CHANGED HIS MIND.
THAT'S ALL I'M ALLOWED TO SAY ABOUT THAT.

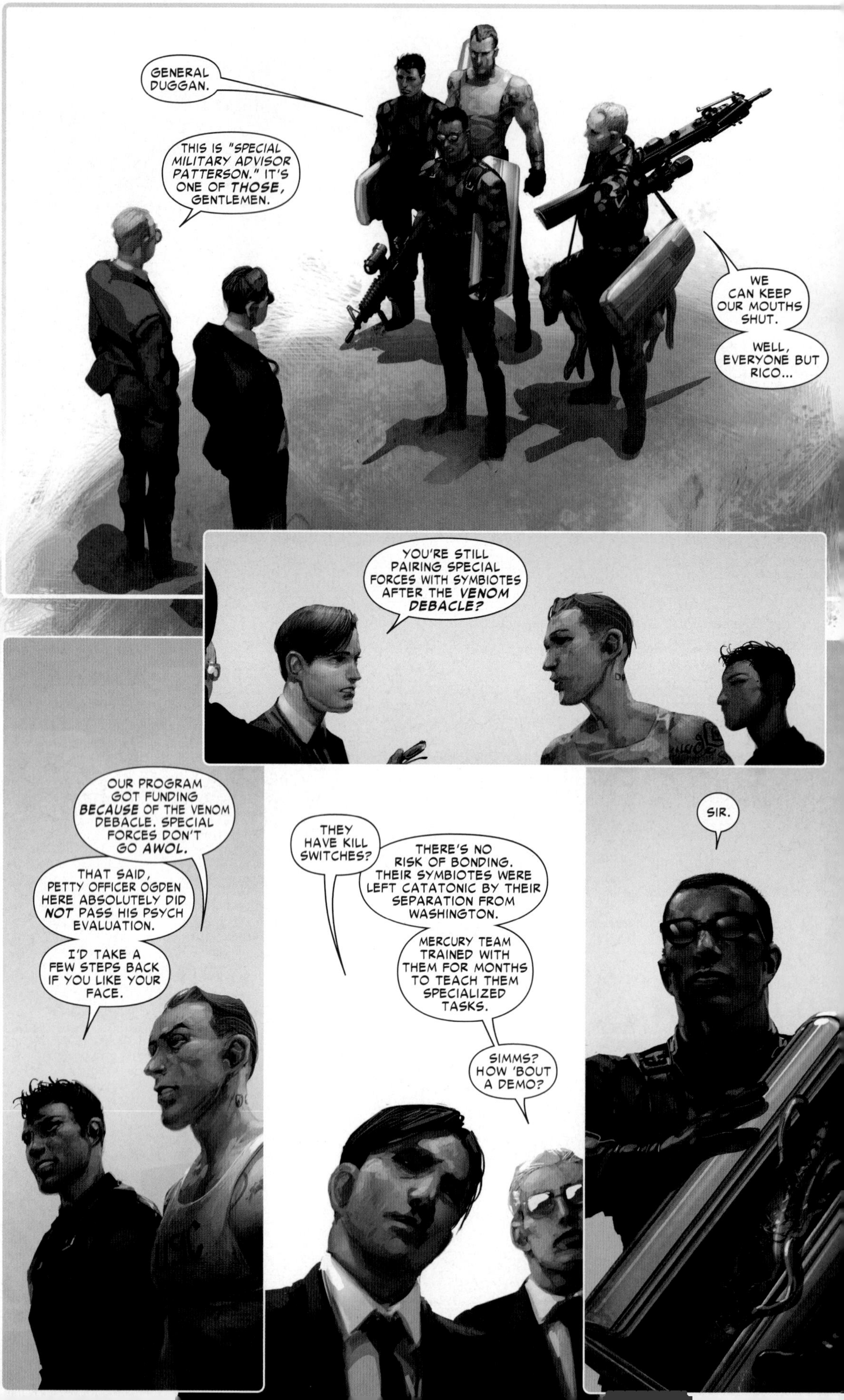
GENERAL DUGGAN.
THIS IS "SPECIAL MILITARY ADVISOR PATTERSON." IT'S ONE OF THOSE, GENTLEMEN.
WE CAN KEEP OUR MOUTHS SHUT.
WELL, EVERYONE BUT RICO...
YOU'RE STILL PAIRING SPECIAL FORCES WITH SYMBIOTES AFTER THE VENOM DEBACLE?
OUR PROGRAM GOT FUNDING BECAUSE OF THE VENOM DEBACLE. SPECIAL FORCES DON'T GO AWOL.
THAT SAID, PETTY OFFICER OGDEN HERE ABSOLUTELY DID NOT PASS HIS PSYCH EVALUATION.
I'D TAKE A FEW STEPS BACK IF YOU LIKE YOUR FACE.
THEY HAVE KILL SWITCHES?
THERE'S NO RISK OF BONDING. THEIR SYMBIOTES WERE LEFT CATATONIC BY THEIR SEPARATION FROM WASHINGTON.
MERCURY TEAM TRAINED WITH THEM FOR MONTHS TO TEACH THEM SPECIALIZED TASKS.
SIMMS? HOW 'BOUT A DEMO?
SIR.

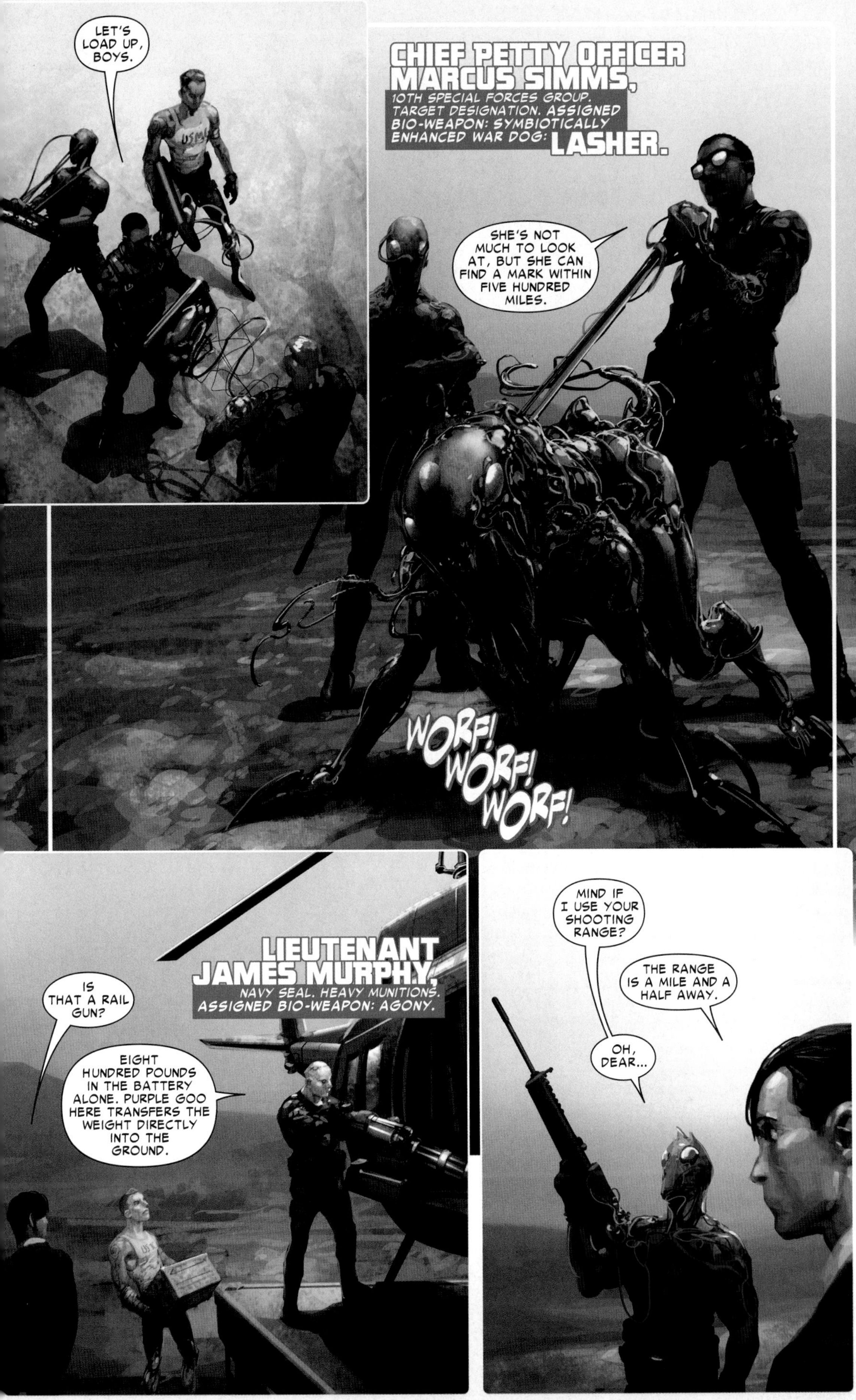
LET'S LOAD UP, BOYS.
CHIEF PETTY OFFICER MARCUS SIMMS,
10TH SPECIAL FORCES GROUP. TARGET DESIGNATION. ASSIGNED BIO-WEAPON: SYMBIOTICALLY ENHANCED WAR DOG: LASHER.
SHE'S NOT MUCH TO LOOK AT, BUT SHE CAN FIND A MARK WITHIN FIVE HUNDRED MILES.
WORF! WORF! WORF!
LIEUTENANT JAMES MURPHY,
NAVY SEAL. HEAVY MUNITIONS. ASSIGNED BIO-WEAPON: AGONY.
IS THAT A RAIL GUN?
EIGHT HUNDRED POUNDS IN THE BATTERY ALONE. PURPLE GOO HERE TRANSFERS THE WEIGHT DIRECTLY INTO THE GROUND.
MIND IF I USE YOUR SHOOTING RANGE?
THE RANGE IS A MILE AND A HALF AWAY.
OH, DEAR...

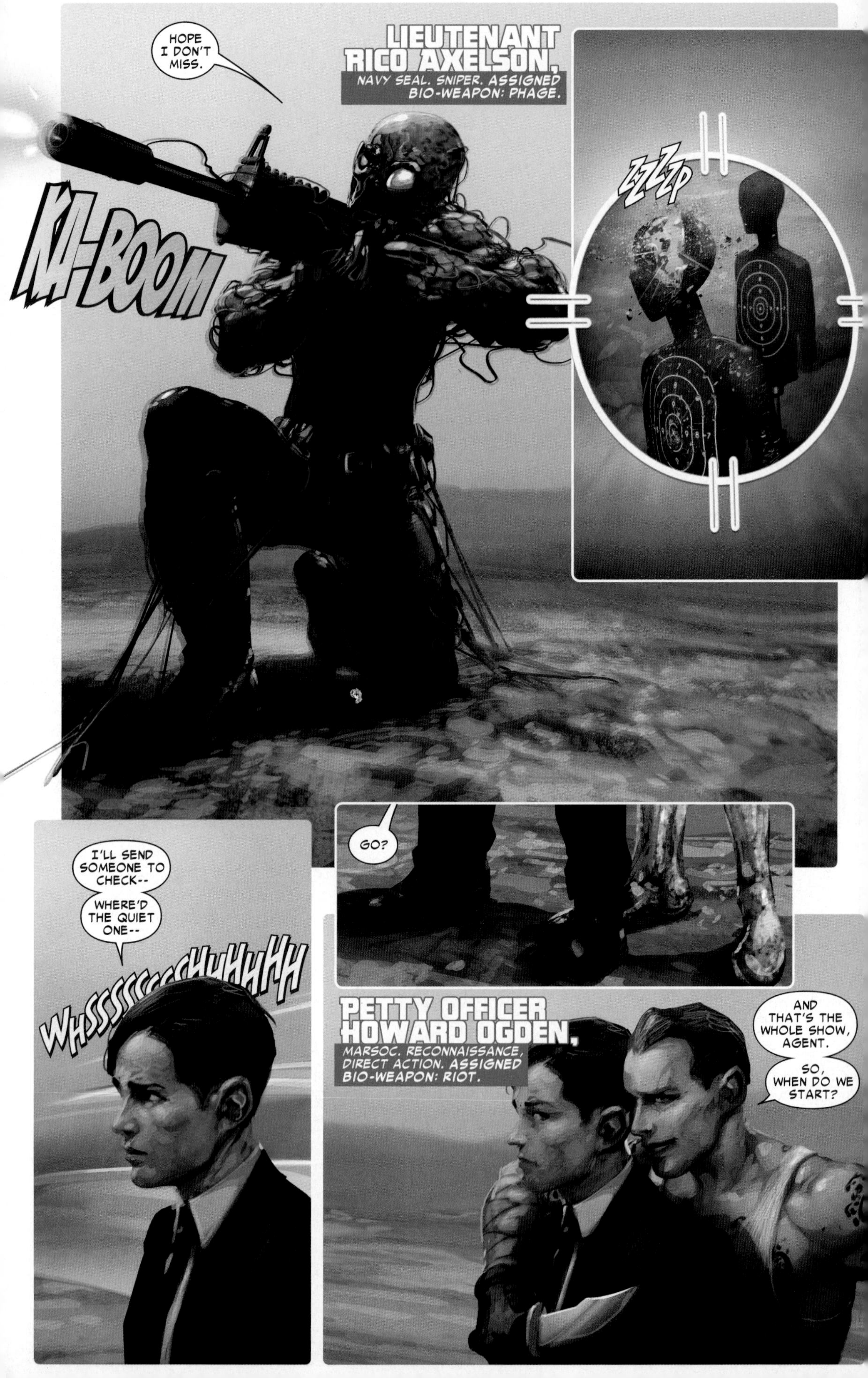
HOPE I DON'T MISS.
LIEUTENANT RICO AXELSON,
NAVY SEAL. SNIPER. ASSIGNED BIO-WEAPON: PHAGE.
KA-BOOM
ZZZZZP
GO?
I'LL SEND SOMEONE TO CHECK--
WHERE'D THE QUIET ONE--
WHSSSSSSCCHHHHHH
PETTY OFFICER HOWARD OGDEN,
MARSOC. RECONNAISSANCE, DIRECT ACTION. ASSIGNED BIO-WEAPON: RIOT.
AND THAT'S THE WHOLE SHOW, AGENT.
SO, WHEN DO WE START?

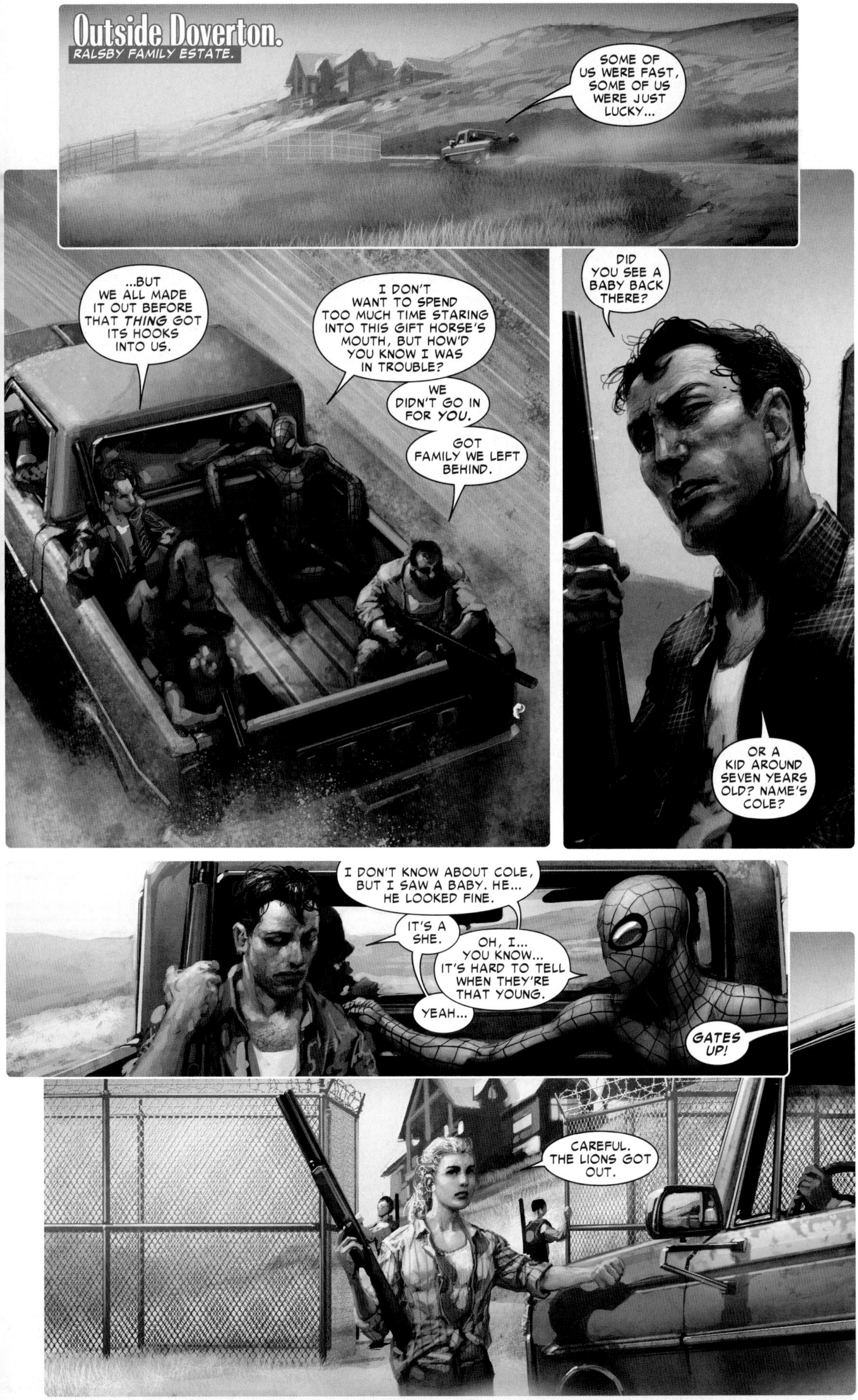

Outside Doverton.
RALSBY FAMILY ESTATE.
SOME OF US WERE FAST, SOME OF US WERE JUST LUCKY...
...BUT WE ALL MADE IT OUT BEFORE THAT THING GOT ITS HOOKS INTO US.
I DON'T WANT TO SPEND TOO MUCH TIME STARING INTO THIS GIFT HORSE'S MOUTH, BUT HOW'D YOU KNOW I WAS IN TROUBLE?
WE DIDN'T GO IN FOR YOU.
GOT FAMILY WE LEFT BEHIND.
DID YOU SEE A BABY BACK THERE?
OR A KID AROUND SEVEN YEARS OLD? NAME'S COLE?
I DON'T KNOW ABOUT COLE, BUT I SAW A BABY. HE... HE LOOKED FINE.
IT'S A SHE.
OH, I... YOU KNOW... IT'S HARD TO TELL WHEN THEY'RE THAT YOUNG.
YEAH...
GATES UP!
CAREFUL. THE LIONS GOT OUT.

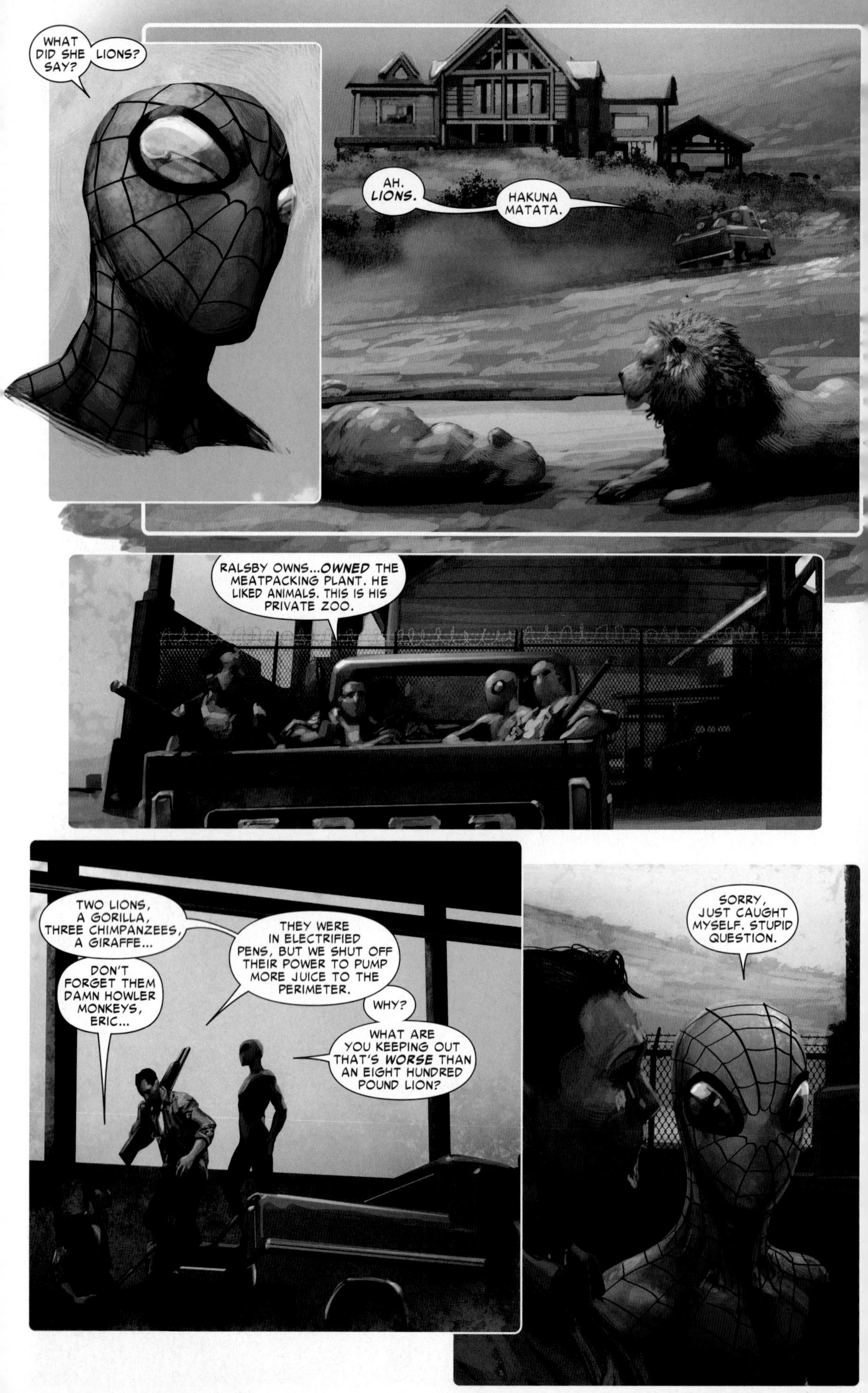

WHAT DID SHE SAY?
LIONS?
AH. LIONS.
HAKUNA MATATA.
RALSBY OWNS...OWNED THE MEATPACKING PLANT. HE LIKED ANIMALS. THIS IS HIS PRIVATE ZOO.
TWO LIONS, A GORILLA, THREE CHIMPANZEES, A GIRAFFE...
DON'T FORGET THEM DAMN HOWLER MONKEYS, ERIC...
THEY WERE IN ELECTRIFIED PENS, BUT WE SHUT OFF THEIR POWER TO PUMP MORE JUICE TO THE PERIMETER.
WHY?
WHAT ARE YOU KEEPING OUT THAT'S WORSE THAN AN EIGHT HUNDRED POUND LION?
SORRY, JUST CAUGHT MYSELF. STUPID QUESTION.

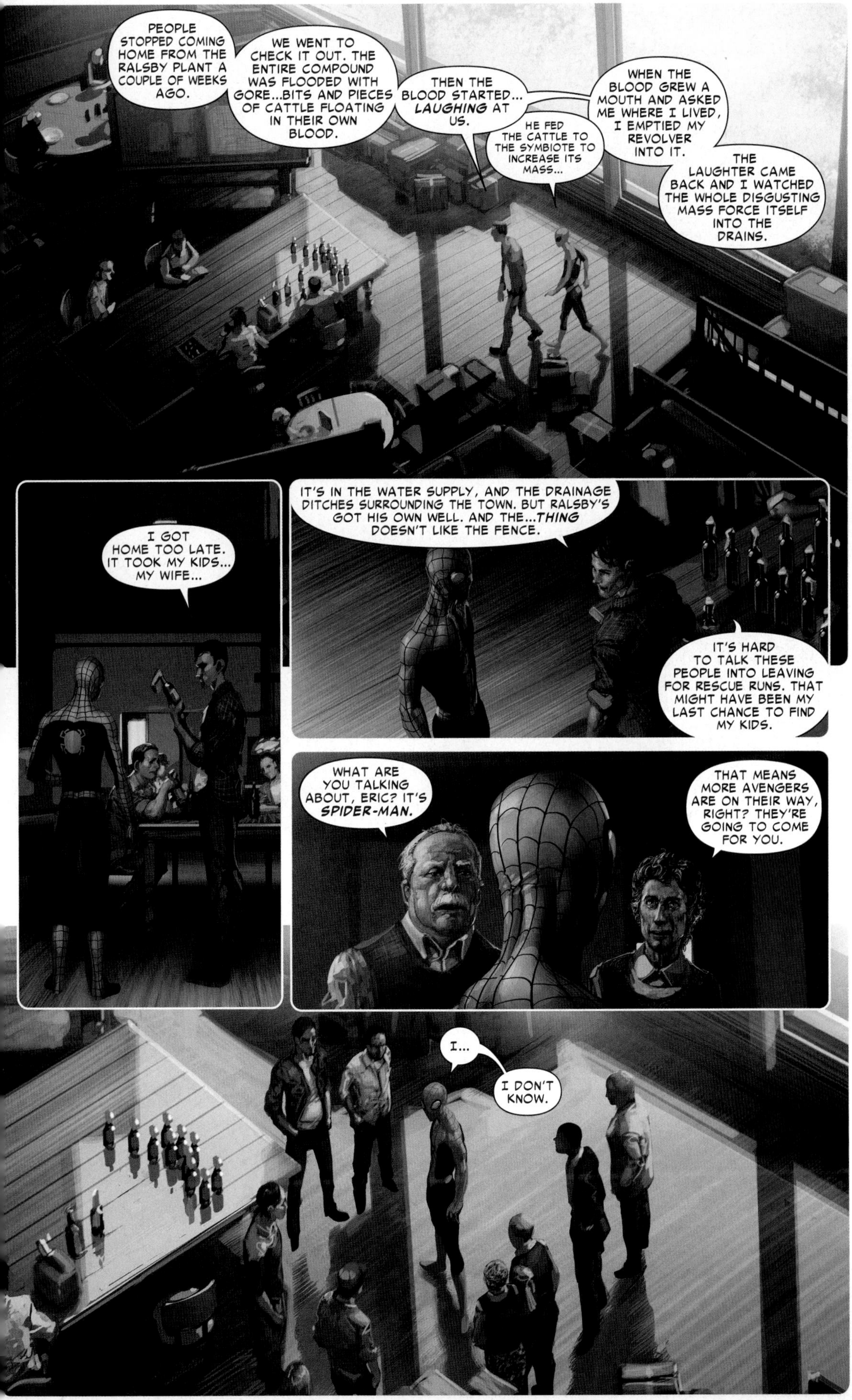
PEOPLE STOPPED COMING HOME FROM THE RALSBY PLANT A COUPLE OF WEEKS AGO.
WE WENT TO CHECK IT OUT. THE ENTIRE COMPOUND WAS FLOODED WITH GORE...BITS AND PIECES OF CATTLE FLOATING IN THEIR OWN BLOOD.
THEN THE BLOOD STARTED... *LAUGHING* AT US.
HE FED THE CATTLE TO THE SYMBIOTE TO INCREASE ITS MASS...
WHEN THE BLOOD GREW A MOUTH AND ASKED ME WHERE I LIVED, I EMPTIED MY REVOLVER INTO IT.
THE LAUGHTER CAME BACK AND I WATCHED THE WHOLE DISGUSTING MASS FORCE ITSELF INTO THE DRAINS.
I GOT HOME TOO LATE. IT TOOK MY KIDS... MY WIFE...
IT'S IN THE WATER SUPPLY, AND THE DRAINAGE DITCHES SURROUNDING THE TOWN. BUT RALSBY'S GOT HIS OWN WELL. AND THE...*THING* DOESN'T LIKE THE FENCE.
IT'S HARD TO TALK THESE PEOPLE INTO LEAVING FOR RESCUE RUNS. THAT MIGHT HAVE BEEN MY LAST CHANCE TO FIND MY KIDS.
WHAT ARE YOU TALKING ABOUT, ERIC? IT'S *SPIDER-MAN.*
THAT MEANS MORE AVENGERS ARE ON THEIR WAY, RIGHT? THEY'RE GOING TO COME FOR YOU.
I...
I DON'T KNOW.

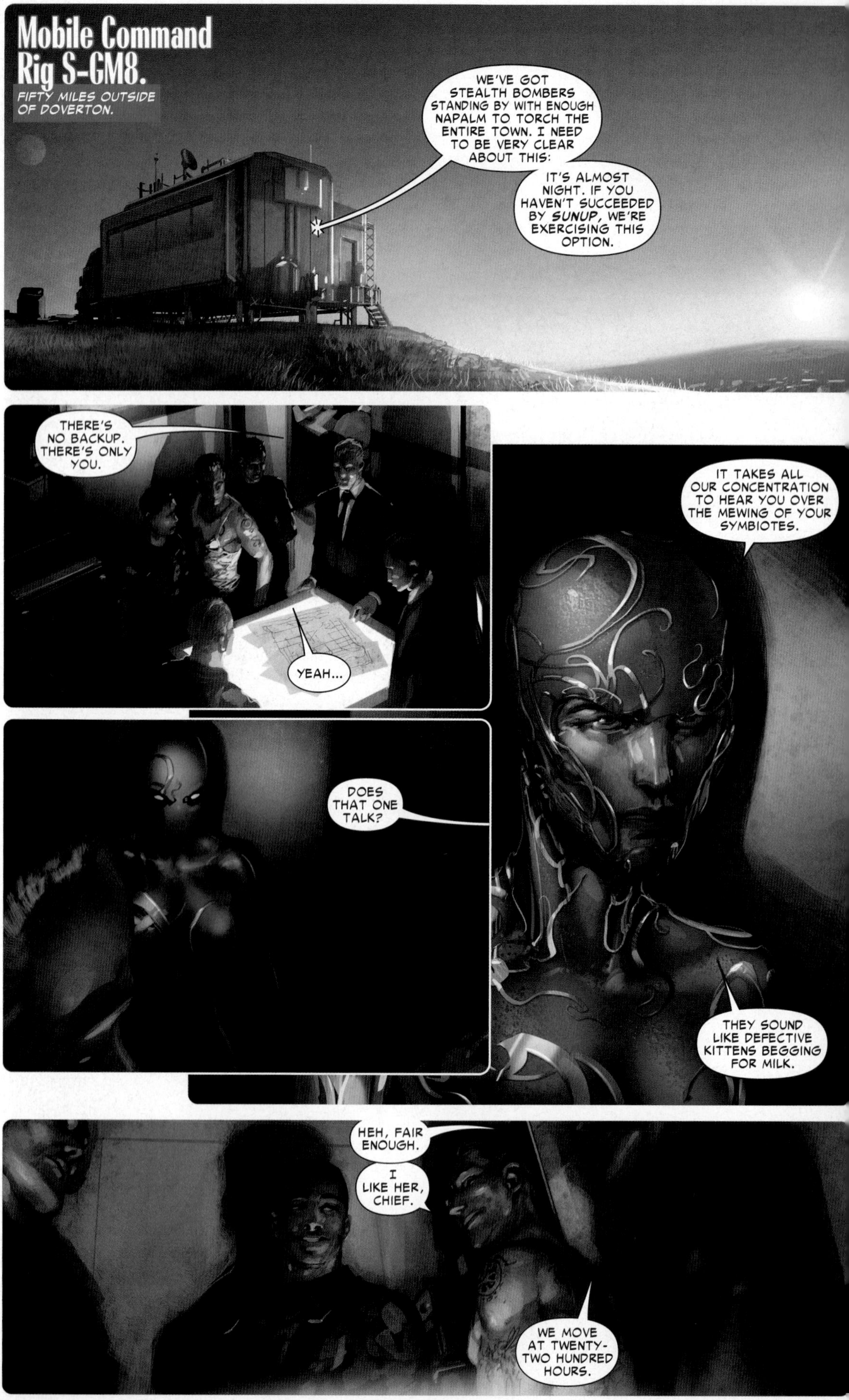
Mobile Command Rig S-GM8.
FIFTY MILES OUTSIDE OF DOVERTON.
WE'VE GOT STEALTH BOMBERS STANDING BY WITH ENOUGH NAPALM TO TORCH THE ENTIRE TOWN. I NEED TO BE VERY CLEAR ABOUT THIS:
IT'S ALMOST NIGHT. IF YOU HAVEN'T SUCCEEDED BY SUNUP, WE'RE EXERCISING THIS OPTION.
THERE'S NO BACKUP. THERE'S ONLY YOU.
YEAH...
IT TAKES ALL OUR CONCENTRATION TO HEAR YOU OVER THE MEWING OF YOUR SYMBIOTES.
DOES THAT ONE TALK?
THEY SOUND LIKE DEFECTIVE KITTENS BEGGING FOR MILK.
HEH, FAIR ENOUGH.
I LIKE HER, CHIEF.
WE MOVE AT TWENTY-TWO HUNDRED HOURS.

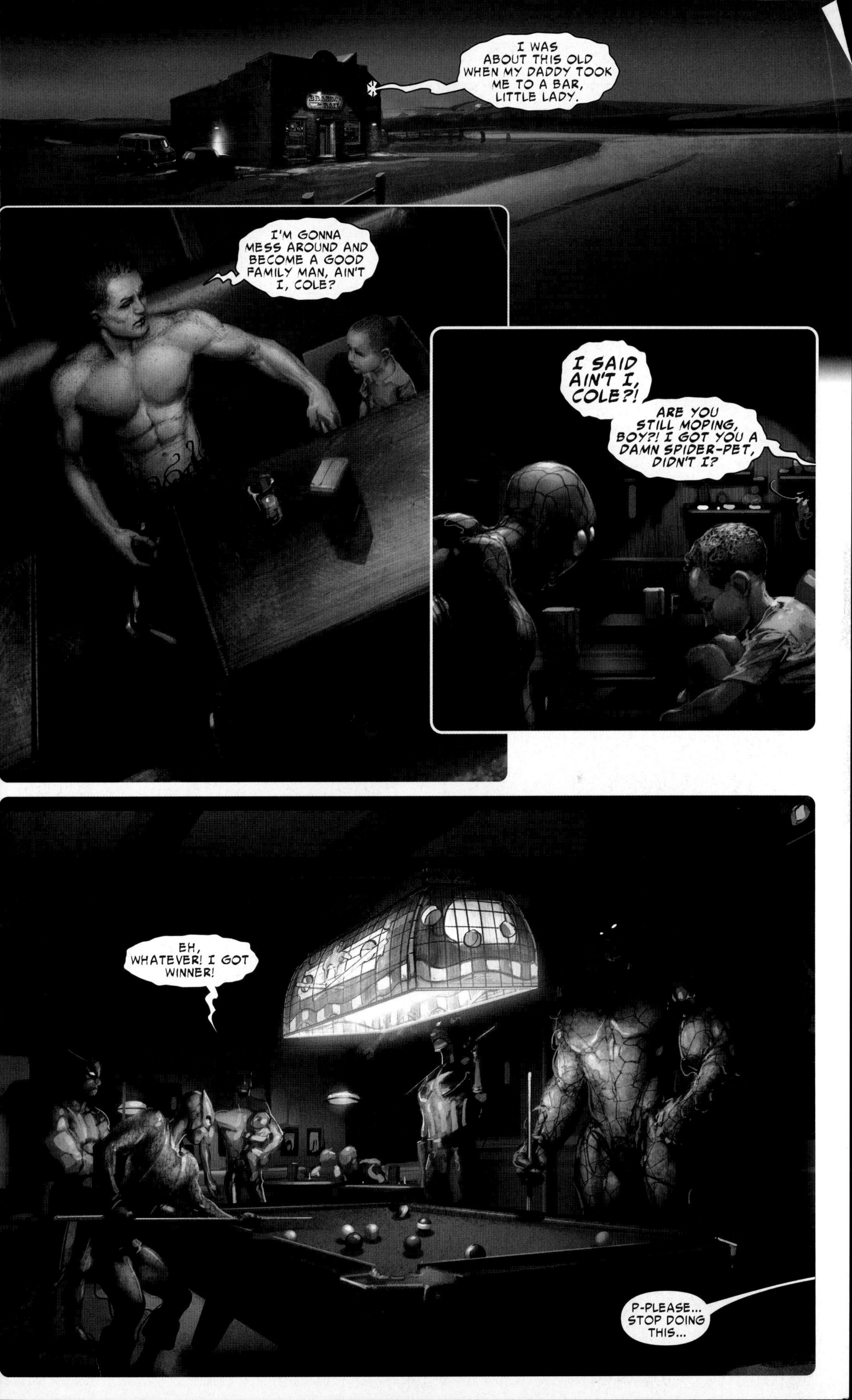
I WAS ABOUT THIS OLD WHEN MY DADDY TOOK ME TO A BAR, LITTLE LADY.
I'M GONNA MESS AROUND AND BECOME A GOOD FAMILY MAN, AIN'T I, COLE?
I SAID AIN'T I, COLE?!
ARE YOU STILL MOPING, BOY?! I GOT YOU A DAMN SPIDER-PET, DIDN'T I?
EH, WHATEVER! I GOT WINNER!
P-PLEASE... STOP DOING THIS...

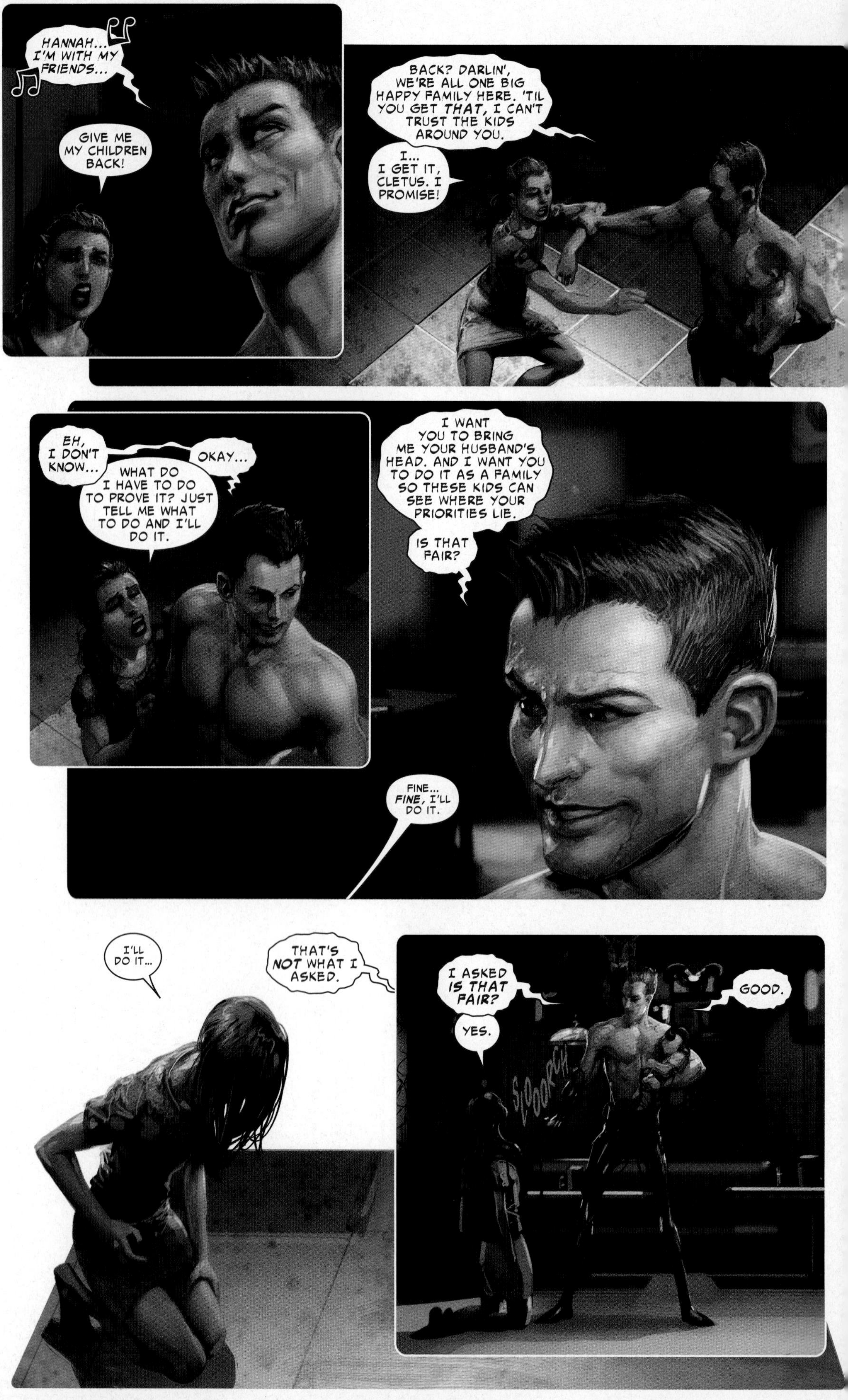
HANNAH... I'M WITH MY FRIENDS...
GIVE ME MY CHILDREN BACK!
BACK? DARLIN', WE'RE ALL ONE BIG HAPPY FAMILY HERE. 'TIL YOU GET THAT, I CAN'T TRUST THE KIDS AROUND YOU.
I... I GET IT, CLETUS. I PROMISE!
EH, I DON'T KNOW...
OKAY...
WHAT DO I HAVE TO DO TO PROVE IT? JUST TELL ME WHAT TO DO AND I'LL DO IT.
I WANT YOU TO BRING ME YOUR HUSBAND'S HEAD. AND I WANT YOU TO DO IT AS A FAMILY SO THESE KIDS CAN SEE WHERE YOUR PRIORITIES LIE.
IS THAT FAIR?
FINE... FINE, I'LL DO IT.
I'LL DO IT...
THAT'S NOT WHAT I ASKED.
I ASKED IS THAT FAIR?
YES.
GOOD.
SLOOORCH

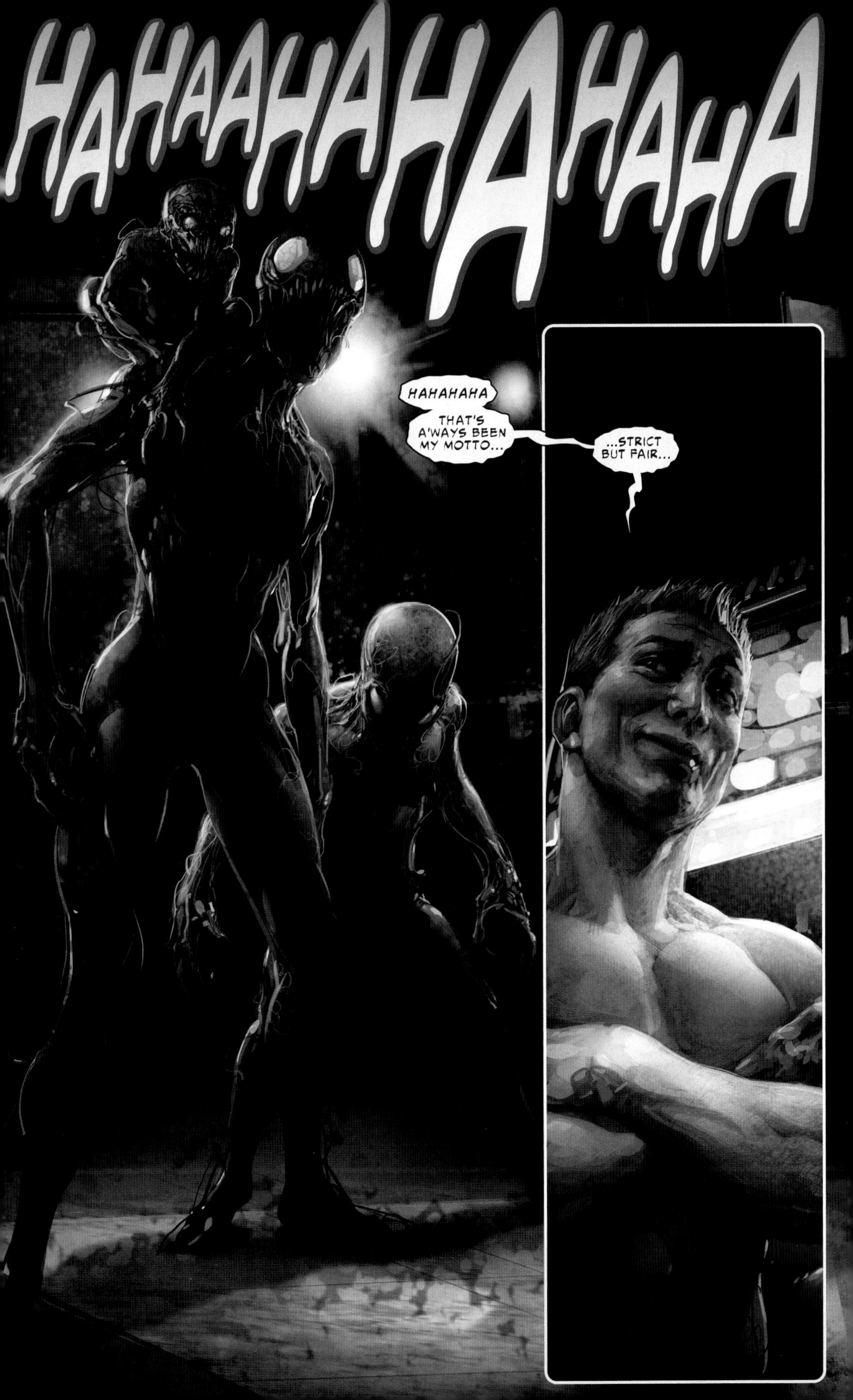
HAHAAAHAHAAHAHAHA
HAHAHAHA
THAT'S A'WAYS BEEN MY MOTTO...
...STRICT BUT FAIR...

Amazing Spider-Man #798-800 connecting variants by Humberto Ramos & Edgar Delgado

Amazing Spider-Man #798 variant by
Javier Garrón & Romulo Fajardo Jr.

Amazing Spider-Man #799 variant by
Ed McGuinness & Morry Hollowell

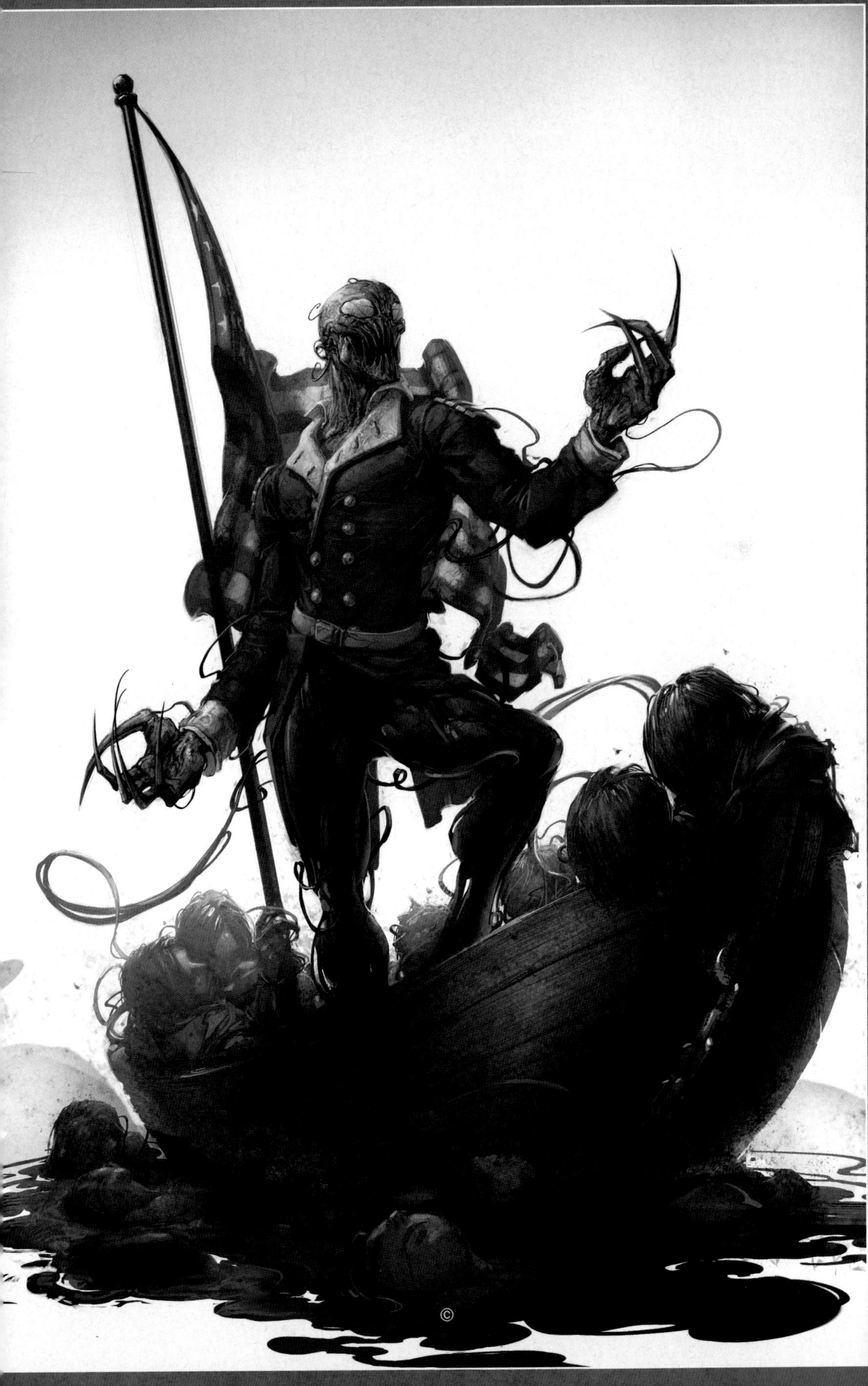

CARNAGE, U.S.A. #3

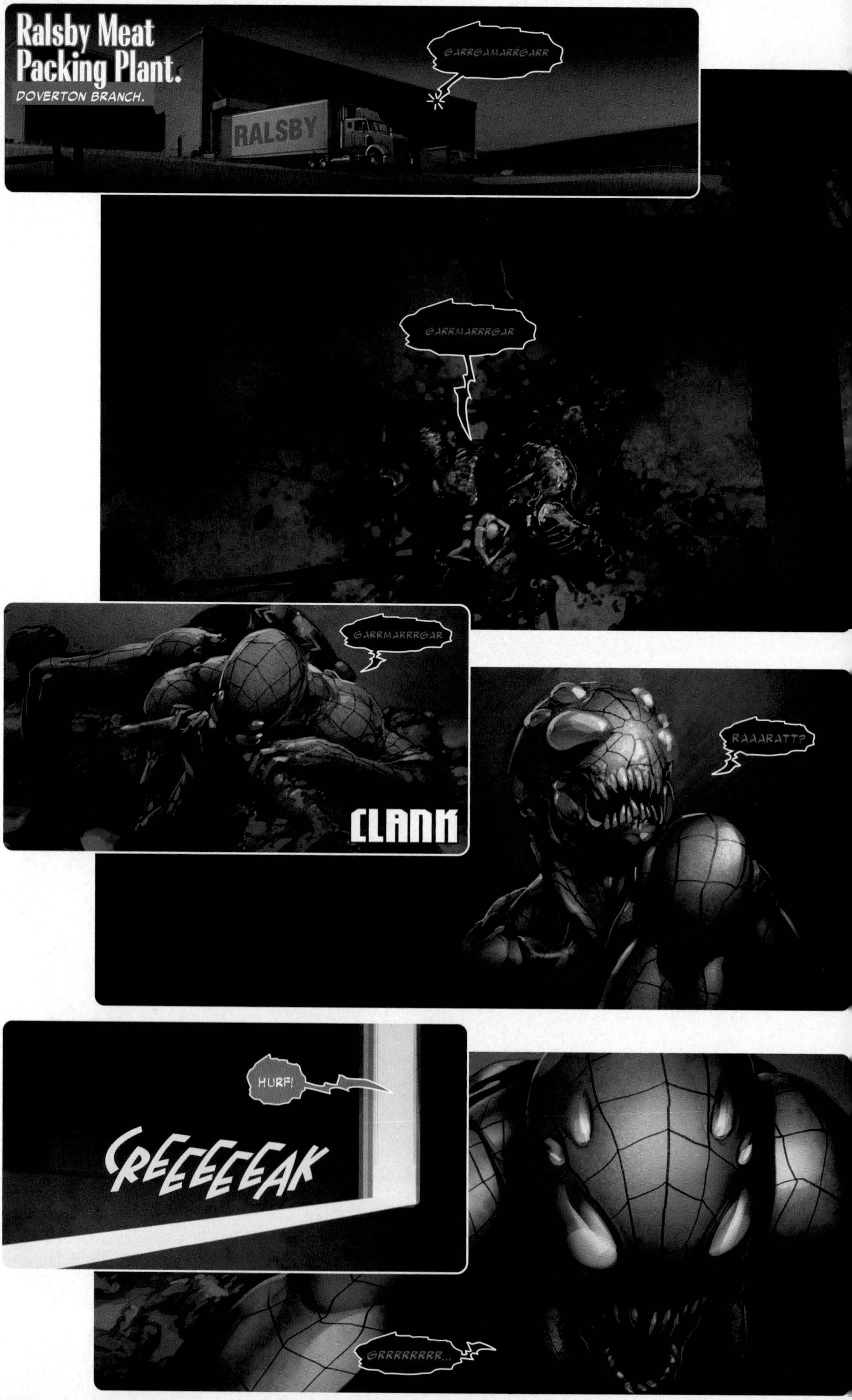
Ralsby Meat Packing Plant.
DOVERTON BRANCH.
GARRGAMARRGARR
RALSBY
GARRMARRRGAR
GARRMARRRGAR
CLANK
RAAARATT?
HURF!
CREEEEEAK
GRRRRRRRR...

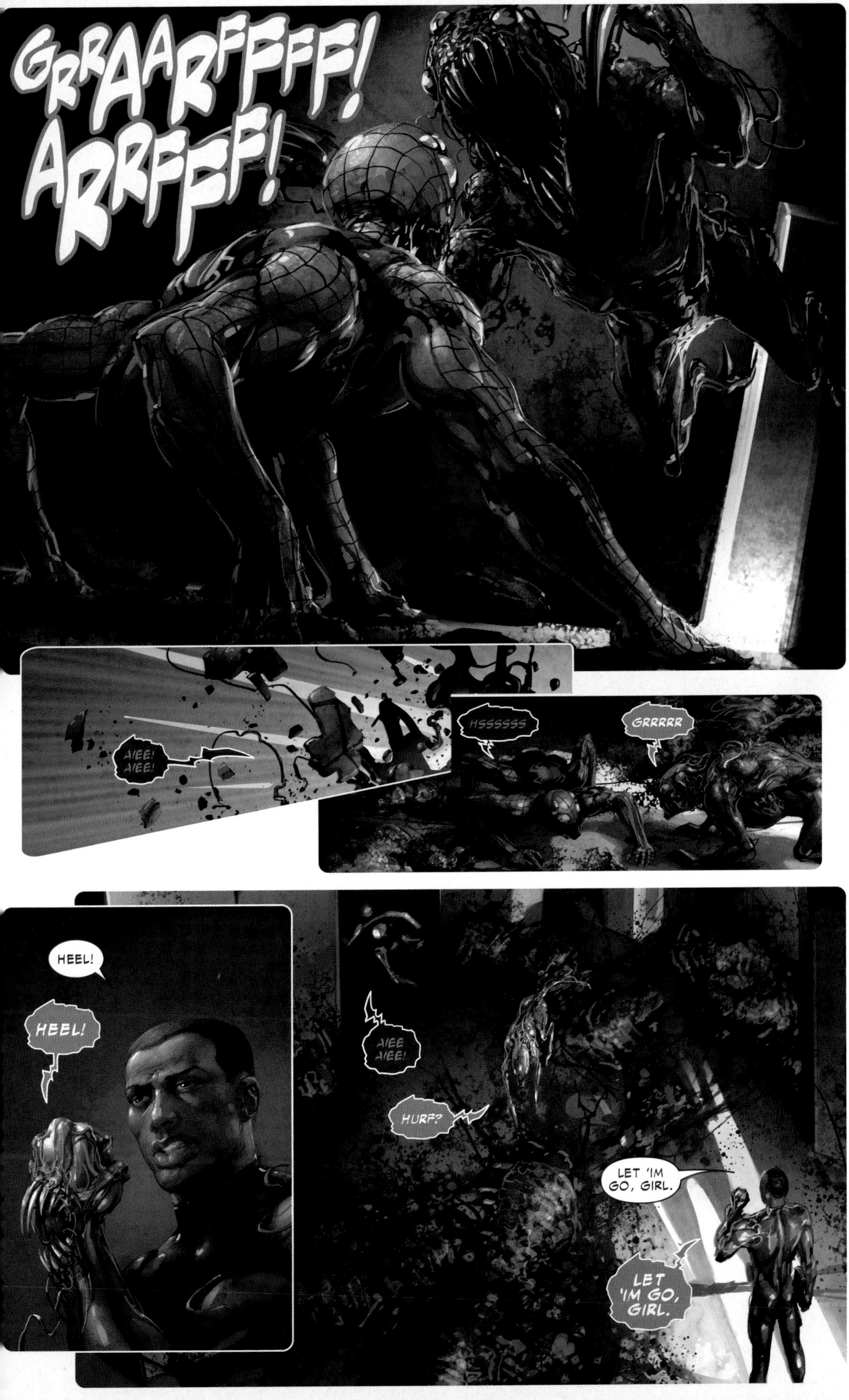
GRRAARFFFF!
ARRFFF!
AIEE!
AIEE!
HSSSSSS
GRRRRR
HEEL!
HEEL!
AIEE
AIEE!
HURF?
LET 'IM GO, GIRL.
LET 'IM GO, GIRL.

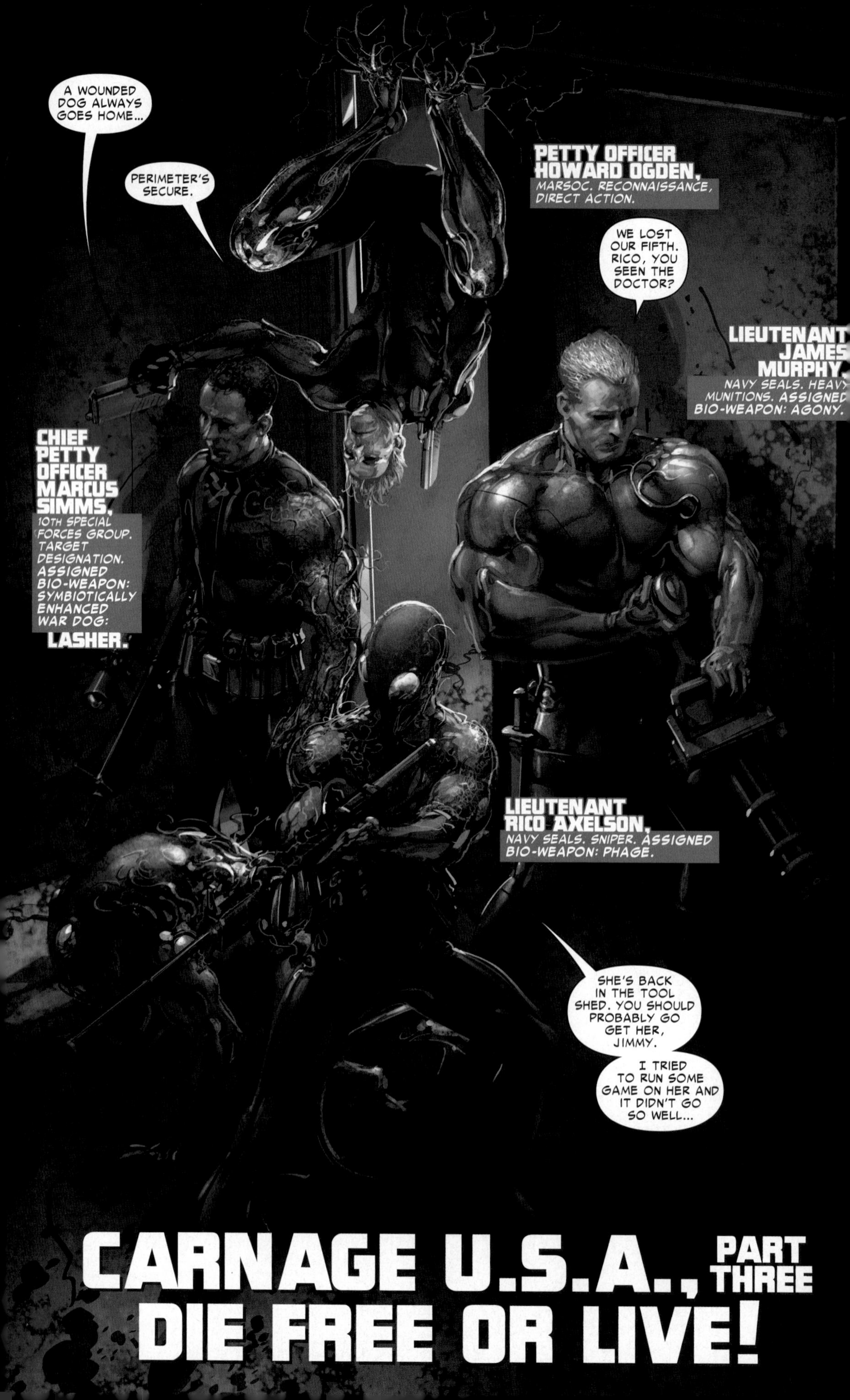
A WOUNDED DOG ALWAYS GOES HOME...
PERIMETER'S SECURE.
PETTY OFFICER HOWARD OGDEN, MARSOC. RECONNAISSANCE, DIRECT ACTION.
WE LOST OUR FIFTH. RICO, YOU SEEN THE DOCTOR?
LIEUTENANT JAMES MURPHY, NAVY SEALS. HEAVY MUNITIONS. ASSIGNED BIO-WEAPON: AGONY.
CHIEF PETTY OFFICER MARCUS SIMMS, 10TH SPECIAL FORCES GROUP. TARGET DESIGNATION. ASSIGNED BIO-WEAPON: SYMBIOTICALLY ENHANCED WAR DOG: LASHER.
LIEUTENANT RICO AXELSON, NAVY SEALS. SNIPER. ASSIGNED BIO-WEAPON: PHAGE.
SHE'S BACK IN THE TOOL SHED. YOU SHOULD PROBABLY GO GET HER, JIMMY.
I TRIED TO RUN SOME GAME ON HER AND IT DIDN'T GO SO WELL...
CARNAGE U.S.A., PART THREE
DIE FREE OR LIVE!

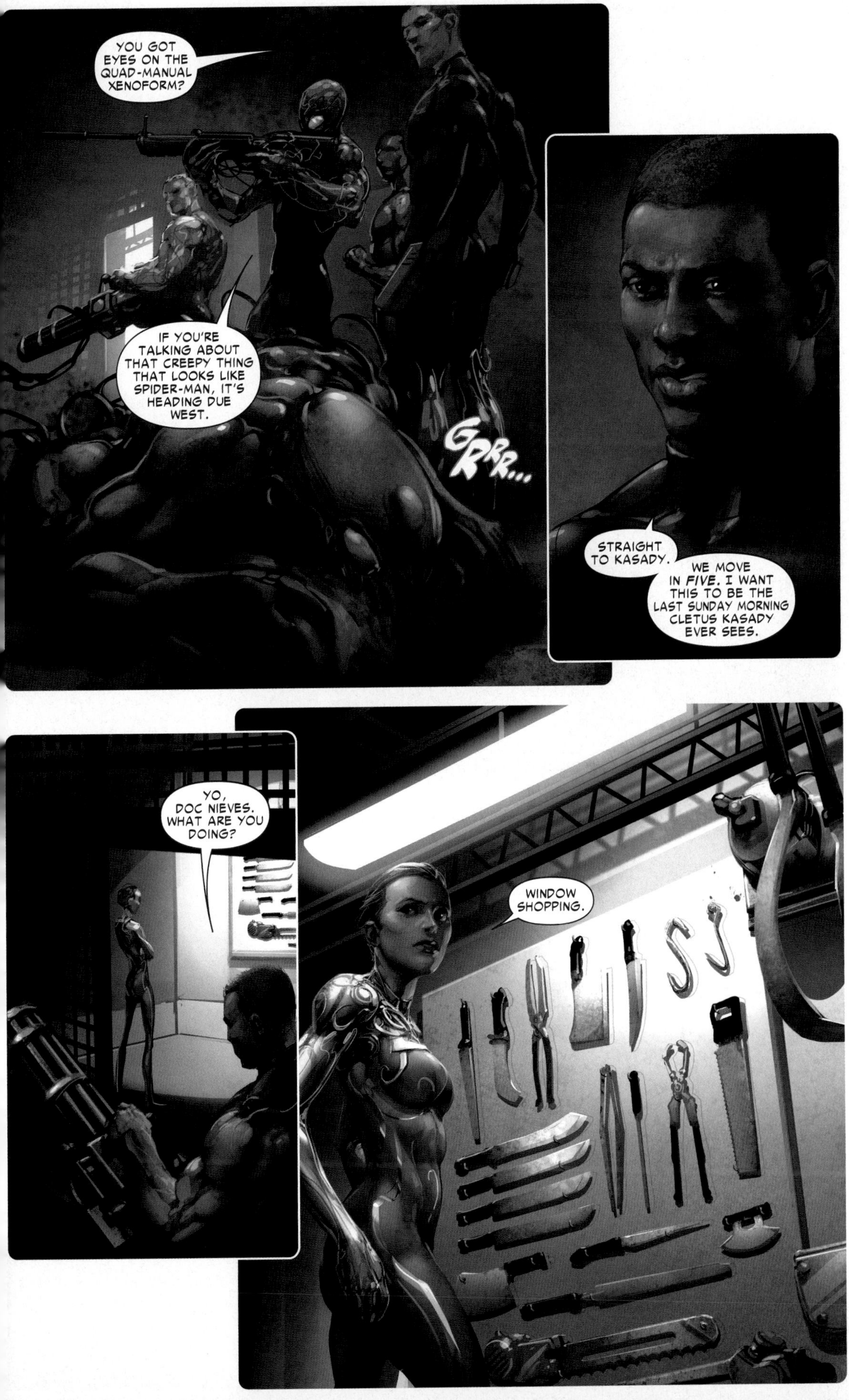
YOU GOT EYES ON THE QUAD-MANUAL XENOFORM?
IF YOU'RE TALKING ABOUT THAT CREEPY THING THAT LOOKS LIKE SPIDER-MAN, IT'S HEADING DUE WEST.
GRRR...
STRAIGHT TO KASADY.
WE MOVE IN *FIVE*. I WANT THIS TO BE THE LAST SUNDAY MORNING CLETUS KASADY EVER SEES.
YO, DOC NIEVES. WHAT ARE YOU DOING?
WINDOW SHOPPING.

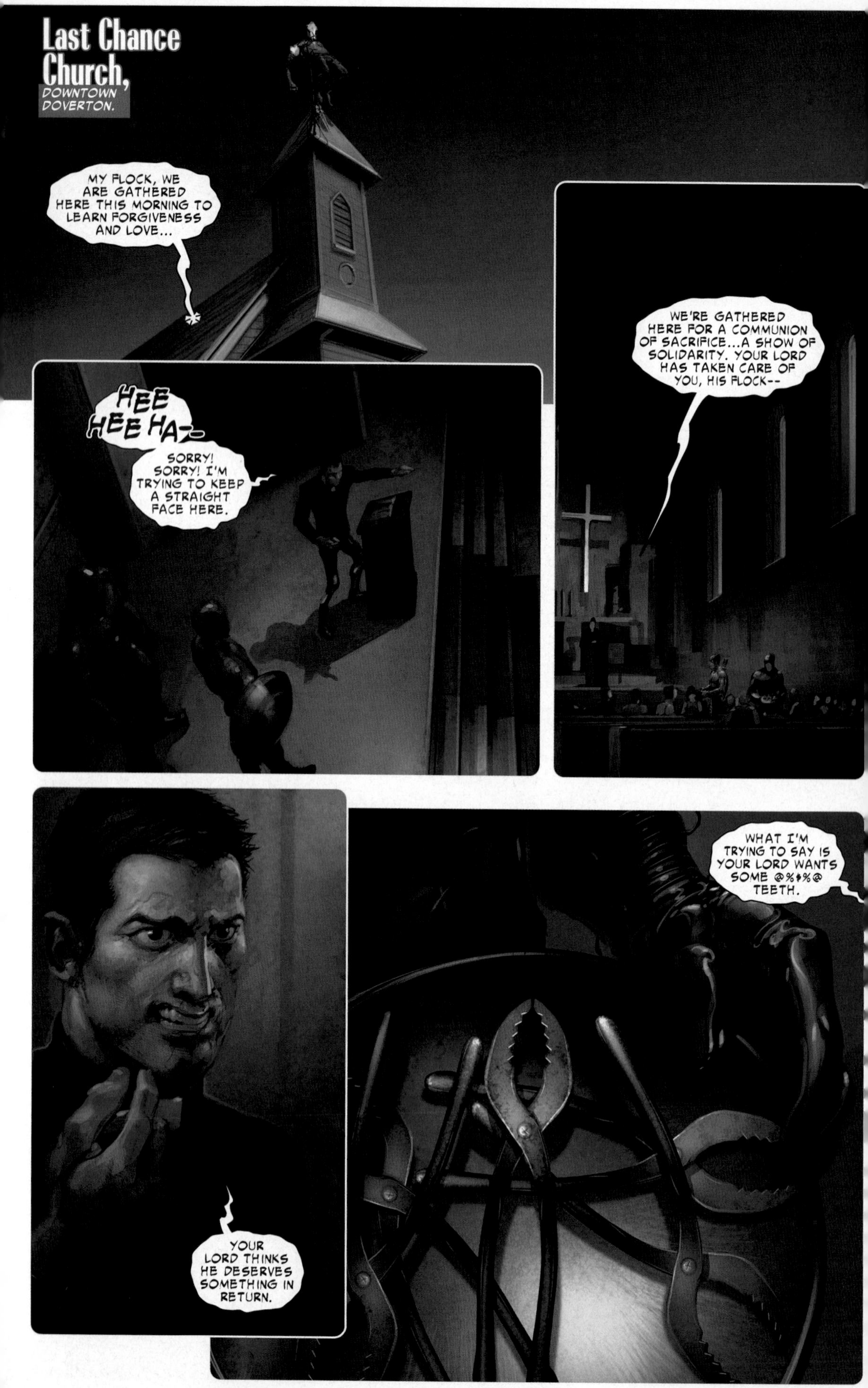
Last Chance Church, DOWNTOWN DOVERTON.
MY FLOCK, WE ARE GATHERED HERE THIS MORNING TO LEARN FORGIVENESS AND LOVE...
WE'RE GATHERED HERE FOR A COMMUNION OF SACRIFICE...A SHOW OF SOLIDARITY. YOUR LORD HAS TAKEN CARE OF YOU, HIS FLOCK--
HEE HEE HA--
SORRY! SORRY! I'M TRYING TO KEEP A STRAIGHT FACE HERE.
YOUR LORD THINKS HE DESERVES SOMETHING IN RETURN.
WHAT I'M TRYING TO SAY IS YOUR LORD WANTS SOME @%#%@ TEETH.

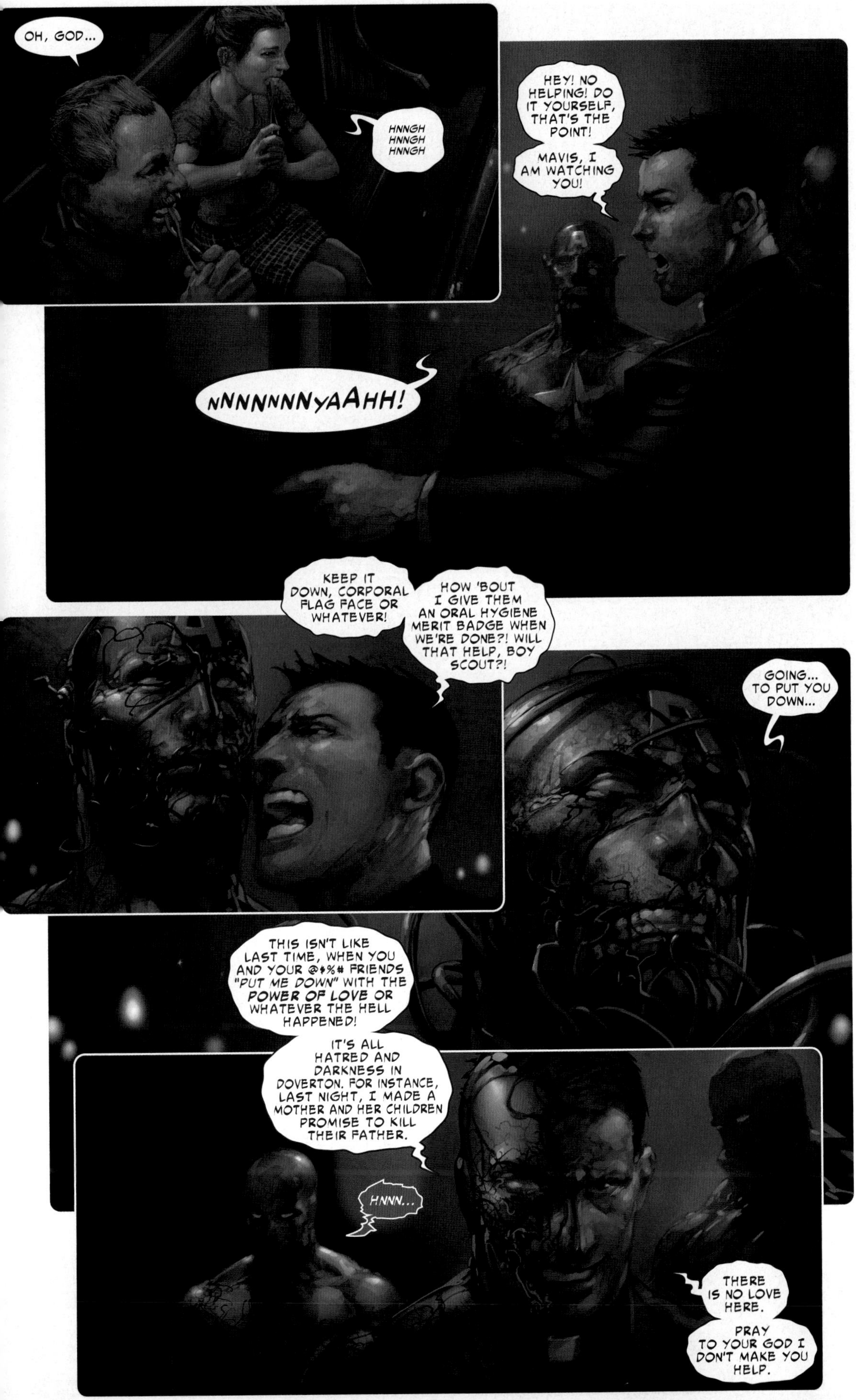
OH, GOD...
HNNGH HNNGH HNNGH
HEY! NO HELPING! DO IT YOURSELF, THAT'S THE POINT!
MAVIS, I AM WATCHING YOU!
NNNNNNNyAAHH!
KEEP IT DOWN, CORPORAL FLAG FACE OR WHATEVER!
HOW 'BOUT I GIVE THEM AN ORAL HYGIENE MERIT BADGE WHEN WE'RE DONE?! WILL THAT HELP, BOY SCOUT?!
GOING... TO PUT YOU DOWN...
THIS ISN'T LIKE LAST TIME, WHEN YOU AND YOUR @$%# FRIENDS "PUT ME DOWN" WITH THE POWER OF LOVE OR WHATEVER THE HELL HAPPENED!
IT'S ALL HATRED AND DARKNESS IN DOVERTON. FOR INSTANCE, LAST NIGHT, I MADE A MOTHER AND HER CHILDREN PROMISE TO KILL THEIR FATHER.
HNNN...
THERE IS NO LOVE HERE.
PRAY TO YOUR GOD I DON'T MAKE YOU HELP.

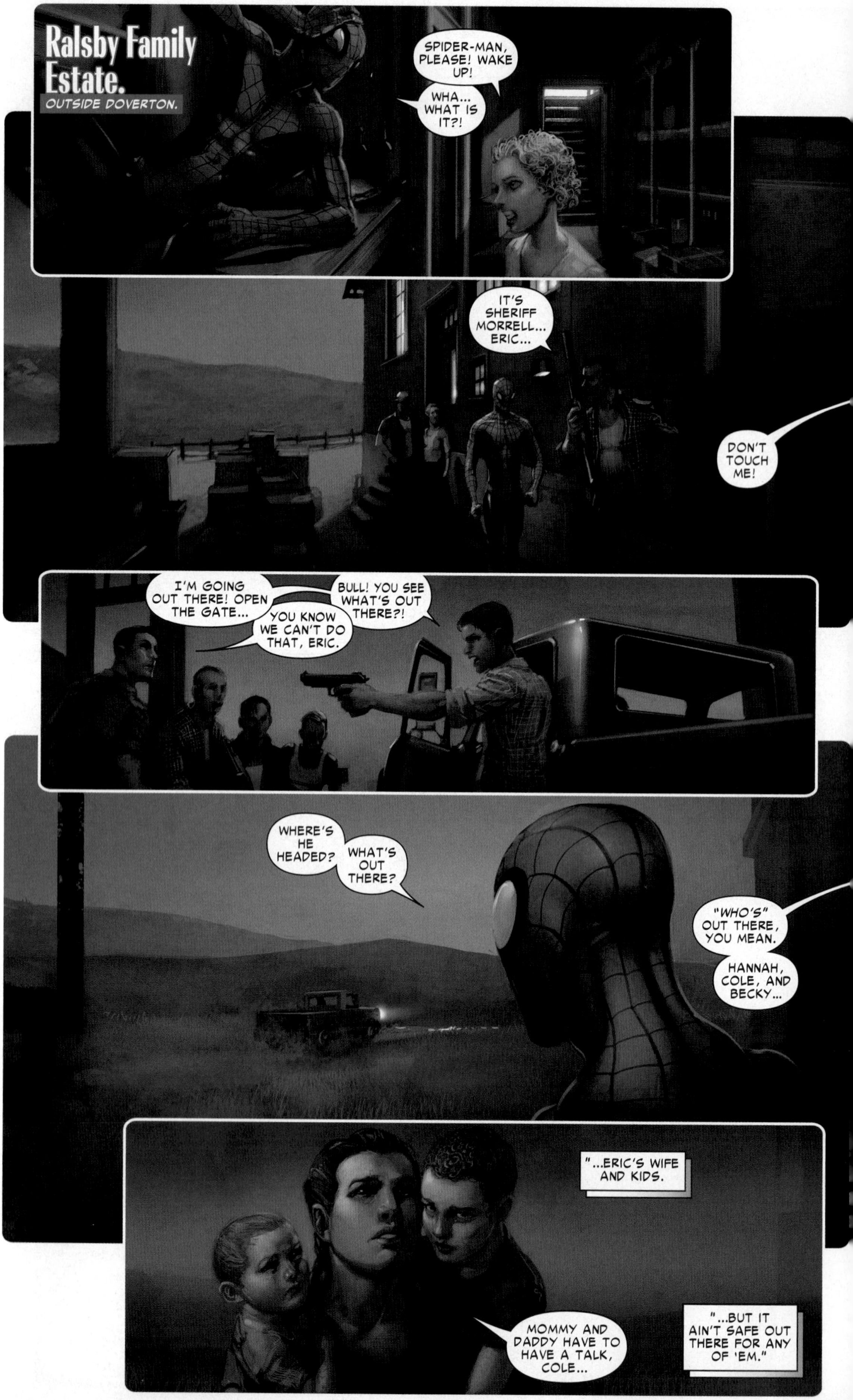

Ralsby Family Estate.
OUTSIDE DOVERTON.
SPIDER-MAN, PLEASE! WAKE UP!
WHA... WHAT IS IT?!
IT'S SHERIFF MORRELL... ERIC...
DON'T TOUCH ME!
I'M GOING OUT THERE! OPEN THE GATE...
BULL! YOU SEE WHAT'S OUT THERE?!
YOU KNOW WE CAN'T DO THAT, ERIC.
WHERE'S HE HEADED?
WHAT'S OUT THERE?
"WHO'S" OUT THERE, YOU MEAN.
HANNAH, COLE, AND BECKY...
"...ERIC'S WIFE AND KIDS.
MOMMY AND DADDY HAVE TO HAVE A TALK, COLE...
"...BUT IT AIN'T SAFE OUT THERE FOR ANY OF 'EM."

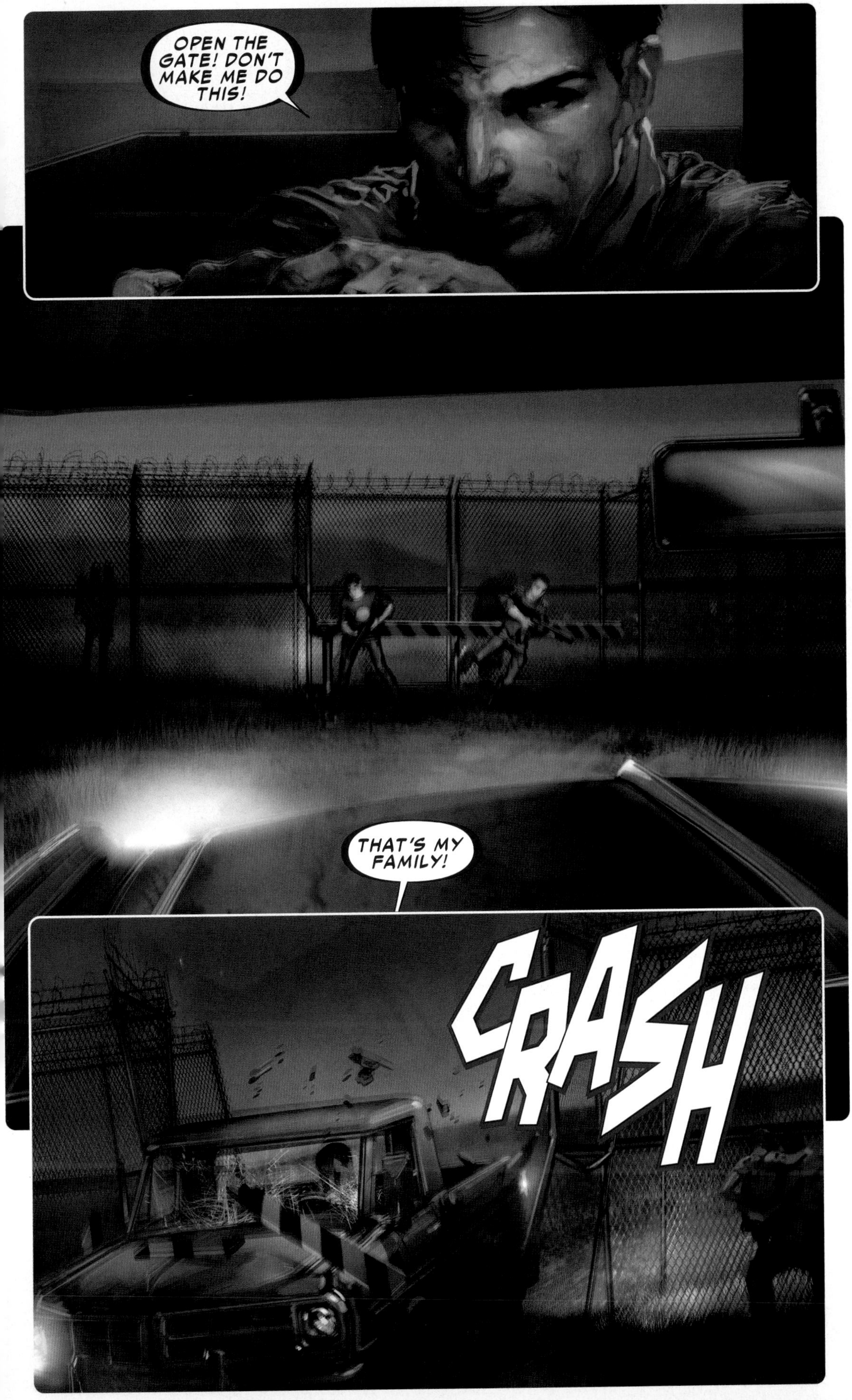
OPEN THE GATE! DON'T MAKE ME DO THIS!
THAT'S MY FAMILY!
CRASH

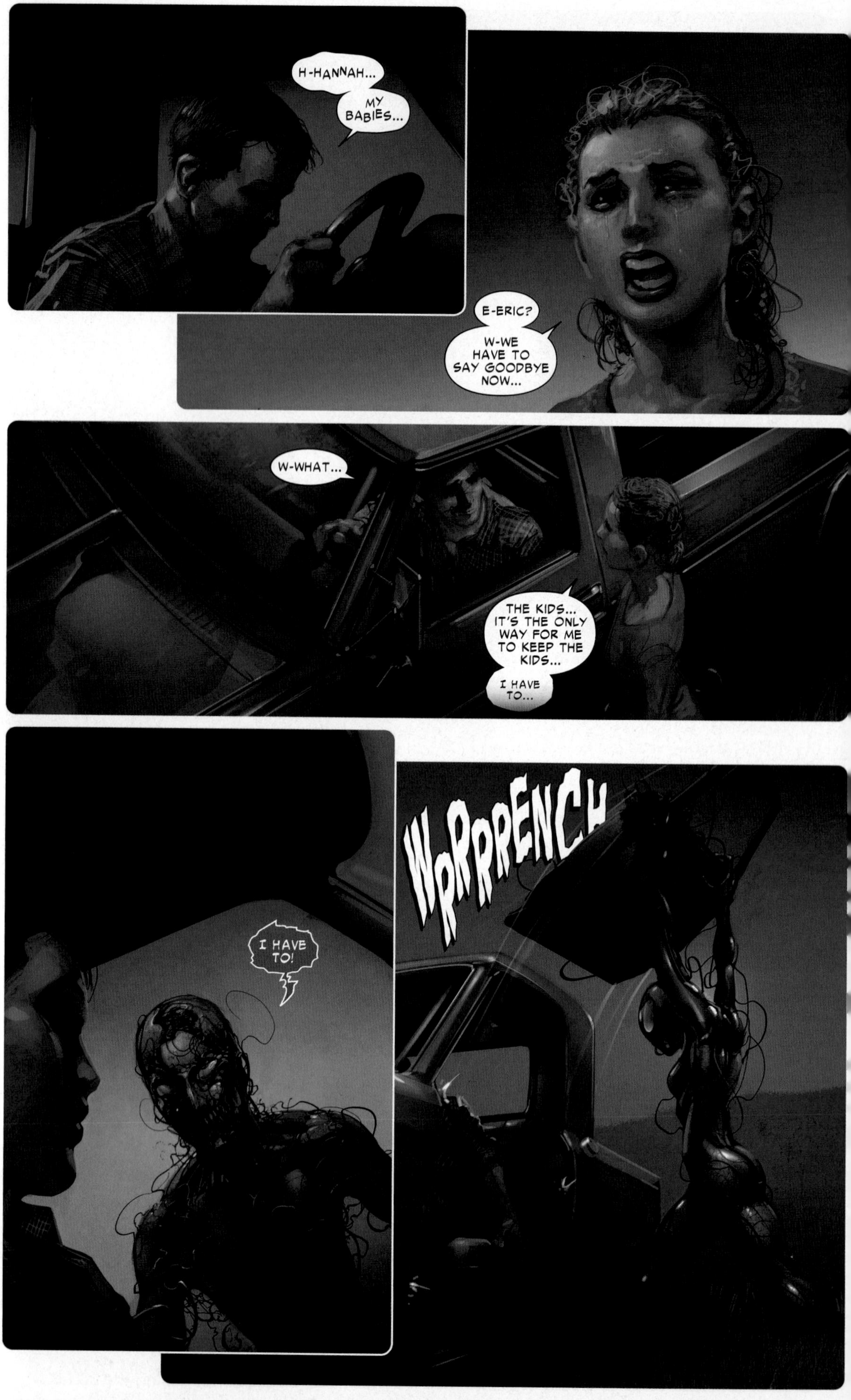
H-HANNAH...
MY BABIES...
E-ERIC?
W-WE HAVE TO SAY GOODBYE NOW...
W-WHAT...
THE KIDS... IT'S THE ONLY WAY FOR ME TO KEEP THE KIDS...
I HAVE TO...
I HAVE TO!
WRRRRENCH

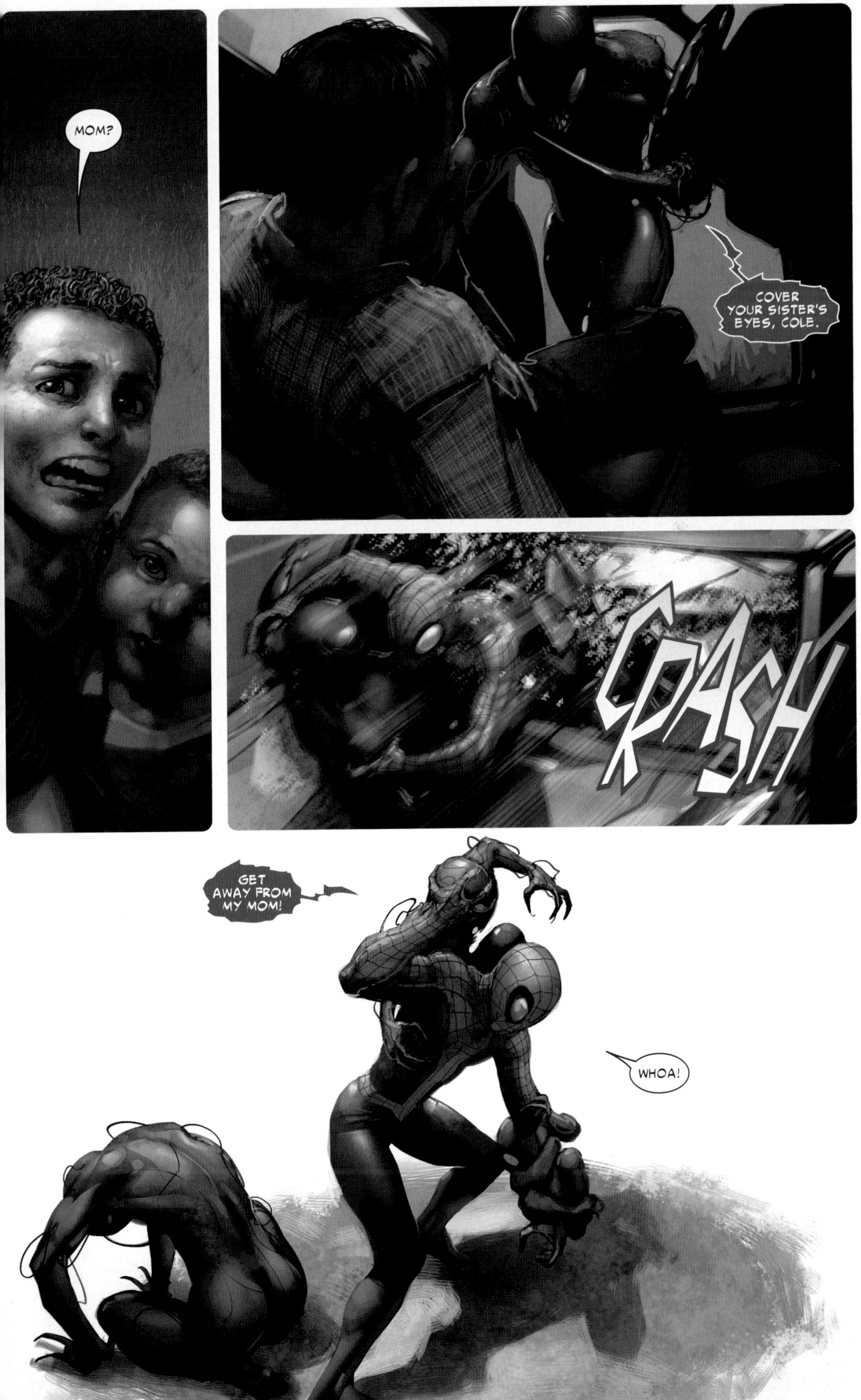
MOM?
COVER YOUR SISTER'S EYES, COLE.
CRASH
GET AWAY FROM MY MOM!
WHOA!

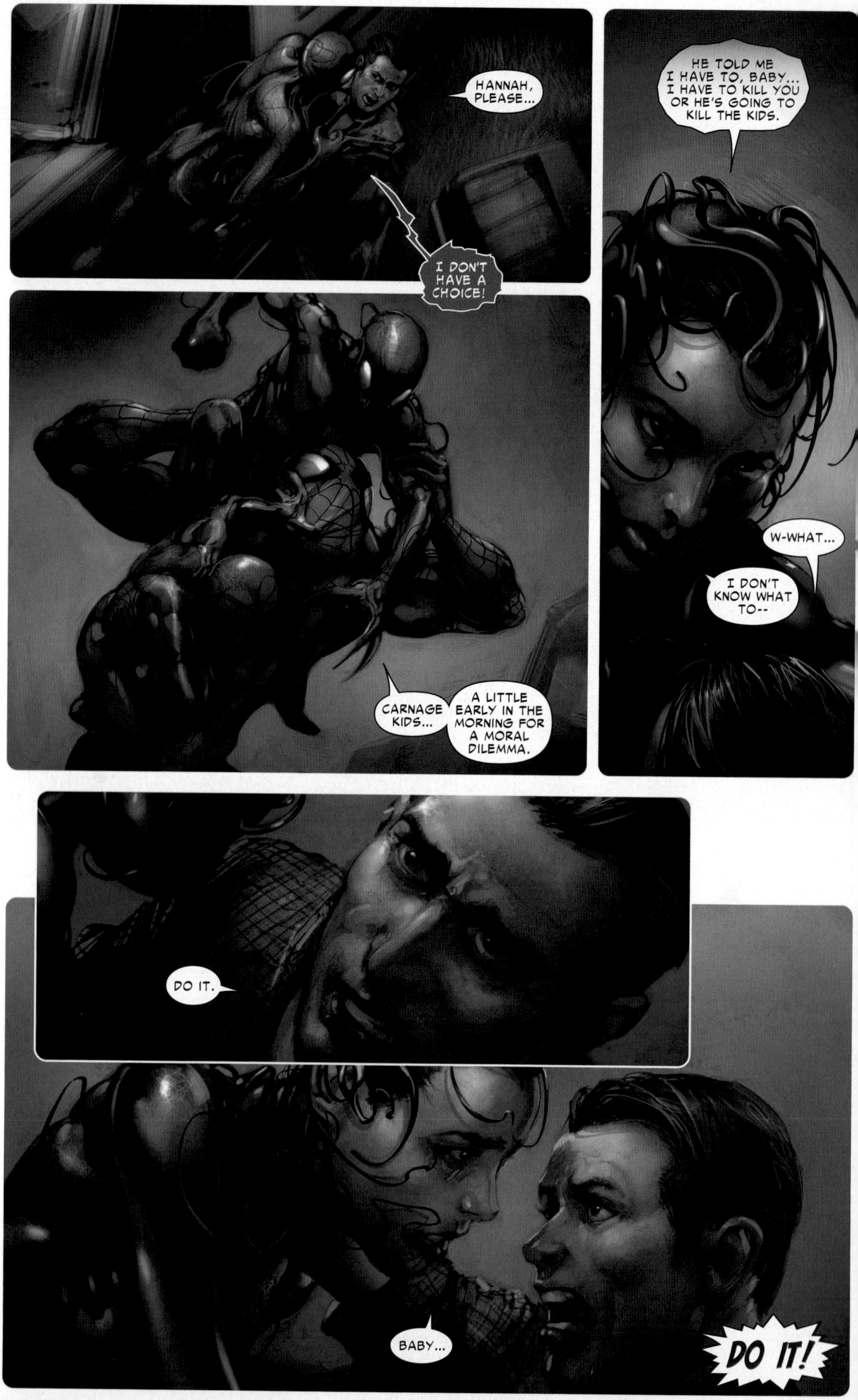
HANNAH, PLEASE...
I DON'T HAVE A CHOICE!
HE TOLD ME I HAVE TO, BABY... I HAVE TO KILL YOU OR HE'S GOING TO KILL THE KIDS.
CARNAGE KIDS...
A LITTLE EARLY IN THE MORNING FOR A MORAL DILEMMA.
W-WHAT...
I DON'T KNOW WHAT TO--
DO IT.
BABY...
DO IT!

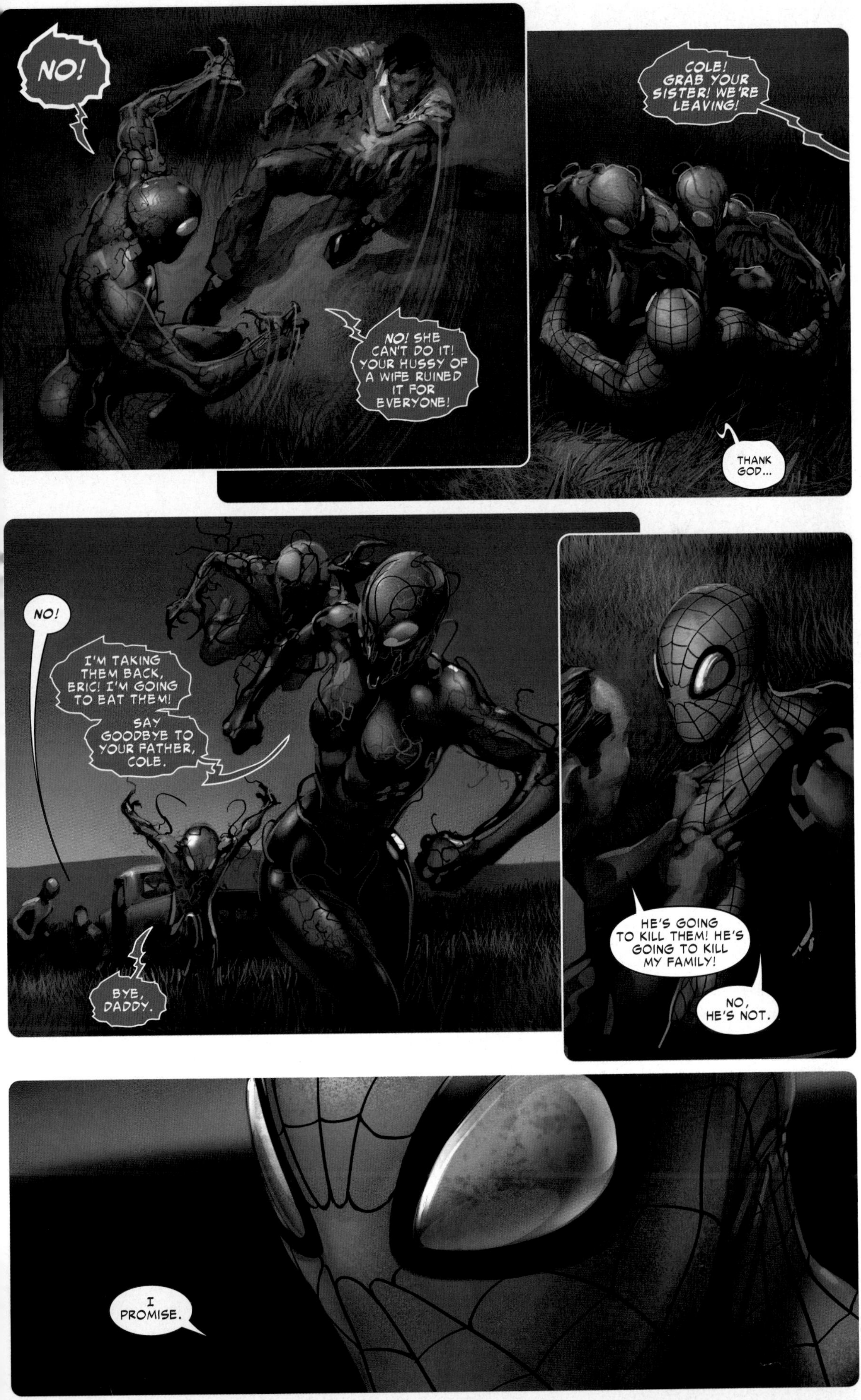
NO!
NO! SHE CAN'T DO IT! YOUR HUSSY OF A WIFE RUINED IT FOR EVERYONE!
COLE! GRAB YOUR SISTER! WE'RE LEAVING!
THANK GOD...
NO!
I'M TAKING THEM BACK, ERIC! I'M GOING TO EAT THEM!
SAY GOODBYE TO YOUR FATHER, COLE.
BYE, DADDY.
HE'S GOING TO KILL THEM! HE'S GOING TO KILL MY FAMILY!
NO, HE'S NOT.
I PROMISE.

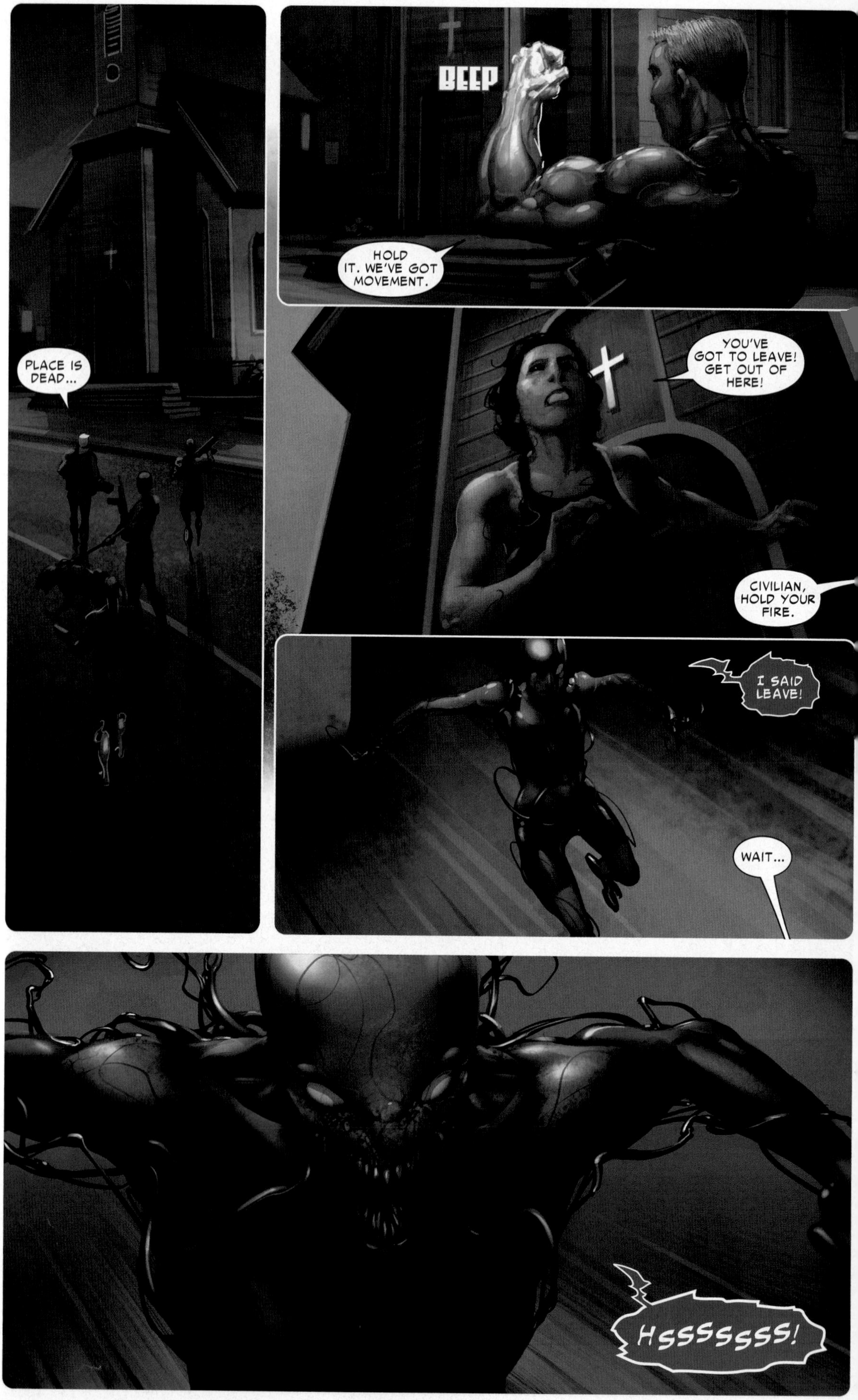
PLACE IS DEAD...
BEEP
HOLD IT. WE'VE GOT MOVEMENT.
YOU'VE GOT TO LEAVE! GET OUT OF HERE!
CIVILIAN, HOLD YOUR FIRE.
I SAID LEAVE!
WAIT...
HSSSSSSS!

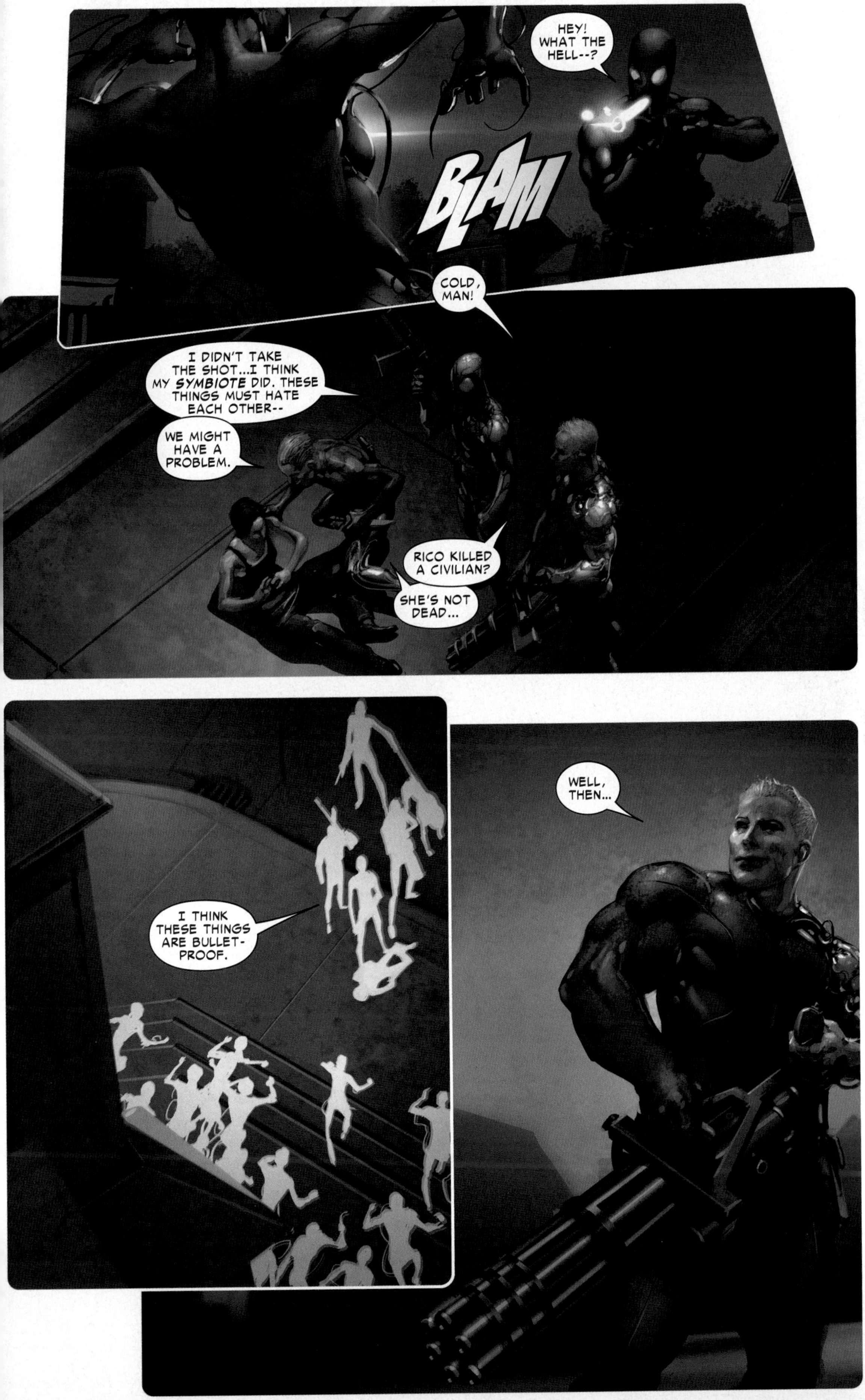

HEY! WHAT THE HELL--?
BLAM
COLD, MAN!
I DIDN'T TAKE THE SHOT...I THINK MY SYMBIOTE DID. THESE THINGS MUST HATE EACH OTHER--
WE MIGHT HAVE A PROBLEM.
RICO KILLED A CIVILIAN?
SHE'S NOT DEAD...
I THINK THESE THINGS ARE BULLET-PROOF.
WELL, THEN...

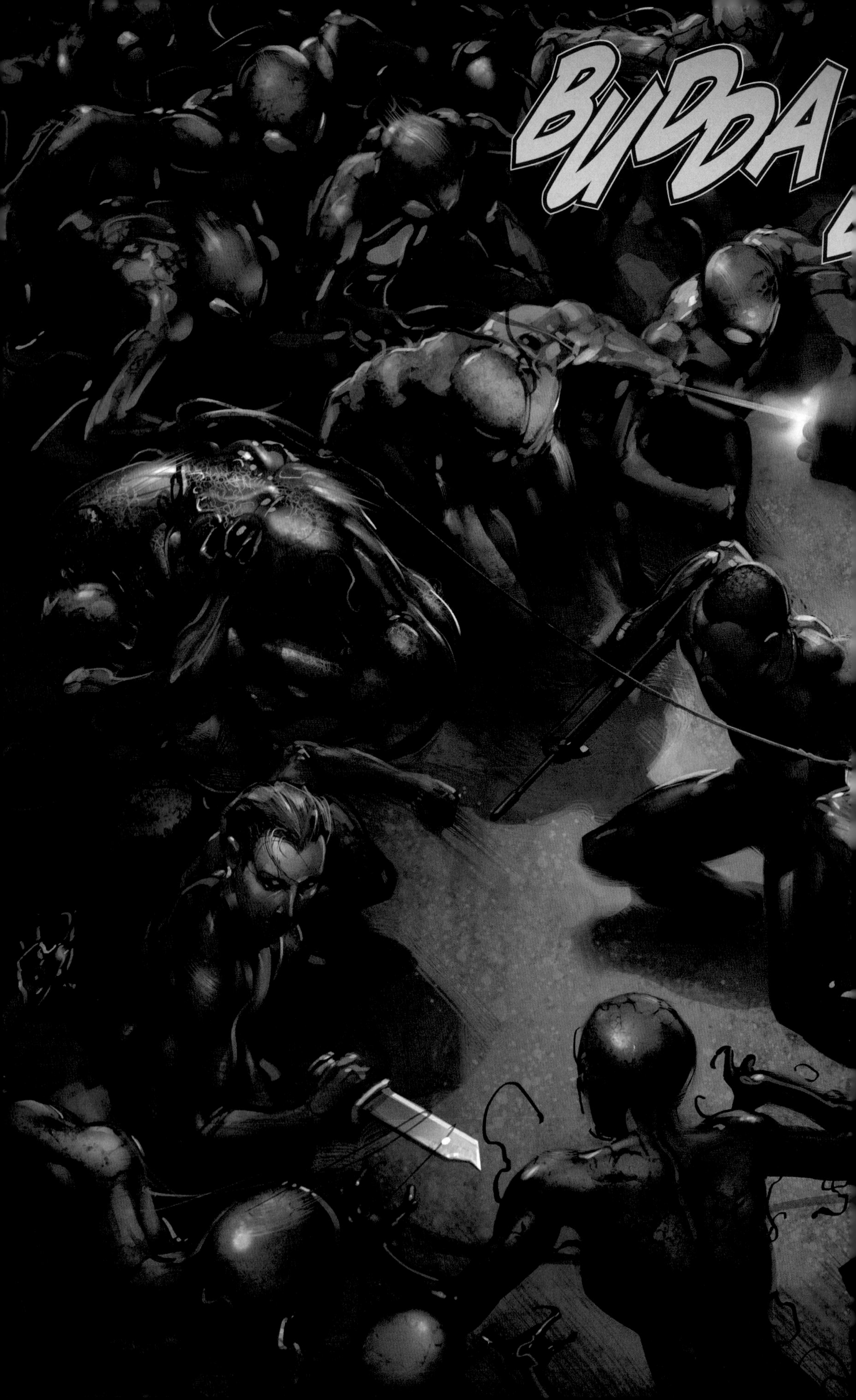
BUDDA

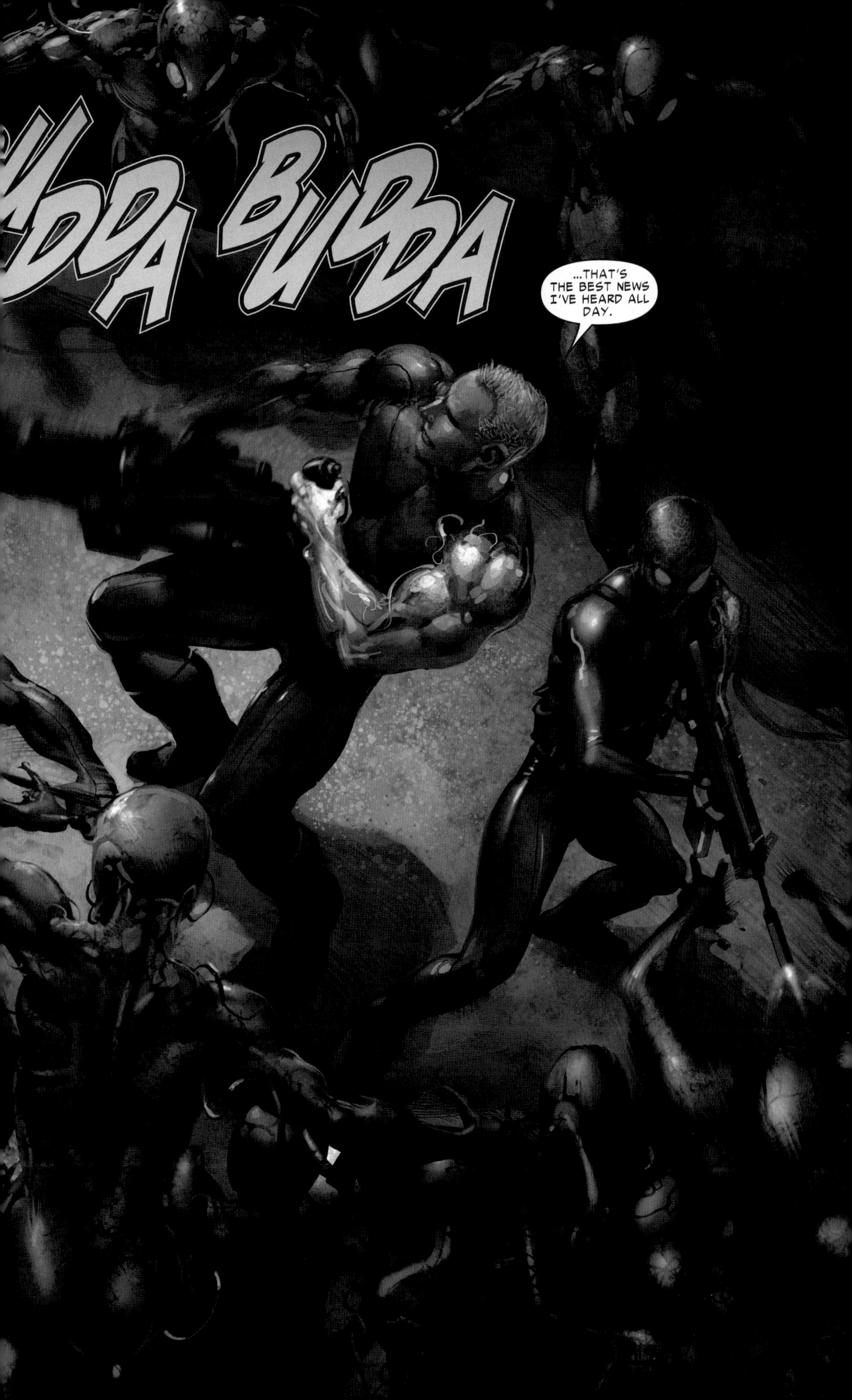

...DDA BUDDA
...THAT'S THE BEST NEWS I'VE HEARD ALL DAY.

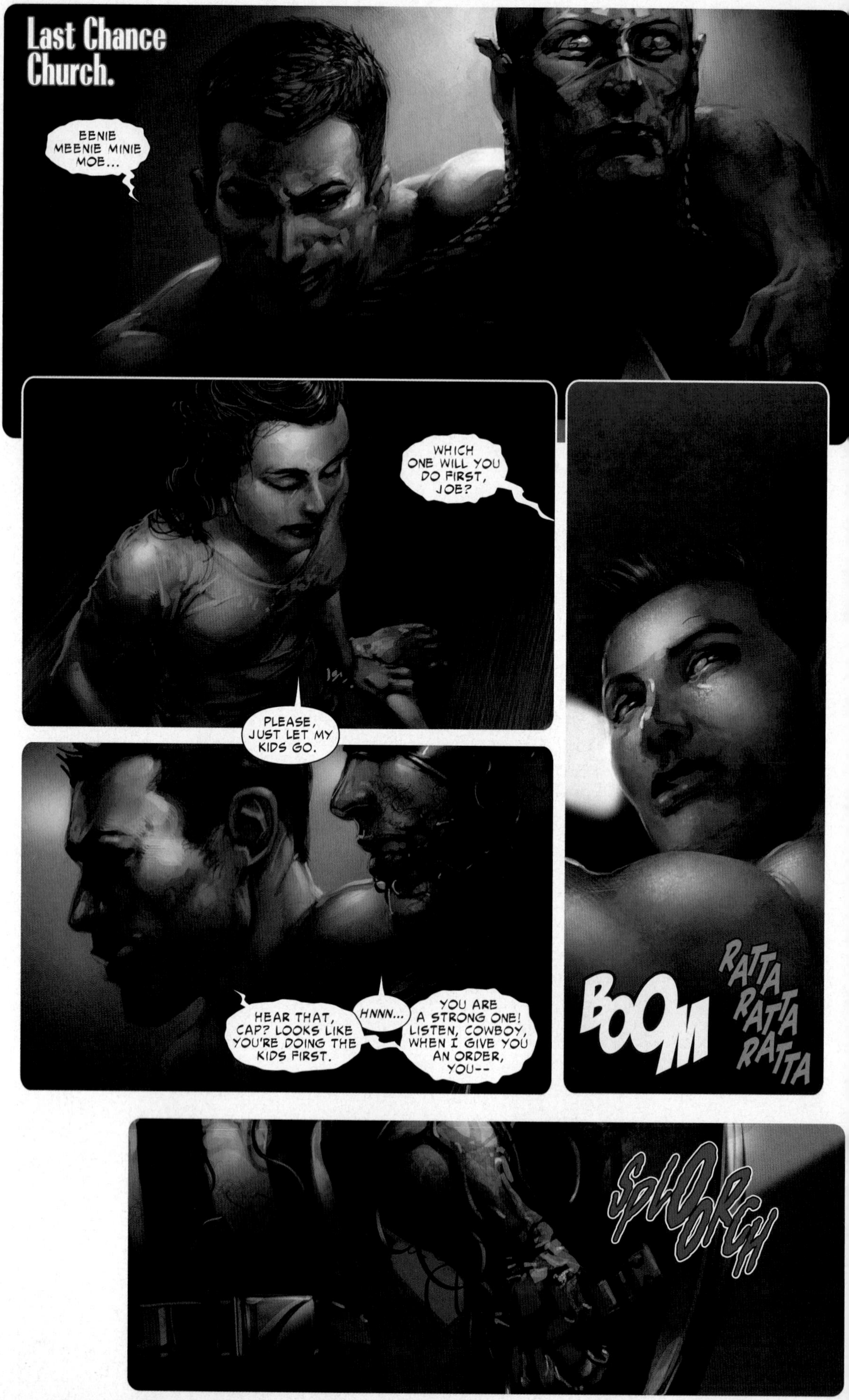
Last Chance Church.
EENIE MEENIE MINIE MOE...
WHICH ONE WILL YOU DO FIRST, JOE?
PLEASE, JUST LET MY KIDS GO.
HEAR THAT, CAP? LOOKS LIKE YOU'RE DOING THE KIDS FIRST.
HNNN...
YOU ARE A STRONG ONE! LISTEN, COWBOY, WHEN I GIVE YOU AN ORDER, YOU--
BOOM
RATTA RATTA RATTA
SPLOORCH

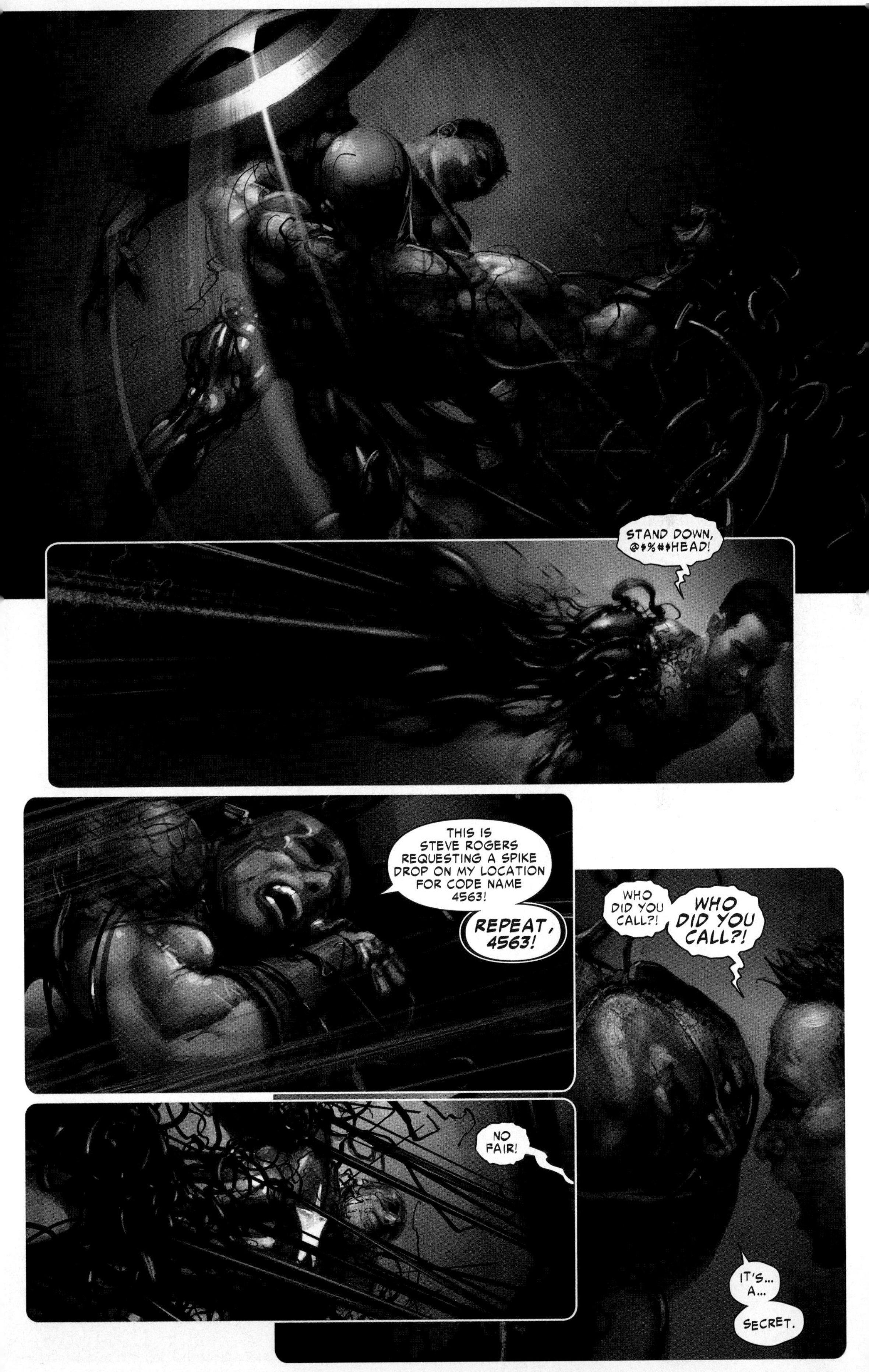

STAND DOWN, @$%##HEAD!
THIS IS STEVE ROGERS REQUESTING A SPIKE DROP ON MY LOCATION FOR CODE NAME 4563!
REPEAT, 4563!
WHO DID YOU CALL?!
WHO DID YOU CALL?!
NO FAIR!
IT'S... A...
SECRET.

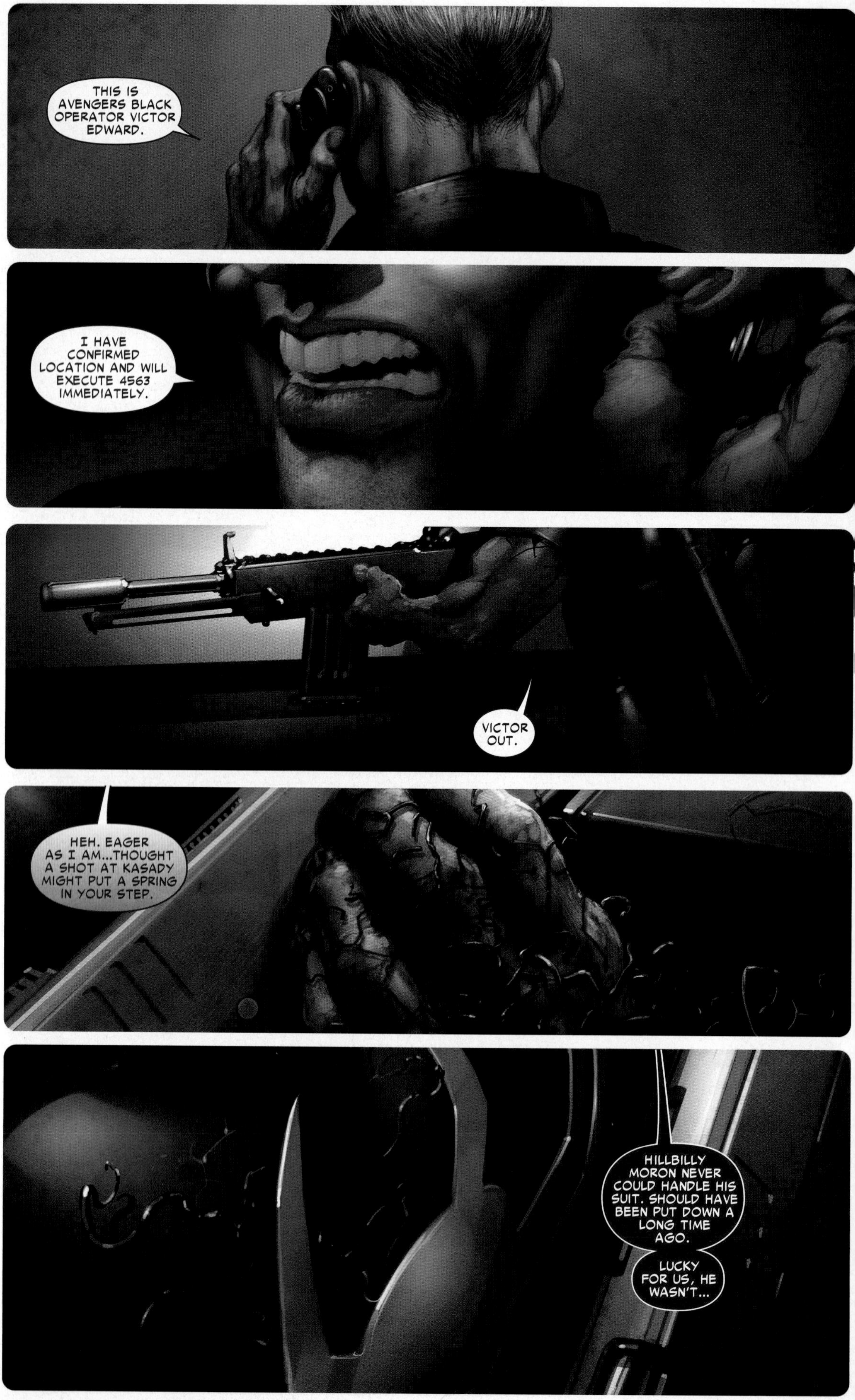
THIS IS AVENGERS BLACK OPERATOR VICTOR EDWARD.
I HAVE CONFIRMED LOCATION AND WILL EXECUTE 4563 IMMEDIATELY.
VICTOR OUT.
HEH. EAGER AS I AM...THOUGHT A SHOT AT KASADY MIGHT PUT A SPRING IN YOUR STEP.
HILLBILLY MORON NEVER COULD HANDLE HIS SUIT. SHOULD HAVE BEEN PUT DOWN A LONG TIME AGO.
LUCKY FOR US, HE WASN'T...

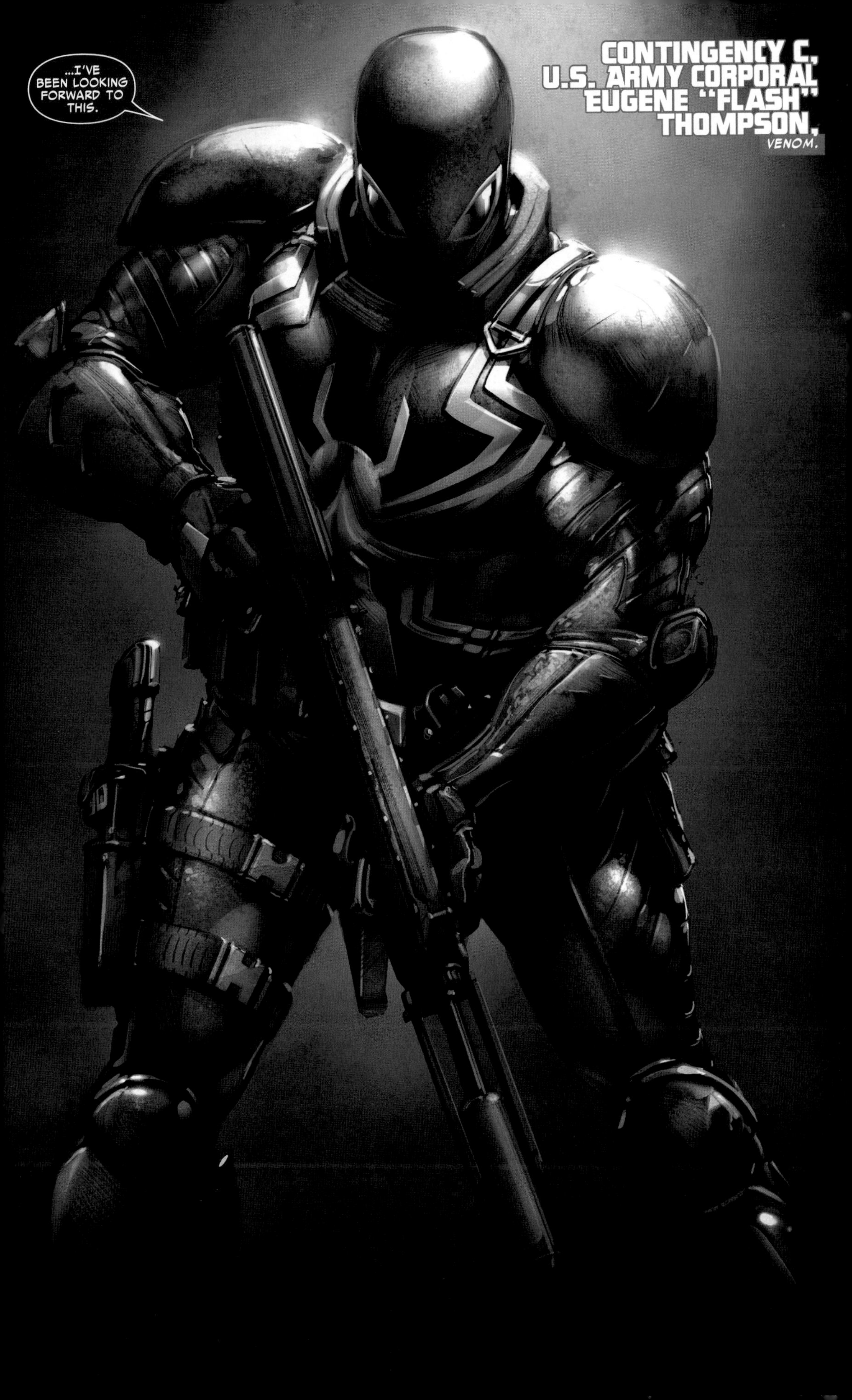
...I'VE BEEN LOOKING FORWARD TO THIS.
CONTINGENCY C, U.S. ARMY CORPORAL EUGENE "FLASH" THOMPSON, VENOM.

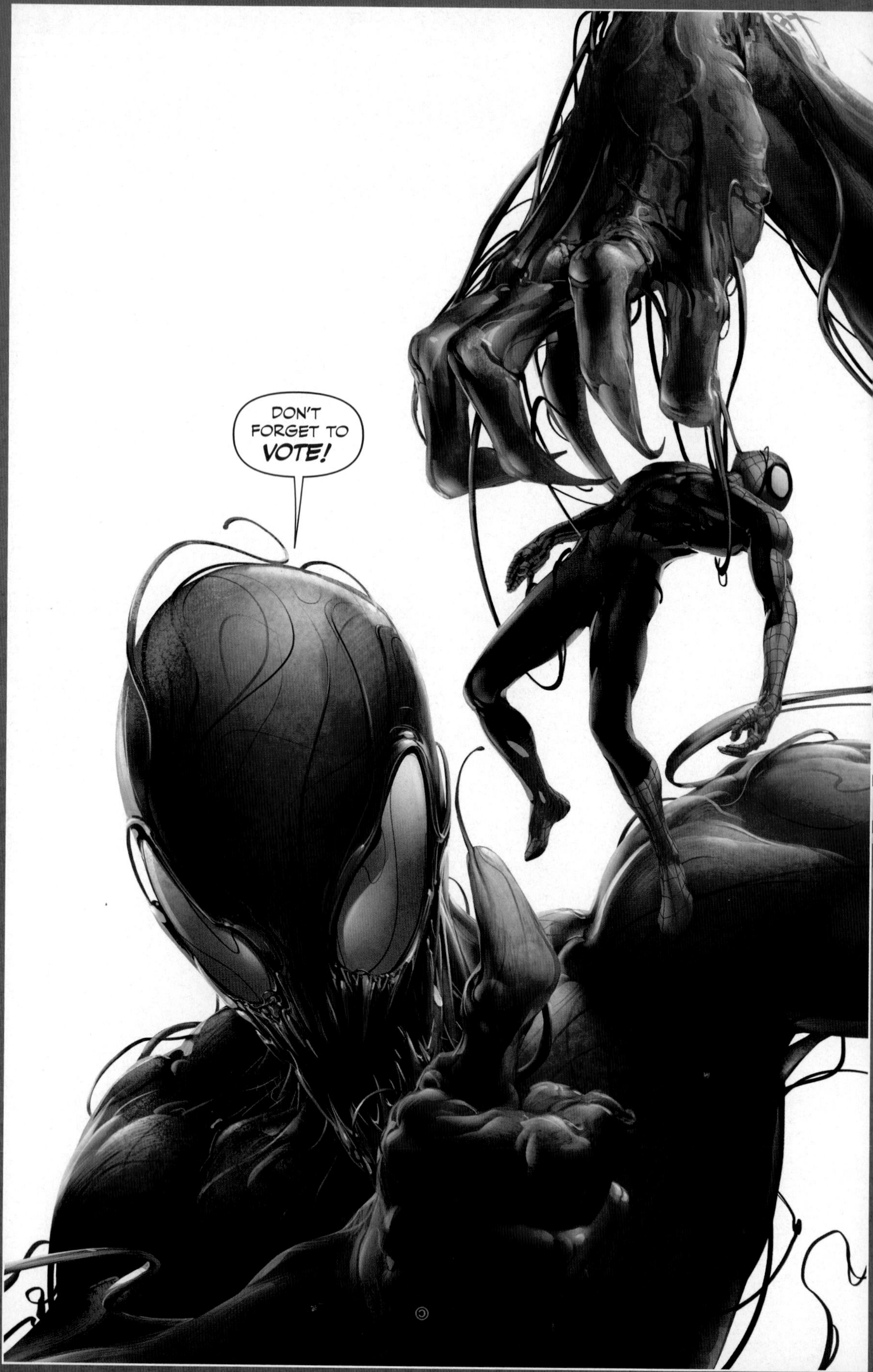
DON'T FORGET TO VOTE!

CARNAGE, U.S.A. #4

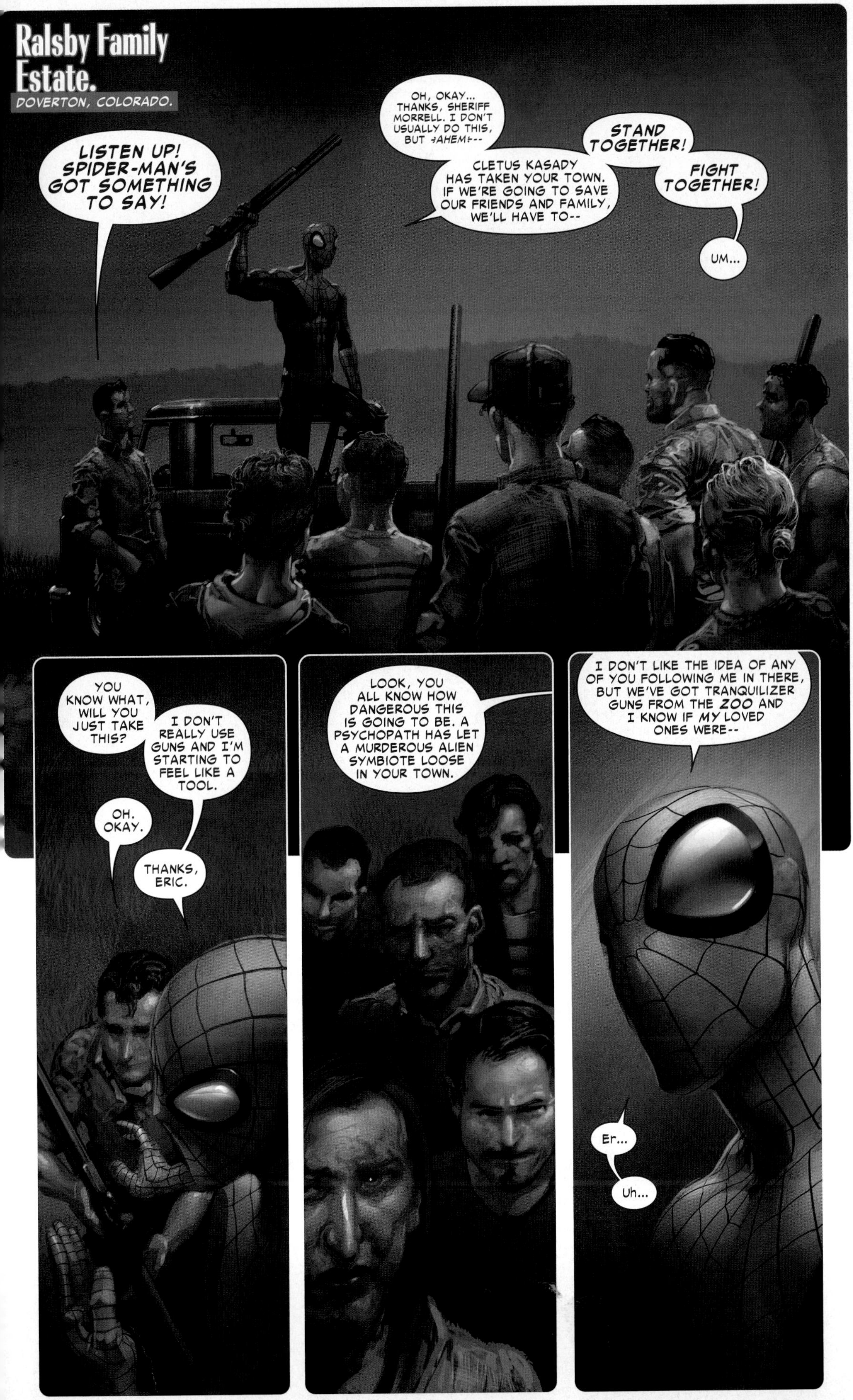
Ralsby Family Estate.
DOVERTON, COLORADO.
LISTEN UP! SPIDER-MAN'S GOT SOMETHING TO SAY!
OH, OKAY... THANKS, SHERIFF MORRELL. I DON'T USUALLY DO THIS, BUT *AHEM*--
CLETUS KASADY HAS TAKEN YOUR TOWN. IF WE'RE GOING TO SAVE OUR FRIENDS AND FAMILY, WE'LL HAVE TO--
STAND TOGETHER!
FIGHT TOGETHER!
UM...
YOU KNOW WHAT, WILL YOU JUST TAKE THIS?
I DON'T REALLY USE GUNS AND I'M STARTING TO FEEL LIKE A TOOL.
OH. OKAY.
THANKS, ERIC.
LOOK, YOU ALL KNOW HOW DANGEROUS THIS IS GOING TO BE. A PSYCHOPATH HAS LET A MURDEROUS ALIEN SYMBIOTE LOOSE IN YOUR TOWN.
I DON'T LIKE THE IDEA OF ANY OF YOU FOLLOWING ME IN THERE, BUT WE'VE GOT TRANQUILIZER GUNS FROM THE ZOO AND I KNOW IF MY LOVED ONES WERE--
Er...
Uh...

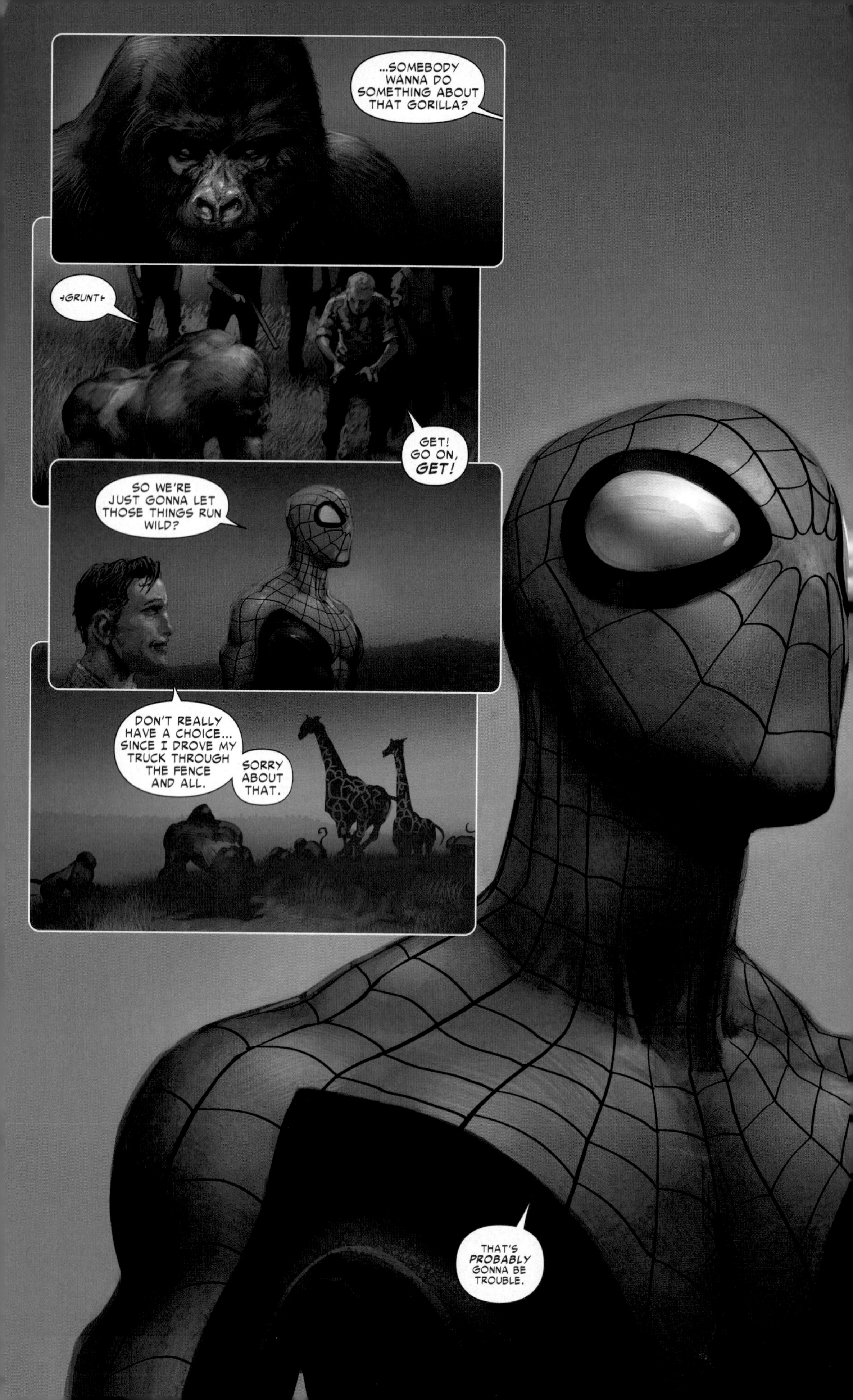
...SOMEBODY WANNA DO SOMETHING ABOUT THAT GORILLA?
+GRUNT+
GET! GO ON, GET!
SO WE'RE JUST GONNA LET THOSE THINGS RUN WILD?
DON'T REALLY HAVE A CHOICE... SINCE I DROVE MY TRUCK THROUGH THE FENCE AND ALL.
SORRY ABOUT THAT.
THAT'S PROBABLY GONNA BE TROUBLE.

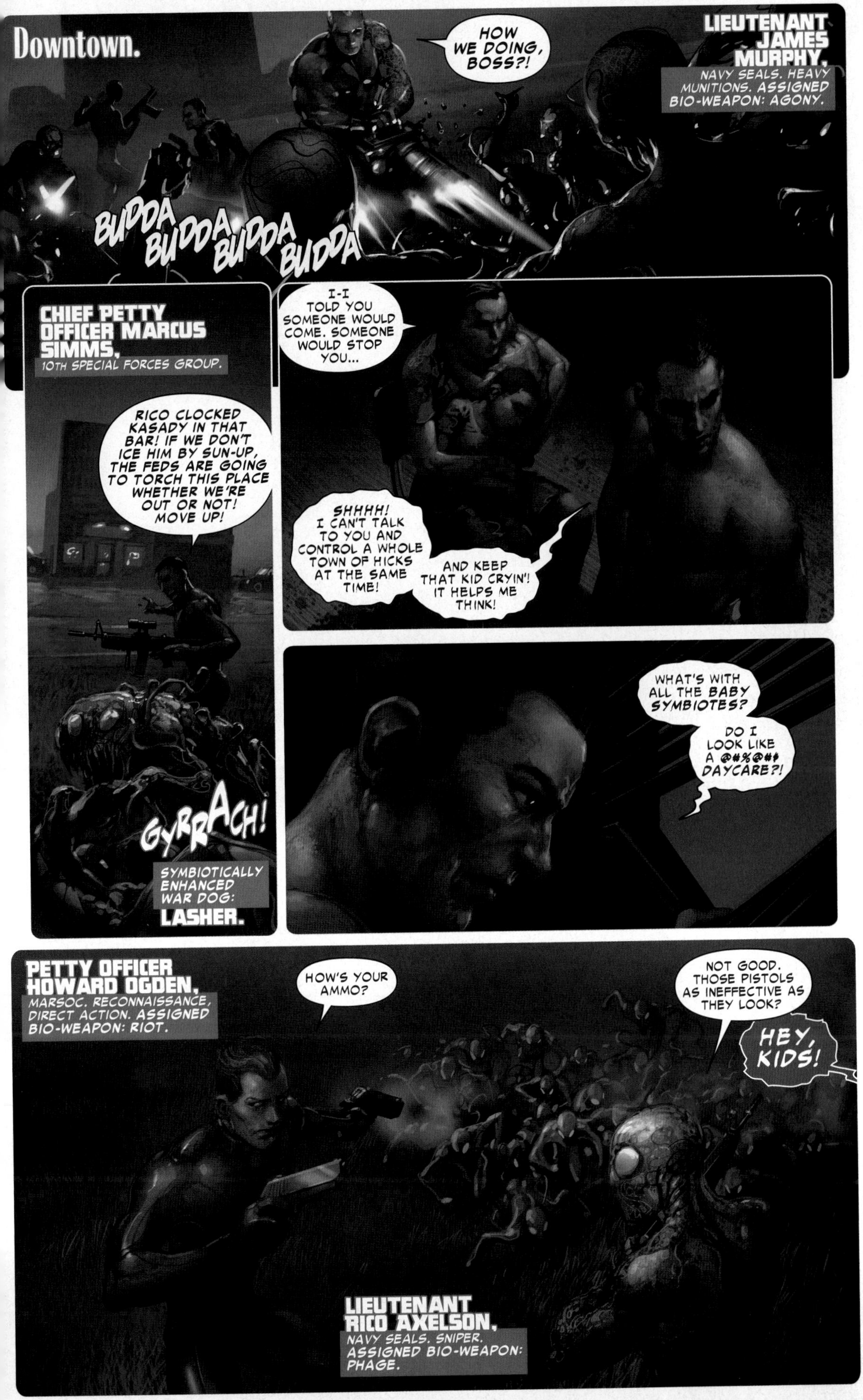
Downtown.
HOW WE DOING, BOSS?!
LIEUTENANT JAMES MURPHY,
NAVY SEALS. HEAVY MUNITIONS. ASSIGNED BIO-WEAPON: AGONY.
BUDDA BUDDA BUDDA BUDDA
CHIEF PETTY OFFICER MARCUS SIMMS,
10TH SPECIAL FORCES GROUP.
RICO CLOCKED KASADY IN THAT BAR! IF WE DON'T ICE HIM BY SUN-UP, THE FEDS ARE GOING TO TORCH THIS PLACE WHETHER WE'RE OUT OR NOT! MOVE UP!
GYRRACH!
SYMBIOTICALLY ENHANCED WAR DOG:
LASHER.
I-I TOLD YOU SOMEONE WOULD COME. SOMEONE WOULD STOP YOU...
SHHHH! I CAN'T TALK TO YOU AND CONTROL A WHOLE TOWN OF HICKS AT THE SAME TIME!
AND KEEP THAT KID CRYIN'! IT HELPS ME THINK!
WHAT'S WITH ALL THE BABY SYMBIOTES?
DO I LOOK LIKE A @#%@#! DAYCARE?!
PETTY OFFICER HOWARD OGDEN,
MARSOC. RECONNAISSANCE, DIRECT ACTION. ASSIGNED BIO-WEAPON: RIOT.
HOW'S YOUR AMMO?
NOT GOOD. THOSE PISTOLS AS INEFFECTIVE AS THEY LOOK?
HEY, KIDS!
LIEUTENANT RICO AXELSON,
NAVY SEALS. SNIPER. ASSIGNED BIO-WEAPON: PHAGE.

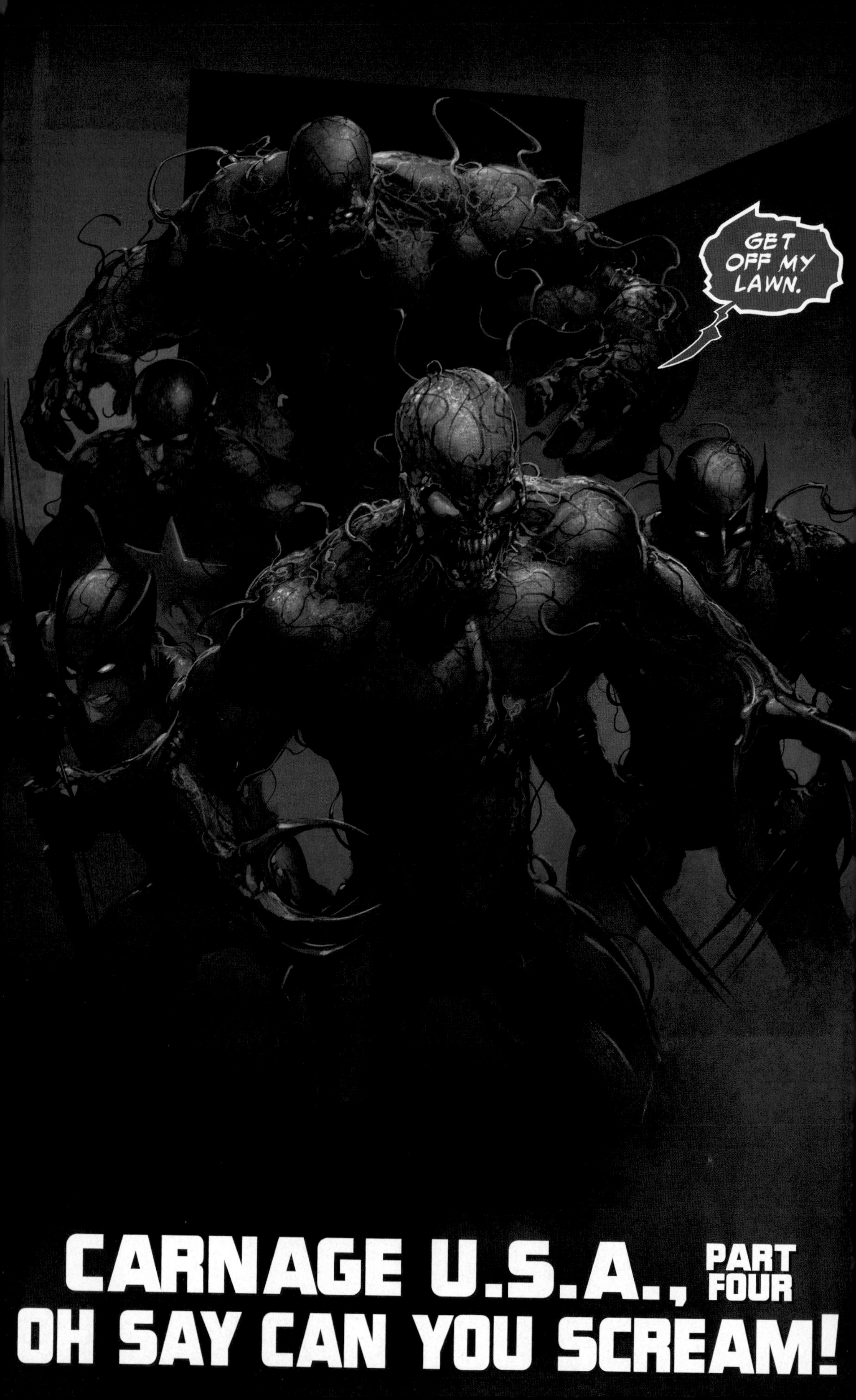
GET OFF MY LAWN.
CARNAGE U.S.A., PART FOUR
OH SAY CAN YOU SCREAM!

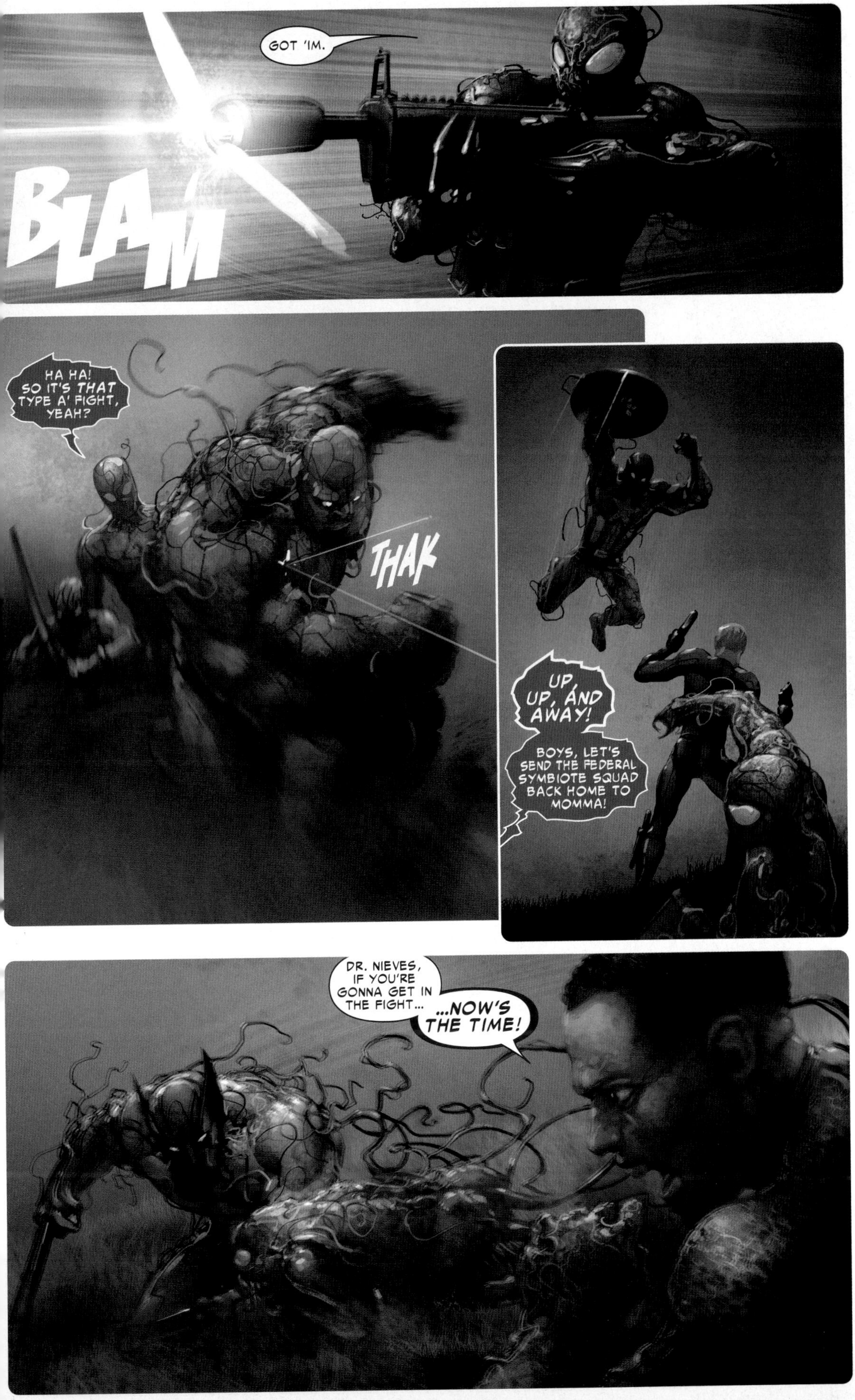
GOT 'IM.
BLAM
HA HA! SO IT'S THAT TYPE A' FIGHT, YEAH?
THAK
UP, UP, AND AWAY!
BOYS, LET'S SEND THE FEDERAL SYMBIOTE SQUAD BACK HOME TO MOMMA!
DR. NIEVES, IF YOU'RE GONNA GET IN THE FIGHT...
...NOW'S THE TIME!

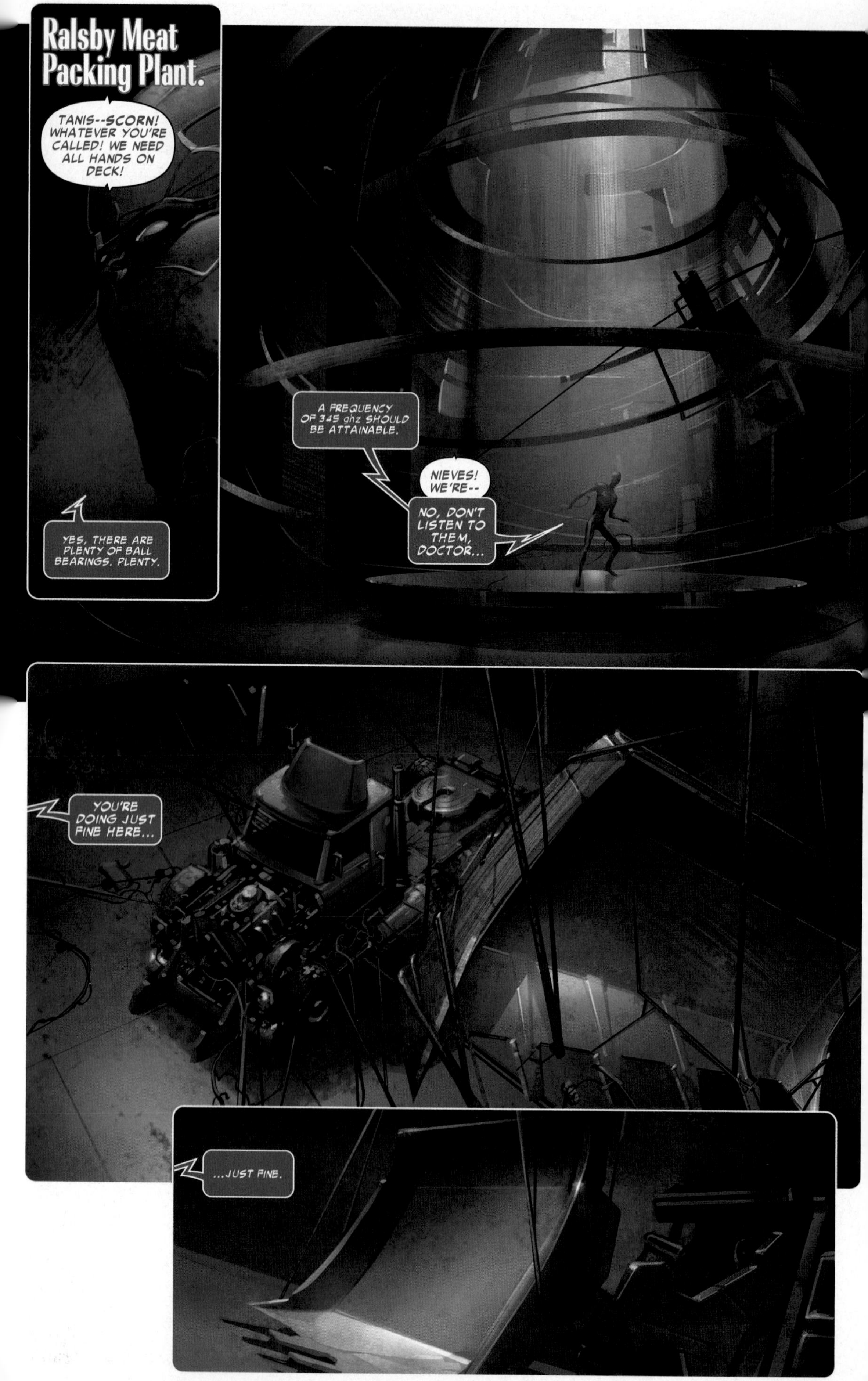
Ralsby Meat Packing Plant.
TANIS--SCORN! WHATEVER YOU'RE CALLED! WE NEED ALL HANDS ON DECK!
YES, THERE ARE PLENTY OF BALL BEARINGS. PLENTY.
A FREQUENCY OF 345 ghz SHOULD BE ATTAINABLE.
NIEVES! WE'RE--
NO, DON'T LISTEN TO THEM, DOCTOR...
YOU'RE DOING JUST FINE HERE...
...JUST FINE.

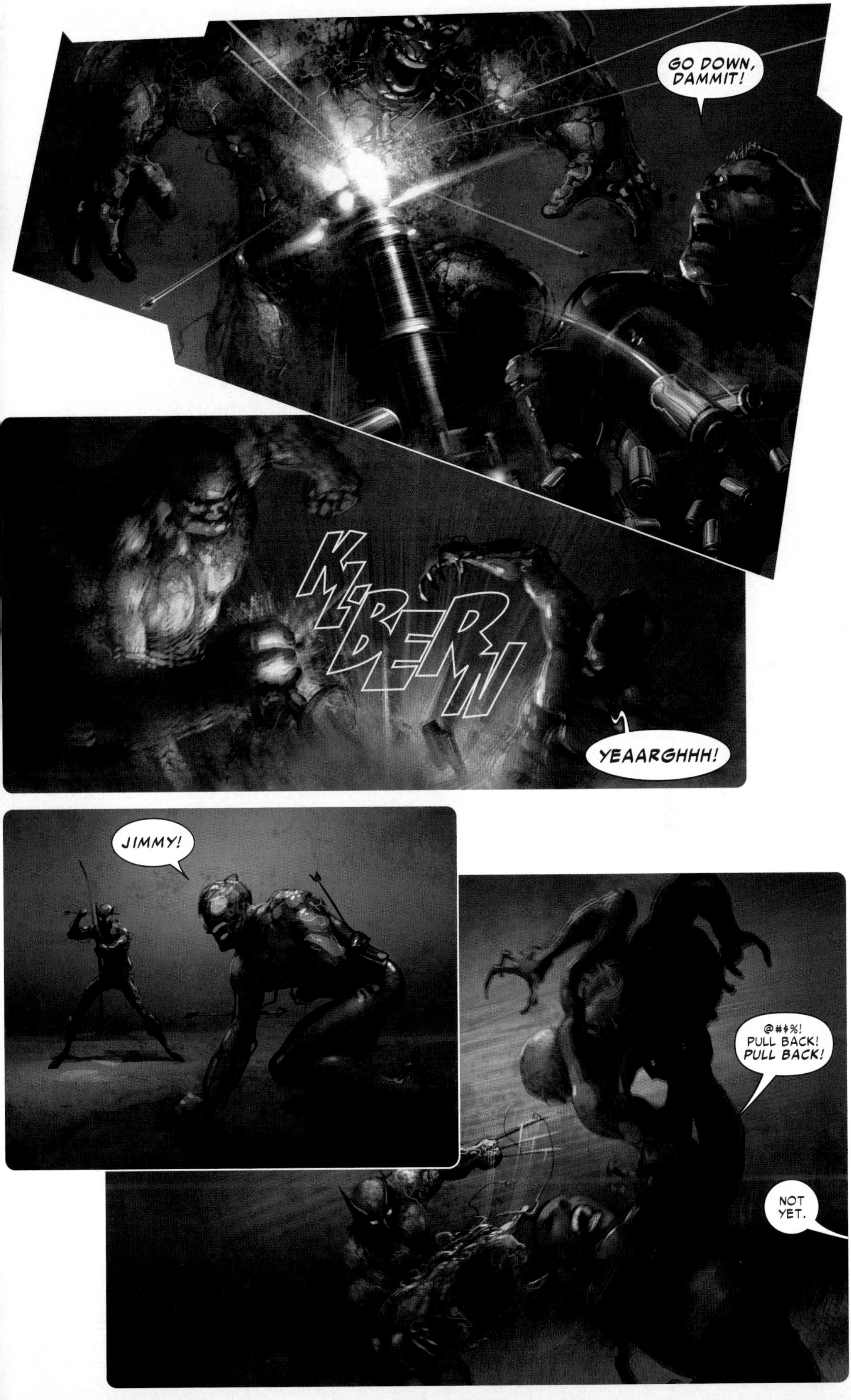
GO DOWN, DAMMIT!
K-BERN
YEAARGHHH!
JIMMY!
@#$%! PULL BACK! PULL BACK!
NOT YET.

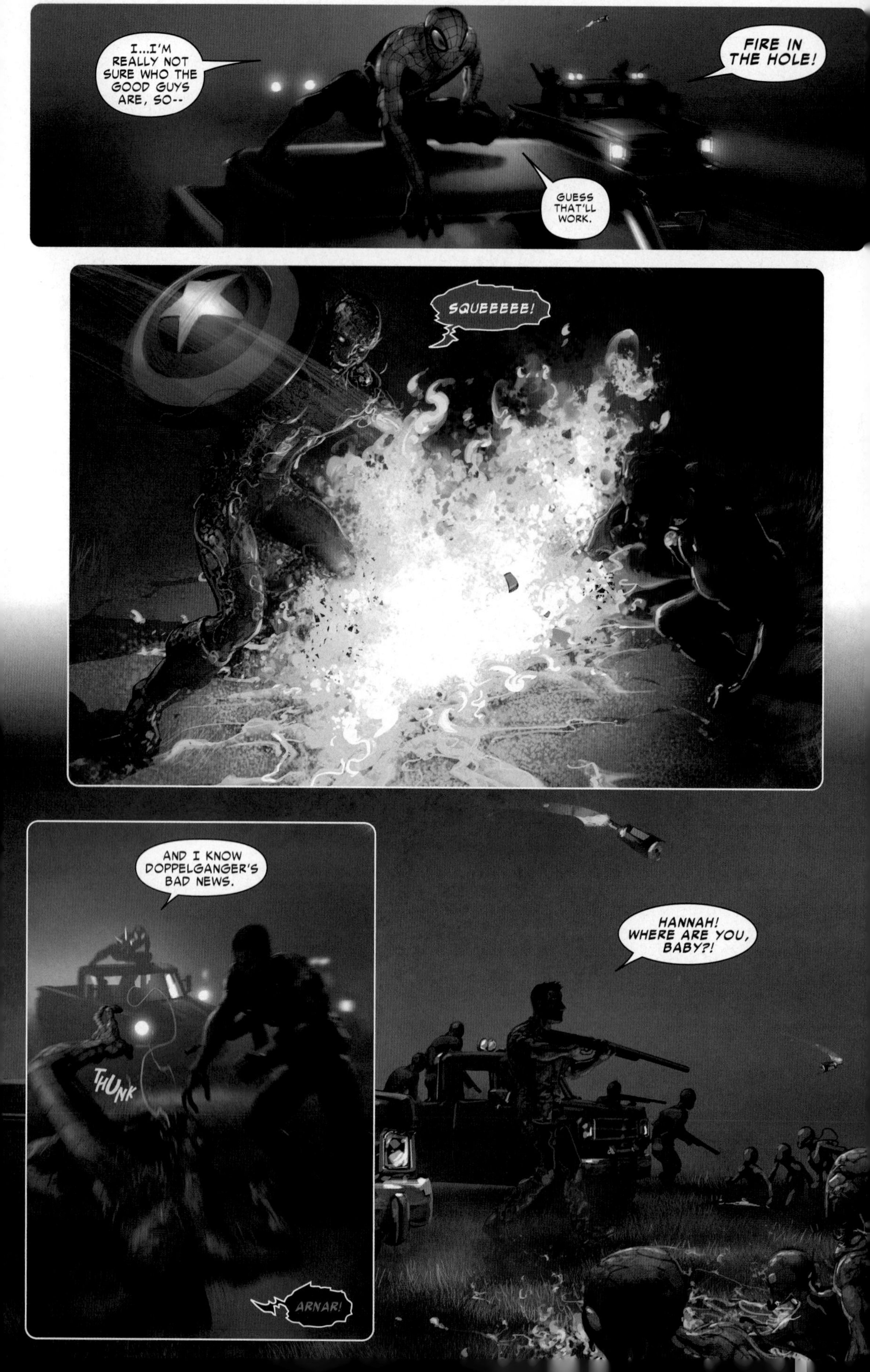
I...I'M REALLY NOT SURE WHO THE GOOD GUYS ARE, SO--
FIRE IN THE HOLE!
GUESS THAT'LL WORK.
SQUEEEEEE!
AND I KNOW DOPPELGANGER'S BAD NEWS.
THUNK
ARNAR!
HANNAH! WHERE ARE YOU, BABY?!

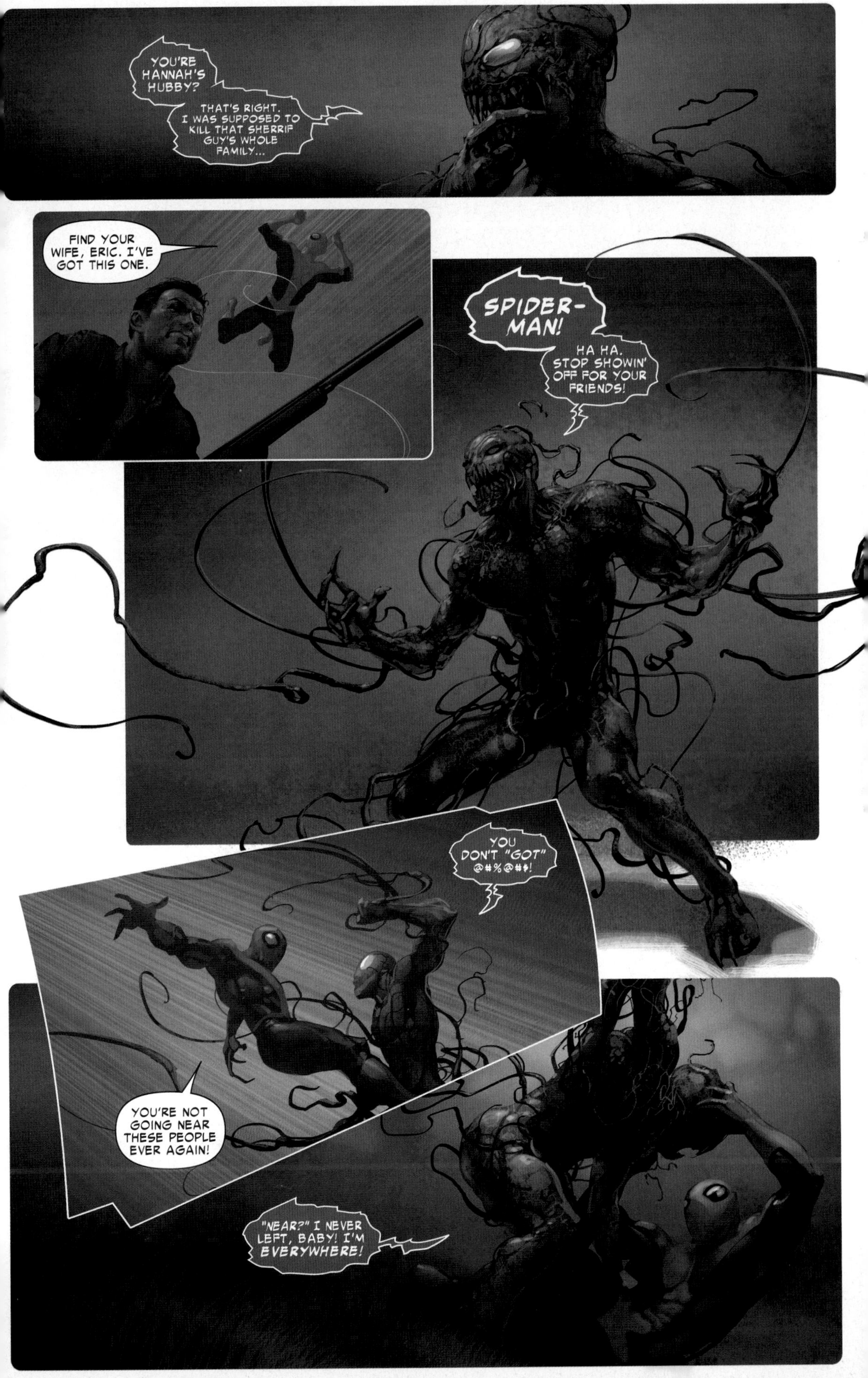

YOU'RE HANNAH'S HUBBY?
THAT'S RIGHT. I WAS SUPPOSED TO KILL THAT SHERRIF GUY'S WHOLE FAMILY...
FIND YOUR WIFE, ERIC. I'VE GOT THIS ONE.
SPIDER-MAN!
HA HA. STOP SHOWIN' OFF FOR YOUR FRIENDS!
YOU DON'T "GOT" @#%@#$!
YOU'RE NOT GOING NEAR THESE PEOPLE EVER AGAIN!
"NEAR?" I NEVER LEFT, BABY! I'M EVERYWHERE!

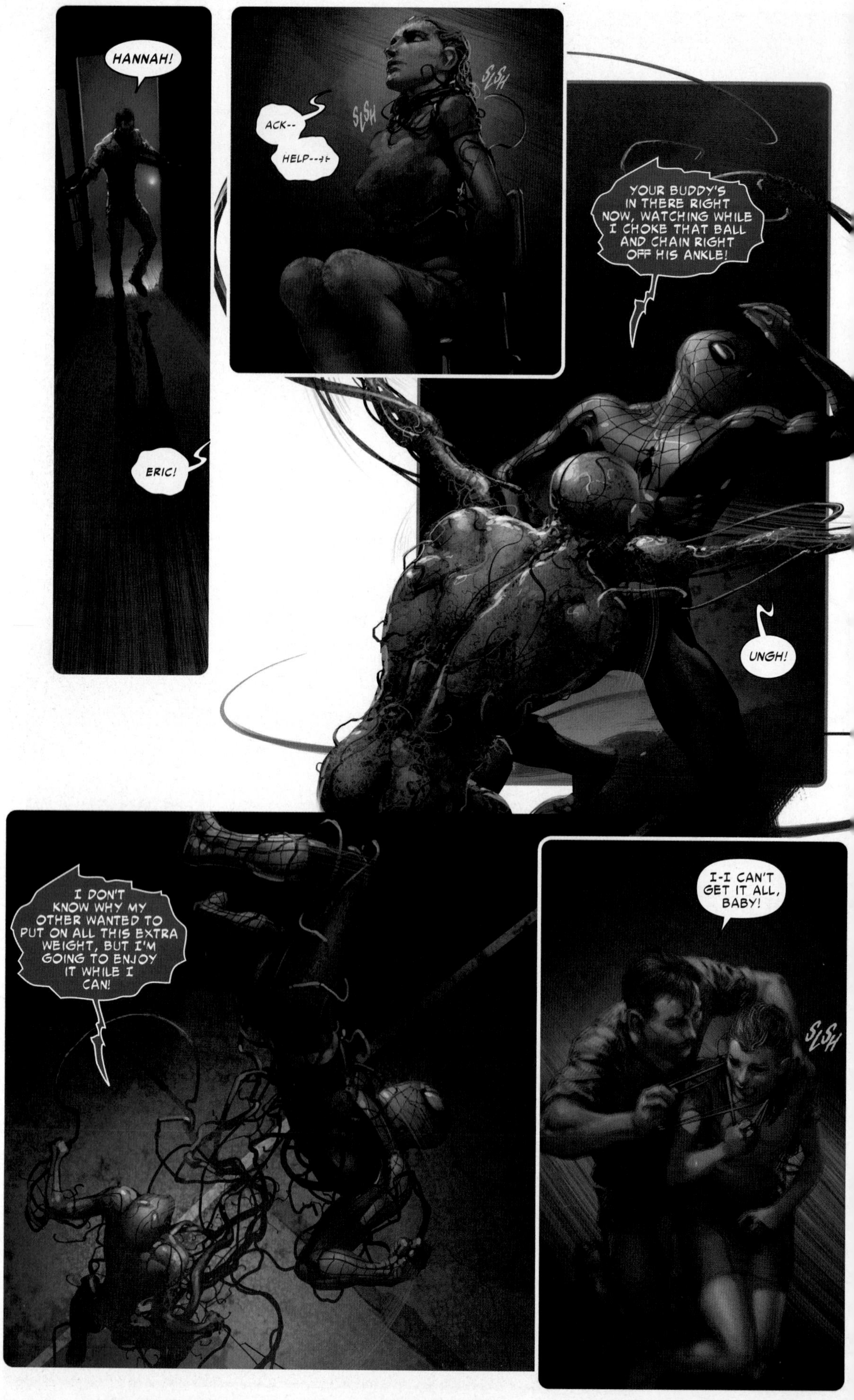
HANNAH!
ACK--
SLSH
SLSH
HELP--
YOUR BUDDY'S IN THERE RIGHT NOW, WATCHING WHILE I CHOKE THAT BALL AND CHAIN RIGHT OFF HIS ANKLE!
ERIC!
UNGH!
I DON'T KNOW WHY MY OTHER WANTED TO PUT ON ALL THIS EXTRA WEIGHT, BUT I'M GOING TO ENJOY IT WHILE I CAN!
I-I CAN'T GET IT ALL, BABY!
SLSH

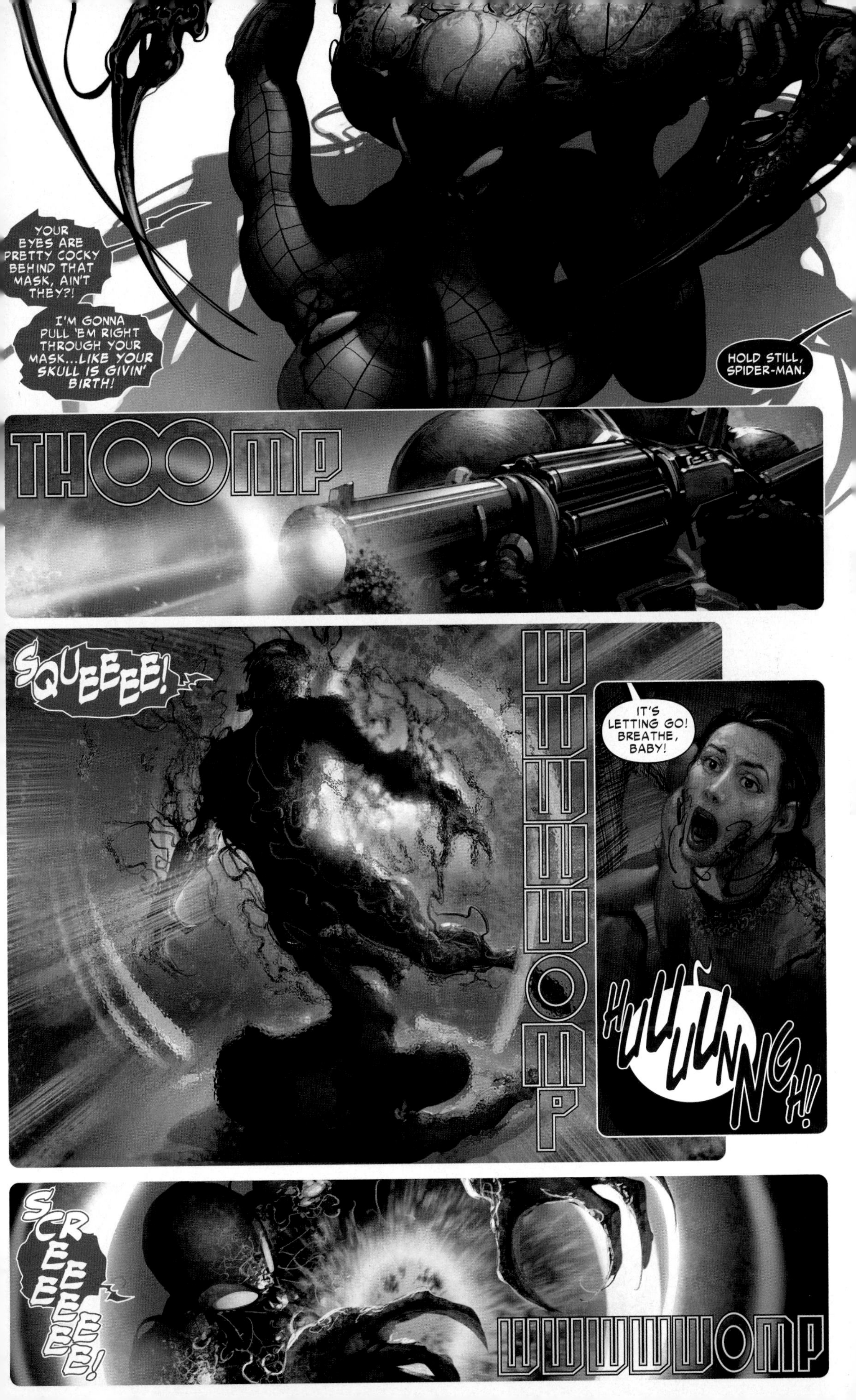
YOUR EYES ARE PRETTY COCKY BEHIND THAT MASK, AIN'T THEY?!
I'M GONNA PULL 'EM RIGHT THROUGH YOUR MASK...LIKE YOUR SKULL IS GIVIN' BIRTH!
HOLD STILL, SPIDER-MAN.
THOOMP
SQUEEEEE!
WWWWWOMP
IT'S LETTING GO! BREATHE, BABY!
HUUUUNNGH!
SCREEEEEEEE!
WWWWWWOMP

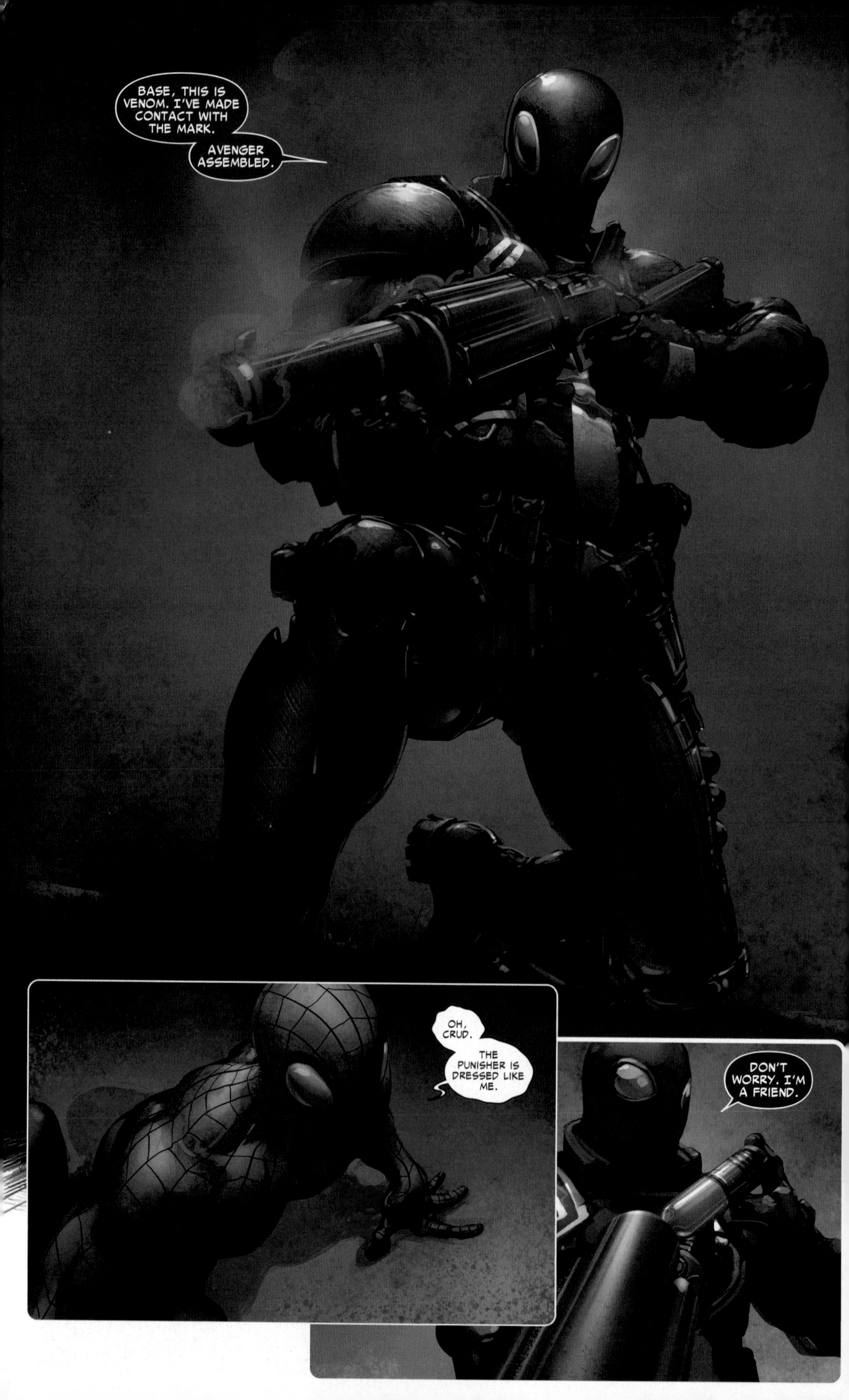
BASE, THIS IS VENOM. I'VE MADE CONTACT WITH THE MARK.
AVENGER ASSEMBLED.
OH, CRUD.
THE PUNISHER IS DRESSED LIKE ME.
DON'T WORRY. I'M A FRIEND.

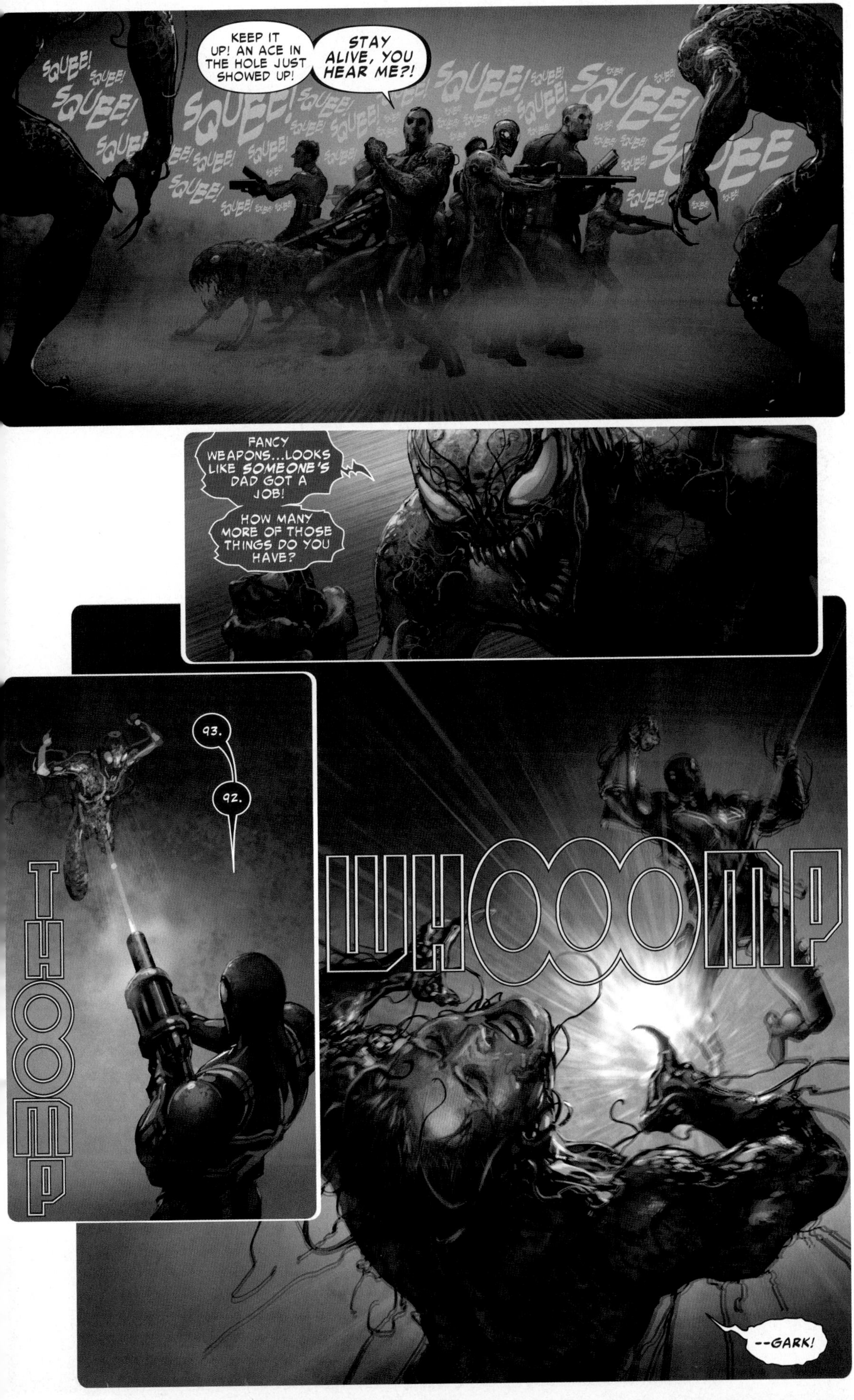
SQUEE! SQUEE! SQUEE! SQUEE!
KEEP IT UP! AN ACE IN THE HOLE JUST SHOWED UP!
STAY ALIVE, YOU HEAR ME?!
FANCY WEAPONS...LOOKS LIKE SOMEONE'S DAD GOT A JOB!
HOW MANY MORE OF THOSE THINGS DO YOU HAVE?
93.
92.
THOOMP
WHOOOOMP
--GARK!

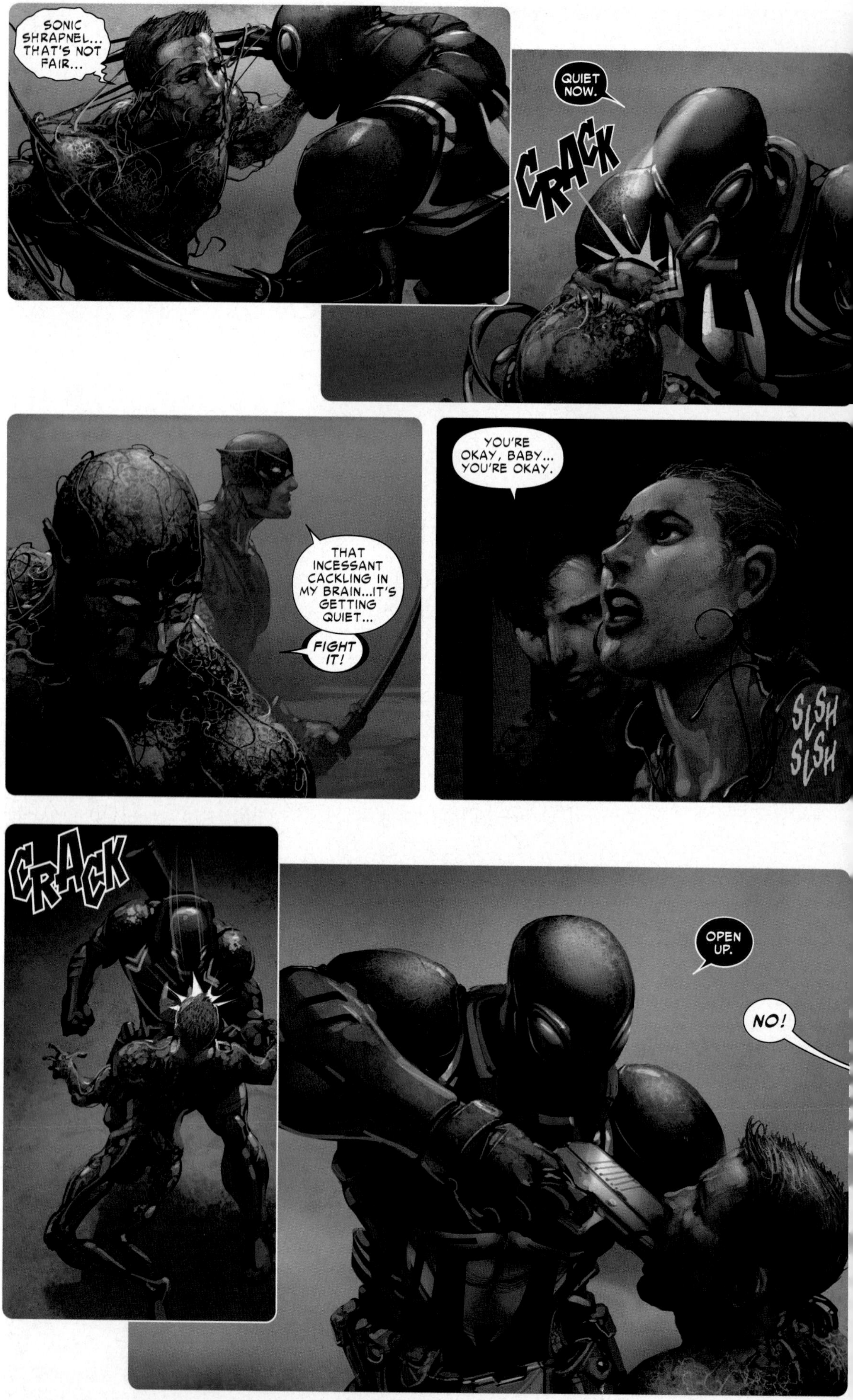
SONIC SHRAPNEL... THAT'S NOT FAIR...
QUIET NOW.
CRACK
THAT INCESSANT CACKLING IN MY BRAIN...IT'S GETTING QUIET...
FIGHT IT!
YOU'RE OKAY, BABY... YOU'RE OKAY.
SLSH SLSH
CRACK
OPEN UP.
NO!

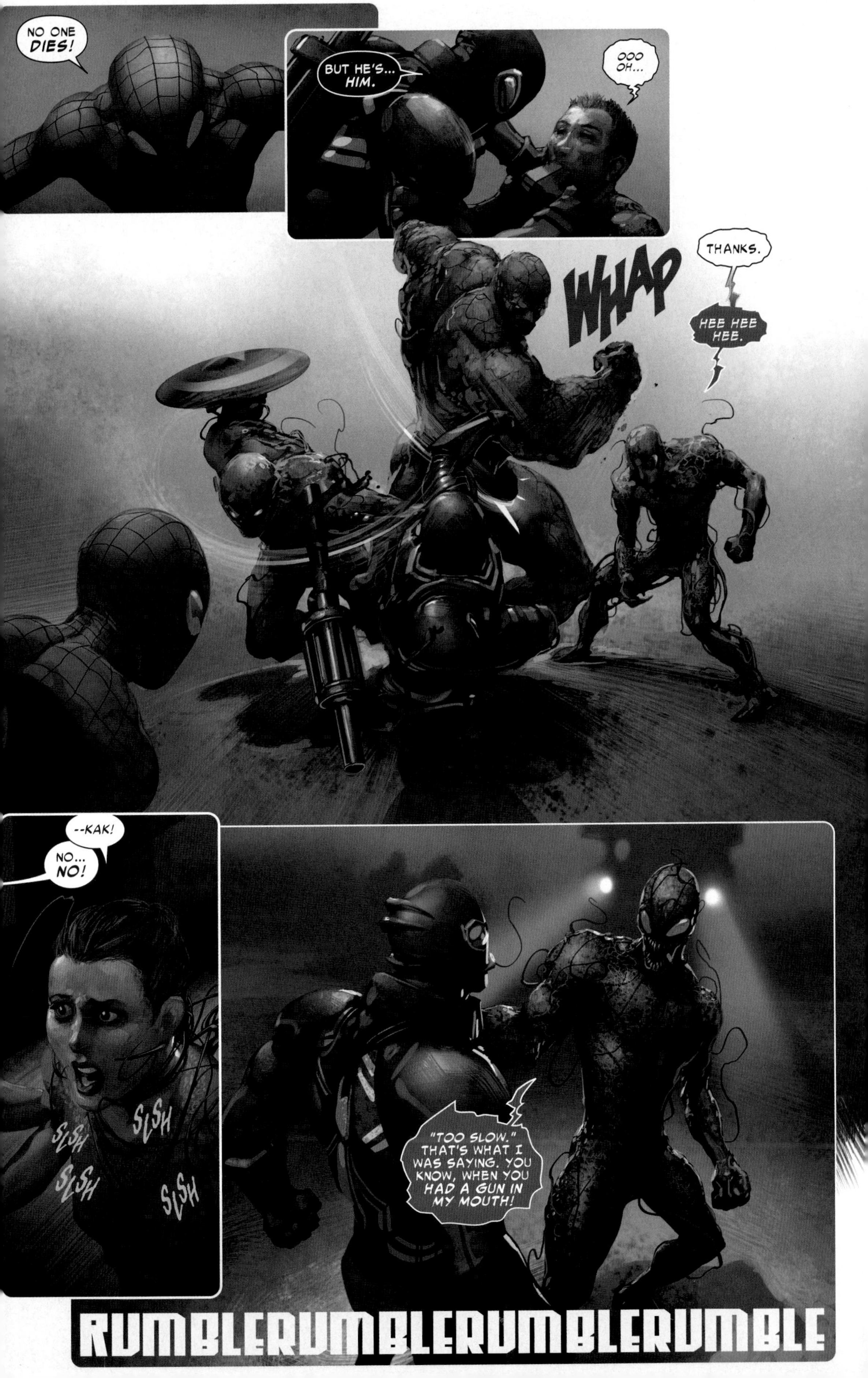

NO ONE DIES!
BUT HE'S... HIM.
OOO OH...
WHAP
THANKS.
HEE HEE HEE.
--KAK!
NO... NO!
SLSH
SLSH
SLSH
SLSH
"TOO SLOW." THAT'S WHAT I WAS SAYING. YOU KNOW, WHEN YOU HAD A GUN IN MY MOUTH!
RUMBLERUMBLERUMBLERUMBLE

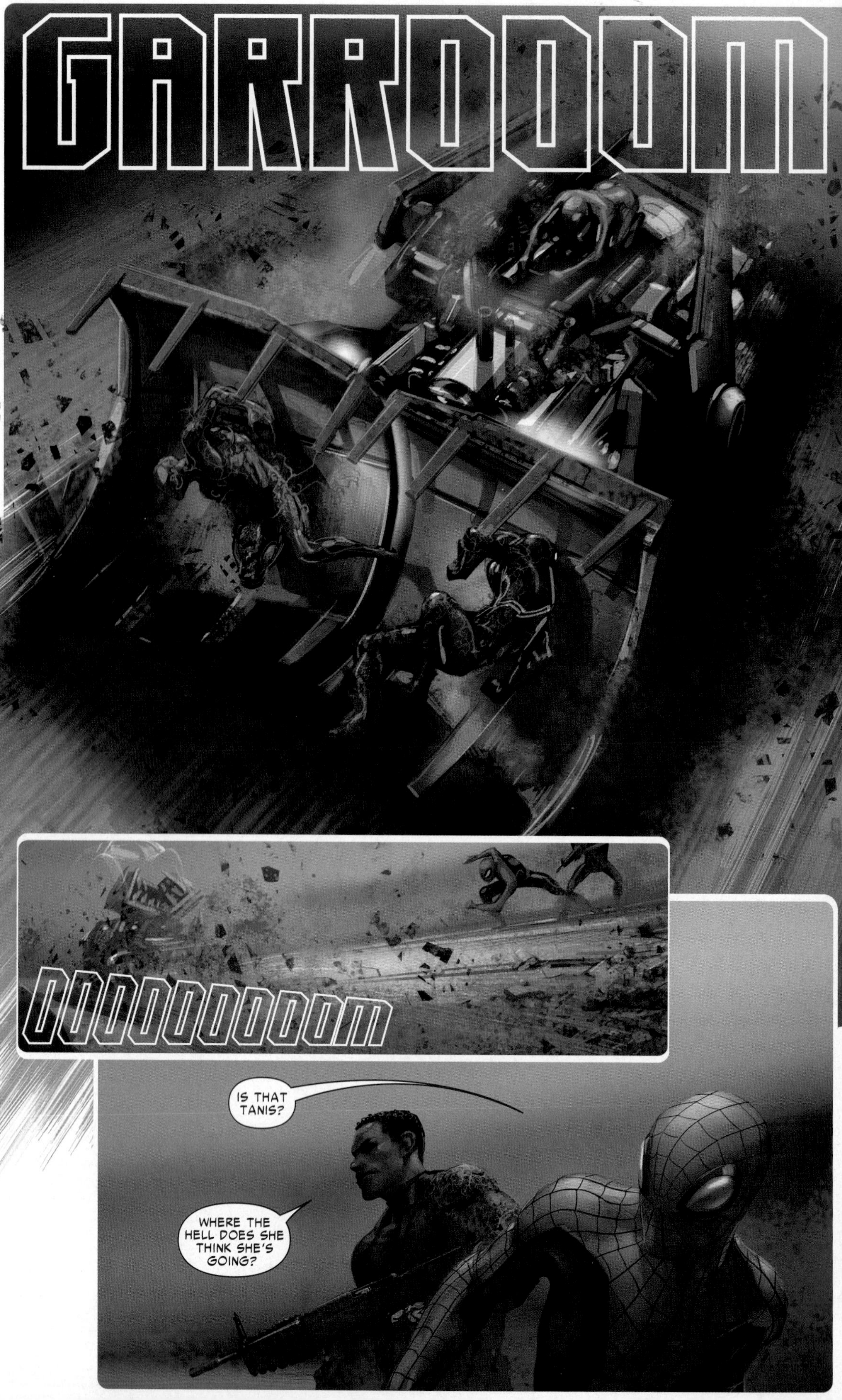
GARROOOM
OOOOOOOOOM
IS THAT TANIS?
WHERE THE HELL DOES SHE THINK SHE'S GOING?

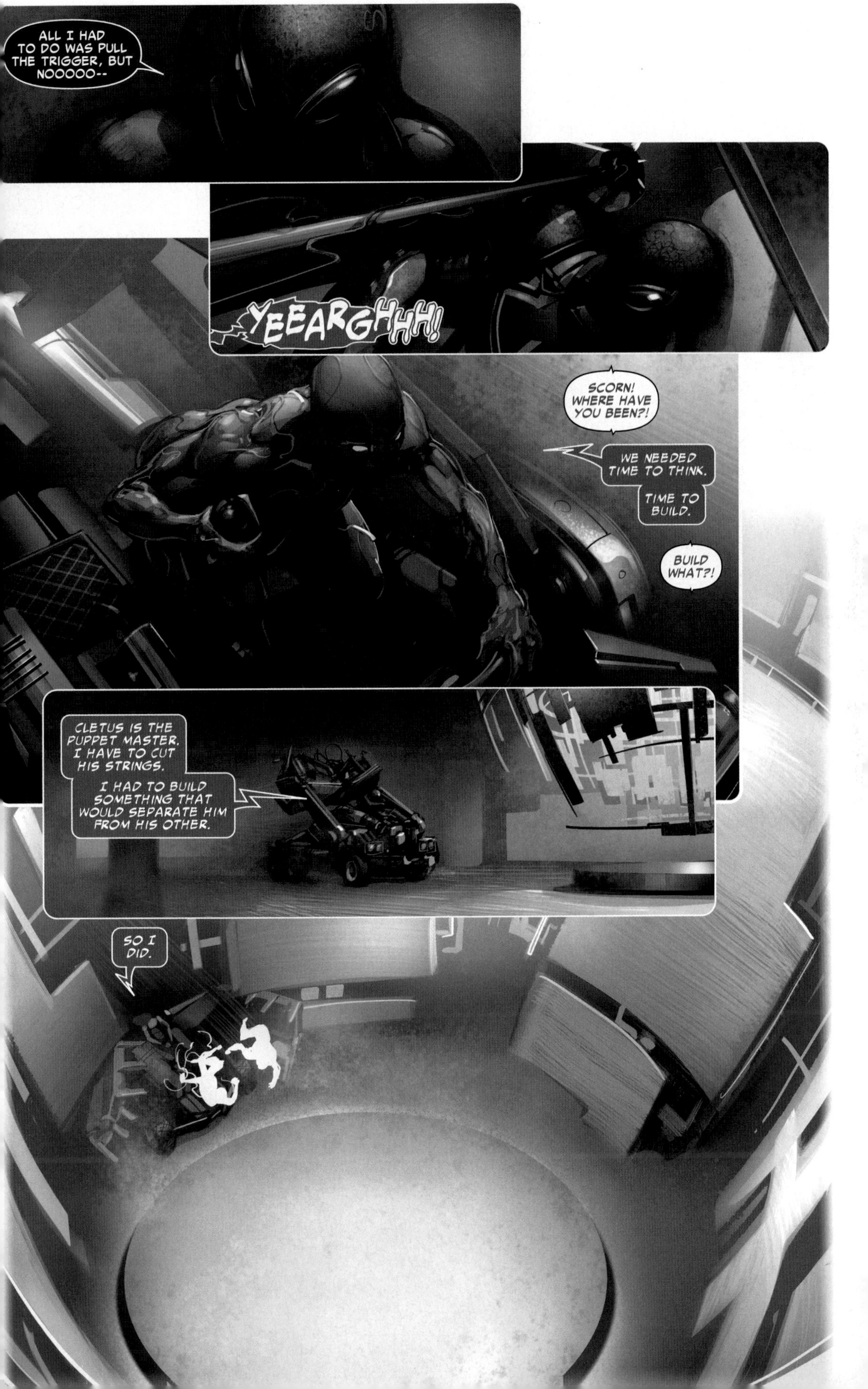
ALL I HAD TO DO WAS PULL THE TRIGGER, BUT NOOOOO--
YEEARGHHH!
SCORN! WHERE HAVE YOU BEEN?!
WE NEEDED TIME TO THINK.
TIME TO BUILD.
BUILD WHAT?!
CLETUS IS THE PUPPET MASTER. I HAVE TO CUT HIS STRINGS.
I HAD TO BUILD SOMETHING THAT WOULD SEPARATE HIM FROM HIS OTHER.
SO I DID.

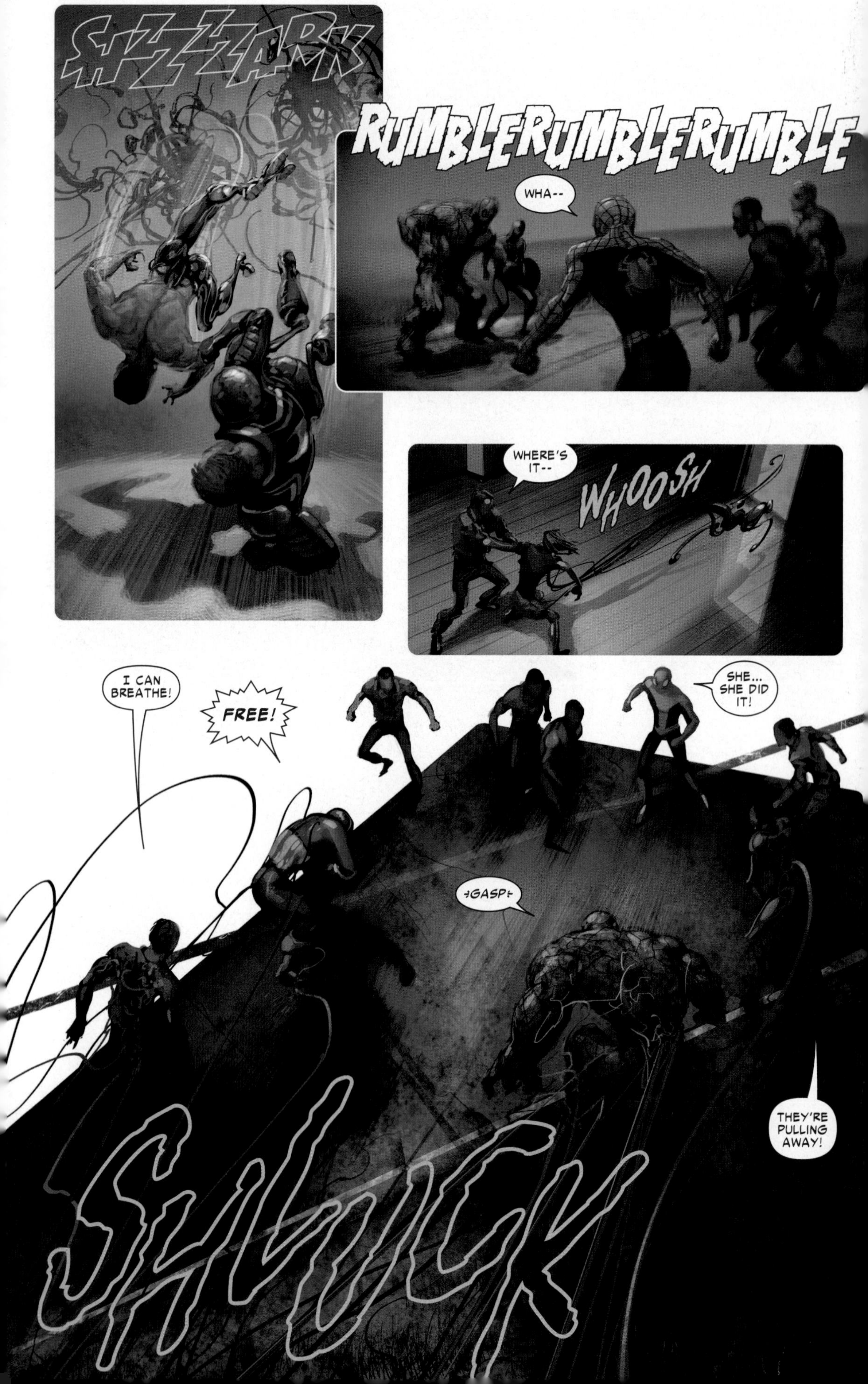
SHZZZARK
RUMBLERUMBLERUMBLE
WHA--
WHERE'S IT--
WHOOSH
I CAN BREATHE!
FREE!
SHE... SHE DID IT!
GASP
THEY'RE PULLING AWAY!
SHLUCK

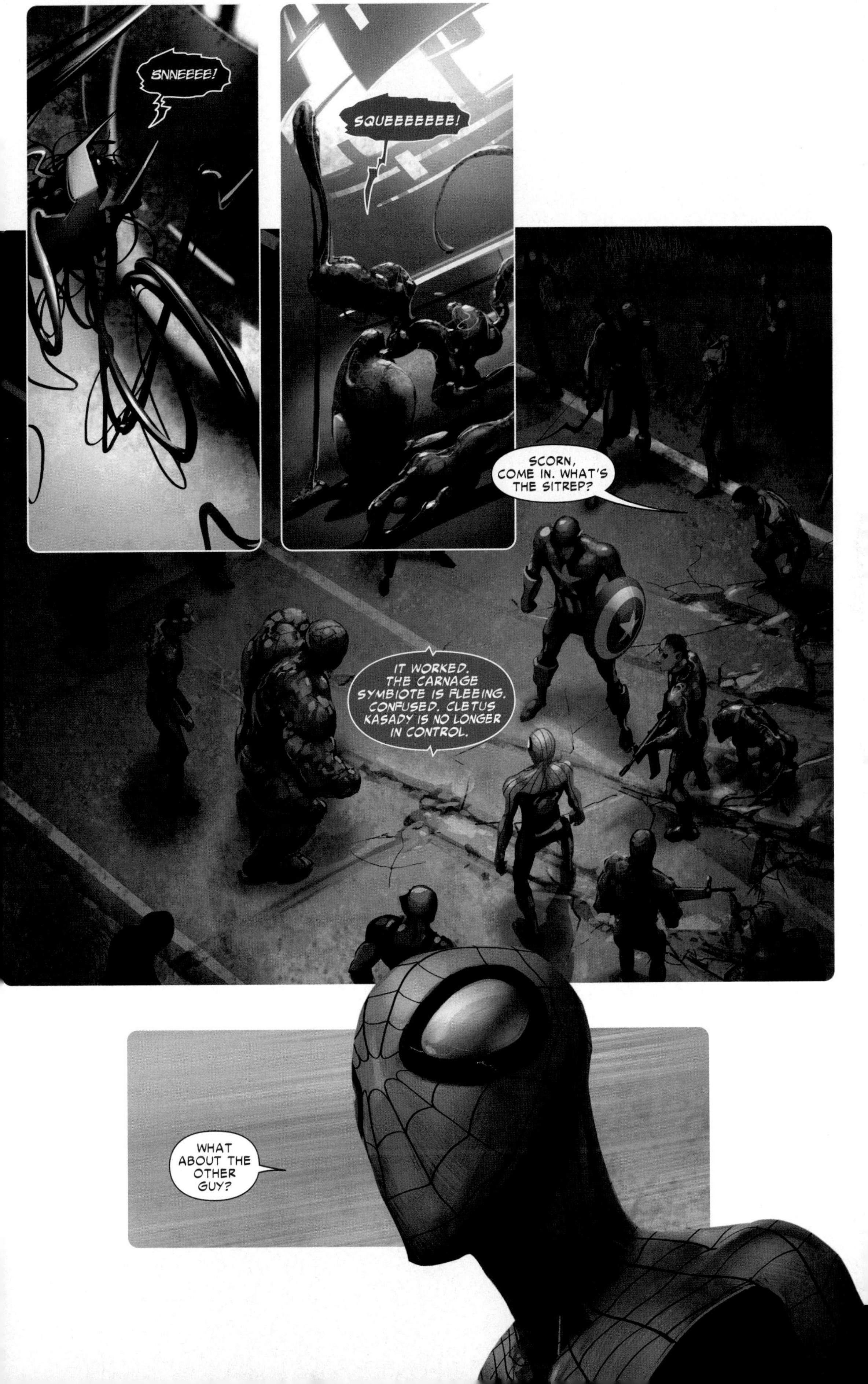
SNNEEEE!
SQUEEEEEEEE!
SCORN, COME IN. WHAT'S THE SITREP?
IT WORKED. THE CARNAGE SYMBIOTE IS FLEEING. CONFUSED. CLETUS KASADY IS NO LONGER IN CONTROL.
WHAT ABOUT THE OTHER GUY?

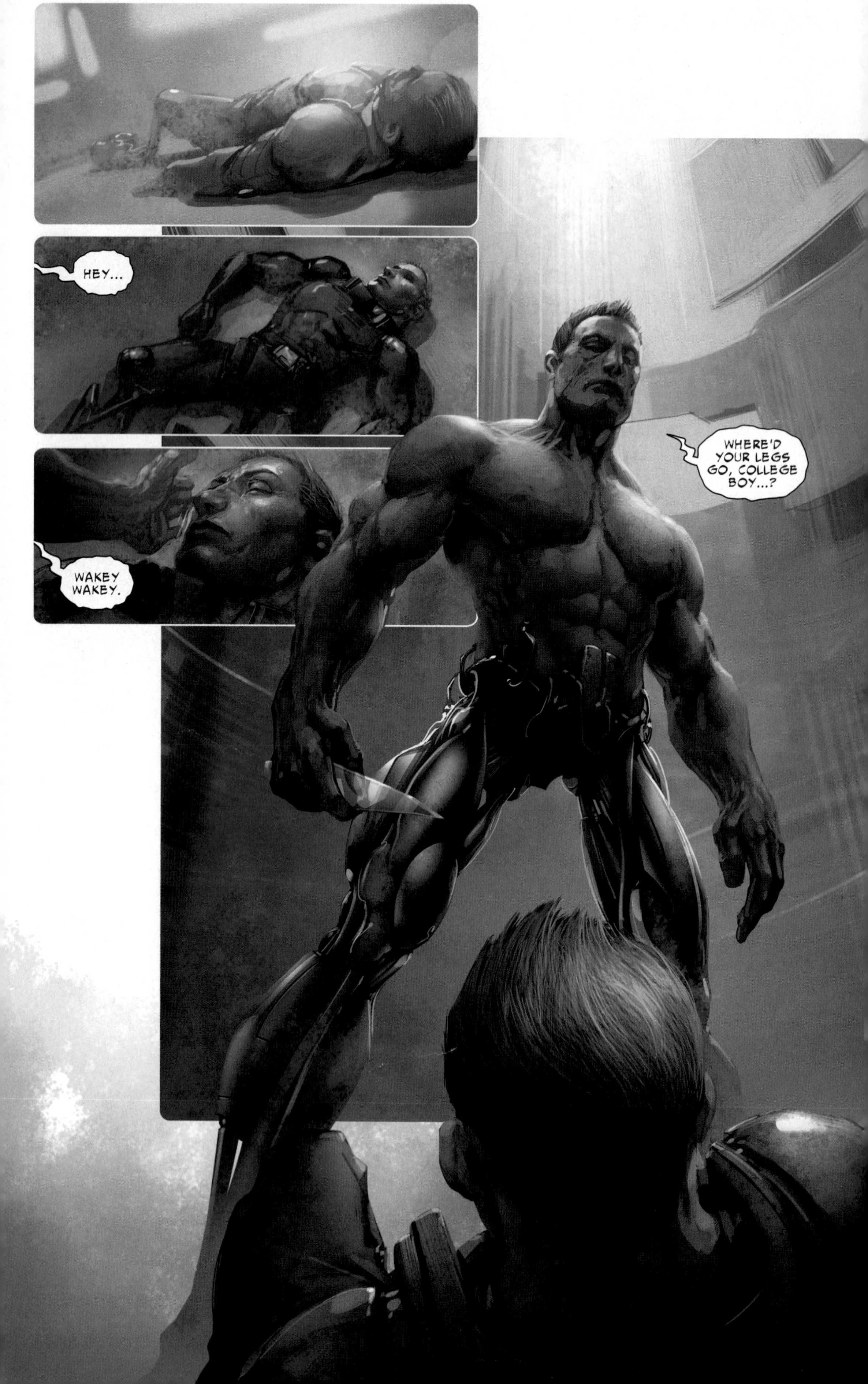
HEY...
WAKEY WAKEY.
WHERE'D YOUR LEGS GO, COLLEGE BOY...?

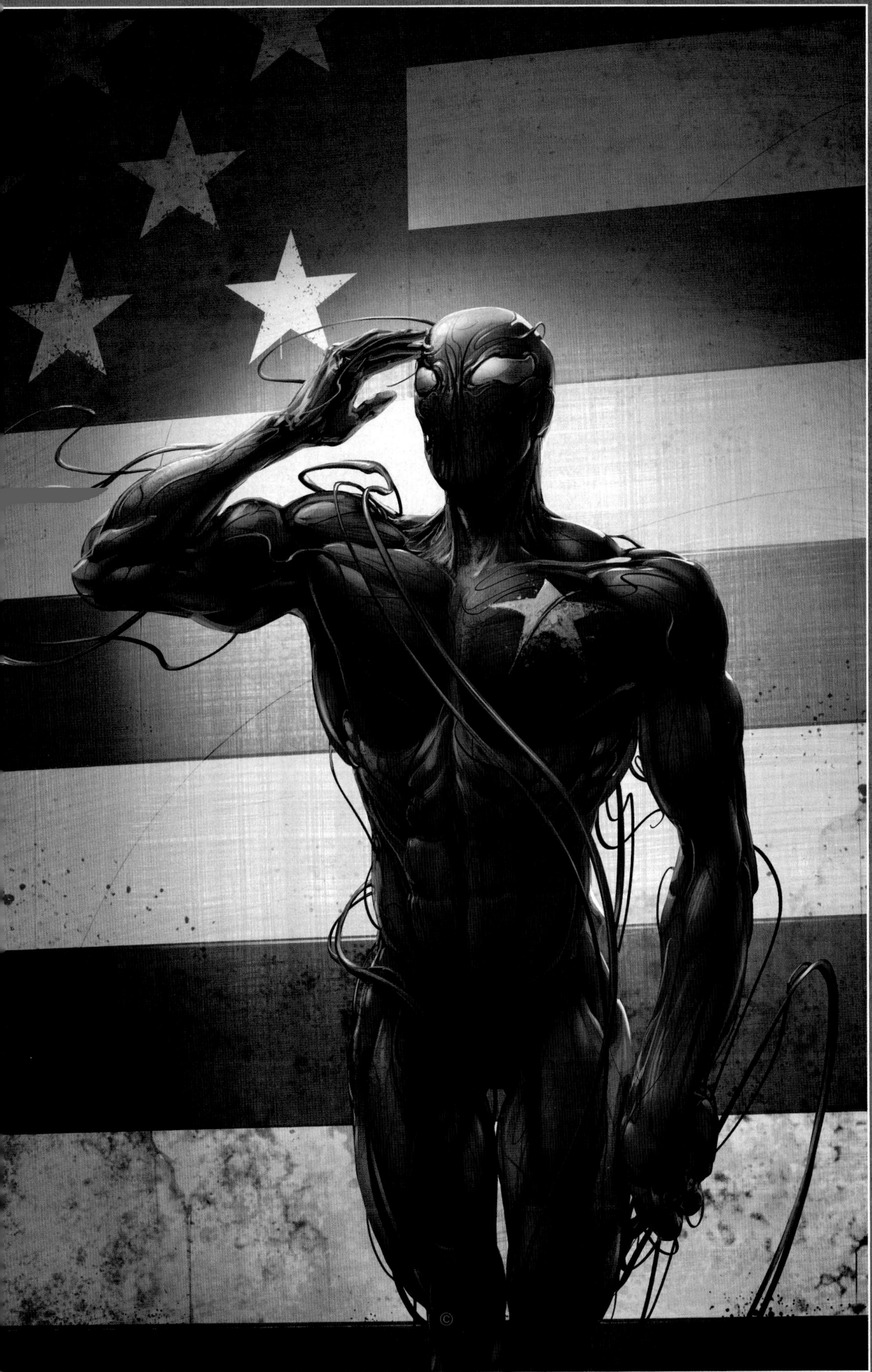

CARNAGE, U.S.A. #5

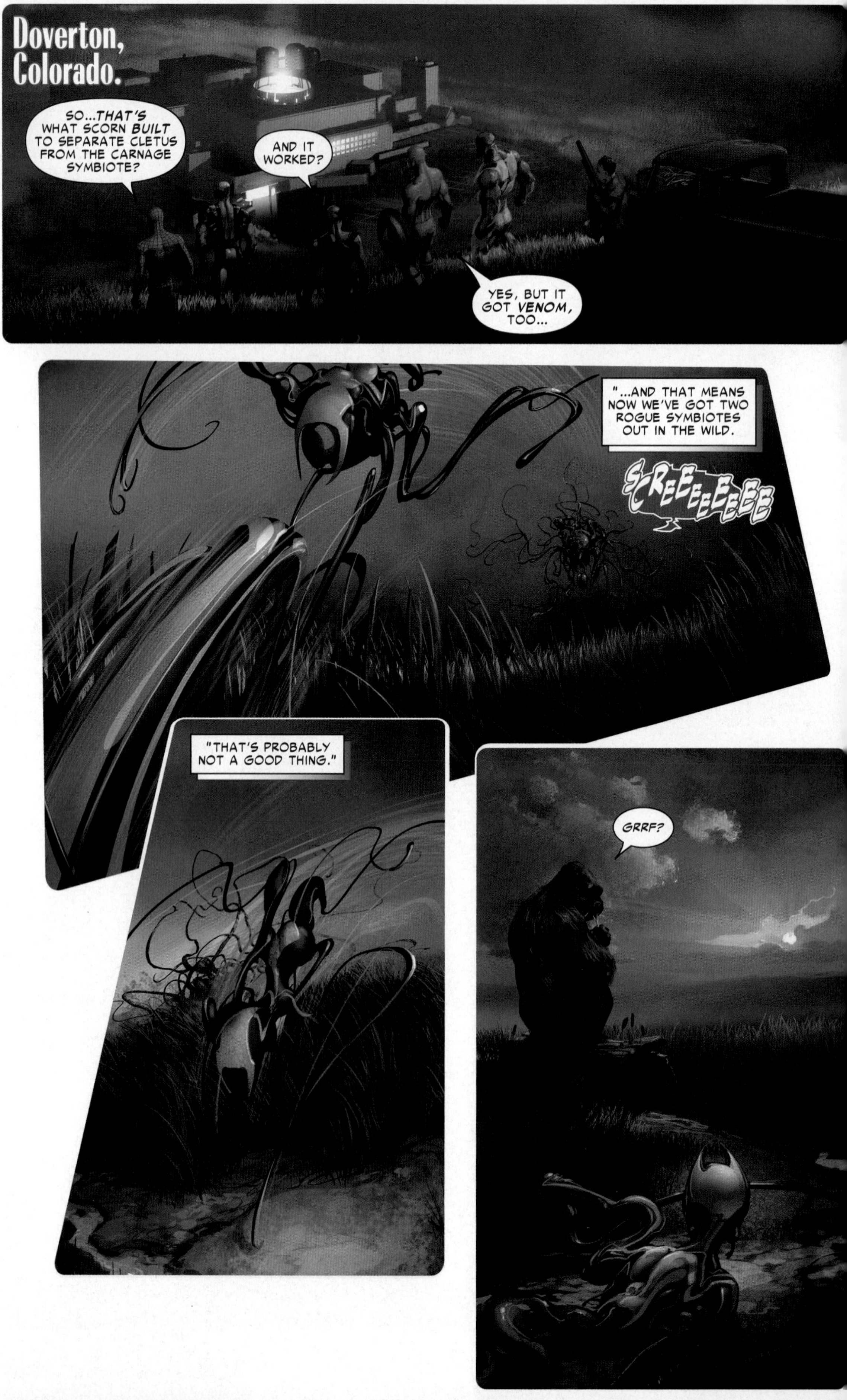
Doverton, Colorado.
SO...THAT'S WHAT SCORN BUILT TO SEPARATE CLETUS FROM THE CARNAGE SYMBIOTE?
AND IT WORKED?
YES, BUT IT GOT VENOM, TOO...
"...AND THAT MEANS NOW WE'VE GOT TWO ROGUE SYMBIOTES OUT IN THE WILD.
SCREEEEEEEEE
"THAT'S PROBABLY NOT A GOOD THING."
GRRF?

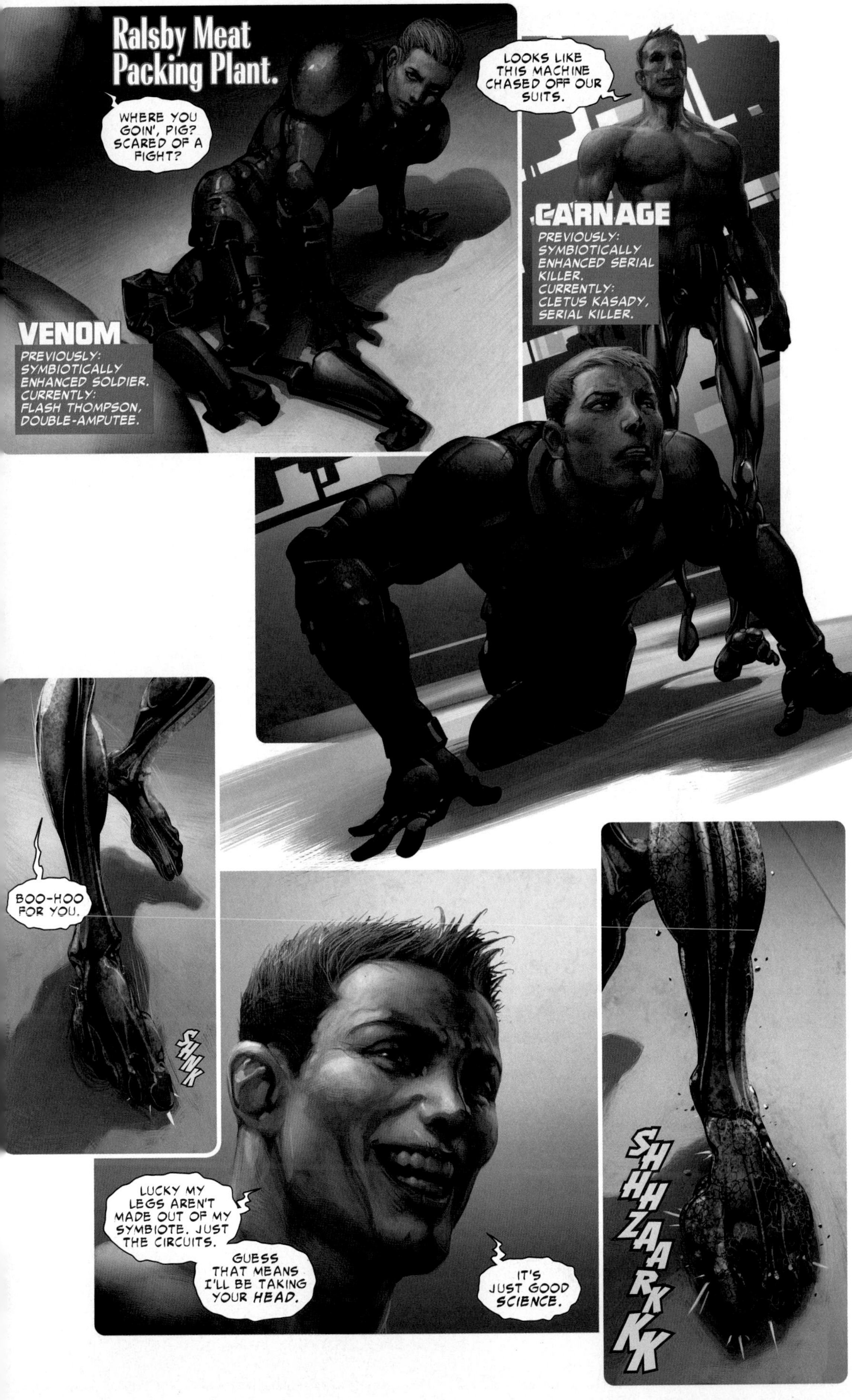
Ralsby Meat Packing Plant.
WHERE YOU GOIN', PIG? SCARED OF A FIGHT?
VENOM
PREVIOUSLY: SYMBIOTICALLY ENHANCED SOLDIER. CURRENTLY: FLASH THOMPSON, DOUBLE-AMPUTEE.
LOOKS LIKE THIS MACHINE CHASED OFF OUR SUITS.
CARNAGE
PREVIOUSLY: SYMBIOTICALLY ENHANCED SERIAL KILLER. CURRENTLY: CLETUS KASADY, SERIAL KILLER.
BOO-HOO FOR YOU.
SHNK
LUCKY MY LEGS AREN'T MADE OUT OF MY SYMBIOTE. JUST THE CIRCUITS.
GUESS THAT MEANS I'LL BE TAKING YOUR HEAD.
IT'S JUST GOOD SCIENCE.
SHHHZAAARKKK

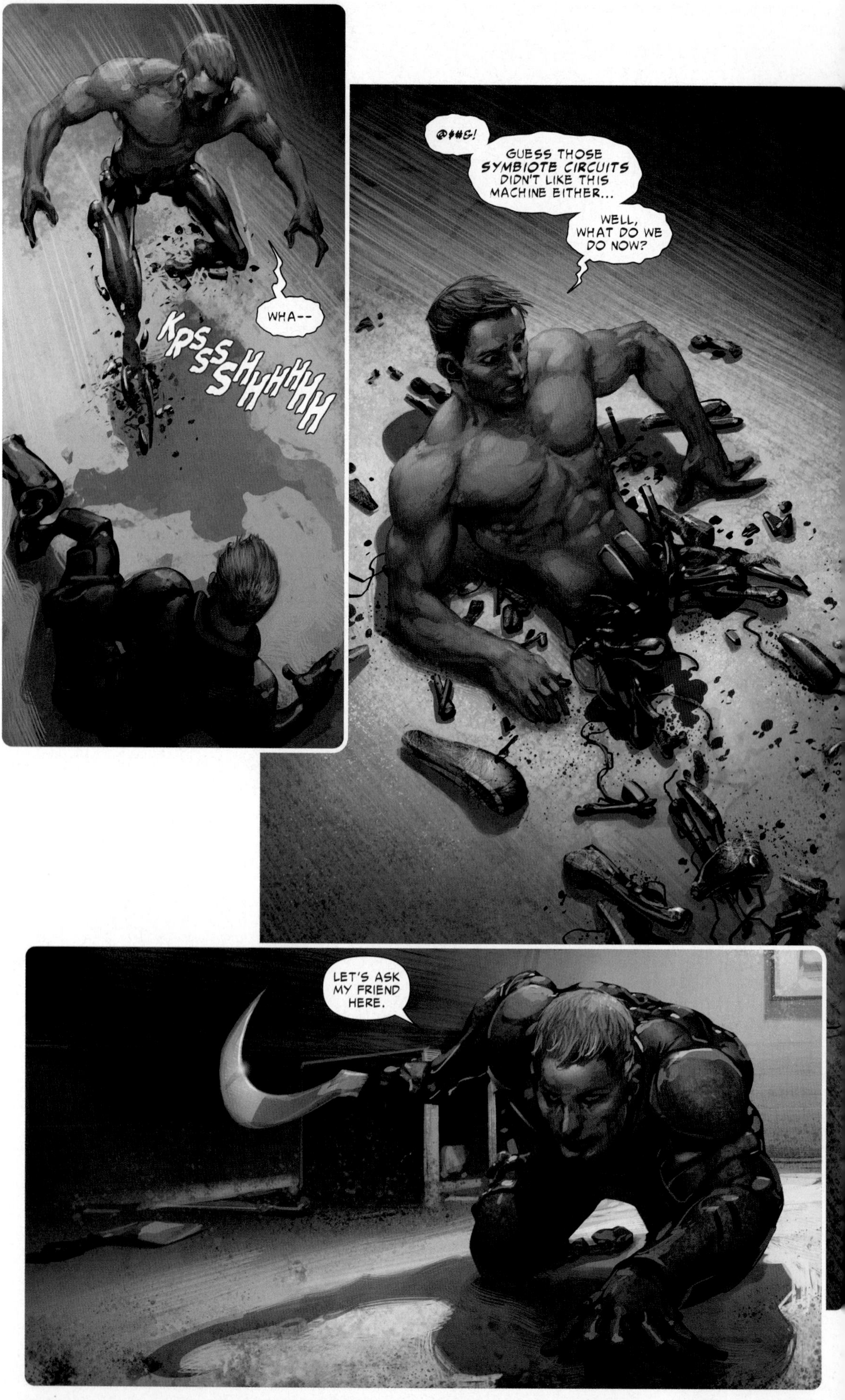
WHA--
KRSSSHHHHHH
@#$G!
GUESS THOSE SYMBIOTE CIRCUITS DIDN'T LIKE THIS MACHINE EITHER...
WELL, WHAT DO WE DO NOW?
LET'S ASK MY FRIEND HERE.

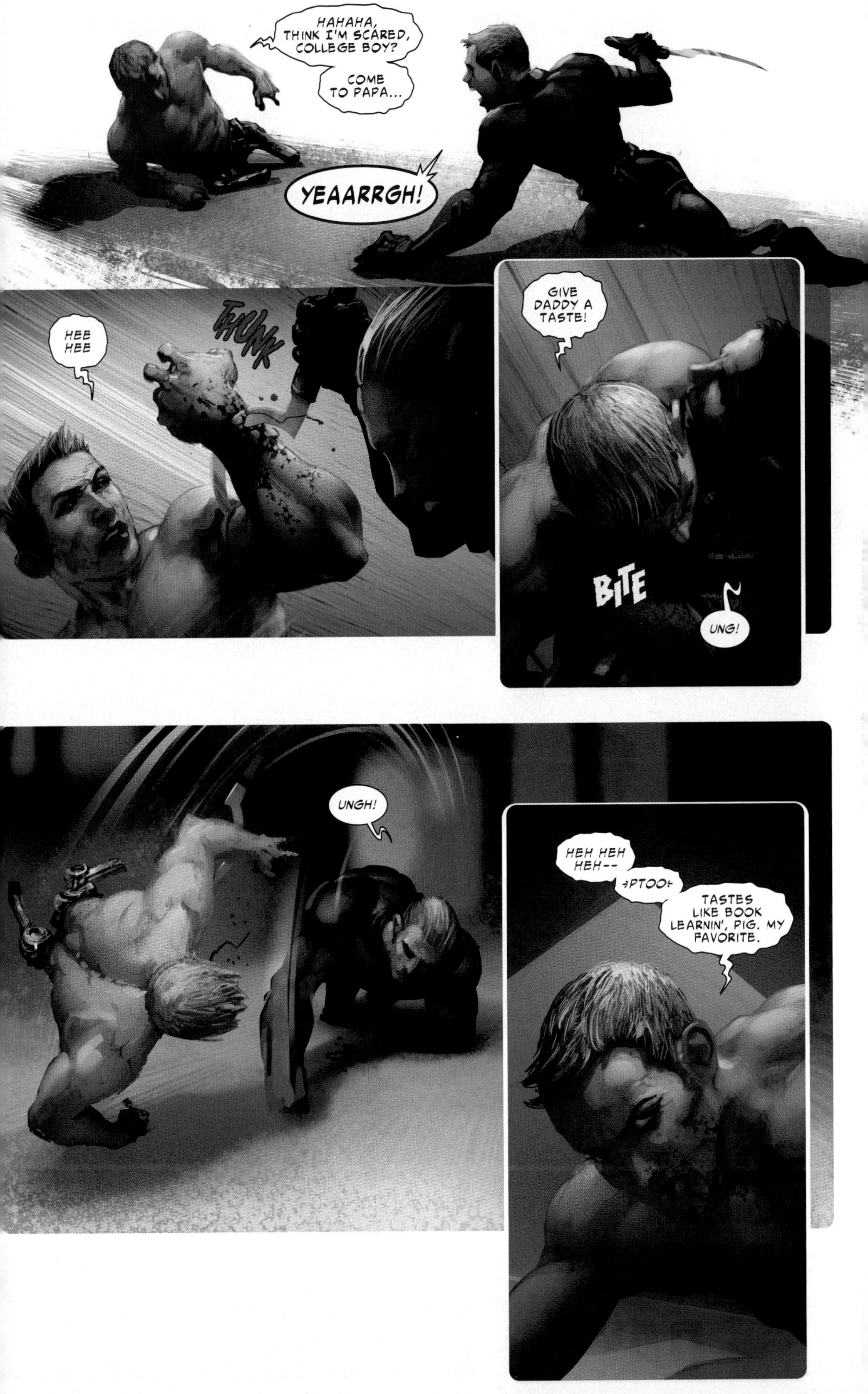
HAHAHA, THINK I'M SCARED, COLLEGE BOY?
COME TO PAPA...
YEAARRGH!
HEE HEE
THUNK
GIVE DADDY A TASTE!
BITE
UNG!
UNGH!
HEH HEH HEH--
PTOO
TASTES LIKE BOOK LEARNIN', PIG. MY FAVORITE.

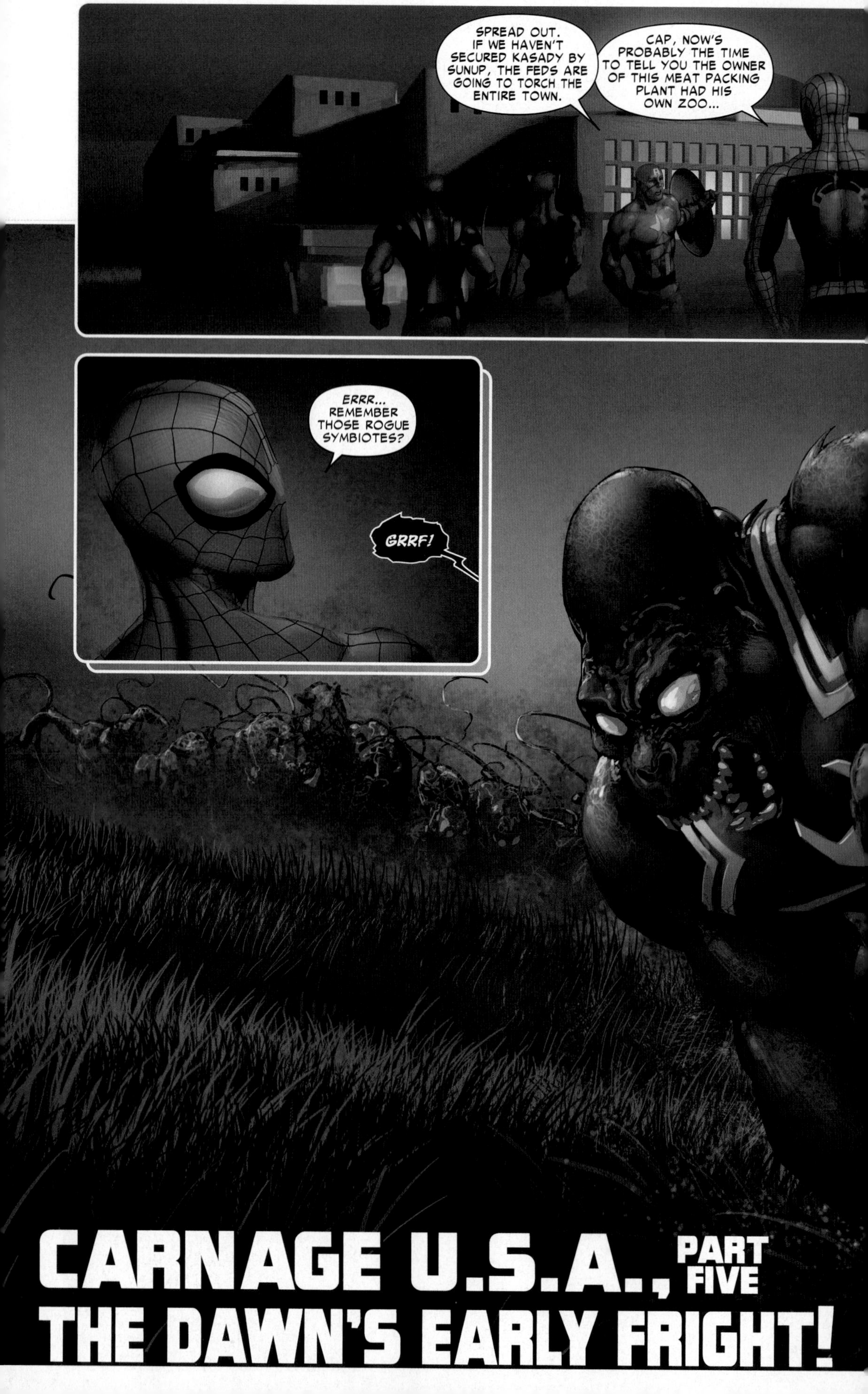
SPREAD OUT. IF WE HAVEN'T SECURED KASADY BY SUNUP, THE FEDS ARE GOING TO TORCH THE ENTIRE TOWN.
CAP, NOW'S PROBABLY THE TIME TO TELL YOU THE OWNER OF THIS MEAT PACKING PLANT HAD HIS OWN ZOO...
ERRR... REMEMBER THOSE ROGUE SYMBIOTES?
GRRF!
CARNAGE U.S.A., PART FIVE
THE DAWN'S EARLY FRIGHT!

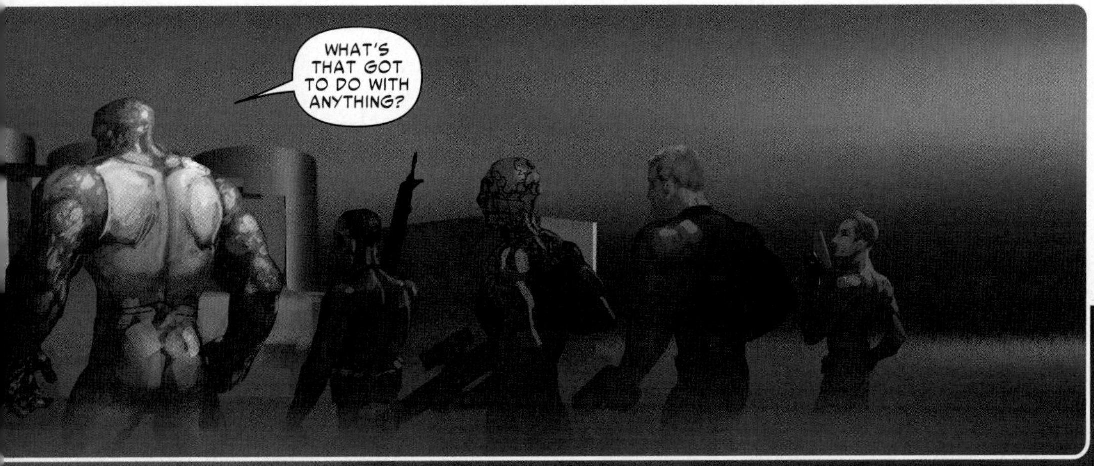
WHAT'S THAT GOT TO DO WITH ANYTHING?

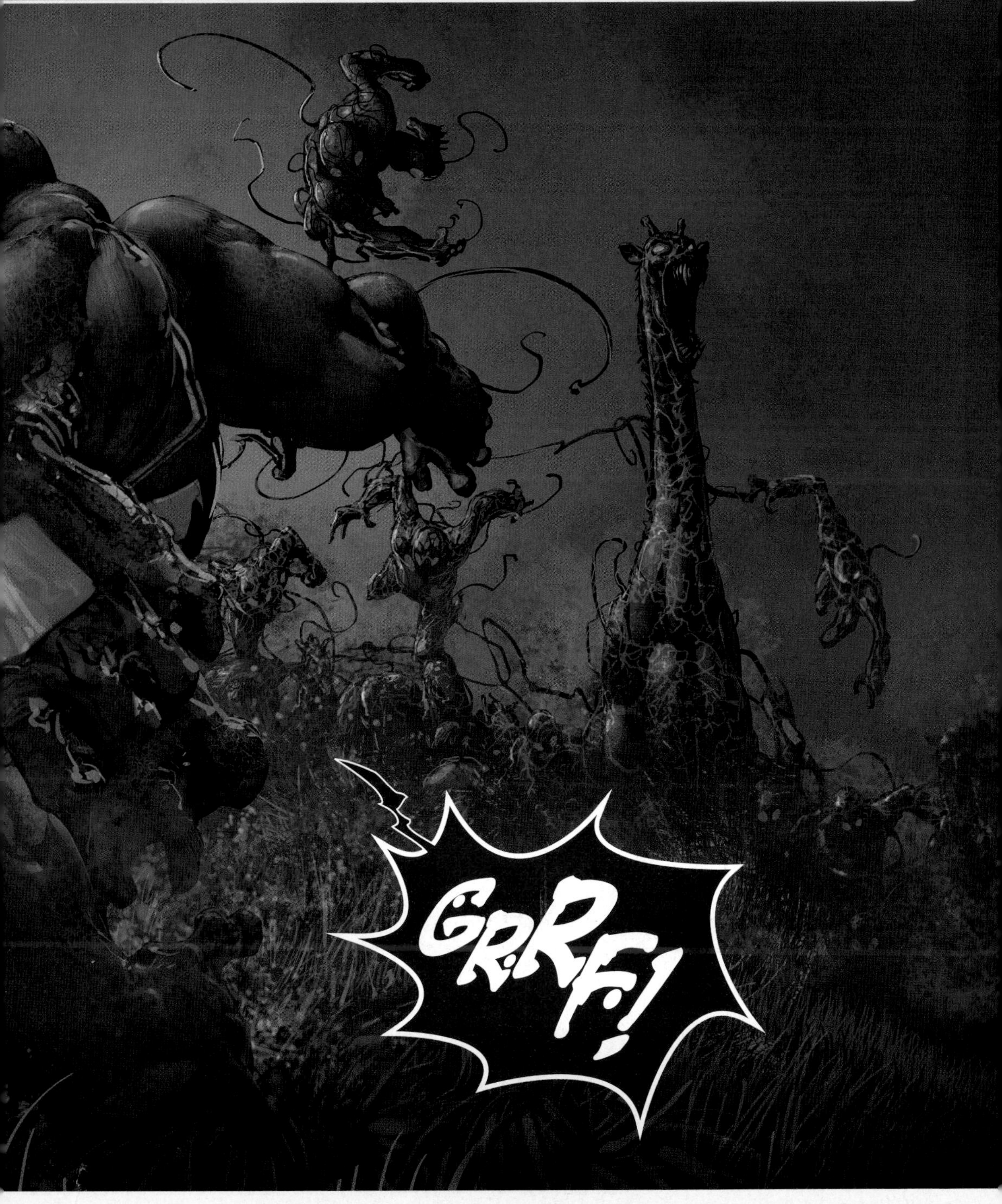
GRRF!

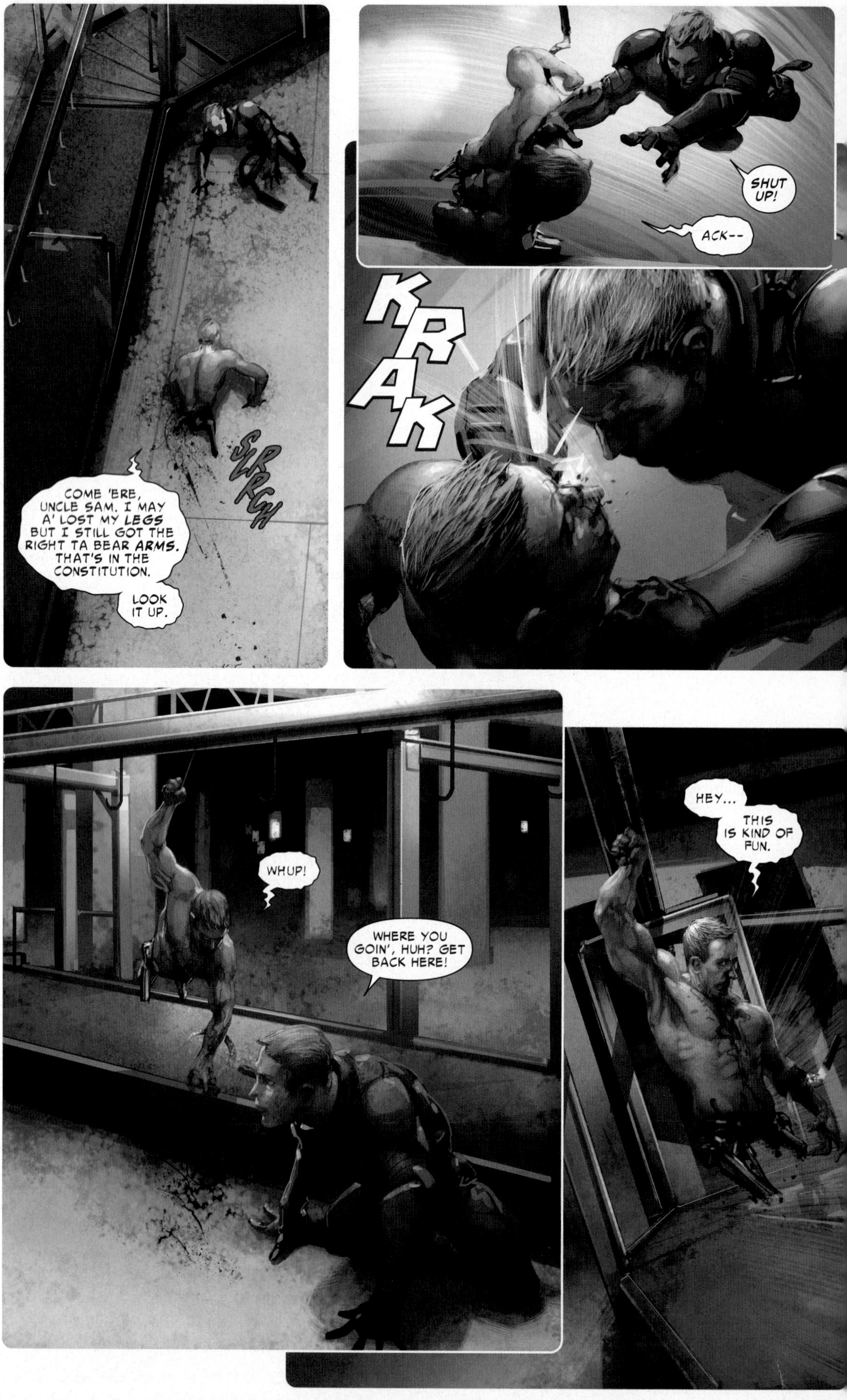
SLRCH
COME 'ERE, UNCLE SAM. I MAY A' LOST MY LEGS BUT I STILL GOT THE RIGHT TA BEAR ARMS. THAT'S IN THE CONSTITUTION.
LOOK IT UP.
SHUT UP!
ACK--
KRAK
WHUP!
WHERE YOU GOIN', HUH? GET BACK HERE!
HEY...
THIS IS KIND OF FUN.

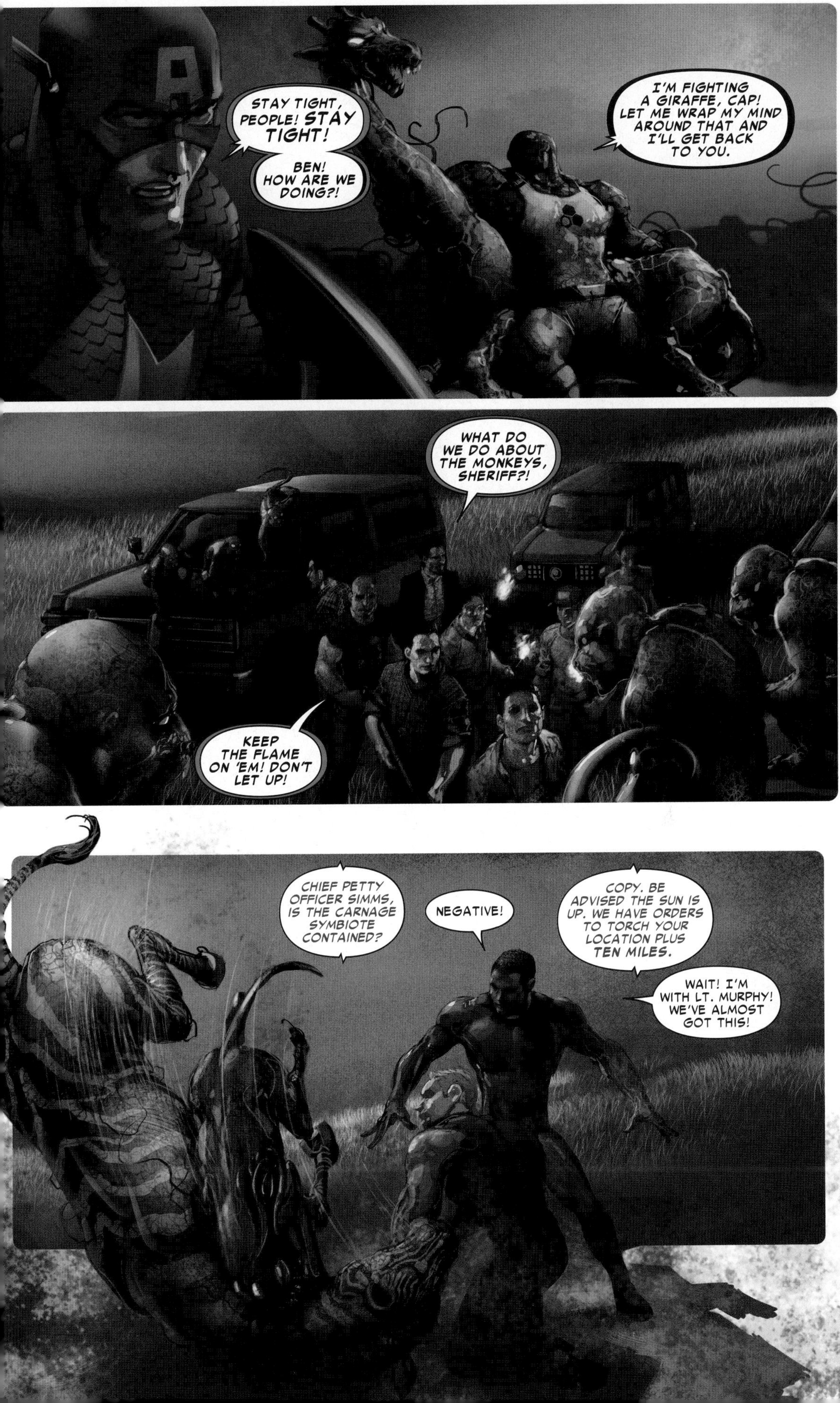
STAY TIGHT, PEOPLE! STAY TIGHT!
BEN! HOW ARE WE DOING?!
I'M FIGHTING A GIRAFFE, CAP! LET ME WRAP MY MIND AROUND THAT AND I'LL GET BACK TO YOU.
WHAT DO WE DO ABOUT THE MONKEYS, SHERIFF?!
KEEP THE FLAME ON 'EM! DON'T LET UP!
CHIEF PETTY OFFICER SIMMS, IS THE CARNAGE SYMBIOTE CONTAINED?
NEGATIVE!
COPY. BE ADVISED THE SUN IS UP. WE HAVE ORDERS TO TORCH YOUR LOCATION PLUS TEN MILES.
WAIT! I'M WITH LT. MURPHY! WE'VE ALMOST GOT THIS!

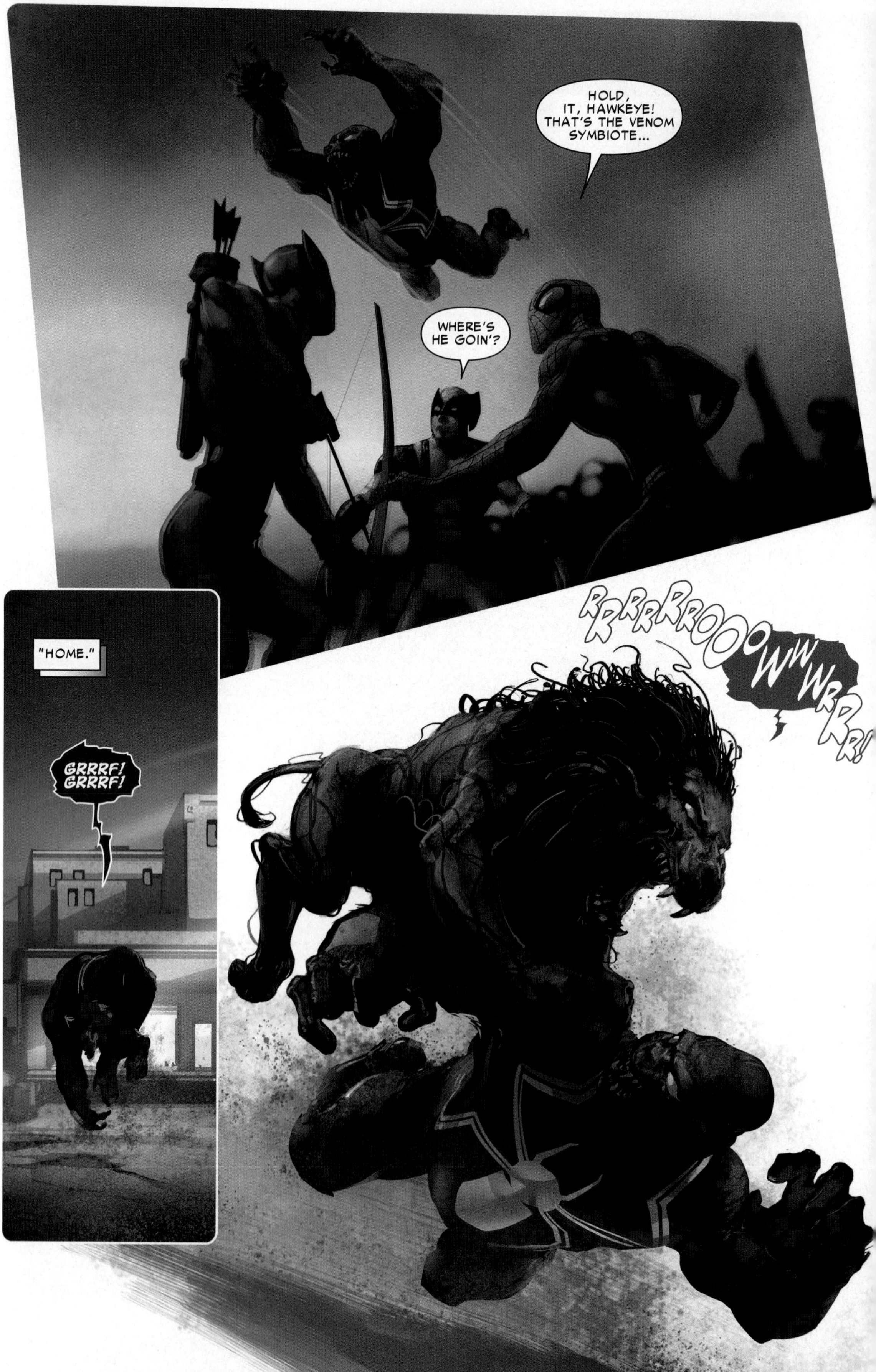
HOLD, IT, HAWKEYE! THAT'S THE VENOM SYMBIOTE...
WHERE'S HE GOIN'?
"HOME."
GRRRF! GRRRF!
RRRRRROOOOWWWRRR!

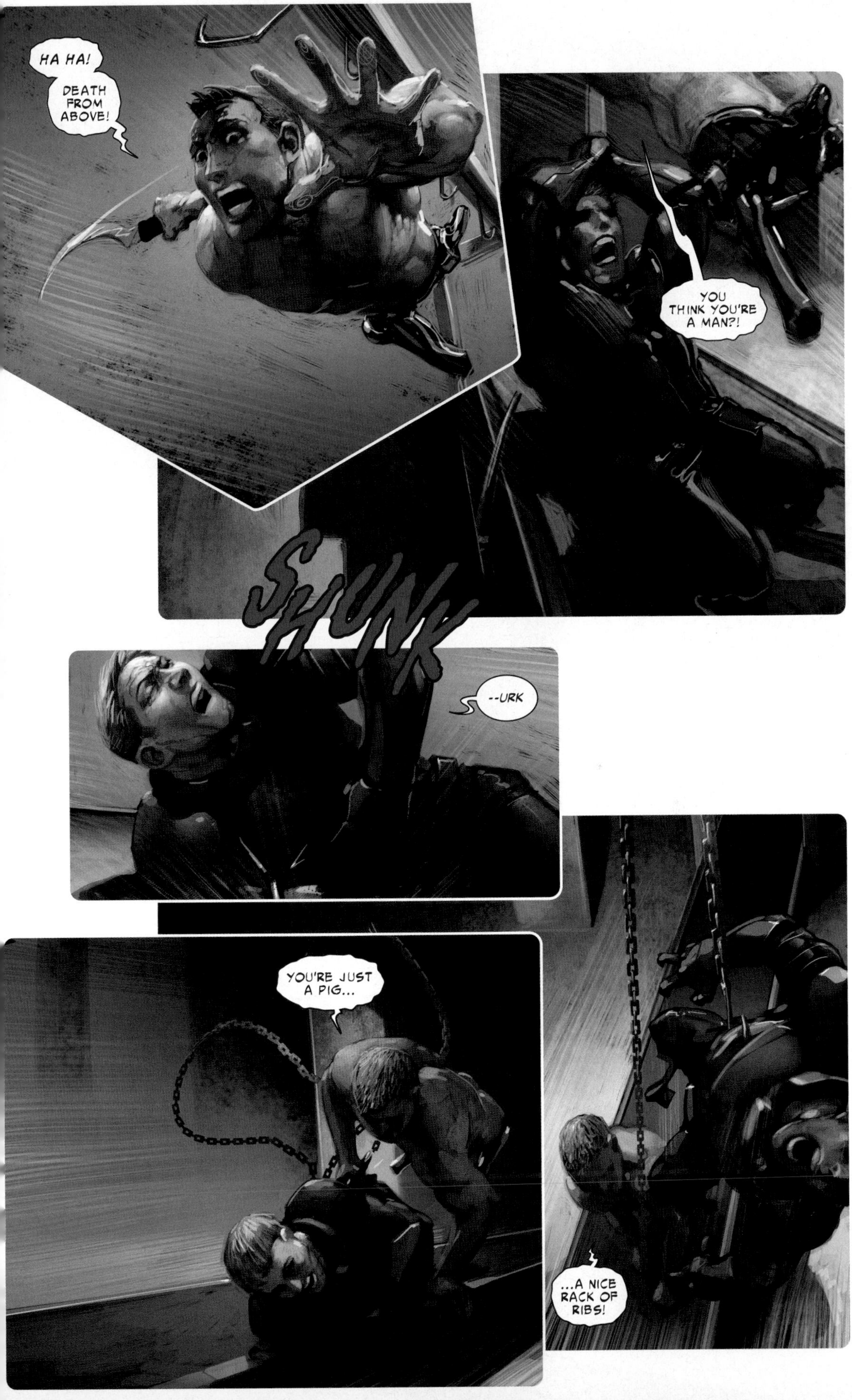
HA HA!
DEATH FROM ABOVE!
YOU THINK YOU'RE A MAN?!
SHUNK
--URK
YOU'RE JUST A PIG...
...A NICE RACK OF RIBS!

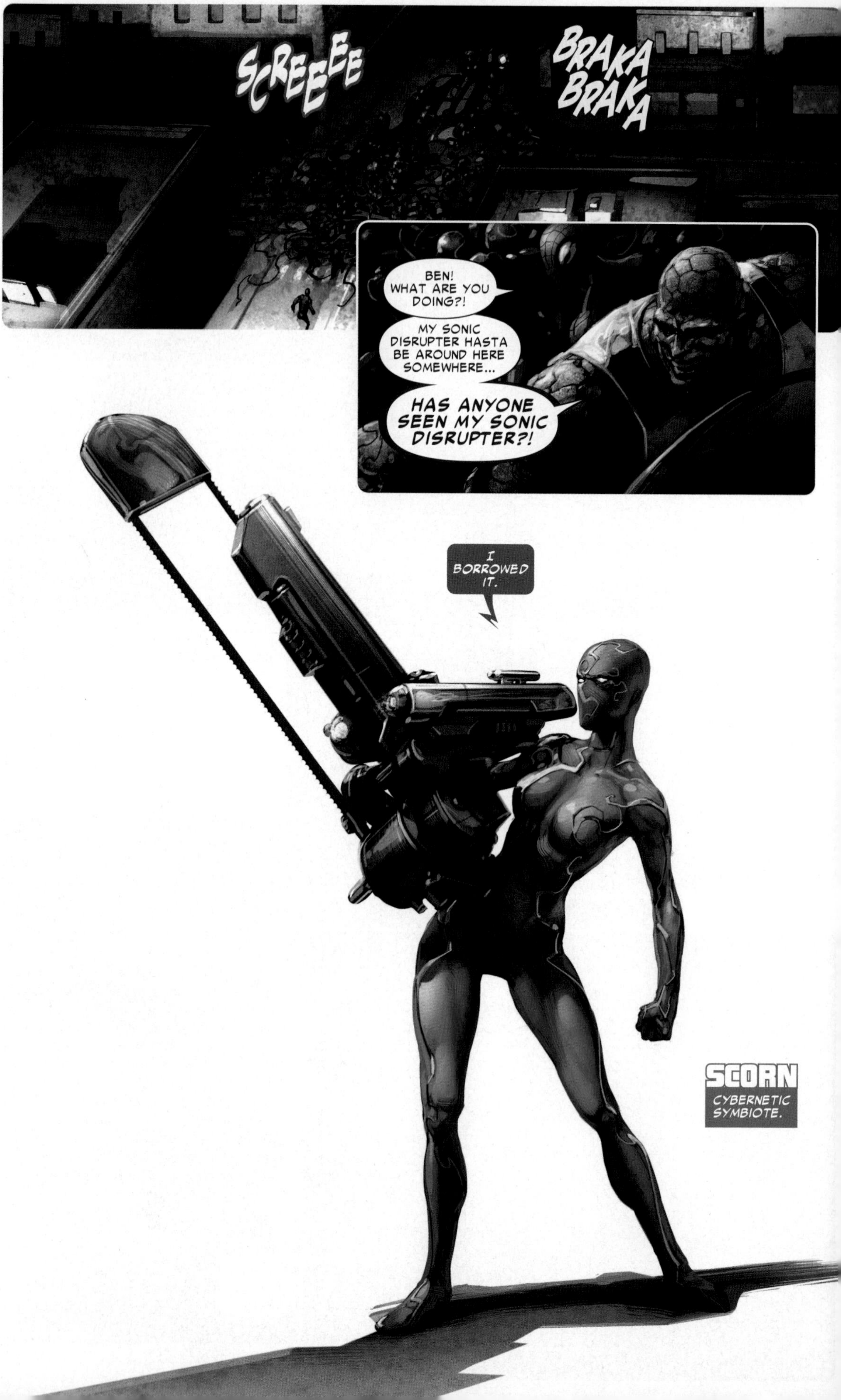
SCREEEEE
BRAKA BRAKA
BEN! WHAT ARE YOU DOING?!
MY SONIC DISRUPTER HASTA BE AROUND HERE SOMEWHERE...
HAS ANYONE SEEN MY SONIC DISRUPTER?!
I BORROWED IT.
SCORN
CYBERNETIC SYMBIOTE.

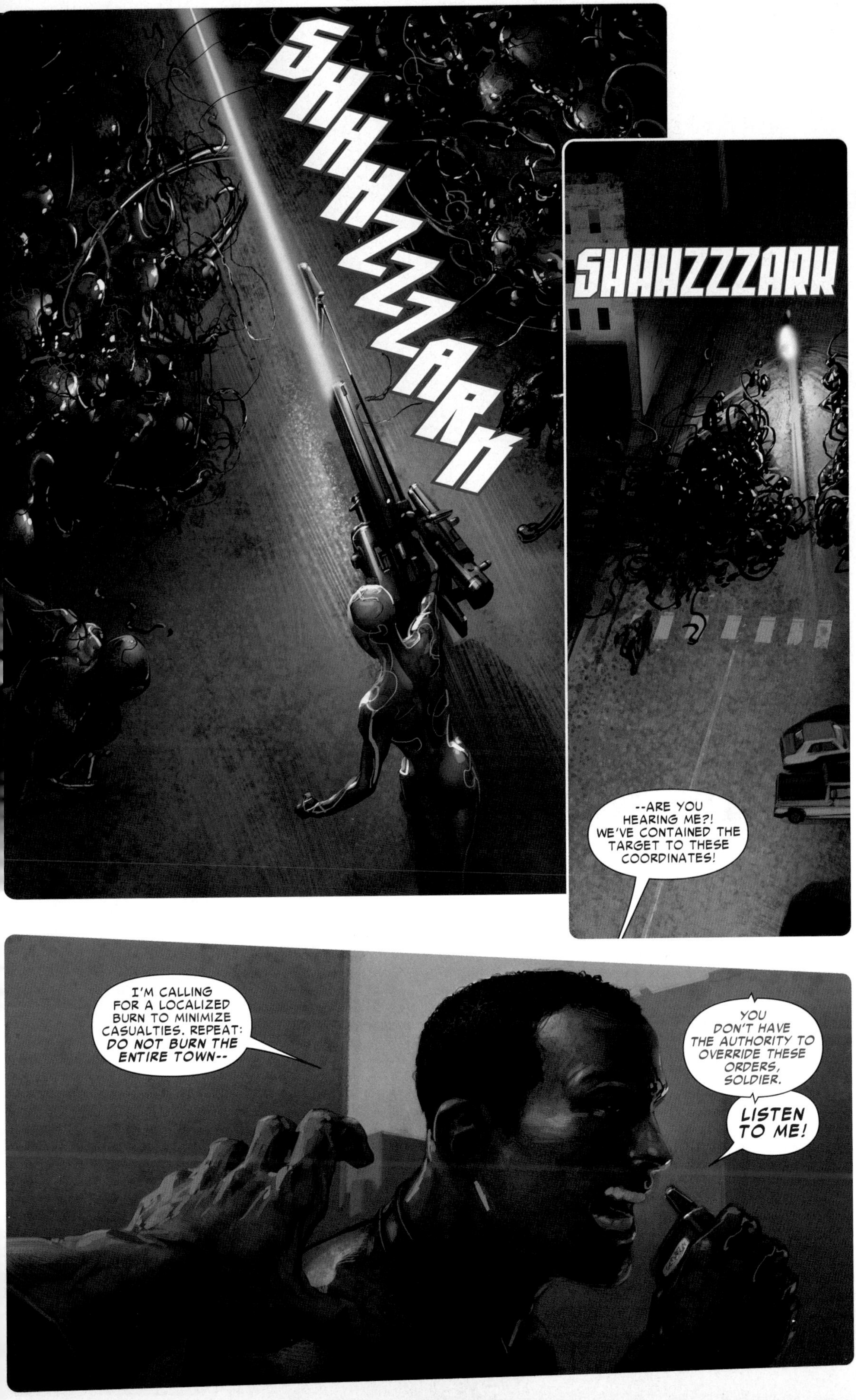
SHHHZZZARK
SHHHZZZARK
--ARE YOU HEARING ME?! WE'VE CONTAINED THE TARGET TO THESE COORDINATES!
I'M CALLING FOR A LOCALIZED BURN TO MINIMIZE CASUALTIES. REPEAT: DO NOT BURN THE ENTIRE TOWN--
YOU DON'T HAVE THE AUTHORITY TO OVERRIDE THESE ORDERS, SOLDIER.
LISTEN TO ME!

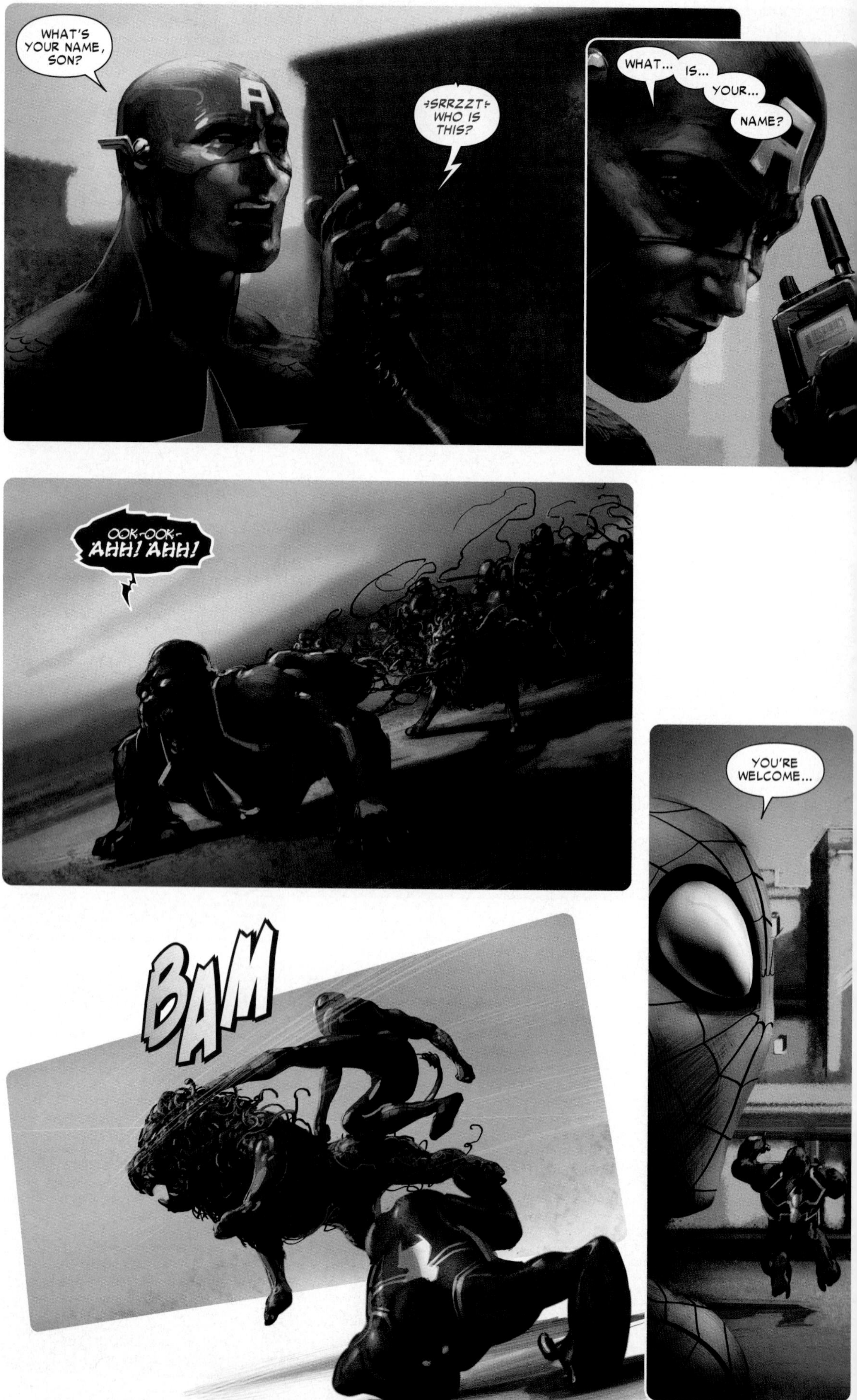
WHAT'S YOUR NAME, SON?
SRRZZT WHO IS THIS?
WHAT...
IS...
YOUR...
NAME?
OOK-OOK-AHH! AHH!
BAM
YOU'RE WELCOME...

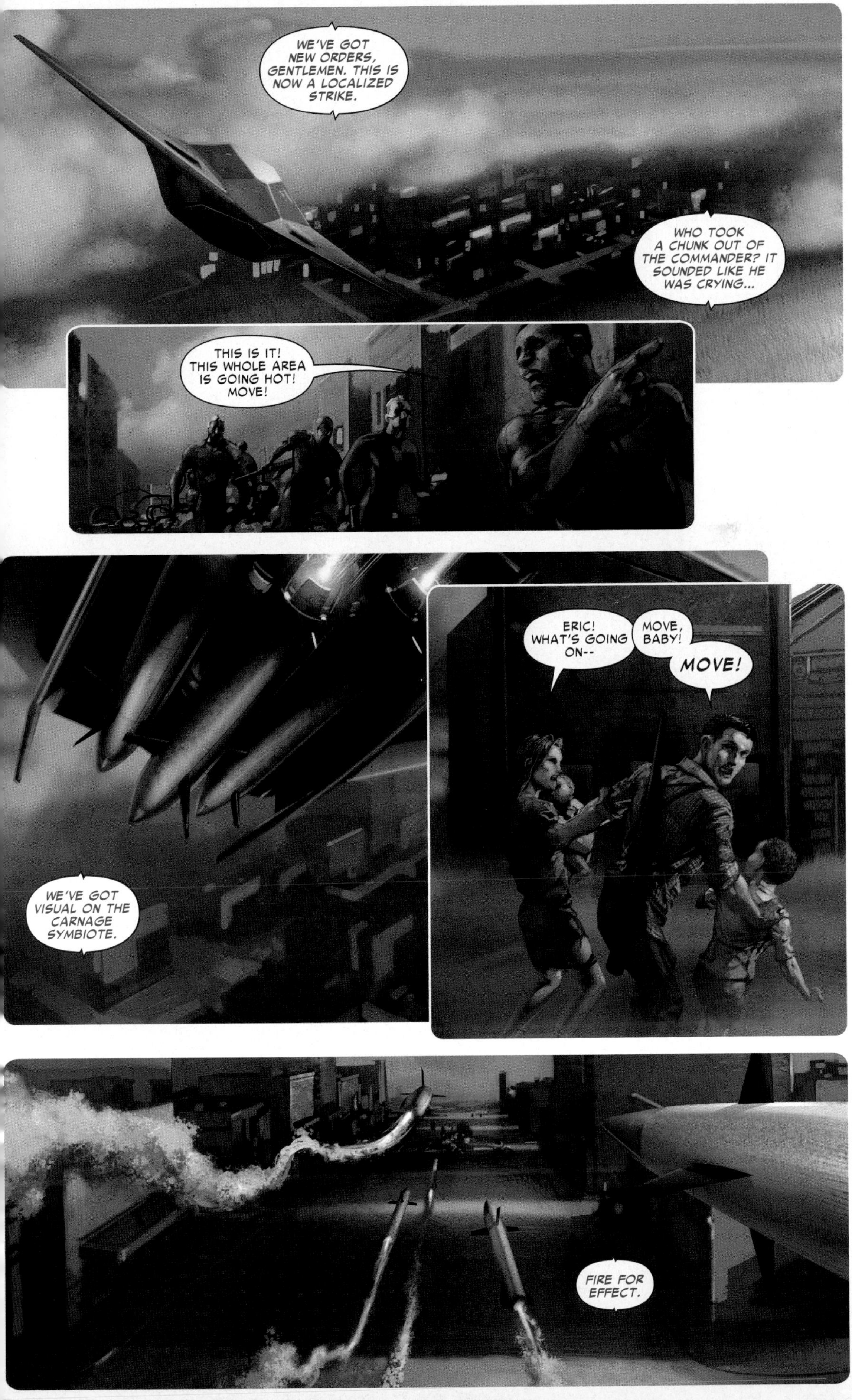
WE'VE GOT NEW ORDERS, GENTLEMEN. THIS IS NOW A LOCALIZED STRIKE.
WHO TOOK A CHUNK OUT OF THE COMMANDER? IT SOUNDED LIKE HE WAS CRYING...
THIS IS IT! THIS WHOLE AREA IS GOING HOT! MOVE!
WE'VE GOT VISUAL ON THE CARNAGE SYMBIOTE.
ERIC! WHAT'S GOING ON--
MOVE, BABY!
MOVE!
FIRE FOR EFFECT.

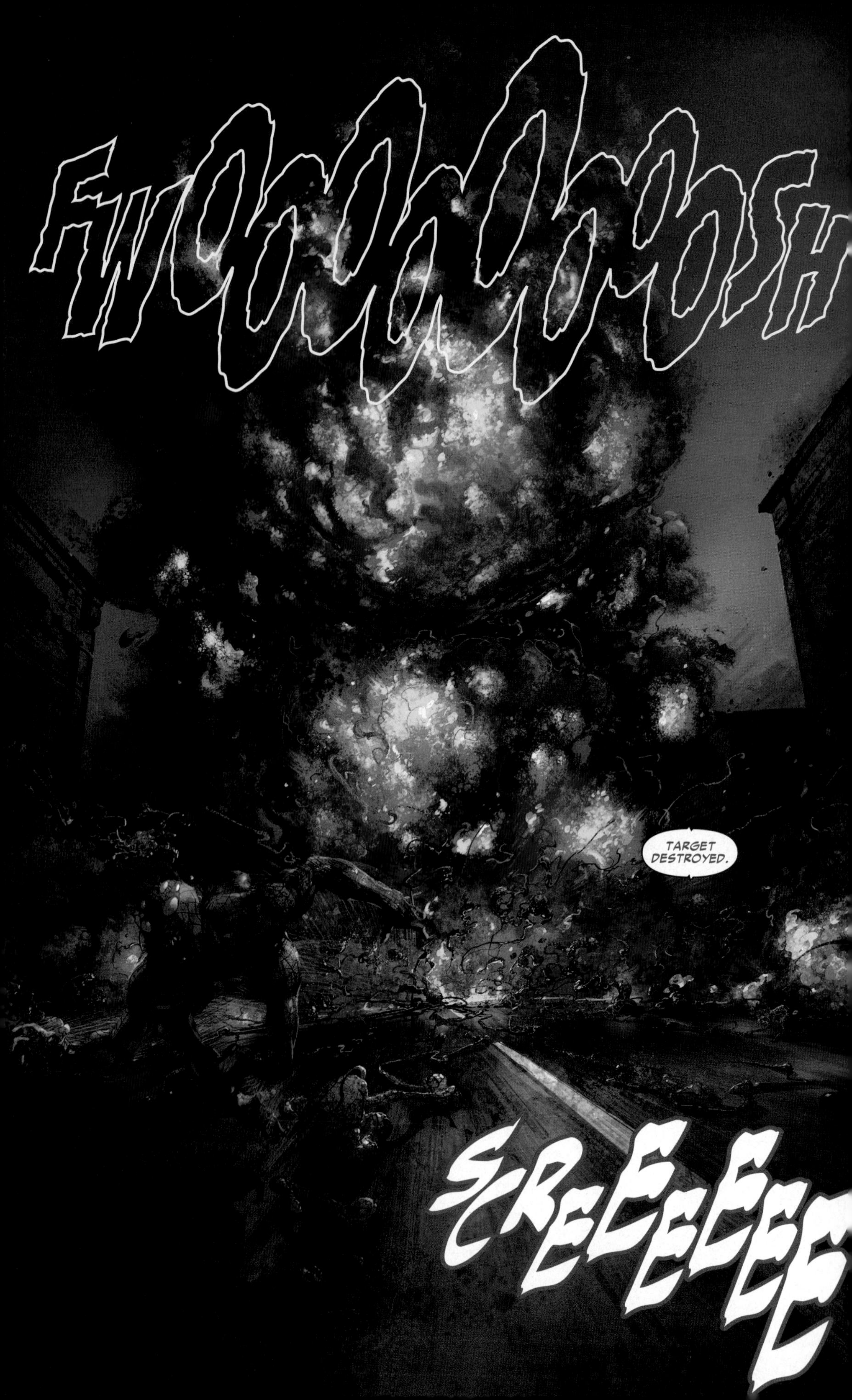
FWOOOOOOOOOSH
TARGET DESTROYED.
SCREEEEEEE

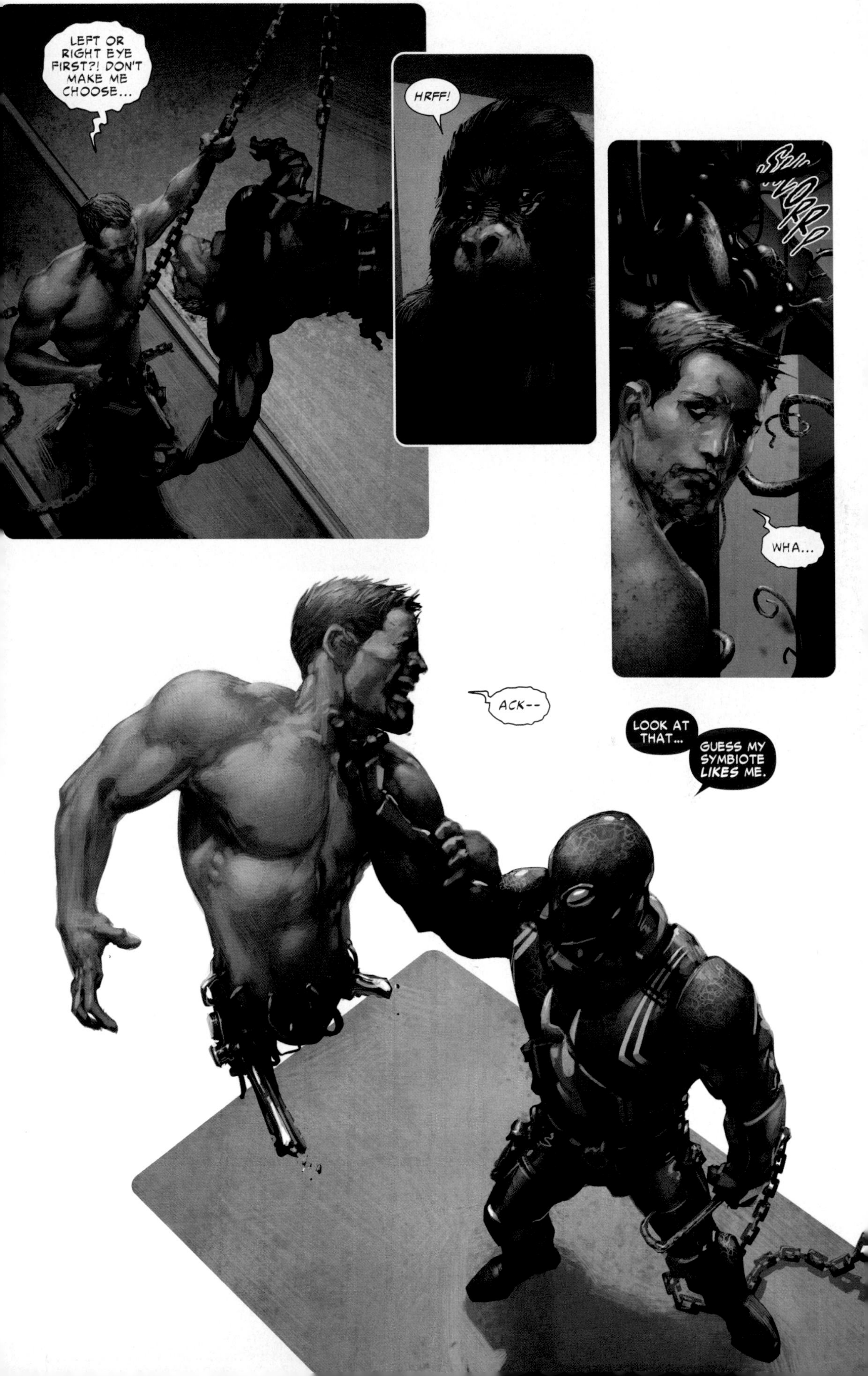
LEFT OR RIGHT EYE FIRST?! DON'T MAKE ME CHOOSE...
HRFF!
WHA...
ACK--
LOOK AT THAT...
GUESS MY SYMBIOTE LIKES ME.

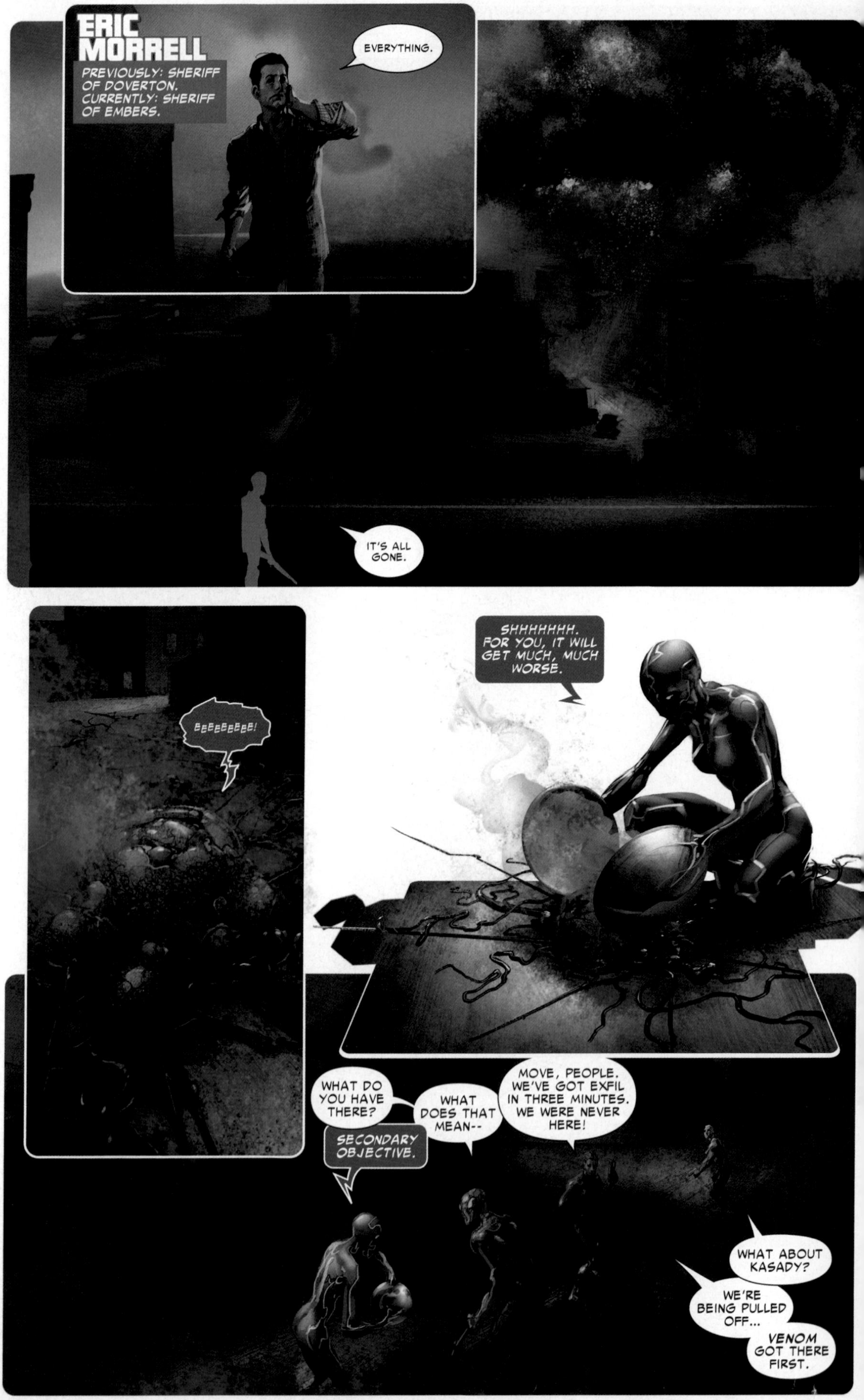
ERIC MORRELL
PREVIOUSLY: SHERIFF OF DOVERTON. CURRENTLY: SHERIFF OF EMBERS.
EVERYTHING.
IT'S ALL GONE.
EEEEEEEEE!
SHHHHHHH. FOR YOU, IT WILL GET MUCH, MUCH WORSE.
WHAT DO YOU HAVE THERE?
SECONDARY OBJECTIVE.
WHAT DOES THAT MEAN--
MOVE, PEOPLE. WE'VE GOT EXFIL IN THREE MINUTES. WE WERE NEVER HERE!
WHAT ABOUT KASADY?
WE'RE BEING PULLED OFF... VENOM GOT THERE FIRST.

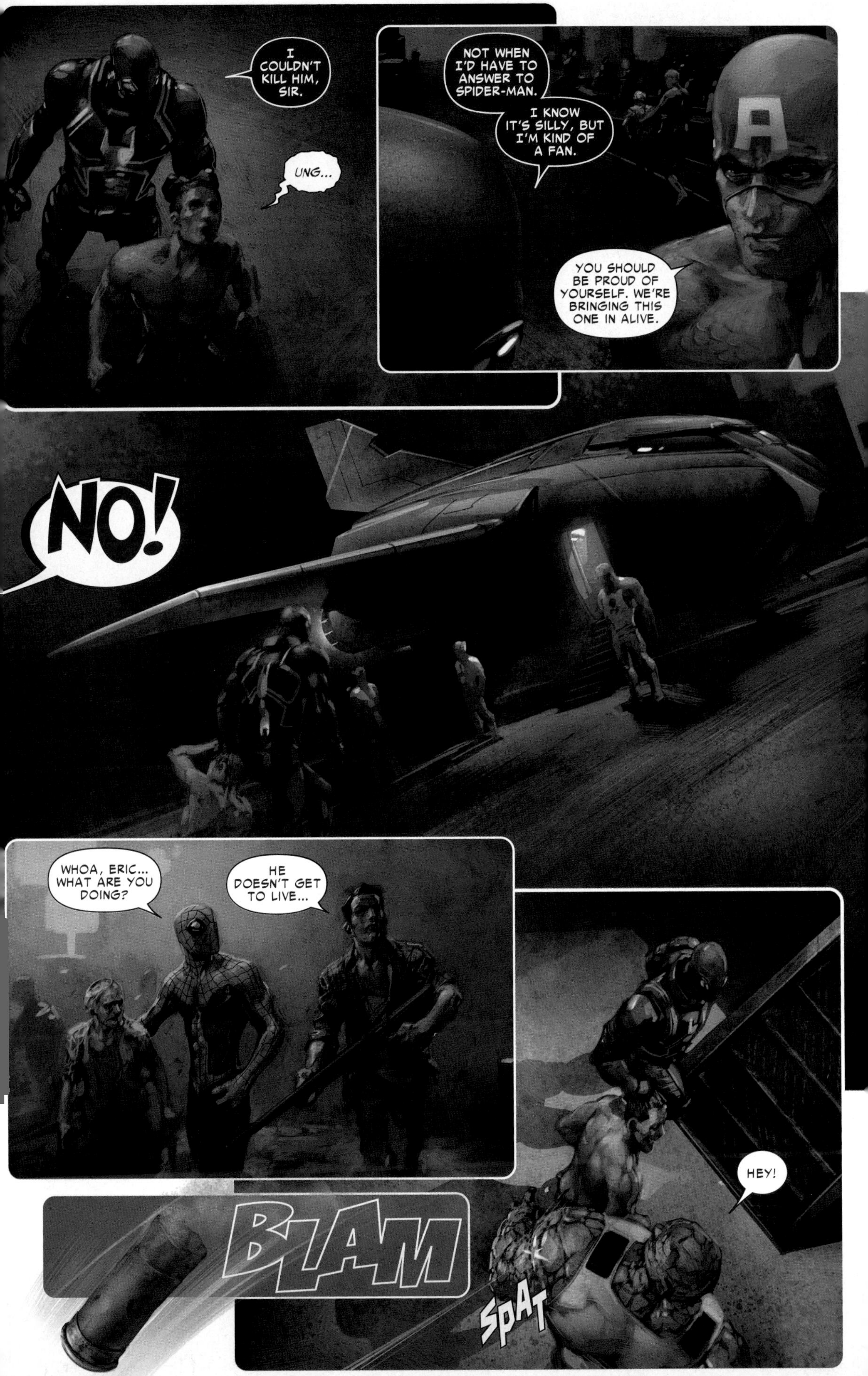
I COULDN'T KILL HIM, SIR.
UNG...
NOT WHEN I'D HAVE TO ANSWER TO SPIDER-MAN.
I KNOW IT'S SILLY, BUT I'M KIND OF A FAN.
YOU SHOULD BE PROUD OF YOURSELF. WE'RE BRINGING THIS ONE IN ALIVE.
NO!
WHOA, ERIC... WHAT ARE YOU DOING?
HE DOESN'T GET TO LIVE...
BLAM
HEY!
SPAT

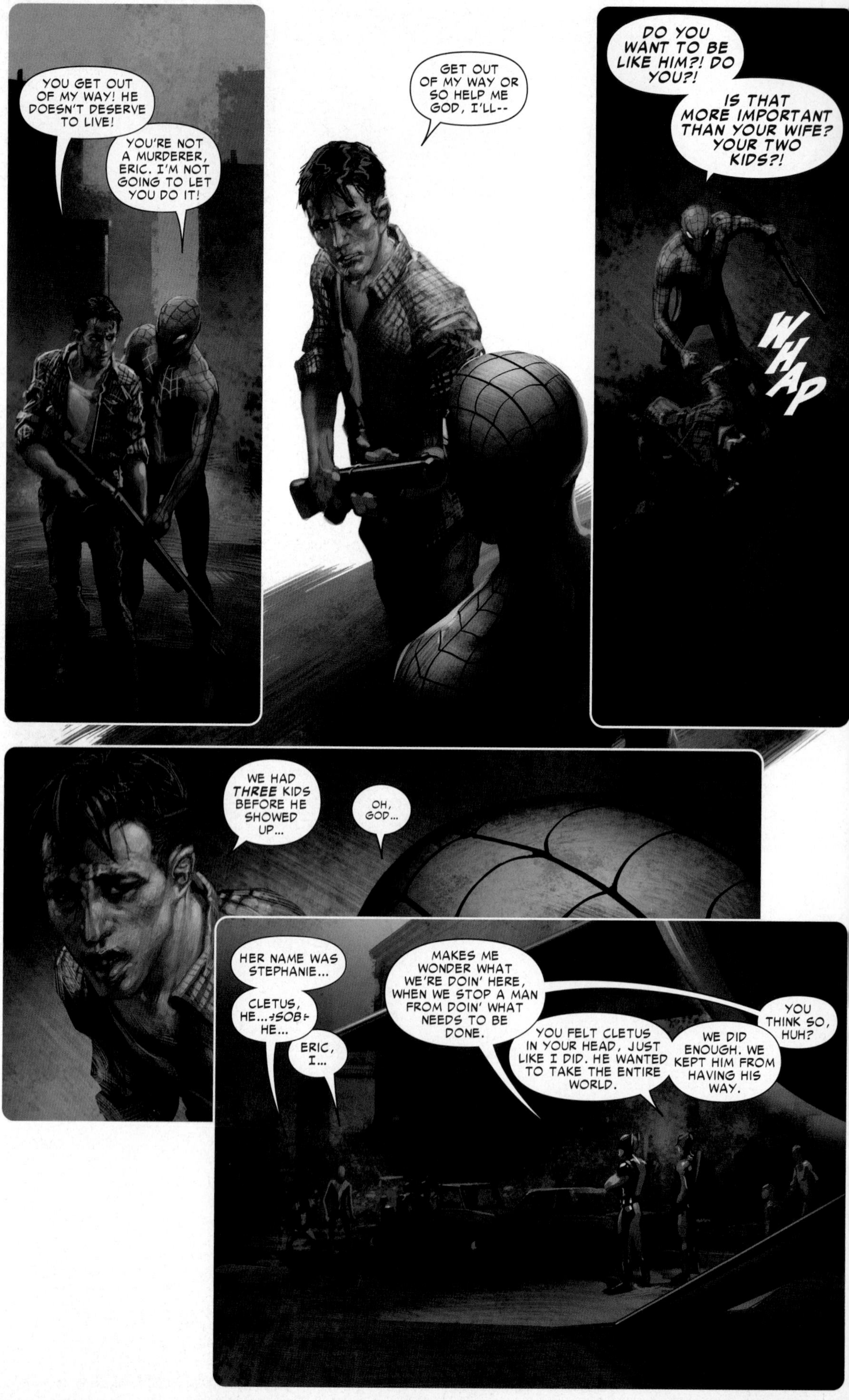

YOU GET OUT OF MY WAY! HE DOESN'T DESERVE TO LIVE!
YOU'RE NOT A MURDERER, ERIC. I'M NOT GOING TO LET YOU DO IT!
GET OUT OF MY WAY OR SO HELP ME GOD, I'LL--
DO YOU WANT TO BE LIKE HIM?! DO YOU?!
IS THAT MORE IMPORTANT THAN YOUR WIFE? YOUR TWO KIDS?!
WHAP
WE HAD THREE KIDS BEFORE HE SHOWED UP...
OH, GOD...
HER NAME WAS STEPHANIE...
CLETUS, HE... SOB HE...
ERIC, I...
MAKES ME WONDER WHAT WE'RE DOIN' HERE, WHEN WE STOP A MAN FROM DOIN' WHAT NEEDS TO BE DONE.
YOU FELT CLETUS IN YOUR HEAD, JUST LIKE I DID. HE WANTED TO TAKE THE ENTIRE WORLD.
WE DID ENOUGH. WE KEPT HIM FROM HAVING HIS WAY.
YOU THINK SO, HUH?

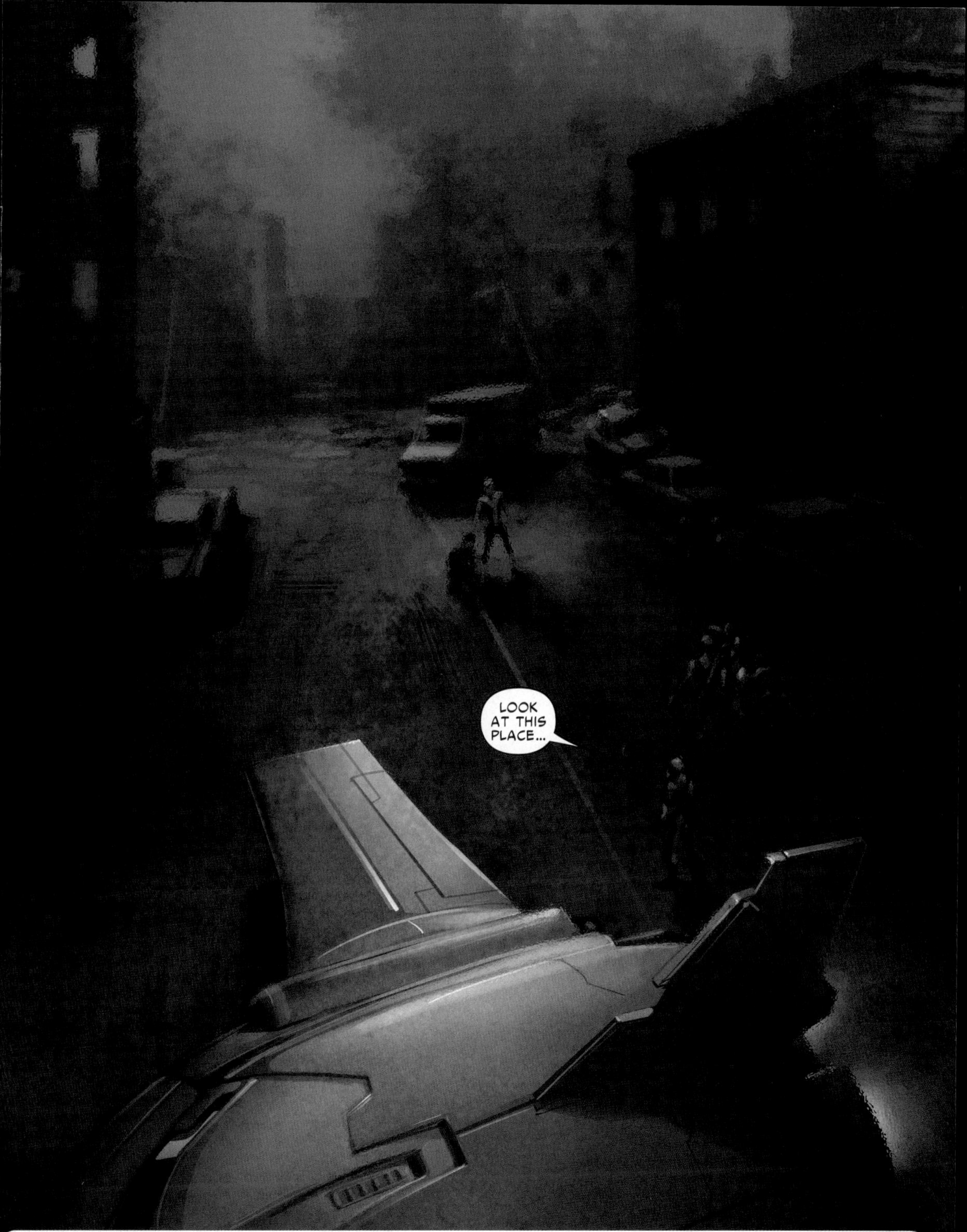
LOOK AT THIS PLACE...

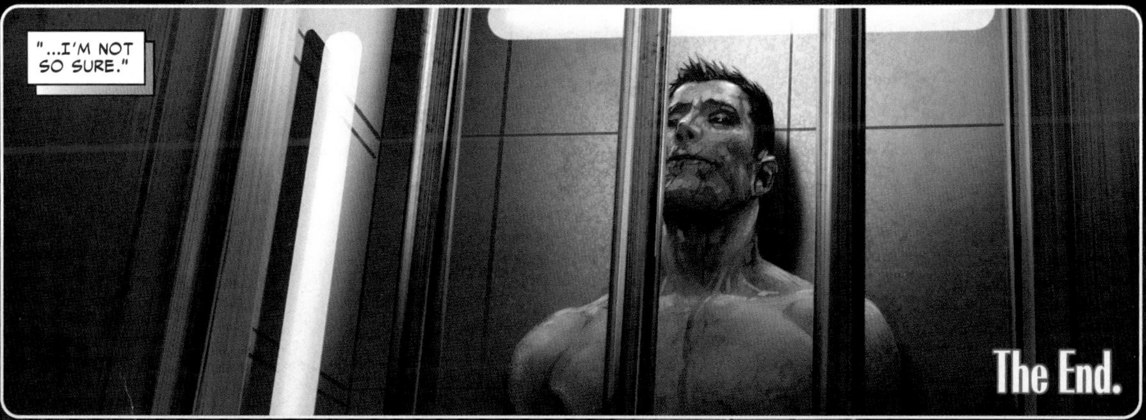
"...I'M NOT SO SURE."
The End.

Cletus Kasady was lobotomized in a later battle. The Wizard, scheming to rebuild the Frightful Four, freed Carnage — but upon discovering Kasady's condition, he decided to forcibly transfer the symbiote to his ally Dr. Karl Malus instead. Meanwhile, J. Jonah Jameson was elected mayor of New York City — and Doctor Octopus transferred his mind into Peter Parker's body, for a time becoming a "superior" Spider-Man!

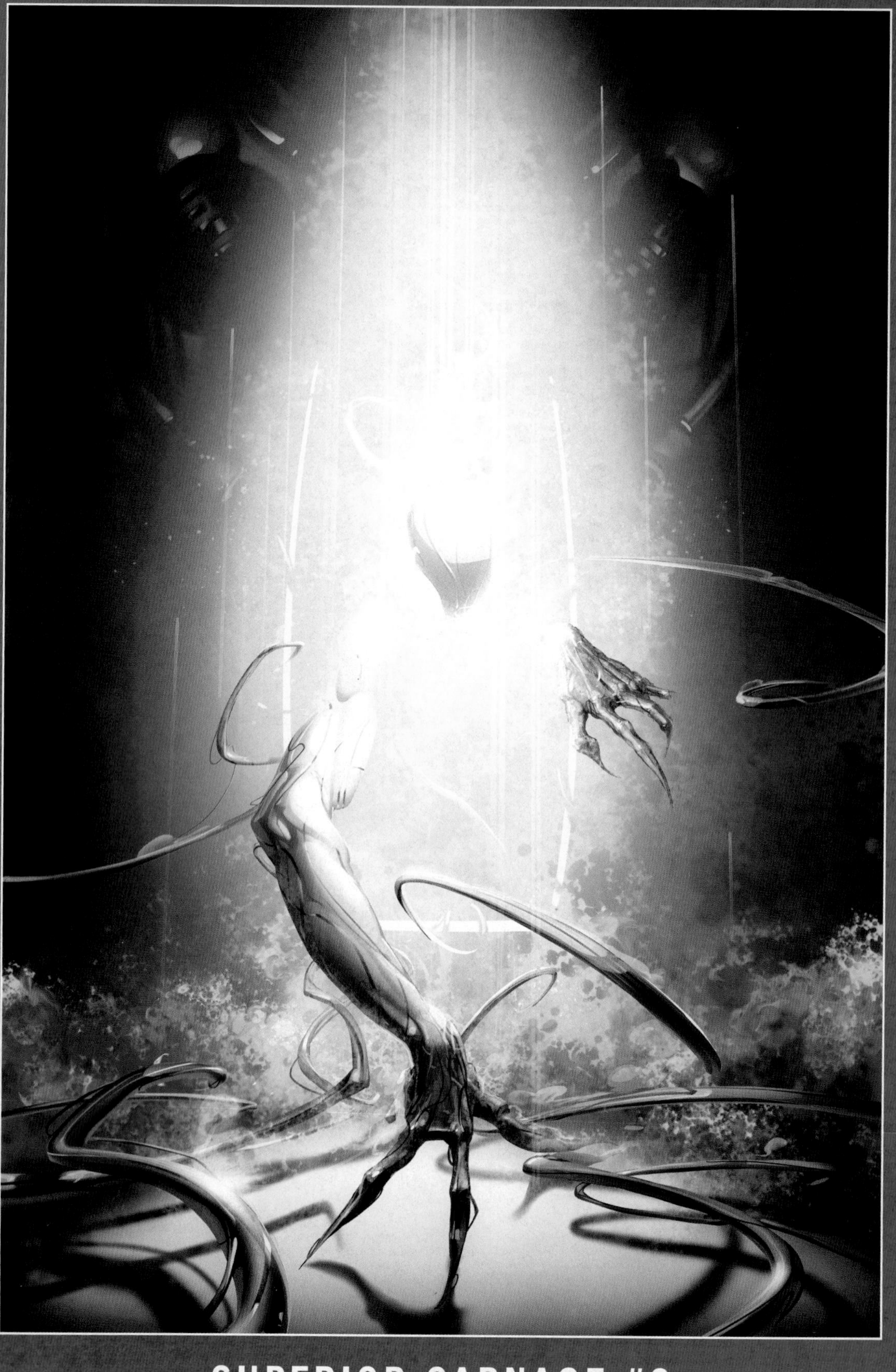

SUPERIOR CARNAGE #3

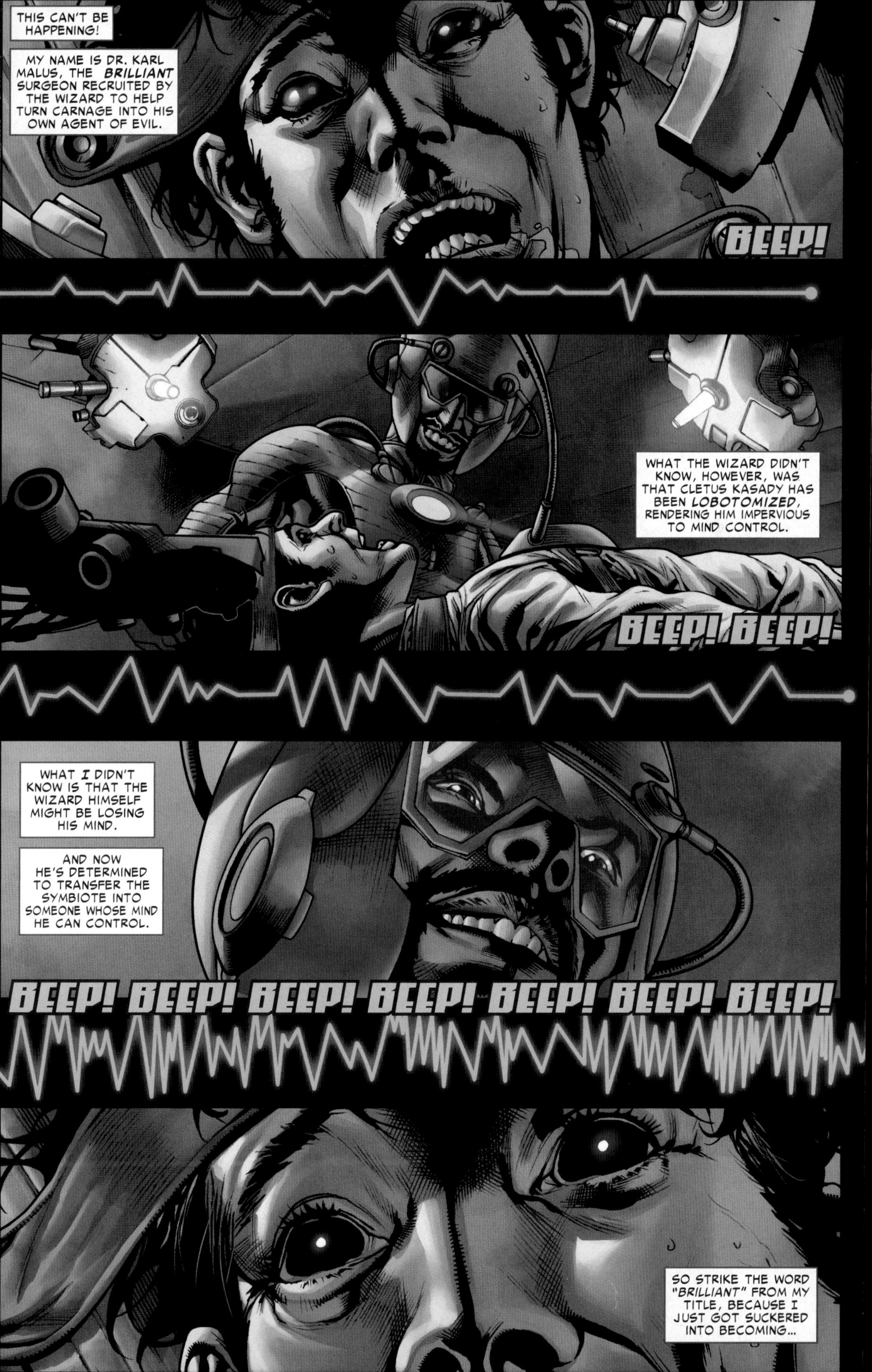
THIS CAN'T BE HAPPENING!
MY NAME IS DR. KARL MALUS, THE *BRILLIANT* SURGEON RECRUITED BY THE WIZARD TO HELP TURN CARNAGE INTO HIS OWN AGENT OF EVIL.
BEEP!
WHAT THE WIZARD DIDN'T KNOW, HOWEVER, WAS THAT CLETUS KASADY HAS BEEN *LOBOTOMIZED*, RENDERING HIM IMPERVIOUS TO MIND CONTROL.
BEEP! BEEP!
WHAT *I* DIDN'T KNOW IS THAT THE WIZARD HIMSELF MIGHT BE LOSING HIS MIND.
AND NOW HE'S DETERMINED TO TRANSFER THE SYMBIOTE INTO SOMEONE WHOSE MIND HE CAN CONTROL.
BEEP! BEEP! BEEP! BEEP! BEEP! BEEP! BEEP!
SO STRIKE THE WORD "*BRILLIANT*" FROM MY TITLE, BECAUSE I JUST GOT SUCKERED INTO BECOMING...

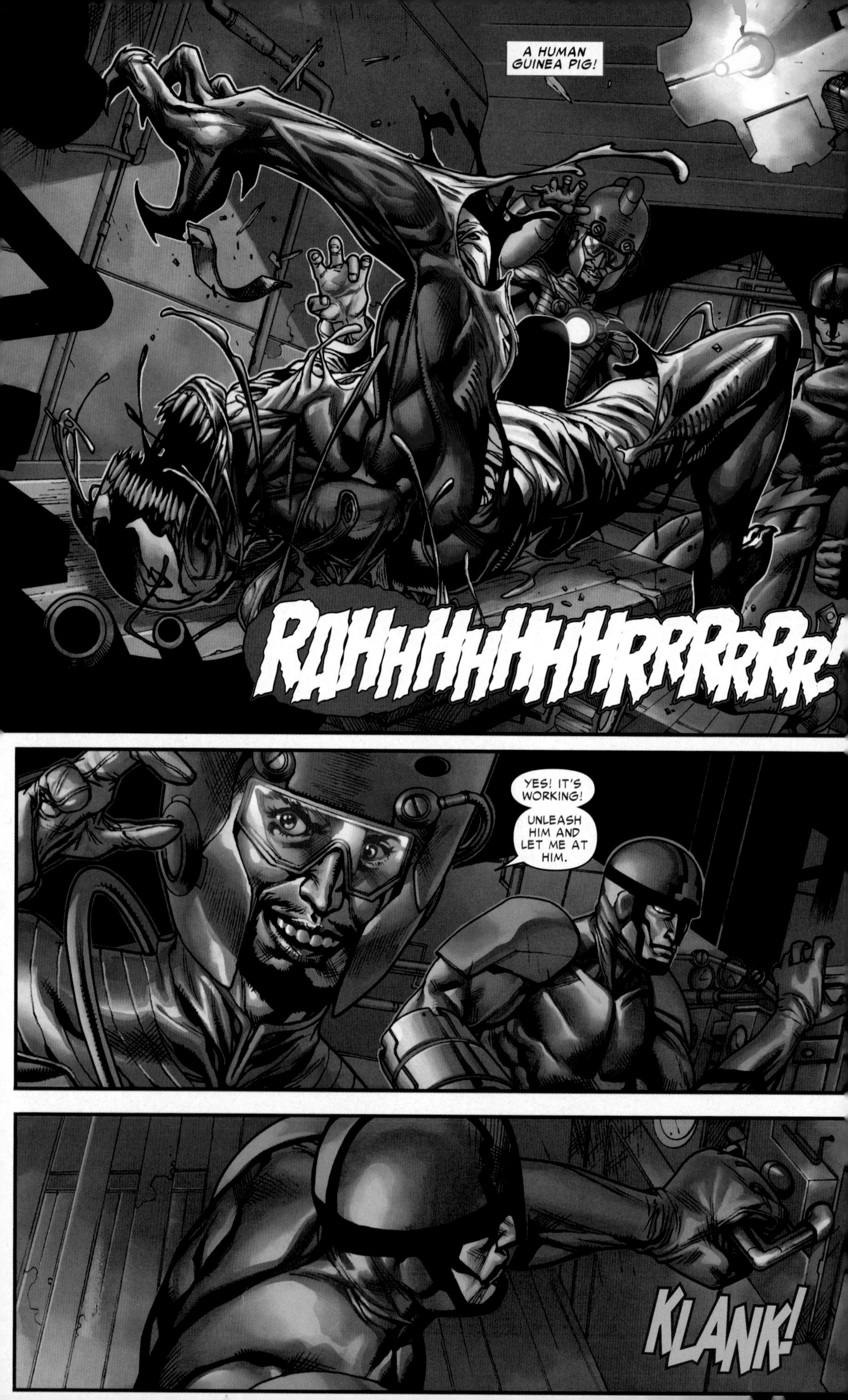

A HUMAN GUINEA PIG!
RAHHHHHHHRRRRRR!
YES! IT'S WORKING!
UNLEASH HIM AND LET ME AT HIM.
KLANK!

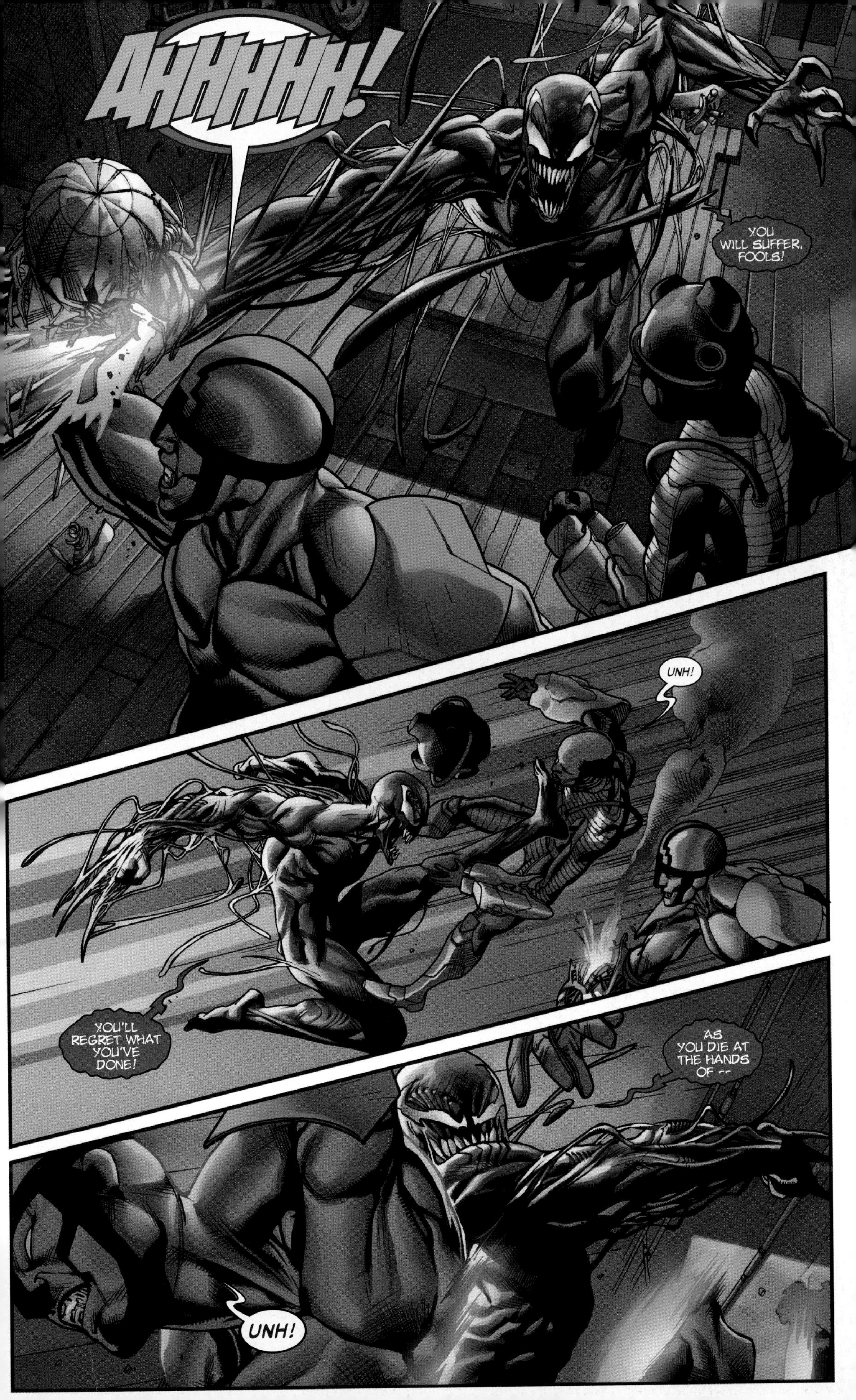
AHHHHH!
YOU WILL SUFFER, FOOLS!
UNH!
YOU'LL REGRET WHAT YOU'VE DONE!
AS YOU DIE AT THE HANDS OF --
UNH!

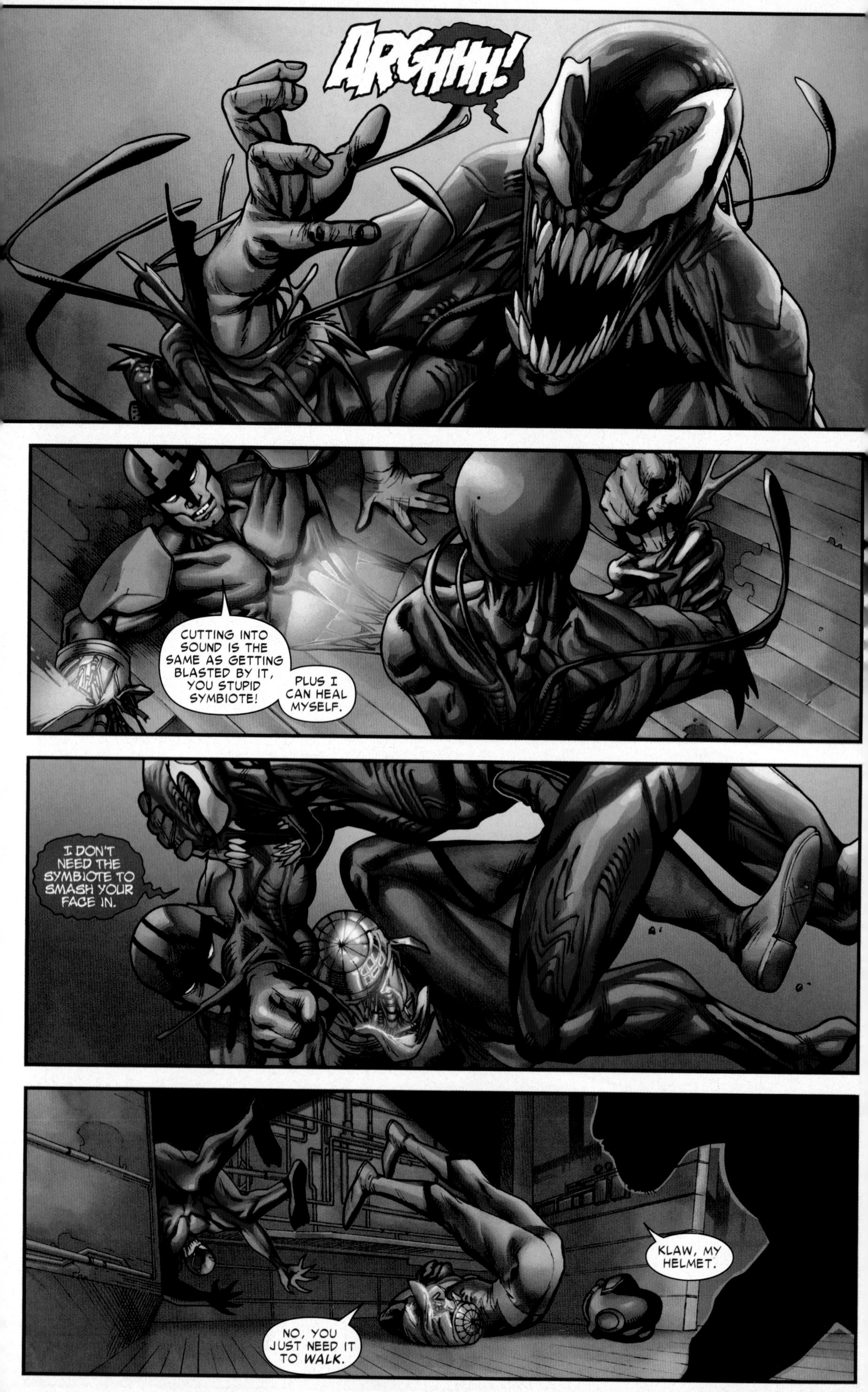

ARGHHH!
CUTTING INTO SOUND IS THE SAME AS GETTING BLASTED BY IT, YOU STUPID SYMBIOTE!
PLUS I CAN HEAL MYSELF.
I DON'T NEED THE SYMBIOTE TO SMASH YOUR FACE IN.
KLAW, MY HELMET.
NO, YOU JUST NEED IT TO WALK.

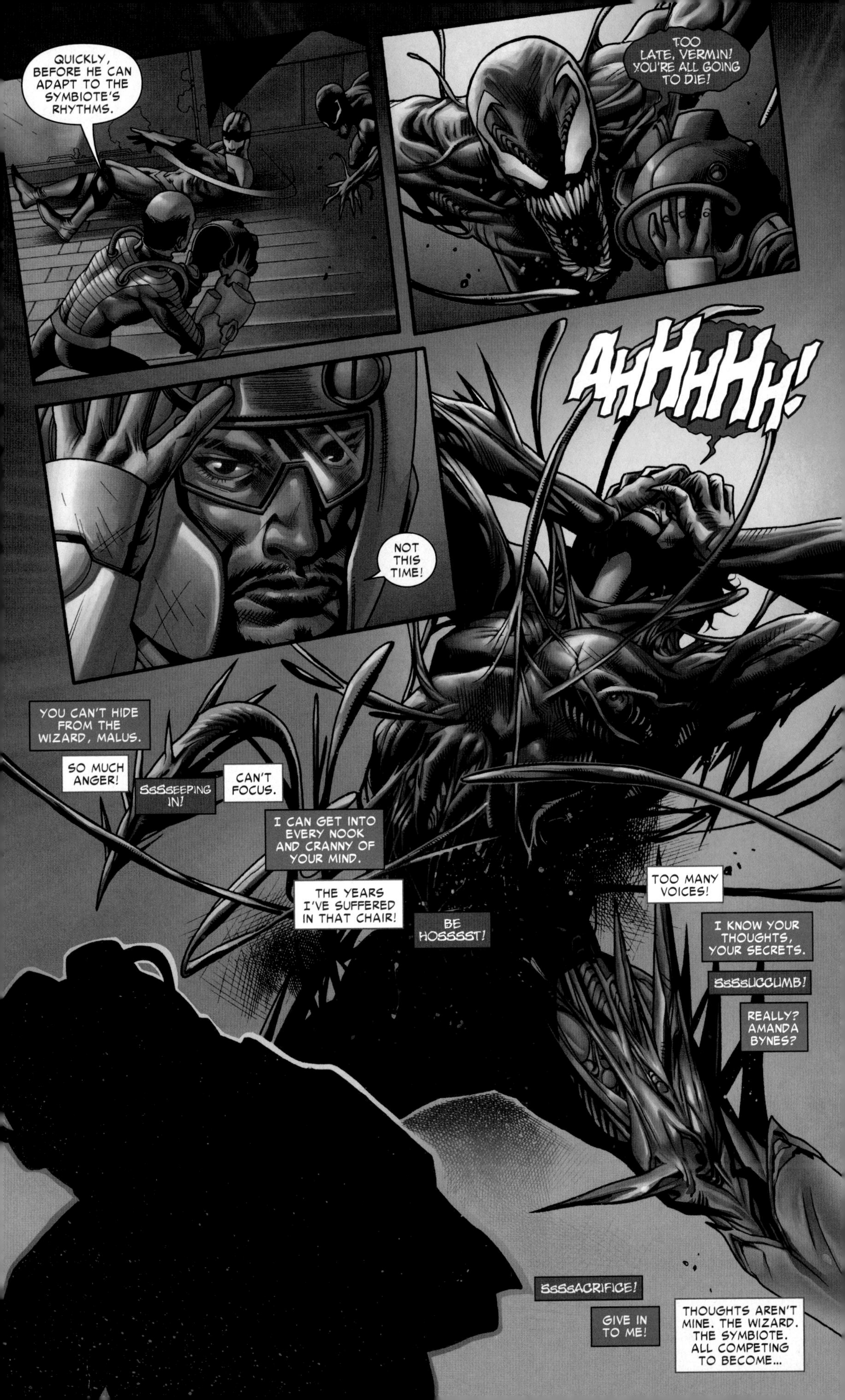
QUICKLY, BEFORE HE CAN ADAPT TO THE SYMBIOTE'S RHYTHMS.
TOO LATE, VERMIN! YOU'RE ALL GOING TO DIE!
NOT THIS TIME!
AHHHHH!
YOU CAN'T HIDE FROM THE WIZARD, MALUS.
SO MUCH ANGER!
SSSSEEPING IN!
CAN'T FOCUS.
I CAN GET INTO EVERY NOOK AND CRANNY OF YOUR MIND.
THE YEARS I'VE SUFFERED IN THAT CHAIR!
BE HOSSSST!
TOO MANY VOICES!
I KNOW YOUR THOUGHTS, YOUR SECRETS.
SSSSUCCUMB!
REALLY? AMANDA BYNES?
SSSSACRIFICE!
GIVE IN TO ME!
THOUGHTS AREN'T MINE. THE WIZARD. THE SYMBIOTE. ALL COMPETING TO BECOME...

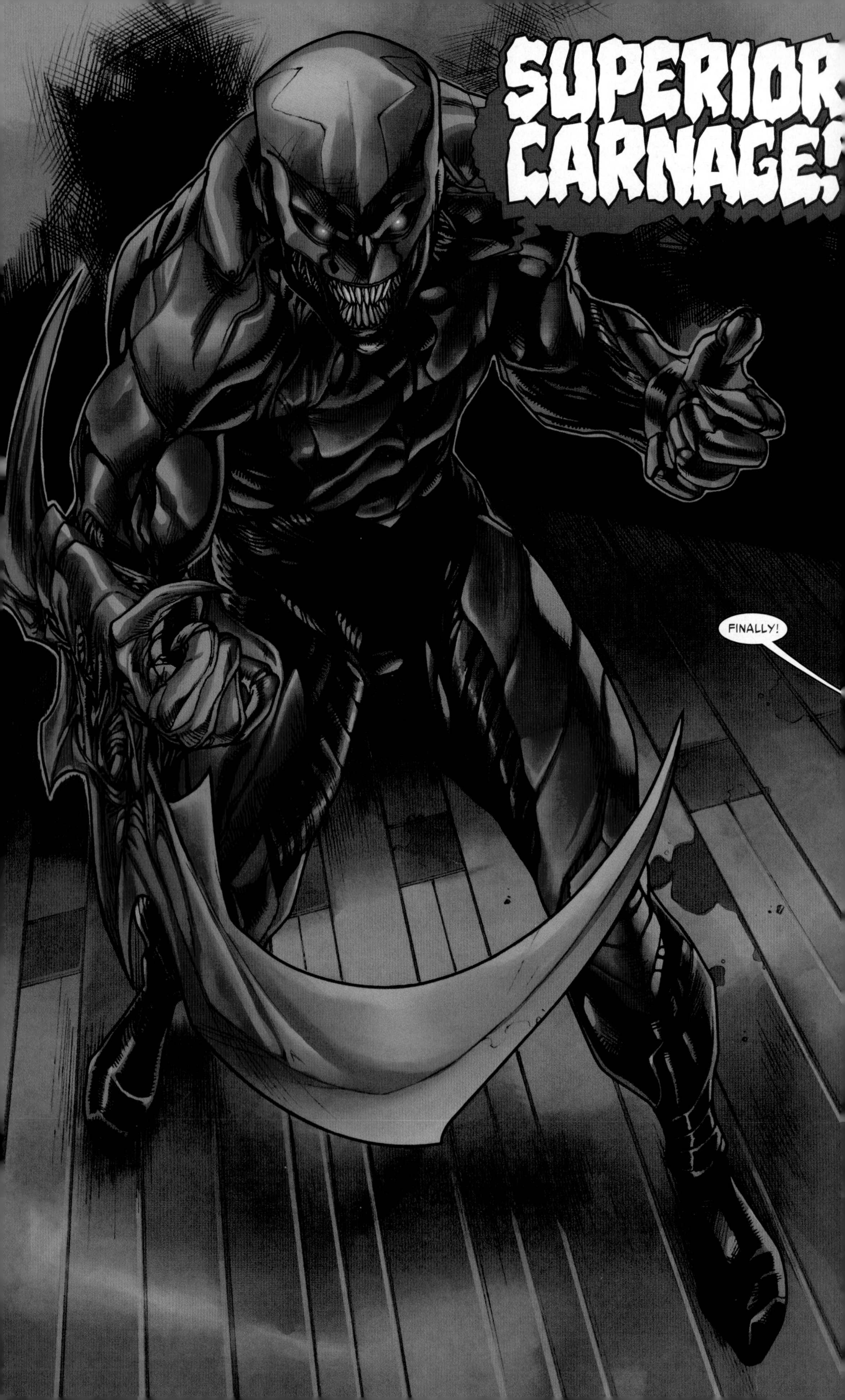
SUPERIOR CARNAGE!
FINALLY!

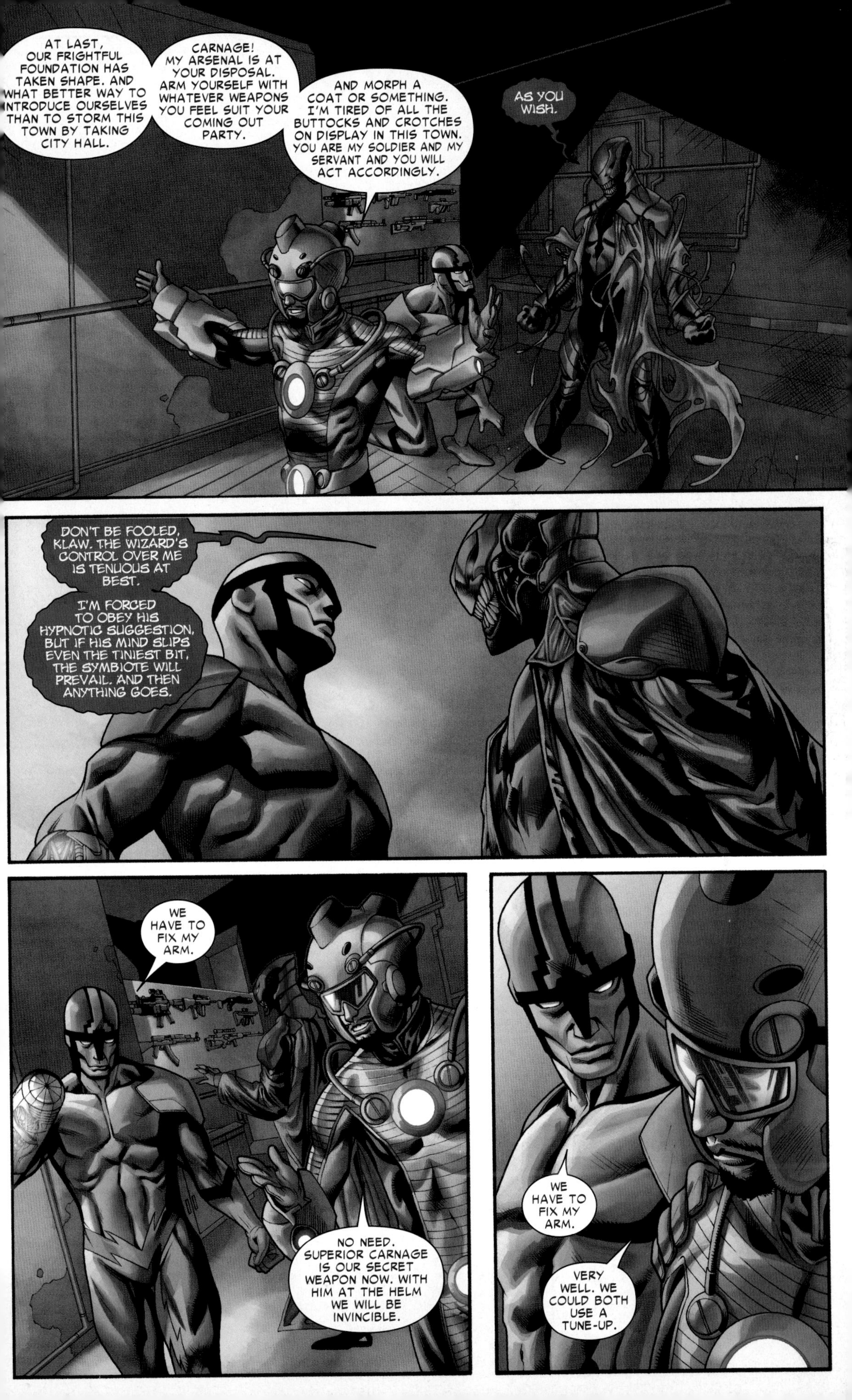
AT LAST, OUR FRIGHTFUL FOUNDATION HAS TAKEN SHAPE. AND WHAT BETTER WAY TO INTRODUCE OURSELVES THAN TO STORM THIS TOWN BY TAKING CITY HALL.
CARNAGE! MY ARSENAL IS AT YOUR DISPOSAL. ARM YOURSELF WITH WHATEVER WEAPONS YOU FEEL SUIT YOUR COMING OUT PARTY.
AND MORPH A COAT OR SOMETHING. I'M TIRED OF ALL THE BUTTOCKS AND CROTCHES ON DISPLAY IN THIS TOWN. YOU ARE MY SOLDIER AND MY SERVANT AND YOU WILL ACT ACCORDINGLY.
AS YOU WISH.
DON'T BE FOOLED, KLAW. THE WIZARD'S CONTROL OVER ME IS TENUOUS AT BEST.
I'M FORCED TO OBEY HIS HYPNOTIC SUGGESTION, BUT IF HIS MIND SLIPS EVEN THE TINIEST BIT, THE SYMBIOTE WILL PREVAIL. AND THEN ANYTHING GOES.
WE HAVE TO FIX MY ARM.
NO NEED. SUPERIOR CARNAGE IS OUR SECRET WEAPON NOW. WITH HIM AT THE HELM WE WILL BE INVINCIBLE.
WE HAVE TO FIX MY ARM.
VERY WELL. WE COULD BOTH USE A TUNE-UP.

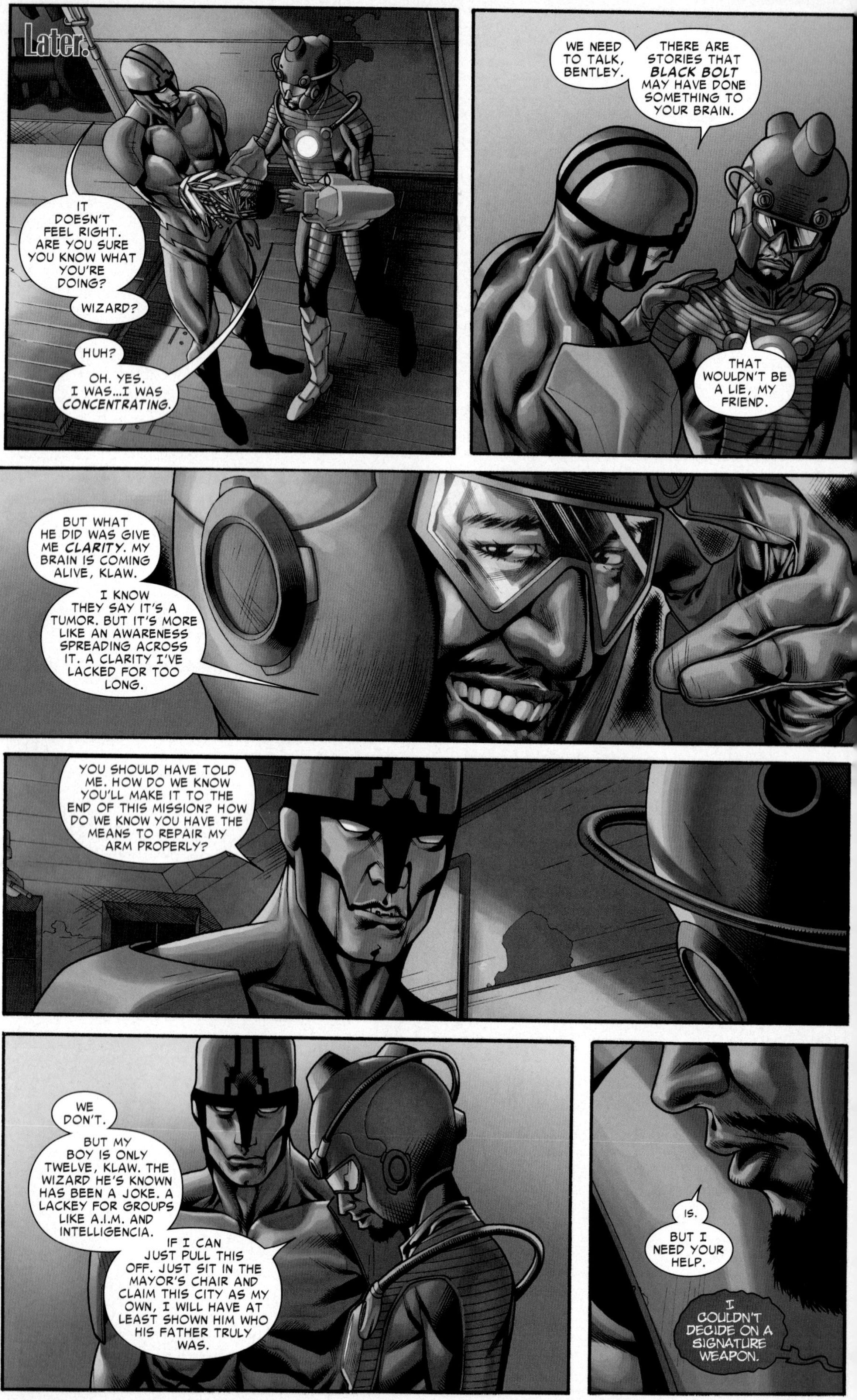

Later.
IT DOESN'T FEEL RIGHT. ARE YOU SURE YOU KNOW WHAT YOU'RE DOING?
WIZARD?
HUH?
OH. YES. I WAS...I WAS CONCENTRATING.
WE NEED TO TALK, BENTLEY.
THERE ARE STORIES THAT BLACK BOLT MAY HAVE DONE SOMETHING TO YOUR BRAIN.
THAT WOULDN'T BE A LIE, MY FRIEND.
BUT WHAT HE DID WAS GIVE ME CLARITY. MY BRAIN IS COMING ALIVE, KLAW.
I KNOW THEY SAY IT'S A TUMOR. BUT IT'S MORE LIKE AN AWARENESS SPREADING ACROSS IT. A CLARITY I'VE LACKED FOR TOO LONG.
YOU SHOULD HAVE TOLD ME. HOW DO WE KNOW YOU'LL MAKE IT TO THE END OF THIS MISSION? HOW DO WE KNOW YOU HAVE THE MEANS TO REPAIR MY ARM PROPERLY?
WE DON'T.
BUT MY BOY IS ONLY TWELVE, KLAW. THE WIZARD HE'S KNOWN HAS BEEN A JOKE. A LACKEY FOR GROUPS LIKE A.I.M. AND INTELLIGENCIA.
IF I CAN JUST PULL THIS OFF. JUST SIT IN THE MAYOR'S CHAIR AND CLAIM THIS CITY AS MY OWN, I WILL HAVE AT LEAST SHOWN HIM WHO HIS FATHER TRULY WAS.
IS.
BUT I NEED YOUR HELP.
I COULDN'T DECIDE ON A SIGNATURE WEAPON.

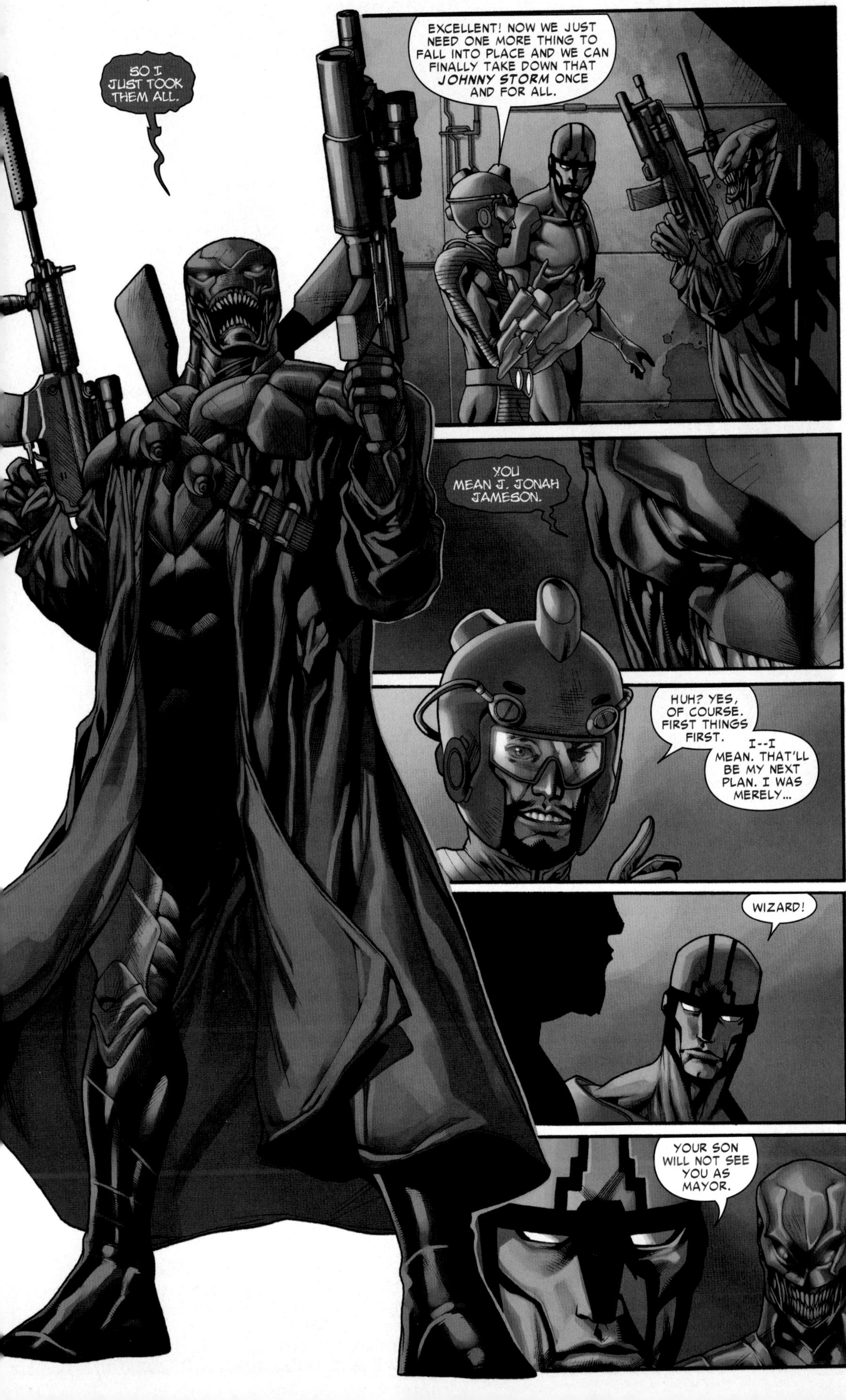
SO I JUST TOOK THEM ALL.
EXCELLENT! NOW WE JUST NEED ONE MORE THING TO FALL INTO PLACE AND WE CAN FINALLY TAKE DOWN THAT JOHNNY STORM ONCE AND FOR ALL.
YOU MEAN J. JONAH JAMESON.
HUH? YES, OF COURSE. FIRST THINGS FIRST.
I--I MEAN. THAT'LL BE MY NEXT PLAN. I WAS MERELY...
WIZARD!
YOUR SON WILL NOT SEE YOU AS MAYOR.

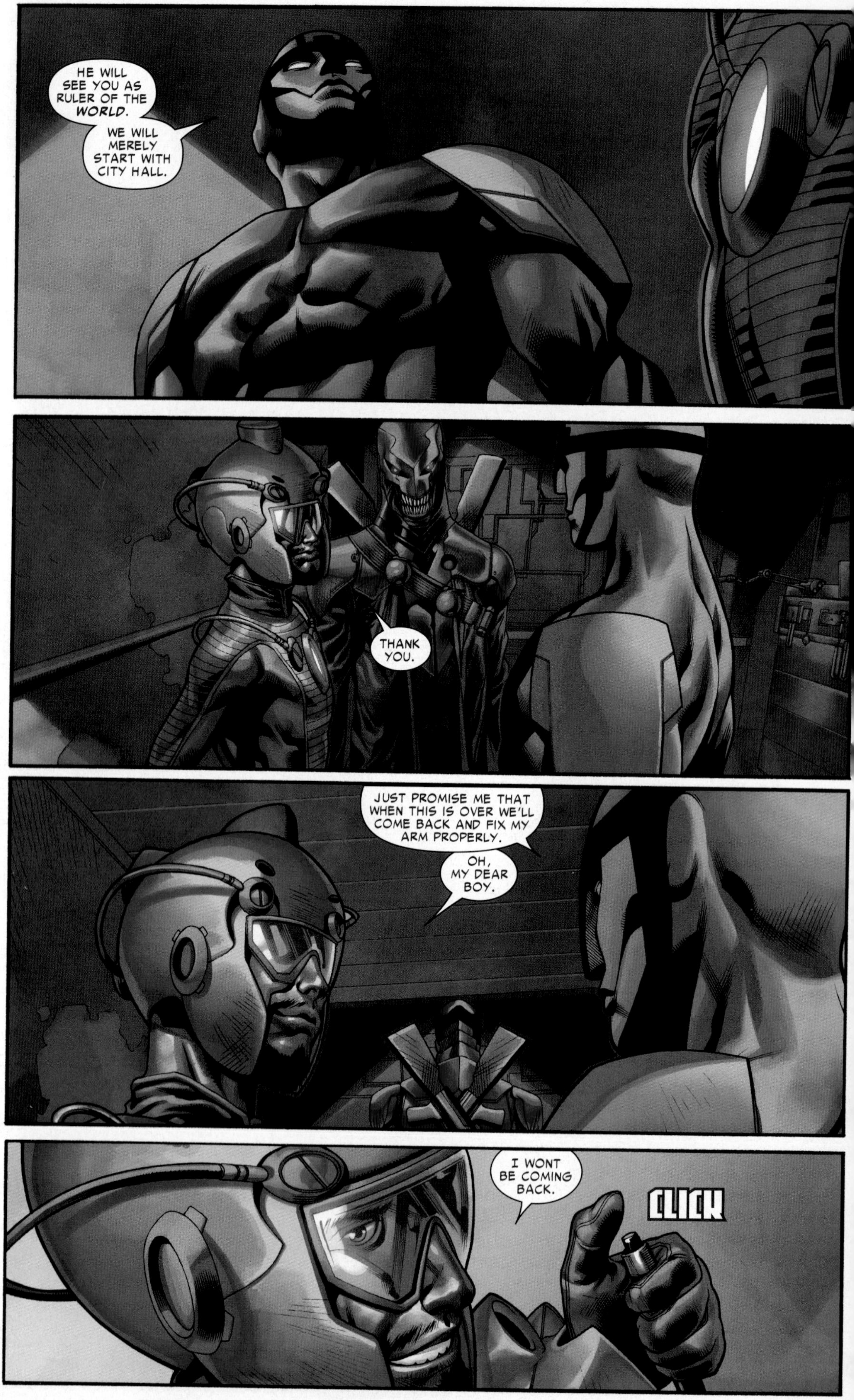
HE WILL SEE YOU AS RULER OF THE WORLD.
WE WILL MERELY START WITH CITY HALL.
THANK YOU.
JUST PROMISE ME THAT WHEN THIS IS OVER WE'LL COME BACK AND FIX MY ARM PROPERLY.
OH, MY DEAR BOY.
I WONT BE COMING BACK.
CLICK

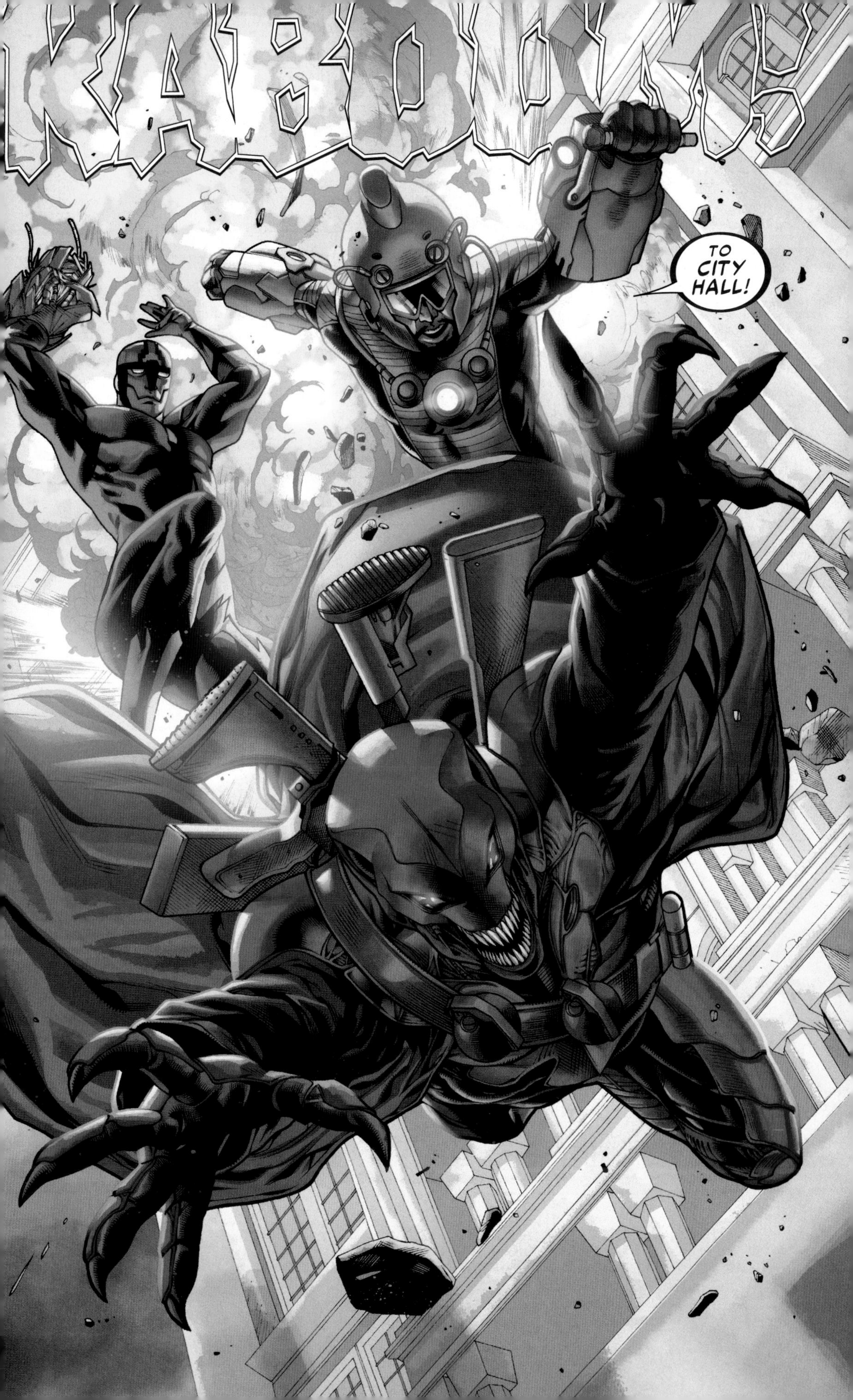
TO CITY HALL!

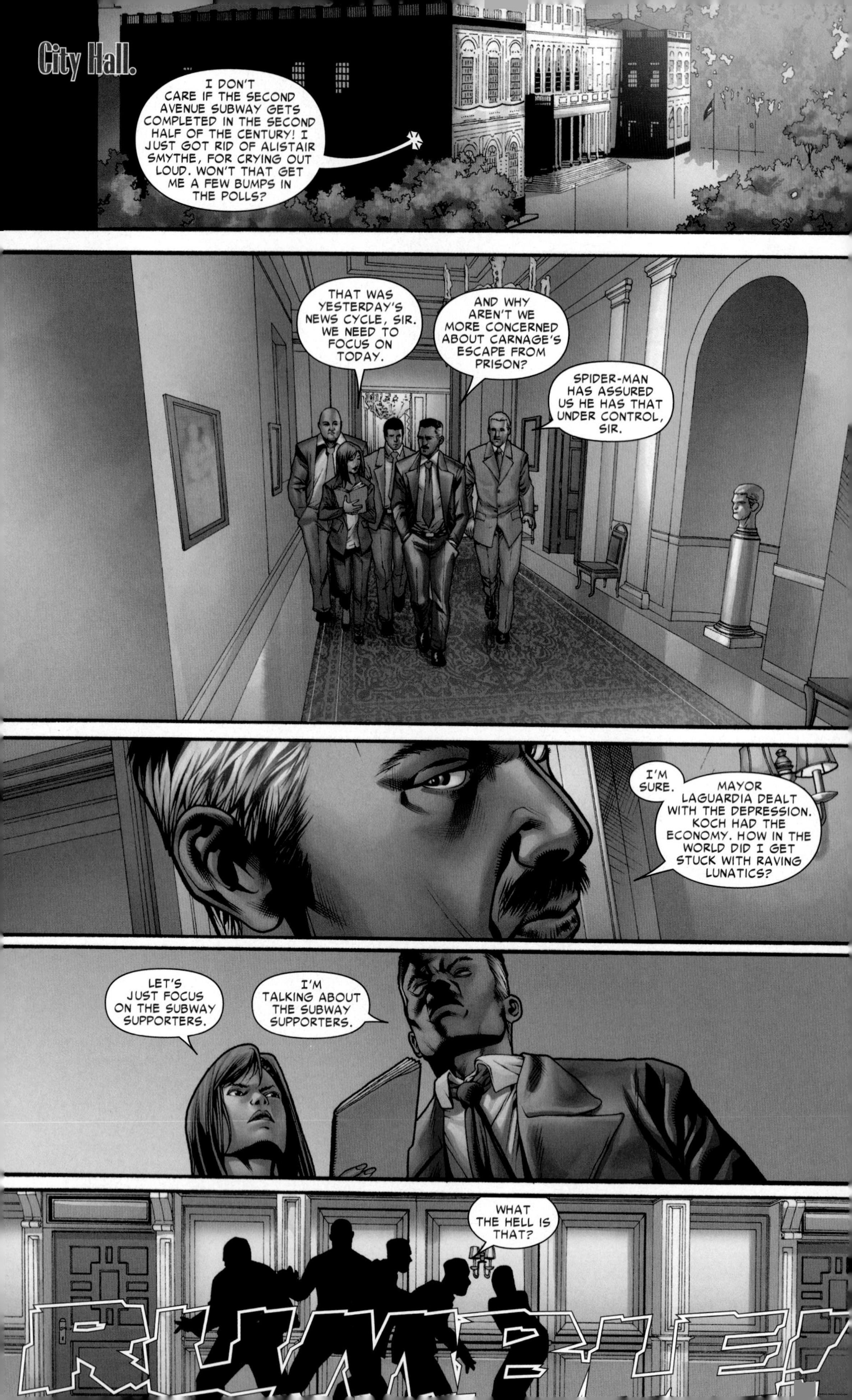
City Hall.
I DON'T CARE IF THE SECOND AVENUE SUBWAY GETS COMPLETED IN THE SECOND HALF OF THE CENTURY! I JUST GOT RID OF ALISTAIR SMYTHE, FOR CRYING OUT LOUD. WON'T THAT GET ME A FEW BUMPS IN THE POLLS?
THAT WAS YESTERDAY'S NEWS CYCLE, SIR. WE NEED TO FOCUS ON TODAY.
AND WHY AREN'T WE MORE CONCERNED ABOUT CARNAGE'S ESCAPE FROM PRISON?
SPIDER-MAN HAS ASSURED US HE HAS THAT UNDER CONTROL, SIR.
I'M SURE.
MAYOR LAGUARDIA DEALT WITH THE DEPRESSION. KOCH HAD THE ECONOMY. HOW IN THE WORLD DID I GET STUCK WITH RAVING LUNATICS?
LET'S JUST FOCUS ON THE SUBWAY SUPPORTERS.
I'M TALKING ABOUT THE SUBWAY SUPPORTERS.
WHAT THE HELL IS THAT?

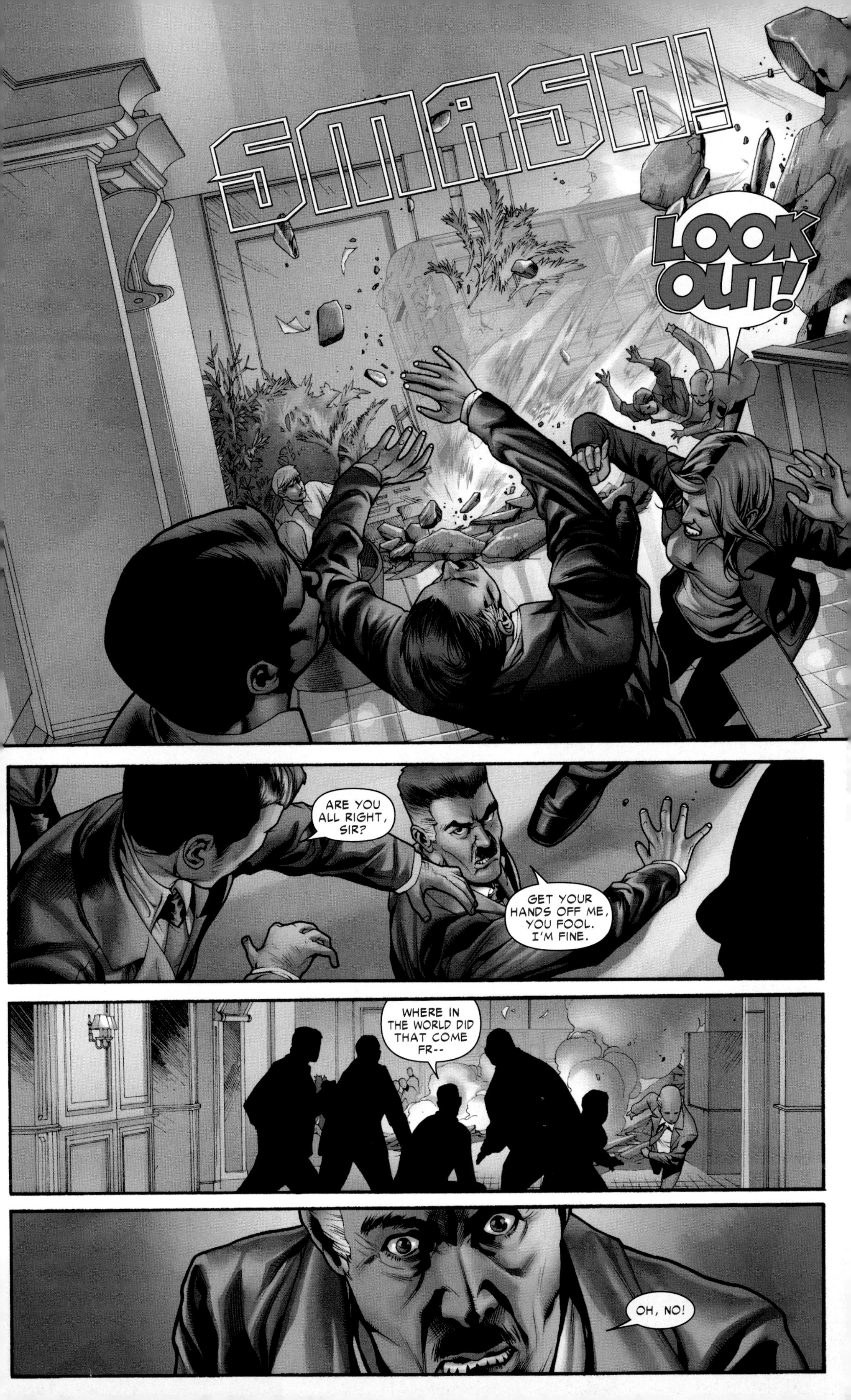
SMASH!
LOOK OUT!
ARE YOU ALL RIGHT, SIR?
GET YOUR HANDS OFF ME, YOU FOOL. I'M FINE.
WHERE IN THE WORLD DID THAT COME FR--
OH, NO!

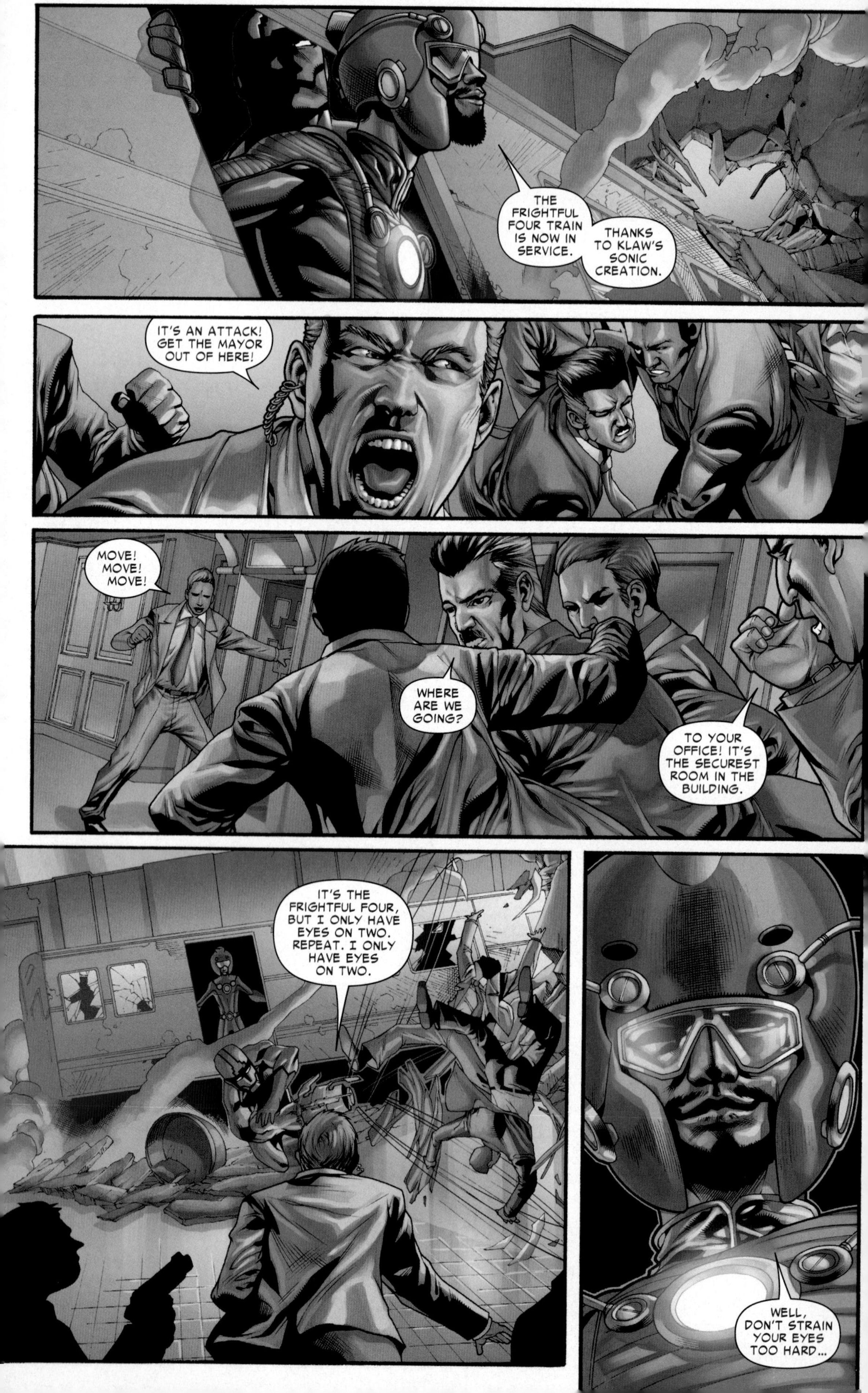
THE FRIGHTFUL FOUR TRAIN IS NOW IN SERVICE.
THANKS TO KLAW'S SONIC CREATION.
IT'S AN ATTACK! GET THE MAYOR OUT OF HERE!
MOVE! MOVE! MOVE!
WHERE ARE WE GOING?
TO YOUR OFFICE! IT'S THE SECUREST ROOM IN THE BUILDING.
IT'S THE FRIGHTFUL FOUR, BUT I ONLY HAVE EYES ON TWO. REPEAT. I ONLY HAVE EYES ON TWO.
WELL, DON'T STRAIN YOUR EYES TOO HARD...

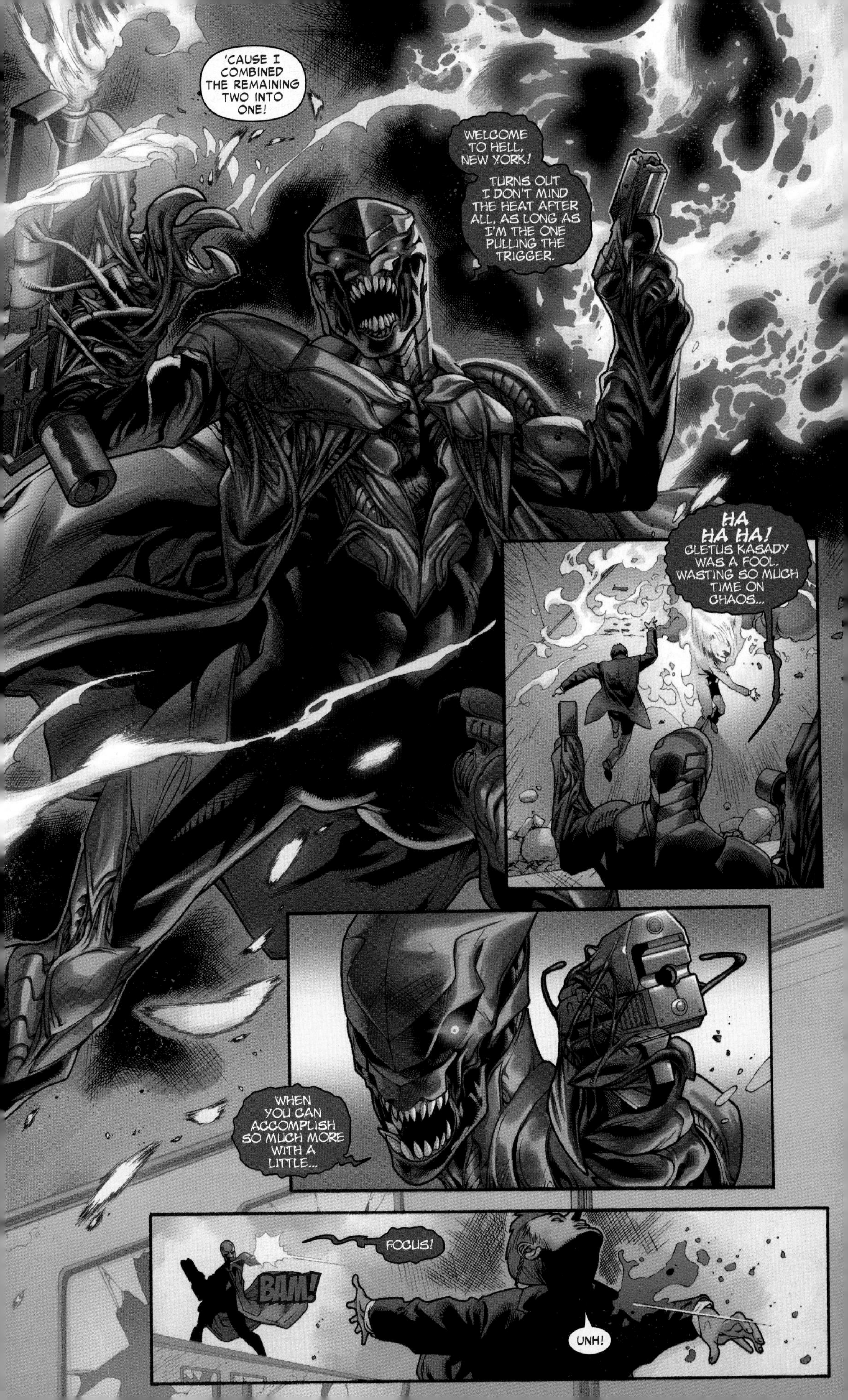
'CAUSE I COMBINED THE REMAINING TWO INTO ONE!
WELCOME TO HELL, NEW YORK!
TURNS OUT I DON'T MIND THE HEAT AFTER ALL, AS LONG AS I'M THE ONE PULLING THE TRIGGER.
HA HA HA!
CLETUS KASADY WAS A FOOL. WASTING SO MUCH TIME ON CHAOS...
WHEN YOU CAN ACCOMPLISH SO MUCH MORE WITH A LITTLE...
FOCUS!
BAM!
UNH!

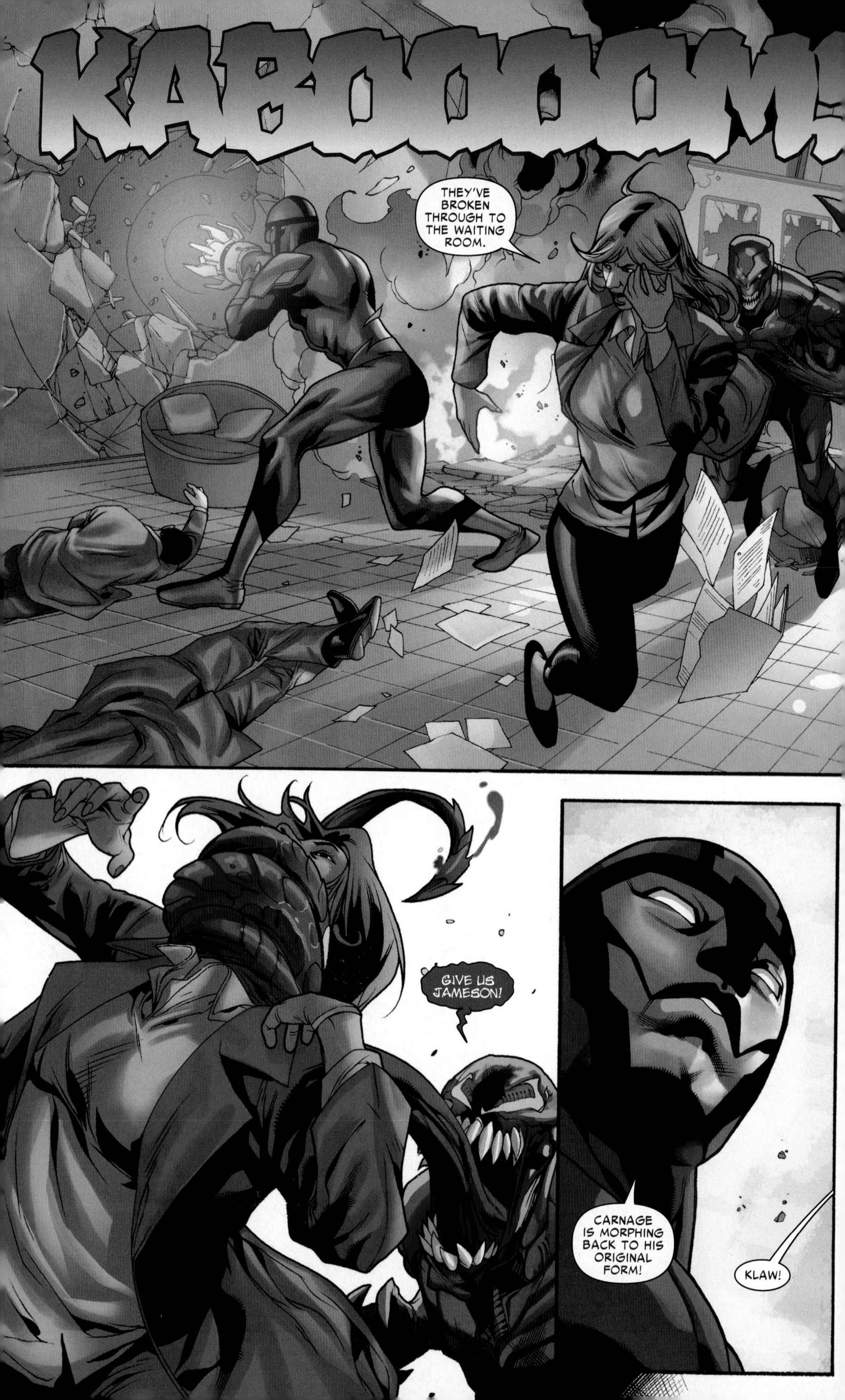
KABOOOOM!
THEY'VE BROKEN THROUGH TO THE WAITING ROOM.
GIVE US JAMESON!
CARNAGE IS MORPHING BACK TO HIS ORIGINAL FORM!
KLAW!

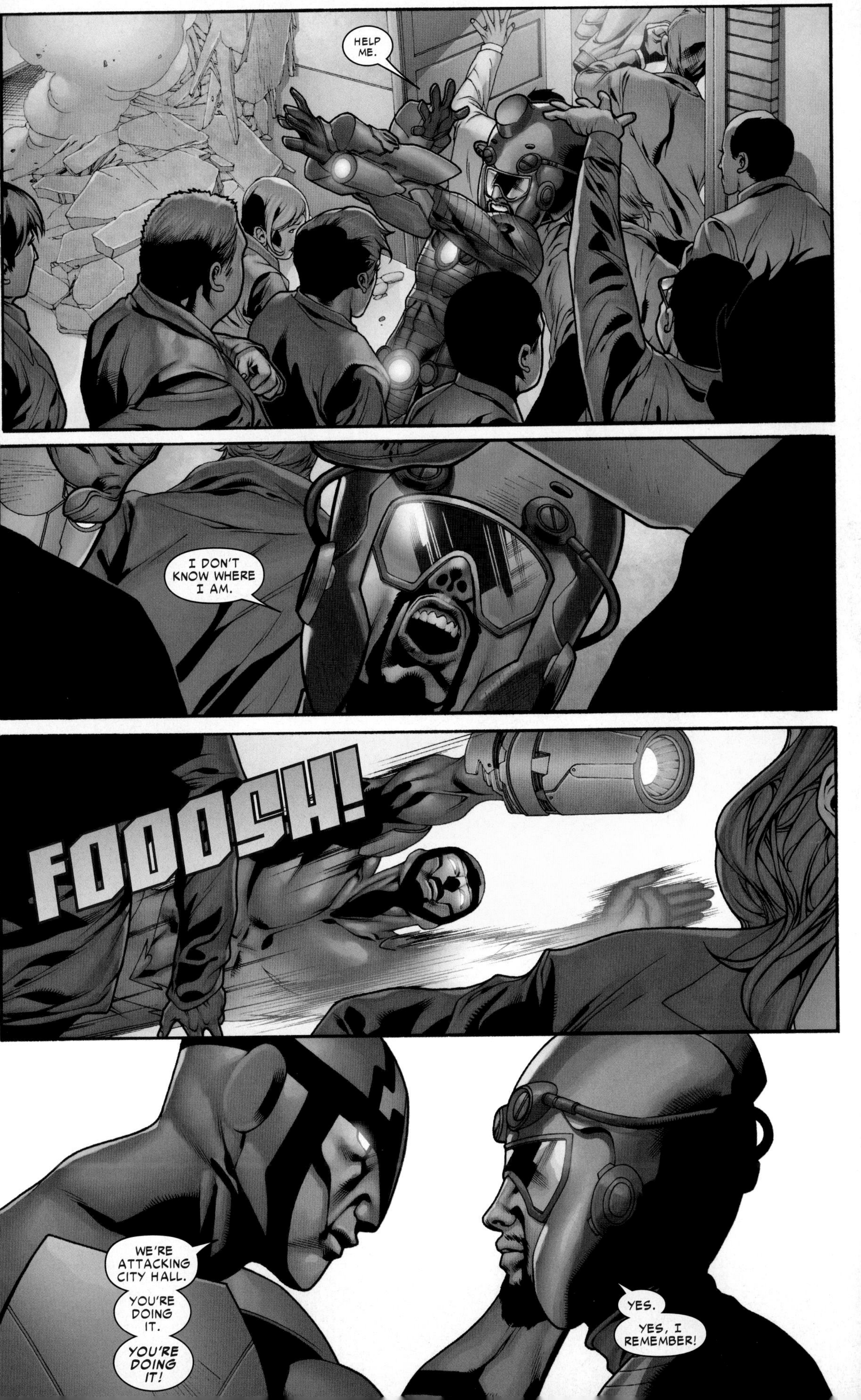
HELP ME.
I DON'T KNOW WHERE I AM.
FOOOSH!
WE'RE ATTACKING CITY HALL.
YOU'RE DOING IT.
YOU'RE DOING IT!
YES.
YES, I REMEMBER!

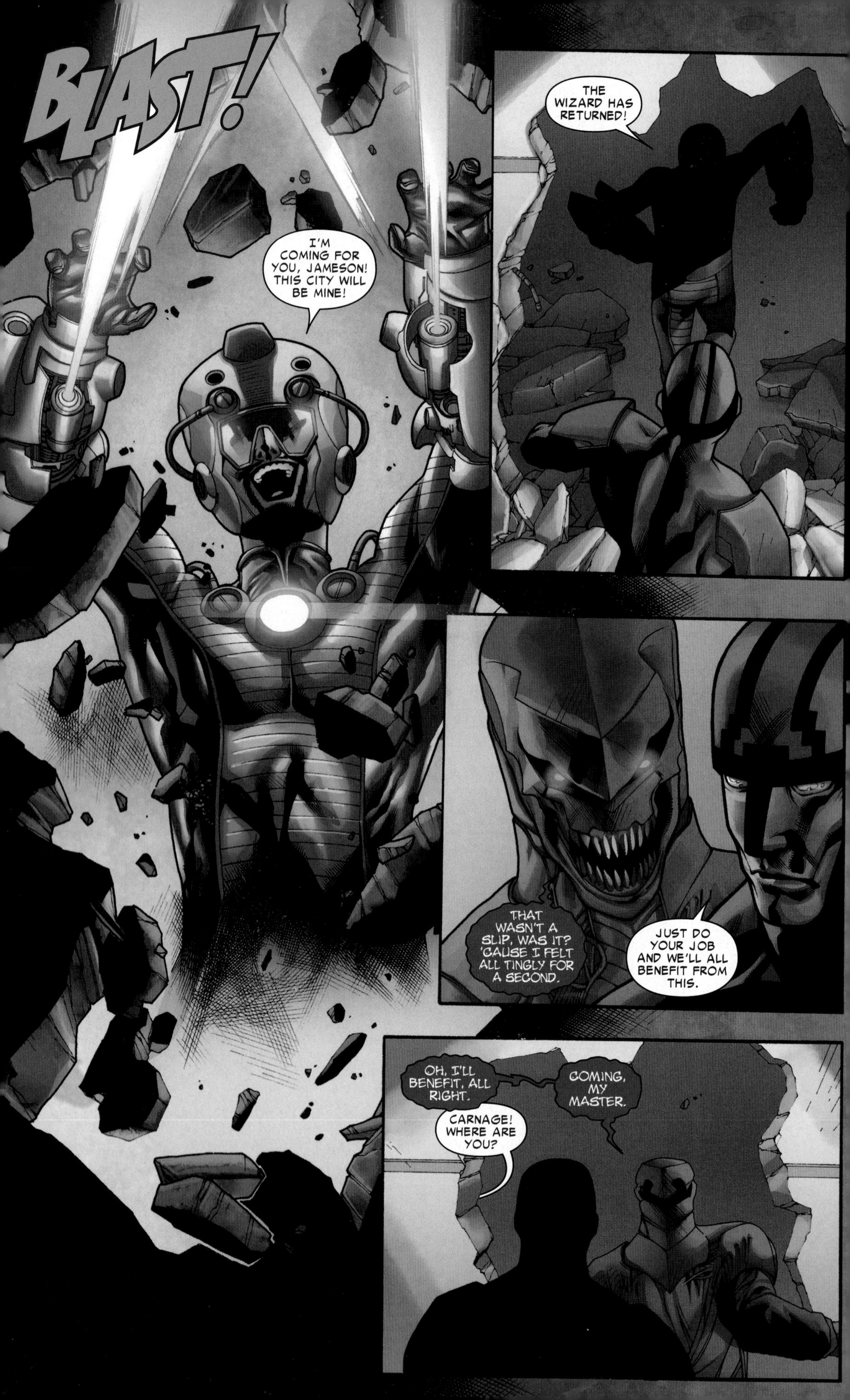
BLAST!
I'M COMING FOR YOU, JAMESON! THIS CITY WILL BE MINE!
THE WIZARD HAS RETURNED!
THAT WASN'T A SLIP, WAS IT? 'CAUSE I FELT ALL TINGLY FOR A SECOND.
JUST DO YOUR JOB AND WE'LL ALL BENEFIT FROM THIS.
OH, I'LL BENEFIT, ALL RIGHT.
COMING, MY MASTER.
CARNAGE! WHERE ARE YOU?

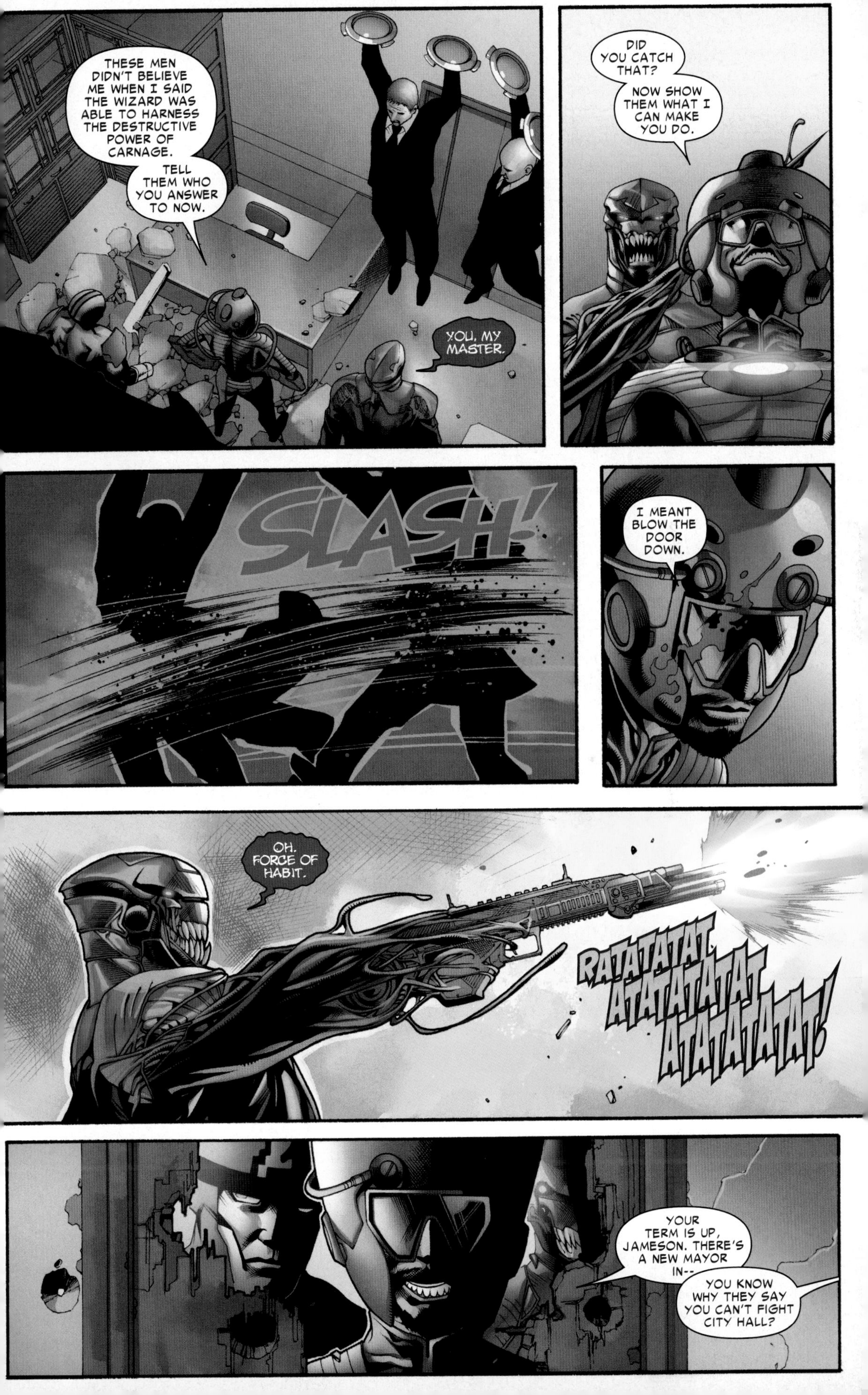
THESE MEN DIDN'T BELIEVE ME WHEN I SAID THE WIZARD WAS ABLE TO HARNESS THE DESTRUCTIVE POWER OF CARNAGE.
TELL THEM WHO YOU ANSWER TO NOW.
YOU, MY MASTER.
DID YOU CATCH THAT?
NOW SHOW THEM WHAT I CAN MAKE YOU DO.
SLASH!
I MEANT BLOW THE DOOR DOWN.
OH. FORCE OF HABIT.
RATATATAT ATATATATAT ATATATATAT!
YOUR TERM IS UP, JAMESON. THERE'S A NEW MAYOR IN--
YOU KNOW WHY THEY SAY YOU CAN'T FIGHT CITY HALL?

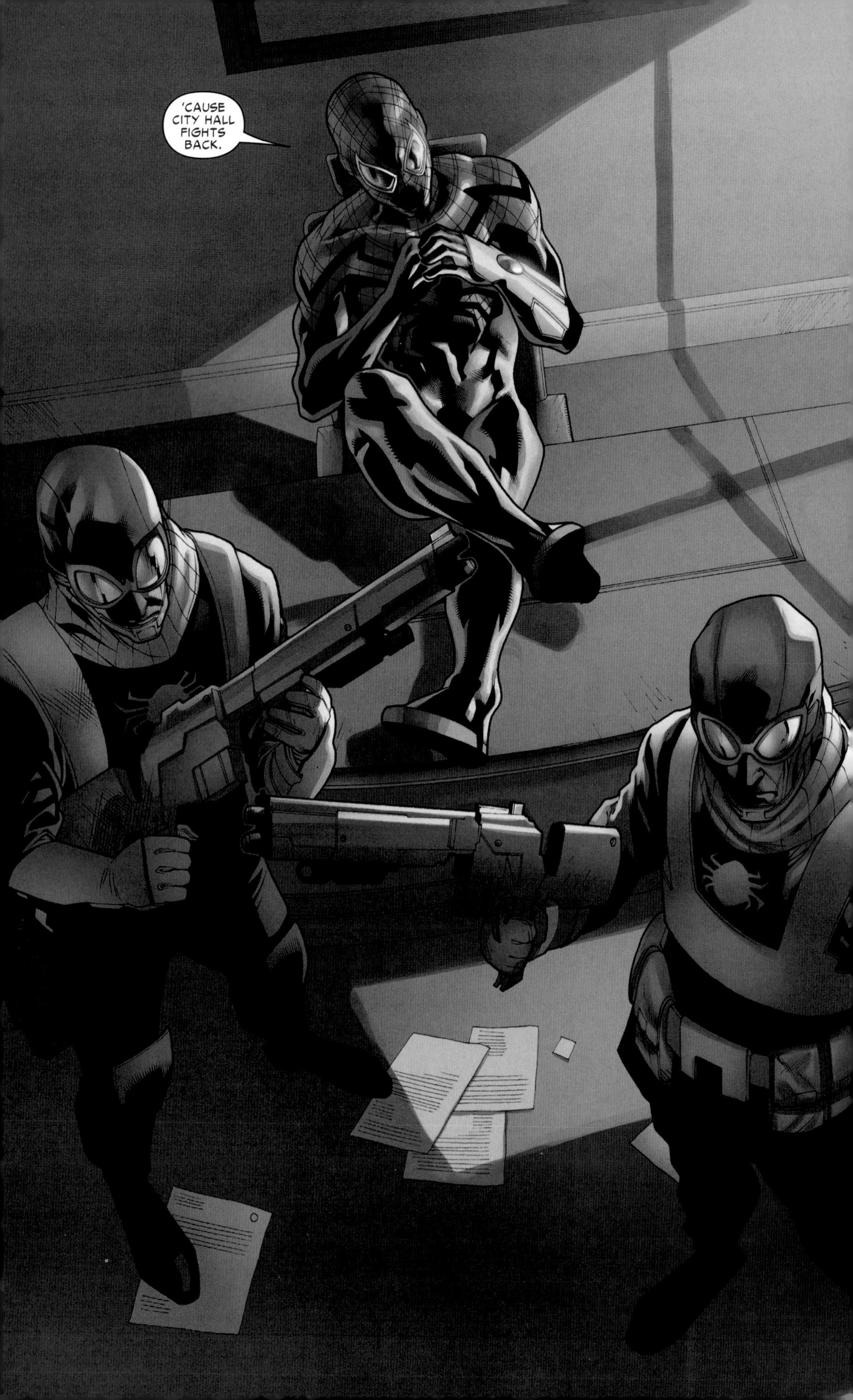
'CAUSE CITY HALL FIGHTS BACK.

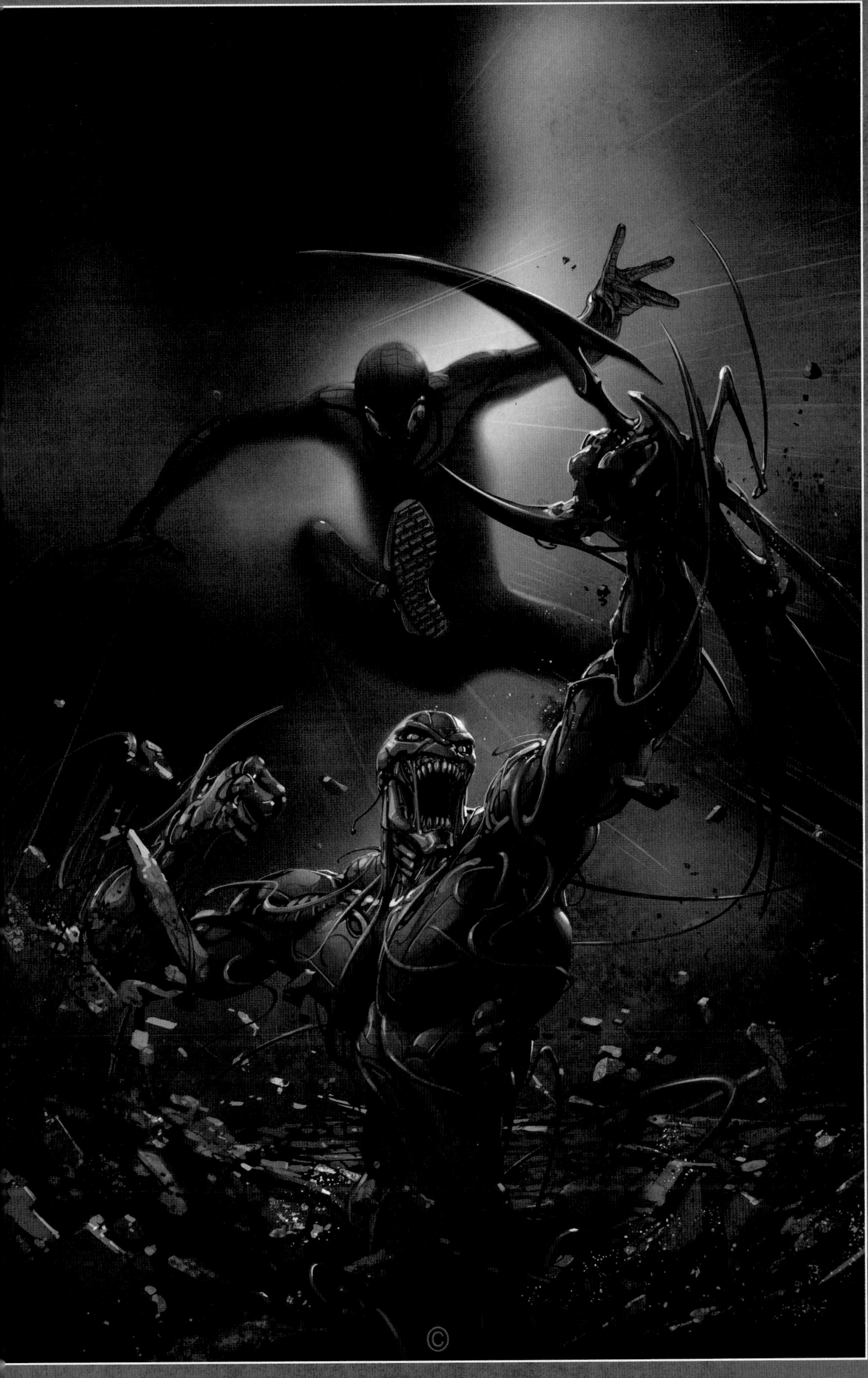

SUPERIOR CARNAGE #4

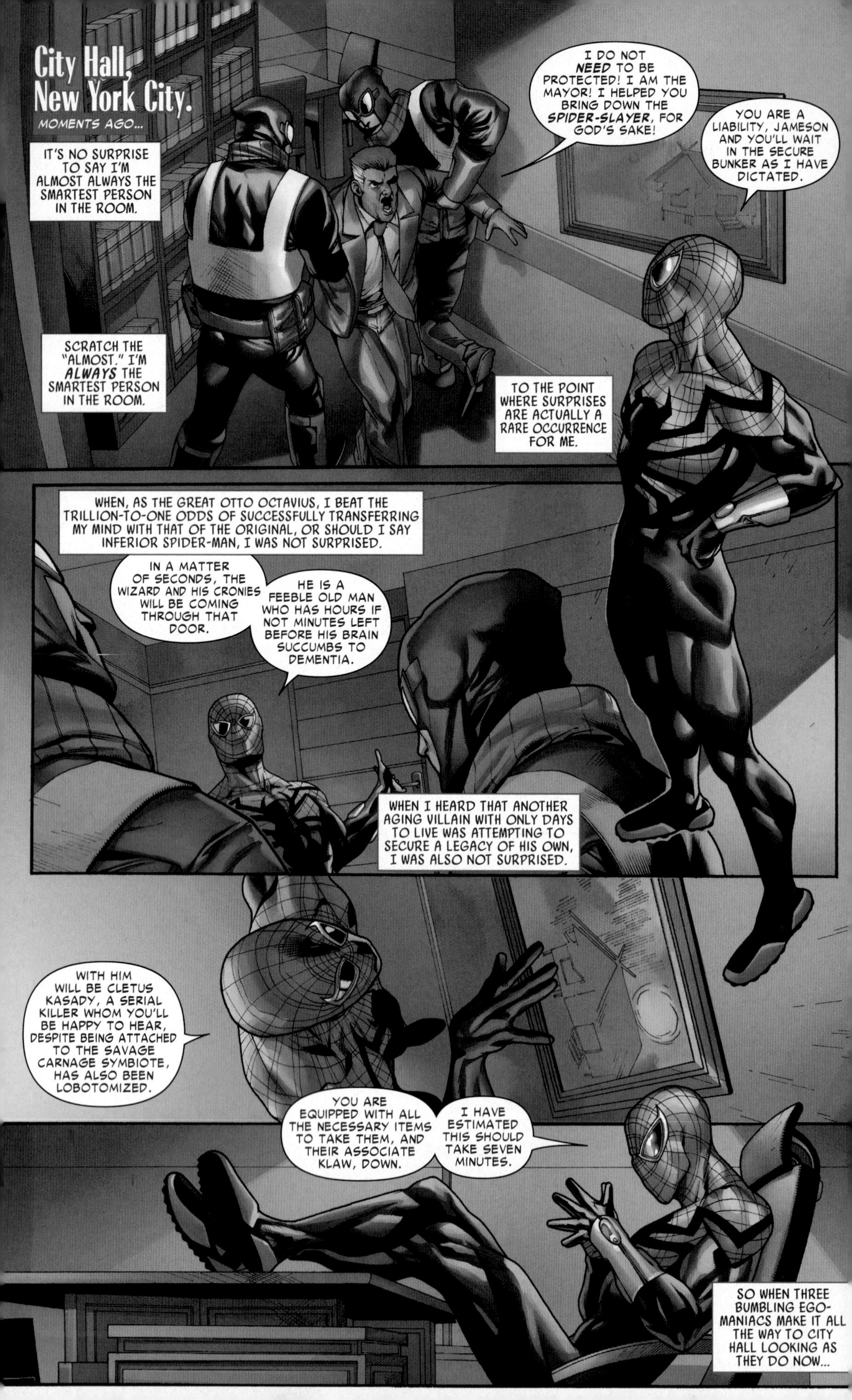
City Hall, New York City.
MOMENTS AGO...
IT'S NO SURPRISE TO SAY I'M ALMOST ALWAYS THE SMARTEST PERSON IN THE ROOM.
I DO NOT NEED TO BE PROTECTED! I AM THE MAYOR! I HELPED YOU BRING DOWN THE SPIDER-SLAYER, FOR GOD'S SAKE!
YOU ARE A LIABILITY, JAMESON AND YOU'LL WAIT IN THE SECURE BUNKER AS I HAVE DICTATED.
SCRATCH THE "ALMOST." I'M ALWAYS THE SMARTEST PERSON IN THE ROOM.
TO THE POINT WHERE SURPRISES ARE ACTUALLY A RARE OCCURRENCE FOR ME.
WHEN, AS THE GREAT OTTO OCTAVIUS, I BEAT THE TRILLION-TO-ONE ODDS OF SUCCESSFULLY TRANSFERRING MY MIND WITH THAT OF THE ORIGINAL, OR SHOULD I SAY INFERIOR SPIDER-MAN, I WAS NOT SURPRISED.
IN A MATTER OF SECONDS, THE WIZARD AND HIS CRONIES WILL BE COMING THROUGH THAT DOOR.
HE IS A FEEBLE OLD MAN WHO HAS HOURS IF NOT MINUTES LEFT BEFORE HIS BRAIN SUCCUMBS TO DEMENTIA.
WHEN I HEARD THAT ANOTHER AGING VILLAIN WITH ONLY DAYS TO LIVE WAS ATTEMPTING TO SECURE A LEGACY OF HIS OWN, I WAS ALSO NOT SURPRISED.
WITH HIM WILL BE CLETUS KASADY, A SERIAL KILLER WHOM YOU'LL BE HAPPY TO HEAR, DESPITE BEING ATTACHED TO THE SAVAGE CARNAGE SYMBIOTE, HAS ALSO BEEN LOBOTOMIZED.
YOU ARE EQUIPPED WITH ALL THE NECESSARY ITEMS TO TAKE THEM, AND THEIR ASSOCIATE KLAW, DOWN.
I HAVE ESTIMATED THIS SHOULD TAKE SEVEN MINUTES.
SO WHEN THREE BUMBLING EGO-MANIACS MAKE IT ALL THE WAY TO CITY HALL LOOKING AS THEY DO NOW...

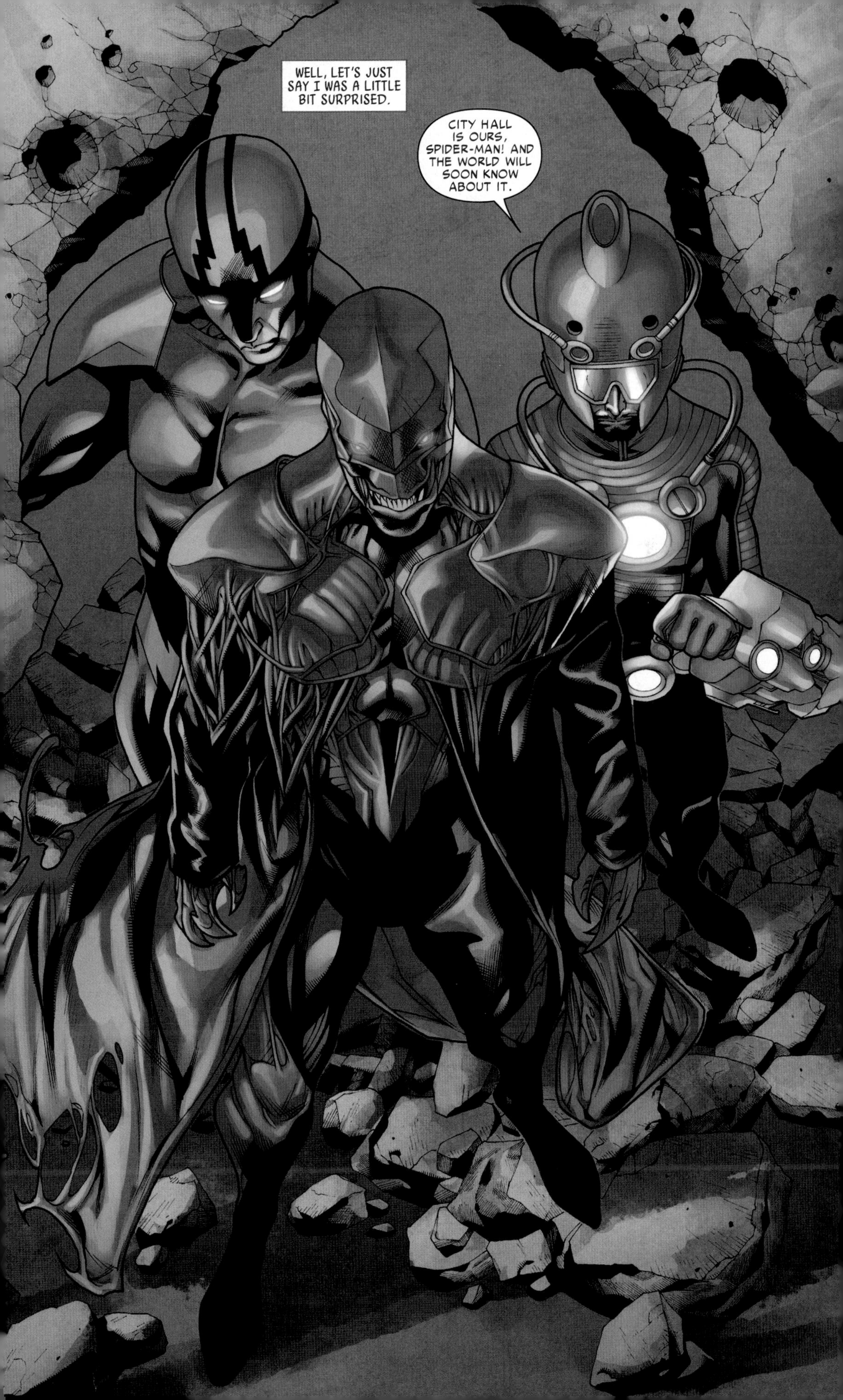
WELL, LET'S JUST SAY I WAS A LITTLE BIT SURPRISED.
CITY HALL IS OURS, SPIDER-MAN! AND THE WORLD WILL SOON KNOW ABOUT IT.

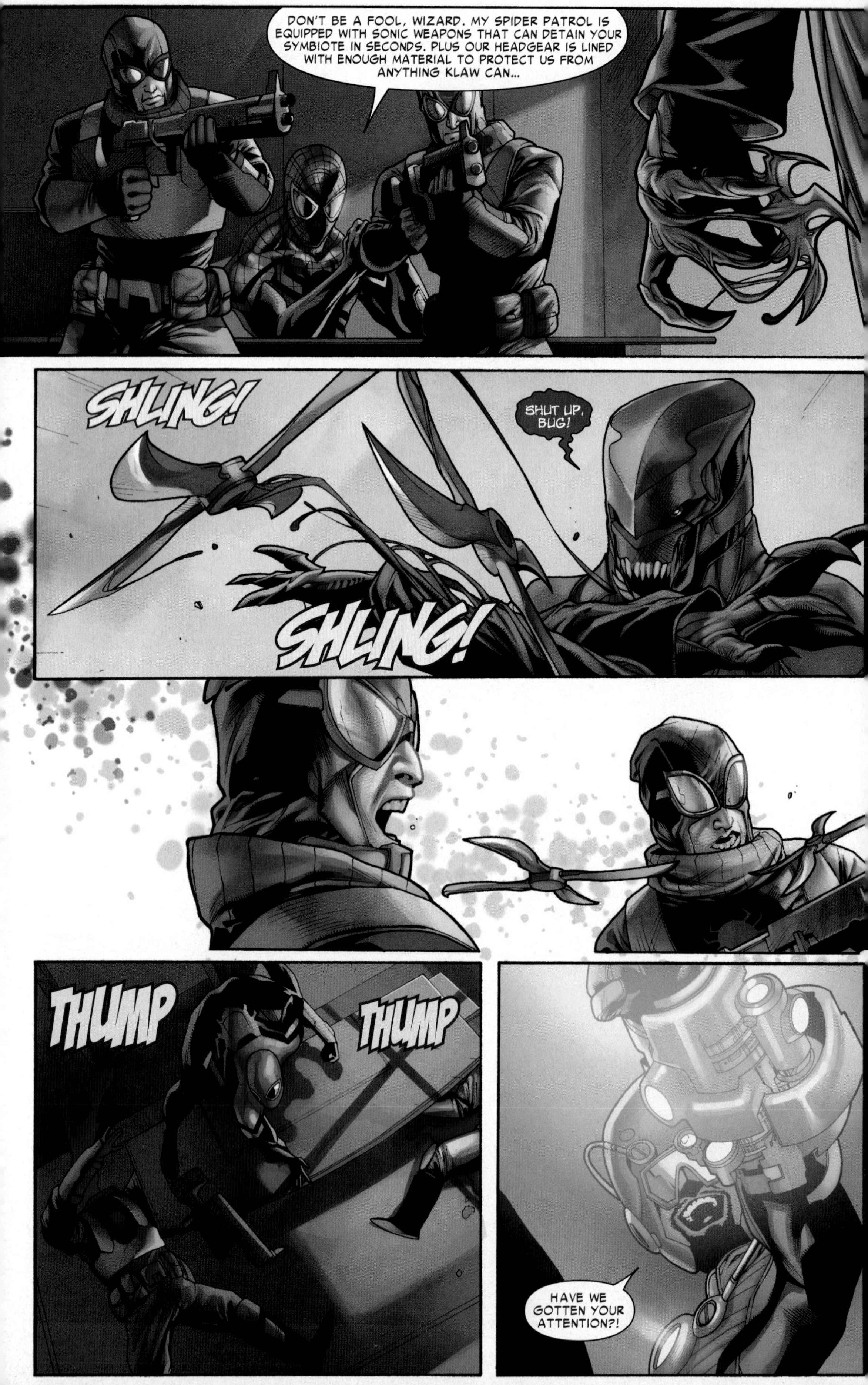
DON'T BE A FOOL, WIZARD. MY SPIDER PATROL IS EQUIPPED WITH SONIC WEAPONS THAT CAN DETAIN YOUR SYMBIOTE IN SECONDS. PLUS OUR HEADGEAR IS LINED WITH ENOUGH MATERIAL TO PROTECT US FROM ANYTHING KLAW CAN...
SHLING!
SHUT UP, BUG!
SHLING!
THUMP
THUMP
HAVE WE GOTTEN YOUR ATTENTION?!

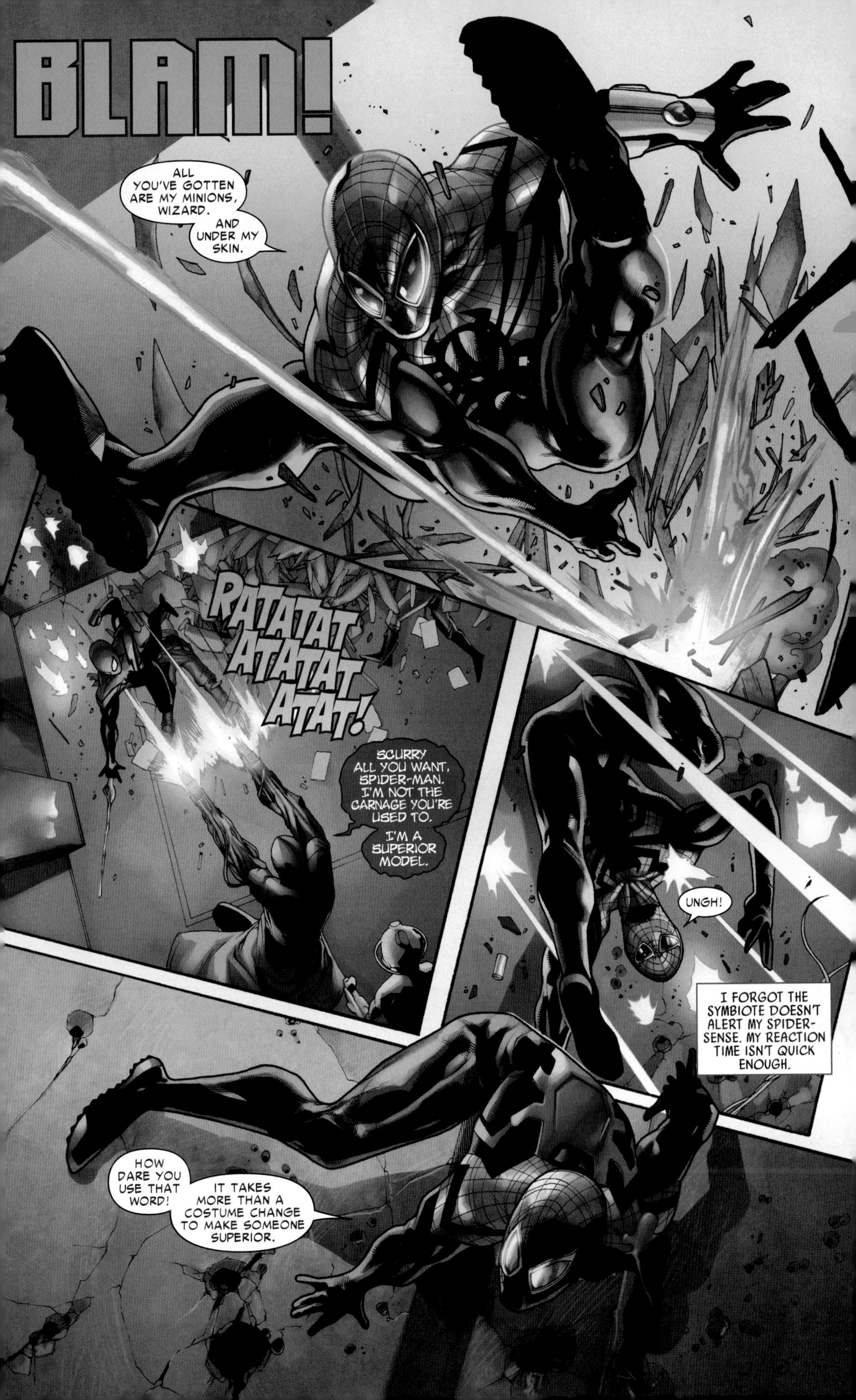

BLAM!
ALL YOU'VE GOTTEN ARE MY MINIONS, WIZARD.
AND UNDER MY SKIN.
RATATAT ATATAT ATAT!
SCURRY ALL YOU WANT, SPIDER-MAN. I'M NOT THE CARNAGE YOU'RE USED TO.
I'M A SUPERIOR MODEL.
UNGH!
I FORGOT THE SYMBIOTE DOESN'T ALERT MY SPIDER-SENSE. MY REACTION TIME ISN'T QUICK ENOUGH.
HOW DARE YOU USE THAT WORD!
IT TAKES MORE THAN A COSTUME CHANGE TO MAKE SOMEONE SUPERIOR.

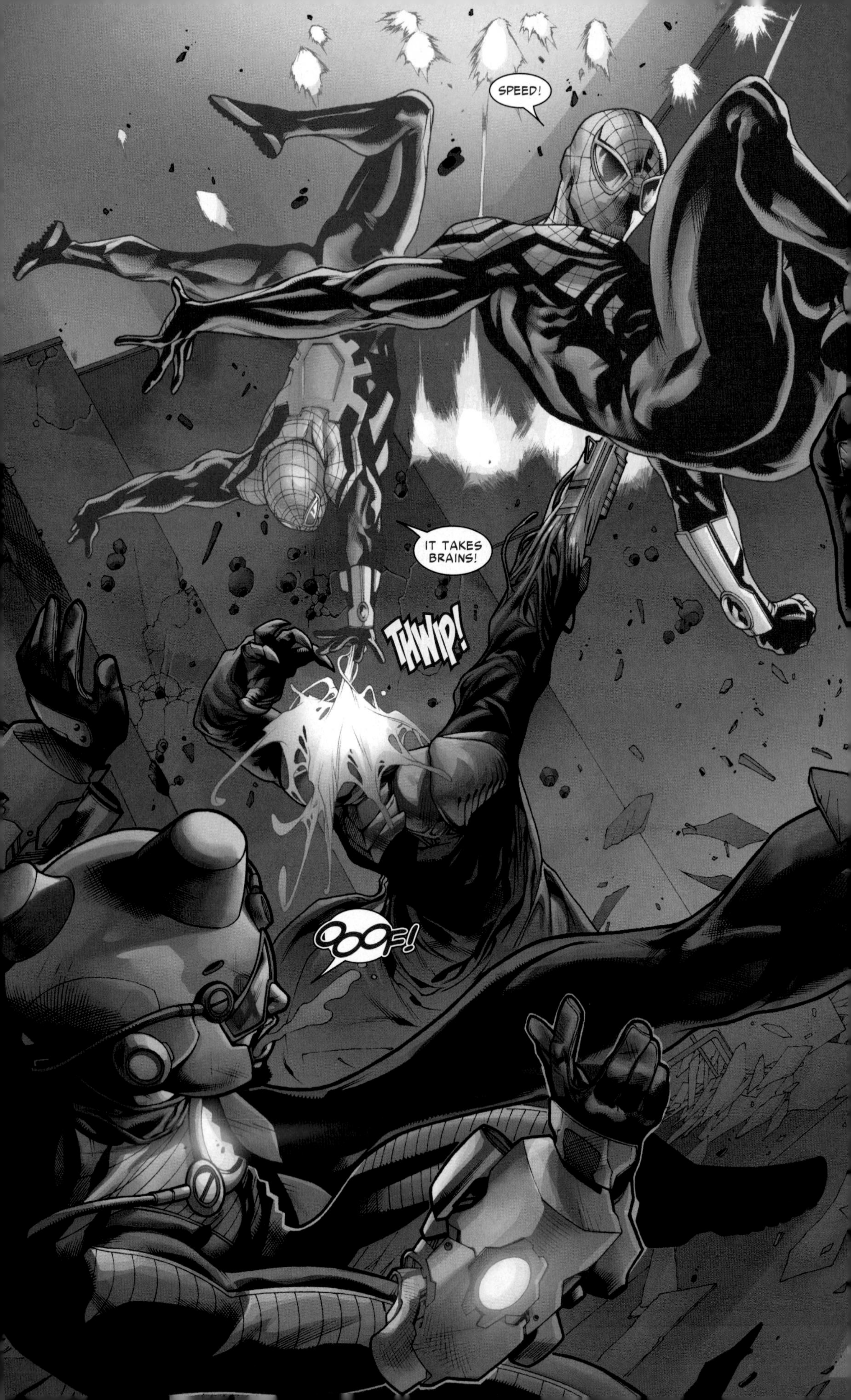
SPEED!
IT TAKES BRAINS!
THWIP!
OOOF!

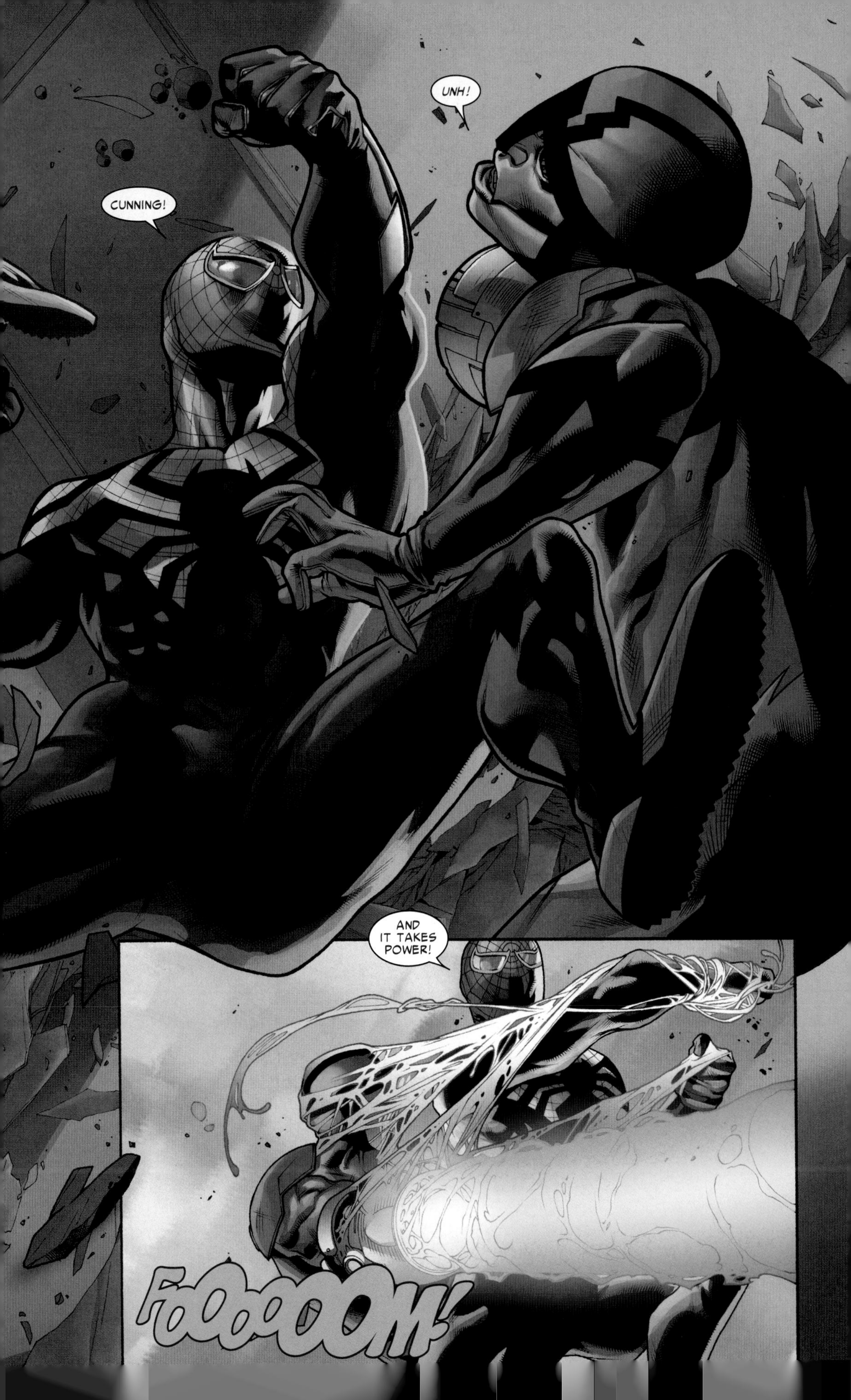
CUNNING!
UNH!
AND IT TAKES POWER!
FOOOOOOM!

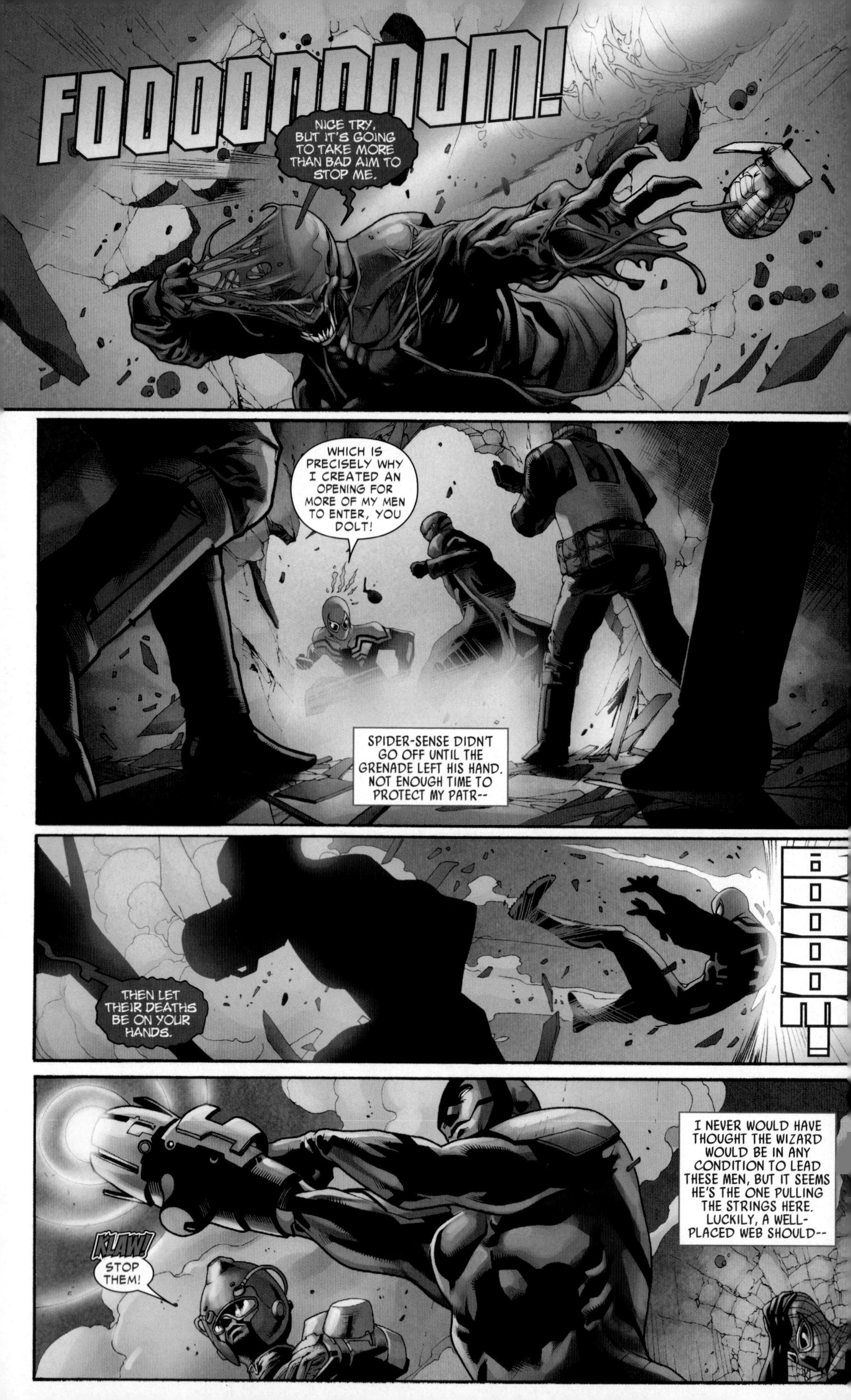
FOOOOOOOOM!
NICE TRY, BUT IT'S GOING TO TAKE MORE THAN BAD AIM TO STOP ME.
WHICH IS PRECISELY WHY I CREATED AN OPENING FOR MORE OF MY MEN TO ENTER, YOU DOLT!
SPIDER-SENSE DIDN'T GO OFF UNTIL THE GRENADE LEFT HIS HAND. NOT ENOUGH TIME TO PROTECT MY PATR--
THEN LET THEIR DEATHS BE ON YOUR HANDS.
I NEVER WOULD HAVE THOUGHT THE WIZARD WOULD BE IN ANY CONDITION TO LEAD THESE MEN, BUT IT SEEMS HE'S THE ONE PULLING THE STRINGS HERE. LUCKILY, A WELL-PLACED WEB SHOULD--
KLAW!
STOP THEM!

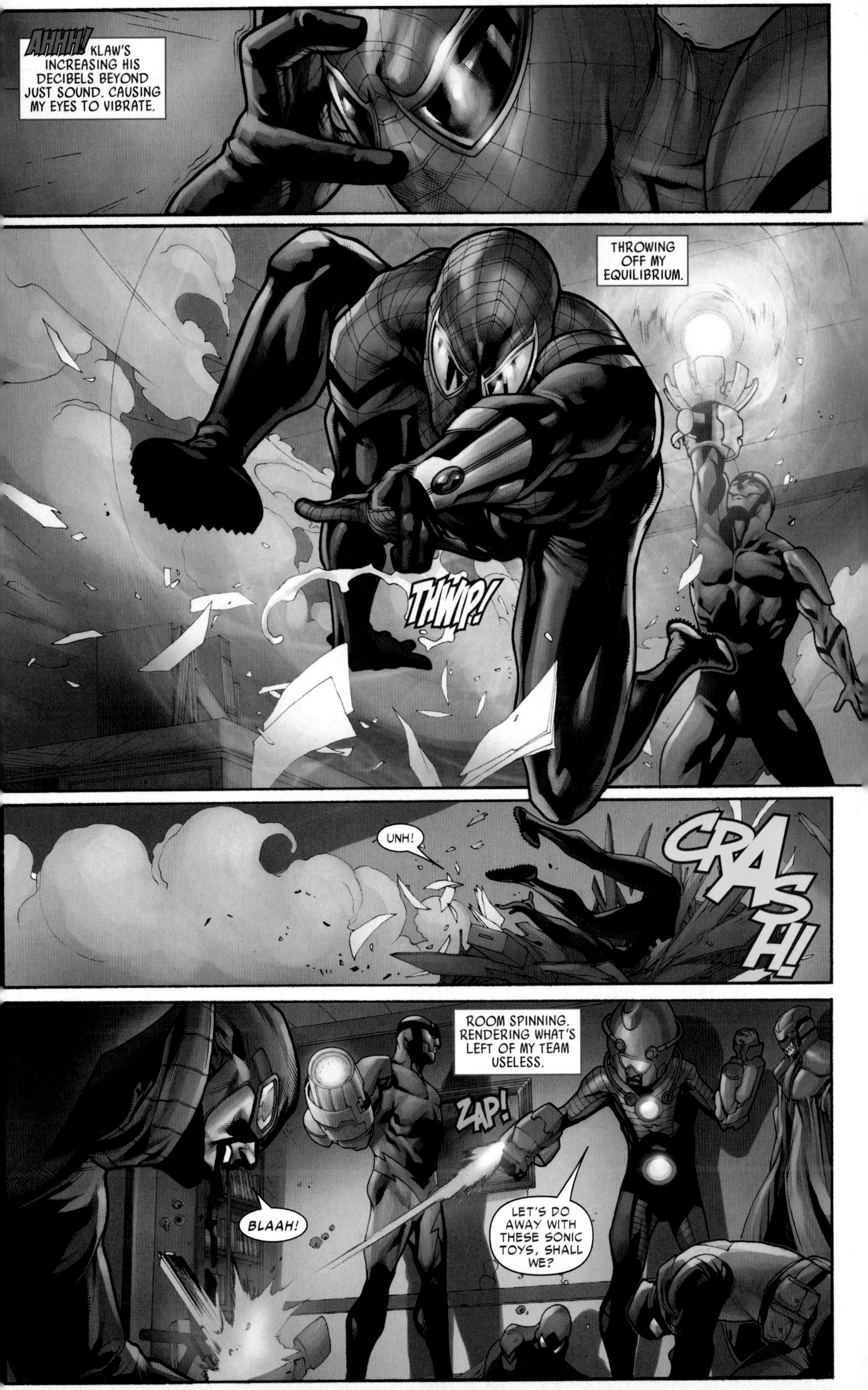

AHHH! KLAW'S INCREASING HIS DECIBELS BEYOND JUST SOUND. CAUSING MY EYES TO VIBRATE.
THROWING OFF MY EQUILIBRIUM.
THWIP!
UNH!
CRASH!
ROOM SPINNING. RENDERING WHAT'S LEFT OF MY TEAM USELESS.
ZAP!
BLAAH!
LET'S DO AWAY WITH THESE SONIC TOYS, SHALL WE?

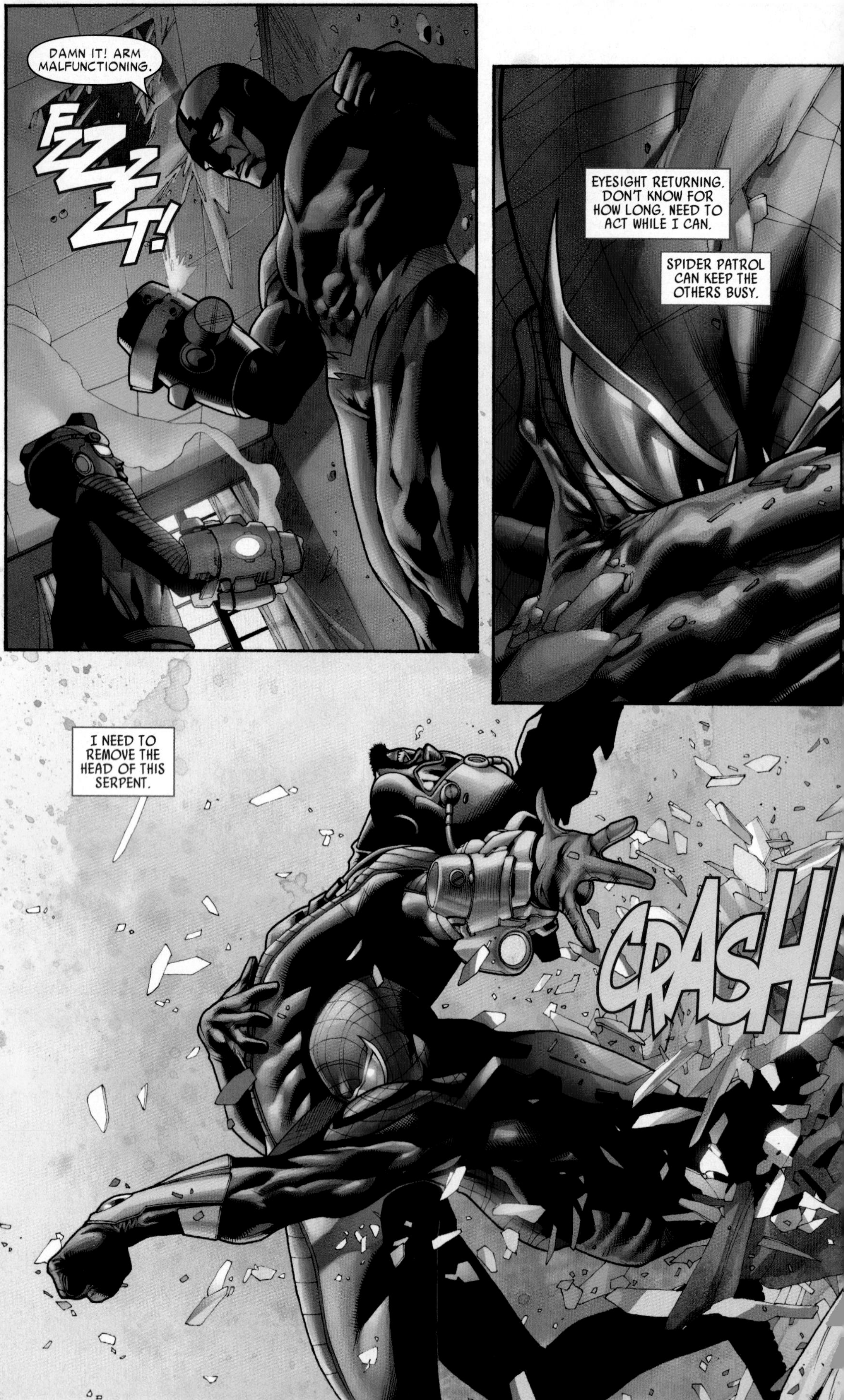
DAMN IT! ARM MALFUNCTIONING.
FZZZZT!
EYESIGHT RETURNING. DON'T KNOW FOR HOW LONG. NEED TO ACT WHILE I CAN.
SPIDER PATROL CAN KEEP THE OTHERS BUSY.
I NEED TO REMOVE THE HEAD OF THIS SERPENT.
CRASH!

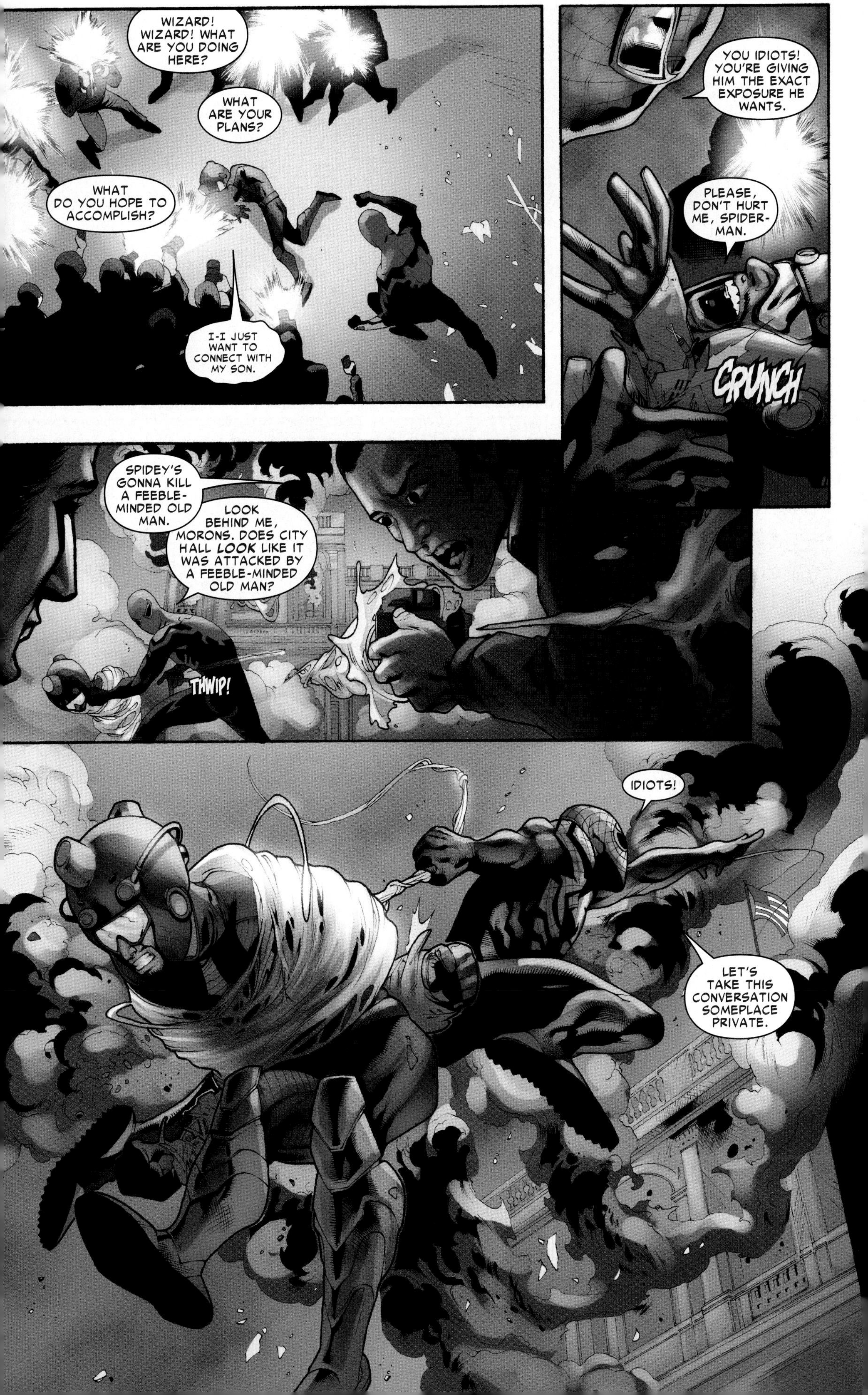
WIZARD! WIZARD! WHAT ARE YOU DOING HERE?
WHAT ARE YOUR PLANS?
WHAT DO YOU HOPE TO ACCOMPLISH?
I-I JUST WANT TO CONNECT WITH MY SON.
YOU IDIOTS! YOU'RE GIVING HIM THE EXACT EXPOSURE HE WANTS.
PLEASE, DON'T HURT ME, SPIDER-MAN.
CRUNCH
SPIDEY'S GONNA KILL A FEEBLE-MINDED OLD MAN.
LOOK BEHIND ME, MORONS. DOES CITY HALL *LOOK* LIKE IT WAS ATTACKED BY A FEEBLE-MINDED OLD MAN?
THWIP!
IDIOTS!
LET'S TAKE THIS CONVERSATION SOMEPLACE PRIVATE.

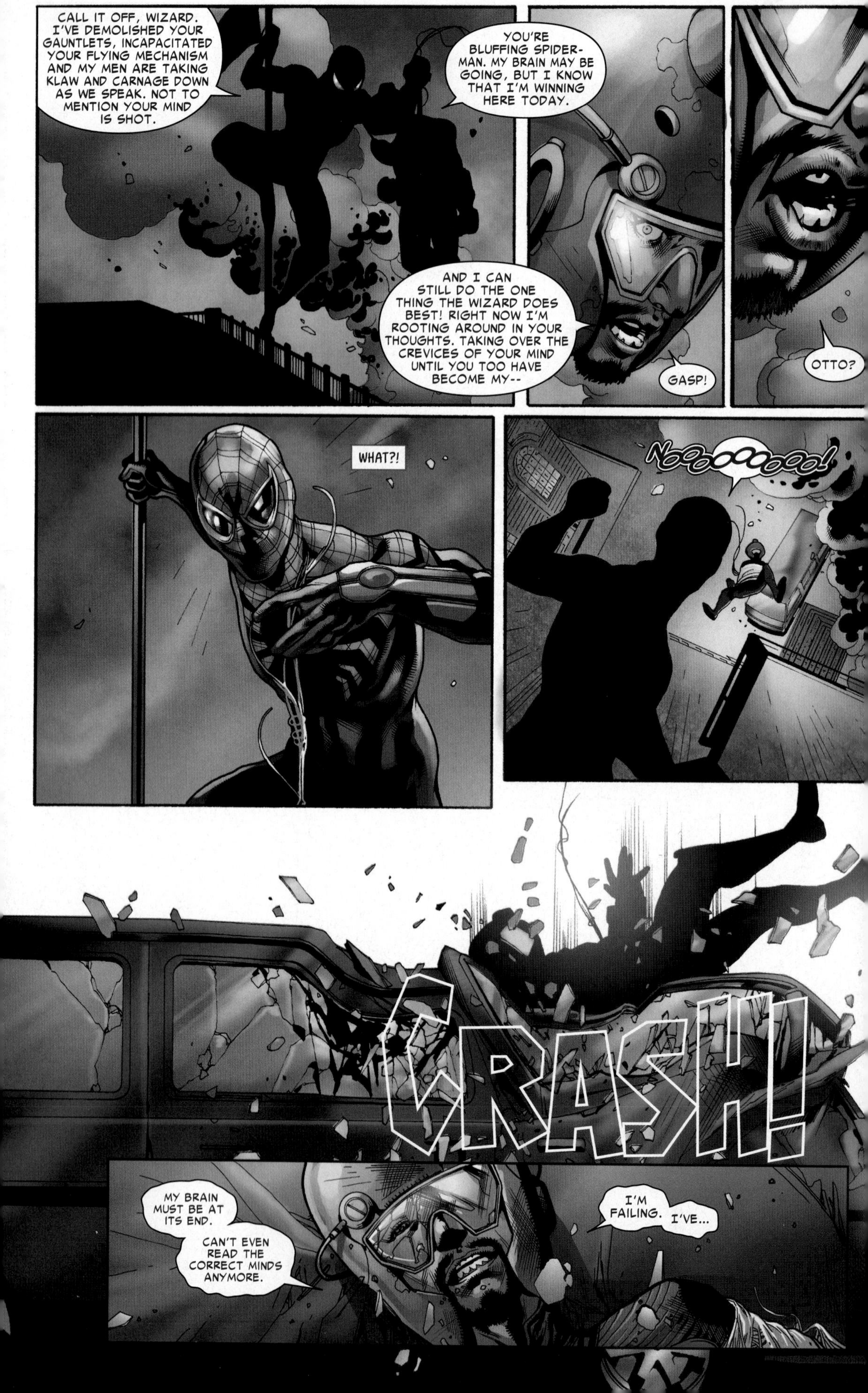
CALL IT OFF, WIZARD. I'VE DEMOLISHED YOUR GAUNTLETS, INCAPACITATED YOUR FLYING MECHANISM AND MY MEN ARE TAKING KLAW AND CARNAGE DOWN AS WE SPEAK. NOT TO MENTION YOUR MIND IS SHOT.
YOU'RE BLUFFING SPIDER-MAN. MY BRAIN MAY BE GOING, BUT I KNOW THAT I'M WINNING HERE TODAY.
AND I CAN STILL DO THE ONE THING THE WIZARD DOES BEST! RIGHT NOW I'M ROOTING AROUND IN YOUR THOUGHTS. TAKING OVER THE CREVICES OF YOUR MIND UNTIL YOU TOO HAVE BECOME MY--
GASP!
OTTO?
WHAT?!
NOOOOOOOOO!
CRASH!
MY BRAIN MUST BE AT ITS END.
CAN'T EVEN READ THE CORRECT MINDS ANYMORE.
I'M FAILING.
I'VE...

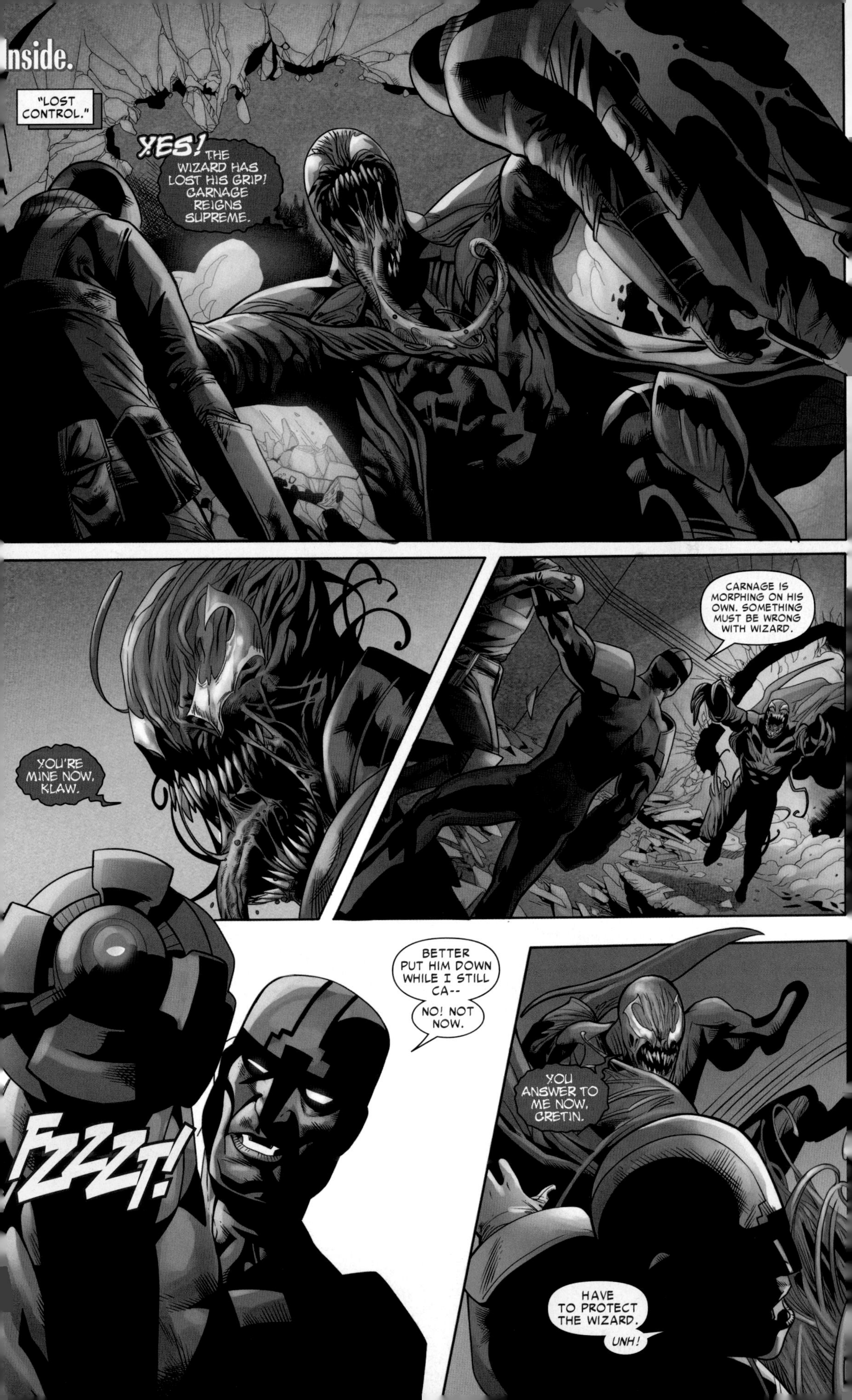
Inside.
"LOST CONTROL."
YES! THE WIZARD HAS LOST HIS GRIP! CARNAGE REIGNS SUPREME.
YOU'RE MINE NOW, KLAW.
CARNAGE IS MORPHING ON HIS OWN. SOMETHING MUST BE WRONG WITH WIZARD.
BETTER PUT HIM DOWN WHILE I STILL CA--
NO! NOT NOW.
FZZZT!
YOU ANSWER TO ME NOW, CRETIN.
HAVE TO PROTECT THE WIZARD.
UNH!

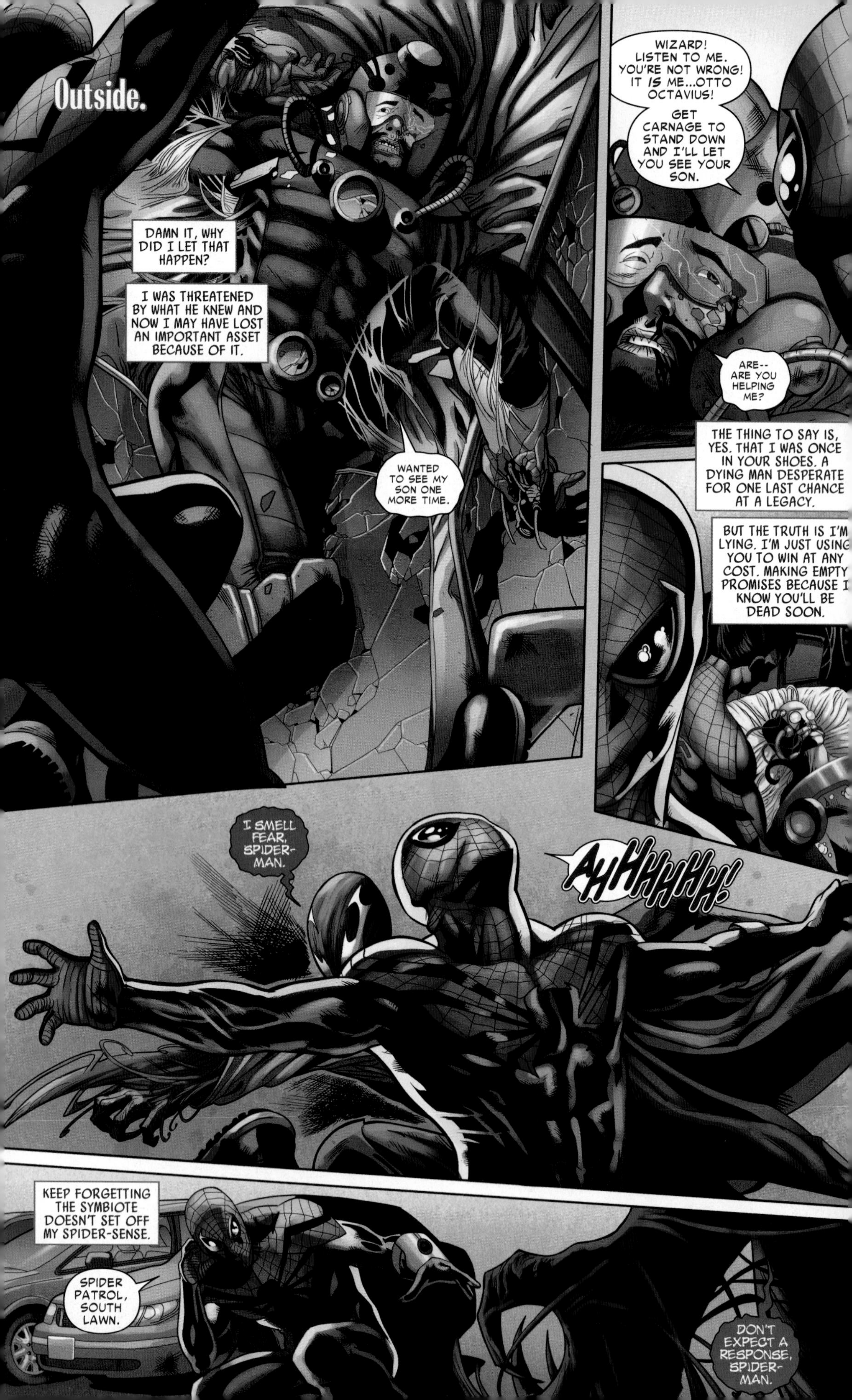
Outside.
DAMN IT, WHY DID I LET THAT HAPPEN?
I WAS THREATENED BY WHAT HE KNEW AND NOW I MAY HAVE LOST AN IMPORTANT ASSET BECAUSE OF IT.
WANTED TO SEE MY SON ONE MORE TIME.
WIZARD! LISTEN TO ME. YOU'RE NOT WRONG! IT IS ME...OTTO OCTAVIUS!
GET CARNAGE TO STAND DOWN AND I'LL LET YOU SEE YOUR SON.
ARE-- ARE YOU HELPING ME?
THE THING TO SAY IS, YES. THAT I WAS ONCE IN YOUR SHOES. A DYING MAN DESPERATE FOR ONE LAST CHANCE AT A LEGACY.
BUT THE TRUTH IS I'M LYING. I'M JUST USING YOU TO WIN AT ANY COST. MAKING EMPTY PROMISES BECAUSE I KNOW YOU'LL BE DEAD SOON.
I SMELL FEAR, SPIDER-MAN.
AHHHHHH!
KEEP FORGETTING THE SYMBIOTE DOESN'T SET OFF MY SPIDER-SENSE.
SPIDER PATROL, SOUTH LAWN.
DON'T EXPECT A RESPONSE, SPIDER-MAN.

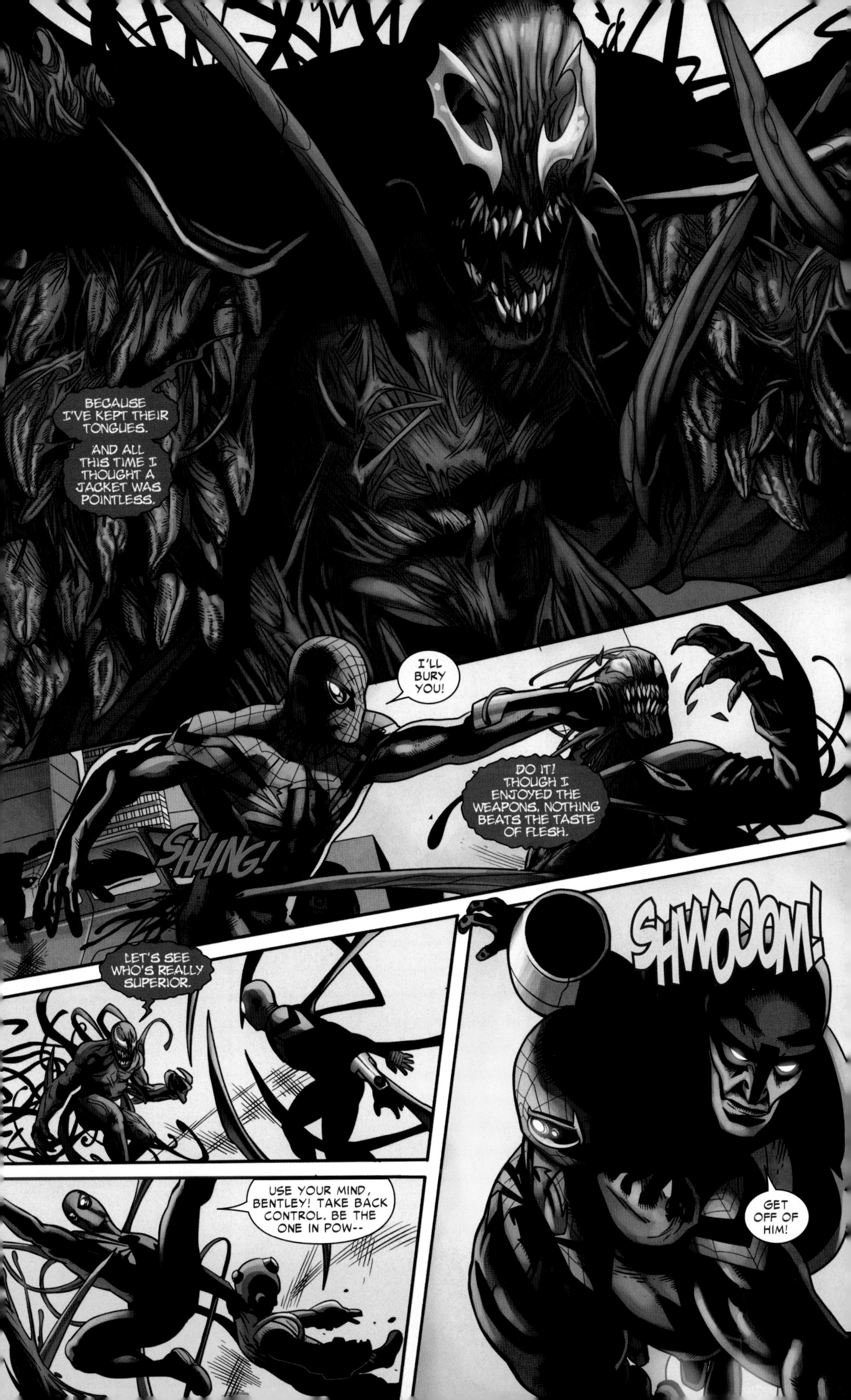
BECAUSE I'VE KEPT THEIR TONGUES.
AND ALL THIS TIME I THOUGHT A JACKET WAS POINTLESS.
I'LL BURY YOU!
DO IT! THOUGH I ENJOYED THE WEAPONS, NOTHING BEATS THE TASTE OF FLESH.
SHLING!
LET'S SEE WHO'S REALLY SUPERIOR.
SHWOOOM!
USE YOUR MIND, BENTLEY! TAKE BACK CONTROL. BE THE ONE IN POW--
GET OFF OF HIM!

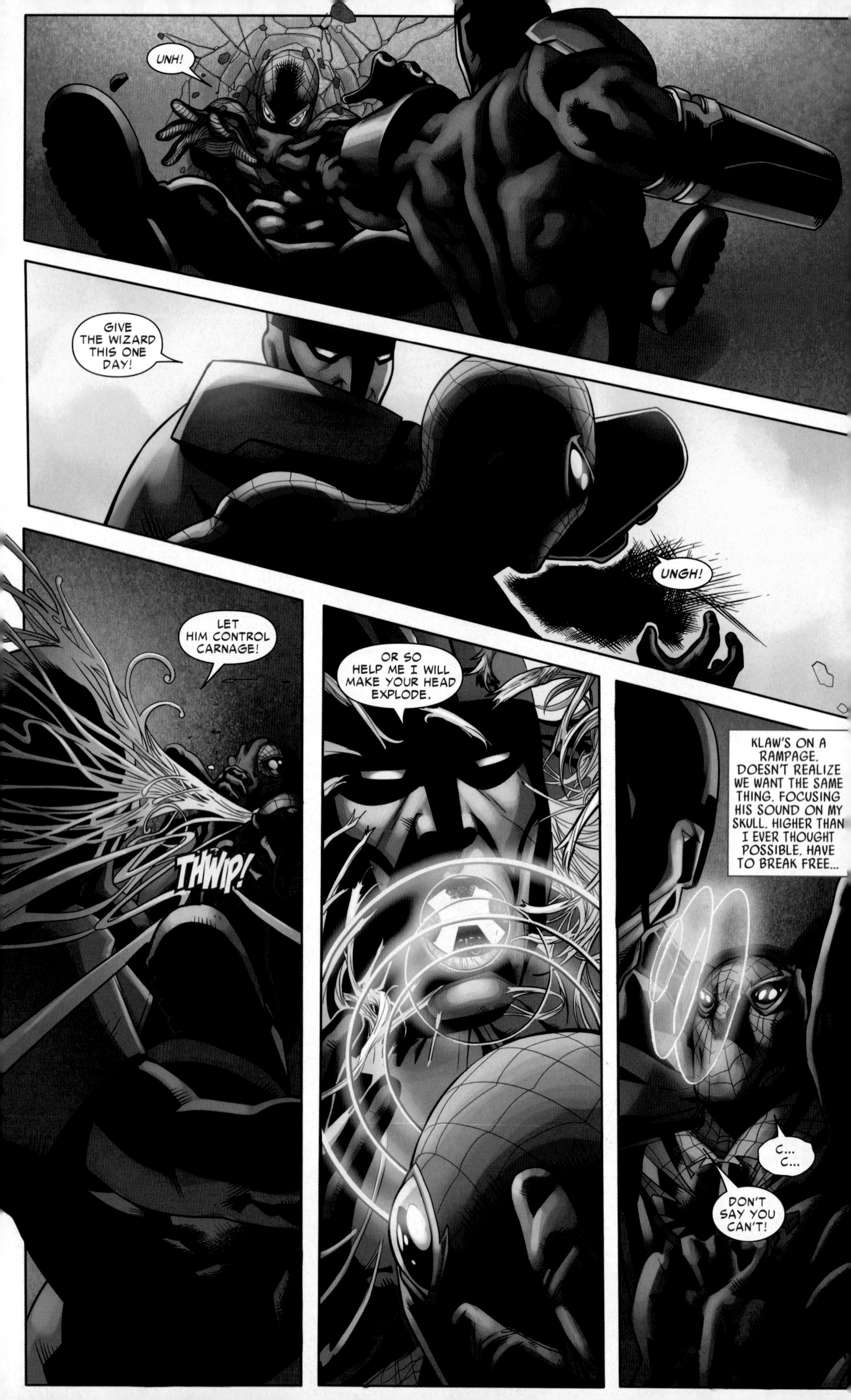
UNH!
GIVE THE WIZARD THIS ONE DAY!
UNGH!
LET HIM CONTROL CARNAGE!
THWIP!
OR SO HELP ME I WILL MAKE YOUR HEAD EXPLODE.
KLAW'S ON A RAMPAGE. DOESN'T REALIZE WE WANT THE SAME THING. FOCUSING HIS SOUND ON MY SKULL, HIGHER THAN I EVER THOUGHT POSSIBLE. HAVE TO BREAK FREE...
C... C...
DON'T SAY YOU CAN'T!

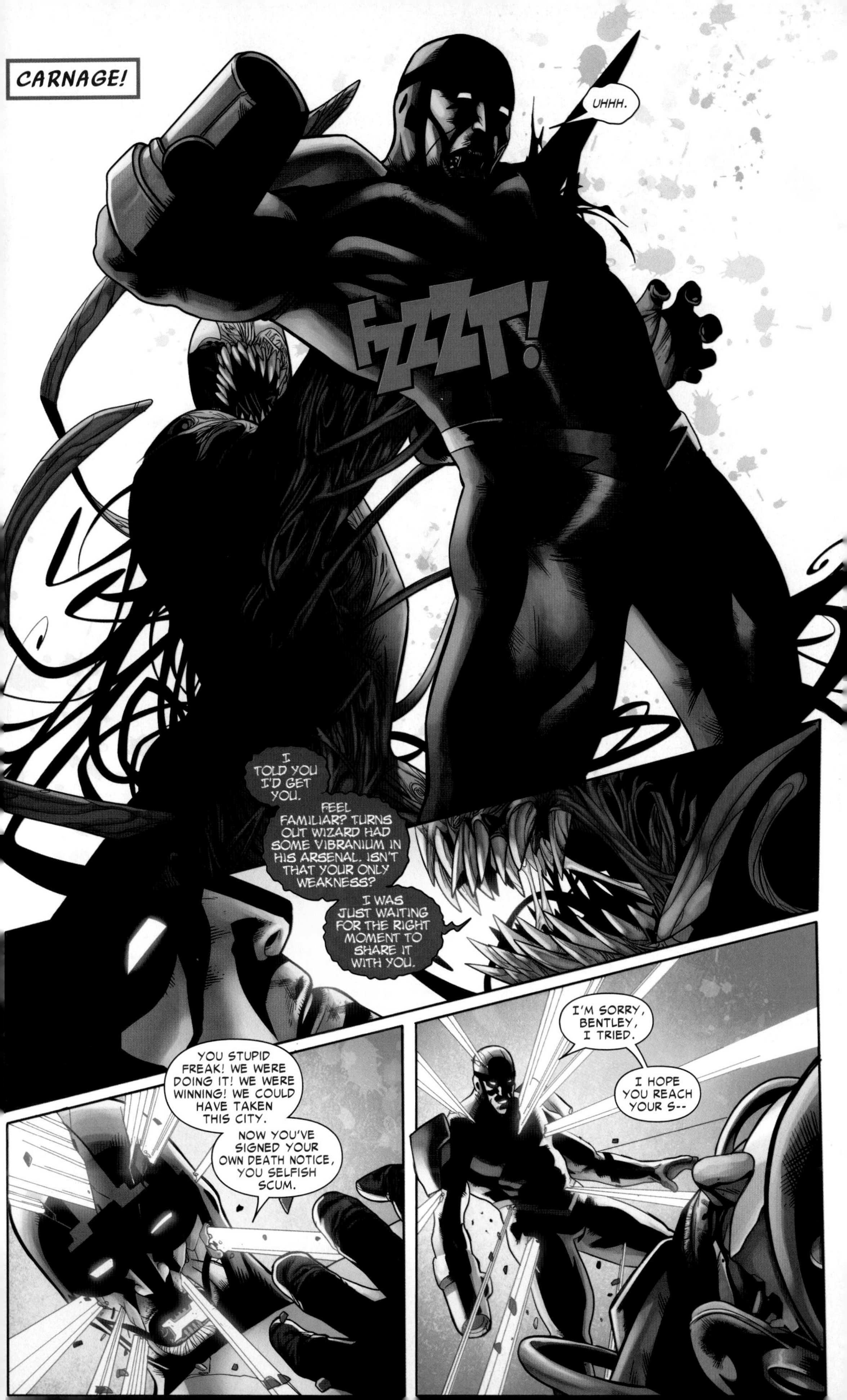
CARNAGE!
UHHH.
FZZZT!
I TOLD YOU I'D GET YOU.
FEEL FAMILIAR? TURNS OUT WIZARD HAD SOME VIBRANIUM IN HIS ARSENAL. ISN'T THAT YOUR ONLY WEAKNESS?
I WAS JUST WAITING FOR THE RIGHT MOMENT TO SHARE IT WITH YOU.
YOU STUPID FREAK! WE WERE DOING IT! WE WERE WINNING! WE COULD HAVE TAKEN THIS CITY.
NOW YOU'VE SIGNED YOUR OWN DEATH NOTICE, YOU SELFISH SCUM.
I'M SORRY, BENTLEY, I TRIED.
I HOPE YOU REACH YOUR S--

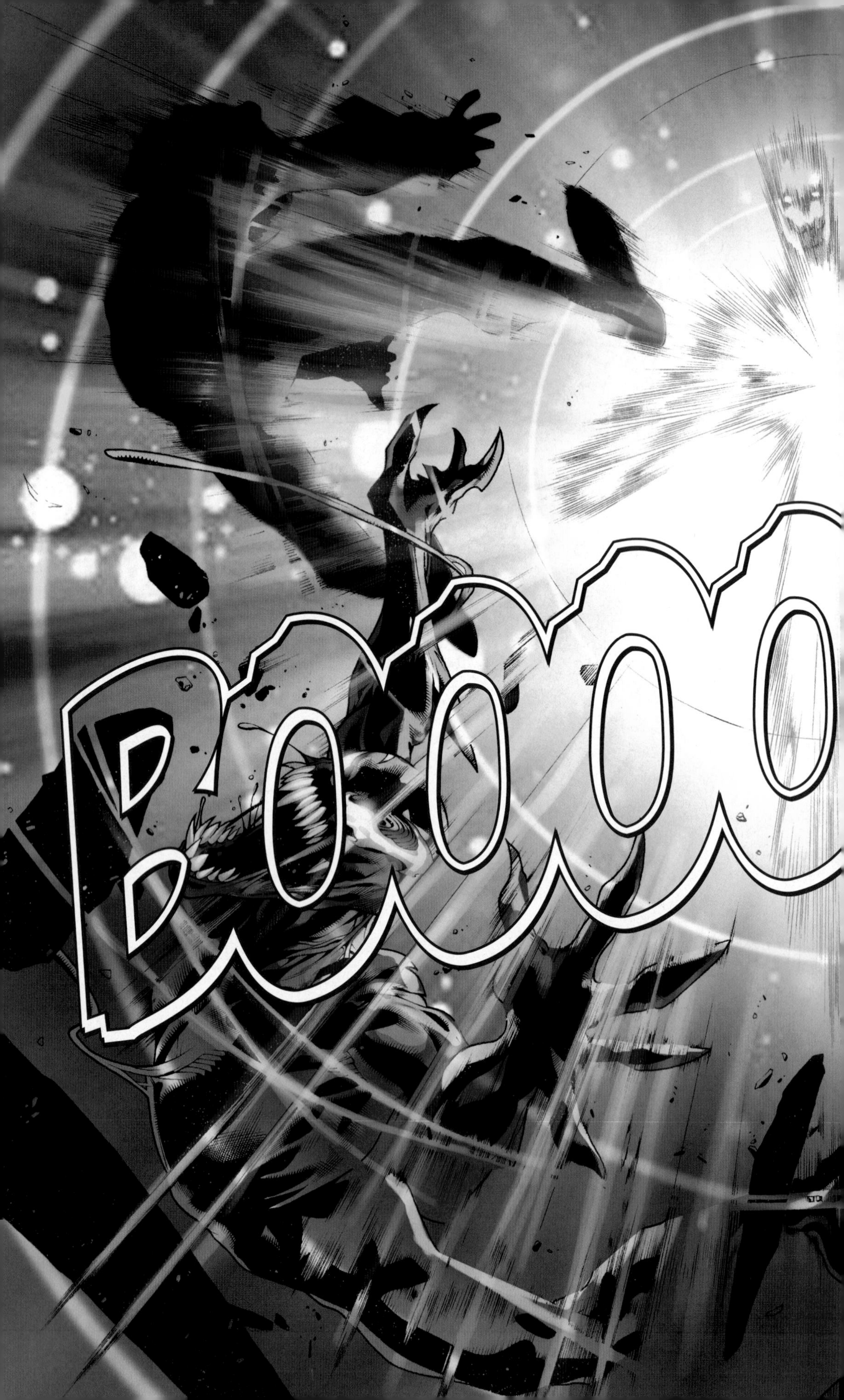
BOOOOO

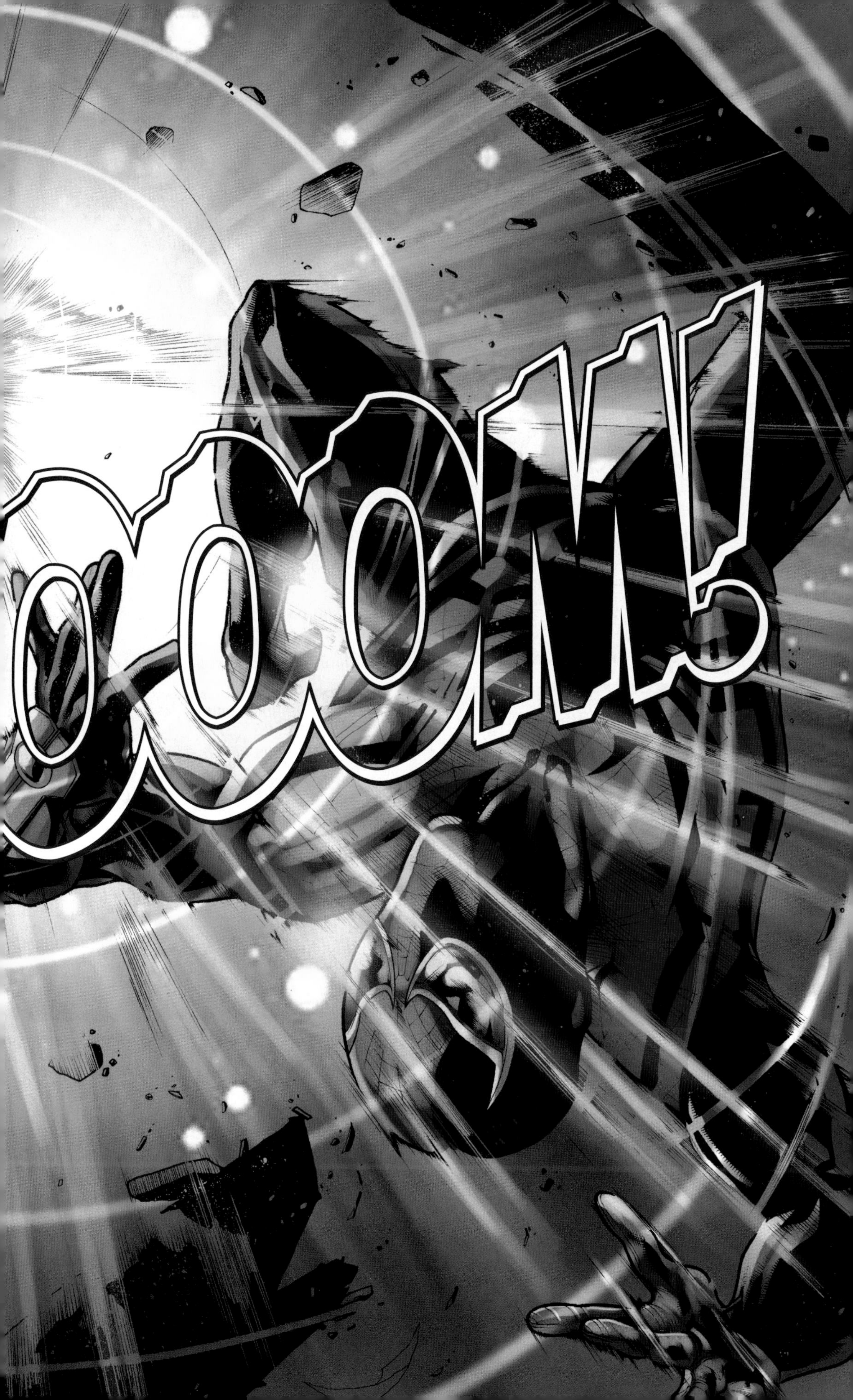
OOOM!

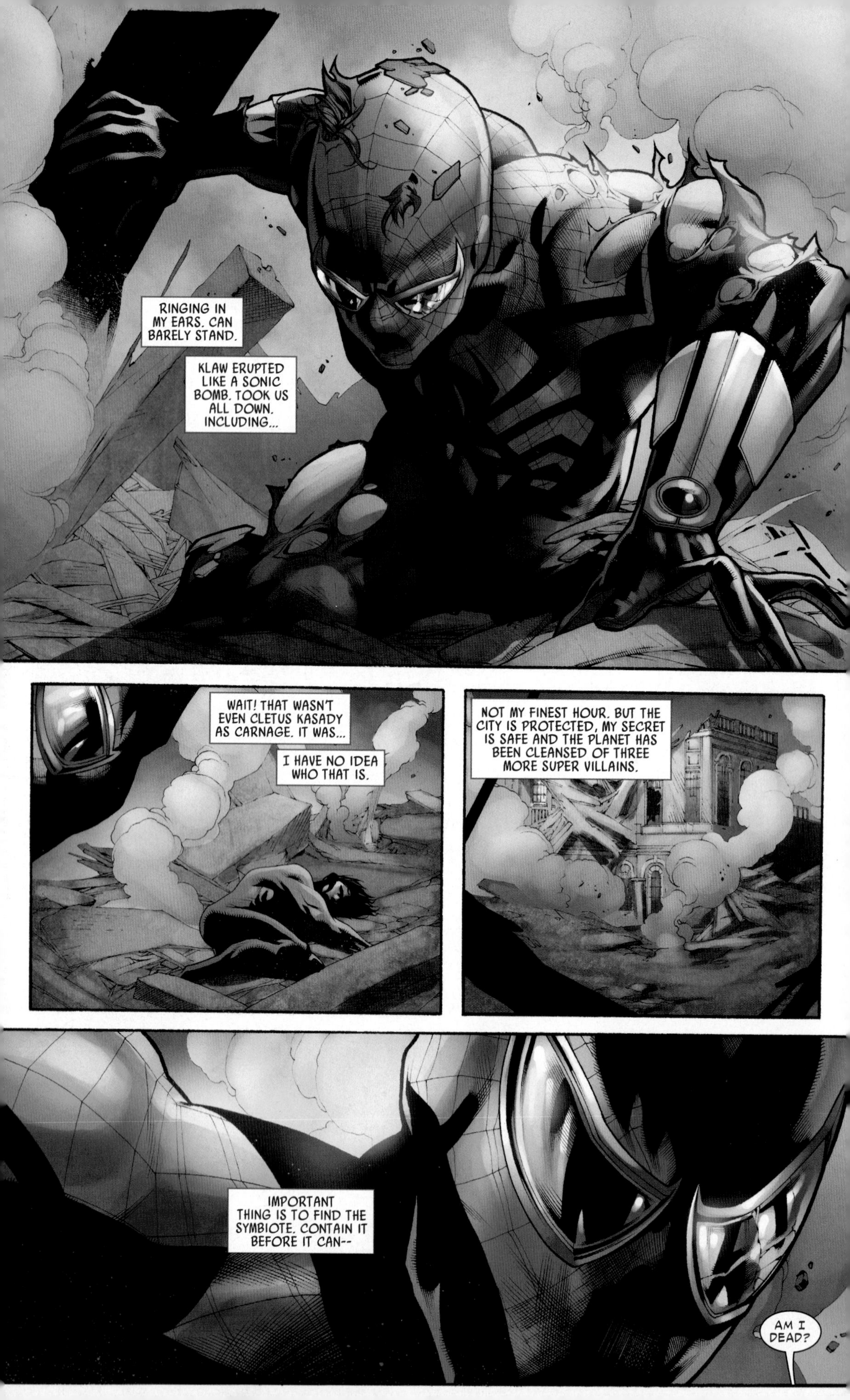
RINGING IN MY EARS. CAN BARELY STAND.
KLAW ERUPTED LIKE A SONIC BOMB. TOOK US ALL DOWN. INCLUDING...
WAIT! THAT WASN'T EVEN CLETUS KASADY AS CARNAGE. IT WAS...
I HAVE NO IDEA WHO THAT IS.
NOT MY FINEST HOUR. BUT THE CITY IS PROTECTED, MY SECRET IS SAFE AND THE PLANET HAS BEEN CLEANSED OF THREE MORE SUPER VILLAINS.
IMPORTANT THING IS TO FIND THE SYMBIOTE. CONTAIN IT BEFORE IT CAN--
AM I DEAD?

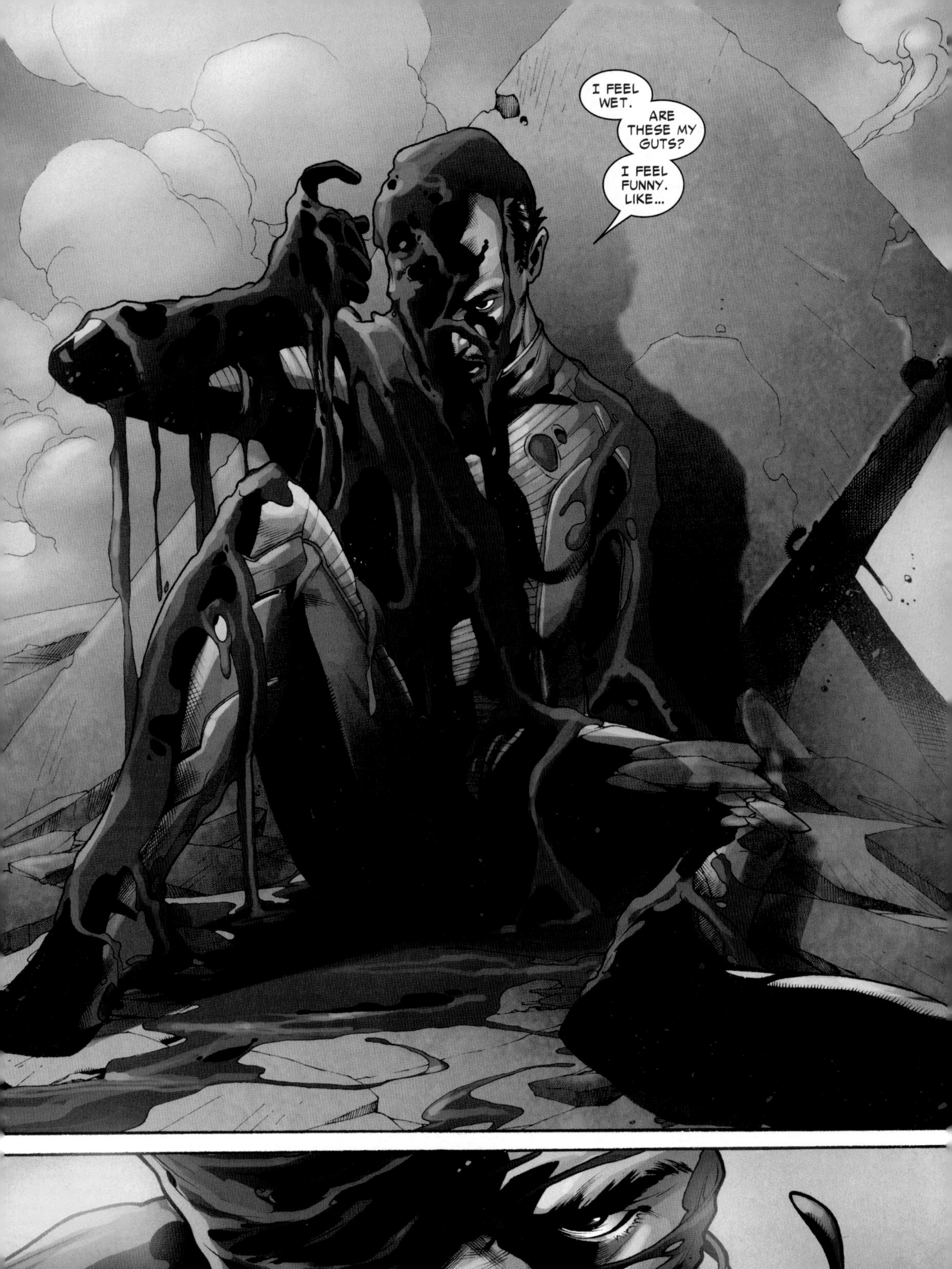
I FEEL WET.
ARE THESE MY GUTS?
I FEEL FUNNY. LIKE...

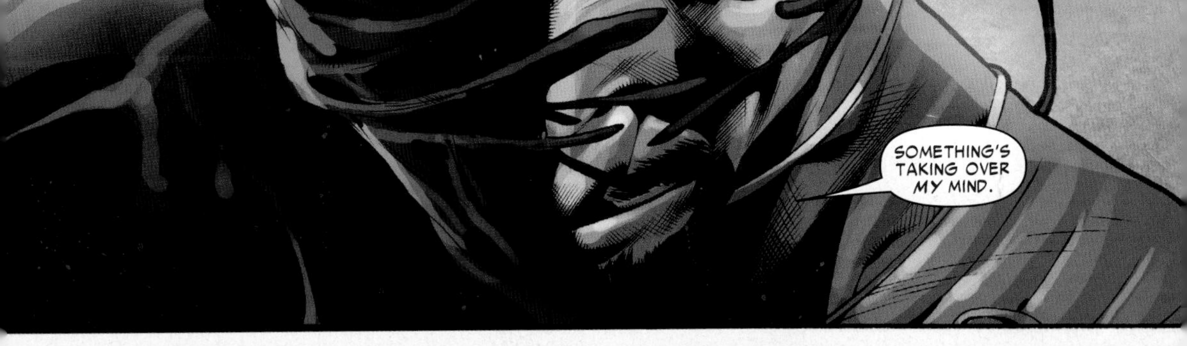
SOMETHING'S TAKING OVER MY MIND.

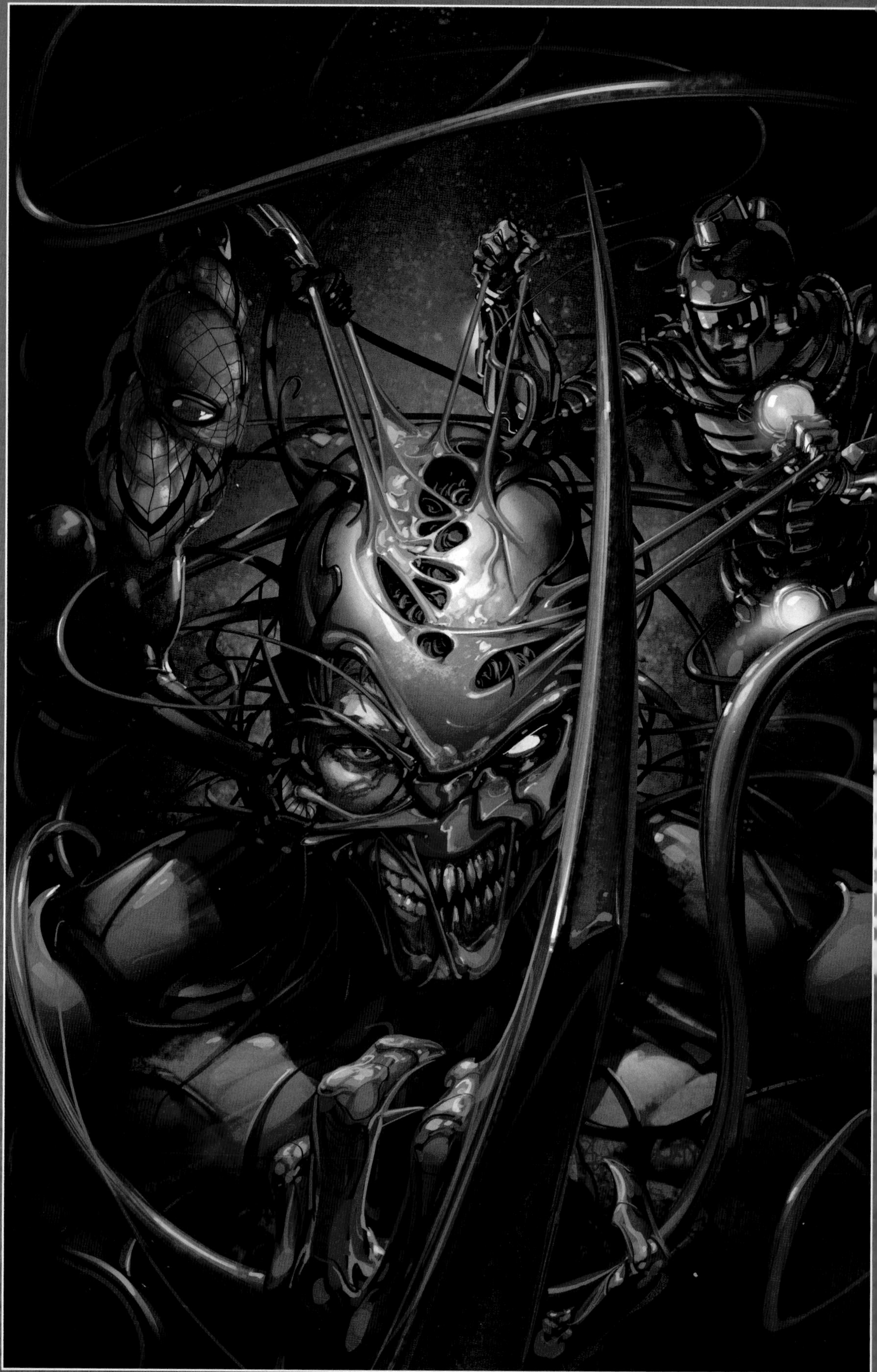

SUPERIOR CARNAGE #5

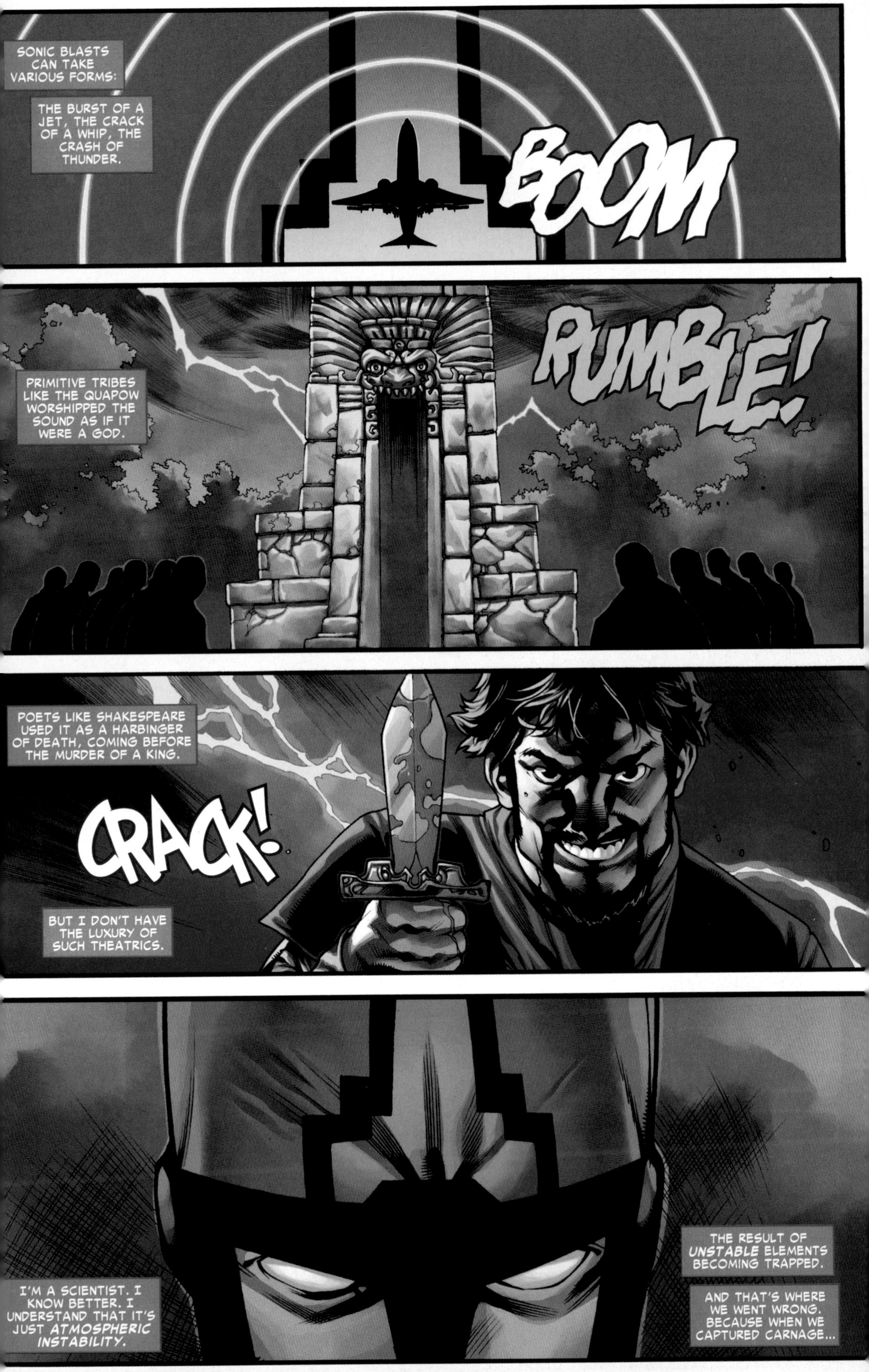
SONIC BLASTS CAN TAKE VARIOUS FORMS:
THE BURST OF A JET, THE CRACK OF A WHIP, THE CRASH OF THUNDER.
BOOM
PRIMITIVE TRIBES LIKE THE QUAPOW WORSHIPPED THE SOUND AS IF IT WERE A GOD.
RUMBLE!
POETS LIKE SHAKESPEARE USED IT AS A HARBINGER OF DEATH, COMING BEFORE THE MURDER OF A KING.
CRACK!
BUT I DON'T HAVE THE LUXURY OF SUCH THEATRICS.
I'M A SCIENTIST. I KNOW BETTER. I UNDERSTAND THAT IT'S JUST *ATMOSPHERIC INSTABILITY.*
THE RESULT OF *UNSTABLE* ELEMENTS BECOMING TRAPPED.
AND THAT'S WHERE WE WENT WRONG. BECAUSE WHEN WE CAPTURED CARNAGE...

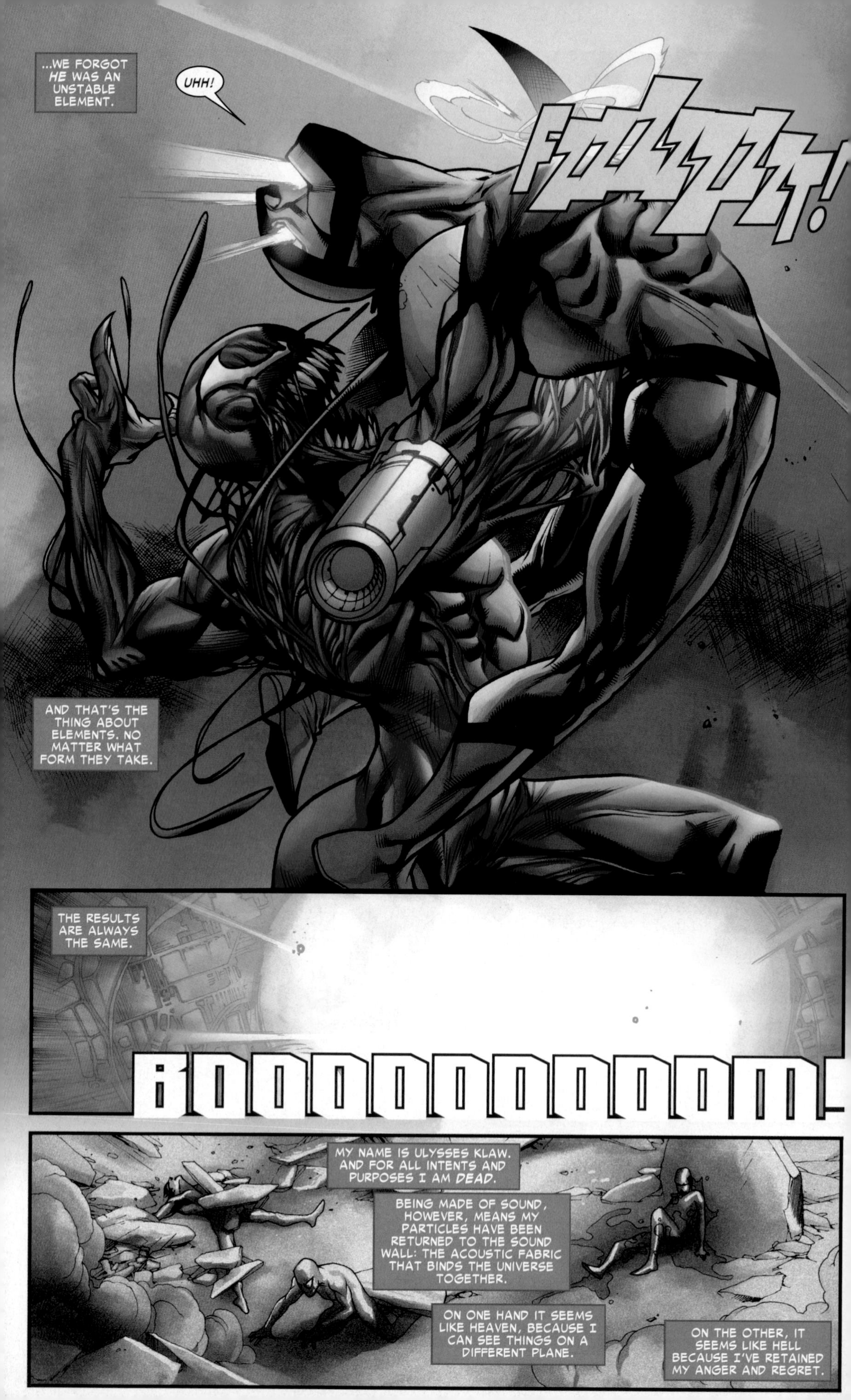
...WE FORGOT HE WAS AN UNSTABLE ELEMENT.
UHH!
FZZAAPZZT!
AND THAT'S THE THING ABOUT ELEMENTS. NO MATTER WHAT FORM THEY TAKE.
THE RESULTS ARE ALWAYS THE SAME.
BOOOOOOOOOOM!
MY NAME IS ULYSSES KLAW. AND FOR ALL INTENTS AND PURPOSES I AM DEAD.
BEING MADE OF SOUND, HOWEVER, MEANS MY PARTICLES HAVE BEEN RETURNED TO THE SOUND WALL: THE ACOUSTIC FABRIC THAT BINDS THE UNIVERSE TOGETHER.
ON ONE HAND IT SEEMS LIKE HEAVEN, BECAUSE I CAN SEE THINGS ON A DIFFERENT PLANE.
ON THE OTHER, IT SEEMS LIKE HELL BECAUSE I'VE RETAINED MY ANGER AND REGRET.

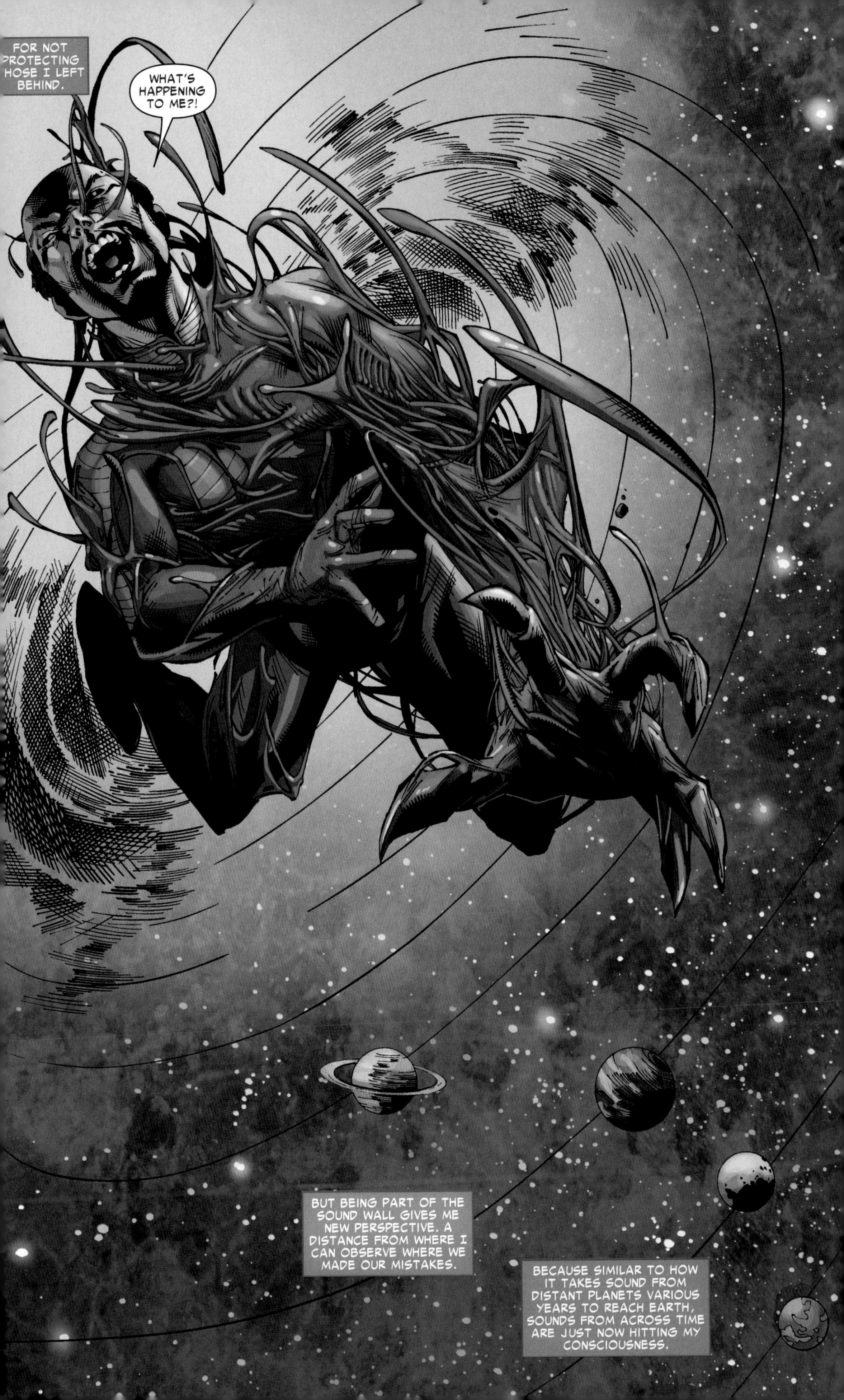
FOR NOT PROTECTING HOSE I LEFT BEHIND.
WHAT'S HAPPENING TO ME?!
BUT BEING PART OF THE SOUND WALL GIVES ME NEW PERSPECTIVE. A DISTANCE FROM WHERE I CAN OBSERVE WHERE WE MADE OUR MISTAKES.
BECAUSE SIMILAR TO HOW IT TAKES SOUND FROM DISTANT PLANETS VARIOUS YEARS TO REACH EARTH, SOUNDS FROM ACROSS TIME ARE JUST NOW HITTING MY CONSCIOUSNESS.

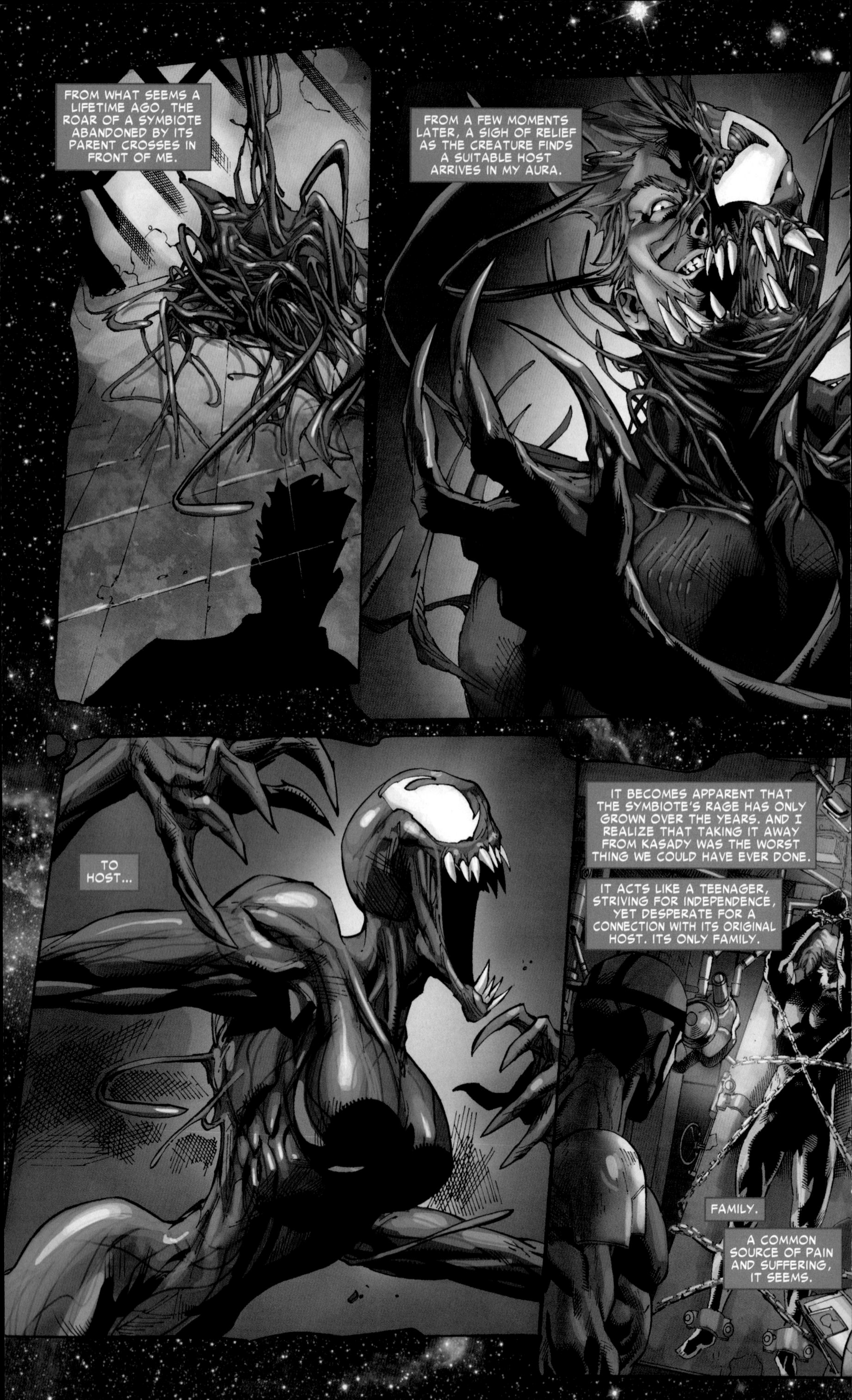
FROM WHAT SEEMS A LIFETIME AGO, THE ROAR OF A SYMBIOTE ABANDONED BY ITS PARENT CROSSES IN FRONT OF ME.
FROM A FEW MOMENTS LATER, A SIGH OF RELIEF AS THE CREATURE FINDS A SUITABLE HOST ARRIVES IN MY AURA.
TO HOST...
IT BECOMES APPARENT THAT THE SYMBIOTE'S RAGE HAS ONLY GROWN OVER THE YEARS. AND I REALIZE THAT TAKING IT AWAY FROM KASADY WAS THE WORST THING WE COULD HAVE EVER DONE.
IT ACTS LIKE A TEENAGER, STRIVING FOR INDEPENDENCE, YET DESPERATE FOR A CONNECTION WITH ITS ORIGINAL HOST. ITS ONLY FAMILY.
FAMILY.
A COMMON SOURCE OF PAIN AND SUFFERING, IT SEEMS.

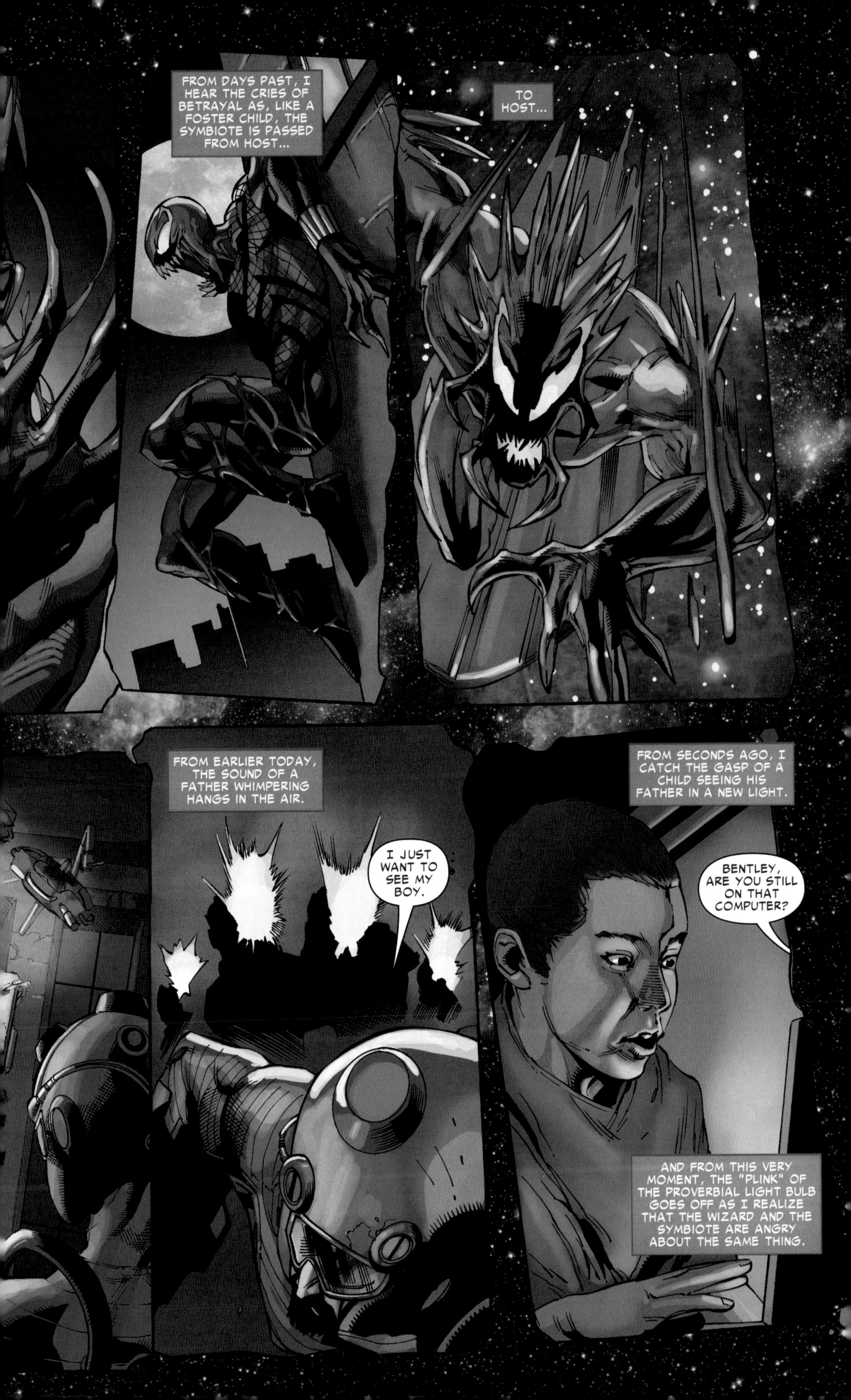
FROM DAYS PAST, I HEAR THE CRIES OF BETRAYAL AS, LIKE A FOSTER CHILD, THE SYMBIOTE IS PASSED FROM HOST...
TO HOST...
FROM EARLIER TODAY, THE SOUND OF A FATHER WHIMPERING HANGS IN THE AIR.
I JUST WANT TO SEE MY BOY.
FROM SECONDS AGO, I CATCH THE GASP OF A CHILD SEEING HIS FATHER IN A NEW LIGHT.
BENTLEY, ARE YOU STILL ON THAT COMPUTER?
AND FROM THIS VERY MOMENT, THE "PLINK" OF THE PROVERBIAL LIGHT BULB GOES OFF AS I REALIZE THAT THE WIZARD AND THE SYMBIOTE ARE ANGRY ABOUT THE SAME THING.

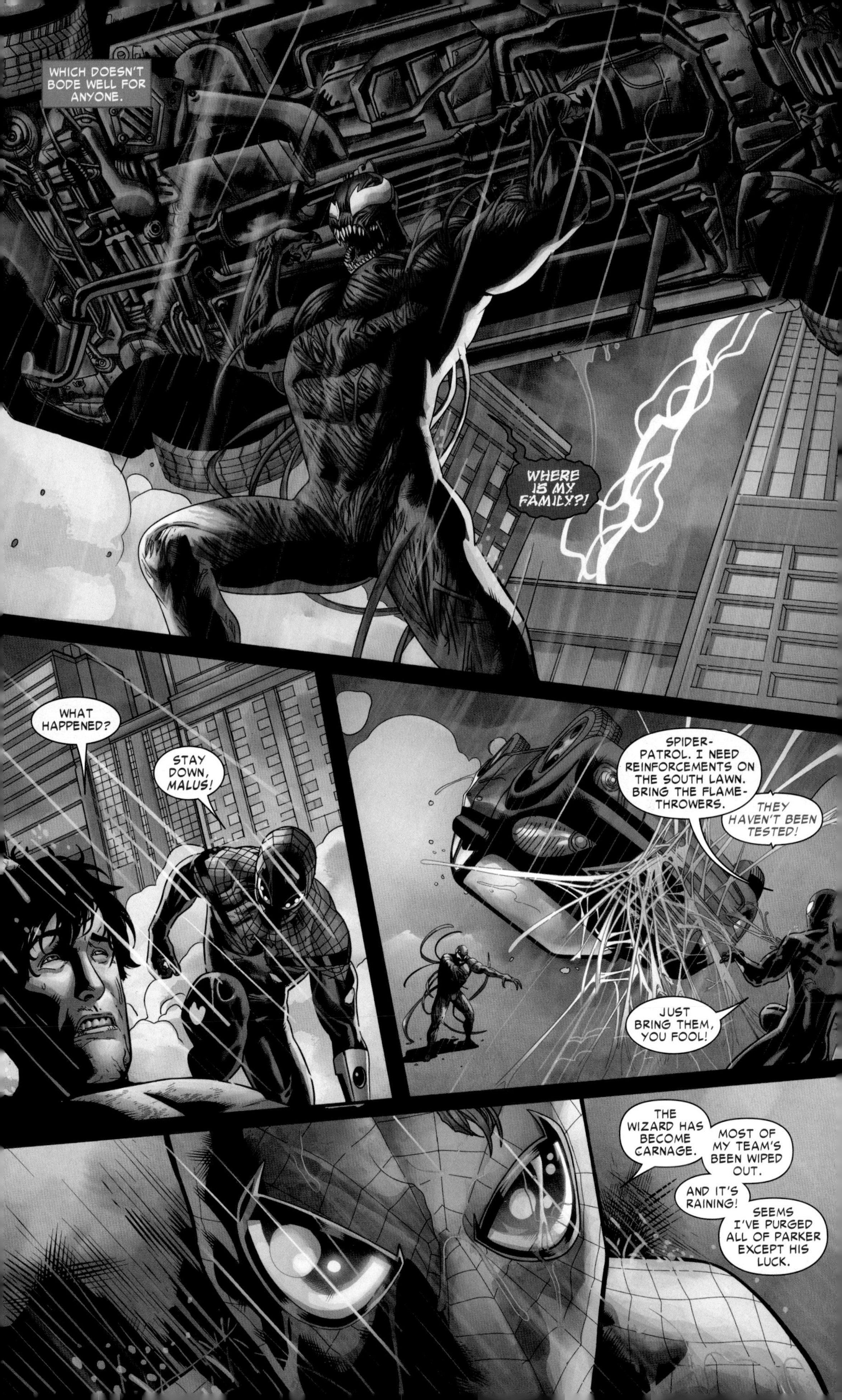
WHICH DOESN'T BODE WELL FOR ANYONE.
WHERE IS MY FAMILY?!
WHAT HAPPENED?
STAY DOWN, MALUS!
SPIDER-PATROL. I NEED REINFORCEMENTS ON THE SOUTH LAWN. BRING THE FLAME-THROWERS.
THEY HAVEN'T BEEN TESTED!
JUST BRING THEM, YOU FOOL!
THE WIZARD HAS BECOME CARNAGE.
MOST OF MY TEAM'S BEEN WIPED OUT.
AND IT'S RAINING!
SEEMS I'VE PURGED ALL OF PARKER EXCEPT HIS LUCK.

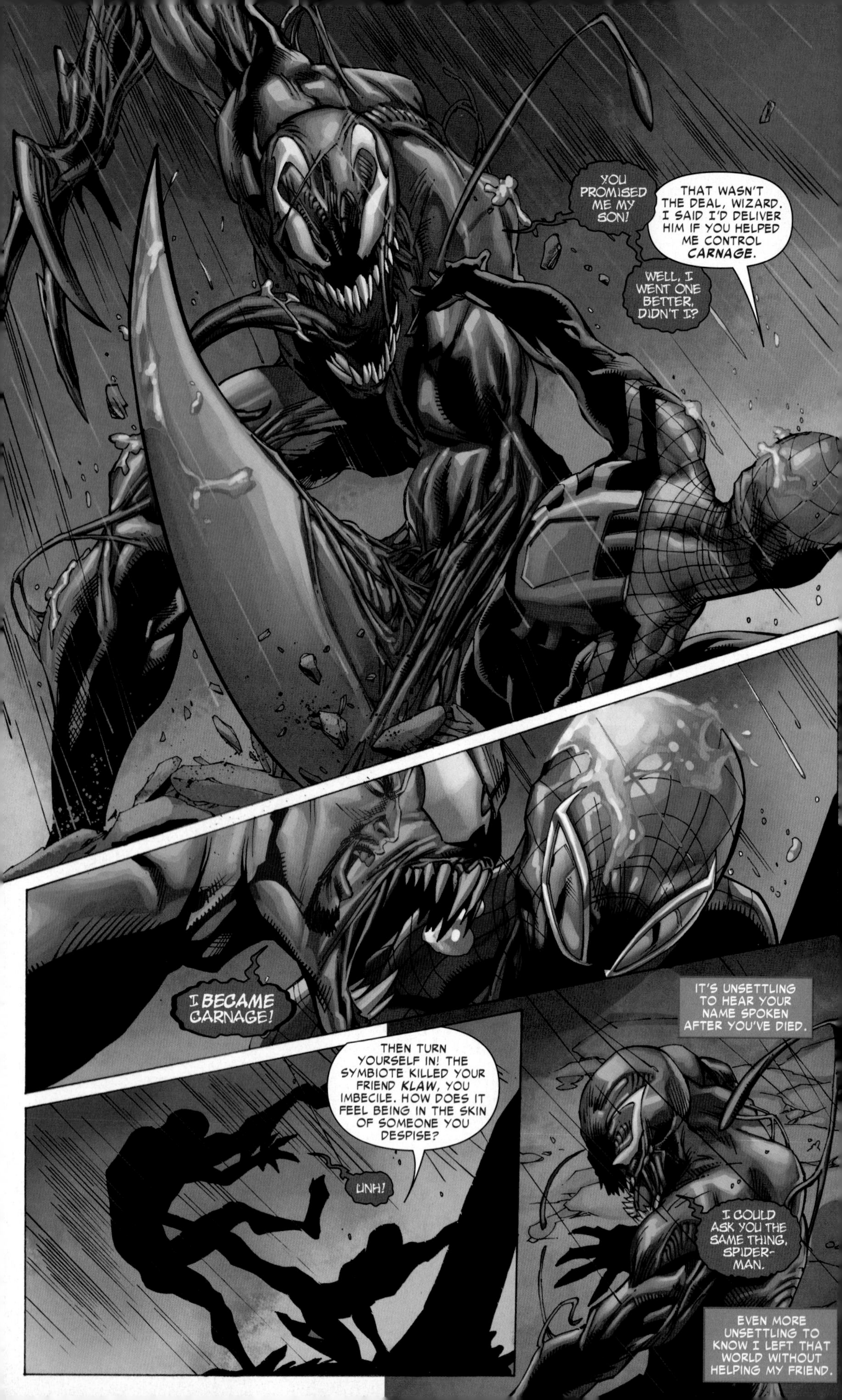
YOU PROMISED ME MY SON!
THAT WASN'T THE DEAL, WIZARD. I SAID I'D DELIVER HIM IF YOU HELPED ME CONTROL CARNAGE.
WELL, I WENT ONE BETTER, DIDN'T I?
I BECAME CARNAGE!
IT'S UNSETTLING TO HEAR YOUR NAME SPOKEN AFTER YOU'VE DIED.
THEN TURN YOURSELF IN! THE SYMBIOTE KILLED YOUR FRIEND KLAW, YOU IMBECILE. HOW DOES IT FEEL BEING IN THE SKIN OF SOMEONE YOU DESPISE?
UNH!
I COULD ASK YOU THE SAME THING, SPIDER-MAN.
EVEN MORE UNSETTLING TO KNOW I LEFT THAT WORLD WITHOUT HELPING MY FRIEND.

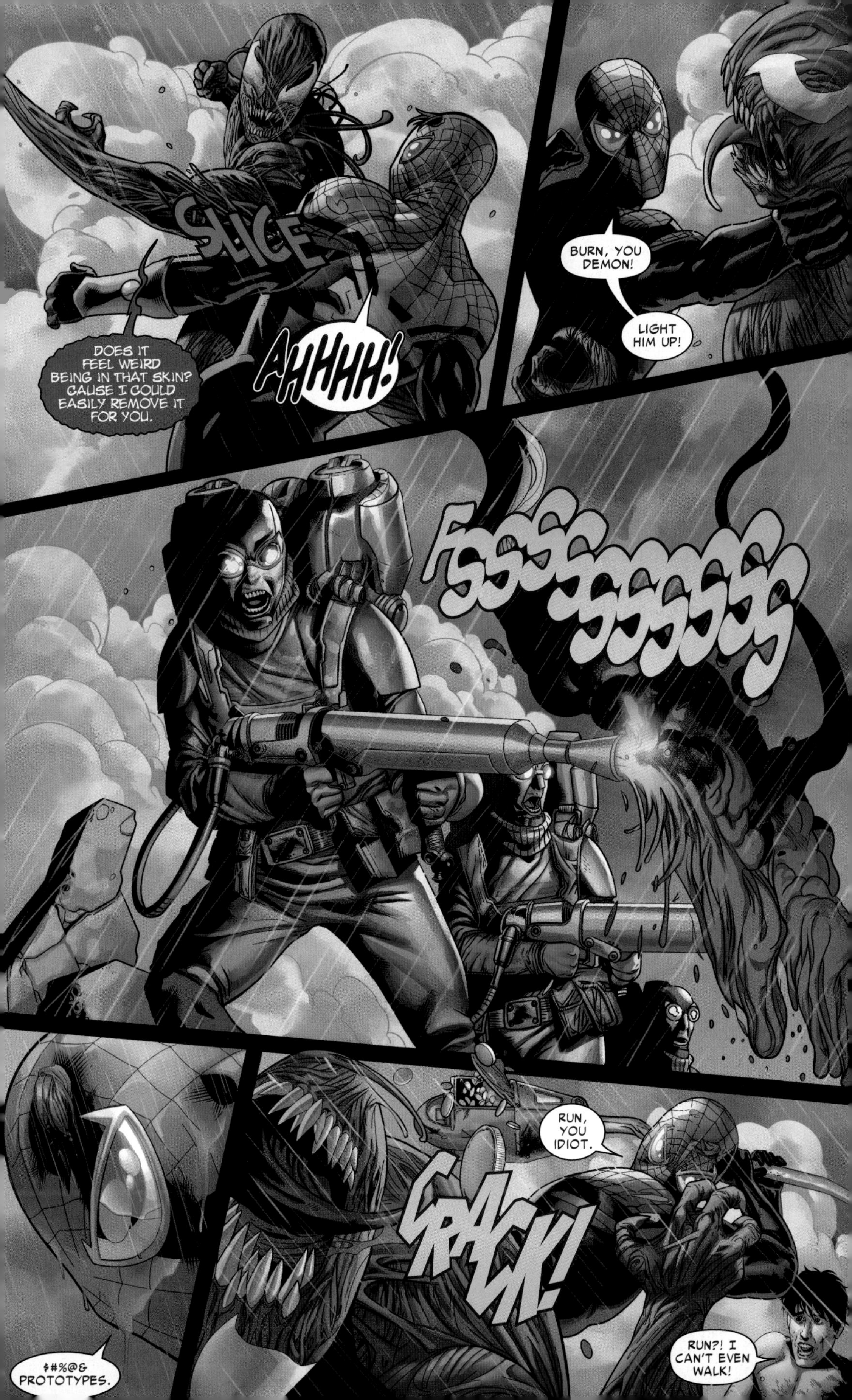
SLICE
DOES IT FEEL WEIRD BEING IN THAT SKIN? CAUSE I COULD EASILY REMOVE IT FOR YOU.
AHHHH!
BURN, YOU DEMON!
LIGHT HIM UP!
FSSSSSSSSSS
$#%@&
PROTOTYPES.
CRACK!
RUN, YOU IDIOT.
RUN?! I CAN'T EVEN WALK!

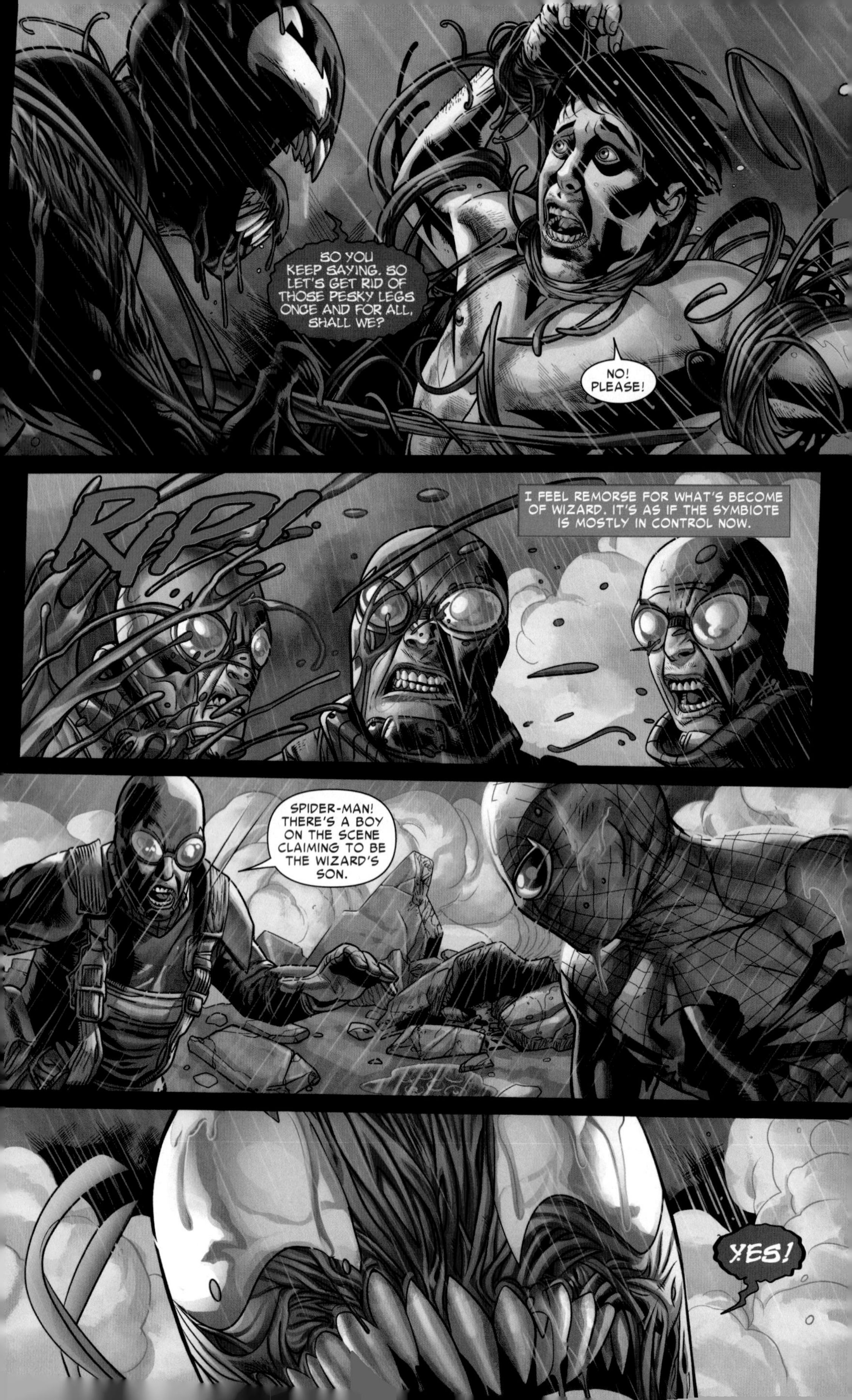
SO YOU KEEP SAYING. SO LET'S GET RID OF THOSE PESKY LEGS ONCE AND FOR ALL, SHALL WE?
NO! PLEASE!
RIP!
I FEEL REMORSE FOR WHAT'S BECOME OF WIZARD. IT'S AS IF THE SYMBIOTE IS MOSTLY IN CONTROL NOW.
SPIDER-MAN! THERE'S A BOY ON THE SCENE CLAIMING TO BE THE WIZARD'S SON.
YES!

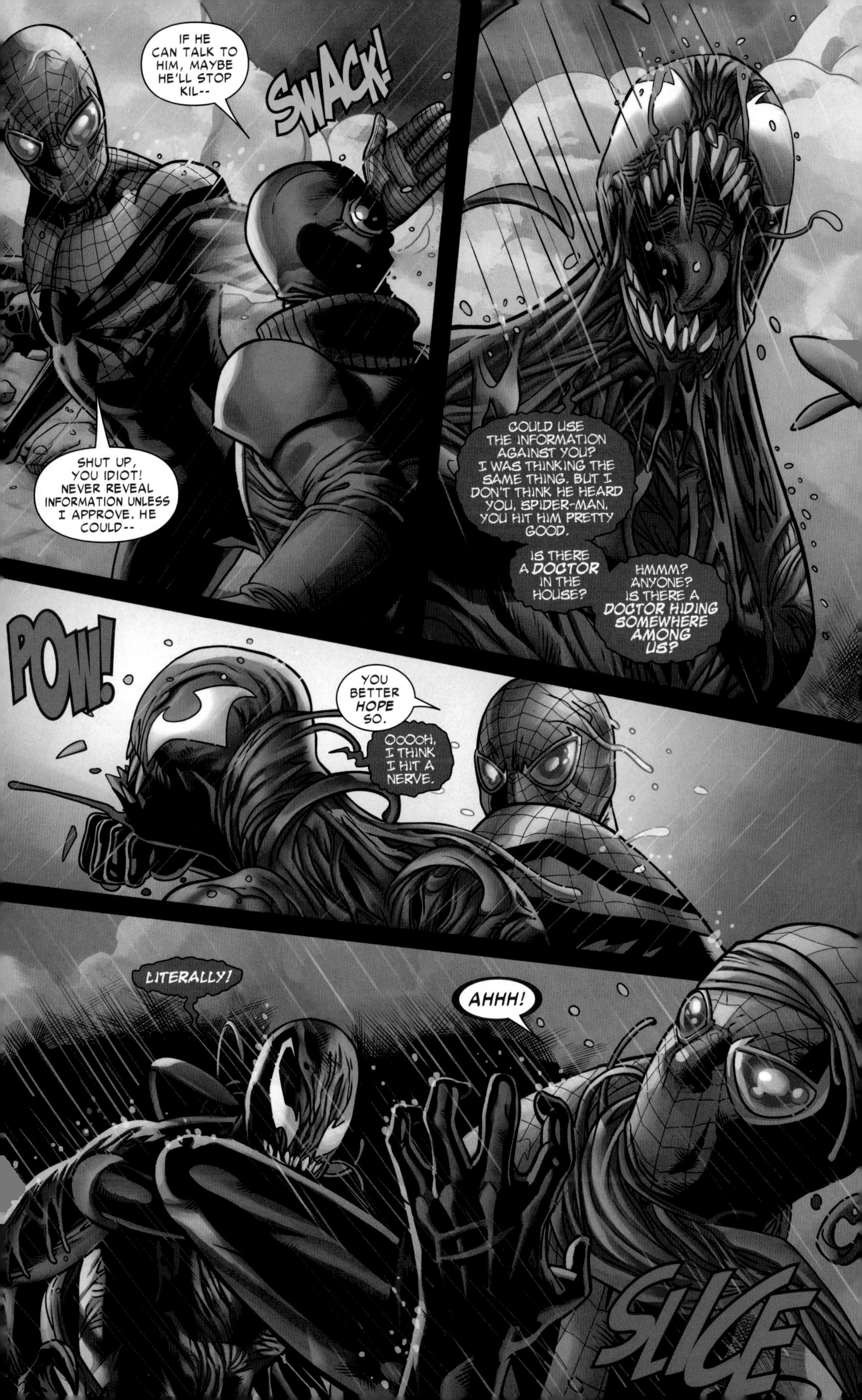
IF HE CAN TALK TO HIM, MAYBE HE'LL STOP KIL--
SWACK!
SHUT UP, YOU IDIOT! NEVER REVEAL INFORMATION UNLESS I APPROVE. HE COULD--
COULD USE THE INFORMATION AGAINST YOU? I WAS THINKING THE SAME THING. BUT I DON'T THINK HE HEARD YOU, SPIDER-MAN, YOU HIT HIM PRETTY GOOD.
IS THERE A DOCTOR IN THE HOUSE?
HMMM? ANYONE? IS THERE A DOCTOR HIDING SOMEWHERE AMONG US?
POW!
YOU BETTER HOPE SO.
OOOOH, I THINK I HIT A NERVE.
LITERALLY!
AHHH!
SLICE

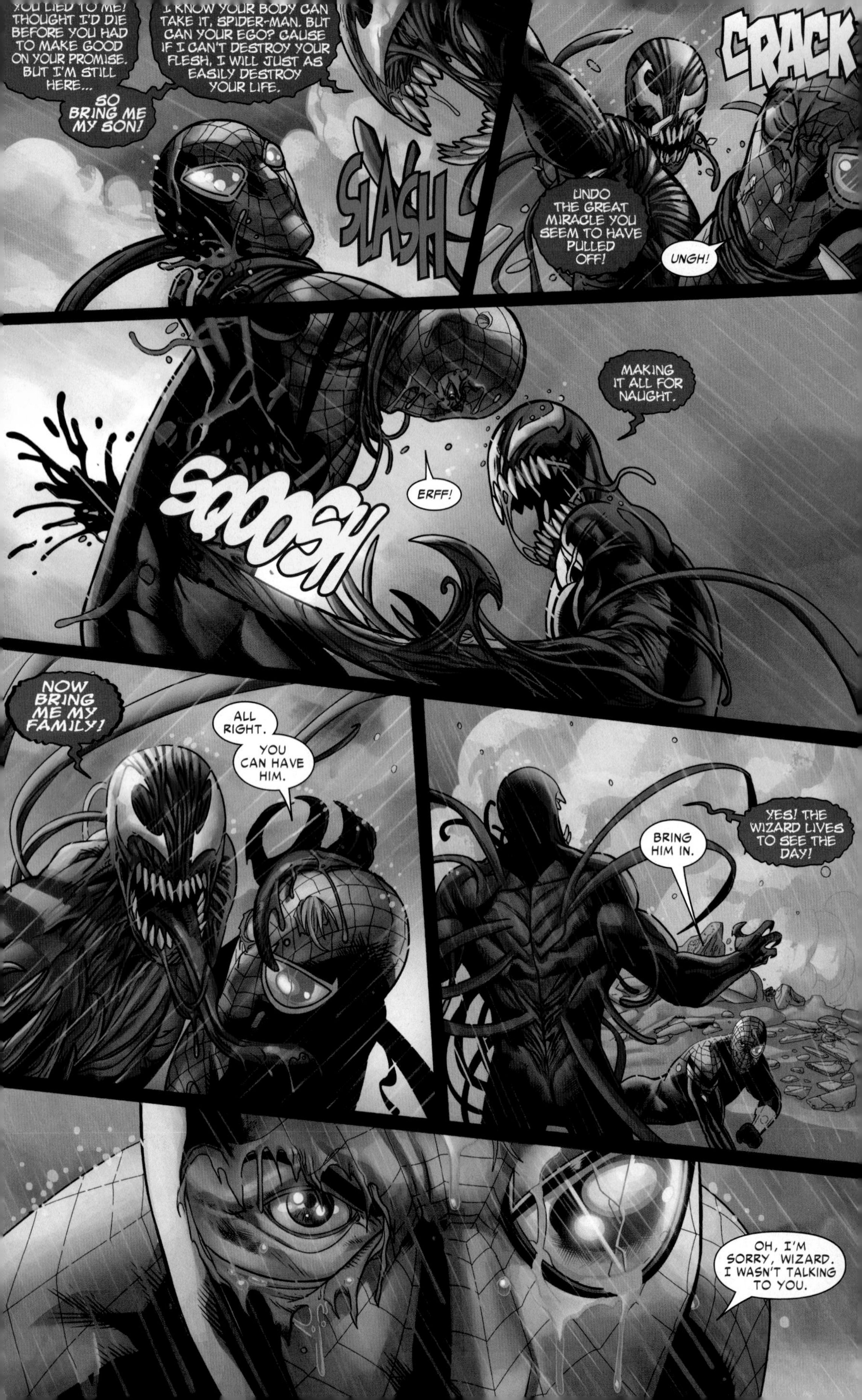
YOU LIED TO ME! THOUGHT I'D DIE BEFORE YOU HAD TO MAKE GOOD ON YOUR PROMISE. BUT I'M STILL HERE...
SO BRING ME MY SON!
I KNOW YOUR BODY CAN TAKE IT, SPIDER-MAN. BUT CAN YOUR EGO? CAUSE IF I CAN'T DESTROY YOUR FLESH, I WILL JUST AS EASILY DESTROY YOUR LIFE.
SLASH
CRACK
UNDO THE GREAT MIRACLE YOU SEEM TO HAVE PULLED OFF!
UNGH!
MAKING IT ALL FOR NAUGHT.
SCOOSH
ERFF!
NOW BRING ME MY FAMILY!
ALL RIGHT.
YOU CAN HAVE HIM.
YES! THE WIZARD LIVES TO SEE THE DAY!
BRING HIM IN.
OH, I'M SORRY, WIZARD. I WASN'T TALKING TO YOU.

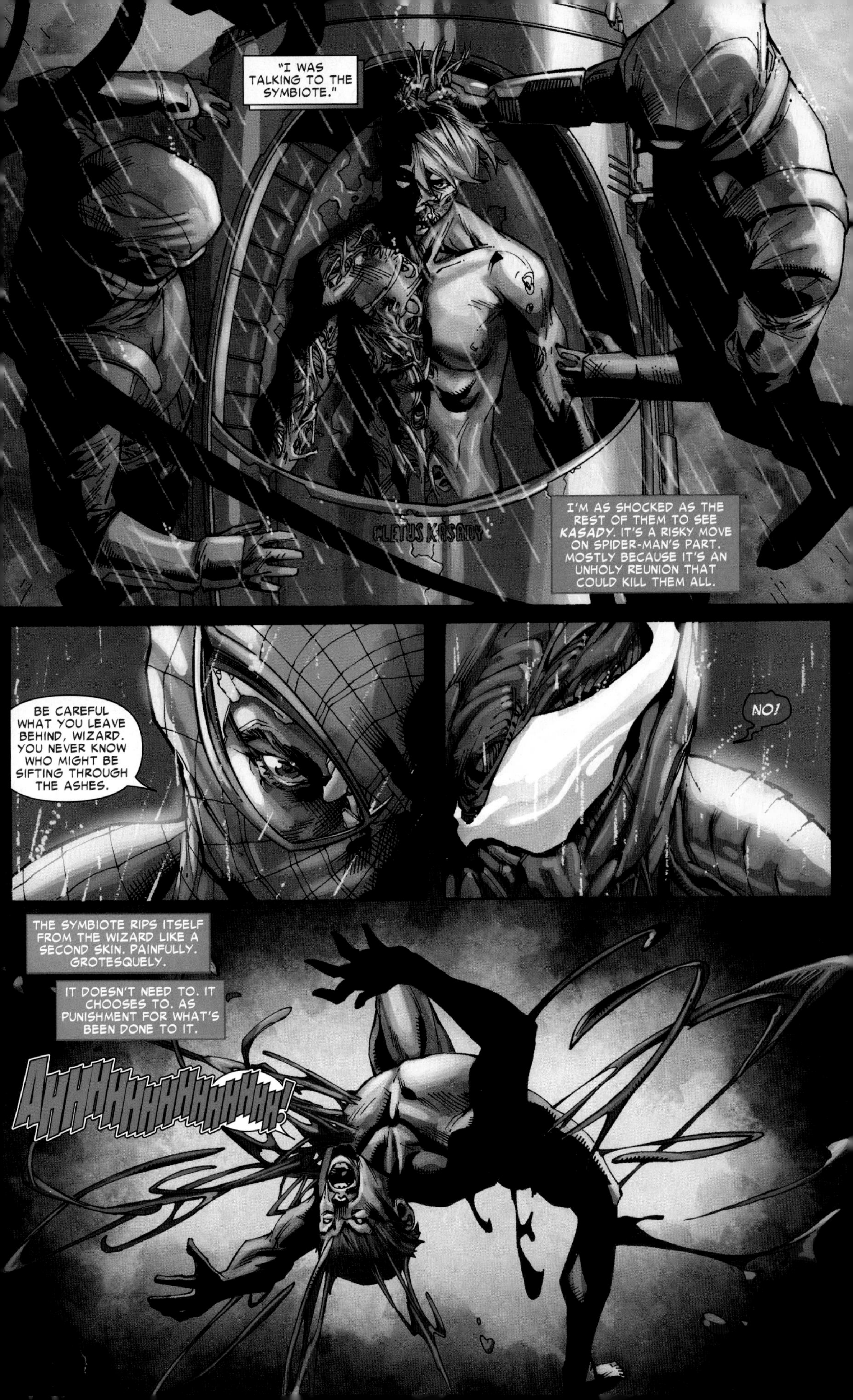
"I WAS TALKING TO THE SYMBIOTE."
CLETUS KASADY
I'M AS SHOCKED AS THE REST OF THEM TO SEE KASADY. IT'S A RISKY MOVE ON SPIDER-MAN'S PART. MOSTLY BECAUSE IT'S AN UNHOLY REUNION THAT COULD KILL THEM ALL.
BE CAREFUL WHAT YOU LEAVE BEHIND, WIZARD. YOU NEVER KNOW WHO MIGHT BE SIFTING THROUGH THE ASHES.
NO!
THE SYMBIOTE RIPS ITSELF FROM THE WIZARD LIKE A SECOND SKIN. PAINFULLY. GROTESQUELY.
IT DOESN'T NEED TO. IT CHOOSES TO. AS PUNISHMENT FOR WHAT'S BEEN DONE TO IT.
AHHHHHHHHHHHHH!

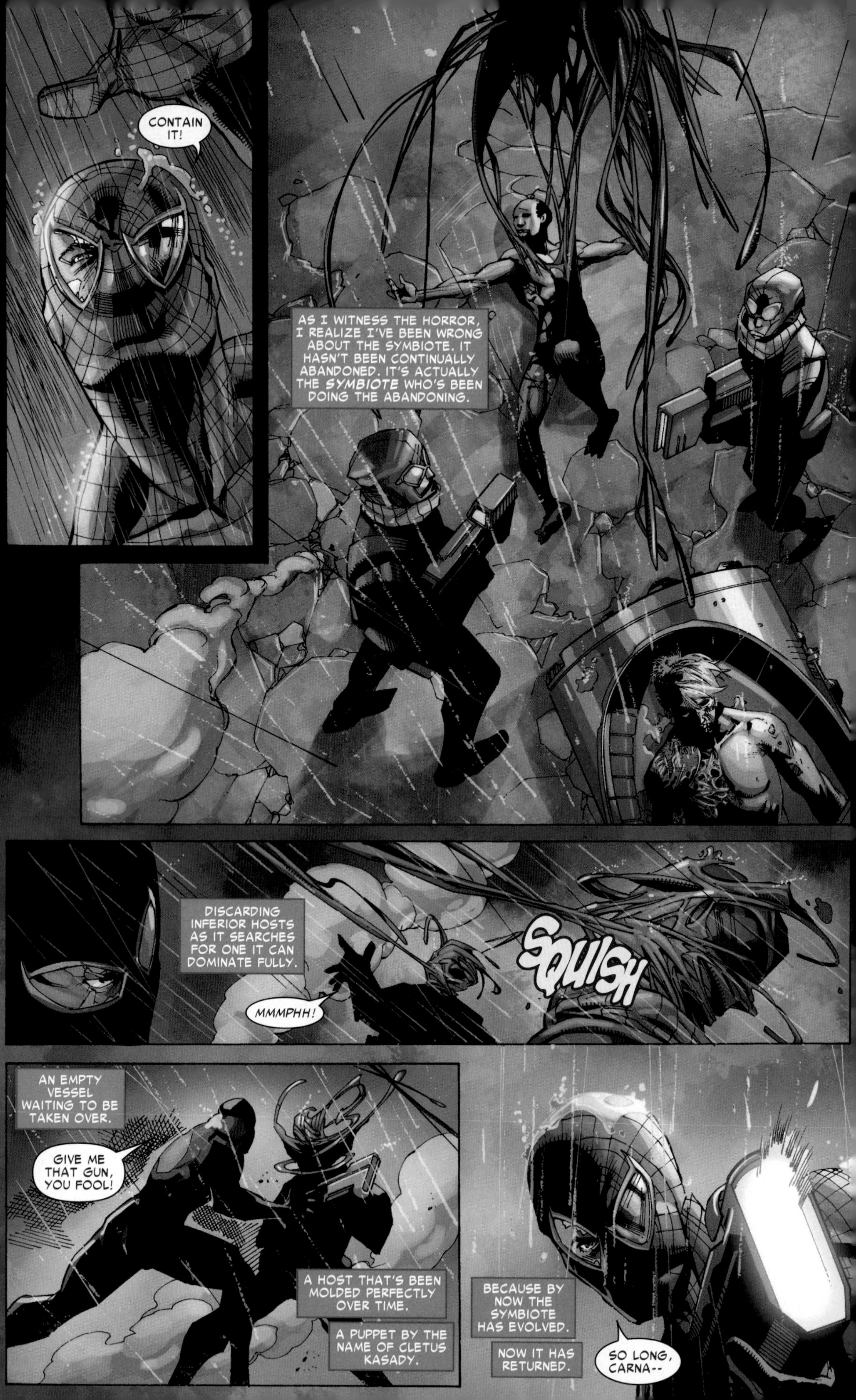

CONTAIN IT!
AS I WITNESS THE HORROR, I REALIZE I'VE BEEN WRONG ABOUT THE SYMBIOTE. IT HASN'T BEEN CONTINUALLY ABANDONED. IT'S ACTUALLY THE *SYMBIOTE* WHO'S BEEN DOING THE ABANDONING.
DISCARDING INFERIOR HOSTS AS IT SEARCHES FOR ONE IT CAN DOMINATE FULLY.
SQUISH
MMMPHH!
AN EMPTY VESSEL WAITING TO BE TAKEN OVER.
GIVE ME THAT GUN, YOU FOOL!
A HOST THAT'S BEEN MOLDED PERFECTLY OVER TIME.
A PUPPET BY THE NAME OF CLETUS KASADY.
BECAUSE BY NOW THE SYMBIOTE HAS EVOLVED.
NOW IT HAS RETURNED.
SO LONG, CARNA--

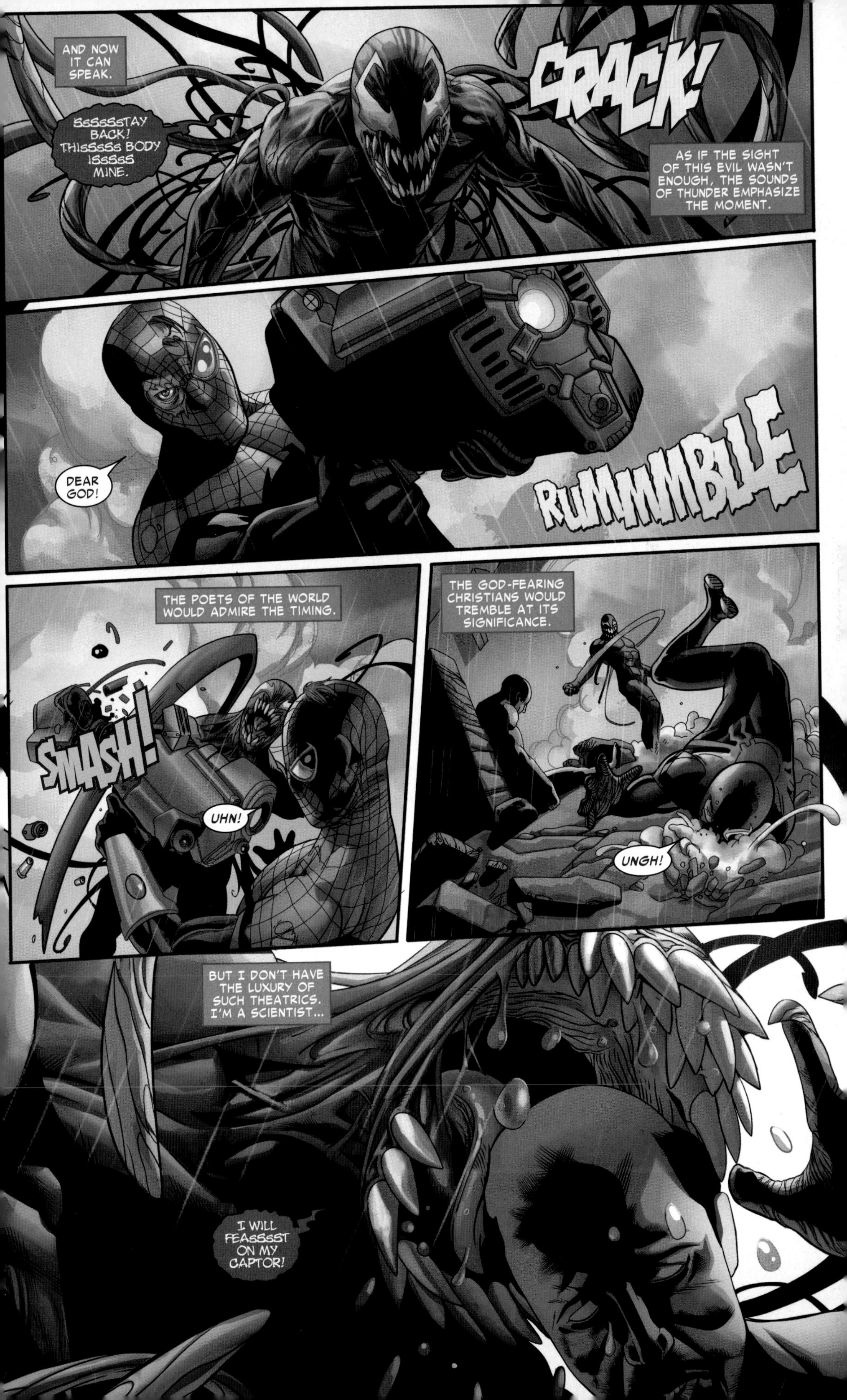
AND NOW IT CAN SPEAK.
SSSSSSTAY BACK! THISSSSS BODY ISSSSS MINE.
CRACK!
AS IF THE SIGHT OF THIS EVIL WASN'T ENOUGH, THE SOUNDS OF THUNDER EMPHASIZE THE MOMENT.
DEAR GOD!
RUMMMBLE
THE POETS OF THE WORLD WOULD ADMIRE THE TIMING.
SMASH!
UHN!
THE GOD-FEARING CHRISTIANS WOULD TREMBLE AT ITS SIGNIFICANCE.
UNGH!
BUT I DON'T HAVE THE LUXURY OF SUCH THEATRICS. I'M A SCIENTIST...
I WILL FEASSSST ON MY CAPTOR!

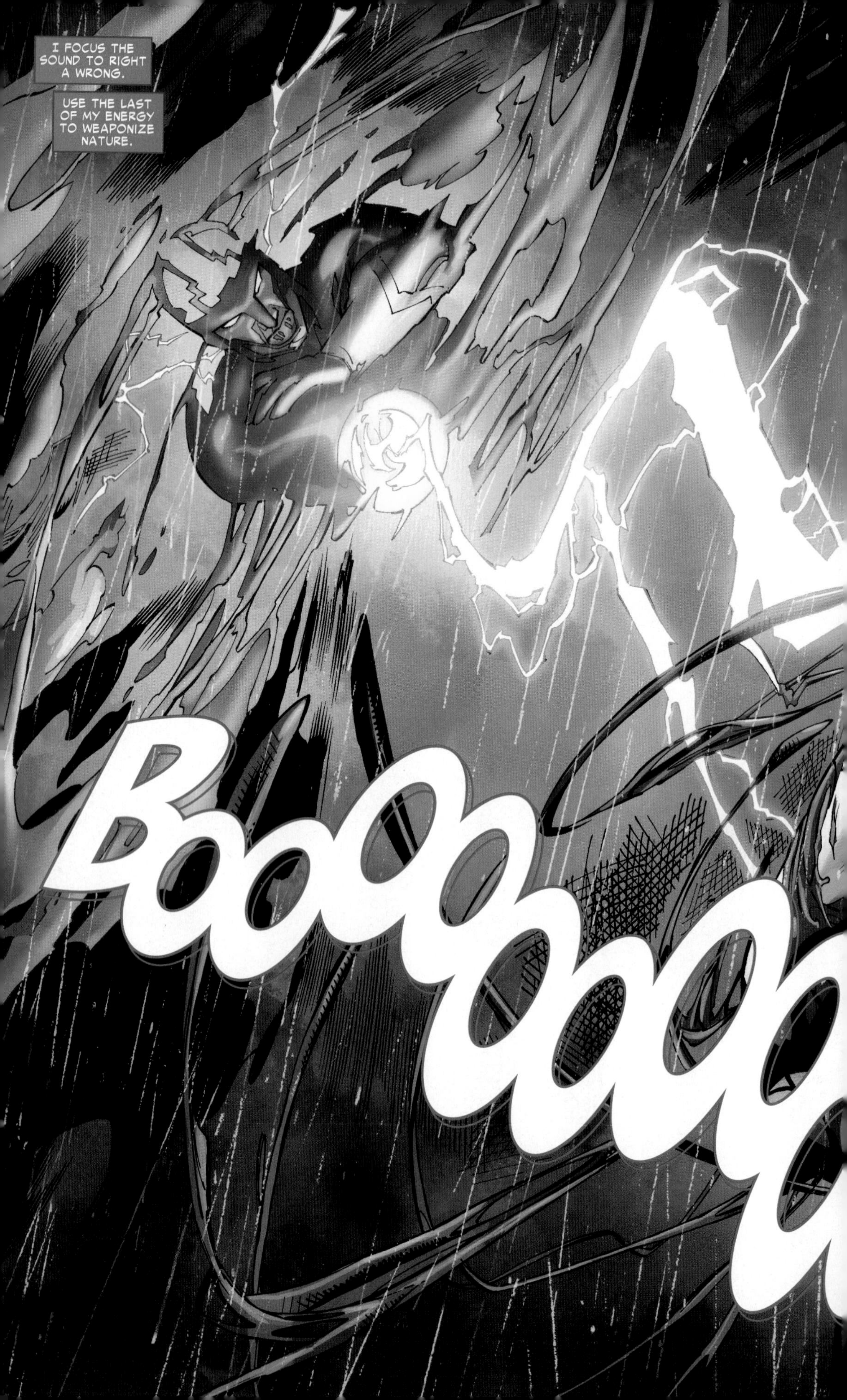
I FOCUS THE SOUND TO RIGHT A WRONG.
USE THE LAST OF MY ENERGY TO WEAPONIZE NATURE.
BOOOOOOOO

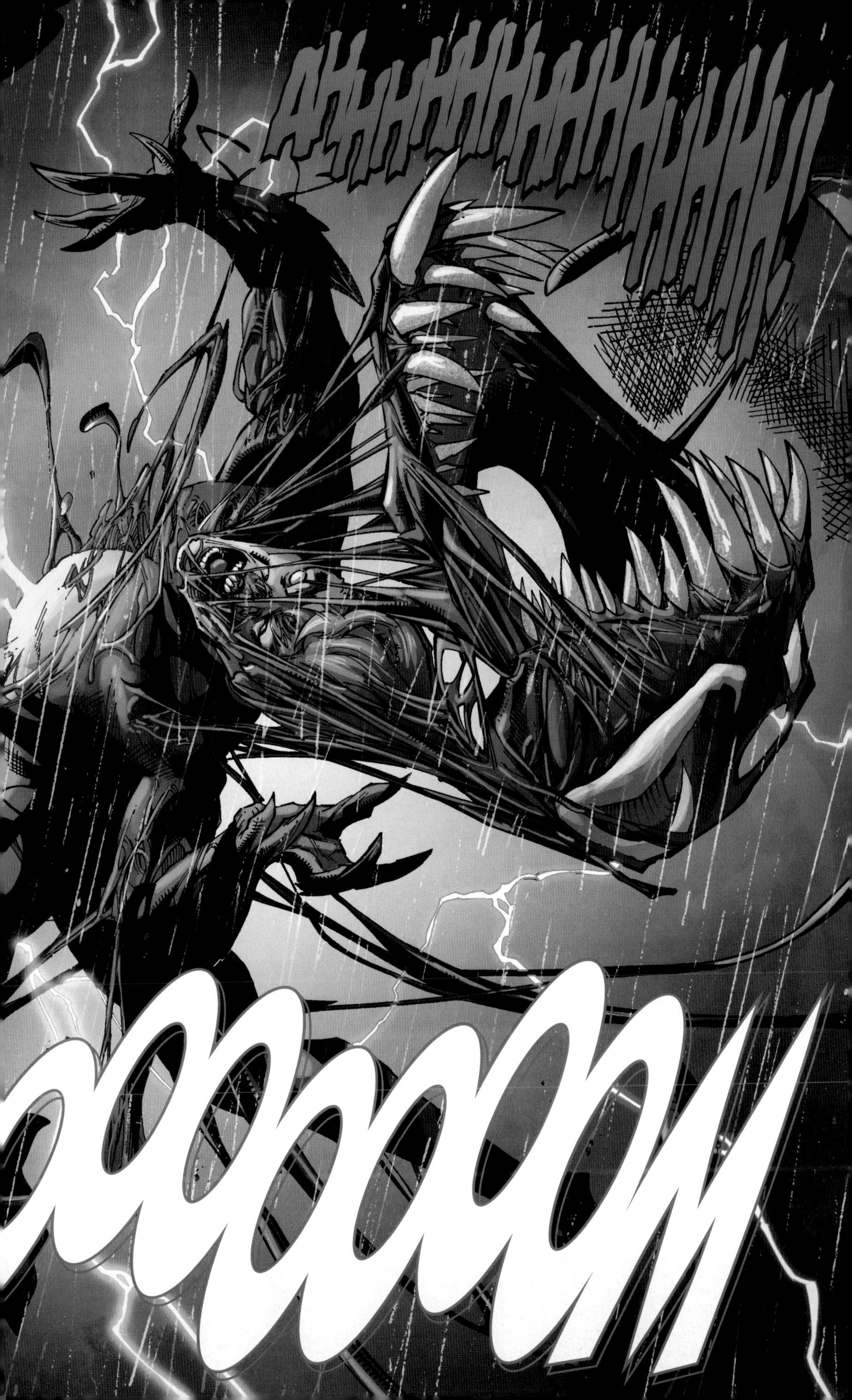
AHHHHHHHHHHHHH!

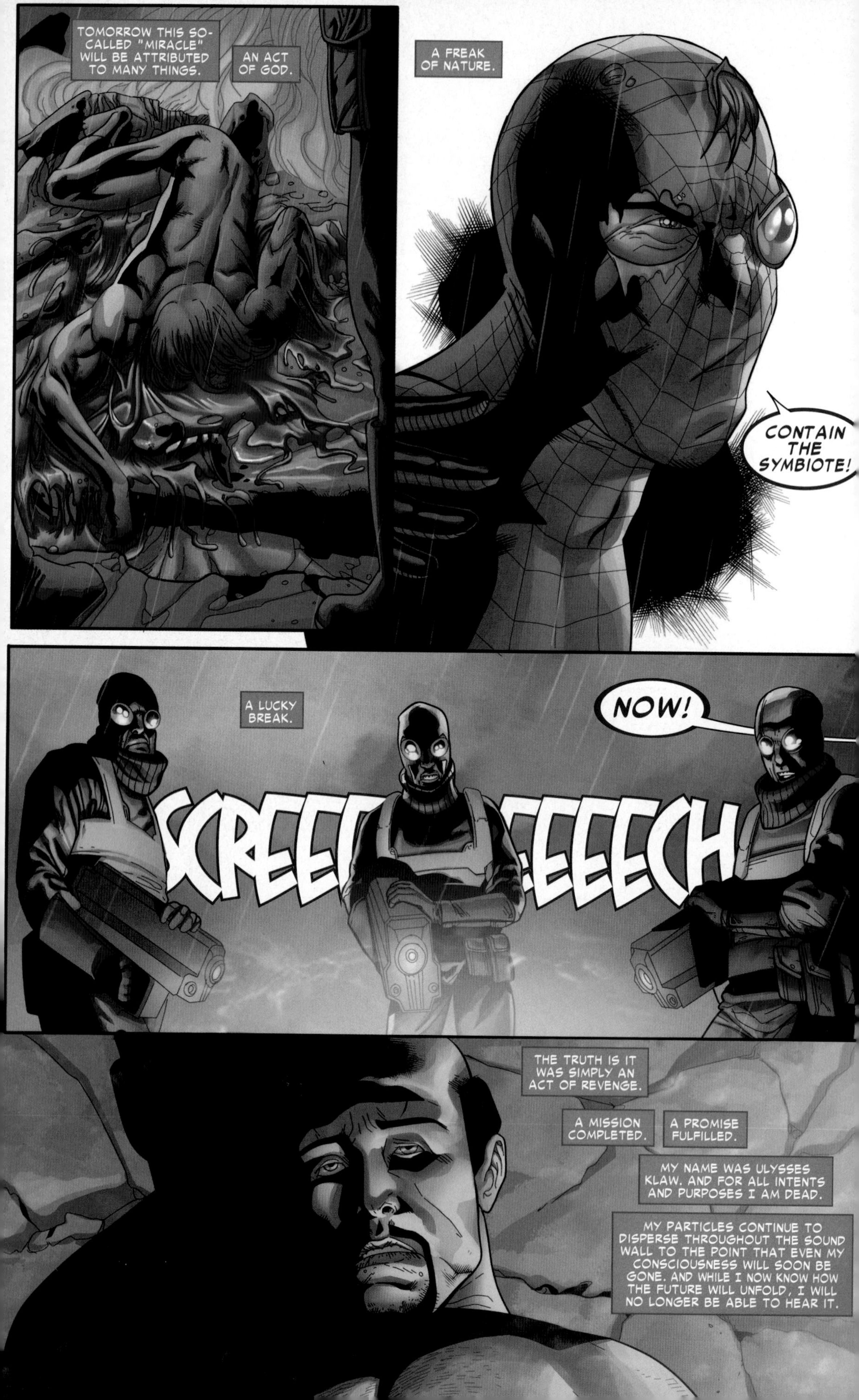
TOMORROW THIS SO-CALLED "MIRACLE" WILL BE ATTRIBUTED TO MANY THINGS.
AN ACT OF GOD.
A FREAK OF NATURE.
CONTAIN THE SYMBIOTE!
A LUCKY BREAK.
NOW!
SCREE... EEEECH
THE TRUTH IS IT WAS SIMPLY AN ACT OF REVENGE.
A MISSION COMPLETED.
A PROMISE FULFILLED.
MY NAME WAS ULYSSES KLAW. AND FOR ALL INTENTS AND PURPOSES I AM DEAD.
MY PARTICLES CONTINUE TO DISPERSE THROUGHOUT THE SOUND WALL TO THE POINT THAT EVEN MY CONSCIOUSNESS WILL SOON BE GONE. AND WHILE I NOW KNOW HOW THE FUTURE WILL UNFOLD, I WILL NO LONGER BE ABLE TO HEAR IT.

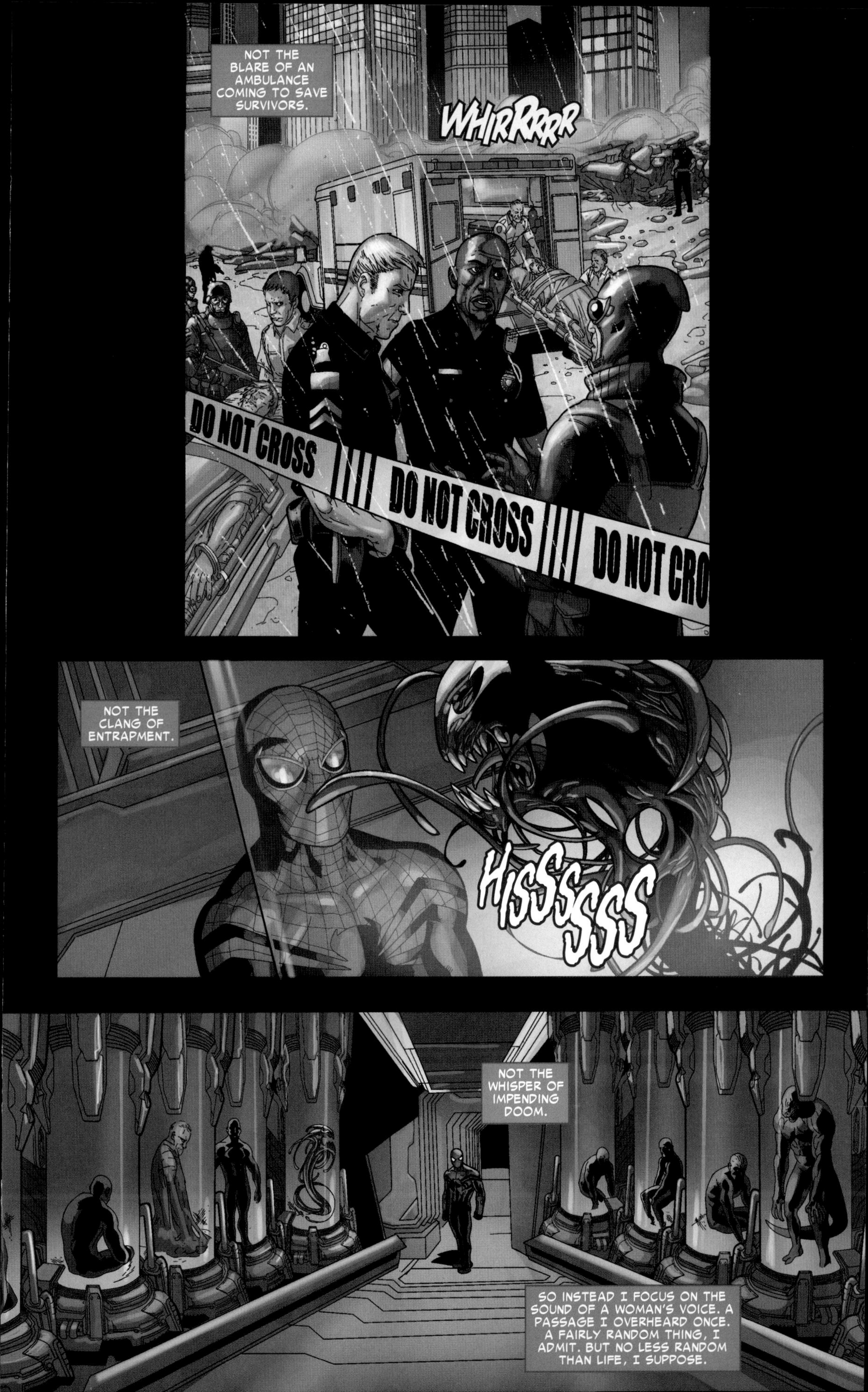
NOT THE BLARE OF AN AMBULANCE COMING TO SAVE SURVIVORS.
WHIRRRRR
DO NOT CROSS
DO NOT CROSS
DO NOT CRO
NOT THE CLANG OF ENTRAPMENT.
HISSSSSS
NOT THE WHISPER OF IMPENDING DOOM.
SO INSTEAD I FOCUS ON THE SOUND OF A WOMAN'S VOICE. A PASSAGE I OVERHEARD ONCE. A FAIRLY RANDOM THING, I ADMIT. BUT NO LESS RANDOM THAN LIFE, I SUPPOSE.

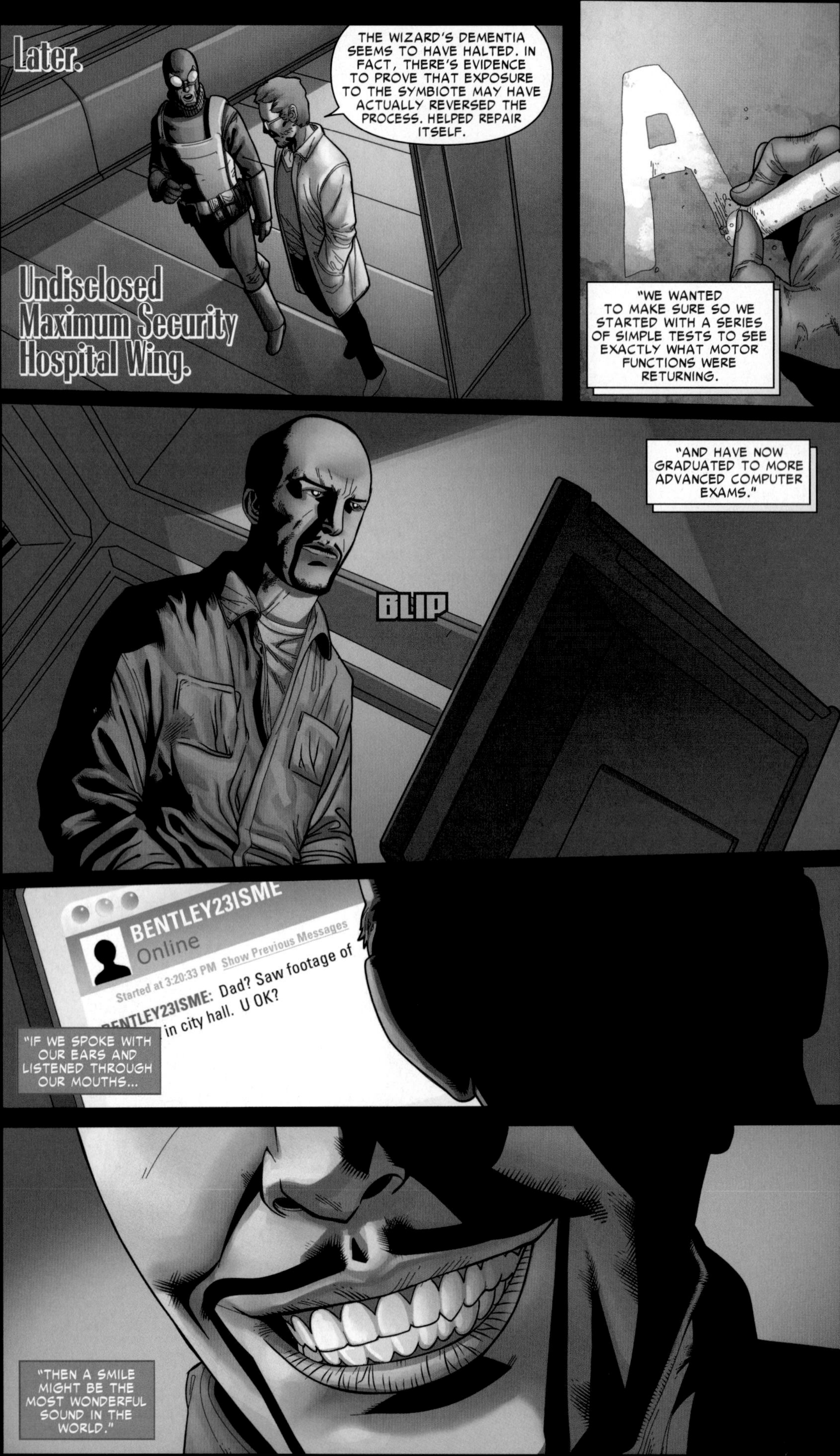
Later.
THE WIZARD'S DEMENTIA SEEMS TO HAVE HALTED. IN FACT, THERE'S EVIDENCE TO PROVE THAT EXPOSURE TO THE SYMBIOTE MAY HAVE ACTUALLY REVERSED THE PROCESS. HELPED REPAIR ITSELF.
Undisclosed Maximum Security Hospital Wing.
"WE WANTED TO MAKE SURE SO WE STARTED WITH A SERIES OF SIMPLE TESTS TO SEE EXACTLY WHAT MOTOR FUNCTIONS WERE RETURNING.
"AND HAVE NOW GRADUATED TO MORE ADVANCED COMPUTER EXAMS."
BLIP
BENTLEY23ISME
BENTLEY23ISME
Online
Show Previous Messages
Started at 3:20:33 PM
BENTLEY23ISME: Dad? Saw footage of in city hall. U OK?
"IF WE SPOKE WITH OUR EARS AND LISTENED THROUGH OUR MOUTHS...
"THEN A SMILE MIGHT BE THE MOST WONDERFUL SOUND IN THE WORLD."

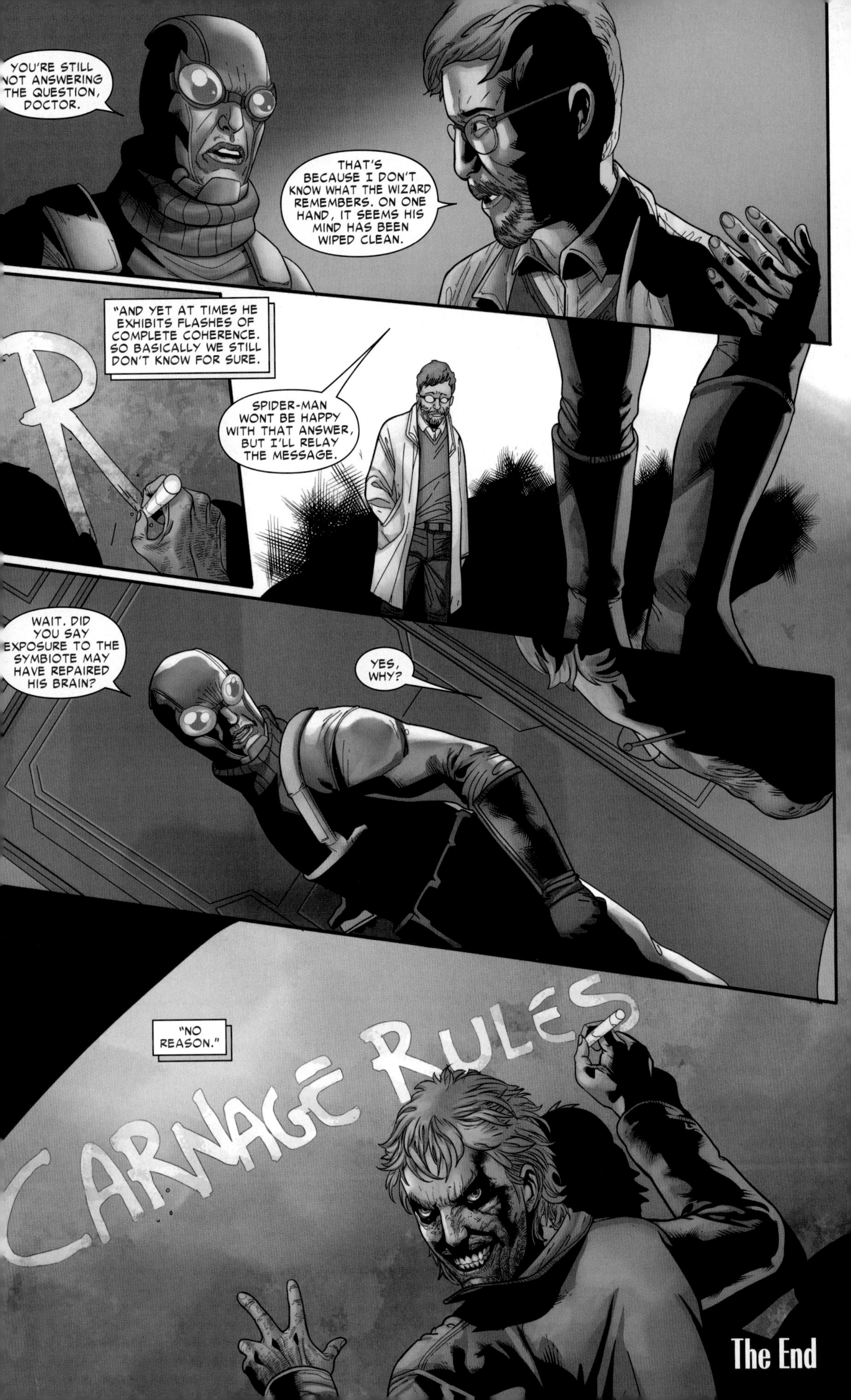
YOU'RE STILL NOT ANSWERING THE QUESTION, DOCTOR.
THAT'S BECAUSE I DON'T KNOW WHAT THE WIZARD REMEMBERS. ON ONE HAND, IT SEEMS HIS MIND HAS BEEN WIPED CLEAN.
"AND YET AT TIMES HE EXHIBITS FLASHES OF COMPLETE COHERENCE. SO BASICALLY WE STILL DON'T KNOW FOR SURE.
SPIDER-MAN WONT BE HAPPY WITH THAT ANSWER, BUT I'LL RELAY THE MESSAGE.
WAIT. DID YOU SAY EXPOSURE TO THE SYMBIOTE MAY HAVE REPAIRED HIS BRAIN?
YES, WHY?
"NO REASON."
CARNAGE RULES
The End

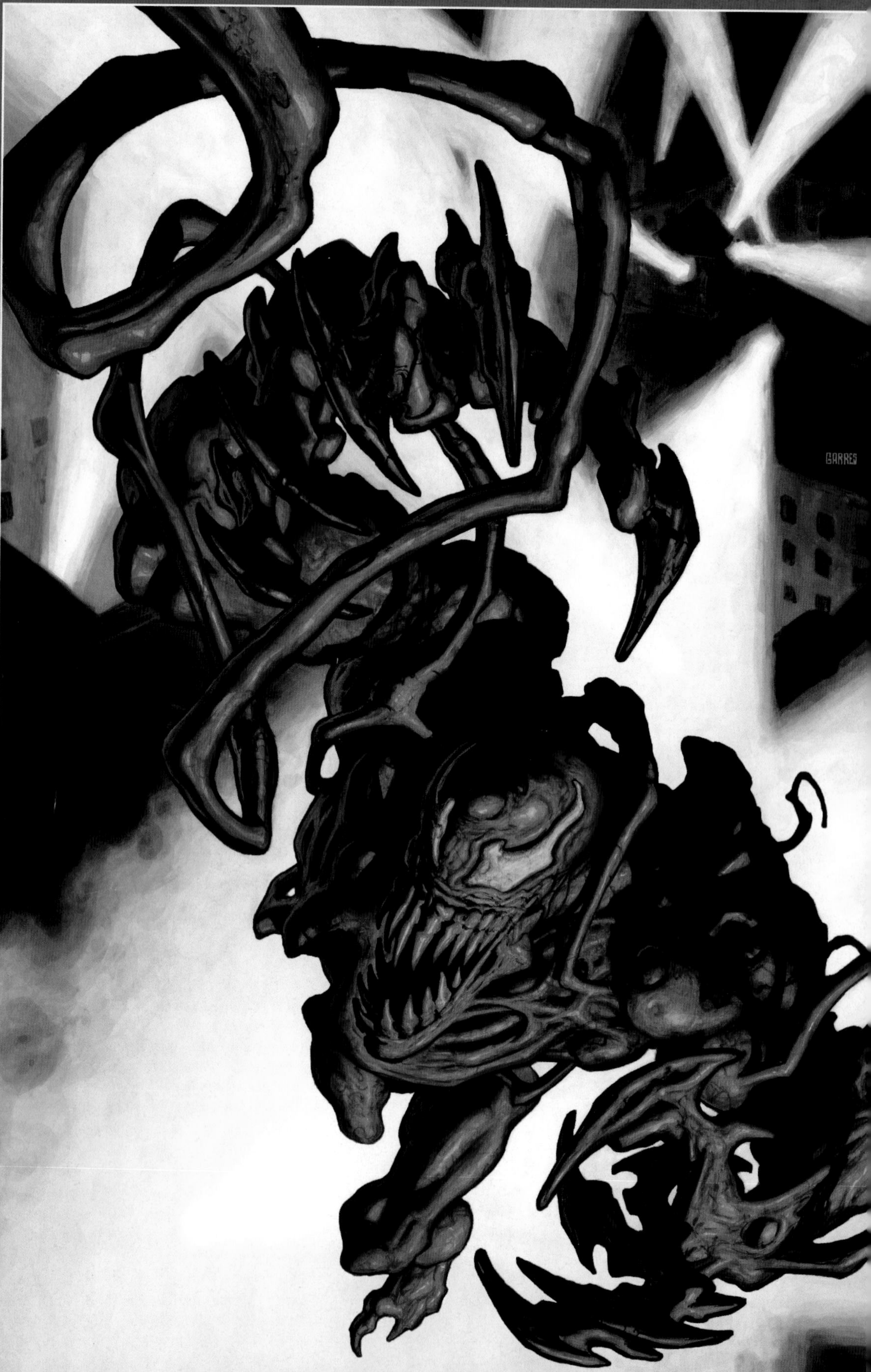
GARRES

SUPERIOR CARNAGE ANNUAL #1

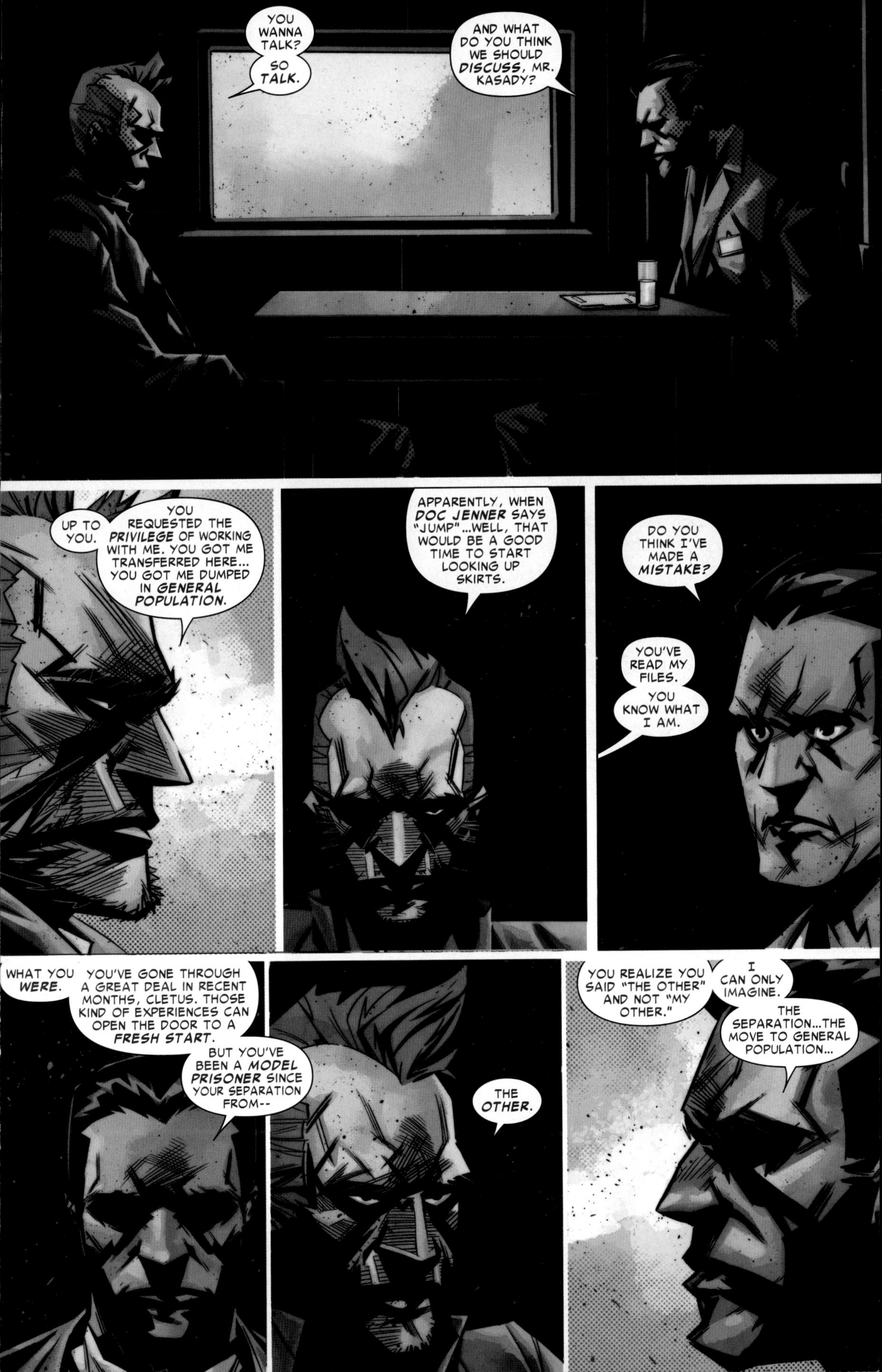

YOU WANNA TALK? SO TALK.
AND WHAT DO YOU THINK WE SHOULD DISCUSS, MR. KASADY?
UP TO YOU.
YOU REQUESTED THE PRIVILEGE OF WORKING WITH ME. YOU GOT ME TRANSFERRED HERE... YOU GOT ME DUMPED IN GENERAL POPULATION.
APPARENTLY, WHEN DOC JENNER SAYS "JUMP"...WELL, THAT WOULD BE A GOOD TIME TO START LOOKING UP SKIRTS.
DO YOU THINK I'VE MADE A MISTAKE?
YOU'VE READ MY FILES. YOU KNOW WHAT I AM.
WHAT YOU WERE.
YOU'VE GONE THROUGH A GREAT DEAL IN RECENT MONTHS, CLETUS. THOSE KIND OF EXPERIENCES CAN OPEN THE DOOR TO A FRESH START.
BUT YOU'VE BEEN A MODEL PRISONER SINCE YOUR SEPARATION FROM--
THE OTHER.
YOU REALIZE YOU SAID "THE OTHER" AND NOT "MY OTHER."
I CAN ONLY IMAGINE.
THE SEPARATION...THE MOVE TO GENERAL POPULATION...

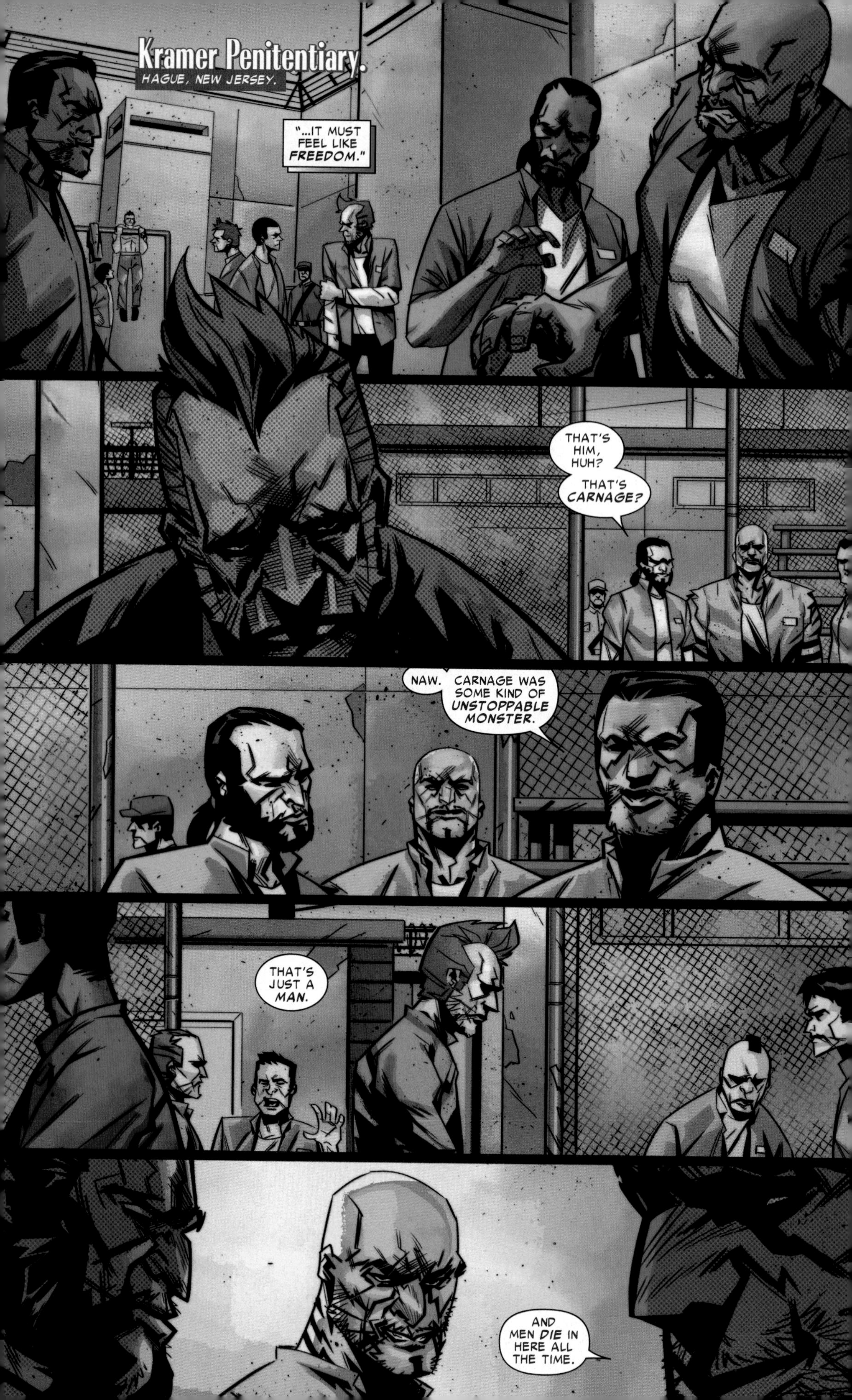
Kramer Penitentiary.
HAGUE, NEW JERSEY.
"...IT MUST FEEL LIKE FREEDOM."
THAT'S HIM, HUH?
THAT'S CARNAGE?
NAW.
CARNAGE WAS SOME KIND OF UNSTOPPABLE MONSTER.
THAT'S JUST A MAN.
AND MEN DIE IN HERE ALL THE TIME.

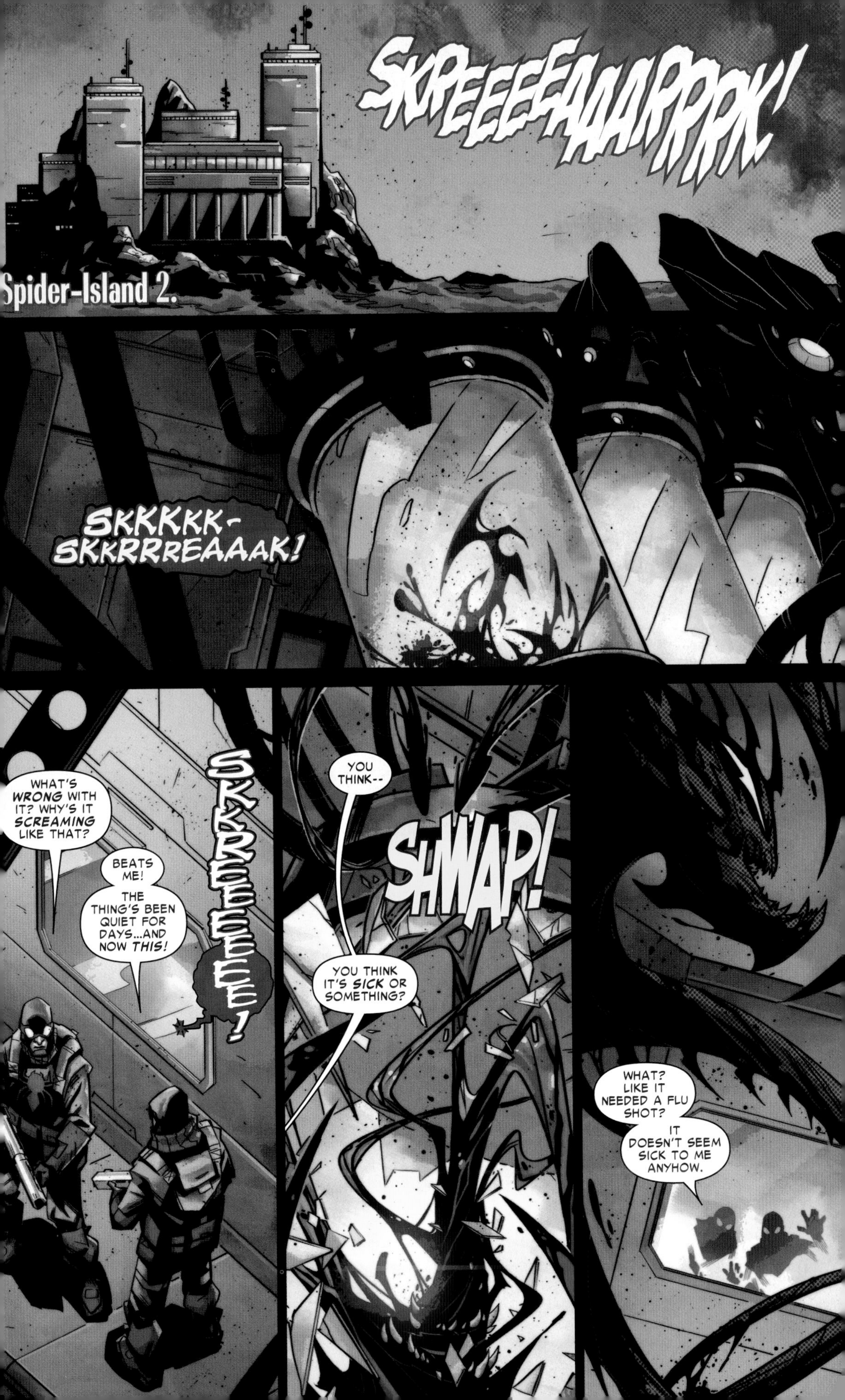
SKREEEEEAAARRRRK!
Spider-Island 2.
SKKKKK-
SKKRRREAAAK!
WHAT'S WRONG WITH IT? WHY'S IT SCREAMING LIKE THAT?
SKKRREEEEEE!
BEATS ME!
THE THING'S BEEN QUIET FOR DAYS...AND NOW THIS!
YOU THINK--
SHWAP!
YOU THINK IT'S SICK OR SOMETHING?
WHAT? LIKE IT NEEDED A FLU SHOT?
IT DOESN'T SEEM SICK TO ME ANYHOW.

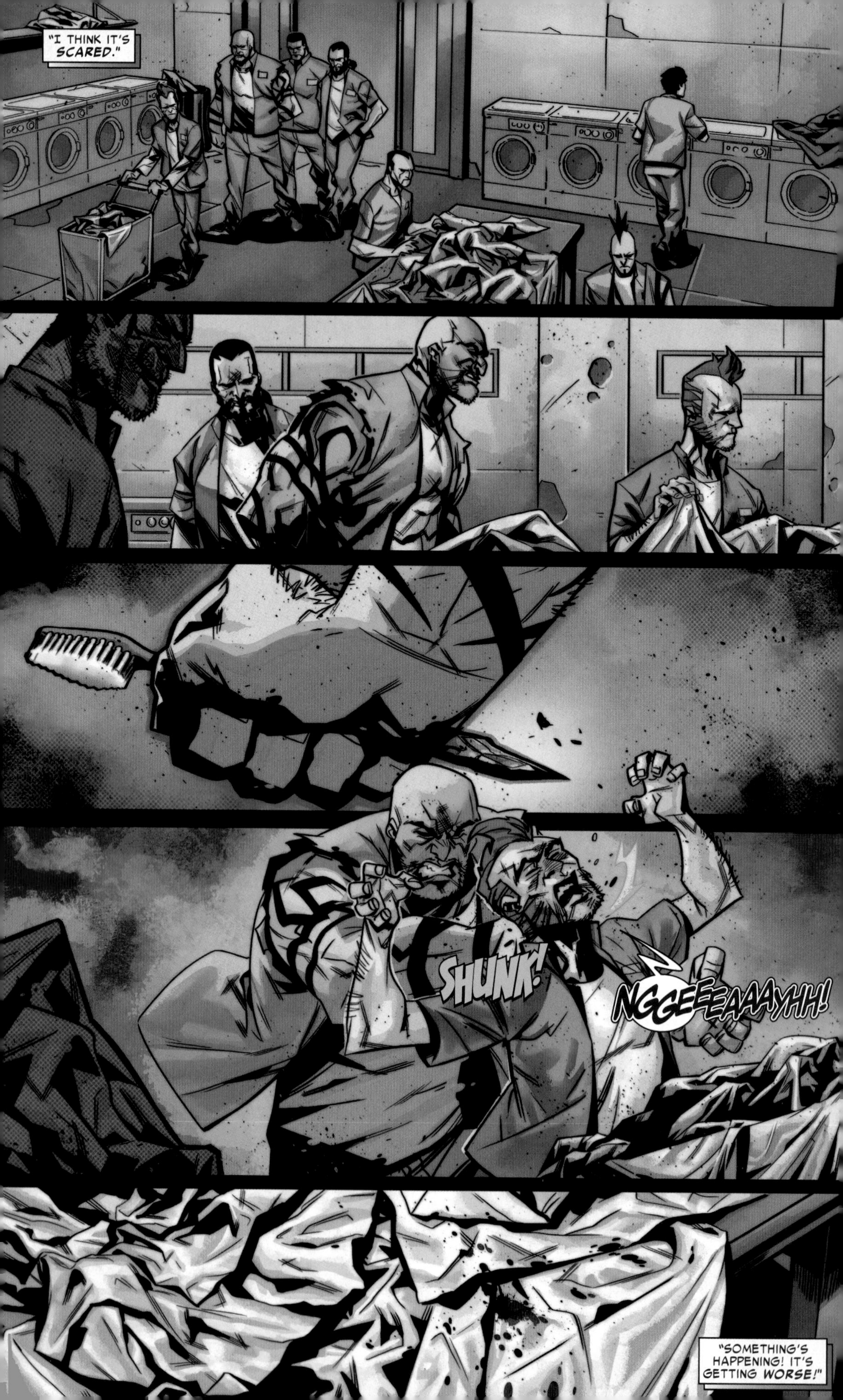
"I THINK IT'S SCARED."
SHUNK!
NGGEEEAAAYHH!
"SOMETHING'S HAPPENING! IT'S GETTING WORSE!"

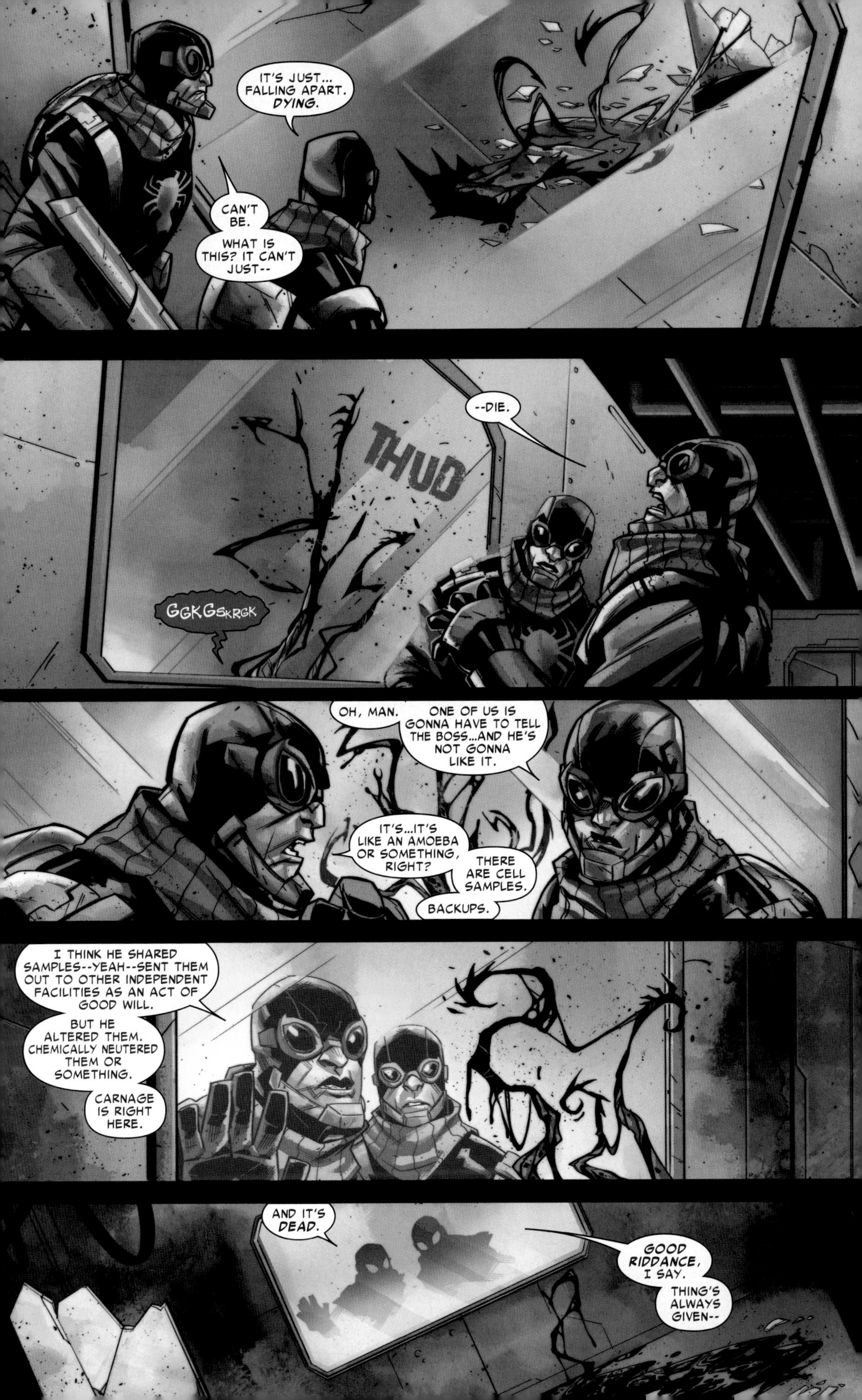
IT'S JUST... FALLING APART. DYING.
CAN'T BE.
WHAT IS THIS? IT CAN'T JUST--
--DIE.
THUD
GGKGSKRGK
OH, MAN.
ONE OF US IS GONNA HAVE TO TELL THE BOSS...AND HE'S NOT GONNA LIKE IT.
IT'S...IT'S LIKE AN AMOEBA OR SOMETHING, RIGHT?
THERE ARE CELL SAMPLES.
BACKUPS.
I THINK HE SHARED SAMPLES--YEAH--SENT THEM OUT TO OTHER INDEPENDENT FACILITIES AS AN ACT OF GOOD WILL.
BUT HE ALTERED THEM. CHEMICALLY NEUTERED THEM OR SOMETHING.
CARNAGE IS RIGHT HERE.
AND IT'S DEAD.
GOOD RIDDANCE, I SAY.
THING'S ALWAYS GIVEN--

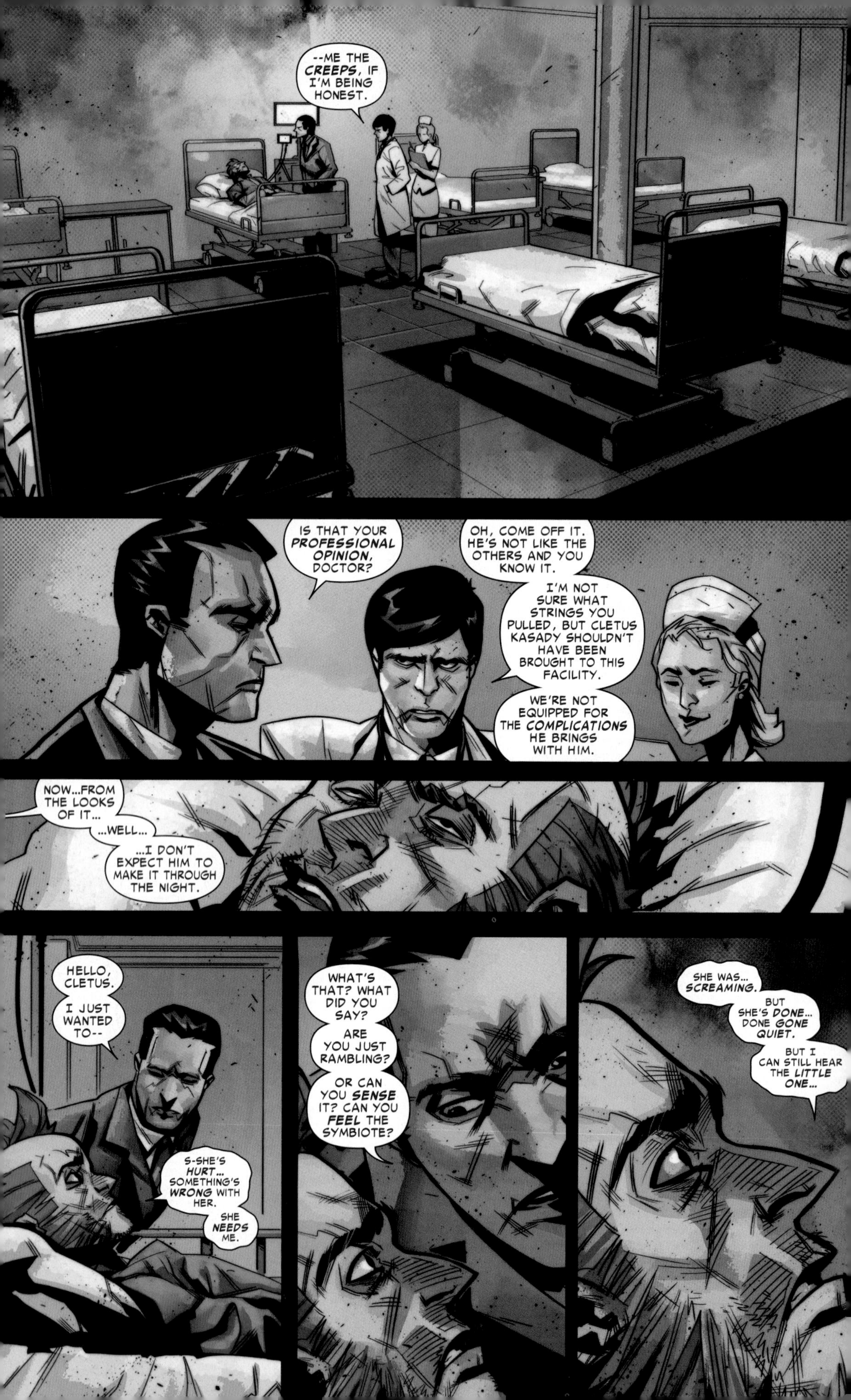
--ME THE CREEPS, IF I'M BEING HONEST.
IS THAT YOUR PROFESSIONAL OPINION, DOCTOR?
OH, COME OFF IT. HE'S NOT LIKE THE OTHERS AND YOU KNOW IT.
I'M NOT SURE WHAT STRINGS YOU PULLED, BUT CLETUS KASADY SHOULDN'T HAVE BEEN BROUGHT TO THIS FACILITY.
WE'RE NOT EQUIPPED FOR THE COMPLICATIONS HE BRINGS WITH HIM.
NOW...FROM THE LOOKS OF IT...
...WELL...
...I DON'T EXPECT HIM TO MAKE IT THROUGH THE NIGHT.
HELLO, CLETUS.
I JUST WANTED TO--
S-SHE'S HURT... SOMETHING'S WRONG WITH HER.
SHE NEEDS ME.
WHAT'S THAT? WHAT DID YOU SAY?
ARE YOU JUST RAMBLING?
OR CAN YOU SENSE IT? CAN YOU FEEL THE SYMBIOTE?
SHE WAS... SCREAMING.
BUT SHE'S DONE... DONE GONE QUIET.
BUT I CAN STILL HEAR THE LITTLE ONE...

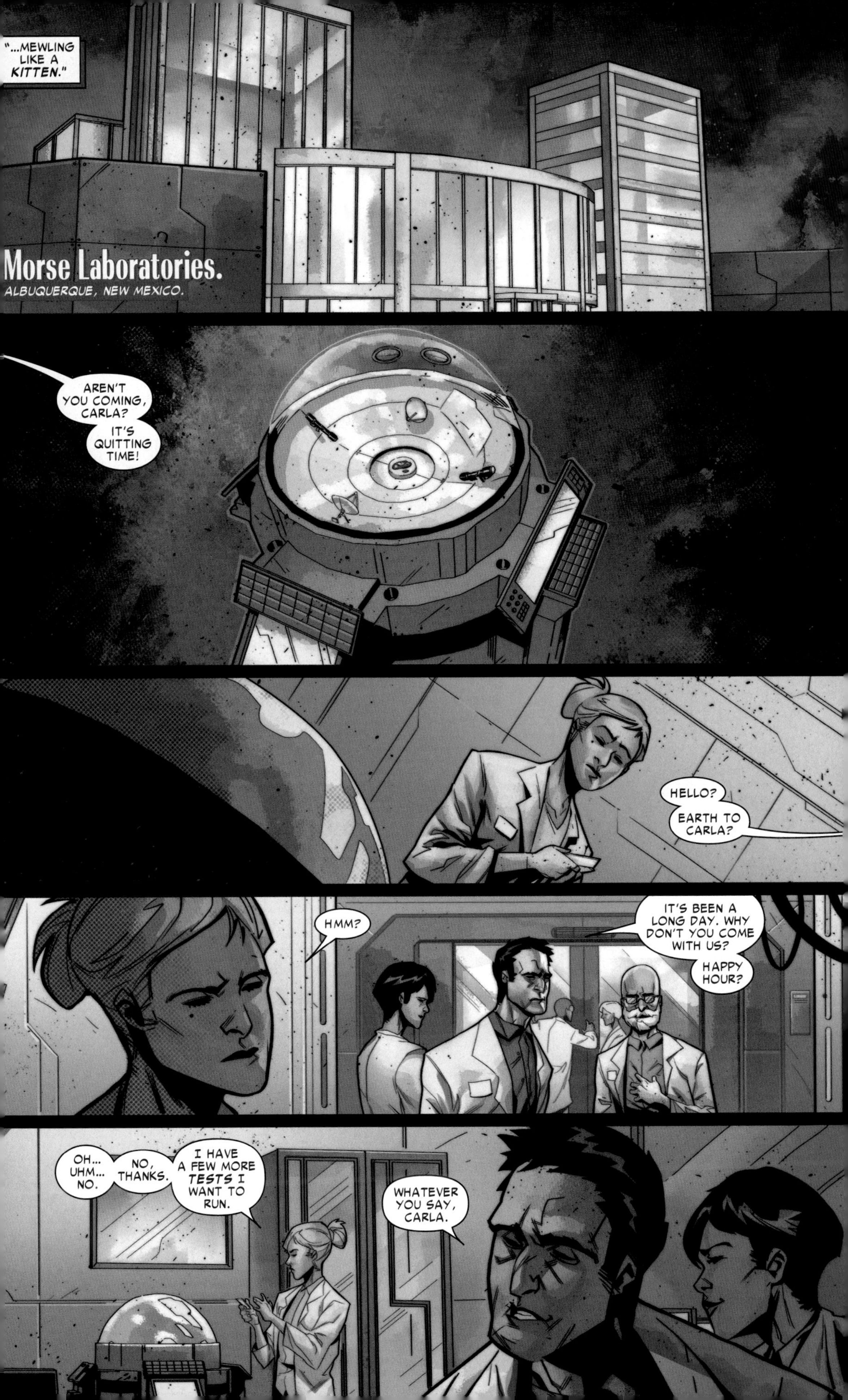
"...MEWLING LIKE A KITTEN."
Morse Laboratories.
ALBUQUERQUE, NEW MEXICO.
AREN'T YOU COMING, CARLA?
IT'S QUITTING TIME!
HELLO?
EARTH TO CARLA?
HMM?
IT'S BEEN A LONG DAY. WHY DON'T YOU COME WITH US?
HAPPY HOUR?
OH... UHM... NO.
NO, THANKS.
I HAVE A FEW MORE TESTS I WANT TO RUN.
WHATEVER YOU SAY, CARLA.

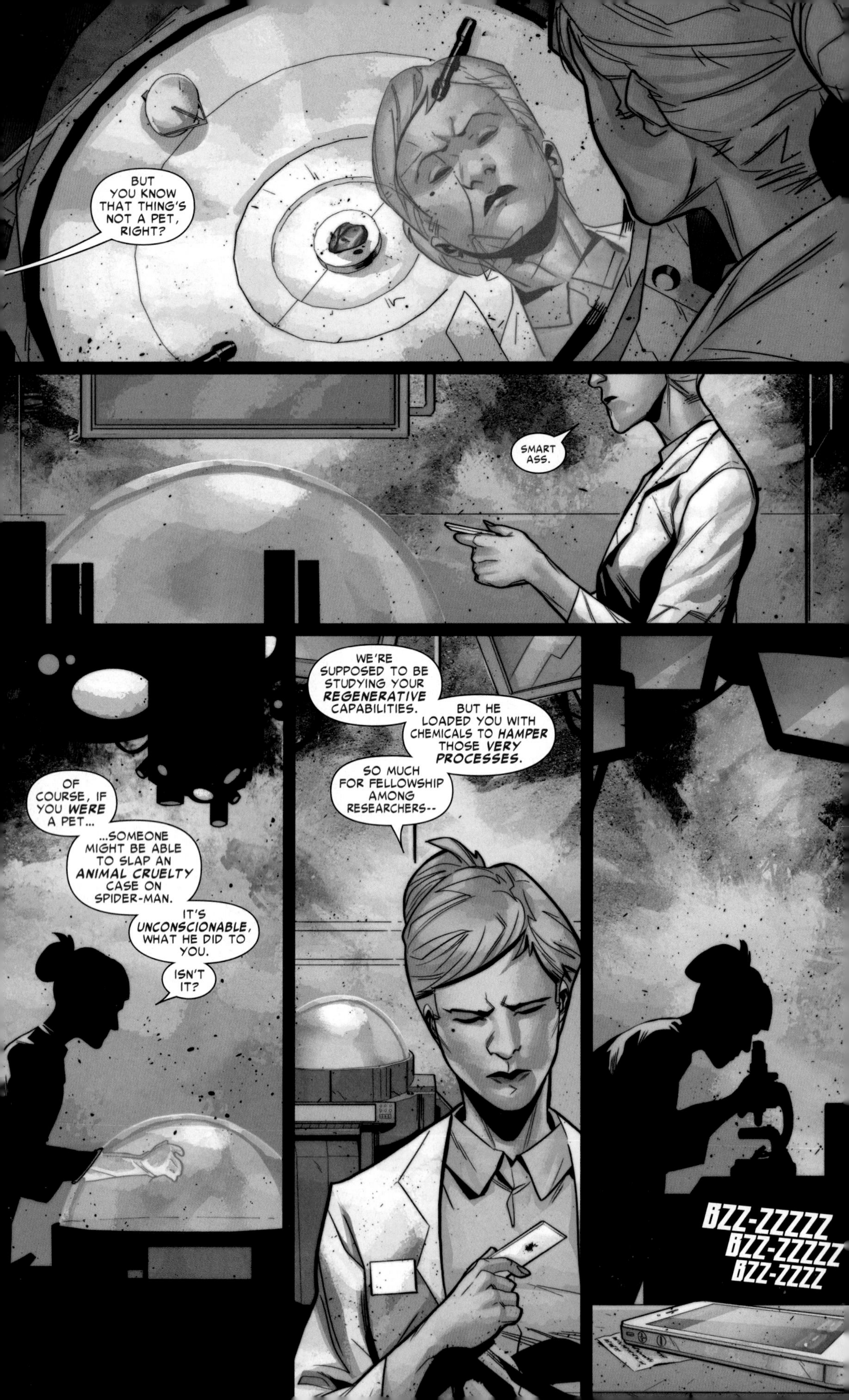

BUT YOU KNOW THAT THING'S NOT A PET, RIGHT?
SMART ASS.
OF COURSE, IF YOU WERE A PET...
...SOMEONE MIGHT BE ABLE TO SLAP AN ANIMAL CRUELTY CASE ON SPIDER-MAN.
IT'S UNCONSCIONABLE, WHAT HE DID TO YOU.
ISN'T IT?
WE'RE SUPPOSED TO BE STUDYING YOUR REGENERATIVE CAPABILITIES.
BUT HE LOADED YOU WITH CHEMICALS TO HAMPER THOSE VERY PROCESSES.
SO MUCH FOR FELLOWSHIP AMONG RESEARCHERS--
BZZ-ZZZZZ
BZZ-ZZZZZ
BZZ-ZZZZ

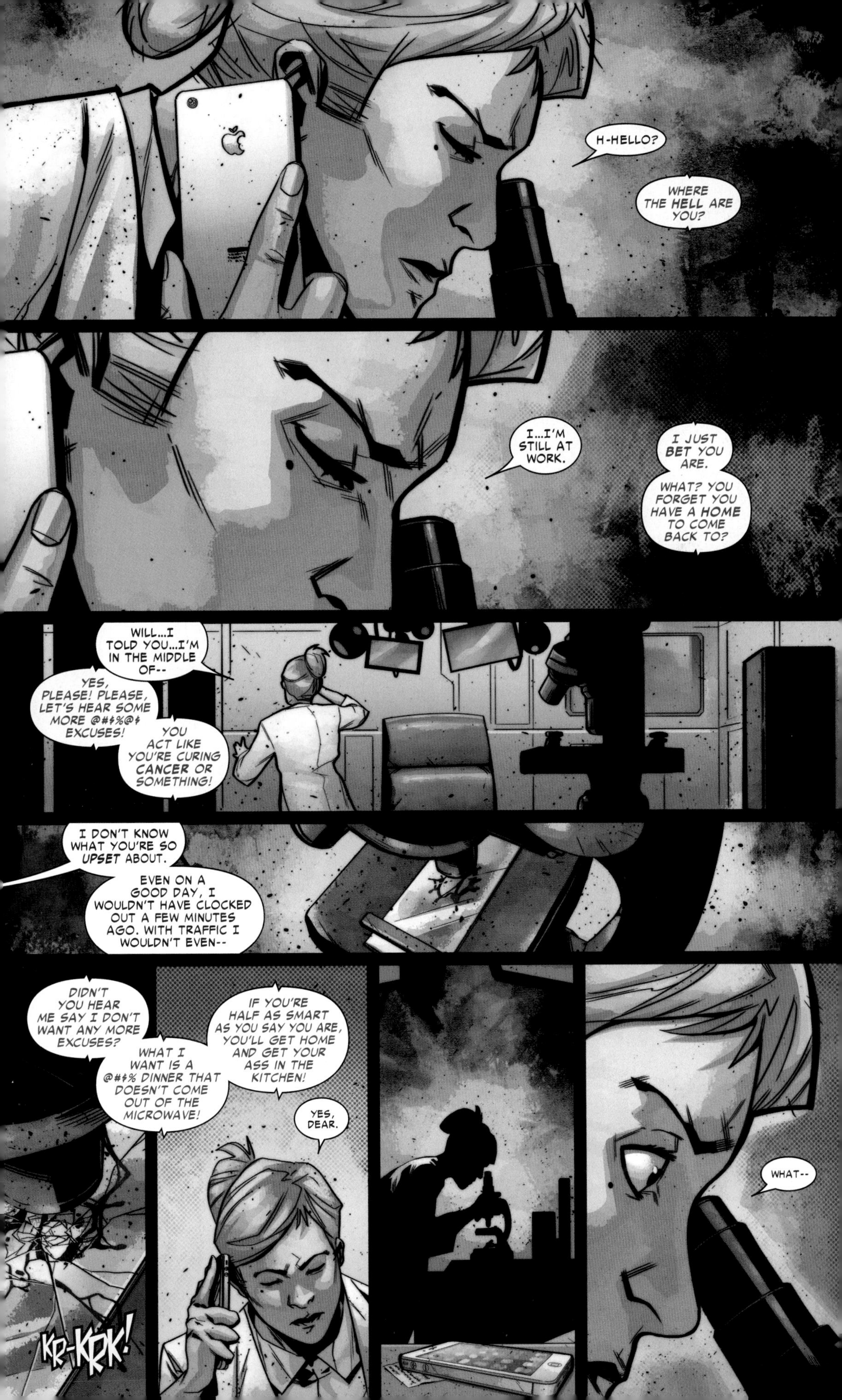
H-HELLO?
WHERE THE HELL ARE YOU?
I...I'M STILL AT WORK.
I JUST BET YOU ARE.
WHAT? YOU FORGET YOU HAVE A HOME TO COME BACK TO?
WILL...I TOLD YOU...I'M IN THE MIDDLE OF--
YES, PLEASE! PLEASE, LET'S HEAR SOME MORE @#$%@$ EXCUSES!
YOU ACT LIKE YOU'RE CURING CANCER OR SOMETHING!
I DON'T KNOW WHAT YOU'RE SO UPSET ABOUT.
EVEN ON A GOOD DAY, I WOULDN'T HAVE CLOCKED OUT A FEW MINUTES AGO. WITH TRAFFIC I WOULDN'T EVEN--
DIDN'T YOU HEAR ME SAY I DON'T WANT ANY MORE EXCUSES?
WHAT I WANT IS A @#$% DINNER THAT DOESN'T COME OUT OF THE MICROWAVE!
IF YOU'RE HALF AS SMART AS YOU SAY YOU ARE, YOU'LL GET HOME AND GET YOUR ASS IN THE KITCHEN!
YES, DEAR.
KR-KRK!
WHAT--

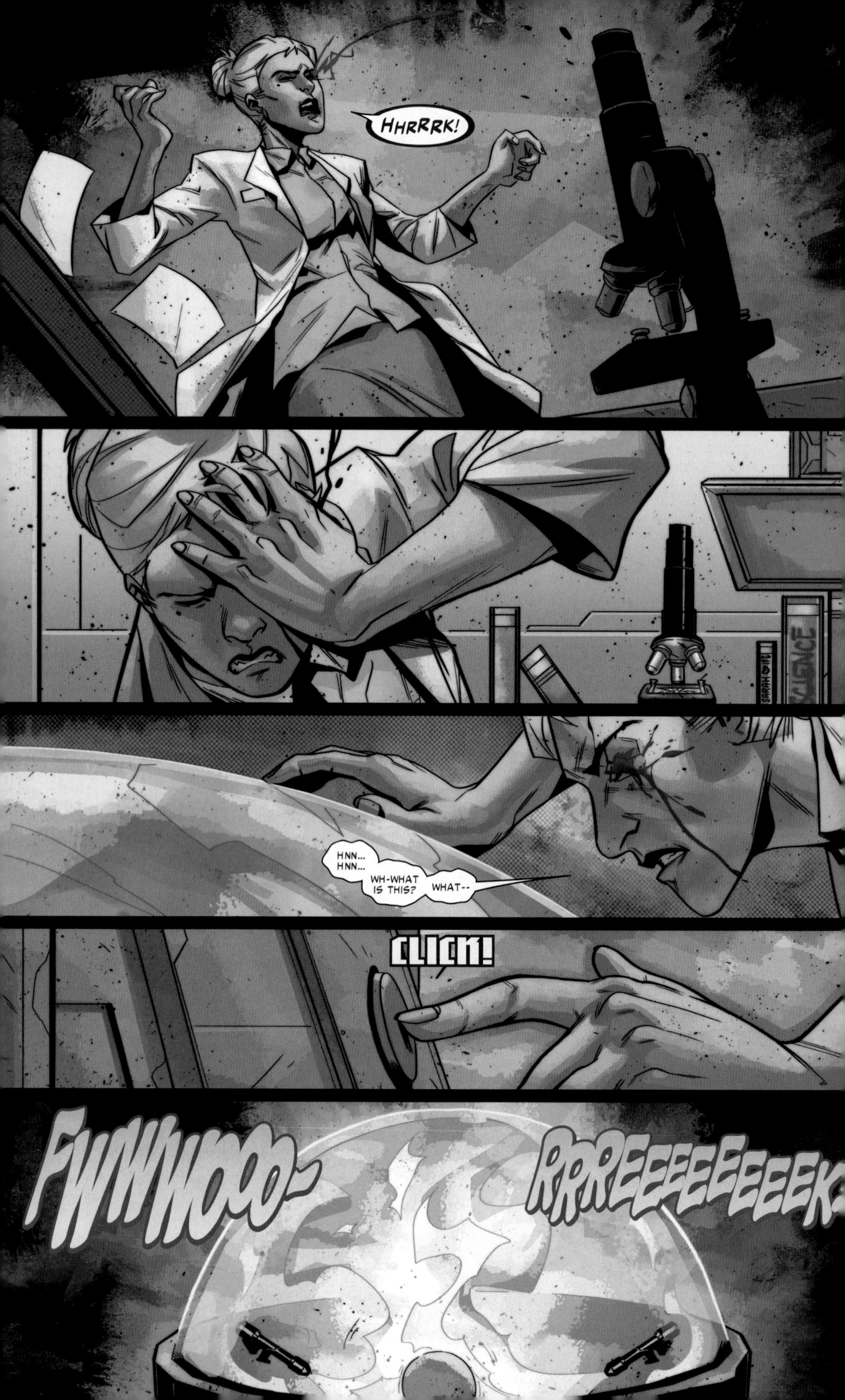
HHRRRK!
HNN... HNN...
WH-WHAT IS THIS? WHAT--
CLICK!
FWWHOOO-
RRRREEEEEEEEEK

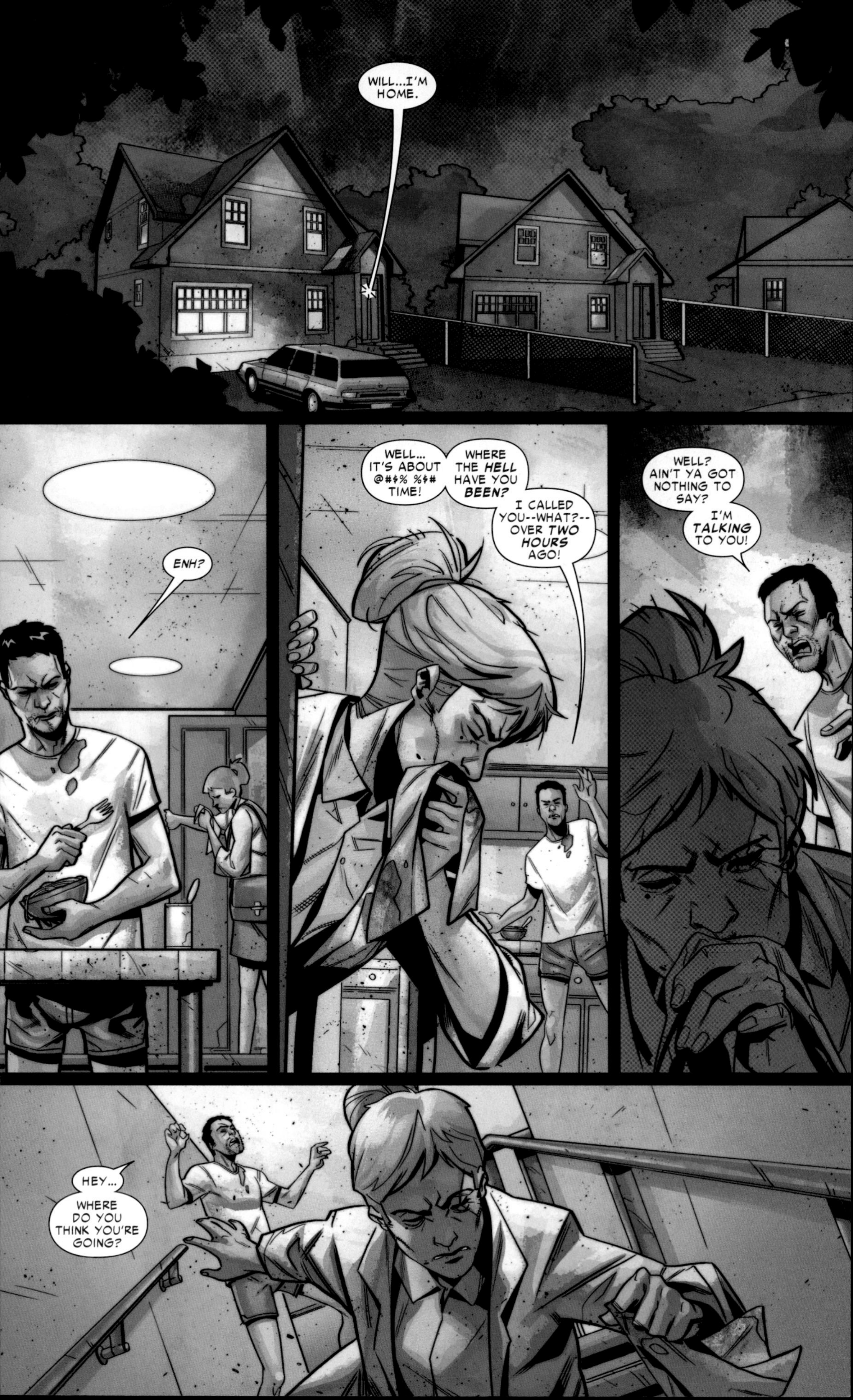
WILL...I'M HOME.
ENH?
WELL... IT'S ABOUT @#$% %$# TIME!
WHERE THE *HELL* HAVE YOU *BEEN?*
I CALLED YOU--WHAT?-- OVER *TWO HOURS* AGO!
WELL? AIN'T YA GOT NOTHING TO SAY?
I'M *TALKING* TO YOU!
HEY...
WHERE DO YOU THINK YOU'RE GOING?

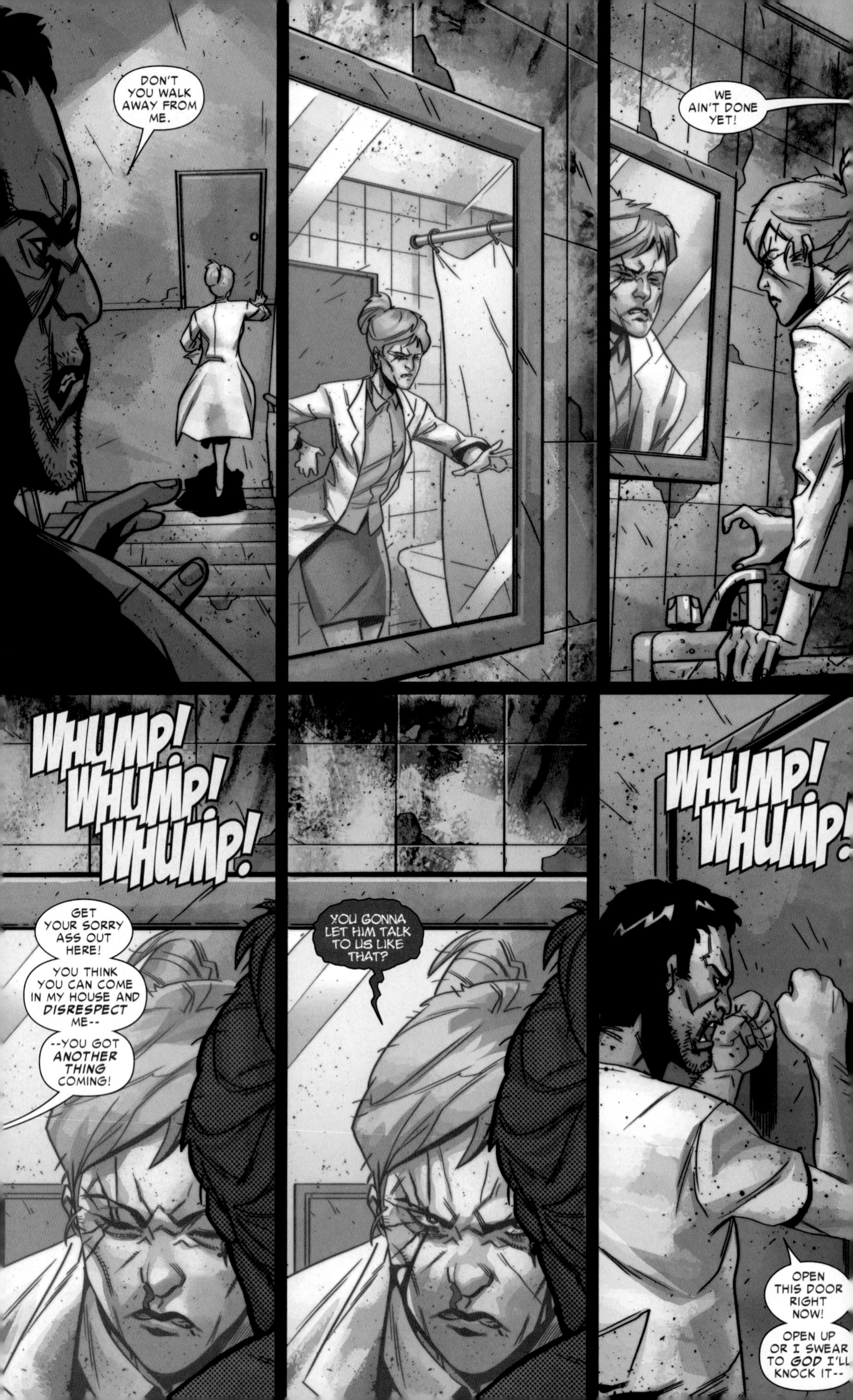
DON'T YOU WALK AWAY FROM ME.
WE AIN'T DONE YET!
WHUMP! WHUMP! WHUMP!
GET YOUR SORRY ASS OUT HERE!
YOU THINK YOU CAN COME IN MY HOUSE AND DISRESPECT ME--
--YOU GOT ANOTHER THING COMING!
YOU GONNA LET HIM TALK TO US LIKE THAT?
WHUMP! WHUMP!
OPEN THIS DOOR RIGHT NOW!
OPEN UP OR I SWEAR TO GOD I'LL KNOCK IT--

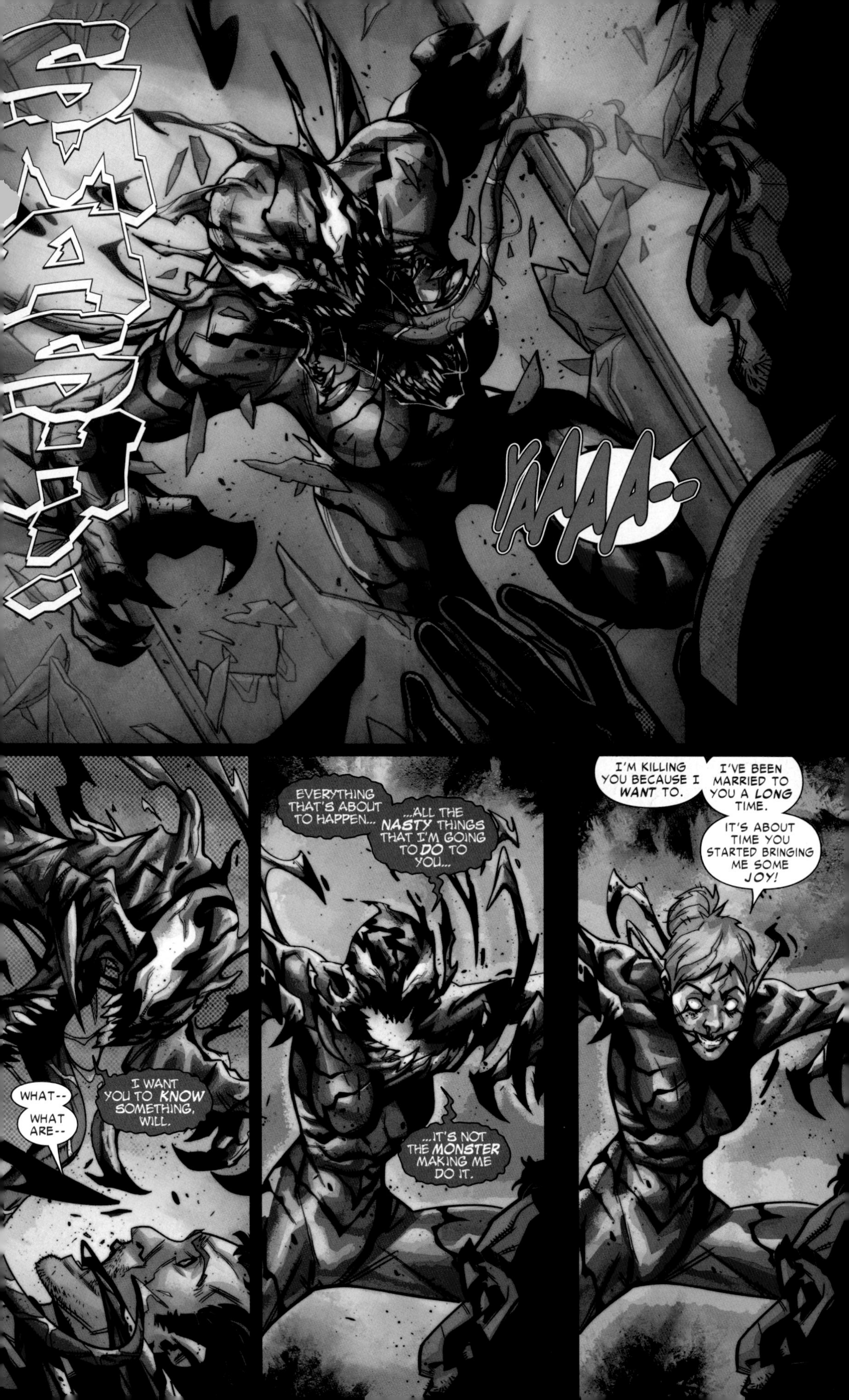
YAAAA--
WHAT--
WHAT ARE--
I WANT YOU TO KNOW SOMETHING, WILL.
EVERYTHING THAT'S ABOUT TO HAPPEN...
...ALL THE NASTY THINGS THAT I'M GOING TO DO TO YOU...
...IT'S NOT THE MONSTER MAKING ME DO IT.
I'M KILLING YOU BECAUSE I WANT TO.
I'VE BEEN MARRIED TO YOU A LONG TIME.
IT'S ABOUT TIME YOU STARTED BRINGING ME SOME JOY!

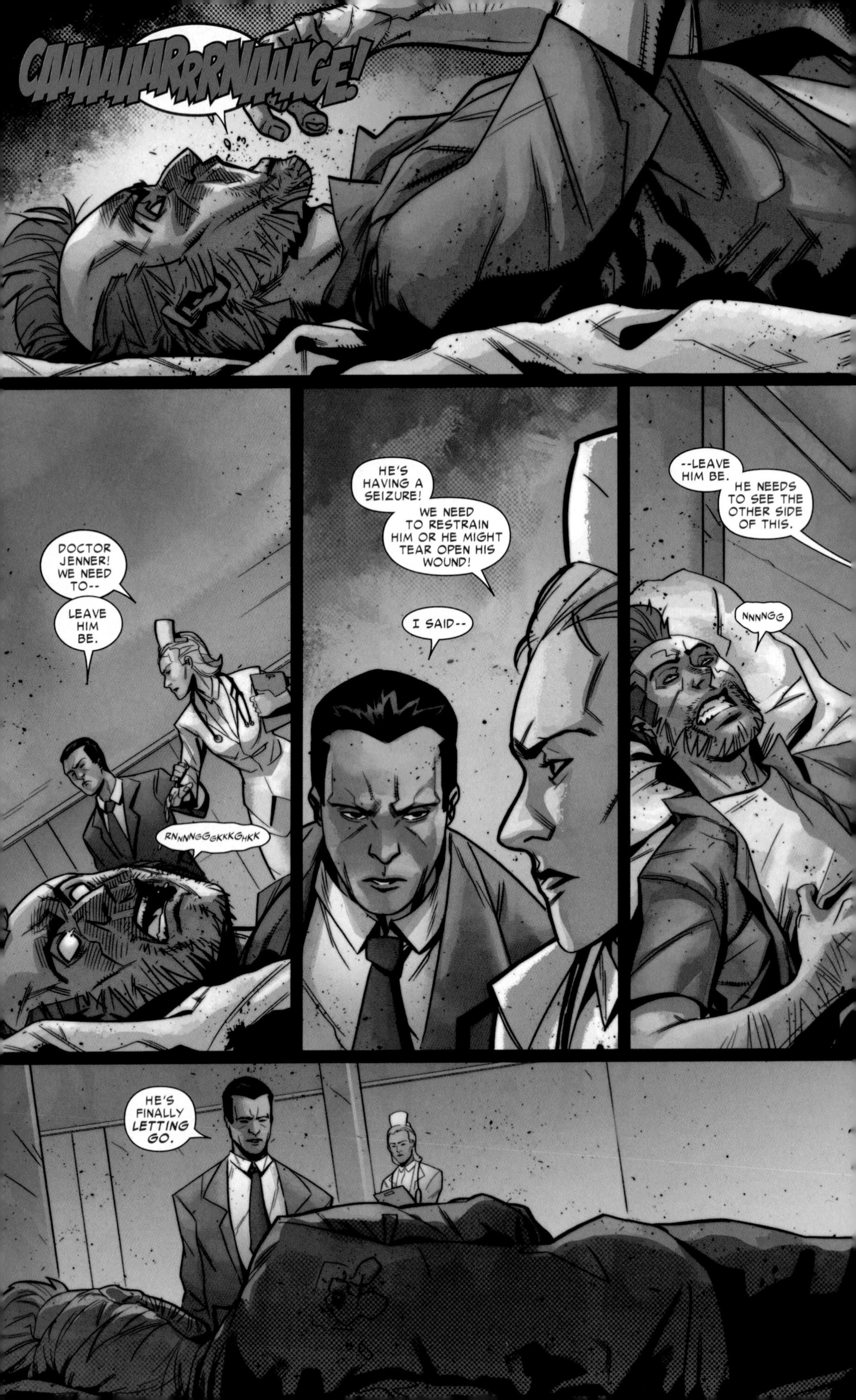
CAAAAAARRRNAAAGE!
DOCTOR JENNER! WE NEED TO--
LEAVE HIM BE.
RNNNNGGGKKKGHKK
HE'S HAVING A SEIZURE!
WE NEED TO RESTRAIN HIM OR HE MIGHT TEAR OPEN HIS WOUND!
I SAID--
--LEAVE HIM BE.
HE NEEDS TO SEE THE OTHER SIDE OF THIS.
NNNNGG
HE'S FINALLY LETTING GO.

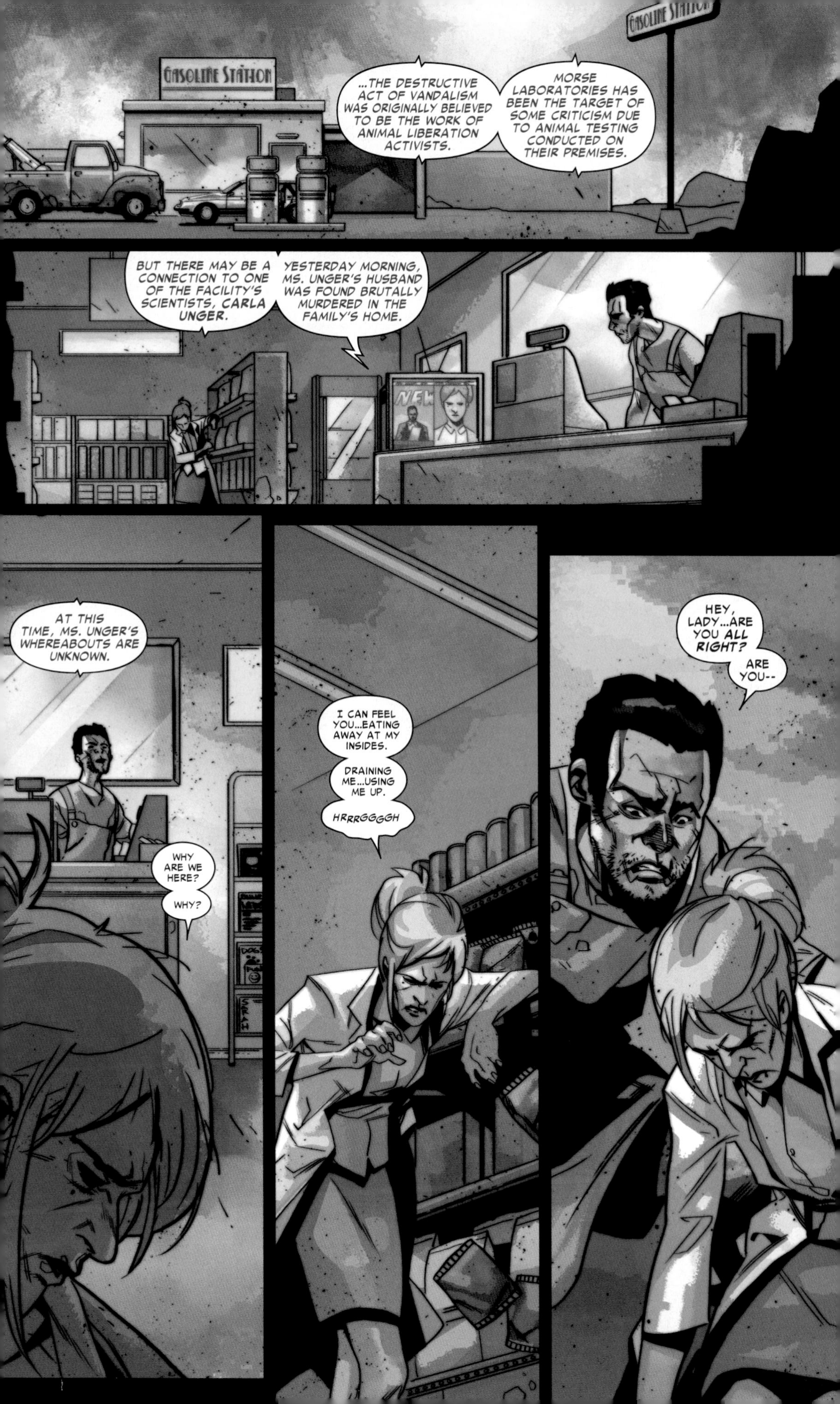
GASOLINE STATION
GASOLINE STATION
...THE DESTRUCTIVE ACT OF VANDALISM WAS ORIGINALLY BELIEVED TO BE THE WORK OF ANIMAL LIBERATION ACTIVISTS.
MORSE LABORATORIES HAS BEEN THE TARGET OF SOME CRITICISM DUE TO ANIMAL TESTING CONDUCTED ON THEIR PREMISES.
BUT THERE MAY BE A CONNECTION TO ONE OF THE FACILITY'S SCIENTISTS, CARLA UNGER.
YESTERDAY MORNING, MS. UNGER'S HUSBAND WAS FOUND BRUTALLY MURDERED IN THE FAMILY'S HOME.
AT THIS TIME, MS. UNGER'S WHEREABOUTS ARE UNKNOWN.
WHY ARE WE HERE?
WHY?
I CAN FEEL YOU...EATING AWAY AT MY INSIDES.
DRAINING ME...USING ME UP.
HRRRGGGGH
HEY, LADY...ARE YOU ALL RIGHT?
ARE YOU--

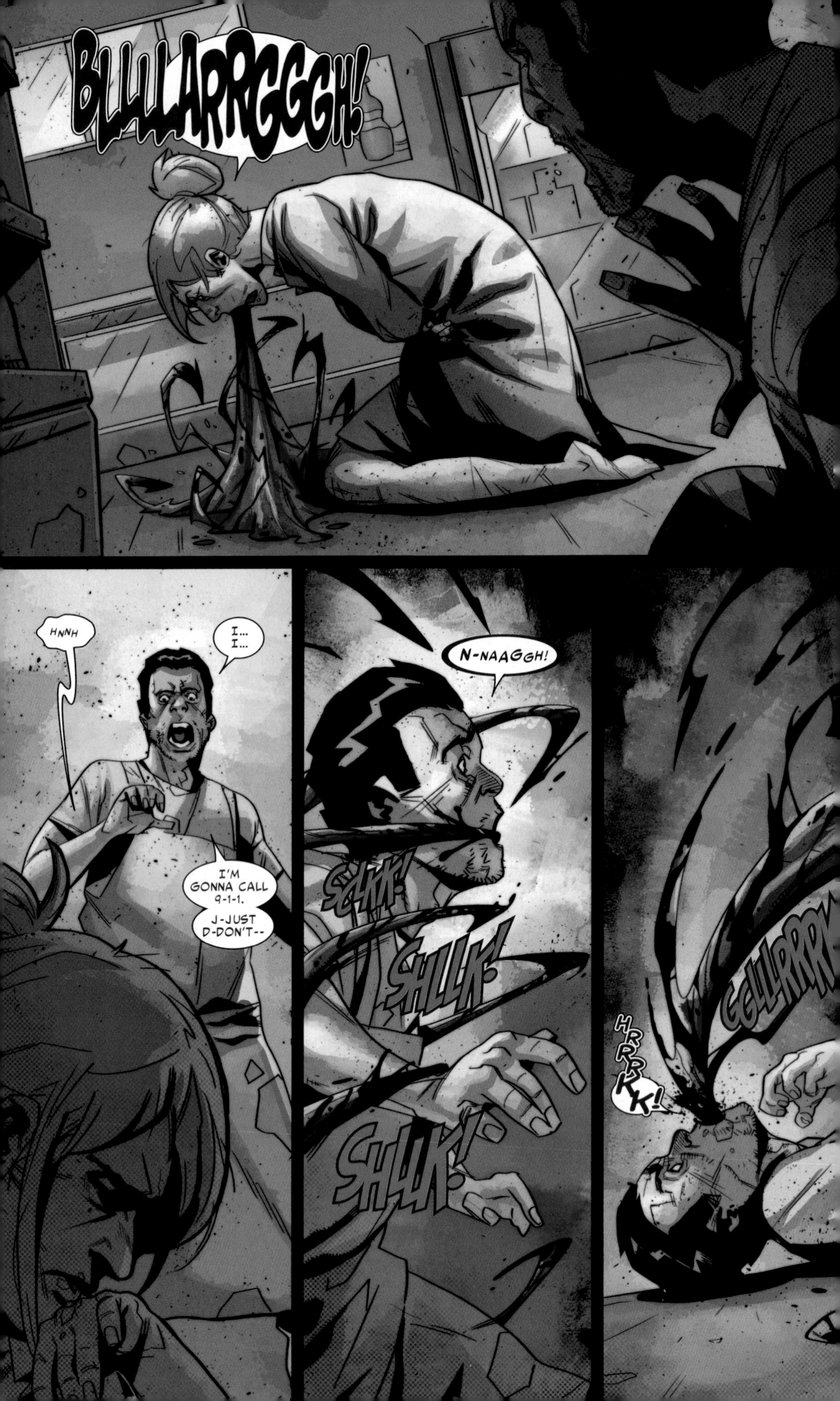
BLLLARRGGGH!
HNNH
I... I...
I'M GONNA CALL 9-1-1.
J-JUST D-DON'T--
N-NAAGGH!
SCLKK!
SHLLK!
SHLK!
HRRRKK!
GELLRRR

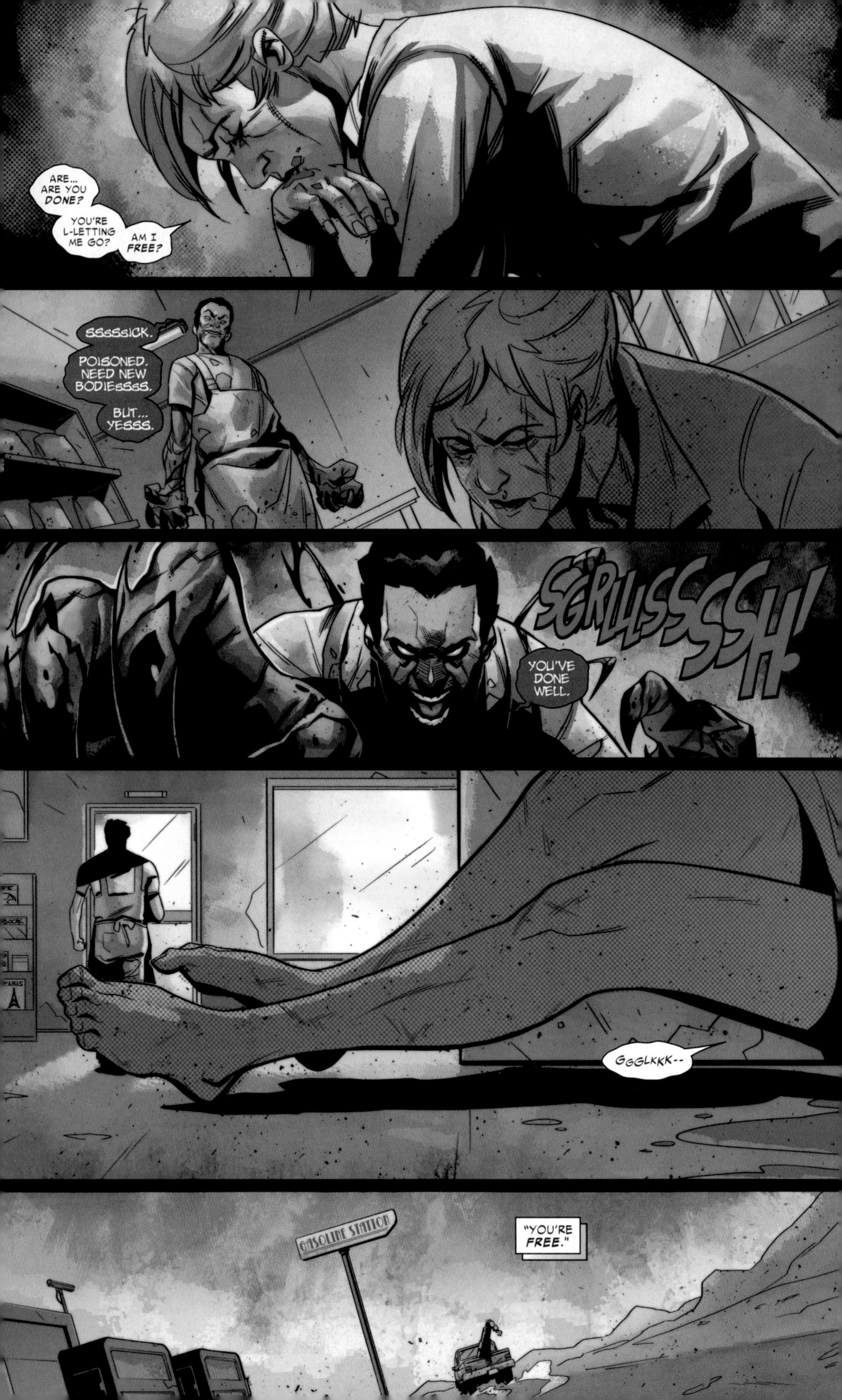

ARE... ARE YOU DONE?
YOU'RE L-LETTING ME GO?
AM I FREE?
SSSSSICK.
POISONED. NEED NEW BODIESSSS.
BUT... YESSS.
SGRLLLSSSSSH!
YOU'VE DONE WELL.
GGGLKKK--
GASOLINE STATION
"YOU'RE FREE."

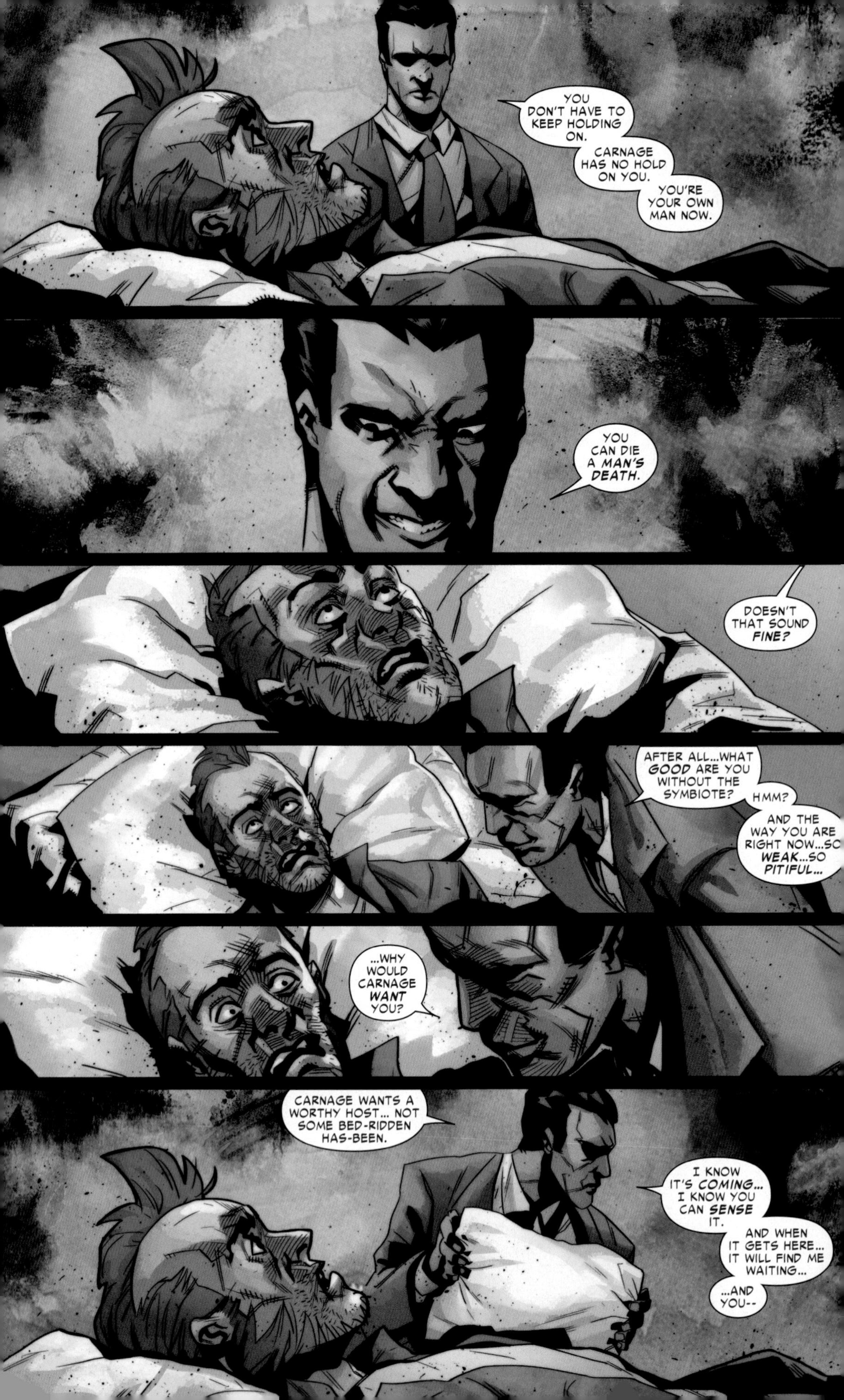
YOU DON'T HAVE TO KEEP HOLDING ON.
CARNAGE HAS NO HOLD ON YOU.
YOU'RE YOUR OWN MAN NOW.
YOU CAN DIE A MAN'S DEATH.
DOESN'T THAT SOUND FINE?
AFTER ALL...WHAT GOOD ARE YOU WITHOUT THE SYMBIOTE?
HMM?
AND THE WAY YOU ARE RIGHT NOW...SO WEAK...SO PITIFUL...
...WHY WOULD CARNAGE WANT YOU?
CARNAGE WANTS A WORTHY HOST... NOT SOME BED-RIDDEN HAS-BEEN.
I KNOW IT'S COMING... I KNOW YOU CAN SENSE IT.
AND WHEN IT GETS HERE... IT WILL FIND ME WAITING...
...AND YOU--

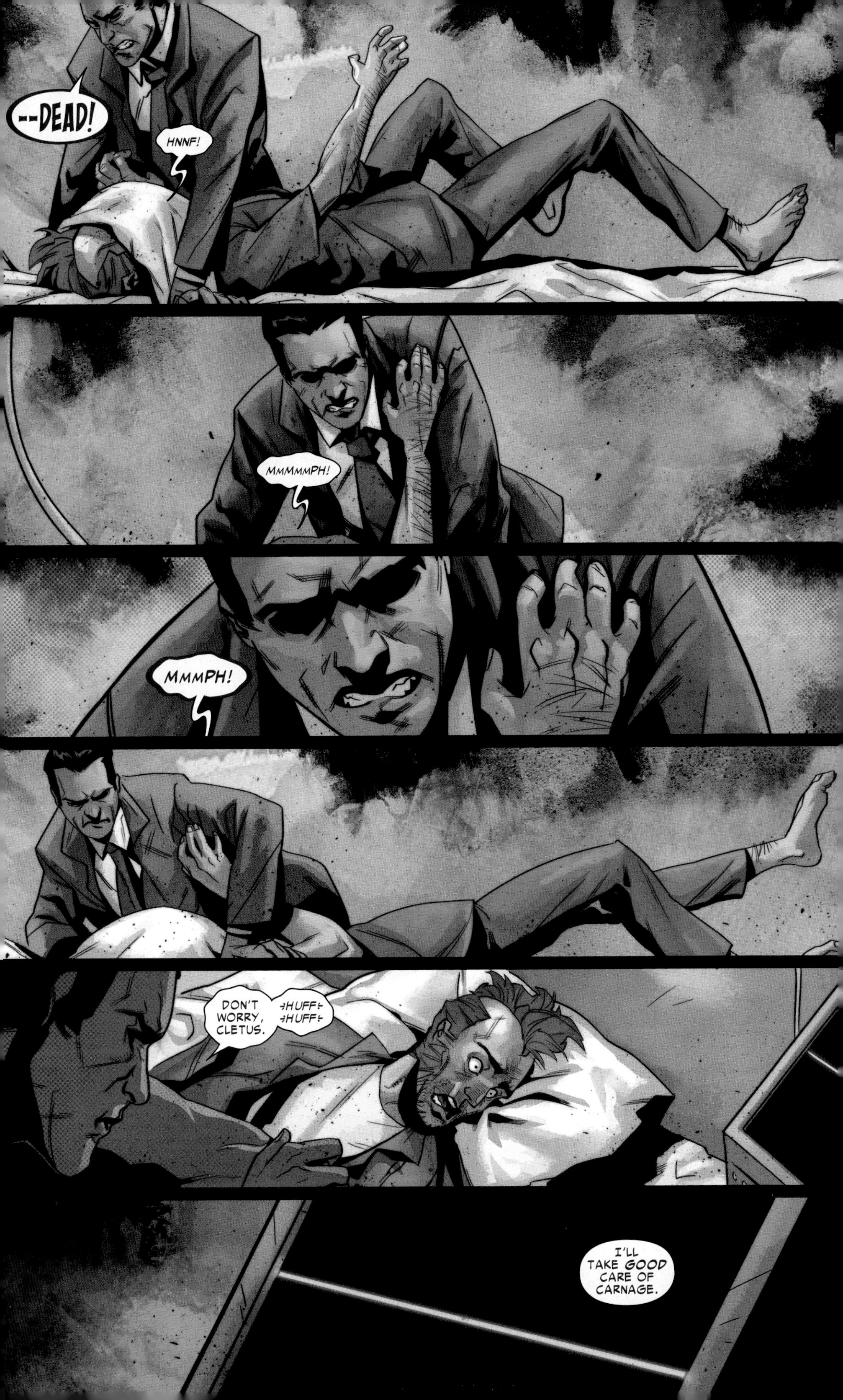
--DEAD!
HNNF!
MMMMMPH!
MMMPH!
DON'T WORRY, CLETUS.
HUFF HUFF
I'LL TAKE GOOD CARE OF CARNAGE.

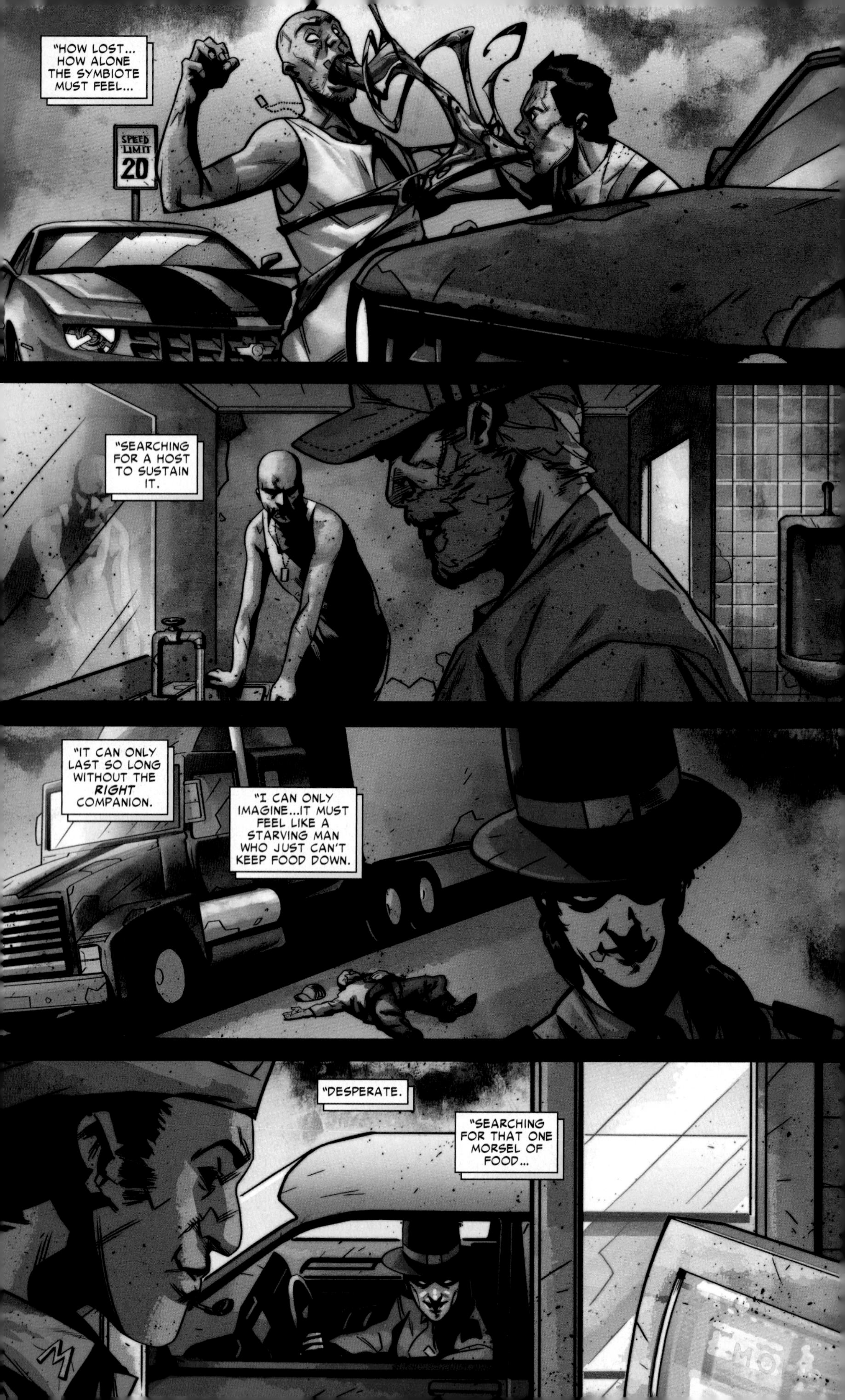
"HOW LOST... HOW ALONE THE SYMBIOTE MUST FEEL...
SPEED LIMIT 20
"SEARCHING FOR A HOST TO SUSTAIN IT.
"IT CAN ONLY LAST SO LONG WITHOUT THE *RIGHT* COMPANION.
"I CAN ONLY IMAGINE...IT MUST FEEL LIKE A STARVING MAN WHO JUST CAN'T KEEP FOOD DOWN.
"DESPERATE.
"SEARCHING FOR THAT ONE MORSEL OF FOOD...

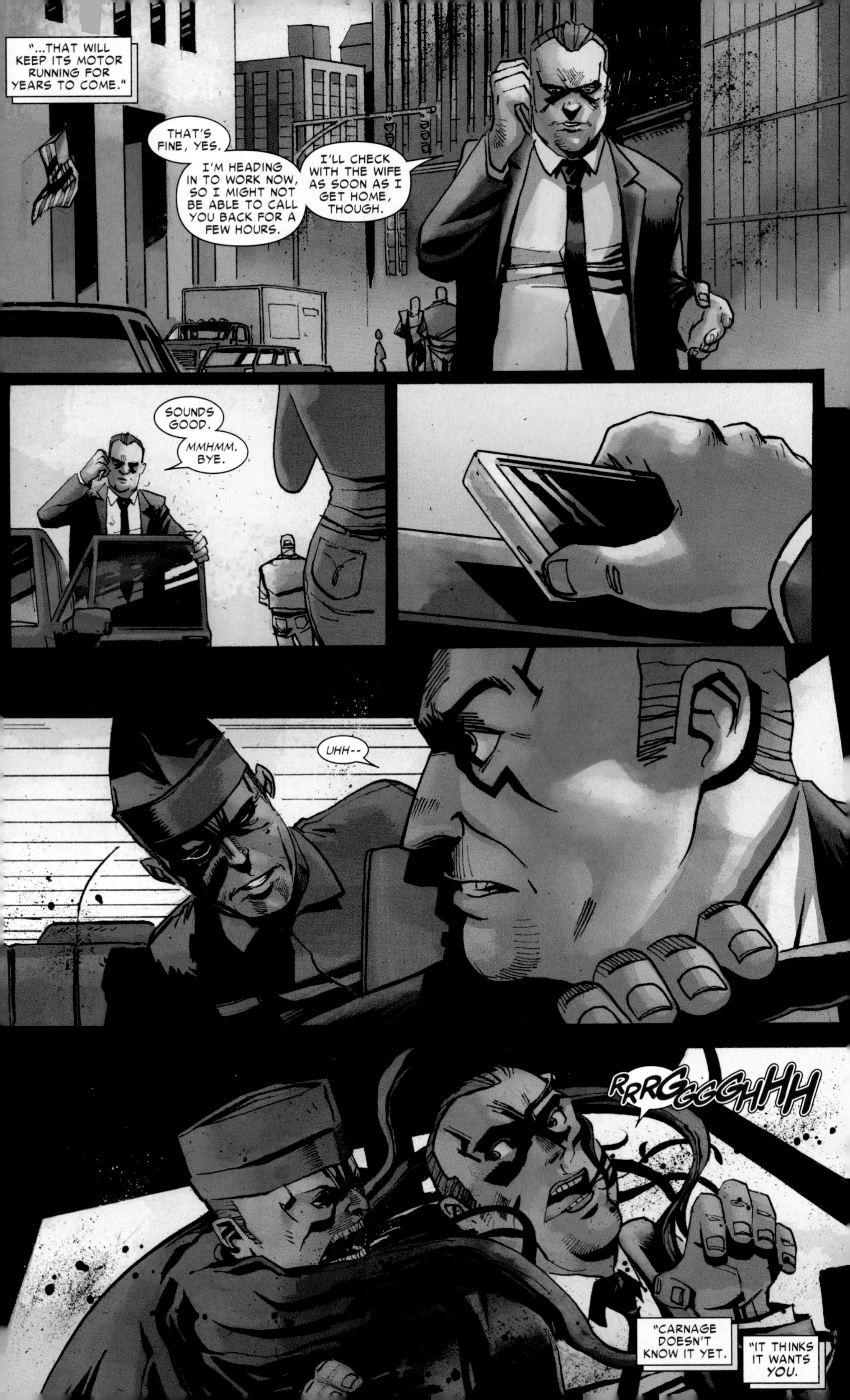
"...THAT WILL KEEP ITS MOTOR RUNNING FOR YEARS TO COME."
THAT'S FINE, YES.
I'M HEADING IN TO WORK NOW, SO I MIGHT NOT BE ABLE TO CALL YOU BACK FOR A FEW HOURS.
I'LL CHECK WITH THE WIFE AS SOON AS I GET HOME, THOUGH.
SOUNDS GOOD.
MMHMM. BYE.
UHH--
RRRGGGGHHH
"CARNAGE DOESN'T KNOW IT YET.
"IT THINKS IT WANTS YOU.

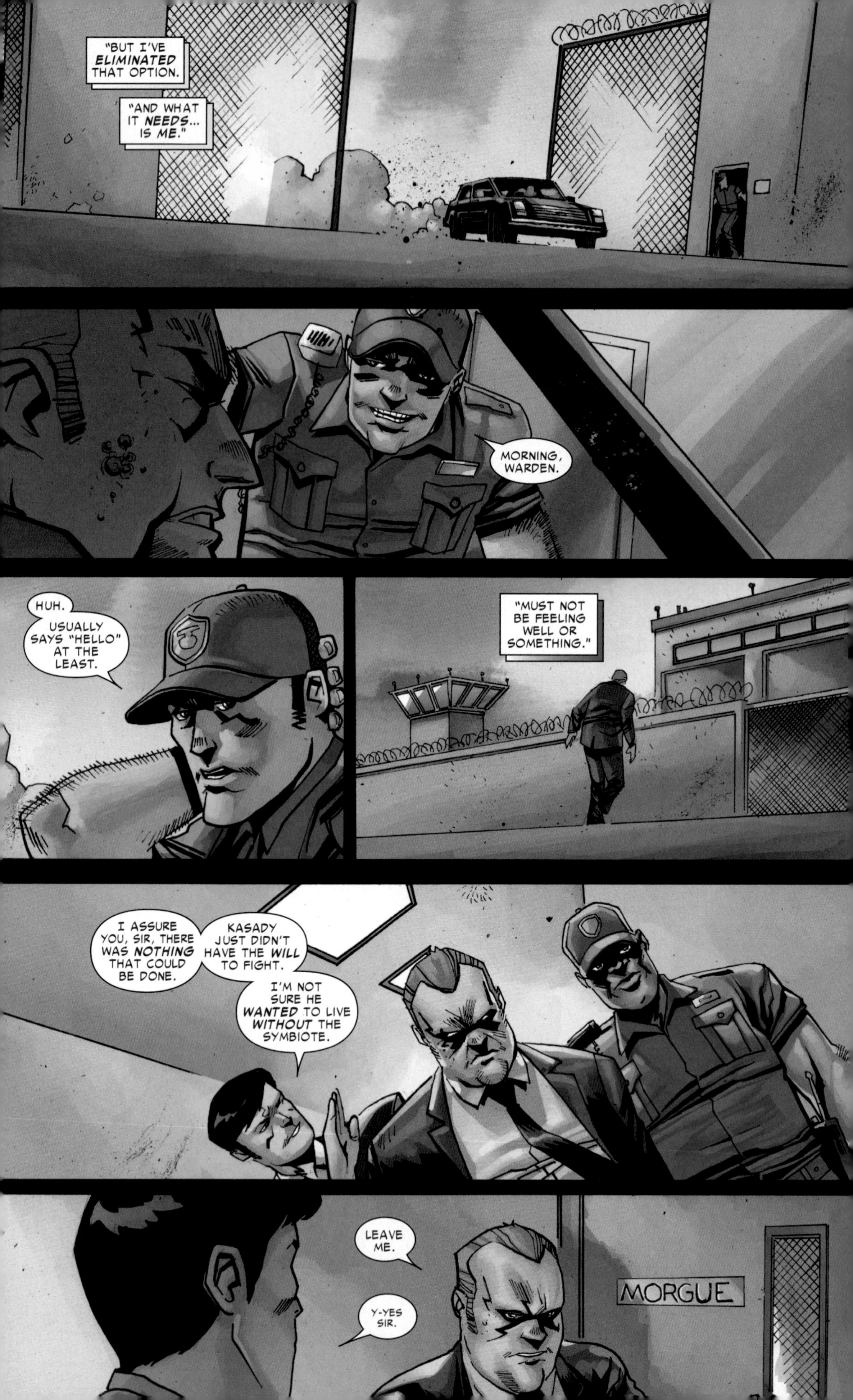
"BUT I'VE ELIMINATED THAT OPTION.
"AND WHAT IT NEEDS... IS ME."
MORNING, WARDEN.
HUH.
USUALLY SAYS "HELLO" AT THE LEAST.
"MUST NOT BE FEELING WELL OR SOMETHING."
I ASSURE YOU, SIR, THERE WAS NOTHING THAT COULD BE DONE.
KASADY JUST DIDN'T HAVE THE WILL TO FIGHT.
I'M NOT SURE HE WANTED TO LIVE WITHOUT THE SYMBIOTE.
LEAVE ME.
Y-YES SIR.
MORGUE

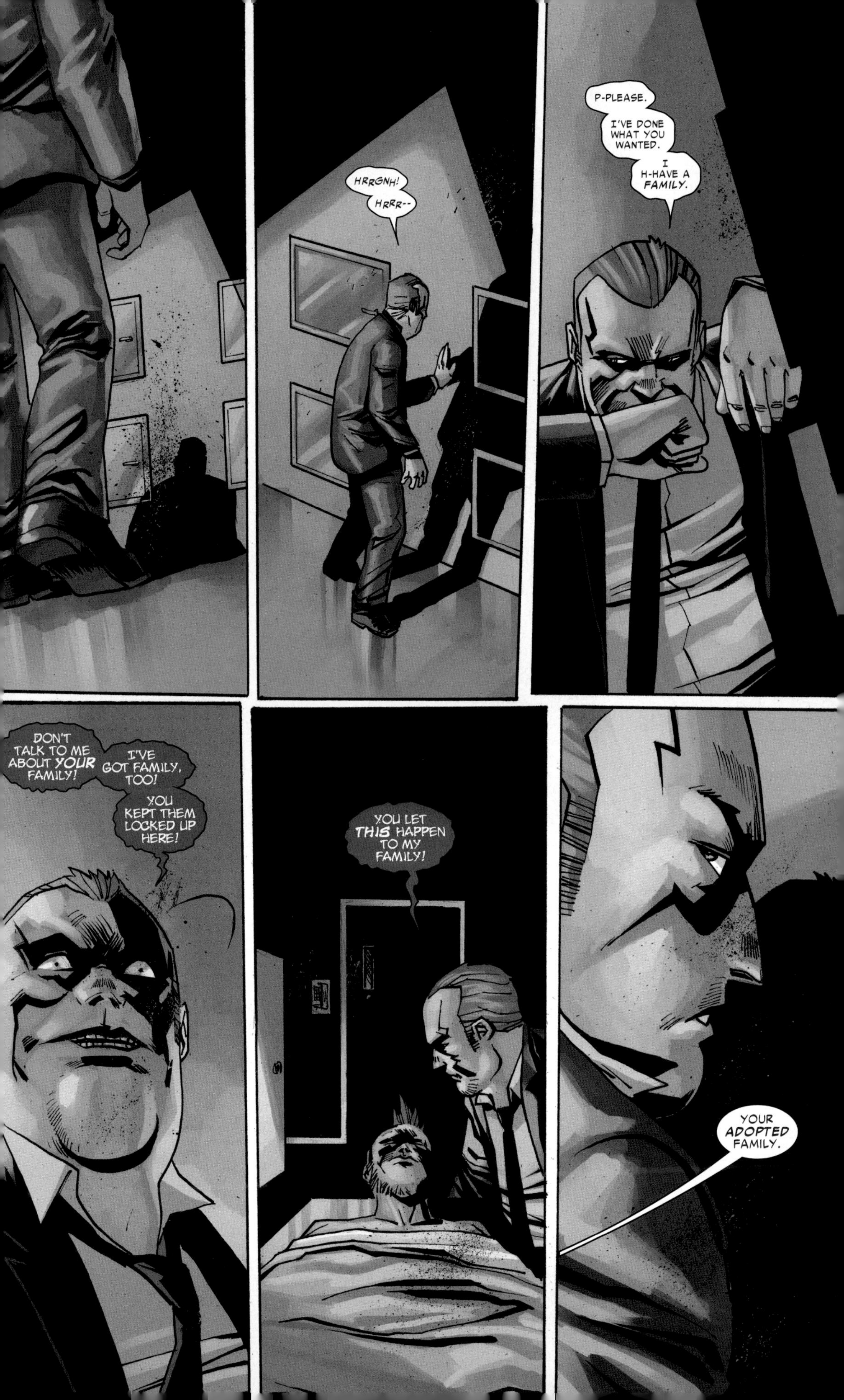
HRRGNH!
HRRR--
P-PLEASE.
I'VE DONE WHAT YOU WANTED.
I H-HAVE A FAMILY.
DON'T TALK TO ME ABOUT YOUR FAMILY!
I'VE GOT FAMILY, TOO!
YOU KEPT THEM LOCKED UP HERE!
YOU LET THIS HAPPEN TO MY FAMILY!
YOUR ADOPTED FAMILY.

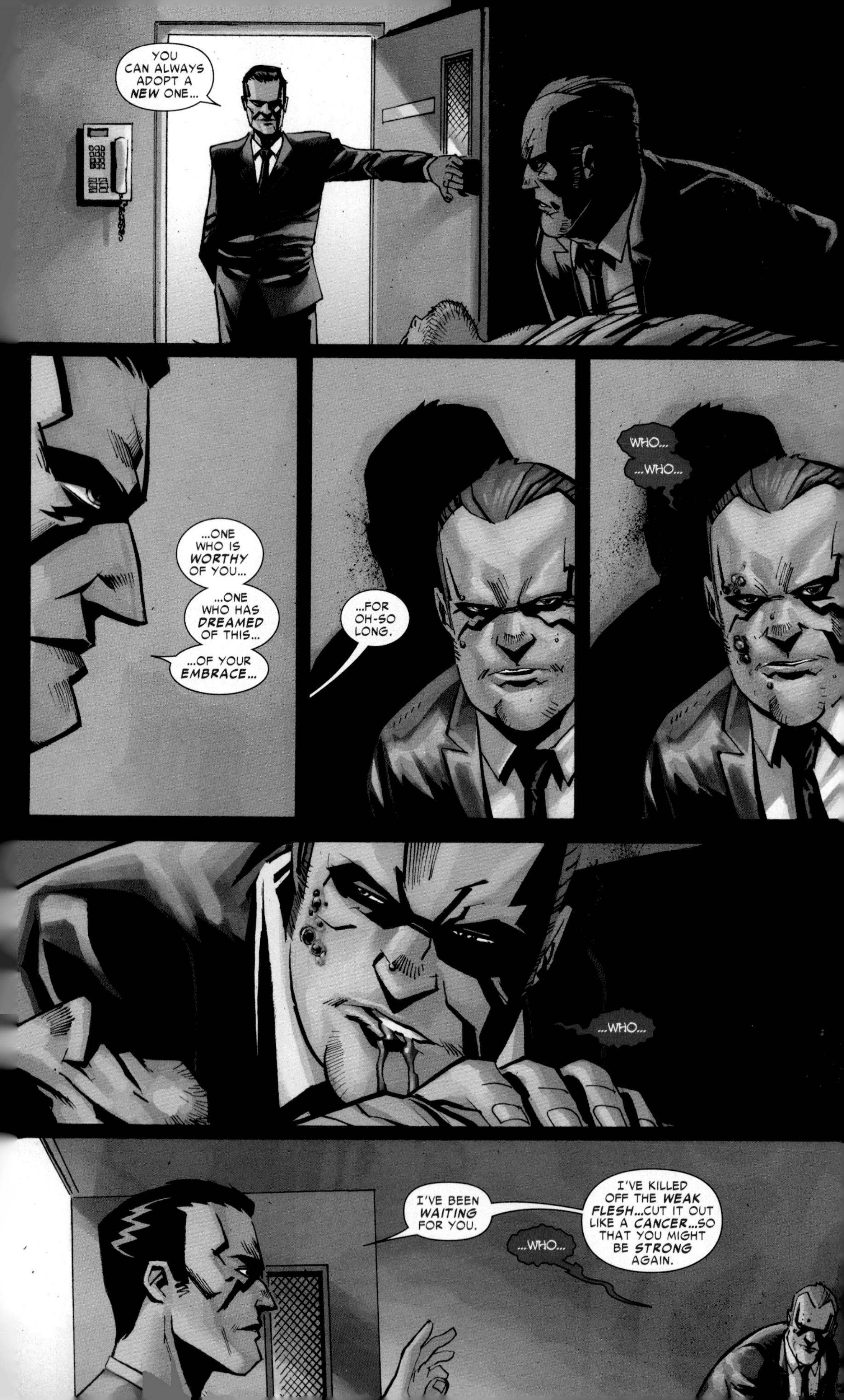
YOU CAN ALWAYS ADOPT A NEW ONE...
...ONE WHO IS WORTHY OF YOU...
...ONE WHO HAS DREAMED OF THIS...
...OF YOUR EMBRACE...
...FOR OH-SO LONG.
WHO...
...WHO...
...WHO...
I'VE BEEN WAITING FOR YOU.
I'VE KILLED OFF THE WEAK FLESH...CUT IT OUT LIKE A CANCER...SO THAT YOU MIGHT BE STRONG AGAIN.
...WHO...

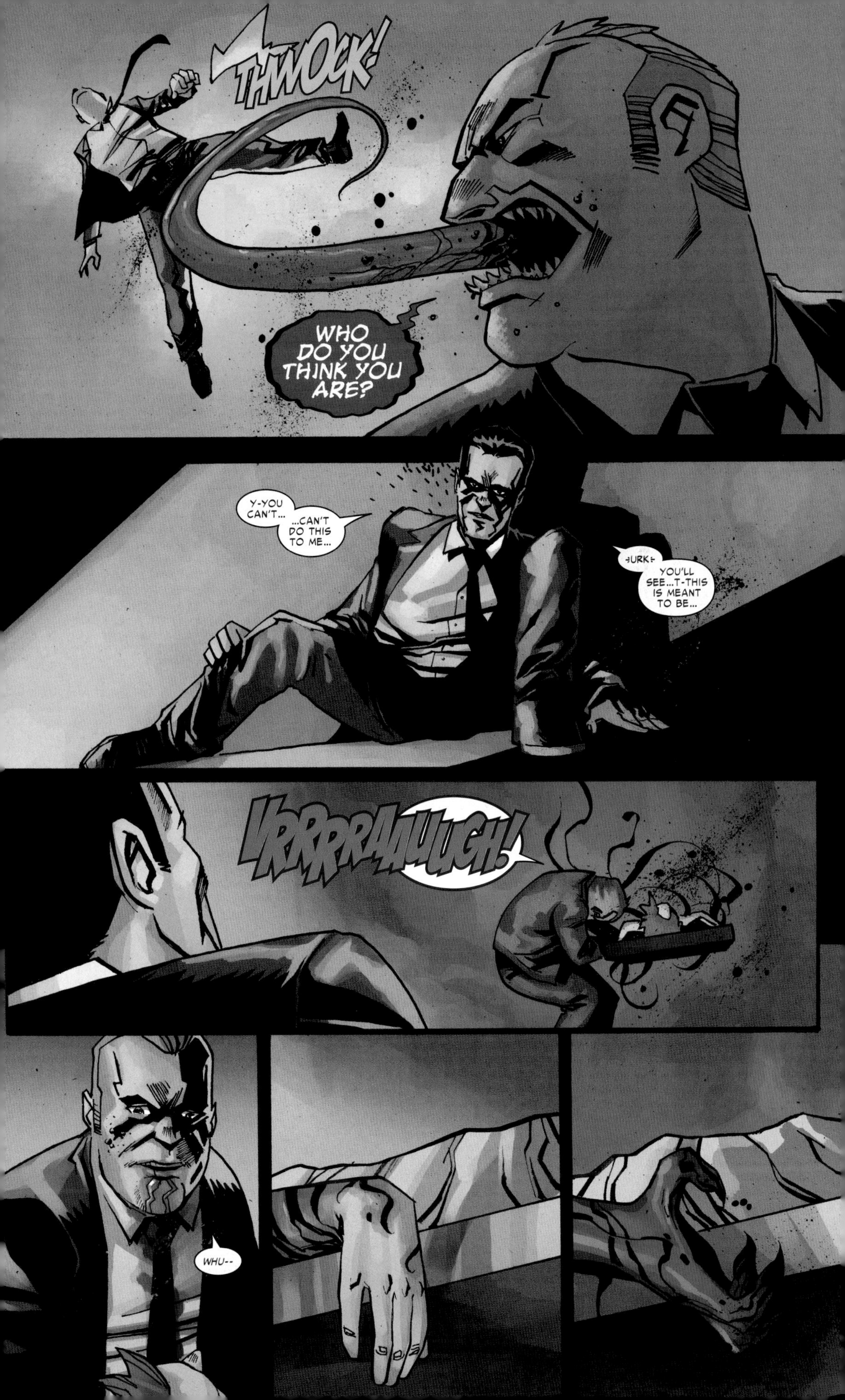
THWOCK!
WHO DO YOU THINK YOU ARE?
Y-YOU CAN'T... ...CAN'T DO THIS TO ME...
=URK= YOU'LL SEE...T-THIS IS MEANT TO BE...
VRRRRAAUUGH!
WHU--

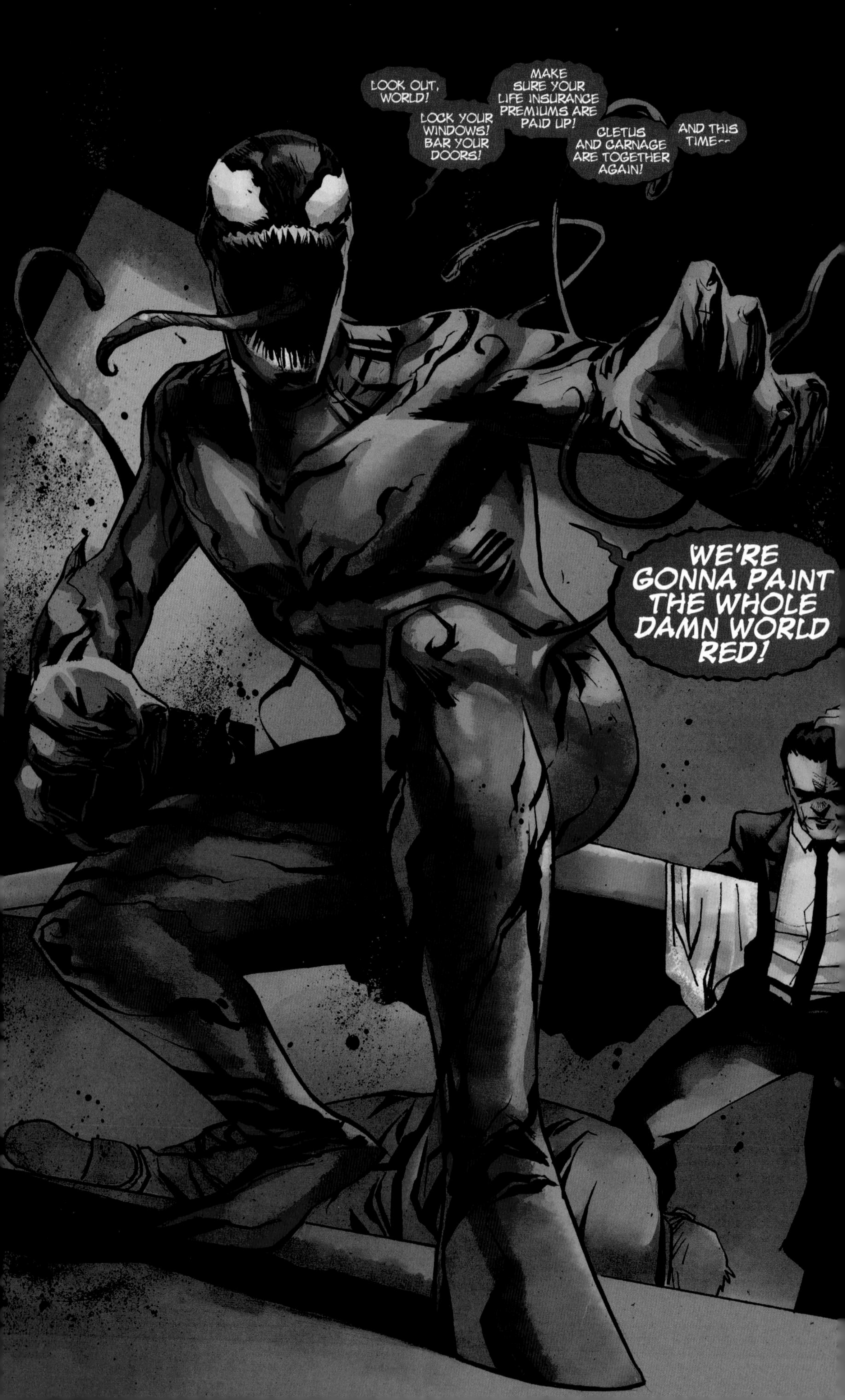
LOOK OUT, WORLD!
LOCK YOUR WINDOWS! BAR YOUR DOORS!
MAKE SURE YOUR LIFE INSURANCE PREMIUMS ARE PAID UP!
CLETUS AND CARNAGE ARE TOGETHER AGAIN!
AND THIS TIME--
WE'RE GONNA PAINT THE WHOLE DAMN WORLD RED!

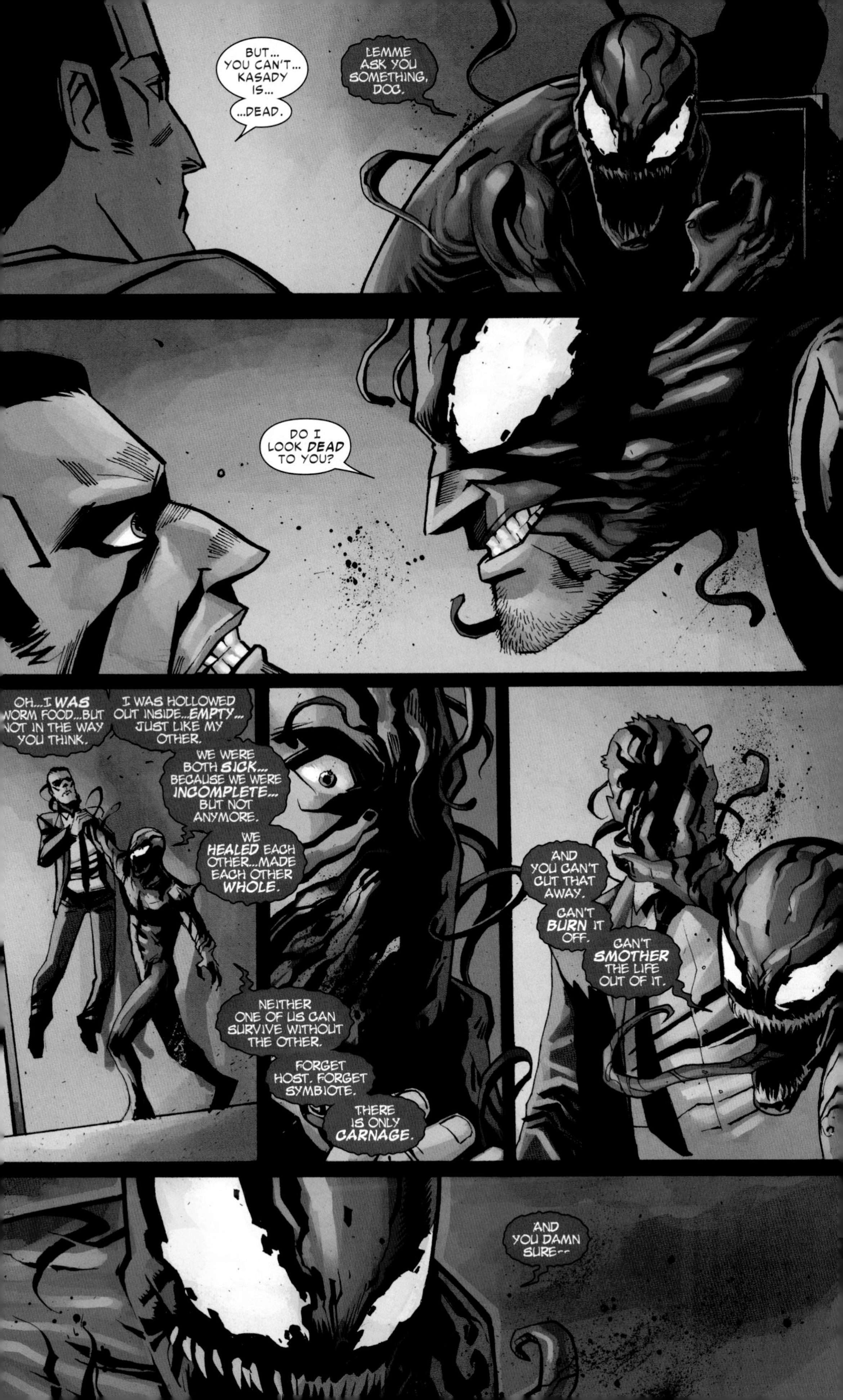
BUT... YOU CAN'T... KASADY IS...
...DEAD.
LEMME ASK YOU SOMETHING, DOC.
DO I LOOK DEAD TO YOU?
OH...I WAS WORM FOOD...BUT NOT IN THE WAY YOU THINK.
I WAS HOLLOWED OUT INSIDE...EMPTY... JUST LIKE MY OTHER.
WE WERE BOTH SICK... BECAUSE WE WERE INCOMPLETE... BUT NOT ANYMORE.
WE HEALED EACH OTHER...MADE EACH OTHER WHOLE.
NEITHER ONE OF US CAN SURVIVE WITHOUT THE OTHER.
FORGET HOST. FORGET SYMBIOTE.
THERE IS ONLY CARNAGE.
AND YOU CAN'T CUT THAT AWAY.
CAN'T BURN IT OFF.
CAN'T SMOTHER THE LIFE OUT OF IT.
AND YOU DAMN SURE--

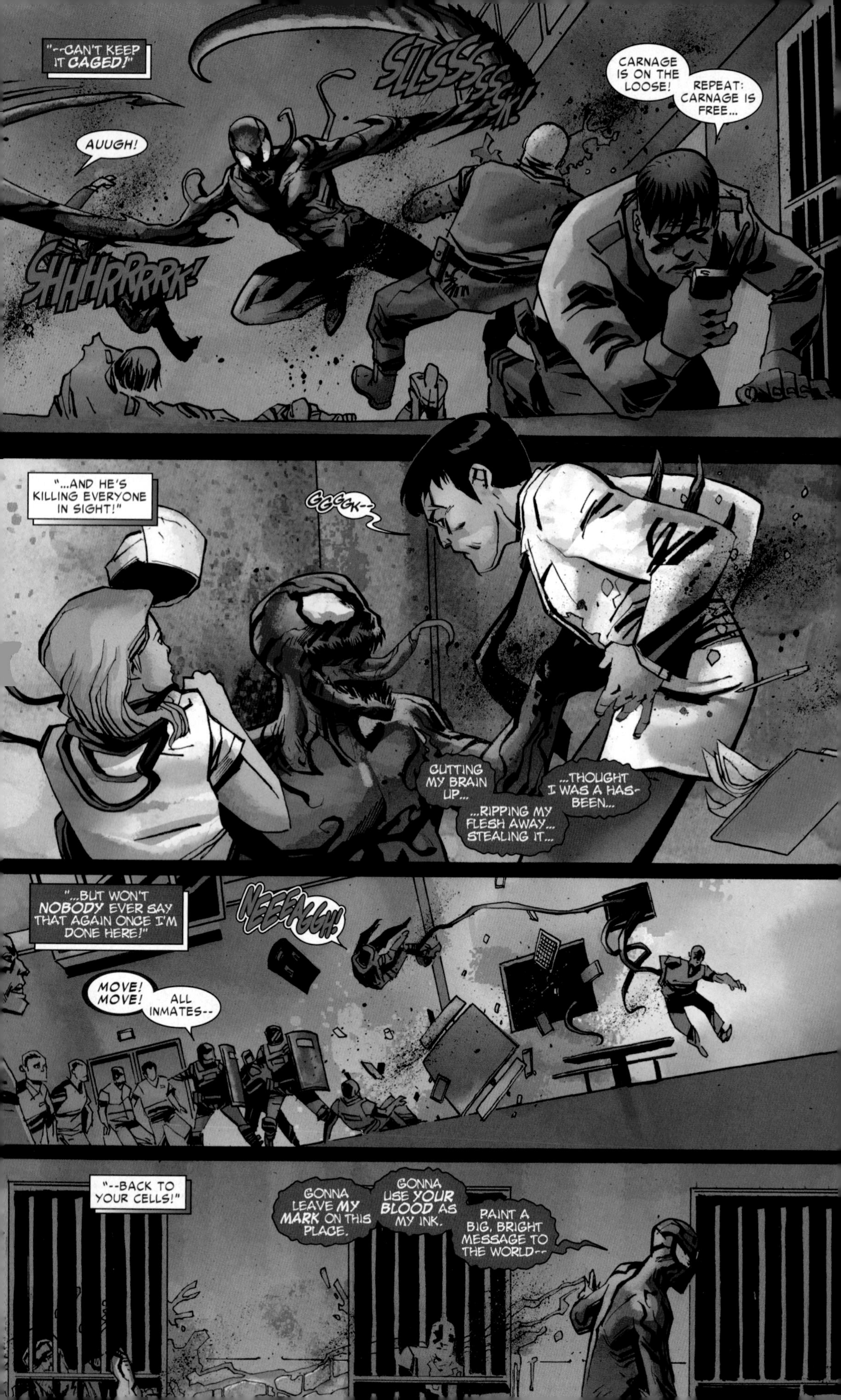

"--CAN'T KEEP IT CAGED!"
SLISSSSSK!
CARNAGE IS ON THE LOOSE!
REPEAT: CARNAGE IS FREE...
AUUGH!
SHHHRRRRK!
"...AND HE'S KILLING EVERYONE IN SIGHT!"
GGGGK--
CUTTING MY BRAIN UP...
...RIPPING MY FLESH AWAY... STEALING IT...
...THOUGHT I WAS A HAS-BEEN...
"...BUT WON'T NOBODY EVER SAY THAT AGAIN ONCE I'M DONE HERE!"
NEEEAGGH!
MOVE! MOVE!
ALL INMATES--
"--BACK TO YOUR CELLS!"
GONNA LEAVE MY MARK ON THIS PLACE.
GONNA USE YOUR BLOOD AS MY INK.
PAINT A BIG, BRIGHT MESSAGE TO THE WORLD--

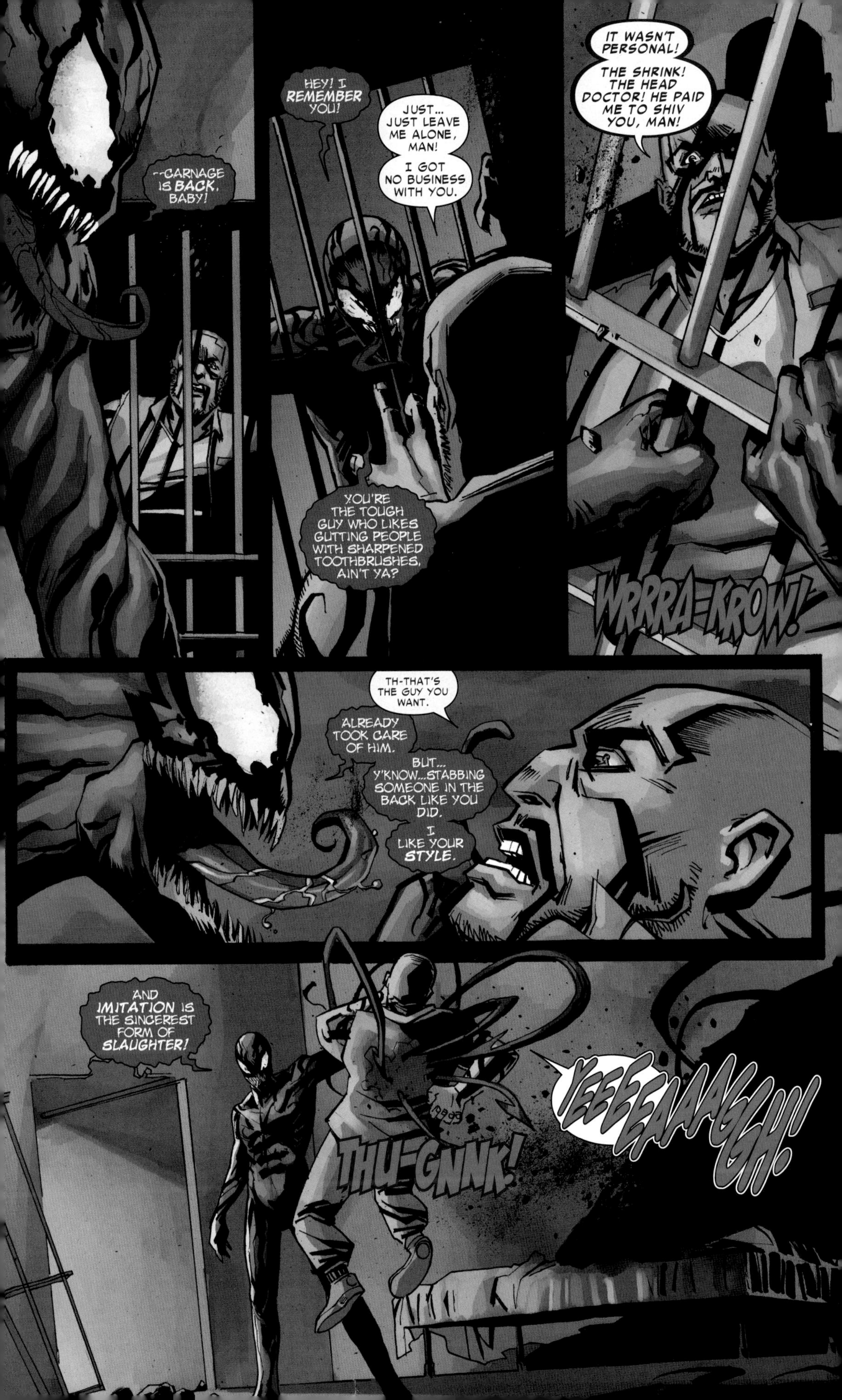

--CARNAGE IS BACK, BABY!
HEY! I REMEMBER YOU!
JUST... JUST LEAVE ME ALONE, MAN!
I GOT NO BUSINESS WITH YOU.
YOU'RE THE TOUGH GUY WHO LIKES GUTTING PEOPLE WITH SHARPENED TOOTHBRUSHES, AIN'T YA?
IT WASN'T PERSONAL!
THE SHRINK! THE HEAD DOCTOR! HE PAID ME TO SHIV YOU, MAN!
WRRRA-KROW!
TH-THAT'S THE GUY YOU WANT.
ALREADY TOOK CARE OF HIM.
BUT... Y'KNOW...STABBING SOMEONE IN THE BACK LIKE YOU DID.
I LIKE YOUR STYLE.
AND IMITATION IS THE SINCEREST FORM OF SLAUGHTER!
THU-GNNK!
YEEEEAAAAGGH!

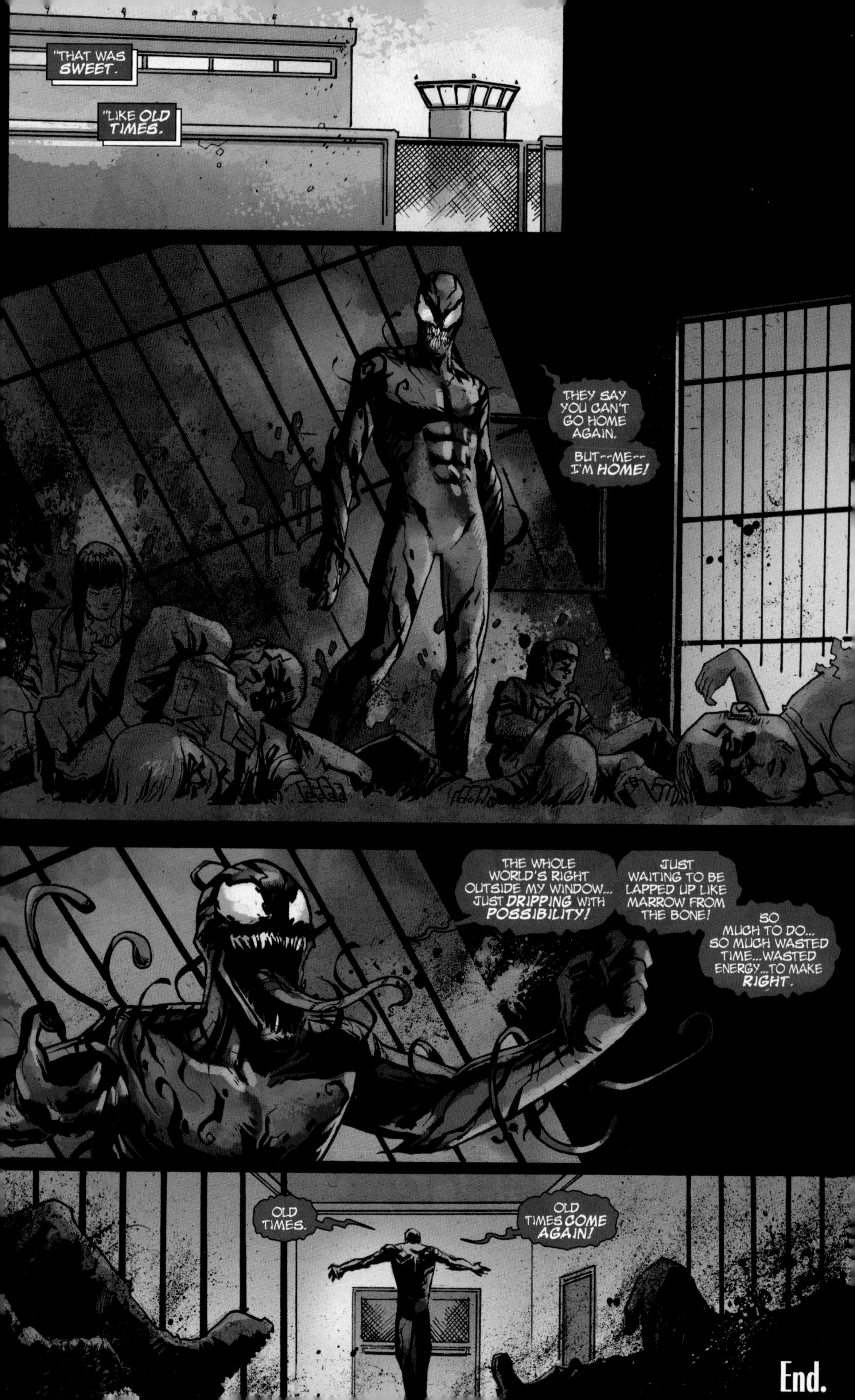
"THAT WAS SWEET.
"LIKE OLD TIMES.
THEY SAY YOU CAN'T GO HOME AGAIN.
BUT--ME-- I'M HOME!
THE WHOLE WORLD'S RIGHT OUTSIDE MY WINDOW... JUST DRIPPING WITH POSSIBILITY!
JUST WAITING TO BE LAPPED UP LIKE MARROW FROM THE BONE!
SO MUCH TO DO... SO MUCH WASTED TIME...WASTED ENERGY...TO MAKE RIGHT.
OLD TIMES.
OLD TIMES COME AGAIN!
End.

Peter Parker soon regained his own body, and the Carnage symbiote was eventually separated from Kasady once again. But its most dangerous host yet was still to come, as seen in these excerpts from *Amazing Spider-Man #795-796*...

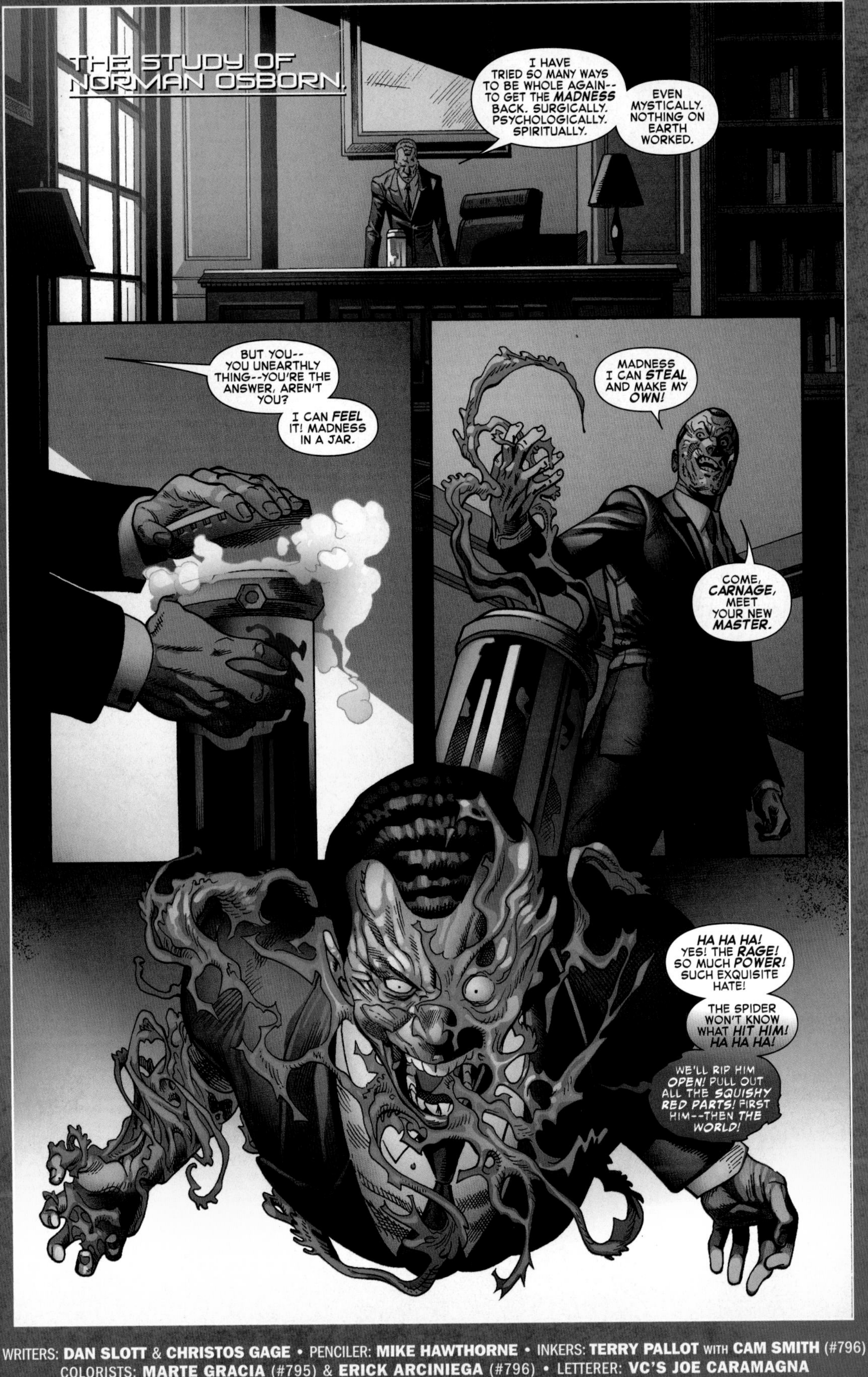
THE STUDY OF NORMAN OSBORN.
I HAVE TRIED SO MANY WAYS TO BE WHOLE AGAIN--TO GET THE MADNESS BACK. SURGICALLY. PSYCHOLOGICALLY. SPIRITUALLY.
EVEN MYSTICALLY. NOTHING ON EARTH WORKED.
BUT YOU--YOU UNEARTHLY THING--YOU'RE THE ANSWER, AREN'T YOU?
I CAN FEEL IT! MADNESS IN A JAR.
MADNESS I CAN STEAL AND MAKE MY OWN!
COME, CARNAGE, MEET YOUR NEW MASTER.
HA HA HA! YES! THE RAGE! SO MUCH POWER! SUCH EXQUISITE HATE!
THE SPIDER WON'T KNOW WHAT HIT HIM! HA HA HA!
WE'LL RIP HIM OPEN! PULL OUT ALL THE SQUISHY RED PARTS! FIRST HIM--THEN THE WORLD!

WRITERS: **DAN SLOTT & CHRISTOS GAGE** • PENCILER: **MIKE HAWTHORNE** • INKERS: **TERRY PALLOT** WITH **CAM SMITH** (#796)
COLORISTS: **MARTE GRACIA** (#795) & **ERICK ARCINIEGA** (#796) • LETTERER: **VC'S JOE CARAMAGNA**
ASSISTANT EDITOR: **TOM GRONEMAN** • ASSOCIATE EDITOR: **DEVIN LEWIS** • EDITOR: **NICK LOWE**

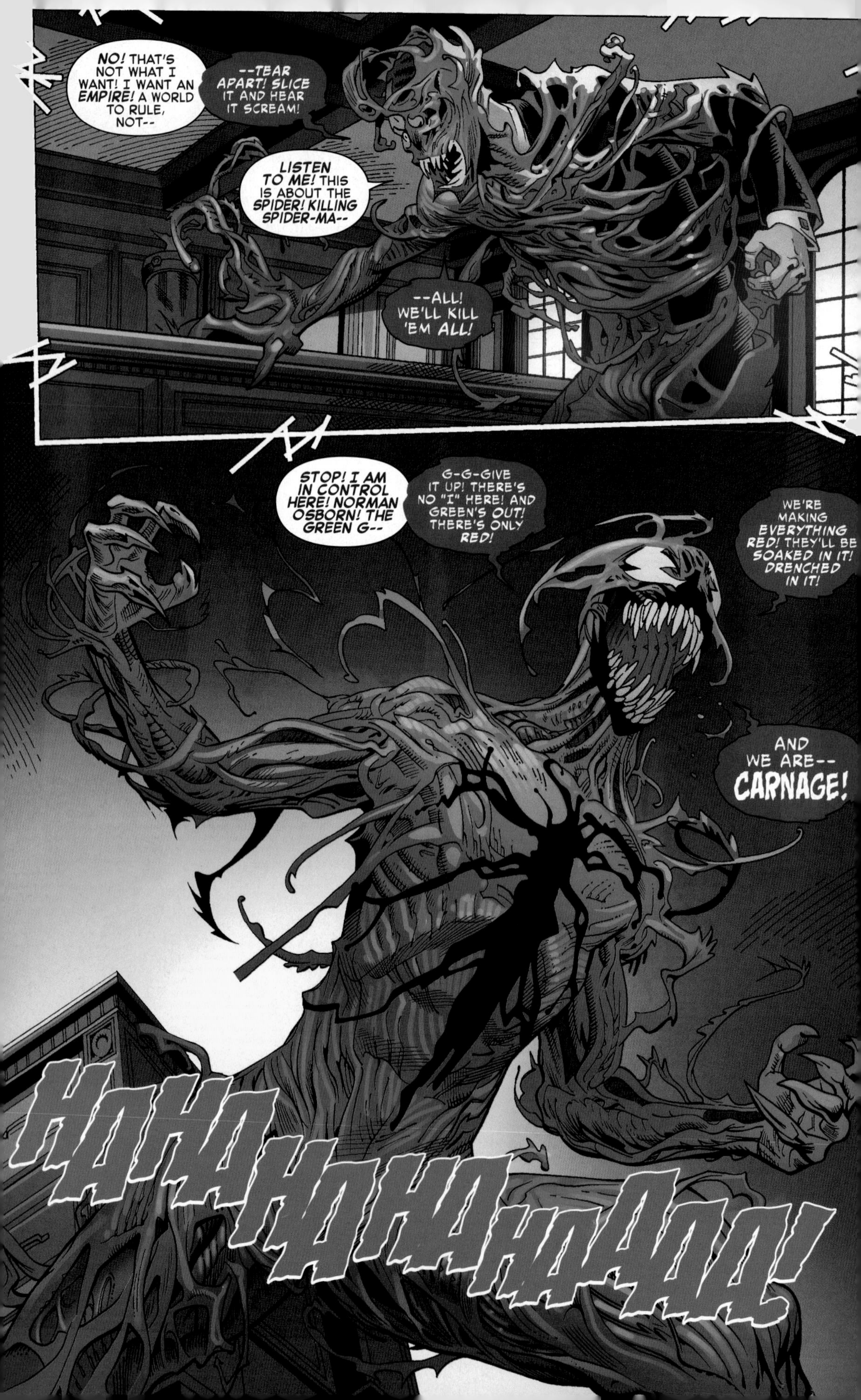
NO! THAT'S NOT WHAT I WANT! I WANT AN EMPIRE! A WORLD TO RULE, NOT--
--TEAR APART! SLICE IT AND HEAR IT SCREAM!
LISTEN TO ME! THIS IS ABOUT THE SPIDER! KILLING SPIDER-MA--
--ALL! WE'LL KILL 'EM ALL!
STOP! I AM IN CONTROL HERE! NORMAN OSBORN! THE GREEN G--
G-G-GIVE IT UP! THERE'S NO "I" HERE! AND GREEN'S OUT! THERE'S ONLY RED!
WE'RE MAKING EVERYTHING RED! THEY'LL BE SOAKED IN IT! DRENCHED IN IT!
AND WE ARE-- CARNAGE!
HAHAHAHAHAHAHAAA!

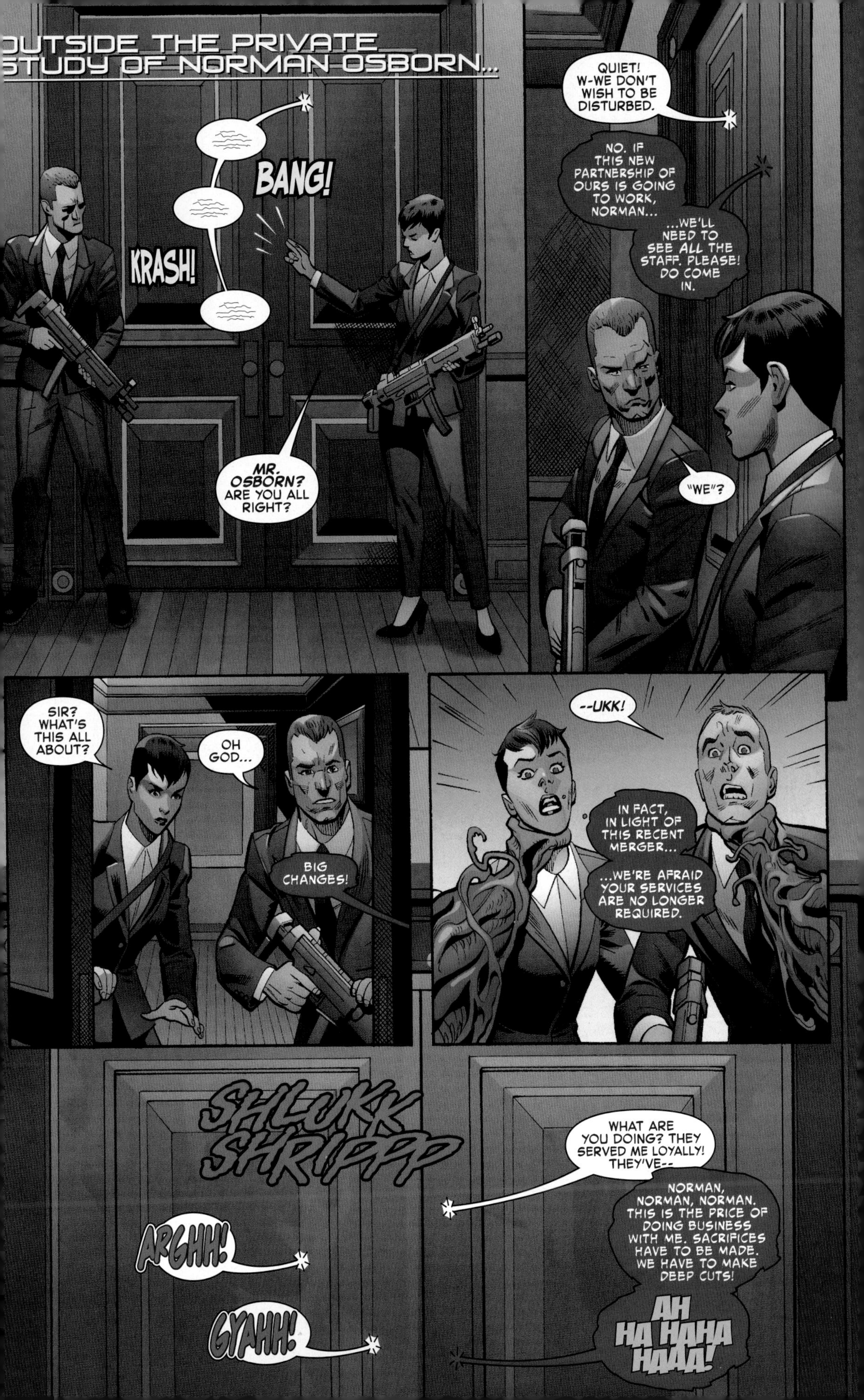
OUTSIDE THE PRIVATE STUDY OF NORMAN OSBORN...
BANG!
KRASH!
MR. OSBORN? ARE YOU ALL RIGHT?
QUIET! W-WE DON'T WISH TO BE DISTURBED.
NO. IF THIS NEW PARTNERSHIP OF OURS IS GOING TO WORK, NORMAN...
...WE'LL NEED TO SEE ALL THE STAFF. PLEASE! DO COME IN.
"WE"?
SIR? WHAT'S THIS ALL ABOUT?
OH GOD...
BIG CHANGES!
--UKK!
IN FACT, IN LIGHT OF THIS RECENT MERGER...
...WE'RE AFRAID YOUR SERVICES ARE NO LONGER REQUIRED.
SHLUKK SHRIPPP
ARGHH!
GYAHH!
WHAT ARE YOU DOING? THEY SERVED ME LOYALLY! THEY'VE--
NORMAN, NORMAN, NORMAN. THIS IS THE PRICE OF DOING BUSINESS WITH ME. SACRIFICES HAVE TO BE MADE. WE HAVE TO MAKE DEEP CUTS!
AH HA HAHA HAAA!

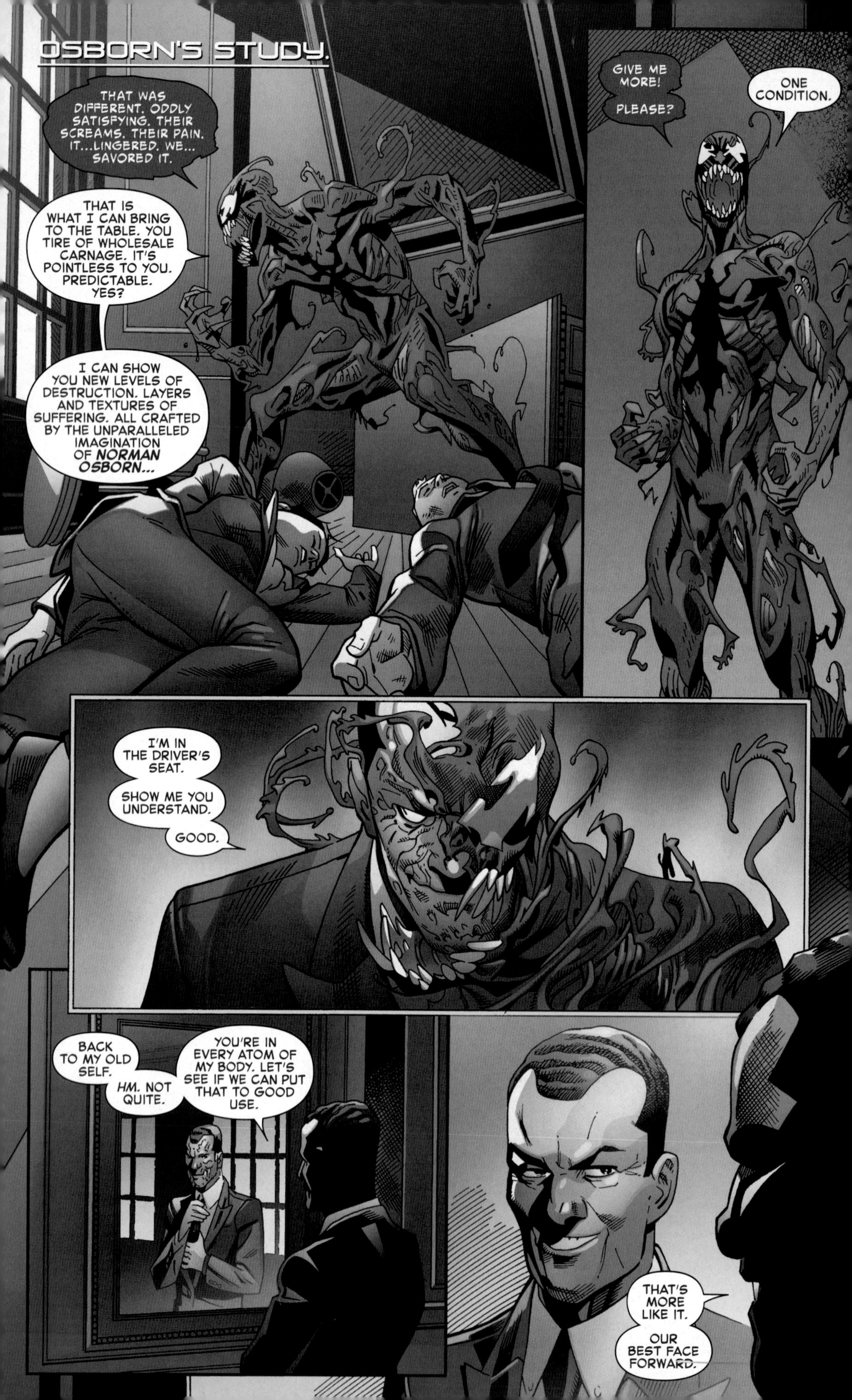
OSBORN'S STUDY.
THAT WAS DIFFERENT. ODDLY SATISFYING. THEIR SCREAMS. THEIR PAIN. IT...LINGERED. WE... SAVORED IT.
THAT IS WHAT I CAN BRING TO THE TABLE. YOU TIRE OF WHOLESALE CARNAGE. IT'S POINTLESS TO YOU. PREDICTABLE. YES?
I CAN SHOW YOU NEW LEVELS OF DESTRUCTION. LAYERS AND TEXTURES OF SUFFERING. ALL CRAFTED BY THE UNPARALLELED IMAGINATION OF NORMAN OSBORN...
GIVE ME MORE!
PLEASE?
ONE CONDITION.
I'M IN THE DRIVER'S SEAT.
SHOW ME YOU UNDERSTAND.
GOOD.
BACK TO MY OLD SELF.
HM. NOT QUITE.
YOU'RE IN EVERY ATOM OF MY BODY. LET'S SEE IF WE CAN PUT THAT TO GOOD USE.
THAT'S MORE LIKE IT.
OUR BEST FACE FORWARD.

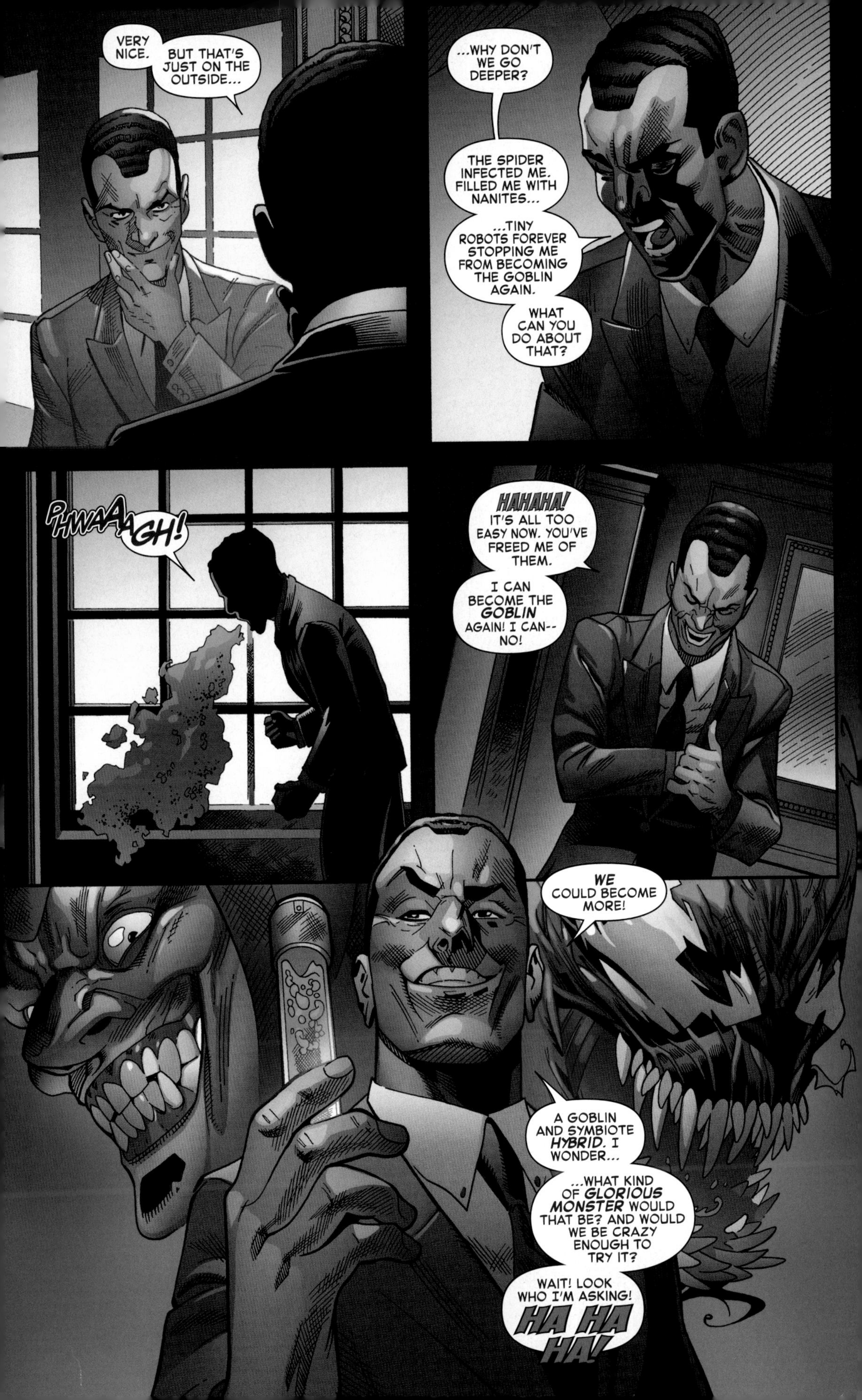
VERY NICE.
BUT THAT'S JUST ON THE OUTSIDE...
...WHY DON'T WE GO DEEPER?
THE SPIDER INFECTED ME. FILLED ME WITH NANITES...
...TINY ROBOTS FOREVER STOPPING ME FROM BECOMING THE GOBLIN AGAIN.
WHAT CAN YOU DO ABOUT THAT?
PHWAAAAGH!
HAHAHA! IT'S ALL TOO EASY NOW. YOU'VE FREED ME OF THEM.
I CAN BECOME THE GOBLIN AGAIN! I CAN--NO!
WE COULD BECOME MORE!
A GOBLIN AND SYMBIOTE HYBRID. I WONDER...
...WHAT KIND OF GLORIOUS MONSTER WOULD THAT BE? AND WOULD WE BE CRAZY ENOUGH TO TRY IT?
WAIT! LOOK WHO I'M ASKING! HA HA HA!

Osborn kidnapped J. Jonah Jameson, no longer mayor but now Spider-Man's ally and confidant. Despite Jameson's bravado, he accidentally revealed Spider-Man's secret identity. Elsewhere, the Venom symbiote has returned to Eddie Brock, and Flash Thompson has become Agent Anti-Venom. He now searches for a stolen, highly explosive chunk of tritium...

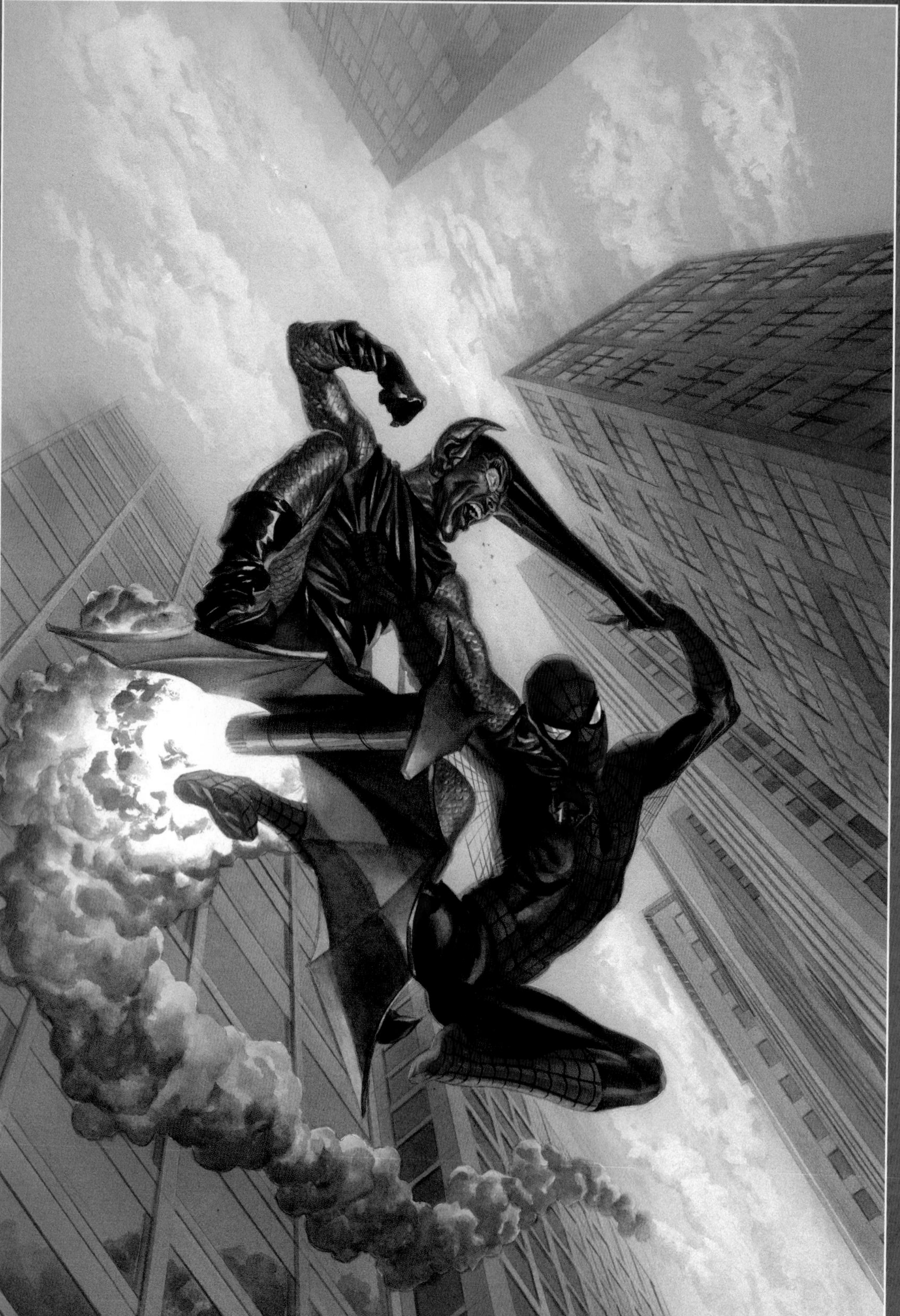

AMAZING SPIDER-MAN #798

GO DOWN SWINGING, PART 2: THE ROPE-A-DOPE

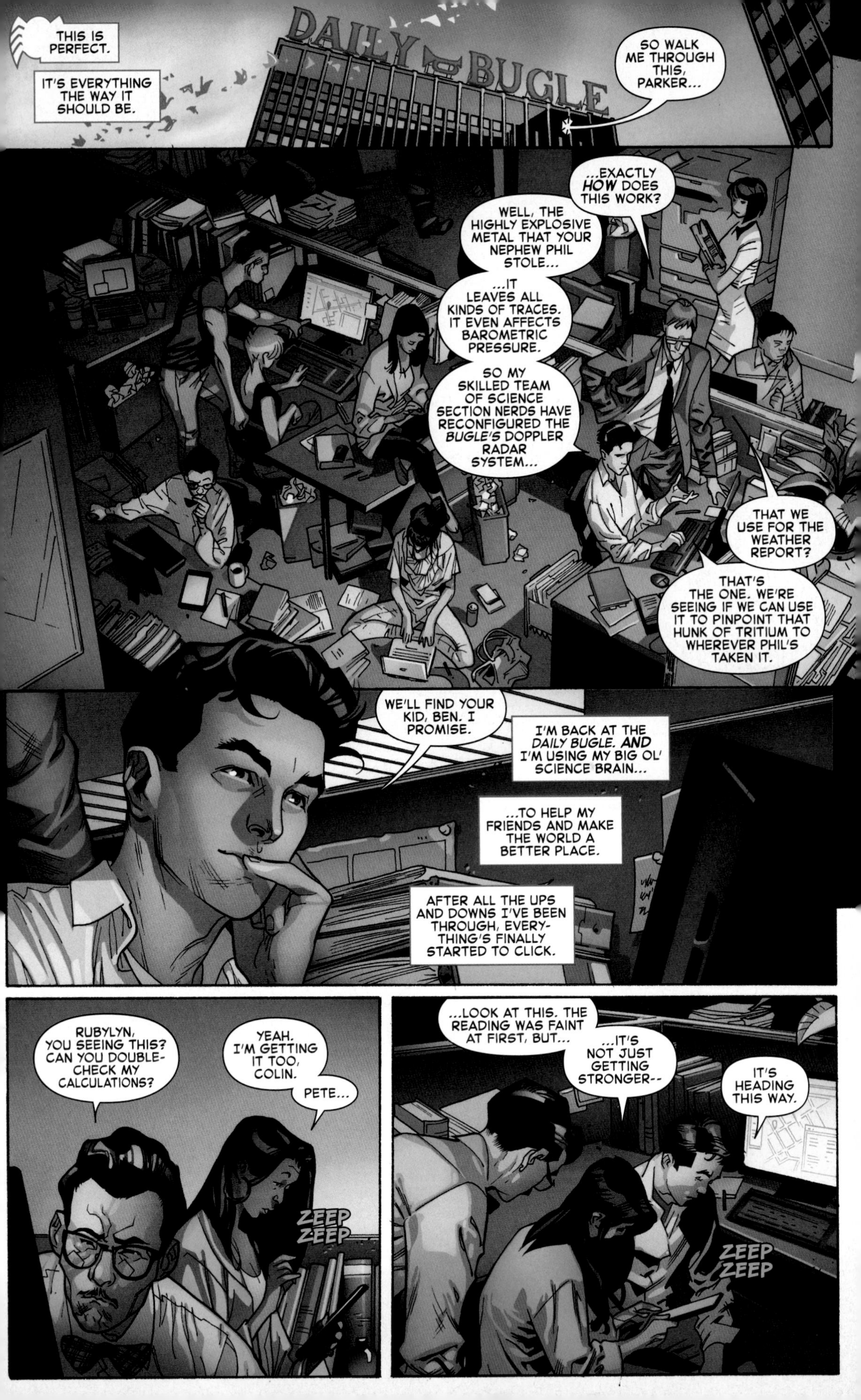

THIS IS PERFECT.
IT'S EVERYTHING THE WAY IT SHOULD BE.
DAILY BUGLE
SO WALK ME THROUGH THIS, PARKER...
...EXACTLY *HOW* DOES THIS WORK?
WELL, THE HIGHLY EXPLOSIVE METAL THAT YOUR NEPHEW PHIL STOLE...
...IT LEAVES ALL KINDS OF TRACES. IT EVEN AFFECTS BAROMETRIC PRESSURE.
SO MY SKILLED TEAM OF SCIENCE SECTION NERDS HAVE RECONFIGURED THE *BUGLE'S* DOPPLER RADAR SYSTEM...
THAT WE USE FOR THE WEATHER REPORT?
THAT'S THE ONE. WE'RE SEEING IF WE CAN USE IT TO PINPOINT THAT HUNK OF TRITIUM TO WHEREVER PHIL'S TAKEN IT.
WE'LL FIND YOUR KID, BEN. I PROMISE.
I'M BACK AT THE *DAILY BUGLE.* **AND** I'M USING MY BIG OL' SCIENCE BRAIN...
...TO HELP MY FRIENDS AND MAKE THE WORLD A BETTER PLACE.
AFTER ALL THE UPS AND DOWNS I'VE BEEN THROUGH, EVERYTHING'S FINALLY STARTED TO CLICK.
RUBYLYN, YOU SEEING THIS? CAN YOU DOUBLE-CHECK MY CALCULATIONS?
YEAH. I'M GETTING IT TOO, COLIN.
PETE...
ZEEP ZEEP
...LOOK AT THIS. THE READING WAS FAINT AT FIRST, BUT...
...IT'S NOT JUST GETTING STRONGER--
IT'S HEADING THIS WAY.
ZEEP ZEEP

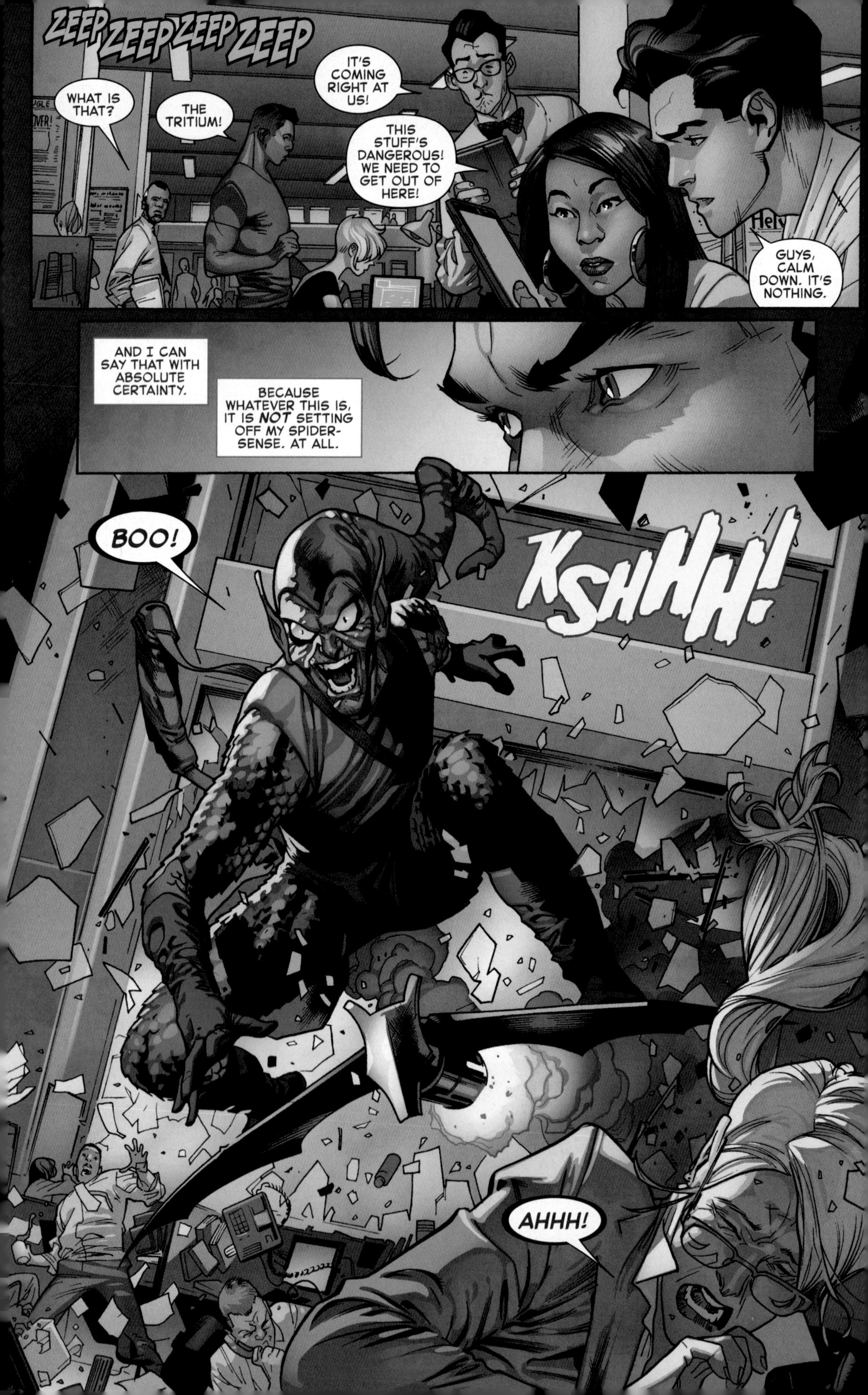
ZEEP ZEEP ZEEP ZEEP
WHAT IS THAT?
THE TRITIUM!
IT'S COMING RIGHT AT US!
THIS STUFF'S DANGEROUS! WE NEED TO GET OUT OF HERE!
GUYS, CALM DOWN. IT'S NOTHING.
AND I CAN SAY THAT WITH ABSOLUTE CERTAINTY.
BECAUSE WHATEVER THIS IS, IT IS *NOT* SETTING OFF MY SPIDER-SENSE. AT ALL.
BOO!
KSHHH!
AHHH!

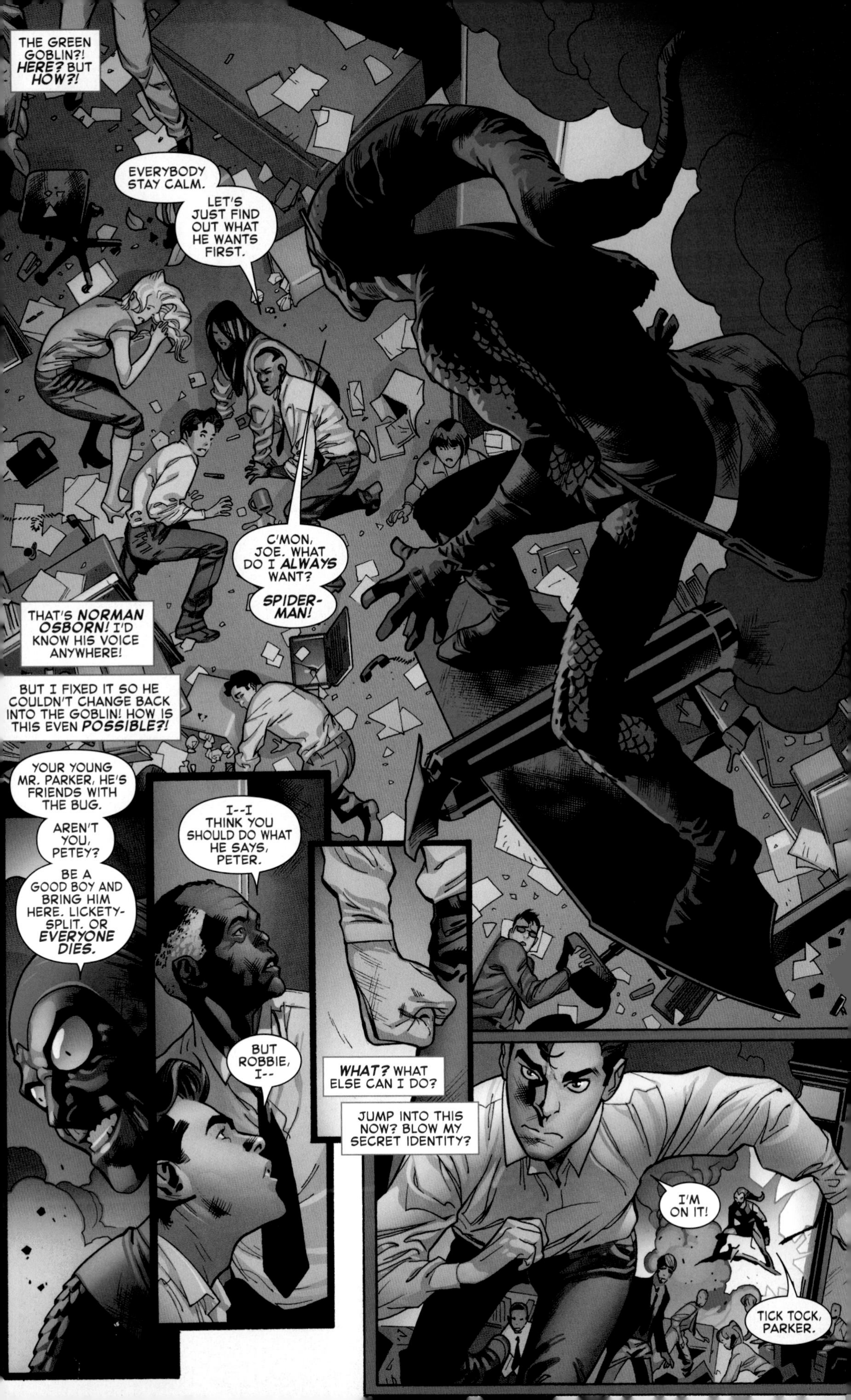
THE GREEN GOBLIN?! HERE? BUT HOW?!
EVERYBODY STAY CALM.
LET'S JUST FIND OUT WHAT HE WANTS FIRST.
C'MON, JOE. WHAT DO I ALWAYS WANT?
SPIDER-MAN!
THAT'S NORMAN OSBORN! I'D KNOW HIS VOICE ANYWHERE!
BUT I FIXED IT SO HE COULDN'T CHANGE BACK INTO THE GOBLIN! HOW IS THIS EVEN POSSIBLE?!
YOUR YOUNG MR. PARKER, HE'S FRIENDS WITH THE BUG.
AREN'T YOU, PETEY?
BE A GOOD BOY AND BRING HIM HERE. LICKETY-SPLIT. OR EVERYONE DIES.
I--I THINK YOU SHOULD DO WHAT HE SAYS, PETER.
BUT ROBBIE, I--
WHAT? WHAT ELSE CAN I DO?
JUMP INTO THIS NOW? BLOW MY SECRET IDENTITY?
I'M ON IT!
TICK TOCK, PARKER.

THE GOBLIN'S LAIR. ACROSS TOWN.

OSBORN'S GOING TO KILL THEM. ALL OF THEM.

HE'LL KILL EVERY SINGLE PERSON PARKER CARES ABOUT.

AND IT'S MY FAULT.

ALL BECAUSE I COULDN'T KEEP MY DAMN FOOL MOUTH SHUT.

HAVE TO *FIX* THIS! HAVE TO--

GNNNH!

I KNOW WHAT IT'S LIKE. TO LOSE EVERYONE. DAD. MARLA. MATTIE.

I--I CAN'T PUT PETER THROUGH THAT. CAN'T HAVE THAT BLOOD ON MY HANDS.

PLEASE. FOR *ONCE*, LET ME BE STRONG ENOUGH.

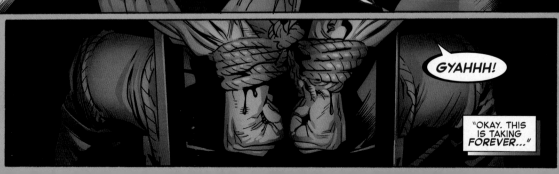

GYAHHH!

"OKAY. THIS IS TAKING *FOREVER*..."

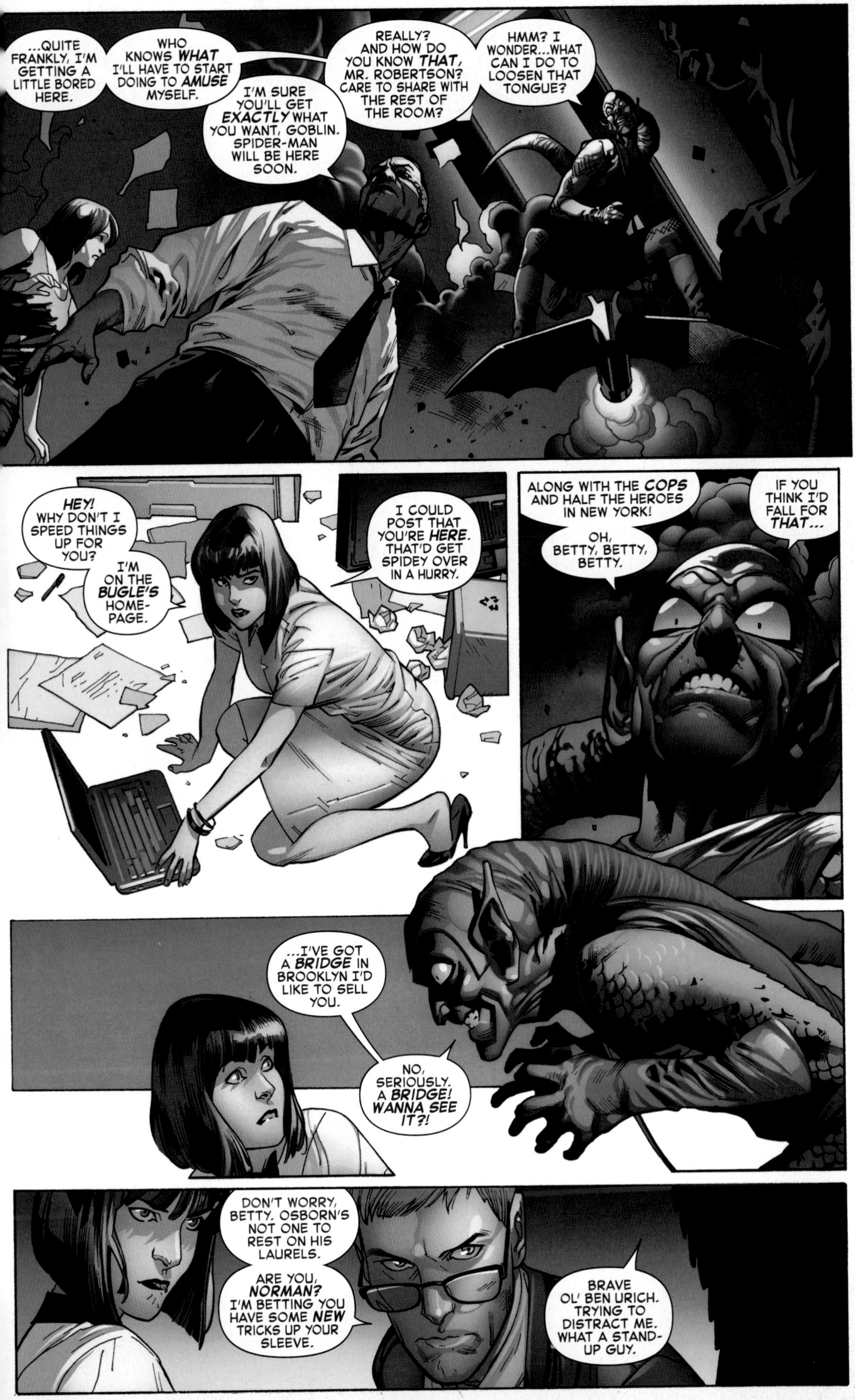
...QUITE FRANKLY, I'M GETTING A LITTLE BORED HERE.
WHO KNOWS WHAT I'LL HAVE TO START DOING TO AMUSE MYSELF.
I'M SURE YOU'LL GET EXACTLY WHAT YOU WANT, GOBLIN. SPIDER-MAN WILL BE HERE SOON.
REALLY? AND HOW DO YOU KNOW THAT, MR. ROBERTSON? CARE TO SHARE WITH THE REST OF THE ROOM?
HMM? I WONDER...WHAT CAN I DO TO LOOSEN THAT TONGUE?
HEY! WHY DON'T I SPEED THINGS UP FOR YOU?
I'M ON THE BUGLE'S HOME-PAGE.
I COULD POST THAT YOU'RE HERE. THAT'D GET SPIDEY OVER IN A HURRY.
ALONG WITH THE COPS AND HALF THE HEROES IN NEW YORK!
OH, BETTY, BETTY, BETTY.
IF YOU THINK I'D FALL FOR THAT...
...I'VE GOT A BRIDGE IN BROOKLYN I'D LIKE TO SELL YOU.
NO, SERIOUSLY. A BRIDGE! WANNA SEE IT?!
DON'T WORRY, BETTY. OSBORN'S NOT ONE TO REST ON HIS LAURELS.
ARE YOU, NORMAN? I'M BETTING YOU HAVE SOME NEW TRICKS UP YOUR SLEEVE.
BRAVE OL' BEN URICH. TRYING TO DISTRACT ME. WHAT A STAND-UP GUY.

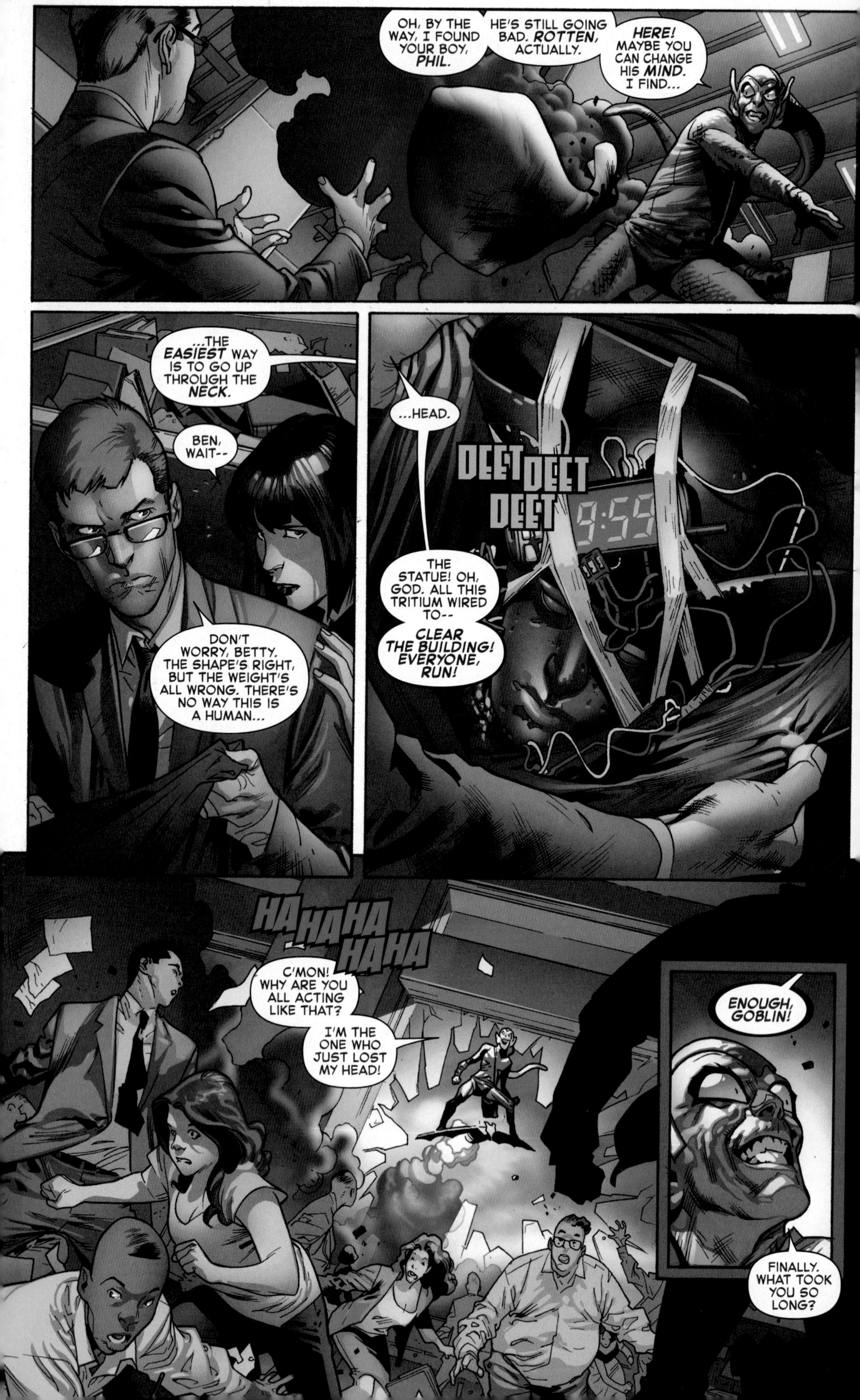
OH, BY THE WAY, I FOUND YOUR BOY, PHIL.
HE'S STILL GOING BAD. ROTTEN, ACTUALLY.
HERE! MAYBE YOU CAN CHANGE HIS MIND. I FIND...
...THE EASIEST WAY IS TO GO UP THROUGH THE NECK.
BEN, WAIT--
DON'T WORRY, BETTY. THE SHAPE'S RIGHT, BUT THE WEIGHT'S ALL WRONG. THERE'S NO WAY THIS IS A HUMAN...
...HEAD.
DEET DEET DEET
9:59
THE STATUE! OH, GOD. ALL THIS TRITIUM WIRED TO--
CLEAR THE BUILDING! EVERYONE, RUN!
HAHAHAHAHA
C'MON! WHY ARE YOU ALL ACTING LIKE THAT?
I'M THE ONE WHO JUST LOST MY HEAD!
ENOUGH, GOBLIN!
FINALLY. WHAT TOOK YOU SO LONG?

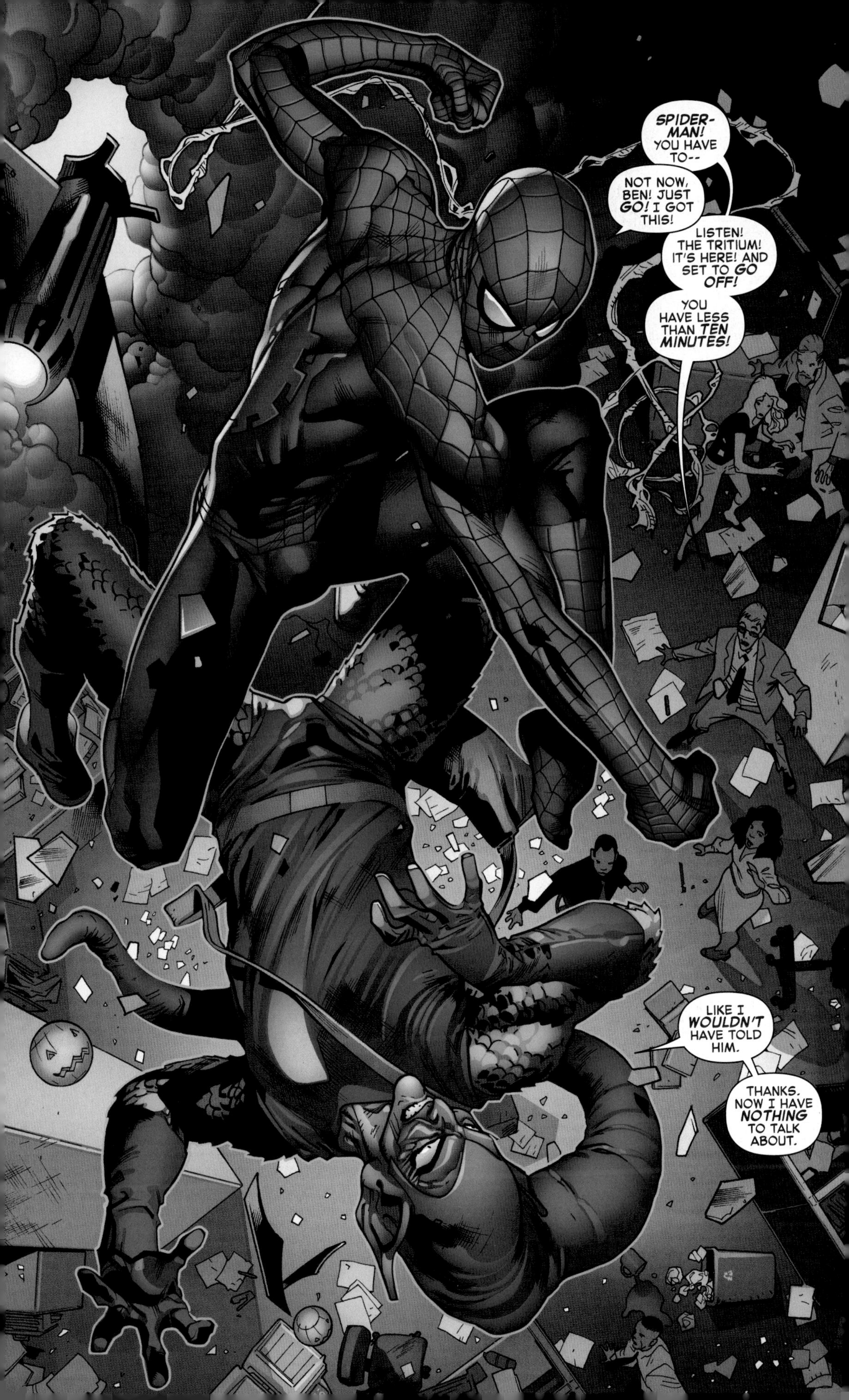

SPIDER-MAN! YOU HAVE TO--
NOT NOW, BEN! JUST GO! I GOT THIS!
LISTEN! THE TRITIUM! IT'S HERE! AND SET TO GO OFF!
YOU HAVE LESS THAN TEN MINUTES!
LIKE I WOULDN'T HAVE TOLD HIM.
THANKS. NOW I HAVE NOTHING TO TALK ABOUT.

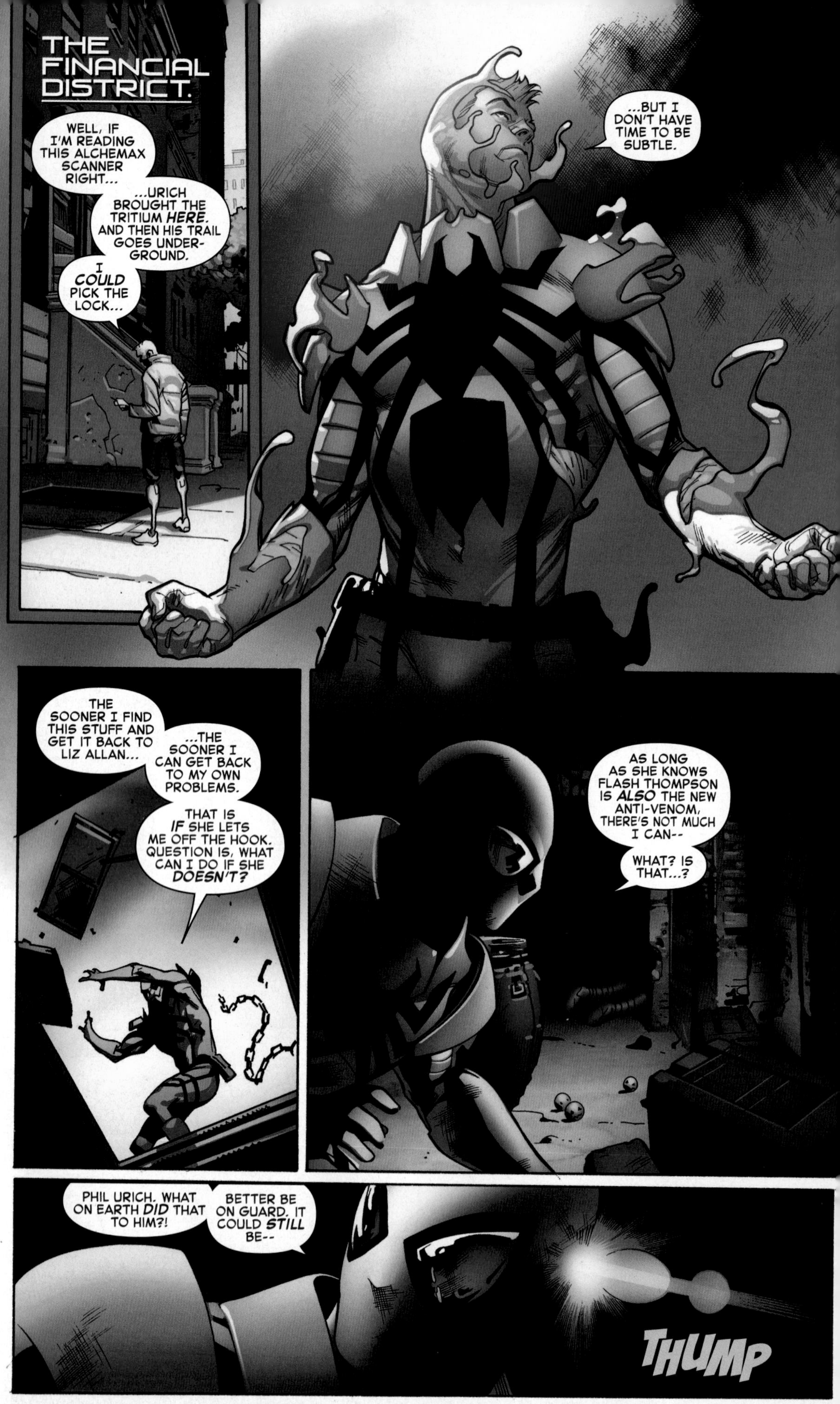
THE FINANCIAL DISTRICT.
WELL, IF I'M READING THIS ALCHEMAX SCANNER RIGHT...
...URICH BROUGHT THE TRITIUM HERE. AND THEN HIS TRAIL GOES UNDER-GROUND.
I COULD PICK THE LOCK...
...BUT I DON'T HAVE TIME TO BE SUBTLE.
THE SOONER I FIND THIS STUFF AND GET IT BACK TO LIZ ALLAN...
...THE SOONER I CAN GET BACK TO MY OWN PROBLEMS.
THAT IS IF SHE LETS ME OFF THE HOOK. QUESTION IS, WHAT CAN I DO IF SHE DOESN'T?
AS LONG AS SHE KNOWS FLASH THOMPSON IS ALSO THE NEW ANTI-VENOM, THERE'S NOT MUCH I CAN--
WHAT? IS THAT...?
PHIL URICH. WHAT ON EARTH DID THAT TO HIM?!
BETTER BE ON GUARD. IT COULD STILL BE--
THUMP

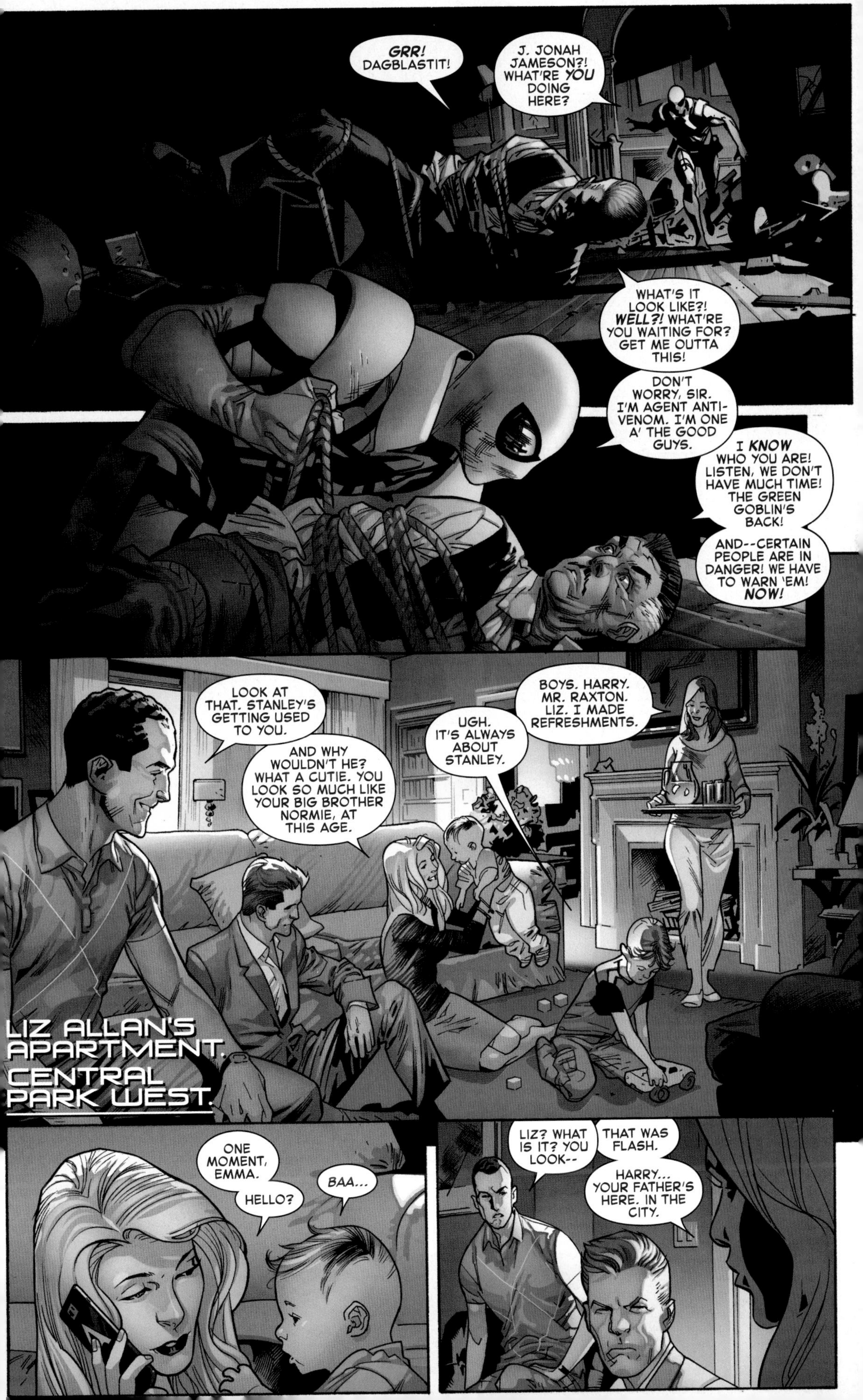
GRR! DAGBLASTIT!
J. JONAH JAMESON?! WHAT'RE YOU DOING HERE?
WHAT'S IT LOOK LIKE?! WELL?! WHAT'RE YOU WAITING FOR? GET ME OUTTA THIS!
DON'T WORRY, SIR. I'M AGENT ANTI-VENOM. I'M ONE A' THE GOOD GUYS.
I KNOW WHO YOU ARE! LISTEN, WE DON'T HAVE MUCH TIME! THE GREEN GOBLIN'S BACK!
AND--CERTAIN PEOPLE ARE IN DANGER! WE HAVE TO WARN 'EM! NOW!
LIZ ALLAN'S APARTMENT. CENTRAL PARK WEST.
LOOK AT THAT. STANLEY'S GETTING USED TO YOU.
AND WHY WOULDN'T HE? WHAT A CUTIE. YOU LOOK SO MUCH LIKE YOUR BIG BROTHER NORMIE, AT THIS AGE.
UGH. IT'S ALWAYS ABOUT STANLEY.
BOYS. HARRY. MR. RAXTON. LIZ. I MADE REFRESHMENTS.
ONE MOMENT, EMMA.
HELLO?
BAA...
LIZ? WHAT IS IT? YOU LOOK--
THAT WAS FLASH.
HARRY... YOUR FATHER'S HERE. IN THE CITY.

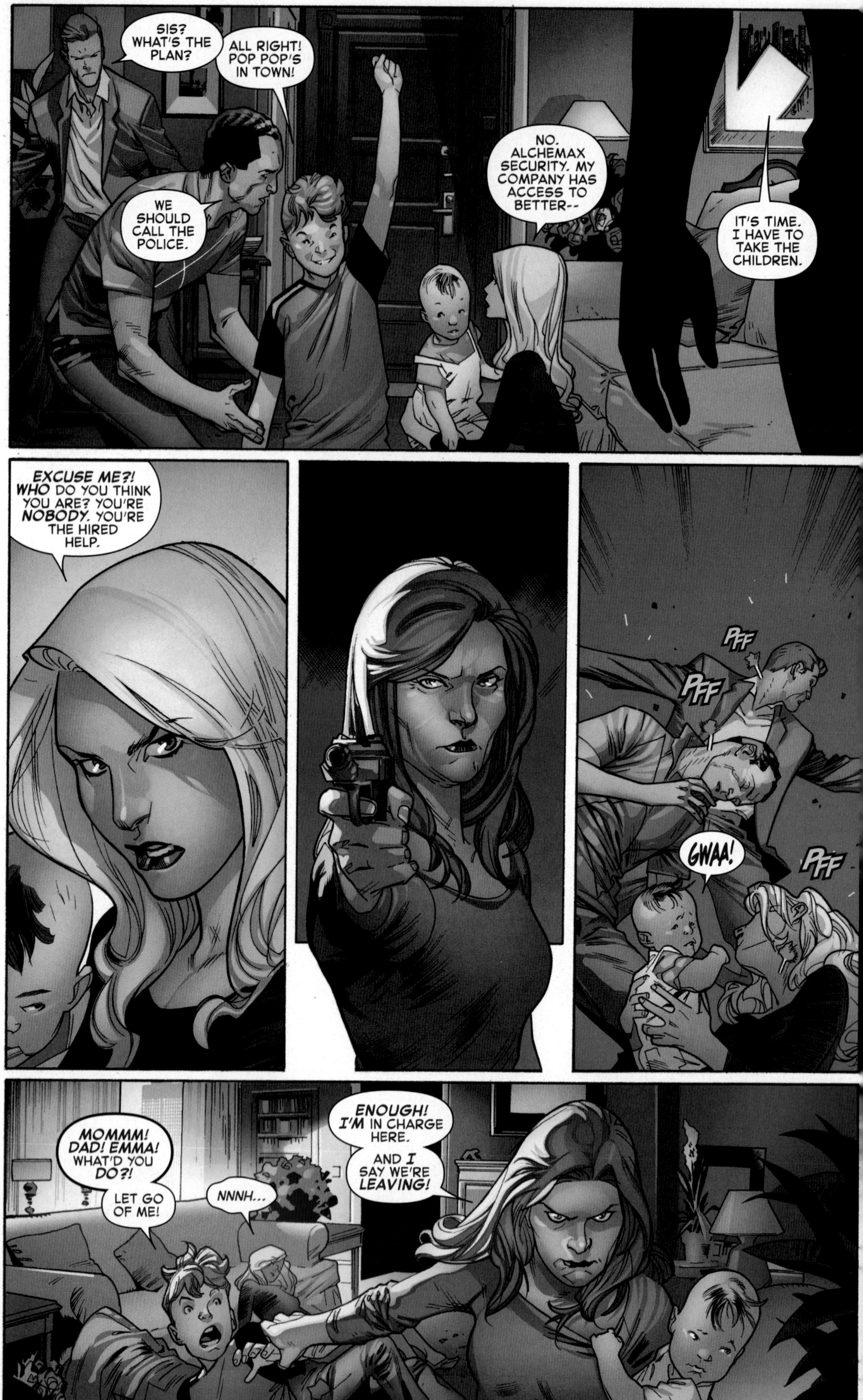

SIS? WHAT'S THE PLAN?
ALL RIGHT! POP POP'S IN TOWN!
WE SHOULD CALL THE POLICE.
NO. ALCHEMAX SECURITY. MY COMPANY HAS ACCESS TO BETTER--
IT'S TIME. I HAVE TO TAKE THE CHILDREN.
EXCUSE ME?! WHO DO YOU THINK YOU ARE? YOU'RE NOBODY. YOU'RE THE HIRED HELP.
PFF
PFF
GWAA!
PFF
MOMMM! DAD! EMMA! WHAT'D YOU DO?!
LET GO OF ME!
NNNH...
ENOUGH! I'M IN CHARGE HERE.
AND I SAY WE'RE LEAVING!

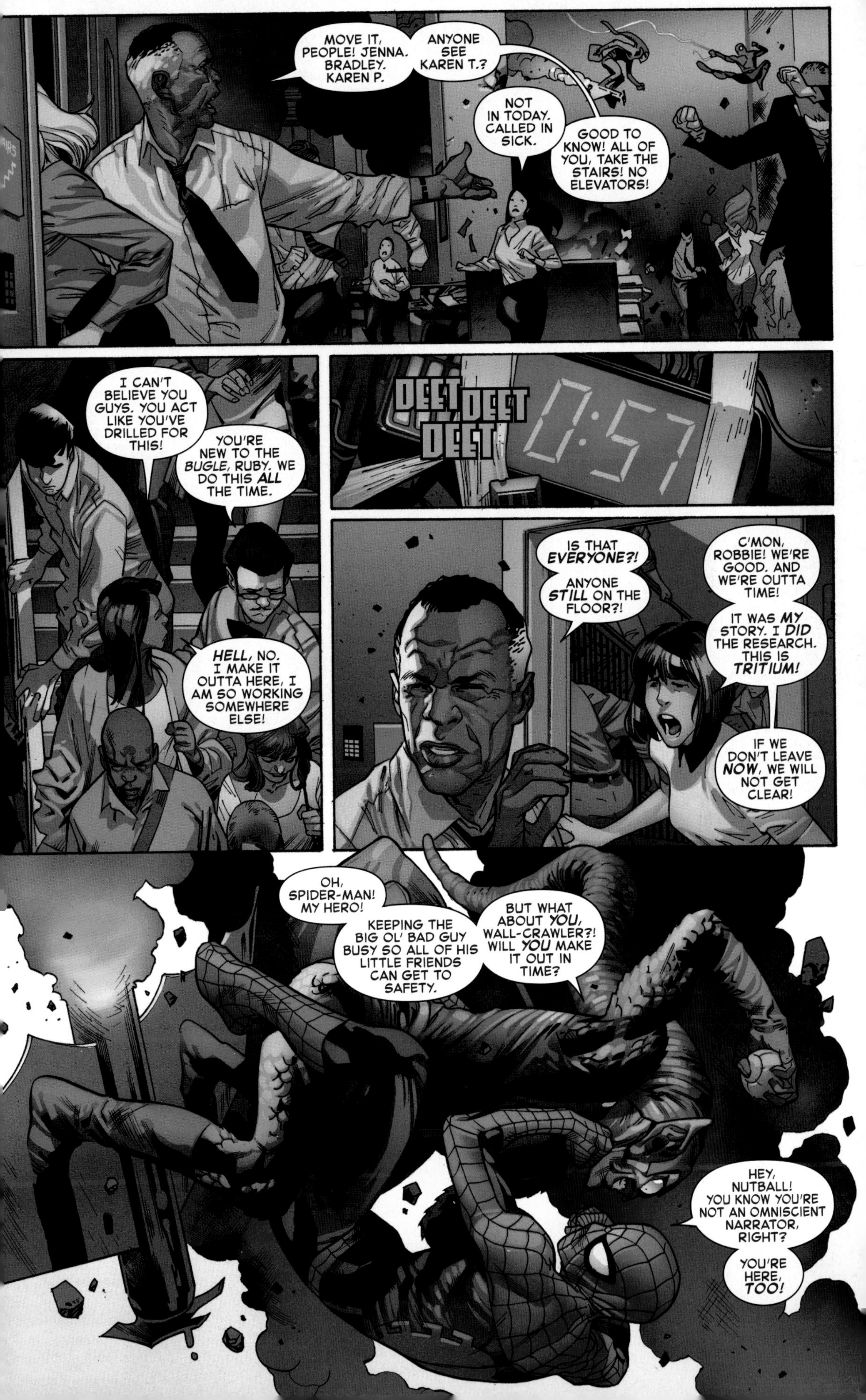
MOVE IT, PEOPLE! JENNA. BRADLEY. KAREN P.
ANYONE SEE KAREN T.?
NOT IN TODAY. CALLED IN SICK.
GOOD TO KNOW! ALL OF YOU, TAKE THE STAIRS! NO ELEVATORS!
I CAN'T BELIEVE YOU GUYS. YOU ACT LIKE YOU'VE DRILLED FOR THIS!
YOU'RE NEW TO THE BUGLE, RUBY. WE DO THIS ALL THE TIME.
HELL, NO. I MAKE IT OUTTA HERE, I AM SO WORKING SOMEWHERE ELSE!
DEET DEET DEET
0:57
IS THAT EVERYONE?!
ANYONE STILL ON THE FLOOR?!
C'MON, ROBBIE! WE'RE GOOD. AND WE'RE OUTTA TIME!
IT WAS MY STORY. I DID THE RESEARCH. THIS IS TRITIUM!
IF WE DON'T LEAVE NOW, WE WILL NOT GET CLEAR!
OH, SPIDER-MAN! MY HERO!
KEEPING THE BIG OL' BAD GUY BUSY SO ALL OF HIS LITTLE FRIENDS CAN GET TO SAFETY.
BUT WHAT ABOUT YOU, WALL-CRAWLER?! WILL YOU MAKE IT OUT IN TIME?
HEY, NUTBALL! YOU KNOW YOU'RE NOT AN OMNISCIENT NARRATOR, RIGHT?
YOU'RE HERE, TOO!

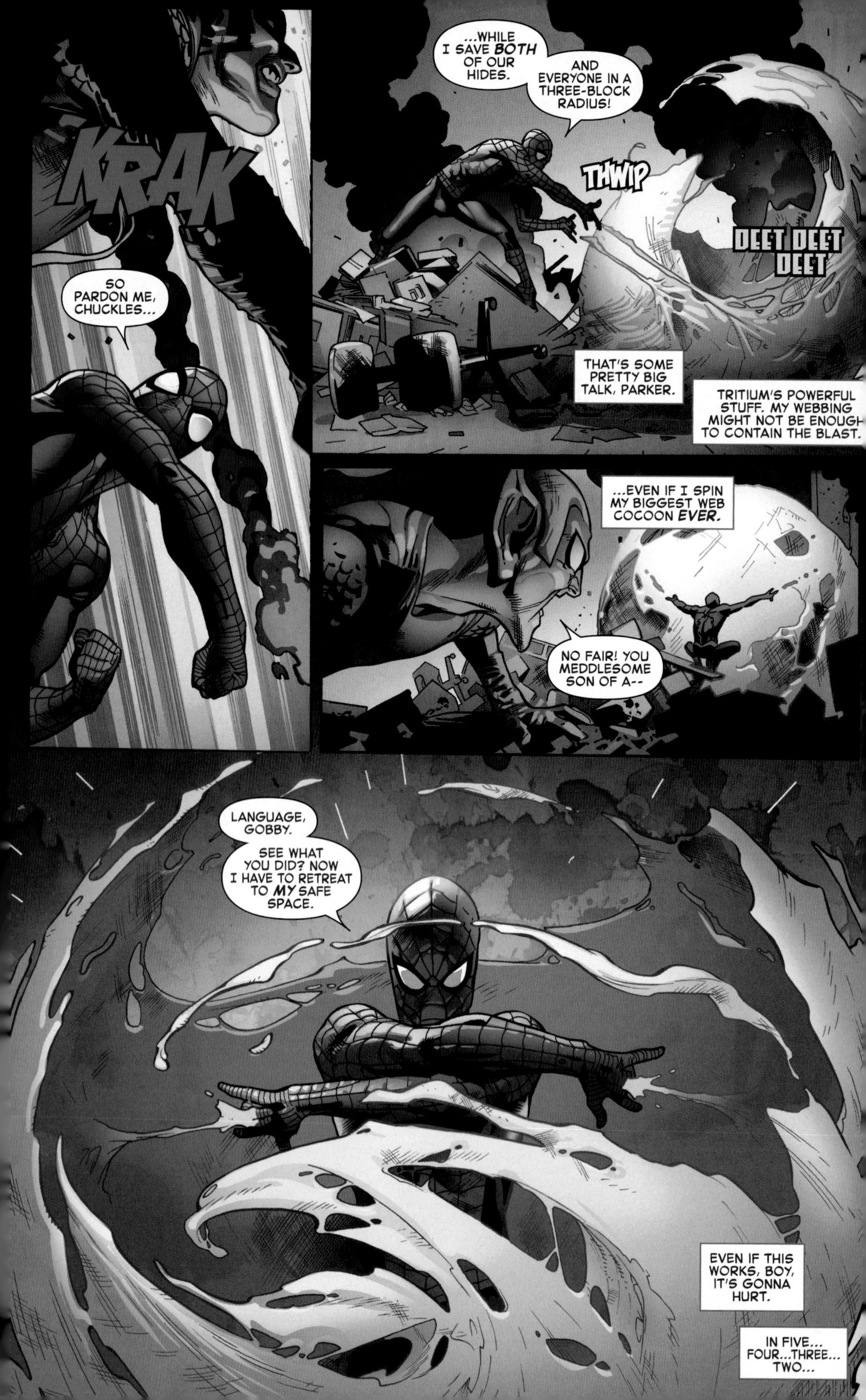
KRAK
SO PARDON ME, CHUCKLES...
...WHILE I SAVE BOTH OF OUR HIDES.
AND EVERYONE IN A THREE-BLOCK RADIUS!
THWIP
DEET DEET DEET
THAT'S SOME PRETTY BIG TALK, PARKER.
TRITIUM'S POWERFUL STUFF. MY WEBBING MIGHT NOT BE ENOUGH TO CONTAIN THE BLAST.
...EVEN IF I SPIN MY BIGGEST WEB COCOON EVER.
NO FAIR! YOU MEDDLESOME SON OF A--
LANGUAGE, GOBBY.
SEE WHAT YOU DID? NOW I HAVE TO RETREAT TO MY SAFE SPACE.
EVEN IF THIS WORKS, BOY, IT'S GONNA HURT.
IN FIVE... FOUR...THREE... TWO...

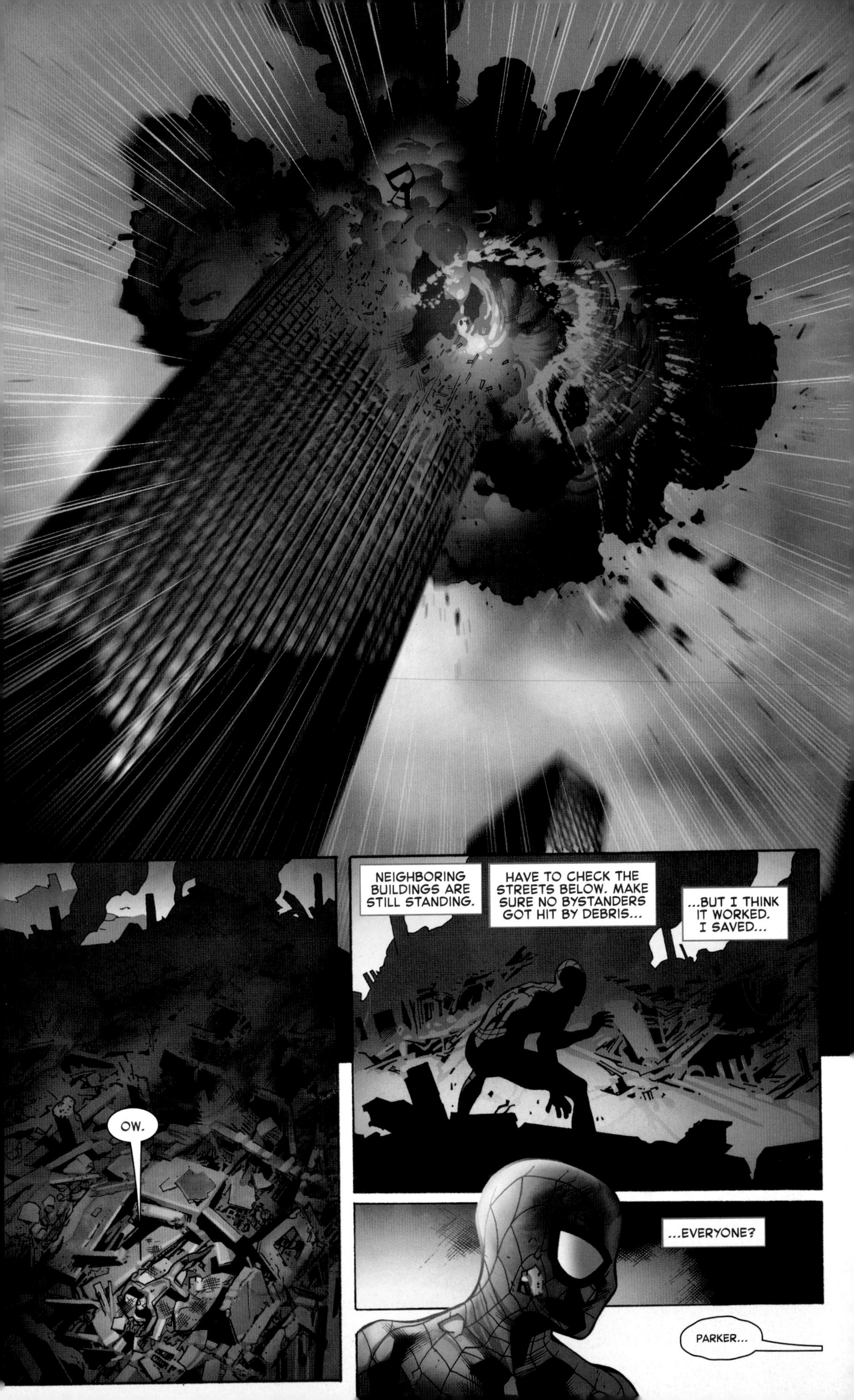

OW.
NEIGHBORING BUILDINGS ARE STILL STANDING.
HAVE TO CHECK THE STREETS BELOW. MAKE SURE NO BYSTANDERS GOT HIT BY DEBRIS...
...BUT I THINK IT WORKED. I SAVED...
...EVERYONE?
PARKER...

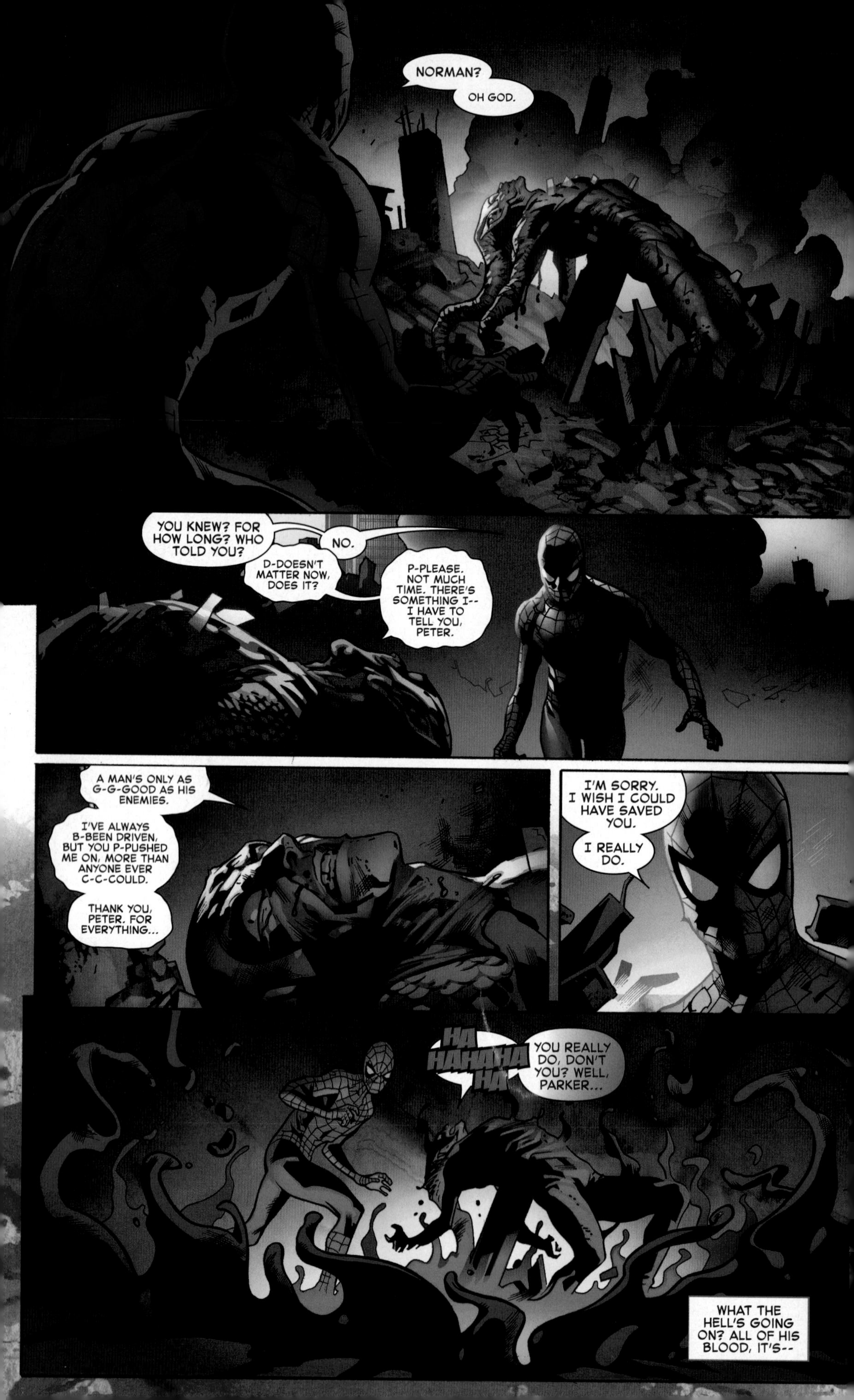
NORMAN?
OH GOD.
YOU KNEW? FOR HOW LONG? WHO TOLD YOU?
NO.
D-DOESN'T MATTER NOW, DOES IT?
P-PLEASE. NOT MUCH TIME. THERE'S SOMETHING I-- I HAVE TO TELL YOU, PETER.
A MAN'S ONLY AS G-G-GOOD AS HIS ENEMIES.
I'VE ALWAYS B-BEEN DRIVEN, BUT YOU P-PUSHED ME ON, MORE THAN ANYONE EVER C-C-COULD.
THANK YOU, PETER. FOR EVERYTHING...
I'M SORRY. I WISH I COULD HAVE SAVED YOU.
I REALLY DO.
HA HAHAHA HA
YOU REALLY DO, DON'T YOU? WELL, PARKER...
WHAT THE HELL'S GOING ON? ALL OF HIS BLOOD, IT'S--

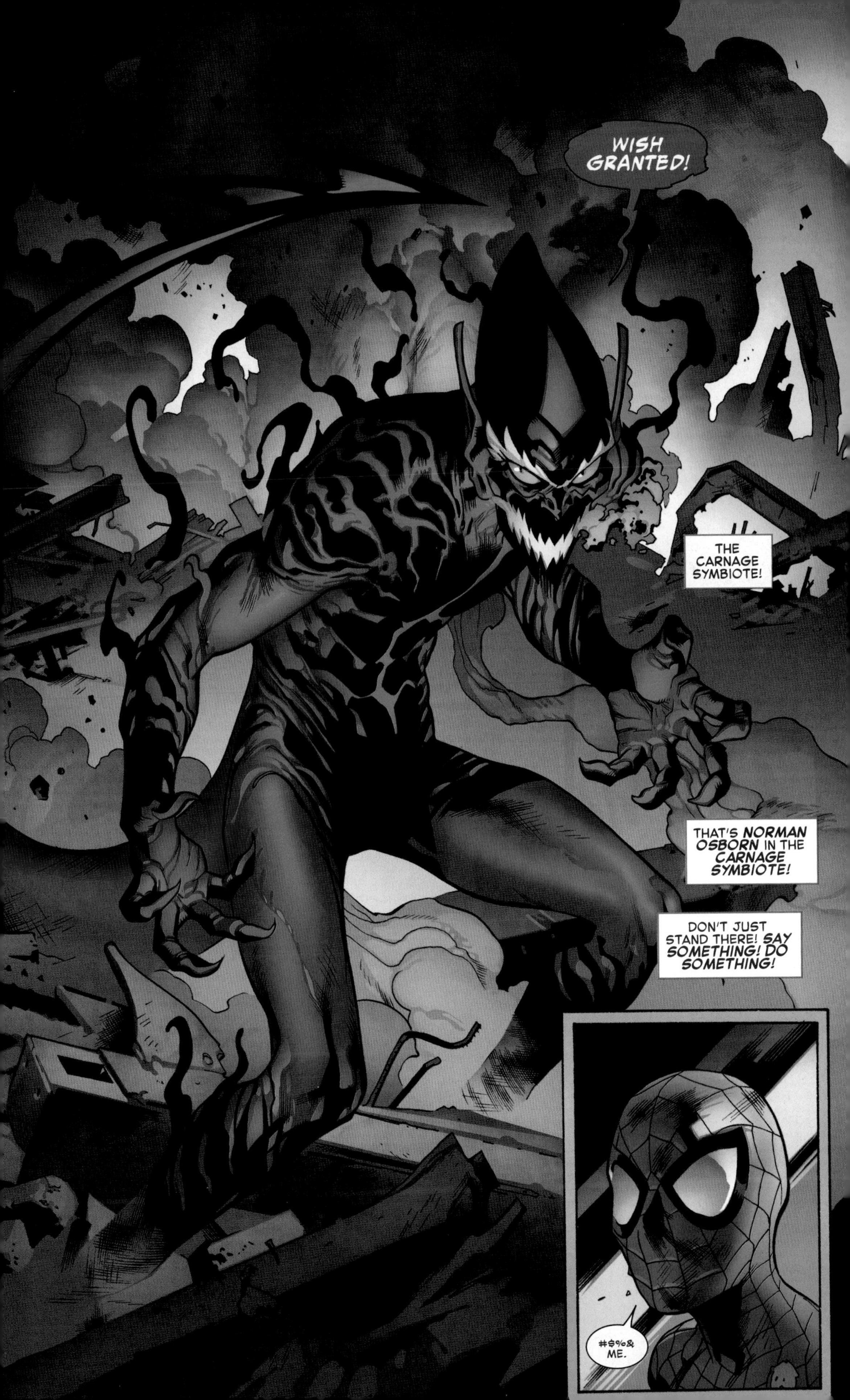
WISH GRANTED!
THE CARNAGE SYMBIOTE!
THAT'S NORMAN OSBORN IN THE CARNAGE SYMBIOTE!
DON'T JUST STAND THERE! SAY SOMETHING! DO SOMETHING!
#$%& ME.

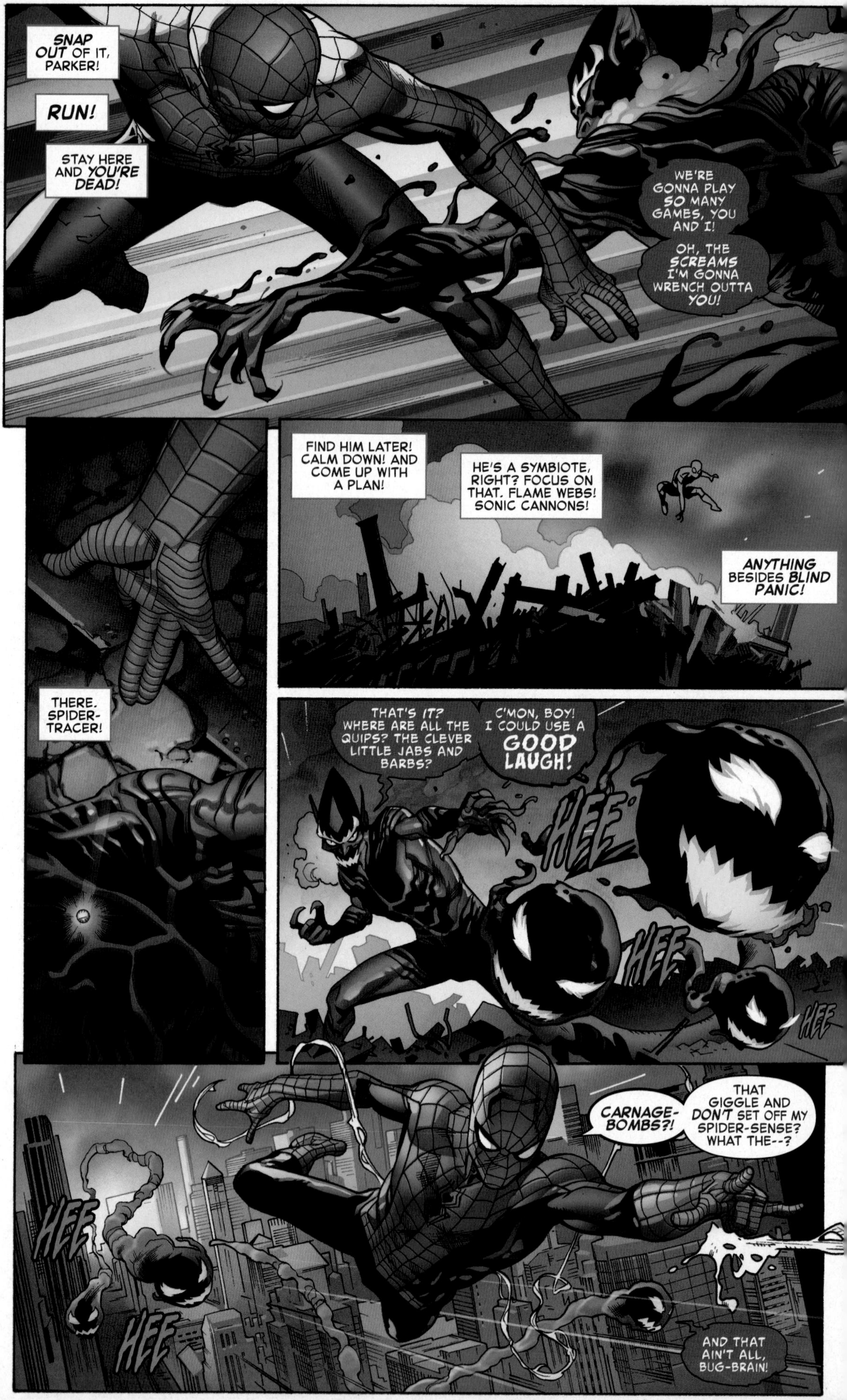
SNAP OUT OF IT, PARKER!
RUN!
STAY HERE AND YOU'RE DEAD!
WE'RE GONNA PLAY SO MANY GAMES, YOU AND I!
OH, THE SCREAMS I'M GONNA WRENCH OUTTA YOU!
FIND HIM LATER! CALM DOWN! AND COME UP WITH A PLAN!
HE'S A SYMBIOTE, RIGHT? FOCUS ON THAT. FLAME WEBS! SONIC CANNONS!
ANYTHING BESIDES BLIND PANIC!
THERE. SPIDER-TRACER!
THAT'S IT? WHERE ARE ALL THE QUIPS? THE CLEVER LITTLE JABS AND BARBS?
C'MON, BOY! I COULD USE A GOOD LAUGH!
HEE
HEE
HEE
CARNAGE-BOMBS?!
THAT GIGGLE AND DON'T SET OFF MY SPIDER-SENSE? WHAT THE--?
HEE
HEE
AND THAT AIN'T ALL, BUG-BRAIN!

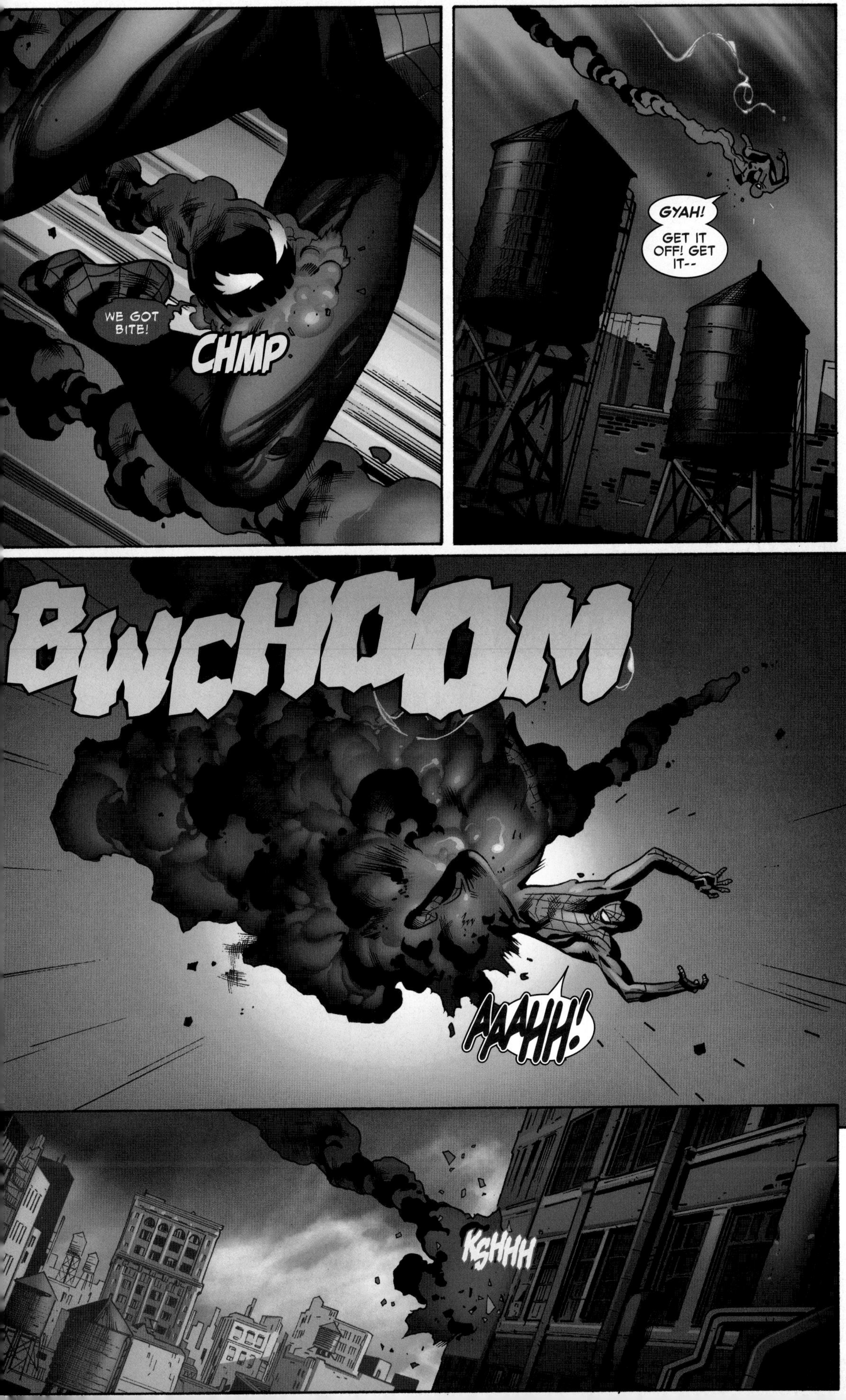
WE GOT BITE!
CHMP
GYAH!
GET IT OFF! GET IT--
BWCHOOM
AAAHH!
KSHHH

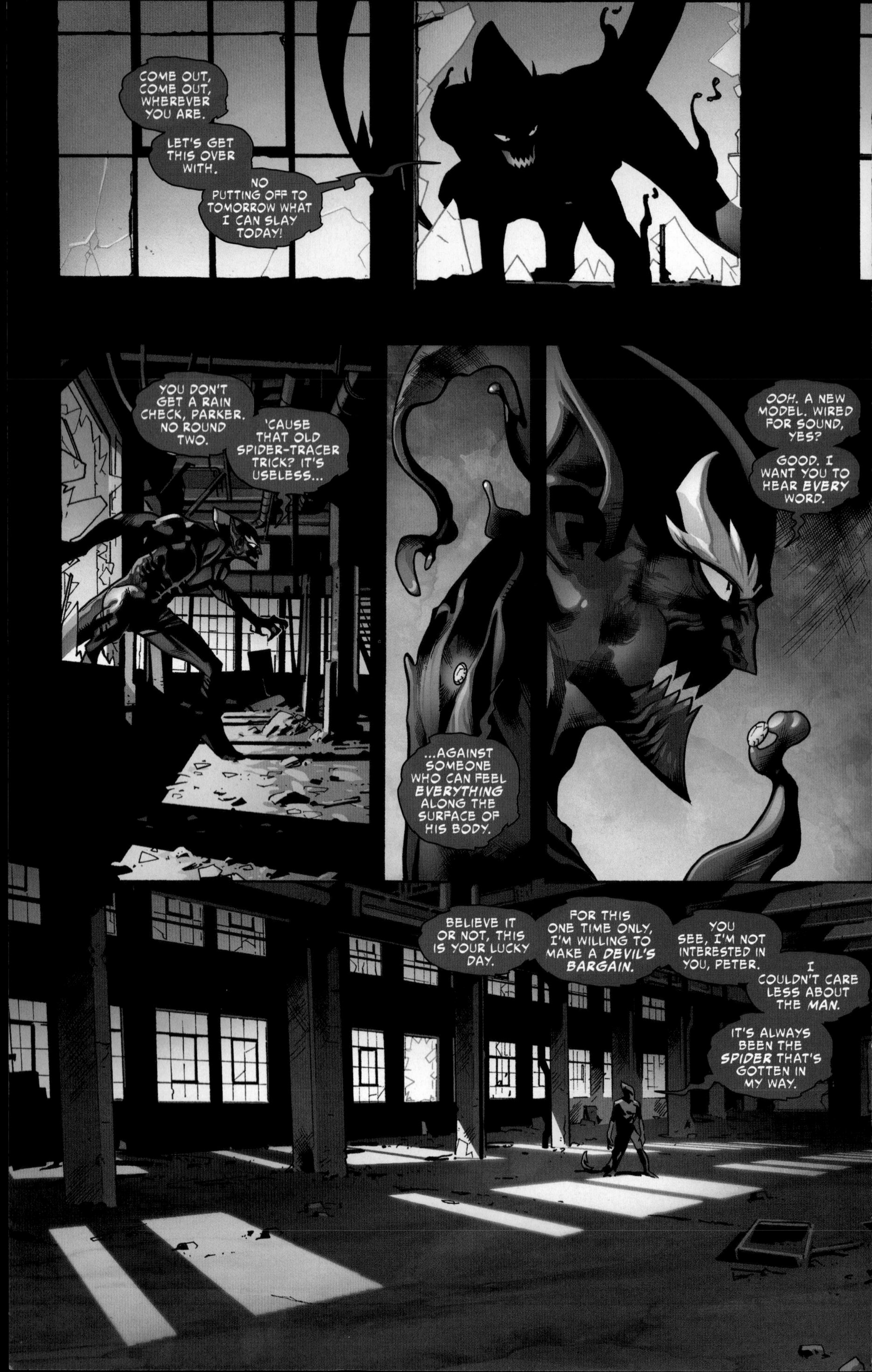
COME OUT, COME OUT, WHEREVER YOU ARE.
LET'S GET THIS OVER WITH.
NO PUTTING OFF TO TOMORROW WHAT I CAN SLAY TODAY!
YOU DON'T GET A RAIN CHECK, PARKER. NO ROUND TWO.
'CAUSE THAT OLD SPIDER-TRACER TRICK? IT'S USELESS...
...AGAINST SOMEONE WHO CAN FEEL EVERYTHING ALONG THE SURFACE OF HIS BODY.
OOH. A NEW MODEL. WIRED FOR SOUND, YES?
GOOD. I WANT YOU TO HEAR EVERY WORD.
BELIEVE IT OR NOT, THIS IS YOUR LUCKY DAY.
FOR THIS ONE TIME ONLY, I'M WILLING TO MAKE A DEVIL'S BARGAIN.
YOU SEE, I'M NOT INTERESTED IN YOU, PETER.
I COULDN'T CARE LESS ABOUT THE MAN.
IT'S ALWAYS BEEN THE SPIDER THAT'S GOTTEN IN MY WAY.

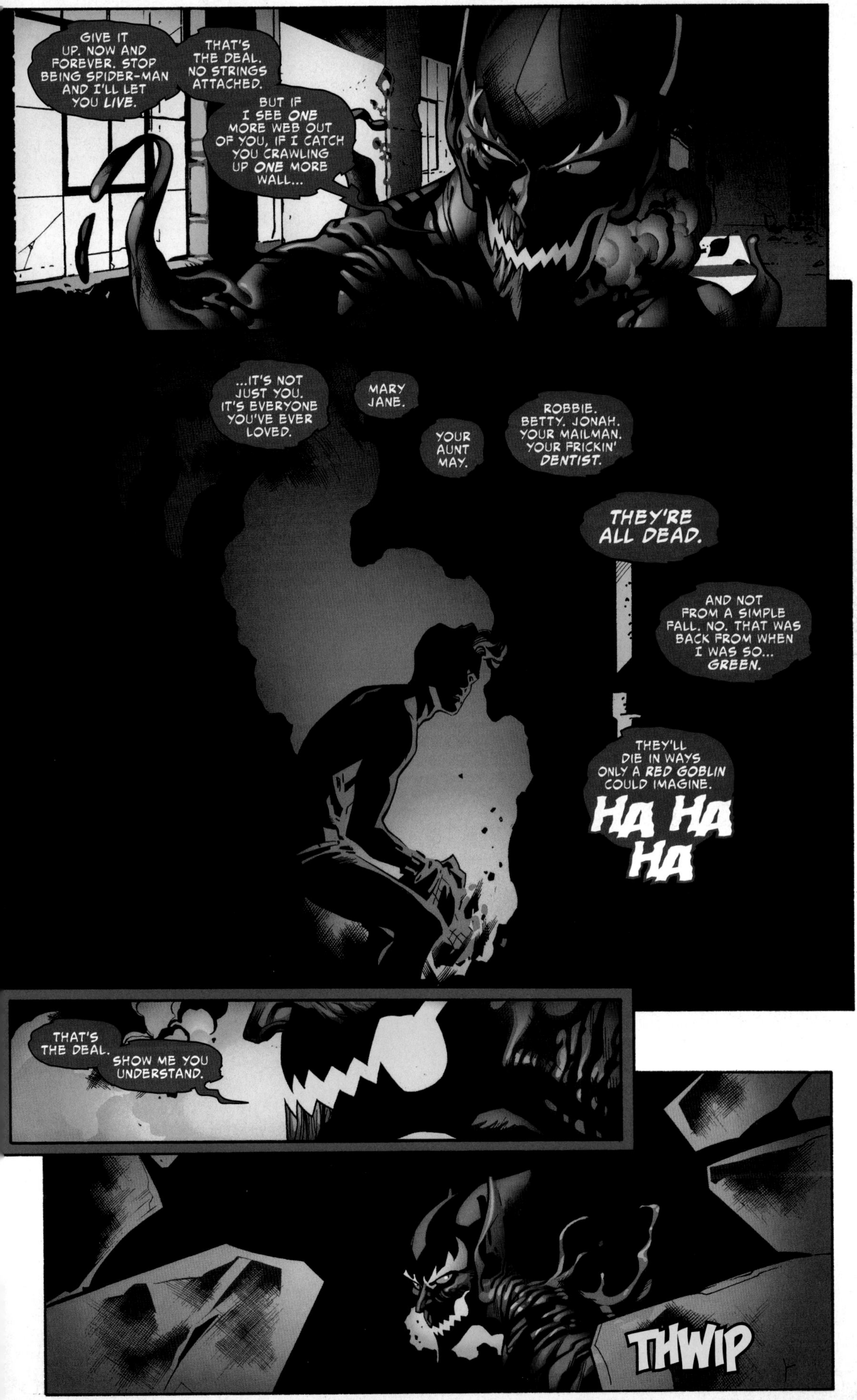
GIVE IT UP. NOW AND FOREVER. STOP BEING SPIDER-MAN AND I'LL LET YOU LIVE.
THAT'S THE DEAL. NO STRINGS ATTACHED.
BUT IF I SEE ONE MORE WEB OUT OF YOU, IF I CATCH YOU CRAWLING UP ONE MORE WALL...
...IT'S NOT JUST YOU. IT'S EVERYONE YOU'VE EVER LOVED.
MARY JANE.
YOUR AUNT MAY.
ROBBIE. BETTY. JONAH. YOUR MAILMAN. YOUR FRICKIN' DENTIST.
THEY'RE ALL DEAD.
AND NOT FROM A SIMPLE FALL. NO. THAT WAS BACK FROM WHEN I WAS SO... GREEN.
THEY'LL DIE IN WAYS ONLY A RED GOBLIN COULD IMAGINE.
HA HA HA
THAT'S THE DEAL.
SHOW ME YOU UNDERSTAND.
THWIP

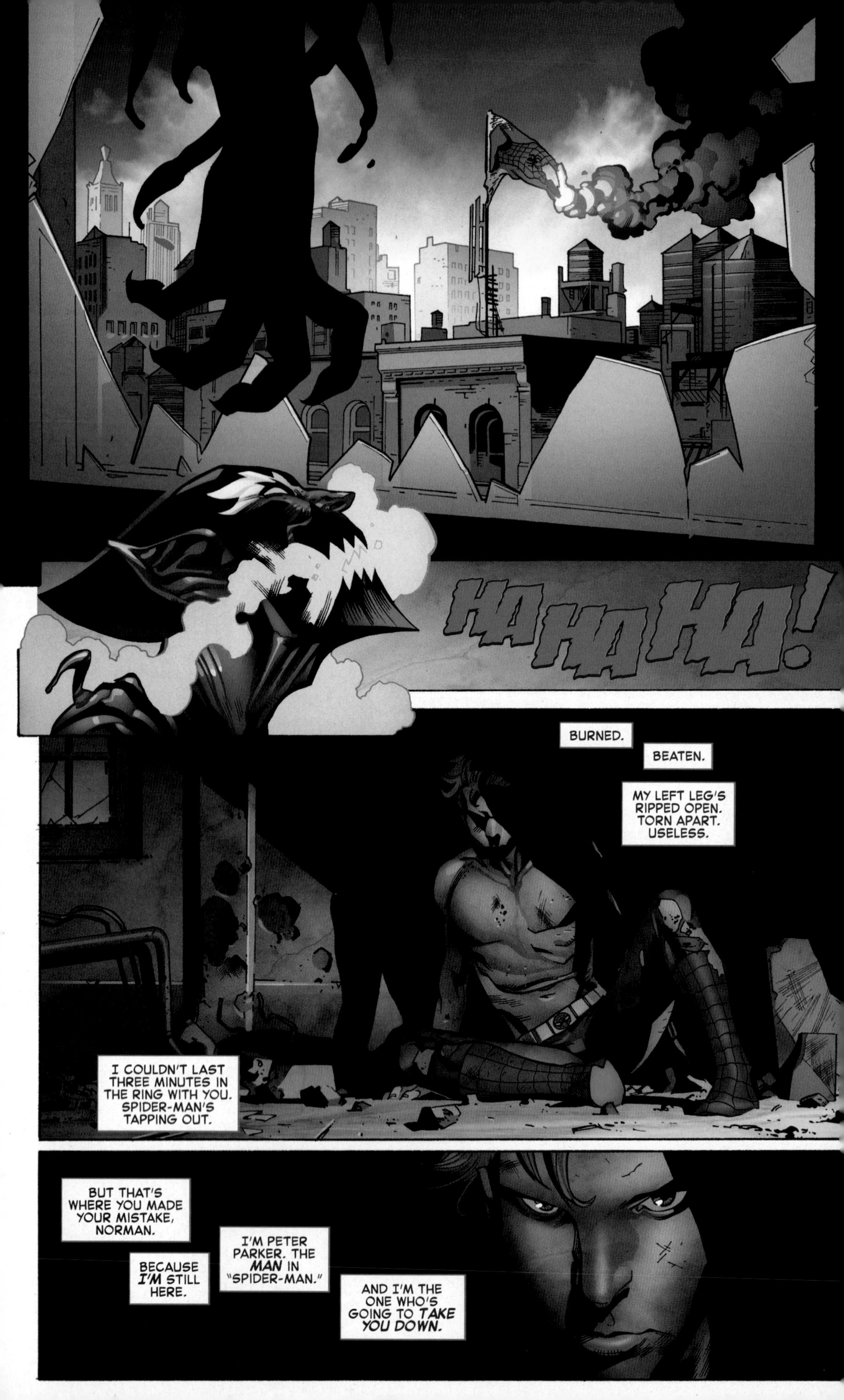
HA HA HA!
BURNED.
BEATEN.
MY LEFT LEG'S RIPPED OPEN. TORN APART. USELESS.
I COULDN'T LAST THREE MINUTES IN THE RING WITH YOU. SPIDER-MAN'S TAPPING OUT.
BUT THAT'S WHERE YOU MADE YOUR MISTAKE, NORMAN.
BECAUSE I'M STILL HERE.
I'M PETER PARKER. THE MAN IN "SPIDER-MAN."
AND I'M THE ONE WHO'S GOING TO TAKE YOU DOWN.

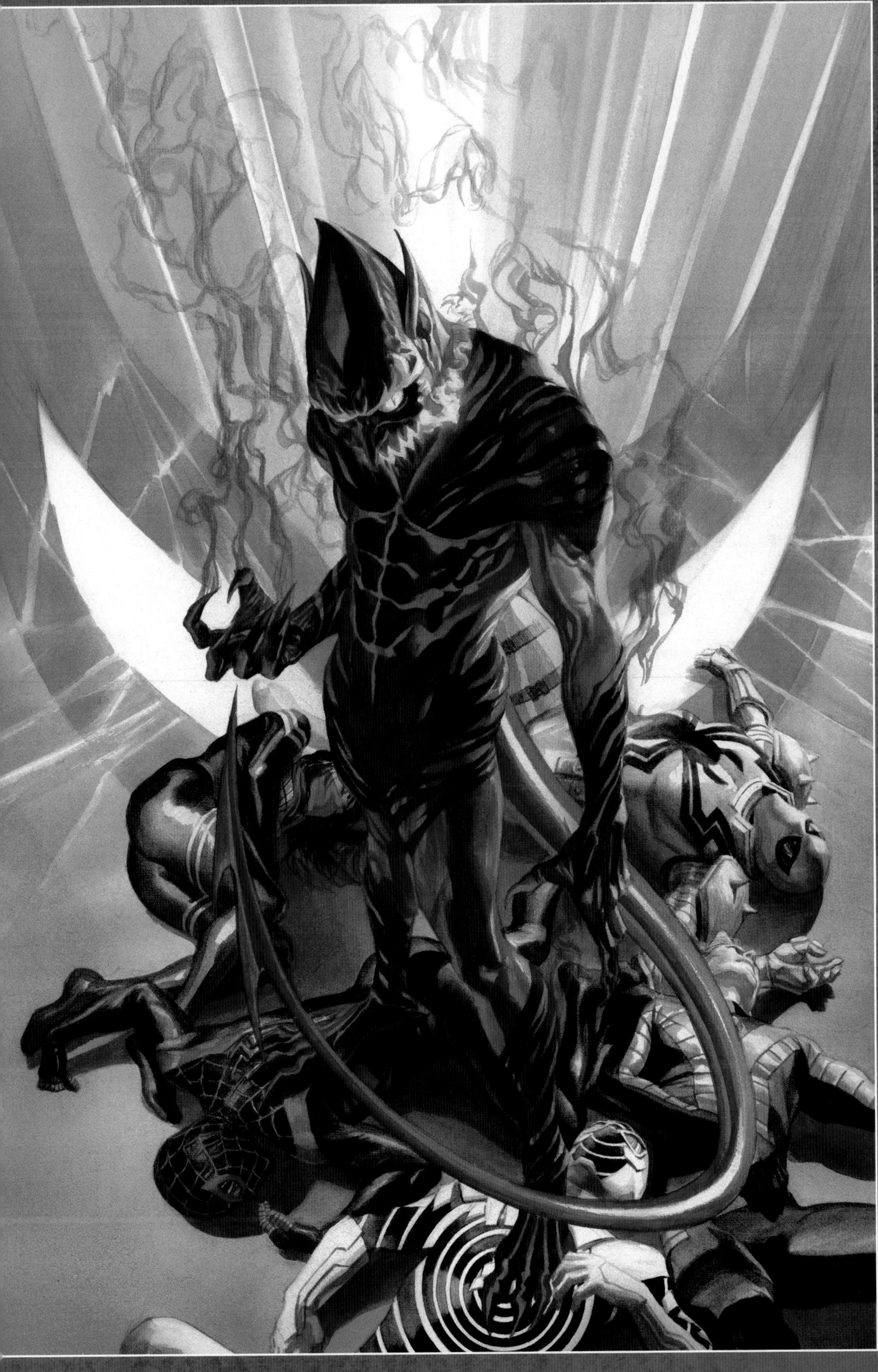

AMAZING SPIDER-MAN #799

GO DOWN SWINGING, PART 3: THE TIES THAT BIND

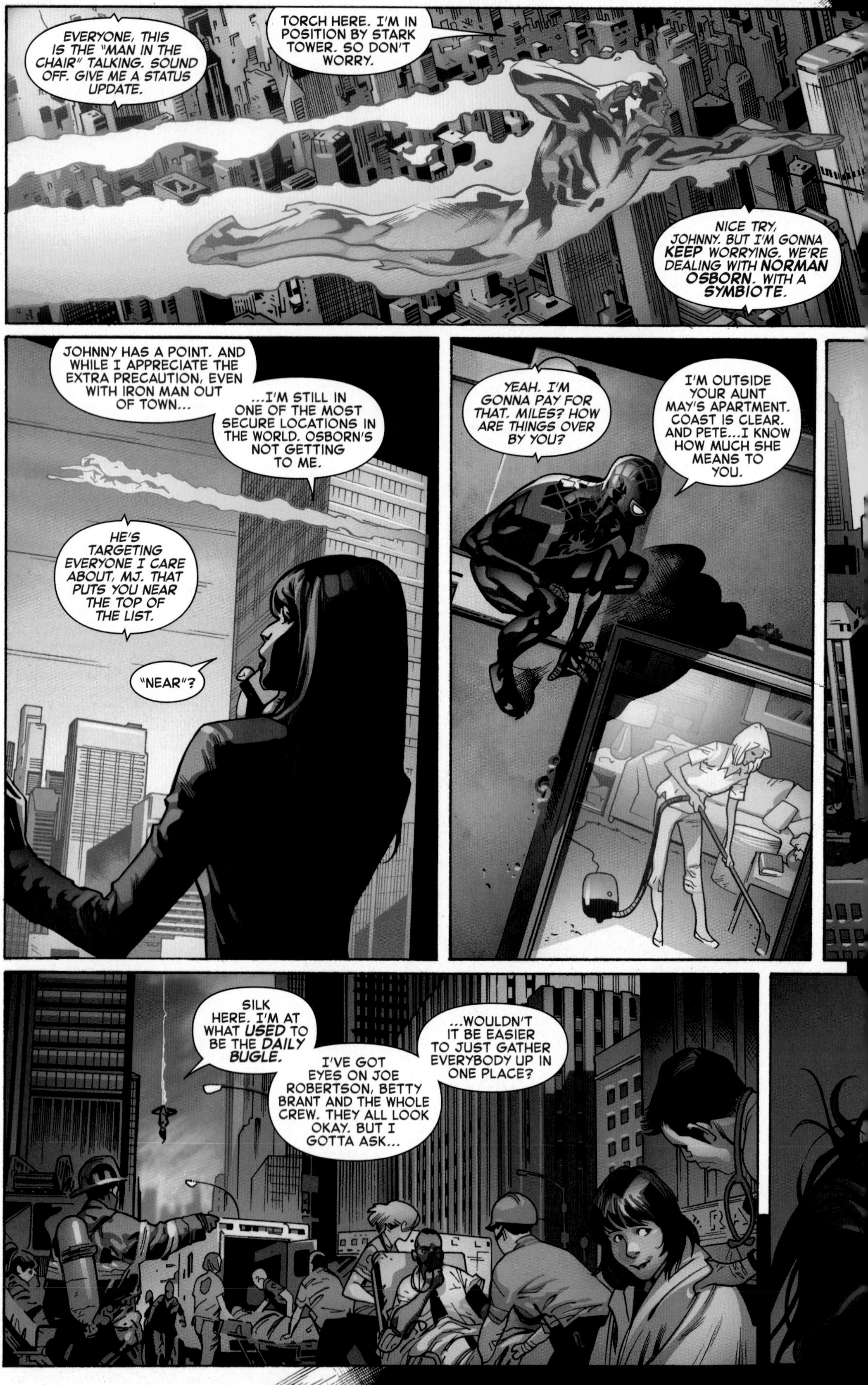
EVERYONE, THIS IS THE "MAN IN THE CHAIR" TALKING. SOUND OFF. GIVE ME A STATUS UPDATE.
TORCH HERE. I'M IN POSITION BY STARK TOWER. SO DON'T WORRY.
NICE TRY, JOHNNY. BUT I'M GONNA KEEP WORRYING. WE'RE DEALING WITH NORMAN OSBORN. WITH A SYMBIOTE.
JOHNNY HAS A POINT. AND WHILE I APPRECIATE THE EXTRA PRECAUTION, EVEN WITH IRON MAN OUT OF TOWN...
...I'M STILL IN ONE OF THE MOST SECURE LOCATIONS IN THE WORLD. OSBORN'S NOT GETTING TO ME.
HE'S TARGETING EVERYONE I CARE ABOUT, MJ. THAT PUTS YOU NEAR THE TOP OF THE LIST.
"NEAR"?
YEAH. I'M GONNA PAY FOR THAT. MILES? HOW ARE THINGS OVER BY YOU?
I'M OUTSIDE YOUR AUNT MAY'S APARTMENT. COAST IS CLEAR. AND PETE...I KNOW HOW MUCH SHE MEANS TO YOU.
SILK HERE. I'M AT WHAT USED TO BE THE DAILY BUGLE.
I'VE GOT EYES ON JOE ROBERTSON, BETTY BRANT AND THE WHOLE CREW. THEY ALL LOOK OKAY. BUT I GOTTA ASK...
...WOULDN'T IT BE EASIER TO JUST GATHER EVERYBODY UP IN ONE PLACE?

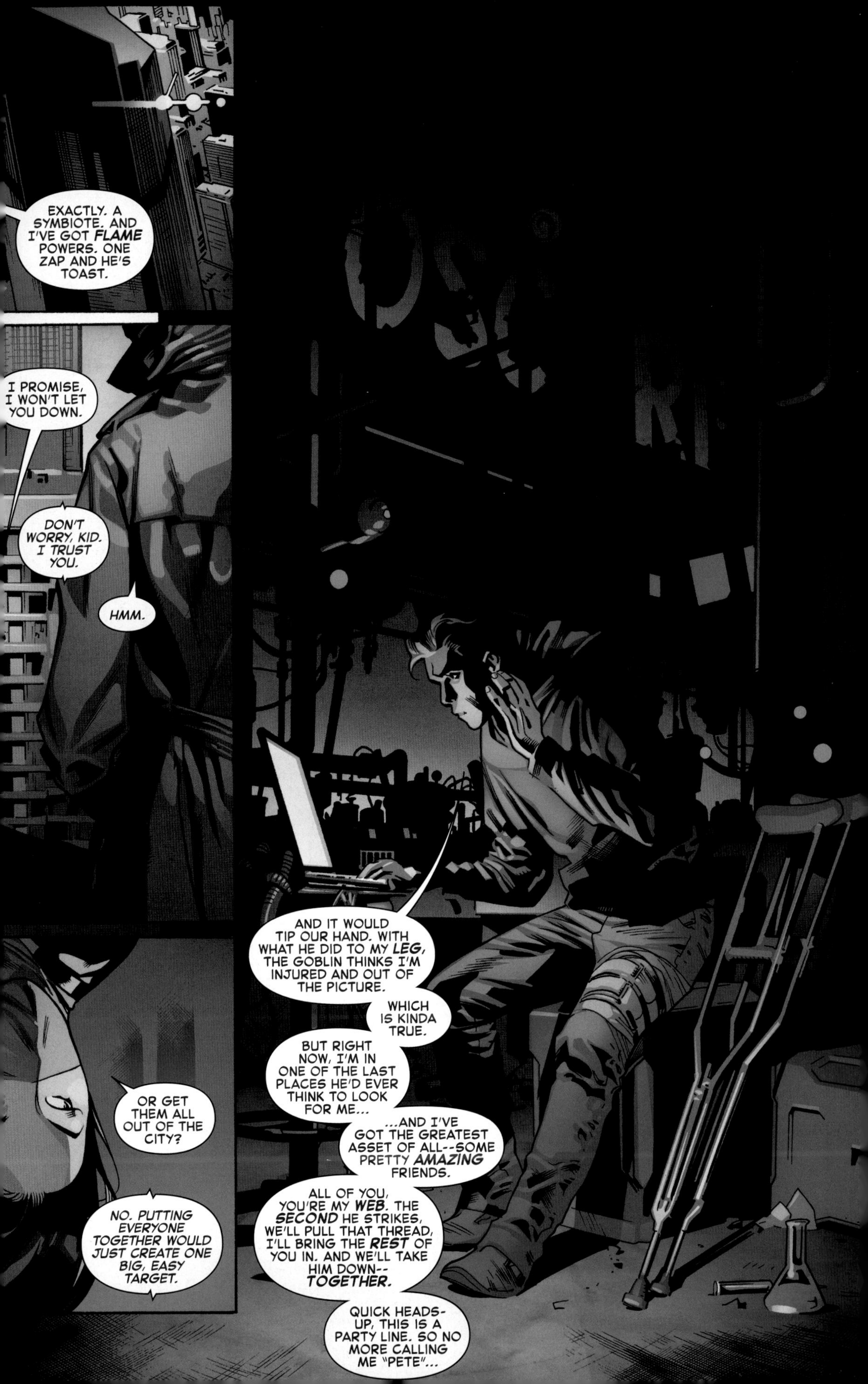
EXACTLY. A SYMBIOTE. AND I'VE GOT FLAME POWERS. ONE ZAP AND HE'S TOAST.
I PROMISE, I WON'T LET YOU DOWN.
DON'T WORRY, KID. I TRUST YOU.
HMM.
OR GET THEM ALL OUT OF THE CITY?
NO. PUTTING EVERYONE TOGETHER WOULD JUST CREATE ONE BIG, EASY TARGET.
AND IT WOULD TIP OUR HAND. WITH WHAT HE DID TO MY LEG, THE GOBLIN THINKS I'M INJURED AND OUT OF THE PICTURE.
WHICH IS KINDA TRUE.
BUT RIGHT NOW, I'M IN ONE OF THE LAST PLACES HE'D EVER THINK TO LOOK FOR ME...
...AND I'VE GOT THE GREATEST ASSET OF ALL--SOME PRETTY AMAZING FRIENDS.
ALL OF YOU, YOU'RE MY WEB. THE SECOND HE STRIKES, WE'LL PULL THAT THREAD, I'LL BRING THE REST OF YOU IN. AND WE'LL TAKE HIM DOWN-- TOGETHER.
QUICK HEADS-UP, THIS IS A PARTY LINE. SO NO MORE CALLING ME "PETE"...

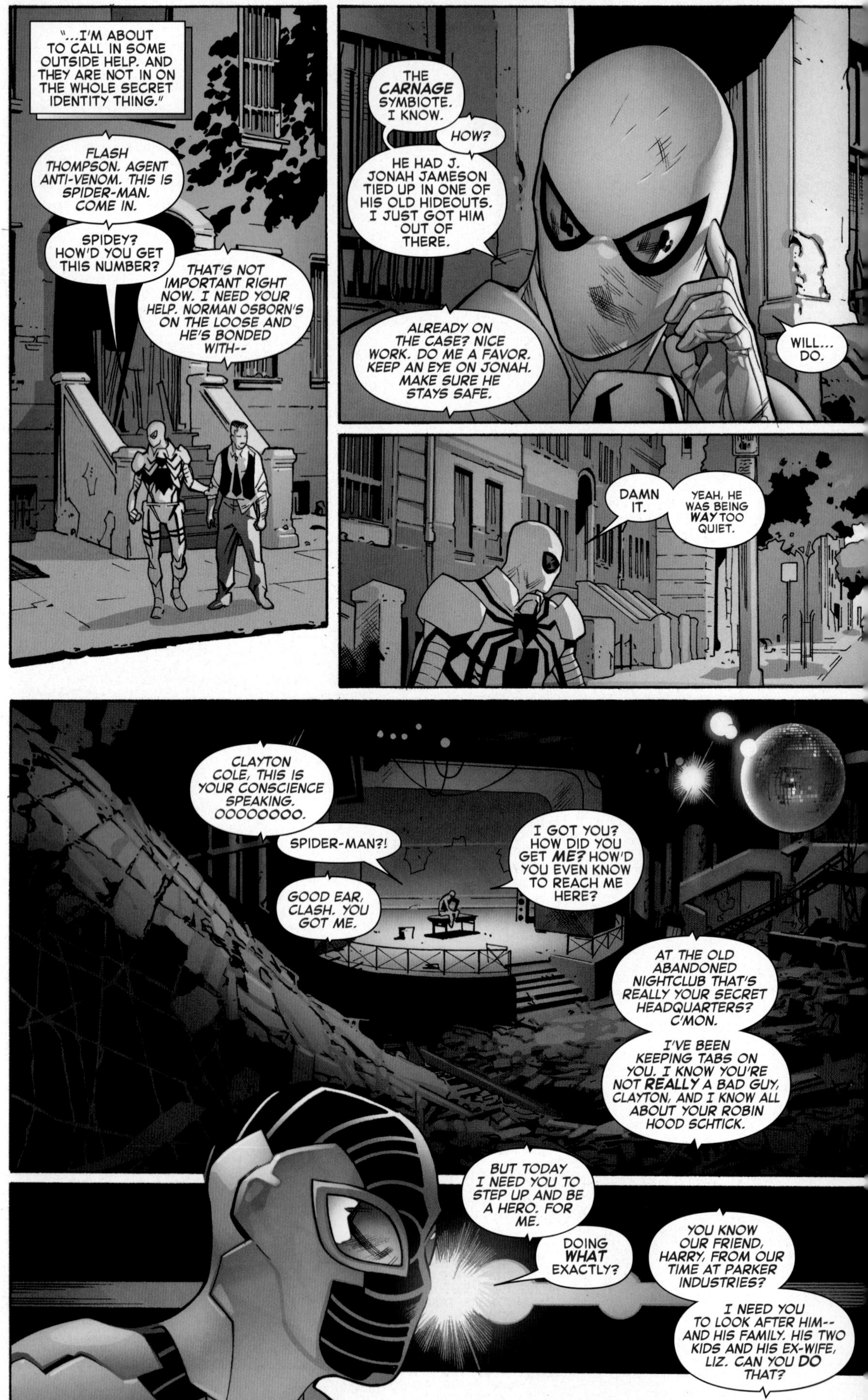

"...I'M ABOUT TO CALL IN SOME OUTSIDE HELP. AND THEY ARE NOT IN ON THE WHOLE SECRET IDENTITY THING."
FLASH THOMPSON. AGENT ANTI-VENOM. THIS IS SPIDER-MAN. COME IN.
SPIDEY? HOW'D YOU GET THIS NUMBER?
THAT'S NOT IMPORTANT RIGHT NOW. I NEED YOUR HELP. NORMAN OSBORN'S ON THE LOOSE AND HE'S BONDED WITH--
THE CARNAGE SYMBIOTE. I KNOW.
HOW?
HE HAD J. JONAH JAMESON TIED UP IN ONE OF HIS OLD HIDEOUTS. I JUST GOT HIM OUT OF THERE.
ALREADY ON THE CASE? NICE WORK. DO ME A FAVOR. KEEP AN EYE ON JONAH. MAKE SURE HE STAYS SAFE.
WILL... DO.
DAMN IT.
YEAH, HE WAS BEING WAY TOO QUIET.
CLAYTON COLE, THIS IS YOUR CONSCIENCE SPEAKING. OOOOOOOO.
SPIDER-MAN?!
GOOD EAR, CLASH. YOU GOT ME.
I GOT YOU? HOW DID YOU GET ME? HOW'D YOU EVEN KNOW TO REACH ME HERE?
AT THE OLD ABANDONED NIGHTCLUB THAT'S REALLY YOUR SECRET HEADQUARTERS? C'MON.
I'VE BEEN KEEPING TABS ON YOU. I KNOW YOU'RE NOT REALLY A BAD GUY, CLAYTON, AND I KNOW ALL ABOUT YOUR ROBIN HOOD SCHTICK.
BUT TODAY I NEED YOU TO STEP UP AND BE A HERO. FOR ME.
DOING WHAT EXACTLY?
YOU KNOW OUR FRIEND, HARRY, FROM OUR TIME AT PARKER INDUSTRIES?
I NEED YOU TO LOOK AFTER HIM-- AND HIS FAMILY. HIS TWO KIDS AND HIS EX-WIFE, LIZ. CAN YOU DO THAT?

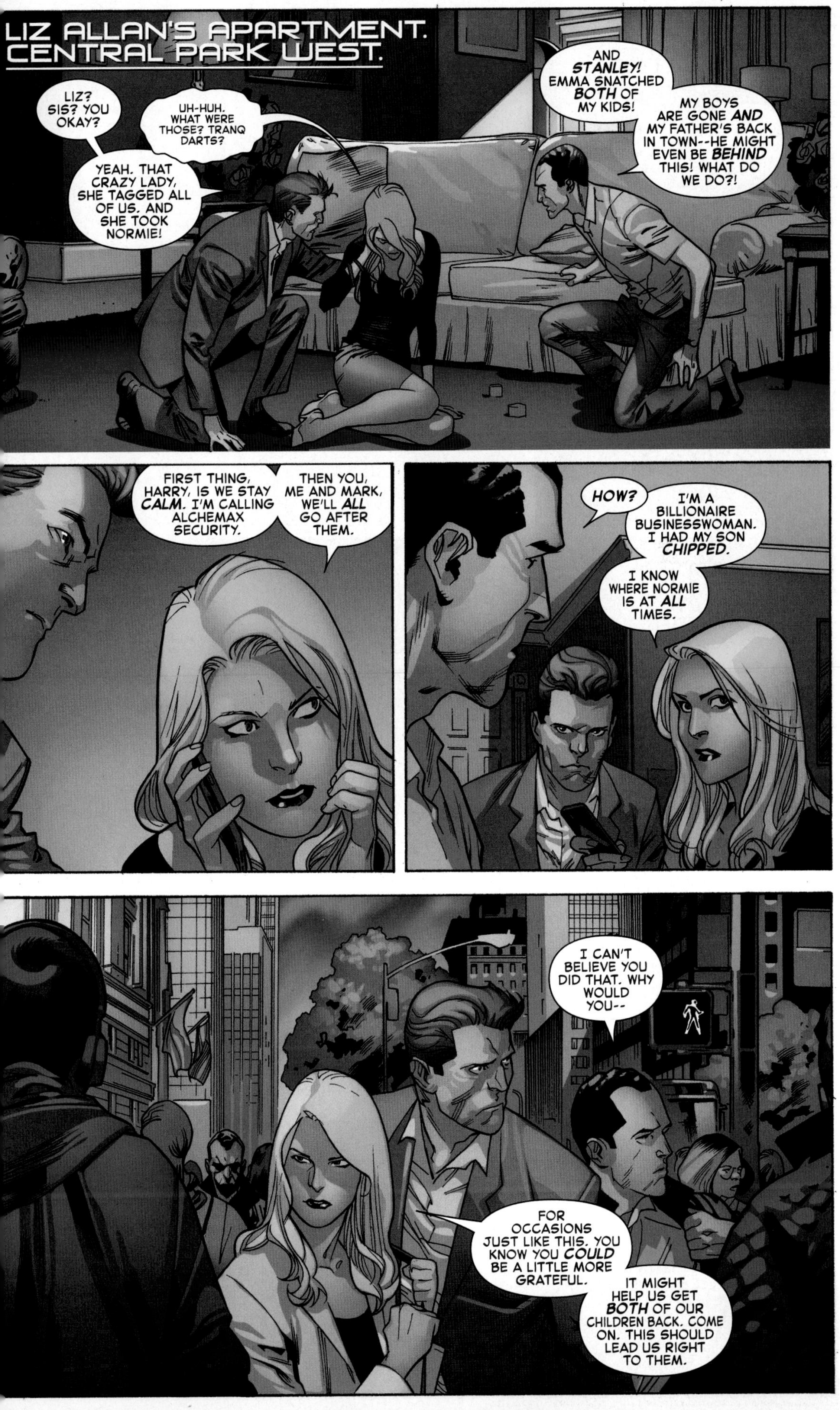
LIZ ALLAN'S APARTMENT. CENTRAL PARK WEST.
LIZ? SIS? YOU OKAY?
YEAH. THAT CRAZY LADY, SHE TAGGED ALL OF US. AND SHE TOOK NORMIE!
UH-HUH. WHAT WERE THOSE? TRANQ DARTS?
AND STANLEY! EMMA SNATCHED BOTH OF MY KIDS!
MY BOYS ARE GONE AND MY FATHER'S BACK IN TOWN--HE MIGHT EVEN BE BEHIND THIS! WHAT DO WE DO?!
FIRST THING, HARRY, IS WE STAY CALM. I'M CALLING ALCHEMAX SECURITY.
THEN YOU, ME AND MARK, WE'LL ALL GO AFTER THEM.
HOW?
I'M A BILLIONAIRE BUSINESSWOMAN. I HAD MY SON CHIPPED.
I KNOW WHERE NORMIE IS AT ALL TIMES.
I CAN'T BELIEVE YOU DID THAT. WHY WOULD YOU--
FOR OCCASIONS JUST LIKE THIS. YOU KNOW YOU COULD BE A LITTLE MORE GRATEFUL.
IT MIGHT HELP US GET BOTH OF OUR CHILDREN BACK. COME ON. THIS SHOULD LEAD US RIGHT TO THEM.

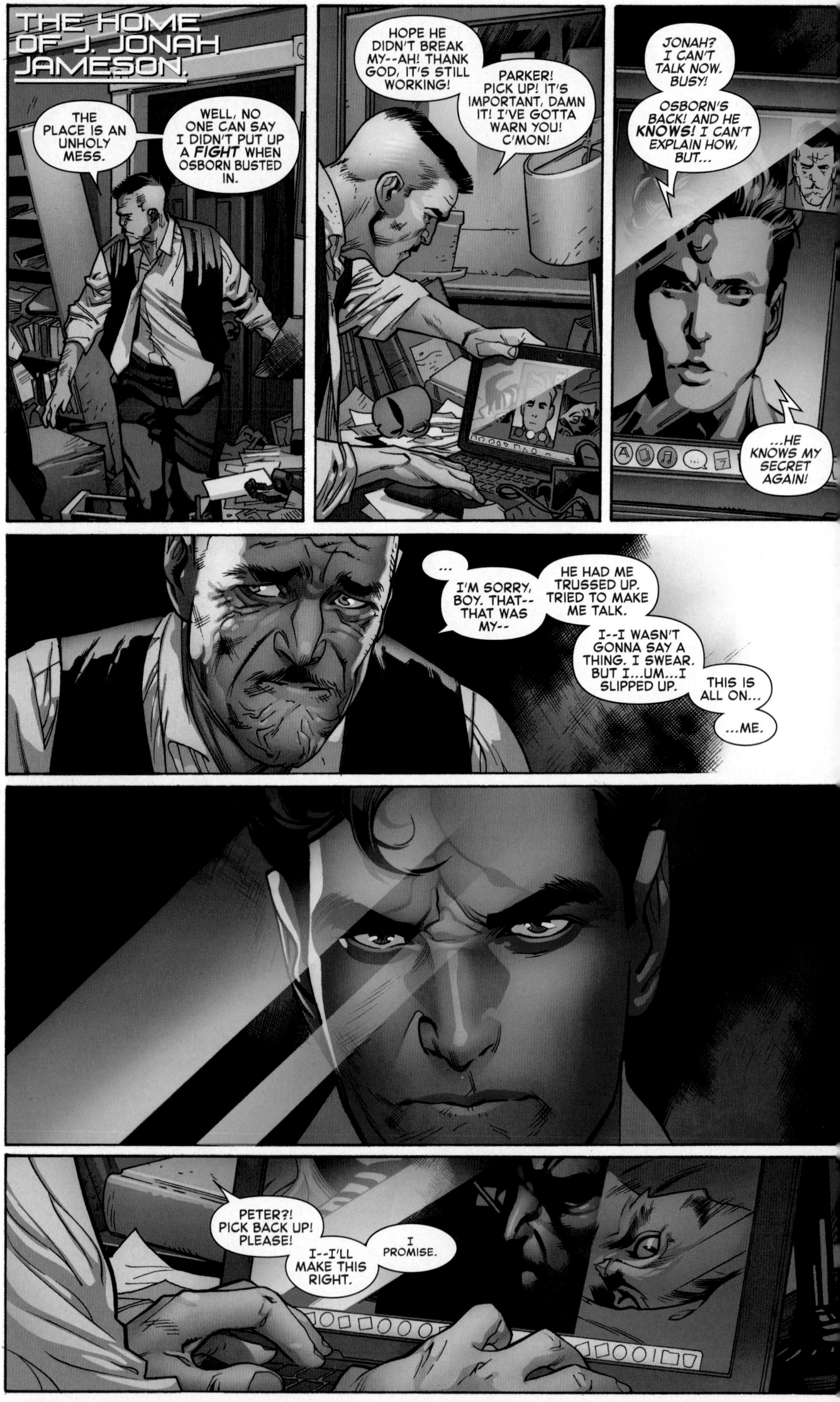
THE HOME OF J. JONAH JAMESON.
THE PLACE IS AN UNHOLY MESS.
WELL, NO ONE CAN SAY I DIDN'T PUT UP A FIGHT WHEN OSBORN BUSTED IN.
HOPE HE DIDN'T BREAK MY--AH! THANK GOD, IT'S STILL WORKING!
PARKER! PICK UP! IT'S IMPORTANT, DAMN IT! I'VE GOTTA WARN YOU! C'MON!
JONAH? I CAN'T TALK NOW. BUSY!
OSBORN'S BACK! AND HE KNOWS! I CAN'T EXPLAIN HOW, BUT...
...HE KNOWS MY SECRET AGAIN!
...
I'M SORRY, BOY. THAT--THAT WAS MY--
HE HAD ME TRUSSED UP. TRIED TO MAKE ME TALK.
I--I WASN'T GONNA SAY A THING. I SWEAR. BUT I...UM...I SLIPPED UP.
THIS IS ALL ON...
...ME.
PETER?! PICK BACK UP! PLEASE!
I--I'LL MAKE THIS RIGHT.
I PROMISE.

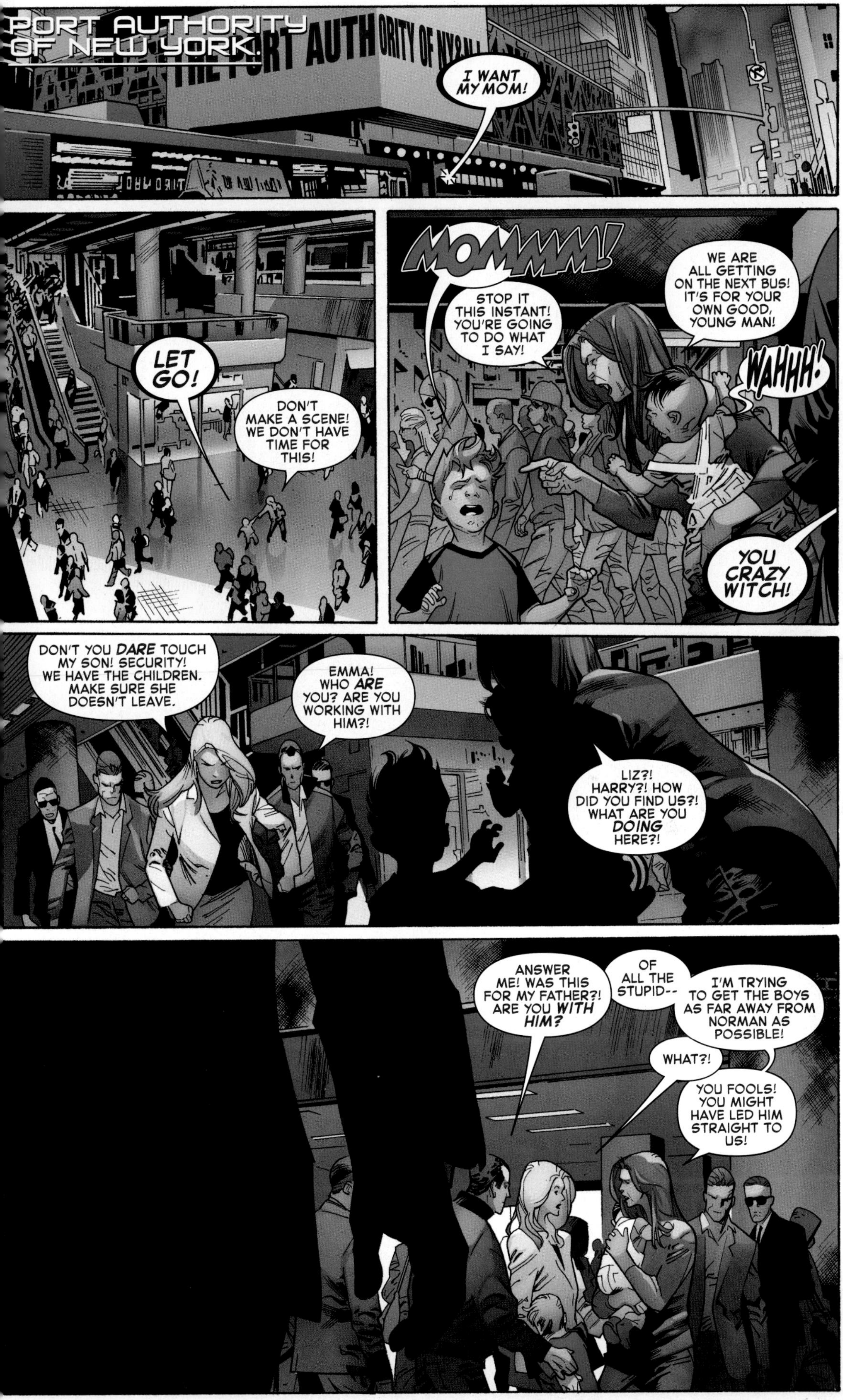

PORT AUTHORITY OF NEW YORK.
I WANT MY MOM!
LET GO!
DON'T MAKE A SCENE! WE DON'T HAVE TIME FOR THIS!
MOMMM!
STOP IT THIS INSTANT! YOU'RE GOING TO DO WHAT I SAY!
WE ARE ALL GETTING ON THE NEXT BUS! IT'S FOR YOUR OWN GOOD, YOUNG MAN!
WAHHH!
YOU CRAZY WITCH!
DON'T YOU DARE TOUCH MY SON! SECURITY! WE HAVE THE CHILDREN. MAKE SURE SHE DOESN'T LEAVE.
EMMA! WHO ARE YOU? ARE YOU WORKING WITH HIM?!
LIZ?! HARRY?! HOW DID YOU FIND US?! WHAT ARE YOU DOING HERE?!
ANSWER ME! WAS THIS FOR MY FATHER?! ARE YOU WITH HIM?
OF ALL THE STUPID--
I'M TRYING TO GET THE BOYS AS FAR AWAY FROM NORMAN AS POSSIBLE!
WHAT?!
YOU FOOLS! YOU MIGHT HAVE LED HIM STRAIGHT TO US!

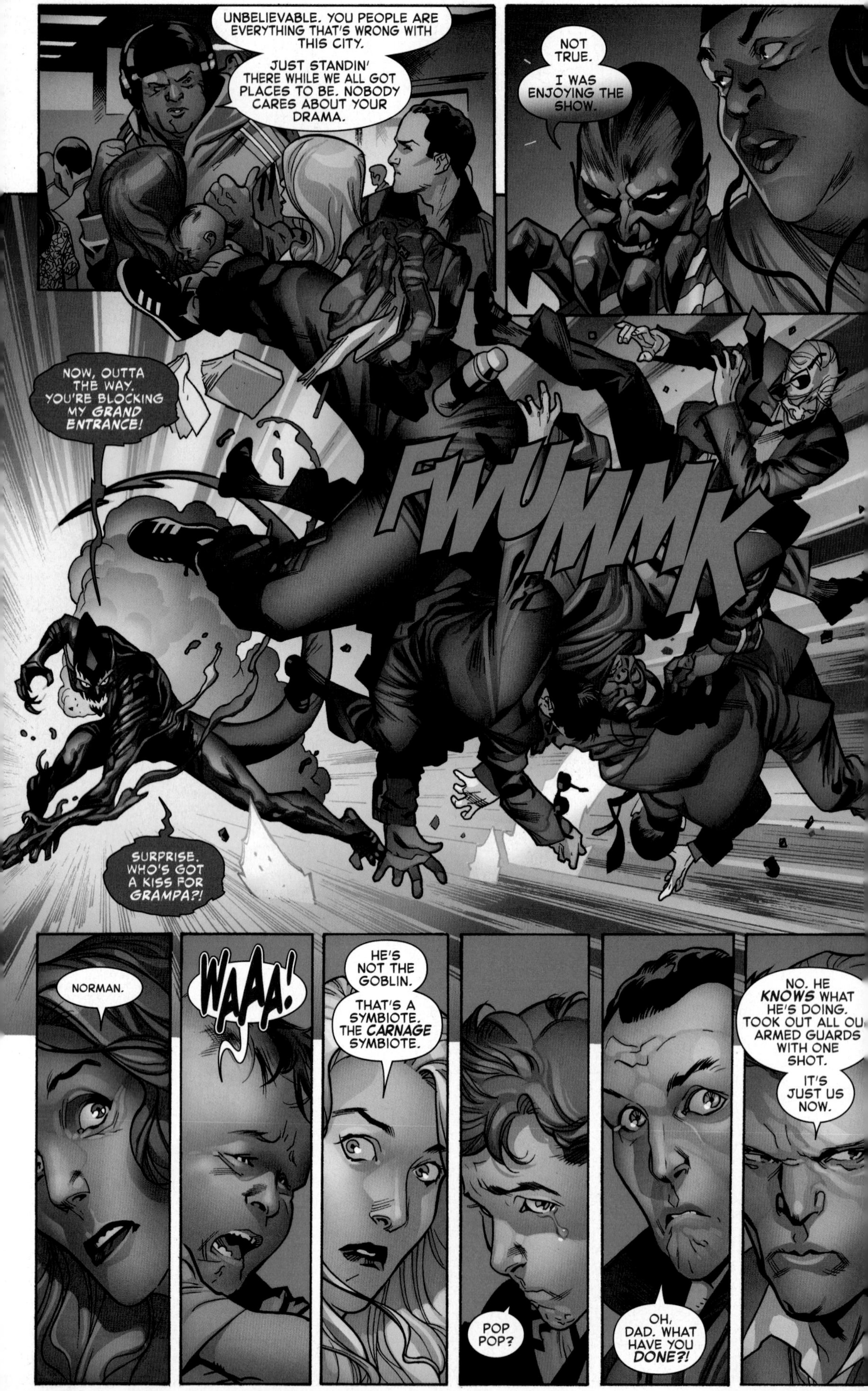

UNBELIEVABLE. YOU PEOPLE ARE EVERYTHING THAT'S WRONG WITH THIS CITY.
JUST STANDIN' THERE WHILE WE ALL GOT PLACES TO BE. NOBODY CARES ABOUT YOUR DRAMA.
NOT TRUE.
I WAS ENJOYING THE SHOW.
NOW, OUTTA THE WAY. YOU'RE BLOCKING MY *GRAND ENTRANCE!*
FWUMMK
SURPRISE. WHO'S GOT A KISS FOR *GRAMPA?!*
NORMAN.
WAAA!
HE'S NOT THE GOBLIN.
THAT'S A SYMBIOTE. THE *CARNAGE* SYMBIOTE.
POP POP?
OH, DAD. WHAT HAVE YOU *DONE?!*
NO. HE ***KNOWS*** WHAT HE'S DOING. TOOK OUT ALL OU ARMED GUARDS WITH ONE SHOT.
IT'S JUST US NOW.

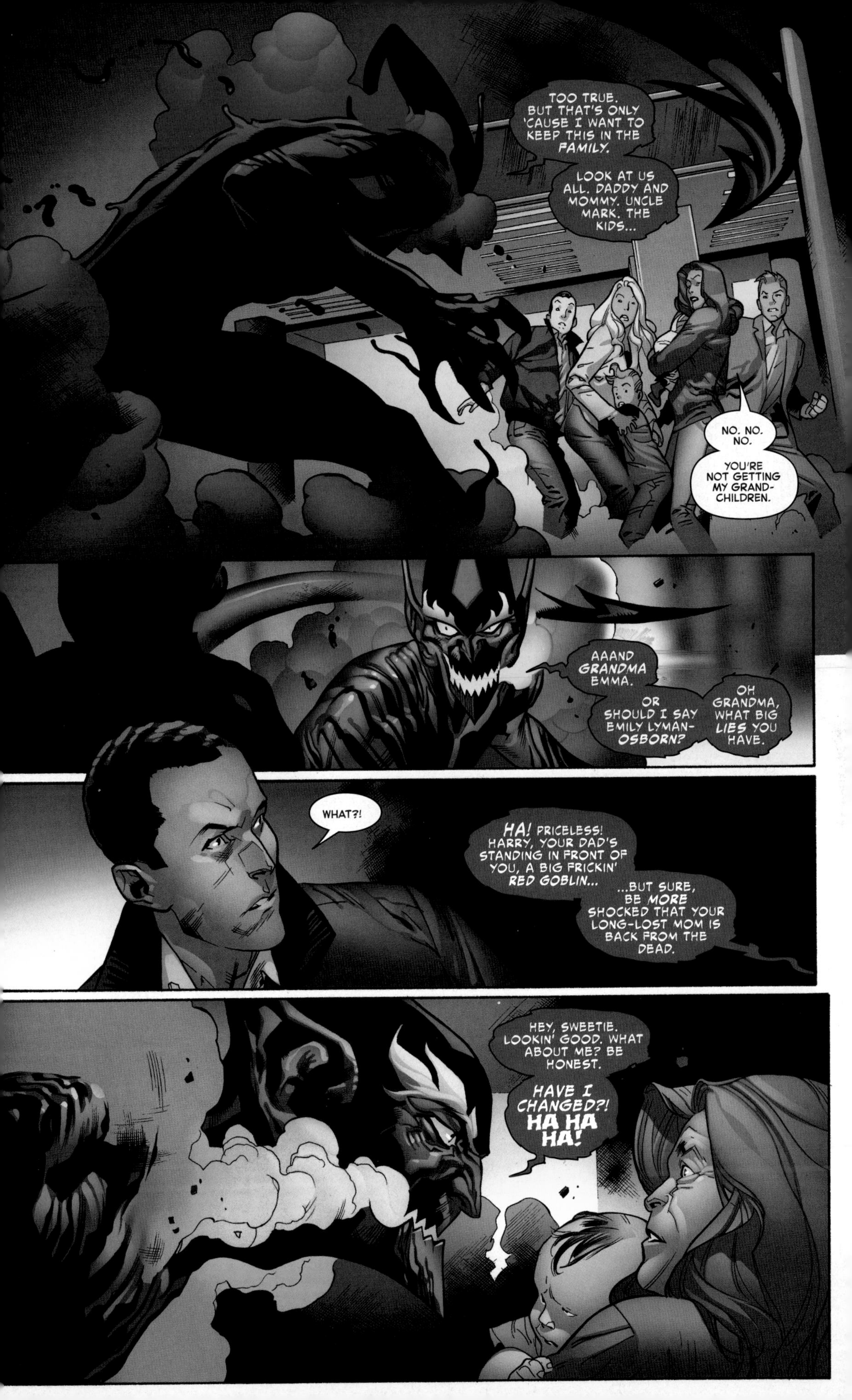
TOO TRUE. BUT THAT'S ONLY 'CAUSE I WANT TO KEEP THIS IN THE *FAMILY.*
LOOK AT US ALL. DADDY AND MOMMY. UNCLE MARK. THE KIDS...
NO. NO. NO.
YOU'RE NOT GETTING MY GRAND-CHILDREN.
AAAND *GRANDMA EMMA.*
OR SHOULD I SAY EMILY LYMAN-*OSBORN?*
OH GRANDMA, WHAT BIG *LIES* YOU HAVE.
WHAT?!
HA! PRICELESS! HARRY, YOUR DAD'S STANDING IN FRONT OF YOU, A BIG FRICKIN' *RED GOBLIN...*
...BUT SURE, BE *MORE* SHOCKED THAT YOUR LONG-LOST MOM IS BACK FROM THE DEAD.
HEY, SWEETIE. LOOKIN' GOOD. WHAT ABOUT ME? BE HONEST.
HAVE I CHANGED?! **HA HA HA!**

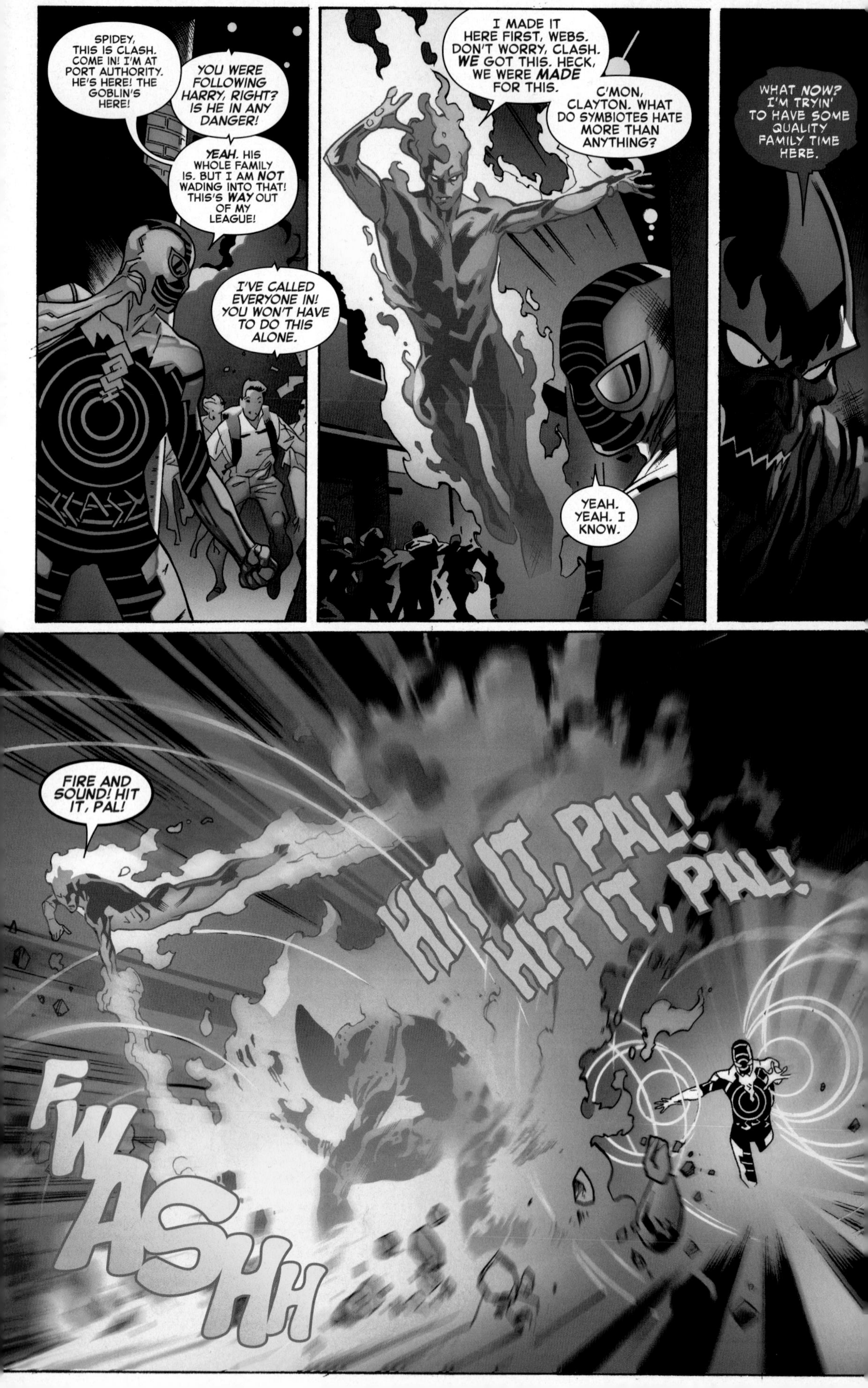
SPIDEY, THIS IS CLASH. COME IN! I'M AT PORT AUTHORITY. HE'S HERE! THE GOBLIN'S HERE!
YOU WERE FOLLOWING HARRY, RIGHT? IS HE IN ANY DANGER!
YEAH. HIS WHOLE FAMILY IS. BUT I AM NOT WADING INTO THAT! THIS'S WAY OUT OF MY LEAGUE!
I'VE CALLED EVERYONE IN! YOU WON'T HAVE TO DO THIS ALONE.
I MADE IT HERE FIRST, WEBS. DON'T WORRY, CLASH. WE GOT THIS. HECK, WE WERE MADE FOR THIS.
C'MON, CLAYTON. WHAT DO SYMBIOTES HATE MORE THAN ANYTHING?
YEAH. YEAH. I KNOW.
WHAT NOW? I'M TRYIN' TO HAVE SOME QUALITY FAMILY TIME HERE.
FIRE AND SOUND! HIT IT, PAL!
HIT IT, PAL! HIT IT, PAL!
FWASHH

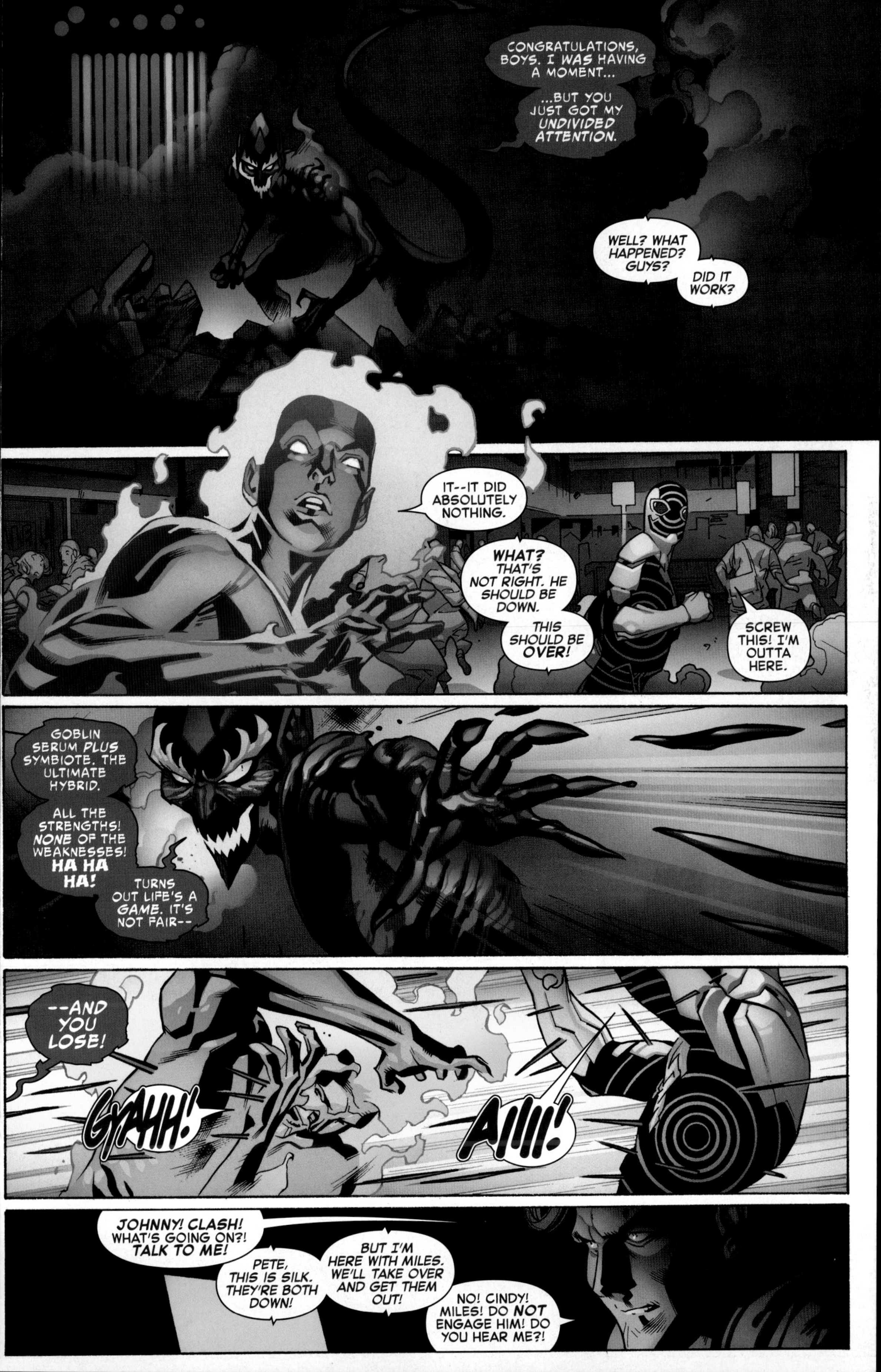
CONGRATULATIONS, BOYS. I WAS HAVING A MOMENT...
...BUT YOU JUST GOT MY UNDIVIDED ATTENTION.
WELL? WHAT HAPPENED? GUYS?
DID IT WORK?
IT--IT DID ABSOLUTELY NOTHING.
WHAT? THAT'S NOT RIGHT. HE SHOULD BE DOWN.
THIS SHOULD BE OVER!
SCREW THIS! I'M OUTTA HERE.
GOBLIN SERUM PLUS SYMBIOTE. THE ULTIMATE HYBRID.
ALL THE STRENGTHS! NONE OF THE WEAKNESSES! HA HA HA!
TURNS OUT LIFE'S A GAME. IT'S NOT FAIR--
--AND YOU LOSE!
GYAHH!
AIIII!
JOHNNY! CLASH! WHAT'S GOING ON?! TALK TO ME!
PETE, THIS IS SILK. THEY'RE BOTH DOWN!
BUT I'M HERE WITH MILES. WE'LL TAKE OVER AND GET THEM OUT!
NO! CINDY! MILES! DO NOT ENGAGE HIM! DO YOU HEAR ME?!

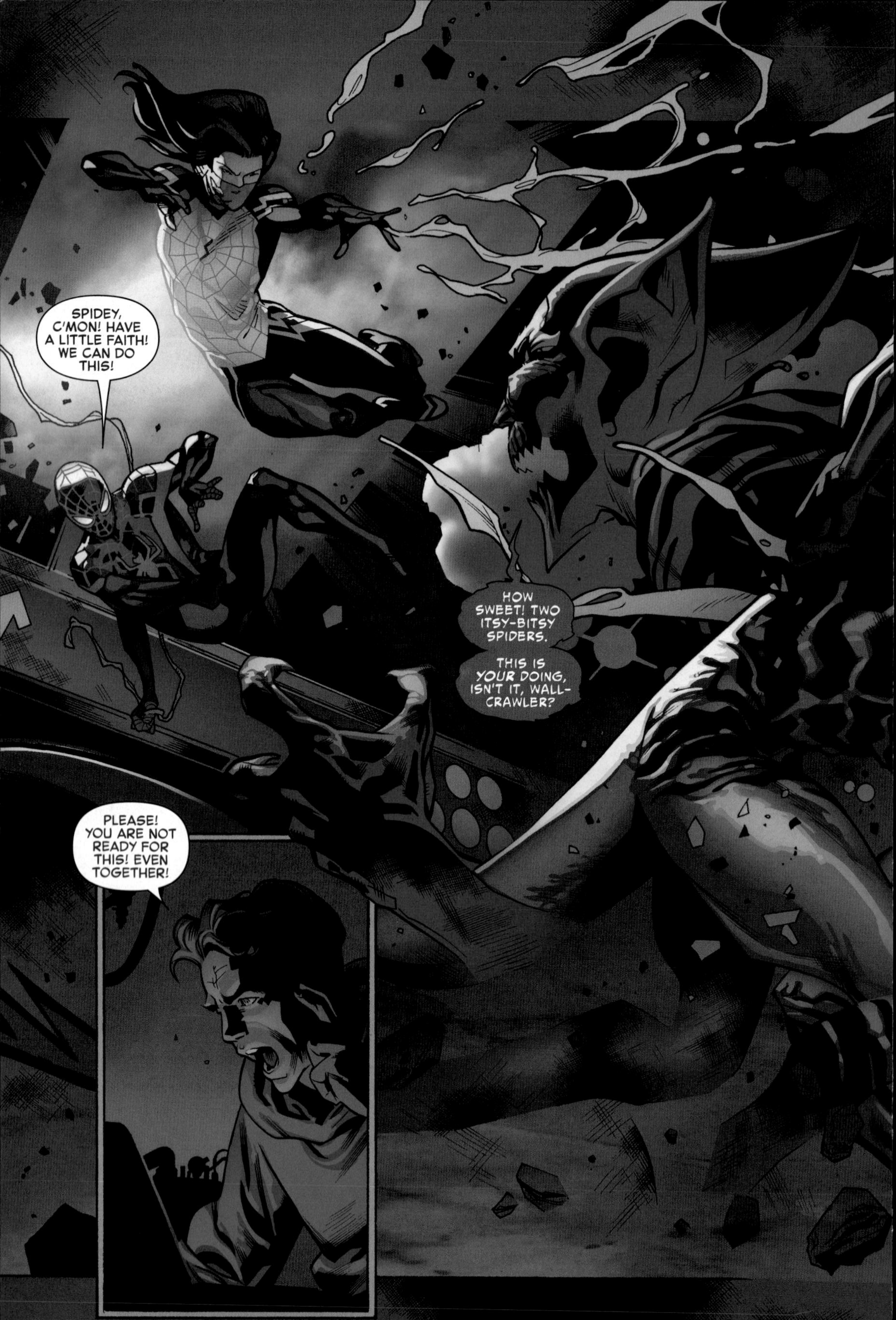
SPIDEY, C'MON! HAVE A LITTLE FAITH! WE CAN DO THIS!
HOW SWEET! TWO ITSY-BITSY SPIDERS.
THIS IS *YOUR* DOING, ISN'T IT, WALL-CRAWLER?
PLEASE! YOU ARE NOT READY FOR THIS! EVEN TOGETHER!

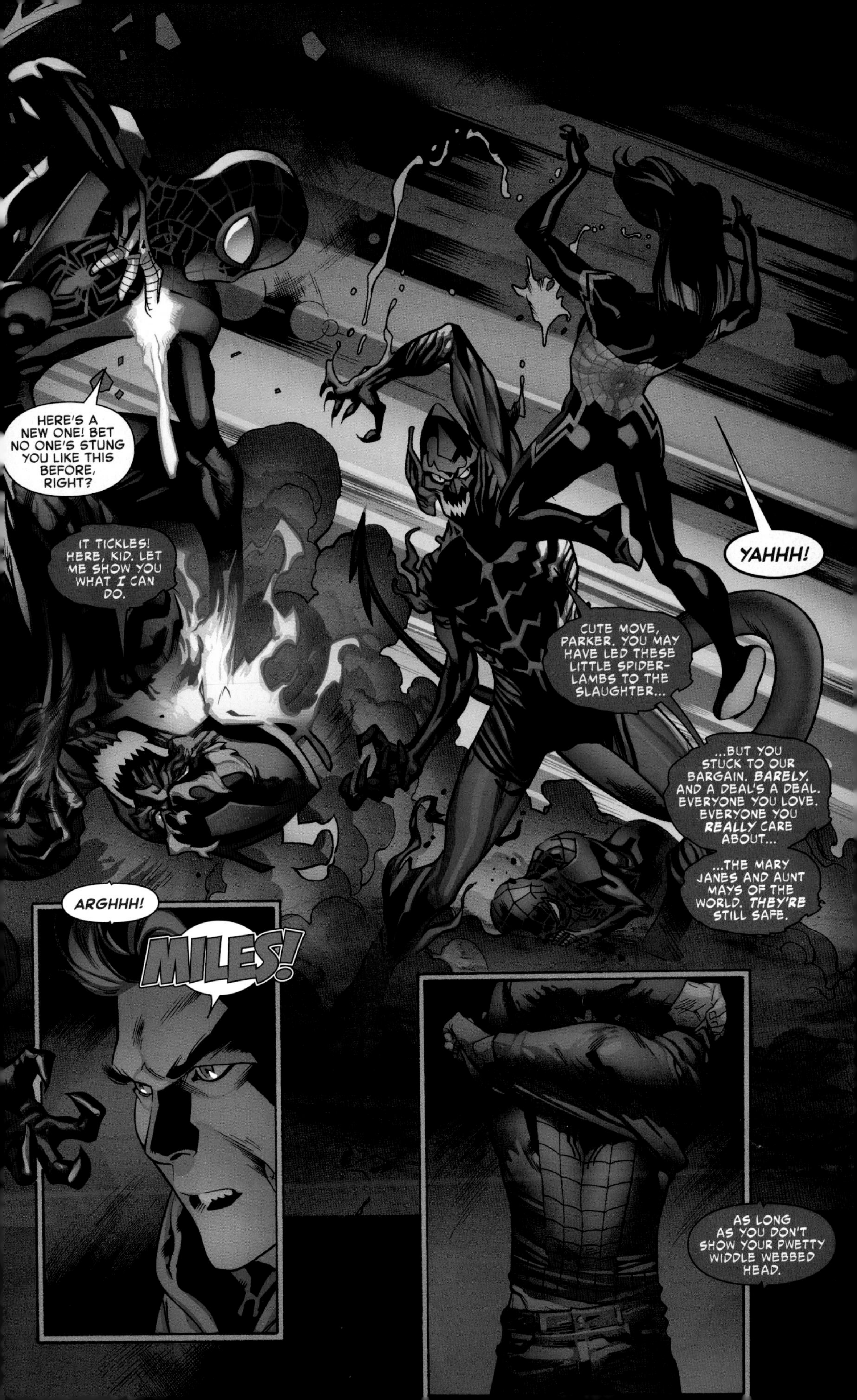
HERE'S A NEW ONE! BET NO ONE'S STUNG YOU LIKE THIS BEFORE, RIGHT?
IT TICKLES! HERE, KID. LET ME SHOW YOU WHAT I CAN DO.
YAHHH!
CUTE MOVE, PARKER. YOU MAY HAVE LED THESE LITTLE SPIDER-LAMBS TO THE SLAUGHTER...
...BUT YOU STUCK TO OUR BARGAIN. BARELY. AND A DEAL'S A DEAL. EVERYONE YOU LOVE. EVERYONE YOU REALLY CARE ABOUT...
...THE MARY JANES AND AUNT MAYS OF THE WORLD. THEY'RE STILL SAFE.
ARGHHH!
MILES!
AS LONG AS YOU DON'T SHOW YOUR PWETTY WIDDLE WEBBED HEAD.

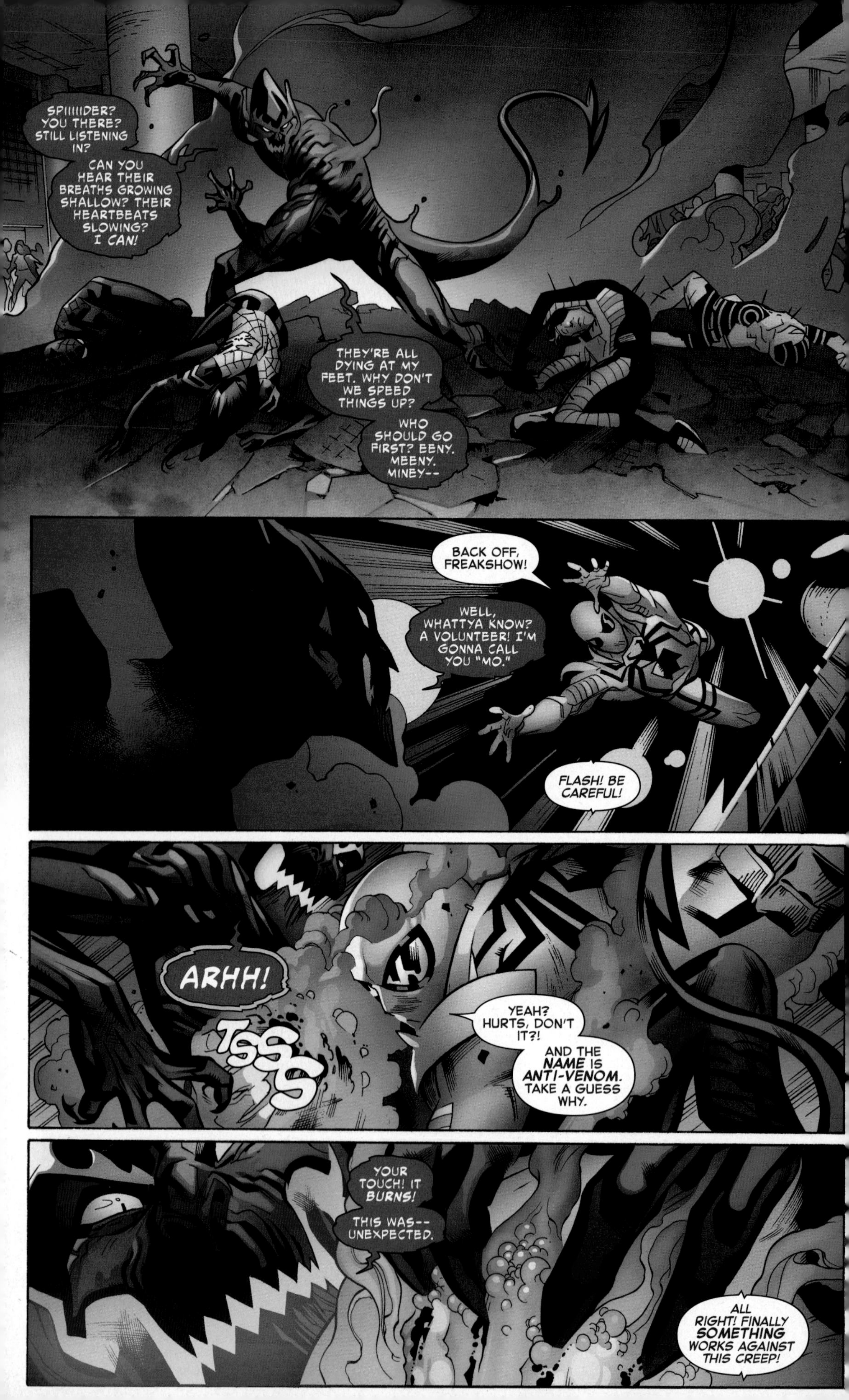
SPIIIIIDER? YOU THERE? STILL LISTENING IN?
CAN YOU HEAR THEIR BREATHS GROWING SHALLOW? THEIR HEARTBEATS SLOWING? I CAN!
THEY'RE ALL DYING AT MY FEET. WHY DON'T WE SPEED THINGS UP?
WHO SHOULD GO FIRST? EENY. MEENY. MINEY--
BACK OFF, FREAKSHOW!
WELL, WHATTYA KNOW? A VOLUNTEER! I'M GONNA CALL YOU "MO."
FLASH! BE CAREFUL!
ARHH!
TSSSS
YEAH? HURTS, DON'T IT?!
AND THE NAME IS ANTI-VENOM. TAKE A GUESS WHY.
YOUR TOUCH! IT BURNS!
THIS WAS-- UNEXPECTED.
ALL RIGHT! FINALLY SOMETHING WORKS AGAINST THIS CREEP!

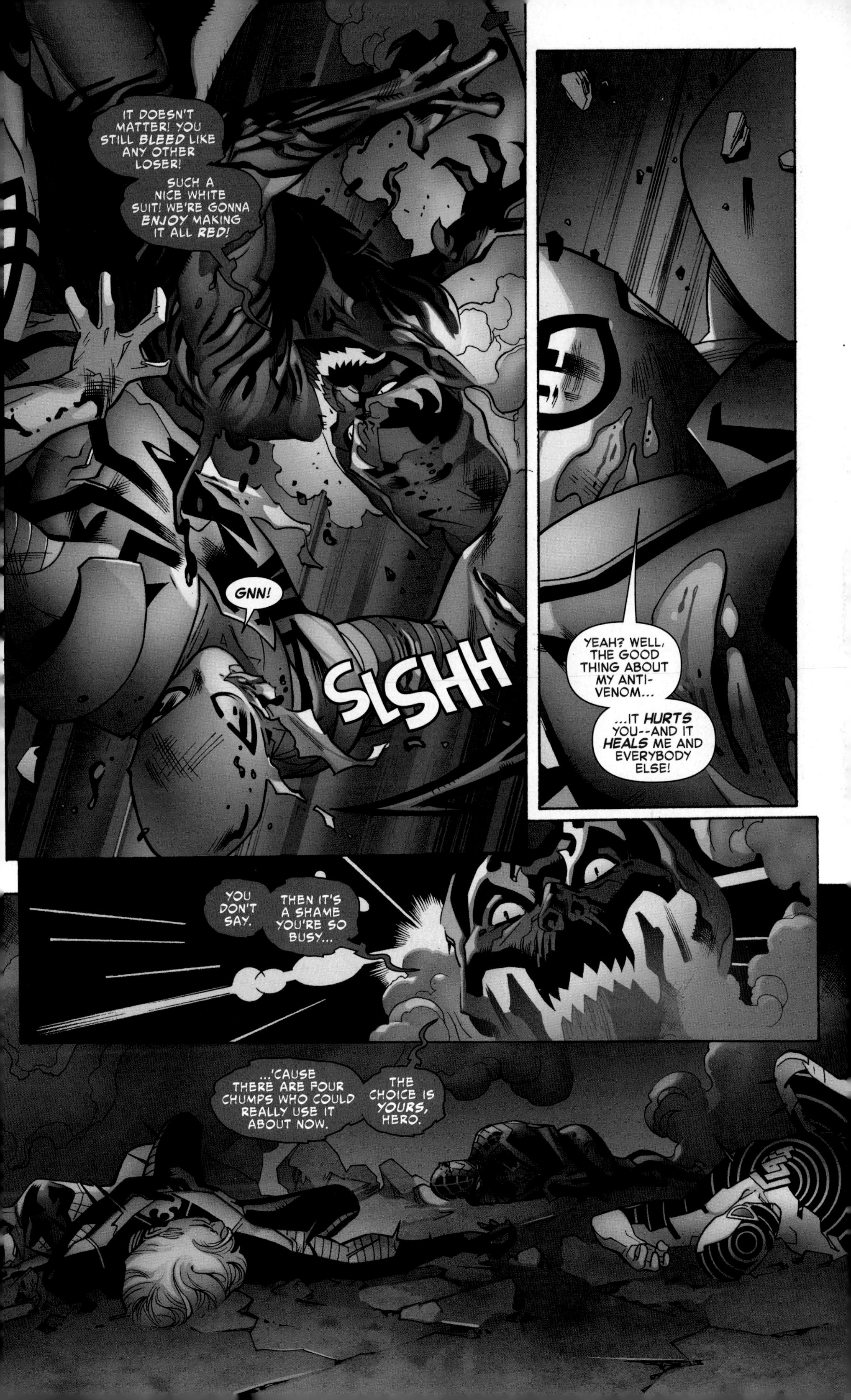
IT DOESN'T MATTER! YOU STILL BLEED LIKE ANY OTHER LOSER!
SUCH A NICE WHITE SUIT! WE'RE GONNA ENJOY MAKING IT ALL RED!
GNN!
SLSHH
YEAH? WELL, THE GOOD THING ABOUT MY ANTI-VENOM...
...IT HURTS YOU--AND IT HEALS ME AND EVERYBODY ELSE!
YOU DON'T SAY.
THEN IT'S A SHAME YOU'RE SO BUSY...
...'CAUSE THERE ARE FOUR CHUMPS WHO COULD REALLY USE IT ABOUT NOW.
THE CHOICE IS YOURS, HERO.

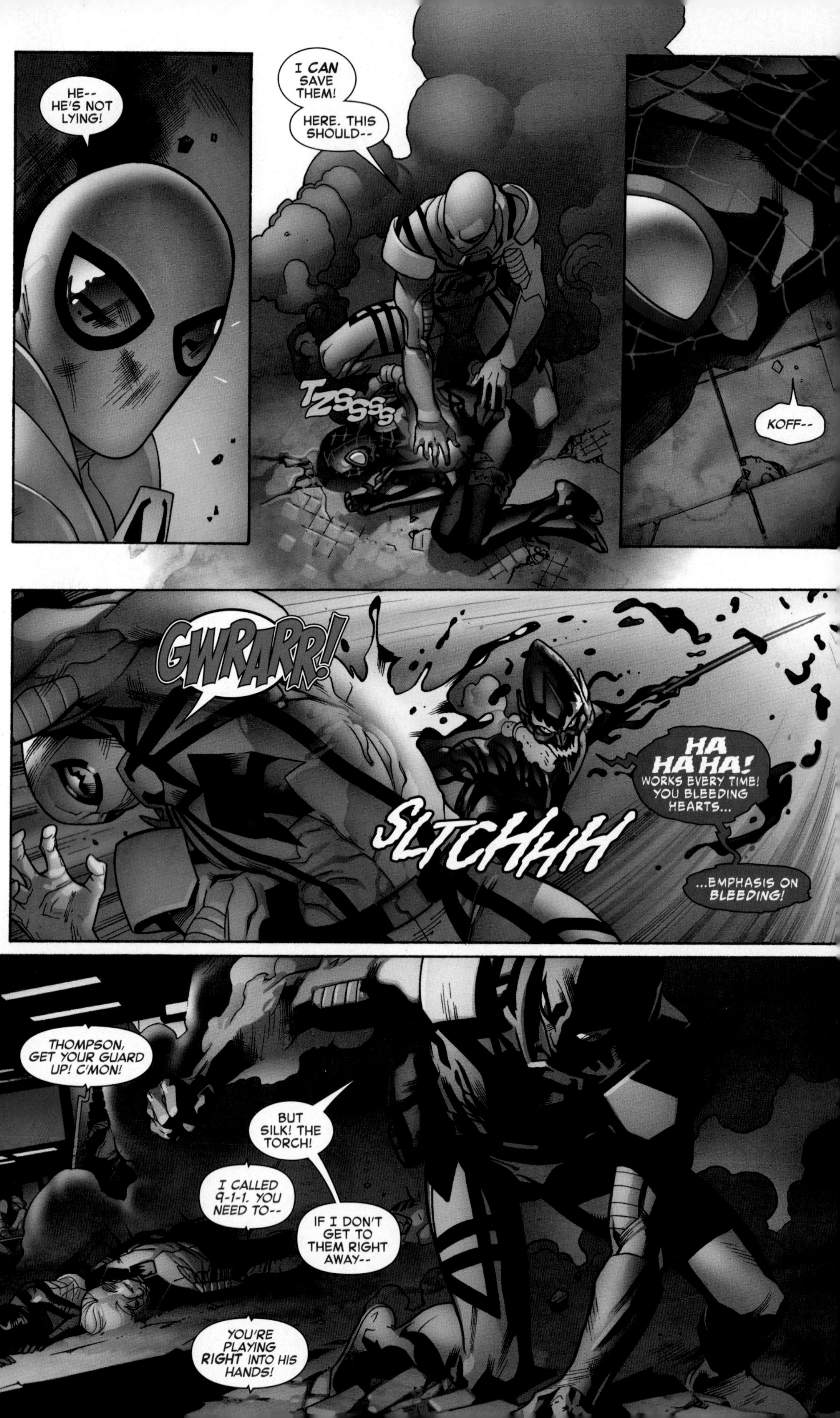
HE--
HE'S NOT
LYING!
I CAN
SAVE
THEM!
HERE. THIS
SHOULD--
TZSSSS
KOFF--
GWRARR!
SLTCHHH
HA HA HA!
WORKS EVERY TIME!
YOU BLEEDING
HEARTS...
...EMPHASIS ON
BLEEDING!
THOMPSON,
GET YOUR GUARD
UP! C'MON!
BUT
SILK! THE
TORCH!
I CALLED
9-1-1. YOU
NEED TO--
IF I DON'T
GET TO
THEM RIGHT
AWAY--
YOU'RE
PLAYING
RIGHT INTO HIS
HANDS!

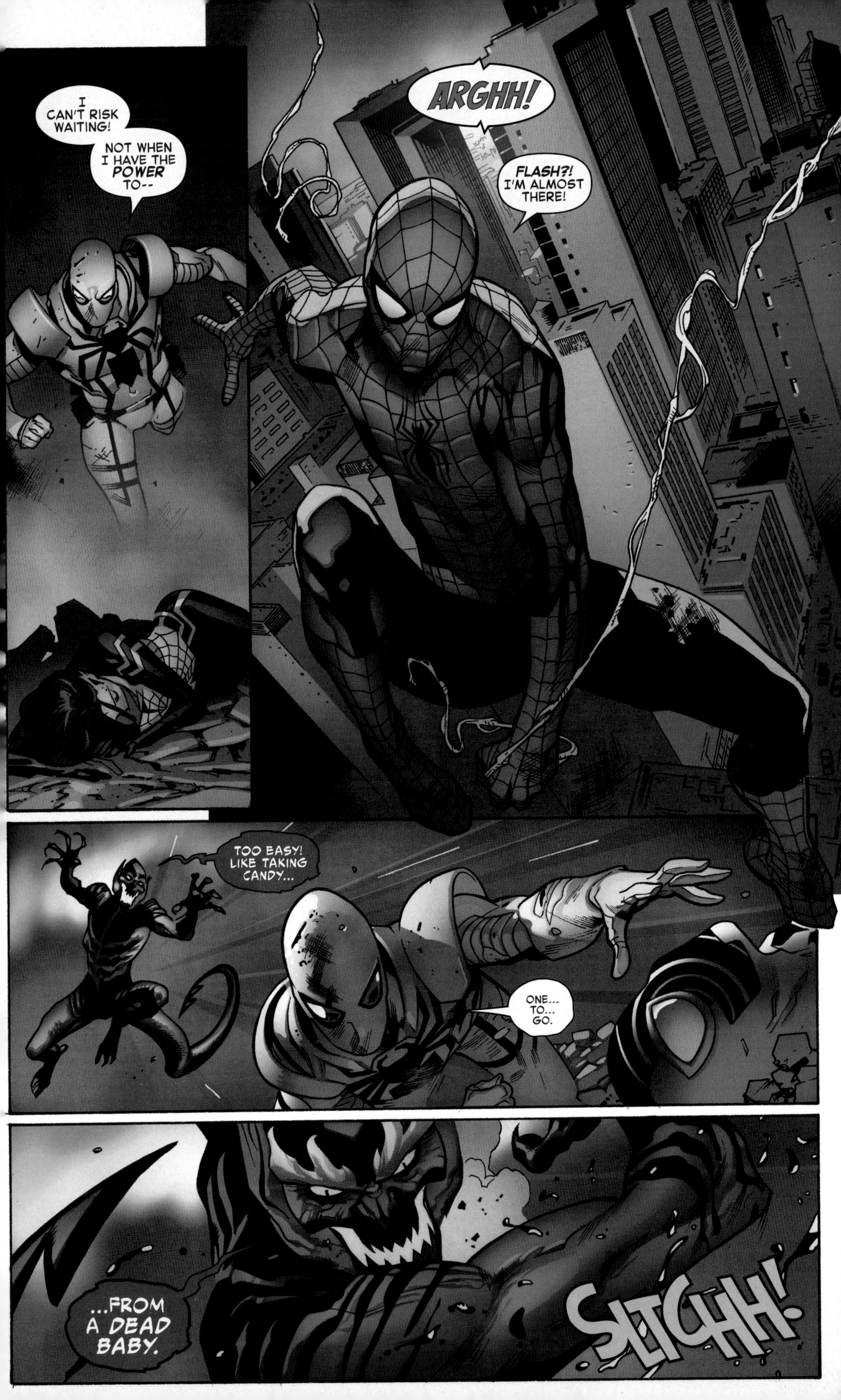
I CAN'T RISK WAITING!
NOT WHEN I HAVE THE POWER TO--
ARGHH!
FLASH?! I'M ALMOST THERE!
TOO EASY! LIKE TAKING CANDY...
ONE... TO... GO.
...FROM A DEAD BABY.
SLTCHH!

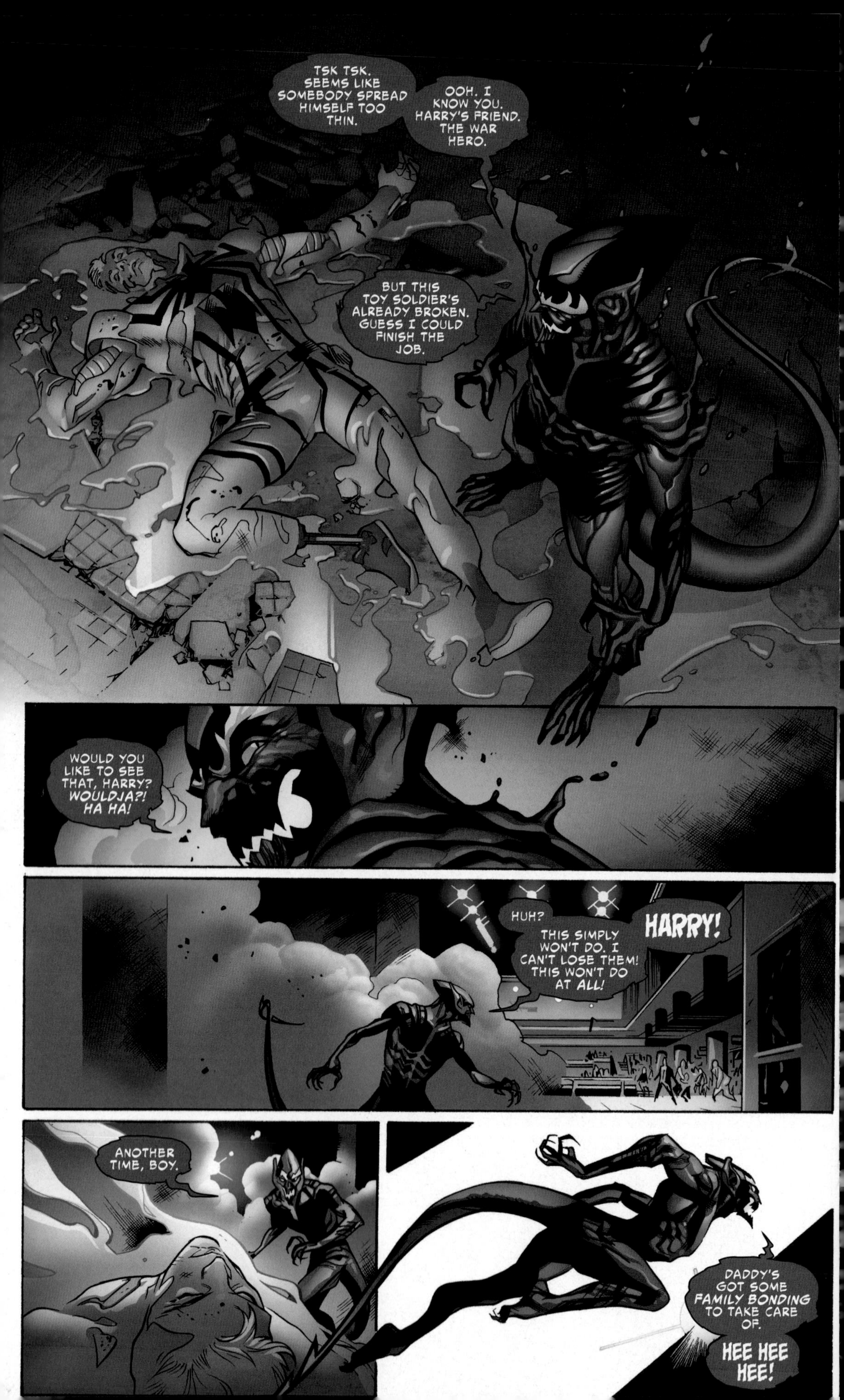
TSK TSK. SEEMS LIKE SOMEBODY SPREAD HIMSELF TOO THIN.
OOH. I KNOW YOU. HARRY'S FRIEND. THE WAR HERO.
BUT THIS TOY SOLDIER'S ALREADY BROKEN. GUESS I COULD FINISH THE JOB.
WOULD YOU LIKE TO SEE THAT, HARRY? WOULDJA?! HA HA!
HUH?
THIS SIMPLY WON'T DO. I CAN'T LOSE THEM! THIS WON'T DO AT ALL!
HARRY!
ANOTHER TIME, BOY.
DADDY'S GOT SOME FAMILY BONDING TO TAKE CARE OF.
HEE HEE HEE!

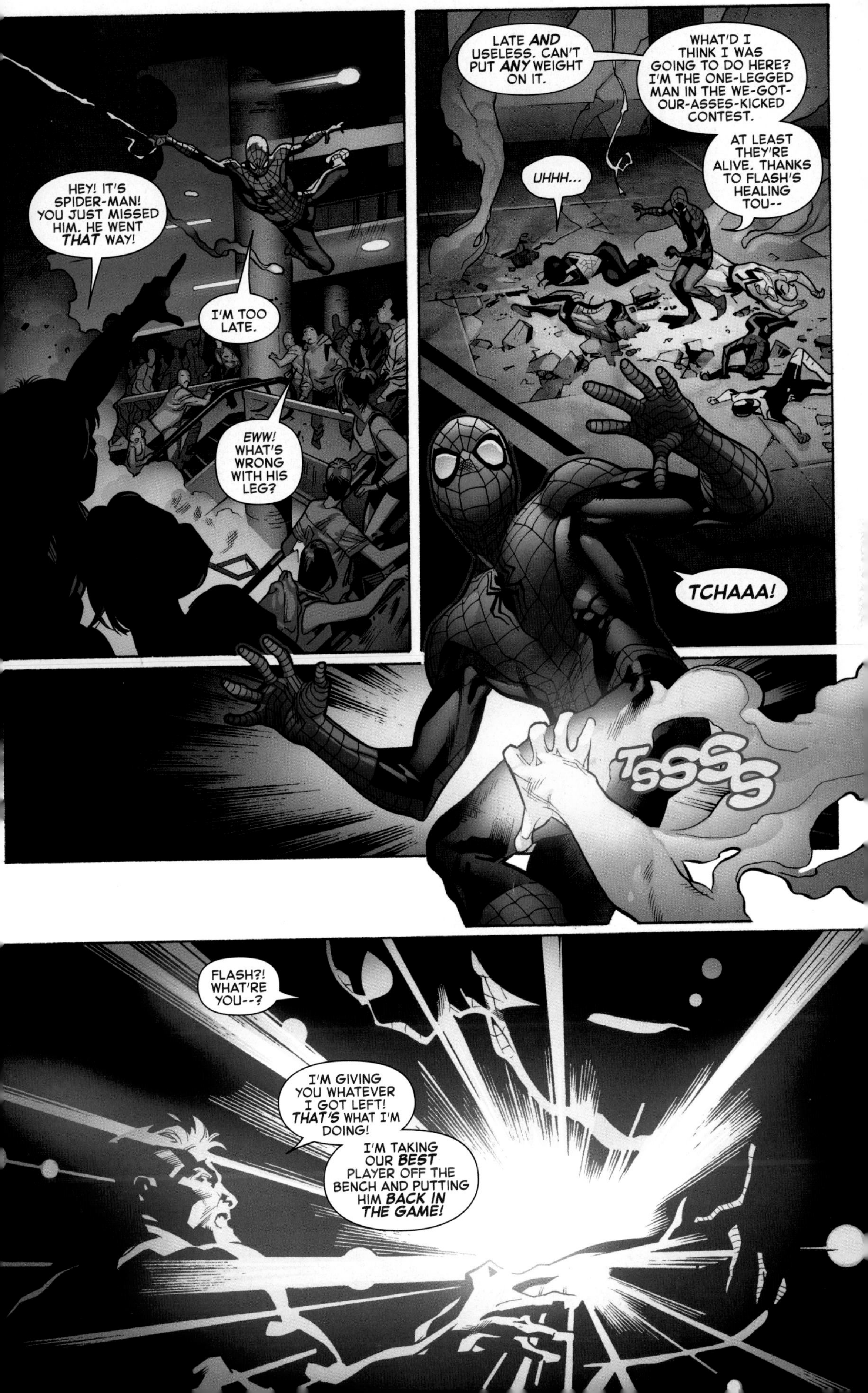

HEY! IT'S SPIDER-MAN! YOU JUST MISSED HIM. HE WENT THAT WAY!
I'M TOO LATE.
EWW! WHAT'S WRONG WITH HIS LEG?
LATE AND USELESS. CAN'T PUT ANY WEIGHT ON IT.
WHAT'D I THINK I WAS GOING TO DO HERE? I'M THE ONE-LEGGED MAN IN THE WE-GOT-OUR-ASSES-KICKED CONTEST.
AT LEAST THEY'RE ALIVE. THANKS TO FLASH'S HEALING TOU--
UHHH...
TCHAAA!
TSSSS
FLASH?! WHAT'RE YOU--?
I'M GIVING YOU WHATEVER I GOT LEFT! THAT'S WHAT I'M DOING!
I'M TAKING OUR BEST PLAYER OFF THE BENCH AND PUTTING HIM BACK IN THE GAME!

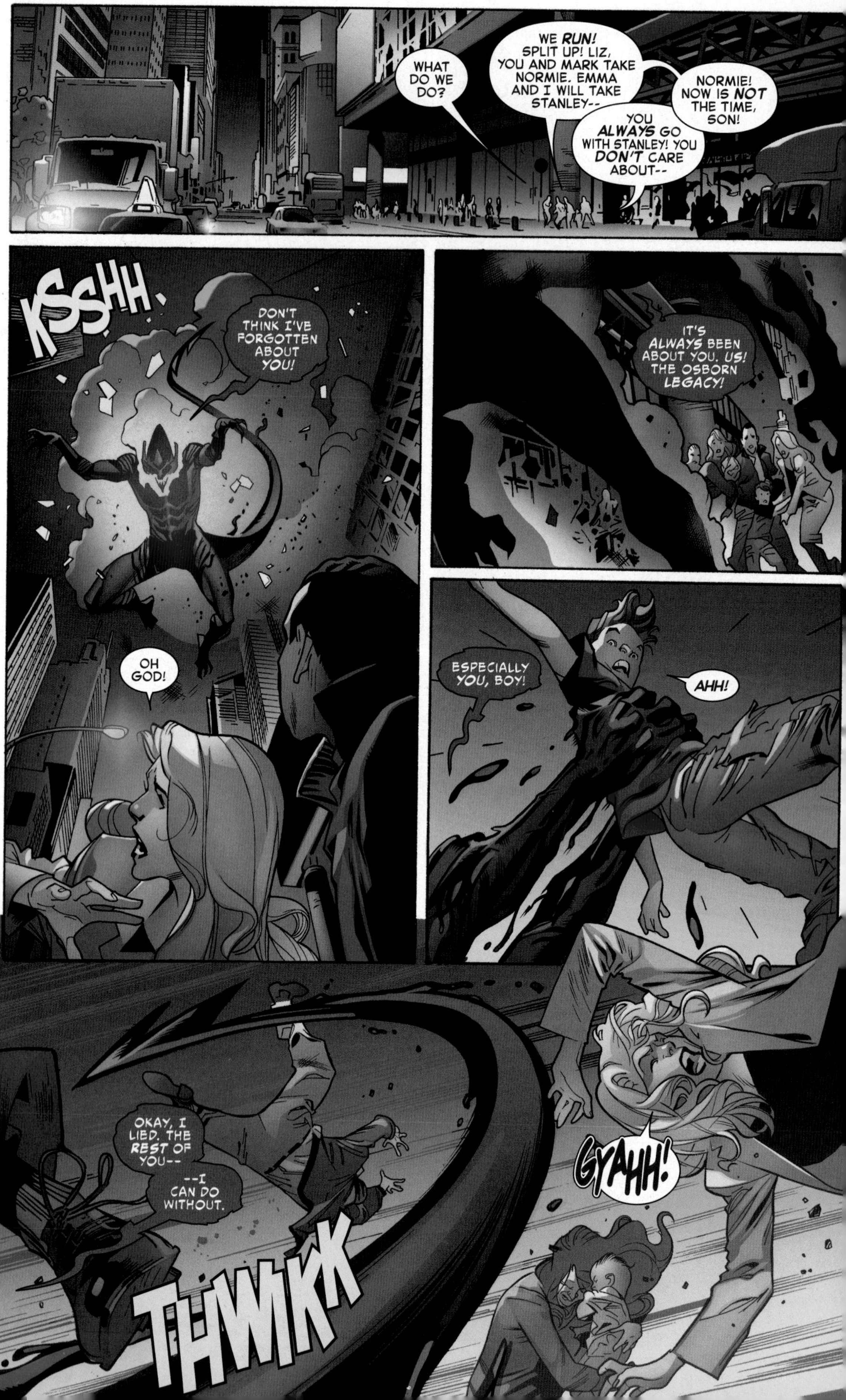
WHAT DO WE DO?
WE RUN! SPLIT UP! LIZ, YOU AND MARK TAKE NORMIE. EMMA AND I WILL TAKE STANLEY--
YOU ALWAYS GO WITH STANLEY! YOU DON'T CARE ABOUT--
NORMIE! NOW IS NOT THE TIME, SON!
KSSHH
DON'T THINK I'VE FORGOTTEN ABOUT YOU!
OH GOD!
IT'S ALWAYS BEEN ABOUT YOU. US! THE OSBORN LEGACY!
ESPECIALLY YOU, BOY!
AHH!
OKAY, I LIED. THE REST OF YOU--
--I CAN DO WITHOUT.
GYAHH!
THWIKK

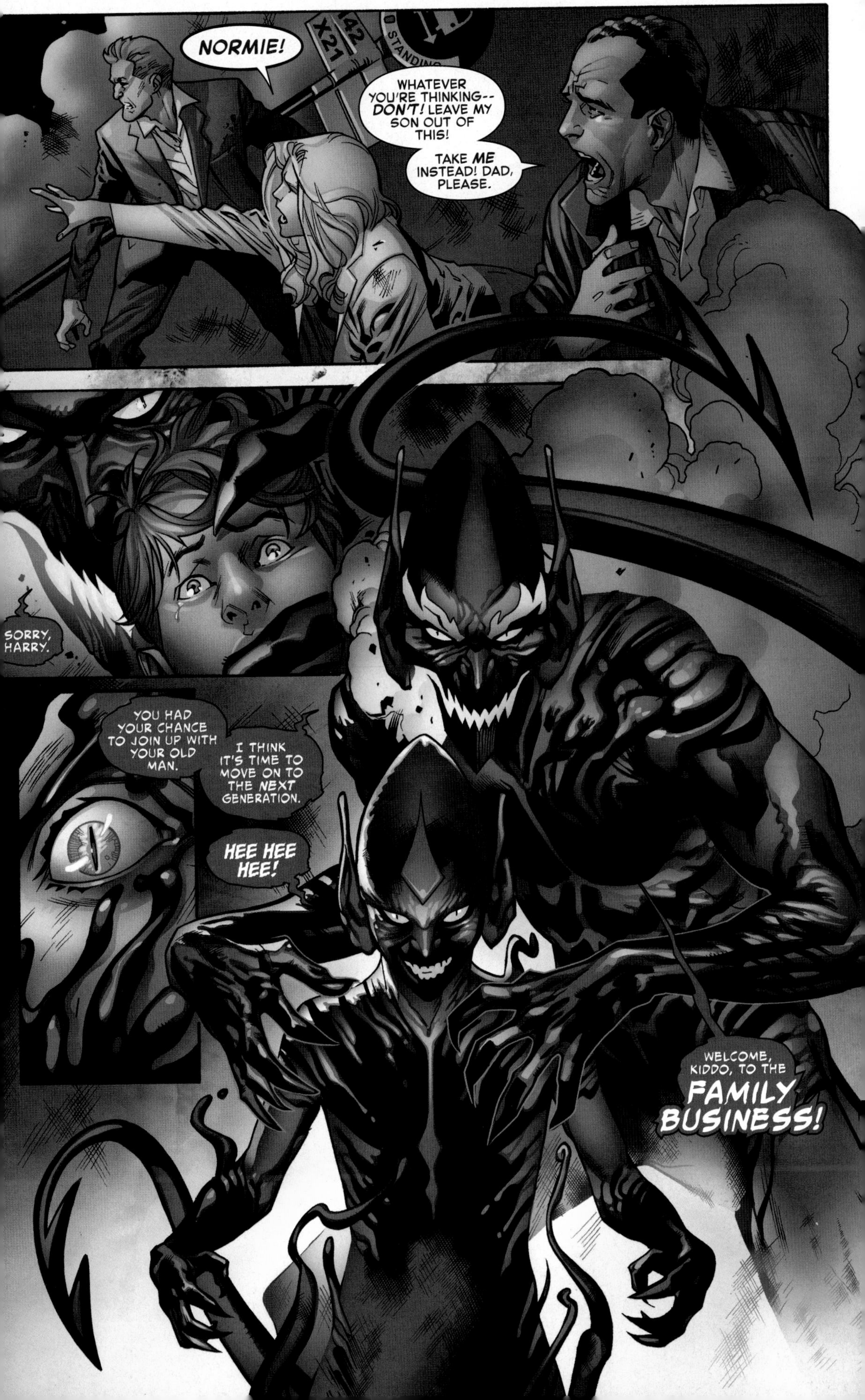
NORMIE!
WHATEVER YOU'RE THINKING-- DON'T! LEAVE MY SON OUT OF THIS!
TAKE ME INSTEAD! DAD, PLEASE.
SORRY, HARRY.
YOU HAD YOUR CHANCE TO JOIN UP WITH YOUR OLD MAN.
I THINK IT'S TIME TO MOVE ON TO THE NEXT GENERATION.
HEE HEE HEE!
WELCOME, KIDDO, TO THE FAMILY BUSINESS!

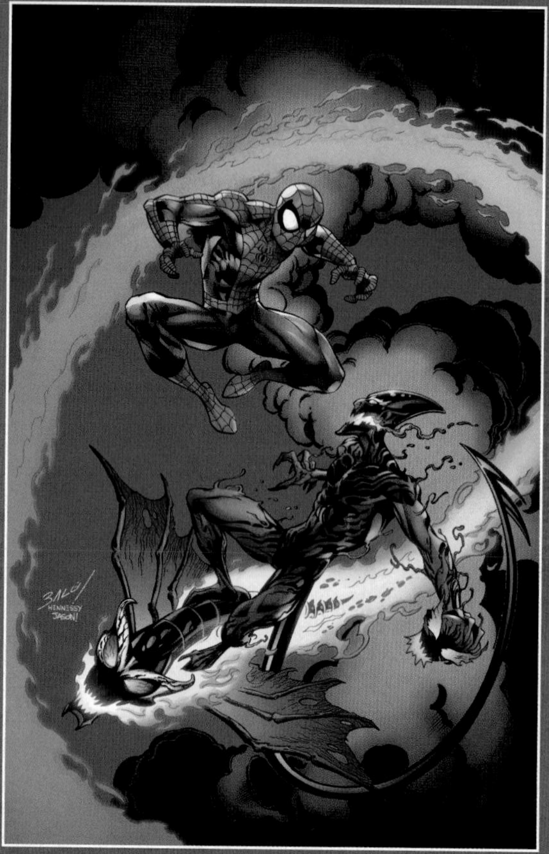

Amazing Spider-Man #800 variant by
Mark Bagley, Andrew Hennessy & Jason Keith

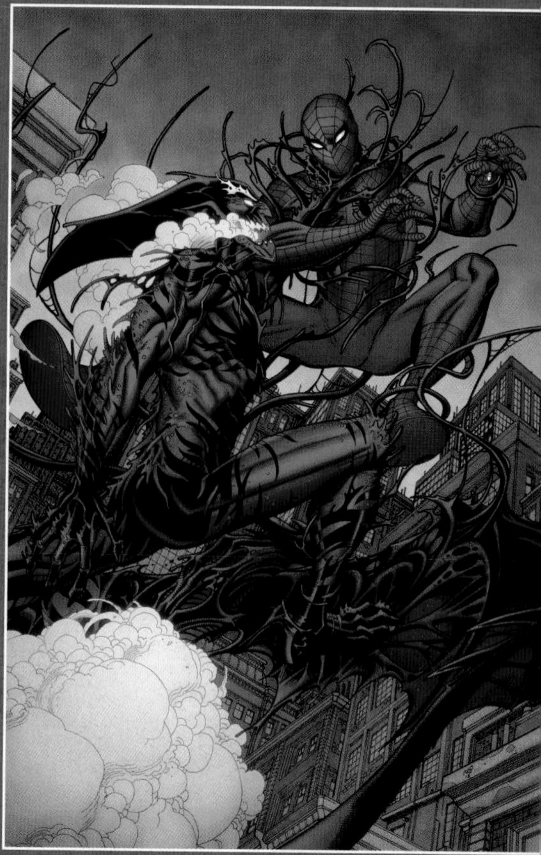

Amazing Spider-Man #800 variant by
Nick Bradshaw & Morry Hollowell

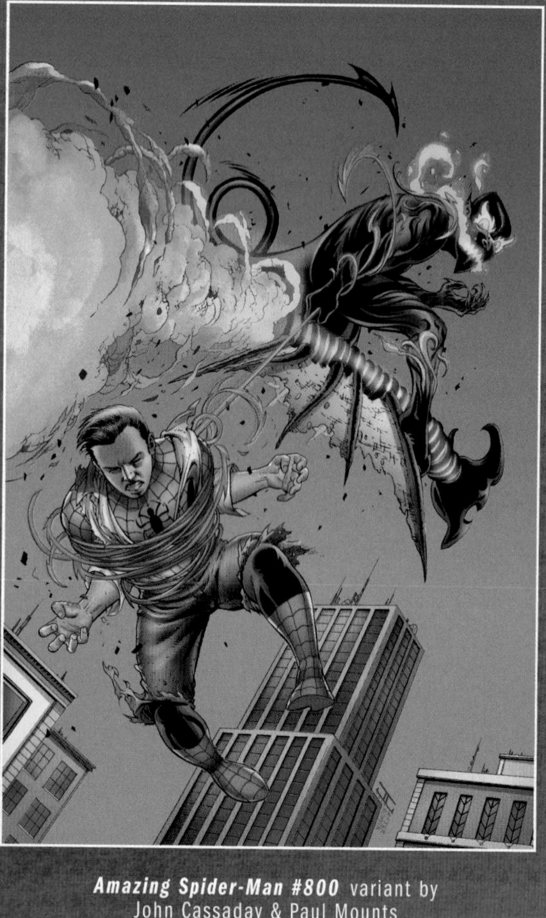

Amazing Spider-Man #800 variant by
John Cassaday & Paul Mounts

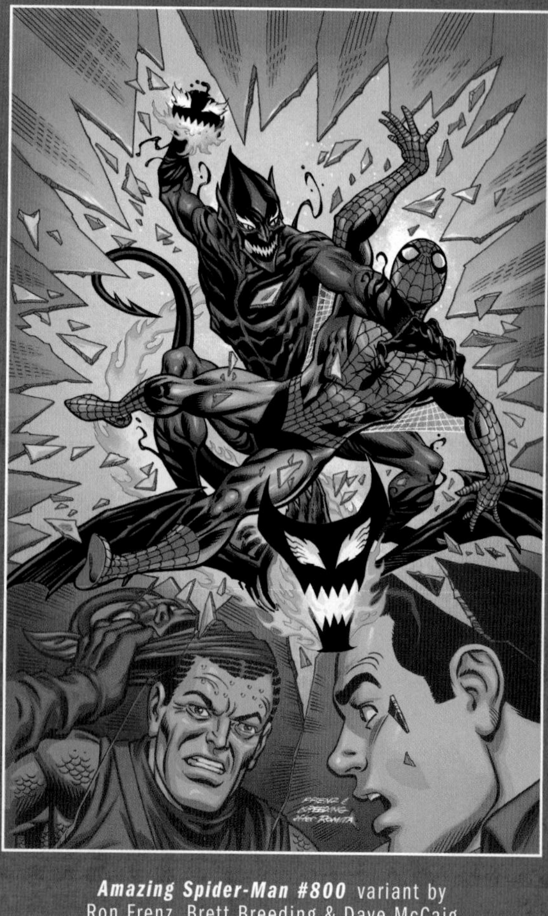

Amazing Spider-Man #800 variant by
Ron Frenz, Brett Breeding & Dave McCaig

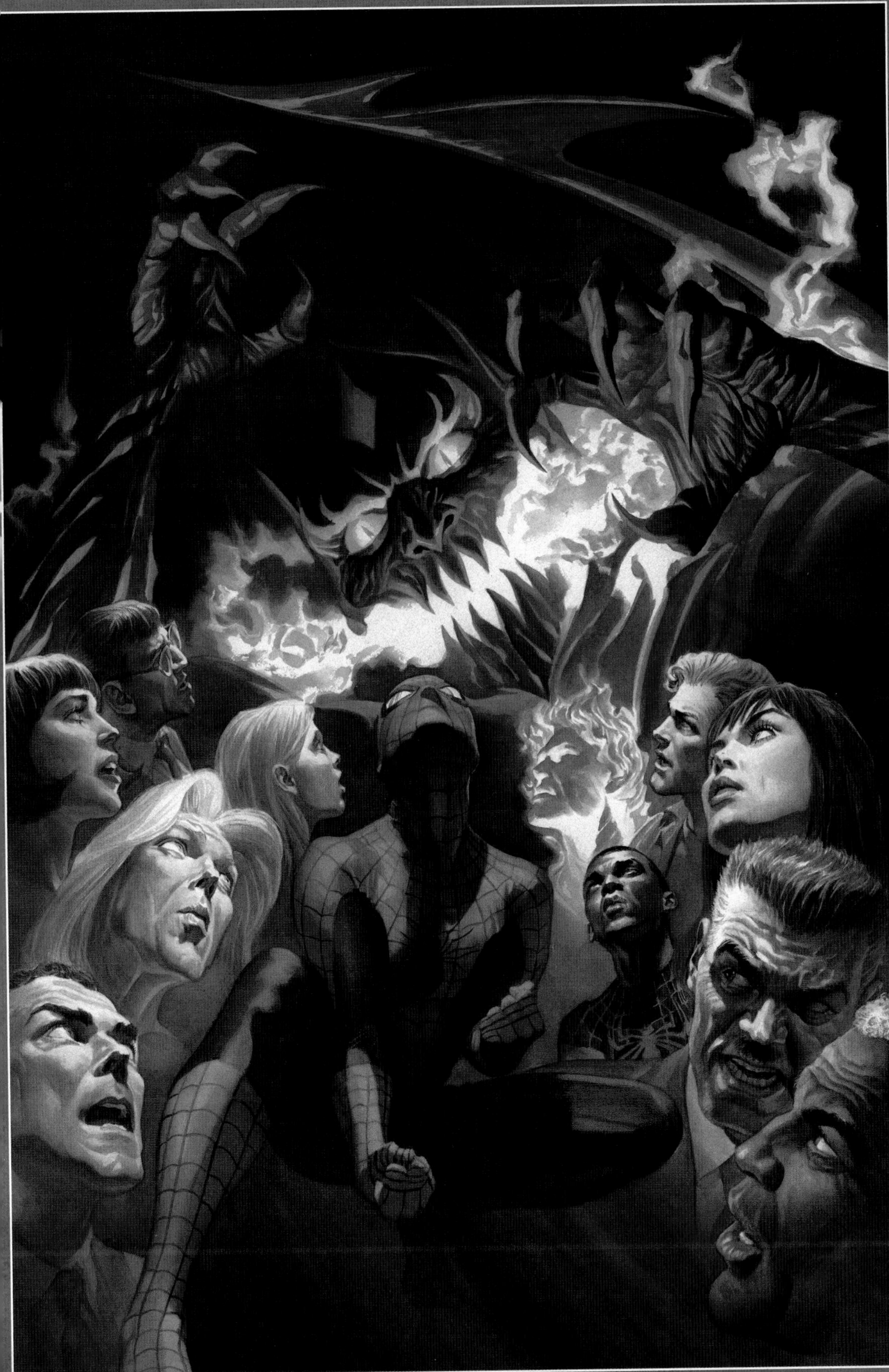

AMAZING SPIDER-MAN #800
GO DOWN SWINGING, CONCLUSION

Chapter 1
Crawling Through the Wreckage

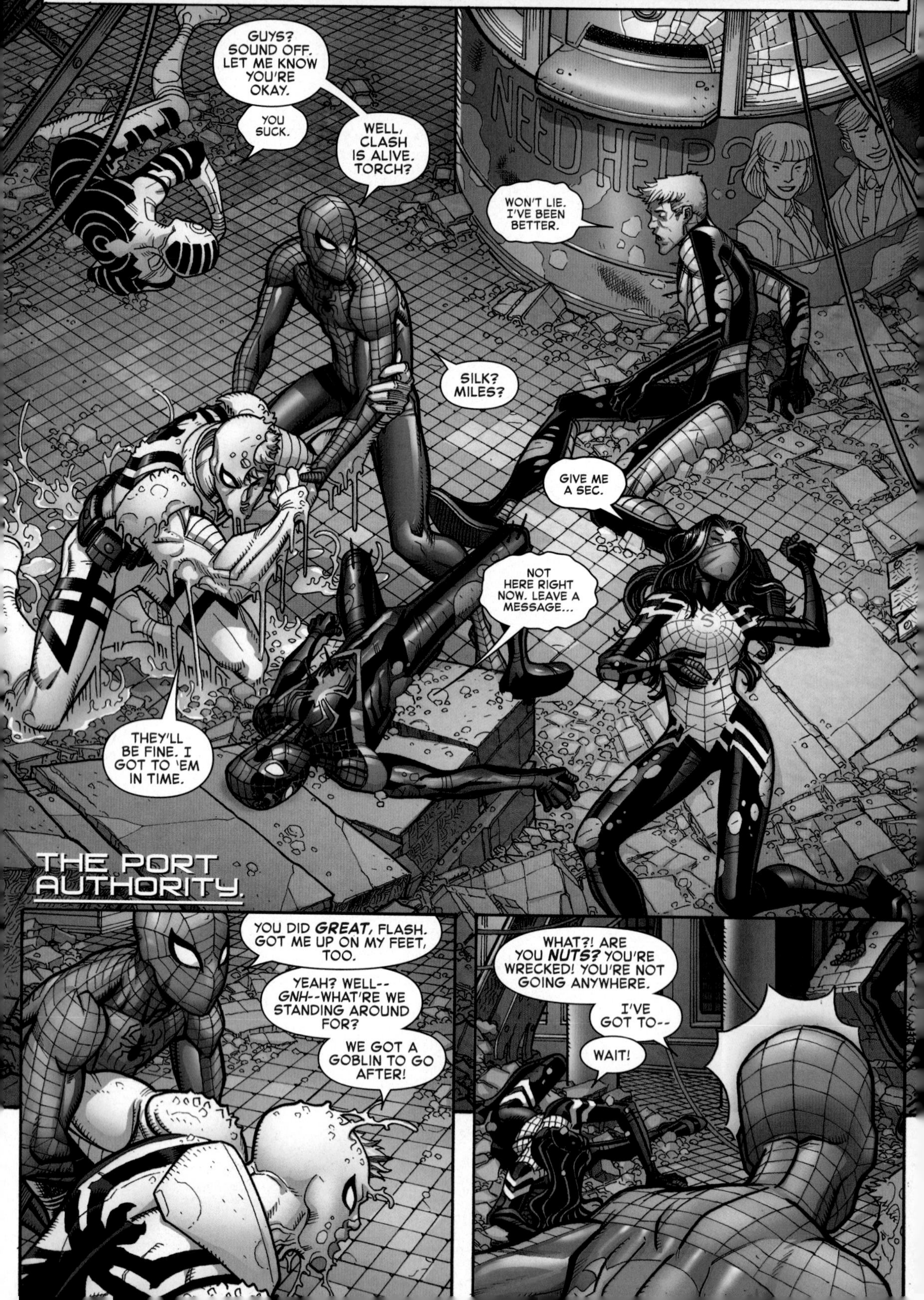
GUYS? SOUND OFF. LET ME KNOW YOU'RE OKAY.
YOU SUCK.
WELL, CLASH IS ALIVE. TORCH?
WON'T LIE. I'VE BEEN BETTER.
SILK? MILES?
GIVE ME A SEC.
NOT HERE RIGHT NOW. LEAVE A MESSAGE...
THEY'LL BE FINE. I GOT TO 'EM IN TIME.
THE PORT AUTHORITY.
YOU DID GREAT, FLASH. GOT ME UP ON MY FEET, TOO.
YEAH? WELL-- GNH--WHAT'RE WE STANDING AROUND FOR?
WE GOT A GOBLIN TO GO AFTER!
WHAT?! ARE YOU NUTS? YOU'RE WRECKED! YOU'RE NOT GOING ANYWHERE.
I'VE GOT TO--
WAIT!

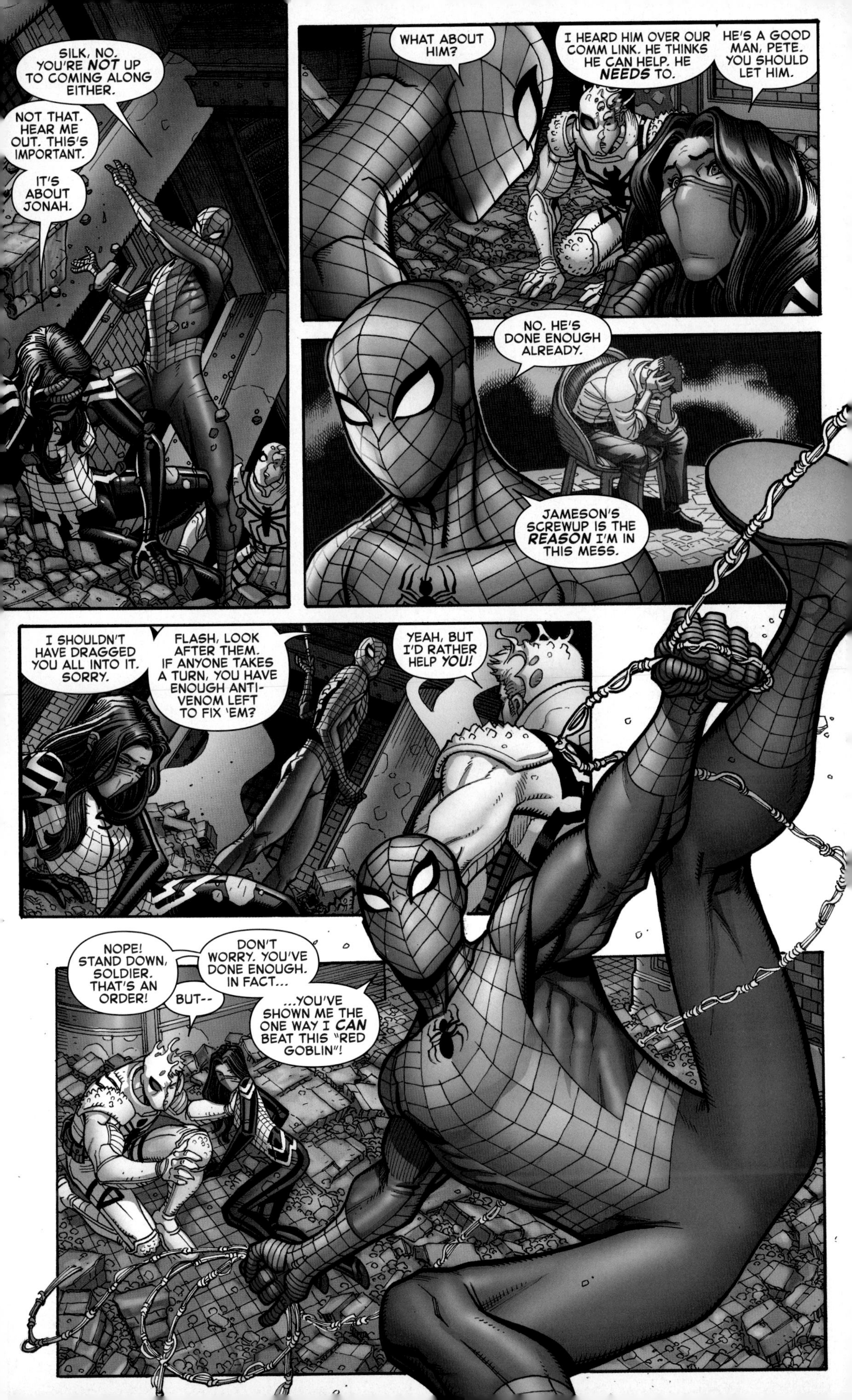

SILK, NO. YOU'RE NOT UP TO COMING ALONG EITHER.
NOT THAT. HEAR ME OUT. THIS'S IMPORTANT.
IT'S ABOUT JONAH.
WHAT ABOUT HIM?
I HEARD HIM OVER OUR COMM LINK. HE THINKS HE CAN HELP. HE NEEDS TO.
HE'S A GOOD MAN, PETE. YOU SHOULD LET HIM.
NO. HE'S DONE ENOUGH ALREADY.
JAMESON'S SCREWUP IS THE REASON I'M IN THIS MESS.
I SHOULDN'T HAVE DRAGGED YOU ALL INTO IT. SORRY.
FLASH, LOOK AFTER THEM. IF ANYONE TAKES A TURN, YOU HAVE ENOUGH ANTI-VENOM LEFT TO FIX 'EM?
YEAH, BUT I'D RATHER HELP YOU!
NOPE! STAND DOWN, SOLDIER. THAT'S AN ORDER!
BUT--
DON'T WORRY. YOU'VE DONE ENOUGH. IN FACT...
...YOU'VE SHOWN ME THE ONE WAY I CAN BEAT THIS "RED GOBLIN"!

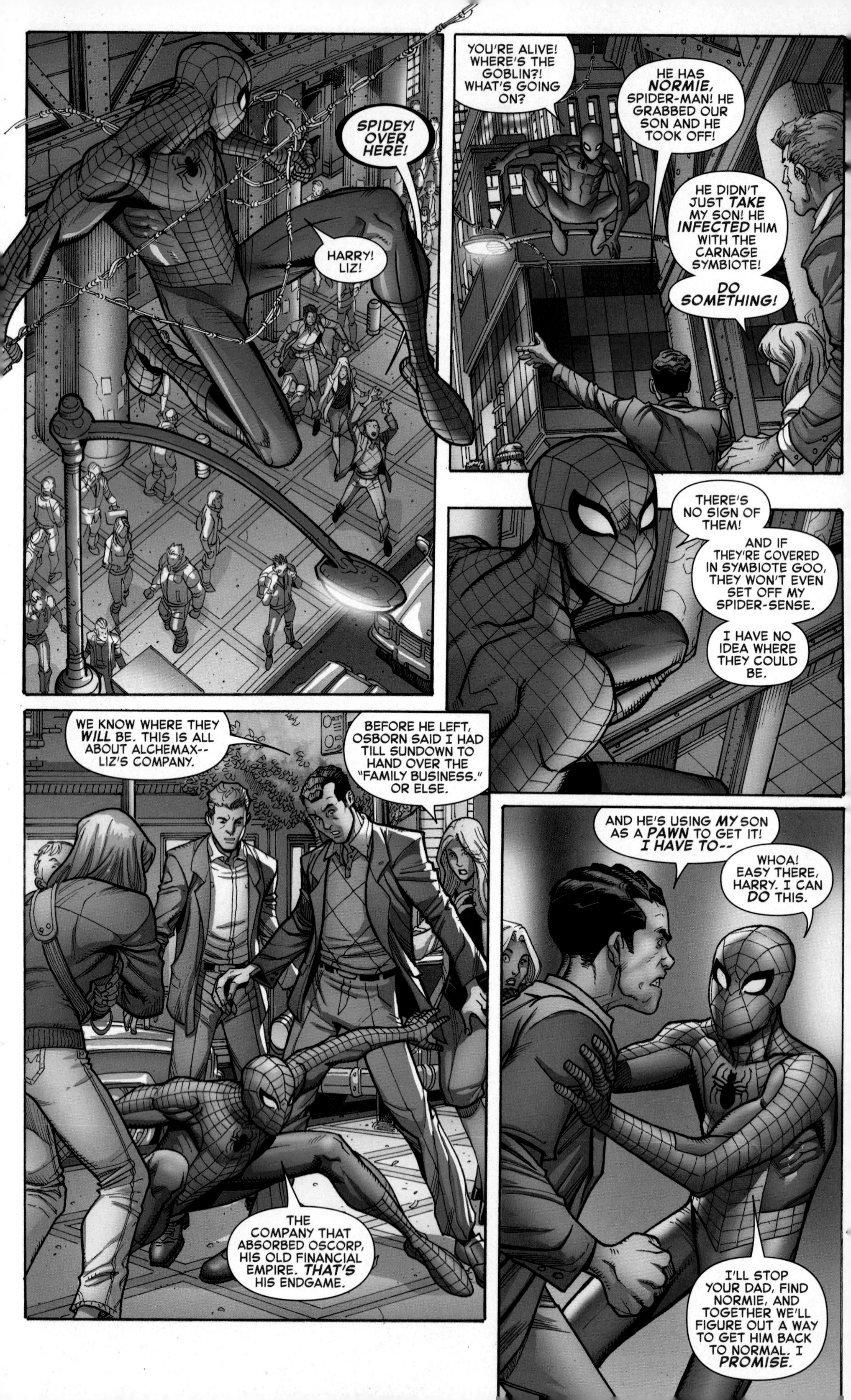
SPIDEY! OVER HERE!
HARRY! LIZ!
YOU'RE ALIVE! WHERE'S THE GOBLIN?! WHAT'S GOING ON?
HE HAS NORMIE, SPIDER-MAN! HE GRABBED OUR SON AND HE TOOK OFF!
HE DIDN'T JUST TAKE MY SON! HE INFECTED HIM WITH THE CARNAGE SYMBIOTE!
DO SOMETHING!
THERE'S NO SIGN OF THEM!
AND IF THEY'RE COVERED IN SYMBIOTE GOO, THEY WON'T EVEN SET OFF MY SPIDER-SENSE.
I HAVE NO IDEA WHERE THEY COULD BE.
WE KNOW WHERE THEY WILL BE. THIS IS ALL ABOUT ALCHEMAX-- LIZ'S COMPANY.
BEFORE HE LEFT, OSBORN SAID I HAD TILL SUNDOWN TO HAND OVER THE "FAMILY BUSINESS." OR ELSE.
THE COMPANY THAT ABSORBED OSCORP, HIS OLD FINANCIAL EMPIRE. THAT'S HIS ENDGAME.
AND HE'S USING MY SON AS A PAWN TO GET IT! I HAVE TO--
WHOA! EASY THERE, HARRY. I CAN DO THIS.
I'LL STOP YOUR DAD, FIND NORMIE, AND TOGETHER WE'LL FIGURE OUT A WAY TO GET HIM BACK TO NORMAL. I PROMISE.

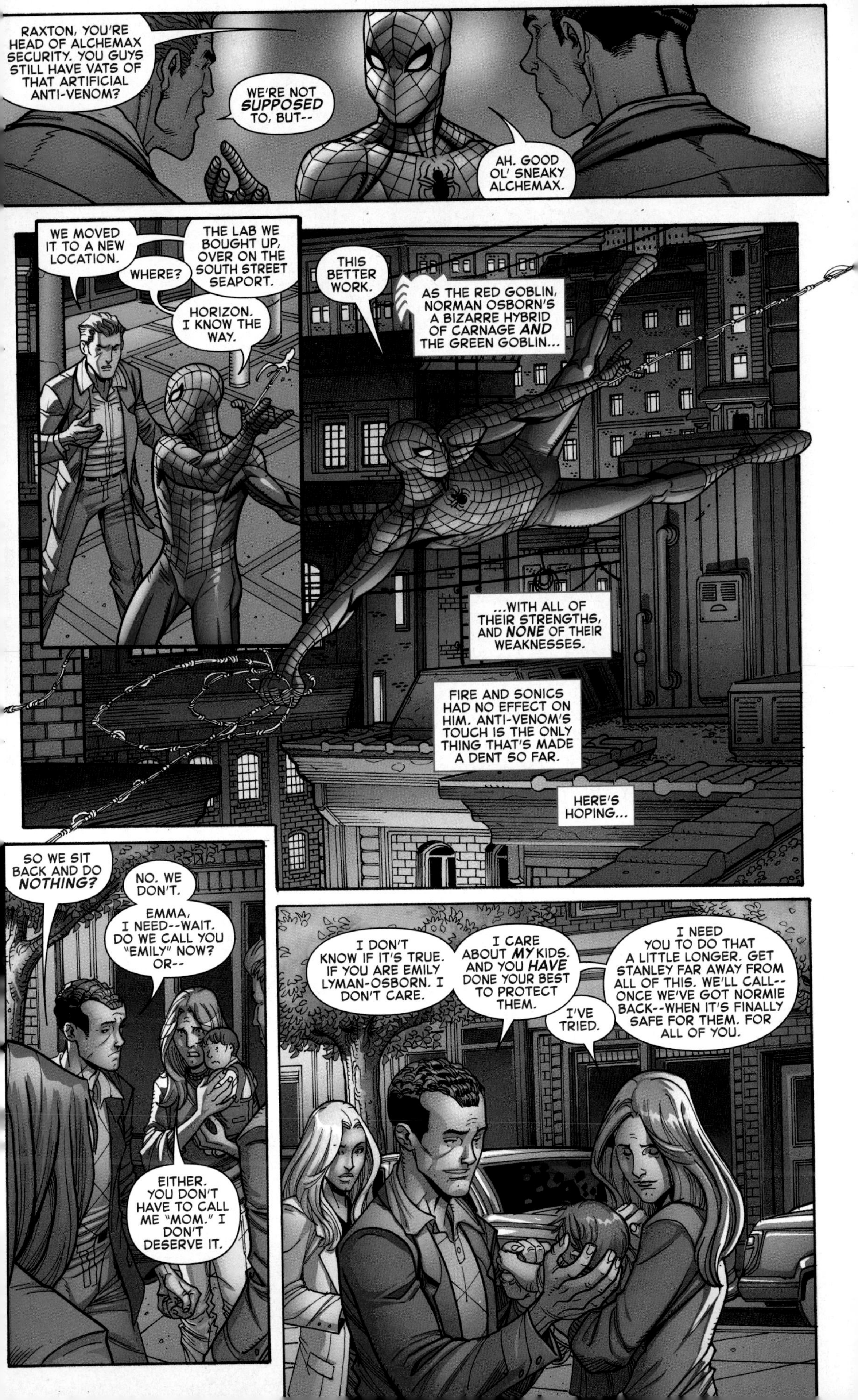
RAXTON, YOU'RE HEAD OF ALCHEMAX SECURITY. YOU GUYS STILL HAVE VATS OF THAT ARTIFICIAL ANTI-VENOM?
WE'RE NOT SUPPOSED TO, BUT--
AH. GOOD OL' SNEAKY ALCHEMAX.
WE MOVED IT TO A NEW LOCATION.
WHERE?
THE LAB WE BOUGHT UP, OVER ON THE SOUTH STREET SEAPORT.
HORIZON. I KNOW THE WAY.
THIS BETTER WORK.
AS THE RED GOBLIN, NORMAN OSBORN'S A BIZARRE HYBRID OF CARNAGE AND THE GREEN GOBLIN...
...WITH ALL OF THEIR STRENGTHS, AND NONE OF THEIR WEAKNESSES.
FIRE AND SONICS HAD NO EFFECT ON HIM. ANTI-VENOM'S TOUCH IS THE ONLY THING THAT'S MADE A DENT SO FAR.
HERE'S HOPING...
SO WE SIT BACK AND DO NOTHING?
NO. WE DON'T.
EMMA, I NEED--WAIT. DO WE CALL YOU "EMILY" NOW? OR--
EITHER. YOU DON'T HAVE TO CALL ME "MOM." I DON'T DESERVE IT.
I DON'T KNOW IF IT'S TRUE. IF YOU ARE EMILY LYMAN-OSBORN. I DON'T CARE.
I CARE ABOUT MY KIDS. AND YOU HAVE DONE YOUR BEST TO PROTECT THEM.
I'VE TRIED.
I NEED YOU TO DO THAT A LITTLE LONGER. GET STANLEY FAR AWAY FROM ALL OF THIS. WE'LL CALL-- ONCE WE'VE GOT NORMIE BACK--WHEN IT'S FINALLY SAFE FOR THEM. FOR ALL OF YOU.

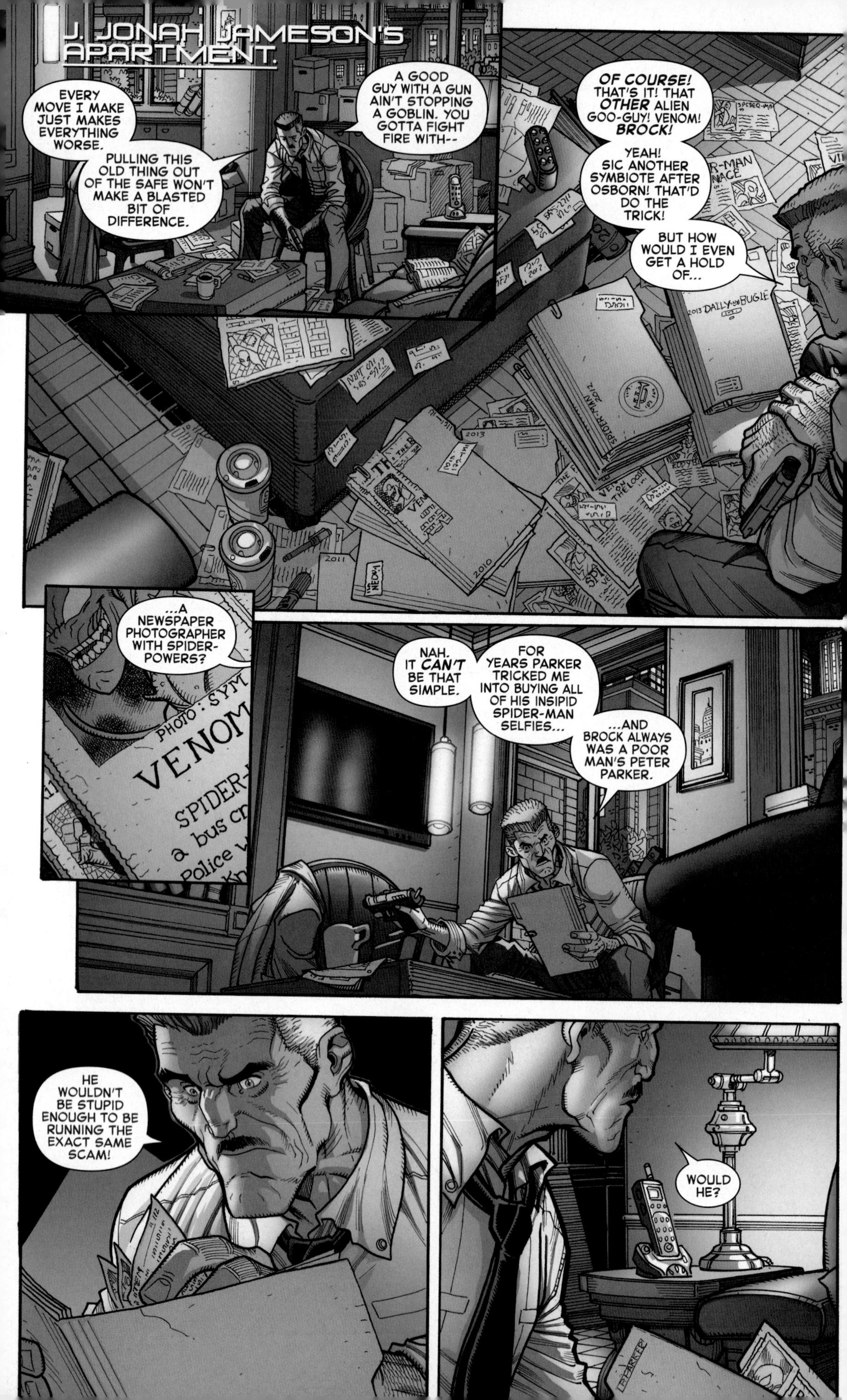

J. JONAH JAMESON'S APARTMENT.
EVERY MOVE I MAKE JUST MAKES EVERYTHING WORSE.
PULLING THIS OLD THING OUT OF THE SAFE WON'T MAKE A BLASTED BIT OF DIFFERENCE.
A GOOD GUY WITH A GUN AIN'T STOPPING A GOBLIN. YOU GOTTA FIGHT FIRE WITH--
OF COURSE! THAT'S IT! THAT OTHER ALIEN GOO-GUY! VENOM! BROCK!
YEAH! SIC ANOTHER SYMBIOTE AFTER OSBORN! THAT'D DO THE TRICK!
BUT HOW WOULD I EVEN GET A HOLD OF...
...A NEWSPAPER PHOTOGRAPHER WITH SPIDER-POWERS?
PHOTO: SYM
VENOM
SPIDER-
a bus c
Police
NAH. IT CAN'T BE THAT SIMPLE.
FOR YEARS PARKER TRICKED ME INTO BUYING ALL OF HIS INSIPID SPIDER-MAN SELFIES...
...AND BROCK ALWAYS WAS A POOR MAN'S PETER PARKER.
HE WOULDN'T BE STUPID ENOUGH TO BE RUNNING THE EXACT SAME SCAM!
WOULD HE?

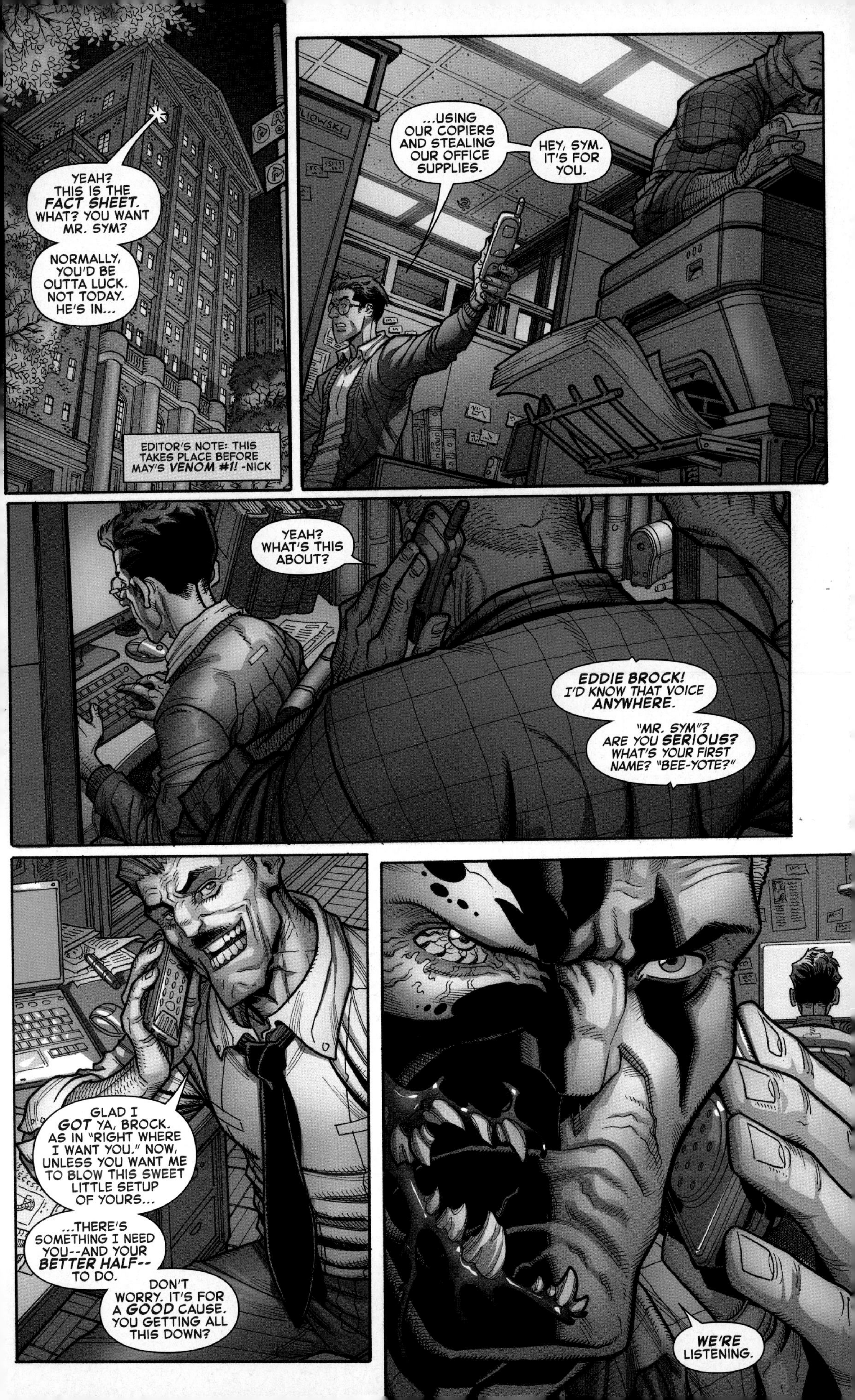
YEAH? THIS IS THE FACT SHEET. WHAT? YOU WANT MR. SYM?
NORMALLY, YOU'D BE OUTTA LUCK. NOT TODAY. HE'S IN...
EDITOR'S NOTE: THIS TAKES PLACE BEFORE MAY'S VENOM #1! -NICK
...USING OUR COPIERS AND STEALING OUR OFFICE SUPPLIES.
HEY, SYM. IT'S FOR YOU.
YEAH? WHAT'S THIS ABOUT?
EDDIE BROCK! I'D KNOW THAT VOICE ANYWHERE.
"MR. SYM"? ARE YOU SERIOUS? WHAT'S YOUR FIRST NAME? "BEE-YOTE?"
GLAD I GOT YA, BROCK. AS IN "RIGHT WHERE I WANT YOU." NOW, UNLESS YOU WANT ME TO BLOW THIS SWEET LITTLE SETUP OF YOURS...
...THERE'S SOMETHING I NEED YOU--AND YOUR BETTER HALF-- TO DO.
DON'T WORRY. IT'S FOR A GOOD CAUSE. YOU GETTING ALL THIS DOWN?
WE'RE LISTENING.

Chapter 2
Too Many Targets

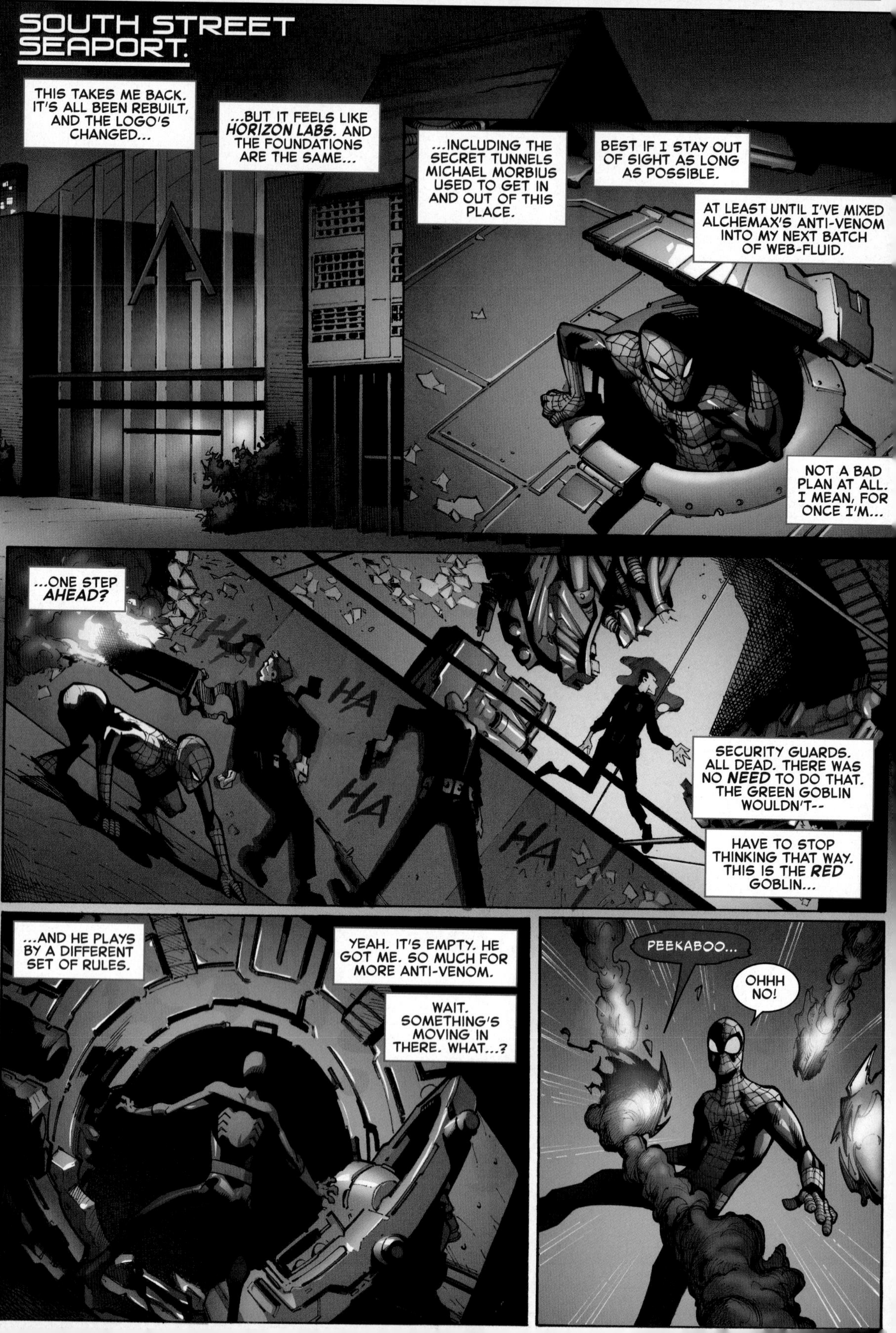
SOUTH STREET SEAPORT.
THIS TAKES ME BACK. IT'S ALL BEEN REBUILT, AND THE LOGO'S CHANGED...
...BUT IT FEELS LIKE HORIZON LABS. AND THE FOUNDATIONS ARE THE SAME...
...INCLUDING THE SECRET TUNNELS MICHAEL MORBIUS USED TO GET IN AND OUT OF THIS PLACE.
BEST IF I STAY OUT OF SIGHT AS LONG AS POSSIBLE.
AT LEAST UNTIL I'VE MIXED ALCHEMAX'S ANTI-VENOM INTO MY NEXT BATCH OF WEB-FLUID.
NOT A BAD PLAN AT ALL. I MEAN, FOR ONCE I'M...
...ONE STEP AHEAD?
HA
HA
HA
HA
SECURITY GUARDS. ALL DEAD. THERE WAS NO NEED TO DO THAT. THE GREEN GOBLIN WOULDN'T--
HAVE TO STOP THINKING THAT WAY. THIS IS THE RED GOBLIN...
...AND HE PLAYS BY A DIFFERENT SET OF RULES.
YEAH. IT'S EMPTY. HE GOT ME. SO MUCH FOR MORE ANTI-VENOM.
WAIT. SOMETHING'S MOVING IN THERE. WHAT...?
PEEKABOO...
OHHH NO!

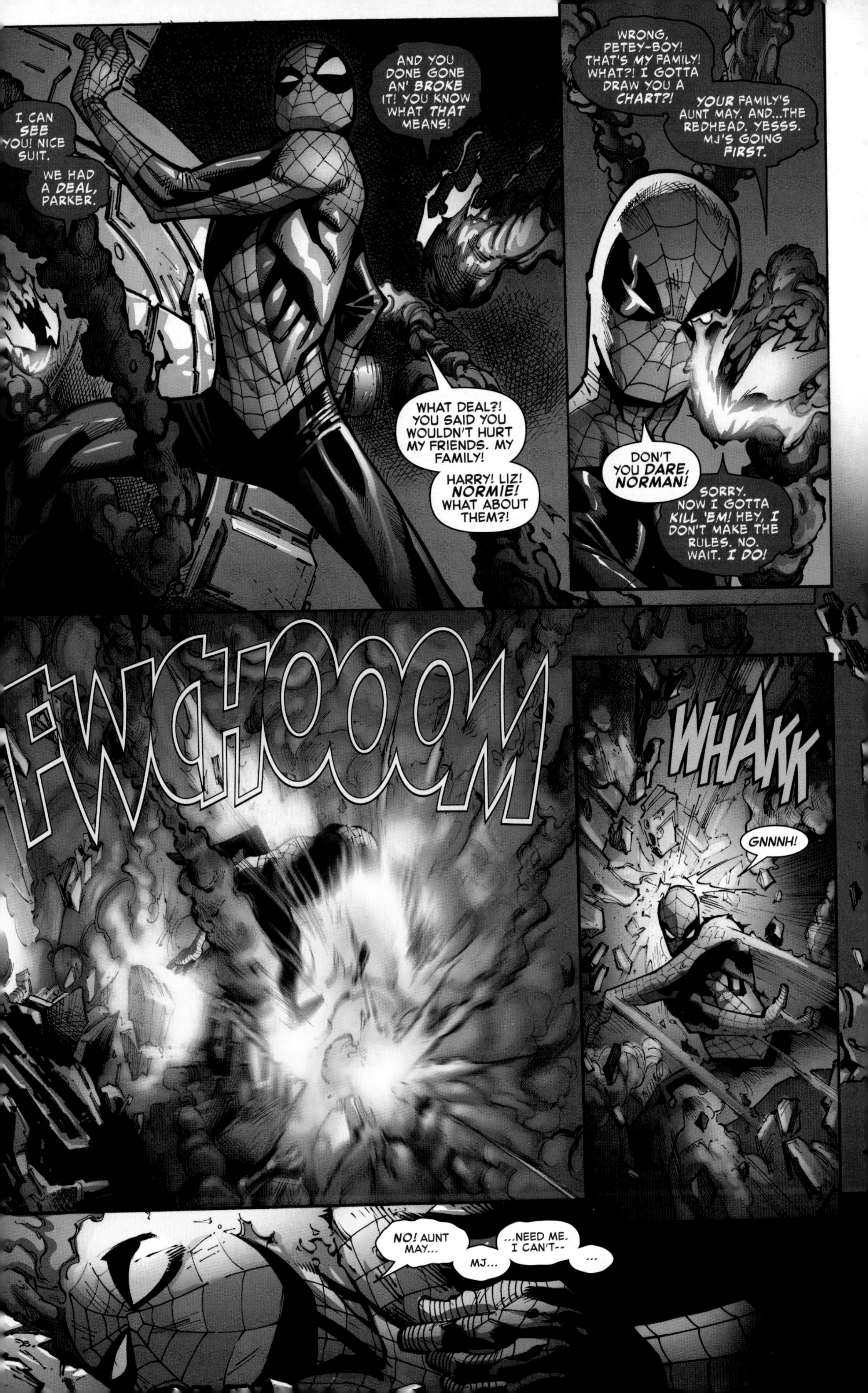
I CAN SEE YOU! NICE SUIT.
WE HAD A DEAL, PARKER.
AND YOU DONE GONE AN' BROKE IT! YOU KNOW WHAT THAT MEANS!
WHAT DEAL?! YOU SAID YOU WOULDN'T HURT MY FRIENDS. MY FAMILY!
HARRY! LIZ! NORMIE! WHAT ABOUT THEM?!
WRONG, PETEY-BOY! THAT'S MY FAMILY! WHAT?! I GOTTA DRAW YOU A CHART?!
YOUR FAMILY'S AUNT MAY. AND...THE REDHEAD. YESSS. MJ'S GOING FIRST.
DON'T YOU DARE, NORMAN!
SORRY. NOW I GOTTA KILL 'EM! HEY, I DON'T MAKE THE RULES. NO. WAIT. I DO!
FWCHOOOM
WHAKK
GNNNH!
NO! AUNT MAY...
MJ...
...NEED ME. I CAN'T--
...

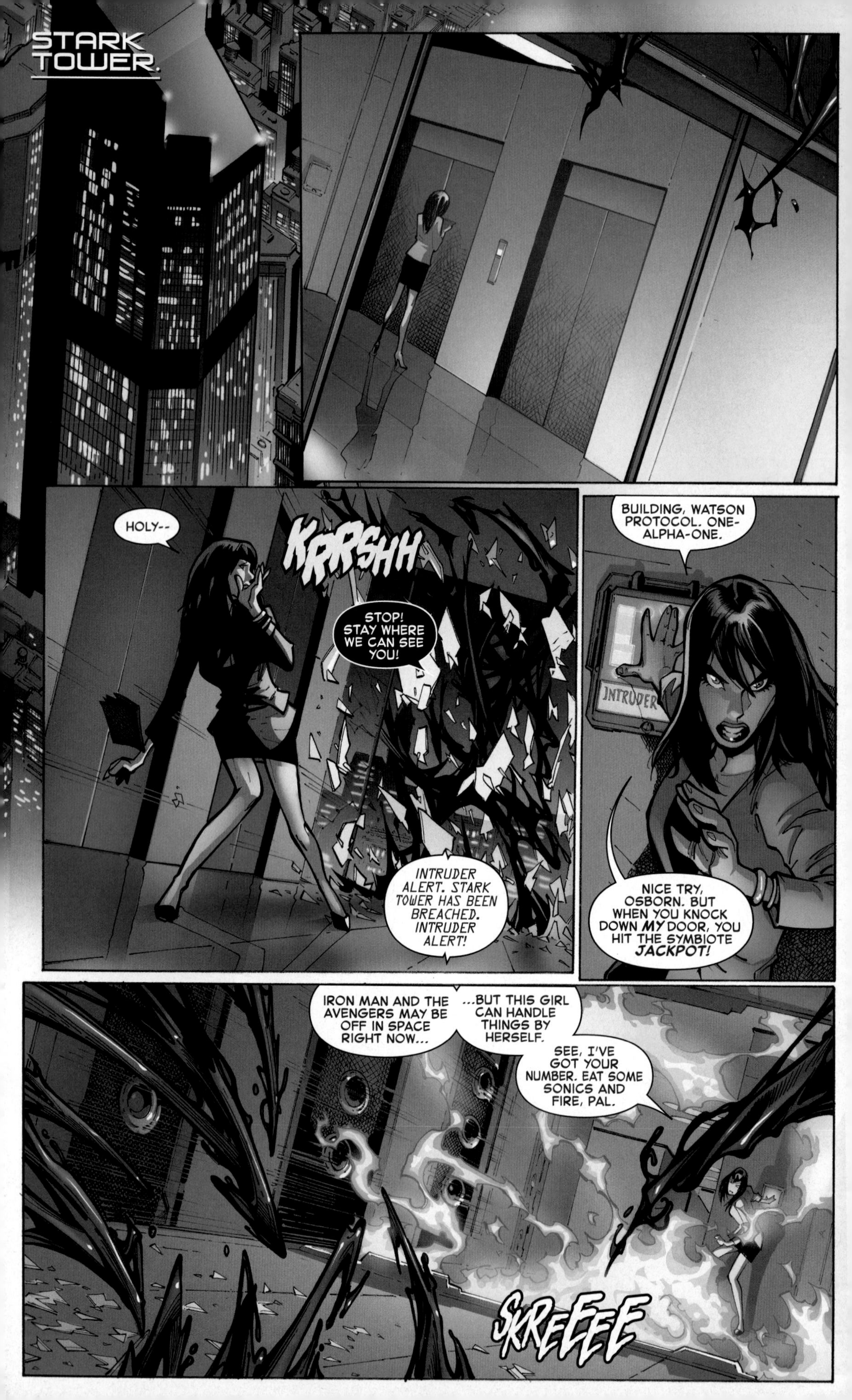
STARK TOWER.
HOLY--
KRRSHH
STOP! STAY WHERE WE CAN SEE YOU!
INTRUDER ALERT. STARK TOWER HAS BEEN BREACHED. INTRUDER ALERT!
BUILDING, WATSON PROTOCOL. ONE-ALPHA-ONE.
INTRUDER
NICE TRY, OSBORN. BUT WHEN YOU KNOCK DOWN MY DOOR, YOU HIT THE SYMBIOTE JACKPOT!
IRON MAN AND THE AVENGERS MAY BE OFF IN SPACE RIGHT NOW...
...BUT THIS GIRL CAN HANDLE THINGS BY HERSELF.
SEE, I'VE GOT YOUR NUMBER. EAT SOME SONICS AND FIRE, PAL.
SKREEEE

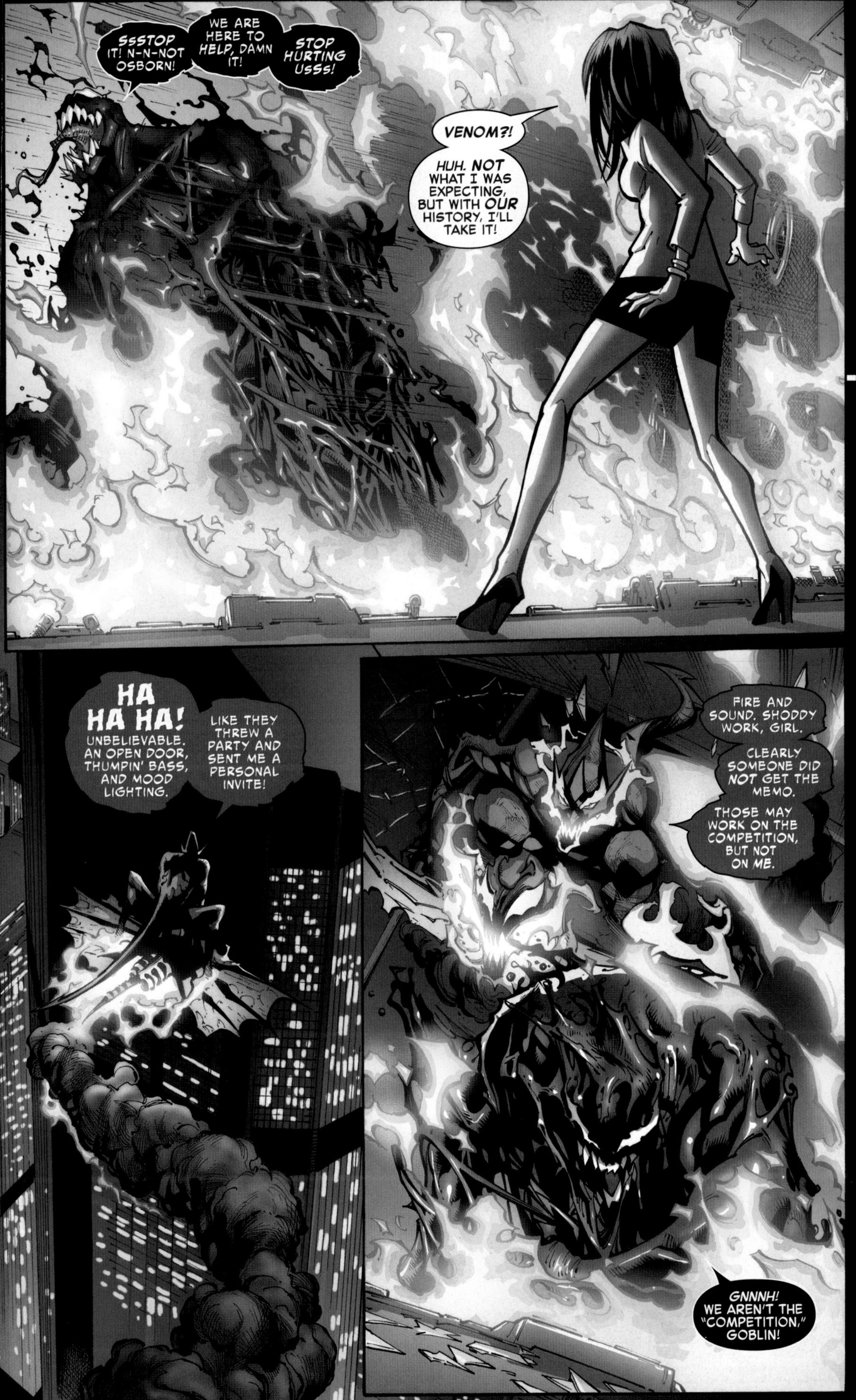
SSSTOP IT! N-N-NOT OSBORN!
WE ARE HERE TO HELP, DAMN IT!
STOP HURTING USSS!
VENOM?!
HUH. NOT WHAT I WAS EXPECTING, BUT WITH OUR HISTORY, I'LL TAKE IT!
HA HA HA! UNBELIEVABLE. AN OPEN DOOR, THUMPIN' BASS, AND MOOD LIGHTING.
LIKE THEY THREW A PARTY AND SENT ME A PERSONAL INVITE!
FIRE AND SOUND. SHODDY WORK, GIRL.
CLEARLY SOMEONE DID NOT GET THE MEMO.
THOSE MAY WORK ON THE COMPETITION, BUT NOT ON ME.
GNNNH! WE AREN'T THE "COMPETITION," GOBLIN!

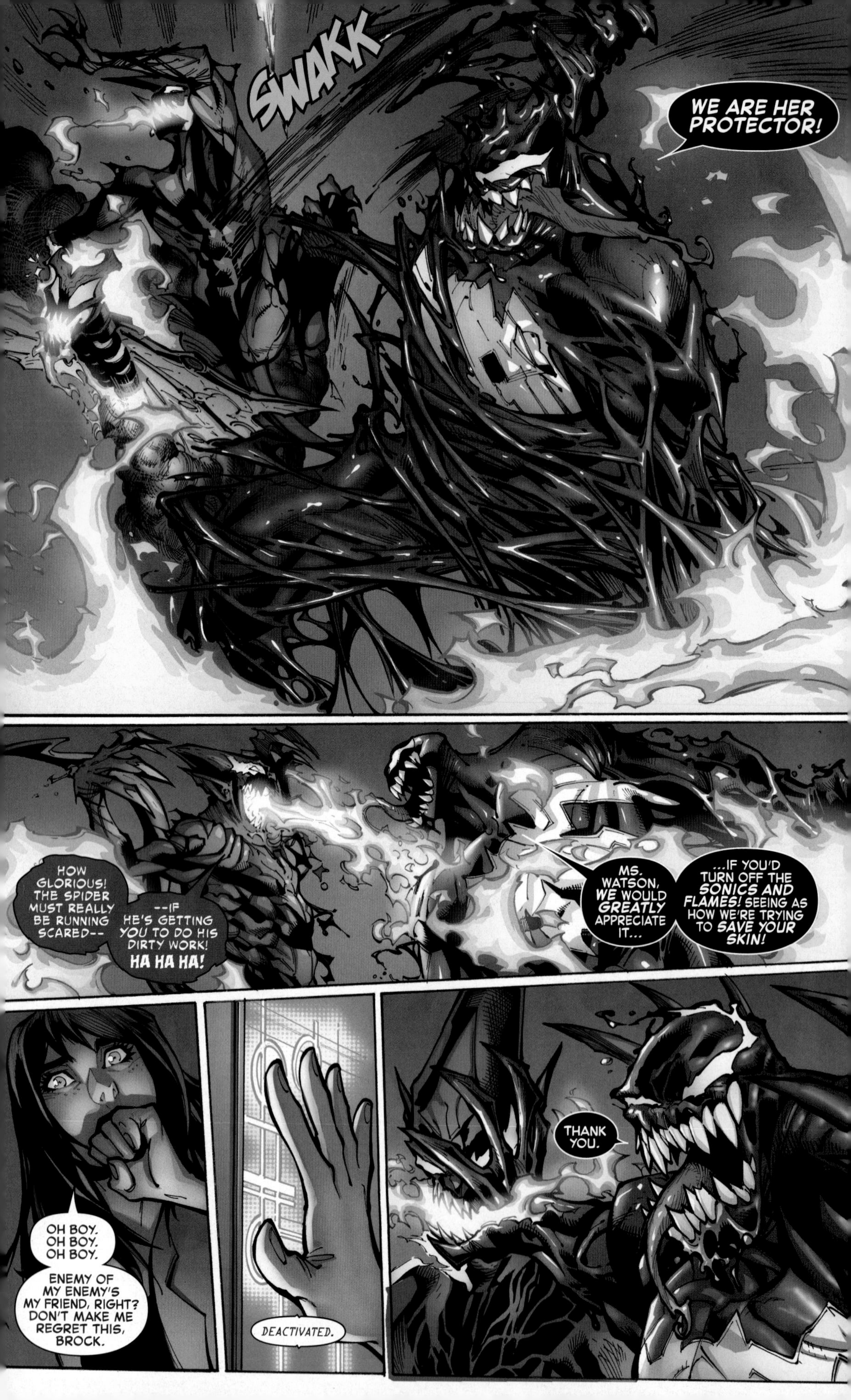
SWAKK
WE ARE HER PROTECTOR!
HOW GLORIOUS! THE SPIDER MUST REALLY BE RUNNING SCARED--
--IF HE'S GETTING YOU TO DO HIS DIRTY WORK! HA HA HA!
MS. WATSON, WE WOULD GREATLY APPRECIATE IT...
...IF YOU'D TURN OFF THE SONICS AND FLAMES! SEEING AS HOW WE'RE TRYING TO SAVE YOUR SKIN!
OH BOY. OH BOY. OH BOY.
ENEMY OF MY ENEMY'S MY FRIEND, RIGHT? DON'T MAKE ME REGRET THIS, BROCK.
DEACTIVATED.
THANK YOU.

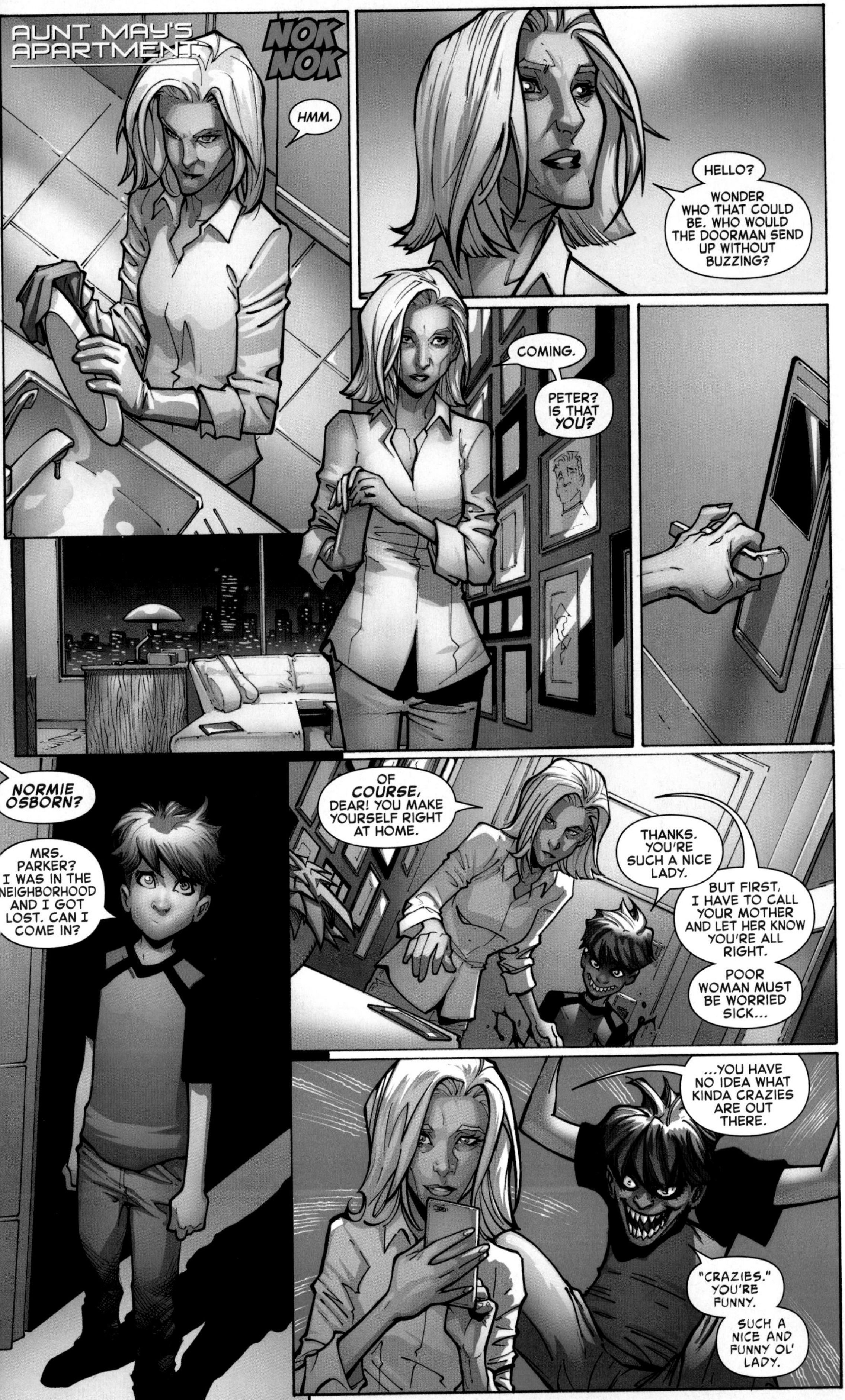
AUNT MAY'S APARTMENT.
NOK NOK
HMM.
HELLO?
WONDER WHO THAT COULD BE. WHO WOULD THE DOORMAN SEND UP WITHOUT BUZZING?
COMING.
PETER? IS THAT YOU?
NORMIE OSBORN?
MRS. PARKER? I WAS IN THE NEIGHBORHOOD AND I GOT LOST. CAN I COME IN?
OF COURSE, DEAR! YOU MAKE YOURSELF RIGHT AT HOME.
THANKS. YOU'RE SUCH A NICE LADY.
BUT FIRST, I HAVE TO CALL YOUR MOTHER AND LET HER KNOW YOU'RE ALL RIGHT.
POOR WOMAN MUST BE WORRIED SICK...
...YOU HAVE NO IDEA WHAT KINDA CRAZIES ARE OUT THERE.
"CRAZIES." YOU'RE FUNNY.
SUCH A NICE AND FUNNY OL' LADY.

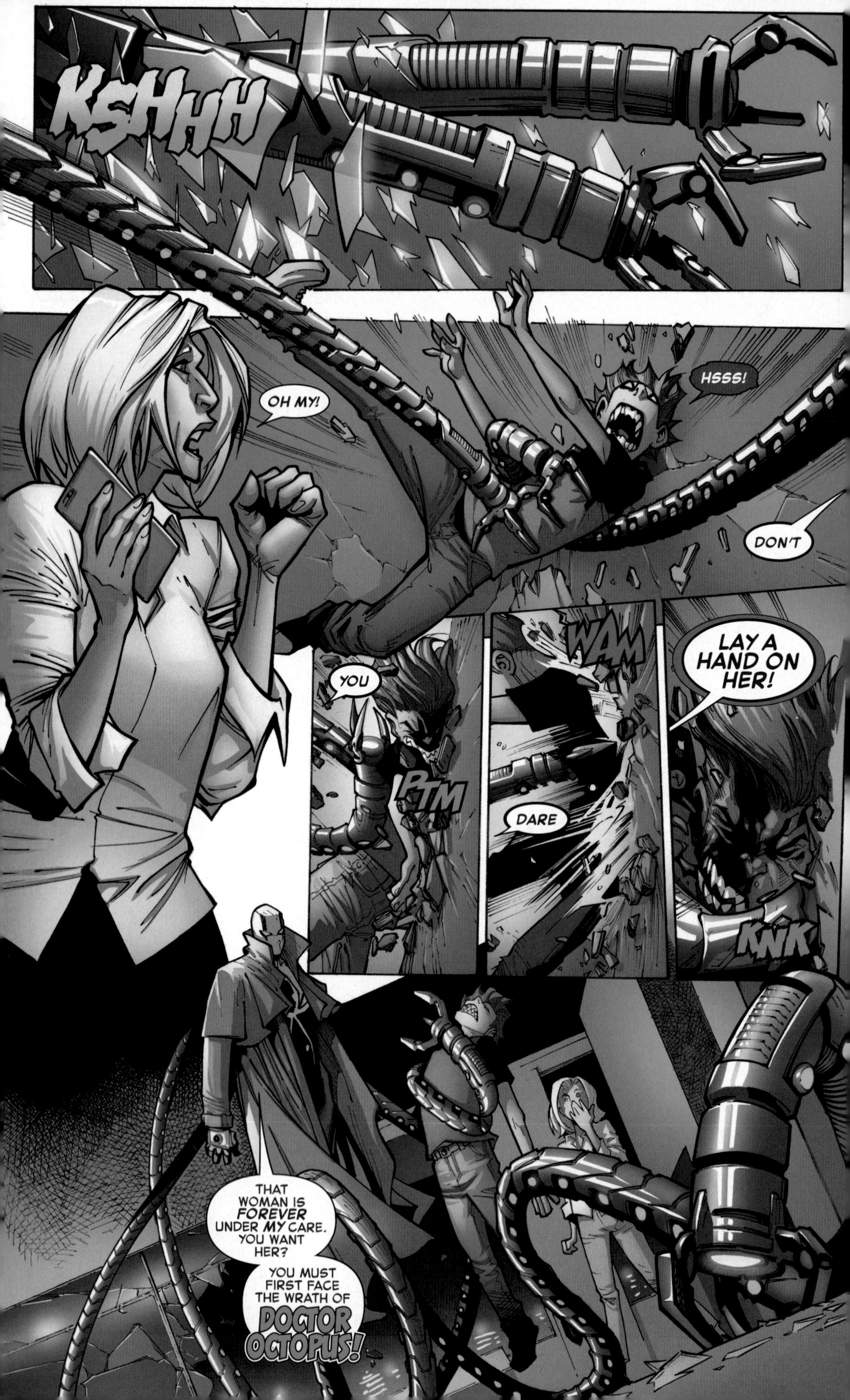
KSHHH
OH MY!
HSSS!
DON'T
YOU
PTM
WAM
DARE
LAY A HAND ON HER!
KNK
THAT WOMAN IS FOREVER UNDER MY CARE. YOU WANT HER?
YOU MUST FIRST FACE THE WRATH OF DOCTOR OCTOPUS!

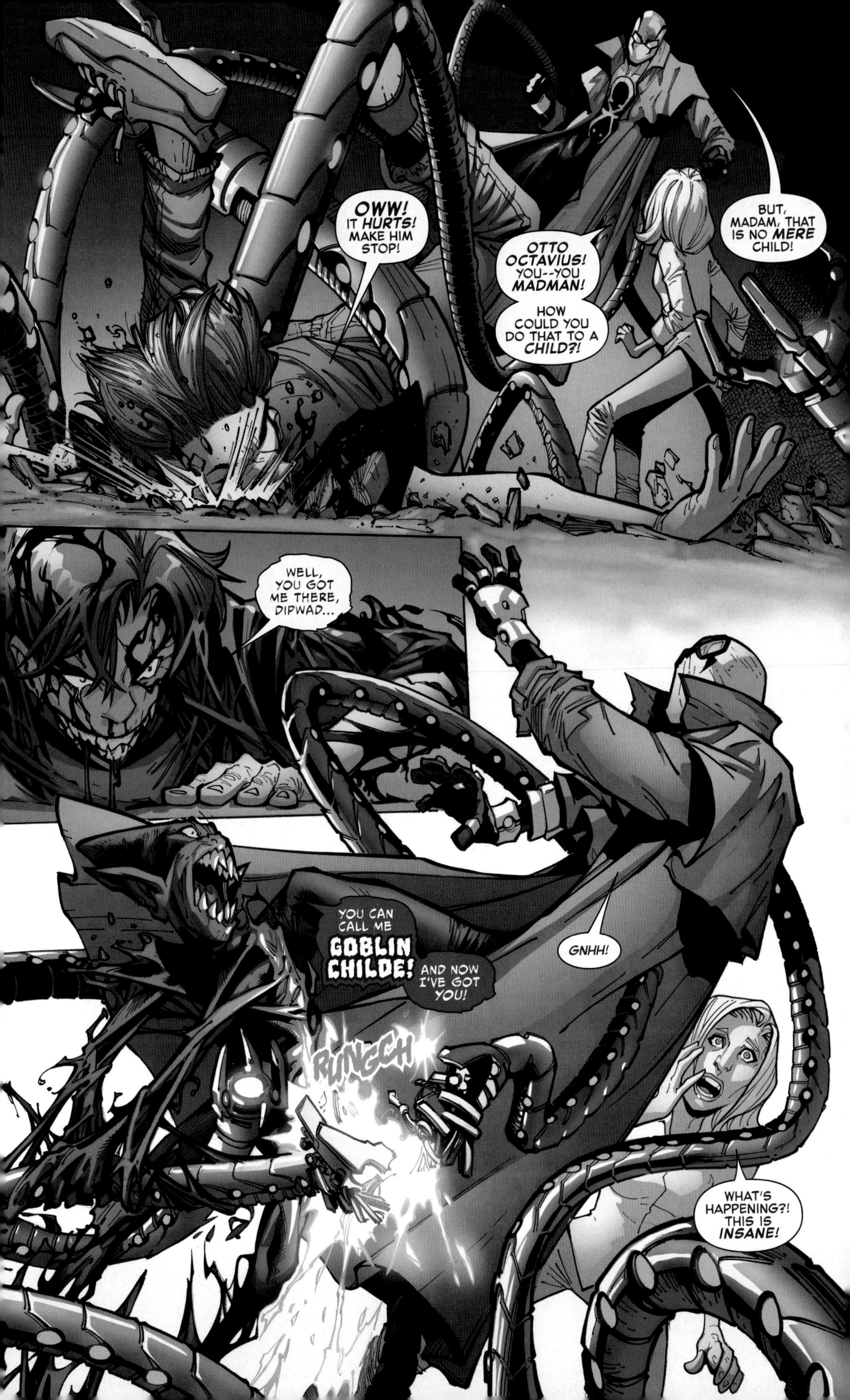
OWW! IT HURTS! MAKE HIM STOP!
OTTO OCTAVIUS! YOU--YOU MADMAN!
HOW COULD YOU DO THAT TO A CHILD?!
BUT, MADAM, THAT IS NO MERE CHILD!
WELL, YOU GOT ME THERE, DIPWAD...
YOU CAN CALL ME GOBLIN CHILDE!
AND NOW I'VE GOT YOU!
GNHH!
KRUNCH
WHAT'S HAPPENING?! THIS IS INSANE!

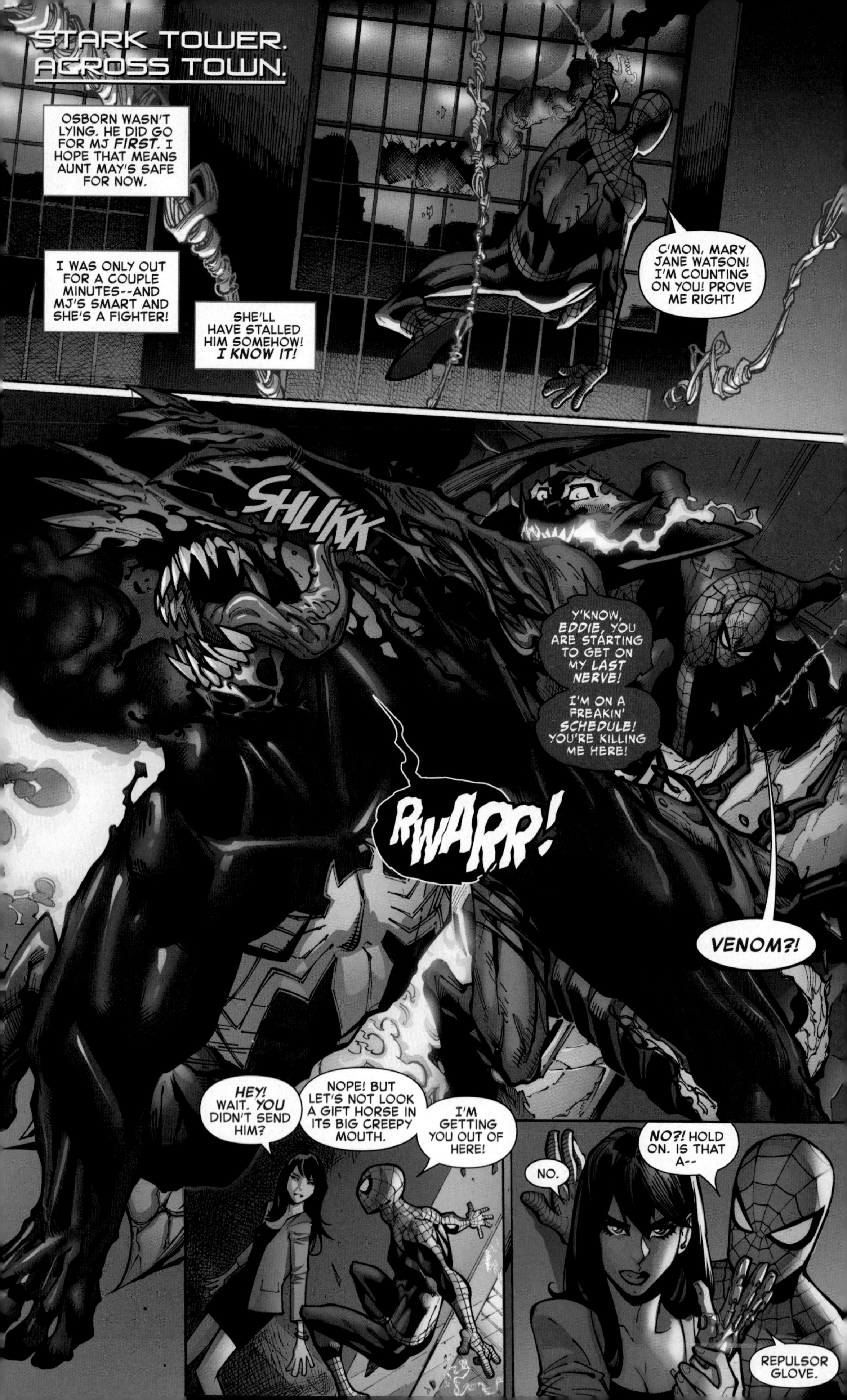

STARK TOWER. ACROSS TOWN.
OSBORN WASN'T LYING. HE DID GO FOR MJ FIRST. I HOPE THAT MEANS AUNT MAY'S SAFE FOR NOW.
I WAS ONLY OUT FOR A COUPLE MINUTES--AND MJ'S SMART AND SHE'S A FIGHTER!
SHE'LL HAVE STALLED HIM SOMEHOW! I KNOW IT!
C'MON, MARY JANE WATSON! I'M COUNTING ON YOU! PROVE ME RIGHT!
SHLIKK
Y'KNOW, EDDIE, YOU ARE STARTING TO GET ON MY LAST NERVE!
I'M ON A FREAKIN' SCHEDULE! YOU'RE KILLING ME HERE!
RWARR!
VENOM?!
HEY! WAIT. YOU DIDN'T SEND HIM?
NOPE! BUT LET'S NOT LOOK A GIFT HORSE IN ITS BIG CREEPY MOUTH.
I'M GETTING YOU OUT OF HERE!
NO?! HOLD ON. IS THAT A--
NO.
REPULSOR GLOVE.

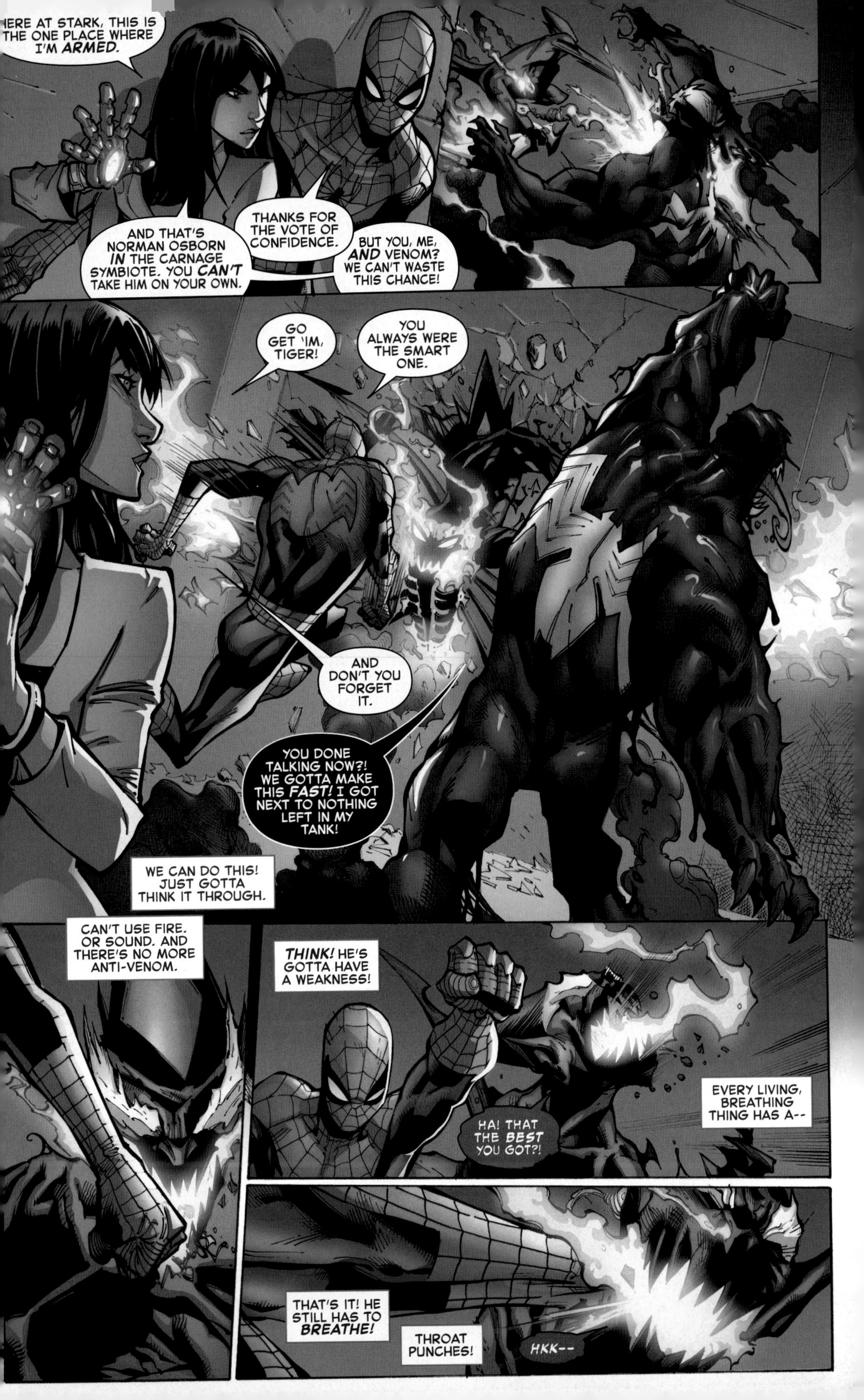

HERE AT STARK, THIS IS THE ONE PLACE WHERE I'M **ARMED.**
AND THAT'S NORMAN OSBORN ***IN*** THE CARNAGE SYMBIOTE. YOU ***CAN'T*** TAKE HIM ON YOUR OWN.
THANKS FOR THE VOTE OF CONFIDENCE.
BUT YOU, ME, ***AND*** VENOM? WE CAN'T WASTE THIS CHANCE!
GO GET 'IM, TIGER!
YOU ALWAYS WERE THE SMART ONE.
AND DON'T YOU FORGET IT.
YOU DONE TALKING NOW?! WE GOTTA MAKE THIS ***FAST!*** I GOT NEXT TO NOTHING LEFT IN MY TANK!
WE CAN DO THIS! JUST GOTTA THINK IT THROUGH.
CAN'T USE FIRE. OR SOUND. AND THERE'S NO MORE ANTI-VENOM.
THINK! HE'S GOTTA HAVE A WEAKNESS!
HA! THAT THE ***BEST*** YOU GOT?!
EVERY LIVING, BREATHING THING HAS A--
THAT'S IT! HE STILL HAS TO ***BREATHE!***
THROAT PUNCHES!
HKK--

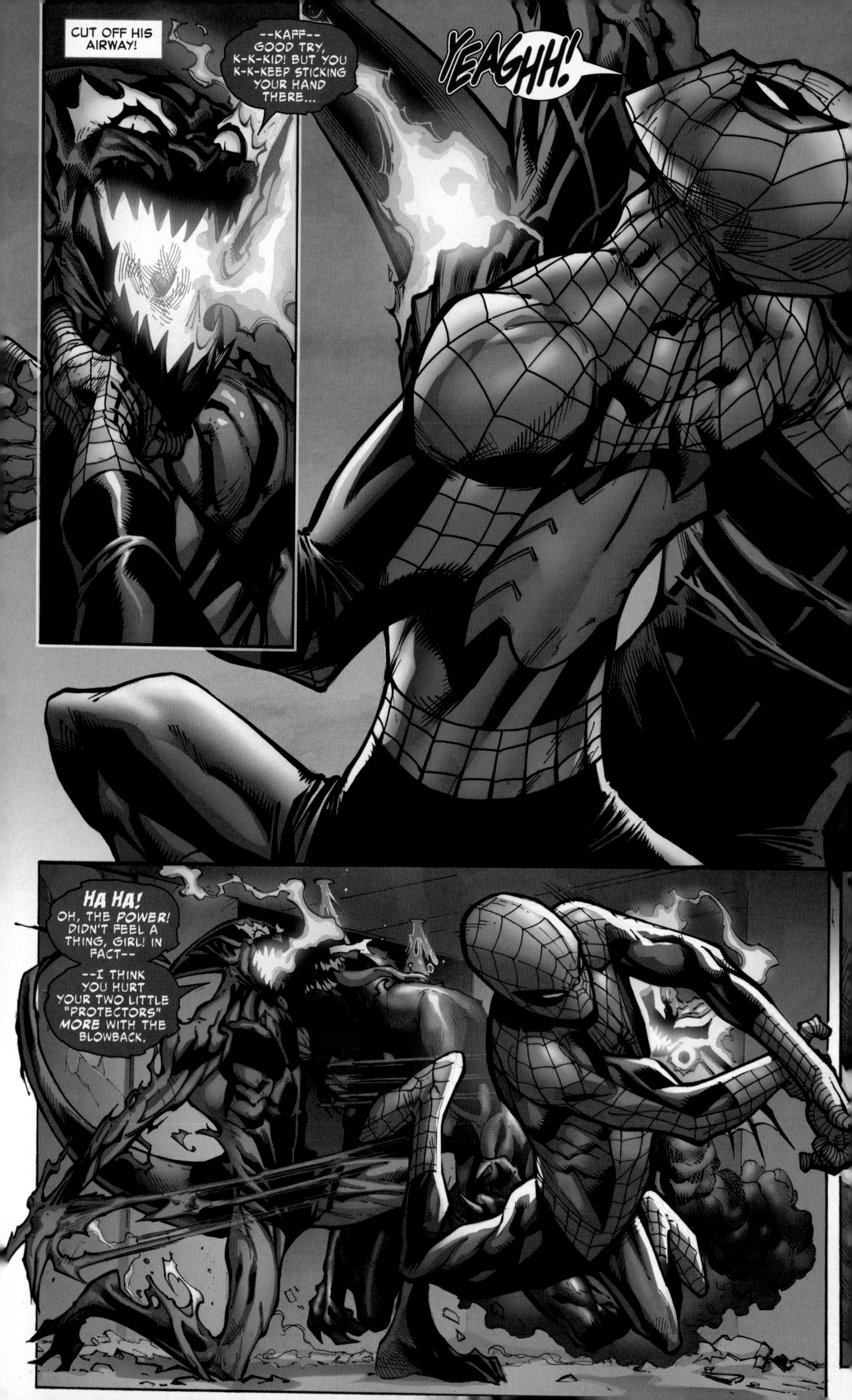
CUT OFF HIS AIRWAY!
--KAFF-- GOOD TRY, K-K-KID! BUT YOU K-K-KEEP STICKING YOUR HAND THERE...
YEAGHH!
HA HA! OH, THE POWER! DIDN'T FEEL A THING, GIRL! IN FACT--
--I THINK YOU HURT YOUR TWO LITTLE "PROTECTORS" MORE WITH THE BLOWBACK.

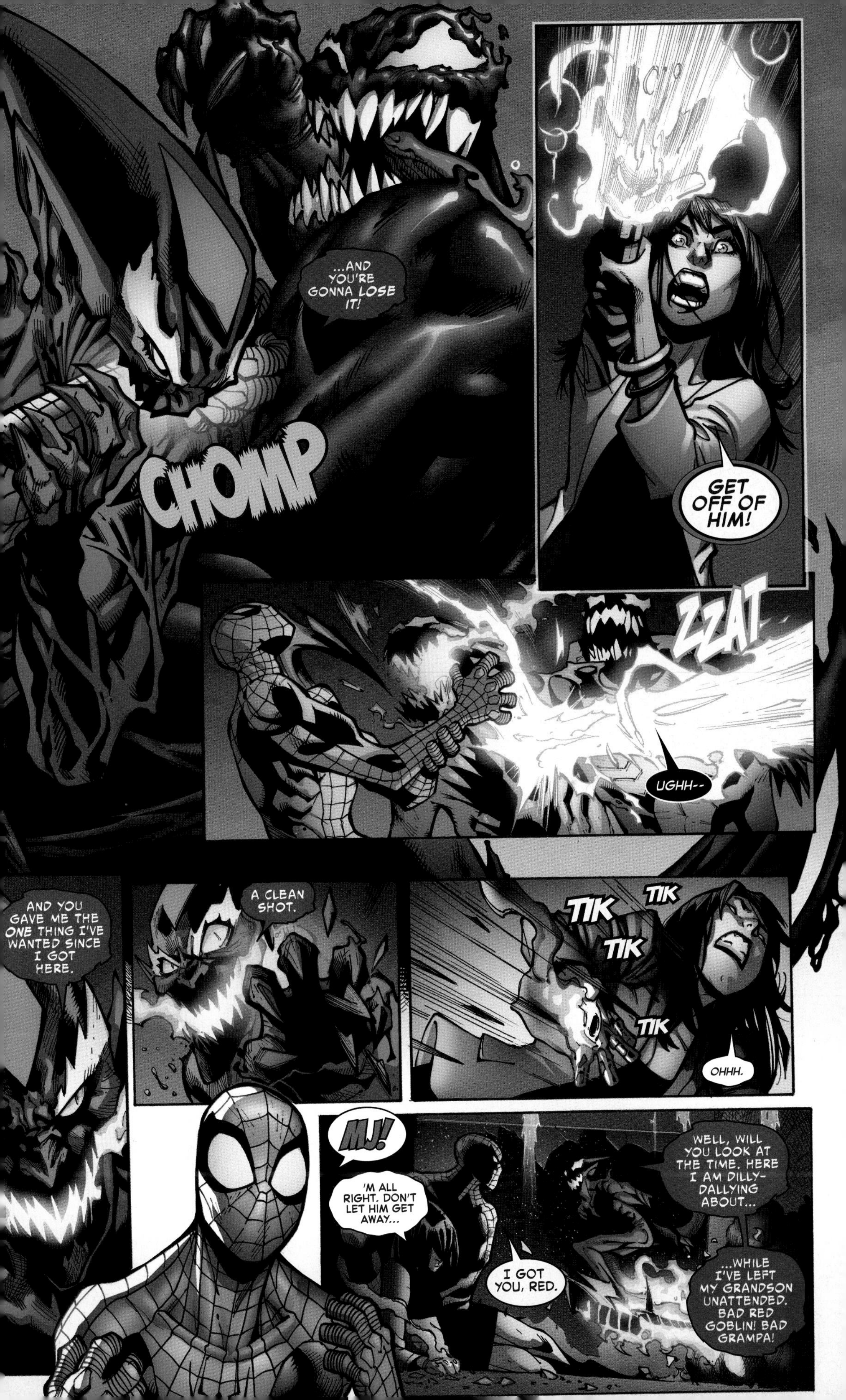
...AND YOU'RE GONNA LOSE IT!
CHOMP
GET OFF OF HIM!
ZZAT
UGHH--
AND YOU GAVE ME THE ONE THING I'VE WANTED SINCE I GOT HERE.
A CLEAN SHOT.
TIK
TIK
TIK
TIK
OHHH.
MJ!
'M ALL RIGHT. DON'T LET HIM GET AWAY...
I GOT YOU, RED.
WELL, WILL YOU LOOK AT THE TIME. HERE I AM DILLY-DALLYING ABOUT...
...WHILE I'VE LEFT MY GRANDSON UNATTENDED. BAD RED GOBLIN! BAD GRAMPA!

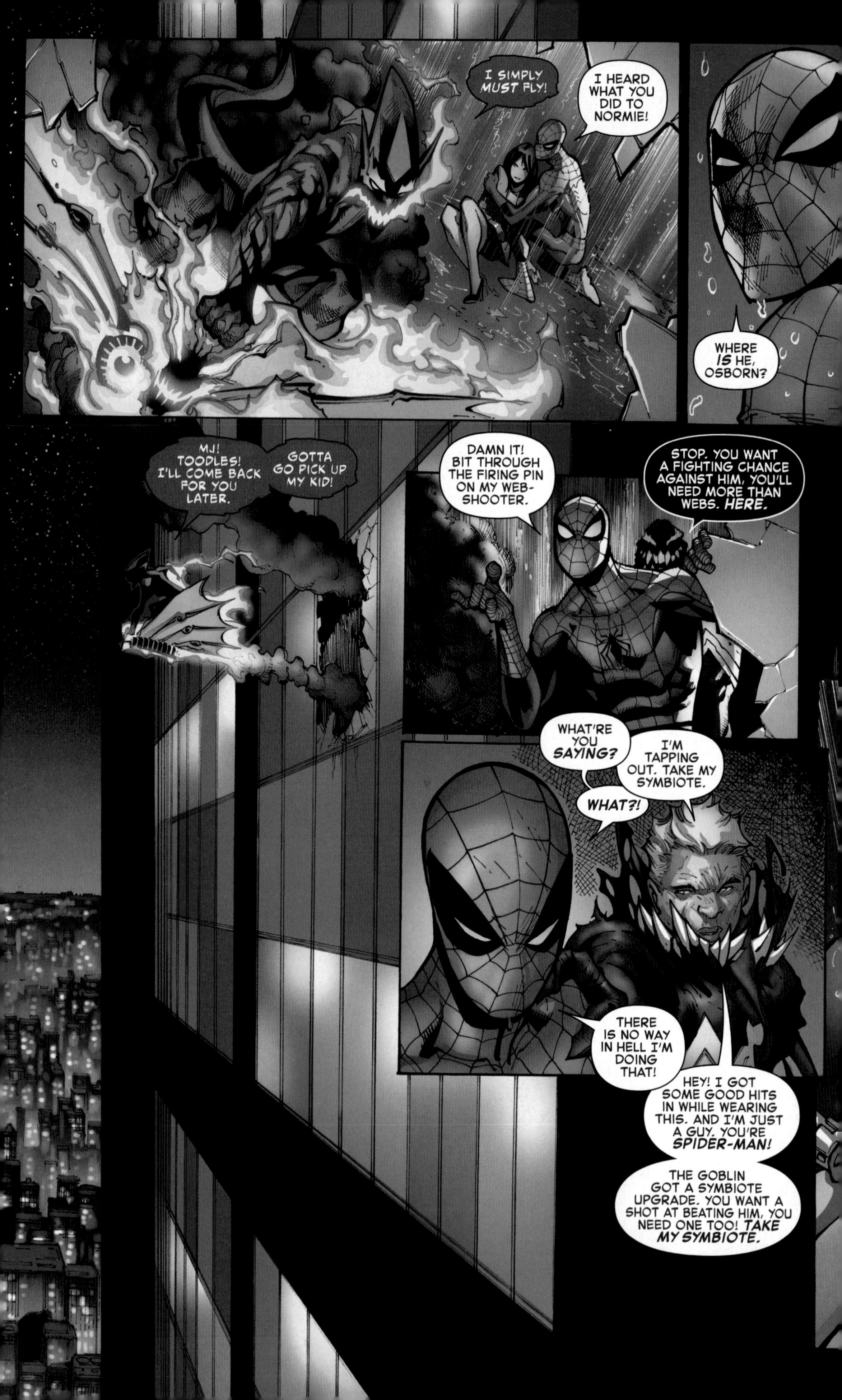
I SIMPLY MUST FLY!
I HEARD WHAT YOU DID TO NORMIE!
WHERE IS HE, OSBORN?
MJ! TOODLES! I'LL COME BACK FOR YOU LATER.
GOTTA GO PICK UP MY KID!
DAMN IT! BIT THROUGH THE FIRING PIN ON MY WEB-SHOOTER.
STOP. YOU WANT A FIGHTING CHANCE AGAINST HIM, YOU'LL NEED MORE THAN WEBS. HERE.
WHAT'RE YOU SAYING?
I'M TAPPING OUT. TAKE MY SYMBIOTE.
WHAT?!
THERE IS NO WAY IN HELL I'M DOING THAT!
HEY! I GOT SOME GOOD HITS IN WHILE WEARING THIS. AND I'M JUST A GUY. YOU'RE SPIDER-MAN!
THE GOBLIN GOT A SYMBIOTE UPGRADE. YOU WANT A SHOT AT BEATING HIM, YOU NEED ONE TOO! TAKE MY SYMBIOTE.

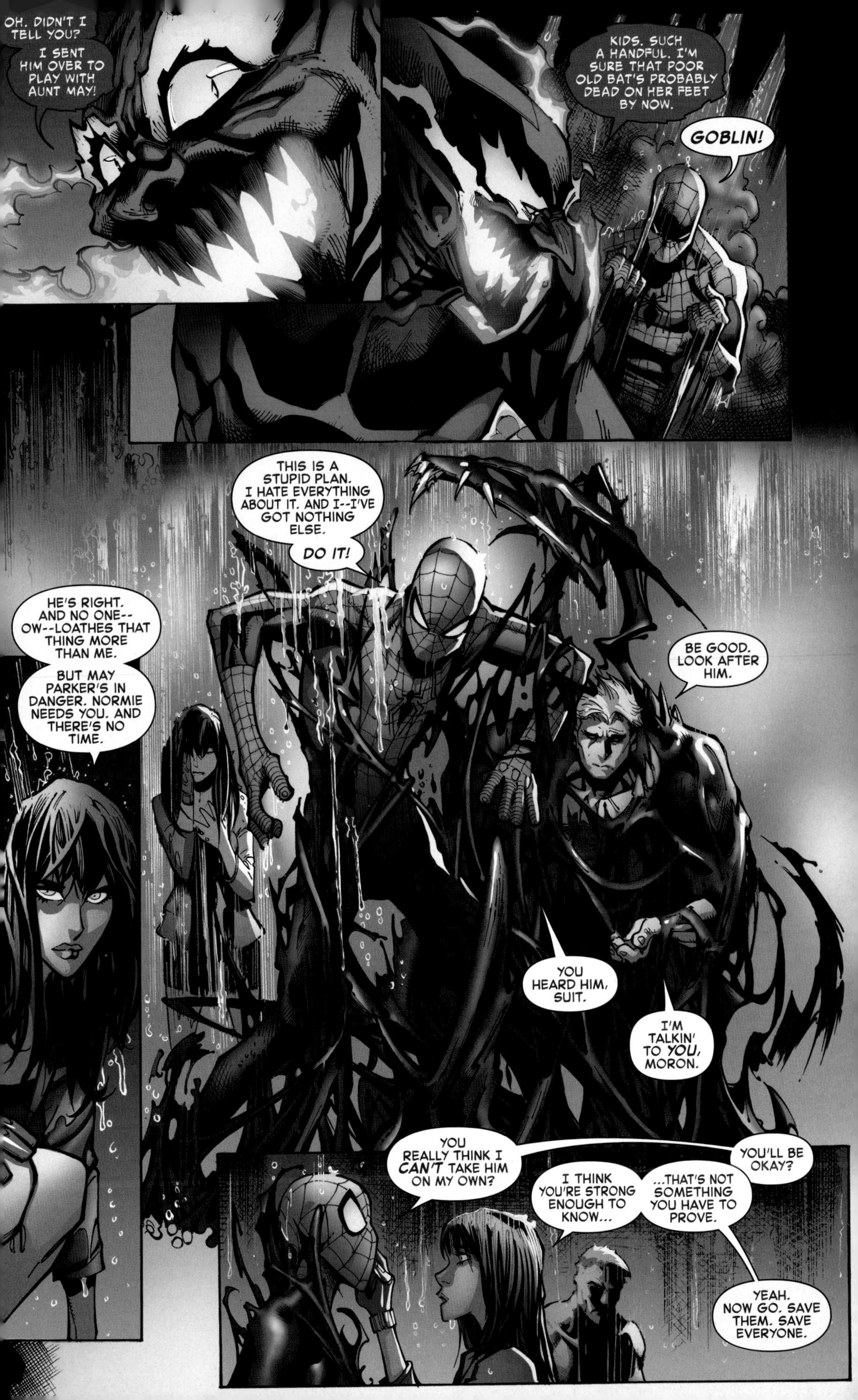

OH. DIDN'T I TELL YOU? I SENT HIM OVER TO PLAY WITH AUNT MAY!
KIDS. SUCH A HANDFUL. I'M SURE THAT POOR OLD BAT'S PROBABLY DEAD ON HER FEET BY NOW.
GOBLIN!
THIS IS A STUPID PLAN. I HATE EVERYTHING ABOUT IT. AND I--I'VE GOT NOTHING ELSE.
DO IT!
HE'S RIGHT. AND NO ONE--OW--LOATHES THAT THING MORE THAN ME.
BUT MAY PARKER'S IN DANGER. NORMIE NEEDS YOU. AND THERE'S NO TIME.
BE GOOD. LOOK AFTER HIM.
YOU HEARD HIM, SUIT.
I'M TALKIN' TO YOU, MORON.
YOU REALLY THINK I CAN'T TAKE HIM ON MY OWN?
I THINK YOU'RE STRONG ENOUGH TO KNOW...
...THAT'S NOT SOMETHING YOU HAVE TO PROVE.
YOU'LL BE OKAY?
YEAH. NOW GO. SAVE THEM. SAVE EVERYONE.

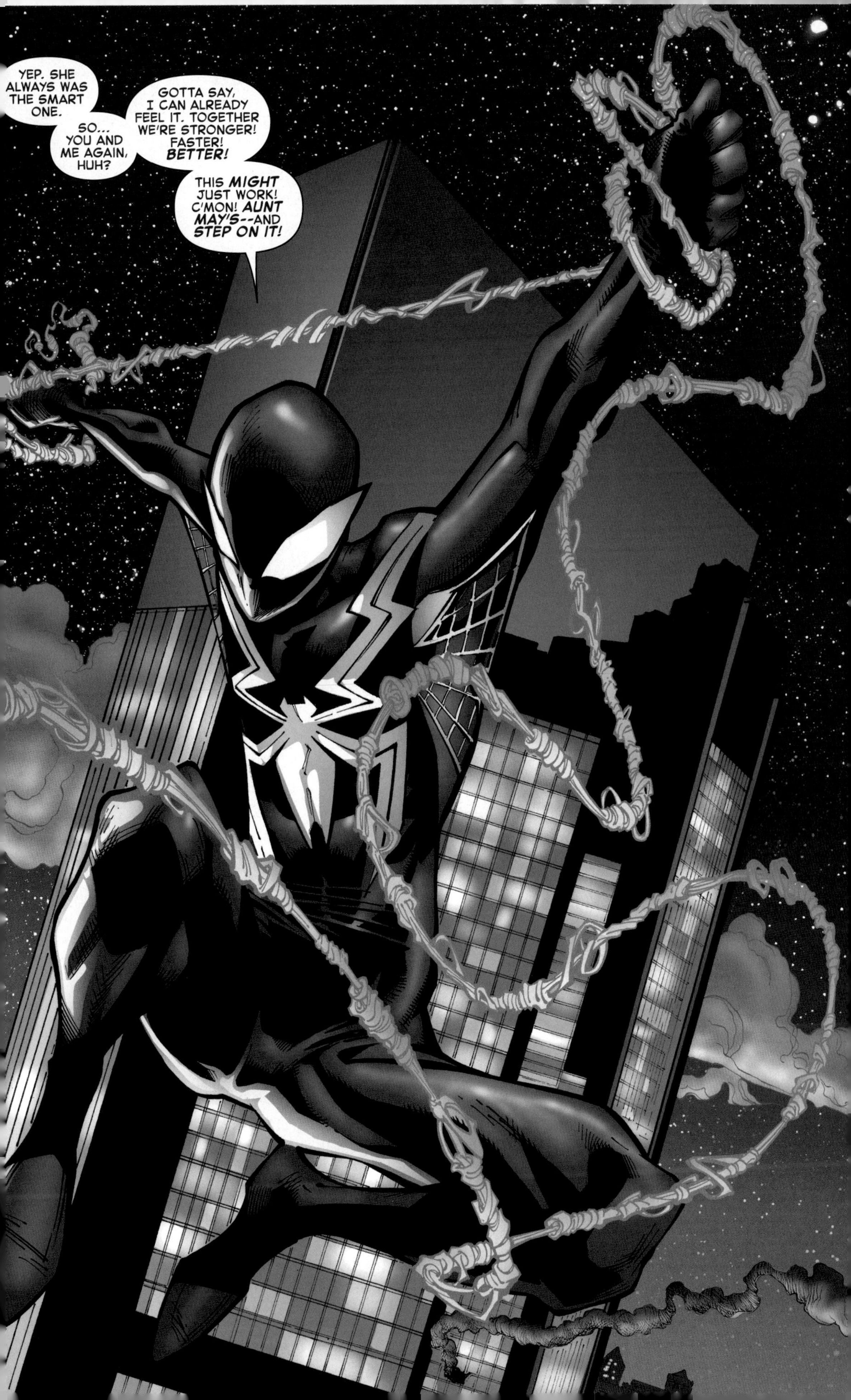
YEP. SHE ALWAYS WAS THE SMART ONE.
SO... YOU AND ME AGAIN, HUH?
GOTTA SAY, I CAN ALREADY FEEL IT. TOGETHER WE'RE STRONGER! FASTER! **BETTER!**
THIS **MIGHT** JUST WORK! C'MON! **AUNT MAY'S**--AND **STEP ON IT!**

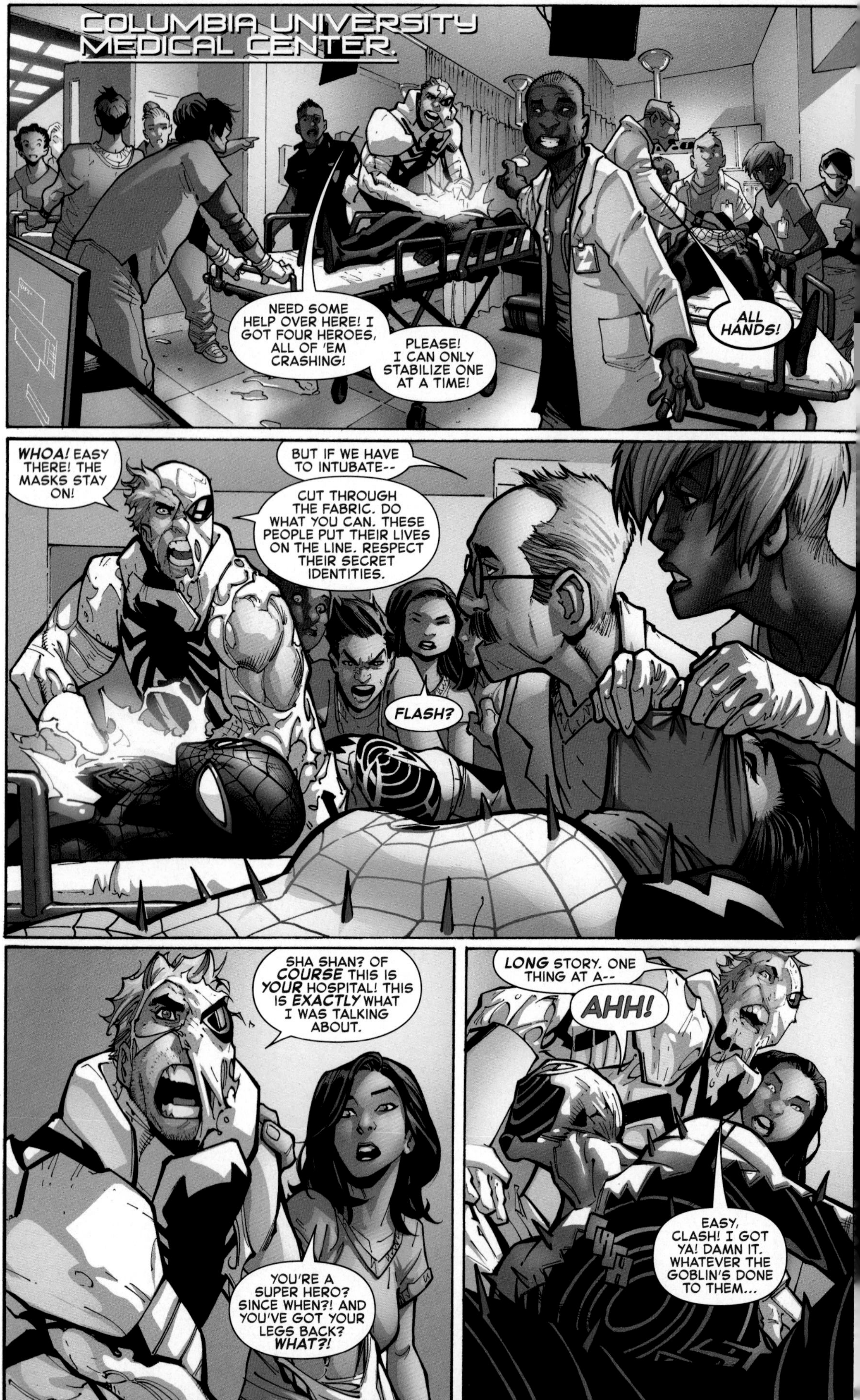
COLUMBIA UNIVERSITY MEDICAL CENTER.
NEED SOME HELP OVER HERE! I GOT FOUR HEROES, ALL OF 'EM CRASHING!
PLEASE! I CAN ONLY STABILIZE ONE AT A TIME!
ALL HANDS!
WHOA! EASY THERE! THE MASKS STAY ON!
BUT IF WE HAVE TO INTUBATE--
CUT THROUGH THE FABRIC. DO WHAT YOU CAN. THESE PEOPLE PUT THEIR LIVES ON THE LINE. RESPECT THEIR SECRET IDENTITIES.
FLASH?
SHA SHAN? OF COURSE THIS IS YOUR HOSPITAL! THIS IS EXACTLY WHAT I WAS TALKING ABOUT.
YOU'RE A SUPER HERO? SINCE WHEN?! AND YOU'VE GOT YOUR LEGS BACK? WHAT?!
LONG STORY. ONE THING AT A--
AHH!
EASY, CLASH! I GOT YA! DAMN IT. WHATEVER THE GOBLIN'S DONE TO THEM...

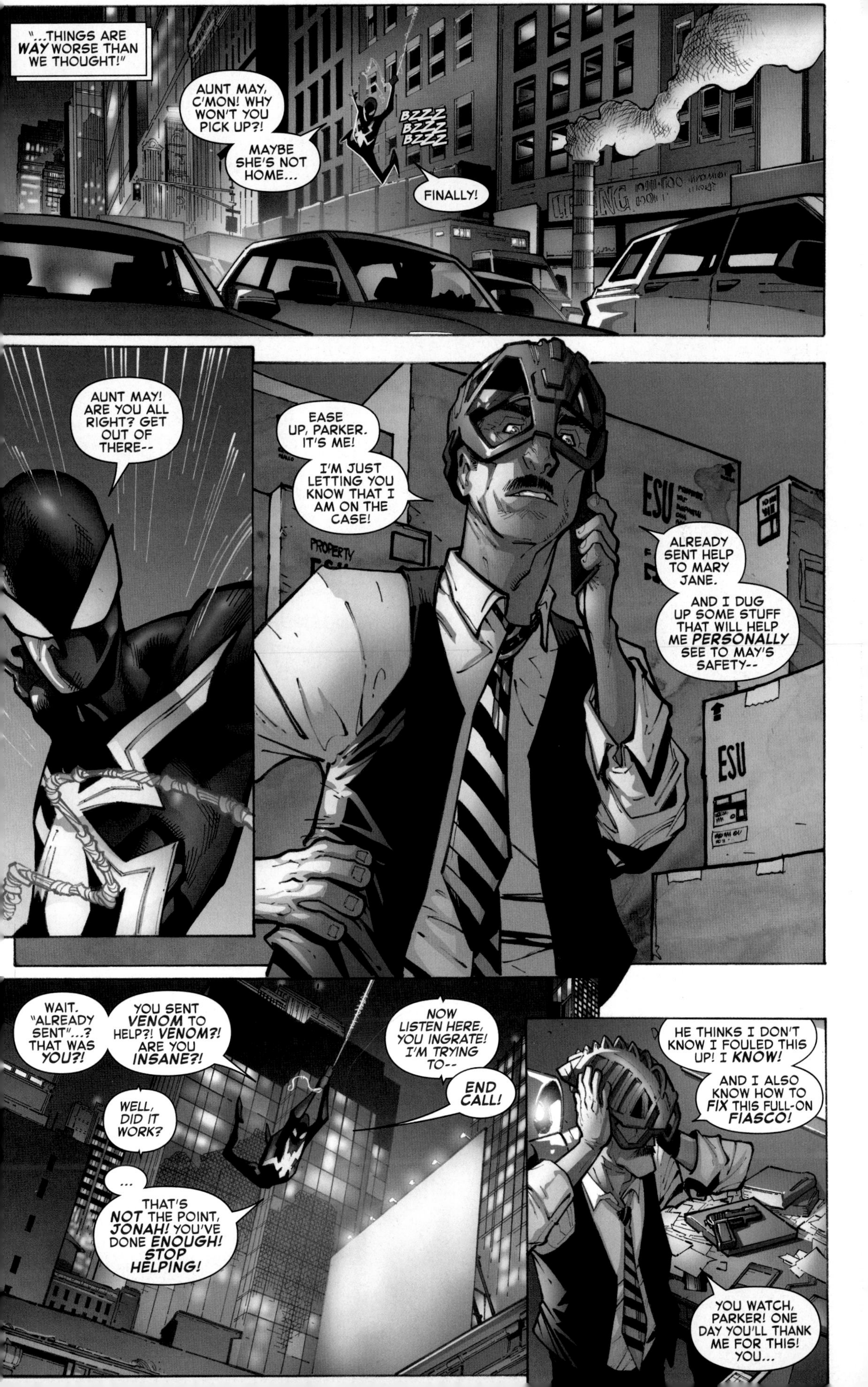
"...THINGS ARE WAY WORSE THAN WE THOUGHT!"
AUNT MAY, C'MON! WHY WON'T YOU PICK UP?!
MAYBE SHE'S NOT HOME...
BZZZ BZZZ BZZZ
FINALLY!
AUNT MAY! ARE YOU ALL RIGHT? GET OUT OF THERE--
EASE UP, PARKER. IT'S ME!
I'M JUST LETTING YOU KNOW THAT I AM ON THE CASE!
ALREADY SENT HELP TO MARY JANE.
AND I DUG UP SOME STUFF THAT WILL HELP ME PERSONALLY SEE TO MAY'S SAFETY--
ESU
WAIT. "ALREADY SENT"...? THAT WAS YOU?!
YOU SENT VENOM TO HELP?! VENOM?! ARE YOU INSANE?!
WELL, DID IT WORK?
...
THAT'S NOT THE POINT, JONAH! YOU'VE DONE ENOUGH! STOP HELPING!
NOW LISTEN HERE, YOU INGRATE! I'M TRYING TO--
END CALL!
HE THINKS I DON'T KNOW I FOULED THIS UP! I KNOW!
AND I ALSO KNOW HOW TO FIX THIS FULL-ON FIASCO!
YOU WATCH, PARKER! ONE DAY YOU'LL THANK ME FOR THIS! YOU...

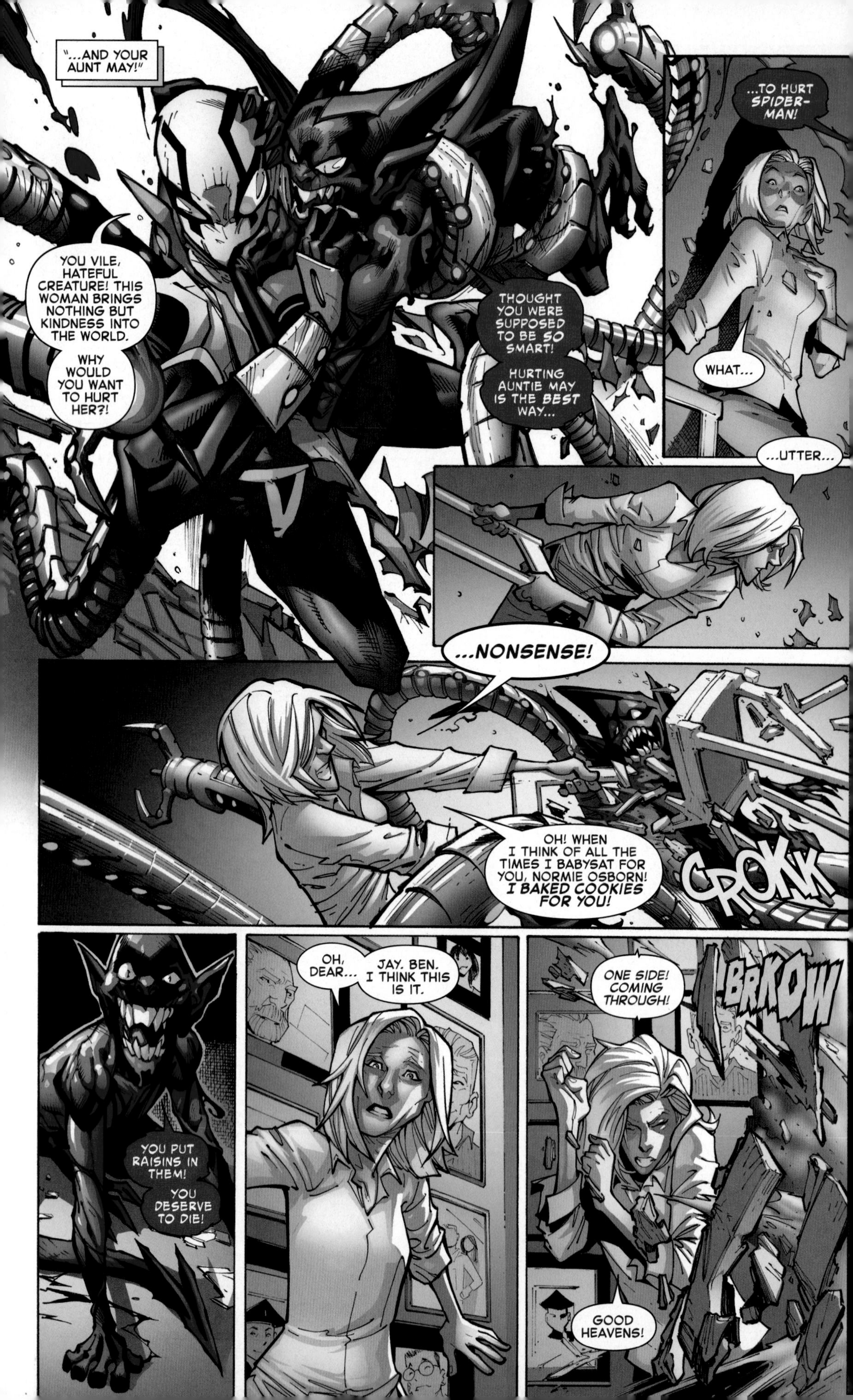
"...AND YOUR AUNT MAY!"
YOU VILE, HATEFUL CREATURE! THIS WOMAN BRINGS NOTHING BUT KINDNESS INTO THE WORLD.
WHY WOULD YOU WANT TO HURT HER?!
THOUGHT YOU WERE SUPPOSED TO BE SO SMART!
HURTING AUNTIE MAY IS THE BEST WAY...
...TO HURT SPIDER-MAN!
WHAT...
...UTTER...
...NONSENSE!
OH! WHEN I THINK OF ALL THE TIMES I BABYSAT FOR YOU, NORMIE OSBORN! I BAKED COOKIES FOR YOU!
CROKK
YOU PUT RAISINS IN THEM!
YOU DESERVE TO DIE!
OH, DEAR...
JAY. BEN. I THINK THIS IS IT.
ONE SIDE! COMING THROUGH!
BRKOW
GOOD HEAVENS!

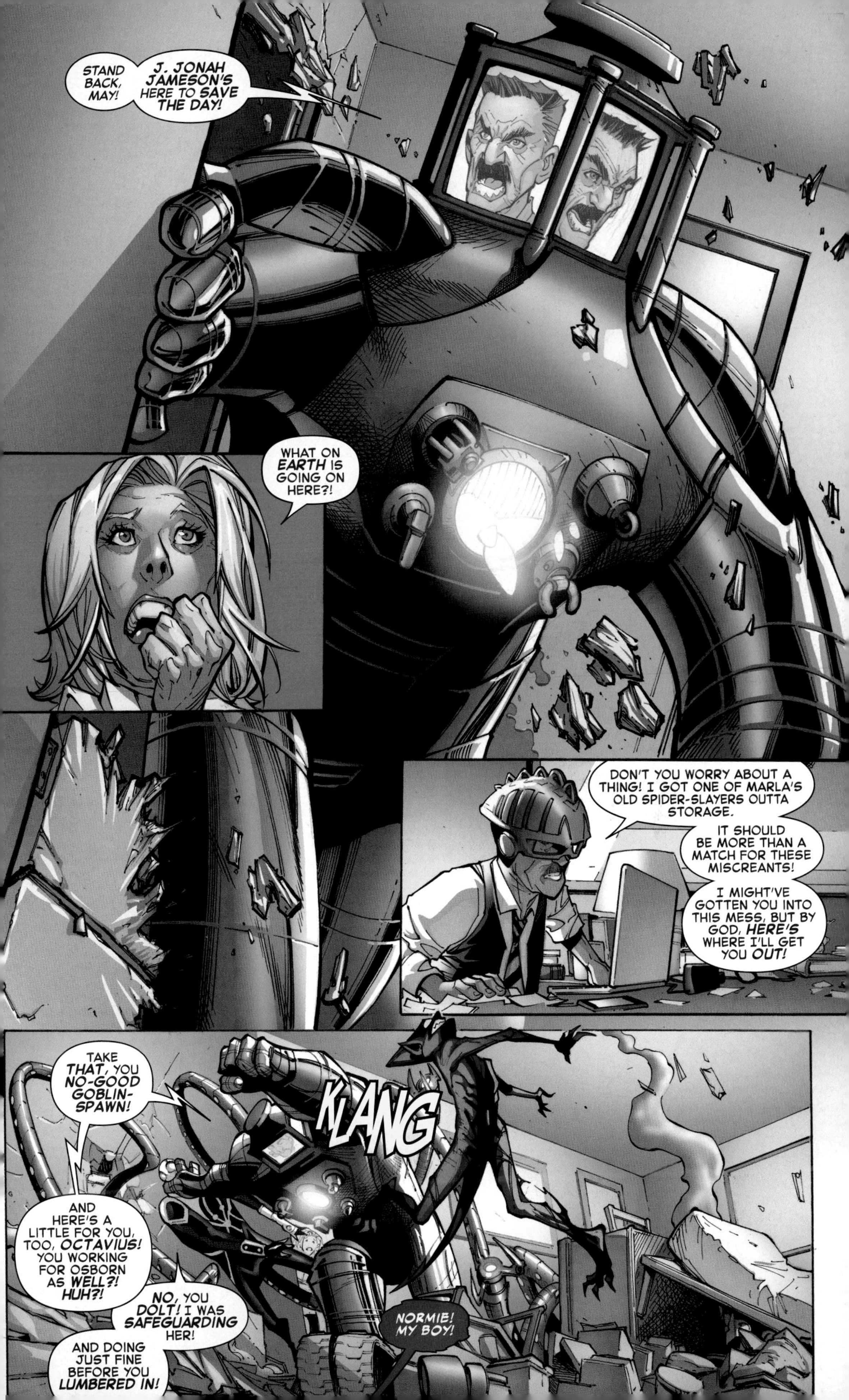
STAND BACK, MAY!
J. JONAH JAMESON'S HERE TO SAVE THE DAY!
WHAT ON EARTH IS GOING ON HERE?!
DON'T YOU WORRY ABOUT A THING! I GOT ONE OF MARLA'S OLD SPIDER-SLAYERS OUTTA STORAGE.
IT SHOULD BE MORE THAN A MATCH FOR THESE MISCREANTS!
I MIGHT'VE GOTTEN YOU INTO THIS MESS, BUT BY GOD, HERE'S WHERE I'LL GET YOU OUT!
TAKE THAT, YOU NO-GOOD GOBLIN-SPAWN!
KLANG
AND HERE'S A LITTLE FOR YOU, TOO, OCTAVIUS! YOU WORKING FOR OSBORN AS WELL?! HUH?!
NO, YOU DOLT! I WAS SAFEGUARDING HER!
AND DOING JUST FINE BEFORE YOU LUMBERED IN!
NORMIE! MY BOY!

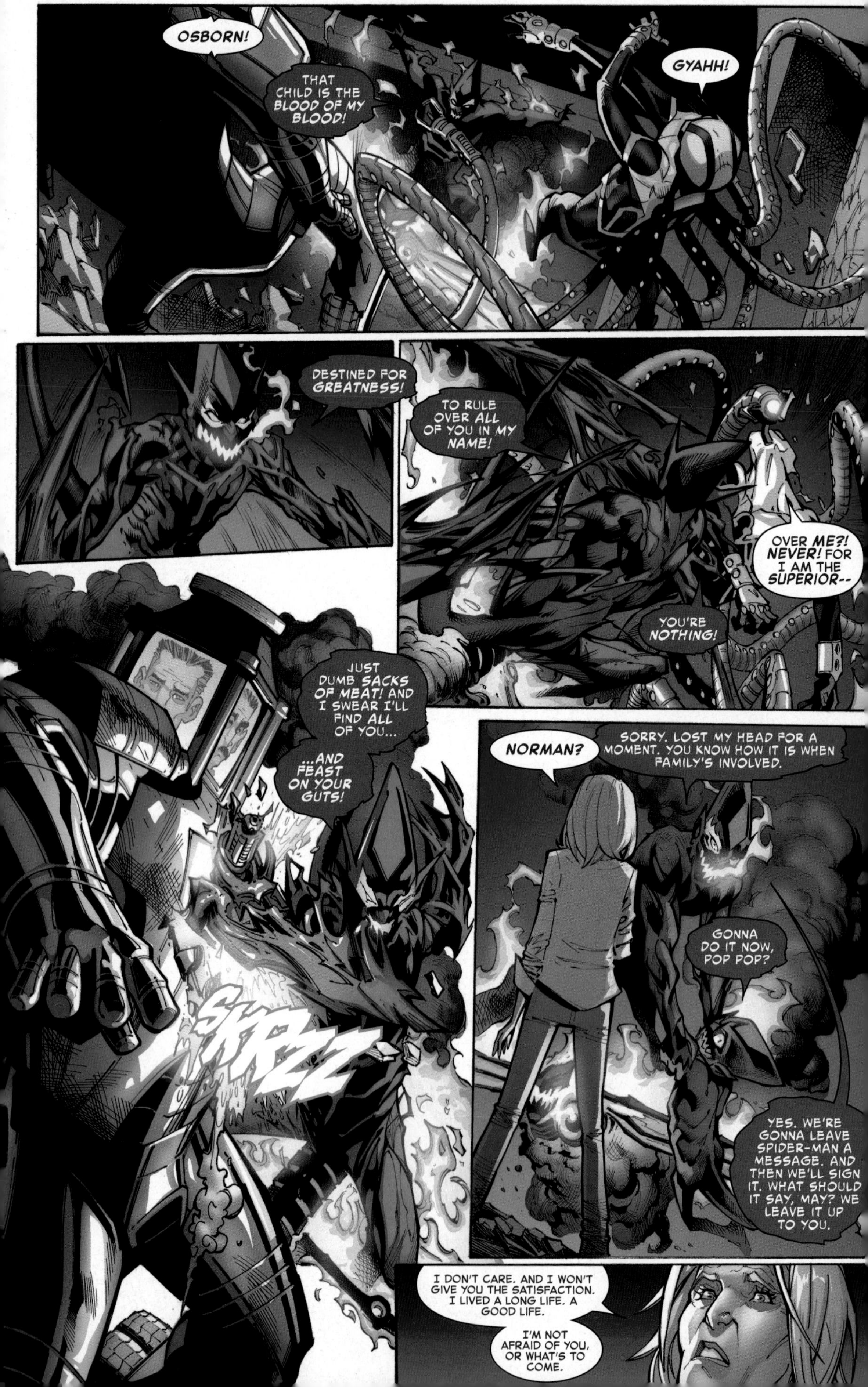
OSBORN!
THAT CHILD IS THE BLOOD OF MY BLOOD!
GYAHH!
DESTINED FOR GREATNESS!
TO RULE OVER ALL OF YOU IN MY NAME!
OVER ME?! NEVER! FOR I AM THE SUPERIOR--
YOU'RE NOTHING!
JUST DUMB SACKS OF MEAT! AND I SWEAR I'LL FIND ALL OF YOU...
...AND FEAST ON YOUR GUTS!
SKRZZ
NORMAN?
SORRY. LOST MY HEAD FOR A MOMENT. YOU KNOW HOW IT IS WHEN FAMILY'S INVOLVED.
GONNA DO IT NOW, POP POP?
YES. WE'RE GONNA LEAVE SPIDER-MAN A MESSAGE. AND THEN WE'LL SIGN IT. WHAT SHOULD IT SAY, MAY? WE LEAVE IT UP TO YOU.
I DON'T CARE. AND I WON'T GIVE YOU THE SATISFACTION. I LIVED A LONG LIFE. A GOOD LIFE.
I'M NOT AFRAID OF YOU, OR WHAT'S TO COME.

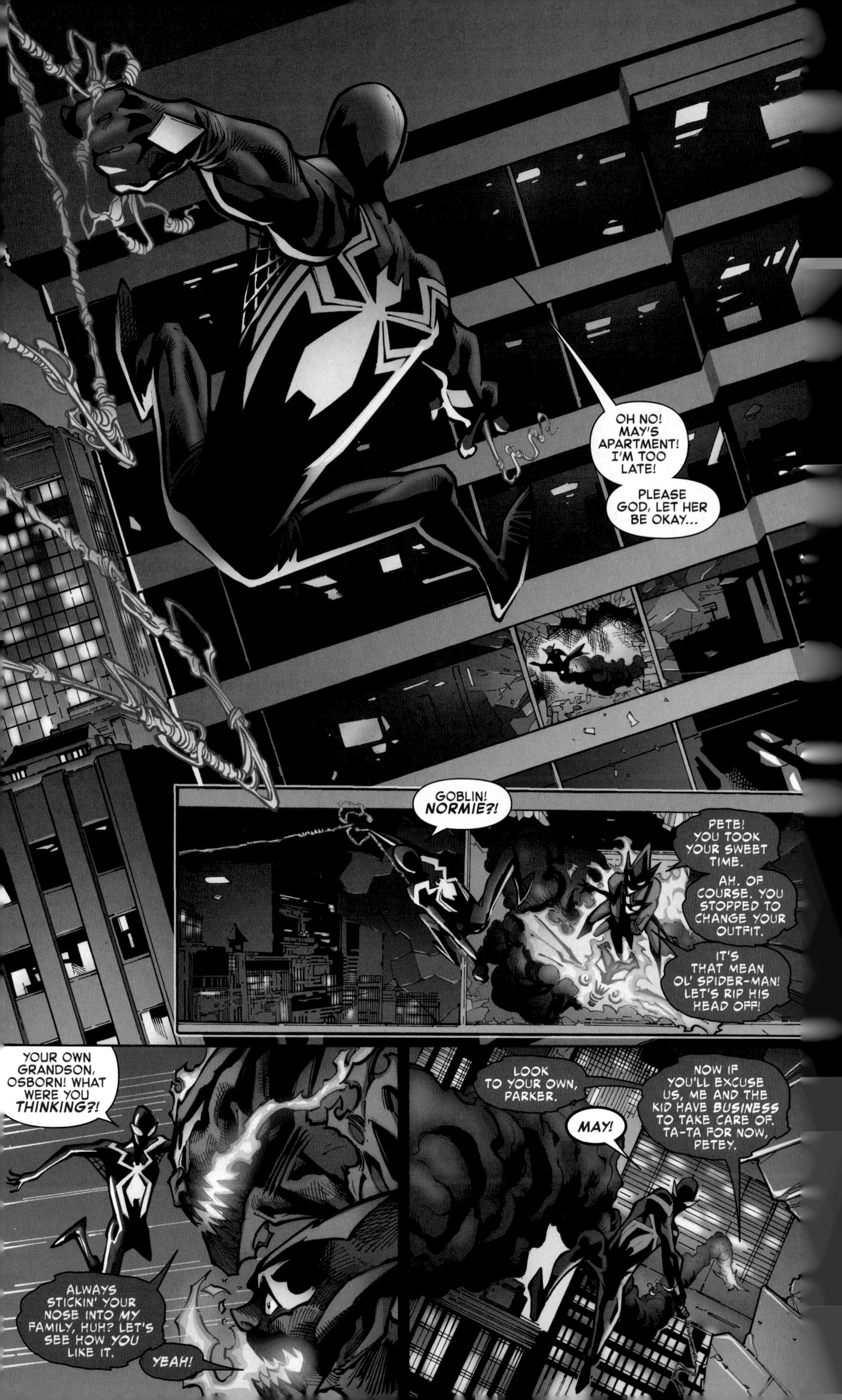

OH NO! MAY'S APARTMENT! I'M TOO LATE!
PLEASE GOD, LET HER BE OKAY...
GOBLIN! NORMIE?!
PETE! YOU TOOK YOUR SWEET TIME.
AH. OF COURSE. YOU STOPPED TO CHANGE YOUR OUTFIT.
IT'S THAT MEAN OL' SPIDER-MAN! LET'S RIP HIS HEAD OFF!
YOUR OWN GRANDSON, OSBORN! WHAT WERE YOU THINKING?!
ALWAYS STICKIN' YOUR NOSE INTO MY FAMILY, HUH? LET'S SEE HOW YOU LIKE IT.
YEAH!
LOOK TO YOUR OWN, PARKER.
NOW IF YOU'LL EXCUSE US, ME AND THE KID HAVE BUSINESS TO TAKE CARE OF. TA-TA FOR NOW, PETEY.
MAY!

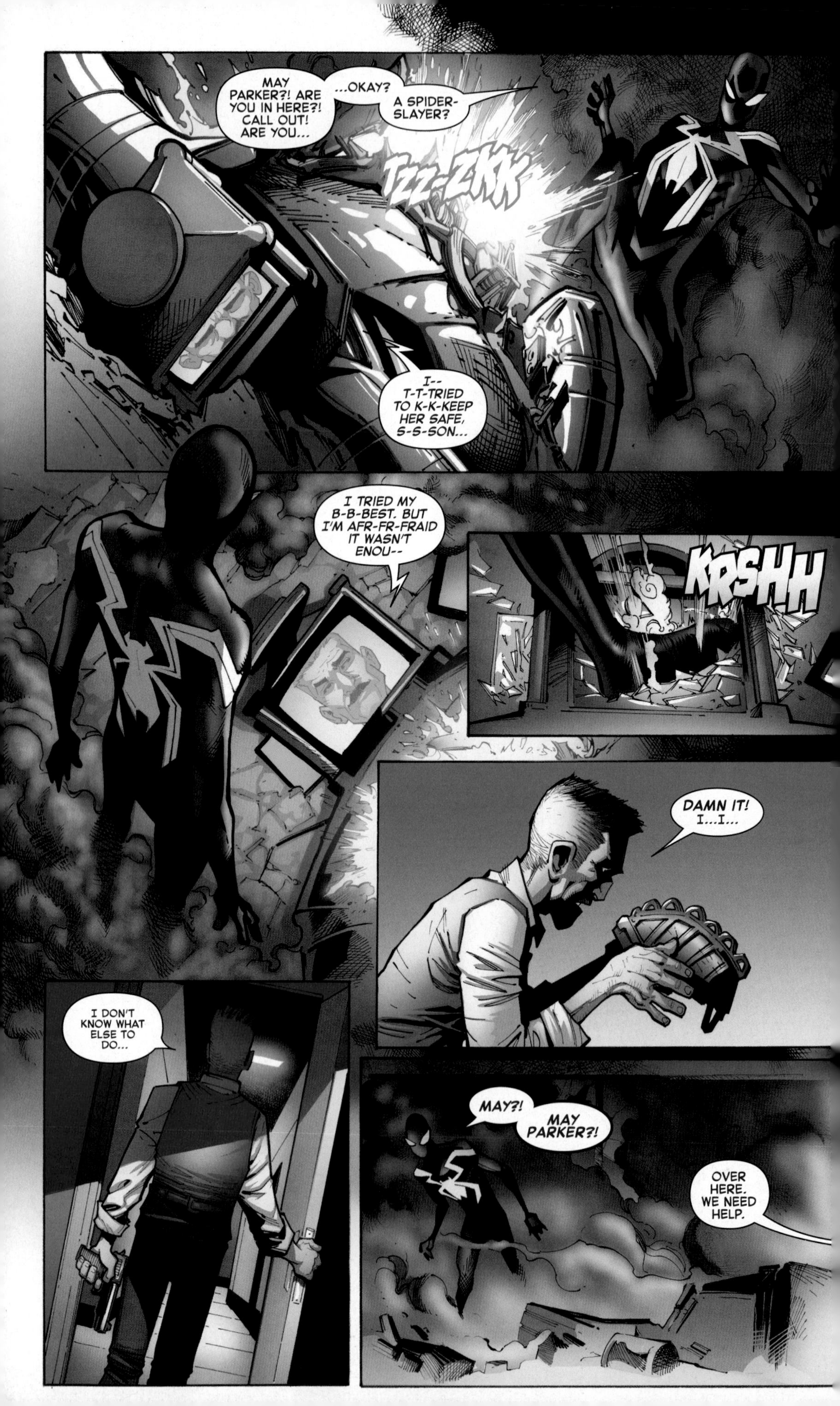
MAY PARKER?! ARE YOU IN HERE?! CALL OUT! ARE YOU...
...OKAY?
A SPIDER-SLAYER?
TZZ-ZKK
I-- T-T-TRIED TO K-K-KEEP HER SAFE, S-S-SON...
I TRIED MY B-B-BEST. BUT I'M AFR-FR-FRAID IT WASN'T ENOU--
KRSHH
DAMN IT! I...I...
I DON'T KNOW WHAT ELSE TO DO...
MAY?!
MAY PARKER?!
OVER HERE. WE NEED HELP.

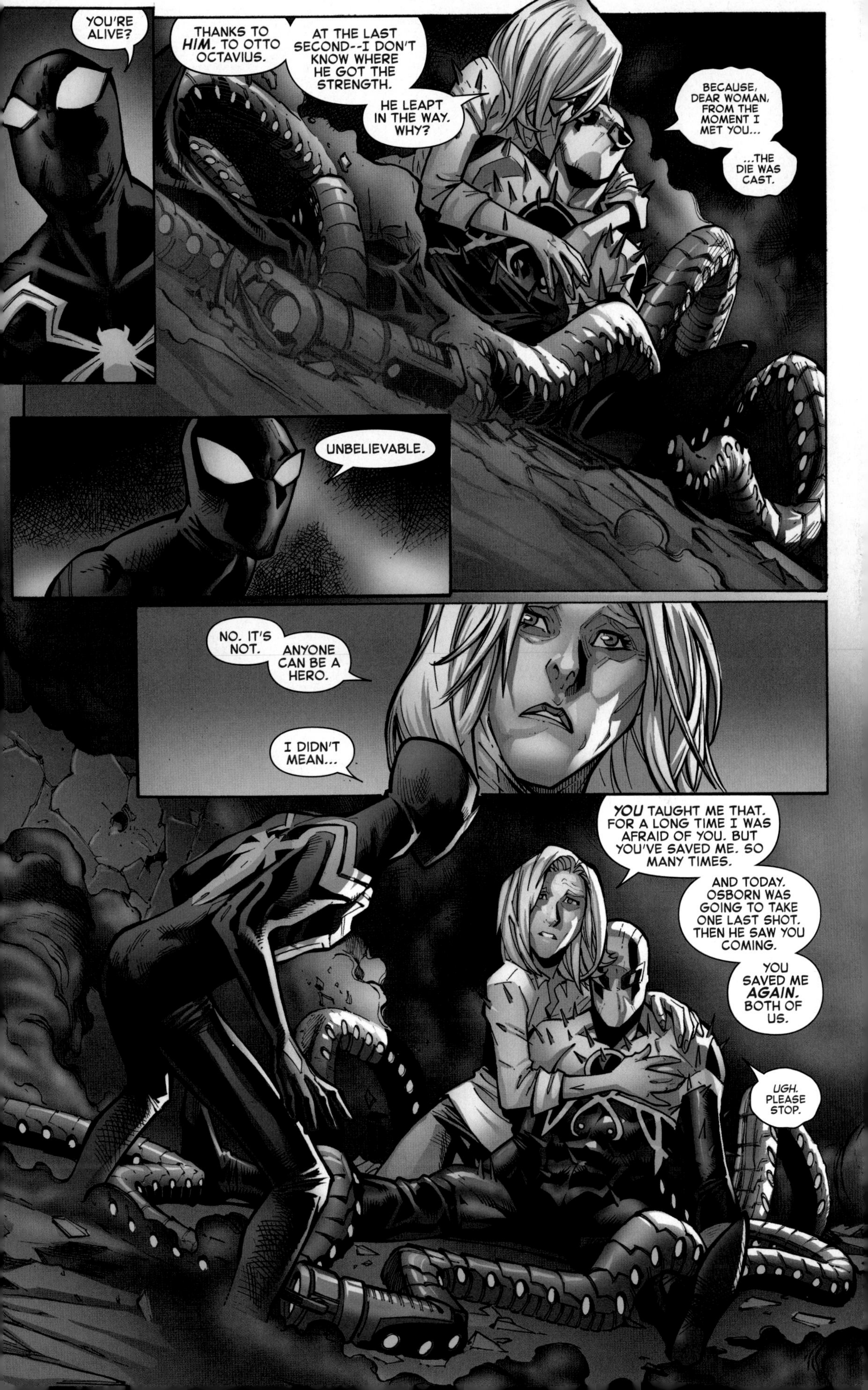

YOU'RE ALIVE?
THANKS TO *HIM.* TO OTTO OCTAVIUS.
AT THE LAST SECOND--I DON'T KNOW WHERE HE GOT THE STRENGTH.
HE LEAPT IN THE WAY. WHY?
BECAUSE, DEAR WOMAN, FROM THE MOMENT I MET YOU...
...THE DIE WAS CAST.
UNBELIEVABLE.
NO. IT'S NOT.
ANYONE CAN BE A HERO.
I DIDN'T MEAN...
YOU TAUGHT ME THAT. FOR A LONG TIME I WAS AFRAID OF YOU. BUT YOU'VE SAVED ME. SO MANY TIMES.
AND TODAY. OSBORN WAS GOING TO TAKE ONE LAST SHOT. THEN HE SAW YOU COMING.
YOU SAVED ME *AGAIN.* BOTH OF US.
UGH. PLEASE STOP.

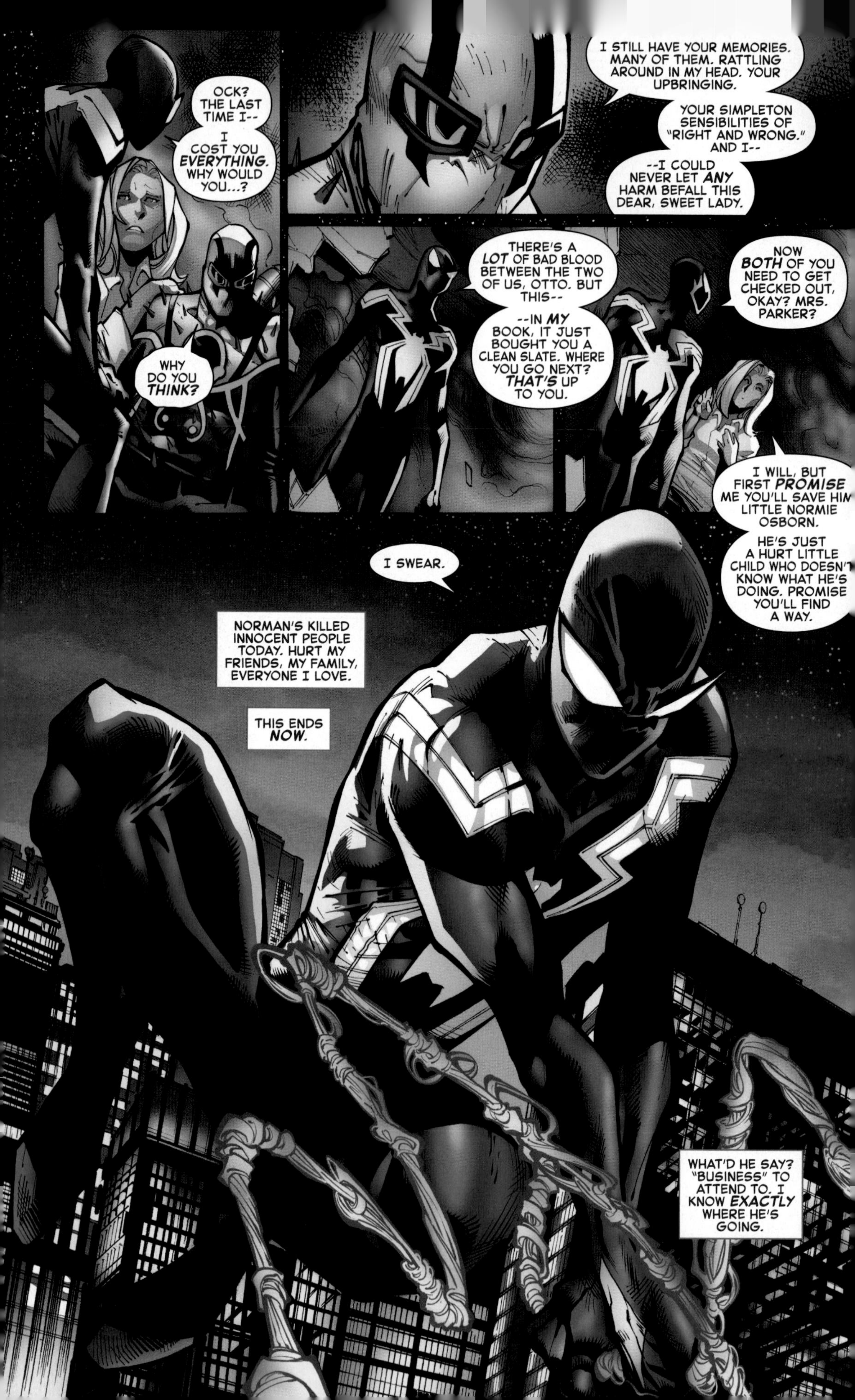
OCK? THE LAST TIME I--
I COST YOU EVERYTHING. WHY WOULD YOU...?
WHY DO YOU THINK?
I STILL HAVE YOUR MEMORIES. MANY OF THEM. RATTLING AROUND IN MY HEAD. YOUR UPBRINGING.
YOUR SIMPLETON SENSIBILITIES OF "RIGHT AND WRONG." AND I--
--I COULD NEVER LET ANY HARM BEFALL THIS DEAR, SWEET LADY.
THERE'S A LOT OF BAD BLOOD BETWEEN THE TWO OF US, OTTO. BUT THIS--
--IN MY BOOK, IT JUST BOUGHT YOU A CLEAN SLATE. WHERE YOU GO NEXT? THAT'S UP TO YOU.
NOW BOTH OF YOU NEED TO GET CHECKED OUT, OKAY? MRS. PARKER?
I WILL, BUT FIRST PROMISE ME YOU'LL SAVE HIM LITTLE NORMIE OSBORN.
HE'S JUST A HURT LITTLE CHILD WHO DOESN'T KNOW WHAT HE'S DOING. PROMISE YOU'LL FIND A WAY.
I SWEAR.
NORMAN'S KILLED INNOCENT PEOPLE TODAY. HURT MY FRIENDS, MY FAMILY, EVERYONE I LOVE.
THIS ENDS NOW.
WHAT'D HE SAY? "BUSINESS" TO ATTEND TO. I KNOW EXACTLY WHERE HE'S GOING.

Chapter 3
Family Infighting

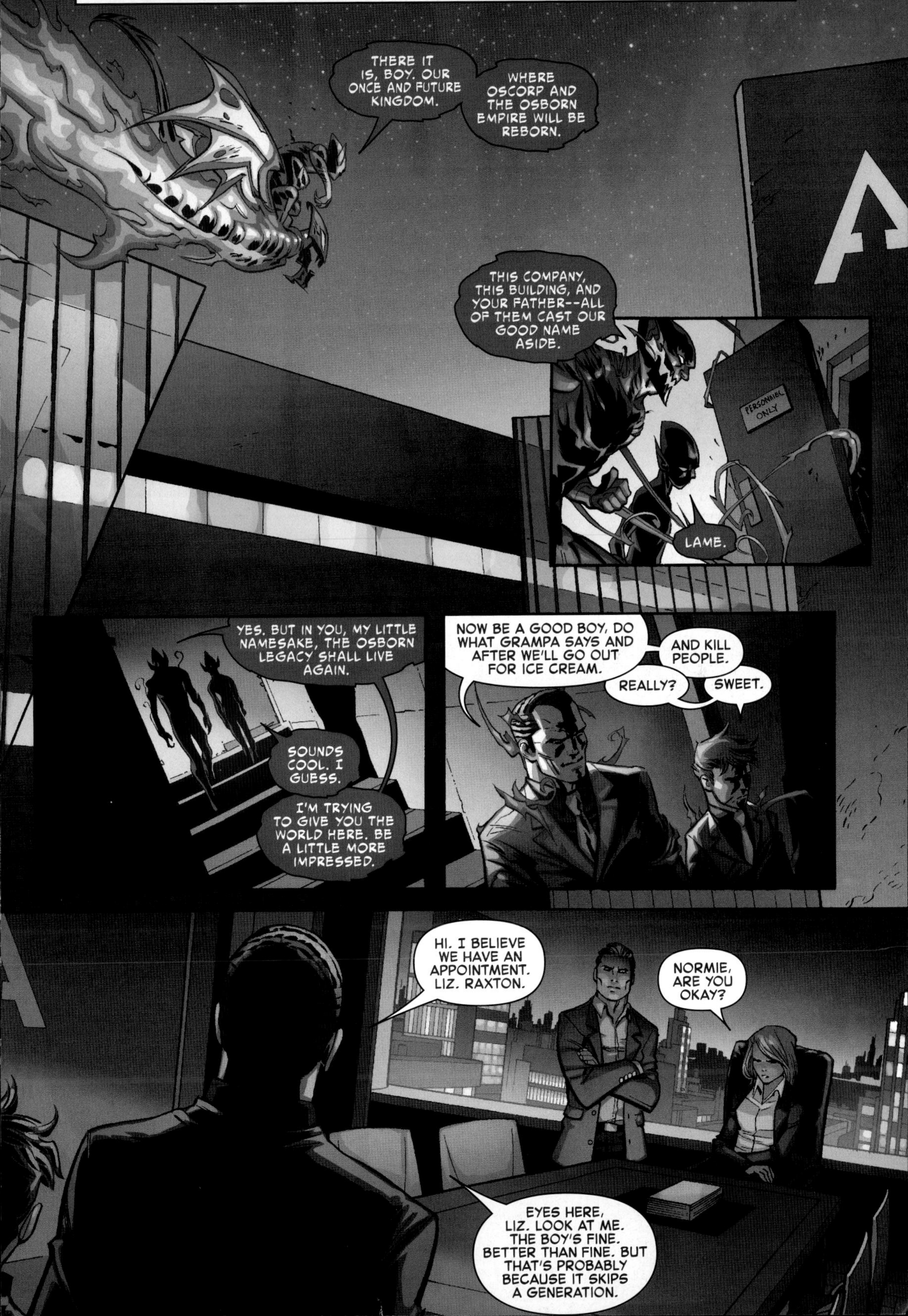

THERE IT IS, BOY. OUR ONCE AND FUTURE KINGDOM.
WHERE OSCORP AND THE OSBORN EMPIRE WILL BE REBORN.
THIS COMPANY, THIS BUILDING, AND YOUR FATHER--ALL OF THEM CAST OUR GOOD NAME ASIDE.
PERSONNEL ONLY
LAME.
YES. BUT IN YOU, MY LITTLE NAMESAKE, THE OSBORN LEGACY SHALL LIVE AGAIN.
SOUNDS COOL. I GUESS.
I'M TRYING TO GIVE YOU THE WORLD HERE. BE A LITTLE MORE IMPRESSED.
NOW BE A GOOD BOY, DO WHAT GRAMPA SAYS AND AFTER WE'LL GO OUT FOR ICE CREAM.
AND KILL PEOPLE.
REALLY?
SWEET.
HI. I BELIEVE WE HAVE AN APPOINTMENT. LIZ. RAXTON.
NORMIE, ARE YOU OKAY?
EYES HERE, LIZ. LOOK AT ME. THE BOY'S FINE. BETTER THAN FINE. BUT THAT'S PROBABLY BECAUSE IT SKIPS A GENERATION.

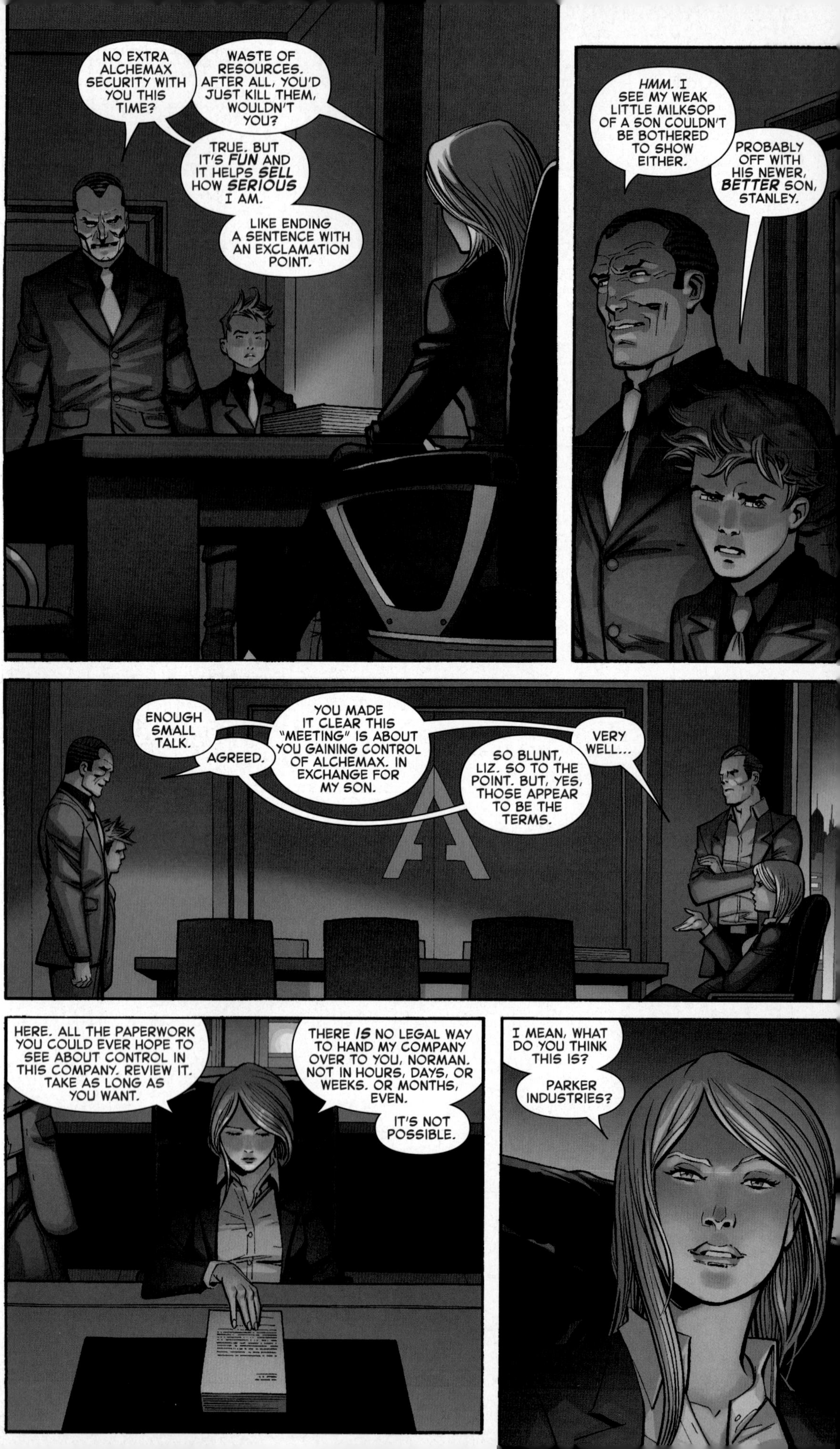
NO EXTRA ALCHEMAX SECURITY WITH YOU THIS TIME?
WASTE OF RESOURCES. AFTER ALL, YOU'D JUST KILL THEM, WOULDN'T YOU?
TRUE. BUT IT'S FUN AND IT HELPS SELL HOW SERIOUS I AM.
LIKE ENDING A SENTENCE WITH AN EXCLAMATION POINT.
HMM. I SEE MY WEAK LITTLE MILKSOP OF A SON COULDN'T BE BOTHERED TO SHOW EITHER.
PROBABLY OFF WITH HIS NEWER, BETTER SON, STANLEY.
ENOUGH SMALL TALK.
AGREED.
YOU MADE IT CLEAR THIS "MEETING" IS ABOUT YOU GAINING CONTROL OF ALCHEMAX. IN EXCHANGE FOR MY SON.
VERY WELL...
SO BLUNT, LIZ. SO TO THE POINT. BUT, YES, THOSE APPEAR TO BE THE TERMS.
HERE. ALL THE PAPERWORK YOU COULD EVER HOPE TO SEE ABOUT CONTROL IN THIS COMPANY. REVIEW IT. TAKE AS LONG AS YOU WANT.
THERE IS NO LEGAL WAY TO HAND MY COMPANY OVER TO YOU, NORMAN. NOT IN HOURS, DAYS, OR WEEKS. OR MONTHS, EVEN.
IT'S NOT POSSIBLE.
I MEAN, WHAT DO YOU THINK THIS IS?
PARKER INDUSTRIES?

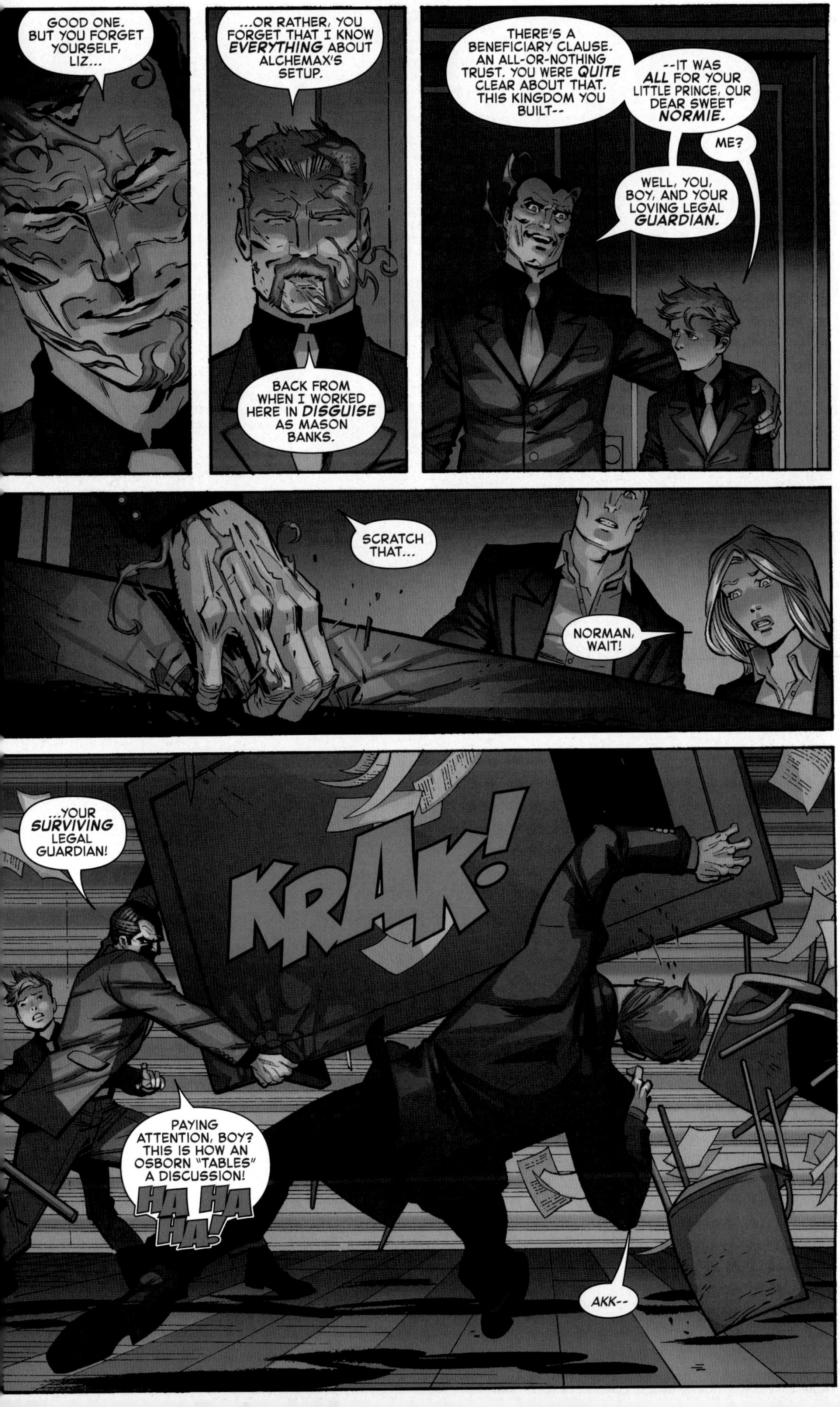
GOOD ONE. BUT YOU FORGET YOURSELF, LIZ...
...OR RATHER, YOU FORGET THAT I KNOW EVERYTHING ABOUT ALCHEMAX'S SETUP.
BACK FROM WHEN I WORKED HERE IN DISGUISE AS MASON BANKS.
THERE'S A BENEFICIARY CLAUSE. AN ALL-OR-NOTHING TRUST. YOU WERE QUITE CLEAR ABOUT THAT. THIS KINGDOM YOU BUILT--
--IT WAS ALL FOR YOUR LITTLE PRINCE, OUR DEAR SWEET NORMIE.
ME?
WELL, YOU, BOY, AND YOUR LOVING LEGAL GUARDIAN.
SCRATCH THAT...
NORMAN, WAIT!
...YOUR SURVIVING LEGAL GUARDIAN!
KRAK!
PAYING ATTENTION, BOY? THIS IS HOW AN OSBORN "TABLES" A DISCUSSION!
HA HA HA!
AKK--

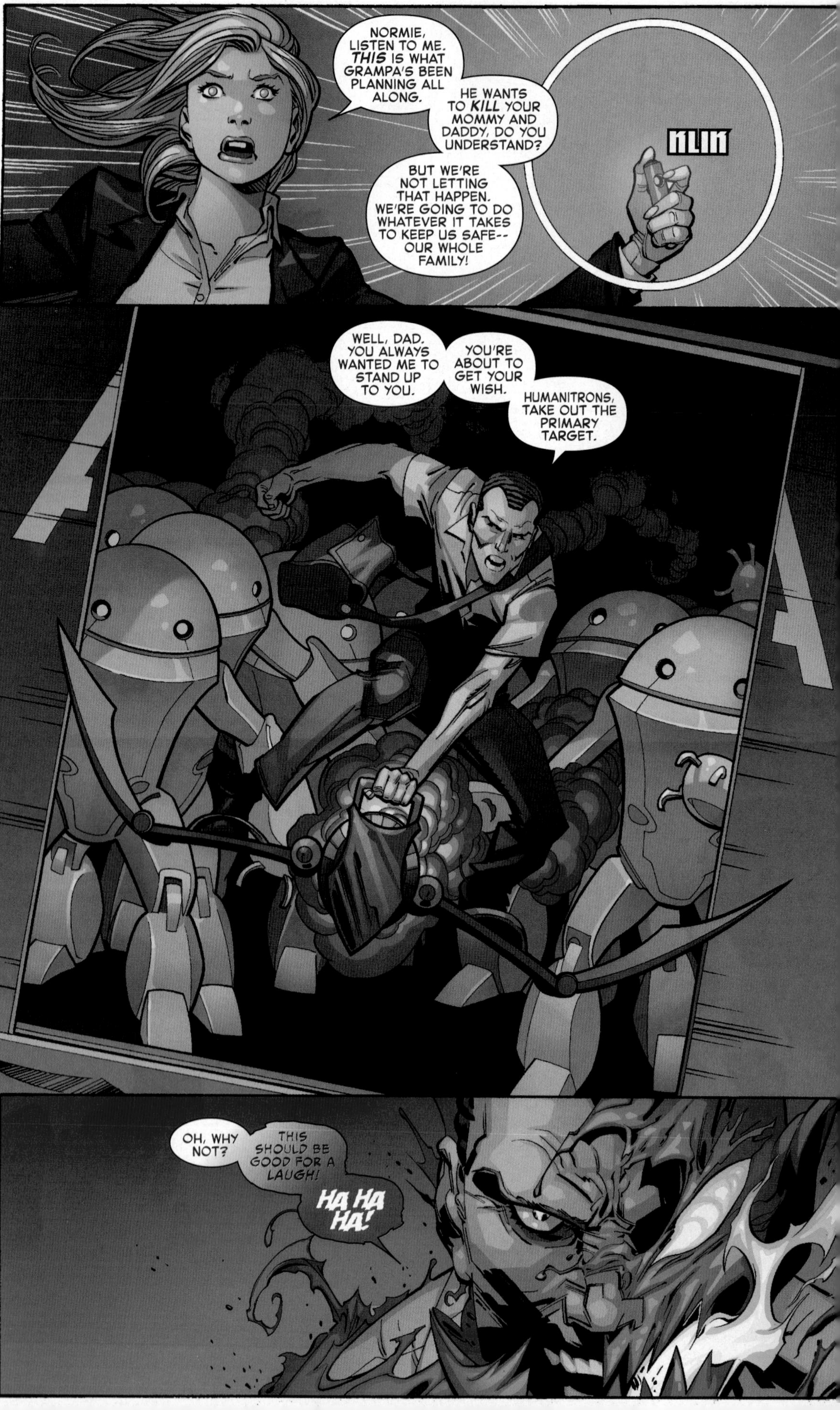

NORMIE, LISTEN TO ME. THIS IS WHAT GRAMPA'S BEEN PLANNING ALL ALONG.
HE WANTS TO KILL YOUR MOMMY AND DADDY, DO YOU UNDERSTAND?
BUT WE'RE NOT LETTING THAT HAPPEN. WE'RE GOING TO DO WHATEVER IT TAKES TO KEEP US SAFE-- OUR WHOLE FAMILY!
KLIK
WELL, DAD. YOU ALWAYS WANTED ME TO STAND UP TO YOU.
YOU'RE ABOUT TO GET YOUR WISH.
HUMANITRONS, TAKE OUT THE PRIMARY TARGET.
OH, WHY NOT?
THIS SHOULD BE GOOD FOR A LAUGH!
HA HA HA!

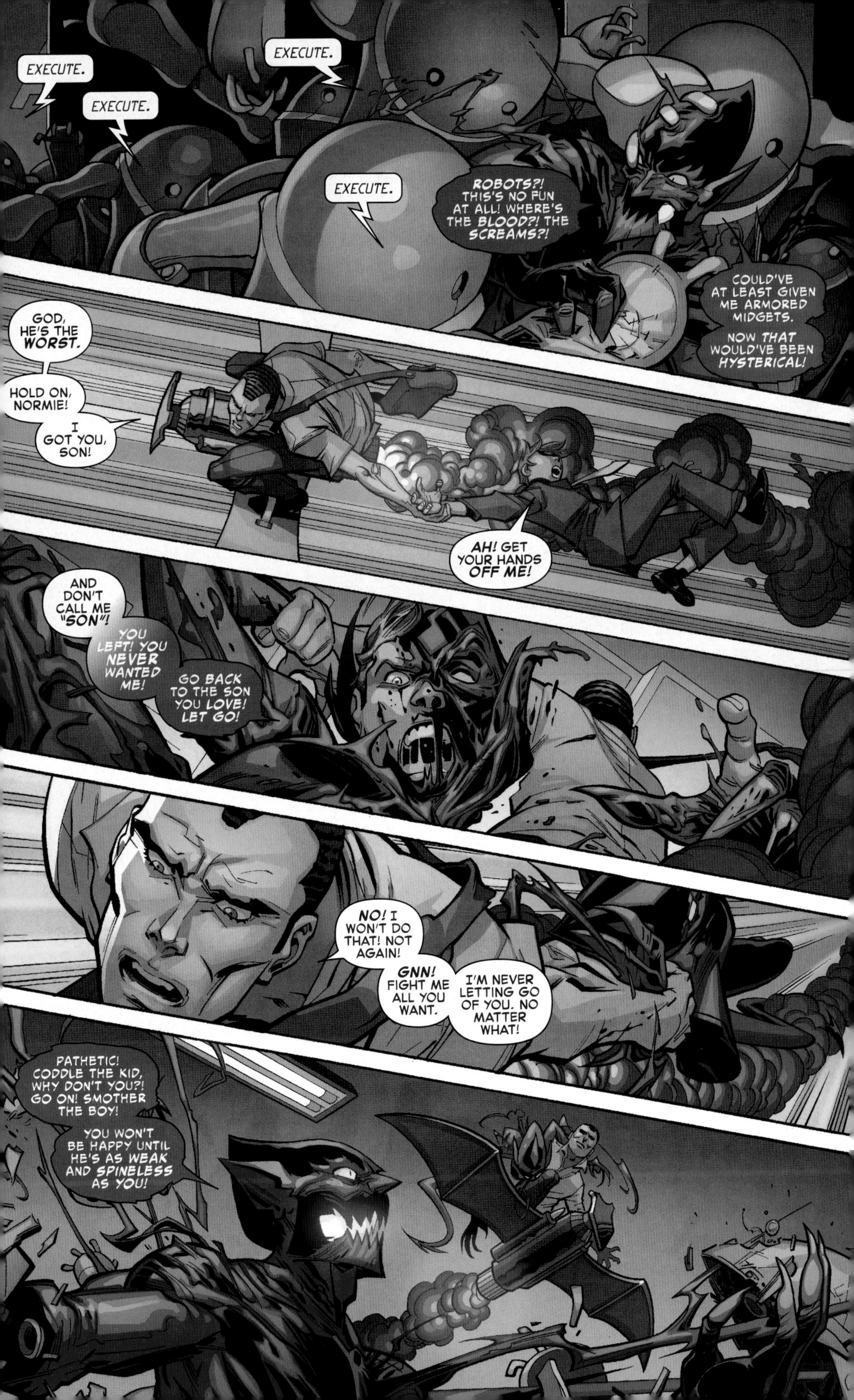
EXECUTE.
EXECUTE.
EXECUTE.
EXECUTE.
ROBOTS?! THIS'S NO FUN AT ALL! WHERE'S THE BLOOD?! THE SCREAMS?!
COULD'VE AT LEAST GIVEN ME ARMORED MIDGETS.
NOW THAT WOULD'VE BEEN HYSTERICAL!
GOD, HE'S THE WORST.
HOLD ON, NORMIE!
I GOT YOU, SON!
AH! GET YOUR HANDS OFF ME!
AND DON'T CALL ME "SON"!
YOU LEFT! YOU NEVER WANTED ME!
GO BACK TO THE SON YOU LOVE! LET GO!
NO! I WON'T DO THAT! NOT AGAIN!
GNN! FIGHT ME ALL YOU WANT.
I'M NEVER LETTING GO OF YOU. NO MATTER WHAT!
PATHETIC! CODDLE THE KID, WHY DON'T YOU?! GO ON! SMOTHER THE BOY!
YOU WON'T BE HAPPY UNTIL HE'S AS WEAK AND SPINELESS AS YOU!

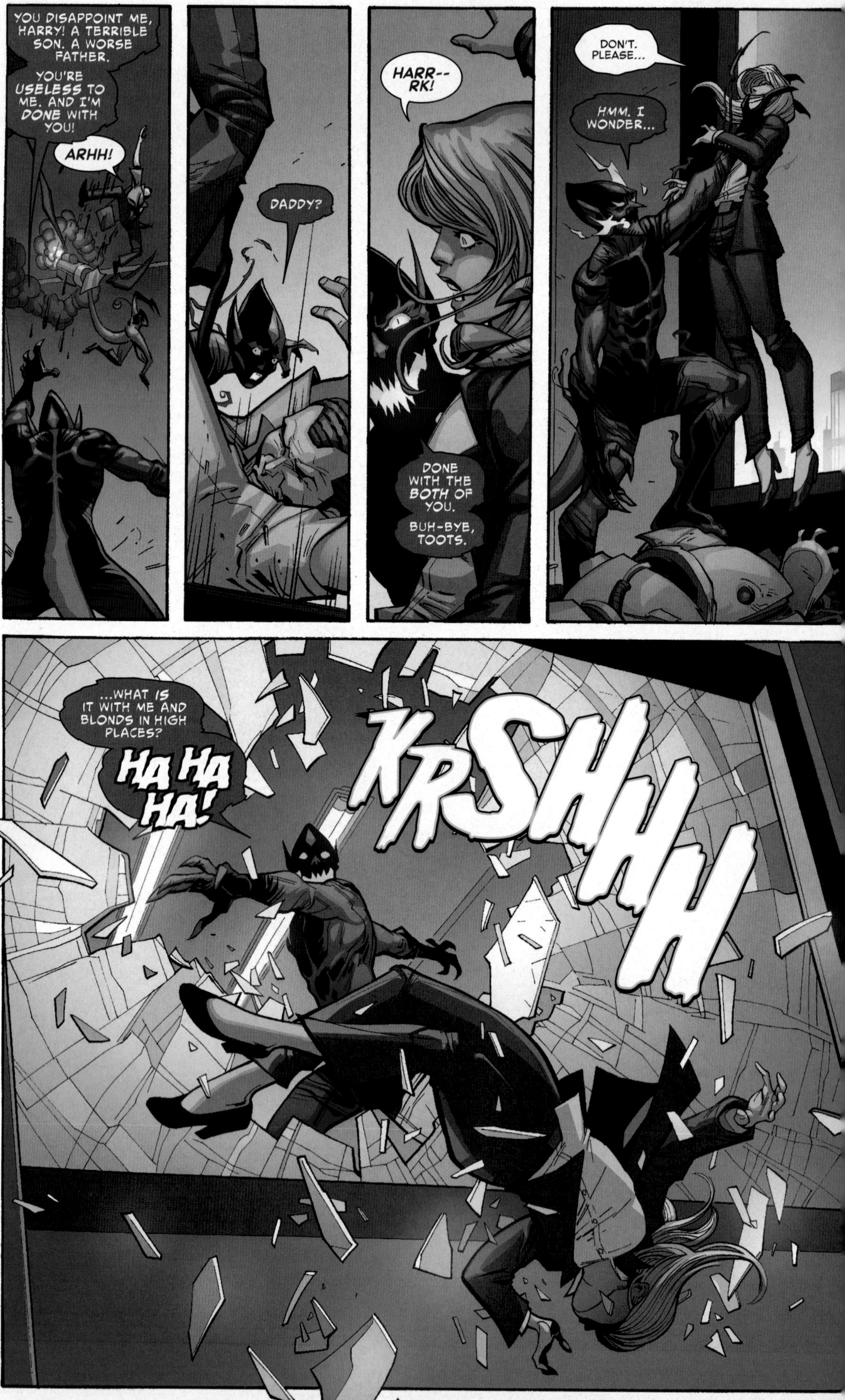
YOU DISAPPOINT ME, HARRY! A TERRIBLE SON. A WORSE FATHER.
YOU'RE USELESS TO ME. AND I'M DONE WITH YOU!
ARHH!
DADDY?
HARR-- RK!
DONE WITH THE BOTH OF YOU.
BUH-BYE, TOOTS.
DON'T. PLEASE...
HMM. I WONDER...
...WHAT IS IT WITH ME AND BLONDS IN HIGH PLACES?
HA HA HA!
KRSHHHH

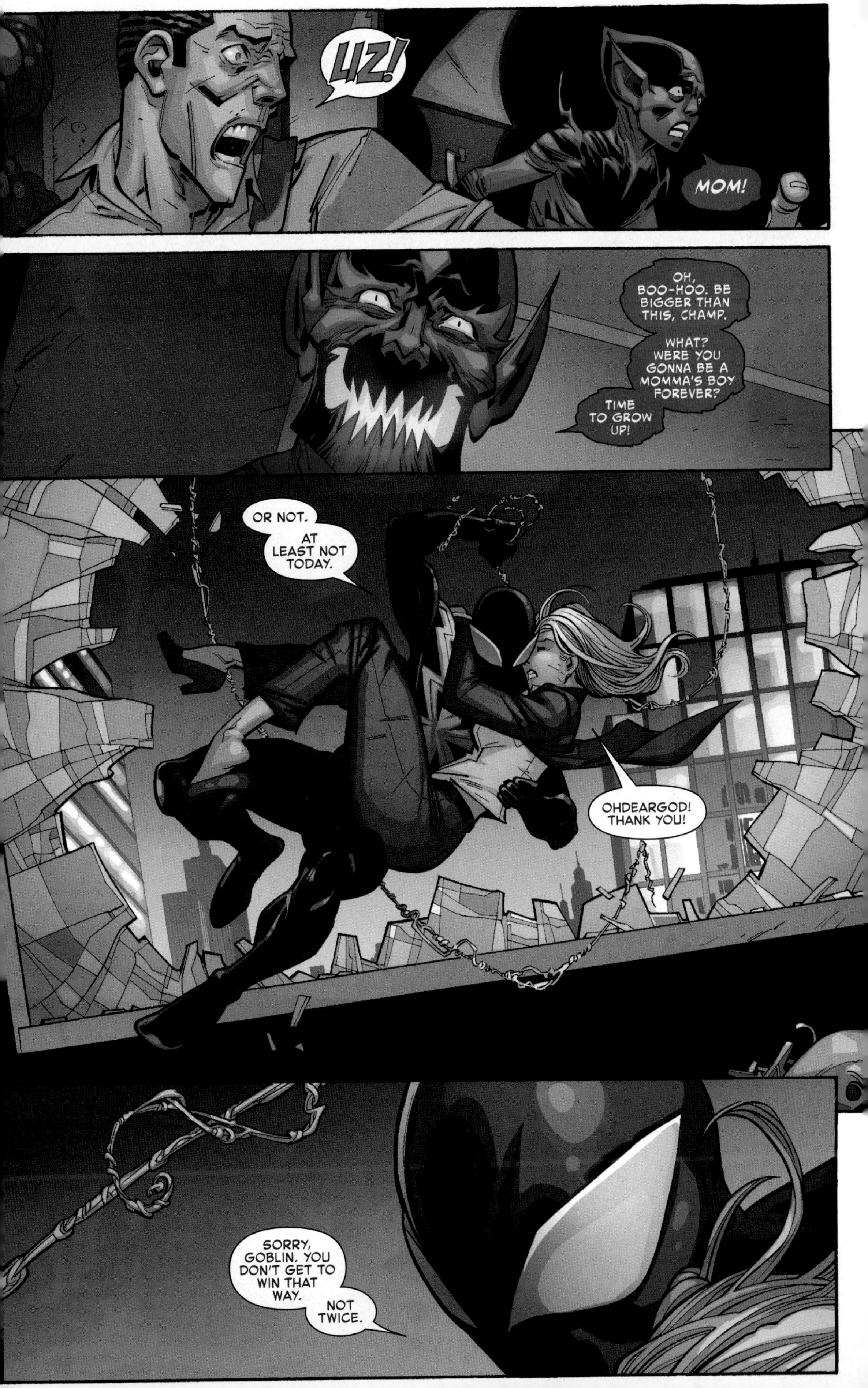
LIZ!
MOM!
OH, BOO-HOO. BE BIGGER THAN THIS, CHAMP.
WHAT? WERE YOU GONNA BE A MOMMA'S BOY FOREVER?
TIME TO GROW UP!
OR NOT. AT LEAST NOT TODAY.
OHDEARGOD! THANK YOU!
SORRY, GOBLIN. YOU DON'T GET TO WIN THAT WAY.
NOT TWICE.

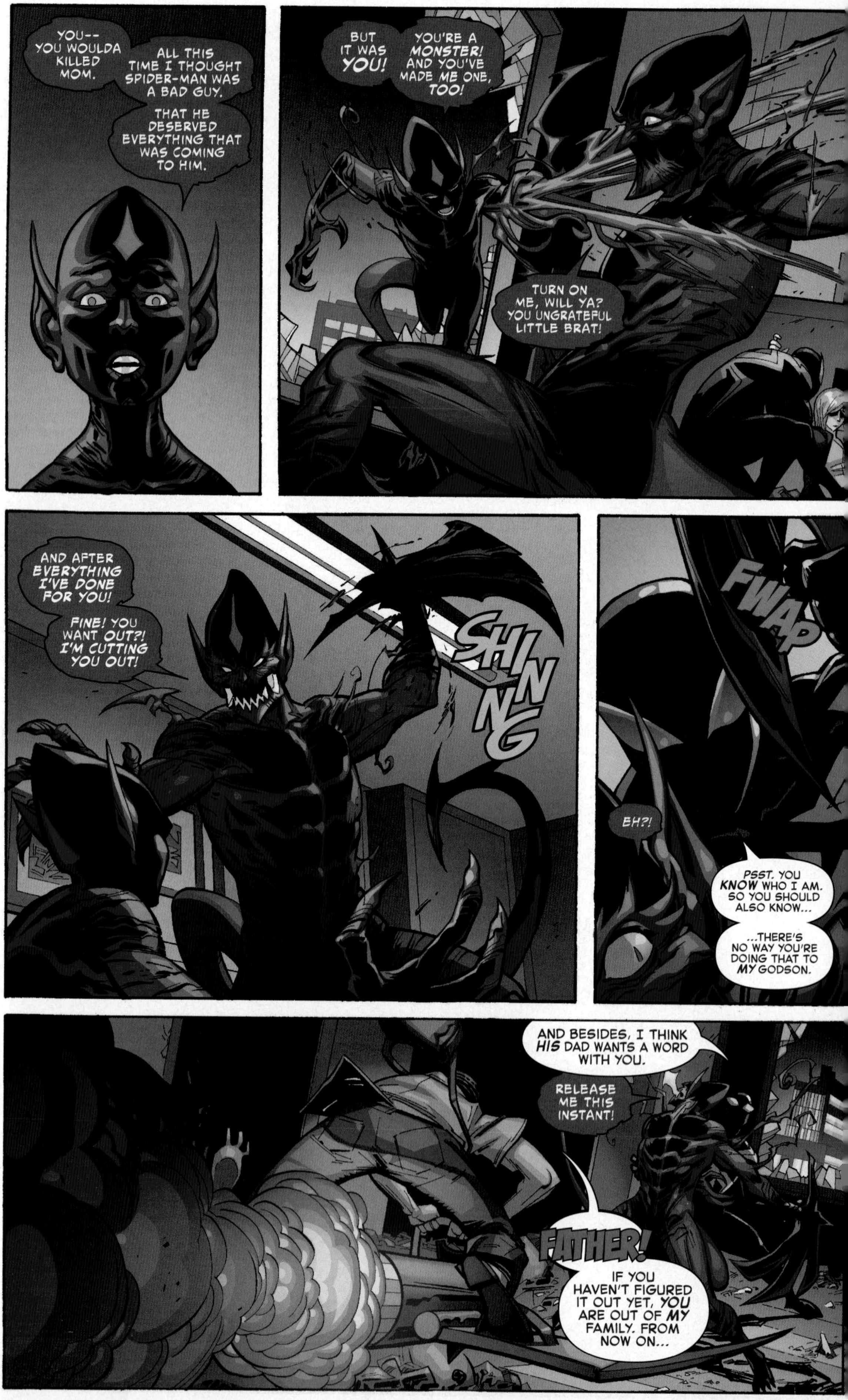

YOU-- YOU WOULDA KILLED MOM.
ALL THIS TIME I THOUGHT SPIDER-MAN WAS A BAD GUY.
THAT HE DESERVED EVERYTHING THAT WAS COMING TO HIM.
BUT IT WAS YOU!
YOU'RE A MONSTER! AND YOU'VE MADE ME ONE, TOO!
TURN ON ME, WILL YA? YOU UNGRATEFUL LITTLE BRAT!
AND AFTER EVERYTHING I'VE DONE FOR YOU!
FINE! YOU WANT OUT?! I'M CUTTING YOU OUT!
SHINNNG
FWAP
EH?!
PSST. YOU KNOW WHO I AM. SO YOU SHOULD ALSO KNOW...
...THERE'S NO WAY YOU'RE DOING THAT TO MY GODSON.
AND BESIDES, I THINK HIS DAD WANTS A WORD WITH YOU.
RELEASE ME THIS INSTANT!
FATHER!
IF YOU HAVEN'T FIGURED IT OUT YET, YOU ARE OUT OF MY FAMILY. FROM NOW ON...

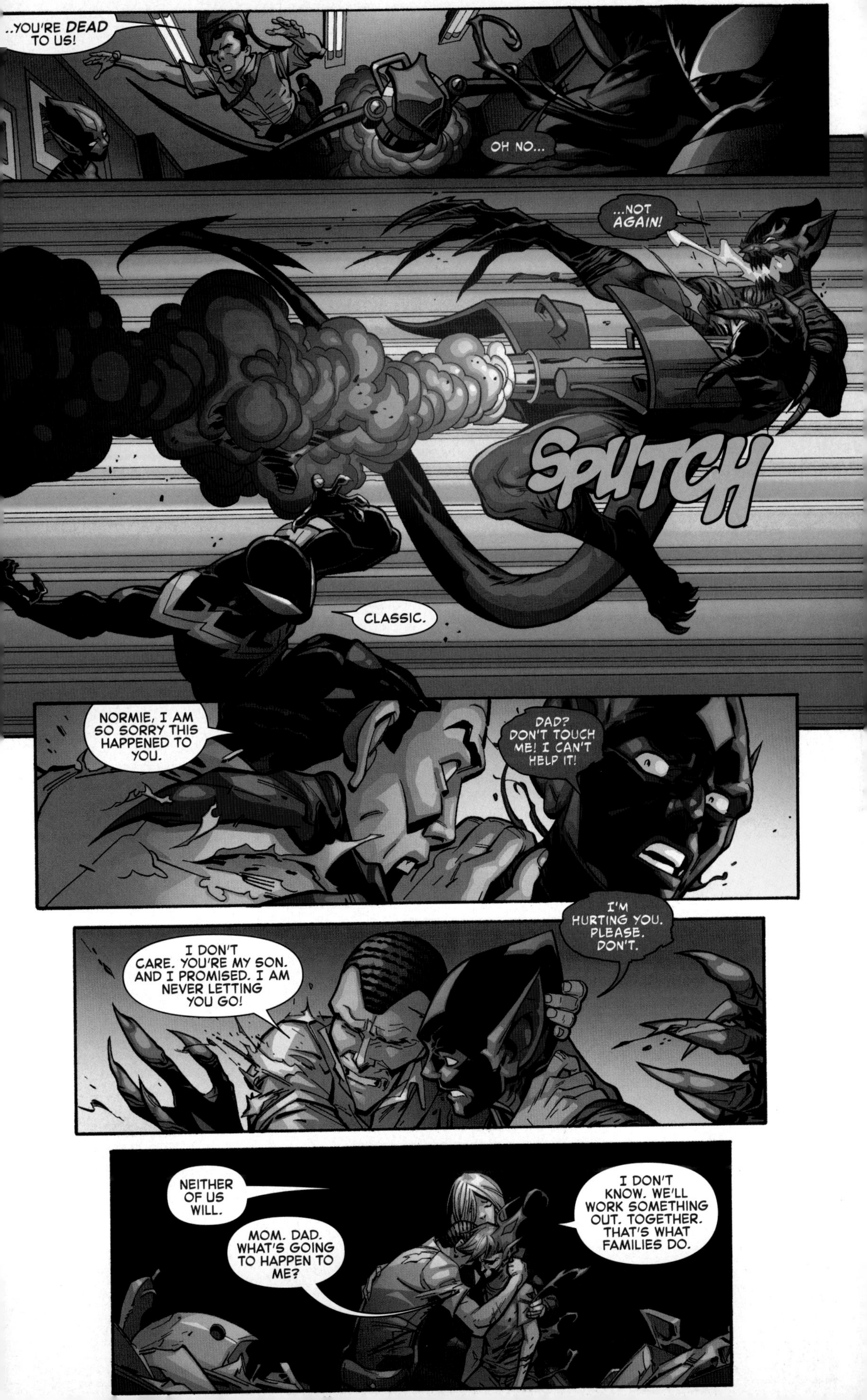
..YOU'RE DEAD TO US!
OH NO...
...NOT AGAIN!
SPUTCH
CLASSIC.
NORMIE, I AM SO SORRY THIS HAPPENED TO YOU.
DAD? DON'T TOUCH ME! I CAN'T HELP IT!
I'M HURTING YOU. PLEASE. DON'T.
I DON'T CARE. YOU'RE MY SON. AND I PROMISED. I AM NEVER LETTING YOU GO!
NEITHER OF US WILL.
MOM. DAD. WHAT'S GOING TO HAPPEN TO ME?
I DON'T KNOW. WE'LL WORK SOMETHING OUT. TOGETHER. THAT'S WHAT FAMILIES DO.

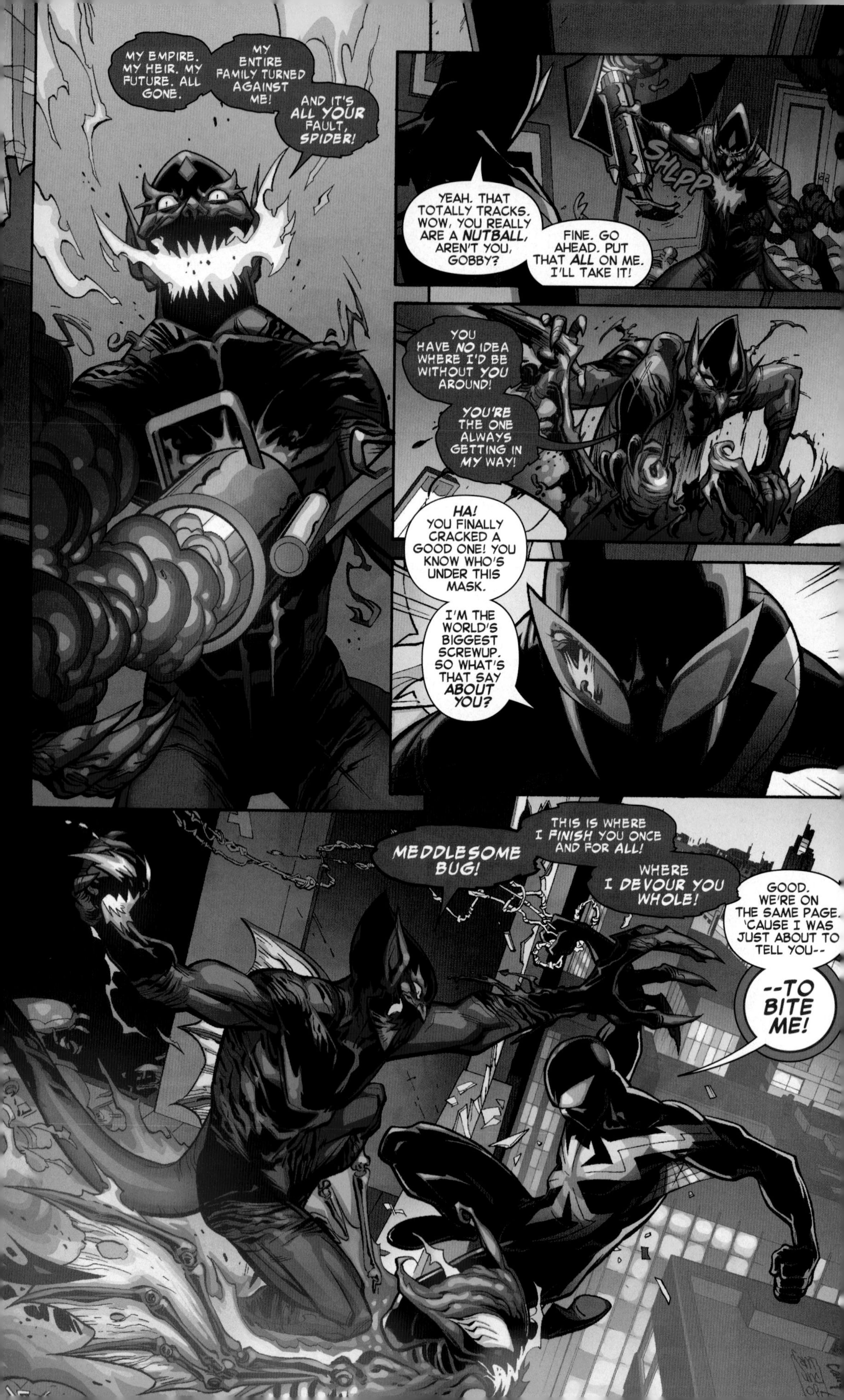
MY EMPIRE. MY HEIR. MY FUTURE. ALL GONE.
MY ENTIRE FAMILY TURNED AGAINST ME!
AND IT'S ALL YOUR FAULT, SPIDER!
SHLPP
YEAH. THAT TOTALLY TRACKS. WOW, YOU REALLY ARE A NUTBALL, AREN'T YOU, GOBBY?
FINE. GO AHEAD. PUT THAT ALL ON ME. I'LL TAKE IT!
YOU HAVE NO IDEA WHERE I'D BE WITHOUT YOU AROUND!
YOU'RE THE ONE ALWAYS GETTING IN MY WAY!
HA! YOU FINALLY CRACKED A GOOD ONE! YOU KNOW WHO'S UNDER THIS MASK.
I'M THE WORLD'S BIGGEST SCREWUP. SO WHAT'S THAT SAY ABOUT YOU?
MEDDLESOME BUG!
THIS IS WHERE I FINISH YOU ONCE AND FOR ALL!
WHERE I DEVOUR YOU WHOLE!
GOOD. WE'RE ON THE SAME PAGE. 'CAUSE I WAS JUST ABOUT TO TELL YOU--
--TO BITE ME!

Chapter 4
The Goblin Triumphant

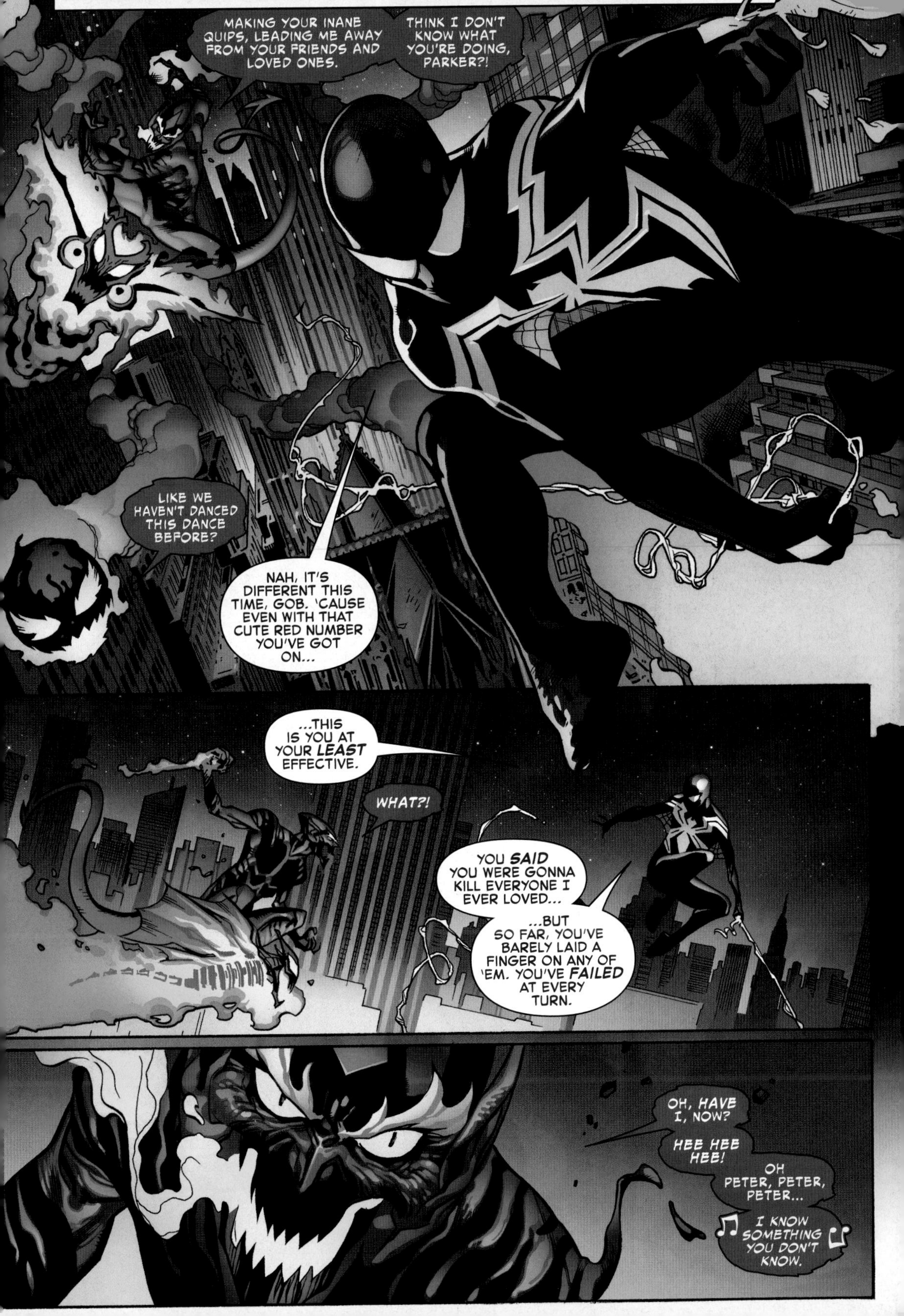

MAKING YOUR INANE QUIPS, LEADING ME AWAY FROM YOUR FRIENDS AND LOVED ONES.
THINK I DON'T KNOW WHAT YOU'RE DOING, PARKER?!
LIKE WE HAVEN'T DANCED THIS DANCE BEFORE?
NAH, IT'S DIFFERENT THIS TIME, GOB. 'CAUSE EVEN WITH THAT CUTE RED NUMBER YOU'VE GOT ON...
...THIS IS YOU AT YOUR LEAST EFFECTIVE.
WHAT?!
YOU SAID YOU WERE GONNA KILL EVERYONE I EVER LOVED...
...BUT SO FAR, YOU'VE BARELY LAID A FINGER ON ANY OF 'EM. YOU'VE FAILED AT EVERY TURN.
OH, HAVE I, NOW?
HEE HEE HEE!
OH PETER, PETER, PETER...
♫ I KNOW SOMETHING YOU DON'T KNOW. ♫

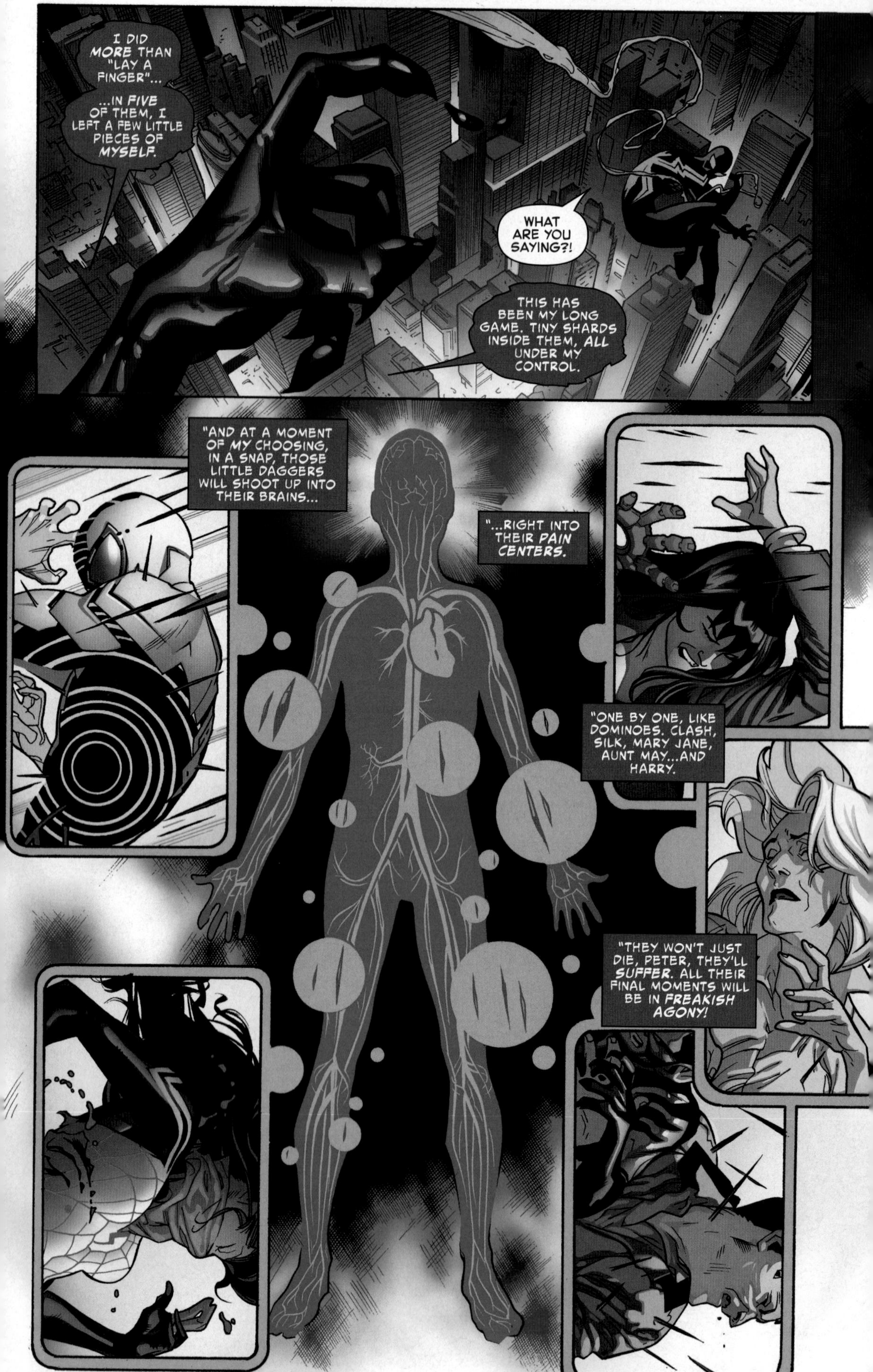
I DID MORE THAN "LAY A FINGER"...
...IN FIVE OF THEM, I LEFT A FEW LITTLE PIECES OF MYSELF.
WHAT ARE YOU SAYING?!
THIS HAS BEEN MY LONG GAME. TINY SHARDS INSIDE THEM, ALL UNDER MY CONTROL.
"AND AT A MOMENT OF MY CHOOSING, IN A SNAP, THOSE LITTLE DAGGERS WILL SHOOT UP INTO THEIR BRAINS...
"...RIGHT INTO THEIR PAIN CENTERS.
"ONE BY ONE, LIKE DOMINOES. CLASH, SILK, MARY JANE, AUNT MAY...AND HARRY.
"THEY WON'T JUST DIE, PETER, THEY'LL SUFFER. ALL THEIR FINAL MOMENTS WILL BE IN FREAKISH AGONY!

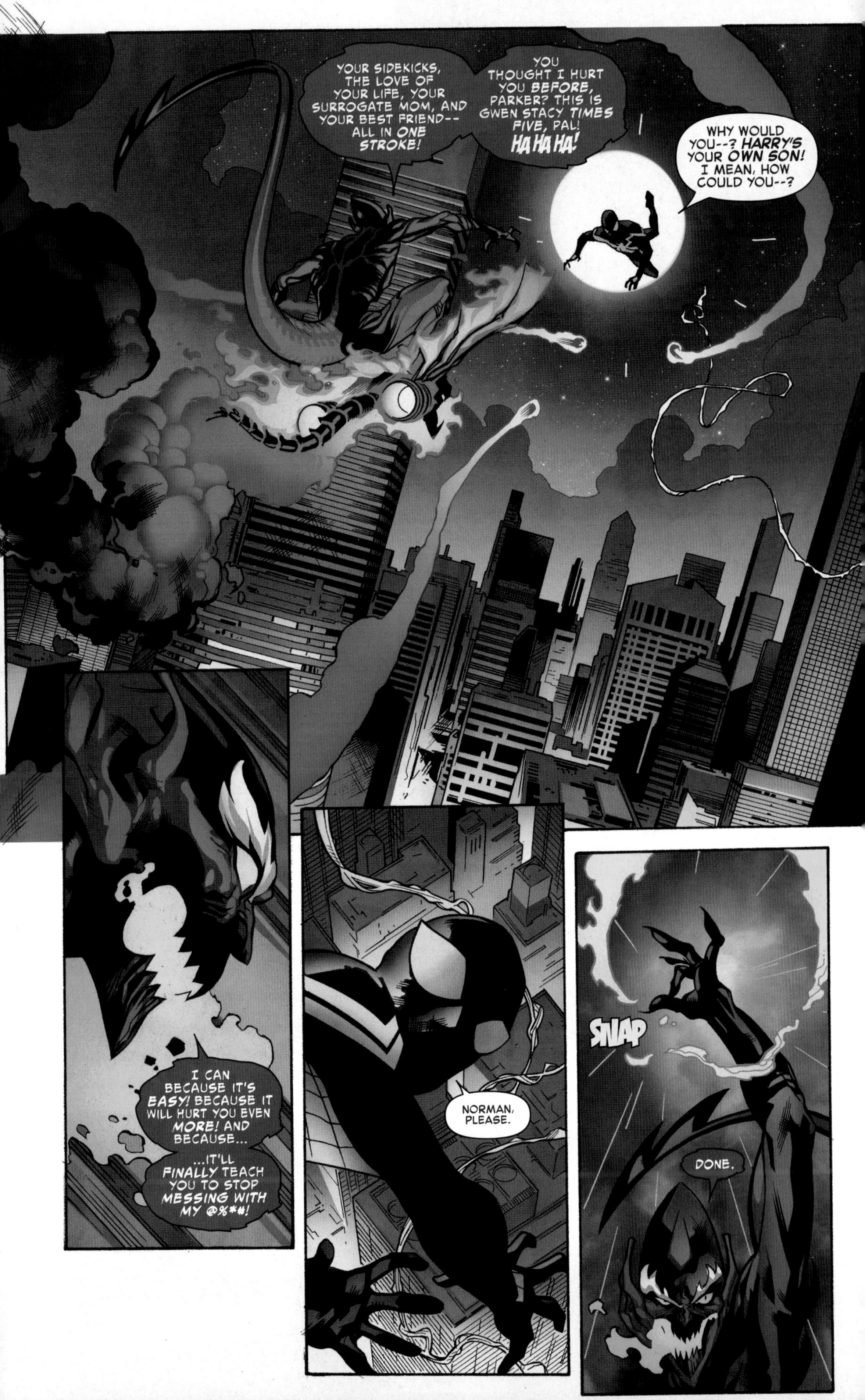
YOUR SIDEKICKS, THE LOVE OF YOUR LIFE, YOUR SURROGATE MOM, AND YOUR BEST FRIEND-- ALL IN ONE STROKE!
YOU THOUGHT I HURT YOU BEFORE, PARKER? THIS IS GWEN STACY TIMES FIVE, PAL! HA HA HA!
WHY WOULD YOU--? HARRY'S YOUR OWN SON! I MEAN, HOW COULD YOU--?
I CAN BECAUSE IT'S EASY! BECAUSE IT WILL HURT YOU EVEN MORE! AND BECAUSE...
...IT'LL FINALLY TEACH YOU TO STOP MESSING WITH MY @%*#!
NORMAN, PLEASE.
SNAP
DONE.

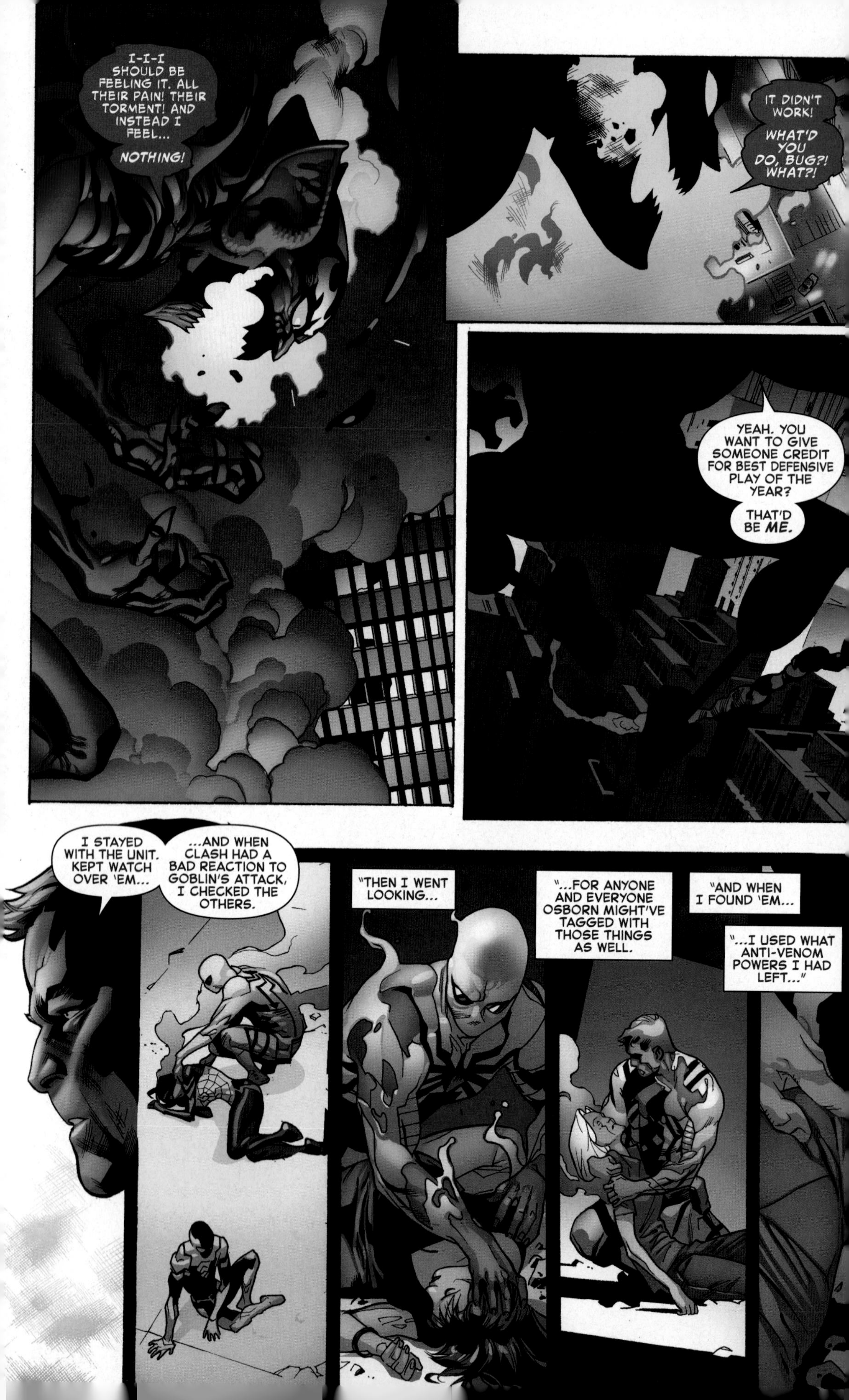

I-I-I SHOULD BE FEELING IT. ALL THEIR PAIN! THEIR TORMENT! AND INSTEAD I FEEL...
NOTHING!
IT DIDN'T WORK!
WHAT'D YOU DO, BUG?! WHAT?!
YEAH. YOU WANT TO GIVE SOMEONE CREDIT FOR BEST DEFENSIVE PLAY OF THE YEAR?
THAT'D BE ME.
I STAYED WITH THE UNIT. KEPT WATCH OVER 'EM...
...AND WHEN CLASH HAD A BAD REACTION TO GOBLIN'S ATTACK, I CHECKED THE OTHERS.
"THEN I WENT LOOKING...
"...FOR ANYONE AND EVERYONE OSBORN MIGHT'VE TAGGED WITH THOSE THINGS AS WELL.
"AND WHEN I FOUND 'EM...
"...I USED WHAT ANTI-VENOM POWERS I HAD LEFT..."

BEATS ME. HEY, I'LL HAPPILY TAKE IT... ...BUT I DIDN'T DO A THING.

WELL, I'LL BE...

...FLASH THOMPSON! OR SHOULD I SAY "AGENT ALMOST ANTI-VENOM."

DUDE, WHAT HAPPENED TO YOU?

WHAT DO YOU THINK? I'M A SOLDIER. I FOLLOWED YOUR ORDERS.

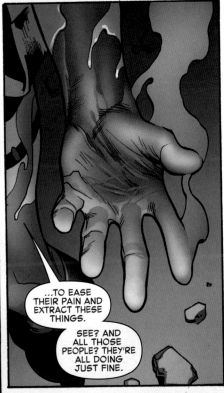

...TO EASE THEIR PAIN AND EXTRACT THESE THINGS.

SEE? AND ALL THOSE PEOPLE? THEY'RE ALL DOING JUST FINE.

ALL RIGHT! CORPORAL EUGENE THOMPSON FOR THE WIN!

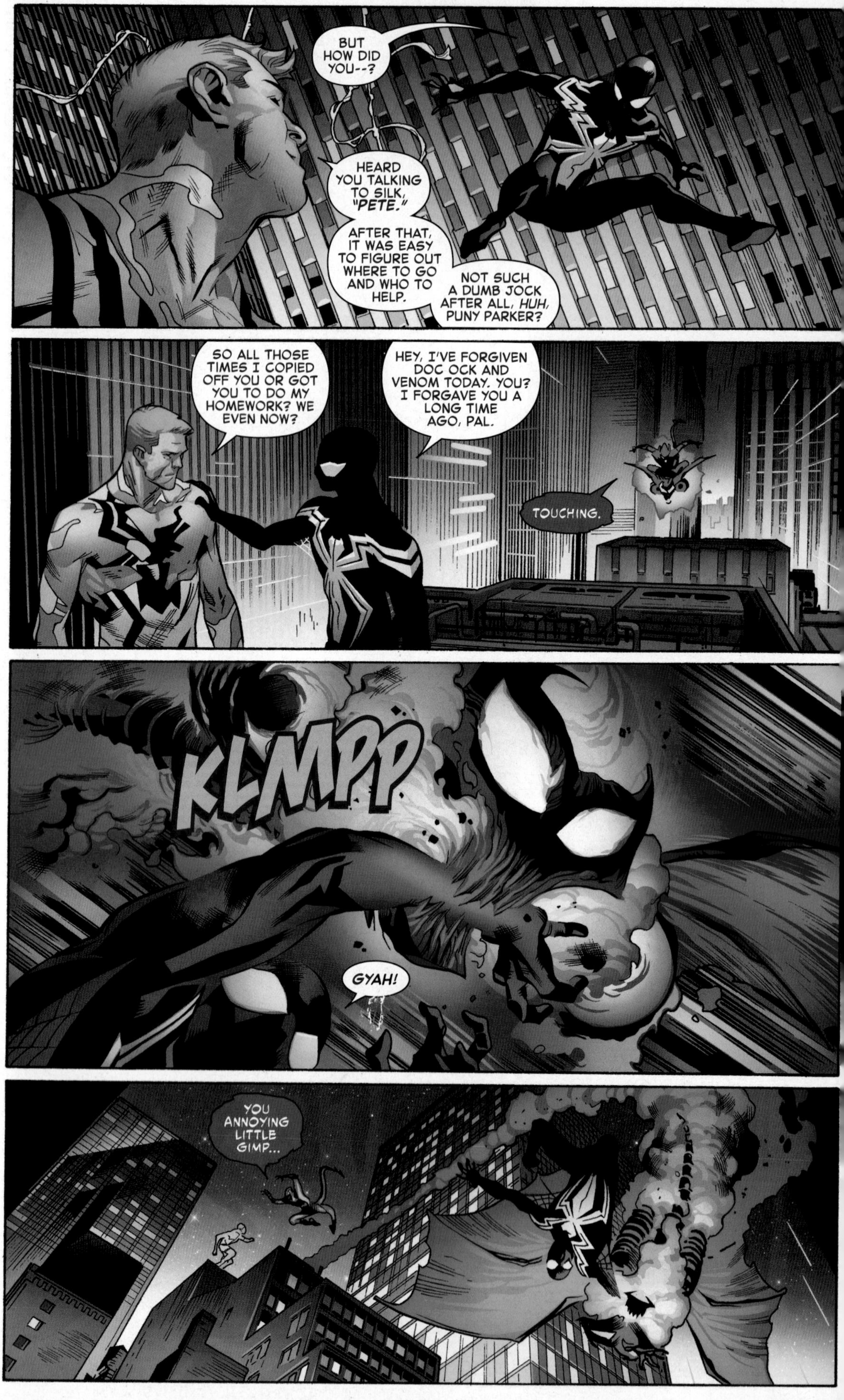
BUT HOW DID YOU--?
HEARD YOU TALKING TO SILK, "PETE."
AFTER THAT, IT WAS EASY TO FIGURE OUT WHERE TO GO AND WHO TO HELP.
NOT SUCH A DUMB JOCK AFTER ALL, HUH, PUNY PARKER?
SO ALL THOSE TIMES I COPIED OFF YOU OR GOT YOU TO DO MY HOMEWORK? WE EVEN NOW?
HEY, I'VE FORGIVEN DOC OCK AND VENOM TODAY. YOU? I FORGAVE YOU A LONG TIME AGO, PAL.
TOUCHING.
KLMPP
GYAH!
YOU ANNOYING LITTLE GIMP...

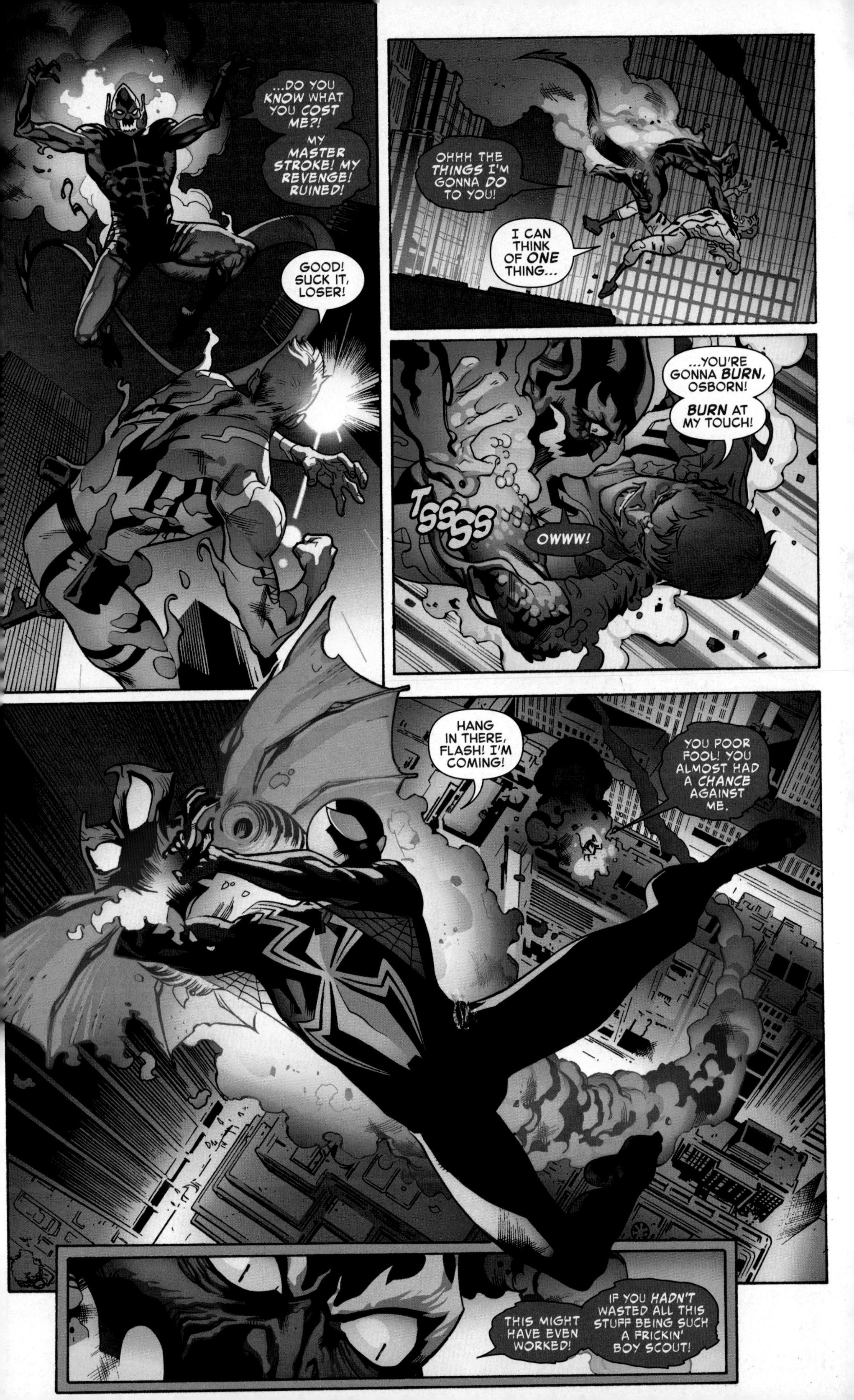

...DO YOU KNOW WHAT YOU COST ME?!
MY MASTER STROKE! MY REVENGE! RUINED!
GOOD! SUCK IT, LOSER!
OHHH THE THINGS I'M GONNA DO TO YOU!
I CAN THINK OF ONE THING...
...YOU'RE GONNA BURN, OSBORN!
BURN AT MY TOUCH!
TSSSS
OWWW!
HANG IN THERE, FLASH! I'M COMING!
YOU POOR FOOL! YOU ALMOST HAD A CHANCE AGAINST ME.
THIS MIGHT HAVE EVEN WORKED!
IF YOU HADN'T WASTED ALL THIS STUFF BEING SUCH A FRICKIN' BOY SCOUT!

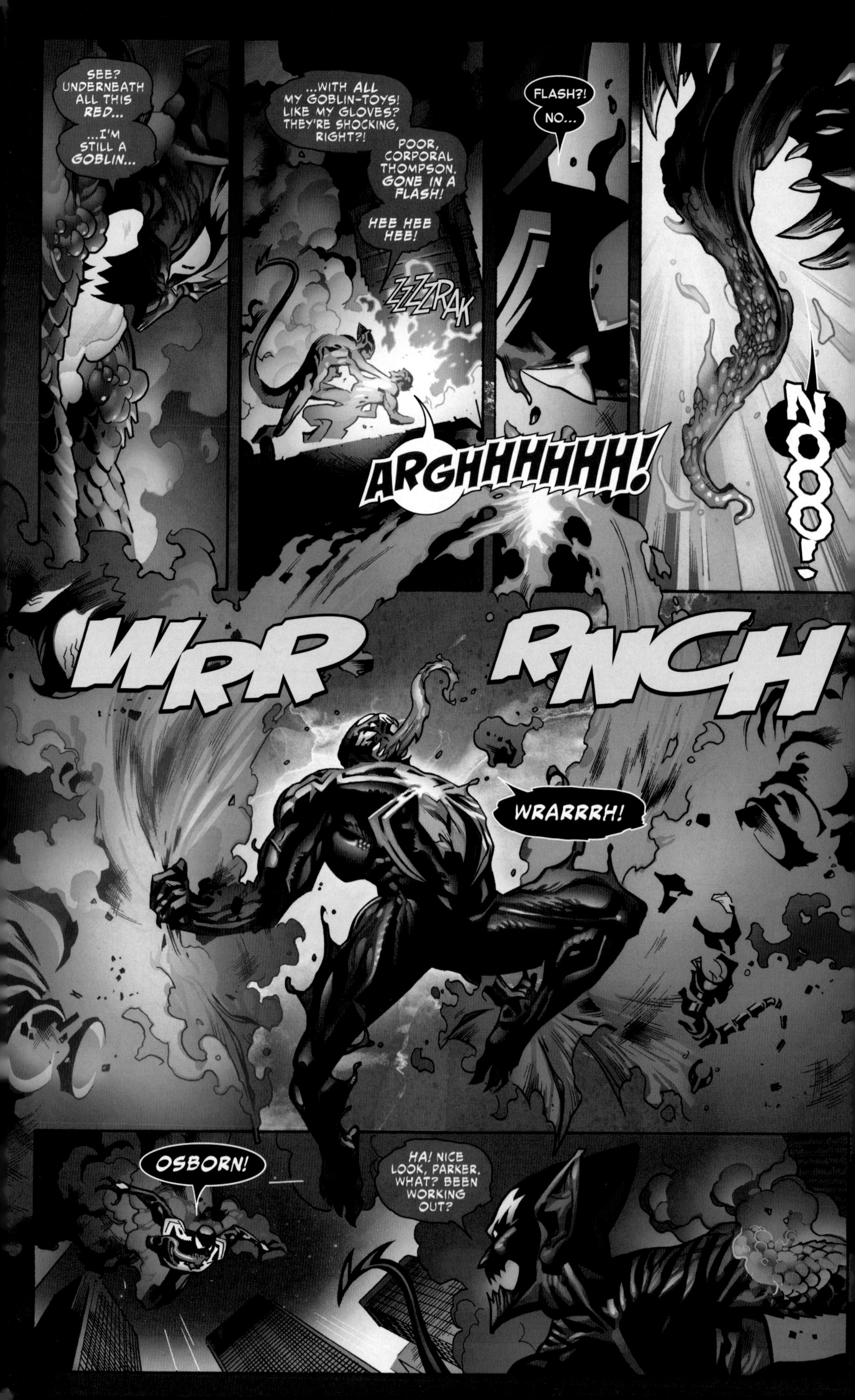
SEE? UNDERNEATH ALL THIS RED...
...I'M STILL A GOBLIN...
...WITH ALL MY GOBLIN-TOYS! LIKE MY GLOVES? THEY'RE SHOCKING, RIGHT?!
POOR, CORPORAL THOMPSON. GONE IN A FLASH!
HEE HEE HEE!
ZZZZRAK
ARGHHHHHH!
FLASH?!
NO...
NOOO!
WRR RNCH
WRARRRH!
OSBORN!
HA! NICE LOOK, PARKER. WHAT? BEEN WORKING OUT?

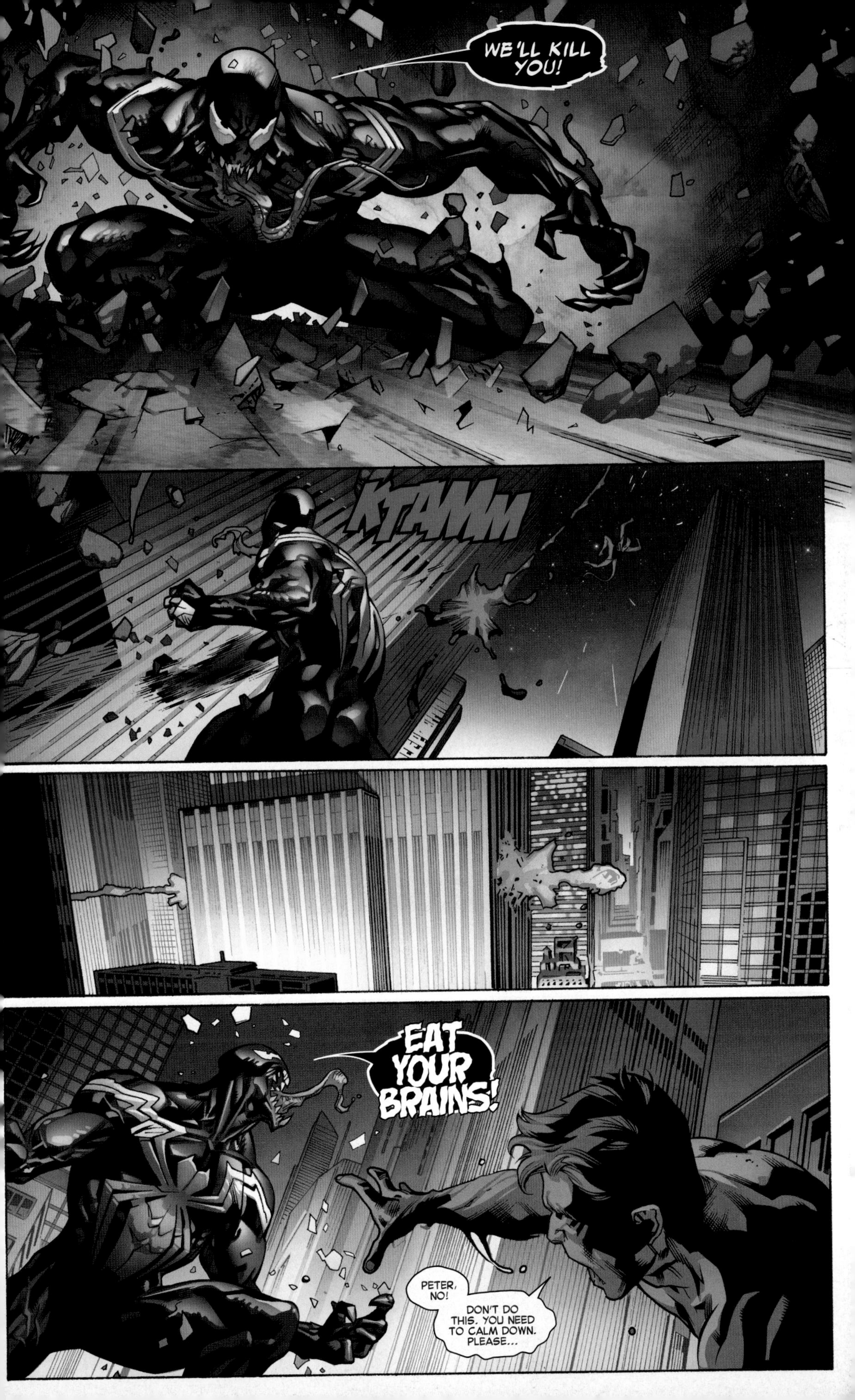
WE'LL KILL YOU!
KTAMM
EAT YOUR BRAINS!
PETER, NO!
DON'T DO THIS. YOU NEED TO CALM DOWN. PLEASE...

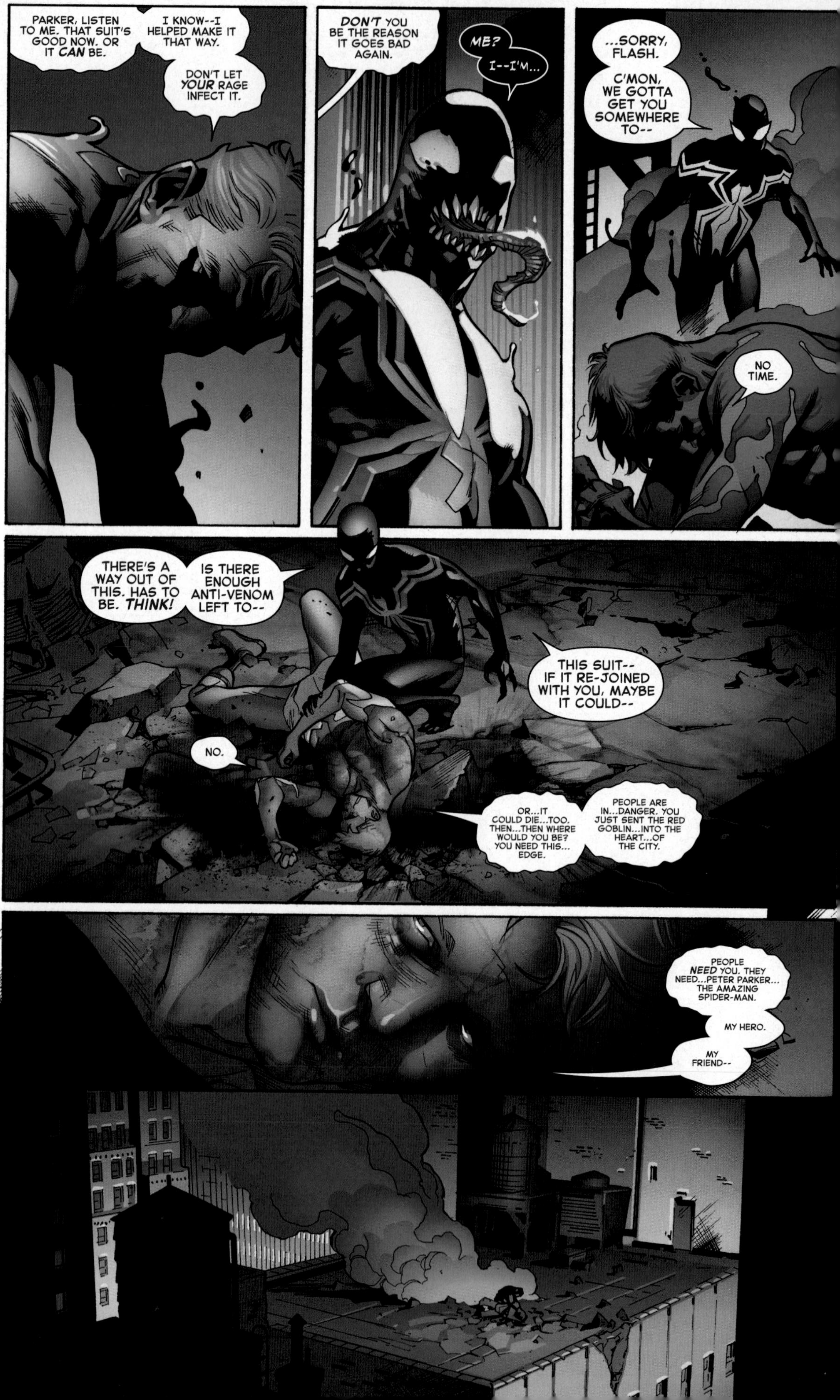
PARKER, LISTEN TO ME. THAT SUIT'S GOOD NOW. OR IT CAN BE.
I KNOW--I HELPED MAKE IT THAT WAY.
DON'T LET YOUR RAGE INFECT IT.
DON'T YOU BE THE REASON IT GOES BAD AGAIN.
ME?
I--I'M...
...SORRY, FLASH.
C'MON, WE GOTTA GET YOU SOMEWHERE TO--
NO TIME.
THERE'S A WAY OUT OF THIS. HAS TO BE. THINK!
IS THERE ENOUGH ANTI-VENOM LEFT TO--
THIS SUIT-- IF IT RE-JOINED WITH YOU, MAYBE IT COULD--
NO.
OR...IT COULD DIE...TOO. THEN...THEN WHERE WOULD YOU BE? YOU NEED THIS... EDGE.
PEOPLE ARE IN...DANGER. YOU JUST SENT THE RED GOBLIN...INTO THE HEART...OF THE CITY.
PEOPLE NEED YOU. THEY NEED...PETER PARKER... THE AMAZING SPIDER-MAN.
MY HERO.
MY FRIEND--

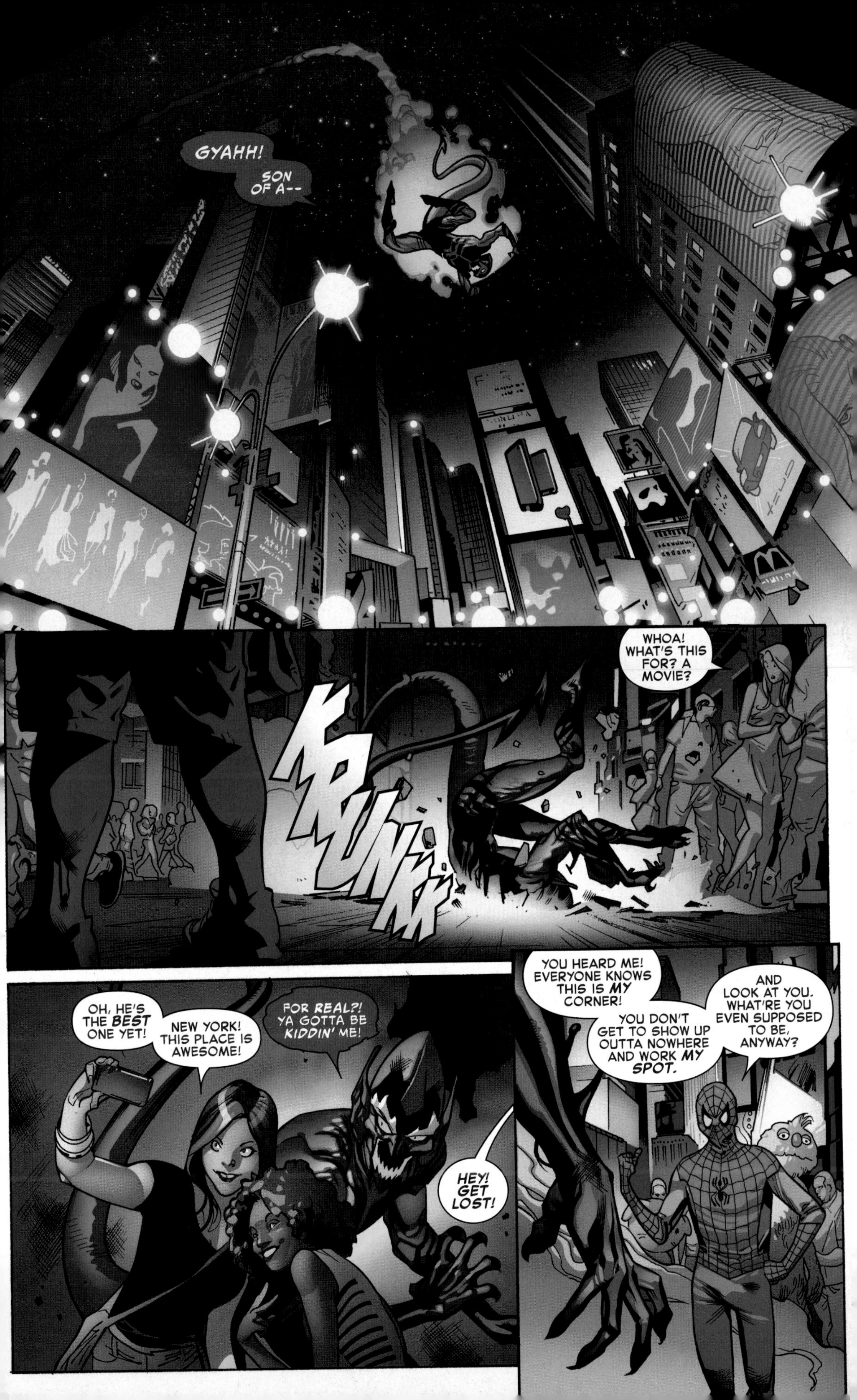
GYAHH!
SON OF A--
KRUNKK
WHOA! WHAT'S THIS FOR? A MOVIE?
OH, HE'S THE BEST ONE YET!
NEW YORK! THIS PLACE IS AWESOME!
FOR REAL?! YA GOTTA BE KIDDIN' ME!
HEY! GET LOST!
YOU HEARD ME! EVERYONE KNOWS THIS IS MY CORNER!
YOU DON'T GET TO SHOW UP OUTTA NOWHERE AND WORK MY SPOT.
AND LOOK AT YOU. WHAT'RE YOU EVEN SUPPOSED TO BE, ANYWAY?

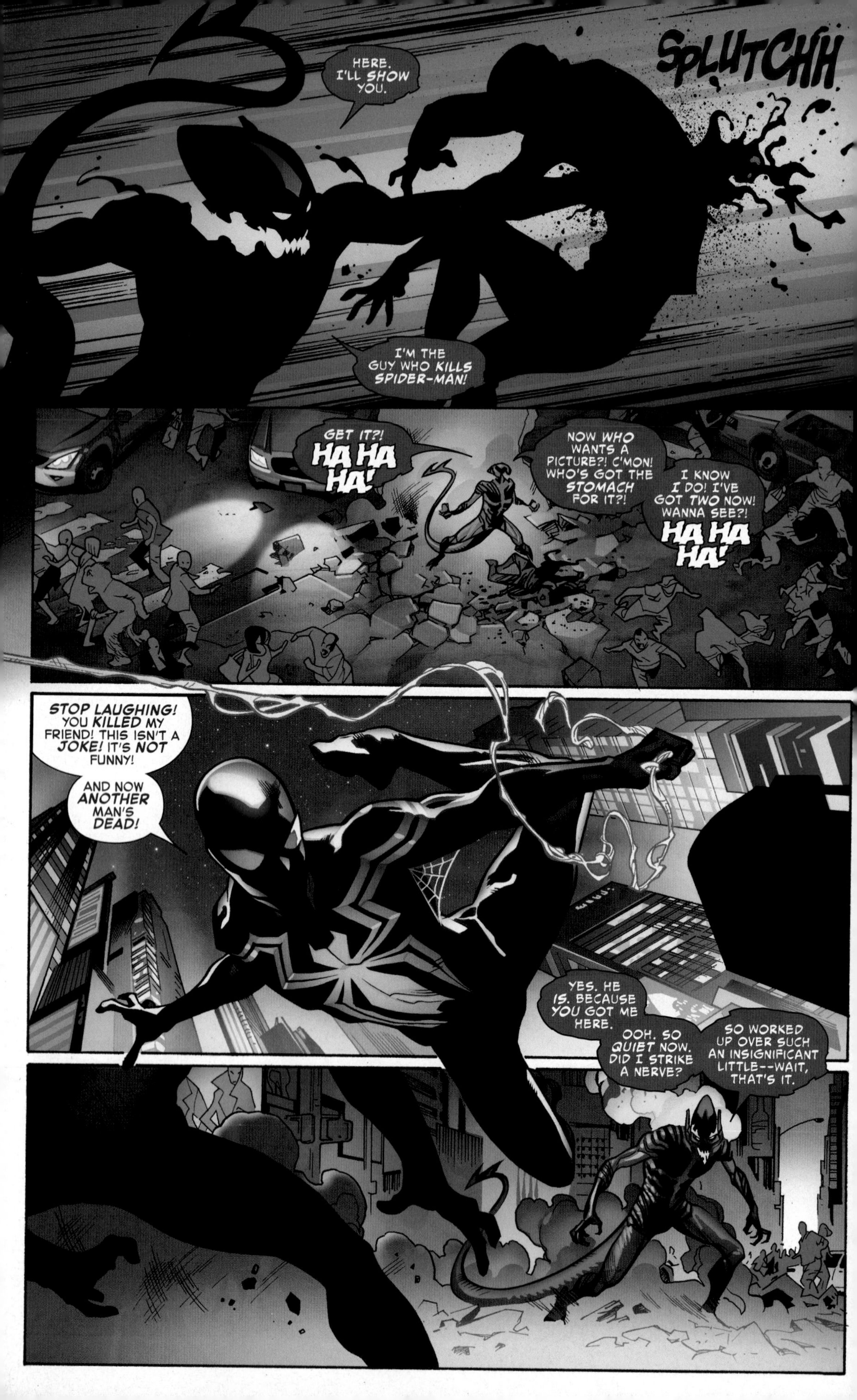
HERE. I'LL SHOW YOU.
SPLUTCHH
I'M THE GUY WHO KILLS SPIDER-MAN!
GET IT?! HA HA HA!
NOW WHO WANTS A PICTURE?! C'MON! WHO'S GOT THE STOMACH FOR IT?!
I KNOW I DO! I'VE GOT TWO NOW! WANNA SEE?! HA HA HA!
STOP LAUGHING! YOU KILLED MY FRIEND! THIS ISN'T A JOKE! IT'S NOT FUNNY!
AND NOW ANOTHER MAN'S DEAD!
YES. HE IS. BECAUSE YOU GOT ME HERE.
OOH. SO QUIET NOW. DID I STRIKE A NERVE?
SO WORKED UP OVER SUCH AN INSIGNIFICANT LITTLE--WAIT, THAT'S IT.

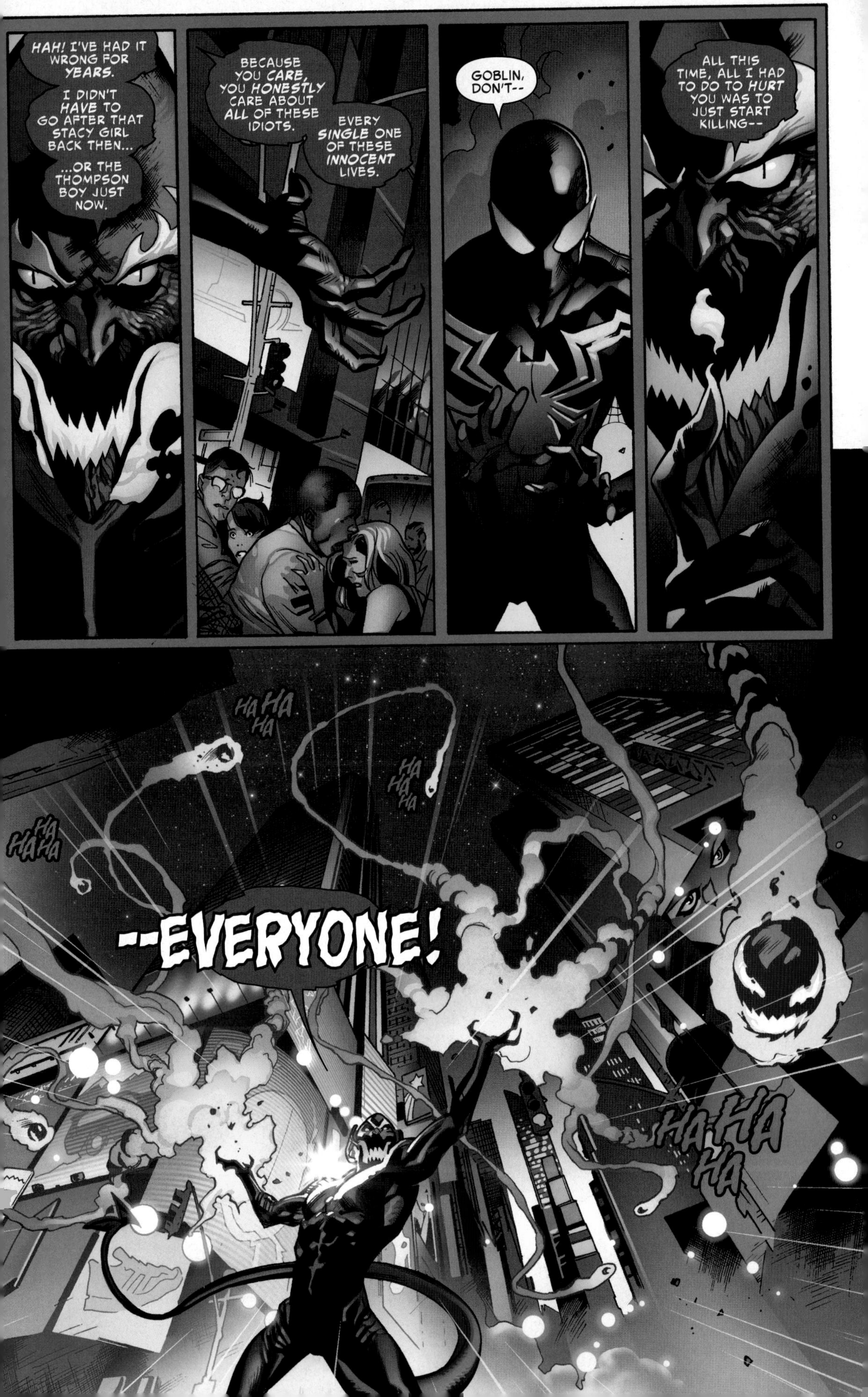
HAH! I'VE HAD IT WRONG FOR YEARS.
I DIDN'T HAVE TO GO AFTER THAT STACY GIRL BACK THEN...
...OR THE THOMPSON BOY JUST NOW.
BECAUSE YOU CARE, YOU HONESTLY CARE ABOUT ALL OF THESE IDIOTS.
EVERY SINGLE ONE OF THESE INNOCENT LIVES.
GOBLIN, DON'T--
ALL THIS TIME, ALL I HAD TO DO TO HURT YOU WAS TO JUST START KILLING--
HA HA HA
HA HA HA
HA HA HA
--EVERYONE!
HA HA HA HA

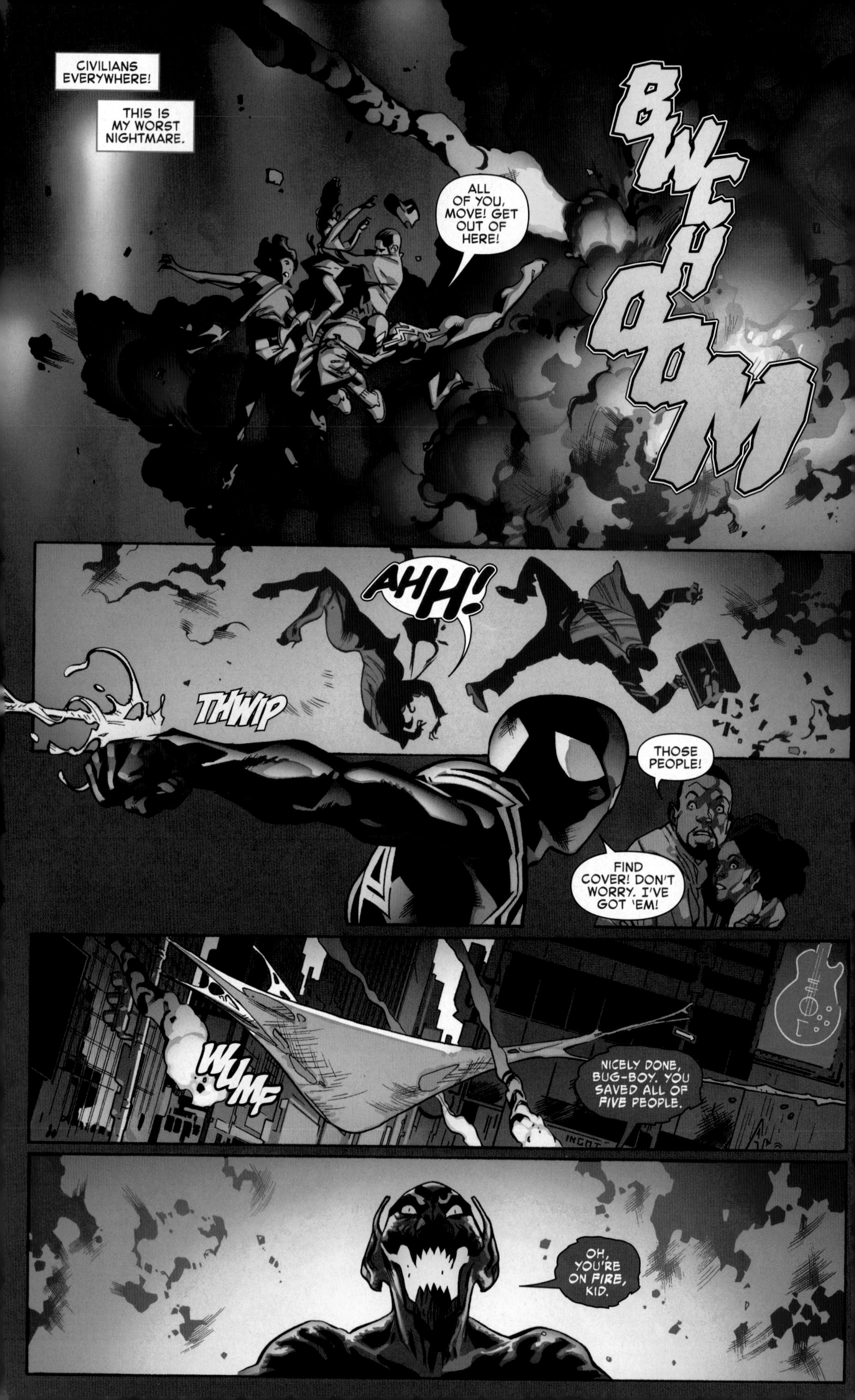
CIVILIANS EVERYWHERE!
THIS IS MY WORST NIGHTMARE.
ALL OF YOU, MOVE! GET OUT OF HERE!
BWOOSH
AHH!
THWIP
THOSE PEOPLE!
FIND COVER! DON'T WORRY. I'VE GOT 'EM!
WUMF
NICELY DONE, BUG-BOY. YOU SAVED ALL OF FIVE PEOPLE.
OH, YOU'RE ON FIRE, KID.

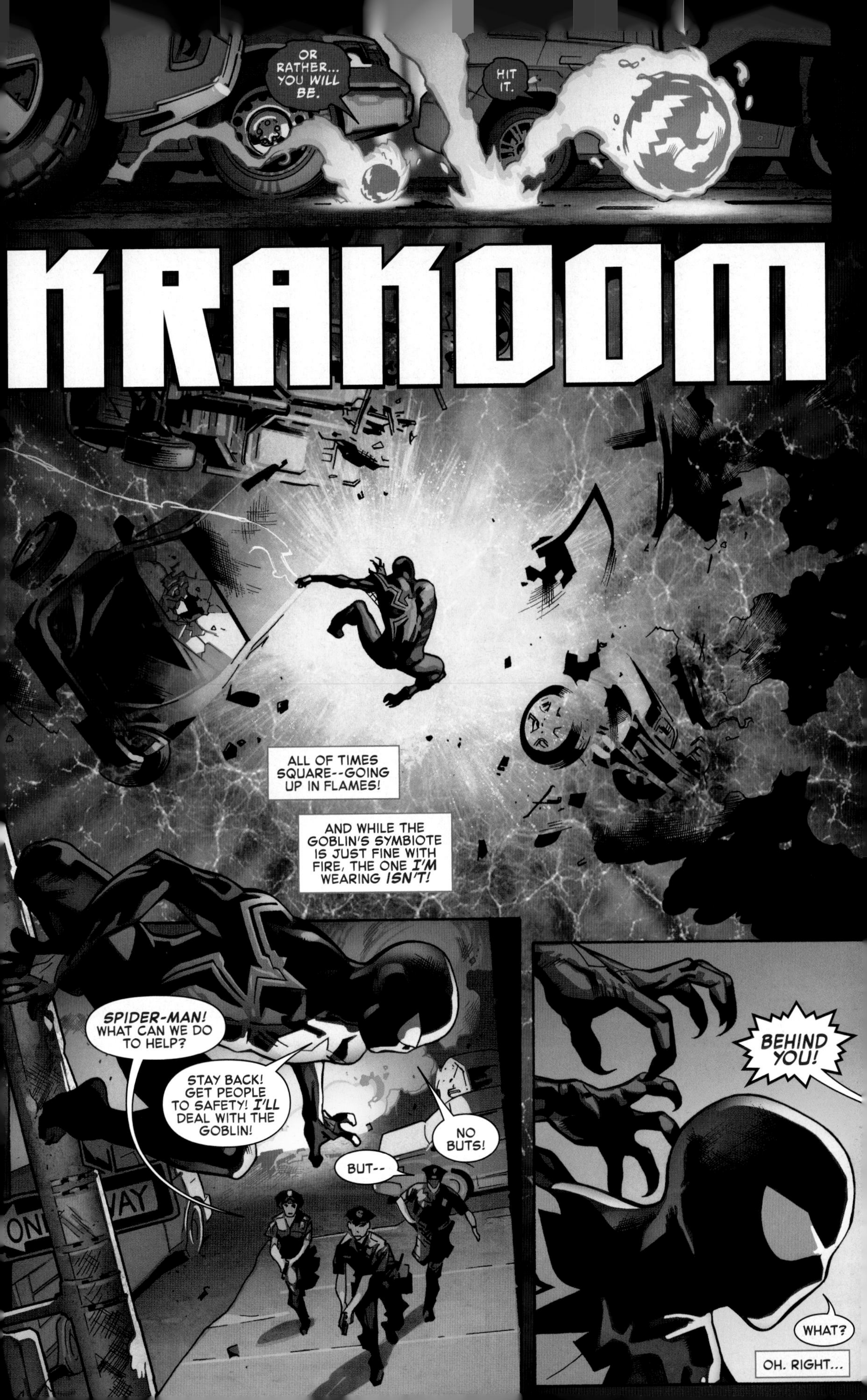
OR RATHER... YOU WILL BE.
HIT IT.
KRAKOOM
ALL OF TIMES SQUARE--GOING UP IN FLAMES!
AND WHILE THE GOBLIN'S SYMBIOTE IS JUST FINE WITH FIRE, THE ONE I'M WEARING ISN'T!
SPIDER-MAN! WHAT CAN WE DO TO HELP?
STAY BACK! GET PEOPLE TO SAFETY! I'LL DEAL WITH THE GOBLIN!
BUT--
NO BUTS!
BEHIND YOU!
WHAT?
OH. RIGHT...

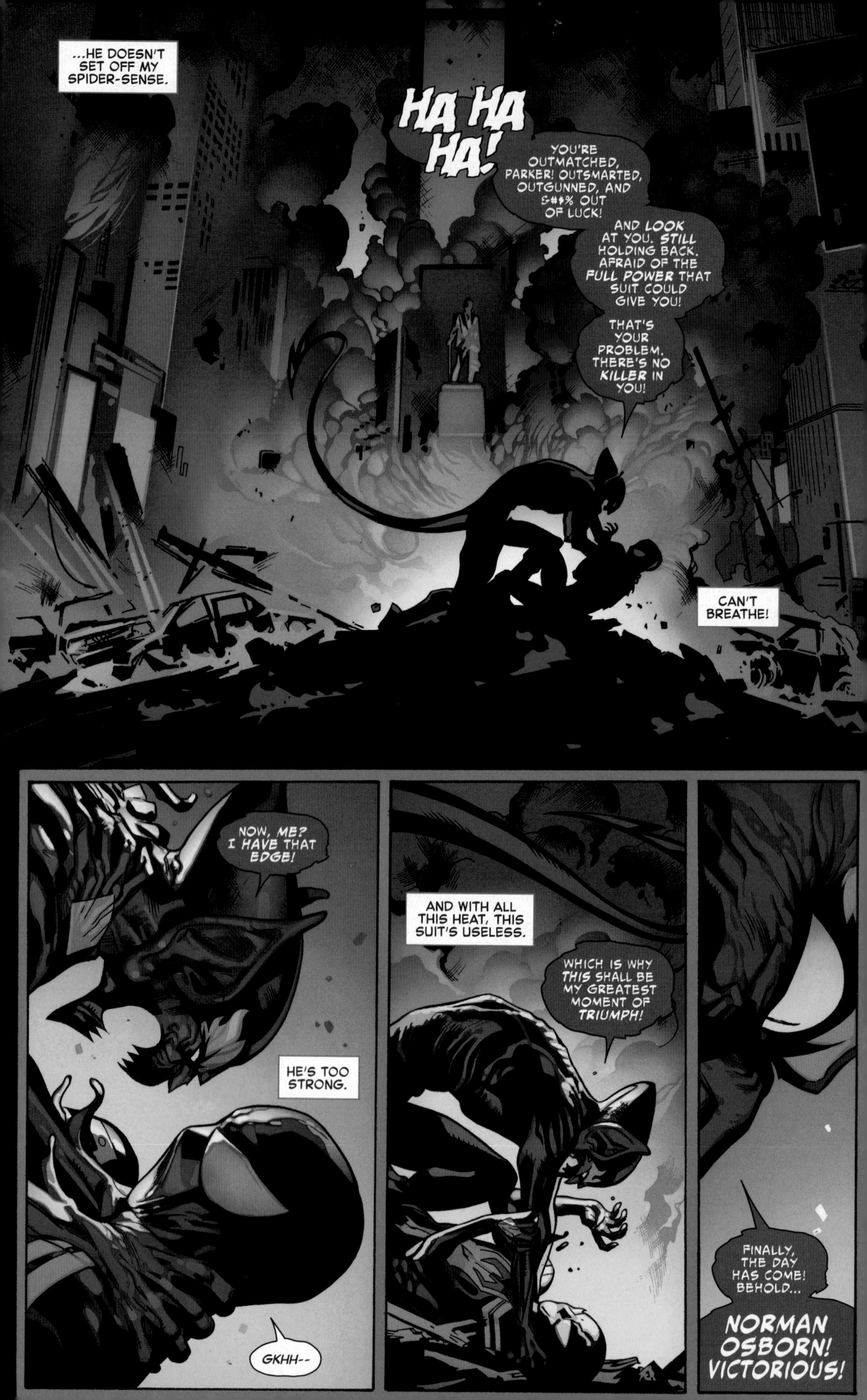
...HE DOESN'T SET OFF MY SPIDER-SENSE.
HA HA HA!
YOU'RE OUTMATCHED, PARKER! OUTSMARTED, OUTGUNNED, AND &#$% OUT OF LUCK!
AND LOOK AT YOU. STILL HOLDING BACK. AFRAID OF THE FULL POWER THAT SUIT COULD GIVE YOU!
THAT'S YOUR PROBLEM. THERE'S NO KILLER IN YOU!
CAN'T BREATHE!
NOW, ME? I HAVE THAT EDGE!
HE'S TOO STRONG.
GKHH--
AND WITH ALL THIS HEAT, THIS SUIT'S USELESS.
WHICH IS WHY THIS SHALL BE MY GREATEST MOMENT OF TRIUMPH!
FINALLY, THE DAY HAS COME! BEHOLD...
NORMAN OSBORN! VICTORIOUS!

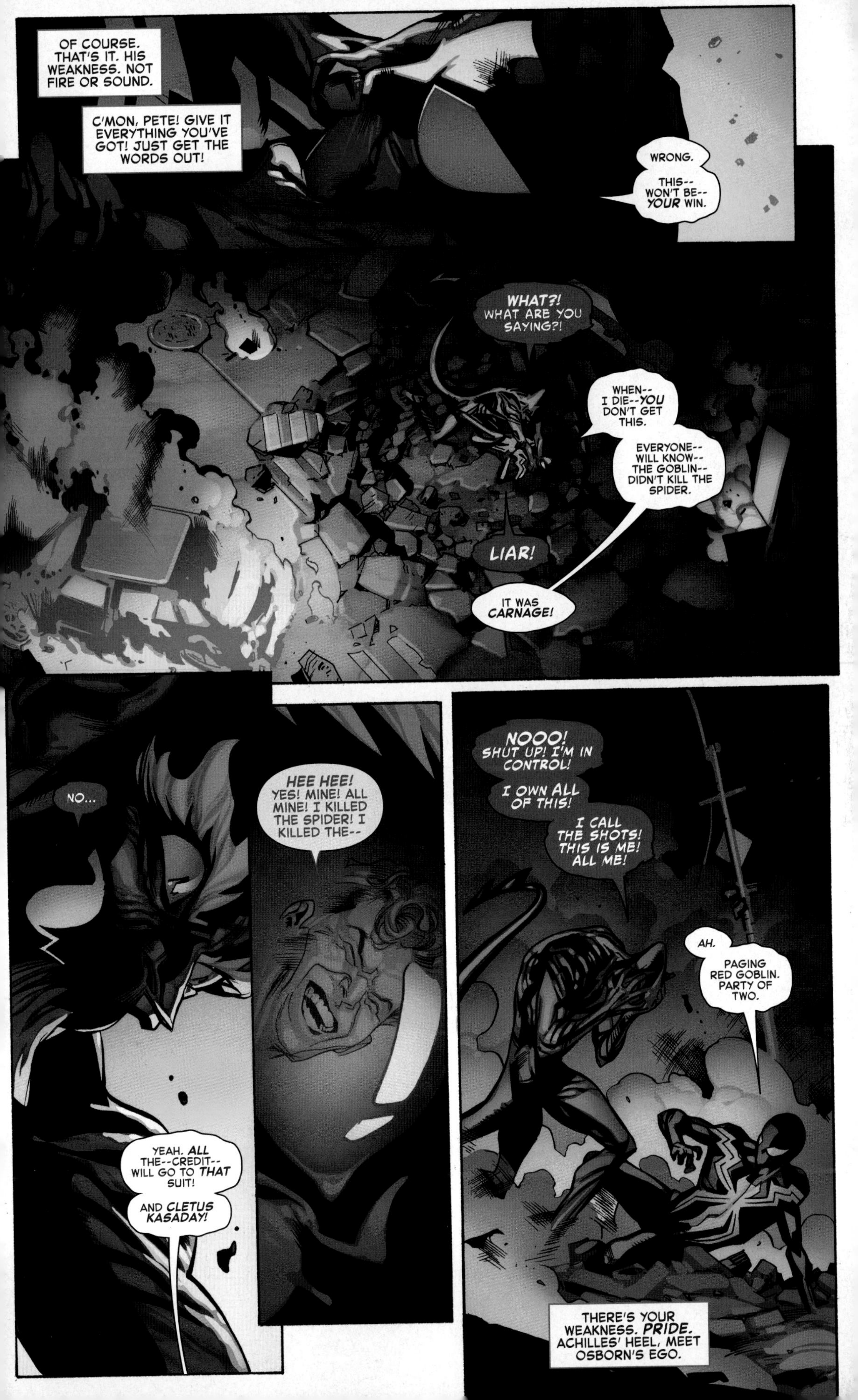

OF COURSE. THAT'S IT. HIS WEAKNESS. NOT FIRE OR SOUND.
C'MON, PETE! GIVE IT EVERYTHING YOU'VE GOT! JUST GET THE WORDS OUT!
WRONG.
THIS-- WON'T BE-- YOUR WIN.
WHAT?! WHAT ARE YOU SAYING?!
WHEN-- I DIE--YOU DON'T GET THIS.
EVERYONE-- WILL KNOW-- THE GOBLIN-- DIDN'T KILL THE SPIDER.
LIAR!
IT WAS CARNAGE!
NO...
YEAH. ALL THE--CREDIT-- WILL GO TO THAT SUIT!
AND CLETUS KASADAY!
HEE HEE! YES! MINE! ALL MINE! I KILLED THE SPIDER! I KILLED THE--
NOOO! SHUT UP! I'M IN CONTROL!
I OWN ALL OF THIS!
I CALL THE SHOTS! THIS IS ME! ALL ME!
AH.
PAGING RED GOBLIN. PARTY OF TWO.
THERE'S YOUR WEAKNESS. PRIDE. ACHILLES' HEEL, MEET OSBORN'S EGO.

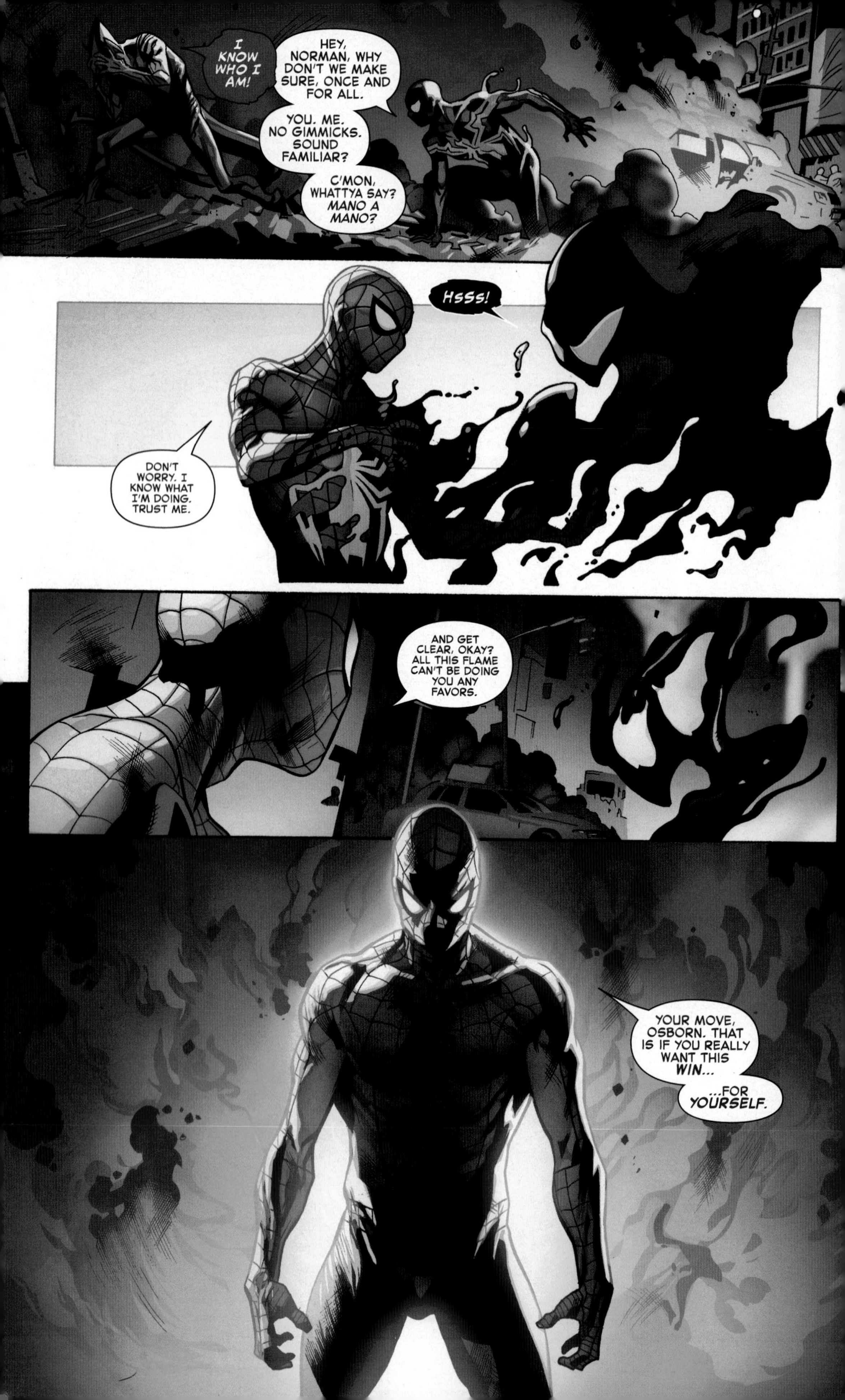
I KNOW WHO I AM!
HEY, NORMAN, WHY DON'T WE MAKE SURE, ONCE AND FOR ALL.
YOU. ME. NO GIMMICKS. SOUND FAMILIAR?
C'MON, WHATTYA SAY? MANO A MANO?
HSSS!
DON'T WORRY. I KNOW WHAT I'M DOING. TRUST ME.
AND GET CLEAR, OKAY? ALL THIS FLAME CAN'T BE DOING YOU ANY FAVORS.
YOUR MOVE, OSBORN. THAT IS IF YOU REALLY WANT THIS WIN...
...FOR YOURSELF.

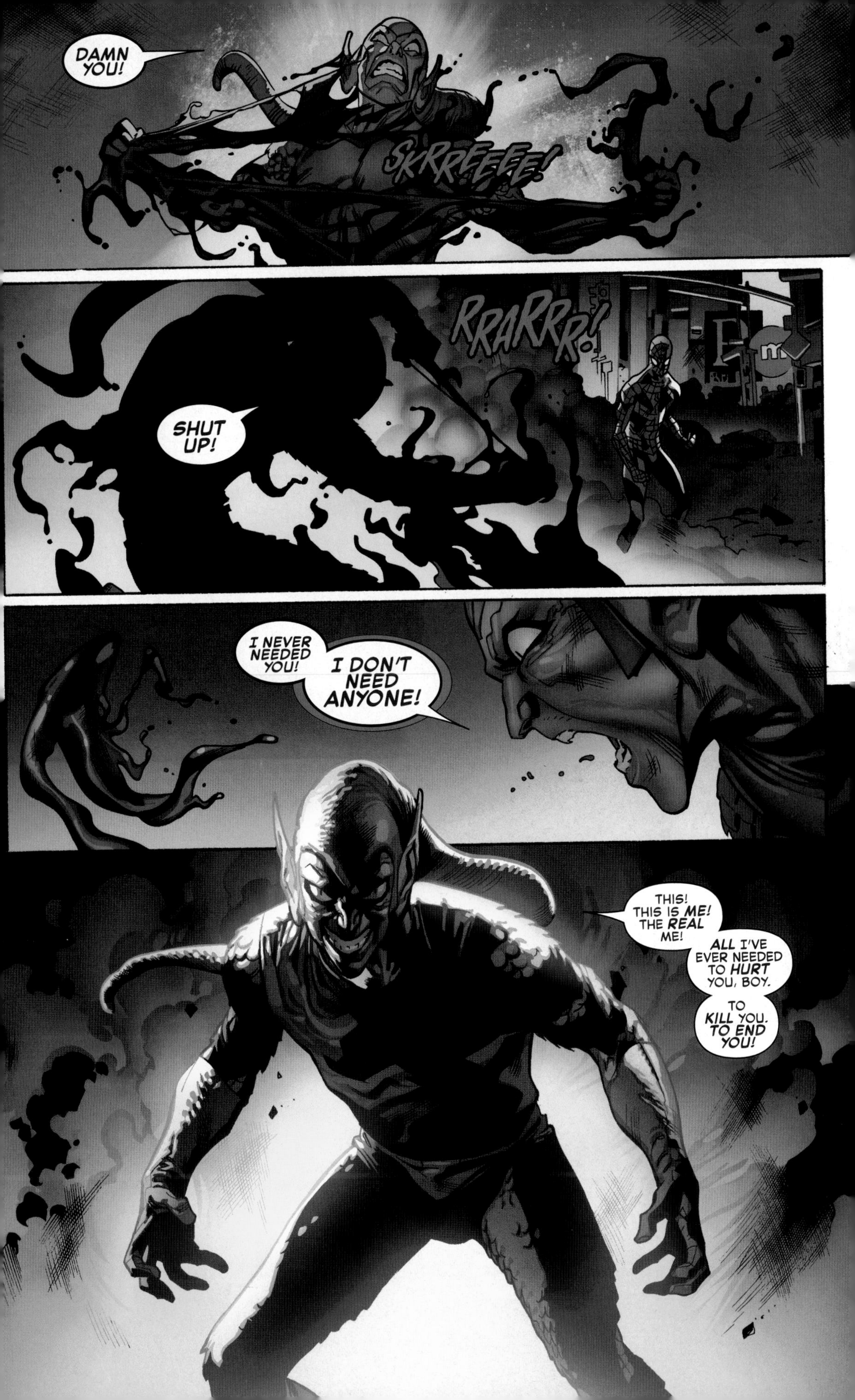
DAMN YOU!
SKRREEEEE!
RRARRRR!
SHUT UP!
I NEVER NEEDED YOU!
I DON'T NEED ANYONE!
THIS! THIS IS ME! THE REAL ME!
ALL I'VE EVER NEEDED TO HURT YOU, BOY.
TO KILL YOU. TO END YOU!

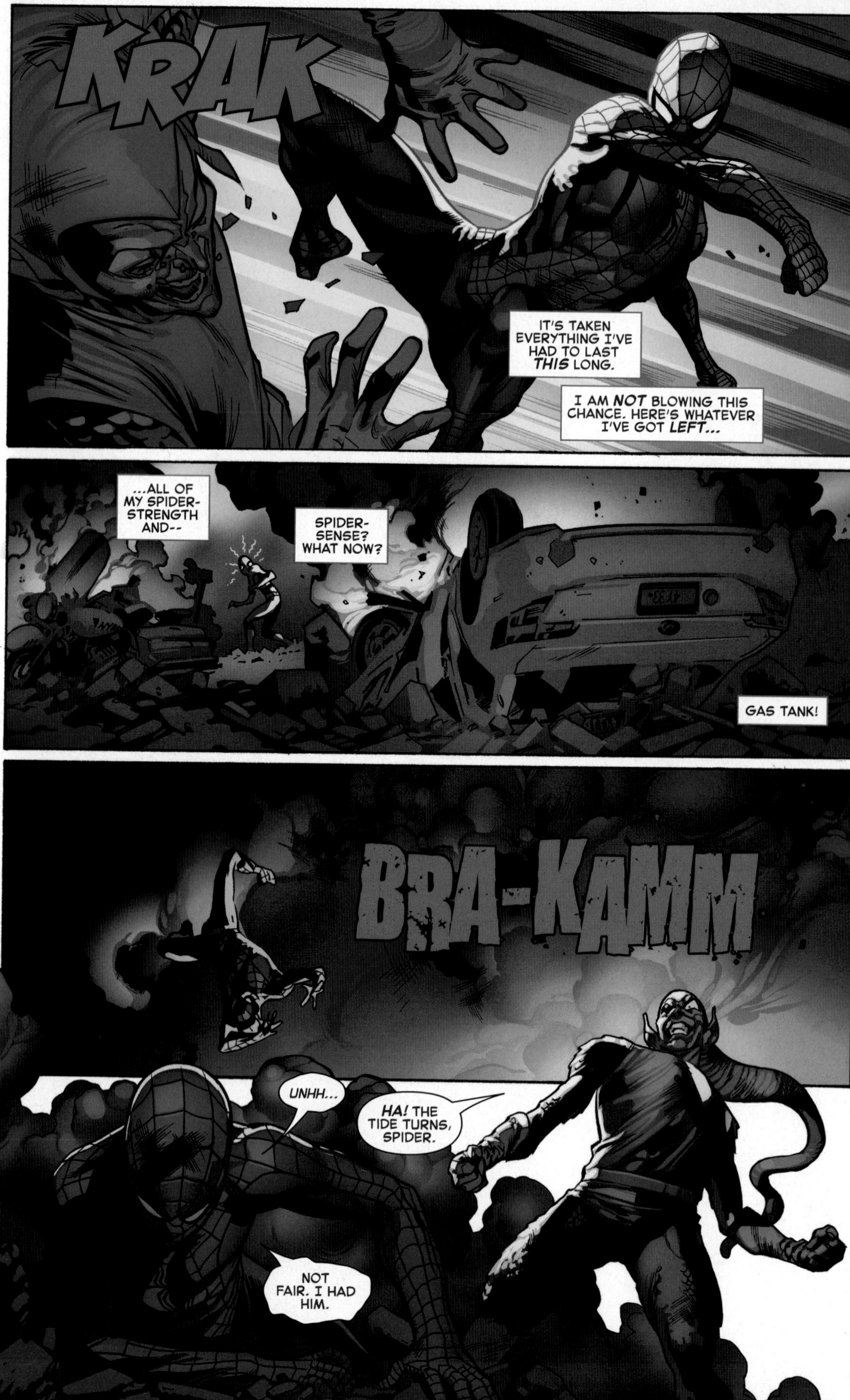
KRAK
IT'S TAKEN EVERYTHING I'VE HAD TO LAST THIS LONG.
I AM NOT BLOWING THIS CHANCE. HERE'S WHATEVER I'VE GOT LEFT...
...ALL OF MY SPIDER-STRENGTH AND--
SPIDER-SENSE? WHAT NOW?
GAS TANK!
BRA-KAMM
UNHH...
HA! THE TIDE TURNS, SPIDER.
NOT FAIR. I HAD HIM.

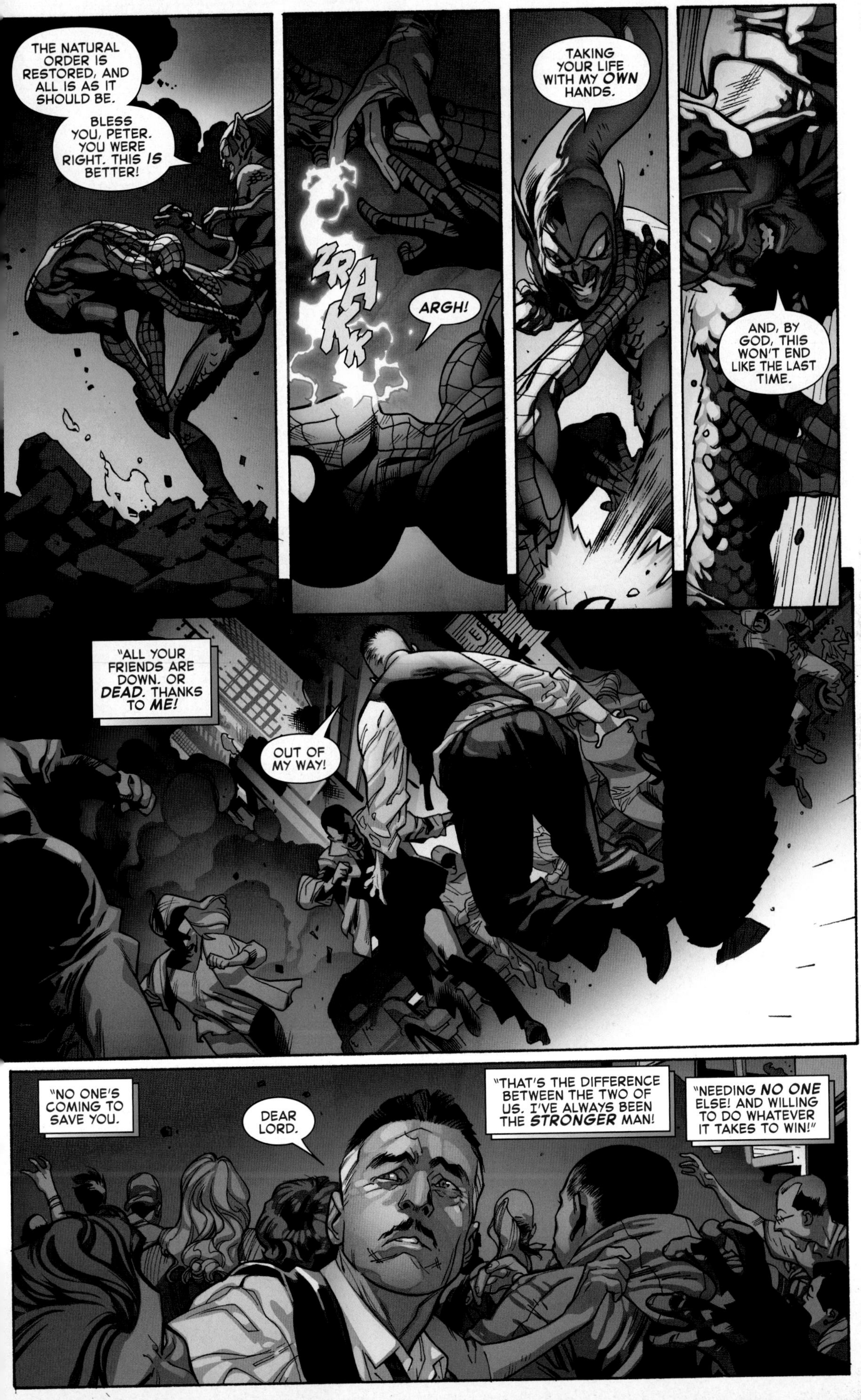

THE NATURAL ORDER IS RESTORED, AND ALL IS AS IT SHOULD BE.
BLESS YOU, PETER. YOU WERE RIGHT. THIS *IS* BETTER!
ZRAKKK
ARGH!
TAKING YOUR LIFE WITH MY *OWN* HANDS.
AND, BY GOD, THIS WON'T END LIKE THE LAST TIME.
"ALL YOUR FRIENDS ARE DOWN. OR *DEAD.* THANKS TO *ME!*
OUT OF MY WAY!
"NO ONE'S COMING TO SAVE YOU.
DEAR LORD.
"THAT'S THE DIFFERENCE BETWEEN THE TWO OF US. I'VE ALWAYS BEEN THE *STRONGER* MAN!
"NEEDING *NO ONE* ELSE! AND WILLING TO DO WHATEVER IT TAKES TO WIN!"

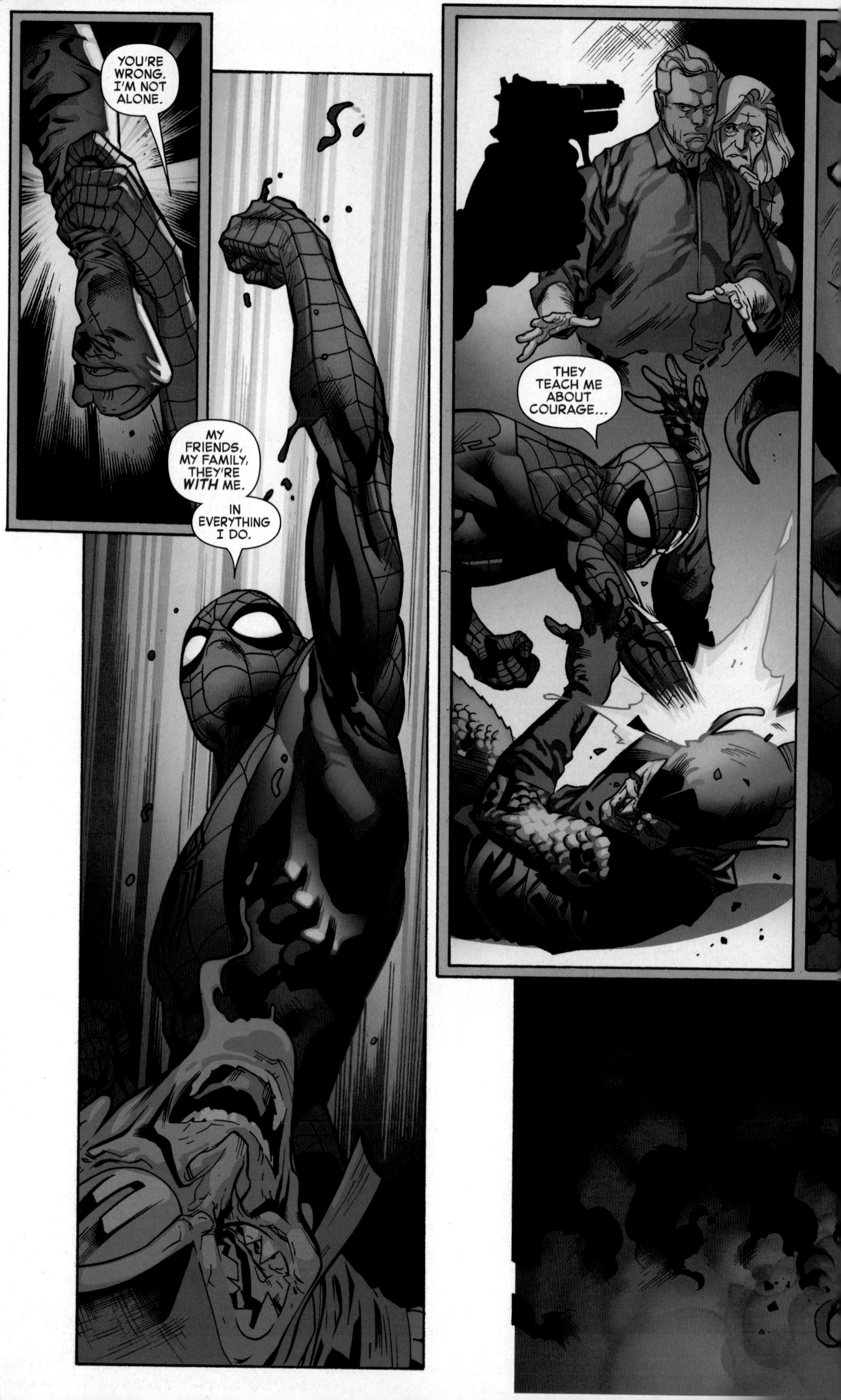
YOU'RE WRONG. I'M NOT ALONE.
MY FRIENDS, MY FAMILY, THEY'RE *WITH* ME.
IN EVERYTHING I DO.
THEY TEACH ME ABOUT COURAGE...

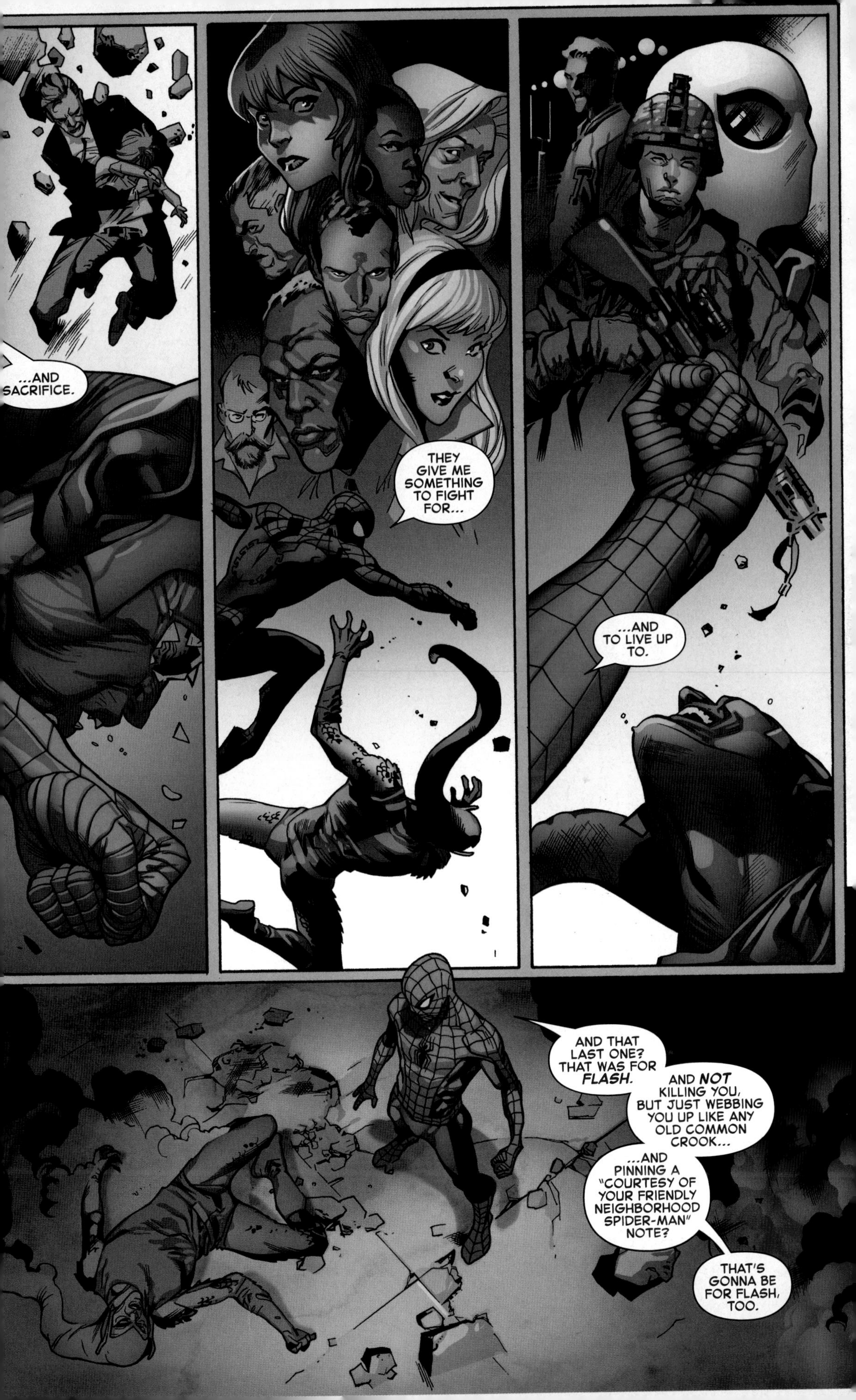
...AND SACRIFICE.
THEY GIVE ME SOMETHING TO FIGHT FOR...
...AND TO LIVE UP TO.
AND THAT LAST ONE? THAT WAS FOR *FLASH*.
AND *NOT* KILLING YOU, BUT JUST WEBBING YOU UP LIKE ANY OLD COMMON CROOK...
...AND PINNING A "COURTESY OF YOUR FRIENDLY NEIGHBORHOOD SPIDER-MAN" NOTE?
THAT'S GONNA BE FOR FLASH, TOO.

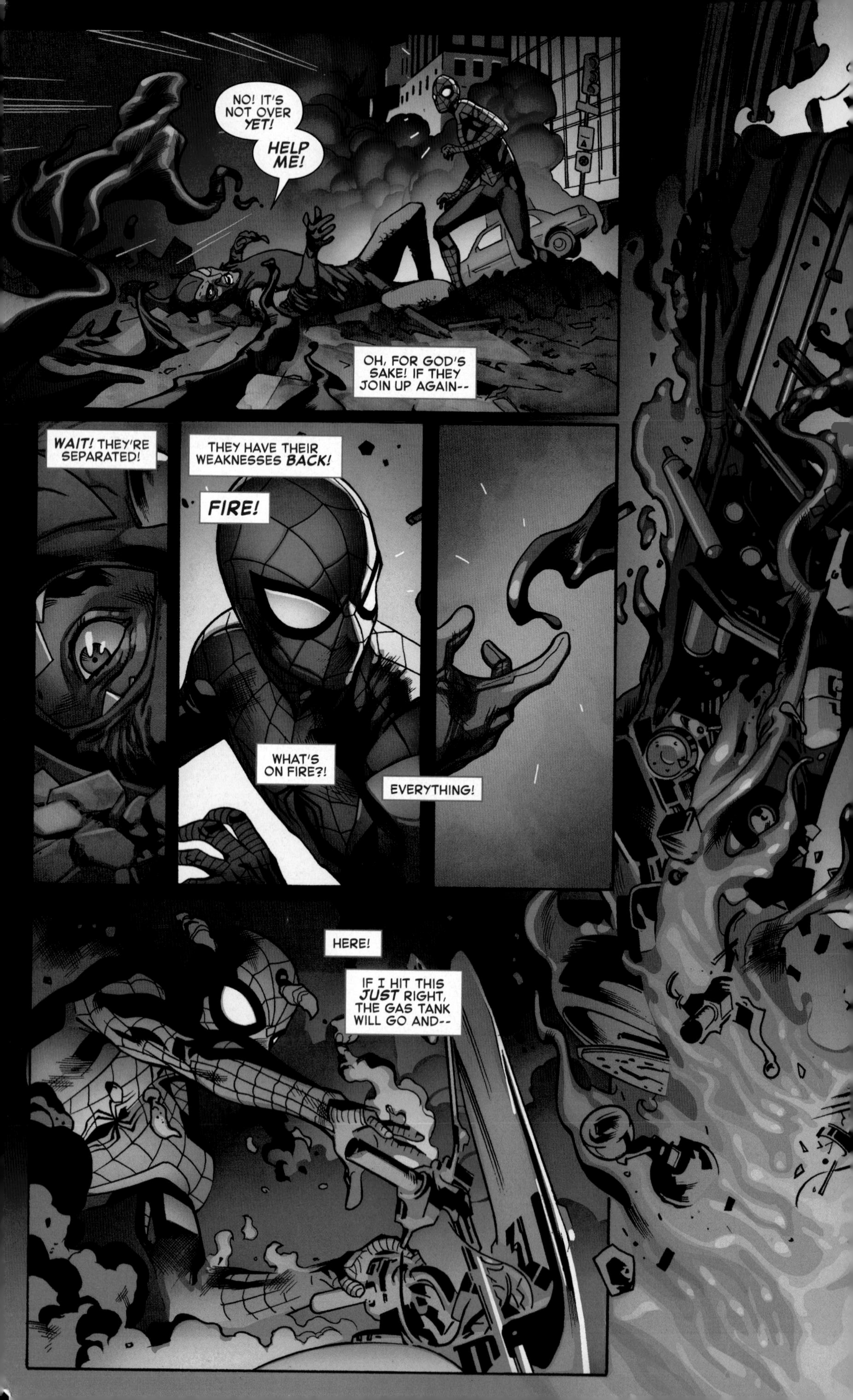
NO! IT'S NOT OVER YET!
HELP ME!
OH, FOR GOD'S SAKE! IF THEY JOIN UP AGAIN--
WAIT! THEY'RE SEPARATED!
THEY HAVE THEIR WEAKNESSES BACK!
FIRE!
WHAT'S ON FIRE?!
EVERYTHING!
HERE!
IF I HIT THIS JUST RIGHT, THE GAS TANK WILL GO AND--

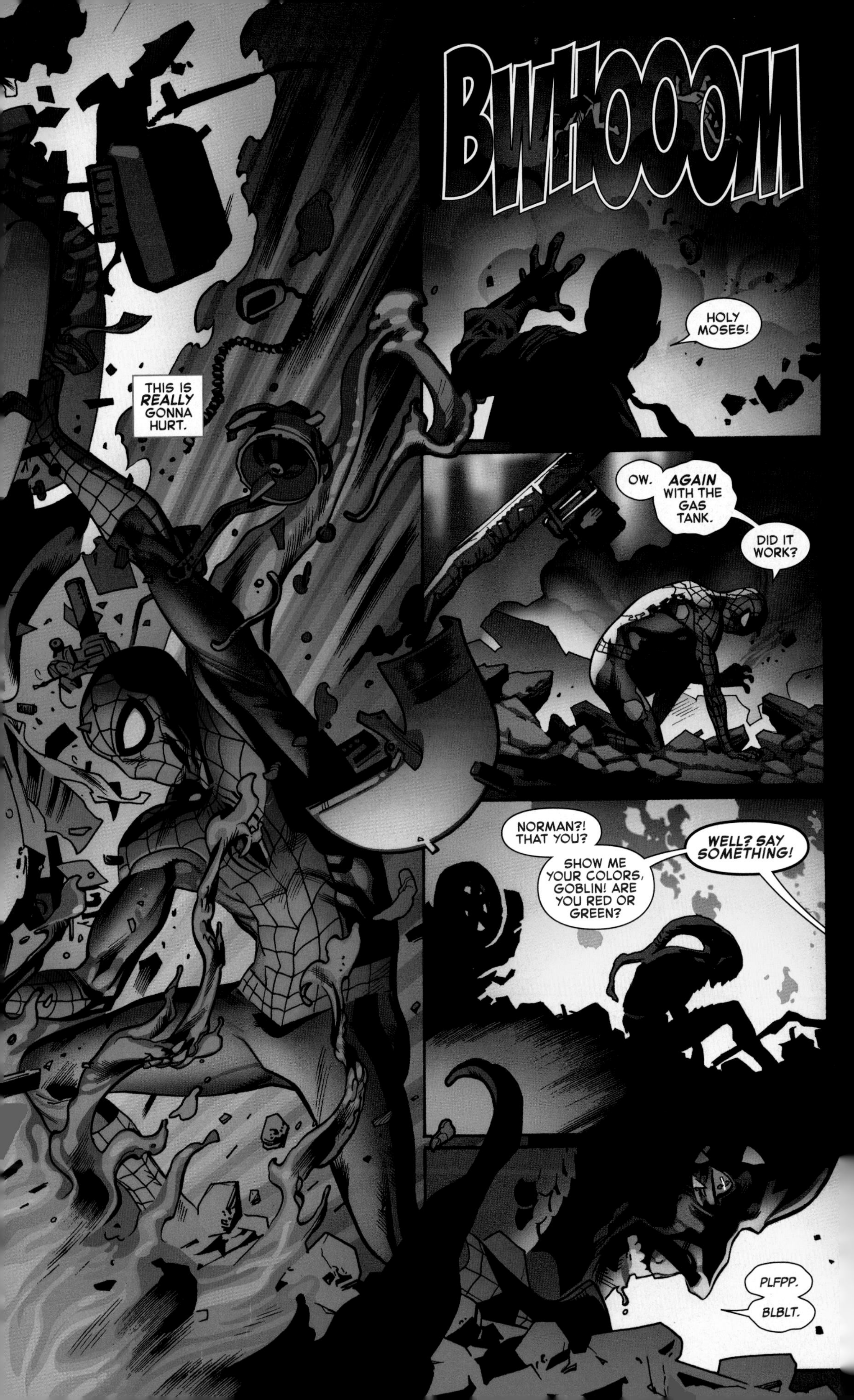
BWHOOOM
THIS IS REALLY GONNA HURT.
HOLY MOSES!
OW. AGAIN WITH THE GAS TANK.
DID IT WORK?
NORMAN?! THAT YOU?
SHOW ME YOUR COLORS, GOBLIN! ARE YOU RED OR GREEN?
WELL? SAY SOMETHING!
PLFPP.
BLBLT.

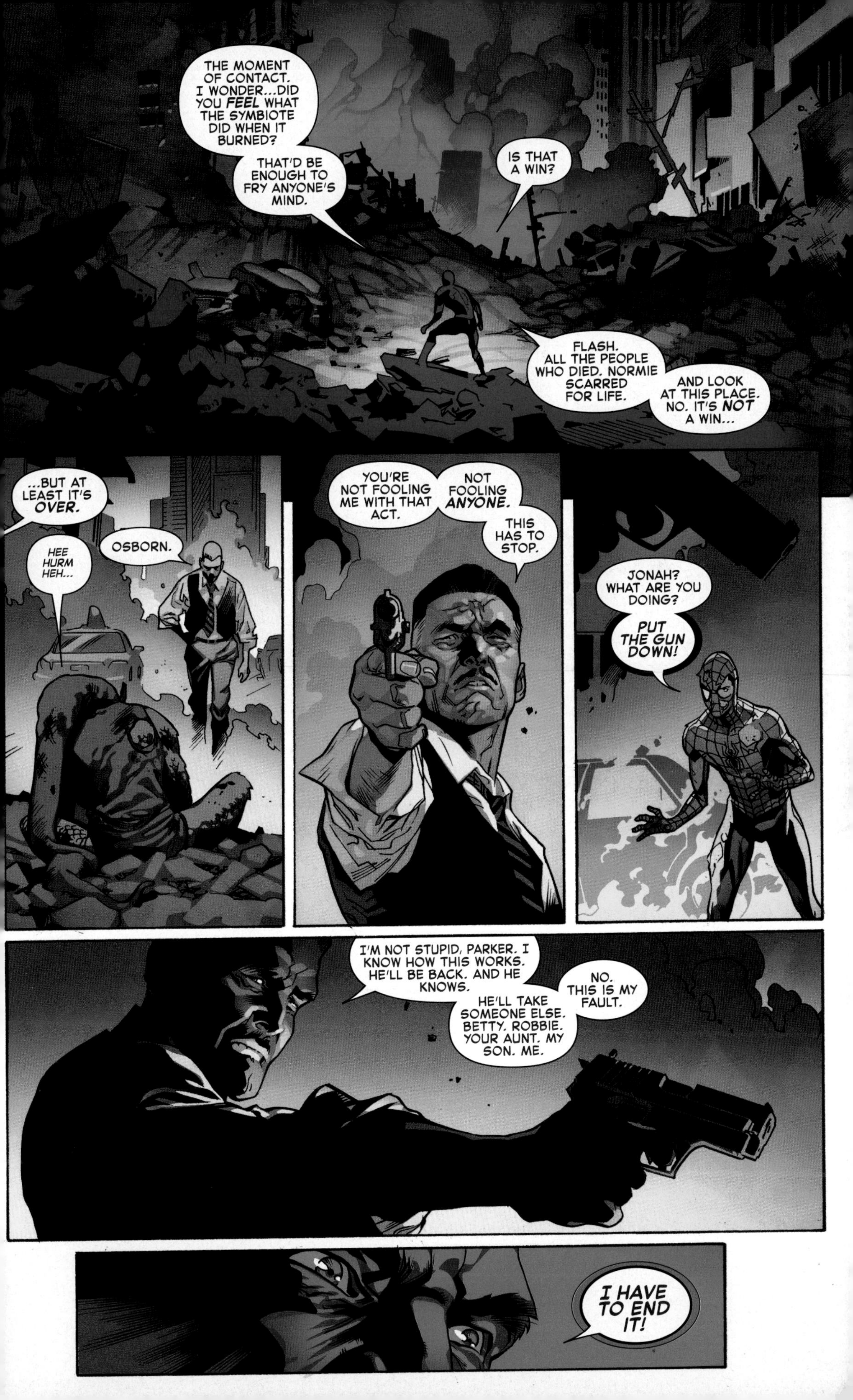
THE MOMENT OF CONTACT. I WONDER...DID YOU FEEL WHAT THE SYMBIOTE DID WHEN IT BURNED?
THAT'D BE ENOUGH TO FRY ANYONE'S MIND.
IS THAT A WIN?
FLASH. ALL THE PEOPLE WHO DIED. NORMIE SCARRED FOR LIFE.
AND LOOK AT THIS PLACE. NO. IT'S NOT A WIN...
...BUT AT LEAST IT'S OVER.
HEE HURM HEH...
OSBORN.
YOU'RE NOT FOOLING ME WITH THAT ACT.
NOT FOOLING ANYONE.
THIS HAS TO STOP.
JONAH? WHAT ARE YOU DOING?
PUT THE GUN DOWN!
I'M NOT STUPID, PARKER. I KNOW HOW THIS WORKS. HE'LL BE BACK. AND HE KNOWS.
HE'LL TAKE SOMEONE ELSE. BETTY. ROBBIE. YOUR AUNT. MY SON. ME.
NO. THIS IS MY FAULT.
I HAVE TO END IT!

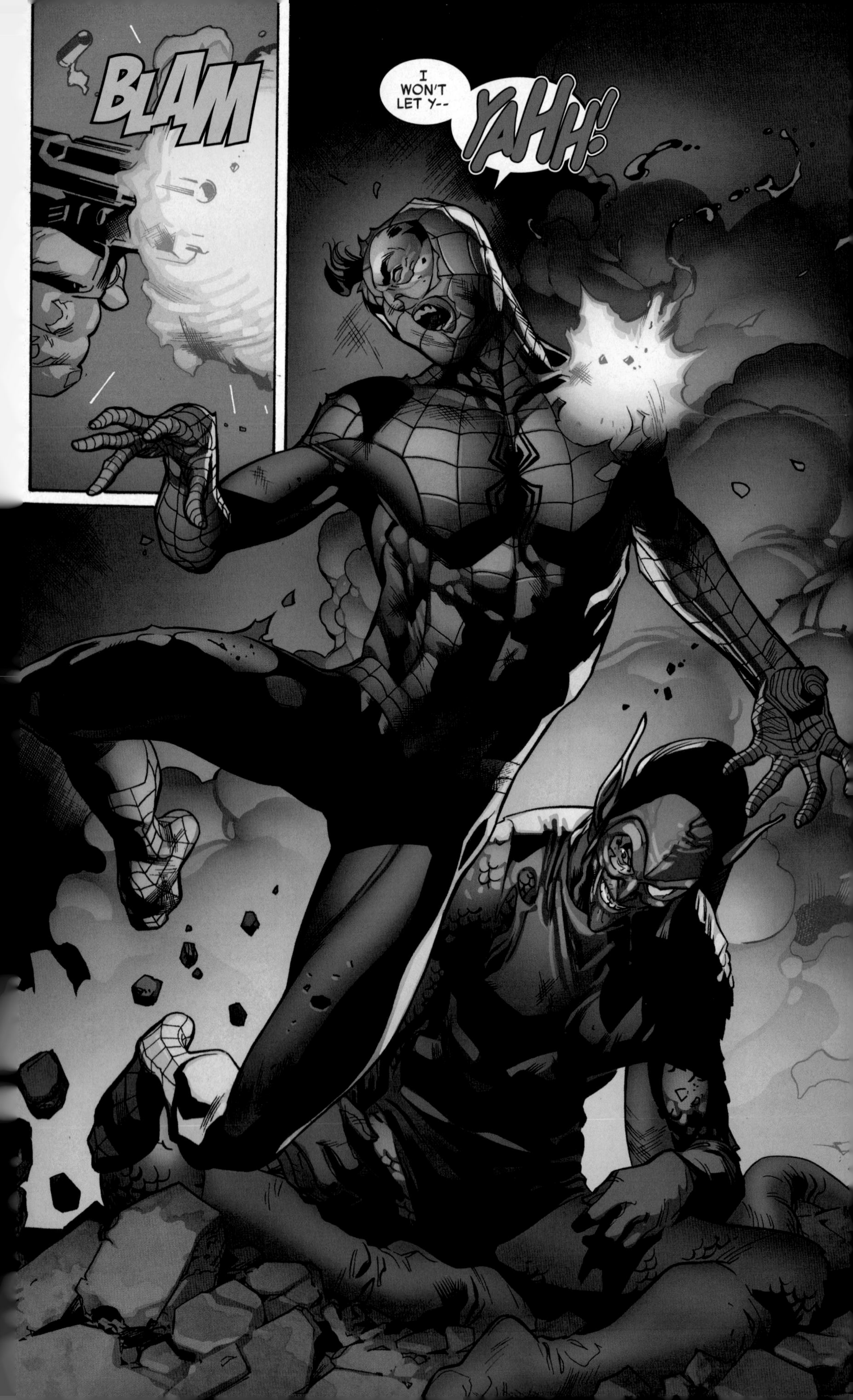
BLAM
I WON'T LET Y--
YAHH!

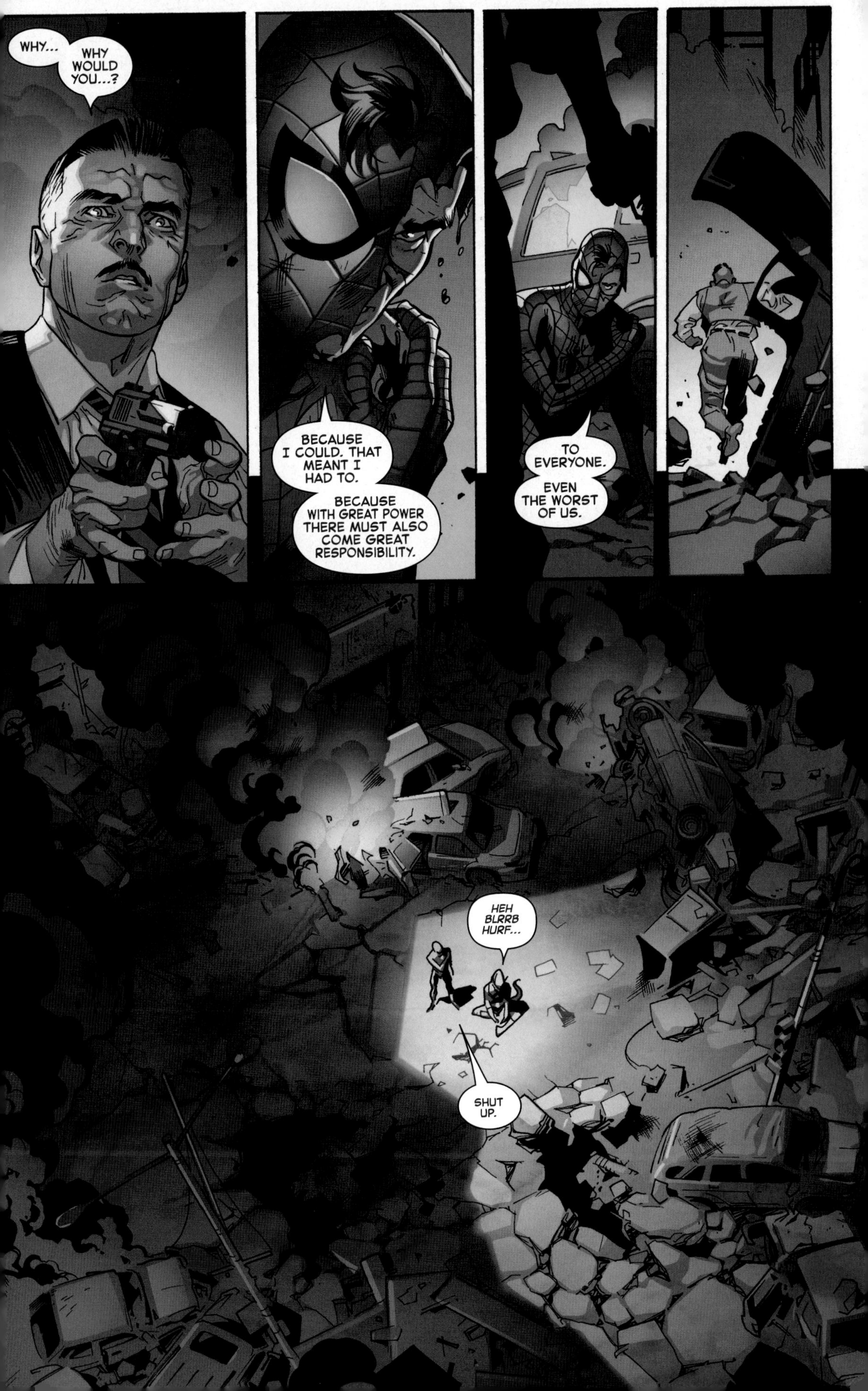
WHY...
WHY WOULD YOU...?
BECAUSE I COULD. THAT MEANT I HAD TO.
BECAUSE WITH GREAT POWER THERE MUST ALSO COME GREAT RESPONSIBILITY.
TO EVERYONE.
EVEN THE WORST OF US.
HEH BLRRB HURF...
SHUT UP.

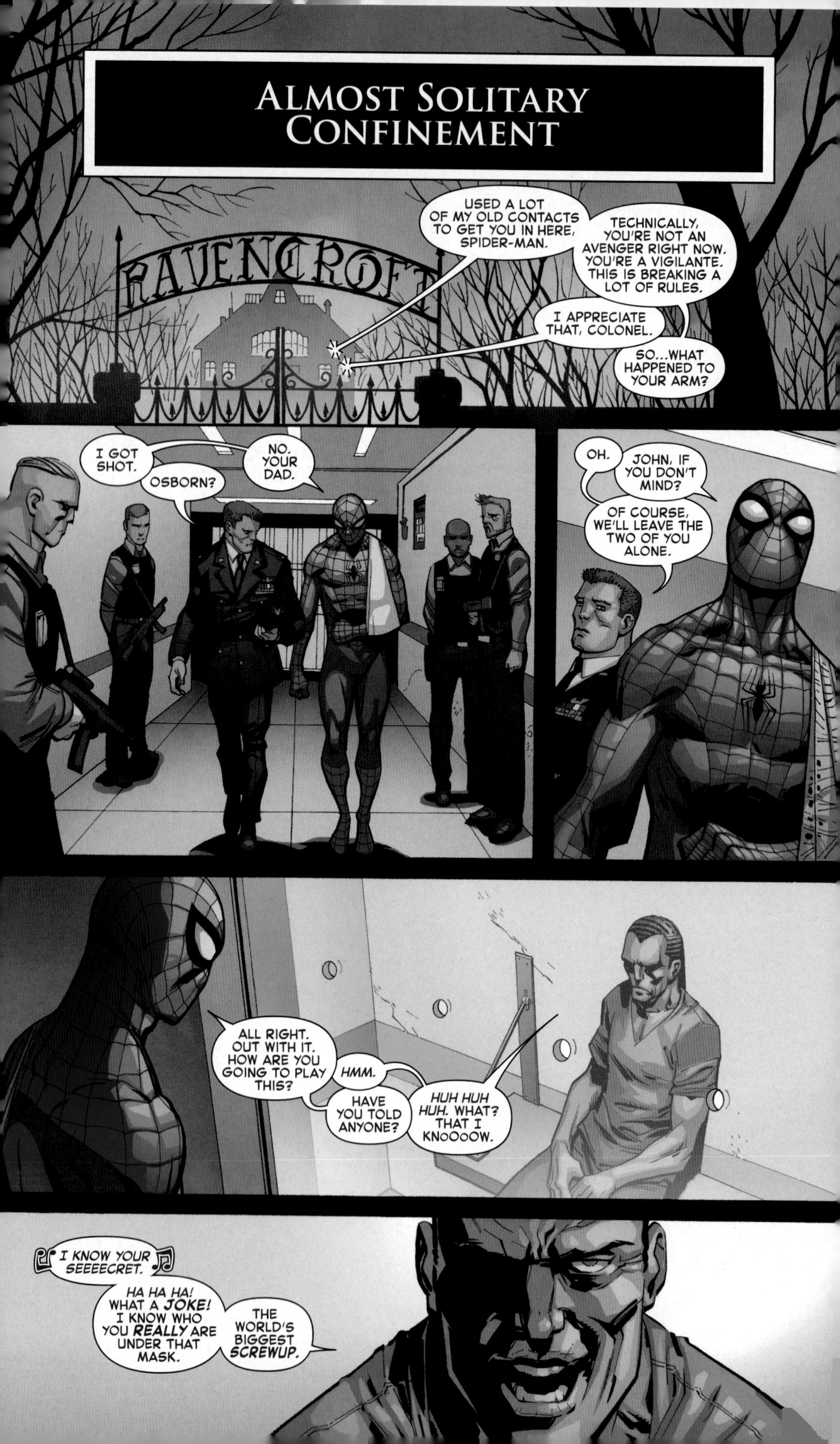
ALMOST SOLITARY CONFINEMENT
RAVENCROFT
USED A LOT OF MY OLD CONTACTS TO GET YOU IN HERE, SPIDER-MAN.
TECHNICALLY, YOU'RE NOT AN AVENGER RIGHT NOW. YOU'RE A VIGILANTE. THIS IS BREAKING A LOT OF RULES.
I APPRECIATE THAT, COLONEL.
SO...WHAT HAPPENED TO YOUR ARM?
I GOT SHOT.
OSBORN?
NO. YOUR DAD.
OH.
JOHN, IF YOU DON'T MIND?
OF COURSE, WE'LL LEAVE THE TWO OF YOU ALONE.
ALL RIGHT. OUT WITH IT. HOW ARE YOU GOING TO PLAY THIS?
HMM.
HAVE YOU TOLD ANYONE?
HUH HUH HUH. WHAT? THAT I KNOOOOW.
I KNOW YOUR SEEEECRET.
HA HA HA! WHAT A JOKE! I KNOW WHO YOU REALLY ARE UNDER THAT MASK.
THE WORLD'S BIGGEST SCREWUP.

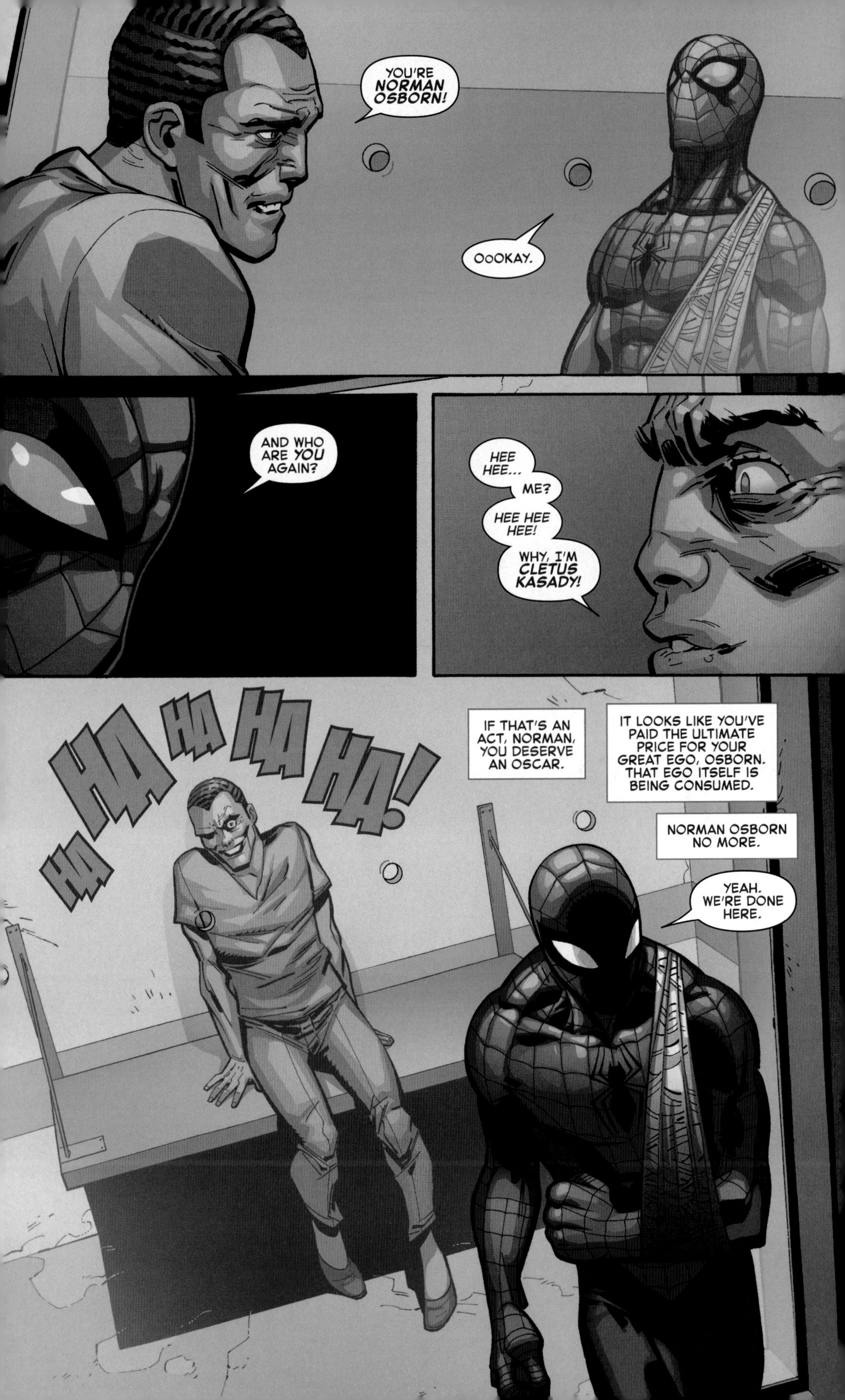
YOU'RE NORMAN OSBORN!
OOOKAY.
AND WHO ARE YOU AGAIN?
HEE HEE...
ME?
HEE HEE HEE!
WHY, I'M CLETUS KASADY!
HA HA HA HA HA HA!
IF THAT'S AN ACT, NORMAN, YOU DESERVE AN OSCAR.
IT LOOKS LIKE YOU'VE PAID THE ULTIMATE PRICE FOR YOUR GREAT EGO, OSBORN. THAT EGO ITSELF IS BEING CONSUMED.
NORMAN OSBORN NO MORE.
YEAH. WE'RE DONE HERE.

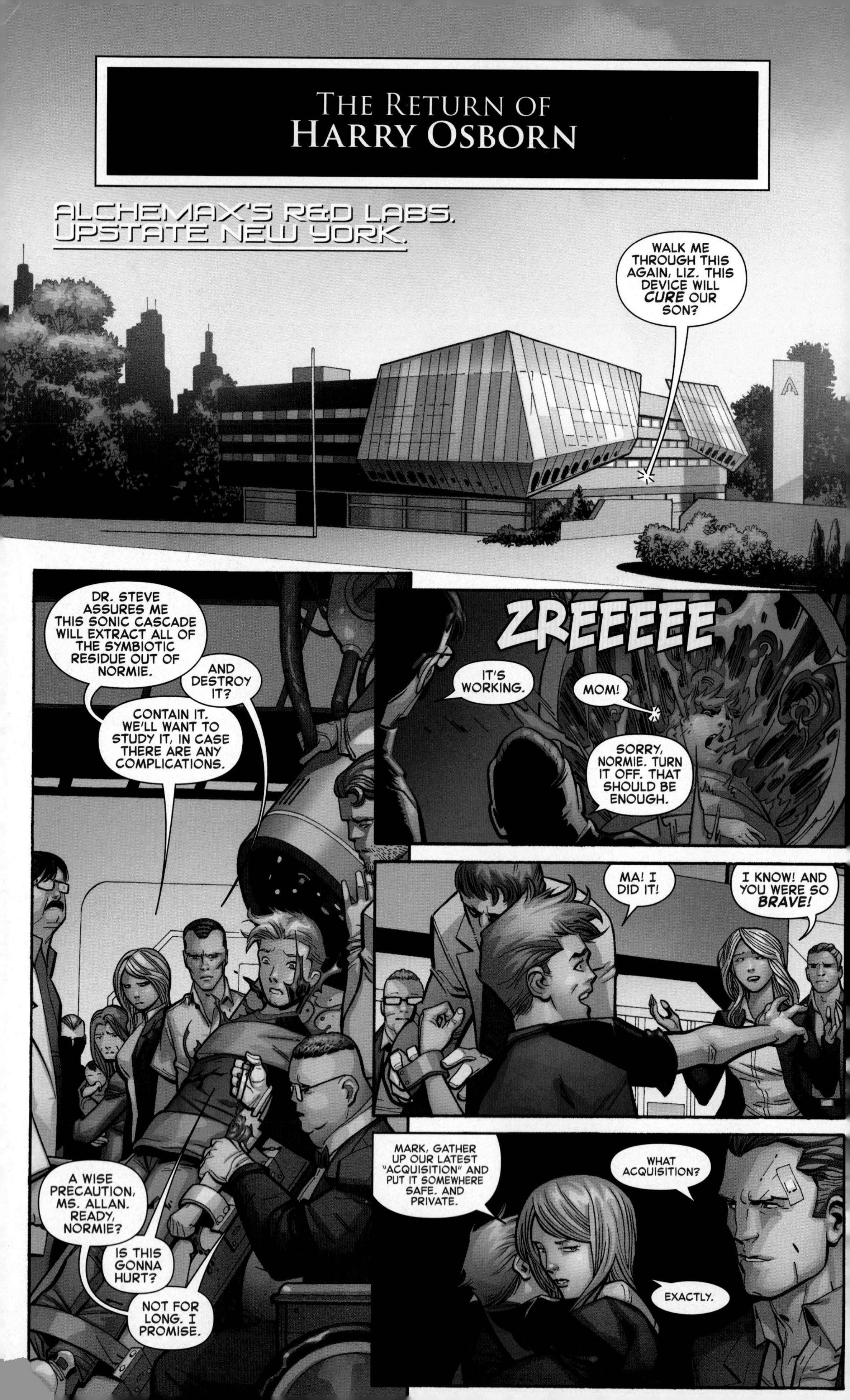
THE RETURN OF HARRY OSBORN
ALCHEMAX'S R&D LABS. UPSTATE NEW YORK.
WALK ME THROUGH THIS AGAIN, LIZ. THIS DEVICE WILL CURE OUR SON?
DR. STEVE ASSURES ME THIS SONIC CASCADE WILL EXTRACT ALL OF THE SYMBIOTIC RESIDUE OUT OF NORMIE.
AND DESTROY IT?
CONTAIN IT. WE'LL WANT TO STUDY IT, IN CASE THERE ARE ANY COMPLICATIONS.
A WISE PRECAUTION, MS. ALLAN. READY, NORMIE?
IS THIS GONNA HURT?
NOT FOR LONG. I PROMISE.
ZREEEEE
IT'S WORKING.
MOM!
SORRY, NORMIE. TURN IT OFF. THAT SHOULD BE ENOUGH.
MA! I DID IT!
I KNOW! AND YOU WERE SO BRAVE!
MARK, GATHER UP OUR LATEST "ACQUISITION" AND PUT IT SOMEWHERE SAFE. AND PRIVATE.
WHAT ACQUISITION?
EXACTLY.

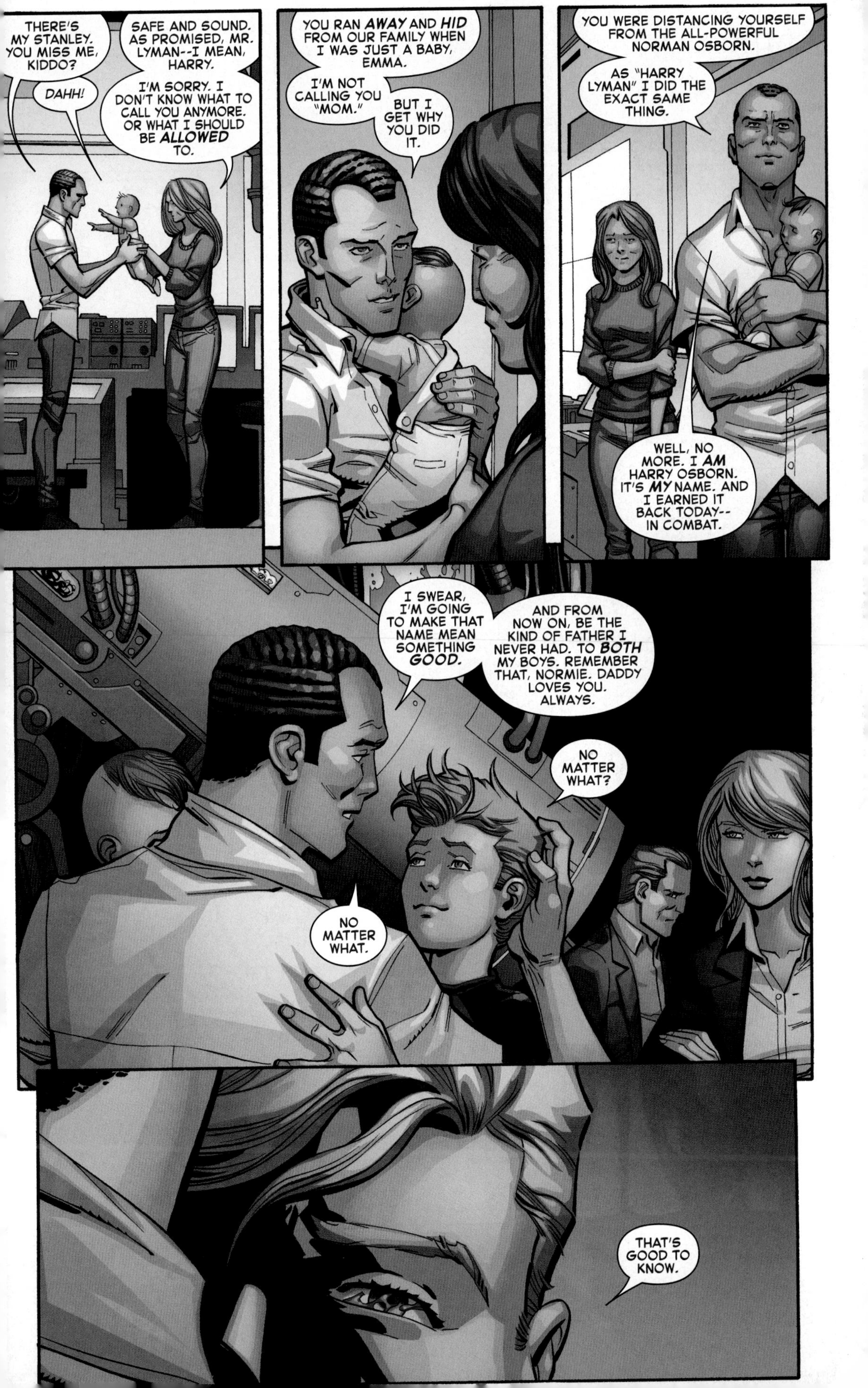
THERE'S MY STANLEY. YOU MISS ME, KIDDO?
DAHH!
SAFE AND SOUND. AS PROMISED, MR. LYMAN--I MEAN, HARRY.
I'M SORRY. I DON'T KNOW WHAT TO CALL YOU ANYMORE. OR WHAT I SHOULD BE ALLOWED TO.
YOU RAN AWAY AND HID FROM OUR FAMILY WHEN I WAS JUST A BABY, EMMA.
I'M NOT CALLING YOU "MOM."
BUT I GET WHY YOU DID IT.
YOU WERE DISTANCING YOURSELF FROM THE ALL-POWERFUL NORMAN OSBORN.
AS "HARRY LYMAN" I DID THE EXACT SAME THING.
WELL, NO MORE. I AM HARRY OSBORN. IT'S MY NAME. AND I EARNED IT BACK TODAY-- IN COMBAT.
I SWEAR, I'M GOING TO MAKE THAT NAME MEAN SOMETHING GOOD.
AND FROM NOW ON, BE THE KIND OF FATHER I NEVER HAD. TO BOTH MY BOYS. REMEMBER THAT, NORMIE. DADDY LOVES YOU. ALWAYS.
NO MATTER WHAT?
NO MATTER WHAT.
THAT'S GOOD TO KNOW.

GOODBYE

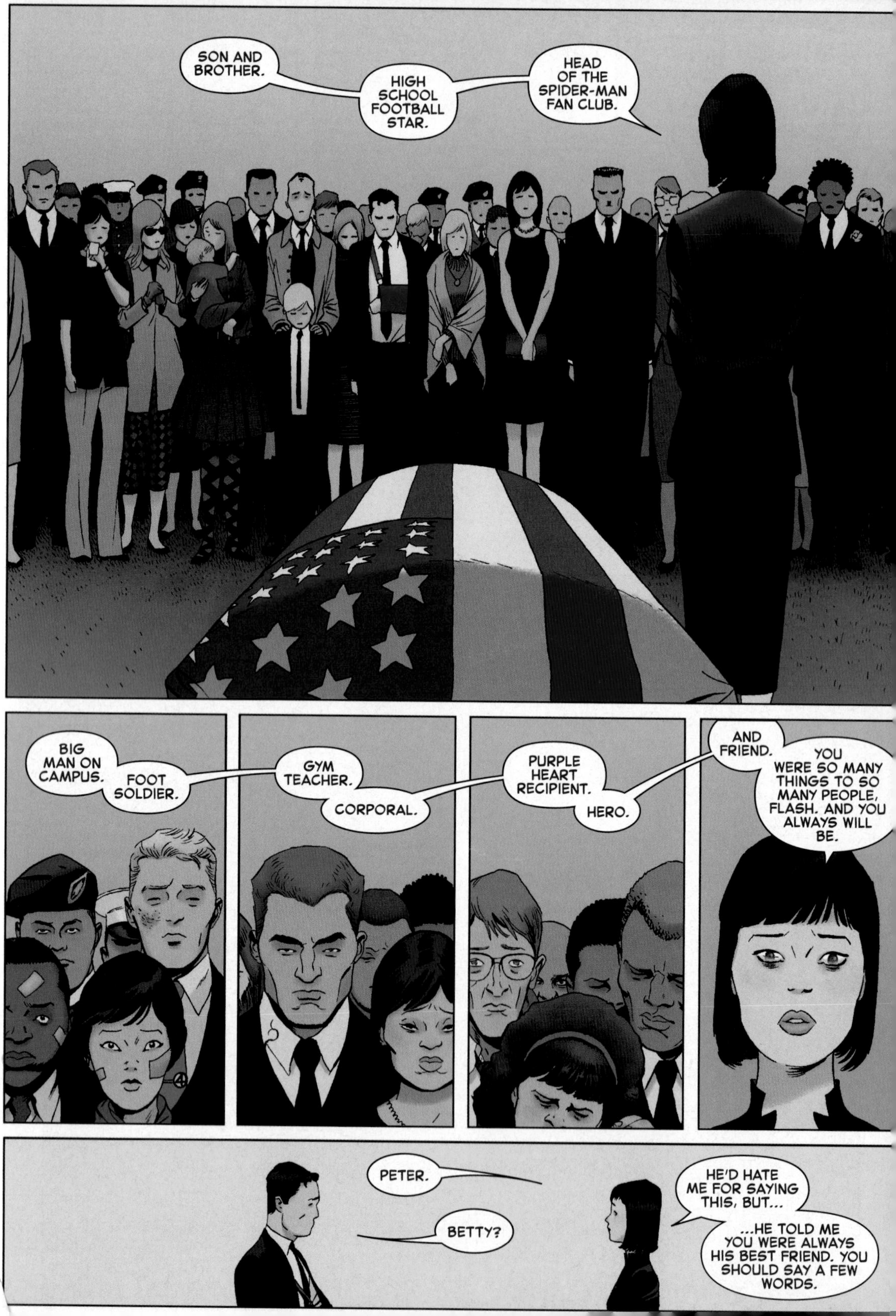
SON AND BROTHER.
HIGH SCHOOL FOOTBALL STAR.
HEAD OF THE SPIDER-MAN FAN CLUB.
BIG MAN ON CAMPUS.
FOOT SOLDIER.
GYM TEACHER.
CORPORAL.
PURPLE HEART RECIPIENT.
HERO.
AND FRIEND.
YOU WERE SO MANY THINGS TO SO MANY PEOPLE, FLASH. AND YOU ALWAYS WILL BE.
PETER.
BETTY?
HE'D HATE ME FOR SAYING THIS, BUT...
...HE TOLD ME YOU WERE ALWAYS HIS BEST FRIEND. YOU SHOULD SAY A FEW WORDS.

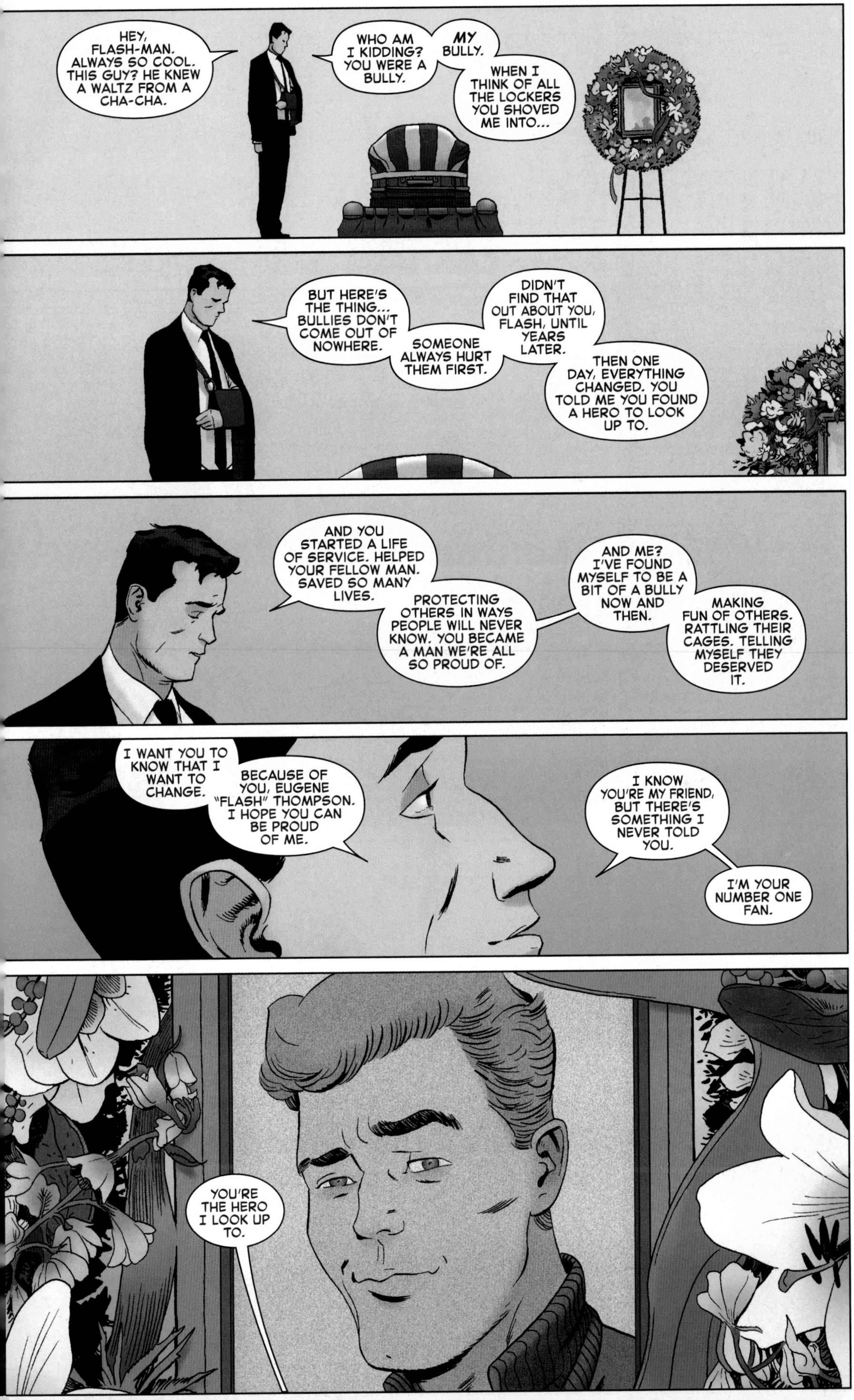
HEY, FLASH-MAN. ALWAYS SO COOL. THIS GUY? HE KNEW A WALTZ FROM A CHA-CHA.
WHO AM I KIDDING? YOU WERE A BULLY.
MY BULLY.
WHEN I THINK OF ALL THE LOCKERS YOU SHOVED ME INTO...
BUT HERE'S THE THING... BULLIES DON'T COME OUT OF NOWHERE.
SOMEONE ALWAYS HURT THEM FIRST.
DIDN'T FIND THAT OUT ABOUT YOU, FLASH, UNTIL YEARS LATER.
THEN ONE DAY, EVERYTHING CHANGED. YOU TOLD ME YOU FOUND A HERO TO LOOK UP TO.
AND YOU STARTED A LIFE OF SERVICE. HELPED YOUR FELLOW MAN. SAVED SO MANY LIVES.
PROTECTING OTHERS IN WAYS PEOPLE WILL NEVER KNOW. YOU BECAME A MAN WE'RE ALL SO PROUD OF.
AND ME? I'VE FOUND MYSELF TO BE A BIT OF A BULLY NOW AND THEN.
MAKING FUN OF OTHERS. RATTLING THEIR CAGES. TELLING MYSELF THEY DESERVED IT.
I WANT YOU TO KNOW THAT I WANT TO CHANGE.
BECAUSE OF YOU, EUGENE "FLASH" THOMPSON. I HOPE YOU CAN BE PROUD OF ME.
I KNOW YOU'RE MY FRIEND, BUT THERE'S SOMETHING I NEVER TOLD YOU.
I'M YOUR NUMBER ONE FAN.
YOU'RE THE HERO I LOOK UP TO.

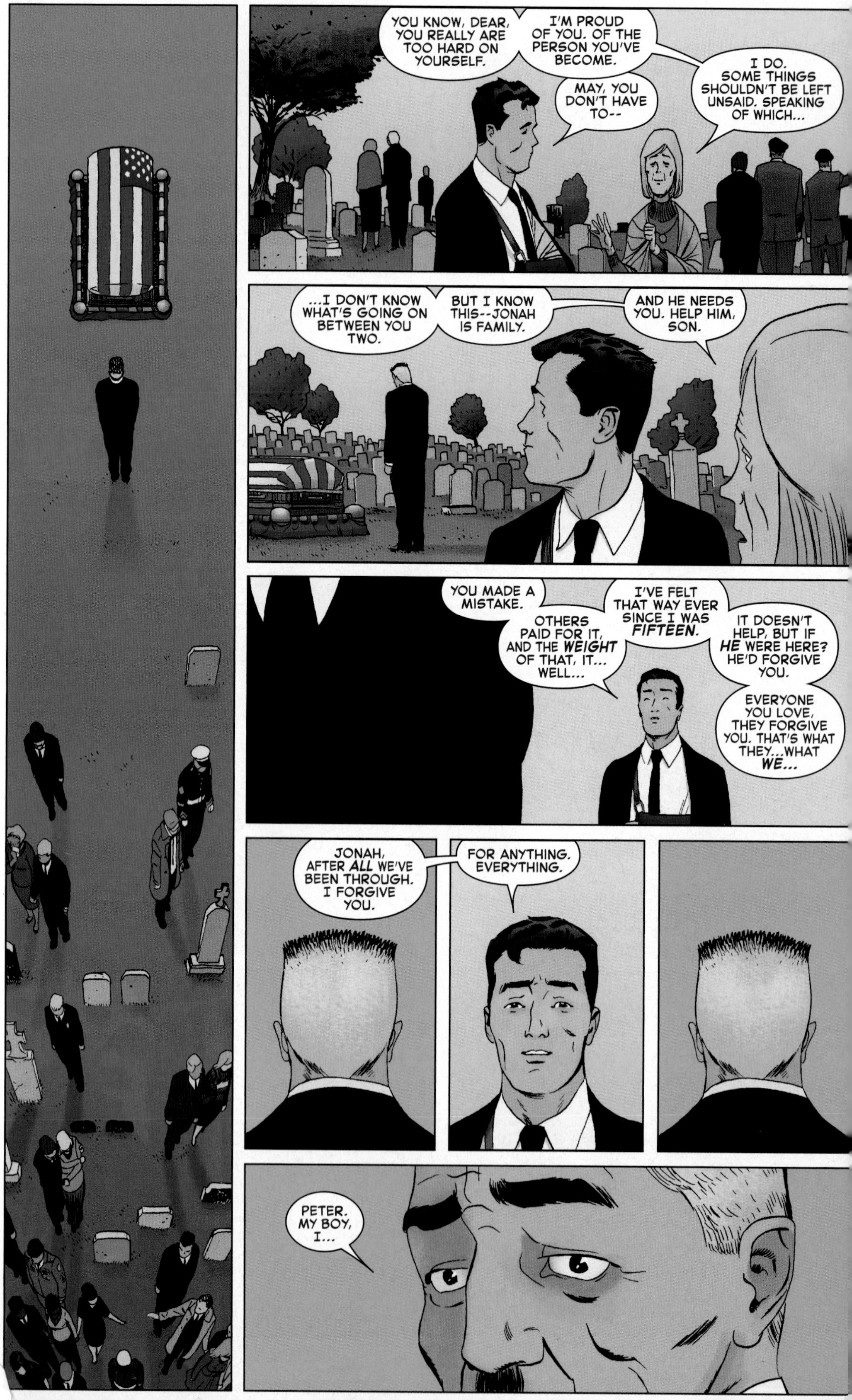
YOU KNOW, DEAR, YOU REALLY ARE TOO HARD ON YOURSELF.
I'M PROUD OF YOU. OF THE PERSON YOU'VE BECOME.
MAY, YOU DON'T HAVE TO--
I DO. SOME THINGS SHOULDN'T BE LEFT UNSAID. SPEAKING OF WHICH...
...I DON'T KNOW WHAT'S GOING ON BETWEEN YOU TWO.
BUT I KNOW THIS--JONAH IS FAMILY.
AND HE NEEDS YOU. HELP HIM, SON.
YOU MADE A MISTAKE.
OTHERS PAID FOR IT, AND THE *WEIGHT* OF THAT, IT... WELL...
I'VE FELT THAT WAY EVER SINCE I WAS *FIFTEEN.*
IT DOESN'T HELP, BUT IF *HE* WERE HERE? HE'D FORGIVE YOU.
EVERYONE YOU LOVE, THEY FORGIVE YOU. THAT'S WHAT THEY...WHAT *WE...*
JONAH, AFTER *ALL* WE'VE BEEN THROUGH. I FORGIVE YOU.
FOR ANYTHING. EVERYTHING.
PETER. MY BOY, I...

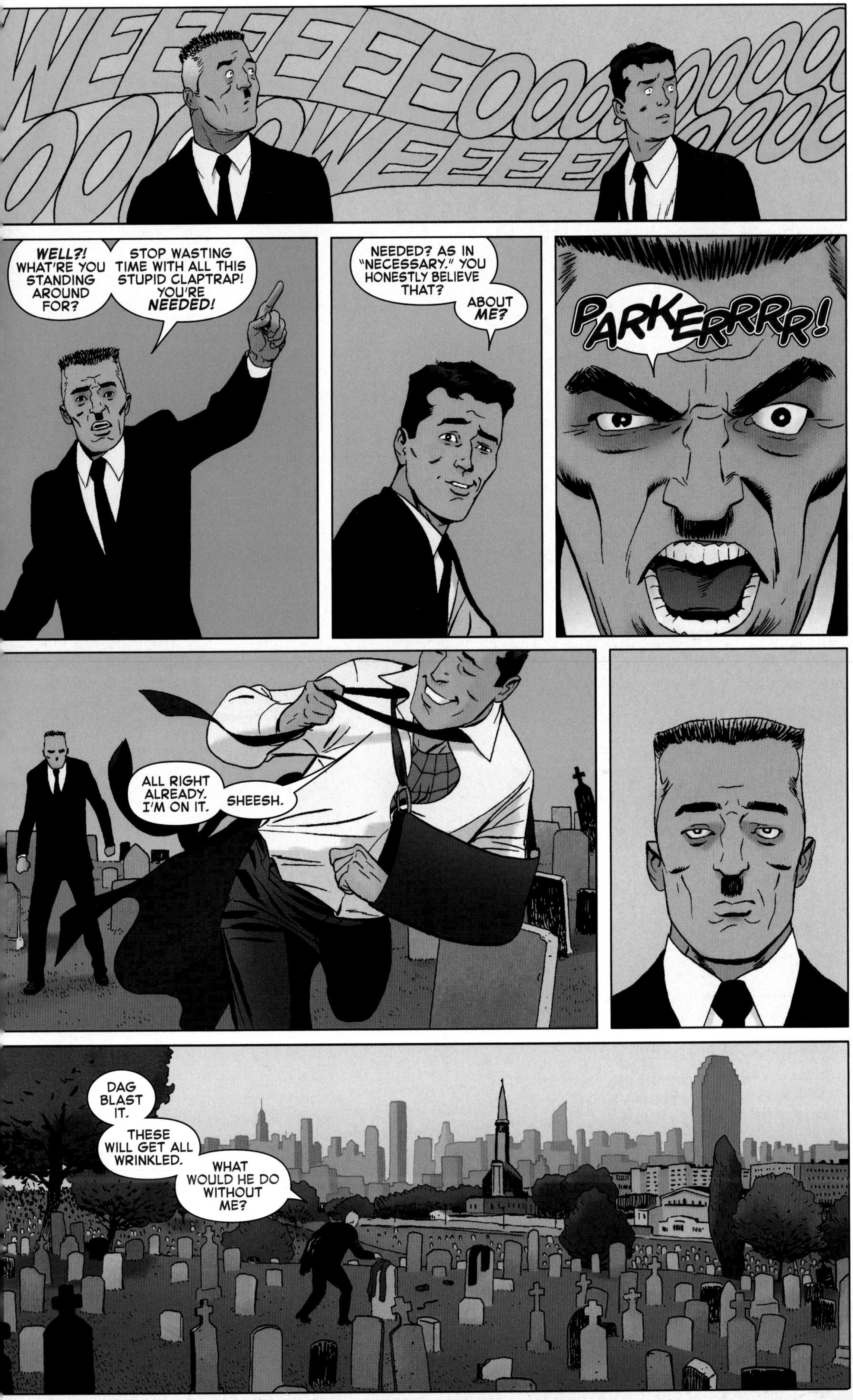
WEEEEEEOooooooooo
OOOOOWEEEEEE
WELL?! WHAT'RE YOU STANDING AROUND FOR?
STOP WASTING TIME WITH ALL THIS STUPID CLAPTRAP! YOU'RE NEEDED!
NEEDED? AS IN "NECESSARY." YOU HONESTLY BELIEVE THAT?
ABOUT ME?
PARKERRRR!
ALL RIGHT ALREADY. I'M ON IT.
SHEESH.
DAG BLAST IT.
THESE WILL GET ALL WRINKLED.
WHAT WOULD HE DO WITHOUT ME?

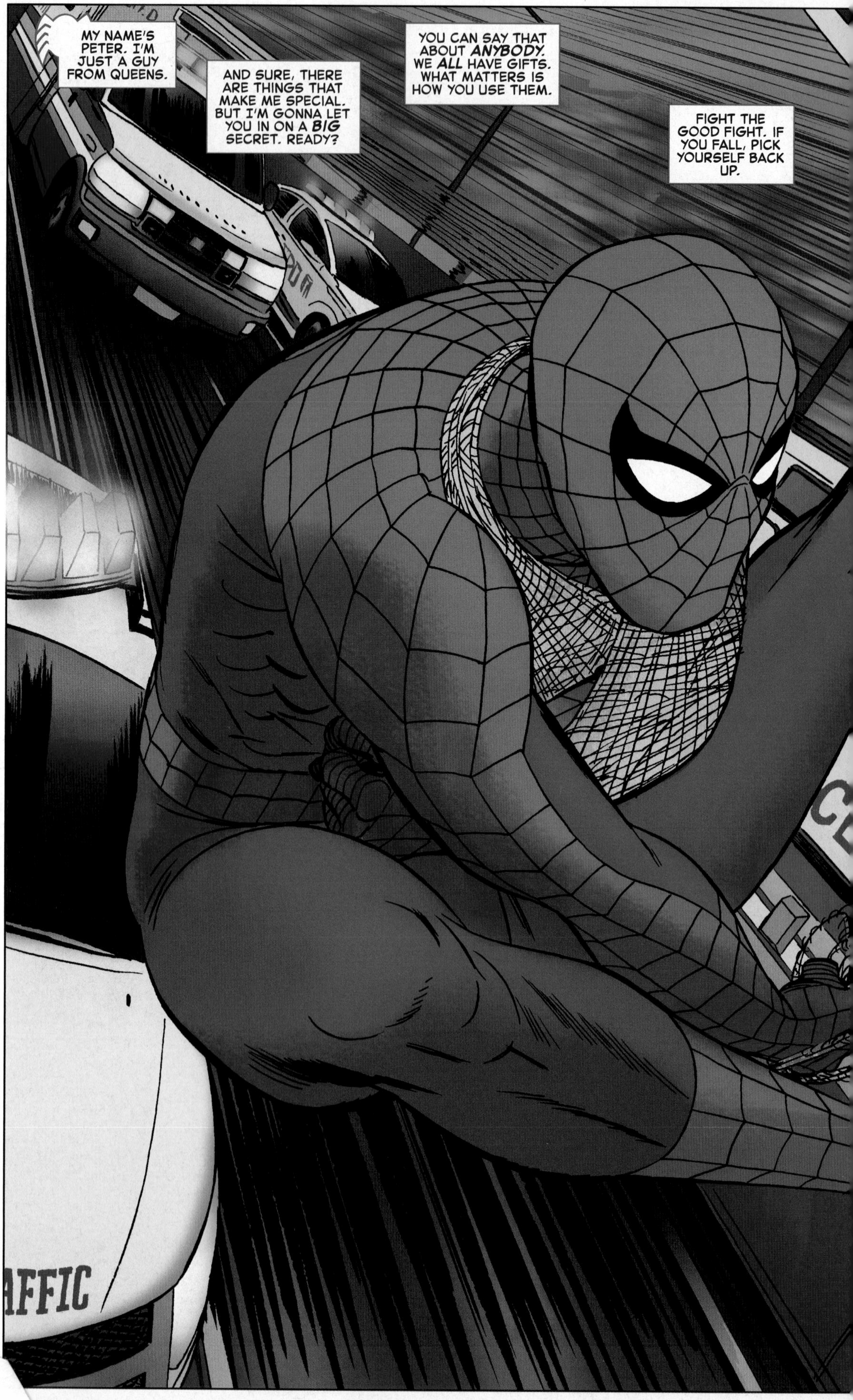
MY NAME'S PETER. I'M JUST A GUY FROM QUEENS.
AND SURE, THERE ARE THINGS THAT MAKE ME SPECIAL. BUT I'M GONNA LET YOU IN ON A BIG SECRET. READY?
YOU CAN SAY THAT ABOUT ANYBODY. WE ALL HAVE GIFTS. WHAT MATTERS IS HOW YOU USE THEM.
FIGHT THE GOOD FIGHT. IF YOU FALL, PICK YOURSELF BACK UP.
AFFIC

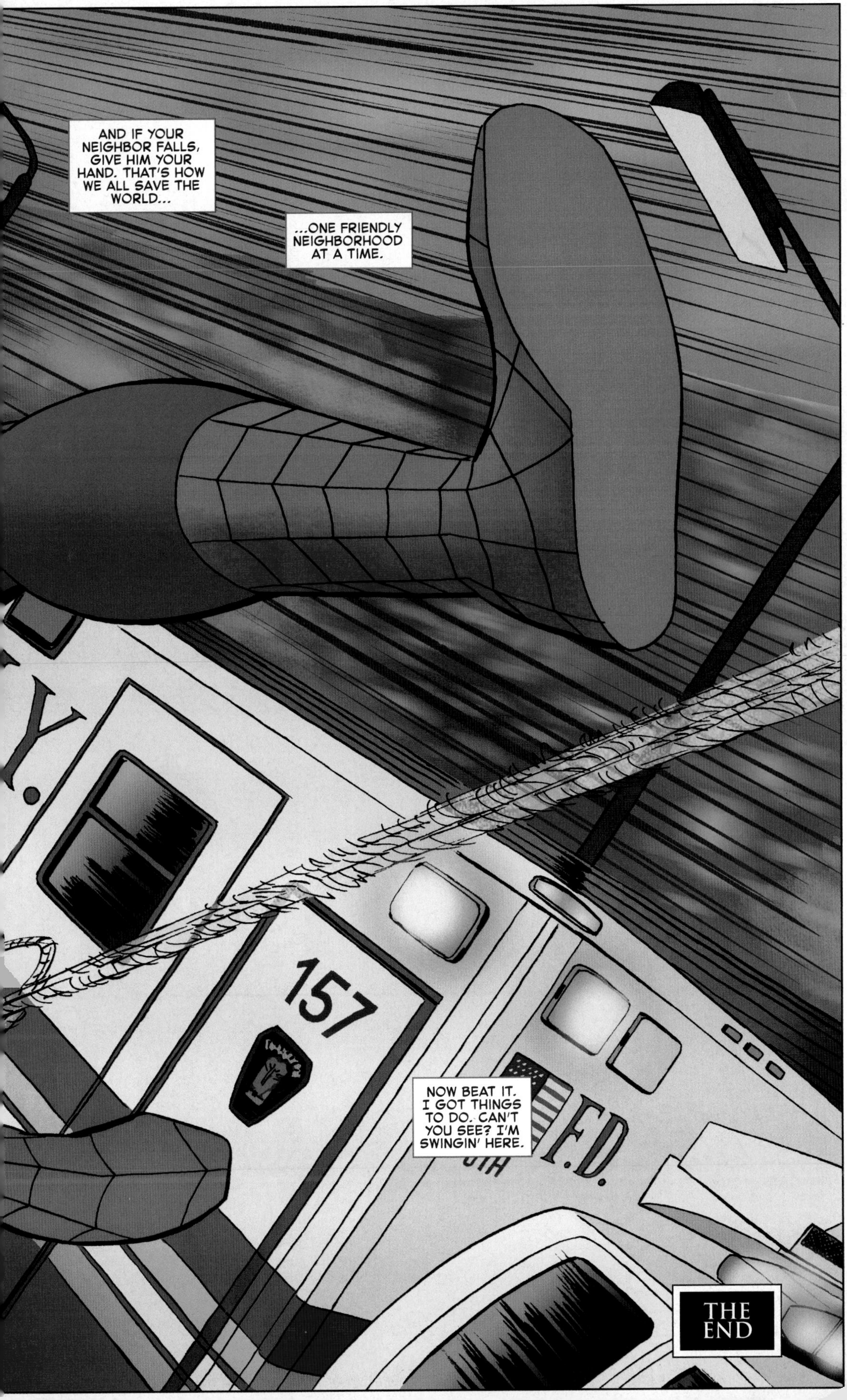
AND IF YOUR NEIGHBOR FALLS, GIVE HIM YOUR HAND. THAT'S HOW WE ALL SAVE THE WORLD...
...ONE FRIENDLY NEIGHBORHOOD AT A TIME.
157
F.D.
NOW BEAT IT. I GOT THINGS TO DO. CAN'T YOU SEE? I'M SWINGIN' HERE.
THE END

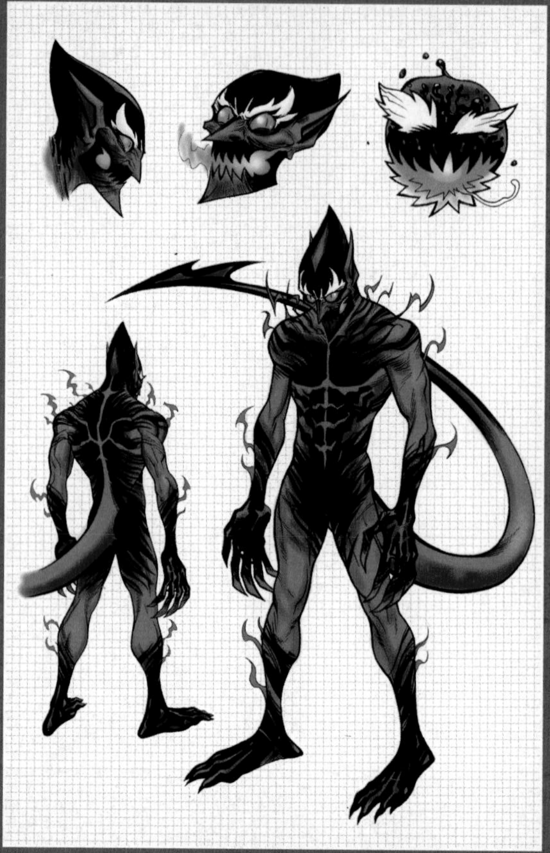

Amazing Spider-Man #797 design variant by Ed McGuinness

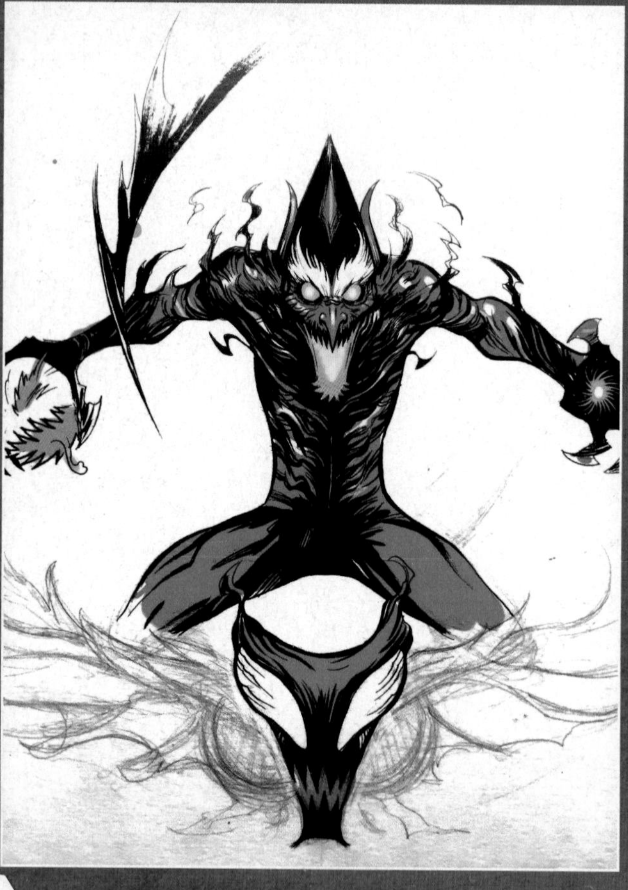

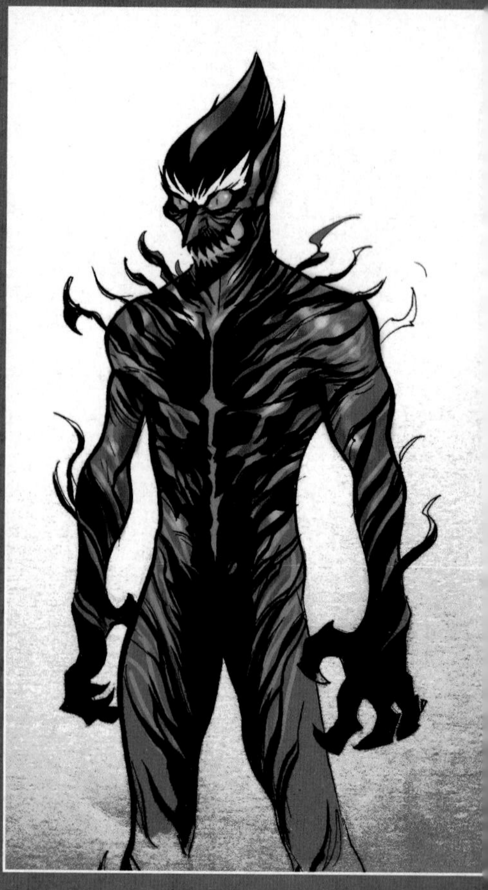

Red Goblin character sketches by Ed McGuinness